Educational Psychology

Reflection for Action

Angela M. O'Donnell
Rutgers, The State University of New Jersey

Johnmarshall Reeve
Korea University

Jeffrey K. Smith
University of Otago

John Wiley & Sons, Inc.

Chapter Opening Graphics, from left to right:
PhotoDisc, Inc./Getty Images
PhotoDisc, Inc./Getty Images
Corbis Digital Stock
PhotoDisc, Inc./Getty Images
Corbis Digital Stock

Chapter Opening Photos:
Chapter 1: PhotoDisc, Inc./Getty Images
Chapter 2: © Media Bakery
Chapter 3: MR © Ellen B. Senisi/The Image Works

Chapter 4: © Media Bakery
Chapter 5: Dynamic Graphics, Inc./Creatas
Chapter 6: PhotoDisc, Inc./Getty Images
Chapter 7: Digital Vision
Chapter 8: Corbis Digital Stock
Chapter 9: Corbis Digital Stock
Chapter 10: © Media Bakery
Chapter 11: © Media Bakery
Chapter 12: Punchstock
Chapter 13: © Amana Productions, Inc./Age Fotostock America, Inc.
Chapter 14: Andrew W. Levine/Photo Researchers
Chapter 15: © Michael Nitzschke/Imagebroker/Age Fotostock America, Inc.

Vice President and Executive Publisher: *Jay O'Callaghan*
Executive Editor: *Christopher Johnson*
Senior Acquisitions Editor: *Robert Johnston*
Senior Development Editor: *Nancy Perry*
Editorial Assistant: *Maura Gilligan*
Marketing Manager: *Margaret Barrett*
Senior Production Editor: *Sujin Hong*
Production Management Services: *Ingrao Associates*
Senior Illustration Editor: *Anna Melhorn*
Senior Photo Editor: *Lisa Gee*
Creative Director: *Harry Nolan*
Cover Designer: *Madelyn Lesure*
Cover Photo: *© Media Bakery*
Text Design Credit: *GGS Book Services*
Media Editor: *Lynn Pearlman*

This book was set in 10.5/12 Minion by Prepare and printed and bound by RRD Von Hoffmann. The cover was printed by RRD Von Hoffmann.

This book is printed on acid free paper. ∞

Founded in 1807, John Wiley & Sons, Inc. has been a valued source of knowledge and understanding for more than 200 years, helping people around the world meet their needs and fulfill their aspirations. Our company is built on a foundation of principles that include responsibility to the communities we serve and where we live and work. In 2008, we launched a Corporate Citizenship Initiative, a global effort to address the environmental, social, economic, and ethical challenges we face in our business. Among the issues we are addressing are carbon impact, paper specifications and procurement, ethical conduct within our business and among our vendors, and community and charitable support. For more information, please visit our website: www.wiley.com/go/citizenship.

Copyright ©2012, 2009, 2007 John Wiley & Sons, Inc. All rights reserved. No part of this publication may be reproduced, stored in a retrieval system or transmitted in any form or by any means, electronic, mechanical, photocopying, recording, scanning or otherwise, except as permitted under Section 107 or 108 of the 1976 United States Copyright Act, without either the prior written permission of the Publisher or authorization through payment of the appropriate per-copy fee to the Copyright Clearance Center, Inc., 222 Rosewood Drive, Danvers, MA 01923, website www.copyright.com. Requests to the Publisher for permission should be addressed to the Permissions Department, John Wiley & Sons, Inc., 111 River Street, Hoboken, NJ 07030-5774, (201) 748-6011, fax (201) 748-6008, website www.wiley.com/go/permissions.

Evaluation copies are provided to qualified academics and professionals for review purposes only, for use in their courses during the next academic year. These copies are licensed and may not be sold or transferred to a third party. Upon completion of the review period, please return the evaluation copy to Wiley. Return instructions and a free of charge return mailing label are available at www.wiley.com/go/returnlabel. If you have chosen to adopt this textbook for use in your course, please accept this book as your complimentary desk copy. Outside of the United States, please contact your local sales representative.

ISBN: 978-1-118-07613-2
          978-1-118-12915-9 (BRV)

Printed in the United States of America

10 9 8 7 6 5 4 3 2 1

About the Authors

Angela M. O'Donnell is a Professor in the Department of Educational Psychology at Rutgers University. She received her PhD in Experimental Psychology from Texas Christian University and has master's degrees in both Experimental Psychology and Special Education. She is a Fellow of the American Psychological Association and the American Educational Research Association. She served as Past-President of Division 15 (Educational Psychology). She received the Early Career Award of Division 15, the New Jersey Psychological Association's Distinguished Teacher Award, and the Scholar/Teacher Award from Rutgers University. Professor O'Donnell serves on numerous editorial boards of journals in educational psychology. She was Secretary of Division C of the American Educational Research Association and served as Program Chair for Division C. Her research interests are in the areas of collaborative learning and learning strategies. She has published extensively in academic journals on the cognitive processes involved in specific types of cooperative learning and the use of visual organizers to support cognitive processing.

Johnmarshall Reeve is a Professor in the Department of Education at Korea University in Seoul, South Korea. He received his PhD from Texas Christian University and completed postdoctoral work at the University of Rochester. Professor Reeve's research interests center on the empirical study of all aspects of human motivation and emotion with a particular emphasis on teachers' motivating styles and students' motivation and engagement during learning activities. He has published three dozen articles on motivation in journals such as the *Journal of Educational Psychology, Educational Psychologist*, and the *Elementary School Journal*. For this work, he received the Thomas N. Urban Research Award from the FINE Foundation and served as past Chair of the Motivation in Education SIG with the American Educational Research Association. He has published two books, *Understanding Motivation and Emotion* and *Motivating Others: Nurturing Inner Motivational Resources*. He is Editor-in-Chief of the journal *Motivation and Emotion*.

Jeffrey K. Smith is a Professor in the College of Education at the University of Otago and the Co-Director of the University's Educational Assessment Research Unit. He received his bachelor's degree from Princeton University and his PhD from the University of Chicago. For three decades, Professor Smith was a member of the faculty at Rutgers University and served as the Chair of the Department of Educational Psychology. He served from 1988 to 2005 as Head of the Office of Research and Evaluation at The Metropolitan Museum of Art. Professor Smith's research interests include psychological factors involved in assessment, classroom assessment and grading, and the psychology of aesthetics. He has published over 50 articles and reviews in these areas and has written or edited five books. Professor Smith is the co-editor of the journal *Psychology of Aesthetics, Creativity, and the Arts* and former editor of the journal *Educational Measurement: Issues and Practice*. He currently sits on the editorial board of four journals and is a former member of the National Advisory Board of Buros' *Mental Measurement Yearbook*. He has won awards for teaching, research, and public service.

Preface

Teachers help students learn, develop, and realize their potential. To become successful in their craft, teachers need to learn how to establish high-quality relationships with their students, and they need to learn how to implement instructional strategies that promote students' learning, development, and potential. This is easier said than done. To prepare pre-service teachers for the profession, the study of educational psychology can help teachers better understand their students and better understand the process of teaching. Such is the twofold purpose of this book—to help you understand your future students better and to help you understand all aspects of the teaching–learning situation. The pursuit of these two purposes leads to the ultimate goal of the book—namely, to help you become increasingly able to promote your students' learning, development, and potential when it becomes your turn to step into the classroom and take full-time responsibility for your own classes.

The Goal of Educational Psychology: Reflection for Action

This book will help preservice teachers become reflective teachers, *reflective practitioners* who can frame classroom-based questions and use a "scientist-practitioner" approach to answer those questions. Each chapter in the book is organized around the goal of helping preservice teachers become more of a reflective practitioner. Each chapter begins by highlighting a set of guiding questions about important classroom-based questions, and each chapter provides an introductory example of one such classroom question. The contents of each chapter then describe the theories and empirical findings that might be drawn on to understand and respond to the situation. It links practical issues with theories and research through illustrations of "what kids say and do," through specific examples of "taking it to the classroom," and through counterintuitive examples of how research contributes new understanding on commonly misunderstood classroom questions. The pages in each chapter model how theory, research findings, and other sources of information can be drawn upon to provide plausible answers to these questions, as students are guided through a process of reflection (summarized as the acronym RIDE). This critical thinking process involves **R**eflection, **I**nformation Gathering, **D**ecision Making, and **E**valuation. By using RIDE, students become increasingly skilled in reflecting on everyday classroom practice. Finally, each chapter concludes with a pair of lesson plans designed to help teachers apply the educational psychology principles in the chapter to the delivery of an actual classroom lesson.

In *Educational Psychology: Reflection for Action*, we provide students with:

1. A clear description of the *theoretical principles* in psychology that have relevance for education, along with an analysis of their current research support.

2. *Practical guidance* about how to link theory and practice in the context of classrooms. We illustrate the opportunities for and limits of application of theoretical principles to classroom practice.

3. *Learning tools* to help preservice teachers develop skills they can build on throughout their teaching careers.

Author Team

The three authors of this text are experts in learning, motivation, and assessment, respectively. Each of us is writing in our special area of substantial experience, providing an advantage over the typical text, in which chapters are written by a single author whose expertise most likely does not fully extend to the range of content needed in an educational psychology text. We are also a global team, as we live, work, and teach students in different parts of the globe, including the United States, South Korea, and New Zealand.

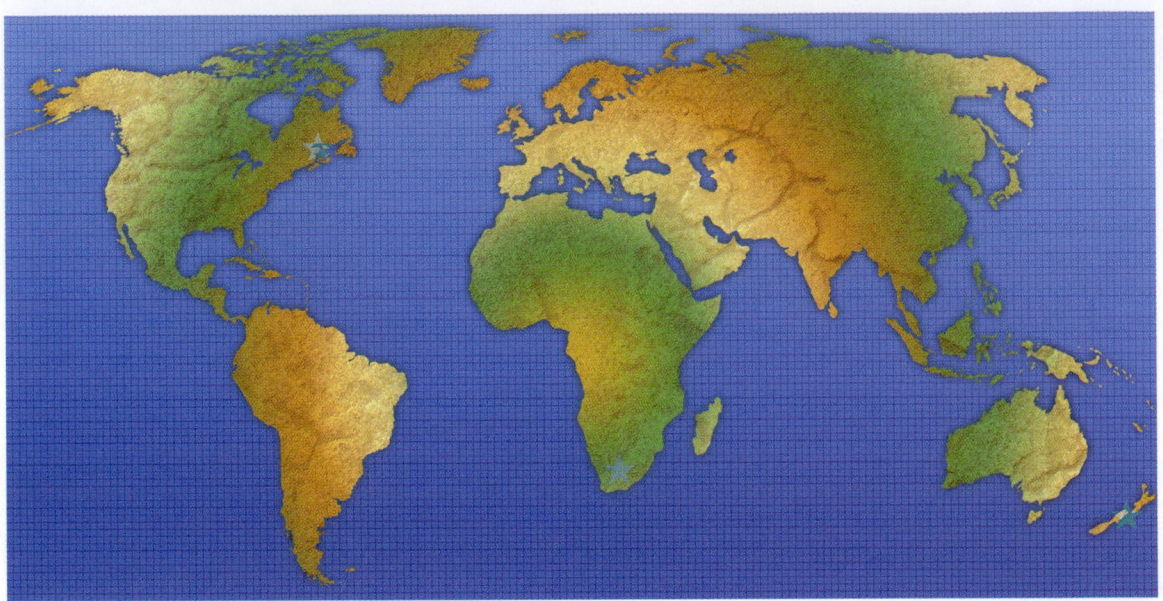

Diversity

Each year, schools become more diverse and issues of diversity become more important. Recognizing this, we treat diversity as one theme within the book and within the study of educational psychology more generally. Chapter 13, entitled "Issues of Diversity," is devoted fully to the issues of diverse learners, multicultural education, and the practical effort of implementing a multicultural approach to teaching. But we have done more. We have chosen to address issues of diversity as part of every chapter. We believe that diversity is a consideration that runs throughout the topics within educational psychology, and that it is not a separate set of concerns. Diversity must be understood, appreciated, and addressed in every aspect of the classroom teacher's activity. In addition, we believe this treatment reflects the day-to-day realities of classroom teachers, in which student diversity is increasingly common.

Special Needs

All students have the right to a free and appropriate education. While practically every teacher will agree that all students deserve this right, making sure that students with special needs, such as autism and intellectual disabilities, experience a free and appropriate education represents a professional challenge on a daily basis. As with diversity, we treat special needs as another theme within the book. Chapter 12, entitled "Individual Differences and Special Needs," is devoted to the issues of variability in the classroom, extremes of intelligence, and prevalent student needs and challenges. Like diversity, we not only provide a separate chapter to highlight the importance of students' special needs, but we further believe that this issue is a consideration that runs throughout the topics within educational psychology, and that it is not a separate set of concerns. So we have chosen to address issues of special needs as part of every chapter. The special needs that interfere with students' learning must be understood, appreciated, and addressed in every aspect of the classroom teacher's activity. In addition, we believe this treatment reflects the day-to-day realities of classroom teachers.

Content and Organization

The textbook consists of six major parts, as summarized here:

- Teaching Chapters 1–2
- Development Chapters 3–4
- Learning Chapters 5–9
- Motivation Chapters 10–11
- Special Needs and Diversity Chapters 12–13
- Assessment Chapters 14–15

The first part of the book (Teaching) discusses the process of teaching, the concerns beginning teachers routinely have, and reflective teaching. The second part (Development) discusses the issues of cognitive and social development. The third part (Learning) discusses behavioral, cognitive, social learning, and social-constructivist approaches to learning. The fourth part (Motivation) discusses the nature of student motivation, teachers' motivating styles, and how teachers can support students' motivation during learning activities. The fifth part (Special Needs and Diversity) discusses the issues of students' special needs and diversity. The sixth part (Assessment) discusses principles of assessment, grading, standardized tests, and standards-based assessments. Collectively, these six sections represent the essential content that students must know as they prepare to become teachers.

Chapter 1: Introducing Educational Psychology and Reflective Practice

Educational psychology is the scientific study of psychology in education. Its goals are to understand learners and to promote their learning. The first part of Chapter 1 introduces educational psychology, and it explains how this dual focus on understanding learners and promoting their learning helps teachers better understand all aspects of the teaching–learning process. The second part of the chapter introduces educational psychology as a scientific field of study. In doing so, we introduce theory, link theory to practice, and explain how classroom teachers can narrow the gap between theory and practice. In the end of Chapter 1, we introduce our model of reflective teaching, called RIDE.

Chapter 2: Teachers and Teaching

The focus of Chapter 2 is on teachers and teaching, and on how thoughtful learning can be fostered by high-quality teaching. We begin the chapter by identifying teachers' most pressing concerns and explain how beginning teachers can quiet their most pressing concerns by developing teaching knowledge, teaching efficacy, teaching expertise, and reflective teaching. In terms of knowledge, we show how teachers' knowledge of the subject matter they are teaching and their beliefs about themselves, their students, and the processes of learning and teaching have important influences on classroom practices and problems. In terms of teachers' concerns, stress, and anxiety, we show how developing teacher efficacy works as an antidote to quiet these concerns. As to teaching itself, Chapter 2 illustrates the instructional process from beginning to end, discussing planning as a key factor in good teaching and examining various general approaches to teaching.

Chapter 3: Cognitive Development

As infants grow into children and as children grow into adolescents, the three interrelated developmental processes of brain development, cognitive development, and language development unfold. Biology and maturation underlie all three developmental processes, but biology provides learners only with their developmental potential. The first part of Chapter 3 focuses on brain development, including a discussion of how the educational process affects brain development. Most of the chapter focuses on cognitive development, including first a Piagetian approach in which teachers provide developing students with richly stimulating and complex classroom environments and second a Vygotskian approach in which teachers provide developing students with wise mentors who can guide their learning and development. The chapter ends with a focus on language development, including a focus on second-language acquisition and bilingualism.

Chapter 4: Social Development

Chapter 4 highlights the role that relationships play in students' social development, and it offers numerous illustrations as to how teachers can help students develop socially. Social development reflects the extent to which students move toward a life of trust, social competence, peer popularity, initiative, competence, identity, moral development, and a prosocial orientation toward others. It also reflects the extent to which students move away from a life of distrust, aggression, bullying, and an antisocial orientation toward others. The extent to which students develop socially depends in part on the quality of the relationships in their lives, including the relationships they have with their teachers. Chapter 4 identifies the aspects of any relationship that allow it to be a high-quality versus a low-quality one. Throughout the chapter, the focus is on how the availability of high-quality relationships allows students to develop social competence whereas the presence of low-quality relationships characterized by neglect and abuse undermine this developmental journey toward social competence.

Chapter 5: Behavioral Learning Theory

Chapter 5 focuses on how students learn the behaviors, skills, and self-regulatory capacity they need to function well in school and in life. To understand how students learn such things, we first define learning and explain how it occurs. We then introduce the basic principles of the behavioral approach to learning, such as positive reinforcement. These principles serve as a foundation for understanding and discussing the everyday problems that teachers face in trying to increase the frequency of desirable behaviors and decrease that of undesirable behaviors. Chapter 5 also discusses how teachers can manage their classrooms for effective learning and how they can support students' capacity for self-management. The chapter concludes by describing the types of instruction that have been inspired by behavioral learning principles.

Chapter 6: Managing Learning in Classrooms

Chapter 6 looks at the opportunities, problems, and concerns associated with creating and managing successful learning communities in classrooms. We begin with the skeleton, discussing concerns that teachers face in designing the physical environment of classrooms. Then we move into the areas that bring the bare bones to life: creating a learning community, establishing and enforcing norms and rules for behavior, managing the tension between freedom and structure, and managing the multidimensional aspects of day-to-day classroom life such as norms, rules, and procedures. The chapter concludes with recommendations for managing day-to-day classroom instruction and for dealing effectively with the most common and the most pressing behavior problems.

Chapter 7: Cognitive Learning Theory

Chapter 7 focuses on the structures and processes of learning from a cognitive perspective. A cognitive view on learning emphasizes information-processing theory. It introduces teachers to the key learning concepts of working memory, long-term memory, encoding, retrieval, and categorization. Throughout this discussion, we pay particular attention to how we can understand the needs of exceptional children, especially the limits students face from the various components of the information-processing system, such as working memory. The chapter also discusses how students' learning can be improved by identifying key learning processes, such as elaboration and organization, and by discussing effective learning strategies. Each section highlights the idea that the more teachers understand the process of learning, the more effective an instructor they will be.

Chapter 8: Social Learning Theory, Complex Cognition, and Social Constructivism

Chapter 8 focuses on social learning, complex cognition, and social constructivism. The first part of the chapter focuses on social learning to illustrate how instructional processes such as modeling promote learning. The second part of the chapter covers topics related to complex cognition, including metacognition, self-explanation, reasoning and argumentation, problem solving, and transfer. The third part of the chapter adds the perspective of social constructivism, as it emphasizes the importance to learning of observing others and of the social context more generally. We provide examples of social constructivist instructional strategies such as scaffolding, cognitive apprenticeships, reciprocal teaching, problem-based learning, and classroom communities. All of these examples of instruction capitalize on a social-constructivist perspective on learning.

Chapter 9: Learning from Peers

Chapter 9 focuses on the peer learning that occurs in contexts such as tutoring and cooperative learning. The first part of the chapter explains why peer learning works so well, as it explains the benefits, mechanisms, and interpersonal processes through which peer learning can lead to the acquisition of students' skills and knowledge in widely differing classroom situations. The first type of peer learning emphasized is tutoring, and it provides both the evidence for why tutoring is effective as well as the processes that are enacted by skilled tutors. The second type of peer learning emphasized is learning in large heterogeneous groups, often referred to as cooperative learning. This section of the chapter considers the key issues in the use of classroom-based peer learning, including the quality of students' discourse, the kinds of tasks that teachers may choose, the role of the teacher in using peer learning, peer mediation, and assessing the outcomes of peer learning. Chapter 9 features several examples of cooperative learning activities, including those involving technology.

Chapter 10: Motivation and Engagement

Chapter 10 focuses on students' motivated engagement during learning activities. We define engagement, explain what it looks like in the classroom, identify where it comes from, explain why it is important, and provide instructional strategies for promoting it. We then introduce the concept of motivation. In doing so, we discuss intrinsic motivation, extrinsic rewards, and types of extrinsic motivation, including the classroom issue of how to use extrinsic motivators in a motivationally constructive way. The chapter also introduces the three psychological needs of autonomy, competence, and relatedness, and it provides instructional strategies to promote them. The last part of the chapter focuses on students' motivational assets versus liabilities. We first discuss curiosity, interest, and positive affect as ways to spark students' engagement, but then discuss the engagement-draining motivational deficits of anxiety, self-worth protection, and self-handicapping. Overall, the chapter identifies engagement-fostering types of student motivation and how to promote them as well engagement-draining types of student motivation and how to understand them and how to provide instruction to avoid them.

Chapter 11: Motivation to Learn

Chapter 11 explains how student motivation is rooted in constructive thinking, and also how students' lack of motivation is rooted in maladaptive thinking. Chapter 11 first discusses the motivational concept of self-efficacy by explaining why it is important and where it comes from. We also identify instructional strategies to increase students' self-efficacy with the goal of energizing students' engagement and persistence. Chapter 11 then discusses outcome-based motivations, including mastery motivation, an optimistic attributional style, and hope with an emphasis on helping teachers prevent helplessness and foster mastery. We then discuss goal setting and how teachers can set up a motivation-fostering goal-setting program in their classroom. We further discuss the related motivational concepts of possible selves, achievement goals, and effective self-regulation. The final section of the chapter examines students' developing self-concept and emphasizes how schooling can enhance students' healthy self-concept. Overall, the chapter presents instructional strategies to reverse students' destructive and maladaptive ways of thinking as well as those that support constructive and adaptive ways of thinking.

Chapter 12: Individual Differences and Special Needs

Chapter 12 focuses on variability in the classroom, and it is concerned specifically with the individual differences among students that affect their learning. The first part of the chapter focuses on intelligence or ability. It describes how the concept of intelligence evolved and introduces several theories of intelligence. The chapter then turns to a discussion of the concept of talent. The emphasis in on how to develop talent and how to provide the sort of instruction that can be expected to develop students' talents. The chapter then discusses extremes of intelligence, including both giftedness and intellectual disabilities. Several instructional strategies are described that are designed specifically to help teachers manage variation in students' ability during instruction. The second part of the chapter focuses on learners with special needs. We explain the law behind special education, including the need for individualized education plans and criteria to identify students with special needs. We also illustrate classroom strategies such as inclusion and within-class ability grouping. The chapter concludes by providing a close-up examination of specific student needs and challenges that are especially prevalent in schools, including learning disabilities, autism, physical and sensory challenges, and attention-deficit disorder.

Chapter 13: Issues in Diversity

Chapter 13 addresses issues in diversity. The first part of the chapter informs teachers of what they can expect to encounter in terms of diverse learners. It discusses the relationships among race, ethnicity, and socioeconomic status, and it explains the role of these student differences in their learning. The second part of the chapter focuses specifically on language diversity and on English language learners in particular. The third part of the chapter overviews multicultural education, and it communicates both the advantages and concerns inherent within multicultural education. The last part of the chapter focuses on the instructional task of implementing a multicultural approach to teaching. This section shows teachers both how they can get started in the effort to implement a multicultural approach to teaching as well as how they can dig deeper to become a teacher of diverse students who works ably in different cultural contexts.

Chapter 14: Assessment for Learning

Chapter 14 examines the critical issues of classroom assessment: purposes, assessment options, principles of grading, constructing classroom assessments, evaluation of results, and the relationship between assessment and instruction. Classroom assessments let students know the extent to which they have learned the class material, and classroom assessments can let students understand what the teacher thinks is of value in the class. They let teachers learn how well students are doing in the class. They can also let teachers learn about the efficacy of their own teaching and let parents know how well their children are doing. Carefully considered and well-constructed assessments promote the notion that classroom assessment is not just assessment *of* learning; it is assessment *for* learning. The chapter also covers the very practical topics of developing and using assessments, developing a grading system, and communicating with parents.

Chapter 15: Standardized and Standards-Based Assessments

Chapter 15 describes standardized and standards-based assessments. We examine what these tests are, what they are used for, and how they are developed. A variety of different types of standardized tests are described, including those used by school testing programs, college admissions testing, and intelligence testing. We also explore the history of such tests and how to understand and interpret the scores, as well as issues related to interpreting scores for students with limited English proficiency or students with special needs. Finally, we consider controversies associated with standardized testing, such as bias in testing and high-stakes testing.

Learning Tools: A Look Inside the Structure of Each Chapter

To help meet the needs of preservice teachers taking this course, we have included the following pedagogical features in each chapter.

Understanding the Context

Reflection for Action The opening of each chapter contains a sample of classroom life by presenting an example of a teaching and learning setting that is particularly relevant to the content of that chapter. The sample of classroom life is taken either from a teacher's actual experience or from a description of a common and important classroom situation (see below for an example). It provides the basis for the reader to engage in Reflection for Action, reflection that can help the reader develop the ability to reflect critically on his or her own work, removed from the immediacy of the particular situation.

Throughout the chapter, we explain how the content of the chapter relates to interpreting, understanding, and solving the classroom situation featured in the opening of the chapter. Each in-chapter reference back to the opening classroom situation is meant to encourage the reader to think about what appears in the text as helpful information to think about the opening segment. At the end of each chapter, a more structured and fully realized analysis is presented to students to think through the problem in a systematic and scholarly fashion (see below for description).

Overall, the Reflection for Action entry can be thought of as two key segments—the opening statement of the learning situation and the closing analysis of that learning situation—that bracket the contents of the chapter. Each invitation for students to engage in reflection for action is denoted in the text with the icon shown here: **RIDE**

Guiding Questions Following the Reflection for Action piece, we present a set of Guiding Questions. These questions form the utility basis for what is to be presented in the chapter, because they tie important classroom issues that will resonate with students to the theories and empirical findings presented in the chapter.

Example: **Chapter 2**

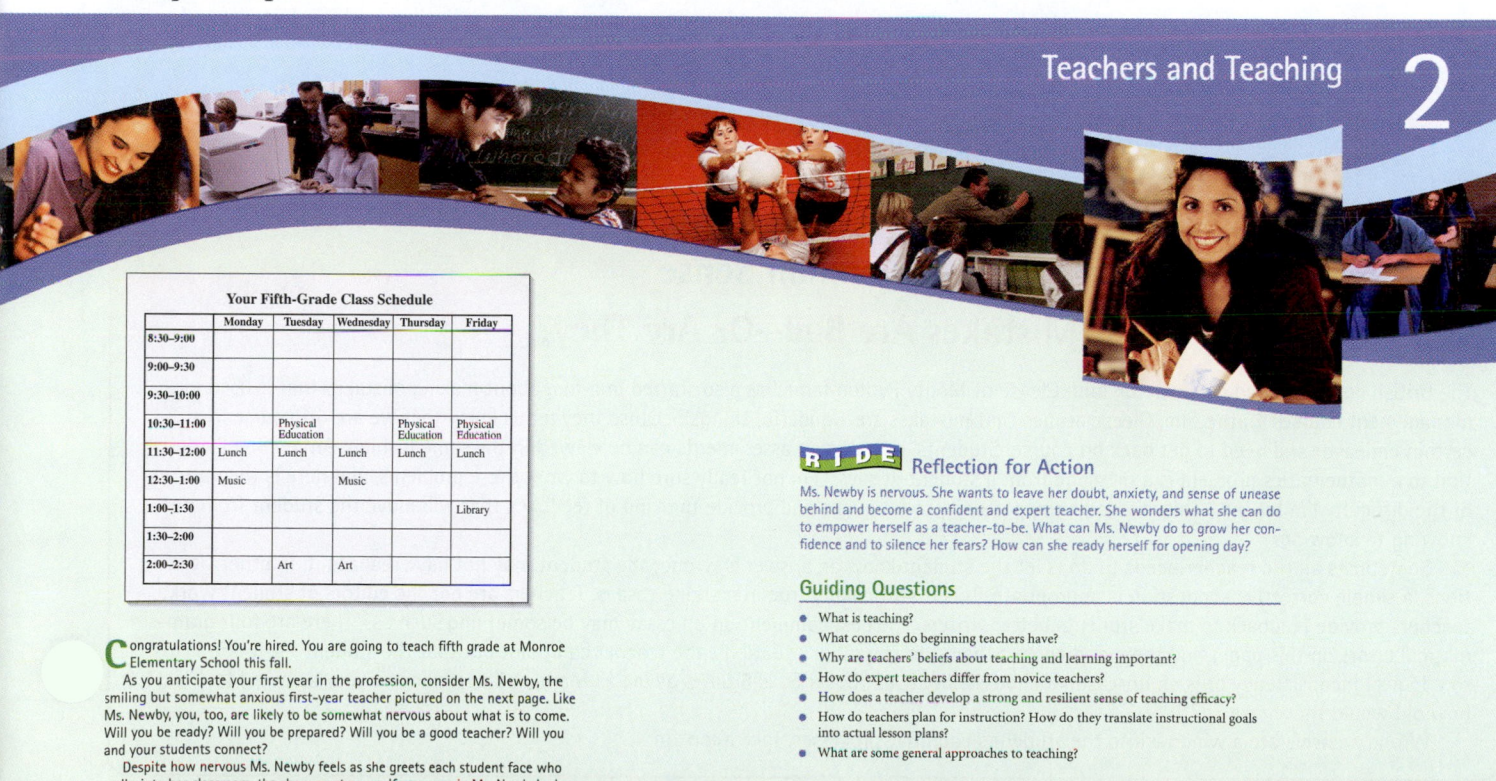

Teachers and Teaching

2

Your Fifth-Grade Class Schedule

	Monday	Tuesday	Wednesday	Thursday	Friday
8:30–9:00					
9:00–9:30					
9:30–10:00					
10:30–11:00		Physical Education		Physical Education	Physical Education
11:30–12:00	Lunch	Lunch	Lunch	Lunch	Lunch
12:30–1:00	Music		Music		
1:00–1:30					Library
1:30–2:00					
2:00–2:30		Art	Art		

RIDE Reflection for Action

Ms. Newby is nervous. She wants to leave her doubt, anxiety, and sense of unease behind and become a confident and expert teacher. She wonders what she can do to empower herself as a teacher-to-be. What can Ms. Newby do to grow her confidence and to silence her fears? How can she ready herself for opening day?

Guiding Questions

- What is teaching?
- What concerns do beginning teachers have?
- Why are teachers' beliefs about teaching and learning important?
- How do expert teachers differ from novice teachers?
- How does a teacher develop a strong and resilient sense of teaching efficacy?
- How do teachers plan for instruction? How do they translate instructional goals into actual lesson plans?
- What are some general approaches to teaching?

Congratulations! You're hired. You are going to teach fifth grade at Monroe Elementary School this fall.

As you anticipate your first year in the profession, consider Ms. Newby, the smiling but somewhat anxious first-year teacher pictured on the next page. Like Ms. Newby, you, too, are likely to be somewhat nervous about what is to come. Will you be ready? Will you be prepared? Will you be a good teacher? Will you and your students connect?

Despite how nervous Ms. Newby feels as she greets each student face who walks into her classroom, the show must go on. If you were in Ms. Newby's shoes, what would you want to know? What sort of experiences would you need before you could feel prepared and ready to go?

Learning the Material

What Kids Say and Do   Samples of children's work or conversation serve as a watershed between theory and practice and a venue for their integration. Teachers depend on students' work to reason about students' achievement and progress, and the availability of such work can be an important contribution to preservice teacher development.

Example: **Chapter 5**

What Kids Say and Do

Describing Caring Teachers

Here are examples of what middle school students in highly diverse schools say when asked to describe caring teachers:

Caring teachers ...

> are fair.
>
> ask me what I think.
>
> hold high expectations for what I can do.

Caring teachers do not ...

> yell.
>
> interrupt me.
>
> criticize me.
>
> hold low expectations for what I can do.

Uncommon Sense   Situations and/or conclusions that are frequently believed by preservice teachers but that are not supported by research are presented for discussion. As an example, students believe that positive reinforcement is always a good practice but are surprised to find that incidents of poor behavior increase in classrooms in which positive reinforcement is provided for good behavior and bad behavior is always ignored. This feature attempts to make students aware of their own misconceptions about predicting and explaining behavior.

Example: **Chapter 14**

Uncommon Sense

Mistakes Are Bad—Or Are They?

The British comedian and comic actor John Cleese of Monty Python fame has also starred in a film about making mistakes that is used in management courses. In the film, Cleese argues that mistakes are wonderful things because they let us know that we are off course in a certain endeavor and need to get back on course. Students' mistakes on assessments can be viewed in the same fashion. An incorrect solution to a mathematics problem is a message from a student. It says, "I'm not really sure how to work these problems, and here is the nature of the difficulty I'm having." This is a golden opportunity to intervene and provide the kind of feedback that will move the student from not knowing to knowing.

Sometimes all the teacher needs to do is let the student know an answer is wrong; the student may not have realized it. In other situations, a simple corrective suggestion is appropriate. This is particularly true in marking essays. Teachers are not the editors of student work; teachers provide feedback to make students better writers. The best comment on an essay may be something such as, "There are four grammatical errors on this page; find them and correct them." In still other situations, the teacher can point out that the student's solution leads to a logical inconsistency or is an unreasonable possibility (e.g., "But if Ed is 6 times as old as Mary, and according to your answer Mary is 34, how old would that make Ed?").

Wrong answers are a window into the student's cognitive processes. Take a look in.

Taking It to the Classroom Guidelines for how to apply the chapter's theoretical principles in everyday classroom practice appear throughout each chapter. The vast majority of students who take educational psychology plan to be teachers. The how-to guidelines embedded within each Taking It to the Classroom entry will help preservice teachers link the theoretical principles they read about in the text to appropriate solutions to classroom problems they will soon face in the classroom. These guidelines will also function as a useful reference when readers engage in their student–teaching experiences.

Example: **Chapter 14**

Taking It to the Classroom

Marking Student Papers: Being Objective, Specific, and Growth-Oriented

Less Desirable Comments	More Desirable Comments
A lot of errors in this area.	See whether you can find four grammatical errors in this section and correct them.
This paragraph is poorly worded and unclear.	I think this paragraph makes the reader work too hard. See whether you can tighten it.
This is hardly your best work.	This looks a little hurried. It doesn't show the care I saw in your last paper.
This is not what we discussed in class.	You're off target somewhat here.
You can't reach the right answer if you are sloppy in your calculations.	You've got the idea, but check your work.
Awkward construction.	Reread this sentence and see whether it says what you want it to.
Redo this.	Try this again.
Excellent job here.	Your use of metaphor here is strong.
Great, I love this.	Think of how much more effective this argument is than in the paper you did last week.

Integrated Primary and Secondary Applications Integrated into each chapter is content specific to both primary education and secondary education, including the middle school level. In each chapter, we deliberately include various discussions of how the theories and research discussed throughout the chapter apply to both primary and secondary age groups.

Integrated Content on Diversity Content related to issues of diversity is distributed among all chapters. K-12 classrooms are significantly more diverse than even a decade ago. We believe that by integrating the content on diversity into each chapter, preservice teachers may have a better grasp of what diversity among their students will mean for their teaching.

Integrated Content on Students with Special Needs Frequently, content about students' individual differences and special needs is separated into a single chapter in a text. As with issues of diversity, the content related to individual differences and special needs is often separated from the issues of instruction/assessment and motivation. By integrating this content into each chapter, preservice teachers may have a more realistic expectation of what differences among their students will mean for their teaching day-to-day.

Integrated Content on Technology Technology has become an increasingly important component of many classrooms at both the elementary and secondary levels. Whether it is the use of simulations to present biology or physics labs, computer-generated manipulables for elementary math instruction, or assistive technology for students with special needs, teachers need to know about technology and how it can be used to promote students' learning. Consistent with our overall approach to instruction, we have chosen to integrate this material across chapters, showing its importance in the particular area under consideration.

Margin Notes Students are given many access points to understanding the theory and applications in the chapter.

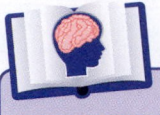

MINDFUL HABITS OF EFFECTIVE TEACHERS

The ability to engage in critical thinking and active reflection about one's practice is a key habit of mind of effective teachers. We describe it as "mindful" because this reflection is deliberate, intentional, and purposeful.

How Can I Use This?
Check out an electronic book (e-book) from your library and ask yourself what instructional uses it affords that a traditional printed book does not.

What Does This Mean to Me?
An SAT verbal score of 650 is a *z*-score of roughly +1.5 (1.5 standard deviations above the mean). Check that against the figure of the normal curve in Figure 15.4, and you can see that this is higher than roughly 93% of the scores.

RIDE Look at Ms. Baldwin's debate assessment at the beginning of the chapter. What skills and knowledge would lead to the highest marks on that assessment? Are they closely related to how you would have taught the material?

Appendix
Learning from Others
Students can learn from others through observation learning and vicarious experience (PRAXIS™, I.A.1; INTASC, Principle 2).

Appendix

PRAXIS™ Exam, INTASC Principles Special margin notes refer students to the Appendix, where they can see the how the contents of the chapter correspond to the Principles of Learning and Teaching (PLT) of the PRAXIS II™ exam and the INTASC principles.

Putting It Together

Reflection for Action End-of-Chapter Activity A Reflection for Action activity consolidates the concepts of each chapter as it models how theory, research findings, and other sources can be drawn upon to provide plausible answers to the question. Students practice *reflecting* on the situation before them, *gathering information* to help them interpret it, *making decisions* on how to handle the situation, and *evaluating* their decisions.

Example: **Chapter 9**

R I D E
REFLECTION FOR ACTION

The Event

A group of third graders have been given a bag of money and asked to find out the total amount of money in the bag. Maria, Carla, Andy, and Wilson are talking to one another. Part of their discussion was presented at the beginning of the chapter. Is the group effective? How would you know?

Reflection R I D E

The group is not acting like a group. The two girls, Maria and Carla, are talking to each other and trying to do the task that the teacher assigned. The two boys, Wilson and Andy, are not doing the task and are talking about a girl. They do not interact with the two girls in their group. What is this an example of? It could be an example of poor classroom management, because two of the children are not paying any attention to the task. It could be an example of ineffective instruction, because the teacher did not assign a task that engages the students. It could also be an example of the operation of status characteristics, because the girls do not interact with the boys. It is an example of a dysfunctional group because the two pairs of students do not interact, and one pair is behaving inappropriately. The students who are working on the task make no effort to engage the other students.

What Theoretical/Conceptual Information Might Assist in Interpreting and Remedying this Situation? Consider the following:

Group Structures

Slavin and the Johnsons describe many of the features of effective group structures. The participants' goals should be interdependent, and each student must be individually accountable for the group's achievement. Perhaps the teacher did not help the students develop a sense of interdependence.

Task Structures

Steiner (1972) describes several types of tasks on which groups work. Some of these tasks are completed by simply having a competent individual solve the problem. Some require coordination of the efforts of several members of a group. Cohen (1994) describes the kinds of cognitive processes that can be promoted using structured and unstructured tasks. The task of finding out how much money is in the bag is a procedural one that is not easily divided among group members.

Classroom Management

The teacher is not attending to the group's interaction and has not noticed the off-task behavior of two of its members. The teacher should draw on theories of reward and scaffolding to correct the problem.

Information Gathering R I D E

How would you decide which of the three possibilities listed above is the correct one? What else would you like to know? The group is not effective in that its four members are not working together. Two members are working on the assigned task, and the other two are off-task. It is almost as though there were two parallel conversations going on. You might like to know whether the two off-task children are typically off-task. You need to be careful if you determine that the two boys are typically off-task. You might attribute the problem to characteristics of the students and not to the nature of the task. It is possible that the teacher always assigns boring tasks that the boys are unlikely to pay attention to or the tasks might be very easy and not require much effort on the part of the boys, leaving them plenty of time to get into trouble.

You might also like to know whether this short segment of conversation is representative of the group's work or just a brief moment of distraction. Depending on the answers to these questions, you might make a different decision about how to solve the problem. If you were the teacher, you might ask the students' previous teacher about their typical behaviors. Do not rely solely on that teacher's comments because they may color your expectations about these students. You might consult the research literature and find out what it says about task structures that promote more effective engagement. You might also look at the literature on motivation to find out what it says about how to get students engaged in a task.

Decision Making R I D E

What is the best interpretation, given the available information? Without more information, you would conclude that the group is not working well. There are problems with the group's structure. The principles of cooperative learning suggest that heterogeneous groups can work effectively, but group members need to experience interdependence, and each member of the group needs to be individually accountable. The two on-task students in this group make no effort to engage the other students and do not try to redirect them, as might be expected if the students believed that their goals were intertwined. There may also be problems with the task structure. The task does not seem to require contributions by all the group's members, and it therefore facilitates cognitive and social loafing on the part of some of the students. To the extent that the two boys are off-task, there is a problem in classroom management, but this problem arises as a consequence of failing to structure the group properly and use a group-worthy task (Lotan, 2003) that would motivate all the members of the group.

Evaluation R I D E

Based on the available information, if you were the classroom teacher, you might decide to assign the students a new task that requires each participant to be involved. You should assign each student a role within the group and require that they all sign a contract that commits them to performing their assigned role. By doing this, you will help them understand the goals of the task and help them become more committed to completing the work. The two students who were on-task might encourage the others to perform their assigned roles. You might also find a more interesting task that requires the students to consider alternative solutions to a problem, and you could create a system of individual accountability that would require each student to be responsible for learning.

If you tried a new task or new procedures, would the group function better? You should monitor the group closely to determine whether the students participate more equally. At the end of the period, you might ask the students to assess how well they played their roles and how attentive to the task they were. If you find that the problem of unequal participation remains unsolved, you should engage in a new cycle of reflection, information gathering, decision making, and evaluation.

Further Practice: Your Turn

Here is a second event for you to consider. In doing so, carry out the processes of reflection, information gathering, decision making, and evaluation.

The Event

You have finally decided to have your sixth-grade students work in groups. You have 26 students in your class, 16 boys and 10 girls. Four of them have special needs. The project on which the children will work will take about two weeks. Tommy is often absent because of illness.

How many groups will you form? What will the composition of the groups be?   R I D E

End-of-Chapter Review and Expansion Each chapter ends with a Summary, list of Key Terms, and several Exercises for thought, discussion, and research.

Lesson Plans The final entry in each chapter is the provision of a pair of lesson plans, one lesson plan used by elementary-grade teachers and a second lesson plan used by secondary-level teachers. The lesson plans on these pages are excerpts from more complete plans. They are included in this form to provide the reader with practice in examining a lesson from the perspective of the content of this chapter. At the end of each lesson plan, we provide reflective Ask Yourself! questions in which we invite you to use the content of the chapter to strengthen the presentation of the lesson plan so as to improve instruction.

Instructor Resources

Instructor's Manual

Designed to help instructors maximize student learning, the Instructor's Manual presents the authors' teaching philosophy, offers teaching suggestions for each chapter of the text, provides several sample syllabi, suggests ways to organize course materials, and offers ideas for teaching each chapter.

Test Bank

The Test Bank is a comprehensive testing package that allows instructors to tailor examinations according to chapter objectives, learning skills, and content. It contains traditional types of questions (i.e., true/false, multiple-choice, matching, and short-answer), as well as open-ended questions.

PowerPoint Slides

The PowerPoint slides aid professors in visually presenting key concepts found in each chapter of the text. Intended as a lecture guide, the slides present material in a concise format that enables easy note-taking.

Teachscape Virtual Classroom Observation Videos

This edition utilizes content from Teachscape that includes video of (1) research-based best practices in action in the classroom; (2) commentaries by noted researchers that are designed to provide a research-based perspective on the practices illustrated; and (3) teacher reflections to promote better understanding of the featured teacher's instructional decisions. Some of this content is referenced, when appropriate, in the text; you will find additional content online.

The Wiley Faculty Network

The Wiley Faculty Network is a faculty-to-faculty network promoting the effective use of technology to enrich the teaching experience. The Wiley Faculty Network facilitates the exchange of best practices, connects teachers with technology, and helps to enhance instructional efficiency and effectiveness. The network provides technology training and tutorials, including online seminars, peer-to-peer exchanges of experiences and ideas, personalized consulting, and sharing of resources. For more information about the Wiley Faculty Network, please contact your Wiley representative; go to www.WhereFacultyConnect.com, or call 1-866-4FACULTY.

Student Resources

The Wiley Resource Kit

The Wiley Resource Kit gives students access to premier, password-protected resources hosted by Wiley. Building upon what they learn in their courses, students can use interactive media, practice quizzes, videos, and more at their own pace to further enhance mastery of key concepts. The Wiley Resource Kit also provides Respondus® Test Banks for many of Wiley's leading titles that instructors can assign and use for assessment through their campus learning management system. The Wiley Resource Kit and other resources can be accessed via the book companion site at www.wiley.com/college/o'donnell.

Acknowledgments

During the course of development of Educational Psychology, the authors benefited greatly from the input of ancillary authors, focus group participants, and manuscript reviewers. The constructive suggestions and innovative ideas of the following people are greatly appreciated.

Ancillary Authors

Lillian Hawkins, *Miami University:* Instructor's Resource Manual

Leah Smith: Instructor's Test Bank

Nicole DiDonato, *Monclair State University*: Reflection for Action Activities and Analysis of Student Work

Susan Parault, *St. Cloud State University*: Student Pre/Post Lecture Questions

Connie Phelps, *Emporia State University*: Web Links and Instructor's PowerPoint Slides

Focus Group Participants

Mary Frances Agnello,
Texas Tech University

Larry Alferink,
Illinois State University

James Allen,
College of Saint Rose

Linda Michelle Baron,
York College

Woan-Jue Jane Benjamin,
Mansfield University

Sandra Bonura,
Chapman University

Scott Brown,
University of Connecticut

Olin Campbell,
Brigham Young University

Li Cao,
State University of West Georgia

Steven Condly,
University of Central Florida

Felicia A. Dixon,
Ball State University

Terri Edwards,
Northeastern State University

Janet Ferguson,
Canisius College

Helen Rose Fives,
Montclair State University

Terry Fogg,
Minnesota State University–Mankato

Linda Garavalia,
University of Missouri–Kansas City

Gregory Goodman,
Clarion University of Pennsylvania

Sherryl Graves,
Hunter College, CUNY

Marlynn Griffin,
Georgia Southern University

Robert Hagstrom,
Northern Arizona University

Michael Heikkinen,
Boise State University

Barbara Hofer,
Middlebury College

Bob Hoffman,
University of Central Florida

Rochelle Hooks,
Community College of Southern Nevada

Brent Igo,
Clemson University

Elana Joram,
University of Northern Iowa

Jeffrey Kaplan,
University of Central Florida

Anastasia Kitsantas,
George Mason University

Nancy Knapp,
University of Georgia

Kurt Kowalski,
California State University–San Bernardino

Joseph Kush,
Duquesne University

Elizabeth Lenell,
University of Colorado–Boulder

Micheline Malow-Iroff,
CUNY–Queens College

Pamela Manners,
Troy State University

Jeff Miller,
California State University, Dominguez Hills

Gayle Mullen,
Midwestern State University

P. Karen Murphy,
The Pennsylvania State University–University Park

Joe Nichols,
Indiana University-Purdue University–Fort Wayne

Eucabeth Odhiambo,
Shippensburg University

Naomi Jeffrey Petersen,
Indiana University–South Bend

John Ramirez,
Middlesex County College

Larry Rogien,
Boise State University

Nanette Schonleber,
Chaminade University of Honolulu

Stephanie Sic,
University of Nebraska–Lincoln

Bruce Smith,
Henderson State University

Rosemarie Stallworth-Clark,
Georgia Southern University

Tehia V Starker,
University of Nebraska–Lincoln

Jessica Summers,
University of Missouri

Phillip Tanner,
Northern Arizona University
Alice K. H. Taum,
University of Hawaii
Taunya Tinsley,
Slippery Rock University of Pennsylvania
Selma Vonderwell,
University of Akron
Carmen Wakefield,
UC Raymond Walters College
Miriam Witmer,
Millersville University

Reviewers

Frank D. Adams,
Wayne State College
Irene Aiken,
University of North Carolina–Pembroke
Funsho Akingbala,
St. Edward's University
Joyce Alexander,
Indiana University–Bloomington
Padma Anand,
Slippery Rock University
Maria Avgerinou,
St. Xavier University
Bambi Bailey,
Midwestern State University
Jacques Benninga,
California State University–Fresno
Shani Beth-Halachmy,
National Louis University
Camille Branton,
Delta State University
Roger Briscoe,
Indiana University of Pennsylvania
Joy Brown,
University of North Alabama
Donna Browning,
Mississippi State University
Steven Burgess,
Southwestern Oklahoma State University
Melva Burke,
East Carolina University
Carolyn Burns,
Eastern Michigan University
Renee Cambiano,
Northeastern State University
Edward Caropreso,
*University of North Carolina–
Wilmington*
Jerrell C. Cassady,
Ball State University
Edward Coates,
Abilene Christian University

Joe Colbert,
Cedar Valley College
Allen Colebank,
Fairmont State University
Chuck Conjar,
Hartford Community College
Anne Cook,
University of Utah
Philip Cooker,
University of Mississippi
Kai Cortina,
University of Michigan–Ann Arbor
Brent Costleigh,
Brookdale Community College
Krista Cournoyer,
Rhode Island College
Andrea Cummings,
Georgia State University
Michael G. Curran,
Rider University
Gypsy M. Denzine,
Northern Arizona University
Robert DiGiulio,
Johnson State College
Jerome B. Dusek,
Syracuse University
Diane Dusick,
University of Southern California
David Estell,
Indiana University–Bloomington
Sue Evans,
University of Arizona
Daniel Fasko,
Bowling Green State University
Harriet Fayne,
Otterbein College
Larry Flick,
Oregon State University
Terry Fogg,
Minnesota State University–Mankato
Michael Gilchrist,
Auburn University–Montgomery
Adina Glickman,
Stanford University
Jennifer Goeke,
Rutgers University
J. Rachel Green,
Northeastern State University
Cheryl Greenberg,
University of North Carolina–Greensboro
Laurie Hanich,
Millersville University
Lillian Hawkins,
Miami University
Joyce Hemphill,
University of Wisconsin–Madison

Alice Herz,
Indiana University–Purdue
Shelly Hiatt,
Northwest Missouri State University
K. C. Holder,
Eastern Oregon University
David Holliway,
Marshall University
Steve Hoover,
St. Cloud State University
Sherri Horner,
Bowling Green State University
John Hummel,
Valdosta State University
Brenda Hurbanis,
Anne Arundel Community College
Jenefer Husman,
Arizona State University–Tempe
Karen Huxtable-Jester,
University of Texas–Dallas
Young Hwang,
*California State University–
San Bernardino*
Brent Igo,
Clemson University
Joyce Juntune,
Texas A&M University
Thomas Kampwirth,
California State University–Long Beach
Douglas Kauffman,
University of Oklahoma–Norman
Frank Keane,
Fayetteville State University
Kurt Kowalski,
*California State University–
San Bernardino*
Brad Kuhlman,
St. Cloud State University
Patricia Lanzon,
Henry Ford Community College
Sandra Lloyd,
University of Texas–El Paso
Edward Lonky,
SUNY–Oswego
Susan Losh,
Florida State University
Anna Lowe,
Loyola University–Chicago
Pamela Manners,
Troy State University
Eric Mansfield,
Western Illinois University
David Matrone,
Central Michigan University
Nancy McBride,
University of Nevada–Reno

Catherine McCartney,
Bemidji State University

Rita McKenzie,
Buena Vista University

Sharon McNeely,
Northeastern Illinois University

Alice H. Merz,
Indiana University-Purdue University–Fort Wayne

P. Karen Murphy,
The Pennsylvania State University–University Park

Vicki Napper,
Weber State University

Ruth Nash-Thompson,
Edinboro University of Pennsylvania

Judi Neufeld,
Lander University

Joe Nichols,
Indiana University-Purdue University–Fort Wayne

Cynthia Northington,
William Paterson University

Christine Nucci,
Florida Memorial College

James O'Kelly,
Rutgers University

Beth Otto,
University of Southern Indiana

Ann Pace,
University of Missouri–Kansas City

Susan Parault,
St. Cloud State University

Ann Pardi,
SUNY—Buffalo

Helen Patrick,
Purdue University–West Lafayette

James Persinger,
Emporia State University

Connie Phelps,
Emporia State University

Evan Powell,
University of Georgia

Judith Puncochar,
University of Minnesota

Shelley Randall,
Bloomsburg University of Pennsylvania

Melinda Ratchford,
Belmont Abbey College

Aaron Richmond,
University of Nevada–Reno

Bambi Riley,
Midwestern State University

Lawrence Rogien,
Boise State University

Paul Rooney,
University of California–Davis

Jeff Sandoz,
University of Louisiana–Lafayette

Gene Schwarting,
Fontbonne University

Ray Scolavino,
University of Wisconsin–Milwaukee

Mary Seaborn,
Indiana Wesleyan University

Marvin Seperson,
Nova Southeastern University

Lawrence Sidlik,
Arizona State University–West

Audrey Skrupskelis,
University of South Carolina–Aiken

Bruce Smith,
Henderson State University

Delany Smith,
Freed-Hardeman University

Robert Sorrells,
Central Washington University

Rayne Sperling,
The Pennsylvania State University

Ken Springer,
Southern Methodist University

Hillary Steiner,
Florida State University

Sapna Taggar,
University of Michigan–Flint

Mary Tallent-Runnels,
Texas Tech University

Kellie Tanner,
Northern Arizona University

Juli Taylor,
University of Wisconsin–Stout

Jennifer L. Titus,
Tarleton State University

Y. I. Tomes,
Eastern Washington University

Michael Verdi,
California State University–San Bernardino

Craig Vivian,
Monmouth College

Brenda Walling,
East Central University

Jann Weitzel,
Lindenwood University

Nambrath Wesley,
Brookdale Community College

Tony Williams,
Marshall University

Sid Womack,
Arkansas Tech University

Jamie Wood,
Pittsburg State University

Martie Wynne,
Loyola University–Chicago

Ming Zhang,
Central Michigan University

Message Test Reviewers

Nancy Adams,
Marshalltown Community College

Alison Barton,
East Tennessee State University

Roger Bass,
Carthage College

Dave Bellini,
Case Western Reserve

Eric Buhs,
University of Nebraska

Don Burwell,
Albertson College

Michael Carr,
Atlantic Cape Community College

Carrie Cate-Cements,
Northwest Indiana Education Service Center

Steve Cockerham,
East Tennessee State University

Elizabeth DeGiorgio,
Mercer County Community College

Darlene Demarie,
University of South Florida–Tampa

Marylee Demeter,
Rutgers University

Mike Desiderio,
Texas A&M Kingsville

Thomas Doyle,
National University

Karen Dreyer,
University of Pittsburgh

Jody Eberly,
The College of New Jersey

Susan Edwards,
Mott Community College

Stewart Ehly,
University of Iowa

Howard Epstein,
Miami University–Hamilton

Julie Evey,
University of Southern Indiana

Beverly Faircloth,
University of North Carolina–Greensboro

Lisa Fiore,
Lesley University

Susan Foltz,
Shippensburg University

Connie Geier,
Northern State University

Richard Hartman,
Loma Linda University

Samuel Heastie,
  Fayetteville State University
Jan Heinitz,
  Concordia University–Wisconsin
Arthur Hernandez,
  University of Texas at San Antonio
Debra Herrera,
  Cisco Junior College
Susan Hersh,
  Otterbein College
Trista Huckleberry,
  University of Washington–Tacoma
Katrina Hunter,
  University of North Alabama
Mona Ibrahim,
  Concordia College
May James,
  Oklahoma State University
Todd Johnson,
  Washington State University
Craig Jones,
  Arkansas State University
Phyllis Jones,
  Laramie County Community College
Pat Keig,
  California State University–Fullerton
Inna Khramtsova,
  Arkansas State University
Jackie Kibler,
  Northwest Missouri State University
Martha King,
  University of West Alabama
David Knowlton,
  Southern Illinois University–
  Edwardsville
Helene Kogos,
  Northeastern University
Brian Leavell,
  Texas Woman's University
Judith Levine,
  Farmington State College
Janet Losser,
  Brigham Young University
Danielle Lusk,
  Virginia Tech University
Angia Macomber,
  Taylor University
Laura Manuel,
  Metropolitan State College
Grace McDaniel,
  Otterbein College
Patricia McElhone,
  St. John's River Community College

Cristal McGill,
  Arizona State University
Shannon McNair,
  Oakland University
Kristen Missall,
  University of Kentucky
Connie Moss,
  Duquesne University
Richard NeSmith,
  North Greenville University
Kristie Neurmeister,
  Ball State University
John Nietfeld,
  North Carolina State University
John Nixon,
  SUNY–Potsdam
Gina Pannozzo,
  Virginia Commonwealth University
Roy Pellicano,
  St. Joseph's College
Lyda Peters,
  Cambridge College
Rebecca Peters,
  Aquina College
Sarah Peterson,
  Duquesne University
Donna Plummer,
  Centre College
Sarah Anne Polasky,
  Arizona State University
Steven Pulos,
  University of Northern Colorado
Diane Raines,
  Roane State Community College
David Rapp,
  Northwestern University
Chris Ray,
  Oklahoma State University
Tamara Richardson,
  Monmouth University
Anne Rinn,
  Western Kentucky University
Jay Samuels,
  University of Minnesota
James Schreiber,
  Duquesne University
Merryellen Schulz,
  College of Saint Mary
David Shannon,
  Auburn University
Bruce Shields,
  Daemen College
Christopher Sink,
  Seattle Pacific University

Patricia Slocum,
  College of Dupage
Emily Smith,
  Fairfield University
Louis Smith,
  The University of West Alabama
Lacey Southerland,
  Atlanta Christian College
Sue Spitzer,
  California State University–San
  Bernardino
Penee Stewart,
  Weber State University
Darrell Stolle,
  University of Montana
Gwen Stowers,
  National University
Mary Ann Swiatek,
  Lafayette Colelge
Debi Switzer,
  Clemson University
Pat Terry,
  Emporia State University
Timothy Van Soelen,
  Dordt College
Doreen Vieitez,
  Joliet Junior College
Rita Weinberg,
  National-Louis University
Reta Whitlock,
  Kennesaw State University
Amanda Williams,
  Texas Tech University
Louise Wine,
  Hagerstown Community College
Steve Wininger,
  Western Kentucky University
Faye Wisner,
  Florida Community College at
  Jacksonville
Robert Wright,
  Widener University
Aaron Yarlas,
  Grand Valley State University
Ellie Young,
  Brigham Young University
Linda Young,
  Brenau University
Laurene Ziegler,
  Finlandia University
Leslie Zorko,
  University of Wyoming

We would first like to thank all the students and teachers from whom we have learned so much over the years. Their insights and concerns have been important to us as we wrote this text.

As the authors of *Educational Psychology: Reflection for Action*, we would like to acknowledge that we are but part of a remarkable team of individuals responsible for the development of this work. The words are ours, but the enthusiasm and dedication for the project, along with endless hours of editing, rewriting, reviewing, revising, and designing are shared with our colleagues at John Wiley and Sons. This has been a true collaboration from the very beginning, and we want to acknowledge our heartfelt gratitude to our friends at Wiley for their professionalism, encouragement, good humor, expertise, and willingness to nudge when necessary. We could not have asked for a better group of people to work with on this endeavor.

The book began with Brad Hanson, who was dedicated to the notion that a text written by scholars in three key areas of educational psychology would provide a new and exciting perspective. His boundless enthusiasm and energy were contagious, and we agreed to venture forth. At every point, Brad was there for us—with encouragement, ideas, and good cheer. His belief in us as an author team exceeded our own.

Optimism was the spirit throughout the Wiley organization. We received great encouragement and support throughout from Debbie Wiley, Bonnie Lieberman, Joe Heider, Anne Smith, and Barbara Heaney. During the development of the book, Jay O'Callaghan and Christopher Johnson stepped into leadership roles in the organization, and from the perspective of the author team, the transition was seamless. We are indebted to them for going out of their way to ensure that our efforts did not miss a beat.

Great ideas are only ideas unless they are realized. We feel we are truly privileged to have been able to work with Nancy Perry as our development editor. She knows this book better than we do. We could say that she is the "fourth author" of *Educational Psychology: Reflection for Action*. Nancy coordinated our efforts, attended to countless details, kept us on track and on schedule (not a simple task), and never lost sight of the vision for the book. At one of our meetings about halfway through our work, one of us said, "Wouldn't it be great if we could have Nancy with us on all of our work?" This book would not have been completed without her.

Sheralee Connors and Carolyn Smith not only provided meticulous editing of our chapters, they taught us much about how to write clearly and succinctly. The book is better and we are better writers because of their care throughout the editorial process.

For the second edition, Robert Johnston joined our team. Lucky for us, as Robert provided excellent organizational skills and focused the author team on the book's big picture. Robert stayed with us for the third edition, and his leadership proved instrumental in advancing the book's clarity and integration from one chapter to the next. If you are reading this as an eBook, you are doing so because of Robert's passion to deliver this book to readers in their preferred format.

We are very proud of the "look and feel" of *Educational Psychology: Reflection for Action*. For that, we thank Harry Nolan and his remarkable design team. Lisa Gee and Hillary Newman have blended creativity with relentlessness at finding great photographs to bring our abstract ideas to classroom life. Sandra Rigby found just the right style for our illustrations and supervised the artists with care. Madelyn Lesure designed a thoughtful and beautiful cover, and Valerie Vargas has done an excellent job in realizing the layout and design of the book. Suzanne Ingrao put this edition together for us and, in doing so, gave the book a better and more inviting look.

Since the beginning of our efforts, we have been dedicated to the notion that this book helps the people who teach educational psychology and the people who learn it. That requires not only our own ideas about educational psychology, but those of our colleagues in the field. Jeffrey Rucker, Danielle Torio-Hagey, and Lynn Pearlman have been exceptionally helpful in bringing the concerns of faculty and students to us and providing us with invaluable feedback from the field on our efforts.

One of the truly outstanding features of working with John Wiley and Sons is the commitment to follow through on details that permeates the organization. We have had the good fortune to work with Mariah Maguire-Fong and Maura Gilligan in our day-to-day interactions and found them to be conscientious, professional, and unfailingly responsive. It's been a pleasure to get to know these talented young people who are on their way to great careers in publishing.

We would like to thank Miranda D'Amico and Richard Schmid of Concordia University for their contribution to the new chapter on diversity. Their insight and perspectives on the topic were invaluable to us as we worked on this edition.

In addition, we'd like to thank Lisa Smith for her advice, support, and encouragement. Her insights on teaching undergraduates and faith in us as a group are greatly appreciated. Thanks to Leah Smith, Kaitlin Wolf, and Benjamin Smith for providing us with a rich source of anecdotes and experiences to draw upon.

We'd also like to thank our dear friend and colleague James O'Kelly for his contributions to our work all along the journey. He not only contributed scholarly material as well as anecdotes about 5 year olds; he provided verisimilitude and reality checks, and occasionally we called on him for counselling and general wisdom. Jim is a great educator and a great friend.

A wonderful group of teachers helped us in the development of one of the key elements of the book, the RIDE component. Some of these teachers also provided example responses to the scenarios presented at the end of each chapter for students to engage in further practice. Many thanks to Stephanie D'Andrea, Tyler W. Post, Shannon Neville, Michael Lawrence, Gayle Wargo, Barbara Goldko, Deborah Kris, Megan Schramm-Possinger, and Debra Brock. Nicole diDonato did a great job on helping coordinate material with regard to Praxis and INTASC standards. In addition we would like to thank the following teachers for their contributions of lesson plans that appear in this edition: Christine Cook, Amy Noack, Nicole Procaccio, and Carrie Tupa.

Lastly, we thank all the preservice teachers who have read and used the book. While this book reflects the work of the author team, we know that you live its content every day in the classroom. We deeply appreciate and respect all the service you will soon provide to the education of our children and adolescents.

Brief Contents

Contents

There is an old saying, "I wish I knew then what I know now." For a beginning teacher, that saying might be rephrased, "I wish I knew in my first year of teaching what I know now in my second year." Such knowledge would be both valuable and reassuring. While it is impossible to sit down and have a cup of coffee with your future self, you can do the next best thing—namely, sit down and chat with a group of second- and third-year teachers.

Statements	Mean
1. I continuously develop as a teacher.	4.48
2. Generally, I enjoy being with my pupils.	4.33
3. We have a good collegial atmosphere in school.	4.32
4. I experience my job as meaningful.	4.31
5. I feel that teaching offers positive challenges.	4.15
6. I enjoy being a teacher.	4.12
7. I am satisfied with my choice of profession.	4.07
8. I am independent in my work as a teacher.	4.02
9. I experience that I influence my pupils.	3.98
10. Generally, I feel I have too much work compared to the time available.	3.88
11. I feel competent in my work as a teacher.	3.87
12. I struggle with unmotivated pupils.	3.41
13. I experience the teaching profession as being too demanding.	2.95
14. I am uncertain about my choice of profession.	2.10

A group of 137 second- and third-year teachers were presented with the list of statements about their teaching shown above and asked if they agreed with each statement (from Roness, 2011). They used a 5-point scale where 1 = *do not agree* to 5 = *strongly agree*. As you glance through the numbers to the right of each statement, you can hear what these teachers have learned. The tone is generally positive, as most teachers said that they felt good about the progress they were making in developing themselves as a teacher, that they enjoyed being with their students, and that they enjoyed their colleagues (statements 1–3). At the same time, the teachers agreed that they had too much to do, that they struggled with unmotivated students, and that—for some—the profession was too demanding (statements 10, 12, and 13).

Introducing Educational Psychology and Reflective Teaching

Guiding Questions

- What is educational psychology?
- What is critical thinking, and how does it contribute to reflective thinking?
- How do educational psychologists use theory and research?
- Which research methods are popular in educational psychology, and what is the purpose of each?
- How can teachers and researchers alike narrow the gap between theory and practice?
- What is reflective teaching, and how does one become a more reflective teacher?

CHAPTER OVERVIEW

The chapter begins by defining educational psychology and by communicating its two objectives: to understand learners and to foster learning. It then introduces the twin tools of the field—theory and research. That is, as a profession, what educational psychology does is build theories to explain educational phenomena and conduct research to test the validity of those theories. The chapter then overviews (with examples) the following four widely used research methods: descriptive research, correlational research, experimental research, and action research. Educational psychologists also work collaboratively with classroom teachers to improve the quality of instruction. The chapter recognizes that all too often a gap exists between what educational psychologists do and value (research) and what classroom teachers do and value (teach), so we explain ways to link theory to practice and practice to theory. The chapter concludes with a focus on reflective teaching. We introduce a model of reflective teaching (the RIDE model) with the goal of providing the reader with a conceptual framework he or she can use throughout the book to develop skills in reflective thinking and reflective teaching.

Educational Psychology
- Critical Thinking and Reflective Teaching
- Educational Psychology as a Scientific Field of Study
- A Focus on Learning

Theories and Research
- What Is a Theory?
- Linking Theory to Practice
- Research Methods

Narrowing the Gap between Theory and Practice

Reflective Teaching
- Levels of Reflection
- Reflection for Action
- A Model of Reflective Teaching: RIDE

Educational Psychology

Welcome to the study of educational psychology. This is a journey that promises you two things and requires another. First, the journey promises to introduce you to a deeply interesting subject matter. Educational psychology concerns all aspects of the teaching–learning process, so what you will find in the pages to come are discussions about what teachers do, how students learn, and how teachers can help students learn. Second, the journey promises to help you ready yourself to become an effective teacher. Educational psychology is an immensely practical field of study. The pages to come will prepare you for the classroom challenges and opportunities to come, introduce a wide range of instructional strategies, explain why some approaches to instruction are more effective than others, and offer recommendations on how to enrich the thousands of student–teacher interactions that lie in your future.

Overall, this book is about how students learn and how teachers can help them learn. It seeks to deepen your understanding of all aspects of the teaching–learning process and, in doing so, improve your capacity to help students learn by pursuing two objectives:

1. To understand learners. As you proceed through this book, you will gain knowledge about learners and how they learn.

2. To foster learning. This book seeks to enhance your understanding of the teaching–learning situation and, hence, your capacity to help others learn.

While the study of educational psychology offers you an interesting and practical subject matter, it also asks something of you in return—namely, critical thinking and active reflection.

Critical Thinking and Reflective Teaching

Critical thinking involves an objective analysis of any claim to determine its accuracy, validity, or worth (Beyer, 1988). It means being able to tell fact from opinion, to see holes in an argument, to spot illogic, to evaluate evidence, and to tell whether or not cause and effect have been established. In practice, critical thinking is your defense against a world of too much information and too many people trying to convince you of one thing or another (Epstein, 2006).

The best way to discuss critical thinking is to talk first about uncritical thinking. To the uncritical mind, what people say, do, and experience is accepted without question. The uncritical mind often wants to believe something is true and looks only for evidence that confirms what the person believes (while ignoring any disconfirming evidence). To the critical mind, however, claims about what works in education need to be evaluated and the evidence examined. Consider three claims often made about effective practice:

- The smaller the class size, the more students learn.
- The more homework students complete, the more they learn.
- Girls learn more in same-sex classes than they do in mixed-sex classes.

Are all these statements true? Are only some of them true? Are none of them true? The role of research is to ask (and answer) the question: Does this claim have support? Is there enough evidence to back it up and accept it as a generally true statement?

The search for answers to questions about teaching and learning often start with common sense. Common sense is then typically supplemented by personal experience. For instance, the claim that students learn more in small classes is consistent with common sense. Personal experience can supplement the analysis that this is a true statement as the teacher reflects on whether her own class size numbers have been an important influence on her students' learning. Teachers can further discuss the accuracy of this claim with colleagues, mentors, and master teachers. These are all helpful sources of information, but they all share the same shortcoming: They are all opinions—they are all *subjective* ways of knowing.

Educational psychology is a scientific field of study created to provide objective, data-based evidence from research studies carefully designed to understand a phenomenon or answer a particular question. In adding objective research findings to supplement subjective ways of thinking, the teacher increases her capacity for critical thinking.

This increased capacity for critical thinking occurs because research relies on the kind of thinking involved in weighing evidence, considering alternative explanations, and making informed decisions (i.e., critical thinking; Halpern, 2003).

Returning to the class size claim, it is appropriate to ask what research can add to what a teacher already knows from common sense, personal experience, and conversations with trusted colleagues. Suppose that these sources suggest that, yes, smaller classes support higher achievement, and they do so because teachers individualize their approach to instruction in small classes to a greater degree than they do in large classes. Classes become more personalized and teachers spend more one-on-one time with students. The problem with this explanation, however, is that it does not seem to be true. Teachers generally do *not* change their teaching styles when moving from larger to smaller classes (Bohrnstedt, Stecher, & Wiley, 2000; Molnar, Smith, & Zahorik, 2000). Instead, as class size decreases, it is the students rather than the teachers that change. As class size decreases, student engagement increases. In small classes, students are more attentive, they participate more, they show greater initiative and effort, they are more likely to follow rules, they interact constructively with the teacher, they collaborate more with peers, and they engage in less disruptive behavior. Hence, greater student engagement explains why smaller classes yield higher achievement (Finn, Pannozzo, & Achilles, 2003). Such a research finding does not contradict teachers' common sense, personal experience, and peer discussions; rather, it adds to them. It does so by holding a subjective way of knowing up to the light of critical thinking to ask: Are you sure?

When put to objective test (as through research), personal experience is sometimes confirmed, sometimes challenged, and sometimes outright contradicted and rejected. It is always, however, enriched. Even the teacher who "already knows" that smaller class size benefits students can walk away from a research report on class size with new insights and a deeper understanding of *why* small class size produces benefits. The Uncommon Sense box on the next page provides a second illustration of the benefits of critical thinking.

critical thinking Critical thinking is the process of telling fact from opinion, seeing holes in an argument, spotting illogic, evaluating evidence, and telling whether or not cause and effect have been established.

Uncommon Sense

Music Training Produces Math Whiz Kids—Or Does It?

Math whiz kids are often gifted musicians. Just as Einstein played the violin, excellence in music seems to pave the way to excellence in math. Before we enroll all our children in music lessons, however, it is worth asking whether research confirms or contradicts this conclusion.

When researchers look at scores on achievement tests, they find that students with musical training do tend to score higher in math than do students without musical training (Cheek & Smith, 1999). But correlation means association, not causation. For causation, we need to dig deeper. We need an experiment. One experiment randomly assigned some children to take piano lessons for 36 weeks, and a control group of similar children took (nonmusical) drama lessons (Schellenberg, 2004). The children who took piano lessons did not score significantly higher on later math achievement tests than did children in the control group.

What can we conclude? Personal experience, Einstein anecdotes, and correlational data suggest a relationship between music and math. But experimental studies do not. When thinking critically, the conclusion seems to be that although the two variables are related, they are not causally related. Instead, they seem to grow out of other shared variables, such as parental support, high expectations, general intelligence, or a love of all things school-related. To nurture math whiz kids, educators do not need to provide music lessons so much as they need to encourage parental support, high expectations, general intelligence, and appreciation for school-related activities.

Developing your capacity for critical thinking is important for many reasons. It gives you the ability to reach sound conclusions based on observations, information, and evidence (Paul, 1988). Reaching sound conclusions is very important, but developing your capacity for critical thinking does more; it helps you develop what this book argues is your most important skill, capacity, and asset as an effective teacher—namely, to think reflectively and to become a reflective teacher.

reflective thinking Questioning why a surprising or negative outcome occurred and then searching for the information one needs to confidently understand why it occurred.

Educational pioneer John Dewey (1933) proposed that **reflective thinking** "involves (1) a state of doubt, hesitation, perplexity, mental difficulty, in which thinking originates, and (2) an act of searching, hunting, inquiring to find materials that will resolve the doubt, settle and dispose of perplexity (p-12)." This quotation makes it clear that developing reflective thinking and becoming a reflective teacher are intellectual struggles that are greatly aided by the following three skills:

- Determining if a conclusion follows logically from the given information or evidence
- Interpreting whether or not a conclusion is warranted or true
- Evaluating an argument as being strong and relevant or weak and irrelevant

These are the skills of critical thinking. In critical thinking, one is exposed to some argument, some conclusion, or some policy decision and is asked to judge if it is true, valid, and accurate. Reflective thinking is simply the application of such critical thinking to one's own unique teaching situation. In reflective thinking, instead of being presented with an argument, conclusion, or policy decision, the teacher is presented with a surprising or negative classroom event. For example, during the normal flow of instruction, the teacher observes that:

- Unexpectedly, this year's students do not respond to a lesson the same way that last year's students responded to it.
- Unexpectedly, your students respond negatively to a classroom event to which you expected them to respond positively.
- Students surprisingly struggle to understand or make sense of a type of math problem you thought they had already mastered.
- Students surprisingly fail to use the basic writing skills they were taught.

In all of these examples, the teacher first experiences what Dewey described as "a state of doubt, hesitation, perplexity, mental difficulty, in which thinking originates" that then leads them to initiate "an act of searching, hunting, inquiring to find materials that will resolve the doubt, settle and dispose of perplexity." This act of searching, hunting, and inquiring to understand why the surprising event occurred and to generate a new, more productive approach to teaching during the next lesson is reflective teaching—teaching in which one questions what went wrong, gathers the information needed to remedy the not-so-effective instruction, and then creates new instruction that can better produce a positive change in the classroom. The last section in this opening chapter will present an extended discussion on what reflective teaching is, how to do it, and why it is so important to professional development and effective classroom teaching.

Educational Psychology as a Scientific Field of Study

Educational psychology came into existence as a field of study through the writings of early psychologists, including Edward Thorndike (1903, 1910, 1913), William James (1912), John Dewey (1910), and others. These pioneers showed how psychological theories, such as the early learning theories, applied to educational settings (Berliner, 2006). The field has grown dramatically in its 100 years, but **educational psychology** remains "the scientific study of psychology in education" (Wittrock, 1992, p. 129).

educational psychology The scientific study of psychology in education.

Contemporary educational psychology has a twofold mission: Enhance theoretical knowledge and improve educational practice. Theoretical knowledge revolves around understanding basic psychological processes, such as how learning occurs, where aggression comes from, and what the nature of motivation is. To enhance their theoretical knowledge, educational psychologists ask many *Why?* questions, such as:

- Why do readers forget so much of what they read?
- Why are some adolescents unusually aggressive?
- Why are some teachers more effective than are other teachers?

Once educational psychologists understand the phenomenon with which they work—once they develop their theories of the nature of memory, aggression, and teaching effectiveness–they then turn to the practical mission of trying to improve educational practice. To improve practice, educational psychologists ask many *How?* questions, such as:

- How can teachers improve students' social skills?
- How can schools prevent teenagers from dropping out?
- How can teachers improve non-English-speaking students' reading abilities?

To gain satisfactory answers to these questions, educational psychologists apply scientifically based research methods to collect the data they need to yield evidence-based answers about how to improve classroom practice. We discuss these research methods in this chapter. We also offer an appendix in this book to help readers see how our discussion of educational psychology reflects PRAXIS™ content and INTASC (Interstate Teacher Assessment and Support Consortium) principles.

A Focus on Learning

The focus of educational psychology is learning (Renninger, 1996). **Learning** is a relatively permanent change in knowledge, skill, or behavior as a result of experience. This focus on learning might seem obvious, but it is actually rather complicated because learning depends on so many factors.

learning A relatively permanent change in knowledge, skill, or behavior as a result of experience.

Learning depends on the quality of instruction. It depends on students' motivation and how engaged students are when they try to learn. It also depends on students' developmental readiness to learn. Learning also occurs better under some conditions than under others. Once learning occurs, how do teachers know that students have learned—how can teachers assess learning to affirm that it has actually taken place? Addressing these issues not only requires a sophisticated understanding of learning itself; it further requires a sophisticated understanding of the multitude of factors that affect learning, including teaching, motivation, development, educational environments, and assessment. This book includes not only several chapters on learning but also separate chapters on each factor that influences learning. Overall, the payoff for one's effort in studying educational psychology is a better understanding of learning and how to promote it (Shuell, 1996).

Theories and Research

One benefit of studying educational psychology is that it can provide preservice teachers with a greater awareness of the principles that underlie learning. One principle, for instance, is that timely and accurate feedback is important for learning. Another is that students learn more cooperatively than they do individually. Another is that motivation is a prerequisite for learning. These principles—and others—do not just emerge from the minds of educational psychologists. Instead, they have deep intellectual roots, and the ground in which these principles grow consists of theory and research, the twin tools of educational psychology.

What Is a Theory?

Like all educators, educational psychologists spend a great deal of time observing and trying to understand how students learn and develop. To understand what they see, educational psychologists develop theories. Theories are created to explain phenomena. Theories are designed to explain how and why a specific phenomenon functions the way it does. The proposed theory may or may not be accurate, so the educational psychologist uses the theory to create a hypothesis, or prediction, about what should happen if the theory is valid. With a hypothesis in hand, researchers collect the data needed to evaluate the accuracy of the hypothesis. If the findings support the theory's hypothesis, researchers gain confidence in their theory.

theory An intellectual framework that organizes a vast amount of knowledge about a phenomenon so that educators can understand and better explain the nature of that phenomenon.

A **theory** is an intellectual framework that can be used to identify and explain the relations that exist among naturally occurring, observable phenomena (Fiske, 2004). One such naturally occurring phenomenon that educators struggle to understand is test anxiety. Figure 1.1 illustrates what a theory of test anxiety might look like. According to the theory depicted in this figure, test anxiety is a multidimensional experience that includes an emotional component (worry), a cognitive component (thoughts of failure), and a physiological component (e.g., heart rate acceleration). The theory further proposes that three classroom variables causally explain the rise and fall of students' test anxiety—time limits, high stakes, and external evaluation. The theory also posits that level of anxiety causally predicts students' test performance and test avoidance (e.g., "Can I write a paper instead of taking the test?"). Each arrow in the figure is important because it represents a separate hypothesis—a testable prediction—to determine the validity or accuracy of the theory.

By providing a better understanding of the nature of an educational phenomenon, the theory should help educators gain new insights that their day-to-day experience might not afford. For instance, much of the impetus behind the movement toward alternative assessment (e.g., using portfolios instead of multiple-choice tests to assess students' learning) comes from a deliberate effort to minimize the sort of anxiety-provoking testing conditions that appear on the left-hand side of the figure.

Consider a second example of a theory of student engagement. According to the theory represented in Figure 1.2, student engagement is a complex, multifaceted

Figure 1.1 A Sample Theory (of Test Anxiety)

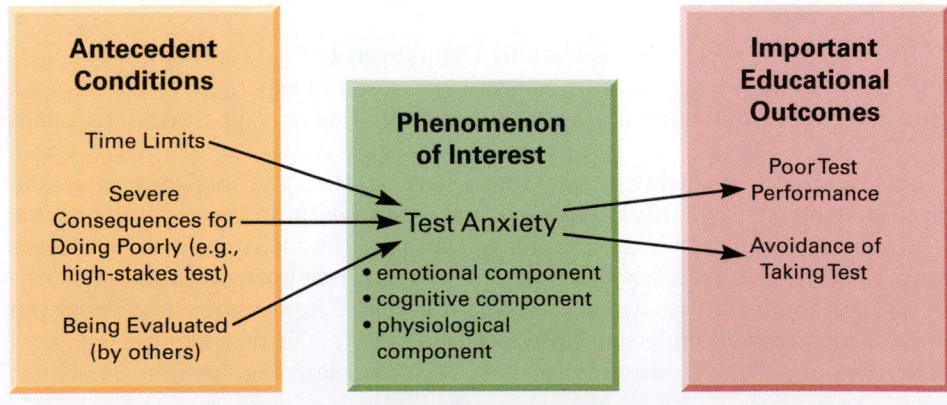

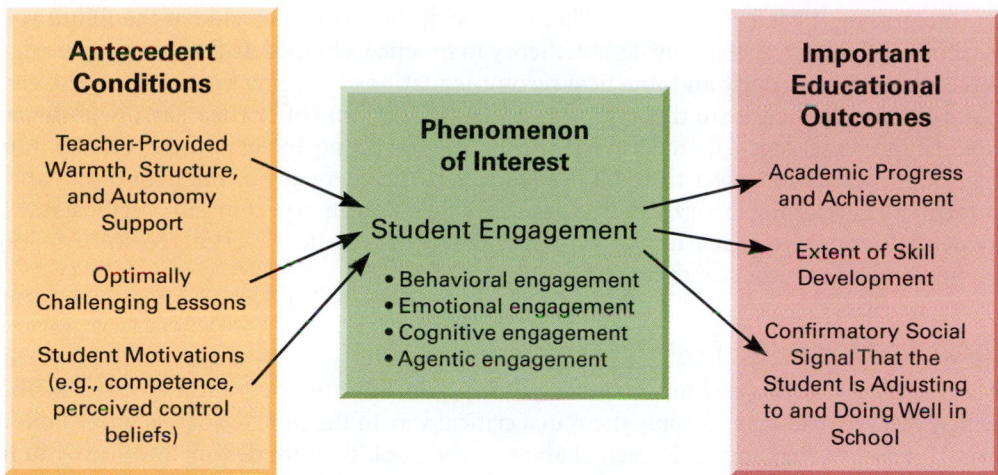

Figure 1.2 A Second Sample Theory (of Student Engagement)

phenomenon consisting of the four distinct yet interrelated aspects of behavioral engagement (concentration, effort), emotional engagement (high enjoyment, low anger), cognitive engagement (sophisticated learning strategies), and agentic engagement (actively contributing to one's own learning). The theory explains why educators care so much about student engagement in that it foreshadows and reliably predicts important educational outcomes such as academic progress, student achievement, and extent of skill development. It is further important because it functions as a confirmatory signal that the student is adjusting to and doing well in school. Further, the theory is very practical in that it addresses the question of from where student engagement and disengagement come. According to the theory represented in the figure, student engagement is a reaction to teacher-provided warmth, structure, and autonomy support; to optimally challenging lessons; and to student motivational resources such as perceived competence and personal control beliefs. It also explains that student disengagement is a reaction to teacher-provided neglect; chaos, and coercion; to lessons that are too easy or overly complicated; and to student motivational deficits such as a sense of helplessness. As with the test anxiety example, a theory of student engagement is well positioned to help educators gain new insights that their day-to-day experience might not afford. A teacher dissatisfied with her students' classroom engagement, for instance, has several attractive, reliable, and previously validated opportunities to enliven her students' engagement through the entries listed on the left-hand side of the figure.

> **How Can I Use This?**
>
> Can you use the information in Figure 1.1 or 1.2 to suggest one strategy a teacher might implement to decrease students' level of anxiety or to increase students' engagement during learning activities?

A good theory should offer recommendations that educators can use to solve classroom problems. In this spirit, Figure 1.3 illustrates the function and utility of any theory (Trope, 2004). Theories help educators understand a complex phenomenon ("Representation" in Figure 1.3), and validated theories are a fruitful ground to offer evidence-based strategies to improve classroom practice ("Practice" in Figure 1.3).

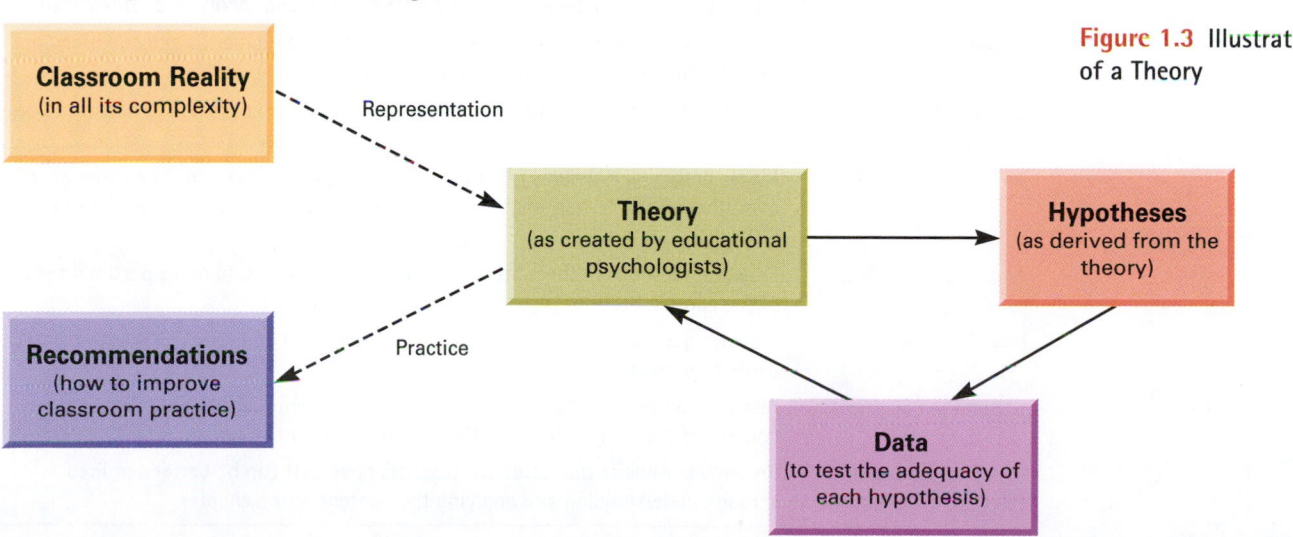

Figure 1.3 Illustration of a Theory

Integrating the left-hand side of Figure 1.3 with the right-hand side of the figure is important, as doing so enables one to link theory to practice. On the left-hand side of the figure are the classroom reality and practical recommendations (i.e., practice), and on the right-hand side of the figure are theory and research. Classrooms offer theorists phenomena to understand. Researchers then develop their theories by proposing hypotheses and by implementing research to collect the data needed to test the adequacy of the hypotheses and to inform the developing theory. At some point, the theorist can expect to gain a critical mass of evidential support to enable him or her to use the theory to offer practical recommendations on how to improve classroom practice.

Linking Theory to Practice

Many features of this text are intended to help you link the theoretical constructs about which you are reading and apply them in a critical way to the practice of teaching. Table 1.1 lists 10 features that appear in each chapter of the book that are designed to help you link theory and research findings with practical application to the classroom experience.

Research Methods

The means through which educational psychologists test, evaluate, and revise their theories is research. In conducting research, they use one or more of the following methods: descriptive studies, correlational studies, experimental studies, and action research.

Each different research method serves its own purpose, as summarized in Table 1.2. The purpose of descriptive research, for instance, is to describe some aspect of the classroom as it naturally occurs. The purpose of correlational research is to determine that a relation between two naturally occurring educational phenomena exists. The purpose of experimental research is to document that a cause-and-effect relation exists between two educational phenomena so as to allow for the possibility of making prescriptive recommendations about what to do as a teacher. And the purpose of action research is to better understand one's own classroom so as to produce a positive change in future instruction. To help communicate the

TABLE 1.1

Ten Features of the Book Designed to Help Link Research with Practical Classroom Applications

Feature	How the Feature Promotes the Relationship between Theory/Research and Practice
Reflection for Action (RIDE)	Provides a classroom scenario and invites you to analyze it through the critical application of the theoretical constructs emphasized in the chapter
Guiding Questions	Focuses your reading so you will be better prepared to apply theory
What Kids Say and Do	Gives students' quotes or actions to represent the practice that expresses a theoretical point in such a way that allows for practice and theory to be integrated
Uncommon Sense	Presents some commonly held beliefs about classroom practice and examines the research to determine whether there is support for the practice
Taking It to the Classroom	Provides theoretically and empirically grounded guidelines for classroom practice
Do You Know Jack?	Makes particular problems real by providing dilemmas that might be experienced by a student and invites you to use your best thinking to try to solve his or her difficulties
What Does This Mean to Me?	Provides questions in the margin that specifically ask you to make personal sense of the content
How Can I Use This?	Provides questions in the margin that specifically ask you how you might use the content in practice
Lesson Plan Segments	Allows practice at analyzing lesson plans (or segments) using the theoretical content of the chapter to make the link from theory to practice
Mindful Habits of Effective Teachers	Presents key habits that effective teachers have that can be better acquired through understanding and applying the content of the chapter

TABLE 1.2

The Purpose of Four Types of Research Methods

Research Method	Purpose, Basic Question, and Example
Descriptive research	*Purpose*: Describe some aspect of naturally occurring classroom practice.
	Basic question: What is happening?
	Example: What are the most common strategies teachers use to motivate and engage their students?
Correlational research	*Purpose*: Determine that a relation exists between two naturally occurring educational phenomena.
	Basic question: What events happen together?
	Example: Is there a meaningful relation between students' socioeconomic status and their school achievement?
Experimental research	*Purpose*: Document that a cause-and-effect relation exists between two educational phenomena.
	Basic question: What events cause other events to happen?
	Example: Does exposure to violent video games cause an increase in adolescents' peer aggression?
Action research	*Purpose*: Produce a positive change in one's own instruction and classroom community.
	Basic question: How can I improve my instruction?
	Example: How do my middle school science students actually use the textbook?

purpose underlying each research method, Table 1.2 also provides the basic question driving that research method (from Cooper, 2006) and an illustrative example of the kind of research question that each method is designed to answer.

Descriptive Studies **Descriptive studies** describe the educational situation as it naturally occurs. Their purpose is to describe the classroom experience and illustrate the way events typically unfold—what happens, how teachers teach, and how students learn and develop. The kinds of questions that researchers attempt to answer through descriptive research include the following:

- What readings strategies do third-grade students use?
- What do adolescents think the purpose of school is?
- What factors explain a highly successful school?

To answer these questions, researchers typically record what they observe in the classroom, then analyze those data in ways that describe what occurred. The researchers might visit the classroom and tally the frequency with which teachers engage in a particular behavior, as in the first research question above (Newby, 1991). Alternatively, researchers might conduct interviews. This interviewing strategy was used in answering the second research question above; researchers learned that the majority of adolescents think the purpose of school is to hang out with their friends (Bacon, 1993). To discover what factors explained a particularly successful African-American school, researchers asked students, "Please tell us in your own words why PSM is such a good school" (Pressley et al., 2004). Researchers then classified the diverse answers from 362 students into nine core factors, such as accountability for high grades, an emphasis on understanding during instruction, schoolwide efforts to motivate students, and selective retention of students that involved weeding out misbehaving students.

Consider an example of a descriptive research study. Researchers wanted to describe the processes of how the goal of becoming a teacher emerges (Schutz, Crowder, & White, 2001). To describe this process, they interviewed 49 preservice teachers, asking questions such as "What influenced you to want to become a teacher?" A summary of the biographical stories provided by five of the preservice teachers appears in Table 1.3. For instance, Molly was inspired to become a teacher through her admiration and respect for her elementary art teacher.

descriptive studies A research method used to describe the educational situation as it naturally occurs—what typically happens, how teachers teach, and how students learn and develop.

TABLE 1.3

Five Preservice Teachers' Explanations of Why They Decided to Become a Teacher

Participant, age	When did you decide?	Grade level and subject interest	What influenced you to want to become a teacher?
Molly, 22	Elementary school	Kindergarten to 12th-grade art	My elementary school art teacher was such an influence to me, I looked up to her as an artist and her ability to pass this to others.
Jane, 19	Elementary school	High school math	I don't know for sure except the fact that I've always liked to help others. When I was little I used to teach my two younger sisters everything I learned. I just like to learn and to teach others what I know.
James, 23	High school	High school history	I found that I liked working with kids. I liked teaching. My favorite players were those who couldn't play, I really enjoyed watching them progress. I enjoyed the fact that I helped them achieve something. I was proud of the player that the boys made fun of when he cleared the bases with a double at the end of the season. When I saw how good he felt about himself, it was then I decided I wanted to become a teacher.
Kerry, 20	High school	Elementary education	Being able to teach my own Sunday school class. I became aware that these children were the basis of our society. I felt that if I wanted them to learn things correctly, I had better teach them and do my part.
Ann, 21	College	Elementary education	I always thought about it, but I wasn't quite sure. I then took a career exploration class and did a field experience with my old third-grade teacher. The minute I walked in my old school, I knew I wanted to become a teacher.

Source: Schultz, P. A., Crowder, K. C., & White, V. E. (2001). The development of a goal to become a teacher. *Journal of Educational Psychology*, 93, 291–308. Copyright © 2001 by the American Psychological Association. Reprinted with permission.

What Does This Mean to Me?

Why do you want to become a teacher? When did you make this decision?

Descriptive research often identifies patterns in participants' behavior or experience. In the study just described, researchers heard 49 different stories, but they were able to identify half a dozen recurring themes that explained how the goal of becoming a teacher emerges (with a brief description and the percentage of teachers nominating each):

Altruism	They desire to help society and children (20%).
Past experiences	Early teaching activity stimulated their interest (19%).
Past teachers	A teaching role model encouraged them to teach (18%).
Personal characteristics	They had the personal characteristics of a teacher (13%).
Parents or family	A family member encouraged them to teach (10%).
Love of children	They wanted to be around children (7%).

Based on their analysis of what these preservice teachers told them, the researchers continued to try to extract meaning from the interviews. In doing so, they uncovered a three-step process that most teachers-to-be go through. First, the person was exposed to a teaching-type experience, as through one-on-one tutoring or teaching Sunday school. Second, the teacher-to-be experienced a positive critical incident—a moving and meaningful experience—during that early teaching encounter. Finally, the teacher-to-be translated this positive critical event into the conscious intention to become a professional teacher.

Descriptive research is sometimes qualitative in nature (Strauss & Corbin, 1998). The term *qualitative* is used to contrast this type of research to *quantitative* research. Data expressed in narrative is qualitative; data expressed in numbers is quantitative. So, when you see a research study that relies on quotations (e.g., what students said word-by-word during an interview, what teachers wrote word-by-word in a journal), it is very likely to be a qualitative study. When you see a research study that relies on numbers (e.g., means, figures, statistical tests to determine group differences), it is very likely to be a quantitative study. In the conduct of **qualitative research**, the researcher embodies herself or himself into the environment of the research, as when a researcher follows a group of English language learners to every one of their language classes for a full academic year to take notes of what happens and to conduct face-to-face interviews after class or perhaps during the lunch hour. Qualitative research observes an educational phenomenon in detail, and the narrative descriptions that

qualitative research A research method in which the researcher collects narrative-based data, such as quotations from interviews, to understand an educational phenomenon or to answer a practical question.

emerge (e.g., quotations) allow researchers to identify the salient issues within that particular educational setting. The types of research questions that are pursued are very often open-ended (rather than hypothesis-driven) questions, such as "What happens when an autistic child is introduced to a regular classroom?" The answer is then determined qualitatively by recording and making sense of quotations provided by the teacher, the trained aide who accompanies the autistic child, and the students in the class.

Correlational Studies **Correlational studies** measure separate variables and summarize in numerical form the nature of the relationship that exists between them. The purpose of correlational research is to articulate the nature and magnitude of the relationship between two naturally occurring variables. The sorts of questions that researchers attempt to answer through correlational research include the following:

- What is the relationship between hours of homework and extent of achievement?
- What is the relationship between class size and student achievement?
- Do bullies have low self-esteem?

Correlational studies begin by measuring the two variables of interest. That is, researchers find ways to measure variables such as bullying and self-esteem. Using these numbers, they calculate the relationship between two variables, which is summarized by a number called the *correlation coefficient*.

The **correlation coefficient** (denoted by the letter *r*) is a statistical value that describes both the *direction* and the *magnitude* of the relationship between two variables. Correlation coefficients can range between −1 and +1. The sign (− or +) before the number indicates the direction of the relationship. A relationship between variables can be positive or negative, or there may be no relationship at all. For example, if students' achievement increases as they increase their hours of homework, the relationship is positive, and the value of *r* will be some positive number between 0 and +1, depending on the strength of the relationship between homework and achievement. If student achievement decreases as class size increases, the relationship is negative, and the value of *r* will be some negative number between 0 and −1, depending on the strength of the inverse relationship between class size and achievement. Finally, the relationship between two variables can be nonexistent; that is, the value of one variable predicts nothing about the value of the second variable. For example, if knowing a student's level of self-esteem tells you nothing about how much of a bully he or she is, there is no relationship between the two variables, and the correlation coefficient will be near zero (*r* = 0).

The absolute value of the number in the correlation coefficient, regardless of whether it is positive or negative, reveals the magnitude, or strength, of the relationship. Values closer to either +1 or −1 indicate strong relationships; they mean that changes in one variable are highly related to changes in the other. Values close to zero indicate weak relationships; they mean that changes in one variable are unrelated to changes in the other.

Consider an example of a correlational research study. Researchers wondered which variables affect students' mathematical proficiency (Byrnes, 2003). They asked nearly 10,000 high school seniors to complete a mathematics test covering geometry, statistics, and algebra. They also asked students about the seven variables listed in Table 1.4. Then they calculated correlation coefficients to summarize the relationship between math proficiency—as measured by each student's score on the math test—and each of the seven variables. As shown in the table, each of the first five variables showed a positive correlation with math proficiency. Notice that some variables (e.g., algebra courses taken) had a stronger positive relationship with math proficiency (as denoted by the higher *r* value) than did other variables (e.g., extent of calculator usage). The sixth variable—relevance of math—showed practically no relationship to math proficiency (*r* is near zero). The seventh variable—math is fact learning—showed a negative correlation, because the more that students thought math was about memorizing facts and formulas, the lower they scored on the proficiency test.

The insights gained from this correlational study can help educators think about possible intervention efforts to boost math proficiency. However, it is important to note that correlational studies show only that two variables are related to each other. They stop short of

correlational studies A research method used to measure two naturally occurring variables and summarize the nature and magnitude of their relationship in numerical form.

correlation coefficient A statistical value that ranges from −1 to +1 to describe both the direction and extent of the relationship between two variables.

TABLE 1.4

Correlations between Math Achievement and Seven Educational Variables

Educational Variable	Correlation with Twelfth–Grade Math Achievement $r(N = 9,499)$
Algebra courses taken Number of courses taken in algebra and calculus	.58*
Geometry courses taken Number of courses taken in geometry and trigonometry	.51*
Extent of homework Number of pages of math homework completed each day	.25*
Calculator usage "How often do you use a calculator?"	.30*
Liking of math Agreement with "I like math"	.37*
Relevance of math Agreement with "Math is useful for solving everyday problems"	.03
Math is fact learning Agreement with "Math is mostly memorizing facts"	−.36*

*$p < .05$.

Source: Adapted from Byrnes, J. P. (2003). Factors predictive of mathematics achievement in White, Black, and Hispanic 12th graders. *Journal of Educational Psychology, 95,* 316–326. Copyright © 2003 by the American Psychological Association.

showing that changes in one variable will lead to a subsequent change in the other. Correlation identifies a relationship, but it does not establish a *causal* relationship. From the data in Table 1.4, we cannot conclude that taking more algebra courses will lead to gains in students' math proficiency. The causal inference is not warranted because high math proficiency might very well cause the student to take more algebra courses. Or some other variable—such as having excellent mathematics teachers—might cause high scores on both variables. Another way to think about correlation and causality is to realize that the winter's cold does not cause the flu, because it is a third variable—the spread of germs from being indoors so much—that actually causes the flu. To address the issue of causality, another type of research method is required—the experiment, which we discuss shortly.

model testing A correlation-based research method in which an entire system of variables included in a theoretical model are intercorrelated and presented pictorially to show the big picture of how all the variables relate to one another.

A sophisticated form of correlational research is **model testing**. Often researchers are not so much interested in the association that one variable might have with a second variable (as in Table 1.4) as they are in the association among all the variables included in a theoretical model. When researchers make predictions of how multiple variables will correlate with one another and when they conduct a correlational analysis of how the entire system of variables intercorrelated simultaneously with one another, they engage in model testing. Model testing is also almost always presented pictorially in an easy-to-understand diagram or figure (recall Figures 1.1 and 1.2). As an example, consider the study depicted in Figure 1.4, which shows how kindergarten students' television viewing was associated with their reading abilities four years later (Ennemoser & Schneider, 2007). To conduct the study, the researchers measured five variables from kindergarten-aged students—socioeconomic status (SES), intelligence (IQ), hours of watching entertainment television (entertainment TV), phonological awareness (a measure of reading readiness), and reading ability three years later (third-grade reading ability). As shown in the figure, SES and IQ were negatively correlated. SES was also negatively correlated with entertainment TV (the higher the children's SES, the fewer hours of entertainment television they watched per week), but SES was positively correlated with phonological awareness (the higher the children's SES, the higher their reading readiness). Most importantly for the study, entertainment TV was correlated negatively with later reading ability, which means that the more hours of television the children watched per week when they were in kindergarten, the lower their reading ability was in the third grade. The important point about Figure 1.4 is that it shows an overall theoretical model designed to explain how five variables of interest all relate to one another. In doing so, a pattern (model) emerges to explain how all the included variables interrelate in the big picture.

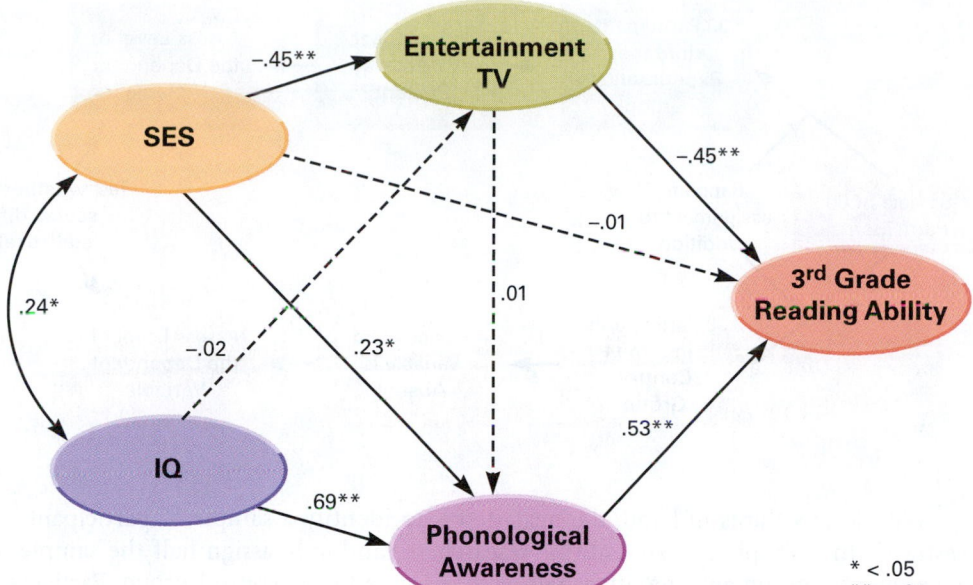

Figure 1.4 Illustration of Model Testing

Source: Ennemoser, M., & Schneider, W. (2007). Relations reading: Findings from a 4–year longitudinal study. *Journal of Educational Psychology,* 99, 349–368. Copyright © 2007 by the American Psychological Association.

Experimental Studies   It is only through **experimental studies** that researchers can obtain the data they need to infer a cause-and-effect relationship between two variables. The unique value of experimental research is that it puts the researcher in a position to make prescriptive statements that if one action is taken, then a particular outcome will occur (Shaw et al., 2010). Such prescriptive statements are offered as *if–then* statements, as in "If students invest hours in deliberate practice, then they will develop greater talent in that domain."

In an experiment, researchers distinguish between two types of variables: independent and dependent. *Independent variables* are hypothesized to cause the change in the dependent variables. The researchers manipulate the independent variable, meaning that they purposely create controlled changes in it. When understood in terms of the aforementioned *if–then* statement, the independent variable is the *if* while the dependent variable is the *then*. For instance, researchers might expose one group of elementary-aged students to instruction on a particular reading strategy while simultaneously not providing exposure to the reading strategy to another group of elementary-aged students (i.e., the researchers would have control over which students did and which students did not receive the reading strategy, which is the independent variable). Once the researchers had control over the independent variable, they would then measure to see whether scores on the dependent variable (e.g., reading comprehension) were different for the two groups of students as a function of exposure to the independent variable. If so, the value of the *dependent variable* depends on the presence versus absence of the independent variable.

Consider three research questions that can be answered through the experimental method. In each question, the first variable (independent variable) can be manipulated by the researcher, and the second variable (dependent variable) is measured at a later time to see whether it has been affected:

- Does participation in a Head Start program accelerate preschool children's academic performance?
- Will exposure to an expert model improve students' subsequent writing skills?
- Do time-outs decrease students' misbehavior?

In a typical experimental study, researchers start with a hypothesis. A **hypothesis** is something that is believed to be true about life. Hypotheses allow us to make predictions about what will happen in experiments, such as how the results of a study will turn out. In the first example above, researchers might predict that a relationship exists between participating in a Head Start program and children's subsequent school achievement. If so, they would propose a hypothesis such as the following: Preschool students who participate in a Head Start program will score higher on a subsequent test of their academic performance than will comparable preschool children who do not participate in the Head Start program.

experimental studies A research method used to test for a cause-and-effect relationship between two variables.

hypothesis A hypothesis is something that is believed to be true about life. Hypotheses allow for predictions about what will happen in an experiment, such as what effect an independent variable will have on a dependent variable.

Figure 1.5 Sequence of Events in an Experiment

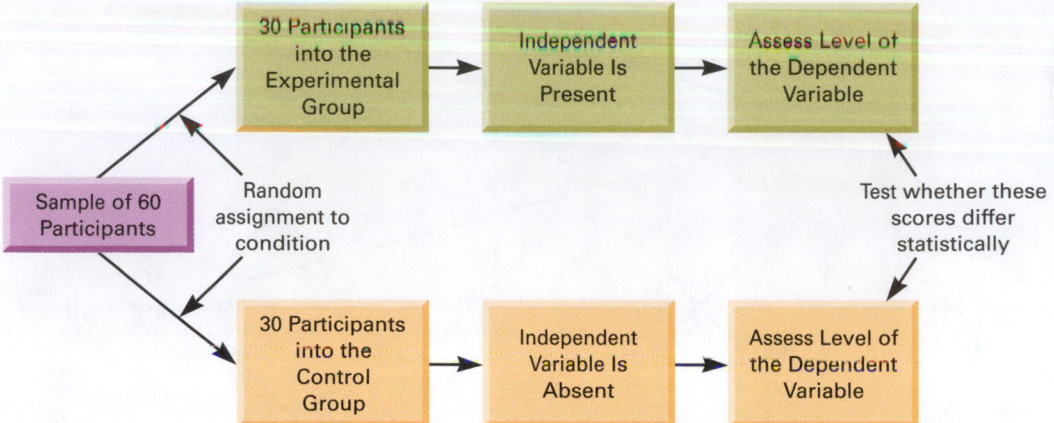

experimental group The group of participants in an experimental study who are randomly assigned to receive exposure to the independent variable.

control group The group of participants in an experimental study who are randomly assigned not to receive exposure to the independent variable.

With a hypothesis in hand, the next step is to identify a sample of participants to investigate. In a simple experiment, the researchers randomly assign half the sample to the **experimental group** and the other half of the sample to the **control group**. Participants in the experimental group are exposed to the independent variable, and participants in the control group are not. Random assignment to conditions is important because it ensures that the two groups will be virtually the same in all characteristics other than the independent variable—characteristics such as age, intelligence, socioeconomic status, and so forth. After some predetermined length of time has passed, researchers assess the level of the dependent variable for all participants. The last step in the experiment is to perform a statistical test to see whether the two groups differ in their levels of the dependent variable. The purpose of the statistical test is to make an objective, numbers-based decision as to whether the presence of the independent variable did or did not cause a difference in participants' scores on the dependent variable. Figure 1.5 graphically summarizes this sequence of steps.

Consider an example of an experimental study. Researchers hypothesized that a middle school student's style of walking would influence his teachers' perception of his aggression, achievement, and need for special education (Neal et al., 2003). To test their hypothesis, researchers prepared four different videotapes:

1. A European-American male walking to class with a stroll
2. An African-American male walking to class with a stroll
3. A European-American male walking to class with standard (no stroll) movement
4. An African-American male walking to class with standard (no stroll) movement

This study actually featured two independent variables: ethnicity and the presence or absence of a stroll. A stroll is a slow, leisurely way of walking that projects a carefree attitude. The experiment also included three dependent measures: perceived aggressiveness, perceived achievement, and perceived need for special education. Results showed that, irrespective of the student's ethnicity, males with strolls were rated as more aggressive, less achieving, and in more need of special education services than were males without strolls. That is, the student's style of walking caused a change in his teachers' perceptions of his likely aggression, underachievement, and need for special education. In a rather alarming way, the findings show how teachers can mistake cultural differences (movement style) for cognitive and behavioral disabilities.

intervention research An experiment-based research design in which a group of participants receive a particular instructional program or type of training to see if their performance on a desired outcome improves in a causal way.

One form of experimental research is **intervention research**. In intervention research, some participants are randomly assigned to receive a type of instructional program or a type of training while other participants are randomly assigned not to receive the instructional program or training. If participants who received the instructional program or training then show improved performance over participants who did not receive the instructional program or training, then a causal relation between the instructional program or training on the outcome is established. That is, the intervention worked in terms of producing improved scores on the dependent variable, as can be seen in a reading program designed to boost elementary-grade students' reading comprehension (Guthrie et al., 2004) or a training program designed to improve teachers' motivating style toward their students (Su & Reeve, 2011). From such research findings, educators can then recommend evidence-based interventions to produce desired outcomes.

Being able to offer evidence-based prescriptive statements about how to causally produce desired outcomes would seem to be such a gold standard for education research as to raise the question of why all educational psychology research is not experimental research. In many circumstances—and probably in most school-based circumstances—intervening in educational settings with random assignment to controlled experimental conditions is neither possible nor feasible. It is very difficult, practically speaking, to randomly assign some students to receive one type of instruction while students in the same class are randomly assigned to not receive that same type of instruction, because the students in the control group will see and hear the instruction being offered to the students in the experimental group simply because they are in the same classroom at the same time. In other words, the reality of complex classrooms is that it is not feasible—or perhaps it is not fair—to implement random assignment of students to experimental versus control conditions. Fortunately, however, educational psychologists have additional research methods that they can rely on to answer the full range of their research questions (see Table 1.2).

Action Research The three research methods presented thus far make it sound as though only educational psychologists conduct research. Research, however, is a part of every teacher's day-to-day experience. In fact, the motto underlying **action research** is *teacher-as-researcher*. As the motto implies, teachers themselves carry out action research, and it takes place in teachers' actual classrooms (Oberg & McCutcheon, 1987; van Manen, 1990).

action research A research method carried out by teachers in their own classrooms to inform and improve their classroom practice.

The three earlier researcher-driven research methods assume that the world can be known objectively and that knowledge can be obtained empirically by using research methods to explain educational phenomena and their causes. In contrast, action research adopts a "participatory paradigm" that assumes that knowledge arises from subjective experience (Heron & Reason, 1997). Action researchers are motivated not by building and testing generalizable theories of phenomena (as in Figures 1.1 and 1.2) but, instead, by the desire to improve practical situations—usually their own classroom situation (Cain & Milovic, 2010).

Action researchers universally ask: How can I improve what I am doing? (Whitehead, 1999). The kinds of questions that teachers-as-researchers attempt to answer through action research include the following:

- Do students enjoy being in my class?
- How engaged in learning are my students during their independent study time?
- Which instructional strategy works best for my lower-achieving students?

As these research questions imply, action research constitutes whatever research projects teachers undertake to better understand and to improve on their own classroom practice. In action research, teachers do not simply import the theories of educational psychology into their classrooms. Instead, they conduct research to see which ideas might be useful for the specific needs of their students. Action research is a recurring spiral of planning, doing, evaluating, and reflecting in the effort to better understand and produce positive change in one's own classroom (Whitehead & McNiff, 2006). In a typical action research project, a teacher will do the following (Kemmis & McTaggart, 1988; Tripp, 1990):

1. Identify a problem.
2. Formulate a plan, using his or her personal theory of teaching.
3. Collect and analyze data to see whether the plan worked.
4. Reflect on what has been learned.
5. Use the new-and-improved personal theory of teaching to revise the plan and repeat steps 2, 3, and 4 until a significant positive change in the problem is observed.

Consider an example of an action research study. A third-grade teacher taught her classes competently—classes began on time, transitions were smooth and quick, and students were consistently on-task (Rogers, Noblit, & Ferrell, 1990). But she felt that something important was missing—the atmosphere in her classroom was not quite right. After taking

(© Media Bakery)

A teacher implements her action research plan—spend more one–on–one time with each student.

a close look at her own approach to instructing students, she planned to spend more one-on-one time with her students, which she hoped would improve the classroom atmosphere. *Spend more one-on-one time with each student* was her *action* to be researched. To assess her action, she kept a nightly journal recording how much time she spent with each child. After a week of doing so, it became apparent that keeping a journal was an ineffective method because she could not remember all the interactions that took place during the day. Her reformulated plan (step 5 above) was to keep a large wall chart with the names of the children listed in rows and the number of interactions listed in columns. Each time she interacted one-on-one with a student, she handed the student a sticker, and the child posted it on the chart beside his or her name. One week later, the chart revealed the data the teacher needed to answer her research question: How much one-on-one time do I spend with my students?

Through this action research project, the teacher improved both her personal theory of what constitutes good teaching and her actual classroom practice. As you read the chapters to come, you will gain information that will help you make similar classroom decisions and, when necessary, conduct your own action research, as discussed in the nearby Taking It to the Classroom box.

Consider a second example of an action research project (Lo & Hyland, 2007). A teacher of English language learners noticed that her students wrote technically acceptable but woefully bland papers. She wanted to motivate and engage her students to write with interest, inspiration, and imagination. So she tried a new writing program in which she encouraged her students to write about topics of interest and relevance to them and to write not to the teacher but to a genuine audience (a person or group who was important to them personally). The new writing program did indeed spark her students' motivation and engagement, but it also took away from their writing accuracy and organization. The teacher was so impressed by her students' new interest and confidence, however, that she decided to reconsider her previous writing instructional strategies, which had made her students successful test-takers but not inspired, flexible, and resourceful writers.

Action research is designed to lead to more effective classroom practice, but it does more than that. It promotes lifelong learning and acts as a valuable and ongoing form of professional development (Cain & Milovic, 2010). The more teachers engage in action research, the more

Taking It to the Classroom

Implementing Action Research in Your Classroom

To conduct action research in your own classroom, first identify a problem to be solved. Then carry out the following four steps: planning, acting, monitoring, and reflecting (Dicker, 1990; Kemmis & McTaggart, 1988).

1. Planning	Once a problem has been identified, state a plan of action to address it. If attendance is poor, make a plan to increase it.
2. Acting	Translate the plan into action. Recognizing the unique circumstances within your classroom, implement your plan to increase attendance.
3. Evaluating	Collect the data necessary to assess whether the plan is working through interviews, journals, classroom observations, and audio or video recordings. You might keep a journal, writing down points of progress and difficulty after each class. Students might also keep a journal—they could be given five minutes at the end of class to write their reactions to the implemented plan. Alternatively, you might make a tape recording, perhaps taping one class before the plan is implemented and another after its implementation.
4. Reflecting	Classroom events rarely unfold as planned. Adjustments almost always need to be made. During reflection, the teacher-as-researcher critiques the plan, revises it, and thinks of new ways to bring the plan to fruition.

knowledge they gain and the more confident in their own teaching they become (Furlong & Sainsbury, 2005; Zeichner, 2003). Further, as teachers learn how to improve their classroom practice, their students become the direct beneficiaries of the teachers' improved instruction.

Narrowing the Gap between Theory and Practice

Some researchers compare the conversations that take place between researchers and teachers to what happens each day at the United Nations (Zirkel, 2007). Although sharing similar goals, educational researchers and classroom teachers often seem to need translators to understand each other—the two simply use different languages (Donmoyer, 1989). Researchers need translators to understand and appreciate what it means to be a teacher, and they also need to know what problems teachers face, what their priorities are, and what sort of questions to which they want answers. Simultaneously, teachers need translators, too, because much research about teaching and learning is written in a way that is hard for nonresearchers to understand (Davis, 2007). In many ways, this book attempts to serve as one such translator between researchers and teachers, and the reader may also find additional translators in professional journals such as *Educational Leadership* and *Phi Delta Kappan*.

Anyone who has spent a good deal of time in a foreign country (the way teachers sometimes feel while reading research, and the way researchers sometimes feel while surrounded by classroom activity) soon learns that it is a good idea to learn the native language. That is essentially what has been happening among researchers and teachers over the last two decades. Educational psychologists no longer work in the laboratory and expect teachers to just import their research findings into the classroom. Contemporary educational psychologists think about authentic classroom problems and issues (Chinn, 2006; Resnick, 1981; Shulman, 1981), and many educational psychologists have been K–12 teachers themselves. Practitioners have also been learning the language of research. As researchers have investigated authentic classroom problems and issues, educators have noticed and have been much more open to the ensuing two-way dialogue. What teachers have learned is that researchers can indeed help them do better what they want to do—understand learners and foster their learning. So while the research/practice divide was once like two people speaking different languages, the contemporary situation is more like a harmonious multicultural family.

When in a foreign country, it is helpful not only to learn the language but also to understand the culture. Researchers examine abstract principles to formulate the knowledge they need to build a theory. Teachers, in contrast, focus less on generalizable knowledge and more on the particular context of their classrooms. Indeed, many teachers are suspicious of the idea that a general theory can help them meet the daunting demands of the classroom (Thomas, 1997). They tend to rely on—and to trust—their own past experience, and they tend to rely on and trust other teachers to develop their classroom skills. So the gap between theory and practice exists. That said, it is immensely helpful to both researchers and teachers to narrow that gap—thereby significantly improving both theory and practice.

To narrow the theory–practice gap, researchers and teachers need to understand and appreciate the other's culture. The teacher's culture values "improve practice," while the researcher's culture values "develop theory." For a sense of what teachers value, consider how teachers rated the importance of the statements shown in Figure 1.6 (based on Lim & Tan, 2010). When it comes to language development, teachers think it is more important to enhance their students' language development than it is to understand language development more generally. When it comes to student aggression, teachers think it is more important to prevent and control student aggression than it is to give reasons for why students are aggressive. And when it comes to student motivation, teachers think it is more important to make learning enjoyable for their particular students than it is to know theories that explain why students in general enjoy learning. In other words, teachers think practice is more important than theory.

Improving practice is certainly important—vital, in fact. But consider the paradoxical insight that one key way to improve practice is to develop greater theoretical knowledge of that which you are trying to put into practice. It is a paradoxical thing to understand that a key way to help students learn is to understand how learning works in general (i.e., a theory of learning), just as it is a paradoxical thing to understand that a key way to prevent and

Figure 1.6 Teachers' Values for Theory versus Practice Concerning Students Language, Aggression, and Motivation
Source: Based on data from Lim, K.-M., & Tan, A.-G. (2010). *Student teachers' perceptions of the importance of theory and practice.* Unpublished manuscript. See Lim, Kam-Ming, and Tan, Ai-Girl, National Institute of Education, Psychological Studies, Nanyang Technological University, 1 Nanyang Walk, Singapore 637616.

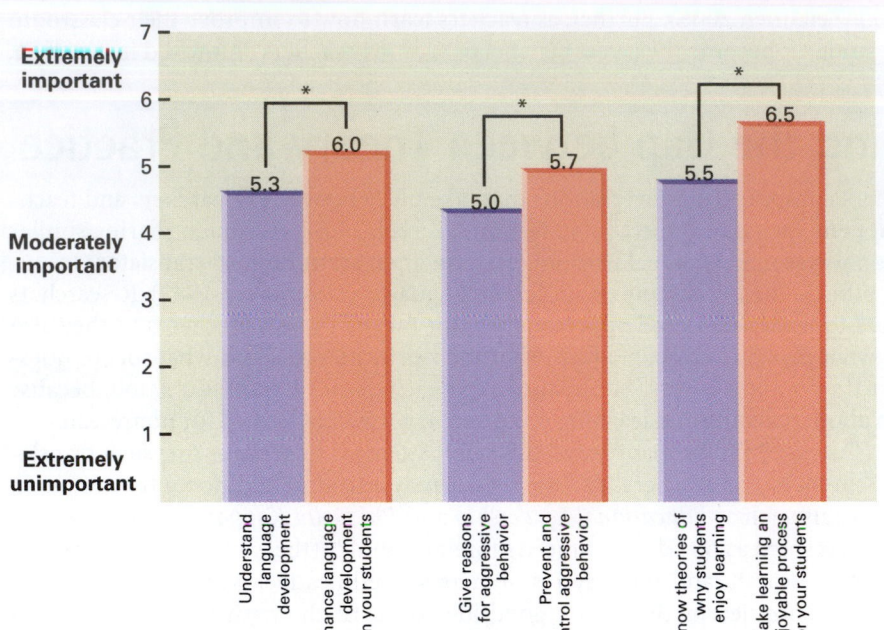

control aggression is to understand why students might become aggressive in the first place (i.e., a theory of aggression), just as it is a paradoxical thing to understand that a key way to make learning enjoyable for students is to understand the conditions that make some tasks more enjoyable than other tasks (i.e., a theory of motivation). The more teachers appreciate these paradoxical truths, the more they will understand the culture of research.

In the same spirit, it is a paradoxical thing to understand that a key way to understand how learning works in general is to understand how to promote learning with one group of students on one particular day by using one particular lesson plan. The same holds true for understanding aggression, as a key way to understand aggression in general is to try to prevent it from breaking out during a specific five-minute period of class. The same holds true for understanding student motivation, as a key way to understand the nature of motivation is to try to make one particular lesson enjoyable for one group of students on one particular day. The more researchers and educational psychologists appreciate these paradoxical truths, the more they will understand the culture of teaching and the culture of practice. Further, it is vital to researchers that they understand the culture of teaching and classroom practice if they seek to avoid presenting only a mechanistic view of teaching to teachers in which the complexity of the teaching situation is neither acknowledged nor deeply appreciated (Doyle, 1990).

Recognizing the benefits that are gained when teachers and researchers understand each other's cultures and values, educational psychology as a scientific field makes the promotion of theory and practice its twofold mission. Recall from the opening pages of this chapter that the twofold mission of educational psychology is (1) to understand learners and (2) to foster learning. When these two priorities are framed within the discussion of narrowing the gap between theory and practice, the twofold mission of educational psychology can be understood as:

● Develop theory—understand learners.

● Improve practice—foster learning.

These two goals are synergistic. The more one develops theoretical understanding and the more one understands learning and related educational phenomena such as language, motivation, development, and assessment, the more able one is to improve practice. Similarly, the more one gains the ability to foster the learning of individual students under particular and sometimes unique circumstances, the more able one is to improve theory and understanding.

Reflective Teaching

Chapter 2 in this book is specifically about teaching. Throughout this book, we encourage you to develop your capacity for and disposition toward being a reflective teacher by providing you with a conceptual framework to think about how to become more reflective. We also provide lots of practice throughout the book to help you develop skills in reflective thinking and reflective teaching. In this section, we put a spotlight on what we mean by reflective teaching, and we explain our model of reflective teaching, which we call RIDE (reflection, information gathering, decision making, and evaluation).

Teaching is a profession filled with uncertainties. Fortunately, some teaching situations can be handled with routine knowledge. Given a set of familiar circumstances, teachers can use their experience and knowledge to provide effective instruction. For instance, given a student's misbehavior, the teacher might implement a time-out procedure. This represents **technical teaching** because a familiar problem surfaced, and the teacher implemented a tried-and-true solution. Lesson plans, prepared demonstrations, scripted activities, and a structured management style represent the nuts and bolts—the everyday planning and problem solving—of technical teaching. Technical teaching is everyday, tried-and-true, by-the-book classroom instruction.

> **technical teaching** Relying on routine knowledge and tried-and-true solutions to manage classroom problems.

In many teaching situations, however, surprises surface. For instance, the teacher might be surprised if the time-out increased, rather than decreased, the student's subsequent misbehavior. Sometimes class does not go according to script, unexpected events occur, and students react to the flow of instruction in unanticipated ways. Sometimes this year's students react negatively to the same lesson that last year's students reacted so positively to.

A teaching surprise leads the teacher to reflect on what is happening, why it is happening, and what adjustments need to be made (Schon, 1987). When instruction does not go as planned, the teacher wonders: What is happening here? How did I get into this mess? What went wrong? How can I get the class back on track? These are reflective questions. Unlike instances of technical teaching, these classroom situations do not lend themselves to tried-and-true solutions. In these instances, a teacher cannot just keep doing what she has been doing. Instead, **reflective teaching** involves generating conjectures to explain the surprising or negative event, then gathering the information needed to make a decision about what might constitute the most effective course of action.

> **reflective teaching** Generating conjectures to explain a surprising or negative event in the teaching situation, then gathering the information needed to make a decision about what would constitute the most effective course of action to pursue.

Figure 1.7 illustrates the two broad ways that teachers translate what they know about teaching into classroom solutions. Predictable classroom events call for the routinely scripted action of technical teaching, while surprising and negative classroom events call for the conjectures of reflective teaching (Dewey, 1910; Loughran, 2002; McAlpine et al., 1999; Schon, 1983, 1987; Zeichner & Liston, 1996). Collectively, the two teaching modes afford teachers the greatest opportunity to offer constructive learning experiences to their students.

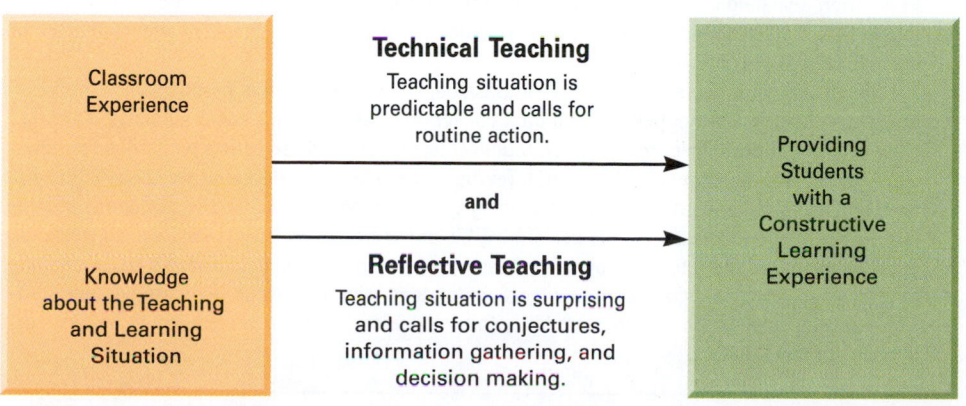

Figure 1.7 Two Modes of Teaching: Technical and Reflective

Throughout this book, many instances of technical teaching will be offered. For instance, Chapter 6 offers a number of tried-and-true instructional strategies for classroom management, Chapter 9 offers a number of tried-and-true instructional strategies to implement cooperative learning, and Chapter 10 offers a number of tried-and-true instructional strategies to motivate and engage students in learning activities. This is very helpful information, because teaching is a profession that plays itself out in the preparation and implementation of instructional strategies. However, teaching is also a profession in which events do not always unfold as planned, and teachers find themselves needing to revise and adjust their instructional strategies.

Many teacher educators lament that what teachers-in-training receive is an overly technical and simplistic view of teaching (Richardson, 1990). They argue that if preservice teachers are really going to be prepared for the classroom, they need both technical teaching and reflective teaching. When training for reflective teaching is added to the curriculum, the goal of reflective teacher education is to develop the reasoning of teachers-in-training about why they use the instructional strategies they use and how they can use both experience and classroom feedback to improve their teaching so to be ever more able to produce positive student outcomes (Lee, 2005). Thus, the goal of reflective teacher education is to place teachers on a trajectory of professional growth after they leave the university and enter the profession. Reflective teaching is not just different from technical teaching; it is a central yet often missing ingredient in effective teaching (Brookfield, 1995; Zeichner & Liston, 1987). The nearby Uncommon Sense box explains how textbooks further assist the teacher's day-to-day decision making in the classroom.

Levels of Reflection

Any teacher walking out of the classroom can reflect on what just happened. That is, say to any teacher, "Tell me about the lesson," and the teacher will be able to do so. But the level of reflection within the responses reveals something important about where the teacher stands in terms of reflective teaching. Three levels of reflection are shown in Table 1.5: recall, analysis, and reflection (based on Lee, 2005). A nonreflective teacher will provide a reenactment of what happened in class by offering a habitual approach to instruction with little awareness of the complexity of the teaching situation and a means–end analysis, as in, "I wanted to produce outcome X so I implemented instructional strategy Y." This teacher will tell you that he or she taught in ways that others teach or in ways that he or she was taught to teach. Recall—level 1 in the levels of reflection—represents technical teaching.

Uncommon Sense

You Learn to Teach by Teaching—Or Do You?

As preservice teachers become beginning teachers and beginning teachers become veterans, most say that they learned how to teach by teaching and by watching others teach (Calderhead, 1989; Zahorik, 1987). Few say that they learned how to teach by reading a textbook (Hall & Loucks, 1982). In addition, teaching is a profession without absolute truths (Broudy, 1980; Floden & Clark, 1988). In a field that lacks universal truths, textbooks cannot provide all the answers. So why read a textbook such as *Educational Psychology*?

When your turn comes to step into the classroom, your instructional practice will express your underlying beliefs. Teacher beliefs are a tacit collection of assumptions about students, learning, classrooms, and the subject matter to be taught (Kagan, 1992); these beliefs will influence how you interact with students (Anning, 1988). Textbooks help teachers develop these beliefs. Reading a textbook can also be instrumental in developing your classroom skills. Like the surgeon who amasses large amounts of knowledge before performing his or her first operation, teachers need to explore, develop, examine, and refine a knowledge-based foundation for teaching. In doing so, textbooks can help teachers anticipate classroom problems, understand why they occur, generate possible solutions, and forecast which solutions are likely to be successful and which are likely to be unsuccessful (Floden & Clark, 1988).

TABLE 1.5

Three Levels of Reflection

Level of Reflection	Level 1: Recall	Level 2: Analysis	Level 3: Reflection
Depth of Thinking	**Technical Teaching**	**Thoughtful Action**	**Reflective Teaching**
Content of Thinking	• Recalls what happened during class without looking for alternative explanations; reflection as reenactment • Attempts to imitate teaching behavior they have observed or were taught	• Searches for "why it was" • Analyzes why particular classroom events occurred • Looks for relations between pieces of the classroom experience (e.g., how context affected learning or behavior)	• Approaches what happened during class with the goal of changing or improving the future • Understands how the teacher impacts students' learning, behavior, and achievement • Analyzes the classroom situation from multiple perspective (one's own, students', another teacher's)

A somewhat reflective teacher will offer a thoughtful analysis of what happened. This teacher will examine the role that his or her beliefs, goals, and expectations played in instruction; show an awareness of the role of context on the teaching situation; and report adapting instruction to meet the needs of the students. The teacher in the analysis level of reflection will search for why events occurred and will analyze the causes and consequences of these events. In doing so, this teacher will look for and identify relations between one aspect of instruction and students' reaction and outcomes. Analysis—level 2 in the levels of reflection—represents thoughtful action.

A highly reflective teacher will discuss what happened with a goal of changing or improving the future. This teacher is preparing for tomorrow's class (and beyond) by focusing on the surprising events that occurred, analyzing multiple explanatory possibilities (often by looking at the same event from multiple perspectives—his or her own, the students', or what another teacher might have done), and stating intentions to collect the data or develop the perspective necessary to ensure that tomorrow's instruction will be more effective than today's. In doing so, this teacher will communicate a solid awareness of the impact his or her instructional decisions have on students' learning, behavior, and achievement. Reflection—level 3 in the levels of reflection—represents reflective teaching.

In considering the three levels of reflection summarized in Table 1.5, one interesting reflective question to ask oneself would be: How do I know at which level of reflection I teach? They are many ways of bringing one's level of reflection to light (Lee, 2005), but consider two—one involving oral reflection and the other involving written reflection. As to oral reflection, imagine how you would respond to an interviewer's questions during a post-teaching face-to-face interview. The interviewer might ask questions such as: (1) Tell me about the lesson. (2) How would you define good teaching in your own words? (3) Why do you want to teach? The first question is an opportunity to reflect on the class, its goals, and your expectations for the next class. The interviewer might also ask you to compare your lesson with either one of your lessons in the past or a lesson given by another teacher. The second question is an opportunity to reflect on your beliefs, values, and goals, such as whether you describe what you do, analyze what you do, or seek to improve what you do. The third question is an opportunity to reflect on your goals and expectations for the future. As to written reflection, keeping a written journal—as in writing two or three entries per week—is another opportunity to reflect on your teaching. Interestingly, researchers recommend teachers engage in multiple forms of reflection because some teachers reflect better orally while other teachers reflect better while writing (Bean & Stevens, 2002; Spalding & Wilson, 2002). Still other teachers reflect best while viewing a videotape of their teaching or that of a peer (Harford & MacRuairc, 2008; Perry & Talley, 2001).

The heart of reflective teaching is simply to question one's own approach to instruction, especially in the effort to transcend one's teaching and see possibilities for change (Revans, 1982, 1984). There are many foci of reflection, however, as a teacher might reflect *in* action, reflect *on* action, or reflect *for* action (Schon, 1987). Reflecting *in* action means reflecting on what one is doing during the act of teaching; it is reflection during action (reflecting while teaching). Reflecting *on* action means reflecting back on what happened and why it happened; it is reflection after action (reflecting for evaluation). Reflecting *for* action means reflecting by looking forward toward future action; it is reflection before future action (reflecting for change). Reflection for action is by far the most important of these three types of reflection (Hatton & Smith, 1995), as it is important for teachers to look ahead and pave the way for their future development as teachers. If one is to develop as a teacher, reflection for action is a necessary part of that development.

Reflection for Action

What Does This Mean to Me?
How can teachers be reflective about their work when so much is going on in the classroom?

The day-to-day decision making of teachers is not unlike that of researchers. From their classroom experiences, teachers reflect on what happened and why it happened; they ask questions, seek explanations, and make conjectures and educated guesses about what is happening and why. To substantiate their conjectures, teachers gather information. They talk to peers, observe mentors, hold conferences with parents, read research reports, subscribe to professional journals, surf Internet Web sites, attend workshops, review videotapes and DVDs, and generally seek information from trustworthy sources. With information in hand, teachers can make an informed decision about what course of action is most likely to constitute effective future practice.

Researchers engage in essentially the same reflective process. Teachers and researchers, however, typically begin their reflective practice at different starting points, as illustrated in Figure 1.8. Teachers typically start with a classroom observation, such as noticing how high-stakes tests are affecting their students' anxiety. They reflect by asking: What am I seeing here? What is this anxiety an example of? From this reflection, conjectures arise: Perhaps this is an example of putting too much pressure on students, or perhaps it is an example of students' insufficient preparation. Researchers, on the other hand, typically start with a theory, such as a general theory of anxiety. They reflect by asking: Why does this event occur? What causes

Figure 1.8 Similarities in the Day–to–Day Work of Teachers and Researchers

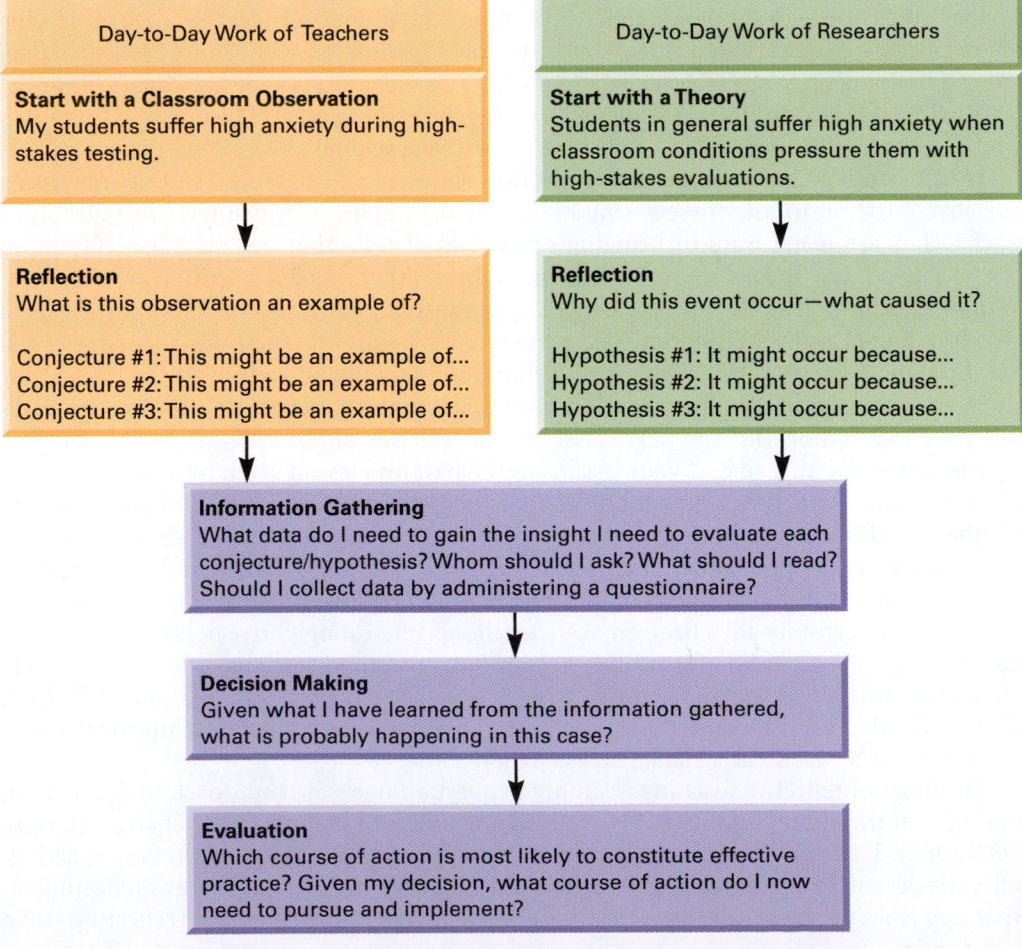

Day-to-Day Work of Teachers

Start with a Classroom Observation
My students suffer high anxiety during high-stakes testing.

Reflection
What is this observation an example of?

Conjecture #1: This might be an example of...
Conjecture #2: This might be an example of...
Conjecture #3: This might be an example of...

Day-to-Day Work of Researchers

Start with a Theory
Students in general suffer high anxiety when classroom conditions pressure them with high-stakes evaluations.

Reflection
Why did this event occur—what caused it?

Hypothesis #1: It might occur because...
Hypothesis #2: It might occur because...
Hypothesis #3: It might occur because...

Information Gathering
What data do I need to gain the insight I need to evaluate each conjecture/hypothesis? Whom should I ask? What should I read? Should I collect data by administering a questionnaire?

Decision Making
Given what I have learned from the information gathered, what is probably happening in this case?

Evaluation
Which course of action is most likely to constitute effective practice? Given my decision, what course of action do I now need to pursue and implement?

anxiety? From this reflection, hypotheses arise: Perhaps anxiety is caused by time pressure; perhaps it arises from individual differences within students' personalities. Aside from these different starting points, however, reflective teachers and researchers think in very similar ways. As shown in the figure, once begun, reflection produces the fruits of information gathering, decision making, and evaluation (Crocker, 1981).

A Model of Reflective Teaching: RIDE

This book will help you become a more reflective teacher. The beginning of each chapter will present a vignette—a brief scenario of a classroom problem—that requires reflective teaching. In Chapter 2, the opening vignette will concern Ms. Newby and her sense of unease about teaching. In each subsequent vignette to come (a new one at the beginning of each chapter), you will be asked to reflect on the event by using the key concepts described in the chapter. Throughout the reading of the chapter, your task is to propose conjectures (educated guesses) as to what the event is an example or illustration of. At the end of each chapter, we present an analysis of the classroom problem under the heading of *Reflection for Action*. *Action* is teaching, and *reflection* is thinking about what is happening, why it is happening, and what might be done better in the future. The goal will be to generate at least three conjectures as to why the classroom problem is happening, then identify the information you need to collect to make a decision about which conjecture best explains and solves the problem.

As shown in Figure 1.9, the model consists of four sequential components: reflection (R); information gathering (I); decision making (D); and evaluation (E). To illustrate the RIDE model, we use the vignette that will be introduced to start Chapter 2 here as a warm-up exercise:

Ms. Newby is nervous. She wants to leave her doubt, anxiety, and sense of unease behind and become a confident and expert teacher. She wonders what she can do to empower herself as a teacher-to-be. What can Ms. Newby do to grow her confidence and to silence her fears? How can she ready herself for opening day?

> **Appendix**
> **Reflective Teaching**
>
> The RIDE scenarios throughout the text are intended to assist you in becoming a reflective practitioner (PRAXIS™, IV. A3; INTASC, Principle 9).

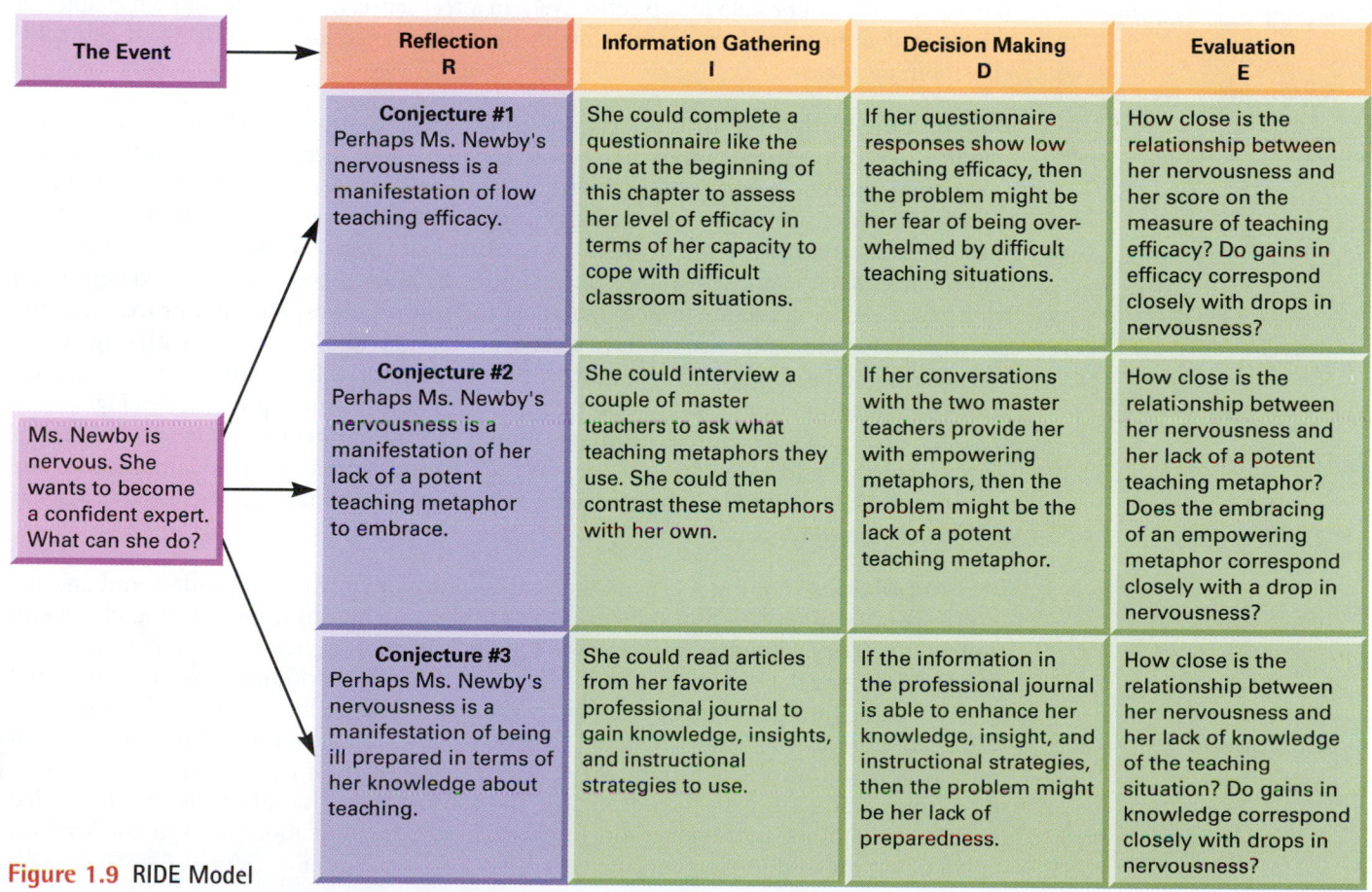

Figure 1.9 RIDE Model

The Event	Reflection R	Information Gathering I	Decision Making D	Evaluation E
Ms. Newby is nervous. She wants to become a confident expert. What can she do?	**Conjecture #1** Perhaps Ms. Newby's nervousness is a manifestation of low teaching efficacy.	She could complete a questionnaire like the one at the beginning of this chapter to assess her level of efficacy in terms of her capacity to cope with difficult classroom situations.	If her questionnaire responses show low teaching efficacy, then the problem might be her fear of being overwhelmed by difficult teaching situations.	How close is the relationship between her nervousness and her score on the measure of teaching efficacy? Do gains in efficacy correspond closely with drops in nervousness?
	Conjecture #2 Perhaps Ms. Newby's nervousness is a manifestation of her lack of a potent teaching metaphor to embrace.	She could interview a couple of master teachers to ask what teaching metaphors they use. She could then contrast these metaphors with her own.	If her conversations with the two master teachers provide her with empowering metaphors, then the problem might be the lack of a potent teaching metaphor.	How close is the relationship between her nervousness and her lack of a potent teaching metaphor? Does the embracing of an empowering metaphor correspond closely with a drop in nervousness?
	Conjecture #3 Perhaps Ms. Newby's nervousness is a manifestation of being ill prepared in terms of her knowledge about teaching.	She could read articles from her favorite professional journal to gain knowledge, insights, and instructional strategies to use.	If the information in the professional journal is able to enhance her knowledge, insight, and instructional strategies, then the problem might be her lack of preparedness.	How close is the relationship between her nervousness and her lack of knowledge of the teaching situation? Do gains in knowledge correspond closely with drops in nervousness?

The first objective of reflective teaching is to identify what the event illustrates; that is, what is Ms. Newby's nervousness a manifestation of? Using the concepts highlighted in Chapter 2, at least three possibilities emerge to help answer that question.

What Theoretical/Conceptual Information Might Assist in Interpreting and Remedying This Situation? Consider the following.

 **Teaching Knowledge**

Ms. Newby may be nervous because she does not yet feel sufficiently prepared for her first day in the classroom. Her nervousness might be a signal that she currently possesses insufficient knowledge about learners, teaching, and the teaching–learning situation in general.

 Teaching Efficacy

Ms. Newby may be nervous because she has low teaching efficacy. It might be the case that because Ms. Newby has low teaching efficacy, she in turn has a high sense of doubt, anxiety, and unease about what will happen when she is actually in the classroom.

Teaching Metaphor

Ms. Newby may lack a potent metaphor to guide her classroom activity. To empower herself and overcome her nagging nervousness, she might embrace a potent metaphor to place herself into a more empowering role.

Reflection   Reflection is the first and most important step in the RIDE model. Reflection rarely occurs until the teacher recognizes that a problem has occurred. Once the teacher recognizes that a surprising classroom event or problem has occurred, the teacher needs to interpret and understand what has happened and why it has happened. Reflection includes the search for alternative explanations. As described above and as presented in Figure 1.9, three conjectures might emerge: lack of knowledge about the teaching situation; low teaching efficacy; and lack of a potent teaching metaphor. Generating these conjectures is the most crucial aspect of the RIDE model, because if these conjectures are intellectual dead ends, the teacher will not be able to cope effectively. In a real sense, the purpose of each chapter in this book is to help teachers generate highly plausible conjectures to understand and solve classroom problems.

Information Gathering   In this step, one gathers information to help determine which of the three conjectures is most plausible. Teachers have access to a wide range of information sources, including colleagues, mentors, master teachers, departmental chairs, principals, parents, one's own students, research reports, professional journals, Web sites, inspirational films, instructional videotapes, DVDs and CDs, workshops, past experiences, and theories such as those featured throughout this book. Looking at the problem from multiple perspectives tends to help stimulate the information-gathering process. As one gathers information, one also needs to consider what information one can trust (e.g., Is my colleague a good source of information for this particular teaching situation? Is the theory about this phenomenon based on solid evidence?). In the example presented in Figure 1.9, we offer three possible sources of information: (1) reading through a favorite journal to gain knowledge and insight about teaching; (2) completing a questionnaire such as the one that will be featured in Table 2.5; and (3) conversing with master teachers to ask what metaphors they embrace.

Decision Making   During this step, the goal is to decide how best to understand and interpret the teaching situation one faces, given the available information. In a classroom context, a teacher will never have access to all the information necessary to make a definitive decision. Any decision will always be tentatively prudent and may need to be revisited at a later date. In the example presented in Figure 1.9, the teacher would (1) consider the practical value of the knowledge and insights offered in the pages of the professional journal, (2) examine the questionnaire responses to score his or her existing level of teaching efficacy, and (3) weigh the advantages and sense of personal fit of the recommended teaching metaphors. In this stage, the teacher makes a decision about what to do, develops a plan of action, and implements it.

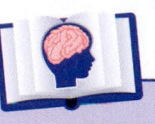

MINDFUL HABITS OF EFFECTIVE TEACHERS

The ability to engage in critical thinking and active reflection about one's practice is a key habit of mind of effective teachers. We describe it as "mindful" because this reflection is deliberate, intentional, and purposeful.

Evaluation The journal readings, questionnaire responses, and conversations with master teachers will yield important information. With this information in hand, Ms. Newby is in a position to evaluate the strength of the relationship between these three sources of information and her nervousness about teaching. If the journal information provides satisfying answers to her questions of what she might do during class, the root of the nervousness is probably a lack of knowledge. If her score on the teaching efficacy measure is low, she may sense a relation between low efficacy and high nervousness. If she feels inspired and empowered by a potent metaphor, she may feel her nervousness slip away and be replaced by a greater sense of confidence or leadership. Frequently, the information collected points the teacher in the right direction. It also allows the teacher to determine what progress has been made in solving the problem and in determining what revisions to her approach to teaching need to be made.

Appendix
Sources of Information
Many sources of helpful information exist to assist your decision making in the classroom (PRAXIS™, IV. A1; INTASC, Principle 9).

SUMMARY

- **What is educational psychology?**

  Educational psychology is the scientific study of psychology in education. Its twofold mission is to understand learners and to foster their learning. Educational psychologists seek to understand all aspects of the teaching–learning process, and they use this knowledge to improve educational practice.

- **What is critical thinking, and how does it contribute to reflective thinking?**

  Critical thinking involves an objective analysis of any claim to determine its accuracy, validity, or worth. It is one's defense against a world of too much information and too many people trying to convince you of one thing or another. Reflective thinking is simply the application of critical thinking to one's own unique teaching situation. Reflective thinking leads to reflective teaching in which one questions what went wrong, gathers the information needed to remedy the not-so-effective instruction, and then creates new instruction that can better produce a positive change in the classroom.

- **How do educational psychologists use theory and research?**

  The twin tools of educational psychology are theory and research. A theory is an intellectual framework to organize a vast amount of knowledge about a phenomenon to understand it better and explain its nature. Theories explain how a phenomenon works, but data are needed to test whether the hypotheses generated by the theory are accurate. In carrying out their research, educational psychologists acquire the data and evidence they need to test, refine, and further develop their theories. At some point, the theorist can expect to accumulate a critical mass of evidential support to enable him or her to use the theory to offer practical recommendations on how to improve classroom practice.

- **Which research methods are popular in educational psychology, and what is the purpose of each?**

  Educational psychologists use four main research methodologies. Descriptive research studies describe some aspect of naturally occurring classroom practice and are designed to answer the basic question: What is happening? Correlational research studies determine that a relation exists between two naturally occurring educational phenomena and are designed to answer the basic question: What events happen together? Experimental research studies document that a cause-and-effect relation exists between two educational phenomena and are designed to answer the basic question: What events cause other events to happen? Action research studies represent the teacher-as-researcher, seek to produce a positive change in a teacher's own instruction, and are designed to answer the basic question: How can I improve my instruction?

- **How can teachers and researchers alike narrow the gap between theory and practice?**

  Some researchers compare the conversation between researchers and teachers to what happens each day at the United Nations, because researchers sometimes need translators to understand and appreciate what it means to be a teacher just as teachers sometimes need translators to understand research because it is often written in a way that is difficult for nonresearchers to understand. To narrow the theory–practice gap, researchers and teachers need to understand and appreciate the other's culture and values, as the teacher's culture values "improve practice" while the researcher's culture values "develop theory." Somewhat paradoxically, teachers find that a good way to improve classroom practice is to understand theory, just as researchers find that a good way to develop theory is to understand practice.

● **What is reflective teaching, and how does one become a more reflective teacher?**

Teachers can approach some teaching situations with routine knowledge and tried-and-true solutions. This approach represents technical teaching. In many situations, however, surprises and setbacks surface that lead teachers to think critically about the teaching situation. Teachers ask: What is happening here? What went wrong? How can I get the class back on track? These are reflective questions. Reflective teaching involves generating conjectures to explain and solve the surprising or negative event. To model the process of reflective teaching, the chapter introduced the RIDE model: reflection, information gathering, decision making, and evaluation. This RIDE model will be used throughout the book to help readers develop skills in reflective thinking and reflective teaching.

Key Terms

action research, p. 15
control group, p. 14
correlation coefficient, p. 11
correlational studies, p. 11
critical thinking, p. 3
descriptive studies, p. 9

educational psychology, p. 5
experimental group, p. 19
experimental studies, p. 13
hypothesis, p. 13
intervention research, p. 14
learning, p. 5

model testing, p. 12
qualitative research, p. 10
reflective teaching, p. 19
reflective thinking, p. 4
technical teaching, p. 19
theory, p. 6

Exercises

1. *Critical Thinking*

   Find a claim that is made about education, or perhaps a claim that is specific to a particular school or to a particular aspect of education. It might be something like "Lower class sizes increase learning" or "Our school has the best music program in the state." Now question that claim. Try to assess just what is meant by the claim and what would constitute good and acceptable evidence to support it. Try to be critical in your approach without being cynical.

2. *Types of Research Methods*

   Four types of commonly used research methods in educational psychology were discussed in the chapter: descriptive, correlational, experimental, and action. One of the claims discussed in the chapter was that smaller class size leads to higher achievement. Such a claim might be investigated using any of these four research methods. Explain how you might gather information that would either support or refute the claim that smaller class size leads to higher achievement using each of the four different research methods. Compare your results with those of a friend in the class.

3. *Theory or Practice?*

   Find a teacher (or two) who teaches full-time in a local K–12 school, and find a researcher (or two) such as a faculty member in the Department of Educational Psychology at your university. Ask them "How important is it to you to understand:" (where 1 = *extremely unimportant* and 7 = *extremely important*) for the following two pairs of questions: (1) Understand why students generally act aggressively/Prevent a particular student from acting aggressively during class; (2) Understand why students generally show strong engagement during learning activities/Engage a particular group of students strongly during one particular classroom activity. In each pair of questions, the first question represents a value for theory and the second represents a value for practice. The purpose of this exercise is to determine if teachers tend to show a stronger valuing for practice while researchers tend to show a stronger valuing for generalizable theory. Do your results parallel those reported in Figure 1.6? It might prove to be very helpful if you also ask the teacher and researcher to explain why they value what they value.

Your Fifth-Grade Class Schedule

	Monday	Tuesday	Wednesday	Thursday	Friday
8:30–9:00					
9:00–9:30					
9:30–10:00					
10:30–11:00		Physical Education		Physical Education	Physical Education
11:30–12:00	Lunch	Lunch	Lunch	Lunch	Lunch
12:30–1:00	Music		Music		
1:00–1:30					Library
1:30–2:00					
2:00–2:30		Art	Art		

Congratulations! You're hired. You are going to teach fifth grade at Monroe Elementary School this fall.

As you anticipate your first year in the profession, consider Ms. Newby, the smiling but somewhat anxious first-year teacher pictured on the next page. Like Ms. Newby, you, too, are likely to be somewhat nervous about what is to come. Will you be ready? Will you be prepared? Will you be a good teacher? Will you and your students connect?

Despite how nervous Ms. Newby feels as she greets each student face who walks into her classroom, the show must go on. If you were in Ms. Newby's shoes, what would you want to know? What sort of experiences would you need before you could feel prepared and ready to go?

R I D E Reflection for Action

Ms. Newby is nervous. She wants to leave her doubt, anxiety, and sense of unease behind and become a confident and expert teacher. She wonders what she can do to empower herself as a teacher-to-be. What can Ms. Newby do to grow her confidence and to silence her fears? How can she ready herself for opening day?

Guiding Questions

- What is teaching?
- What concerns do beginning teachers have?
- Why are teachers' beliefs about teaching and learning important?
- How do expert teachers differ from novice teachers?
- How does a teacher develop a strong and resilient sense of teaching efficacy?
- How do teachers plan for instruction? How do they translate instructional goals into actual lesson plans?
- What are some general approaches to teaching?

CHAPTER OVERVIEW

This chapter focuses on teachers and on how confident, reflective, and planful teaching defines effective teaching and paves the way to positive student outcomes. The chapter begins by identifying the concerns beginning teachers have that worry them as well as the goals that inspire them. It highlights the beliefs that beginning teachers enter the profession with—beliefs about themselves, their students, and the process of learning. We illustrate the importance of these beliefs and how they influence classroom practice by comparing novice and expert teachers and by comparing confident and anxious teachers. The chapter then adopts a developmental perspective to track how teacher expertise, teaching effectiveness, and teaching efficacy develop through the early years of a teaching career. The latter part of the chapter considers the events that take place during successful teaching. The emphasis is on planning and how teachers translate their instructional goals into actual lesson plans. The chapter ends with an overview of three general approaches to teaching.

The Teaching Life

Most people think of January 1 as the beginning of the year. But for schoolteachers, the beginning of the year occurs in late summer and early fall, whenever school starts again. That's the beginning of the year! For most teachers, teaching is not just a job or even a career; it is part of their identity—who they are as persons. Teachers view events with teachers' eyes: How could I turn this into a lesson? What would my students make of this? I wonder if I can get a complete class set of these?

Jane Mitchell, a primary school teacher in Dunedin, New Zealand, has the following list of things that are different about her life because she is a teacher:

● I can't play a board game without organizing everyone involved.
● If I see children misbehaving in the street, I can't hold myself back from talking to them.
● I explain things in detail.
● I can make up a song about any activity.

- I make the most of the "teachable" moment whenever I can.
- I am good at multitasking.

The teaching life: It's a way of looking at who you are.

What Is Teaching?

Teaching is one person's interpersonal effort to help others acquire knowledge, develop skill, and realize their potential. To accomplish these goals, teachers explain, demonstrate, listen, guide, support, assess, offer feedback, and otherwise structure a learning opportunity to help learners advance from a state of having less knowledge, skill, and potential to a state of enhanced knowledge, skill, and potential.

Outstanding teaching combines knowledge about the teaching–learning process and a host of other attributes, including the following:

- Expertise in the subject matter being taught
- Belief in one's ability to teach and students' abilities to learn
- Sensitivity to the needs of different kinds of learners
- Planning and organizational skills
- Interpersonal and leadership skills
- A great deal of hard work

But what do these attributes mean? How do teachers acquire them? The attributes of exceptional teaching have long been a focus of researchers in educational psychology as well as related disciplines. This chapter examines what these skills and traits are as well as how they work both individually and together to result in exceptional teaching. It not only looks at the nuts and bolts of teaching, such as planning; it also presents the research on how expert and novice teachers differ, how beliefs about efficacy influence teacher behavior, and the difference between content knowledge and pedagogical content knowledge. It is an inside look into the development of effective teaching.

What do teachers actually do when teaching? How can you tell whether someone is teaching or not? Jackson (1968) once asked: "If a person were doing all the acts commonly associated with teaching in front of a mirror rather than in front of a class, would it still be considered teaching?" The answer that comes to mind is: Of course not. It is immediately followed by the question: Why not? The answer is clear: Teaching is not something one can do alone. It is reciprocal by its very nature: Teaching implies learning; teachers imply students. (Students can, of course, be *virtual*, as in the case of an instructional video intended for students to see at a later date. But by making the videotape, the teacher is intending to promote learning.)

Classroom teaching generally involves four components: presage variables, context variables, process variables, and product variables (Duncan & Biddle, 1974). Presage variables relate to characteristics of teachers such as their own formative experiences as students, their training, and their beliefs and motivations. Presage variables constitute the focus of the present chapter. Context variables relate to the nature of the students being taught, the community, the school, and the cultural context more generally. Process variables concern what sorts of behaviors occur in the classroom. Product variables are outcomes such as student learning and personality development. Borrowing from the more elaborate model of Duncan and Biddle (1974), these variables might be conceptualized as in Figure 2.1.

teaching The interpersonal effort to help learners acquire knowledge, develop skill, and realize their potential.

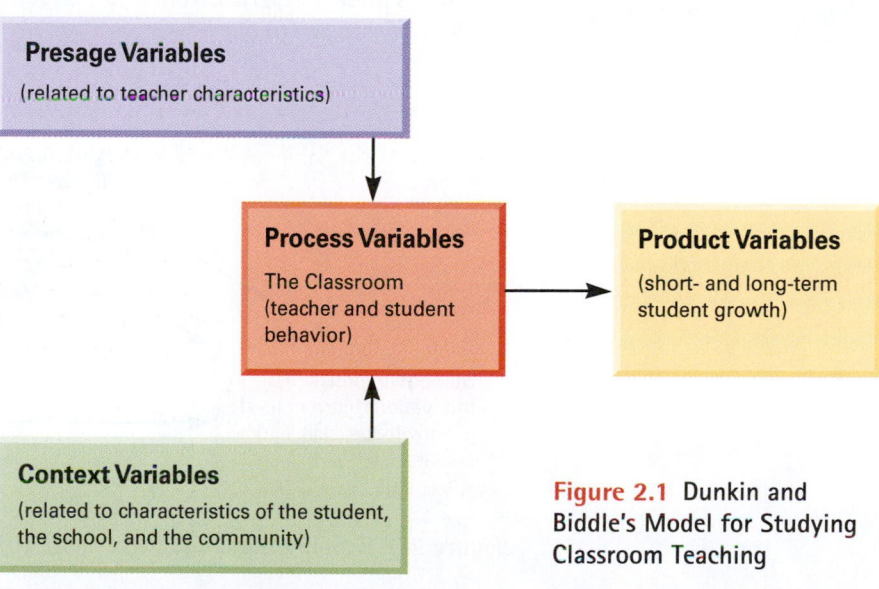

Figure 2.1 Dunkin and Biddle's Model for Studying Classroom Teaching

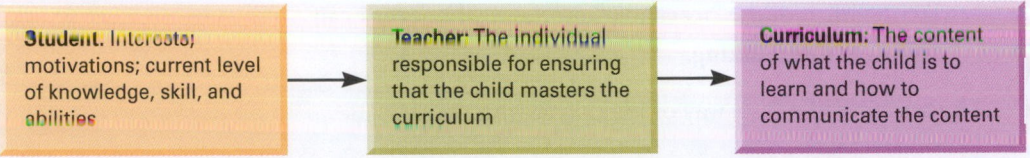

Figure 2.2 An Initial Model Relating Students, Teachers, and the Curriculum

However, teaching involves more than just an interaction between a teacher and students; teaching also involves content. The content being taught, and the way it is organized—that is, the *curriculum*—is the third component of teaching. There are a variety of ways of thinking about, or representing, the three components of teaching. One approach is linear, with the teacher acting as a link or mediator between the student and the curriculum (Figure 2.2).

This view of teaching, however, suggests that the teacher's task is to bring students to the curriculum, that the only way students can learn the curriculum is through the intervention of the teacher. A more interactive approach, therefore, is to consider the relationship in terms of a triangle, with the teacher guiding students' efforts to master the curriculum (Figure 2.3).

This depiction indicates that the teacher and students interact and that both are influenced by the curriculum. But it does not suggest that either students or the teacher can influence the curriculum or make decisions about what is to be learned. Moreover, it suggests that what is to be taught and how it is taught are determined by the curriculum and that the teacher has little or no influence over that process. It does not yet seem satisfactory as a model for teaching and learning in classrooms. Figure 2.4 represents a more interactive approach.

This view of the relationships among students, teacher, and curriculum is more realistic in that it acknowledges that there is some overlap among the three components of the process. Figure 2.4 shows that although all three components are distinct, the interactions among the three are important. As the educational philosopher John Dewey wrote (Dewey, 1971/1990):

Abandon the notion of subject-matter as something fixed and ready-made in itself, outside the child's experience; cease thinking of the child's experience as also something hard and fast; see it as something fluent, embryonic, vital; and we realize that the child and the curriculum are simply two limits which define a single process. Just as two points define a straight line, so the present standpoint of the child and the facts and truths of studies define instruction. It is continuous reconstruction, moving from the child's present experience out into that represented by the organized bodies of truth that we call studies. (p. 11)

MINDFUL HABITS OF EFFECTIVE TEACHERS

The ability to develop instructional plans based on knowledge of students, subject matter, and curriculum goals is a key habit of mind of effective teachers. This ability allows them to promote learning by their students.

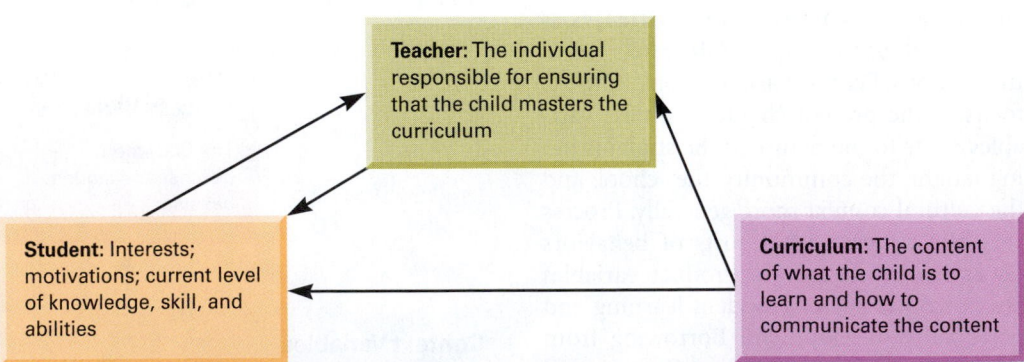

Figure 2.3 Refining the Student/Teacher/Curriculum Model

Teacher Development

Concerns of Beginning Teachers

Beginning to teach is exciting and rewarding. Finally, you have the opportunity to put your ideas and plans into practice. But it is not easy being a beginning teacher. To illustrate the point, here are the remembrances of Jim, a first-year fifth-grade teacher:

I came up here thinking, "Elementary education, what an easy degree." I worked with kids all the time, so I wondered what the big mystery was about it.[1] (p. 136)

Two weeks into his teaching career, Jim noticed some unexpected problems:

I am constantly, constantly having to discipline the entire class. . . . It's a constant battle to maintain order, and it's exhausting. The energy I use in management takes away from the energy I have for curriculum. (p. 139)

The problems grew to include concerns about motivation or lack thereof:

I got really frustrated at their lack of passion. So I told them, "You know, it really frustrates me to stand up here and see you just slouching in your seats looking at me, half of you not really paying attention. . . . The things we talk about in here give you the knowledge, but you've got to care, you've got to care about something." (p. 139)

Unfortunately, the problems did not stop there. One month into his career, Jim felt near despair about his students' disrespectful comments to one another:

The thing that really distracts me is the lack of respect they show, not just to me, but to each other. (p. 140)

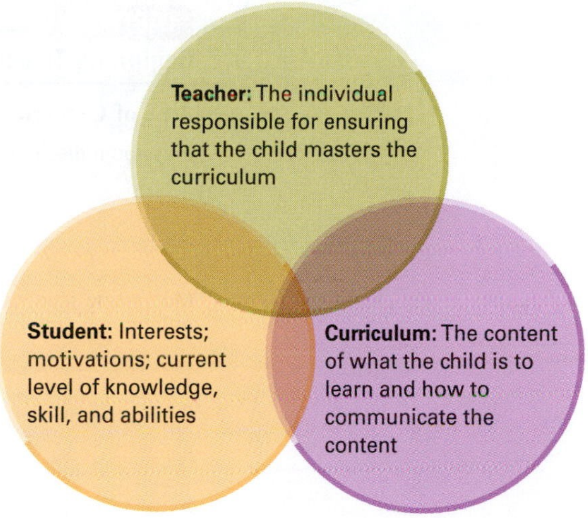

Beginning teachers face a host of doubts and uncertainties, as do their students. To appreciate which problems beginning teachers consider to be most pressing, researchers asked elementary and secondary school teachers from nine different countries to report the most serious concerns they encountered during their first three years of teaching (Veenman, 1984). Two dozen concerns emerged, but the most attention-getting problems were maintaining classroom discipline, motivating students, dealing with special needs, and assessing students' work. Concrete examples of these concerns appear in Table 2.1. Additional follow-up research expanded this list of beginning teachers' concerns beyond the four shown in Table 2.1 to further include developing high-quality relationships with parents, organizing class work, overcoming a lack of instructional resources such as insufficient materials and supplies, and dealing constructively with the problems caused by individual students (Berliner, 2001; Tschannen-Moran & Woolfolk Hoy, 2007).

Another group of educators who have concerns over beginning teachers are principals. When principals are asked what concerns they have about teacher effectiveness, they cite worries such as poor lesson-implementation skills, inability to establish rapport with students, and subpar classroom management skills (Torff & Sessions, 2005). Poor lesson-implementation skills occur as teachers plan learning experiences but fail to execute them during the instructional period; inability to establish rapport involves poor communication and interpersonal relationship skills with students; and subpar classroom management skills center around the inability to keep students attentive and on-task.

Teacher: The individual responsible for ensuring that the child masters the curriculum

Student: Interests; motivations; current level of knowledge, skill, and abilities

Curriculum: The content of what the child is to learn and how to communicate the content

Figure 2.4 An Integrated Model of Student/Teacher/Curriculum

What Does This Mean to Me?
Do you have any of the same concerns of beginning teachers listed in Table 2.1?

How Can I Use This?
One way to track your professional progress as a teacher is to reflect on how well you have found ways to solve these concerns.

[1]Quotations from Bondy, E., & McKenzie, J. (1999). Resilience building and social reconstructionist teaching: A first-year teacher's story. *Elementary School Journal, 100*(2), 136, 139, 140. Reprinted with the permission of the University of Chicago Press.

TABLE 2.1

Beginning Teachers' Top Concerns

Area of Concern	Examples
Classroom discipline	• How can I best cope with students' misbehavior? • What can I do to prevent acts of aggression before they occur? • Should I set classroom rules at the beginning of the year, or should the students make their own rules?
Motivating students	• How can I engage students more during learning activities? • What is intrinsic motivation, and can I trust it to promote learning? • How should I react to students who protest with "I can't"?
Special needs	• What are the benefits and costs of an inclusive classroom? • How can I best teach slow learners? • Will I be able to accommodate my instruction to students with special needs?
Assessment and grading	• What criteria should I use to develop a grading system? • Should I use portfolios to assess students' work? • How can I assess students' progress?

RIDE Could a sense of uncertainty as to how she will solve the teaching problems and concerns listed in Table 2.1 explain why Ms. Newby feels nervous?

Voicing beginning teachers' concerns is important because teaching success, teaching satisfaction, and professional development are all tied to finding ways to solve these problems (Caprara et al., 2003). Beginning teachers often question their adequacy as teachers. They worry about their professional survival, and they want desperately to be evaluated positively by the principal, their students, parents, and fellow teachers (Bullough, 1989). Finding solutions to the problems listed in Table 2.1 is one way of developing oneself as a teacher. In fact, professional development can be viewed as the successful progression from first being overwhelmed by these problems to later being able to solve them consistently and effectively (Borich, 1988; Fuller & Brown, 1975).

Stages of Teachers' Concerns The basic flow of concerns for almost any teacher is a shift from self-related concerns through task-related concerns to student- or impact-related concerns (Conway & Clark, 2003; Watzke, 2007). How this flow of concern plays itself out in the life of a teacher is that "Job 1" is often the self-focused phase of survival. That is, beginning teachers often have an idealized representation of what effective teaching is, and they typically feel a sense of personal inadequacy as they fail to live up to that ideal. During the task-focused phase, teachers begin to focus on planning, instruction, delivering the curriculum, implementing teaching strategies, and grading. "Job 2" is therefore to deliver the curriculum. During the student or impact phase, teachers develop a personal style, and they are most concerned about whether they can adjust their instruction to meet the academic and emotional needs of their students in ways that advance their intellectual and emotional development. Research studies that have followed teachers throughout their early careers do indeed tend to show that teachers' self-related concerns decrease over time and that task-focused and impact-focused concerns then emerge over the course of one's professional development (Pigge & Marso, 1997).

Beginning teachers not only have concerns, they also have goals and aspirations (Conway & Clark, 2003; Hagger & Malmberg, 2011). Like concerns, beginning teachers' goals align with self-related, task-related, and student- or impact-related goals (Hagger & Malmberg, 2011), as shown in Table 2.2. The important message from Table 2.2 is that while teachers do have concerns that they struggle to overcome, they also simultaneously have goals, aspirations, and targets for themselves that put the stages of teachers' concerns into a more proactive light of positive professional development. Beginning teachers both worry over the professional concerns they will face *and* set goals and strive to become the professionals they hope to become.

TABLE 2.2

Beginning Teachers' Top Goals

Category of Goals	Examples	Percentage of Preservice Teachers Mentioning the Goal
Self-related teaching goals	• Improve oneself as a teacher	31%
	• Manage classroom behavior well	27%
	• Apply for and get a job	25%
	• Establish positive relations with colleagues and community	8%
Task-related teaching goals	• Plan and organize lessons	30%
	• Master specific instructional strategies	23%
	• Understand the subject matter taught	17%
Impact-related teaching goals	• Produce desired learning outcomes	30%
	• Engage students in learning	28%
	• Establish positive relationships with students	17%

Source: Based on data from Hagger, H., & Malmberg. L.-E. (2011). Preservice teachers' goals and future-time extension, concerns, and well-being. *Teaching and Teacher Education, 28,* 1–11. Reprinted with the permission of Elsevier.

Phases of Professional Growth

As they begin their teaching careers, preservice teachers routinely emulate the effective teachers they observed as students (Calderhead & Robson, 1991). Thus, an admired role model is typically the starting point for a beginning teacher's idea about what constitutes good teaching. This is a reasonable starting point, of course. With actual classroom experience, however, preservice teachers' ideas evolve. Most of the time, beginning teachers become experts by advancing through the following four phases of professional growth (Kagan, 1992):

1. Decreased focus on self-as-teacher; increased focus on the needs of learners

2. Enhanced knowledge about learners

3. Automation of classroom routines and procedures

4. Growth in problem-solving skills

For an illustration of how these phases of professional growth unfold in the lives of most teachers, consider what Ms. Newby's experiences are likely to be. In her first year of teaching, she will constantly ask herself the question: Am I a good teacher? She will worry about what her colleagues, her students, her departmental chair, her principal, and students' parents think of her. She will also be trying to master the curriculum. In her second and third years, her focus will likely shift toward her students and what they need. She will ask herself whether her students are learning and how she can help them learn further. She will probably discover ways to transform the once-frequent classroom crises into rare events. By her fourth and fifth years of teaching, she will not even have to think about how to cope with classroom crises because her solutions to problems such as dealing with disruptive behavior and making transitions will become fairly automatic. Instead of just reacting to the various kinds of problems that arise during instruction, Ms. Newby will begin to anticipate them, and she will be able to call on a large repertoire of tried-and-true solutions to solve them, often before they have a chance to occur.

These four areas of professional growth highlight two key differences between beginning and expert teachers. First, as reflected in the first two phases, novice teachers focus strongly on themselves as teachers, whereas expert teachers focus strongly on their students as learners. Second, as reflected in the last two phases, novice teachers often possess an oversimplified picture of what constitutes classroom practice, often embracing a one-size-fits-all approach to instruction. Experts, on the other hand, have acquired a wealth of classroom experience and professional reflection that allows them to automate classroom routines and procedures. They manage classroom situations in ways that are context- and student-specific—the opposite of a one-size-fits-all approach. In a sense, experts operate on automatic pilot. They can retrieve the knowledge and strategies they need in a given teaching situation with minimal cognitive effort. The more they are able to do so, the more time and energy they have available for developing the rich problem-solving skills they need to meet the individual needs of their students (Berliner, 1986).

In addition, expert teachers distinguish themselves in another important way—by their vast knowledge. Here is a sampling of what expert teachers know (Shulman, 1987):

- Broad and deep subject-matter knowledge (English literature, algebra)
- How-to instructional strategies (how to capture students' interest)
- Knowledge about learning environments (how to organize students for group work)
- Knowledge about educational materials (curriculum, testing materials)

Beliefs about Teaching and Learning

Consider the following two propositions:

1. Students learn best when they are taught in classes in which students at different ability levels are mixed together.

2. To maximize learning, students should be sorted into classes based on their ability or prior achievement.

Which do you believe is true? How did you acquire your belief? What evidence do you have to support your position? How would your belief affect your approach to teaching? What would make you change your current position?

Teachers' beliefs are propositions that they believe to be true (Green, 1971). The beliefs that teachers hold to be true stem from three main sources (Richardson, 1996):

- Personal experience—the activities, events, and understandings that are a part of everyday life
- Experience with schooling and instruction—the experiences that teachers had when they were students
- Experience with formal knowledge—including knowledge gained from academic subjects and pedagogical knowledge gained in teacher education programs

Thus, what you believe about the efficacy of ability grouping would depend in part on your own experience in life, what happened to you in school, and what you were taught about grouping in your teacher education courses (Hallam & Ireson, 2003).

Beliefs affect the ways in which people process information. A research study whose findings are consistent with one's beliefs, for example, is much more likely to be accepted uncritically than is a study that challenges one's beliefs. Beliefs shape expectations of what will happen, and we prepare to respond to events based on those expectations. Errington (2004) argues that teachers' beliefs are probably the most important factor in determining the success or failure of a new approach to teaching, mostly because teachers act on their beliefs about what good teachers do and resist acting on their beliefs about what bad teachers do (Beijaard, Meijer, & Verloop, 2004). If you firmly believe in mixed-ability grouping, how receptive would you be to an instructional program based on ability grouping?

Teacher educators see changing the beliefs of teachers as essential to educational reform. Classroom experience, particularly the student-teaching experience, has a powerful influence on beliefs about teaching; once established, those beliefs are highly resistant to change. In a study of elementary school teachers, it was very difficult to persuade these teachers to change their beliefs about their students' abilities (with regard to writing; Wolf & Gearhart, 1997). Though it is difficult to convince teachers to change their beliefs, programs that emphasize an experiential approach in which students have opportunities for reflective field experiences hold promise (Richardson, 1996).

Content Knowledge, Pedagogical Knowledge, and Pedagogical Content Knowledge

content knowledge Knowledge about the subject matter being taught.

pedagogical knowledge Knowledge about how to teach.

Content knowledge—knowledge of the subject matter one teaches—is critical not only at the high school level, where there are history teachers and mathematics teachers, but also at the elementary school level, where most teachers teach all subjects (Hollon et al., 1991; Leinhardt et al., 1991). **Pedagogical knowledge**—knowledge about how to teach—is also

TABLE 2.3

Examples of Content Knowledge, Pedagogical Knowledge, and Pedagogical Content Knowledge

Content Knowledge	Pedagogical Knowledge	Pedagogical Content Knowledge
• Science: The causes of seasons, how gravity works • Math: Factoring quadratic equations, probability • English: Punctuation rules, sonnets • History: The Kansas-Nebraska Act, the Sacco and Vanzetti case	• Development: When children move from concrete-operational to formal-operational thinking • Peer learning: Group structures that work better for social development purposes or work better for learning • Self-regulation: The ability to organize and carry out one's work • Cognition: Overcoming ingrained misperceptions • Classroom organization: Students will have some overlapping and some distinct abilities, interests, and interaction styles	• Knowing that differences in students' backgrounds will require a thorough understanding of the students' current level of knowledge in order to teach them about the Sacco and Vanzetti case • Knowing how to set up groups to work on peer editing of essays • Understanding that science instruction at the elementary school level benefits from larger blocks of time in which activities such as experiments can be completed (even if that means fewer blocks per week)

critically important to facilitate students' learning (Newton & Newton, 2001). And the point where content knowledge and pedagogical knowledge intersect is also important (Shulman, 1986, 1986). This point of intersection is called **pedagogical content knowledge.**

Pedagogical content knowledge identifies the distinctive bodies of knowledge for teaching. It represents the blending of content and pedagogy into an understanding of how particular topics, problems, or issues are organized, represented, and adapted to the diverse interests and abilities of learners, and presented for instruction. (Shulman, 1987, p. 4)

Pedagogical content knowledge is not the sum of content knowledge and pedagogical knowledge but is, instead, an understanding of the nexus between the two—that is, of what it takes to translate content knowledge into a set of activities that will help students understand that content (Paulsen, 2001). This may consist of coming up with a strong analogy that the students can build on (Hulshof & Verloop, 2002), the ability to break down a complex task into its component parts (Jonassen et al., 1999), or the realization that students need to engage in activities that will illustrate a common misconception and lead them to correct it (Berg & Brower, 1991). Table 2.3 illustrates the relationships among the three kinds of knowledge that are important for good teaching.

pedagogical content knowledge Knowledge about how to make a particular subject matter understandable to particular students.

Taking It to the Classroom

Pedagogical Content Knowledge

It's break time in a nursery school and the teacher comes out with a tray of sliced vegetables and fruits. The children run up to the tray and rapidly consume the offerings. A visitor to the school asks, "Do you always give them such a healthy snack and are they always so receptive to it?" The teacher responds with a smile, "They haven't eaten since breakfast. You've got to give them the good stuff while they're hungry. They'll eat anything right now. They'll get something a little more like a treat later, but this helps them learn that fruits and vegetables are really good, too." Pedagogical content knowledge comes in many forms.

Figure 2.5 Combining
Content Knowledge and
Pedagogical Knowledge into
Pedagogical Content
Knowledge

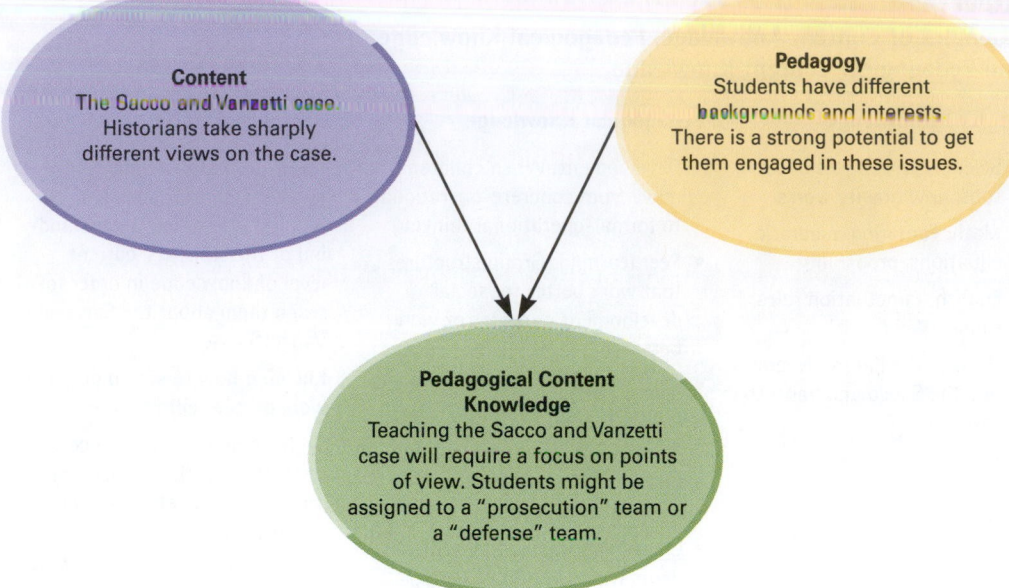

Figure 2.5 Combining
Content Knowledge and
Pedagogical Knowledge into
Pedagogical Content
Knowledge

An example of how content knowledge and pedagogical knowledge come together in terms of pedagogical content knowledge is presented in Figure 2.5. The development and application of pedagogical content knowledge requires the necessary subject-matter knowledge, awareness of any pedagogical issues associated with the students being taught, and the ability to bring the two together through appropriate instructional activities.

It is not surprising that experienced teachers have a greater stock of pedagogical content knowledge than do beginning teachers. Fortunately, widespread access to the Internet has made it much easier to share this knowledge. Lederman (2001), for example, has published a list of literature on teaching science that includes hundreds of entries and is accessible online. Becoming familiar with Web sites that focus on pedagogical content knowledge, lesson planning, and instructional activities is essential for professional development, especially for new teachers. Examples of these can be found on the Web site that accompanies this book.

Differences in Knowledge between Experts and Novices

Take a look at the chessboard in Figure 2.6. Spend about a minute and try to remember where all the pieces are. Then look away and think about how well you could re-create the arrangement of the pieces on the board.

Figure 2.6 Recognizing Chess Patterns

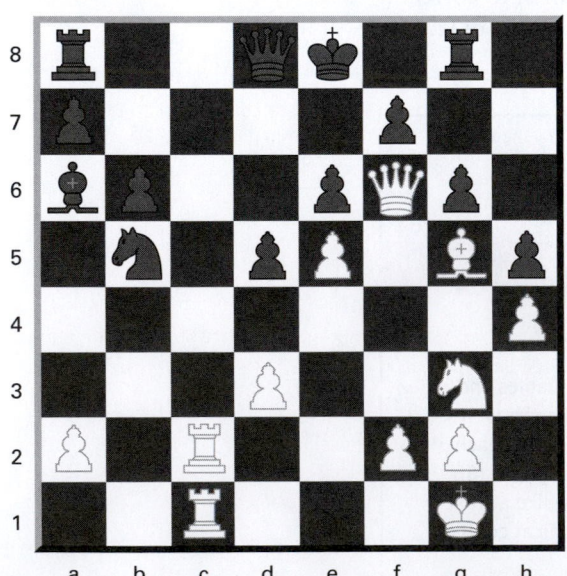

Most likely you would not be able to do so because, unless you are a chess expert, it is an extremely difficult task. However, if you *are* a chess expert, it is not difficult because the locations of the pieces mean something to a chess expert. It is not just a random arrangement of pieces on squares; it is a specific point in a reasonably well-played game of chess. As is evident from this example, experts see things differently than novices. A person who is knowledgeable about football is likely to be able to predict the next play a team will make. A radiologist will know how to identify a fracture and what subtle differences in an X-ray's shading mean.

Research on differences between experts and novices began with the work of Nobel laureate Herbert Simon and his colleague William Chase (Chase & Simon, 1973). They studied differences between experts' and novices' perceptions of chessboards, such as the one in the figure. They found that experts processed the information on the board in larger perceptual chunks than did novices. That is, not only is the king seen as occupying a space on the board, but its location is also processed in terms of potential threats against it in its current position and the protection provided by other pieces. This finding has been extended to many other areas, ranging from physics (Chi et al., 1981) to physical education (Chen, 2002).

While teachers do not generally strive to become experts at chess, they do strive to become experts at providing their students with warm, well-organized, and cognitively stimulating interactions. Many studies have compared expert and novice teachers (Berliner, 1992, 1994; Livingston & Borko, 1989a). In general, expert teachers do the following:

- View the classroom as a collection of individuals as opposed to a generic whole (Housner & Griffey, 1985; Kolis & Dunlap, 2004)
- Plan more globally and for longer periods (Livingston & Borko, 1989b)
- Have a more complex view of instructional options (Clermont et al., 1994)
- Run a more smoothly operating classroom (Leinhardt & Greeno, 1986)
- Evaluate student learning more often (Newton & Newton, 2001; Sanchez et al., 1999)
- Attribute failure in a given lesson to problems with planning, organization, or execution rather than to disruptive behavior on the part of students (Gonzalez & Carter, 1996)
- Make significant use of students' existing knowledge during instruction (Meyer, 2004)

Table 2.4 presents some key findings from a review of the literature on expert/novice differences in teaching (Hogan et al., 2003). Some differences are clearly just gains in

---

TABLE 2.4

Differences between Expert and Novice Teachers

Area	Novice Teachers	Expert Teachers
Curriculum planning	Plan for the class as a whole	Differentiate individual differences among students
	Focus more on short-term planning, with highly structured plans	Focus on both long-term and short-term planning, with more loosely structured plans
Instruction	Simpler view of instructional process and fewer instructional strategies	More complex views of the instructional process; better able to shift among methods
Teaching routines	Difficulty in shifting from one activity to another	Smooth transitions between activities
	Present fewer ideas in a given amount of time	Present more ideas in a given amount of time
	Difficulty in questioning for comprehension	Ease and consistency in probing for comprehension
Demonstrations	Less variety and detail	More variety and detail
	Lack of appreciation of areas of possible misperception or misunderstanding	Solid appreciation of areas of possible misperception or misunderstanding
Feedback	Focus more on student interest level than on understanding	Focus on student comprehension
Perceptions and reflections	Focus on behaviors and efficacy; concern with classroom management	Focus on student learning
	Less elaborate representation of classroom events/activities	More elaborate representation of classroom events
	Effective instruction believed to be focused on clear communication to students	Effective instruction focused on concepts such as advanced organization, examples and analogies, and assessment of progress
Classroom management	Focus on solving problems in the here and now	Focus on anticipating and defining management problems, generating multiple interpretations of behavior and possible approaches
	More likely to focus on teacher behavior	More likely to focus on student behavior
	Attribution of success or failure to problems or lack of problems with students	Attribution of success or failure to planning, organization, and execution of instructional strategies and lesson plans
	Less able to recall events of instruction	Better able to recall events of instruction
Communication	Less well organized and thematic	Organized around a central theme
	Does not incorporate ongoing evaluation of student progress	Evaluation of progress incorporated into discourse

Source: Hogan, T., Rabinowitz, M., & Craven, J. A. (2003). Problem representation in teaching: Inferences from research of expert and novice teachers. *Educational Psychologist, 38,* 235–247.
Copyright © 2003 by the Taylor and Francis Group.

skill, such as "smooth transitions between activities" that come with time, practice, and experience. But some differences might surprise a beginning teacher, such as focusing more on student comprehension than on student interest during instruction and focusing more on student learning than on student behavior and classroom management.

How does one become an expert teacher? One obvious first place to look is experience, but teaching experience alone does not make an expert teacher (Torff, 2003), as years of experience is a poor predictor of classroom expertise (Marsh, 2007). In fact, a small trend exists for teaching effectiveness to decline with more years of experience, though the relation between years of experience and teaching effectiveness is more complex than that. A reliable pattern of findings is that (1) beginning teachers display an impressive rise in teaching effectiveness during the first few years of teaching, (2) teaching effectiveness then levels off rather quickly in one's career, (3) teaching effectiveness stays stable for years, before (4) gradually declining later in one's career, at least to the extent that veteran teachers begin to reject innovations and changes in educational policy (Barnes, 1985).

While teaching expertise generally rises early in one's career, levels off, stabilizes, and then gradually declines, teacher expertise can be broken down by specific aspects of teaching. The teaching skill of providing organization—managing behavior, making sure class time is well-spent, and skillfully presenting learning opportunities—grows with experience (Malmberg et al., 2010). That is, teachers tend to get better and better in organizing their classrooms with each passing year. However, the teaching skill of emotionally supporting students—meeting the social and developmental needs of students, being responsive to their needs, and offering an enjoyable and positive classroom climate in which to learn—shows an inverted-U-shaped pattern in that teachers rapidly increase their expertise in this area, level off, and show a gradual decline with more years of experience (Malmberg et al., 2010).

If experience does not make the expert, then it seems important to ask: What does? It is not enough simply to teach prospective teachers the skills, knowledge, and abilities of expert teachers. Instead, various forms of experience are necessary, including supervised experience with a mentor or advisor, detailed feedback that allows teachers to monitor the progress they are trying to make, and vicarious experiences in which one envisions what one would do in certain situations (Klein & Hoffman, 1993; Landry et al., 2009). Experience needs to be combined with expert consultation (a coach, mentor), timely feedback, and active reflection (Artzt & Armour-Thomas, 1999; Landry et al., 2009; Ward & McCotter, 2004). A model for the kind of active reflection necessary to gain expertise can be found in the Reflection for Action exercises presented throughout this text.

Professional Development

Expertise is a high bar for a preservice teacher to meet, but developing teaching effectiveness through professional development is a common aspiration for all beginning teachers. In professional development, teachers ready themselves for their role and responsibilities in supporting children's and adolescents' learning in the classroom. Mentoring in the form of in-classroom coaching enhances professional development (Spodek, 1996). It is through such mentoring and guidance that beginning teachers have opportunities to try new approaches to instruction, and it is through mentoring and guidance that is personally tailored to the needs of one particular teacher-in-training that beginning teachers develop effective skills such as arranging their classrooms physically, planning lessons, delivering lessons, and assessing learning. Professional development best sparks gains in teaching effectiveness when teachers work and practice collaboratively rather than in isolation (Putnum & Burko, 2000; Spodek, 1996), as might occur either in small-group learning or in online teacher communities.

Online Teacher Communities Teachers are often quite isolated from other adults when teaching. This can be particularly difficult for new teachers, who need opportunities to discuss issues and problems and to learn from more experienced teachers. The Internet offers a partial solution by making extensive resources, such as vast stores of lesson plans, teaching ideas, and a variety of online teacher communities, available. One example of an online community is Tapped In, which includes educators at every level of the education system from around the world. The goal of Tapped In is to assist teachers in supporting one another through peer online networks. Teachers can participate in discussions and mentor other teachers. Another online community, Proteacher, has over 30 active discussion boards and many teaching resources for a variety of subjects. (See the Web site of this text for current Web addresses.)

Online teacher communities can provide ideas and suggestions for how to manage the various phases of professional growth and development. Many online teacher communities provide discussion boards specifically for new teachers. Many of them also deal with the kinds of concerns that beginning teachers have about managing classrooms, maintaining discipline, motivating students, and teaching children with special needs.

Teaching Efficacy

Too often, the first year of teaching is a dramatic one. Beginning teachers feel considerable anxiety and doubt over their ability to cope with the teaching situation. In fact, so potentially overwhelming is the transition from teacher education to full-time responsibility that it is sometimes referred to as *the reality shock*. The name is apparently deserved because schools lose 40% to 50% of their new K–12 teachers in the first five years of teaching (Budig, 2006; Roness, 2011). (The good news is that teacher attrition is relatively rare after five years; Tye & O'Brien, 2002.) So years 1 through 5 are a critical period in the life of a teacher, and it will serve the reader well to understand how to cope effectively with the reality shock and its aftermath.

Teaching is a highly demanding occupation that requires a commitment to achieve goals in the face of sometimes daunting odds. It requires high levels of mental, physical, and interpersonal energy. Without a strong belief in one's ability to achieve one's instructional goals, it would be easy to give up and pursue a less strenuous career.

To counter professional fears and feelings of anxiety and doubt, beginning teachers need to develop a sense of coping confidence, or teaching efficacy. **Teaching efficacy** is a teacher's judgment of his or her capacity to cope with the teaching situation in ways that bring about desired outcomes (Tschannen-Moran & Hoy, 2001; Woolfolk Hoy, 2004).

teaching efficacy A teacher's judgment of, or confidence in, his or her capacity to cope with the teaching situation in ways that bring about desired outcomes.

When classroom situations are simple and routine, most teachers judge themselves to be sufficiently, if not highly, efficacious. They see the mild demands of the classroom and the manageable obstacles before them and rightly judge that they have what it takes to cope accordingly. It is when things go wrong and during times of unexpected difficulties and setbacks that confidence begins to slip and give way to doubt, anxiety, and negative emotionality that is the very antithesis of teaching efficacy (Bandura, 1988).

Providing a sampling of which classroom situations most commonly test teachers' sense of efficacy, Table 2.5 lists items from the Teachers' Sense of Self-Efficacy Scale. As shown in the table, three teaching domains define most of what constitutes the emotional struggle between feeling efficacious versus feeling overwhelmed: classroom management, student engagement, and instructional strategies. Notice how well these three teaching situations correspond to the concerns voiced by beginning teachers in Table 2.1. Teachers need a sense of efficacy—a sense of *I can do this*—for classroom management to solve problems of classroom discipline. They need a sense of efficacy for student engagement to solve problems of student motivation. And they need a sense of efficacy for instructional strategies to solve a range of instructional concerns, including how to assess students' learning and how to adjust their lessons to deal with students' individual differences and special needs.

Beginning teachers worry most about how they will solve day-to-day problems associated with discipline, motivation, assessment, and students' special needs.

A study involving prospective teachers in Turkey asked teachers-to-be to complete a pair of questionnaires—one assessing the same top concerns as depicted in Table 2.1 broken

TABLE 2.5

Questionnaire Items to Assess Teaching Efficacy

Factor 1: Efficacy for classroom management

1. How much can you do to control disruptive behavior in the classroom?
2. How much can you do to get children to follow classroom rules?
3. How much can you do to calm a student who is disruptive or noisy?
4. How well can you keep a few problem students from ruining an entire lesson?

Factor 2: Efficacy for student engagement

5. How much can you do to get students to believe they can do well in schoolwork?
6. How much can you do to help your students value learning?
7. How much can you do to motivate students who show low interest in schoolwork?
8. How much can you do to foster student creativity?

Factor 3: Efficacy for instructional strategies

9. To what extent can you use a variety of assessment strategies?
10. To what extent can you provide an alternative explanation or example when students are confused?
11. To what extent can you craft good questions for your students?
12. How much can you do to adjust your lessons to the proper level for individual students?

Note: The above items are from the Teachers' Sense of Self-Efficacy Scale.

Source: Reprinted from *Teaching and Teacher Education*, Vol. 17, Tschannen-Moran, M., & Hoy, A. W., "Teacher efficacy: Capturing an elusive construct," 783–805. Copyright © 2001, reprinted with permission from Elsevier.

RIDE Could a sense of teaching inefficacy explain Ms. Newby's anxiety and nervousness? If so, is the primary source of that anxiety inefficacy toward classroom management? Inefficacy toward student engagement? Or inefficacy toward instructional strategies?

down by self-, task-, and impact-related concerns and a second assessing the same aspects of teaching efficacy depicted in Table 2.5. The relation between teachers' concerns and teachers' efficacy appears in Figure 2.7. The figure shows a meaningful relation between the concerns teachers have and the efficacy they perceive. The large negative number immediately above the bold double-headed arrow (−.43) indicates a rather strong inverse relation between having many concerns and low teaching efficacy or having few concerns and high teaching efficacy. The more teachers have of one, the less they seem to have of the other.

Taking It to the Classroom

Do You Know Jack: How Many Jacks Are There?

Mr. Ramsey, the physics teacher, and Ms. Ramón, the Spanish teacher, have just discovered that they both have Jack as a student, although they cannot believe it is the same child. Mr. Ramsey finds Jack a conscientious and attentive student, whereas Ms. Ramón finds Jack to be a constant irritant and a poor student in Spanish. What can Ms. Ramón do to find Mr. Ramsey's Jack? Here are two suggestions related to each of the three aspects of teaching efficacy (classroom management, student engagement, and instructional strategies):

- Have him sit at the front of the room so it is easier for him to pay attention.
- Ask Jack's friend to work with and help him during class.
- Talk to Jack. Does he like Spanish? Does he understand the utility it has for his life?
- Ask Jack what strategies he uses when trying to learn Spanish and help him advance from superficial strategies (memorization) to sophisticated strategies (elaboration).
- Observe Jack's differential responsiveness to your variety of instructional strategies—lecture, paired learning, whole-class discussion, time with language software, and so on.
- Prepare a special and individualized question that Jack will find especially interesting and optimally challenging.

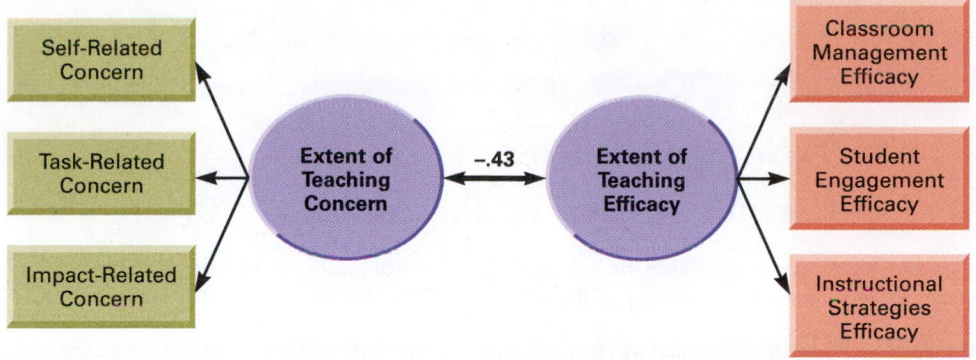

Figure 2.7 Negative Relation between Teachers' Concerns and Teaching Efficacy

Source: Adapted from Boz, Y., & Boz, N. (2010). The nature of the relationship between teaching concerns and sense of efficacy. *European Journal of Teacher Education, 33,* 279–291. Copyright © 2010 by the Taylor and Francis Group.

Beginning teachers generally have lower teaching efficacy than do veteran teachers (Hoy & Woolfolk, 1993). Fortunately, positive teaching experiences are associated with greater teaching efficacy (Bruinsma & Jansen, 2010). This is an important point to make note of because striving to develop a sense of teaching efficacy is well worth the effort. Compared with teachers with relatively low efficacy, teachers with high efficacy are more enthusiastic during teaching (Allinder, 1994; Guskey, 1984), more committed to teaching (Coladarci, 1992; Evans & Tribble, 1986), more open to new ideas and more willing to experiment with new teaching methods (Ross, 1992), more satisfied with their job (Klassen & Chiu, 2010), and more likely to stay in the profession (Bruinsma & Jansen, 2010; Glickman & Tamashiro, 1982). Also, during instruction, teachers with high efficacy invest greater effort in and spend more time planning and organizing instructional activities (Allinder, 1994). When things go wrong, they persist in the face of setbacks rather than give up. They are also less critical of the errors their students make (Ashton & Webb, 1986). For all these reasons, this is the sort of teacher you want to become, because teachers with high efficacy are better able to foster positive outcomes for their students, including gains in students' thinking (Anderson, Greene, & Loewen, 1988), motivation (Midgley, Feldlaufer, & Eccles, 1989), and achievement (Ashton & Webb, 1986; Ross, 1992).

Developing Teaching Efficacy

The early years of the profession are a critical time in the life of a teacher in terms of developing strong and resilient teaching efficacy. This is so because teaching efficacy beliefs are deeply rooted in personal mastery experiences of being able versus unable to produce valued student outcomes such as student engagement and classroom management (Bandura, 1997). A consistent and optimistic finding in teacher education is that teaching efficacy increases during teacher preparation and during student-teaching experiences (Wenner, 2001). An equally consistent but pessimistic finding is that teaching efficacy decreases during the first year of teaching (Woolfolk Hoy & Spero, 2005).

While the above findings might appear contradictory at first, they are actually important points of data to embrace if one wants to understand the process of developing teaching efficacy throughout one's teaching career. As the teacher-to-be gains experience, benefits from mentoring and timely feedback, and engages in active reflection about how to improve and solve tomorrow's problems, teaching efficacy generally grows. That is, beginning teachers benefit from the experience of mastery, a positive school climate, encouragement and support during difficult times, and strong mentoring by more experienced teachers (Brennan et al., 1999; Darling-Hammond & McLaughlin, 1995; Jenlink et al., 1996; Rimm-Kaufman & Sawyer, 2003; Woolfolk Hoy & Spero, 2005; Yost, 2002). (See the nearby Uncommon Sense box.)

Yet experience also makes one increasingly aware of the obstacles to producing valued student outcomes. According to Woolfolk Hoy and Spero (2005), beginning teachers often underestimate the complexity and sheer difficulty of the teaching task and often make mistakes such as being too harsh (trying to manage behavior) or too lenient (trying to relate

Uncommon Sense

Veteran Teachers Are Not Nervous on the First Day of School—Or Are They?

Jim O'Kelly has a doctorate in education and many years of experience. He is recognized as a skilled teacher and is often asked to mentor new teachers. He has taught kindergarten for many years. In a discussion of the first day of school, Jim related the following story:

You know, I've been teaching kindergarten for 24 years now, and it was only about 3 years ago that I was able to sleep through the night for the week before school started. My wife used to say, "Jim, are you crazy? You've been teaching kindergarten all of your life. You love the kids and they love you. Why are you losing sleep over the beginning of the school year?" I told her that I was about to meet 20 people whom I had never met before and with whom I was about to spend an entire year. Furthermore, their start in school depended on me. They were counting on me, and so were their parents. I didn't know what they would be like this year.

It is normal to be anxious about getting started on a new adventure, and that is what each school year is. Jim lets us know that even a highly experienced teacher is nervous at the beginning of the school year. Experts and novices (and students and parents) may not be so different when it comes to first-day-of-school jitters.

warmly to students). Beginning teachers also lose the source of support they enjoyed during teacher training and come to realize the gap that typically exists between anticipating that one can cope well with the teaching situation and the reality of actually coping well. Basically, the optimistic teaching efficacy of beginning teachers sometimes—perhaps often—becomes tarnished when confronted with the realities and complexities of teaching (Rushton, 2000). Fortunately, teachers typically snap back from the first year's reality shock (which decreases their teaching efficacy) so that teaching efficacy generally returns to a rising trajectory during the early career period before taking root in a stable way and becoming firmly established by mid-career (Tschannen-Moran & Woolfolk Hoy, 2007; Wolters & Daugherty, 2007). Further, this snapback and gradual rise in teaching efficacy to a mid-career peak holds true for all three aspects of teaching efficacy—namely, teaching efficacy for classroom management, teaching efficacy for student engagement, and teaching efficacy for instructional strategies (Klassen & Chiu, 2010).

referral Educators' shorthand for the recommendation that a child be evaluated for possible special education classification.

Teaching Efficacy and Learners with Special Needs Teaching efficacy is particularly important in working with students with special needs. Efficacy-confirming positive feedback is not an everyday experience as teachers relate to children with autism, students who are deaf, and adolescents with a conduct disorder. There is a strong tendency for teachers to send students they perceive to be troublesome to be evaluated for **referral** and a high probability that a referred student will become a classified student (Algozzine et al., 1982; Gelzheiser, 1990). Teachers with a high sense of teaching efficacy are less likely to refer students for evaluation than are teachers with a low sense of efficacy (Soodak & Podell, 1993). This is so because high teaching efficacy gives teachers the confidence they need to work ever harder to manage any student's behavior, engage any student in learning, and enact instructional strategies that help any student learn. Further, when high and strong, teaching efficacy is resilient against what might appear to be momentary failure feedback. If, as the research indicates, referral almost always leads to classification, it follows that classification depends to some degree on the teacher's efficacy in the classroom. (See the nearby Taking It to the Classroom box.)

Teaching Efficacy and Diverse Students Teaching efficacy is also important in working with diverse students. This is so for the same reason that teaching efficacy is so important when working with learners with special needs—namely, that doubt-inducing negative feedback may be a more common experience for a beginning teacher than is efficacy-confirming positive feedback. It takes effort, experimentation, reflection, and patience to figure out how to best manage behavior and how to spark students' engagement when interacting with students whom one may not understand well, such as students who do not

Taking It to the Classroom

Teaching Efficacy and Special Education Teachers

Brownell (1997) provides some advice for teachers of students with special needs:

- Set high but realistic expectations. Ask successful colleagues—especially those with a good deal of experience in special education—to help you set goals.

- Use best practices. Do not forget to be a professional. You should be in constant pursuit of the best practices to apply in your classroom.

- Track student progress. This is something you almost certainly will ask your students to do. It is a good idea for you to do so, too. If you record your students' progress, it will give you a better sense of perspective when you encounter the rough days that all teachers have from time to time.

- Employ professional discretion and personal autonomy. It may sometimes seem that everything you do as a teacher is predetermined, but in fact you can have a great deal of flexibility.

- Do not rely on praise. People (your principal, your colleagues, your supervisor) may *or may not* tell you what a great job you are doing. Your professional satisfaction has to stem from the progress you see in your students.

speak English well, students in poverty, or students with very different backgrounds from the teacher's. But that is the essential feature of teaching efficacy, as all teachers will experience a hint of doubt in their teaching efficacy when their instructional efforts do not seem to work. What matters most with teaching efficacy, however, is how quickly the teacher's confidence snaps back to its former high and strong levels. Teachers with high efficacy recover their confidence quickly after a setback, whereas teachers with low efficacy tend to take a surprisingly long time to recover their confidence after a setback and perhaps do not recover it at all (Bandura, 1997). Hence, the resiliency of one's teaching efficacy is as important as is the level of one's teaching efficacy. A good way to diagnose how resilent your own teaching efficacy is might be is to assess your teaching efficacy in the context of working with both learners with special needs and diverse learners.

Metaphors for Teaching

Visualize yourself in the role of a full-time teacher, and ask yourself how you would complete the following phrase: "The teacher as a(n) _____." In the blank, write a metaphor to capture the spirit of what you would like to accomplish in the classroom. Some possible responses might include *entertainer, coach, lion tamer, choreographer, party host, circus master, traffic cop, ship captain*, and *air traffic controller* (Bullough, 1991; Carter, 1990; Marchant, 1992). For purposes of illustration, Table 2.6 lists the metaphors generated by one group of high school teachers.

TABLE 2.6

Teaching Metaphors for Eight High School Teachers

Teacher	Years Experience	Subject Matter Taught	Metaphor for "The Teacher as a(n) ____"
Amy	0	Social studies	Motivator
Betsy	4	History, psychology	Chameleon
Cal	5	Geography, history	Cowboy
Don	5	Geography, history	Boat captain
Evelyn	7	Spanish	Ringmaster
Francine	7	Journalism	Gardener
Gregory	9	Biology	Team leader
Howard	9	Economics	Coach

Source: Reprinted from *Teaching and Teacher Education*, Vol. 12, Stofflett, R. T., "Metaphor development by secondary teachers enrolled in graduate teacher education," 577–589. Copyright © 1996, reprinted with permission from Elsevier.

What Does This Mean to Me?
What metaphor for a teacher would you use? How would it influence your behavior in the classroom?

Generating metaphors for teaching can help teachers improve their classroom practice in three ways (Tobin, 1990). First, metaphors facilitate reflection. By generating metaphors, teachers gain greater personal understanding of how they view themselves as teachers (Berliner, 1990; Bullough, 1991). As a case in point, elementary school teachers often generate a metaphor that emphasizes the caring and nurturing aspects of teaching (e.g., the teacher as gardener or facilitator). Secondary school teachers often generate a metaphor that emphasizes the dispensing of knowledge (e.g., the teacher as information giver or ship captain).

Second, a metaphor can serve as a standard by which teachers can evaluate their current practice. By treating metaphors as standards, teachers can identify points of conflict that might exist between their teaching ideals and their actual practice. For instance, one beginning teacher adopted the metaphor of *gardener*, which he explained as:

> *I see my role as teacher being most importantly one of providing the very best climate in the classroom for the maximum growth and development of each student . . . who needs more or less light, more or less water, or who needs to have weeds pulled up from around them.* (Bullough, 1991, p. 45)

During his first year of teaching, this teacher decided to audiotape several class periods. After listening to the tapes, the *gardener* felt deeply disturbed. What he heard was not the nurturing gardener he conceptualized himself to be but, instead, a teacher who engaged in lengthy monologues that imposed his own agenda on a group of passive listeners. Rather than living up to the standard of a gardener, his teaching reflected curricular demands for content coverage, the need to achieve high standardized test scores, and the accepted norms at his school about what constitutes effective teaching (teaching as telling). By reflecting on the metaphors they hold, teachers may realize, as this teacher did, that their metaphors are inadequate to help them cope effectively with their actual classroom conditions.

How Can I Use This?
Generating a metaphor of your own can give you an ideal to strive for, a standard to judge your current way of teaching, and an opportunity to reflect on yourself as a teacher.

Third, generating a new metaphor can help initiate a desired change in one's current way of teaching. If one's current way of teaching is personally unsatisfactory, one can generate a potentially more appropriate metaphor that represents an ideal goal to strive for. For instance, a teacher might seek to change an adversarial *traffic cop* metaphor to a more collaborative *protector of the learning environment* (Marshall, 1990). In the example provided earlier, the *gardener* developed a second, complementary metaphor. He began to think of teaching as a conversation and himself as a *dialogist*. In this way, a well-chosen metaphor can serve as a conceptual springboard from which to expand and to improve one's way of teaching (Tobin, 1990).

Because successful teachers generally have richer and more conceptually complex metaphors than do less successful teachers (Bullough & Stokes, 1994) and because the effort to uncover one's metaphors can lead to meaningful change in how one teaches (Tobin, 1990; Tobin & LaMaster, 1995), it might be a good idea to pause for a moment and ask yourself what metaphor or metaphors for teaching you currently hold. To gain such insight, you might want to do what one group of qualitative researchers did and pull out the Personal Statement you submitted in your admission application to the College of Education (Pinnegar et al., 2011). These researchers read many such Personal Statements and extracted from these essays each teacher's own definition of what a teacher is and each teacher's sense of what a teacher's roles, responsibilities, and obligations were. From these essays, the researchers extracted 12 common metaphors held by preservice teachers—celebrity, creator, expert, friend, leader, learner, mentor, nurturer, performer, redeemer, scaffolder, and self-sacrifice.

R I D E Does the lack of a powerful teaching metaphor explain why Ms. Newby feels nervous about her coming teaching responsibilities? If she reconceptualized herself into the role of a leader or a captain, would that metaphor silence her fears and offer her a sense of empowerment?

For purposes of illustration, Table 2.7 focuses on two of these metaphors—celebrity and scaffolder (for a detailed description of all 12 metaphors, see Pinnegar et al., 2011). The teacher-as-celebrity is one who is exciting and admired. The celebrity has charisma and is never dull. The celebrity expects students to be admirers and to imitate. The teacher-as-scaffolder is one who strives to teach students at the correct level in their development and skill. The scaffolder encourages students to reach a level of independence in their own learning. A scaffolder expects students to be responsible and independent.

TABLE 2.7

Two Sample Teaching Metaphors with Definition, Teacher Obligations, and Student Role

Metaphor	Definition	Teacher's Obligations	Students' Role
Celebrity	Teachers have charisma. They teach exciting and new things to their students. Every part of teaching should be fun and exciting. Teachers are important figures in students' lives, setting an example, influencing, and impacting their students. They are people who students look up to and admire immensely. Students want to be like their teachers. Teachers must be well-liked by students in order to make a difference in their lives.	• Have charisma • Be fun • Entertain, never repeat or be dull, appeal to sense of "play" • Teach "exciting and new" concepts • Gain the admiration of students • "Make a difference" in students' lives because of the admiration they inspire in students	• Imitate and admire teacher • Aspire to become like teacher
Scaffolder	Teachers simplify concepts and teach at the correct level of the learners. Teachers teach through building on concepts. A teacher is encouraging and shows students how to do things on their own and tries to be kind.	• Simplify concepts • Teacher at correct level (implicit: understand child developmental levels) • Build on concepts • Encourage students • Help students reach a level of independence in their learning • Try to be kind (implicit: the teacher must pretend to be kind even when he/she doesn't feel like it)	• Be responsive • Work independently under teacher's guidance

Source: Reprinted from *Teaching and Teacher Education*, Vol. 27, Pinnergar, S., Mangelson, J., Reed, M., & Groves, S. "Exploring preservice teachers' metaphor plotlines," 639–647. Copyright © 2011, reprinted with permission from Elsevier.

Contrasting these two metaphors suggests that the beginning teacher who sees herself as a scaffolder is very likely more ready for the classroom challenge than is one who sees herself as a celebrity, because the celebrity does not yet really understand the relational nature of teaching and the crucial role that students need to play in their own learning. In contrast, the scaffolder foresees multiple roles for both teacher and students. The celebrity will also likely reject attempts to teach her to plan and enact difficult work, while the scaffolder will likely embrace these aspects of her teacher education experience (Pinnegar et al., 2011).

The Payoff: Enjoying Your Work, Finding Passion, and Having Societal Trust

Is all this work to anticipate beginning teachers' concerns, develop high teaching efficacy, and generate teaching metaphors worth it? If so, what is the payoff? Experienced teachers report that their efforts to develop expertise are unambiguously worth the sweat and tears. As one teacher explains, effective teaching can be highly rewarding (Brunetti, 2001, p. 60):

. . . [Seeing] one of these kids [from] two years ago and watching him graduate. These kids were going nowhere; they weren't even going to school. We couldn't get 'em to spend two days in class together in a row, and now they're graduating. And they're graduating because of me. That's the most rewarding of all.

When done well, teaching can be highly rewarding—not only for students but for teachers as well (Brunetti, 2001, p. 56):

I just love what I do. It's fun. I was out for long periods of time because I had serious eye problems . . . drove the doctors crazy because I wanted the operation right away so I could get back to the classroom.

Quotations such as these help explain why passion is so widespread throughout the teaching profession, as 93% of one large and diverse group of Canadian teachers reported at least a moderate—if not high—level of passion toward teaching (Carbonneau, Vallerand, Fernet, & Guay, 2008). Indeed, most teachers are passionate about what they do (Day, 2004).

The general public also recognizes the excellent and caring work that teachers do. When people rated over 100 different professions in the United States on a survey in terms of trustworthiness and credibility, teachers scored second highest among all professionals, behind only U.S. Supreme Court justices (Budig, 2006).

Planning

Appendix
Effective Planning

To be a good teacher, you must plan your instruction carefully and link your instructional goals to your teaching strategies (PRAXIS™, II.B.1; INTASC, Principles 4, 7).

Thus far, we have examined the notion of becoming an effective teacher by looking at teachers from a developmental perspective. Now we turn to consider the actual activities and events of successful teaching. This section begins with instructional goals and lesson planning, which is the planning that takes place before teaching begins. Then it considers the activities that occur in the classroom, where the excitement, the interaction with students, and the reward of watching children make progress take place.

As we will see, outstanding teachers have well-developed planning and organizational skills. Effective teachers first define what is to be taught and what is to be learned, as they set goals and objectives for the lesson. The process of teaching begins as teachers translate these instructional goals and objectives into lesson plans, instructional units, and projects and activities.

Instructional Goals

instructional goal A statement of desired student outcomes following instruction.

It is difficult to know whether progress is being made toward an **instructional goal** if the goal is not clearly defined. Instructional goals have been called *objectives, achievement targets, desired outcomes, standards,* and *learning intentions.* They have been defined in very broad terms and in terms that are so narrow as to be almost microscopic, ranging from "Students will develop a sense of citizenship" to "Students will be able to link 10 state capitals with their states in a matching task in a maximum of 20 seconds." No matter how they are phrased, instructional goals state the desired outcomes of instruction. They are an essential component of the educational process and have been the focus of a great deal of educational research and theory.

educational objectives Explicit statements of what students are expected to be able to do as a result of instruction.

taxonomy A classification of objects according to a set of principles or laws.

Educational Objectives: Bloom's Taxonomy Drawing on the pioneering work of Tyler (1949), who developed behavioral objectives in military training, Bloom and colleagues developed a taxonomy of **educational objectives** for use in constructing courses and the assessments to go with them (Bloom et al., 1956). They wrote objectives to reflect what students would be able to do as a result of instruction and classified them according to their level of complexity. The result is widely known as *Bloom's taxonomy.* (The term **taxonomy** is taken from biology, where it is the system for the classification of plants and animals.) Bloom's goal was to organize educational objectives according to the level of cognitive complexity and thought required.

Bloom's taxonomy, shown in Table 2.8, has been one of the most influential ideas in education over the past half-century. Bloom wanted educators to think seriously about what they want to achieve in their classes. He advised teachers to develop a small set of broad statements about what they want students to be able to do as a result of the planned instruction. By developing a taxonomy that showed what **higher-order thinking skills** looked like, he encouraged teachers to make sure that they were not simply requiring students to recall information. In Bloom's model, the goals for a course became a blueprint for developing instruction and assessment.

higher-order thinking skills Skills and abilities that go beyond recall and comprehension, including the ability to apply ideas and concepts, analyze and synthesize information, and evaluate complex information.

As you examine Bloom's taxonomy, you may have the same reaction that other teachers have had in the past. That is, the first three levels of the taxonomy all seem reasonable and highly applicable to classroom instruction—knowledge, comprehension, and application. The three higher levels of the taxonomy—analysis, evaluation, and synthesis—might not

TABLE 2.8

Bloom's Taxonomy of Educational Objectives

Level	Description	Examples
Knowledge	Recall of facts, dates, and general information about a subject	Identifying trees from the shapes of their leaves Reciting multiplication facts
Comprehension	Understanding information, ideas, or skills	Restating the ideas in a paragraph in the student's own words Explaining how the future tense is formed in regular French verbs
Application	Applying skills to new situations	Using an algebra skill such as simultaneous equations to solve a novel math problem Performing an analysis of water from a local stream
Analysis	In-depth consideration of an idea or concept	Comparing and contrasting possible causes of the Great Depression Explaining the underlying tenets of Cubist art
Synthesis	Taking two ideas and concepts and seeing what the intersection or *synthesis* of these ideas would be; this involves generating a new (to the student) idea	Projecting what would happen if Toni Morrison rewrote the concluding scene from Shakespeare's *Hamlet* Inventing a set of rules for wheelchair baseball
Evaluation	Critical consideration of a concept or theory in some definable context—not simply a judgment of whether one likes or dislikes something and the reasons why (in Bloom's taxonomy, the most sophisticated mental activity)	Evaluating the potential of Piaget's stage theory for explaining conflicts that occur among children on the playground Writing a critical assessment of the impact of the First Amendment protection of freedom of speech on Internet blogs

seem distinct enough or might not seem obviously useful in assessing different students' abilities or progress. To enhance the ability of the taxonomy to speak more clearly to teachers, two colleagues of Bloom, Anderson and Krathwohl, adapted the nouns Bloom used into action verbs, as follows:

What Does This Mean to Me?
Think of a course you are currently taking. What levels of cognitive objectives are identified in the syllabus of the course?

Bloom	**Anderson**
Knowledge	Remembering
Comprehension	Understanding
Application	Applying
Analysis	Analyzing
Evaluation	Evaluating
Synthesis	Creating

This adapted scheme has a logical appeal to it, primarily in employing terms that are more closely related to classroom life, such as *creating* instead of *synthesis*.

New Approaches to Goals   The use of goals or objectives in planning instruction and assessment has been both in and out of favor over the years. Today, instructional goals are once again popular, but in new forms. The first of these is **standards**, which are discussed later in this section and more fully in Chapter 15. Standards are a set of objectives that define what should be learned in a given subject area by students at specific grade levels. In the United Kingdom, objectives are often referred to as learning intentions (Clarke, 2005).

Another new form of instructional goals is **achievement targets** (Stiggins, 2001). Achievement targets are specific statements of what teachers want to accomplish in a particular lesson or set of lessons. The use of the word *target* implies a goal for the instruction and, therefore, for the assessment that goes with it. Stiggins's (1997) approach, shown in

standards A comprehensive set of educational objectives organized by subject matter and grade level.

achievement targets Well-specified statements of what teachers want to accomplish in a particular lesson or set of lessons.

TABLE 2.9

Stiggins's Taxonomy

Target	Description	Examples
Knowledge	• Declarative knowledge: facts, terms, concepts and generalizations • Procedural knowledge: procedures or problem-solving methods	• Declarative: information, facts, dates, relationships, etc. • Procedural: steps involved in a science procedure; the algorithm for a particular mathematics problem
Reasoning	• The process of answering questions through analytical problem solving	• Story problems in mathematics
Skills	• The abilities necessary to put procedural knowledge to use in a fluent fashion and in the appropriate context	• At the elementary school level, the ability to come into school on a winter day, take off outdoor clothes, and get ready for school • At the high school level, the ability to write haiku in the proper form
Products	• Things students create that reflect their current skill and ability levels	• A science experiment lab report • A map detailing U.S. imports and exports
Attitudes and dispositions	• Interests in certain areas; the desire to learn more about a topic	• Purchasing a book about a topic in a lesson • Attendance at a concert

Table 2.9, might be thought of as a set of specifications for what students should learn or do, in contrast to the broader objectives of Bloom's taxonomy.

Stiggins's target category of **products** represents a substantial break from Bloom's thinking. Products are things created by students that reflect their skills and abilities as well as their ability to create something brand new. Bloom would probably consider products to be forms of assessment rather than an objective or a target; Stiggins believes that the ability to combine those skills and abilities into a successful product is a worthwhile target in itself. Consider, for example, a book report. What does a book report represent?

products Student creations that reflect their skills and abilities as well as their ability to create something new.

- The underlying skills of being able to comprehend a book one has read, synthesize the ideas contained in the book into a concise report, and communicate those ideas in a clear fashion (Bloom) OR
- A goal in and of itself, the ability to produce a report under certain constraints and guidelines that requires pulling together a variety of abilities (Stiggins)

The first of these represents a focus on process, whereas the latter focuses on the product.

Another key area of difference between Bloom's taxonomy and Stiggins's classification is that Stiggins includes attitudes and dispositions—because, for example, it does not do a person much good to learn how to read if he or she never reads. For Stiggins, the development of positive attitudes is another achievement target, as skill itself may not be enough for learning and transfer to occur (Salomon & Globerson, 1987). Mindfulness, or the purposeful use of thought and effortful processes, is also necessary for learning and transfer of skills. Unless the tasks in which students are engaged are valued by the students, it is unlikely that they will engage in such effortful processing. Bloom also believed in the importance of attitudes and dispositions. He and his colleagues developed a second taxonomy solely for attitudes and dispositions that they called the taxonomy of the "affective domain."

Using Goals in Classroom Teaching

Twenty years ago, teachers were often trained in how to develop and communicate instructional goals and objectives. To a great extent, that is no longer true. The instructional standards movement in assessment at the state and national levels has generated a much more *top-down* model for setting instructional goals. In all likelihood, the instructional goals, objectives, or standards you use in your classroom will have been established at the state or national level. These might be quite broad or very specific. In either case, you will need to work to translate those goals into your classroom goals and planning.

You will still have a number of decisions to make, however, about the kinds of instruction and assessment needed for students to meet the standards set for them. Figure 2.8 provides some examples of instructional goals from various statewide programs. Choose one that is close to the level and subject matter you think you might be teaching, and

Figure 2.8 Samples of Statewide Instructional Goals

Grade 3 Reading Standards for California Public Schools

1.0 Word Analysis, Fluency, and Systematic Vocabulary Development

Students understand the basic features of reading. They select letter patterns and know how to translate them into spoken language by using phonics, syllabication, and word parts. They apply this knowledge to achieve fluent oral and silent reading.

Decoding and Word Recognition

1.1 Know and use complex word families when reading [e.g., *-ight*] to decode unfamiliar words.
1.2 Decode regular multisyllabic words.
1.3 Read aloud narrative and expository text fluently and accurately and with appropriate pacing, intonation, and expression.

Vocabulary and Concept Development

1.4 Use knowledge of antonyms, synonyms, homophones, and homographs to determine the meanings of words.
1.5 Demonstrate knowledge of levels of specificity among grade-appropriate word and explain the importance of these relations [e.g., *dog/mammal/animal/living things*].
1.6 Use sentence and word context to find the meaning of unknown words.
1.7 Use a dictionary to learn the meaning and other features of unknown words.
1.8 Use knowledge of prefixes [e.g., *un-, re-, pre-, bi-, mis-, dis-*] and suffixes [e.g., *-er, -est, -ful*] to determine the meaning of words.

Source: California Department of Education http://www.cde.ca.gov/be/st/ss/.

Grade 8 Mathematics Standards for Texas Public Schools

8.5 Patterns, relationships, and algebraic thinking. The student uses graphs, tables, and algebraic representations to make predictions and solve problems. The student is expected to:
(A) predict, find, and justify solutions to application problems using appropriate tables, graphs, and algebraic equations; and

(B) find and evaluate an algebraic expression to determine any term in an arithmetic sequence with a constant rate of change

Source: (2006) Texas Administrative Code (TAC), Title 19, Part II, Chapter 111. Texas Essential Knowledge and Skills for Mathematics. Retrieved August 16, 2007, from http://www.tea.state.tx.us/rules/tac/chapter111/ch111b.html.

Grade 11 Ohio Content Standards

Life Sciences Characteristics and Structure of Life

1. Describe how the maintenance of a relatively stable internal environment is required for the continuation of life, and explain how stability is challenged by changing physical chemical and environmental conditions as well as the presence of pathogens.
2. Recognize that chemical bonds of food molecules contain energy. Energy is released when the bonds of food molecules are broken and new compounds with lower energy bonds are formed. Some of this energy is released as thermal energy.
3. Relate how birth rates, fertility rates and death rates are affected by various environmental factors.
4. Examine the contributing factors of human population growth that impact natural systems such as levels of education, children in the labor force, education and employment of women, infant mortality rates, costs of raising children, birth control methods, and cultural norms.

Source: Ohio Department of Education, Academic Content Standards (2002). Retrieved June 22nd, 2011, from http://education.ohio.gov/GD/Templates/Pages/ODE/ODEDetail.aspx?page=3&TopicRelationID=1705&ContentID=834&Content=100394.

think about what it means. How specific is it? How would you go about trying to teach the standard? What questions would you have about what might or might not be included as part of that standard or goal?

Consider the standards for eleventh-grade students in Ohio. They seem to be fairly clear and worthwhile objectives for eleventh-grade students. But what kinds of experiences, activities, explorations, explanations, group work, analogies, examples, or experiments would help students understand this material? How should an understanding of how chemical bonds of food molecules contain energy (content knowledge) and an understanding of eleventh-grade students in a science class (pedagogical knowledge) be combined to help students gain the knowledge and skills included in the standard (pedagogical content knowledge)? The answer will not be the same for all classrooms. Help, however, is readily available: Curriculum guides have ideas; colleagues and supervisors have suggestions; and veteran teachers offer guidance on the Internet. As a teacher, you will need to make intelligent choices among the options, try them out, and reflect on the results obtained for purposes of expanding and refining your pedagogical content knowledge.

Translating Goals into Plans

Translating instructional goals into lessons and units of instruction is a critical juncture in the process of instruction. Planning is so critical that we have developed a special feature of the text to help develop these skills. Beginning with this chapter, at the end of each chapter you will find lesson plans that emphasize one or more of the important aspects of the chapter. It might be useful to stop at this point and take a look at the first set of plans.

Planning for instruction is somewhat similar to planning for other activities, such as a vacation, a party, or how to spend a free Saturday. Planning begins with a set of givens and anticipations.

Planning: An Overview   How is planning for instruction like planning a vacation? Each involves the following:

- Setting objectives or goals
- Choosing a way to achieve those goals
- Making decisions concerning the details of the approach, possibly consulting people who have more experience
- Making changes as the plan is carried out
- Evaluating the plan after it has been carried out in order to be better prepared the next time around

In teaching, there are several layers of plans, with smaller plans nested within larger ones (Sardo-Brown, 1988a, 1988b; Yinger, 1980). A plan for a particular lesson (e.g., a plan for a lesson on the structure of a Shakespearean sonnet) is embedded within a larger plan to teach students various sonnet structures. The plans for teaching about the structures of sonnets may be embedded within a larger unit plan for teaching about common poetic forms. There are various approaches to these subunits. Many elementary school teachers like to take a seasonal approach to the year, emphasizing changes in the seasons and holidays or other events associated with them. With the seasons, they will have units that are often thematic in nature. Thus, in the fall, there might be a unit on the changing of the leaves and, in the winter, there might be a unit on Valentine's Day. Within units, some teachers plan by the day, whereas others plan by the week, then by the day within the week. Teachers usually look for natural break points in their planning, such as time off for a holiday. Secondary teachers' planning is often broken down into instructional units related to the texts that they are using. They need to develop the flexibility to adjust their planning according to the perceived progress of the students in their classes.

Planning On and Planning For: Instructional Time and Scheduling   When an event is far in the future or might not even occur, the impetus to plan—and to plan realistically—is not as great (except perhaps as a pleasant diversion). The rule here is simple: The more you plan *on* something, the more you plan *for* it. A daily lesson plan for a period that is more than three months away does not really have to be *in the book* right now, but a plan for the day after tomorrow really does.

Elementary school teachers must plan about 1,000 hours of instructional time for one group of children (180 school days times 5 to 6 hours a day). High school teachers must plan 150 to 200 hours for each of four or five classes, some of which may be in the same subject and at the same grade level.

Elementary school teachers need to organize the day and the week in their classrooms. They have to make room for *specials*, such as gym, art, and music, which are scheduled for specific times, as well as for lunch and possibly recess. In addition, individual students may be pulled out of class for speech therapy, gifted programs, and the like. Teachers typically come to terms with these interruptions by developing a daily or weekly instructional schedule that lays out when each subject or activity will take place each day. An example of such a schedule is presented in Figure 2.9.

This teacher puts language arts and math in the morning and social studies, science, and foreign language (Spanish) in the afternoon. She has allocated an hour and a half each day for language arts and an hour and 15 minutes for math. Science and social studies each get two hours per week. Clearly, her instructional goals lean more heavily toward language arts and math than to other subjects. Also note that she has left an hour slot open on Wednesdays. This allows her to place other activities in that time slot or use it to catch up if need be. Her planning is now more controlled: She has allocated the available hours to various subject areas, and her planning will take place within the structure she has created.

At the secondary school level, there is no need for this kind of schedule. The times when teachers meet with students are decided well in advance of the school year, and teachers usually have little say in those decisions. Even if a math teacher feels that students learn math better early in the morning than in the afternoon, he or she will still have to have some classes in the afternoon. Another factor that secondary school teachers have to deal with is the amount of time they have for each class each day. In a typical high school, this will probably be 40–50 minutes. Some high schools have **block scheduling**, which structures the academic time for students during a school day in larger blocks of time for particular subjects. For example, science might be taught in two blocks of two hours each instead of five 45-minute classes; the amounts could be much greater.

Within the structures that elementary school teachers create and that secondary school teachers are given, teachers build their plans for the year broadly, for seasons or thematic units somewhat more specifically, and for the upcoming weeks and days even

MINDFUL HABITS OF EFFECTIVE TEACHERS

Effective teachers are organized and follow through. They don't lose papers or materials they need for class. They plan ahead and know what they are going to do. They follow through—on promises, on getting assignments graded thoroughly and on time, and on commitment to their students.

block scheduling An approach to scheduling at the middle and high school levels that allows for larger (but fewer) blocks of time to be scheduled for subjects.

Figure 2.9 Mrs. Johnson's Class Schedule

	Monday	Tuesday	Wednesday	Thursday	Friday
Fifth-Grade Class Schedule					
8:30-10:00	Language Arts	Language Arts	Language Arts	Language Arts	Language Arts
10:00-10:15	Recess	Recess	Recess	Recess	Recess
10:15-11:30	Mathematics	Mathematics	Mathematics	Mathematics	Mathematics
11:30-12:15	Phys Ed	Art	Lunch	Phys Ed	Art
12:15-12:45	Lunch	Lunch	Writers' Workshop	Lunch	Lunch
12:45-1:30	Science	Social Studies		Science	Social Studies
1:30-2:00	Music	Phys Ed	Open	Music	Phys Ed
2:00-2:30	Spanish	Spanish		Spanish	Spanish

How Can I Use This?

Are you someone who is highly organized and keeps a tight schedule, or do you tend to be less organized and take things as they come? How might these tendencies translate into teaching?

www.wiley.com/college/odonnell

more specifically. Table 2.10 presents a visual model of the planning process and the issues that need to be considered in developing instructional planning. The results of each day's teaching will lead to changes in the plans for the next day, and sometimes plans at broader levels will have to be adjusted. Flexibility without losing sight of long-term goals is the key. Often, beginning teachers feel that if they do not make it through their plans for the day, the lesson was a failure. Such "failures" probably have more to do with errors in estimating the amount of time it will take to do something than with what went on in the classroom. Veteran teachers are much more likely to evaluate their lessons in terms of students' engagement and responses to the instructional activities that took place.

Looking at Lesson Plans Individual lesson plans usually have several different elements, including objectives or standards, lists of materials needed, descriptions of activities, and assessment procedures. We look at a lesson plan in depth in this section. There are lesson plans at the end of each chapter that you can examine as well. Also, a variety of Web sites offer lesson plans. You can find some of these in the Web site associated with this text. Examine the lesson plan in Figure 2.10, and ask yourself the following questions:

● What is the teacher trying to accomplish?

TABLE 2.10

Levels of Planning for Instruction and Issues Involved in Developing Plans

Level of Planning	Specific Considerations
Plan for the year in language arts Yearly plans are statements of the overall approach to teaching language arts for the year that clearly address the goals/standards/objectives set for the class.	● Where are my students now? (Test scores, last year's performance, informal assessments) ● What resources are available to me? (Expertise, curriculum materials, funds) ● What are my students' interests? How can I accommodate diversity in my planning? (Previous year's students, discussions) ● What are the overall goals for the year? (Statewide and district standards, my goals, student input) ● Are there students with special needs? (What kinds of needs, help available?)
Seasonal plans for the year: mid-fall Teachers usually like to break the year down into smaller units and relate their lessons to seasonal events and holiday times, such as Thanksgiving and President's Day.	● What is going on this time of year that I can highlight? (Changing leaves, getting colder, Thanksgiving) ● Where should we be now in terms of goals? (Experience from previous years, informal assessments) ● What seems to be working well with this class? (Student responses, parent/teacher conferences) ● Where can I find some good thematic units? (The Internet, teachers' magazines, colleagues)
Instructional units Instructional units are pieces of the planning process that might last for a week or several weeks. They are a cohesive whole made up of a number of parts. A unit in language arts might focus on reading a particular book, working on haiku, or constructing a good paragraph.	● How will students react in terms of motivation in this unit? (Relationship to students' interests) ● How will this unit work toward overall goals? (What will students be learning in this unit?) ● How will I assess student learning? (Getting the needed information, helping students with self-assessment) ● How can I accommodate learners with special needs in this unit? (Modifications, highlighting abilities, getting help from special education teacher)
Daily lesson plans Daily lesson plans are guides for day-to-day activities in the classroom. They include motivational activities, instructional activities, materials needed, and assessments. Beginning teachers tend to be more elaborate and more likely to stick to daily plans than are veteran teachers.	● What should today consist of? (Presenting new material, student activities, group work) ● How can I engage student interest? (Student interests, relevance to current events, benefits to students) ● How will I know if it is going well? (Informal assessments, student engagement) ● What can I do if the lesson "is a disaster"? (Moving on, cycling back, moving to another subject)

Lesson Plan—Ocean Observation

SUMMARY

This activity will help familiarize students with methods scientists use to study the coastal ocean in the Pacific Northwest, and will encourage them to pose and investigate their own questions about the ocean.

SUBJECT AREA: Physical Science/Earth science

GRADE LEVEL: 6–12

KEY CONCEPTS

- Technology enables scientists to study global and local ocean characteristics over long periods of time.
- Scientists use technology to help them answer questions about the ocean.

OBJECTIVES: Students will be able to

- *Describe* the various methods used by NANOOS researchers to study ocean characteristics, events, and ecology.
- *Apply* information found on the NANOOS Web Portal to answer questions.

MATERIALS

- Computer lab with Internet access or projection screen
- Science journal or notebook for each student

PROCEDURE

1. Engage students in a class discussion, considering the following questions:
   - How do scientists study the ocean?
   - How can they "see underwater"?
   - Why is the ocean studied?
   - What do we need to know about the ocean?
   - What are some things you would like to know about the ocean or things that live in the ocean?

2. Ask students to make their own list of questions, write them in their science journal, and share them with a partner.

3. Have students visit the NANOOS Web Portal (http://www.nanoos.org) and work with a partner to explore the various data and visual products and decision tools available.
   - On the left menu, click *About NANOOS*, and from there, *Ocean Observing* to find out about ocean observing systems and what questions scientists are trying to answer about the ocean.
   - On the left menu, click *About NANOOS* then *Sensor Platforms* to discover some of the tools NANOOS researchers use to explore the oceans.
   - On the left menu, click *Data*, then *Data Explorer* and *NANOOS Estuarine and Shoreline Data*. Examine the map to see the various locations ocean observing data are being collected. Clicking the different colored thumbnails, and from there, the station, will bring you to data from that specific platform. What are some of the types of data being collected?

4. Have students explore the NANOOS Web Portal to determine which data or visual product or tools could help answer the questions they recorded earlier in their science journals.

5. Have students keep a record in their journal of things they notice and things the wonder about during their exploration. These questions can be used later as possible investigation topics.

6. Keep a chart of student questions and refer to them as answers or connections come up during class study. This helps students see that research begins with questions and helps them recognize the value of asking questions.

ASSESSMENT

- **Performance**—Did students participate in discussion and web investigation sessions and demonstrate an understanding of how scientists study the ocean?
- **Product**—Did students compose appropriate questions for investigation in their science journal? Did students accurately describe some of the research projects and technology involved in studying the oceans? Did students apply the information found on the NANOOS Web Portal to answer their questions?

RESOURCES

- "Bridge" Ocean Observing Resources: http://www2.vims.edu/bridge/search/bridge1output_menu.cfm?q=oos
- Coastal and Ocean Observing System Primer: http://web.vims.edu/bridge/Bridge_OOS_Primer.pdf
- Rutgers Coastal Ocean Observation Laboratory: http://rucool.marine.rutgers.edu/
- NOAA IOOS website: http://ioos.noaa.gov/about/basics.html

Figure 2.10 Example of a Lesson Plan

Source: From the Pacific Northwest Regional Ocean Observing system.

- What assumptions does this plan make about the students as learners?
- Could I teach this lesson from these plans? Would I want to?
- Are the assessment procedures adequate?
- How likely are students to respond positively to this plan?
- How might I improve this plan?
- How difficult would it be to carry out this lesson plan?

www.wiley.com/college/odonnell

Not all lesson plans look alike. The lesson plans at the end of the chapter are excerpts from more complete plans. They are included in this form to provide you with practice in examining a lesson from the perspective of the content of this chapter. The complete lesson plans are available at www.pbs.org. To get the most use out of the lesson plans at the end of each chapter, it is recommended that you first read each excerpt and then respond to the questions related to Bloom's and Stiggin's taxonomies at the end in the Ask Yourself! section.

Research on Teacher Planning   Research on planning generally shows that as teachers become more experienced, they tend to rely more on routine and do less formal planning (Leinhardt, 1983). This is not to say that teachers do not plan, but it appears that veteran teachers' planning often takes the form of mental rehearsal of what is to be done in class (McCutcheon & Milner, 2002; Morine-Dersheimer, 1979). Teachers often rely on textbooks and curriculum guides as sources of information for planning (McCutcheon, 1980; Smith & Sendelbach, 1979). They focus on what is needed to fill the instructional time available to them (Leinhardt, 1983; Sardo-Brown, 1988a, 1988b, 1990). Teachers are also influenced by external factors, such as district or school requirements or recommendations about how much time to allocate to various subject areas and what areas of the curriculum to emphasize (Sardo-Brown, 1990). Therefore, the extensive approach to planning at all levels that is presented here and in other works on teacher preparation may not be what first-year teachers see when they observe their more experienced peers. Two points are worth mentioning here: It is better to create more detailed plans at first, and it is almost always better to plan thoroughly.

Lesson Study   An interesting new approach to looking at planning and the execution of those plans in classrooms comes from Japan and is called *lesson study*. In lesson study, a team of teachers who are teaching the same curriculum work together collaboratively to think about how best to approach the lesson. Then one member of the team teaches the lesson while the other members observe the lesson and collect data and impressions of how the lesson went. They gather together to analyze the data, reflect on the lesson, and discuss what they have learned. The fourth step in the process is to refine and reteach the lesson, perhaps with a different team member, and to consolidate what they have learned about that lesson specifically and what they might generalize to new lessons. This is but a very brief description of this exciting idea. An excellent reference to learn about lesson study is *Lesson Study: A Handbook of Teacher-Led Instructional Change* by Catherine C. Lewis (2002).

www.wiley.com/college/odonnell

Planning and Technology   Advances in technology can benefit teachers looking for help in planning in several ways. As mentioned earlier in the chapter, there is abundant advice concerning planning on the Internet. There is a Web site for almost any area in which a teacher might develop a lesson. A general search on the Internet using keywords such as "teachers' lesson plans" should produce a large number of Web sites. You will need to carefully evaluate the quality of lesson plans you find because, over time, some of these sites become obsolete. The Web site for this text includes a list of useful sites.

Planning for Students with Special Needs

Planning for students with special needs within the context of overall instructional planning poses special challenges. The research in this area suggests that general education teachers at the elementary school level have difficulty adapting their lesson plans for such students or using individualized education programs (IEPs) in making their decisions (Schumm et al., 1995; Venn & McCollum, 2002). At the middle and high school levels, there is little evidence that differential planning to accommodate the special needs of classified students included in regular classrooms actually occurs (Schumm & Vaughn, 1992; Vaughn & Schumm, 1994).

Planning for classrooms that include students with special needs is certainly more complicated than planning for classrooms without such students, but *not* planning for such students is irresponsible. If you are working with students with special needs, you must decide how to include them in ways that address their needs while fostering the productivity and caring nature of all the students in the class.

In such planning, first consider your instructional goals or objectives. Your task is to bring together the goals and activities you are considering for the class as a whole and the goals and educational assistance required by each special needs student, as documented in the IEP, to form a cohesive instructional plan. This may be challenging, but help is available. Your school's faculty will include special education teachers who are trained to help you with this task. Next, there are written resources and resources on the Web that can help in your planning and even provide practical tips for modifying plans (see the Web site for this text for current URLs). Next, think about the resources you have available for working with students with special needs. You may have an in-class paraprofessional or teacher's aide. You may have resource room help (which will require working with the resource room teacher to coordinate planning). You can give students with special needs extra time to complete assignments or allow them to work on assignments at home with their parents. You can make modifications in assignments that are more in line with the instructional goals for a particular student. You can have students with special needs work with other students, either one-on-one or in group settings.

The key to planning for inclusion is to keep in mind the goals that have been laid out for students in their IEPs, the resources available to you, and the in-class options and modifications that can be made to maximize growth for each student and for the class as a whole.

General Approaches to Teaching

Over the course of their professional development, teachers build up a set of strategies and tactics that they employ in their day-to-day teaching. *Strategies* are broad approaches to teaching and learning. They may include an approach to introducing new or difficult material to children, how to review material before an assessment, or how to organize adolescents into groups for cooperative learning activities. Broad strategies are typically embedded within a general approach to teaching, typically either a teacher-centered or a student-centered approach. In the brief introductions that follow, we provide an overview of expository teaching, discovery learning, and direct instruction. The discussion here is intended as a framework for thinking about teaching in general. There are a host of various approaches to teaching, and each of these will be discussed in the coming chapters of the text.

Ausubel (1961) distinguished between rote and meaningful learning. Rote learning involves verbatim memorization. The information has little connection to what the learner already knows. In contrast, meaningful learning involves connecting new information to what the learner already knows and understands, and it involves three necessary conditions: (1) The learner must approach the task at hand with a learning strategy appropriate for extracting meaning; (2) the task must be potentially meaningful to the learner; and (3) the relationship of what the learner knows and the new information must be clear.

Paralleling this distinction between rote and meaningful learning, Ausubel further distinguished between **reception learning** and **discovery-based learning**. In reception learning, "the entire content of what is to be learned is presented to the learner in its final form" (Ausubel, 1961, p. 16). Reception learning is similar to **expository teaching**. The teacher provides an *exposition* of how knowledge of a particular content is structured and organized. In discovery learning, learners must integrate information with existing information and reorganize cognitive structures. They *discover* principles by actively engaging in experiences that prompt their exploration of principles underlying these experiences.

reception learning A type of learning in which the learner acquires the structure of knowledge set forth by the teacher.

discovery-based learning Students work on their own to grasp a concept or understand a lesson.

expository teaching A type of teaching in which the teacher provides an exposition of how a particular set of information is structured and organized.

(© Stockbyte, Inc./Getty Images)

The teacher provides support for the students' inquiry as they engage in guided discovery.

Expository Teaching

An expository lesson involving reception learning begins with the presentation of a concept. The teacher presents a rule, then illustrates it with examples. For example, a high school social studies teacher may be teaching about the origins of war and may begin by presenting the conclusion to be drawn from the lesson: "Wars are caused by a set of interacting factors that include economic and social forces, including prior history." This statement is an advance organizer in that it provides the students with an overall statement of the intent of the lesson and a broad statement of what is to be learned during the lesson. An **advance organizer** is always introduced early in expository teaching so that it may serve "to bridge the gap between what the learner already knows and what he needs to know before he can meaningfully learn the task at hand" (Ausubel et al., 1978, pp. 171–172). It helps students organize new information that is presented.

Types of advance organizers exist. Advance organizers can be either **comparative organizers**, which remind students of what they already know, or **expository organizers**, which provide students with new knowledge.

One of the misconceptions related to expository teaching is that it is entirely teacher-centered. Clearly, the teacher plays a key role. However, an important aspect of the progress of a lesson is the presentation of examples by both students and teacher to illustrate the general principle under study. Students, for example, might activate prior knowledge of World War I by giving examples of how economic forces helped to cause the war. They might further illustrate some of the social forces that contributed, such as the animosity between various nations. In studying World War II, students will have a framework for encoding new information by relating it to material they already know. They will compare the similarities and differences between the causes of the two wars. The teacher helps the students to connect their examples back to the original advance organizer. Research on the use of advance organizers suggests that they are most effective for learners who lack prior knowledge (West & Fensham, 1976).

Discovery Learning

Discovery learning is characterized by **inductive reasoning**, or the abstraction of general principles from a variety of examples. It involves *bottom-up processing* in contrast to reception learning, which involves *top-down processing*. Students may, for example, attempt to categorize a set of rocks based on criteria they decide on. Their goal is to find the underlying structure of a body of knowledge that would allow them to categorize the rocks correctly on the basis of an underlying principle (e.g., density).

Discovery learning often requires some teacher direction or support so that it is actually **guided discovery**. In the previous example, the teacher may help students focus on key attributes by asking them to consider which rocks are heavier or bigger. In research on students learning to program in Logo using discovery learning methods, children were found to have difficulty learning even the fundamentals of Logo programming (Dalbey & Linn, 1985; Kurland & Pea, 1985; Mayer, 1988). Left to their own devices to uncover underlying principles related to programming, students are more often than not largely unsuccessful. There is little evidence that unguided discovery learning is the most effective instructional strategy for the majority of students, while the evidence for guided discovery learning is substantial (Mayer, 2004).

Direct Instruction

Direct instruction is explicit teaching. Direct instruction is a systematic form of instruction that is used for the mastery of basic skills and facts. It involves an ordered set of six sequential activities (Rosenshine, 1979, 1987, 1988; Rosenshine & Stevens, 1986) in which the teacher does the following:

1. **Review the previous material**. Reviewing prior material allows the teacher to help students activate appropriate schemas for the task at hand. A schema is an organized set of knowledge about a topic. For example, one of the authors of this book asked a

advance organizer A broad introductory statement of the information that will be presented in a lesson.

comparative organizer A broad statement that reminds the student of what he or she already knows.

expository organizer A broad statement of what is to be learned in a lesson.

inductive reasoning The abstraction of a general principle from a variety of examples.

guided discovery Students work under the guidance of a capable partner to grasp a concept or understand a lesson.

direct instruction A systematic form of instruction that is used for mastery of basic skills and facts.

12-year-old whether he had ever heard of Socrates. The boy answered, "Yes, he used to play for Brazil." For the author, Socrates was a philosopher who was the subject of a fine painting in an art gallery. For the child, Socrates was a soccer player. When the teacher reviews previous material, he or she helps ensure that the teacher and students have activated the same organized set of information. The students are thus ready for additional information. Reviewing previous material can also provide the teacher with an opportunity to detect any residual misunderstandings that students may have.

2. **Present new material.** The teacher links the new material explicitly to the material learned previously. He or she communicates goals for the new material and presents it in small segments, providing lots of examples.

3. **Provide guided practice.** The teacher should check students' understanding by asking questions, providing examples that were solved and other problems for practice. The teacher needs to check for misconceptions and misunderstandings and provide additional practice as needed.

4. **Provide feedback.** The teacher should provide students with information about the correctness of their efforts and provide corrective information to clarify students' understanding.

5. **Provide independent practice.** A key element in providing guidance as in step 3 is being able to withdraw it. The student needs an opportunity to practice the new skills alone to ensure that he or she has mastered the skill. Independent practice can be provided through the use of groups, seatwork, and homework.

6. **Review weekly and monthly.** It is important to review the material in a distributed fashion. Distributed practice or practice at irregular intervals is more effective than massed practice or practice performed all at once, perhaps just before a test.

Part of the reason that direct instruction is effective is because it presents small amounts of information and provides sufficient practice to attain mastery of the targeted skill. It is also very predictable, which may help some students organize their own learning strategies to fit the task. Direct instruction, however, may not be appropriate for all kinds of tasks, particularly those that do not involve certainty in the outcomes. It is an effective approach to teaching, though its effectiveness lies mostly in cultivating mastery of basic skills and facts.

REFLECTION FOR ACTION

The Event

Ms. Newby is nervous. She wants to leave her doubt, anxiety, and sense of unease behind and become a confident and expert teacher. She wonders what she can do to empower herself as a teacher-to-be. What can Ms. Newby do to grow her confidence and to silence her fears? How can she ready herself for opening day?

Reflection RIDE

She is nervous and wants to empower herself to become a confident and expert teacher. Why is she nervous? Is being nervous really a problem? It makes her feel uneasy, but will the sense of doubt, anxiety, and unease really interfere with her performance as a teacher? If it will undermine her effectiveness, what steps might she take before the first day of class to empower herself? What should she do?

What Theoretical/Conceptual Information Might Assist in Interpreting and Remedying This Situation? Consider the following.

Teaching Knowledge

Ms. Newby may be nervous because she does not yet feel sufficiently prepared for her first day in the classroom. Her nervousness might be a signal that she currently possesses insufficient knowledge about learners, teaching, and the teaching–learning situation in general.

Teaching Efficacy

Ms. Newby may be nervous because she has low teaching efficacy. It might be the case that because Ms. Newby has low teaching efficacy, she, in turn, has a high sense of doubt, anxiety, and unease about what will happen when she is actually in the classroom.

Teaching Metaphor

Ms. Newby may lack a potent metaphor to guide her classroom activity. To empower herself and overcome her nagging nervousness, she might embrace a potent metaphor to place her into a more empowering role.

Information Gathering RIDE

Is Ms. Newby nervous because of a lack of teaching knowledge? To determine if this is the case, she could read articles from her favorite professional journal to gain more knowledge, insights, and instructional strategies that she could use. She might consult other teachers to inquire about their knowledge, insights, and instructional strategies. *Is Ms. Newby nervous because of a lack of teaching efficacy*? To determine if this is the case, she could complete a questionnaire like the one in Table 2.5 to assess her level of teaching confidence in terms of her capacity to cope with potentially difficult classroom situations. *Is Ms. Newby nervous because she lacks a potent metaphor to guide her identity as a teacher*? To determine if this is the case, she could initiate conversations with master teachers to ask about the empowering metaphors they use to define their identities as teachers. She needs to diagnose why she is nervous.

Decision Making RIDE

If the information she gains from reading professional journals and talking with other teachers is able to enhance her knowledge, then the source of her nervousness might indeed be a lack of teaching knowledge. Does her nervousness decline as she gains more teaching knowledge? If her questionnaire responses show low teaching efficacy, then the source of her nervousness might indeed be her fear of being overwhelmed by the potentially difficult teaching situations that she will soon face. Do responses to the questionnaire items seem to hit the mark on why she is nervous? If her conversations with the two master teachers provide her with empowering metaphors, then her nervousness might indeed be the lack of a potent teaching metaphor. Does her nervousness slip away as she shifts her identity toward a new teaching metaphor?

Evaluation RIDE

Through evaluation, Ms. Newby will be able to put her finger on the cause of her nervousness. The key question in this evaluation is how close a relation there is between her sense of doubt, anxiety, and fear on the one hand and her lack of teaching knowledge, responses to the Teaching Efficacy scale that indicate low self-efficacy, and lack of a potent metaphor on the other hand. As she gains teaching knowledge, does her anxiety move toward confidence? As she gains teaching efficacy, does her anxiety move toward confidence? As she embraces a new metaphor for herself as a teacher, does her anxiety move toward confidence? By changing each of these three aspects of her teaching—teaching knowledge, teaching efficacy, and teaching metaphors—she will be able to observe the causal factor underlying her nervousness. Once identified, she will be very well positioned for change—for future empowerment.

Further Practice: Your Turn

Here is a second event for consideration and reflection. In doing so, implement the processes of reflection, information gathering, decision making, and evaluation.

The Event

You are in your first year of teaching and things are going pretty well. Your colleague is also a new teacher but is having great difficulty. He has not planned well and does not have clear instructional goals. He also does not seem to have a strategic approach to teaching or a general approach to teaching. Your colleague has come to you for assistance.

What key elements of effective teaching and the process of teaching does your colleague seem to lack? How could you help him become a more effective teacher?

SUMMARY

- **What is teaching?**

  Teaching is one person's interpersonal effort to help others acquire knowledge, develop skill, and realize their potential. It involves everything that teachers do to help learners advance from a state of having less knowledge, skill, and potential to a state of enhanced knowledge, skill, and potential.

- **What concerns do beginning teachers have?**

  Beginning teachers have many concerns, but the four at the top of the list are maintaining classroom discipline, motivating students, dealing with individual differences and special needs, and assessing students' learning. These concerns tend to shift from self-related concerns in the first year of teaching toward task-related and impact-related concerns in subsequent years.

- **Why are teachers' beliefs about teaching and learning important?**

  Teachers' beliefs come from personal experience, experience with education, and experiences with formal knowledge. Beliefs shape expectations of what will happen, and we prepare to respond to events based on those expectations. Teachers act on their beliefs about what good teachers do and those beliefs are probably the most important factor in determining the success or failure of a new approach to teaching. However, the beliefs teachers have about themselves and their students may not be accurate. Classroom experience, particularly the student-teaching experience, has a powerful influence on beliefs about teaching, and once established, those beliefs are highly resistant to change.

- **How do expert teachers differ from novice teachers?**

  Expert and novice teachers differ along a variety of dimensions. Compared to novices, experts are better able to do the following:
  - View the classroom as a collection of individuals
  - Plan more globally and for longer periods
  - Have a more complex view of instructional options
  - Run a more smoothly operating classroom
  - Evaluate student learning more often
  - Attribute failure in a given lesson to problems with planning, organization, and execution
  - Use complex ideas about the role of students' existing knowledge and make use of it during instruction

- **How does a teacher develop a strong and resilient sense of teaching efficacy?**

  Teaching efficacy is a teacher's judgment of his or her capacity to cope with the teaching situation in ways that bring about desired outcomes. As teachers find ways to cope ever more effectively with all aspects of the teaching situation, they develop teaching efficacy that is both strong and resilient against failure feedback. Developing teaching efficacy allows teachers to silence their professional fears and concerns and to lessen their emotional worry and anxiety. Both the level of teaching efficacy (how high?) and the resilience of teaching efficacy (how quickly does confidence return after a setback?) are good predictors of a teacher's enthusiasm for teaching; commitment to teaching; and capacity to produce positive student outcomes such as learning, motivation, and achievement.

- **How do teachers plan for instruction? How do they translate instructional goals into actual lesson plans?**

  Outstanding teachers have well-developed planning and organizational skills. They first define what is to be taught and what is to be learned, and they then translate those instructional goals and objectives into specific lesson plans, instructional units, and projects and activities. A very useful framework teachers can use to create instructional goals is Bloom's taxonomy. In Bloom's taxonomy of educational objectives, teachers have a helpful blueprint for developing instruction and for assessing learning. The output of such planning is often a lesson plan with objectives, standards, lists of materials needed, description of activities, and assessment procedures.

- **What are some general approaches to teaching?**

  There are a large variety of ideas to teaching. These approaches can be generally organized by distinguishing instructional strategies designed to promote role and reception learning from those designed to promote meaningful and discovery-based learning. Expository teaching promotes reception learning by first offering students an advance organizer followed by many examples to illustrate and confirm the prepared-in-advance conclusion statement. Discovery learning and guided discovery ask students to learn or discover the meaning in a lesson on their own or with the help of a facilitator. Direct instruction is explicit teaching that is used for mastery of basic skills and facts.

Key Terms

achievement targets, p. 49
advance organizer, p. 58
block scheduling, p. 53
comparative organizer, p. 58
content knowledge, p. 36
direct instruction, p. 58
discovery-based learning, p. 57
educational objectives, p. 48

expository organizer, p. 58
expository teaching, p. 57
guided discovery, p. 58
higher-order thinking skills, p. 48
inductive reasoning, p. 58
instructional goal, p. 48
pedagogical content knowledge, p. 37
pedagogical knowledge, p. 36

products, p. 50
reception learning, p. 57
referral, p. 44
standards, p. 49
taxonomy, p. 48
teaching, p. 31
teaching efficacy, p. 41

Exercises

1. *Concerns and Goals of a Beginning Teacher*

   Find a teacher-in-training and ask him or her two questions. First, ask what he or she is most worried about in terms of future teaching. Second, ask what he or she most wants to accomplish in future teaching. Encourage the teacher-in-training to reflect a bit so as to be able to express several such concerns and goals. Write down these expressed concerns and goals and see if you can classify each concern and each goal as being either self-related, task-related, or impact-related. As you look over the classified list, at which level is the teacher most focused—self, task, or impact? Is the teacher more negatively focused on concerns or more positively focused on goals?

2. *Differences between Experts and Novices*

   Think of two of your high school teachers. Choose one who was a veteran teacher and excelled at the craft of teaching. For the second one, choose someone who was just starting out as a teacher. Now look at the summary of expert/novice differences in Table 2.4. Compare your two teachers on each of the categories. Which of the differences listed was most evident for the two teachers you are considering? Does it seem that there are one or two areas of dramatic difference, or was the veteran teacher better in almost all respects? Are there any areas in which the novice teacher was better than the experienced teacher?

3. *Discovering the Roots of Teaching Anxiety*

   Many, perhaps all, teachers suffer some doubt and anxiety about their teaching. Often this sense of anxiety is a diffuse one, as the teacher says, "I'm anxious about teaching, but I can't tell you specifically why I feel so anxious." Try this exercise to pinpoint the source of any anxiety you currently feel about teaching. Rate yourself on the following three questions, each of which corresponds to one of the three dimensions of teaching efficacy listed in Table 2.5. Use a 1-to-7 scale in which 1 means *not at all confident* while 7 means *highly confident*. How confident are you that you will be able to control disruptive behavior in the classroom? How confident are you that you will be able to motivate a student who shows low interest? How confident are you that you will be able to adjust your lesson to meet the individual needs of all your students? By working through this exercise, you can begin to isolate the underlying and specific source of your teaching anxiety.

4. *Generating Metaphors for Teaching*

   Generate half a dozen metaphors to complete the following sentence: The teacher as _____. Once you have several different metaphors to choose from, select one that best describes the way you think about yourself as a teacher. Reflect on what that metaphor implies about your own views of teaching and learning. Ask yourself whether this metaphor represents an ideal role for you as a teacher. If not, can you generate another metaphor that successfully captures the essence of your ideal teaching role?

5. *Developing Lesson Plans*

This exercise can be done with a classmate. Each of you should prepare a lesson for a particular curricular goal. Have the lesson plan involve two or three days' worth of classroom work. When you have each developed your lesson plan, answer the following questions:

- How much time (total clock time) do you think it will take to complete this lesson?
- What will be the most exciting aspect of this lesson from the perspective of the children?

Lesson Plans

Lesson #1: "Nature Journaling"

GRADES: 2–4

SUBJECT AREAS: Science and Technology

I. TOPICS: Classification, Life Science, Botany

II. SUMMARY: The study of natural history encompasses the whole world, including the life contained in a backyard. It operates on all scales, from the panoramic sweep of a mountaintop view to a patch of weedy grass next to a sidewalk; living things are present at all levels of habitat. To better experience their own patch of earth, students in grades kindergarten through fourth grade can learn to observe closely one small area and record what they observe through nature journaling in their own backyards. The student is directly involved in the observation because the illustrator literally re-creates what he sees; the illustrator often expresses the feeling of having really "seen" the natural subject for the first time. Nature journaling refines future drawing and observational skills, creates a connection to a specific place over a discrete time, and fosters an appreciation of the outside world.

The lesson will combine outdoor observation, classroom discussions, and online activities. Students will observe and illustrate their own backyards, compare and contrast their backyard discoveries with classmates, and share their findings with others via the Backyard Jungle Web site.

III. OBJECTIVES: The students will be able to:

- Identify a natural subject they find interesting to observe.
- Record relevant observations about the subject, such as date, time, weather, cloud pattern, sounds, smells, and location.
- Choose the most appropriate among a variety of art materials to illustrate their subject.
- Observe their subject over time (one sitting or multiple.)
- Create a layout and presentation of ideas and observations in a nature journal.
- Accurately render the subject through drawing, painting, or coloring.

- Write, discuss, and share their thoughts on the subject.

IV. SOURCES:

- Walker-Leslie, Clare and Charles E. Roth, *Nature Journaling*. Pownal, VT: Storey Books, 1998.
- Walker-Leslie, Clare, *Nature Drawing: A Tool for Learning*. Upper Saddle River, NJ: Prentice-Hall, 2002.

V. ESTIMATED COMPLETION TIME: 3 to 4 hours (minimum: 1 hour classroom discussion, 1 hour computer lab, 1 hour outside)

VI. MATERIALS NEEDED:

- Art supplies
- Drawing paper/nature journal/downloaded worksheet
- Ruler
- Thermometer
- Digital camera (optional)

VII. PROCEDURES: (are continued)

Ask Yourself!

1. Classify the objectives of this lesson using Bloom's and Stiggins's taxonomies.
2. What difficulties might a novice teacher have in attaining these objectives?

Reprinted with permission from Forum One Communications.

- What aspect might be somewhat boring for the children?
- How effective do you think this lesson will be in achieving your instructional goals?
- How difficult will it be to carry out this plan?

When you have completed your lesson plans and your answers to the questions, exchange lesson plans with your classmate and answer the questions for his or her plan. Then meet with your classmate to compare your assessments.

Lesson Plans

Lesson #2: "A Meal of Endurance"

This is one of a series of lessons to help students understand more about Ernest Shackleton's expedition to the Antarctic.

GRADES: 5–8

SUBJECT AREAS: Life Science, Mathematics

I. LESSON OBJECTIVES: By the end of this activity, students will be able to:

- Understand the nutritional value of the explorers' meals.
- Describe the trend in the diet changes that the explorers experienced over the two-year expedition and explain the physiological consequences that these changes implied.
- Analyze caloric intake versus caloric expenditure and recognize the pattern of slow starvation of the explorers.
- Analyze the nutritional balance and caloric intake of the student's own diet.

II. RELATED NATIONAL STANDARDS: NATIONAL SCIENCE EDUCATION STANDARDS (NATIONAL RESEARCH COUNCIL)

III. GRADES: 5–8

IV. SCIENCE STANDARD C: Life Science

V. REGULATION AND BEHAVIOR

- All organisms must be able to obtain and use resources, grow, reproduce, and maintain stable internal conditions while living in a constantly changing environment.
- Regulation of an organism's internal environment involves sensing the internal environment and changing physiological activities to keep conditions within the range required to survive.

CURRICULUM AND EVALUATION STANDARDS FOR SCHOOL MATHEMATICS (NATIONAL COUNCIL OF TEACHERS OF MATHEMATICS)

VI. GRADES: 5–8

VII. STANDARD 7: Computation and Estimation

VIII. TOOLS AND MATERIALS NEEDED:

- Blue and red pens
- Copy of *Meals of Endurance* activity sheet
- Reference for calorie content of food
- Access to the Internet

IX. ESTIMATED TIME TO COMPLETE LESSON

The activity should take one class period to complete.

X. TEACHING STRATEGY

Background Information: The food Calorie (written with an uppercase C) discussed in this guide and other nutritional references is in reality a kilocalorie, which is 1,000 calories. The daily amount of calories an individual requires is based on numerous factors. Chief among them are body build, height, gender, age, rate of metabolism, and level of activity. If an individual is in a very cold climate, he or she will need more calories to maintain body temperature. Due to these variations, it is necessary to use calorie estimates when making comparisons of calories consumed versus calories expended.

It is estimated that at the beginning of the Shackleton journey (December 1914) the explorers had sufficient calories and a variety of foods to meet their nutritional needs at their level of activity. A year later—when they were stranded on the ice floes—the demands on them for physical labor increased and they probably expended more energy than they consumed. Also, the proportion of their diet that comprised carbohydrates was reduced (carbohydrates are essential for normal metabolic function). At the end of the journey—when the men basically had no carbohydrates left to eat—they had trouble performing physical labor. They subsisted mainly on seal, penguin, and seaweed.

A normal diet is approximately 35% fat, 10% protein, and 55% carbohydrates; the explorers' diet at the end contained just protein and fat. At this point they did not consume enough calories, nor did they have the variety (carbohydrates and certain vitamins) in their diet necessary to fulfill basic nutritional needs.

XI. PROCEDURES: (are continued).

Ask Yourself!

1. Classify the objectives of this lesson using Bloom's and Stiggins's taxonomies.
2. How do the lesson objectives relate to the standards set forth by the National Research Council (http://www.nap.eddingroom/booku/reas/nses/) and the National Council of Teachers of Mathematics (http://standards.nctm.org/)?

From Nova/WGBH Education Foundation Copyright © 2002 WGBH/Boston.

Source: Gettman, D. (1987). *Basic Montessori.* New York: St. Martin's Press. Reprinted with permission.

Fractions Activity

This apparatus is a fractions activity (Gettman, 1987). It helps elementary school students understand the concept of fractions—the division of a whole into equal parts. How might you, the teacher, help students develop such a concept? One way might be to use a hands-on approach. You could invite the children to play freely with the trays and inserts. Using the attached knobs, the children could pick up the inserts, manipulate them, compare them, mix and sort them, count them, and so on. Through exploration, students could discover the concept that a whole can be divided into any number of equal parts.

A second way might be to sit beside the children and tutor them. You might explain what fractions are and coach the children on how to use the tray as a tool to understand fractions, perhaps starting with the simpler first tray and working your way up to the more complicated second tray. Once the children start to show signs that they have the hang of it, you could put your hands in your lap and even ask them to explain the concept of fractions to you.

Cognitive Development

3

RIDE **Reflection for Action**

What is the most effective instructional approach to help students learn concepts such as fractions? Does learning through exploration and self-discovery work best? Does learning through mentoring and social guidance work best? Which instructional approach would work with a child with special needs?

Guiding Questions

- How does education enrich brain development?
- How does Piaget explain cognitive development?
- What are the stages of cognitive development?
- How can teachers apply Piaget's theory in the classroom?
- How does Vygotsky explain sociocognitive development?
- How can teachers apply Vygotsky's theory in the classroom?
- How does language develop?
- How can teachers use their knowledge of brain, cognitive, and language development when working with diverse learners and students with special needs?

CHAPTER OVERVIEW

The plan of this chapter is to overview the three interrelated processes of brain development, cognitive development, and language development as infants grow into children and as children grow into adolescents. Biology and maturation underlie all three capacities, but biology provides learners with only their developmental potential. For a student's brain, cognitive, and language development to be fully realized, appropriate growth-promoting experiences must also occur. The first part of the chapter explains how brain development depends on exposure to richly stimulating learning environments. The second part discusses cognitive development from two perspectives—Piaget's four-stage model and Vygotsky's apprenticeship model. For Piaget, cognitive development occurs as low-level mental structures are enriched and transformed into higher-level mental structures. From this perspective, teachers can learn how to offer classroom environments that are stimulating, interesting, and complex enough to develop higher-order thinking. For Vygotsky, cognitive development is a socially mentored activity that occurs in a context of social interaction. From this perspective, teachers can learn how to offer social guidance to develop the skills students need to become effective participants in the culture. The third part discusses language development, including second-language learning and bilingualism.

Brain Development
- Brain Structure and Function
- How Experience (Education) Affects Brain Development

Cognitive Development
- Adaptation and Schemas: Piaget's Theory
- Stages in Cognitive Development
- Classroom Applications
- Limitations

Sociocognitive Development
- Cognitive Development as an Apprenticeship: Vygotsky's Theory
- Scaffolding in the Zone of Proximal Development

- Instructional Conversations
- Role of Language
- Cultural Tools
- Importance of Peers
- Classroom Applications
- Which Theory Should Teachers Apply?

Language Development
- How Language Develops
- Technology Support for Young Readers and Students with Special Needs
- Second-Language Acquisition and Bilingualism

Brain Development

The human brain, an organ the size of a coconut with the texture of cold butter, is the part of the body that thinks, learns, remembers, and solves problems. To study what the brain does, neuroscientists identify its parts or structures (Kandel et al., 1991). Once they have done this, their next step is to identify each structure's underlying function or purpose. They learn, for example, that most thinking and planning occurs in the frontal and prefrontal lobes of the cortex, and that emotions such as fear and anger begin in the amygdala and limbic area. Educators take a special interest in the study of the brain at this point because they want to understand how the brain generates educational phenomena, such as learning, memory, intelligence, language, and emotion. Figure 3.1 identifies the brain structures associated with these functions.

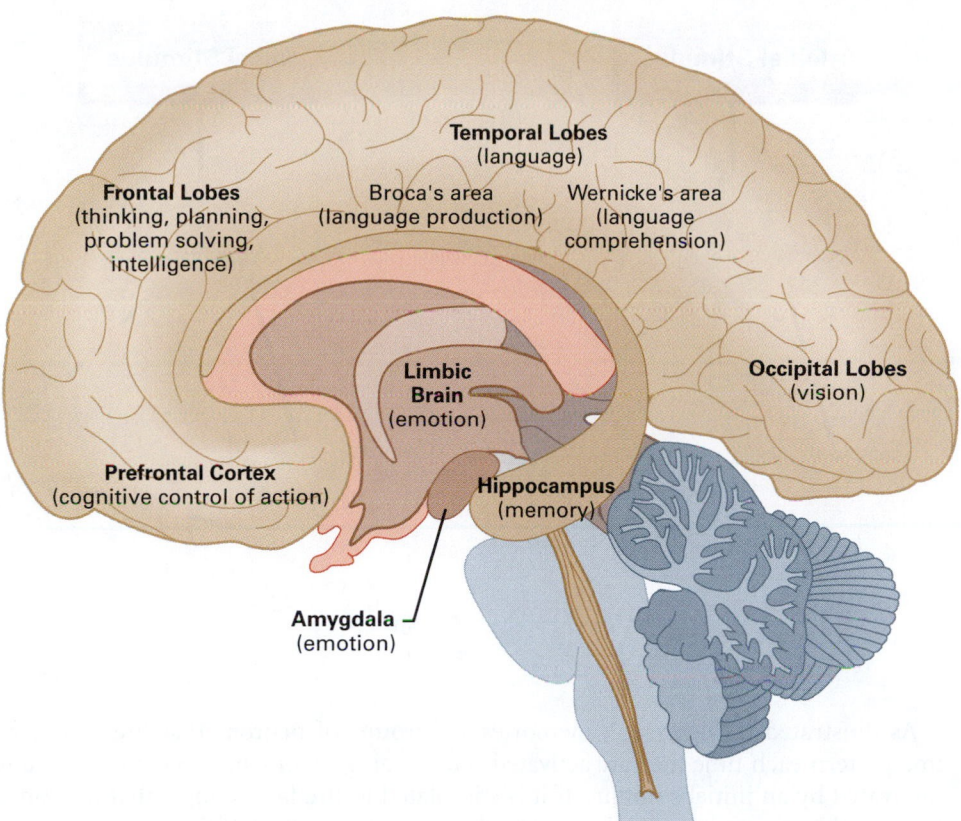

Figure 3.1 Brain Structures and Their Functions

Brain Structure and Function

By the time a child enters the first grade, the brain is 90% to 95% of its adult size. The human brain does not fully mature, however, until formal schooling ends (age 20–25), and it continues to change and develop throughout the full lifespan, including old age. Most of what happens in brain development does not consist of brain size growth but, rather, consists of the development of its neurons and support cells. Before we outline this developmental story, consider examples of how one brain structure (the hippocampus) and one brain area (prefrontal cortex) regulate brain functions such as memory and the control of action.

The **hippocampus** is the brain structure that processes a person's new experiences in order to construct memories. Only after the hippocampus processes and makes sense of new information is a memory created and eventually stored as long-term knowledge. As a case in point, when a student manipulates the fractions activity described at the beginning of the chapter, the hippocampus's dense network of neurons processes the resulting sensory information (sights, sounds, touch, maybe even smells from the wooden tray); holds that sensory information in memory for a brief time; and, while doing so, works to forge new connections between these new experiences and prior knowledge that has been stored in the brain from previous learning experiences. Generating connections between what is new and what is already known is the basis of learning and memory.

The **prefrontal cortex** is the frontmost part of the brain that lies right behind the forehead. It is responsible for the cognitive control of action (Fuster, 2008), which is the ability to coordinate thought and action in ways that reflect the person's goals, as in planning and considering the feelings associated with goals and actions, such as "Do I want to visit my friend Joey?" The prefrontal cortex also regulates attention, plans complex behavior, makes decisions between conflicting thoughts, and predicts future events. As the brain's executive control center, the prefrontal cortex is closely connected with most areas of the brain, as it projects two-way communication fibers that function as information highways. One connection, for instance, is with the amygdala. Because of this two-way connection, emotions like fear and anger can influence and change thinking just as thinking can influence and calm negative emotionality.

hippocampus Seahorse-shaped structure in the limbic area of the brain involved in the formation of new memories.

prefrontal cortex Cortical area of the brain lying behind the forehead that is responsible for the cognitive control of action and the planning of complex behaviors.

Figure 3.2 A Model of How a Learning Experience Becomes a Memory

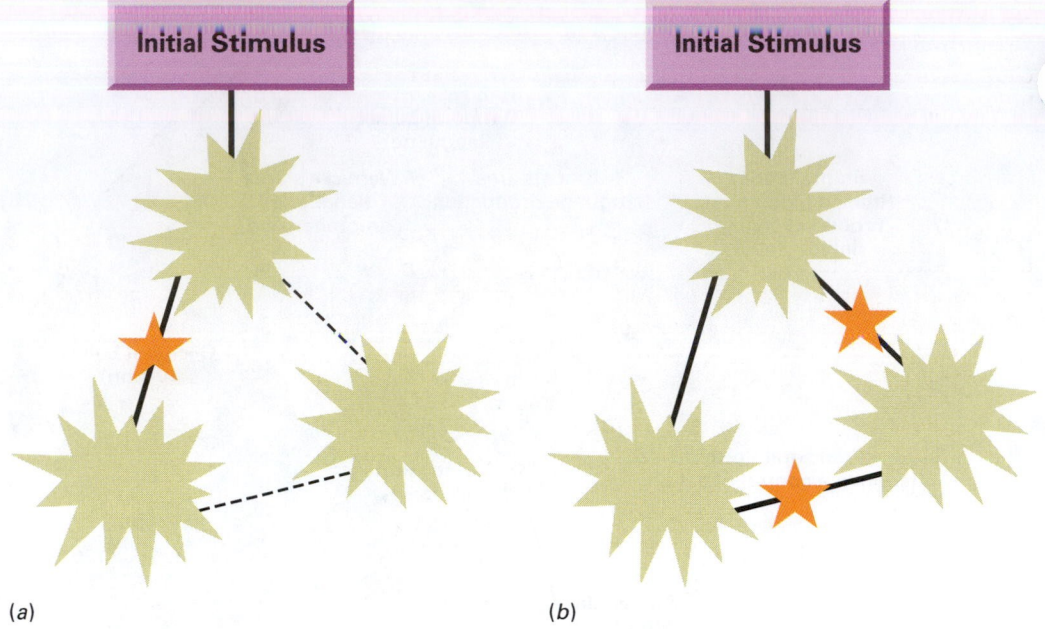

(a)   (b)

R I D E How does knowledge of the hippocampus clarify why discovery learning helps children understand the concept of fractions?

As illustrated in Figure 3.2, memories are groups of neurons that fire together in the same pattern each time they are activated. The forging of a memory begins when a neuron is activated by an initial stimulus. If it is stimulated to fire fast enough, that neuron will set off its neighboring neuron, as denoted by the star in Figure 3.2*a*. If the cells fire in synchrony enough times, a connection is formed between them. The dashed lines represent a lack of connections with the third neuron. Through future encounters with the initial stimulus (e.g., the fractions activity), the bonded pair of neurons will gain enough strength to trigger their neighboring neurons, as represented by the two stars in Figure 3.2*b*. If this stimulation occurs frequently enough, then the three neurons will bond together and, in doing so, create a new memory. Hence, the person learns to remember the stimulus event as that particular pattern of neural activation.

neurons Nerve cells that receive and transmit the neural impulses underlying thinking.

Neurons are nerve cells that make all brain functions possible. At birth, the brain possesses about 100 billion neurons (Carter, 1998). Impressive as that number is, the brain forges about 100 *trillion* connections that join neurons together, as depicted in Figure 3.2*b*. That means that the average neuron connects with about 1,000 of its neighboring neurons. Some connections exist at birth, but most connections between neurons depend on experience and learning. These connections are forged in the following manner (Greenough & Black, 1992; Greenough et al., 1987; Nelson & Bloom, 1997):

- Exposure to an enriched learning environment stimulates neurons.

- When stimulated, neurons reach out to neighboring neurons by growing *dendrites*, the part of the neuron that extends out like branches off a tree to connect to neighboring neurons.

- With repeated stimulation, the number of connections between neurons increases.

How Experience (Education) Affects Brain Development

Stimulated neurons reach out and connect with other stimulated neurons, whereas inactive and understimulated neurons degenerate and die out (Huttenlocher, 1994). The result is that experience leaves a unique mark on brain development.

plasticity The brain's capacity for structural change as the result of experience.

The concept that unites experience (e.g., education) and brain development is neural **plasticity** (or neuroplasticity), which is essentially the brain's capacity to change its structure in response to experience (Greenough et al., 1987). The *experience* that drives experience-induced plasticity includes environmental stimulation, thoughts, and actions (such as occurs in music and athletics). Such stimulation causes changes in neural activity, especially in the growing of dendrities and in the synaptic changes between neurons (e.g., see Figure 3.2), but also in the additions of new neurons (neurogenesis), increased myelination of axons, and changes in the size and shape of a neuron. Through such experience-induced plasticity, the brain adapts itself to that stimulation (Garlick, 2002).

Stimulation leads to greater neural interconnectivity, whereas a lack of stimulation leads to pruning. Education supports greater neural interconnectivity, but pruning is also important. For instance, many neuroscientists believe that insufficient or abnormal pruning just before birth causes autism. Neural interconnectivity occurs rapidly between 6 and 12 years of age. After age 12, the developing brain tends to focus on speeding up its existing neural connections. Improving the speed of these connections throughout adolescence produces meaningful benefits and explains adolescents' ever-increasing attention span and capacities to think ahead, control impulses, answer hypothetical questions, and understand the future consequences of their actions (Fischer & Rose, 1995; Nelson & Bloom, 1997).

The sensitivity of the developing brain to experience can be seen, for example, in blind students who read Braille. The area of the brain that senses touch from the right index finger is much larger in people who are blind than it is in people who see because the index finger is used to read Braille (Schwartz & Begley, 2002). The same effect occurs among musicians. Among lifelong violinists, the part of their brains that controls the four fingers of the left hand involved in playing a stringed instrument becomes larger (Elbert et al., 1995). Perhaps the clearest empirical test of the plasticity hypothesis involved young adults learning to juggle (Draganski et al., 2004). After they had tried to learn how to juggle for three months, the brain regions involved in the coordination of motor activity increased significantly. Interestingly, however, months after the training and juggling ended, these enlarged brain regions returned to their baseline levels, illustrating that brain stability is sometimes just as adaptive as is brain growth (Piaget, 1980). So what the brain is doing is adaptive (rather than growing per se) in response to experience.

If factors such as practice, stimulation, and training affect brain development in musicians, jugglers, and people who are blind, it seems reasonable to ask whether schooling affects brain development. Certainly, schooling boosts intelligence, reasoning ability, learning strategies, and talent. Further, education-based intervention programs, such as Head Start, which are designed to provide preschool children with stimulating and complex environments, produce educational gains. But do interventions such as formal schooling and Head Start actually change the structure and function of the brain? Those who study the brain have concluded that they do, though the effect is probably small (Greenough et al., 1987).

The main reason educational programs produce academic gains is that stimulating environments give the brain a great deal of information to process, store, remember, and later use to solve problems. This greater reservoir of stored knowledge explains one key developmental benefit of education. But brain neuroplasticity is key as well. Brain neuroplasticity is greater neuronal interconnectivity, as illustrated in Figure 3.3. Figure 3.3 shows brain development ranging from relatively little neuronal interconnectivity on the left-hand side to greater interconnectivity on the right-hand side (more complex neural circuitry, more dendritic expansion, more synapses, and thicker myelin). Increased interconnectivity expands one's information-processing capacity, speed, and efficiency.

Experience (or education) therefore provides the developing brain with the stimulation it needs to connect more and more neurons together. But neuroplasticity, like knowledge acquisition, does not just happen automatically. Rather, it occurs when environmental demands (e.g., learn a foreign language, learn how to read) are noticeably greater than they were in the past (sixth grade is more demanding than is the fifth grade) and when these demands occur over an extended period of time. The following sequence summarizes the relation between experience and brain development:

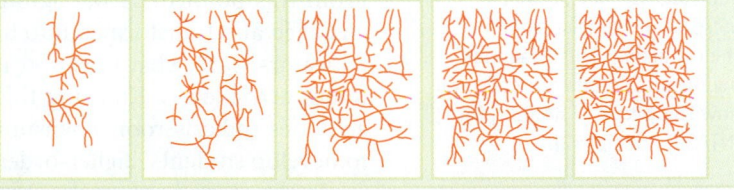

Figure 3.3 Brain Development as Greater Neural Interconnectivity (Neuroplasticity)

Source: Comer, R. and Gould, E. (2011). *Psychology Around Us*, p. 67. Copyright © John Wiley & Sons, Inc.

- Stimulating experiences, especially those that are new, more demanding, and prolonged over time, occur.

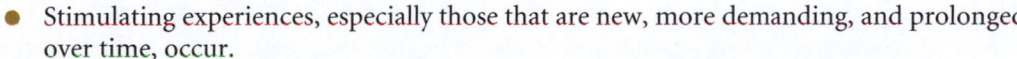

- Those demands set in motion the process of neuroplasticity (as represented in both Figures 3.2 and 3.3) that change the structure of the brain.
- Developing neuroplasticity sets the stage for future learning and cognitive development.

Enrichment and Brain Development   A very practical question about brain development is: Does environmental enrichment lead to advanced brain development? To answer this question, consider two pieces of this intellectual puzzle. First, young brains mature and develop naturally. As a rule, brain areas that process lower-level information (i.e., sensory information) mature earlier than those that process higher-level information (i.e., reading words on a page; Scherf et al., 2007). Brain development takes time and does not reach maturity until early adulthood, as mentioned previously, but it does progress and develop rather naturally. Second, environments can be classified, roughly, as deprived, expected, and enriched. Deprived environments clearly undermine brain development, as children institutionalized at birth have noticeably low intelligence quotients (IQs). Placing these same children in high-quality foster care before the age of two leads to a dramatic increase in IQ up to the normal range, and it greatly improves these children's linguistic and emotional capacities as well (Ghera et al., 2009; Windsor et al., 2007). So, there exists a night-and-day difference between deprived and expected environments. But a separate question is whether there exists a large difference between expected and enriched environments—that is, does excessive enrichment beyond typical or expected stimulation help? On this point, cognitive capacities generally follow the growth curve of the human body such that enriched environments enable children's brains to attain their natural biological growth trajectory but not to exceed that natural trajectory (Fox, Levitt, & Nelson, 2010). The surest prescription for optimal brain development seems to be this (Fox et al., 2010, p. 35):

> *Rich early experience must be followed by rich and more sophisticated experience later in life, when high-level circuits are maturing, in order for full potential to be achieved.*

Cognitive Development

As children make their way through the school curriculum, they become ever more capable and sophisticated in their thinking. In examining the mental processes that emerge during cognitive development, we will consider two theoretical approaches. Both explain how students become sophisticated thinkers, and both offer concrete advice for teachers who are trying to develop their students' thinking.

In the first approach—Piaget's theory—students are viewed as naturally curious explorers who constantly try to make sense of their surroundings. By manipulating objects and by exploring what is new and unfamiliar, they discover and adapt to the world around them. From this point of view, cognitive development occurs as low-level mental structures are enriched and transformed into higher-level mental structures. By examining Piaget's theory, educators learn what to expect in terms of children's and adolescents' thinking across different grade levels. Knowing this, teachers can offer students developmentally appropriate activities and classroom environments that are stimulating, interesting, and complex enough to develop students' higher-order thinking.

In the second approach—Vygotsky's theory—students are viewed as young apprentices who benefit from the relationships they have with competent mentors. Through social guidance and cooperative dialogue, students acquire skills and knowledge. From this point of view, cognitive development is the gradual acquisition of skills, knowledge, and expertise. By examining Vygotsky's theory, educators learn that cognitive growth is a socially mentored activity that occurs in a context of social interaction. Knowing this, teachers can offer students social guidance to help them develop the kind of thinking they need to become effective participants in their culture.

Appendix
Learning Theories

As children grow and become adolescents, they become increasingly sophisticated in their thinking skills. Piagetian and Vygotskian theories describe how this occurs (PRAXIS™, I.A.1; INTASC, Principle 2).

Adaptation and Schemas: Piaget's Theory

Jean Piaget was a Swiss psychologist who conducted a lifelong study of children's cognitive development. He observed children and adolescents in natural situations. Sometimes he would just observe a child; other times he would pose a problem for the child or adolescent to solve. Upon hearing their solutions, Piaget would ask them to explain their reasoning. From what these children and adolescents told him, Piaget began to understand how young people think and understand the world around them.

One problem Piaget posed was the flower problem. As shown in the nearby What Kids Say and Do box, the flower problem introduces five daisies and two carnations bunched together into a single vase. Children are asked to observe and manipulate the flowers until they feel comfortable with them. The point of the flower problem—and the point of all such Piagetian tasks—is to bring out the child's reasoning while he or she attempts to solve the problem. This is important because the child's reasoning reveals his or her underlying mental operations. Six-year-old Jenny evidently lacks the mental capacity for two-dimensional classification, instead relying on what her eyes tell her to say: that there

What Kids Say and Do

Two Children Solve the Flower Problem

(Photo by Johnmarshall Reeve)

Teacher: Here are a bunch of pretty flowers. As you look them over, which would you say is true— are there more daisies than flowers, more flowers than daisies, or are there about the same number of daisies and flowers?

Six-year-old Jenny	Ten-year-old Maria
"More daisies."	"More flowers."
"See how many there are!"	"There are many daisies, but there are even more flowers."

are more daisies than flowers—after all, there are so many daisies. Ten-year-old Maria evidently understands what Jenny does not—namely, that objects can be grouped two dimensionally into classes and subclasses in which the class (flowers) is greater than any of its subclasses (daisies).

Piaget studied cognitive development because he viewed intelligence as a basic life process that helps the person adapt to the environment. Hence, the function of thought—its purpose—is to facilitate adaptation. Piaget's definition of intelligence was adaptation to the environment. **Adaptation** is the process of adjusting to the demands of the environment. A person adapts when he or she successfully copes with challenges, solves problems, and displays sophisticated ways of thinking. Adaptation occurs through the two complementary processes of assimilation and accommodation as well as the motivational process of disequilibrium, as explained below.

adaptation Adjusting to the demands of the environment.

The basic building blocks for thinking are schemas (or schemes). **Schemas** are the basic structure for organizing information. Piaget identified three types. **Behavioral schemas** are mental representations of physical actions. Infants *literally* think in actions, as actions (behavioral schemes) such as grasping, banging, and shaking are used to explore, respond to, and make sense of and adapt to the objects around them. **Symbolic schemas** are language-based mental representations of objects and events. By interacting with animals and by writing letters, children create symbolic (mental) representations of environmental objects such as cats and sentences. As development progresses, symbolic schemas become more numerous and more complex. For instance, an early symbolic schema of *sentence* soon differentiates into several types of sentences, such as the basic sentence, the run-on sentence, and the incomplete sentence. Much of what is meant by cognitive development is growth in the number and complexity of one's symbolic schemas.

schemas The basic mental structure for organizing information.

behavioral schemas Mental representations of physical actions.

symbolic schemas Language-based representations of objects and events.

The third type of schema is the operational schema. An **operation** is a mental action. It is a manipulation not carried out with one's hands but in one's mind. Classification, for instance, is an operation 10-year-old Maria was able to use to reason logically about the flower problem. All operations are mentally reversible acts; that is, they can be carried out in one's mind in either one direction or the opposite direction. Addition is a mental operation that involves adding objects together. Subtraction is the reversal of addition; it is the same mental operation, carried out in the opposite direction (Piaget, 1970). For Piaget, the sophistication of one's mental operations determines the level of cognitive development (e.g., pre-operations, concrete operations, or formal operations).

operation A mental action or a mental manipulation carried out to solve a problem or to reason logically.

Assimilation Adaptation occurs through assimilation and accommodation. **Assimilation** is a process of incorporation in which some outside event (e.g., the fractions activity) is brought into a person's way of thinking. Assimilation involves adaptation to the extent that the student must grow or expand an existing schema to make room for the new information. Children have schemas for *cat*, adolescents have schemas for *rap music*, and teachers have schemas for *standardized tests*. Assimilation occurs when one applies what one knows about cats, rap music, and standardized tests in the effort to fit newly encountered objects into one's way of thinking. Teachers make sense of the Iowa Test of Basic Skills that they have just been introduced to by thinking, "Oh, it's a standardized test." The new object is distorted somewhat at the price of understanding it. Through assimilation, schemas grow—in number and in complexity—and knowledge expands.

assimilation An incorporation process in which an outside event is brought into one's way of thinking.

Accommodation **Accommodation** is a process of change in which an existing schema is changed or modified to make sense of something that is new and different. It occurs when the mild distorting process within assimilation is not satisfying—assimilation works only up to a point. To make sense of the new object, thinking must sometimes be reorganized, and a lower-level schema is transformed into a higher-level one, as might typically happen when the child's schema for *cat* proves inadequate to make sense of new animals encountered at the zoo (e.g., a leopard). When a student's existing schema proves inadequate, one of two things must occur: The student can modify the existing schema into a new and better way of thinking or create a whole new schema (De Lisi & Golbeck, 1999). Through accommodation, schemas are overhauled or created anew. With each accommodation, thinking advances to a more sophisticated level.

accommodation A modification process in which lower-level schemas are transformed into higher-level schemas.

Figure 3.4 Origins and Consequences of Cognitive Conflict

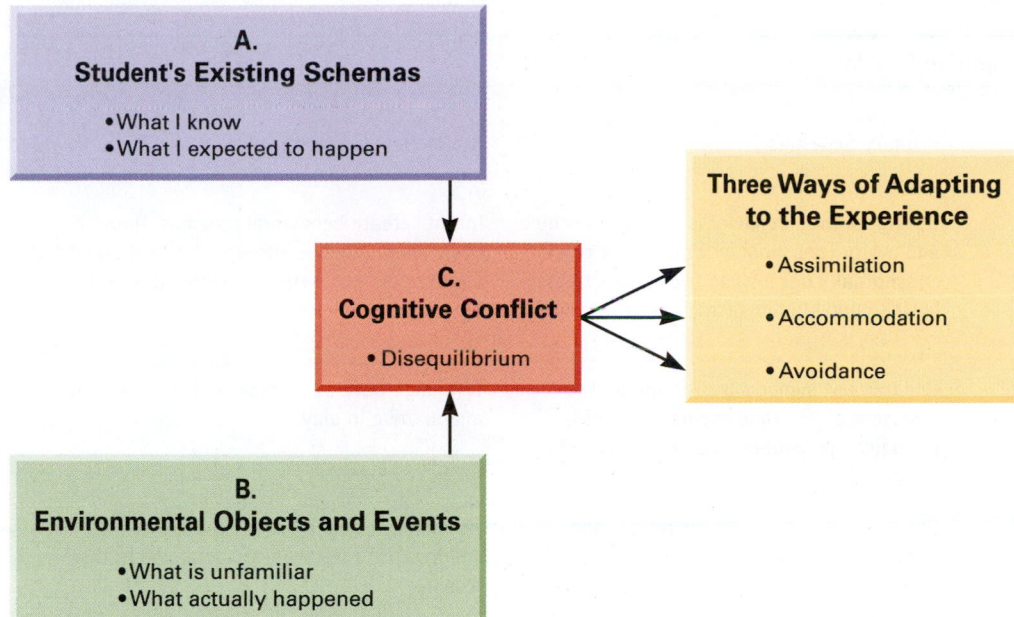

Disequilibrium According to Piaget (1954), learning is always an interaction between the student and the environment. Children do not learn passively from experience. Rather, the student enters into a learning activity with an existing way of thinking—that is, with schemas, expectations, and predictions about what should happen during the learning experience (box A in Figure 3.4). Classroom activities, in turn, provide objects and events to be understood and problems to be solved. As learning activities unfold, the student observes what actually happens in reality (box B in Figure 3.4). For instance, a high school student might come to an English literature class with a schema that poems are short, rhyme, and are about love. The English teacher, however, might present a poem that is long, does not rhyme, and is about a social issue. The resulting mismatch between *what I expected to happen* versus *what actually happened* is shown in box C in Figure 3.4 as cognitive conflict, or disequilibrium.

Disequilibrium is a state of cognitive conflict that arises when experience is contradicted by one's existing way of thinking. It is the motivational engine for learning and adaptation. When it occurs, disequilibrium typically yields an openness to experience, as in "I want and need more information to make sense of this." Equilibrium, in contrast, follows after accommodation has produced a state of cognitive congruence in which one's new way of thinking has been advanced and now adequately reflects one's experience. It typically results in a closed way of thinking, as in "Okay, now I understand this; I'm satisfied." (Piaget, 1971).

As shown in Figure 3.4, a third possibility is that students respond to the cognitive conflict with frustration, avoidance, and abandonment of the effort to think. With avoidance, the student does not profit from the learning experience, and adaptation does not occur. Instead, negative emotions—frustration, anxiety, confusion—overwhelm the desire to accommodate the information to be learned, and the student avoids the learning opportunity by ignoring it—physically or mentally walking away from it (De Lisi & Golbeck, 1999).

Teachers can contribute to students' learning and adapting by providing environmental objects and events that create cognitive conflict (box B in Figure 3.4) and by giving students the time, opportunity, and support to explore and make sense of what is new, interesting, and different. After an overview of Piaget's stage theory of cognitive development, we will discuss the how-to underlying classroom practice guided by Piaget's theory.

What Does This Mean to Me?
Would you describe your learning experience in reading this chapter as one of assimilation, accommodation, or both?

disequilibrium A state of cognitive conflict in which one's existing schema or way of thinking is not confirmed by experience.

TABLE 3.1

Piaget's Hypothesized Stages of Cognitive Development

Approximate Age and Grade Level	Stage	Primary Schemas	Major Developments
0–2 years			
Infancy	Sensorimotor	During infancy, behavior is sensory (touching) and motor (grasping). Infants do not think conceptually but instead use actions to gain a basic understanding of their environment.	Infants create behavioral schemas. Through object permanence, infants learn that objects continue to exist when they are out of sight.
2–7 years			
Preschool, early elementary school	Preoperational	Children use symbols (words, images) to represent objects and events. Thought is prelogical, perception bound, and egocentric.	Language develops rapidly. Children become imaginative in play.
7–11 years			
Late elementary school	Concrete operations	Children acquire mental operations and apply them to solve concrete problems in front of them. Logic replaces perception.	No longer misled by physical appearances, children use their mental operations to think and reason.
11 years and older			
Middle school and high school	Formal operations	Adolescent thought becomes logical and abstract. Adolescents use mental operations to imagine what is possible, consider unseen hypotheses, and solve abstract problems.	Adolescents become capable of systematic, deductive, and inferential reasoning. Such scientific reasoning allows adolescents to formulate a hypothesis and test it, including testing many possible solutions to a problem to choose the most appropriate one.

Stages in Cognitive Development

According to Piaget, cognitive development unfolds in a structured and universal sequence consisting of four stages: sensorimotor, preoperational, concrete operations, and formal operations. In this view, each stage of development represents a qualitatively different way of thinking and a fundamentally different view of the world. Notice the word *operation* within the name of the stages, because cognitive development revolves around acquiring ever more sophisticated mental operations. Table 3.1 summarizes the primary schemas that students rely on during each stage as well as the major developments that occur during each stage. The table also provides the ages and grade levels commonly associated with each stage.

Sensorimotor Stage Cognitive development begins in infancy with the sensorimotor stage. As mentioned earlier, infants literally think in actions. They grasp, they suck, and they pull, and in doing so they coordinate these actions with sensory experiences of seeing what happens and what changes. Actions coordinated with sensory information and feedback create behavioral schemes. Soon after birth, simple reflexes become more complex, more intentional, and more organized, as represented in the following five substages:

- *Primary circular reactions* (1–4 months): By chance, infants discover that some actions—such as sucking and arm waving—are satisfying. They then repeat these behavioral schemes over and over (hence, they are circular).
- *Secondary circular reactions* (4–8 months): Infants discover that some actions have interesting ("secondary") effects on the environment (e.g., squeezing a noise-producing ball).
- *Goal-directed behavior* (8–12 months): Intentions replace reflexes. The infant grasps an object, then shakes it intentionally to realize the goal of producing a noise simply for the sake of producing a noise.

- *Tertiary circular reactions* (12–18 months): Curiosity leads the infant to experiment with objects to discover new and interesting properties of these objects. Knowing that the rattle makes a pleasing sound, the infant experiments to see what additional ("tertiary") effects it might produce if dropped (bounces) or mouthed (tastes bad).

- *Symbolic problem solving* (18–24 months): Infants begin to construct symbolic images of environmental objects. The emergence of symbolic operations marks the end of the sensorimotor stage, as illustrated by the mastery of object permanence.

Object permanence is the understanding that objects in the environment continue to exist even when they cannot be seen, felt, or heard. Adults who leave their houses know that their houses are still there even when they are out of sight. In contrast, if you show a one-year-old infant an attractive stuffed animal and then hide it behind some object, such as a curtain, the infant acts as though the stuffed animal ceased to exist (i.e., out of sight, out of mind). Two-year-olds, however, can remember that the hidden object still exists, and they can use mental inferences (guesses, hypotheses) to guide their search for the toy. Because they are able to create a symbolic representation of the object in memory (i.e., represent the physical object with a mental representation of that same object), infants can understand that objects have permanence. This intellectual achievement—the understanding of object permanence and the beginning of symbolic mental representations—marks the end of the sensorimotor stage and the beginning of the preoperational stage.

Preoperational Stage In the preoperational stage, children create symbolic schemas to represent the objects and events in the world around them. A *symbol* is a word or image that stands for something else (DeLoache, 1987, 1991). For instance, a globe is a symbolic representation of the earth, just as is the word *earth*. Piaget used the term *semiotic function*, or symbolic function, to refer to this new cognitive ability in the preoperational mind. The most striking use of mental symbols is language, and children's use of language increases very rapidly during this stage.

A second hallmark of the preoperational stage is pretend play (Piaget, 1951). During pretend play, children use one object, such as a broom, to represent another object, such as a horse. Such play fosters cognitive development. For instance, preschool children who engage in a good deal of pretend play perform better on tests of language, creativity, cognitive development, and social maturity than do preschool children who engage in less pretend play (Connolly & Doyle, 1984). Pretend play fosters social development, too, as it nurtures social referencing (using one person's response as a guide for one's own response), reading the intentions of others, role and turn taking, and social competencies such as negotiation, as pretend play is often preceeded by negotiating turns, what the plot of the play will be, and what objects will be involved (Lillard, Pinkham, & Smith, 2011). The pretend play of the preoperational child typically gives way to games with rules in the concrete-operational child. The nearby Uncommon Sense box addresses the question of whether or not "games with rules" play is important enough to warrant its place in the school curriculum.

By adult standards, the preoperational stage is mostly characterized by immature cognitive capacity. *Preoperational* means that preschool children have not yet gained the operational schemas they need in order to think logically. Instead of thinking logically, preschool children think intuitively and use perception, not reason, to understand the world and to solve problems, just as six-year-old Jenny did in the flowers problem. Another illustration of perception-bound thinking can be illustrated by the three-mountains task shown in Figure 3.5. The preoperational child sits in one chair and looks at the three mountains while a teddy bear sits in a second chair that offers a different view. The child is first asked to describe what the view looks like from his or her perspective. Next, the

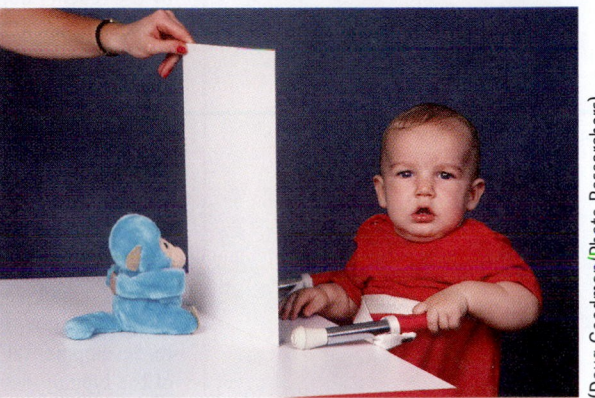

(Doug Goodman/Photo Researchers)

Infants who have not yet mastered object permanence cannot remember hidden environmental objects (i.e., out of sight, out of mind).

object permanence Understanding that objects continue to exist even when they cannot be seen or detected by other senses.

Uncommon Sense

Play and Recess Are Wasted School Time—Or Are They?

Recess is often part of the curriculum in preschool and elementary school, and teachers often insert play into their lesson plans (e.g., a phonics game), but few educators think of play as important school time in the same way that they think of math or language arts. This raises the key questions of whether children benefit from their play and whether play time should be in the curriculum.

By definition, play is child-initiated and not purposive (Burghardt, 2005). So anything engineered by the teacher during a lesson is not play (because it is not voluntarily initiated by the child), and what children do during play is not immediately useful in the way other school subjects are (because it does not boost achievement or standardized test scores). Play does, however, build peer relationships, and it helps children maintain their attention and interest for the post-recess part of the school day (Pellegrini, 2005; Pellegrini & Smith, 1998). But its core benefits are deferred (post-childhood) in that play helps children respond creatively and flexibly to novel and challenging environments and provides a safe environment in which to build life skills such as role taking, social dominance, and how to enjoy an activity simply for the sake of the activity itself.

So are play and recess wasted school time? Play offers unique benefits for children in the preoperational stage of cognitive development—preschool through the first or second grade—and this is true for object play (building a block tower), pretend play (playing the role of the teacher), social play (play fighting with pencils as swords), and locomotor play (a game of tag). But the need for play and its developmental benefits are less apparent after the preoperational stage, with the one exception of the type of locomotor play that occurs during recess, which enriches the motor skills and cardiovascular fitness (Pellegrini & Smith, 1998) that are important to the later school subject of physical education.

child is asked to describe what the view looks like from the teddy bear's perspective. Preoperational thinkers will say that the teddy bear sees the mountains from the same view as does the child (e.g., the biggest mountain is still on the left-hand side). In other words, the preoperational child shows an inability to take the perspective of the teddy bear. It is actually quite a cognitive achievement to put aside one's own perceptions (what one sees) and mentally construct another person's perspective. To be able to do so, the child needs the capacity to mentally manipulate a schema, such as moving the mountains around in one's mind, which is the essence of what a mental operation is (Flavell et al., 1993).

Concrete Operations Stage The emergence of concrete operations allows the child to revise or alter a symbol or image to reach a logical conclusion (Flavell et al., 1993). Mental manipulations allow the elementary school student's thinking to become dynamic (rather than static), decentered (rather than centered on only one dimension), and logical (rather than perceptual). Table 3.2 summarizes and defines seven emerging capacities of concrete-operational thinking: **animism**, **centration**, **transductive reasoning**, **egocentrism**, **reversibility**, **classification**, and **seriation**. To illustrate what a concrete operation is, we will discuss the latter two operations—namely, classification and seriation.

As elementary-grade children physically manipulate objects that might be grouped into different categories, they begin to recognize that objects vary on more than one dimension and thus may be grouped in many different ways. For instance, children mentally classify their treasured objects, such as dolls, Beanie Babies, stamps, stickers, and baseball cards, in many different ways. Collections include objects; they therefore provide an ideal means for enriching children's classification operation. By trying to organize their collected objects, children richly develop the concept of

Figure 3.5 The Three-Mountains Problem
Source: Kowalski, R. N., & Westen, D. *Psychology,* Fourth Edition. Copyright © 2005 John Wiley & Sons, Inc.

TABLE 3.2

Comparison of Seven Mental Operations during the Preoperational and Concrete-Operational Stages

Concept	Preoperational Thought	Concrete-Operational Thought
Animism	The belief that all things are living (e.g., the sun sets because it is tired).	
	Children assume that moving objects have lifelike qualities. A table hurts if it is scratched.	Children distinguish between animate and inanimate objects and know not to ascribe lifelike qualities to inanimate objects.
Centration	Focusing on an object's most salient perceptual feature, such as its height, while neglecting other important features that are not as perceptually salient, such as width and depth.	
	Children rely on perception-bound judgment and focus on a single, salient aspect of an object when trying to solve a problem or answer a question.	Children can discount misleading physical appearances and focus on more than one aspect of an object at a time (e.g., considering not only an object's height but also its width and depth).
Transductive reasoning	A causality belief in which children think that when two events occur simultaneously, one must have caused the other.	
	Children assume that when two events occur at the same time, one caused the other.	Children have a better understanding of temporal cause-and-effect relationships.
Egocentrism	Viewing the world from one's own perspective while failing to recognize that other people might have a different perspective or point of view.	
	Children typically assume that others share their point of view. "The world is as it looks to me."	Children are more aware of others' perspectives and understand that they can be different from their own. "The world can be seen both from my perspective and from yours."
Reversibility	The ability to reverse an action by mentally performing its opposite, such as mentally putting a piece of paper back into its original state after it has been torn into pieces.	
	Children cannot mentally undo an action they have witnessed. They cannot understand that adding $2 + 3 = 5$ can be undone, such that $5 - 2 = 3$.	Children can mentally undo an action they witnessed and return the object back to its original state: 2 beads can be added to 3 to make 5, and 2 can be subtracted from 5 to return to the original 3.
Classification	Grouping objects into categories. An understanding of whole/part relationships among objects, such as understanding that Texas is a part of the whole United States.	
	Children use one-dimensional classifications, because they include all objects that share a common attribute in the same single category.	Children use two-dimensional classifications, because they distinguish between whole classes and underlying subclasses by recognizing that objects have more than one attribute.
Seriation	The ability to order or arrange a set of objects along a quantifiable dimension, such as height or weight of the objects.	
	Lacking the ability to seriate, children given a set of six sticks of varying lengths will arrange them in a random or haphazard way.	Children arrange objects such as the six sticks of differing lengths in serial order, starting with the shortest and finishing with the longest.

relationships between classes and subclasses, and even subclasses within subclasses. In a card collection, for instance, *baseball cards* is the whole, and *National League* and *American League* might be subclasses, or *my favorite team* and *all other teams* might be subclasses.

With seriation, the concrete-operational child can mentally arrange, or order, a set of objects along a quantifiable dimension, such as height. Understanding operations such as *greater than* (>) and *less than* (<) allows children to arrange objects in a serial order, such as arranging the 20 students in their class by height in terms of shortest to tallest. Because concrete-operational thinkers can seriate, they begin to recognize that attributes of people can also be arranged on a quantifiable dimension, such as grades, running speed, physical attractiveness, and so forth. Such judgments have important consequences for the child's developing sense of self-worth, because seriation makes social comparisons possible. Because of their capacity to seriate, late-elementary school children begin to realize that "I am faster than Joe but slower than Jill and José. Maybe I'm not the fastest after all."

The ultimate operational schema that defines the concrete operations stage is **conservation**, the realization that the properties of an object do not change even if its appearance is altered in some way. Lacking the capacity to conserve, preoperational thinkers use their perceptions to judge an object whose appearance has been altered. Concrete-operational children realize that the change in one attribute is compensated by

conservation Understanding that appearance alterations (e.g., an object's length, height, or width) do not change the essential properties of an object (e.g., its amount).

Figure 3.6 Three Piagetian Tests of a Child's Capacity to Conserve
Source: Kowalski, R. N., & Westen, D. *Psychology,* Fourth Edition. © 2005 John Wiley & Sons. Reprinted by permission of John Wiley & Sons, Inc.

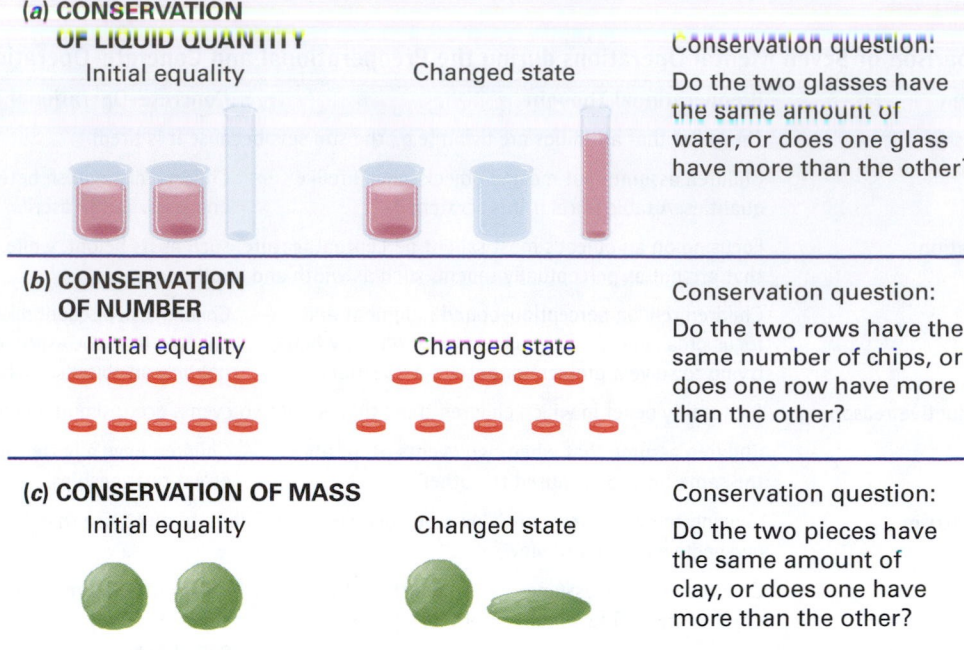

(a) CONSERVATION OF LIQUID QUANTITY

Initial equality   Changed state

Conservation question: Do the two glasses have the same amount of water, or does one glass have more than the other?

(b) CONSERVATION OF NUMBER

Initial equality   Changed state

Conservation question: Do the two rows have the same number of chips, or does one row have more than the other?

(c) CONSERVATION OF MASS

Initial equality   Changed state

Conservation question: Do the two pieces have the same amount of clay, or does one have more than the other?

How Can I Use This?

Try one of the tasks in Figure 3.6 with an elementary-grade child and ask: How are the two objects different? How are they the same? What do the child's responses tell you about his or her cognitive development?

a corresponding change in another attribute. Figure 3.6 shows three illustrations of Piagetian conservation tasks involving the conservation of liquid, number, and mass. In each test of the child's mental ability to conserve, some perceptual property of the object has been changed—its height, width, or surface area, for instance. Preoperational thinkers follow their eyes and say that each object has changed—more water, more chips, and more clay. Concrete-operational thinkers use the conservation mental operation to follow their logic and say that the objects contain the same amount, despite their altered appearances. The Taking It to the Classroom box on next page offers six ways teachers can enrich their students' concrete operations.

If you examine the six recommended ways to enrich children's concrete operations in the Taking It to the Classroom box, you may notice that the most obvious one is missing—namely, using concrete materials in learning. After all, it is common practice to help children learn math concepts by using physical manipulatives (concrete materials) such as beads, blocks, fraction tiles, Popsicle sticks, or their computer animation counterparts while not using abstract materials such as numerals or equations. Four coins are easier to

(MR © Ellen B. Senisi/The Image Works)

In the test of conservation of a liquid quantity, the preoperational thinker believes the tall, skinny glass has more juice than the shorter (but wider) glass.

Taking It to the Classroom

Ways to Enrich Concrete Operations

Promote exploration	Provide children with interesting objects to manipulate and explore.
Promote discovery	Instead of telling students about a concept, create the opportunity for them to discover it. To discover *taxonomy*, have children explore leaves of different shapes, colors, and spiral patterns, then ask why some leaves would be grouped together.
Keep discovery going	The teacher's role is to get things started (collect a sample of leaves), then to keep discovery going by supporting students' curiosity and interest. (If a student invents a dubious taxonomy, ask how the student reached that conclusion and point out differences the child does not yet see.)
Ask for predictions	Ask students to predict what might happen next. Before turning the page in a book, first ask the child to predict what might happen next.
Encourage thinking about relationships	As students explore and manipulate objects, ask about relationships: In what ways are these two trees similar to each other? In what ways are they different?
Resist telling or showing students the right answer	Resist telling a child something, because telling prevents children from discovering that knowledge by themselves. The problem with telling students answers is that they learn without understanding. Through invention, students learn with understanding.

understand than is the numeral *4*. This practice is highly consistent not only with Piaget (1970) but with other famous educators such as Montessori (1917) and Bruner (1966). The reasoning is that young children's thinking is inherently concrete, they are intrinsically motivated to manipulate concrete objects, and they cannot interpret the world in any way other than concretely. This is surely true of preoperational children, but late-elementary children in the concrete operations stage can benefit greatly from instructional help designed to advance their concrete thinking toward abstract thinking. As an example of such instructional help, students may have difficulty seeing the objects in the fractions activity introduced on page 66 as anything other than wooden tiles or pizza slices when presented to them in the way depicted there. To help concrete-operational children see the pizza slices as symbolic representations of fractions, it is best to dump out the individual pieces on a table and have students reason about where each piece might be placed into the tray (Martin, 2009), while enacting the recommendations introduced in the Taking It to the Classroom box—namely, promoting exploration and discovery, keeping discovery going, asking for predictions, encouraging thinking about relations, and resisting the telling or showing of the right answers. What matters is not whether children use concrete materials but, instead, whether teachers facilitate the **dual representation** of seeing objects as both what they are and what they represent (e.g., numbers, maps, models, and the symbols that occur in algebra, science, and mythology; DeLoache, 2000; Uttal, Scudder, & DeLoache, 1997). The capacity for dual representation opens the cognitive-developmental door to the formal operations stage.

dual representation All symbolic objects have a dual nature, as they are simultaneously objects in their own right and representations of something else.

Formal Operations Stage As impressive as the cognitive repertoire of concrete-operational thinkers is, operations can be applied only to *concrete* (tangible) objects and events that lie immediately in front of them. With formal-operational thinking, preadolescents and adolescents consider unseen possibilities. They generate hypotheses, and they think logically and systematically about ideas and possibilities. The *form* in formal operations refers to the capacity to follow the form of an argument, not just its content. Parables, metaphors, ironies, proverbs, analogies, and satire—such as those found in the books *Animal Farm* and *Gulliver's Travels*—illustrate this feature. Concrete thinkers understand *Animal Farm* to be a story about farm animals, whereas formal thinkers understand the story is a satire on government. With formal-operational thinking, thinking can be independent of concrete reality. For example, actors say, "Break a leg"; parents say, "Money doesn't grow on trees"; and television sportscasters say, "That ball was a frozen rope."

Most classroom-based tasks involve both real facts and possible hypotheses, as discussed with dual representations in the previous section. In an art class, for instance, the task might be to draw or paint a still life. Concrete-operational thinkers generally draw what is in front of them (flowers, landscapes), whereas formal-operational thinkers think about what is possible (imagined events, abstract art). In a math class, concrete-operational thinkers count beads and coins, whereas formal-operational thinkers reason with abstract concepts such as letters and numbers (e.g., if $4x + 10 = 26$, what does x equal?).

Two ways of thinking hypothetically are inductive and deductive reasoning (Goswami, 2011). With **inductive reasoning**, adolescents reason from a number of specific observations to generate a general conclusion. The adolescent has some given information (an example, an analogy) and is asked to "go beyond the information given" to make an inference. For instance, Mark may observe that Jeff likes basketball, tennis, and water skiing, and conclude (i.e., induce) that Jeff probably likes sports in general. With **deductive reasoning**, adolescents draw information out of evidence and general premises to reason a single logically valid answer. For instance:

> **inductive reasoning** The abstraction of a general principle from a variety of examples.

> **deductive reasoning** Drawing a valid conclusion out of a general premise or a sample of evidence.

- *What I know*: Friday is always test day.
- *What I know*: Today is Friday.
- *What I deduce*: Therefore, we probably have a test today.

The conclusion that *we probably have a test today* is deduced information, as it goes beyond what is known (Friday is test day; today is Friday) to generate a single valid answer (i.e., we have a test today). The important point is that adolescents think like the famous detective from literature, Sherlock Holmes, as they use both inductive and deductive thinking to go beyond the information in front of them to induce new insights and to deduce logical conclusions.

Systematic problem solving (scientific thinking) represents another important formal operation (Kuhn, 2011). Scientific thinking is not just for scientists, as knowledge seeking and the weighing of evidence is something that almost all adolescents and adults do, as the opening chapter's discussion on critical thinking hopefully communicated. But some people are more systematic in their thinking than are others. Concrete-operational thinkers generally use a trial-and-error approach to problem solving as they search haphazardly (unsystematically) for a solution. Formal-operational thinkers are more likely to think systematically during problem solving. To illustrate this difference, consider the pendulum problem in Figure 3.7 (from Inhelder & Piaget, 1958). A weight suspended on a string and set into motion acts as a pendulum. In the pendulum problem, the student is asked to determine which factor explains how fast the pendulum swings. Concrete-operational thinkers are unable to separate the four variables—lengths, weights, elevations, and pushes—to determine or isolate the separate effect of each. For instance, concrete thinkers might change the length of the string but at the same time also change the object's weight and the force of the initial push. Only systematic formal-operational thinkers who generate and test reasonable hypotheses can come to a conclusion such as the following (Inhelder & Piaget, 1958, p. 75):

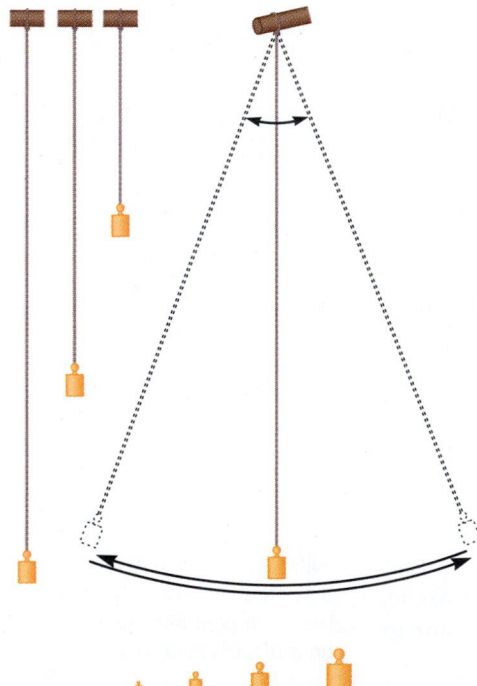

Figure 3.7 The Pendulum Problem
Source: Figure 3 from Inhelder, B., & Piaget, J. (1958). *The Growth of Logical Thinking from Childword to Adolescence.* Copyright © 1958 by Basic Books, Inc. Reprinted by permission of Basic Books, a member of Perseus Books, L.L.C.

After having selected 100 grams with a long string and a medium length string, then 20 grams with a long and a short string, and finally 200 grams with a long and a short, [the student] concludes: "It's the length of the string that makes it go faster or slower; the weight doesn't play any role." She discounts

Taking It to the Classroom

Ways to Enrich Formal Operations

Ask for possibilities	Request a statement of all the possibilities relating to a particular event.
Analyze logic	Ask students to state an opinion, such as that democracy is the best form of government, and then to explain why that opinion is valid. Help students use inferential and deductive logic.
	Identify and challenge invalid (illogical) arguments, including:
	a. Appeals to the masses (everyone else does it).
	b. Appeals to pity/feelings (persuasion via emotion, not reason).
	c. Illegitimate appeals to authority (citing a source with no topic expertise in the subject, such as a celebrity's endorsement).
	d. Arguing against the individual (name-calling).
Encourage scientific thinking	Create classroom projects that require students to isolate variables, imagine unseen possibilities, and generate hypotheses.
Act as a consultant	As students solve problems, act as a consultant to their exploration, not as an authority who has the answers. As one educator phrased it, "Not a sage on the stage but a guide on the side."
Use peer learning	Because teachers have greater knowledge and status than students do, teachers' answers often come across as definitive. An egalitarian relationship is easier to achieve among peers, so peer learning provides a better opportunity for students to experience cognitive conflict.

likewise the height of the drop and the force of her push. [Quote from adolescent who solves the problem using formal operations]

While the pendulum problem is an artificial task, the same scientific reasoning is used in daily life, as by high school seniors trying to decide which college to attend or why a piece of machinery is not working properly. In each case, several factors play a possible determining role, and an adaptive solution requires systematic thinking in which hypotheses are formulated, variables are isolated, confounding factors are controlled, and key influences are identified.

Developing formal-operational thinking does not happen automatically (Neimark, 1979), and adolescents and adults frequently do not reason in formal-operational ways (Byrnes, 1988). Instead, formal-operational thinking requires the kinds of cognitive challenges that schools provide (Cole, 1990), as in algebra (e.g., solve for x in the following equation: $8 = 2x - 2$), science (e.g., the pendulum problem), literature (e.g., interpreting imagery, satire, metaphors), and politics (e.g., what would happen if a country's political structure changed from socialism to capitalism?). Teachers and schooling can clearly help students develop their formal-operational thinking (De Lisi & Staudt, 1980; Fischer et al., 1990), as discussed in the nearby Taking It to the Classroom box.

Classroom Applications

Educators generally react positively to Piaget's ideas (Gallagher & Easley, 1978; Ginsburg & Opper, 1988; Wadsworth, 1996). Here are three guidelines for classroom applications (based on Piaget, 1971, 1973).

1. **Be sensitive to individual differences**

   All children proceed sequentially through the Piagetian stages of cognitive development, yet they do so at different rates. Because this is so, not all children are

What Does This Mean to Me?
After your first exam in a college course, try to determine which one factor most influenced your grade (hours studied, exam difficulty, etc.).

What Does This Mean to Me?
Perhaps you are currently enrolled in a collage course in introductory philosophy. If so, glance through the textbook's table of contents and you will see that the study of logic is a basic training ground for the development and use of formal operations (e.g., inference, deduction, syllogisms, and probabilities).

intellectually ready to learn the same lesson. To be sensitive to differences in students' readiness to learn, plan learning activities for individual students or for small groups of students, rather than for the whole class. For instance, teachers can set up interest areas for students to explore, and they can have students work on personal projects or portfolios of their work.

2. *Motivate by stimulating curiosity*

Students come to school wanting to learn. They come with existing schemas, and they come to school wanting to enhance their existing knowledge to better understand and adapt to the world around them. Hence, all students possess a natural motivation to learn. To help teachers capitalize on students' natural curiosity, Table 3.3 offers three curiosity-inducing instructional strategies that teachers can use during instruction: guessing and feedback, suspense, and controversy. With these disequilibrium-creating experiences, students are inherently motivated to seek out new knowledge and are open to learning and to revising their existing knowledge (Loewenstein, 1994).

3. *Promote discovery-based learning*

Piaget advised teachers to avoid instructional strategies that place students in a passive mode of learning (e.g., lecturing, telling, demonstrating, showing). He believed strongly that the mind is *not* a passive receptacle. Instead of being asked to watch and listen to the teacher, students should be encouraged to explore the objects and activities around them (Bruner, 1961). For example, instead of watching a math teacher show on a chalkboard how to add and subtract, students should combine and separate objects. Similarly, a science teacher might lecture on the metric system, but students would be better served by activities involving measuring various classroom objects of interest. To promote discovery-based learning, teachers can provide classroom environments that are rich in stimulation, complexity, and objects of interest—books, computers, art, animals or pets, construction paper, puzzles, libraries, science laboratories, musical instruments, and all sorts of wall-hangings.

RIDE How would Piaget suggest a teacher help students understand the concept of fractions?

TABLE 3.3

Three Curiosity–Inducing Instructional Strategies

1. *Guessing and feedback*

The teacher asks students a difficult question based on the day's lesson plan. Students then generate an answer by writing it down or saying it aloud. The teacher gives right/wrong feedback. Wrong answers crucially expose gaps in students' understanding. Students are allowed a second answer, and if this, too, is incorrect, disequilibrium grows.

- An elementary school teacher brings the topic for discussion into class wrapped in a brown paper bag. She asks students to guess what it might be.

- A history teacher writes the names of five presidents on the board and asks, "What do these presidents have in common? Why should they be grouped together?"

2. *Suspense*

The teacher introduces a learning activity and asks students to try to predict its outcome. Students then collect the data they need to test the validity of their prediction. Students use this outcome-revealing information to assess the adequacy of their prior knowledge.

- One-third book report: Students read the first third of a book and stop to write a brief report consisting of predictions about what will likely happen in the book's remaining pages. As they read, students find out whether their predictions are correct.

- Demonstration: A physics teacher has two objects—a golf ball and a Ping Pong ball. Students are asked to predict which object will hit the ground first when dropped side by side. Students watch the demonstration, hoping their prediction will be confirmed.

3. *Controversy*

Students are introduced to an issue with more than one possible answer and asked to take a position on it. Using these position statements, the teacher divides the students into pairs or small groups and communicates the value of different perspectives, rather than a right or best answer. During the ensuing discussion, students become aware of their peers' differing perspectives, which instigates disequilibrium and the search for additional information to defend their perspective and to critique their peers' perspectives.

- A controversy: Where did the moon come from? Perhaps a textbook offers three different explanations and students debate those explanations.

- An open-ended question: What is the theme of *The Adventures of Huckleberry Finn*?

Limitations

Piaget's ideas have had a lasting impact on the practice of education (Beilin, 1992). But several of his key ideas have been challenged (Miller, 2011), and these challenges have led to new ways of thinking about cognitive development (Lourenco & Machado, 1996). One limitation is that Piaget sometimes underestimated the intellectual capacities of infants, preschoolers, and elementary school students (Baillargeon, 1987; Bjorklund, 1995). When children are given problems to solve that are simpler and more familiar to them than those used by Piaget, they sometimes show greater problem-solving skills.

A second limitation concerns Piaget's insistence that cognitive development is *qualitatively* different for students of different ages (Bjorklund, 1995). Those who study cognitive development from an information-processing perspective (see Chapter 7) argue that cognitive development unfolds in small *quantitative*, rather than large qualitative, changes (Case & Okamoto, 1996). The idea is that ongoing and very gradual maturation of the brain and central nervous system explains why older children are more complex thinkers than younger children (Fischer & Rose, 1995; Nelson & Bloom, 1997). Students with more physically mature brains will be better at sustaining attention, interpreting information, planning ahead, answering hypothetical questions, holding information in memory, and thinking abstractly. This greater biological capacity allows adolescents to use more sophisticated *strategies* to solve problems. For instance, adolescents can solve Piagetian tasks like the pendulum problem by remembering what they have and have not done, by processing information faster, by using more efficient problem-solving strategies, and by tapping into their domain-specific prior knowledge (Bjorklund et al., 1997; Case, 1992; Kuhn & Phelps, 1982). Hence, thinking speed, memory capacity, effective strategies, and prior knowledge can—and do—explain some advances in cognitive development (Halford & Andrews, 2011).

A third limitation concerns the practice of **discovery–based learning**, a general approach to teaching that was introduced at the close of Chapter 2 and featured earlier as a Piagetian classroom application. In science, algebra, and computer programming, for instance, direct instruction in which teachers explicitly teach and show students information often works better than does discovery learning (Klahrl & Nigam, 2004). In addition, **guided discovery** generally produces better learning outcomes than does pure discovery (Mayer, 2004).

A final limitation of Piaget's theory is his relative neglect of the importance of culture and mentoring in the advancement of cognitive development. For Piaget, students develop cognitively when acting as independent explorers who interact in a stimulating and supportive environment. However, this view of cognitive development leaves out the important role of social guidance and mentoring. Often, children's understanding and skills—how to read, how to cook, how to plan, how to build something—benefit if they have access to and guidance from a competent adult. The view that cognitive development occurs largely through social guidance is the subject of the next section.

discovery–based learning Students work on their own to grasp a concept or understand a lesson.

guided discovery Students work under the guidance of a capable partner to grasp a concept or understand a lesson.

Sociocognitive Development

Sociocognitive development is the study of how other people (*socio-*) help develop our thinking (*cognitive*). The term might better be represented as *socio → cognitive development*, such that social interaction precedes and causes later individual cognitive development.

To capture the essential flavor of *socio*cognitive development, consider the experience of traveling to a foreign country, one with a different language and different customs from your own. If you have traveled abroad, you probably felt unsure of yourself and wanted to travel with someone who already knew the language and customs rather well. If so, this is how you probably learned your way around: Stay near the trusted guide, watch closely and mimic what the guide does, ask the guide whether what you are doing is okay, and attend very closely to any instruction he or she provides. When we find ourselves in uncharted territory, it helps to have a mentor to guide us along the way. For Russian developmental psychologist Lev Vygotsky, students who are asked to learn how to read, play a musical instrument, or solve algebra problems are like travelers in a foreign land who want, need, and benefit from access to a trusted guide.

Cognitive Development as an Apprenticeship: Vygotsky's Theory

About the same time that Piaget was formulating his ideas on cognitive development, Lev Vygotsky was doing the same, though he reached very different conclusions. Vygotsky argued that cognitive development emerges mostly out of the child's social interactions with parents, teachers, peers, and other competent members of society. For Vygotsky, cognitive growth developed from collaborative dialogues with skilled members of the culture (Vygotsky, 1978,1987).

From this brief introduction, it might already be apparent that Vygotsky had a different answer from Piaget's to the question: What develops during cognitive development? For Piaget, cognitive development involved enrichment of general mental operations (e.g., object permanence, conservation) that can be used to solve problems. For Vygotsky, cognitive development involved enrichment of task-specific skills and knowledge (Fischer, 1980). What students need to learn task-specific skills and knowledge is not exploration and discovery but, instead, guidance and mentoring.

Guided participation occurs when one engages in learning activities alongside a skilled partner who provides the support and encouragement needed to acquire new skills and new understanding (Rogoff, 1998). Children and adolescents seek out opportunities for social guidance in any number of daily activities, including getting dressed, preparing a nutritious breakfast, crossing the street, working on a computer, learning a sporting activity, learning a foreign language, submitting applications to colleges, and so on. They do so because cognitive processes often occur in conversation on the social level before they are internalized and transformed on the individual level. Thus, because learning is so often embedded within social interaction, cognitive development requires an apprenticeship (Rogoff, 1990).

guided participation Having one's engagement in a learning activity encouraged, supported, and tutored by a skilled partner.

Scaffolding in the Zone of Proximal Development

A student faces every educational task with a certain range (a bandwidth) of domain-specific competence, as shown in Table 3.4. At the left-hand side of this range is *predevelopment*, a level of competence at which the student is unable to solve problems in that domain, even with assistance. The difficulty of the task overwhelms the student's problem-solving capacities. In the middle of the table is the **zone of proximal development**, the level at which students can solve problems, provided that they receive sufficient support while doing so. A high school student might be able to write a persuasive 500-word essay, but the extent to which he or she will be able to do so depends on the teacher's supportive tips and feedback while the student is drafting topic sentences, making transitions between paragraphs, and the like. At the right-hand side of the range is *actual development*, the level at which students are capable of solving problems independently. For example, if a biology teacher asks students to identify a specimen under a microscope, students in the zone of predevelopment will hesitate and stare blankly. Students in the zone of proximal development will express readiness but also require help and support to get through the exercise successfully. Students in the zone of actual development will be fully able to carry out the task on their own.

zone of proximal development A level of competence at which a student cannot yet master a task on his or her own but can accomplish it with appropriate guidance from a more capable partner.

In Vygotsky's theory, the zone of proximal development is of particular importance because this is the critical zone in which cognitive development occurs. Relatively little learning occurs in the zones of either predevelopment or actual development. Instead, learning occurs as teachers help students narrow the gap between their potential development (what they can do with assistance) and their actual development (what they can do alone). For Vygotsky (1987), instruction is useful only when it moves ahead of the student's development.

How do teachers do this? How do teachers help students achieve that which they cannot yet achieve on their own? For example, how do English teachers advance would-be writers

> **What Does This Mean to Me?**
> For a teaching task such as creating a test, would you place your current competence in the zone of predevelopment, proximal development, or actual development?

TABLE 3.4

The Zone of Proximal Development as a Range of Competence

Predevelopment	Zone of Proximal Development	Zone of Actual Development
Students lack the competencies needed to learn from the task, even with guidance.	Students can learn from the task if they receive another's expert guidance and support.	Students have the competencies needed to learn from the task on their own.

toward becoming proficient writers? Essentially, they provide instruction that moves ahead of what students can currently do while simultaneously providing the support they need to move ahead (Vygotsky, 1987).

Scaffolding is the guidance, support, and assistance a teacher provides to students during social interaction that allows students to gain skill and understanding. Just like a newly planted tree needs the support of a stake and ropes to hold it upright during its first year of growth, students, too, need teachers' scaffolding until they gain the developmental roots of the skill that will allow them to learn on their own. Such a scaffold serves at least four functions:

- It provides support.
- It extends the range of what the learner can do.
- It allows the learner to accomplish tasks that would otherwise not be possible.
- It is used only when needed.

Because students have a difficult time knowing where to begin a new lesson, scaffolding typically begins with the teacher's planning and structuring of the lesson, such as setting up the learning activity, defining the learning goal, and modeling what an idealized performance might look like. Once the lesson begins, scaffolding involves instructional acts, such as providing hints, tips, reminders, examples, directions, challenges, explanations, prompts, and well-timed questions and suggestions. In a nutshell, scaffolding is the teacher's effort to support the student's learning in the zone of proximal development by providing what the student needs most but cannot yet provide for him- or herself—namely, expert planning, strategies, skills, and knowledge.

The following is an example of the scaffolding provided by a teacher to an elementary-grade student during a geography lesson:

TEACHER: Here is a map of the United States.

STUDENT: *[Saying nothing, she just stares at the map, then looks at the teacher.]*

TEACHER: *[Shifting her glance toward the map.]* Can you identify any of the states?

STUDENT: *[The student continues to stare at the map, saying nothing.]*

TEACHER: *[Points to one particular state.]* Do you recognize this one?

STUDENT: Yeah, that's where we live—Texas.

TEACHER: *[Showing excitement.]* That's right! What cities are in Texas?

STUDENT: Dallas and Houston.

TEACHER: *[Taking her hands off the map and placing them in her lap.]* Can you show me where Dallas and Houston are on the map?

STUDENT: *[Pointing to each city.]*

TEACHER: What else is in Texas?

scaffolding The guidance, support, and tutelage provided by a teacher during social interaction designed to advance students' current level of skill and understanding.

MINDFUL HABITS OF EFFECTIVE TEACHERS

Adapting lesson plans to stimulate curiosity and maximize the time students spend working within their zones of proximal development is a key habit of mind of effective teachers.

(Dynamic Graphics/Creatas)

With guidance and support from a capable mentor, students learn complex, culturally valued skills.

Appendix
**Supporting Students'
Learning**

Teachers need to know a variety of instructional strategies and techniques so that they can support students' learning (PRAXIS™, II.A.2; INTASC, Principle 4).

STUDENT: *[The student points to and names additional points of interest. Finally, without any further prodding from the teacher, the student begins to identify other states and other points of interest.]*

TEACHER: *[Adjusts her tutelage by becoming less directive and pausing more often to give the student more chances to talk and take the lead in the learning process.]*

Scaffolding is not just for children. The same process applies equally well for interactions with adolescents, as in the following example of the scaffolding provided by a Spanish teacher to a high school student in a mock-restaurant setting:

TEACHER: You are in a restaurant, and you want to place an order.

STUDENT: *[Saying nothing, the student sits in the chair in the imaginary restaurant, shrugs, and looks at the teacher.]*

TEACHER: Here comes the waiter: What would you say as a greeting?

STUDENT: *[The student continues to sit at the table, looking at the teacher, hesitating, and wanting the teacher to take responsibility for the conversation.]*

TEACHER: *[Smiling, pausing, and looking with anticipation at the student, finally asking.]* What might a friendly greeting be?

STUDENT: ¿Hola, cómo está usted? *[Hello, how are you?]*

TEACHER: *[Showing excitement.]* That's right! What do you say to request a menu?

STUDENT: ¿Puedo ver un menú? *[May I see a menu?]*

TEACHER: *[Backing away from the table so that the student and "waiter" can talk.]* Where might the conversation go from there?

STUDENT: *[Points to the menu item, and speaks.]* La papa al horno, por favor. *[Baked potato, please.]*

WAITER: ¿Y para beber? *[And to drink?]*

STUDENT: La gaseosa, por favor. *[Soda pop, please.]*

TEACHER: *[Coming back toward the table.]* Okay, see whether you can say it all together—greeting, menu request, order.

STUDENT: *[Turning to the waiter, the student strings together a greeting and an order. Finally, without any further prodding from the teacher, the student begins to engage in a more casual conversation, asking the waiter whether the restaurent serves desserts and whether there will be any music during dinner.]*

TEACHER: *[Adjusts her tutelage by asking open-ended questions and pausing more often to give the student more chances to talk and take the lead in the learning process.]*

Transfer of Responsibility Initially, communication between the teacher and the student is asymmetrical. The teacher selects the activity, models expert performance, sets goals, and explicitly teaches the student. In other words, the teacher takes full responsibility for the task. As the student gains and displays skill and shows fewer nonverbal signs of hesitance and frustration, the teacher begins the subtle process of assessing the student's readiness to take on more responsibility in the endeavor.

In part, transfer of responsibility is initiated by the teacher. The teacher might, for instance, increase the length of pauses in conversation to give the student an opportunity to step in and take more responsibility (Fox, 1988). The teacher might up the ante in terms of performance expectations. The teacher might also begin to replace directive communications with more open-ended questions. In the same spirit, the teacher might ask the student to explain what she is doing and why she is doing it that way. But transfer is also initiated by the student. As students grow their skills and knowledge, they learn how to send signals that they are ready to take on greater responsibility and decision making. Instead of just receiving hints, the student begins to ask for them (Rogoff & Gardner, 1984). The student also shows increased levels of leadership. As the student asks for and takes on more responsibility, the teacher provides fewer instructions and instead spends most of his time monitoring the student's progress and remaining alert for student-initiated cues indicating that the student seeks additional responsibility.

Eventually, the student achieves self-regulation, in which she takes on the full responsibility for the task—choosing activities, structuring the task, setting goals, regulating emotion, implementing task strategies, providing self-reminders, deciding when and whether outside help is needed, and basically assuming full responsibility for managing the endeavor. Students who are able to take full responsibility for the task operate within the zone of actual development.

Instructional Conversations

Scaffolding is a one-on-one tutoring process by which teachers assist one student's learning and cognitive development. When teachers apply these same scaffolding principles to a group of learners, the mentoring is called an *instructional conversation*.

Traditional instruction (i.e., direct instruction) typically relies on a one-way conversation in which teachers talk and provide information as students listen. Instructional conversations are different; they are open discussions in which a group of learners collectively attempt to make sense of the topic of conversation, often by informing, debating, and persuading one another. Overall, the goal of an instructional conversation is to have students learn within the context of a community of learners (Rogoff et al., 2002).

Traditional instruction utilizes the *IRE discourse model* (initiate, respond, evaluate), whereas instructional conversations utilize the **PQS discourse model** (probe, question, scaffold). IRE begins as the teacher *initiates* a question—Which planet is closest to the sun?—continues as the student *responds* with an answer—Mercury!—and ends as the teacher *evaluates* the correctness of the response—Yes, that's right. In this *I teach, you learn* model, the teacher provides information and uses IRE discourse to check that students have indeed learned the information. PQS begins as the teacher *probes*, or investigates, what students think—What do you think? Can you explain it to me?—*questions* the basis of that thinking—Why do you believe that? What is your evidence?—and *scaffolds* students toward a deeper understanding—What sort of evidence do we need to answer this question? In an instructional conversation, the teacher typically encourages students to reflect on their thinking, develop their logic or reasoning, and obtain the evidence they need to defend or justify their thinking.

Traditional, IRE-based classroom conversations are very common (Mehan, 1979), mostly because teachers place a higher priority on covering a lot of content during the lesson than on providing students with opportunities to voice alternative perspectives on the content (Alvermann et al., 1990). In addition, classroom teachers find IRE to be relatively easy and PQS to be relatively difficult (Alvermann & Hayes, 1989). To help implement the PQS discourse model, some teachers find it useful to come to the class prepared with question frames, such as: Explain why _____. What is a new example of _____? How would you use _____ to _____? How does _____ affect _____? (King, 1989, 1991). Making the effort to add PQS-based instructional conversations to one's teaching repertoire is important for three reasons: (1) Students generally find instructional conversations more interesting than they find traditional IRE-based conversations; (2) more students get involved and participate in instructional conversations than they do in traditional instruction; and (3) socially shared cognition has a chance to take root and emerge.

Socially shared cognition is meaning, understanding, or a solution to a problem that emerges during a group discussion that would not have been achieved by any individual member alone (Resnick et al., 1991). For instance, during a class discussion about the meaning of a literary work, students bring different perspectives and prior knowledge into the conversation as they (and the teacher) probe, question, and scaffold one another's thinking so that all participants gain an understanding of the book that they could not have gained individually. Such a phenomenon supports the Vygotskian truism that, often, two heads are better than one. Indeed, Vygotsky did not limit his ideas to just two heads (mentor and mentee) but suggested that groups, institutions, and whole communities also act in the role of the mentor (i.e., a thousand heads are better than one).

Intersubjectivity is a unique product that arises out of the socially shared experiences that occur within expert–novice interactions. It occurs as two people converse and come to a shared understanding of how to manage the problem-solving situation (Gauvain & Rogoff, 1989). If the pair is to achieve a measure of intersubjectivity within the relationship, the student must do more than just mimic the expert's language, strategies, and answers. To achieve intersubjectivity, the pair must work collaboratively to formulate a shared focus

PQS discourse model Conversation during instruction in which the teacher follows a script of probe, question, and scaffold.

socially shared cognition A shared understanding of a problem that emerges during group interaction that would not have been achieved by any individual member of the group acting alone.

intersubjectivity The unique product that arises from social interaction in which the interaction partners come to a shared understanding of how to manage the problem-solving situation.

of attention, shared intentions, shared strategies, mutual engagement, shared emotions—a joint and socially shared understanding of how to develop skill and solve problems. In short, intersubjectivity is not something the student lacks, nor is it something the teacher has. It is a mutual understanding, a co-construction that exists at the socially shared level to extend the student's understanding (Vygotsky, 1987).

Role of Language

Piaget and Vygotsky came to different conclusions about the role of language in cognitive development. For Piaget, language is a by-product of cognitive development, one that reflects the individual's level of cognitive maturity. Instead of language facilitating cognitive development, a mental schema must exist *prior* to the expression of language. In other words, thought precedes language. As a case in point, children use the word *gone* only after they have first mastered object permanence (Gopnik, 1984).

For Vygotsky, speech is a tool for thinking. On this point, Vygotsky agreed with Plato, the ancient philosopher who believed that truth and understanding emerged only through dialogue. In Vygotsky's understanding, the learner first receives the mentor's speech as an external aid, which is then internalized into *inner* or *private speech*. **Private speech** is spoken-aloud thought whose purpose is to communicate with oneself while trying to understand and solve a problem, as occurs with self-guidance (Vygotsky, 1962).

Table 3.5 lists three types of private speech that have been shown to advance children's problem solving and cognitive development: self-guidance, reading aloud, and inaudible muttering (Berk & Garvin, 1984).

Cultural Tools

Sociocognitive development occurs at two levels (Vygotsky, 1978). The first level is through face-to-face, one-on-one interaction in which a competent member of the culture mentors a less competent member, as discussed earlier. The second level is through the culture's history and technology. Because past members of the culture have developed effective tools (or "artifacts") for solving problems, students learn more easily when they use these cultural tools. For instance, while learning to read, the would-be reader benefits greatly not only from having a trusted mentor but also from having access to the alphabet, the language, a book, a library, eyeglasses, and so on. All these cultural products were invented to help people develop their thinking through reading. Other cultural artifacts include diagrams, maps, systems for counting, works of art, mnemonic techniques, algebraic symbols, and so on.

Each culture defines which problems are most important, and each culture creates its own tools for solving these problems. In the United States, for instance, writing papers and making engaging classroom presentations are important problems, and tools such as computers and PowerPoint software help students become proficient writers and presenters. Literacy and mathematics are also **cultural tools**. With literacy, students develop their ideas through written material; with mathematics, they develop ideas related to numbers and calculations (Nunes, 1999; Rogoff, 2003; Serpell, 1993). Teachers provide students with tools such as books and newspapers to help students solve the problem of understanding printed

private speech Spoken-aloud thought, especially during the engagement of a learning activity.

cultural tools Products created and designed by advanced members of a culture to help less advanced members of the culture learn and solve problems.

TABLE 3.5

Three Types of Private Speech Associated with Gains in Cognitive Development

1. Self-guidance	Remarks about one's own activity that are public but not directed to anyone in particular: "I want to read something. Let's see. I need a book. Where are the books? Oh yeah, there. Now, which one? What did I read last time . . . ?"
2. Reading aloud	Reading books or other materials aloud, sounding out words, or silently mouthing words: "Sum-time. Sum-e-time. Sum-mer-time."
3. Inaudible muttering	Quiet remarks that cannot be heard by an observer. Child moves his or her lips and makes sounds, but the sounds are incomprehensible.

material and tools such as calculators and statistical software programs to help students solve the problem of understanding and working with numbers. In another culture, the central problems might be farming, tracking prey, or carrying water. Such a culture will provide its members with the tools they need to learn about and successfully solve those problems.

In any culture, members do not generally learn to use tools through exploration and self-discovery. Rather, they learn to understand, manipulate, and use tools through a process of social transmission. It is hard to imagine using an unfamiliar tool effectively without first benefiting from the spoken or written words of a mentor. Tools such as the metric system, the periodic table of the elements, and multifunction cell phones are typically introduced by a mentor, who might be a knowledgeable peer.

Importance of Peers

When it comes to promoting sociocognitive development, peers can be every bit as helpful as teachers. True, peers can be as unskilled and confused as is the novice student, and when novices work together, they are often a source of distraction (Tudge, 1992). However, when novices work with a more able peer, they routinely show the same sort of advances in cognitive development that they show when working with a teacher (Tudge, 1992). Like teachers, competent peers can scaffold a student forward (Vygotsky, 1978). This is so because novices pick up new strategies when they observe the performances of their more able peers (Azmitia, 1988). Able peers also make ideal collaborators because they are uniquely sensitive to the novice's zone of proximal development. That is, after the more able peer has learned a skill such as how to solve a particular algebra problem, he is keenly aware of the critical needs of the novice and can concentrate his guidance on that critical skill area. Hence, able peers are uniquely qualified to offer tailored instruction and guidance to the less able learner.

Classroom Applications

Educators generally react positively to Vygotsky's ideas (Rogoff, 1990; Tudge, 1989). Here are four guidelines for classroom applications:

1. **Teacher as guide, mentor**

   Whereas Piaget recommended that students learn by engaging in independent, discovery-based activities, Vygotsky favored a more interventive role for the teacher. The teacher helps by structuring the learning activity, providing instructions, offering guidance, monitoring and correcting the student's progress, probing and questioning what the student knows, staying out in front of students' existing competencies, and gradually turning responsibility for the task over to the student.

2. **Peers as guides, mentors**

   A core premise of the Vygotskian approach to instruction is that *two heads are better than one* (Azmitia, 1988). Generally speaking, students who work cooperatively with a more able peer show better subsequent performance and greater problem-solving skills than do students who work alone (Gauvain & Rogoff, 1989; Johnson & Johnson, 1987). The sociocognitive view endorses cooperative learning settings. It also endorses multi-age classrooms, in which younger children (e.g., third graders) benefit from their older and more able peers (e.g., fourth graders).

3. **Culture as guide, mentor**

   To see how knowledge and skill can be viewed as occurring within a specific cultural context, consider the following letter. It was written more than two centuries ago by the leaders of the Indians of the Five Nations in response to a recruitment letter from William and Mary College:

   You who are wise must know, that different nations have different conceptions of things; and you will therefore not take it amiss, if our ideas of this kind of education happen not to be the same with yours. We have had some experience of it: several of our young people were formally brought up at the colleges of the northern provinces; they were instructed in all your sciences; but when they came back to us . . . [they were] ignorant

Appendix
Cultural Experiences

Understanding that individual students come from disparate backgrounds and cultural experiences will assist you in tailoring your instruction to capitalize on those experiences (PRAXIS™, I.B.6.; INTASC, Principle 3).

R I D E How would Vygotsky suggest a teacher help students understand the concept of fractions?

of every means of living in the woods . . . neither fit for hunting, warriors, or counselors; they were totally good for nothing. We are, however, not the less obliged by your kind offer . . . and to show our grateful sense of it, if the gentlemen of Virginia will send us a dozen of their sons, we will take great care of their education, instruct them in all we know, and make men of them. (Drake, 1834)

What Does This Mean to Me?

Assess your current skill level as a prospective teacher. Did your skill arise from discovery learning? Mentoring? Cultural guidance?

4. *A new view of motivation*

Proponents of discovery learning presume that students are active, interested explorers of their surroundings. This is often the case. They further presume that discovery learning breeds curiosity, interest, and positive emotion. This is only partly true. Learning on one's own can also conjure up a range of negative emotions, such as confusion, frustration, and helplessness (Linn, 1986). If one is to learn, negative emotions need to be managed, and face-to-face scaffolding provides an ideal arena for teachers to do this. Through scaffolding, teachers can help students manage their motivation, mood, and expectations. Whereas Piaget emphasized curiosity and positive emotion as the motivational springs to cognitive development, Vygotsky emphasized perseverance, commitment, and goal setting (Hickey, 1997). This new view of motivation does not argue against interest and curiosity; instead, it adds the idea that learning requires not only sparking positive motivations and emotions but also putting the breaks on negative ones.

Which Theory Should Teachers Apply?

Both the Piagetian and the Vygotskian perspectives on cognitive development offer important contributions to the practice of education. Table 3.6 summarizes each perspective's position on eight issues of interest to teachers.

TABLE 3.6

Summary of Piaget's and Vygotsky's Theories of Cognitive Development

Educational Issue	Piaget's Cognitive-Developmental Perspective	Vygotsky's Sociocognitive-Developmental Perspective
What develops during cognitive development?	Domain-general mental operations that can be used to solve problems in various contexts.	Domain-specific skill, knowledge, and expertise that is specific to a culturally valued problem.
How does learning occur?	Through discovery, invention. Learning is the internal process of making sense of the external world.	Through social transmission. Learning is a cognitive apprenticeship in which knowledge is passed from more able members of the culture to less able ones.
Is cognitive development universal, or is it culturally specific?	Universal. Cognitive development unfolds in an invariant sequence.	Culturally specific. Students develop skills and understanding that are valued by the culture but do not develop skills and understanding in nonvalued domains.
What is the source of gains in cognitive development?	Rich, stimulating, challenging, and responsive environments. Given these conditions and active, independent exploration, students construct knowledge.	Social interaction and guidance from highly competent members of the culture. Students co-construct knowledge with competent partners through a process of guided participation.
What is the role of the teacher?	To provide students with rich, stimulating, challenging, and responsive environments. Create cognitive conflicts. Ask questions about relationships (same? different?).	To select culturally valued problems to solve, introduce the tools of the culture, provide scaffolding within students' zone of proximal development, probe–question–scaffold students' thinking during dialogue.
What is the role of peers?	To stimulate cognitive conflict so as to create disequilibrium.	To act as a mentor and guide in much the same ways as the teacher.
How important is language development to cognitive development?	Largely unimportant. Language is a by-product of thought.	Crucial. Language is the most important tool for thought.
What are recommended instructional strategies?	Discovery-based learning; Montessori classrooms; interest areas; project-based learning; curiosity-inducing strategies.	Scaffolding in the zone of proximal development; dialogue within an instructional conversation; cooperative learning.

As for which theory teachers should apply, it seems that both have merit and that both offer useful recommendations. While there is some merit to keeping the theories separate (Duncan, 1995), many educators recommend that teachers combine the two theories so that Piaget's ideas help teachers formulate instructional strategies to promote disequilibrium and self-discovery, and Vygotsky's ideas help them formulate instructional strategies to promote social guidance and instructional conversations (Glassman, 1994). From this point of view, it is possible to embrace both approaches. In reading this book, for instance, you might ask whether you are exploring an interesting and challenging environmental activity or whether you are benefiting from the social guidance of three veteran authors who are willing to pass along a trick or two.

Language Development

Educators are interested in **language** and its development for three reasons. First, they seek to promote language development because of its enabling and facilitating role in cognitive development. Second, they seek to promote language-based outcomes, such as literacy, oral communication, vocabulary development, writing composition, and so forth. Third, educators seek to help students learn one or more additional languages, as with foreign-language and bilingual education.

> **language** The use of agreed-on rules to combine a small number of symbols (sounds, letters, gestures) to produce a large number of meaningful messages.

How Language Develops

Is language a naturally inherited process or does its emergence and development depend on instruction? If language is a naturally inherited process, it should flower naturally as children mature, which it does. This natural process occurs because children have an innate biological preparedness for language.

Innate Language Acquisition Device More than 4,000 languages exist today, and any one of them is far too complex for children to learn through trial and error or formal instruction. Despite the overwhelming complexity of language, all children learn to talk and by the time they enter school are quite proficient in doing so. This is so because children seem to possess an inborn linguistic processor called a **language acquisition device** (LAD; Chomsky, 1959,1968) or a *language-making capacity* (LMC; Slobin, 1985).

According to Chomsky (1980), the knowledge of how language works and that it is made of words, has nouns and verbs, and also rules on how words are to be moved around (i.e., syntax, grammar) is innate and the core of the LAD. Naturally occurring verbal input appears to be sufficient to activate the LAD so that children learn the language of their culture rather naturally, mostly by listening. What they hear are words and sentences, and what they come to understand and produce are meaning and grammar. Something is going on that allows children to transform words into meaning and sentences into grammar, and it is not formal instruction.

> **language acquisition device** Inborn capacity that enables children to understand grammar and produce language.

To appreciate children's remarkable natural ability to understand language, try the following exercise. Listen to a conversation between people who speak a foreign language with which you are not familiar. As you listen, can you identify where sentences end? Can you decipher the language's syntax? Generally speaking, adults walk away from such an experiment bewildered. Children, on the other hand, come to understand what they hear—the sounds, syllables, words, and syntax. The critical period during which the LAD is highly sensitive to language input occurs between 18 months and 6 years of age.

The part of language for which people have a biological preparedness is called *syntax*. **Syntax** refers to the structure of language, such as word order and sentence formation rules (e.g., noun–verb–object). Syntax emerges in an orderly and predictable pattern:

> **syntax** The structure of a language, including sentence formation rules, such as noun–verb–object.

- One-word stage: holophrases, such as "doggie" (1 to $1\frac{1}{2}$ years).
- Two-word stage: telegraphic speech, such as "milk gone" (1 to $2\frac{1}{2}$ years).
- Conversational stage: Sentence length increases as children learn rules of sentence formation (3 years and older).

No matter what language they speak, all children start with single words, or holophrases, usually nouns such as animals, body parts, and toys (Bornstein et al., 2004). These are typically in the form of intonated utterances such as "Give!" and "Dollie!" (to draw attention to it). They then add verbs to produce two-word, or telegraphic, speech. At first, the two words typically have equal status in the telegraphic communication, such as "ball table," before one word begins to anchor the communication, such as "more milk!" By two years of age, children universally use about 300 nouns, 100 verbs, and 30 pronouns. Around four years of age, children add adjectives, prepositions, and quantifiers to learn grammar and sentence structure—that is, syntax.

In addition, phonology and semantics develop rapidly from age two through preschool. *Phonology* refers to sounds and pronunciation (e.g., pronouncing letters and words). English-speaking children generally read and can produce sounds such as *p*, *n*, and *b* at age two and more complex sounds such as *th* by preschool. *Semantics* refers to the meaning of words and sentences. From age two to preschool, vocabulary grows rapidly, increasing from about 400 words (age four) to about 2,000 (preschool age).

Although language qualities such as syntax and phonology are largely innate endowments, children still benefit from support, guidance, and instruction. As they constantly point to objects and ask the names of things, environmental support—instruction—helps them to learn the meaning of words. They also need environmental support to learn how to engage in the social aspects of speech, such as what gestures mean, how to take turns talking, and what to say to whom and when. Reading and writing do not come naturally, either. Reading and writing require not only language but also visual understanding and fine motor production. Longitudinally designed research studies confirm that there exists considerable continuity between the language fluency of the preschooler and his or her reading capacities in elementary school (Storch & Whitehurst, 2002).

Role of a Teacher   Even though children and adolescents learn language rather automatically, educational supports for language development are important. After all, the functional purpose of language is to communicate—to get one's message across and to understand the messages that others are trying to get across (Tomasello, 1992, 1995). Thus, language is developed within social interaction as students seek ways to make requests, share information, bond with others, make assertions, make denials, and so forth. Social interaction—not just exposure to speech—is therefore important. In particular, children benefit most when they use language during social interactions that are responsive and linguistically complex (Bloom et al., 1996), and they benefit relatively little from passive reception of language, such as when watching television (Snow et al., 1976). Socially embedded language also occurs in a context of affect and emotion, and children's language growth is enriched by their exposure to affectively positive verbal input (Hart & Risley, 1995).

Learning to speak any language is mostly a task of comprehension. Thus, the quality of the language input is critical to learning a new language (Padilla, 2006). In this spirit, the role of the teacher in helping students learn language is to provide, first, high-quality language input that invites active listening and, second, opportunities for language learners to interact socially and to produce communications (Connor, Morrison, & Slominski, 2006; Penner, 1987; Pianta, Nimetz, & Bennett, 1997; Rice, 1986; Rogoff, 2003; Schuele, Rice, & Wilcox, 1995), such as the following examples:

- Teach phonics, as by introducing a letter, saying what the letter stands for, and inviting children to repeat the sound.

- Provide explicit language-decoding activities, such as an alphabet activity or handwriting practice to facilitate letter–sound connections.

- Paraphrase, extend, expand, and elaborate on what the child says.

- Use rare words. Provide labels and explanations.

- Interact with children in a conversational manner about objects and events that have their attention. Provide opportunities for sustained, multiple-turn conversations.

- Provide pauses in conversations to give children opportunities to generate language, rather than just be exposed to language.

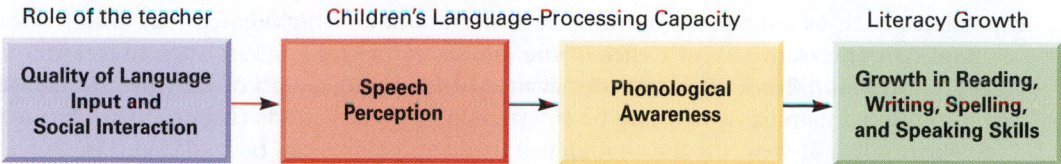

Figure 3.8 A Phonological Awareness Model of Growth in Children's Language Development

- Provide opportunities for peer-to-peer conversations by using the redirect strategy in which the child says to the teacher, "I want to draw", so the teacher replies, "Okay, tell Shin, 'I want to draw.'"

To integrate the role of the teacher and the language capacity of children, Figure 3.8 presents a model to explain the growth rate at which children develop their language (i.e., growth in reading, spelling, and speaking). To the extent that children receive high-quality language input, they learn to perceive the elements of speech. Those speech perception experiences then enable the crucial predictor of children's language development—namely, phonological awareness. **Phonological awareness**—the ability to identify units of speech and connect them with letters, such as connecting the sound "bee" to the written letter *b*—is the best predictor of literacy growth (Badian, 1998; Schatschneider et al., 2004), and it is a better predictor than other factors such as breadth of vocabulary (Chiappe et al., 2007). Importantly, the model depicted in Figure 3.8 has been shown to apply equally as well to monolingual children learning their native language and bilingual children learning a second language (Chiappe et al., 2007). Hence, the crucial role of the teacher in children's language development is to provide instruction that facilitates phonological awareness.

phonological awareness The ability to identify the specific sound units in spoken language.

Genie's Story *Genie* is the pseudonym given to a young girl who grew up in Los Angeles, California, without access to the normal linguistic input that we all take for granted. Rymer (1993) described Genie as "the most damaged child I've ever seen" (linguistically speaking). She was locked away and isolated from language and social interaction from birth through early adolescence. After being rescued from a domineering and abusive father, 13-year-old Genie entered a hospital and worked daily with a linguist to acquire language. When she entered the hospital, Genie could say only a few words, *stopit* and *nomore*. Two pressing questions were: (1) Could she, as a postpubescent adolescent, learn language? (2) What did the language areas of her brain look like?

As to whether she could learn language, experts worked with Genie for years. She was able to increase her vocabulary, but she could not understand grammar and syntax. For Genie, the critical period in which language acquisition needs to occur had passed. A *critical period* is a sensitive developmental duration of time in which the absence of an experience results in irreversible damage. After puberty, if the language-sensitive areas of the brain have not been stimulated with appropriate linguistic input, people learn language only laboriously, if at all. As to what the language areas of Genie's brain looked like, nonintrusive brain imaging showed that her language areas had atrophied. When she finally did encounter words during her adolescence, Genie processed the words in an area of the brain that only picks up noises.

Technology Support for Young Readers and Students with Special Needs

Literacy is the ability to read and write. It is the means through which most education and learning take place. Consequently, the more developed students' language and literacy skills are, the better they function and perform in school (Cummins, 1981). Young children and students with reading disabilities often need technology-based accommodations and external supports to cope successfully with this basic academic task (Lever-Duffy, McDonald, & Mizell, 2005).

Talking Books for Young Readers CD-ROM storybooks, also known as *talking books*, are digital or computerized versions of traditional picture storybooks (Doty et al., 2001). Part of the appeal of these electronic texts is that they add multimedia capabilities to the traditional storybook—

How Can I Use This?
Check out an electronic book (e-book) from your library and ask yourself what instructional uses it affords that a traditional printed book does not.

capabilities such as animation, sound effects, narration, and highlighted text. Many talking books are interactive. With a click of the mouse, young readers can listen to a narrator read the text aloud, listen over and over again to the pronunciation of difficult words, see definitions for unfamiliar words, and be entertained by special effects (Labbo, 2000). From a Vygotskian point of view, these technology-embedded features can be considered *electronic scaffolds*, used at the young reader's discretion (McKenna et al., 1996).

Talking books promote young readers' phonological awareness (Chera & Wood, 2003), word recognition (McKenna et al., 1996), and vocabulary development (Higgins & Hess, 1999). Whether talking books promote reading comprehension to a greater extent than do traditional books remains an open question (Matthew, 1997), though talking books do promote reading comprehension when stories are relatively long or complex (Moore & Smith, 1996). The problem with talking books seems to be that their special effects can be so appealing that readers' attention is diverted away from the text material and toward the electronic entertainment of sights and sounds (Trushell et al., 2001). Because multimedia capabilities can act as a two-edged sword, the nearby Taking It to the Classroom box offers some recommendations for elementary school teachers who utilize CD-ROM storybooks (based on McKenna et al., 1996).

Electronic Books for Students with Special Needs Electronic books can also function as assistive technology to enhance the literacy and classroom participation of students with special needs. Like talking books for young readers, e-books offer literacy-enhancing multimedia features. For instance, e-books offer audio and text-to-speech capabilities (Boyle et al., 2002), extralarge print for students with visual impairments (Cavanaugh, 2002), and highlighted words and text for students with specific reading disabilities, such as dyslexia (Lockard & Abrams, 2004). Figure 3.9 illustrates what these multimedia features look like when integrated into an e-book used by high school students with reading disabilities to define and elaborate on unfamiliar words.

What Does This Mean to Me?
Examine an e-book or Web site with hypertext and ask yourself what role multimedia features play in your reading comprehension.

Appendix
Supporting Readers with Special Needs

Teachers have a variety of resources (e.g., technology) to support them in adapting their instruction for students with special needs (PRAXIS™, I.B.4; INTASC, Principles 1, 3).

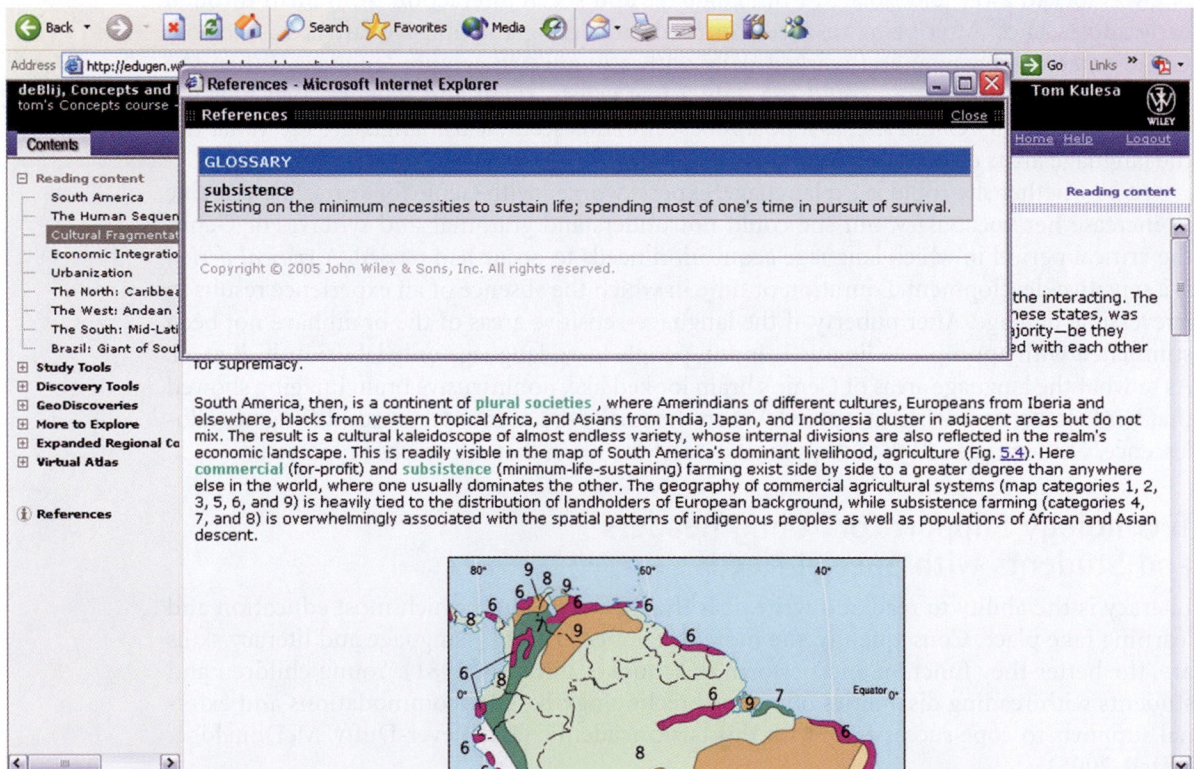

Figure 3.9 Illustration of Assistive Technology to Promote Reading Comprehension for Students with Special Needs
Source: de Blij, H. J., & Muller, P. O. *Concepts and Regions in Geography,* Second Edition. © 2005 H. J. de Blij and John Wiley & Sons, Inc. Reprinted by permission of John Wiley & Sons, Inc.

Taking It to the Classroom

Maximizing the Literacy-Enhancing Potential of Electronic Storybooks

- **Choose appropriate books**
  Talking books for young readers are best for relatively long and complex stories. Printed text is more appropriate for easily understood material because electronic scaffolds are less needed.

- **Encourage attention to print**
  The audiovisual effects of electronic storybooks may distract young readers from attending to the text material. It is sometimes prudent to disable certain features of the program.

- **Plan carefully; clarify your goals**
  Consider using printed material for highly structured reading assignments, and use electronic storybooks during free time. Also use specific features of electronic storybooks to develop specific literacy skills, such as decoding text.

- **Consider different contexts for encounters with books**
  Introduce a projection device to use an electronic storybook like a big book. Establish reading centers where students can read and explore the electronic storybooks.

Text-based scaffolding devices act as embedded resources within reading material to enhance students' reading comprehension and learning (Anderson-Inman & Horney, 1999). Examples within e-books include the following:

- *Transitional resources* that convert text into something more comprehensible to the student, such as speech or definitions

- *Illustrative resources* that help the reader elaborate on and better understand the text, such as pictures, charts, and video

- *Summarizing resources* that provide an overview of the text, such as a concept map or a chapter outline

- *Notational resources* that promote interaction with the text, such as note-taking and outlining tools

- *Enrichment resources*, such as informational sidebars, historical background information, and links to primary resources

Second-Language Acquisition and Bilingualism

If learning one's native language depends on exposure to linguistic input during a childhood critical period, is the same true for learning a second language? Stated in another way, the language question for second-language acquisition asks whether there is a critical period for second-language learning.

Second-Language Acquisition The earlier one begins to learn a second language, the greater is his or her chance of developing fluency in that language. For example, one group of researchers studied immigrants from South Korea and China, focusing on *when* they began to learn English and how successful they were in doing so (Johnson & Newport, 1989). When preschool immigrants tried to learn English, they were able to gain significantly better syntactical competence than were elementary-grade immigrants. Further, the elementary-grade immigrants showed greater fluency than did adolescents. Adolescent immigrants, in turn, were able to gain linguistic competence to a greater degree than were adult immigrants. These data show that second-language proficiency is relatively easy to acquire during childhood, possible but not to the point of native fluency before puberty, and noticeably more difficult after puberty. This shows that second-language acquisition occurs best within a "sensitive period" but is not precluded by the passing of a childhood "critical period." The nearby Taking It to the Classroom box lists several instructional strategies to support second-language learners' English proficiency.

Appendix
Second-Language Learning

Most teachers will encounter students who are learning English as their second language. Knowing some strategies for how to support their learning will be very helpful to you (PRAXIS™, I.B.5; INTASC, Principle 3).

What Does This Mean to Me?
If you speak a second language, how much of an accent do you have? A person who learned before puberty will likely sound like a native speaker. A person who learned after puberty will likely have a noticeable accent. Is this true for you?

These findings raise the practical question of why schools routinely teach foreign languages in high school and college, rather than in elementary school. Research on language acquisition shows that this is clearly a curricular blunder. The best time to acquire a second language is before puberty, not after (Bialystok, 2001). Fortunately, the trend is toward students learning a second language in elementary school and away from learning a second language taught as a separate subject in high school (i.e., foreign-language class), as evidenced by the following range of contemporary formal approaches to second-language learning commonly seen in elementary school (Padilla, 2006):

1. *Immersion Education*: Instruction is provided only in the second language (usually English) so students have no recourse but to learn the new language.

2. *English as a Second Language (ESL)*: English language learners (ELLs) learn the new language in a pullout-type program or during a special class period designed for ELLs to acquire sufficient language proficiency to function well in an otherwise English-speaking school.

3. *Bilingual Instruction*: Some school subjects are taught in the students' native language with the goal of making the transition so that future instruction can occur in English once the student is ready.

The newer elementary school–based approaches to second-language acquisition have grown in popularity and usage partly because so many more students are English language learners (ELLs). About 5 million students in the U.S. public school system speak a language other than English at home, and schools have been enrolling about 5% more ELLs each school year. This is so largely because English is not the first language of 18% of all individuals living in the United States. By far, the greatest number of ELLs speak Spanish, and many states have very large percentages of ELLs (e.g., California, Texas, Florida, Illinois, Arizona), just as many states have high percentages of students who speak a language other than English in the home, and many large urban school districts have students who are mostly from non-English-speaking homes.

Taking It to the Classroom

Do You Know Jack? Helping Students Learn English

Jack is a student with limited English proficiency. Jack was born in Mexico and has been in this country for two years. Though more proficient in Spanish than in English, he speaks English fairly well. Jack was held back a grade during his first year, but he has begun to pick up English rather well. Given his rapid progress, you resist recommending that Jack take an English proficiency class that would require him to leave your regular class. What practical and immediate approaches can you take to assist Spanish-speaking Jack?

- Use synonyms to clarify the meaning of unknown words.
- When necessary, use Spanish to convey a word or concept that Jack doesn't understand, but then continue in English.
- To make English more comprehensible, use concrete materials, visuals, and body-language cues.
- Paraphrase questions and statements to allow for different levels of proficiency.
- Let all students know that there is nothing wrong with an accent, perhaps by playing a recording of famous people with accents.
- Ask Jack to interpret some communication or text that is in Spanish for the rest of the class, therefore showing the value of being bilingual.

Bilingualism Bilingualism is the regular use of two (or more) languages, and bilinguals are students who use two (or more) languages in their everyday lives (Grosjean, 1992). A key reason non-English-speaking children and adolescents need a second language is that English is the language of schooling. A pressing question in American education is whether learning two languages (rather than just one, English) hinders the child's proficiency in either language (see the nearby Uncommon Sense box). The practical question is whether students who speak a language other than English in the home would be best served by an English-only classroom.

bilingualism The use of two or more languages in everyday life.

Evidence shows that learning two languages at the same time during childhood generally results in excellent proficiency in both the classroom language (English) and the native language (Cummins, 1979; Lanza, 1992; Reich, 1986). In fact, there is a benefit to learning two languages simultaneously, because bilinguals generally outperform monolinguals on tests of language fluency, concept formation, and nonverbal intelligence (Diaz, 1983, 1985; Proctor et al., 2006). Findings such as these suggest that students benefit from bilingual education and that the time to acquire a second language is before puberty, not after (Bialystok, 2001).

Uncommon Sense

Non-English-Speaking Children Should Use Only English in the Classroom—Or Should They?

Public opinion polls show that most U.S. citizens favor English-only classrooms. They believe that learning a second language places a mental burden on children. If this is so, the thinking goes, then children need to be relieved of this burden and educated in only the language of the host country, English. Does research support this thinking? Do languages compete with one another? Is bilingualism a mental burden?

The research-based answer to these questions seems to be no. Using one's native language in school does not interfere in any meaningful way with the learning of English. This is so because different languages are not stored in different parts of the brain. Rather, learning a second language uses the same cognitive system that learning the first language uses (Francis, 1999; McLaughlin, 1987). Hence, proficiency in one language is highly related to proficiency in a second. So *English-only classrooms* is a political stance, not a developmental one.

REFLECTION FOR ACTION

The Event

A teacher wants to help her students learn a new concept, such as the concept of fractions. Prior to the lesson, the concept is foreign or only vaguely familiar to the majority of her students. What would be an effective instructional approach to help students understand the new concept and grow more sophisticated and capable in their thinking?

Reflection RIDE

Imagine that you are the teacher wanting to help elementary-grade students learn the concept of fractions. Would a disequilibrium-inducing, exploration-based approach work best? The children could pick up the fraction inserts, manipulate them in their hands, move them around to see what fits and what does not fit, and hence discover the underlying concept of fractions. Another way might be to sit beside the children and tutor them. Would such social guidance and teacher mentorship work better?

What Theoretical/Conceptual Information Might Assist in Interpreting and Remedying This Situation? Consider the following:

Create Disequilibrium

A concept such as fractions is best learned by discovering or inventing. Instructional strategies such as exploration, discovery, and making predictions about what might happen next would yield the kinds of experiences children need to develop this concept.

Offer an Apprenticeship

Unfamiliar concepts are best learned through social transmission. Cultural representatives, such as the teacher, already have a sophisticated understanding of such concepts, so an instructional strategy that involves social interaction, guidance, and collaboration would yield the kinds of social experiences children need to develop this concept.

Disequilibrium and Apprenticeship

Perhaps a teacher can use both strategies. Perhaps some students would respond to a hands-on, discovery-based learning experience, and others would respond to a collaborative, mentor–novice experience. Also, students who understand the concept could coach their peers who do not yet grasp the concept.

Information Gathering RIDE

You will need several pieces of information. Is the concept of fractions a domain-general mental operation that students can use to solve problems in various contexts, such as math, science, and economics, or is this concept a domain-specific skill, knowledge, or expertise that is specific to a particular problem? Is students' motivation strongly positive and something to be supported, or is it prone to negativity, fragile, and something to be soothed? Can you find access to other manipulatives to supplement the fraction titles? Can some students act as able peers to tutor the less able students? How do students react to peer-learning opportunities? You might also consult another teacher in the same grade level for his or her perspective on these two instructional methods. A videotape that illustrates a Piagetian or Vygotskian approach to teaching such a lesson could also provide useful information. Several articles and books contain discussions and classroom applications of the Piagetian and Vygotskian approaches as well.

Decision Making RIDE

You need to decide what students are to learn—a domain-general concept or a domain-specific skill. You need to decide whether the motivation you are most concerned with is how to promote interest or how to soothe negative emotions, such as confusion and frustration. You will need to decide whether you have the resources that can promote a manipulatives-based lesson or a social guidance–based lesson. From your own teaching philosophy, from your readings of articles and books, and from your conversations with trusted colleagues, you will need to decide whether you prefer a Piagetian exploration-based approach or a Vygotskian social guidance–based approach. You will also need to decide how compatible or incompatible those two approaches are, both in ideology and in practical application.

Evaluation RIDE

You will need to monitor and assess the quality of students' understanding, motivation, initiative, and collaboration. You will also need to listen carefully to students' language and activity to gain a sense of whether their thinking is becoming more sophisticated. You will need to evaluate how students are reacting to a purely Piagetian, a purely Vygotskian, or a blended approach. You will also need a post-lesson assessment measure ready.

Further Practice: Your Turn

Here is a second event for consideration and reflection. In doing so, implement the processes of reflection, information gathering, decision making, and evaluation.

The Event

Mr. Heartland is a high school economics teacher who knows a lot about capitalism, interest rates, and how the economy works. His students, however, do not. By the end of the semester, he wants his students to understand complex concepts such as supply and demand, the stock market, and gross domestic product.

What might this teacher do? How can he help his students develop these concepts? In reflecting on how Mr. Heartland might best foster cognitive development, what approach would you recommend?

SUMMARY

- **How does education enrich brain development?**

  The brain is the organ of learning. The concept that unites education with brain development is neural plasticity, which is the brain's capacity to change its structure in response to experience. Education provides the developing brain with the stimulation it needs to connect more and more neurons together, and this greater neuroplasticity sets the stage for future learning and cognitive development.

- **How does Piaget explain cognitive development?**

  According to Piaget, students are naturally curious explorers who constantly try to make sense of their surroundings. Through exploration, students interact with their surroundings; they discover the world around them and develop three types of schemas—behavioral, symbolic, and operations. New information requires that the student adapt to it, as occurs through the cognitive processes of assimilation and accommodation. Assimilation grows and expands an existing schema to make room for the new information, while accommodation transform the low-level schema into a higher-level one that advances thinking. The motivation to advance one's thinking occurs through the experience of disequilibrium that arises from encountering a cognitive conflict.

- **What are the stages of cognitive development?**

  Four sequential stages provide the structure for cognitive development. During the sensorimotor stage, infants think in actions. Object permanence paves the way for the second stage. During the preoperational stage, language develops rapidly but thought is prelogical, perception-bound, and egocentric. During the concrete-operational stage, children can use mental operations such as conservation to reason about the objects before them and learn to represent concrete objects not only for what they are but also for what they represent, which paves the way for the final stage. During the formal-operational stage, adolescents use mental operations to consider unseen hypotheses and solve abstract problems; reasoning is systematic, deductive, and inferential—that is, adultlike and sophisticated.

- **How can teachers apply Piaget's theory in the classroom?**

  Piaget's approach offers three recommendations for instruction. First, be sensitive to individual differences—plan learning activities (such as interest areas and portfolio projects) specifically around individuals rather than generally around the whole class. Second, motivate students' exploration and activity by stimulating curiosity and interest. Third, promote discovery-based learning. To do so, provide classrooms that are richly stimulating, complex, and interesting enough to invite and sustain exploration.

- **How does Vygotsky explain sociocognitive development?**

  According to Vygotsky, students are young apprentices who benefit from conversations with competent members of their culture. Through mentoring and social guidance, students acquire the skills and knowledge they need to solve the problems that are most important in their culture. Cognitive development is the gradual acquisition of new skills and knowledge, and it occurs in the context of guided participation and cooperative dialogue with peers, adults, and cultural tools.

- **How can teachers apply Vygotsky's theory in the classroom?**

  Vygotsky's approach offers four recommendations for instruction. First, the teacher acts as a guide, scaffolding students as they work within their zones of proximal development. Second, because two heads are better than one, peers can act as guides and mentors, as exemplified by cooperative learning and multi-age classrooms. Third, culture can guide and scaffold students, such as through the offering of its tools. Fourth, teachers can use scaffolding, the PQS discourse model, and instructional conversations to both advance students cognitively and to soothe their motivation during potentially frustrating episodes.

● **How does language develop?**

The essential language question is whether language is a naturally inherited process or whether its development depends on instruction. Children show a remarkable natural ability to understand and use language, presumably because they have an innate language acquisition device. To the extent that children receive high-quality language input, they develop greater phonological awareness, which predicts language development and literacy growth. This natural ability to understand syntax extends not only to the child's primary language but also to second languages and to bilingualism. The role of the teacher is primarily to provide high-quality language input to facilitate students' phonological awareness.

● **How can teachers use their knowledge of brain, cognitive, and language development when working with diverse learners and students with special needs?**

Many students enter classrooms with a different language and a different cultural background from those of their teacher and peers. Research on bilingualism shows that learning two languages simultaneously produces excellent proficiency in both the native and classroom languages. Assistive technology such as talking books and electronic books supports both young readers and students with special needs.

Key Terms

accommodation, p. 74
adaptation, p. 74
animism, p. 79
assimilation, p. 74
behavioral schemas, p. 74
bilingualism, p. 99
centration, p. 79
classification, p. 79
conservation, p. 79
cultural tools, p. 90
deductive reasoning, p. 82
discovery-based learning, p. 85
disequilibrium, p. 75

dual representation, p. 81
egocentrism, p. 79
guided discovery, p. 85
guided participation, p. 86
hippocampus, p. 69
inductive reasoning, p. 82
intersubjectivity, p. 89
language, p. 93
language acquisition device, p. 93
neurons, p. 70
object permanence, p. 77
operation, p. 74
phonological awareness, p. 95

plasticity, p. 70
PQS discourse model, p. 89
prefrontal cortex, p. 69
private speech, p. 90
reversibility, p. 79
scaffolding, p. 87
schemas, p. 74
seriation, p. 79
socially shared cognition, p. 89
symbolic schemas, p. 74
syntax, p. 93
transductive reasoning, p. 79
zone of proximal development, p. 86

Exercises

1. *Toys as Developmentally Appropriate Learning Activities*

With your knowledge of Piaget's stages of cognitive development, make a trip to a mega toy store to examine the developmental appropriateness of the different toys on the shelves. Many toys will have a suggested age on the package label, but for this field trip, ignore the manufacturer's age recommendations and choose the level of cognitive development at which each toy is most appropriate. Ask yourself questions such as: At what age would this toy be most interesting? Most fun? Also examine which mental operations and cognitive skills are required to interact effectively with each toy. For instance, does this toy stretch and challenge the child's counting skills? Classification skills? Find toys that would be most enjoyable for children of the following four ages: 1, 6, 10, and 15. Explain why.

2. *Asking Hypotheticals*

Concrete-operational thinkers rely on reality thinking, whereas formal-operational thinkers rely on possibility thinking. Interview several children and adolescents by asking these questions: What would the world be like if human beings were extinct? What would it be like to have a third eye? What would it be like if you lived in the year 2100? Listen for the extent to which their thinking, reasoning, and problem solving reflect reality thinking or possibility thinking. Concrete thinkers will generally find these questions uninteresting, even stupid. Formal thinkers, however, will find these questions interesting, perhaps even asking for more possibilities to think about.

3. *Using Curiosity-Inducing Strategies as Motivational Strategies*

Look over the three curiosity-inducing strategies introduced in Table 3.3: guessing and feedback, suspense, and controversy. As you present information to another person, explicitly use one of these strategies to spark his or her curiosity about the information you are providing. As you use the strategy, closely monitor the other person's sense of curiosity and willingness to obtain more information. As you use the curiosity-inducing strategy and as the person experiences disequilibrium from the cognitive conflict you have created, does the person seem to truly and earnestly *want* new information?

4. *Peer Tutoring*

Provide tutoring for another person in an area in which you are an expert and the other is a novice. As you tutor, closely monitor all the different ways in which you provide social guidance and scaffolding. How subtle or explicit is your scaffolding? After your own

Lesson Plans

The lesson plans on these pages are excerpts from more complete plans. They are included in this form to provide you with practice in examining a lesson from the perspective of the content of this chapter. The complete lesson plans are available at www.pbs.org. For both lesson plans, read the lesson plan excerpt and respond to the questions related to cognitive development in the Ask Yourself! section at the end.

Lesson #1: "Talk About A Hero/ Heroine!" [elementory education]

GRADES: 1–4

SUBJECT AREAS: Reading, Language, Geography

ESTIMATED TIME: 30 minutes per book selection

I. OBJECTIVES:
- Students will practice conversational English skills to demonstrate comprehension.
- Students will become familiar with the terms *hero*, *heroine*, *role model*.
- Students will experience a variety of books about multicultural heroes/heroines.
- Students will cooperatively compose a written description of book characters.

II. MATERIALS:
- Map/globe
- Lesson printout: Map It!
- Books: *Cesar Chavez: A Hero for Everyone* by Gary Soto (ages 7–10), *Remember the Ladies: 100 Great American Women* by Cheryl Harness (age 8), *Gandhi* by Hitz Demi (ages 7–10), and *Escape North!: The Story of Harriet Tubman* by Monica Kulling (ages 5–8)

III. PROCEDURE:

1. What is a hero (male) or heroine (female)? A hero/heroine is an ordinary person that has done something extraordinary! For example: Roman Catholic nun Mother Teresa (1910–1997) spent her life in India caring for people living in the slums. Her only possessions were a bucket and two saris (Indian clothing). She was awarded the Nobel Peace Prize for her humanitarian work and is remembered as a true heroine for the many years she dedicated her life to serving the poor and dying.

2. Explain that many heroes/heroines are not famously known or materially wealthy, never seen on television or read about in books. Encourage students to identify someone in their own lives that they regard as having heroic status. Share with students that a hero or heroine may also be called a "role model."

tutoring experience, observe a teacher you consider to be a terrific instructor. Watch what this teacher does as he or she provides social guidance and scaffolding. In what ways was your scaffolding the same as the expert's? In what ways was your scaffolding different?

5. *Contrasting Electronic and Printed Books*

Visit a toy store, a bookstore, or a library to locate an e-book (a computer-based version of a printed book that has multimedia features, such as hypertext and drop-down menus) or a talking book (a colorful electronic storybook with multimedia features, such as sound effects and animation). Find a book for which you can also find a regular printed version. Compare the two versions of the book, page by page. Ask yourself what the advantages and disadvantages of the electronic and printed versions are for young readers. Ask yourself what the advantages and disadvantages of the two versions are for students with reading disabilities.

Lesson Plans

3. Encourage students to make predictions. For example: Before reading about Cesar Chavez, create interest by sharing with students that this cultural role model was born in Arizona in 1927. He was named after his grandfather, who migrated to the United States from Mexico. Continue by adding that this person worked hard as a child on the family farm and grew up to become a famous labor leader for migrant workers.

4. Using a map or globe, help students locate physical points relating to a story or particular character. (Example: For Cesar Chavez, locate Mexico, where his grandfather came from, and Arizona, Chavez's birthplace.)

5. Read a book selection, then check for understanding by encouraging students to recall details. Conclude each reading by cooperatively composing a brief two- to three-sentence character description of each hero/heroine on the board. Invite students to participate by offering story details for composition.

6. Read aloud the character description. Practice for fluency and rhythm. Ask students to contribute ideas on how to improve the composition. Note: It's important for students to see that in the process of writing, it's normal to make changes, additions, or deletions to a working com-

position. Make adjustments to the composition. Adjust the composition until everyone is satisfied that it expresses a good character description.

Ask Yourself!

1. How would you adapt this lesson plan to better fit a Piagetian framework for cognitive development?
2. How would you adapt this lesson plan to better fit a Vygotskian framework for cognitive development?
3. Maya and Miguel are 10-year-old twins. Based on what you have learned in this chapter, what cognitive or linguistic challenges might you expect them to experience?

www.pbs.org/parents/mayaandmiguel/english/lessonplans/hero.html

Lesson Plans

Lesson #2: "Identifying Civil Rights" [secondary education]

GRADES: 9–12

SUBJECT AREAS: Social Studies

ESTIMATED TIME: 35 minutes (additional time needed for further exploration)

I. OBJECTIVES: Students will be able to:

- Define the terms *civil rights* and *civil liberties*.
- Identify basic civil liberties.
- Describe how the Supreme Court decided two cases when individual rights conflicted with societal goals: *Minersville School District v. Gobitis* (1940) and *West Virginia State Board of Education v. Barnette* (1943).

II. MATERIALS:

- PBS series *The Supreme Court*, Episode 3: "A Nation of Liberties"
- DVD player/television
- Overhead projector or blackboard
- Handout #1: Civil Liberties and Civil Rights
- Handout #2: Viewer's Guide for "A Nation of Liberties"

III. PROCEDURE: Introductory Activity (10 Minutes)

1. Show the following prompt on the board.... *with liberty and justice for all.*

As class begins, ask students to spend five minutes writing a short-response essay about what this phrase means to them. Write the ending time on the board.

2. At the end of five minutes, ask students to switch papers with a neighbor and to discuss the short essays.

You can help guide students by suggesting the following items for discussion:

- As you read your neighbor's paper, ask your neighbor any questions you have about it, and tell your neighbor what new ideas his or her paper gave you.

LEARNING ACTIVITIES: Identifying Liberties (10 minutes)

1. In a large-class discussion, ask students the following questions and record their answers on the board.

- Where do you think these liberties and freedoms come from?

Some people believe that we are born with certain undeniable political, social, and economic freedoms. These are often known as our human rights.

Some people believe that our rights and freedoms are derived from our democratic form of government—a government that sets out our rights in the Constitution and limits the power of government to trample our rights. Note: If you wish to extend this lesson to teach about human rights or the Universal Declaration of Human Rights,

Lesson Plans

this would be a good time to do so. Most government or practical law textbooks contain a copy of the declaration.

- How do you define *liberty* or *civil liberty*?

Answers will vary but will likely center on the ideas of freedoms or rights. If students do not mention the ideas below, raise them:

Liberty is the right and power to act, believe, or express oneself in a manner of one's own choosing. Having liberty means being free from restrictions or control, particularly from excessive or unfair government control.

Civil liberties are the rights that are guaranteed in the Bill of Rights, the Constitution, or the laws made by elected officials and decisions made by courts.

- Can you list specific civil liberties people have in the United States?

Answers will vary but may include:

- Freedom of speech, religion, press, assembly, etc.
- Freedom from cruel and unusual punishment, unreasonable searches and seizures, self-incrimination, discrimination, etc.
- Rights to speedy trial, attorney, due process, privacy, marry, vote, etc.

2. Tell students that many people use the terms *civil liberties* and *civil rights* interchangeably. Distribute Handout and Transparency #1: Civil Liberties and Civil Rights.

After reviewing the rest of the handout, check to be sure students understand the concept of the "constitutional floor" for rights and liberties.

Ask Yourself!

1. What does the teacher's expectations of varied answers tell you about the teacher's theory or theories of cognitive development?

2. Does the teacher provide scaffolding for cognitive development?

Courtesy of Thirteen/WNET New York.

Ms. Hernandez's
Fourth-Grade Class

(© Media Bakery)

Here are 15 members of Ms. Hernandez's fourth-grade class. It is early fall, and Ms. Hernandez just received this photograph taken during the first week of class. As she looks at each face, something stirs within her. She becomes determined to build a constructive sense of community with this group of students. She would like to help them become friends. She would like to see her students helping, sharing, and trusting one another. She wants to keep disrespect, put-downs, and acts of aggression out of her classroom. In these early days of September, Ms. Hernandez has noticed some potential obstacles to her goal. One student seems hyperaggressive; another appears to have a short temper. Many possess immature social skills. Still, as she looks at these smiling faces, she wonders what she can do to help them develop socially.

Social Development

4

 **Reflection for Action**

Ms. Hernandez wants to enrich her students' social development, and she wants to build a strong sense of community in her classroom. How can she help her students develop the skills they need to make friends and to cope with conflict? What might she do?

Guiding Questions

- What characterizes a high-quality student–teacher relationship?
- What are mental models, and why are they important to social development?
- How can teachers nurture psychosocial development, especially students' initiative, competence, and identity?
- What are the stages of moral development?
- How does social competence develop, and how can teachers nurture students' pro-social behaviors?
- How does aggression develop, and how can teachers help students resolve conflicts amicably?
- What makes a bully? What makes a victim? Do antibully interventions work?
- How do students' special needs interfere with their social development?

CHAPTER OVERVIEW

Social development reflects the extent of one's social competence, peer popularity, interpersonal trust, personal initiative, sense of competence, identity formation, moral development, prosocial orientation, and character. The extent to which students develop socially depends in part on the quality of the relationships in their lives, including the relationships they have with their teachers and peers. The first part of this chapter identifies the aspects of a relationship that allow it to be characterized as a high-quality relationship. The second part discusses specific social-developmental outcomes, especially psychosocial development, social competence, and moral development. A particular emphasis is placed on aggression and the question of what teachers such as Ms. Hernandez can do to help students build the social competencies they need to manage their anger and frustration. The final part discusses bullying and peer victimization. Taken as a whole, the chapter highlights the role that relationships play in students' social development, and it offers numerous illustrations of how teachers can help students develop socially.

Relationships
- Mental Models—Self and Others
- Quality of Relationships
- Culture, Diversity, and Special Needs
- Trust: The Beginning of Positive Social Development
- Students' Attachment Styles with Teachers
- Attachment for Learners with Special Needs

Psychosocial Development
- Erikson's Framework

Moral Development
- Stages of Moral Development
- The Ethic of Care

- Character and Conscience: Doing the Right Thing for the Right Reason

Social Competence
- Social Competence in Special Education

Aggression
- Instrumental and Hostile Aggression
- Video Game Technology and Aggression
- Bullying

Social-emotional development concerns students' abilities to establish positive relationships, solve interpersonal problems, and express and regulate their emotions effectively. Such positive development does not just happen, as its fruition depends on a caring, supportive, and responsive surrounding social context. The instructional effort to provide such care is well worth the effort, as students who attain social-emotional skill flourish in so many important ways, including getting along with peers, being cooperative, being able to resolve conflicts amicably, displaying good communication skills, being popular and well accepted, being highly engaged in learning activities, being highly motivated to learn, being better behaved and less likely to engage in aggressive or problematic behavior, and performing better in school in terms of classroom grades and standardized test scores (Zins, Weissberg, Wang, & Walberg, 2004).

Relationships

Relationships are the soil in which social development grows. Each student who walks through the school's front door brings in a unique history of relationships. The quality of students' past and present relationships explains a lot about their subsequent social development—why they trust or mistrust others, why they feel competent or incompetent, why they are cooperative or aggressive, and so forth. In essence, high-quality relationships are the means by which students develop the social competence they need to make friends and be successful in school (Birch & Ladd, 1997; Hamre & Pianta, 2001).

When kindergartners form high-quality relationships with their teachers, they function more positively during kindergarten, both socially and academically (Pianta & Steinberg, 1992), and the benefits of this early relationship continue with the child through elementary school and even into the middle school years (Hamre & Pianta, 2001). Positive early relationships have enduring effects because children use these high-quality relationships to develop socially—they learn how to cooperate, how to cope constructively with frustration, and how to develop good work habits. This chapter highlights social-developmental outcomes such as these and explains their development throughout the school-age years.

At the center of evaluating the quality of a teacher–student relationship is the dimension of closeness versus conflict (Pianta & Steinberg, 1992). To capture the flavor of a close versus conflictual child–teacher relationship, Figure 4.1 presents some questionnaire items researchers use to ask teachers to assess how close versus conflictual their relationship with a student is (from Hightower et al., 1986). In general, teachers promote close relationships by being responsive to students' needs and by acting as an all-purpose support system as children and adolescents try to develop the competencies they need to adjust to the varied demands of school.

From their daily interactions, children learn what other people think of them and how other people tend to treat them. Once these expectations are formulated (e.g., "Overall, my experience has taught me that other people are nice and helpful—you can trust them"), children use these relationship-grown expectations to figure out how to respond to the new people they meet. These expectations form very early (in infancy, for instance; Johnson, Dweck, & Chen, 2007), and affect social development constantly from "the cradle to the grave" (Bowlby, 1984). Another term for these expectations is *mental models*.

> **Close relationship indicators**
>
> - If upset, this child will seek comfort from me.
> - This child spontaneously shares information about him- or herself.
>
> **Conflictual relationship indicators**
>
> - This child and I always seem to be struggling with each other.
> - This child easily becomes angry at me.

Figure 4.1 Questionnaire Items for Kindergarten Teachers to Ask about Their Close versus Conflictual Relationships with Children

Mental Models—Self and Others

Mental models are students' enduring beliefs and expectations about what they are like and what other people are like (Ainsworth et al., 1978; Bowlby, 1982; Bretherton, 1990; Collins et al., 2004; Main, Kaplan, & Cassidy, 1985). *Mental models of the self* represent students' answers to questions such as: Am I lovable? Am I a good person? Am I worthy of other people's attention and care? *Mental models of others* represent students' answers to questions such as: What are other people like? Can you trust others? Will they be there when you need them? Are others nice and helpful, or are they mostly mean and selfish? (Collins, 1996).

Figure 4.2 illustrates the central role that mental models play in understanding and predicting students' future social development. As shown on the left-hand side of the figure, some relationships are of high quality and produce feelings of security, whereas others are of low quality and produce feelings of insecurity. With high-quality relationships, children experience warm, responsive caregivers. Through experience, these children have learned that their caregivers are accessible, dependable, trustworthy, and responsive. They feel secure because they feel loved, accepted, and valued—by parents, teachers, day-care providers, and so forth. With low-quality relationships, children experience cold and unresponsive caregivers. Their experience has taught them that their caregivers are inaccessible, undependable, untrustworthy, and unresponsive. They feel insecure because they feel unloved, rejected, or ignored.

Over time, students transform the history of their interactions with these social partners into mental models of themselves and of others. They may say to themselves, "Because my parents are so warm and caring for me, I must be lovable" or "My parents are always there

mental models Students' enduring beliefs and expectations about what they are like and what other people are like.

Figure 4.2 Antecedents and
Developmental Outcomes of
Students' Mental Models of
Self and Others

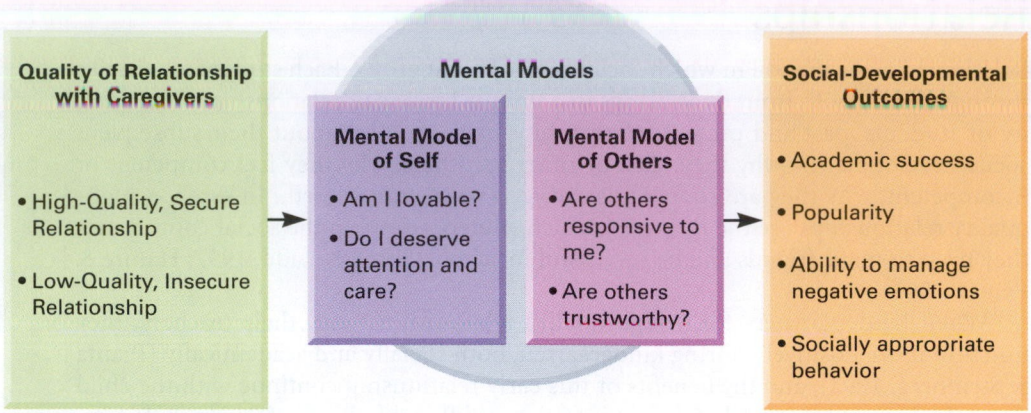

when I need them—I can count on them to be there when I need them." If these experiences
are consistent enough, children's mental models become entrenched. Mental models then
gain the capacity to affect students' future feelings, thoughts, and behaviors and thus exert
a significant effect on their future social development (Belsky & Cassidy, 1994; Rothbard &
Shaver, 1994). As shown on the right-hand side of the figure, four key social-developmental outcomes are (1) academic success, (2) peer popularity, (3) ability to manage negative
emotions, and (4) capacity to enact socially appropriate, rather than socially inappropriate,
behaviors (Allen et al., 1998; Thompson, 1998,1999).

Quality of Relationships

relationship Interaction between
two people in which the
actions of one person affect the
thoughts, feelings, and actions of
the other person and vice versa.

A **relationship** involves two people, each affecting the other. The quality of a relationship,
therefore, always depends on the contributions of both parties (Kochanska et al., 2004). That
said, some ways of relating to students are more likely than others to promote their well-
being and social development (Ainsworth et al., 1978; Allen et al., 2003; De Wolff & Van
Ijzendoorn, 1997; Kochanska, 2002).

What Constitutes a High-Quality Relationship? Figure 4.3 identifies four characteristics of a high-quality way of relating to students (Reeve, 2006). Although these characteristics
overlap, research shows that each contributes to students' social development in a unique
and positive way (Allen et al., 2003).

attunement Sensing and reading another's state of being and
adjusting one's own behavior
accordingly.

    Attunement is sensing and reading a student's state of being and adjusting one's own
behavior accordingly (Stern et al., 1983). A synonym for attunement is *sensitivity* (De Wolff
& Van Ijzendoorn, 1997; Haft & Slade, 1989). When teachers are highly attuned to their
students, they have a good sense of what their students are thinking and feeling, how engaged they are during a learning activity, and whether they understand what they are trying

Figure 4.3 Four Charac-
teristics of a High-Quality
Relationship

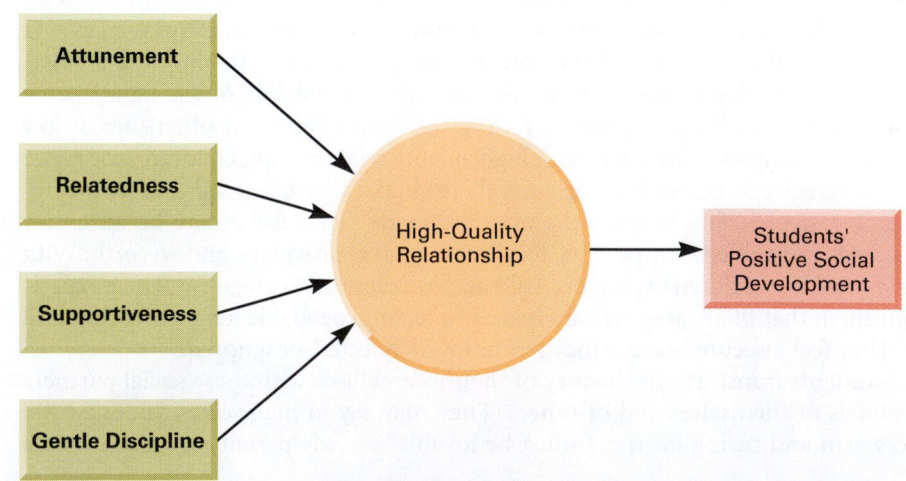

(Media Bakery)

Relatedness is a sense of being close to another person.
It calms negative emotions
and sparks a willingness to
participate.

to learn. Highly attuned teachers have a good idea about these things because they listen closely to what their students say and because they read students' facial expressions and body language to sense and predict what students will do next. They also make a special effort to be aware of what their students want and need. This sensitivity enables teachers to be highly responsive to students' words, behaviors, needs, preferences, and emotions. It also allows teachers to deal with problems before they occur, because attuned teachers sense the coming storm and diffuse it proactively.

Relatedness is a sense of being close to another person; it entails feeling special and important to that person (Furrer & Skinner, 2003). Because it involves a sense of warmth, affection, and acceptance by the other person, relatedness is sometimes referred to as *belongingness*
(Goodenow, 1993) or *intimacy* (Berndt, 2004). Establishing a sense of relatedness within the
teacher–student (or peer–peer) relationship is important because it gives students a sense
of security about themselves and about being with others. This sense of
security calms negative emotions that may arise during the school day,
such as anxiety or frustration. It also has an energizing effect that sparks
students' enthusiasm and willingness to participate. For these reasons,
relatedness is an especially good predictor of students' high classroom
engagement (Furrer & Skinner, 2003) and low classroom disruptiveness
(Murdock, 1999).

relatedness The psychological
sense of having close emotional
bonds and attachments with
other people.

> **How Can I Use This?**
>
> Awareness of these relationship qualities provides
> beginning teachers with a set of standards to strive for
> in their day-to-day relationships with students.

Supportiveness is affirmation of the other person's capacity for self-direction. When
teachers support their students, they accept students for who they are, express their faith
that students can self-regulate their behavior, and assist students as they try to realize the
goals they set for themselves. Supportive teachers provide their support in ways that preserve students' autonomy rather than in ways that make students dependent on the teacher's help (Grolnick, 2003; Noddings, 1984; Rogers, 1969). Supportiveness is important to students' success in school
because the more supportive teachers are, the greater students feel in
control of their learning and the more engaged they are during learning
activities (Reeve, 1996; Ryan & Grolnick, 1986).

supportiveness An affirmation
of the other person's capacity for
self-direction and contribution
to help realize his or her self-set
goals.

> **How Can I Use This?**
>
> Can you use one of the qualities in Figure 4.3 to improve
> the quality of an existing relationship in your life?

Gentle discipline is a socialization strategy that involves explaining why a particular way
of thinking or behaving is right or wrong. Its opposite is *power assertion*, a socialization
strategy that includes forceful commands and a no-nonsense insistence that students comply
with the teacher's requests (Kochanska, Aksan, & Nichols, 2003). Gentle discipline is a verbal,
relationship-based approach to discipline that begins with a conversation to draw attention
to the hurtful effect the student's misbehavior had on others (Grusec & Goodnow, 1994). The
teacher then explains why that behavior is wrong and should be changed. The conversation
continues with a two-way problem-solving effort as to what action the student might take to

gentle discipline A socialization
strategy that revolves around
explaining why a way of thinking
or behaving is right or wrong.

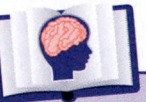

RIDE How can Ms. Hernandez capitalize on these four relationship qualities to promote her students' social development?

undo the harm, such as apologize or share. Students with caregivers who use gentle discipline rather than power assertion show more positive social development (Brody & Shaffer, 1982).

What Constitutes a Low-Quality Relationship? Low-quality relationships are those characterized by relatively high neglect (indifference, permissiveness, lack of support, lack of involvement) and abuse (insensitivity, rejection, hostility). Children who come to school with a relationship history that includes either chronic neglect or chronic abuse often show delays in their cognitive and social development (Tower, 1996).

Neglect in the home can come from poverty, parental depression, divorce, and similar circumstances that take parents away from caring for their children; abuse can come from conflict in the home, parental substance abuse, and a variety of traumatic experiences (Whitbourne et al., 1992). Neglect and abuse lead children to form negative mental models, because they describe themselves as being unlovable (Tower, 1996) and their caregivers as being unresponsive (Gondoli & Silverberg, 1997). Cognitively, these children tend to exhibit poor academic progress, low grades, low scores on standardized tests, and a tendency to be held back a grade (Trickett & McBride-Chang, 1995). Emotionally, these children are prone to anger and chronic emotional difficulties (Newman, 1981). Socially, these children often show a striking absence of social competencies (Trickett & McBride-Chang, 1995). Behaviorally, these children are more aggressive and less cooperative (Pianta, Steinberg, & Rollins, 1995). These poor social-developmental outcomes can be seen in students across all grade levels and reflect neglect and abuse not only from parents but from peers and teachers as well (Conger et al., 1993).

Verbal abuse and neglect are not strangers to the classroom. Verbal abuse from teachers includes chronic ridiculing and teasing, scolding, name-calling, public humiliation in front of others, or yelling at the student, while neglect includes ignoring the student (Brendgen et al., 2007; Hart, Brassard, & Germain, 1987). About 15% of students—mostly boys and mostly those showing behavior problems—report suffering verbal abuse from teachers (Brendgen, Wanner, & Vitaro, 2006). More commonly, however, it is students' perceptions of a teacher's lack of fairness (unusually harsh discipline, lower-than-deserving grades), rigidity (toward behavior problems), or disrespectfulness (of their race, gender, or academic ability) that lead them to perceive a low-quality relationship with a teacher. Bias (lack of fairness), discrimination, rigidity, and disrespectfulness lead students not only to conflictual teacher–student relationships but also to decreased interest in school and elevated behavior problems (Brand et al., 2003; Di Lalla, Marcus, & Wright-Phillips, 2004; Fisher, Wallace, & Fenton, 2000; Graham, Bellmore, & Mize, 2006; Juvonen, 2006).

Relationships Are Always Two-Sided All relationships require work and depend on the constructive contribution of both partners. Some students, such as those with autism or emotional difficulty, may lack the capacity to contribute fully and constructively to a relationship. Other students vary in their willingness to relate to teachers. For instance, some students bring a chronic negative attitude or an array of defiant behaviors into the classroom and, therefore, show an unwillingness to be in a relationship with the teacher (Eisenberg, Fabes, et al., 1997; Gallagher, 2002; Kochanska et al., 1997; Tramontana, Hooper, & Selzer, 1988). Other students are simply more aggressive or more socially withdrawn (Ladd, Kochenderfer-Ladd, & Rydell, 2010). The more resistance the student shows, the less motivated teachers tend to be to display qualities such as attunement, relatedness, supportiveness, and gentle discipline.

A Teacher's Responsibility If all relationships are always two-sided, then it seems unfair to place the burden of responsibility to form a high-quality relationship on the teacher's shoulders. After all, research confirms that children's prosocial versus antisocial behavior is as much a source of relationship conflict as is the teacher's provision of a low-quality relationship with that child (Birch & Ladd, 1998). Still, the responsibility to get the relationship started off on the right foot does belong to the teacher—here is why. When interaction partners differ in perceived status or power (based on age, authority, social position, expertise, or the ability to influence others), the higher-status person (teacher) is expected, even somewhat obligated, to initiate the conversation, to talk, and to make suggestions for the lower-status person (student, especially the young student) to follow (Magee, Galinsky, & Gruenfeld, 2007). So the inherent difference in social status between teachers and students puts the social burden on teachers to take the initiative to get the relationship started off on

What Does This Mean to Me? Think of a close relationship in your life. How would you rate the other person in terms of attunement, relatedness, supportiveness, and gentle discipline?

MINDFUL HABITS OF EFFECTIVE TEACHERS

The value of establishing and working constantly to maintain a high-quality relationship with all students is a key habit of mind of effective teachers.

the right foot. Plus, teachers know what is at stake during their teacher–student interactions in a way that students are more naive about, as research shows that the quality of a current teacher–student relationship has surprisingly long-term and enduring ramifications on the student's later school functioning and achievement (Hamre & Pianta, 2001).

Culture, Diversity, and Special Needs

Students benefit when teachers provide attunement, relatedness, supportiveness, and gentle discipline. But a student's cultural background will affect how successful these aspects of a relationship will be. Figure 4.3 is based on the assumption that teachers seek to promote students' social development. Sometimes, however, other socialization goals take precedence. Parents in authoritarian families, for instance, emphasize strict discipline to such an extent that their children come to view strict discipline as more appropriate than gentle discipline (Deater-Deckard et al., 1996; Miller, Fung, & Mintz, 1996). Other families might heavily prioritize school success and academic achievement over social success and social development (Schneider & Lee, 1990). Likewise, some cultures strongly value respect for one's elders and, therefore, want to see relationships characterized by adult direction rather than by adult supportiveness.

As society grows more diverse, teachers' knowledge about students' cultural backgrounds grows in importance. Asian-American students are sometimes believed to display social skill deficits, at least to the extent that they focus on academics and forgo opportunities to interact socially with their peers (Reglin & Adams, 1990; Schneider & Lee, 1990). African-American students are sometimes believed to display behavioral disorders, at least to the extent that they enact an energetic, behaviorally intense style (Irvine, 1992). Generally speaking, these behaviors reflect cultural priorities rather than social skill deficits or behavioral disorders (Feng, 1996). Hence, rather than offering relationships in a cultural void, teachers can promote social development through open-ended classroom dialogues (rather than teacher-generated recommendations) about how students can use their own cultural opportunities to accomplish social tasks valued in all cultures, such as the following (Doll, 1996):

- Maintain a good relationship with others
- Avoid trouble with peers and adults
- Pursue equity and justice

Trust: The Beginning of Positive Social Development

All infants have an emotional need for relatedness, which motivates them to seek close, affectionate bonds with their caregivers. All infants also seek protection in times of distress, which leads them to seek proximity to their stronger and wiser caretaker (Bowlby, 1984). Caregivers, in turn, provide varying levels of **care** and protection that produce different degrees of interpersonal sensitivity, relatedness satisfaction, and felt security. Some adults provide warm, responsive, sensitive, predictable, and nurturing care, and this high-quality care allows children to form secure **attachments** with them. Other children receive care that leads them to form insecure attachments, because adults are out of synch with the child and provide care that is inconsistent (sometimes loving, sometimes rejecting), impatient, unresponsive, and generally frustrating to the child's need to feel safe and secure. Based on the quality of this early care, children develop the kinds of mental models of self and others introduced in Figure 4.2 (Mikulincer, 1998).

The basic psychological issue related to a child's mental model of others is trust; the basic psychological issue related to a child's mental model of self is self-esteem.

Trust is one's confidence that the other partner in the relationship cares, is looking out for one's welfare, and will be there when needed (Tschannen-Moran & Hoy, 2000). When students trust their teacher, they know that the teacher will be responsive to their bids for attention, signals of distress, and need for assistance. *Mistrust*, on the other hand, involves being suspicious and expecting to be disappointed. When students mistrust, they stay on alert for signs of betrayal. Out of this sense of mistrust flow negative emotions, such as fear, anger, anxiety, and sadness.

care An emotional concern and sense of responsibility to protect or enhance another person's welfare or well-being.

attachment A close emotional relationship between two persons that is characterized by mutual affection and the desire to maintain proximity with the other.

trust Confidence that the other person in the relationship cares, is looking out for your welfare, and will be there when needed.

Figure 4.4 Assessing Attachment Classification with a Questionnaire
Source: Hazan, C., & Shaver, P. (1987). Romantic love conceptualised as an attachment process. *Journal of Personality and Social Psychology, 52,* 511–524. Copyright © 1987 by the American Psychological Association. Reprinted with the kind permission of Cambridge University Press.

Check *one* of the following:

_____ I find it relatively easy to get close to others and am comfortable depending on them and having them depend on me. I don't worry about being abandoned or about someone getting too close to me.

_____ I find that others are reluctant to get as close as I would like. I worry that others don't really love me or want to stay with me. I want to merge completely with others, especially love partners, and this desire sometimes scares others away.

_____ I am somewhat uncomfortable being close to others. I find it difficult to trust others completely, difficult to allow myself to depend on them. I become nervous when anyone gets too close, and others often want me to be more intimate with them than I feel comfortable being.

What Does This Mean to Me?
Which of the three attachment styles describes you best?

self–esteem Trust applied to oneself; an attitude that one is worthy of a positive rather than a negative self-evaluation.

In response to how much they trust their caregivers, students develop one of three attachment styles: secure, resistant, or avoidant (Ainsworth, 1989; Ainsworth et al., 1978). The *secure style* reflects high trust and confidence in the availability of attachment figures in times of need. The *resistant style* reflects a strong desire for relatedness together with mistrust, a fear of rejection, and insecurity about how attachment figures will respond in times of need. The *avoidant style* reflects high mistrust and a preference to maintain one's emotional distance from other people (i.e., low desire for relatedness). Figure 4.4 helps clarify the nature of these three attachment styles by providing the beliefs that adolescents with each attachment style might agree with and say aloud during conversation (Hazan & Shaver, 1987). From top to bottom, the three attachment classifications are secure, resistant, and avoidant. Using different terminology, these attachment styles might also be labeled as close, clingy, and conflictual, respectively (Birch & Ladd, 1997).

Self-esteem is trust applied to oneself. It is a self-evaluation that one is worthy of a positive rather than a negative evaluation (Baumeister, Tice, & Hutton, 1989). From the perspective of attachment theory (Bartholomew & Horowitz, 1991; Bowlby, 1982), self-esteem in childhood reflects a sense of being worthy of love—a sense of lovability. That is, a child's level of self-esteem is a mirror of how much or how little warm care he or she has received from others. The more children feel rejected or ignored by others, the more they come to feel that they are worthless and of little value. Thus, securely attached students have higher self-esteem than do insecurely attached ones (Bylsma, Cozzarelli, & Sumer, 1997; Mikulincer, 1995).

If trust and care are the beginning of positive social development, then mistrust and rejection are the beginning of negative social development. Just as it is a developmental asset/resource to experience trust and high self-esteem, it is a developmental liability for children and adolescents to experience mistrust, rejection, or low self-esteem.

Students' Attachment Styles with Teachers

A child's attachment style is formed during early interactions with primary caregivers. Once the child leaves the home, however, additional relationships emerge to affect his or her mental models of self and others (Ainsworth, 1989; Bowlby, 1988; Howes, 1999). As they encounter caregiving relationships outside the home, children develop relationship-specific beliefs with specific interaction partners, such as their teachers (Al-Yagon & Mikulincer, 2004). The positive benefits of a high-quality relationship with one's teacher have been shown to occur above and beyond (in addition to) the positive benefits of a high-quality relationship with one's parents (Meehan, Hughes, & Cavell, 2003). Children therefore develop a mental model of what their parents are like, but they also develop a mental model of what their teacher is like. Even when the attachment figure changes (e.g., from parent to teacher), the basic attachment-related questions remain:

- Can I trust this person to be available and responsive in times of need?
- With this person's support, what can I accomplish?

Effective attachment relationships serve two crucial and complementary purposes: (1) provide a safe haven in times of uncertainty and (2) provide a secure base one can use

Taking It to the Classroom

Do You Know Jack?
Sensing Maladaptive Attachments by Sensing Anxiety and Avoidance

Teachers cannot directly see students' psychologically based attachment styles. Rather, teachers see publicly observable behaviors that children and adolescents display in times of stress and uncertainty. In a general sense, what teachers see in students with maladaptive attachment styles is either anxiety or avoidance (in times of stress and uncertainty). Here are sample indicators of Anxious Jack and Avoidant Jack.

Anxious Jack

- Worries about rejection, abandonment
- Seeks comfort yet resists it at the same time
- Other students are reluctant to get close to Anxious Jack
- Disorganized behavior (e.g., freezing) in the presence of the teacher

Avoidant Jack

- Does not seek proximity with the teacher
- Avoids the teacher after a separation
- Worries when the teacher tries to get too close
- Uncomfortable when depending on others

to explore the world. The first attachment question asks whether the student sees the teacher as a safe haven when upset and in times of uncertainty. The second attachment question asks whether the student sees the teacher as a secure base from which to launch his or her initiatives for exploration and social development more generally. As highlighted in the nearby Taking It to the Classroom box , teachers can use students' displays of anxiety and avoidance to answer these two pivotal questions that drive students' attachment styles with them.

Attachment in Childhood Familiarity with the three attachment styles is important for elementary school teachers because attachment styles explain not only students' trust and self-esteem but also their school functioning, popularity, ability to manage negative emotions, and prosocial/antisocial orientation toward peers (see Figure 4.2). A secure attachment with a teacher provides the child with a *safe haven* to go to when afraid, a strong and wise confidant who can soothe away negative feelings, and a *secure base* from which to explore and investigate the surrounding environment (Bowlby, 1988; Kochanska, Coy, & Murray, 2001). Resistant and avoidant children lack access to such a safe haven, a wise confidant, and a secure base and are, therefore, easily overwhelmed by threatening or distressing events, such as encountering a stranger or having a toy taken away by another child.

Secure attachments in childhood and adolescence give students the steady social foundation they need to develop social competencies and to make progress toward the positive developmental outcomes listed on the right-hand side of Figure 4.2, while insecure attachments in childhood leave students vulnerable to develop social incompetencies and academic setbacks, such as academic failure, peer rejection, overwhelming negative emotionality, and socially inappropriate behavior (Waters, Wippman, & Sroufe, 1979).

With this much at stake, it is important for teachers to know what to expect in terms of students' attachment styles. Figure 4.5 shows the attachment categorizations of boys and girls ages 6 to 16 who were included in a large sample of students across the United States. Half of all students in this sample were rated as securely attached, one-in-eight were rated as

(Stephanie Maze/Woodfin Camp & Associates)

When children encounter threatening events, it helps to have access to a safe haven, a wise confidant, and a secure base—the teacher.

Figure 4.5 Percentage of Students Rated in Each of the Three Attachment Styles in a Large U.S. Sample

Source: Based on data from Bakermans-Kranenburg, M. J., & Van IJzendoorn, M. H. (2009). No reliable gender differences in attachment across the lifespan. *Behavioral and Brain Sciences, 32*, 22–23. Reprinted with the kind permission of Cambridge University Press.

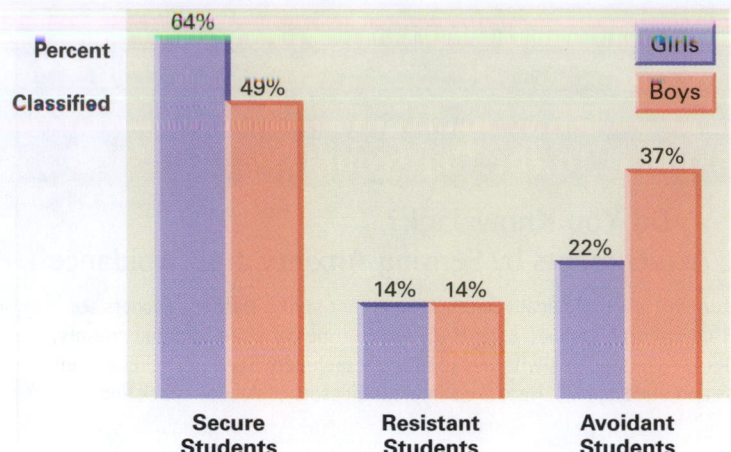

resistant—they wanted attachment but experienced insecurity in relationships, and one-in-three were rated as avoidant—they were mistrusting and emotionally distant in relationships (Bakermans-Kranenburg & Van IJzendoorn, 2009). Figure 4.5 also breaks the attachment categorizations down by gender to show that, among girls, two-thirds were secure, one-eighth were resistant, and one-fourth were avoidant and also to show that, among boys, half were secure, one-eighth were resistant, and one-fourth were avoidant.

Attachment in Adolescence Adolescents make domain-specific evaluations of their competence, such as "I'm good in school, but not so good in athletics." Through these self-evaluations, they gain a second source of self-esteem beyond their relationship-based childhood mental models of self (Mikulincer, 1995; Park, Crocker, & Mickelson, 2004). In addition to high or low self-esteem emanating from one's relationships with others, adolescents further base their self-esteem judgments on other factors, such as their physical appearance, the approval of others, and spirituality. Among secure adolescents, self-esteem tends to be high, as it was in childhood. Among resistant adolescents, self-esteem tends to be low, as it was in childhood. Among avoidant adolescents, self-esteem actually tends to turn positive. This positive self-esteem, however, is rooted in a defensive denial of their need for relatedness, as their peers actually perceive them to be cold and hostile (Bartholomew & Horowitz, 1991). To achieve their high self-esteem, avoidant teenagers use nonrelationship bases of self-esteem as their primary way of evaluating the self positively.

Attachment for Learners with Special Needs

Children with learning disabilities typically report greater dissatisfaction in their relationship with teachers than do children without learning disabilities (Murray & Greenberg, 2001). Students with emotional disturbances and students with mild mental retardation are especially likely to report being dissatisfied with their student–teacher relationship. These students are also less likely to be securely attached to their teachers. Because of this, they are at risk for socioemotional problems and maladjustment (Culbertson, 1998).

Students with learning disabilities are sensitive to the way their teachers relate to them because they feel that their teachers are less available, less accepting, and more rejecting than do students without learning disabilities. For instance, students with learning disabilities frequently *disagree* with the first two of the following statements but *agree* with the third:

- When I need the teacher's help, she is always there.
- The teacher makes me feel welcome in the class.
- The teacher makes me feel that I'm unnecessary in the class.

These data suggest that one reason students with special needs show poorer social development is that they do not believe they have high-quality relationships with their teachers. When they do have high-quality relationships with their teachers, however, they are significantly

Appendix
Understanding Students' Social Histories

Attachment categories help teachers summarize students' social histories and then offer the types of high-quality relationships students need to grow socially (PRAXIS ™, I. B. 6; INTASC, Principles 1, 2, 3).

Taking It to the Classroom

Am I a Supportive Teacher?

One way to assess your own supportiveness toward students is to monitor the extent to which you engage in two relationship-maintaining behaviors during a conflict or disagreement: relatedness and autonomy support (Allen & Hauser, 1996; Allen & Land, 1999). With relatedness, the teacher expresses acceptance, shows empathy for the student's point of view, and shows constant signs of engagement—with few signs of disengagement—throughout the conflict and disagreement. With autonomy support, the teacher presents his or her reasoning in an open and flexible way while encouraging the student to do the same. The message is that both points of view have validity and deserve to be heard (as opposed to a more dogmatic "my way or the highway").

Of course, it is tempting to use one's status or position as teacher to override the student's sense of autonomy. It is also tempting to express relationship-disrupting emotions, such as anger or disgust. But doing these things during a disagreement undermines the student's assurance that teacher and student can work together not only to solve the problem but also to maintain the high-quality relationship.

more likely to show meaningful gains in their social, emotional, and academic adjustment (Murray & Greenberg, 2001). The nearby Taking It to the Classroom box provides two telltale signs of a supportive teacher.

Psychosocial Development

Psychosocial development is a broad term used to describe the quality of a person's development as a function of how other people have treated that person in the past. To make sense of the term, consider each part separately. *Psycho* represents the student's sense of self, *social* represents the quality of the relationships in the person's life, and *development* represents the extent to which one's social development thrives or flounders. Stated differently, teachers (social) affect students' sense of self (psycho), which, in turn, expresses itself through a host of developmental outcomes. For instance, when teachers provide gentle discipline, students tend to develop a positive sense of self and interact cooperatively with peers; when teachers provide harsh discipline, students tend to develop a negative sense of self and interact aggressively with peers (Hoffman, 1975; Kochanska, Aksan, & Nichols, 2003). Hence, self-development depends on social relationships.

psychosocial development A broad term to describe the quality of a person's social development as a function of past relationships in that person's life.

Erikson's Framework

The essence of social development is the student's progression toward psychological growth, personal adjustment, emotional maturity, a prosocial orientation toward others, and a capacity for autonomous and competent functioning (Loevinger, 1976). Perhaps no theory better communicates the role of teachers and schools in students' ongoing social development than Erik Erikson's (1959, 1963, 1964, 1968). As shown in Table 4.1, Erikson described eight developmental turning points (or "crises") that all people face, the approximate age at which each emerges, and the relationships that most influence the resolution at each turning point.

Erikson argued that social development "has a ground plan" in which development and personal growth proceed through the series of eight successive turning points, shown in Table 4.1. The phrase *turning point* connotes a critical period in which the student moves in a direction of either greater strength and adjustment or greater vulnerability and maladjustment. Each turning point is related to all seven others, because a positive resolution at one stage increases the individual's strength and potential to cope with future turning points, whereas a negative resolution leaves the person more vulnerable to later maladjustment. Stages 3–5 emerge during the K–12 years; therefore, they deserve special emphasis. Stage 7 also deserves attention, because it applies to teachers.

TABLE 4.1
Erikson's Lifespan Developmental Framework

Developmental Turning Point	Approximate Age Range	Most Important Social Agents
1. Trust vs. mistrust	Infancy	Caretakers
2. Autonomy vs. shame, doubt	Early childhood	Parents, siblings, grandparents
3. Initiative vs. guilt	Preschool	Teachers
4. Competence vs. incompetence	Elementary school	Role models, peers
5. Identity vs. role confusion	Middle and high school	Partners in love, work
6. Intimacy vs. isolation	College	Students, one's own children
7. Generativity vs. stagnation	Teaching career	
8. Integrity vs. despair	Retirement years	

initiative The child's capacity to use a surplus of energy to plan and constructively carry out a task.

Developing Initiative The developmental turning point that preschool children face above all others involves moving toward either greater initiative or greater hesitance and guilt. **Initiative** is the capacity to use a surplus of energy to plan and constructively carry out a task. Children tap into their reservoir of initiative when they explore the objects around them, draw with crayons, pretend they are a princess, and make things out of paper, blocks, or the stuff in mom's purse. As summarized in Figure 4.6, preschool children become increasingly experimental in exercising their physical, linguistic, and imaginative skills, and their curiosity is endless. Equipped with such energy and curiosity, children test the limits that teachers impose on them to see what is and is not permissible.

The teacher's task during preschool is to provide some direction to students' zest—to nurture initiative while at the same time communicating classroom rules and limits. When teachers find ways to support and encourage preschoolers' curiosity and vigor—even while imposing a structure on classroom activity—children develop initiative, a willingness to explore, and a sense of purpose within their activity. When teachers suppress preschoolers' curiosity, however, children develop guilt, hesitance, and a tendency to sacrifice their initiative so as to live within the imposed limits. To find a balance between supporting initiative and structuring appropriate behavior, the nearby Taking It to the Classroom box offers several useful guidelines.

(Digital Vision)

The developmental turning point in preschool children's lives is moving toward greater initiative or toward hesitance.

Taking It to the Classroom

Guidelines for Supporting Preschoolers' Initiative

- Set rules and limits, but offer children some freedom within those limits.
- Explain the *why* behind an imposed rule or limit.
- Explain the *why* behind an instruction not to do something.
- Be tolerant of mistakes and accidents, affirming students' initiative and enthusiasm even while correcting their behavior.
- When children are engrossed in an activity, avoid interrupting them or asking them to change to a different activity.
- Allocate some time during the day for free play.

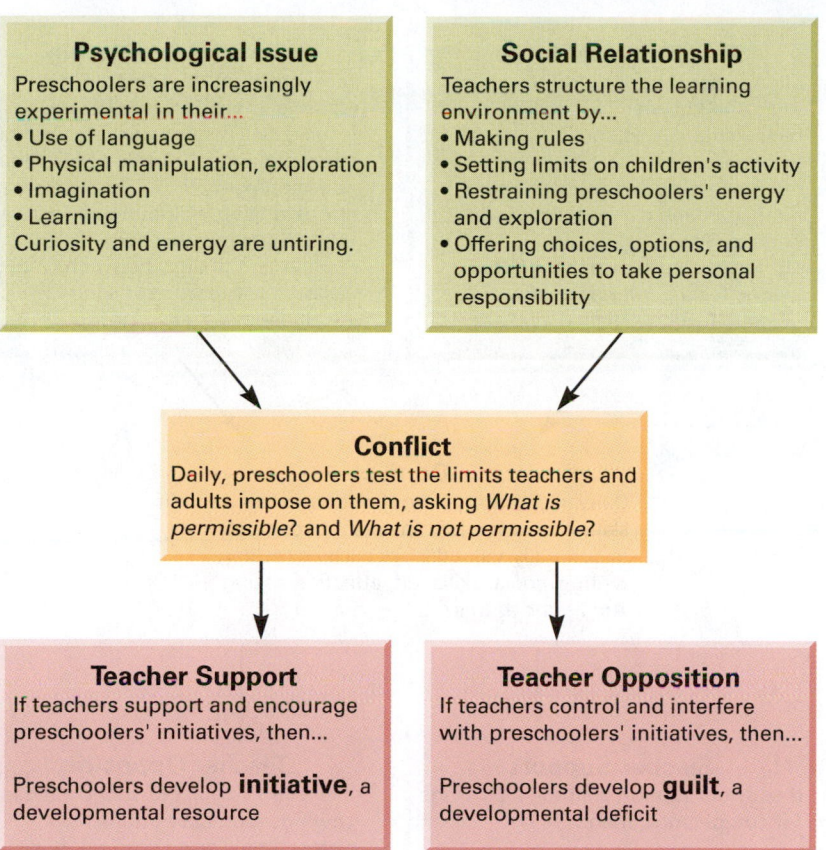

Psychological Issue
Preschoolers are increasingly experimental in their...
• Use of language
• Physical manipulation, exploration
• Imagination
• Learning
Curiosity and energy are untiring.

Social Relationship
Teachers structure the learning environment by...
• Making rules
• Setting limits on children's activity
• Restraining preschoolers' energy and exploration
• Offering choices, options, and opportunities to take personal responsibility

Conflict
Daily, preschoolers test the limits teachers and adults impose on them, asking *What is permissible?* and *What is not permissible?*

Teacher Support
If teachers support and encourage preschoolers' initiatives, then...

Preschoolers develop **initiative**, a developmental resource

Teacher Opposition
If teachers control and interfere with preschoolers' initiatives, then...

Preschoolers develop **guilt**, a developmental deficit

Figure 4.6 The Role of Teachers in Supporting Preschoolers' Initiative

Developing Competence The turning point that elementary school students face above all others involves developing a sense of competence rather than incompetence. The nearby Taking It to the Classroom box offers several guidelines for promoting competence in elementary school students. **Competence** is the self-assurance that one can successfully accomplish culturally valued tasks. It involves understanding the relationship between trying hard and experiencing the pleasure of a job well done. As summarized in Figure 4.7, elementary school students engage in learning a multitude of skills that will be necessary for their lives,

competence The psychological need to be effective as one interacts with the surrounding environment.

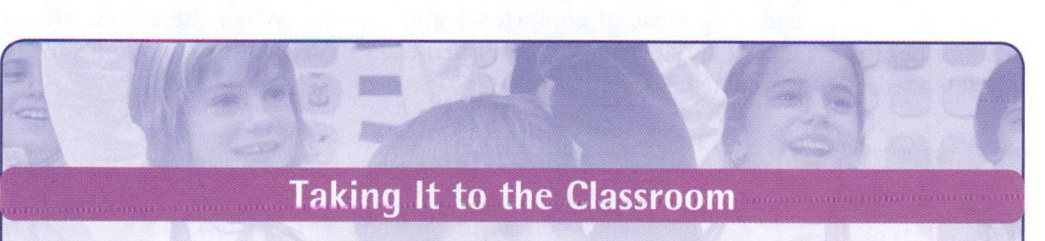

Taking It to the Classroom

Guidelines for Supporting Elementary-Grade Children's Competence

• Provide developmentally appropriate challenges to students' skills, and avoid tasks that are too easy or too difficult.

• As students work on these optimally challenging tasks, provide scaffolding—hints, tips, reminders, encouragement, and similar supports for learning.

• After students perform, provide constructive and skill-building feedback.

• Highlight points of progress in the child's skill development.

• Discuss the links among effort, perseverance, and the eventual pleasure of a job well done.

• Take time to recognize the products of a child's work.

• Provide support for discouraged students. For instance, keep samples of their earlier work on hand so they can see that they are indeed making progress.

Figure 4.7 The Role of Teachers in Supporting Elementary School Students' Competence

Psychological Issue
Elementary school children acquire skills and knowledge that are valued by the culture and apply those skills through...
• Behaviors, such as concentration, engagement, perseverance, work habits
• Emotions, such as enjoying the work, feeling interest, feeling useful, feeling satisfied

Social Relationship
Teachers do or do not provide...
• Developmentally appropriate challenges (vs. too easy, too difficult)
• Scaffolding in the zone of proximal development
• Constructive, skill-building feedback
• Praise of a job well done
• Discussion of links between child's effort and pleasure of a job well done

Conflict
Daily, elementary school children exercise their skills and strive for mastery and competence in culturally valued tasks such as reading, writing, social skills, art, athletics, asking *Am I good at this?*

Teacher Support
If teachers support children's strivings for competence, then...

Children develop **competence** (or a work ethic), a developmental resource

Teacher Opposition
If teachers neglect to support these strivings (don't communicate expectations, don't scaffold, don't provide constructive feedback), then...

Children develop **incompetence**, a developmental deficit

How Can I Use This?
The next time you impose a restriction on another person, see whether you can do so without undermining that person's sense of initiative.

including academic skills such as reading, penmanship, and the capacity to enjoy work (Kowaz & Marcia, 1991). Erikson placed particular emphasis on developing a "work ethic," or the emotional capacity to take pleasure in a job well done. When efforts on challenging tasks produce positive feedback and completed tasks, the student begins to develop an enduring sense of competence and mastery. When these same efforts produce negative feedback and a string of unfinished tasks, however, the student begins to develop a sense of incompetence and inferiority.

The developmental turning point in elementary school students' lives is developing a sense of competence or incompetence.

(© Media Bakery)

The teacher's task during elementary school is to offer students developmentally appropriate challenges, provide positive but authentic feedback to communicate a job well done, and engage in ongoing discussions about the relationship between perseverance and the pleasure of work. From this point of view, a lesson in penmanship, singing, or painting is not just about writing, singing, or painting, and playground attempts to hit a softball are about more than merely trying to hit the ball. The content of the day's lesson is important, but elementary school lessons are always embedded within an ever-present subtext of developing competence.

Developing Identity   The transition from adolescence into adulthood involves a progressive strengthening of one's sense of identity (Waterman, 1982), which in practice means finding "something to do" and "someone to be" (Waterman, 1983). Hence, as shown in Figure 4.8, the turning point that secondary school students face above all others is the need to develop a sense of identity within the larger society rather than suffering from role confusion. **Identity** is the sense of being a distinct and productive individual within the larger social framework. Adolescence is a time of exploring occupational and ideological commitments, and students construct a sense of identity when they are able to fit themselves into the adult social system (Baumeister, 1986, 1987; Marcia, 1994). When adolescents search for, find, and eventually commit to a particular set of adult roles and ideological beliefs, they develop a sense of identity; when they fail to do so, they suffer from role confusion and a sense of uncertainty about themselves and their future (Meilman, 1979).

The search for identity begins with awareness of social demands in terms of what one should be as well as social opportunities in terms of what one can be (Grotevant, 1987). The teacher's task during middle and high school is to create classroom (and schoolwide) opportunities in which students explore and test their aspirations, personal beliefs, possible future selves, and conceivable occupations. One way to do this is to give adolescents a steady stream of opportunities to explore and try out approaches for themselves in various aspects of life,

identity The sense of being a distinct and productive individual within the larger social framework.

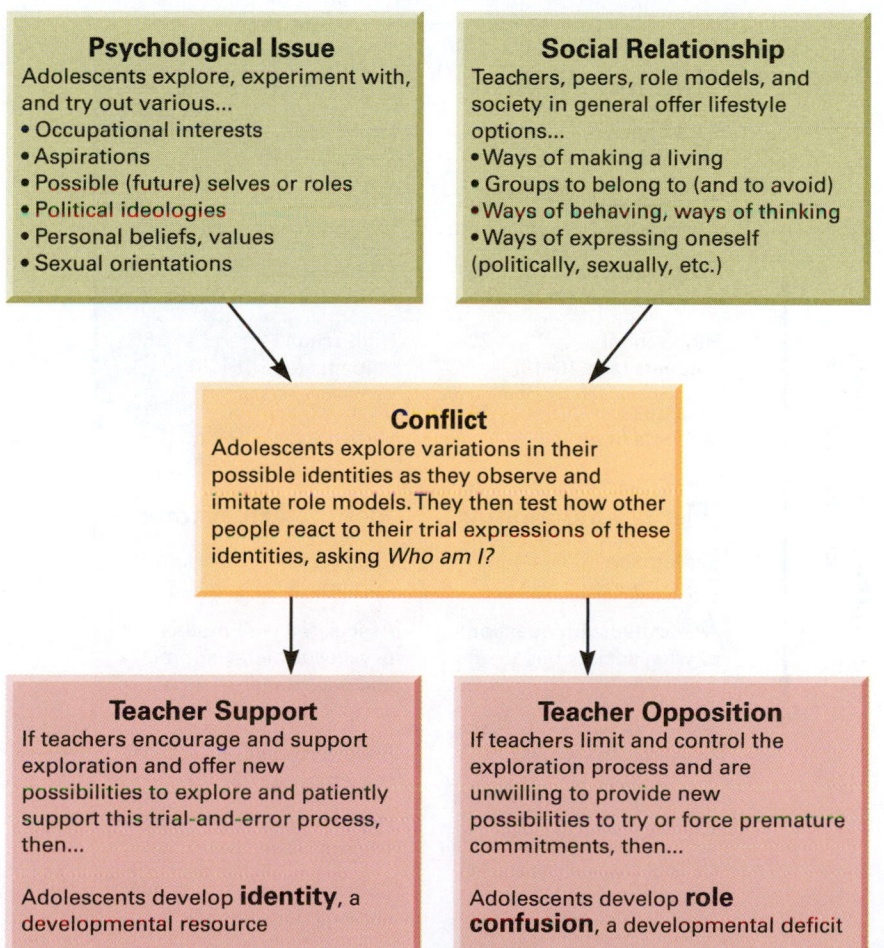

Figure 4.8 The Role of Teachers in Supporting Adolescents' Identity

(© Media Bakery)

The developmental turning point in adolescents' lives is developing identity or suffering role confusion.

such as vocation, personal values, political orientation, and perspectives on marriage and parenting. When presenting such opportunities, teachers need to do so in a classroom climate characterized by openness to change. Overall, the two critical sources of support teachers can provide during this identity-versus-role-confusion struggle are exploration of alternatives and openness to change (Bosma & Kunnen, 2001), as discussed in the nearby Taking It to the Classroom box.

As students become aware of societal roles, explore these roles, and make decisions about which roles to commit to and which ones to avoid, four identity statuses unfold: diffused, foreclosed, moratorium, and achieved (Marcia, 1966,1994). With *diffused identity*, the adolescent has not searched, explored, or committed to adult roles. Both exploration and commitment are low. With *foreclosed identity*, the adolescent has not explored yet has committed to adult roles. Identity foreclosure is common when the adolescent simply takes on and assumes (without exploration) the values, ideology, and occupation of his or her parents. A teenager might say, "My mother was a nurse, my grandmother was a nurse, so I'm going to be a nurse, too." With *moratorium*, the adolescent has explored but has not yet committed to adult roles. Exploring roles while withholding personal commitments results in the well-known *identity crisis*, which is a synonym for identity moratorium. With *achieved identity*, the adolescent has actively explored and made personal commitments to a way of life (ideology, occupation). Figure 4.9 summarizes these four identity statuses and indicates the percentages of middle school, high school, and college-age students occupying each

Figure 4.9 Four Identity Statuses Related to Occupational Choice (and the Percentages of Students at Different Grade Levels Who Occupy Them)

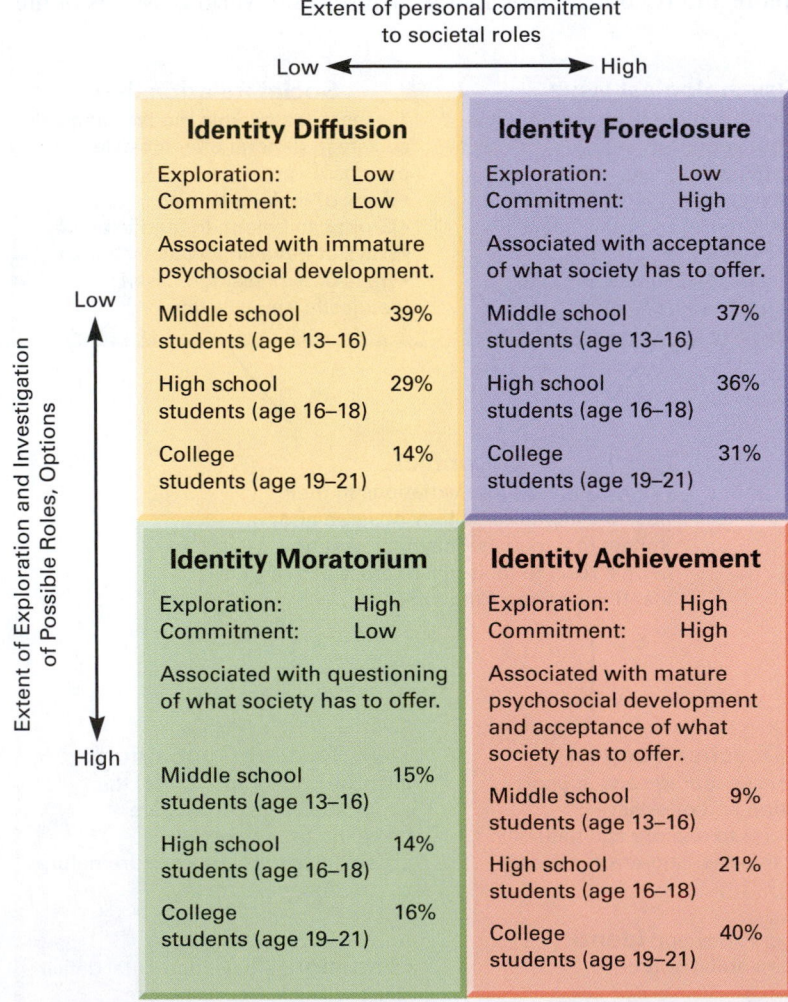

Extent of personal commitment to societal roles

Low ◄──────► High

Extent of Exploration and Investigation of Possible Roles, Options

Low

High

Identity Diffusion

| Exploration: | Low |
| Commitment: | Low |

Associated with immature psychosocial development.

Middle school students (age 13–16)	39%
High school students (age 16–18)	29%
College students (age 19–21)	14%

Identity Foreclosure

| Exploration: | Low |
| Commitment: | High |

Associated with acceptance of what society has to offer.

Middle school students (age 13–16)	37%
High school students (age 16–18)	36%
College students (age 19–21)	31%

Identity Moratorium

| Exploration: | High |
| Commitment: | Low |

Associated with questioning of what society has to offer.

Middle school students (age 13–16)	15%
High school students (age 16–18)	14%
College students (age 19–21)	16%

Identity Achievement

| Exploration: | High |
| Commitment: | High |

Associated with mature psychosocial development and acceptance of what society has to offer.

Middle school students (age 13–16)	9%
High school students (age 16–18)	21%
College students (age 19–21)	40%

Taking It to the Classroom

Guidelines for Supporting Adolescents' Identity

Expand Students' Awareness of Social Opportunities

- Raise awareness of a wide range of identity opportunities.
- Invite guest speakers into the class.
- Identify possible role models to emulate.

Support Exploration of Possible Identities

- Encourage open discussions of ideological possibilities.
- Provide supplemental information for the societal roles in which students express an interest.
- Identify apprenticeship opportunities in the local community.

Communicate Value and Support for School-Based Clubs and Organizations

- Encourage students to explore interest groups and to join clubs and organizations.
- Understand the positive role that membership in a small club within an otherwise large high school can play in adolescents' identity development.

Support Open-Ended Decision Making about Possible Identities

- Work collaboratively with students to find the resources they need to make decisions about their future.
- Be sensitive to adolescents' familial priorities, especially tension between the family's press for connectedness and the student's desire for individuality.

of them (Waterman, 1982, 1985). The nearby What Kids Say and Do box indicates what adolescents at each status actually said about their own identity search.

Emerging Adulthood Erikson proposed that adolescence was followed by young adulthood, and this model of psychosocial development represented the life course rather well when Erikson was writing. Today, however, people marry later, delay parenthood, move often, participate in lengthy postsecondary school education, and change jobs frequently.

Appendix
Meeting Students' Developmental Needs

Students' developmental needs vary according to age. Erikson's theory identifies which psychosocial needs are most pressing for students of different ages (PRAXIS™, I.B.1; I.C.1; INTASC, Principles 2, 3, 5).

What Kids Say and Do

Adolescents Speak about Identity Status

A group of high school seniors were asked about their likely occupation after high school in the following way (after each nominated a preferred occupation): So, you might become a(n) _____. Okay, but if something better comes along, how willing would you be to change and give up this occupation?

Achieved Identity
I might, but I doubt it. This is something I've thought about, and I know I want to become an artist. I can't really see what "something better" would be for me.

Moratorium
Maybe. I don't know for sure. If I knew for sure, then I could answer your question better [*laughs*]. I would have to look into it—find out more about it. A definite maybe.

Foreclosed Identity
No, not very willing. My parents are happy with it and so am I. It's what I've always wanted to do.

Diffused Identity
Sure. Why not? Who knows what will happen? If something good comes along, I might take it.

Young people in their late teens and mid-20s continue to experiment with and try out choices in love, work, and ideology. The period of emerging adulthood is now more than just a time of transition from one stage to another—from adolescence to young adulthood. It is a developmental period in its own right (Arnett, 2000, 2004, 2007).

Emerging adulthood is the age of identity explorations, the age of instability, the self-focused age, the age of feeling in-between, and the age of possibilities (Arnett, 2004). The implication of this newly proposed stage of life is that adolescence is now a time of exploration, young adulthood is a time of commitment, and emerging adulthood is a time of changes in love, work, and ideology that allow people to settle into richly informed choices, decisions, and styles of life to which they can confidently commit.

Developing Generativity The primary developmental challenge that experienced teachers face is that of being productive and able to guide the next generation successfully (Erikson, 1963; McAdams et al., 1997; McAdams & du St. Aubin, 1992). (Beginning teachers in their 20s, however, are more likely to be concerned with issues of identity and intimacy.) **Generativity** is the sense of being productive in one's work and in looking after and guiding others, particularly one's students and one's own children. It is an active concern for the growth of self and others, a sense of responsibility for sharing skills and knowledge (Bradley, 1997).

In daily life, generativity involves actions such as creative work (e.g., writing, teaching), training those who are less skilled, meeting the needs of one's students, raising one's own children, integrating work with family life to balance self-care with other-care, making contributions to the community (e.g., through volunteer work), and basically "making a difference" in people's lives. Difficulty in achieving a sense of generativity can lead to stagnation and self-indulgence (Levinson, 1986). The key to generativity appears to be the experience of career consolidation, in which the teacher gains the self-assurance needed (e.g., through academic tenure) to worry less and less about the self and more and more about the next generation (Vaillant & Milsofsky, 1980). As an overview, the nearby Uncommon Sense box discusses the overall developmental goal of positive psychosocial mental health.

generativity The sense of being productive in one's work and in looking after and guiding others.

> **What Does This Mean to Me?**
> Which developmental crisis is currently the most pressing one in your life: Identity? Intimacy? Generativity?

Uncommon Sense

Healthy Development Requires High Trust, Initiative, Competence, Identity, and Generativity—Or Does It?

To develop trust is better than to develop mistrust, to develop autonomy is better than to develop shame, and so on for all eight of Erikson's stages of psychosocial development. It makes sense, then, to assume that the ideal developmental trajectory throughout the lifespan would be the steady accumulation of personal strengths such as trust, autonomy, initiative, competence, identity, intimacy, generativity, and integrity.

According to Erikson (1982), however, it is preferable to develop a certain degree of tension between each stage's polar alternatives, with an emphasis on the more positive alternative. In this way, the student sustains basic trust but does not eliminate mistrust, particularly in situations where mistrust may be more appropriate (e.g., the overly naive student gets taken advantage of). In addition, human potential needs an internalized system of checks and balances. Initiative needs a conscience to keep it in check (guilt); competence needs a dose of reality (incompetence); and identity needs healthy skepticism (role confusion). In other words, the psychosocial-developmental goal is not to eliminate all traces of mistrust, shame, guilt, and so on, so much as it is to develop more trust than mistrust, more initiative than guilt, and so forth through the eight stages.

Moral Development

Morality concerns judgments of right and wrong, while **moral development** concerns changes in one's reasoning as to why one action is right and another is wrong. For instance, is it right to share your lunch with a classmate? If it is right, *why* is it right? Is it wrong to hurt others? If it is wrong, *why* is it wrong?

moral development Changes in students' reasoning as to why one action is right and another is wrong.

Stages of Moral Development

According to Lawrence Kohlberg (1963, 1975, 1981, 1984), moral reasoning is the application of principles to solve moral dilemmas. The principles applied to solve moral dilemmas reveal students' underlying level of moral development. These principles as to why some acts are right while others are wrong develop throughout the school years in a predictable pattern, as shown in Table 4.2.

At the preconventional level, children's moral reasoning is immature; the term *preconventional* connotes a period before the development of moral principles. Students in this stage determine right and wrong only through a lens of self-interest and an understanding of the personal consequences of their actions. At the *conventional* level, students begin to use principles to reason morally. Conventional reasoning is rooted in social convention, such as doing the right thing so as to live up to the expectations of others. At this level, being good means doing what others approve of. At the *postconventional* level, students understand and embrace moral principles, and these principles are differentiated from social convention, an authority figure, or a group norm. Instead, what is right is what has stood up to one's own personal critical examination, been reflected on, revised as appropriate, and determined to be just and fair by oneself. The nearby What Kids Say and Do box provides some quotations from high school students who reason at these three levels of moral reasoning when asked whether cheating is wrong. Within the quotations, you can hear morality as self-interest

TABLE 4.2

Stages of Moral Development (Kohlberg's Theory)

Preconventional

Understands neither social convention nor moral rules.

Stage 1:	Moral judgments are based on a punishment-and-obedience orientation. What is good or right is that which avoids punishment and defers to authority.
Stage 2:	Moral judgments are based on what satisfies one's own needs. What is right is what I need; what is wrong is what I get punished for. A pragmatic "you scratch my back and I'll scratch yours" orientation prevails.

Conventional

Understands and embraces social convention.

Values living up to the expectations of the family, group, or culture.

Conforms to group norms and acts to maintain them.

Stage 3:	Moral judgments are based on a good boy—nice girl orientation. What is good or right is what pleases others and gains their approval.
Stage 4:	Moral judgments are based on a law-and-order orientation. What is good or right is doing one's duty, following fixed rules, and acting to maintain the social order.

Postconventional

Understands and embraces moral rules.

Moral rules are defined apart from group norms.

Instead of just accepting the social order, the individual adopts his or her own perspective on what is right.

Stage 5:	Moral rules are created from socially agreed-upon standards that have been critically examined and revised to meet the needs and values of the society.
Stage 6:	Moral rules exist as self-chosen ethical principles, such as justice, equal rights, respect for the individual, fairness, and reciprocity.

Figure 4.10 Stages of Moral Development for Males Ages 10–20

Source: Based on Colby, A., Kohlberg, L., Gibbs, J., & Lieberman, M. (1983). A longitudinal study of moral development. *Monographs of the Society for Research in Child Development, 48*(1–2, Serial No. 200). Reprinted with the permission of Wiley/Blackwell.

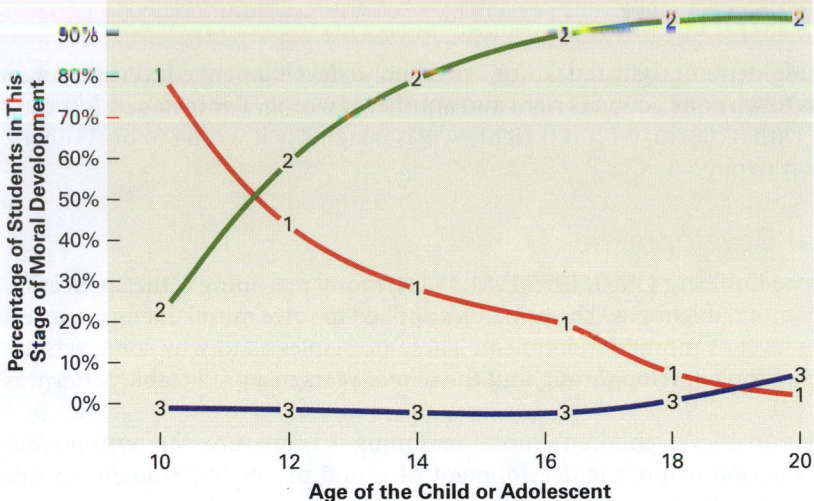

(preconventional), morality as social convention (conventional), and morality as justice (postconventional).

The level of moral development displayed by males of different ages (10–20 years) appears in Figure 4.10 (Colby et al., 1983). The figure rather strikingly shows that most elementary school males rely on preconventional moral reasoning (10-year-olds: 73%). By middle school, most males rely on conventional moral reasoning (14-year-olds: 78%). By high school, most males continue to rely on conventional moral reasoning (18-year-olds: 84%). Postconventional moral reasoning is rare during the school years. It is also rare in adulthood (Kohlberg, 1984). Based on these data, teachers can expect that most males' moral reasoning will involve either immature moral principles (preconventional) or conventional principles, in which an act is right because "it's what everybody else does."

Personal Morality and Social Convention Morality focuses on issues of harm to the self and to others. A moral judgment is that the harm brought to oneself or to others is wrong. But the issue of what is wrong and harmful is larger than the concept of personal morality,

What Kids Say and Do

Moral Reasoning about Cheating

Question asked of tenth- and eleventh-grade students: Most students say that cheating on a test is wrong. Do you agree? If so, could you explain why cheating is wrong?

A Student Using Preconventional Reasoning

Cheating on a test? Yeah, that's wrong. It's bad. You can't just cheat because you want to. If you do, you'd be like a criminal or something.

A Student Using Conventional Reasoning

Duh. I guess it's natural for students to want to cheat—to get ahead, you know. But it is still always wrong to cheat. You have to follow the rules, and that is true regardless of whether you have studied enough or not. That's just the way it is.

A Student Using Postconventional Reasoning

Most of the time cheating is wrong—almost always. Before you say cheating is morally wrong, you've got to consider the whole situation. There is just so much pressure placed on students to excel that cheating might be reasonable. It's wrong, sure, but so is putting so much pressure on students to be number one.

because what is wrong is also a matter of social convention—rules set by social expectations and authority figures, including manners and such societal norms as that women wear dresses and students should call their teachers by their last names. Manners, etiquette, and matters of social convention lie outside personal morality (Turiel, 1983, 2008). Morality does not apply to such questions as: Is it the norm? Is it the rule? Is it what the authority figure says needs to be done in order to maintain order? Instead, personal morality applies specifically to such issues as: Is it wrong to harm? Is it right to help? Is it fair? Is it equal? Is it equitable? Is it equal and equitable?

Moral Development and Cognitive Development In many respects, moral reasoning reflects students' underlying cognitive development. As Kohlberg pointed out, "Since moral reasoning clearly is reasoning, advanced moral reasoning depends on advanced logical reasoning; a person's logical stage puts a certain ceiling on the moral stage he can attain" (Kohlberg, 1975, p. 671). Preoperational thinking (to use Piaget's terminology) limits children to egocentric thinking and, thus, cognitively paves the way toward preconventional moral reasoning. Concrete-operational thinking allows the child to overcome egocentrism and recognize other people's points of view. The child understands what others might judge to be good and morally acceptable versus bad and morally unacceptable. Postconventional moral reasoning requires formal-operational thinking, because it is based on abstract principles, not on rules that hang concretely on the classroom wall for everyone to see (Schlaefli, Rest, & Thoma, 1985). That said, while many high school students can use formal-operational thinking, few actually show signs of postconventional moral reasoning. Thus, cognitive development is necessary but not sufficient for moral reasoning (Kuhn et al., 1977; Tomlinson-Keasey & Keasey, 1974).

If they are to advance their moral reasoning to a level that reflects their cognitive development, students need opportunities to discuss moral issues in an open and nonthreatening way. That is, moral reasoning advances through discussions within high-quality relationships and a sense of community in which misdeeds and conflicts are resolved through fairness and perspective taking (Eisenberg, Lennon, & Roth, 1983). Students who are consistently given rationales for why something is right or wrong (i.e., gentle discipline) show greater advances in their moral development than do students who are disciplined harshly with forceful commands (Brody & Shaffer, 1982; Eisenberg et al., 1983). Thus, the development of moral reasoning requires both cognitive development and supportive social dialogue (Kruger & Tomasello, 1986).

Does Moral Reasoning Predict Moral Behavior? The day-to-day relationship between moral reasoning and moral action is a weak one (Blasi, 1980; Kohlberg & Candee, 1984; Underwood & Moore, 1982). This is so because many opportunities to help and share are low-cost situations. When helping or sharing costs the person very little, most people—regardless of their moral development—lend a helping hand. When the costs of helping are high in terms of time, energy, or money, however, a person's level of moral development does predict whether he or she will help (i.e., do what is right).

In one study, for instance, children could donate an unattractive or an attractive possession to hospitalized children. When they were asked to donate low-cost, unattractive possessions, level of moral reasoning did not predict which children donated their possessions; but when they were asked to donate high-cost, attractive possessions, only children with higher levels of moral reasoning made a donation (Eisenberg & Shell, 1987). Thus, level of moral development predicts moral action, but only when the costs are high. This is so because high costs create moral conflicts (self-interest versus the needs of others), and for morally immature students, self-interest routinely trumps social concern.

The Ethic of Care

In Kohlberg's theory, the highest level of moral reasoning reflects the individual's level of cognitive development and expresses itself in a personal commitment to abstract principles such as justice and fairness. Morality centers on the question: Is it fair? According to a second perspective, however, moral reasoning grows out of relationship concerns. That is, decisions about right and wrong can be based on compassion, social duties and

Figure 4.11 The Ethic of Care Depicted as Concentric Circles

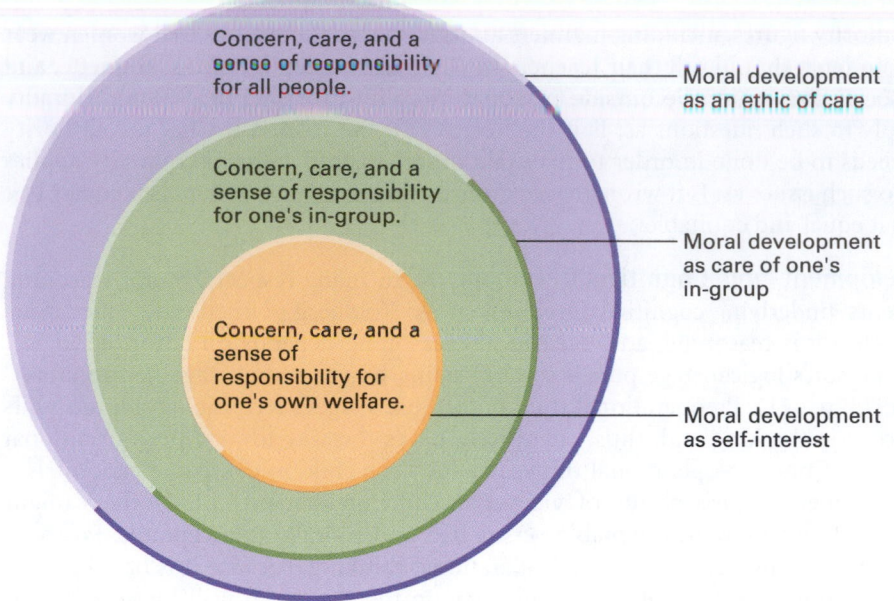

Concern, care, and a sense of responsibility for all people. ——— Moral development as an ethic of care

Concern, care, and a sense of responsibility for one's in-group. ——— Moral development as care of one's in-group

Concern, care, and a sense of responsibility for one's own welfare. ——— Moral development as self-interest

obligations, responsibility to others, and concern for the welfare of others. In short, moral judgments can be based on an *ethic of care* (Gilligan, 1993). Morality centers on the question: Is someone in need?

To appreciate how an ethic of care can distinguish among different levels of moral reasoning, Figure 4.11 shows three concentric circles. At the center is a sense of concern, care, and responsibility only for the needs of oneself. Self-interest represents the most immature level of moral reasoning—the inner circle. At a more advanced level is the wider second circle, in which one's range of care expands to include concern for one's in-group, such as friends, family, and "people like me." This level of moral reasoning is more mature than the first because one's ethic of care includes not only oneself but others as well. At the outer boundary is a sense of concern, care, and responsibility for the needs of "all people." One's sense of responsibility and compassion extends beyond oneself and one's in-group to include a general *ethic of care*. Thus, according to this view, moral maturity advances from concern for the needs of the self through concern for the needs of one's in-group to a concern for the needs of all.

R I D E How might Ms. Hernandez expand her students' ethic of care to include all class members?

Caring is an emotional concern and sense of responsibility to protect another's well-being.

(Jeffrey Greenberg/Photo Researchers, Inc.)

Gender Differences in Moral Development Carol Gilligan (1993) proposed her relationship-based ethic of care as a theory of moral development because she felt that existing theories were gender biased. She titled her book on this subject *In a Different Voice* because she wanted to voice what she believed to be the female perspective on morality. To formulate her ideas, she began with the assumption that gender socialization leads boys and girls to internalize different moral voices. Boys are encouraged to be independent and assertive and to see moral dilemmas as conflicts of interest. Hence, boys learn a morality of justice that asks: What is fair? What is equal? What is equitable? Girls, however, are encouraged to be empathic, to be concerned about others, and to see moral dilemmas as relationship issues. Hence, girls learn a morality of care that asks: Is someone in need? How interpersonally connected with the person-in-need am I?

Research actually did not support this assumption, but the theory was nevertheless a milestone in the study of moral development because it argued persuasively that moral development can be based on both a morality of justice and a morality of care. Contemporary research is now clear that both boys and girls reason morally based on justice *and* care (Brabeck, 1983; Jaffee & Hyde, 2000; Walker, 2006).

Character and Conscience: Doing the Right Thing for the Right Reason

When teachers ask students to "do this" or "don't do that," students tend to comply, at least if they have a positive relationship with the teacher. But students comply for two different reasons (Kochanska, Aksan, & Koenig, 1995), referred to as *situational compliance* and *committed compliance*. With **situational compliance**, students are cooperative but lack a sincere commitment to the action, instead, they act out of obligation. With **committed compliance**, students eagerly and willingly embrace the request and carry it out in a volitional, self-regulated way rather than in a have-to, teacher-regulated way.

These two types of compliance are negatively correlated, meaning that the more students engage in situational compliance, the less they engage in committed compliance, and vice versa (Kochanska et al., 1995). These two types of compliance have different developmental origins and different implications for students' social competence, morality, and conscience. As shown in Figure 4.12, committed compliance grows out of a high-quality relationship with the teacher. The more teachers show attunement, relatedness, supportiveness, and gentle discipline, the more likely it is that students will respond with committed rather than situational compliance (Kochanska et al., 2001). Students are more likely to show situational compliance, however, when they have a low-quality relationship with the teacher, because the teacher relies only on the assertion of power to gain students' compliance.

Power assertion is a socialization strategy designed to gain compliance through coercion, pressure, forceful insistence, and a negative or critical interaction style; it is associated with situational compliance, impaired self-regulation, and increased aggression (Deater-Deckard

situational compliance Cooperatively carrying out a teacher's "do this" or "don't do that" request with a sense of obligation rather than a sincere commitment to the action.

committed compliance Cooperatively carrying out a teacher's request to "do this" or "don't do that" with an eager, willing, and sincere commitment to the action.

power assertion A socialization strategy designed to gain compliance through coercion, pressure, forceful insistence, and a negative or critical interaction style.

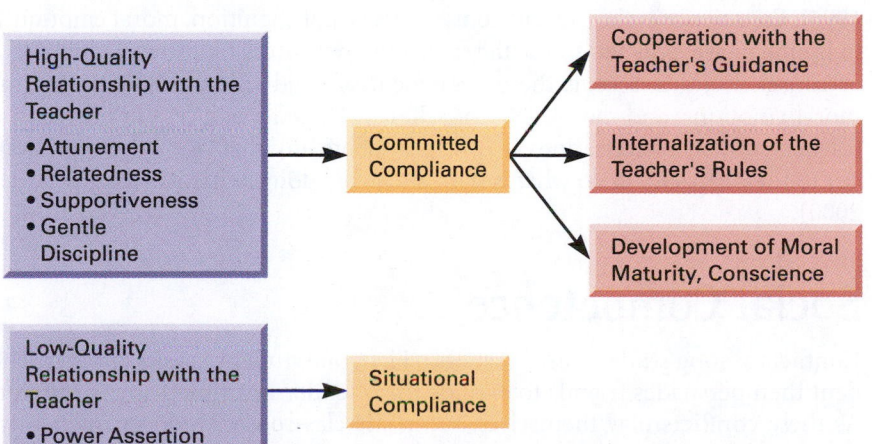

Figure 4.12 Origins and Developmental Implications of Two Types of Compliance

Figure 4.13 Integration of Four Systems in the Development of Character or Conscience

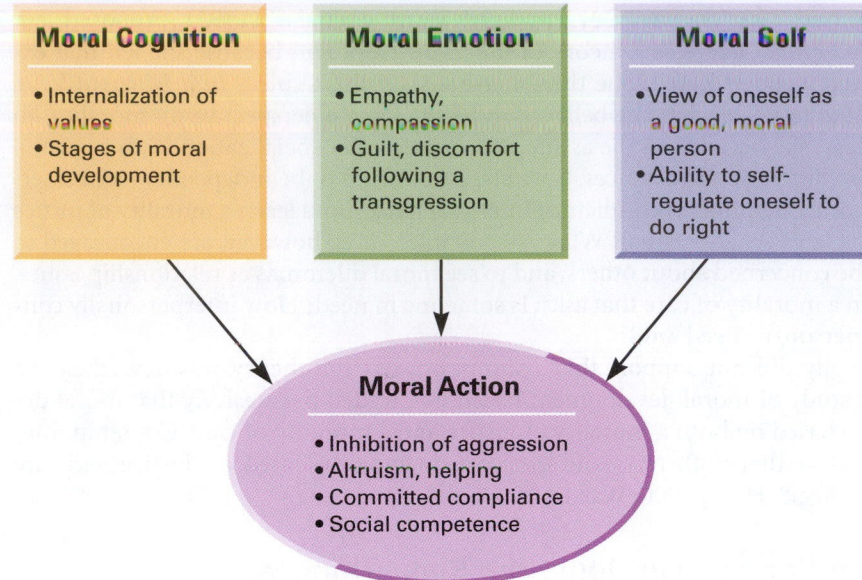

Figure 4.13 Integration of Four Systems in the Development of Character or Conscience

et al., 1996; Gershoff, 2002a; Kochanska et al., 2003; McCord, 1995). The problem with power assertion is that it arouses anger and hostility in students, thus generating an inner resistance against complying with the teacher's wishes. The distinction between these two types of compliance is important, because only committed compliance is associated with ongoing cooperation with the teacher's requests, internalization of rules, gains in moral maturity, and development of a conscience (Kochanska et al., 1995; Kochanska & Thompson, 1997), as shown in Figure 4.12. Situational compliance is not associated with any gains in students' ongoing social development.

Figure 4.13 frames the chapter's discussion of moral development under the umbrella of character or conscience (Grusec, 1997; Kochanska & Aksan, 2004). At the base of the figure is *moral action*, which represents the relative absence of aggression and relative presence of altruism, committed compliance, and social competence. Above moral action are the three sources that foster prosocial behavior and inhibit aggression. *Moral cognition* is essentially one's thoughts and values about prosocial and antisocial behavior, because it includes the internalization of values and the stages of moral development. *Moral emotions* are those, such as empathy, that foster care and prosocial action and those, such as guilt, shame, disgust, and discomfort following a transgression, that inhibit harm and aggression (Ferguson, Stegge, & Damhuis, 1991; Haidt, 2001; Hoffman, 1982; Kochanska et al., 2002). *Moral self* is the person's mental model in which the self is viewed as a good and moral person who cares for others (Hart & Fegley, 1995).

The extent to which these four systems are correlated with one another reflects the student's character (Rushton, Brainerd, & Pressley, 1983) or conscience (Kochanska, Padavich, & Koenig, 1996). **Conscience** is the capacity to use one's moral cognition, moral emotions, and moral self to inhibit aggression and to use the same inner resources to initiate helping. The development of conscience, therefore, is the development of children's and adolescents' moral cognition, moral emotions, and moral sense of self. It is helped along by the provision of high-quality teacher–student conversations that help students link their thoughts, emotions, and sense of self to their capacity to do what is right and avoid doing what is wrong (Kochanska & Murray, 2000).

Social Competence

Conflicts among students are inevitable. First, one student insults another. The offended student then persuades friends to exclude the offender from their social activities (as revenge). As these conflicts play themselves out in the classroom, students frequently feel emotions

Appendix
Social–Emotional–Moral Development

Teachers who support students in one domain of social, emotional, or moral development subsequently enhance students' development in the other two domains of social development as well (PRAXIS™, I.A.2; INTASC, Principle 2).

conscience The capacity to use one's moral cognition, moral emotions, and moral self to inhibit aggression and to initiate altruism and helping.

such as anger and frustration. How children and adolescents manage their negative emotions leads to displays of social competence versus aggression, which are the next two topics of the chapter.

Social competence is how skilled children and adolescents are at managing the often frustrating and challenging experiences they have with other people. For example, conflicts with peers often generate anger and frustration; social competence reflects the capacity to respond to the conflict in a socially appropriate manner even while feeling angry and frustrated. The two primary benefits of social competence are the capacity to resolve social conflict amicably and popularity with peers (Eisenberg et al., 1993; Eisenberg, Guthrie, et al., 1997; Hubbard & Cole, 1994).

Several factors explain which students lack social competence (Repetti, Taylor, & Seeman, 2002). Students from homes with high levels of conflict and aggression display more aggression and less social skill during conflict (Crockenberg & Lourie, 1996; Pettit, Dodge, & Brown, 1988). Students living in homes with parents who are cold, unsupportive, or neglectful also exhibit more aggression and less social skill (Brody & Flor, 1998; Weiss et al., 1992). What these students lack is the knowledge and capacity to manage their negative emotions so as to generate constructive, prosocial responses during conflict (Caspi et al., 1995,1996). They let their negative emotion get the best of them, so to speak. The capacity to manage negative emotions constructively is so central to the concept of social competence that some researchers prefer the term *emotion regulation*. **Emotion regulation** is the capacity to modulate—or calm—upsetting internal emotional reactivity during stressful situations (Thompson, 1994).

Emotions arise and change over time. Whether a specific emotion arises and whether a specific emotion changes is a matter that people have some control over. When students lack the capacity to regulate their emotions, especially their negative emotions, emotions just automatically happen to them. When students have the capacity to regulate their emotions, however, emotions are managed or regulated strategically. Figure 4.14 illustrates the many opportunities students have during an emotional episode to regulate their emotionality. Students can predetermine which emotion they experience by selecting situations that are likely to yield, say, joy rather than anger (e.g., spend time with a friend, avoid the bully). Once the situation activates a particular emotion, students can modify that emotion by modifying the situation that caused its emergence (e.g., after cutting in line and causing a commotion, apologize and go to the back of the line). Students can further manage their cognitions—their appraisals of the situation—to change the meaning of the situational event (e.g., think of waiting in line not as lost time but as an

social competence How skilled children and adolescents are at managing the often frustrating and challenging experiences they have with other people.

emotion regulation The capacity to modulate or calm internal emotional reactivity during stressful situations.

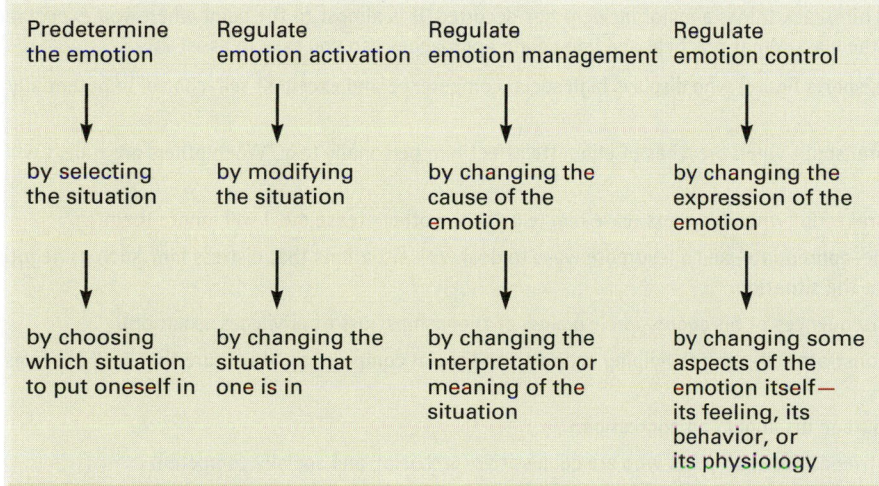

Figure 4.14 The Many Opportunities to Self-Regulate an Emotional Experience

opportunity to meet someone or spend time with a friend). And students can modify some aspect of their emotional experience itself by managing their physiology (e.g., taking a deep breath or counting to 10 when angry). In all four of these ways, students can manage the quality of their emotional life.

As highlighted in the nearby Taking It to the Classroom box, teachers can promote students' social competence and emotion regulation in three ways. First, they can use gentle discipline, such as explaining and problem solving, rather than harsh disciplinary strategies. Students who are disciplined gently show greater social competence and prosocial behavior than do students who are disciplined harshly (Weiss et al., 1992). Second, teachers can help students lessen their anger and deepen their empathy toward others by providing them with secure, high-quality relationships (Einsenberg & Fabes, 1998). Relatedness helps soothe negative emotions, and empathy can be developed, as discussed in the second Taking It to the Classroom box on the next page (Eisenberg, 1992, 2000; Schulman & Mekler, 1986). When teachers help students feel empathic toward their peers, students respond by showing more prosocial and less antisocial behavior (Carlo et al., 1999). Third, a more indirect strategy is to encourage participation in extracurricular activities. The more students participate in such activities, the more naturally occurring opportunities they have to grow their social competence; this is especially true for adolescents with low social competence (Mahoney, Cairns, & Farmer, 2003).

Helping Others Prosocial behavior includes not only resolving conflict with others but actually helping and assisting them. Students who are prosocial help, comfort, and defend others, and they share and cooperate with them as well.

The desire to help others takes root in the prosocial emotions of empathy and sympathy. *Empathy* is responding to another's distress with a similar emotion; *sympathy* is responding to another's distress with feelings of sadness and concern. Empathy and sympathy serve as a powerful emotional basis for helping because they are unpleasant emotional states (because of the felt distress) that can be reduced if the distress of the other is reduced. Thus, by help-

Taking It to the Classroom

Do You Know Jack? Promoting Social Competence

Jack is easily angered, annoyed, or upset. Jack seems to have a chip on his shoulder. A minor joke at his expense unleashes his fury. If a classmate commits a minor offense toward him, Jack thinks a major incident has occurred. It is almost to the point where you *expect* Jack will show his temper at some point during the class. What practical and immediate approaches can you take to assist Jack?

- Expose Jack to a model (peers, videotape, sports figure) who displays high social competence and excellent self-control in potentially aggressive situations.
- Provide Jack with a constructive behavioral script when breaches of etiquette affect him personally (e.g.,"When others are rude, I will ask them to be polite").
- Provide Jack with a constructive behavioral script when his peers tease him (e.g.,"When others tease me, I will ignore them").
- Teach Jack nonaggressive, alternative, age-appropriate, and all-purpose ways to deal with situations that distress him, such as negotiation, counting to 10, or withdrawing from the situation.
- Make sure that Jack understands the consequences of his aggression (e.g., loss of friendships, loss of privileges, isolation).
- Reinforce students in the class who demonstrate self-control, helping behavior, and social competence. Make sure that Jack observes the reinforcement.
- Separate Jack from classmates who encourage his anger and aggression.
- Create opportunities for Jack to develop friendships with peers who are cooperative, prosocial, and socially competent.
- Communicate with Jack's parents to share information concerning his progress so they can reinforce Jack at home for demonstrating self-control and social competence.

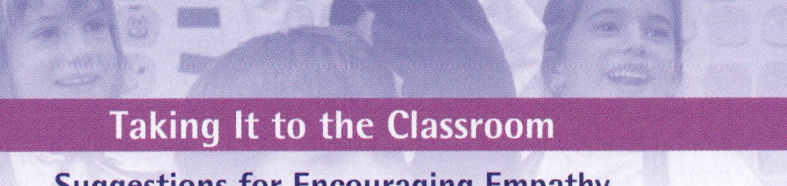

Taking It to the Classroom

Suggestions for Encouraging Empathy

1. Foster empathy:
   - Let students know what impact their actions have on other people's feelings.
   - Teach them to imagine themselves in the other person's place.
   - Help students understand other people's feelings by reminding them of similar experiences in their own lives.

2. Expect empathy, praise it, and explain how to show it:
   - Let students know that you expect them to be considerate—it is important to you.
   - Recognize occasions when students show empathy for others, and offer your praise and admiration.
   - Explain what actions students can take that would be more considerate.

3. Explain the benefits of empathy:
   - Point out the good feelings that come from caring for others, including a good mood.
   - Point out the relationship benefits that come from caring, including trust and friendship.

RIDE Would greater social competence allow Ms. Hernandez's students to make friends and diffuse conflicts?

ing others, one reduces one's own discomfort. Of the two, empathy is the more fundamental of the two, as people can react to sympathy by avoiding the other person, while empathy relief requires that the other person's distress actually be reduced (Eisenberg et al., 2006).

Social Competence in Special Education

When teachers are asked what social competencies they consider most important, they generally list cooperating with peers, following directions, maintaining self-control, responding constructively to peer pressure, and avoiding such behaviors as aggression and disrupting the class (Hersh & Walker, 1983; Walker et al., 1992). These competencies are emphasized by both elementary teachers (Lane, Givner, & Pierson, 2004a) and secondary school teachers (Lane, Givner, & Pierson, 2004b). Teachers value these social competencies not only for their own sake but also because they believe that they enable students to succeed in school. Special education teachers frequently place a premium on a narrower band of competencies. They rate cooperation with others and social assertiveness as important, but they rate *maintaining self-control* as the essential social competence for students with special needs (Lane et al., 2004b). Taking this lead from special education teachers, elementary school and secondary school teachers can make the social competence of emotion regulation for their students with special needs a priority (and, hence, utilize gentle discipline strategies to foster empathy, explain how students can show it, and explain its value in their lives, as discussed above).

A Teacher's Guide to Social Competence Concerns for Students with Disabilities The following paragraphs are offered as a guide for teachers to use in gaining insights into why students in special education sometimes have more difficulty in the realm of social competence and peer interaction than do their peers without disabilities.

Students with learning disabilities sometimes display difficulties in communication skills and social initiative. Relative to their peers, they show conversational skill deficits and difficulties using peer-appropriate interaction strategies (Hartas & Donahue, 1997). For instance, they may shove or pull on a peer in a bid for attention. These deficits sometimes make them less preferred playmates and friends and more likely targets of teasing and bullying (Mishna, 2003).

Students with intellectual disabilities are sometimes less responsive to others than are their peers. When students with severe intellectual disabilities are enrolled in self-contained special classes with peers who also have severe disabilities, their opportunities for peer interactions are limited by the nature of each child's disability. Even at lunch, students with severe intellectual disabilities and typically developing students rarely interact with one another (Hughes et al., 1999). When they do interact, the interactions are often asymmetrical, as the typically developing peer tends to direct the interaction, whereas the student with intellectual disabilities tends to follow (Diamond, Huang, & Steed, 2010). That said, when students with intellectual disabilities are enrolled in general education classes, they receive more social support and achieve more durable friendship networks than do students with intellectual disabilities who are enrolled only in self-contained classes.

Students with Down syndrome typically display cognitive and communication (especially language) deficits that undermine their social competence. For instance, they are not as expressive as their peers, and they are not as accurate in interpreting the social signals that others are sending them (e.g., when to take turns, expressing a subtle intention to end the conversation). They do, however, show a sociable style, and this social initiative pays off for them, as their peers generally accept about 70% of their social initiatives (e.g., to play) and they themselves accept about 70% of social initiations that are directed toward them from their peers (Sigman & Ruskin, 1999). It is also not unusual for them to have a best friend or to participate in clubs, such as the Girls Scouts, though most of their social lives are spent with their families.

Students with autism (autism spectrum disorders) typically display several social and communicative deficits. Some of these social competencies are quite basic to successful interaction, such as making eye contact and being responsive to the social initiatives others show. Socially inappropriate verbalizations, gestures, and facial expressions are also common. These displays are often unexpected by their peers and are thus confusing as well as being negative (Strain, Schwartz, & Bovey, 2008). Peers therefore report being confused by what students with autism want. During interaction, students with autism also have difficulty with the reciprocal back-and-forth that is normal in successful conversions. However, when students with autism are given regular opportunities to interact with typically developing peers (or perhaps their typically developing siblings), they do make significant gains in their social skills and competencies (Roeyers, 1996).

Students with physical disabilities may be at risk for developing social competence difficulties because of social isolation (e.g., they require assistance from others for locomotion), independent of their intrinsic social competence (Harper & McCluskey, 2002). Children with visual impairments may develop social competence difficulties to the extent that they are unaware of subtle social and emotional cues that provide important information about the interaction, such as how the other person feels.

Aggression

aggression Any intentional behavior designed to harm another person or group physically or psychologically.

Aggression is any intentional behavior designed to harm another person or group physically or psychologically (Parke & Slaby, 1983). Students trip each other in the hallway, hit and kick, take each other's possessions, tease and annoy, utter threats such as "I'll beat you up," and call each other names; they spread rumors, tell lies, and defame each other's character; they exclude others from their groups; and they vandalize property (Crick, Bigbee, & Howes, 1996). The nearby Uncommon Sense box lists common aggressive behaviors from both boys and girls.

When one student deliberately and intentionally engages in such actions with the purpose of harming another, almost irrespective of how much harm subsequently ensues, the behavior is aggressive. Behavior that causes accidental harm, however, is not aggressive because the harm was not intentional.

When teachers are asked why they want to understand the developmental roots of students' aggression, they say it is because they want the sense of security that comes from being able to predict—and hence avoid—danger and disruption in their classrooms (Muehlenhard & Kimes, 1999). In that spirit, we, too, will try to understand why students

Uncommon Sense

Boys Are More Aggressive than Girls—Or Are They?

After spending a lot of time in schools, most educators see that boys are more likely than girls to shove, take things, curse, hit, kick, and trip others (Leagerspetz, Bjorkquist, & Peltonen, 1988). But these same educators will also see that girls are more likely to gossip, argue, talk behind another's back, and say to others, "Let's not be friends with her." This difference highlights the distinction between direct and indirect aggression. Boys are more direct in their aggression, girls more indirect. This point is worth emphasizing because teachers are more likely to notice direct aggression and conclude that boys are more aggressive than girls. When they look for indirect displays of aggression, teachers become more likely to conclude that girls are just as aggressive as boys.

are aggressive so that teachers can prevent aggression from creeping into their classrooms and finding a home there.

Instrumental and Hostile Aggression

Aggression comes in two types—instrumental and hostile. It is important to distinguish between these types because they have different developmental origins and different classroom remedies (Anderson & Bushman, 2002).

Instrumental Aggression One type of aggression is **instrumental aggression**, which is strategic behavior to obtain something the aggressor desires, such as a possession, a toy, attention, "my way," or respect from others. During infancy, a developmental period in which aggression hits its peak, instrumental aggression is common, as infants often try to overpower others for toys, possessions, and attention. Among preschoolers, physical acts of aggression generally give way to verbal ones, including teasing, tattling, and name-calling. As children enter school, their coping skills during conflict situations expand to include not only physical and verbal aggression but also noncoercive ways of coping, including negotiation. Throughout elementary school, acts of aggression usually give way to these alternative ways of getting what one wants as children develop their social skills.

> **instrumental aggression** Strategic behavior to obtain something one desires that results in harm inflicted on another person.

What can teachers do to help students make this transition from instrumental aggression to social skill? Approaches involving punishment, behavior modification, and medication generally fall short as intervention strategies, largely because they fail to teach students the social skills they need to resolve conflicts amicably. Two more productive approaches are helping students cope constructively with their anger, and building and refining students' prosocial problem-solving skills and strategies (Lochman et al., 1984). Conflicts are difficult situations for children to handle, especially when the conflict makes them feel angry. Teachers can help by showing students how to cope in a way that is both more effective and more prosocial.

Hostile Aggression The second type of aggression is **hostile aggression**, or aggression in which harm is sought as a goal itself. The intent is not to cope but to harm. Hostile aggression is typically impulsive, thoughtless, and driven by anger (Anderson & Bushman, 2002). During infancy, hostile aggression emerges in proportion to the extent to which infants' needs are frustrated—for example, through parental abuse and neglect. Among preschoolers, infantile rage expresses itself through such acts as stubborn defiance, annoying others, and bullying. Some children learn that aggression has value for its own sake, because it enables the child to dominate and control others. Throughout middle and high school, hostile aggression expresses itself in such acts as verbal assault: fighting; property damage; shoplifting; frequent lying; and violent acts such as attacks, strong-arming others, rape, and homicide

> **hostile aggression** The anger-driven impulse to inflict intentional harm on another person.

(Loeber & Hay, 1994). By adolescence, hostile aggression manifests itself in the classroom in three principal ways (Olweus, 1980):

1. Starting fights—unprovoked physical aggression
2. Verbal protests—verbal aggression directed at teachers
3. Verbal hurt—verbal aggression directed at peers

The roots of hostile aggression are (1) having mental models that others are untrustworthy—others are not to be trusted and, in fact, are assumed to be hostile; (2) having friends and a peer group who accept, value, and expect aggression as an interpersonal style; and (3) a disciplinary history with adults who relied on coercion and ridicule (punishment and power assertion) rather than empathy and perspective taking (gentle discipline) (Olweus, 1980). As for what teachers can do to cope with students' hostile aggression, prevention works better than remediation. As for prevention, students who shun hostile aggression are those who (1) have a history of having their psychological needs met (a mental model that others can be trusted); (2) have friends and peers who discourage, rather than encourage, hostile aggression; and (3) develop strong capacities for empathy and perspective taking. As for remediation, it is probably wise to enlist the assistance of professionals (e.g., school psychologist) who are trained to deal effectively with hostile aggression.

What Does This Mean to Me?

Recall a recent display of aggression and judge what type it was—instrumental or hostile? How could you tell?

Constructive Response to Aggression   When students break rules, instigate fights, or cruelly tease their classmates, teachers' most common reaction is to provide discipline immediately following the student's misbehavior. There is little wrong with discipline and classroom management strategies—except for one thing. After years of research, educators now realize that this is not the only, or even the best, approach to curbing aggression.

The long-held view that students' misbehavior should be immediately followed by discipline has given way to a focus on the ongoing quality of the teacher–student relationship (Kochanska, 2002; Zhou et al., 2002). This change of emphasis reflects the understanding that the student is an agent in his or her own moral socialization, one who actively processes a teacher's moral messages and exercises a sense of autonomy regarding how to behave (Grusec & Goodnow, 1994; Maccoby, 1992). The quality of the teacher–student relationship is important because it affects the student's willingness to embrace the teacher's rules, values, and requests (Kochanska & Thompson, 1997). The quality of the teacher–student relationship not only affects the student's openness to the teacher's socialization efforts but also determines the effectiveness of specific discipline strategies. Just about any discipline strategy will backfire in the context of a negative, adversarial relationship (Patterson, Debaryshe, & Ramsey, 1989). It seems reasonable to conclude that teachers need to develop both effective discipline strategies and high-quality relationships with their students.

What Kids Say and Do

A Constructive Response to Aggression

When I was a kid, a bunch of my friends and I were goofing off after high school, and we went over to a public tennis club. We were hiding behind some bushes near a court and were throwing clods of dirt at the players, who were adults. Two of them snuck around the bushes and took us by surprise. Instead of yelling at us, they said, "We don't have any high school players for our tournament and we need some. Come on around and let's see what you guys can do instead of just throwing dirt." None of us had played before, as we thought it was a wealthy person's game. But we all gave it a try, all became members of the club (for $1 each), and we all became lifelong tennis players. It was all in how those two men decided to respond to a bunch of hooligans.

Video Game Technology and Aggression

Many towns have recently suffered deadly shootings by students in their schools, including the 13 murders committed by Eric Harris and Dylan Klebold at Columbine High School. Is it just coincidence that these two boys, like boys who committed violent shootings in other schools, liked to play the video game Doom? One of the Columbine boys customized the Doom game so that it featured two shooters, extra weapons, and defenseless victims—features all too similar to the actual shooting scenario.

Exposure to violent video games does increase viewers' aggression and violence. The more viewers are exposed to violent video games, the more violence they display; this is true for girls as well as boys and for children as well as teenagers and young adults (Anderson & Bushman, 2001). Exposure to violent video games does more than just stir viewers to violence. It also leads viewers to think more aggressively, feel more aggressively, and experience heightened arousal. Exposure also decreases helping and prosocial behavior.

Why? What role does repeated exposure to violent video games (even violent cartoons) play in the forging of a violence-prone personality whereby students become significantly less helpful and significantly more aggressive? Exposure to violence changes how students think. Repeated exposure gives viewers aggressive social expectations (others will be aggressive, not cooperative) and aggressive behavioral scripts (when insulted, one retaliates). Students who take these aggressive social expectations and behavioral scripts into the schools will be more aggressive and less helpful (Anderson, 1983; Anderson & Dill, 2000).

Bullying

Conflicts are commonplace in peer interactions. Sometimes, however, students add a second layer on top of their disagreements in the form of taunts, threats, and acts of aggression and social exclusion. These are acts of harassment and bullying, and they routinely cause emotional stress in those who are subjected to them, as they experience emotions such as anger, anxiety, distress, rejection, and loneliness.

Bullying is a distinct form of aggression. It features three defining characteristics (Salmivalli, Peets, & Hodges, 2010):

- It intends to harm and socially dominate another.
- It is repeated over time.
- It features a power or strength differential between aggressor and victim.

Like other types of aggression (instrumental, hostile), **bullying** involves a physical, verbal, or psychological attack on another, and these attacks (e.g., hitting, pushing, name-calling, uttering threats, socially excluding others) are intended to intimidate and cause fear, distress, or harm to the victim (Olweus, 1993).

To be considered bullying, the aggression must be unprovoked. It does not flow out of negative emotion, like anger, and instead is unprovoked and persistent or recurring. It always involves an unequal distribution of power, as the bully seeks social dominance over another who is perceived to be weaker. Indeed, the main reason to bully is a need to gain control or dominance over another (Kaiser & Rasminsky, 2003). While the most common manifestation of bullying is a verbal attack, bullies inflict harm and exert social dominance in a wide variety of ways, as they hit, shove, slap, name-call, insult, tease, threaten, socially exclude, make sexual comments, start rumors, damage the other's social status, and so forth. New technologies such as cell phones and Internet Web pages have expanded bullying into cyberbullying, as some students harm others through emails, chat rooms, video images, and Web sites (Kowalski, Limber, & Agatston, 2007).

Bullying is a developmental problem for both bully and victim. Victims of bullying are more likely than nonvictims to become anxious and insecure, lonely, depressed, and to perform worse in school—including lower grades and higher absences (Gladstone, Parker, & Malhi, 2006; Hanish & Guerra, 2002; Hawker & Boulton, 2000; Juvonen & Graham, 2001; Kochenderfer & Ladd, 1996; Nishina et al., 2006; Schwartz et al., 2006). Bullies might not appear to suffer in the moment, but they do show severe later developmental difficulties, including dropping out of school, a high likelihood of criminal conviction, substance abuse problems, psychiatric problems such as depression and suicidal ideation, and difficulty in romantic relationships (Hourbe et al., 2006; Kaiser & Rasminsky, 2003; Klomek et al., 2008; Pepler et al., 2006; Sourander et al., 2006).

From these research findings, it is clear that both bullies and victims are at risk of developmental difficulties. It is also worth noting that this at-risk status applies to many students, as roughly one-quarter of all students report being involved in bullying (either as bully or as bullied; Seals & Young, 2003), though more males are involved than are females (Nansel et al., 2001). If participants include bystanders, then the number of students involved in bullying zooms to about 90% (Gini et al., 2008). Bystanders are not unaffected by what they see, as their inaction and even laughter provide a reinforcing social environment for the bully. Their inaction also tends to induce feelings of guilt and helplessness, as they are afraid to report incidences of bullying so as not to be bullied themselves or to be labeled a snitch.

bullying An unprovoked physical, verbal, or psychological attack on a peer that is intended to harm, repeated over time, and involves a power differential between bully and victim.

What Makes a Bully? Bullying arises out of one part personality, one part development, and one part social context. In terms of individual characteristics, bullies lack empathy (Endresen & Olweus, 2002). In fact, a lack of empathy is both a cause and a consequence of bullying (Stavrinides, Georgiou, & Theofanous, 2010), as nonempathic students are more likely to bully and bullies fail to develop a capacity for empathy. Bullies are not socially incompetent, however, as they often show high social intelligence (Kaukiainen et al., 1999) and are routinely more well liked by their peers than are their victims (Alsaker & Nagele, 2008). What bullies show is low empathy and a high need for social dominance and peer admiration. Developmentally, bullying tends to peak in early adolescence, making bullying a key issue in middle school. It is also clear that bullies do not "grow out of it," as who is a bully is highly stable throughout childhood and adolescence. In terms of social context, a lack of social support—from both peers and adults—is associated with bullying, as students who are disconnected from teachers, peers, and others are more likely to bully. Students who attend schools with high crime rates are more likely to bully, but the reason is because they are less likely to benefit from a network of supportive social relationships (Nansel et al., 2001).

What Makes a Victim? Victims of bullying—students who report being bullied two or three times per month—cannot be predicted by physical characteristics, such as weight, clothing, and wearing eyeglasses. Instead, the best predictor of who is bullied is the student's difficulty in making new friends, thereby leaving the student socially isolated without a protective social network to defend against bullies (Nansel et al., 2001). Socially withdrawn, shy, and inhibited students are the prime targets of bullies (Juvonen, Graham, & Schuster, 2003). Hence, bullies do not target all their classmates but, rather, select those victims who are perceived to be easy targets. Somewhat surprisingly, when students are asked what makes a victim, they commonly say that the victims brought the bullying on themselves—that is, the victims themselves are to blame or partly to blame (Oliver, Hoover, & Hazler, 1994).

How Can Teachers and Schools Stop Bullying? Regrettably, most school-based interventions to counter bullying produce no positive effects (Merrell et al., 2008). What is clear, however, is that a rather strong negative relationship exists between bullying and empathy, suggesting that low a level of empathy is a risk factor for future bullying (Jolliffe & Farrington, 2006). Some researchers claim that high empathy inhibits students from harming others (Zhou et al., 2002). Based on this reasoning, many educators (e.g., school psychologists) consider the development of empathy to be an essential component for intervention programs.

Given that it is difficult to stop a bully (when supervising adults are not present), students sometimes ask rather directly for help. Indeed, probably all victims, when harassed by peers, face a dilemma of whether to ask the teacher for help. Teacher-provided assistance may be helpful, and perhaps it is necessary to cope with the harassment. However, in asking the teacher for help, the student might experience social costs, as students are generally expected (rightly or wrongly) to resolve peer conflicts on their own. So, three options exist when students ask the teacher for help (Newman, 2008), one of which is adaptive (seeking help when it is necessary) and two of which are not (seeking help when it is unnecessary, not seeking help when it is necessary).

Just as bullies lack empathy, victims lack social allies and social coping skills to deter and defend against social aggression. Children and adolescents need to develop skills to defend themselves, such as how to resolve conflicts, how to assert one's rights (e.g., when one child takes the possession of another). Friends are also very important, as they can provide help and support, both directly in the bullying episode and indirectly in contributing positively to the victim's social reputation, status, or popularity. But help from a teacher is unique in that the teacher has greater status and power than the bully and can therefore balance the unequal power that exists between bully and victim. The two most effective ways that teachers can help is by not being overly protective but, rather, (1) helping the victim learn effective coping strategies and (2) providing a learning environment in which all students are supported and safe—psychologically, emotionally, and physically. As to helping students learn more effective coping strategies, developing and role-playing assertiveness skills is especially effective. Victims who react assertively to a bullying experience significantly reduce the likelihood of being victimized in the future (Hazler, 1996; Rigby, 2002; Roberts & Coursol, 1996). The nearby Taking It to the Classroom box offers additional ways that teachers can intervene.

In this same spirit, the most effective way the school at large can help is to communicate and enforce a school culture in which bullying and coercive behavior more generally are simply not tolerated (Clarke & Kiselica, 1997). Acknowledging that bullying occurs and communicating the school's commitment that it will not be tolerated is a key step. Some research suggests that schoolwide antibullying intervention programs that aim to change the social norms of student-to-student conduct and focus on prevention and emotional safety are the most effective approaches (Salmivallie, Kaukiainen, & Voeten, 2005).

Taking It to the Classroom

Classroom Intervention Strategies to Stop Bullying

1. Establish clear rules against bullying, defining what bullying is and making clear that it will not be tolerated.

2. Model desirable behaviors. To help victims, model what an assertive coping response to a bully would be (perhaps practicing these skills through role playing). To help bullies, illustrate what prosocial behavior is and that it is expected.

3. Foster a caring peer culture and a climate of emotional safety by enacting, for instance, greater opportunities for collaborative learning and volunteer or helping opportunities.

4. Hold regular (e.g., weekly) discussions with students to review or even revise classroom rules and to discuss the classroom climate in terms of what is working and what is not working.

5. Help students understand what bullying is, and also what successful interaction with peers is.

6. Tell students that they are never alone against a bully and who is there to help (e.g., teacher, support group of students).

REFLECTION FOR ACTION

The Event

Ms. Hernandez looks at the photograph shown at the beginning of this chapter. She wants to enrich her students' social development, and she wants to build a strong sense of community within her classroom. She wants to see her students trusting each other, forming friendships, sharing, helping, and cooperating with one another; and she wants to defuse conflicts and keep disrespect, put-downs, and acts of aggression out of her classroom.

Reflection RIDE

Where do positive social-developmental outcomes such as trust, moral development, and social competence come from? Where do negative social-developmental outcomes such as mistrust and aggression come from? How can Ms. Hernandez help her students develop socially? What might she do?

What Theoretical/Conceptual Information Might Assist in Interpreting and Remedying This Situation? Consider the following:

High-Quality Relationships

To what extent does positive social development grow out of having access to high-quality relationships? If she provided greater attunement, relatedness, supportiveness, and gentle discipline, would her students develop social competencies?

Ethic of Care

How can she help her students expand their narrow circle of care that includes only themselves and their best friends to a wider circle that includes care for all class members?

Social Competence

Should Ms. Hernandez concentrate her attention on those classroom situations that involve conflict, aggression, and bullying? What skills do her students need to handle frustrating and harassing interactions, and how can she help them develop the skill to resolve their differences amicably? How can she make empathy and helping staples in her classroom?

Information Gathering RIDE

In what ways do Ms. Hernandez's students express their positive social development? In what ways do they express their negative social development? She will need to collect data on the following:

- How frequently her students engage in behaviors such as trusting each other, forming friendships, sharing, helping, cooperating, disrespecting, and aggressing
- The quality of her relationship with students
- Her students' existing ethic of care
- Her students' existing social competencies, such as empathy, perspective taking, and emotion regulation capacities
- The level of bullying that occurs

To collect these data, she might ask her students to complete a questionnaire. Perhaps a teacher's aide, parent volunteer, or colleague can make observational ratings for her.

A conversation with colleagues and master teachers might also shed light on these issues. She might ask her colleagues for suggestions on how to create a caring classroom community. She might also read articles and books about specific topics, such as on empathy development or aggression or bullying. Several videotapes on social development exist, and these videotapes frequently address the question of how to help students develop socially.

Decision Making RIDE

Ms. Hernandez needs to decide whether her students simply lack social-developmental resources, such as trust and care for others, or whether the problem is deeper in that they not only lack these resources but also possess liabilities, such as tendencies toward aggression and little capacity to regulate negative emotions like anger. She needs to decide whether she has a high-quality relationship with her students and how possible it will be to improve on that relationship. She needs to determine how widely or how narrowly her students extend their circle of care—to include only best friends or to include all classmates? She also needs to decide whether she has the time, skill, and access to the resources she will need to teach her students social skills in the same way she teaches her other lessons—with high expectations, modeling, explaining, and practice.

Evaluation RIDE

Ms. Hernandez needs to evaluate the quality of the relationships she provides to her students, the extent of her students' circle of care, and the extent of her students' positive and negative social-developmental outcomes. She needs to evaluate how important her relationship to students is—does she notice any increase in their sociability and any decrease in their aggressiveness when she provides attunement, relatedness, supportiveness, and gentle discipline? She needs to evaluate whether her students relate positively to classmates inside their circle of care but negatively to those outside their circle of care. She needs to evaluate whether the improved social competencies she sees in her students reflect committed compliance or only situational compliance.

Further Practice: Your Turn

Here is a second event for consideration and reflection. In doing so, implement the process of reflection, information gathering, decision making, and evaluation.

The Event

Mr. Cooper is a tenth-grade teacher. For the most part, today has been a good day. His students are learning, and most are actively engaged in the lesson. The classroom calm suddenly comes to a screeching halt as a fight breaks out between two boys. One wrote an insulting remark on the other's desk, and the second boy—after reading it—jumped out of his seat and onto the other boy. Insults and fists start flying.

What might this teacher do? Could these events have been prevented? Now that these behaviors have occurred, how might Mr. Cooper best cope with the aggression? What would you recommend?

SUMMARY

- **What characterizes a high-quality student–teacher relationship?**

  Relationships are the soil in which social development grows. Therefore, the better the quality of the relationship between student and teacher, the more positive the student's social development is likely to be. Four qualities define a high-quality relationship—namely, teacher-provided attunement, relatedness, supportiveness, and gentle discipline.

- **What are mental models, and why are they important to social development?**

  Mental models are students' enduring beliefs and expectations about what they are like (Am I a good person?) and what other people are like (Can others be trusted?). These beliefs reflect how other people have treated the student in the past, as represented by the three attachment styles of secure, resistant, and avoidant. Secure attachment reflects high trust in self and others and is associated with positive social-developmental outcomes, such as academic success, popularity, emotion regulation, and prosocial behavior. Resistant and avoidant attachments reflect mistrust in others and are associated with poor social-developmental outcomes.

- **How can teachers nurture psychosocial development, especially students' initiative, competence, and identity?**

  According to Erikson's model, children develop initiative, competence, and identity when teachers find ways to encourage and support these developmental resources. Initiative is the use of surplus energy to plan and constructively carry out a task, and preschool teachers can nurture initiative by encouraging exploration even while communicating limits. Competence is the self-assurance that one can successfully accomplish culturally valued tasks, and elementary school teachers can nurture competence by offering developmentally appropriate challenges, positive feedback, and discussions about the pleasure of a job well done. Identity is the sense of being a distinct and productive individual within the larger social framework. Middle school and high school teachers can nurture identity by helping students become aware of and explore possible societal roles, such as various occupations.

- **What are the stages of moral development?**

  Moral development concerns judgments about what is right or wrong as well as reasons why one action is right and another is wrong. At a preconventional level, children's moral reasoning is immature and reflects self-interest. At the conventional level, moral reasoning follows social conventions—what is right is what others approve of. At the postconventional level, adolescents' moral reasoning reflects self-chosen principles. Moral development also reflects one's ethic of care. Preconventional children care for the self; conventional children and adolescents extend care to include their in-group; and postconventional adolescents extend their ethic of care to include all people.

- **How does social competence develop, and how can teachers nurture students' prosocial behavior?**

  Social competence reflects how skilled children and adolescents are at managing the negative emotions they experience during social conflicts so as to produce amicable outcomes. Teachers can promote social competence by using gentle discipline strategies, such as reasoning, and by emphasizing interpersonal skills, such as empathy.

- **How does aggression develop, and how can teachers help students resolve conflict amicably?**

  Aggression is any intentional behavior that is designed to harm another person or group physically or psychologically. There are two types: instrumental and hostile. With instrumental aggression, which is strategic behavior to obtain a desired object, teachers can help students learn more effective and prosocial ways of getting what they want. With hostile aggression, which is impulsive behavior intended to inflict harm, prevention works better than remediation.

● **What makes a bully? What makes a victim? Do antibullying interventions work?**

Students who bully lack an empathic concern for others, though they are often socially competent. They also lack a network of socially supportive relationships. The best predictor of who will be a victim is difficulty in making new friends, a social shortcoming that leaves victims as easy targets for bullies, especially if those victims are socially withdrawn, shy, or inhibited. The two most effective ways that teachers can counter bullying is to help victims learn effective coping strategies, such as being assertive, and providing a learning environment that communicates and enforces a culture in which bullying is simply not tolerated to the point that antibullying social norms develop.

● **How do students' special needs interfere with their social development?**

All students benefit when their teachers provide them with high-quality relationships characterized by attunement, relatedness, supportiveness, and gentle discipline. Students with special needs, such as autism or an emotional disorder, often have difficulty contributing their part to a relationship. For this reason, interaction partners sometimes feel less close to students with special needs; therefore, they are less likely to develop high-quality relationships with their teachers and peers. Students with special needs also typically report lower self-esteem than students without special needs.

Key Terms

aggression, p. 136
attachment, p. 115
attunement, p. 112
bullying, p. 139
care, p. 115
committed compliance, p. 131
competence, p. 121
conscience, p. 132
emotion regulation, p. 133

generativity, p. 126
gentle discipline, p. 113
hostile aggression, p. 137
identity, p. 123
initiative, p. 120
instrumental aggression, p. 137
mental models, p. 111
moral development, p. 127
power assertion, p. 131

psychosocial development, p. 119
relatedness, p. 113
relationship, p. 112
self-esteem, p. 116
situational compliance, p. 131
social competence, p. 133
supportiveness, p. 113
trust, p. 115

Exercises

1. *Understanding the Elements of a High-Quality Relationship*

   Identify a teacher who has an excellent interaction style with students. Ask permission to visit this teacher's class and observe the ensuing student–teacher interactions during instruction. Rate this teacher in terms of attunement, relatedness, supportiveness, and gentle discipline. Do those four factors explain why this teacher has such a positive and constructive relationship with students? Repeat the same exercise with a teacher who has a poor interaction style with students. Does the absence of those four factors explain why the second teacher does not have a positive and constructive relationship with students?

2. *Providing a High-Quality Relationship of Your Own*

   Recall a recent interaction you had with someone in which you were in the role of a teacher, such as trying to show a friend how to do something. Recall how that interaction went and how much or how little your friend benefited from your teaching. Think about what role your provision of attunement, relatedness, supportiveness, and gentle discipline played in helping your friend learn. The next time you have another teaching chance, intentionally try to provide high attunement, relatedness, supportiveness, and gentle discipline and notice what changes, if any, occur in the learner.

3. *Assessing Attunement*

   How attuned are you to a student? Find a questionnaire (or construct a brief one of your own) that assesses a student's self-perceptions during a learning activity (e.g., It was fun, I was nervous, I felt competent). After conducting a learning actively with another person, ask the other person to complete the questionnaire. Also, independently complete the same questionnaire yourself and try to answer each question the way you think the other person answered it. Place the two completed questionnaires side by side, then compare how much the answers overlapped (high attunement) or diverged (low attunement).

4. *Conducting an Eriksonian Life Review*

Interview a student or a teacher by conducting an Eriksonian life review. A life review is a process in which the person looks back on the developmental influences and milestones that have shaped his or her life. Ask the following questions related to that person's trust, initiative, competence, and identity:

- Who were the most important people who contributed to or interfered with your development?
- In general, would you say that you trust or mistrust other people?
- What memories come to mind when you think about trusting or mistrusting others?
- Recall doing new things, such as starting school or traveling by yourself. As you recall these events, did you show mostly initiative or mostly inhibition? Why?
- Recall a vivid experience in which you received negative feedback, such as an academic failure. How did you react in terms of effort and perseverance? Did you work harder, or did you give up and do something else?

Lesson Plans

The lesson plans on these pages are excerpts from more complete plans. They are included in this form to provide you with practice in examining a lesson from the perspective of the content of this chapter. The complete lesson plans are available at www.wiley.com/college/odonnell. For both lesson plans, read the lesson plan excerpt and respond to the questions related to social development in the Ask Yourself! section at the end.

Lesson #1: "Mirror Image"

GRADES: 3–8

ESTIMATED COMPLETION TIME: one 45-minute class period

LEARNING AREAS: self-image, respect for self and others

SUBJECT AREAS: Social Studies, ELA

I. OBJECTIVES: Students will be able to:
- Focus on positive aspects of others
- Consider others' views of them
- Reflect on how they view themselves

II. MATERIALS:
- Paper labeled with student's name
- Self-image chart (pre-made or student-created as follows):

How I see myself	How others see me
Things I was surprised to learn	Things I was expecting

III. PROCEDURE:

1. Students will identify their "passing partner" whom they will pass to through the entire exercise.

It would be helpful for students to be in a circle as their paper needs to rotate through the entire class, but not entirely necessary.

2. Have students fill in the first square on their chart, "How I see myself."

3. Students will pass their paper to their passing partner once, and with the paper they currently have they will identify one positive trait about this person.

Let students know that while their trait **must** *be positive, it can be as simple as "they have very neat handwriting."*

- Who are you? List any five words or phrases that describe who you are in terms of occupation and beliefs.
- Last, looking back, how satisfied versus dissatisfied are you with your life? Have other people mostly supported your development, or have they mostly frustrated and thwarted it?

5. *Who Am I?*

On a single piece of paper, make a list from 1 through 20 down the left-hand side of the page. At the top of the page, write the question, Who am I? Take about 10 minutes to generate 20 different answers to this single question. Use single words, phrases, or complete sentences. After you are done, rate your responses in terms of realism, abstraction, and differentiation.

Lesson Plans

4. Students will continue to rotate papers, repeating step 3 until they have their own paper back. **Each trait must be original!**

5. Give students time to read their sheet, and then have them fill in the remaining squares on their chart.

6. Have students in a large or small group share, focusing on the following reflection questions:

- What were you surprised to see on your sheet? Did this make you feel good or bad and why?
- Did people not say something about you that you were expecting?

7. Have students do a reflective writing/journal entry about their experience. You can use the share-out questions from above or new questions.

Ask Yourself!

1. Which aspects of a high-quality relationship might this activity promote, and which aspects might it not promote (i.e., attunement, relatedness, supportiveness, and gentle discipline)?

2. How might children's self-concept change as a result of this lesson?

3. Explain why participating in this activity might be expected to enrich students' moral development and social competence.

Lesson Plans

Lesson #2: "In My Neighborhood"

GRADES LEVEL: 7–12

ESTIMATED COMPLETION TIME: eight to ten 50-minute class periods

SUBJECT AREA: Social Studies

I. OVERVIEW: This lesson was originally performed as part of an "urban environment" study. Here it has been written for completion in an urban setting; however, it can easily be adjusted to work in a suburban area. *Note: This task requires inference skills and estimation skills. Not all data found will be 100% accurate, but students con still generate ideas based on their findings.*

II. OBJECTIVES: Students will be able to:

- Become informed about the area that they live in
- Recognize the cause and effect of problems and actions in a neighborhood
- Create informed opinions about why problems in their neighborhood exist
- Create solutions for recognized problems

III. MATERIALS:

- Computers with Internet access
- Neighborhood maps
- Markers
- Chart paper

IV. PROCEDURE:

Day 1:

1. Students recognize a problem in their neighborhood (e.g., there is a lot of graffiti).

2. Students recognize another problem in their neighborhood that they think might be related (e.g., where there is more graffiti, there will be an increase in auto theft).

3. Ask the students: Why do you think these items are related? What predictions can you make about what your research will find?

Day 2:

1. This is "field trip" day. Students will be taken on a walk of about a 3-4 block radius (depending on size, what can be completed in a single or double class period); students will choose which item they can look for on their walk

Lesson Plans

(in this case, graffiti). They will mark on their map every instance of graffiti.

Days 3–5:

1. Students will use the Internet to research the other item they are studying (in this case, auto theft).

2. They will mark on their maps instances of this item in a different color

3. For students who finish researching early, have them create a large version of their map using chart paper for display

Days 5–10:

1. Students will analyze their results:
   - *Was there a connection between the two things?*
   - *Do you think that these two items are actually related or could it have been coincidence? (For older students, you can bring in the Roe Effect Theory)*

2. Imagine that these items are related: Which item would it be easier to fix and why?

3. Have students begin an action plan to fix one of the problems.

V. RESOURCES: Neighborhood maps: http://maps.google.com. Crime statistics: vary based on city; most cities have a "public safety" link from their main, .gov site

Ask Yourself!

1. How would a student's attachment style influence his or her response to this lesson?

2. How might adolescents' sense of identity and self-concept change as a function of participating in this activity?

3. How might you adjust this activity toward the goal of building students' character and conscience (i.e., doing the right thing for the right reason)?

"punishment"   "reward system"

"privileges"
"rules and procedures"
"suspension"   "detention"
"role models"

"**M**ore ideas, please?" asked Allan Duba, director of guidance, as he scribbled another idea on the chalkboard. The principal had appointed him to head a faculty committee whose task was to figure out how to deal with the undesirable behaviors occurring during the middle school lunch periods. Tossing of food ... offensive language ... confrontations between students ... taunting of lunchroom aides—such behaviors were occurring more and more often. It was becoming increasingly difficult for teachers to supervise the lunch period or get students back to their classrooms in an orderly manner.

Behavioral Learning Theory

R I D E Reflection for Action

The problem faced by the committee is not an easy one. What should the committee members recommend? Do you think that punishing the students will work? What kind of punishment might be appropriate? Would it be possible to solve the problem without resorting to punishment? What about ignoring what the students are doing? Will it be difficult to get them to change their behavior?

Guiding Questions

- How do teachers who adhere to behavioral, cognitive, and social-constructivist approaches describe learning?
- What kinds of learning can be described by behavioral learning theory?
- How do different forms of reinforcement affect behavior and performance?
- How can teachers increase the frequency of desirable behaviors and decrease that of undesirable behaviors?
- How can teachers help students learn self-management?
- How can teachers use behavioral learning principles in instruction?
- How might teachers use behavioral learning theory with diverse learners and learners with special needs?
- What are some limitations of behavioral learning theory?

CHAPTER OVERVIEW

In this chapter, we focus on students' behavior. We ask how students learn the behaviors, skills, and self-regulatory abilities they need to function well in school and in life. To understand how students learn such things, we first define learning and explain how it occurs. We then introduce the basic principles of the behavioral approach to learning. These principles serve as a foundation for understanding and discussing the everyday problems that teachers face in trying to increase the frequency of desirable behaviors and decrease that of undesirable behaviors. We also describe the types of instruction that have been inspired by behavioral learning principles.

Explaining Learning

On an early October morning, Mrs. Johnson, a middle school teacher, walks down the hall to her first class of the day. She enjoys first period and her students appear to be learning, but she worries about how they behave toward one another. Too often they are inconsiderate, even rude. She has talked to her students about this, but the put-downs and insults keep coming back like weeds in a garden. So today, she has invited the school psychologist to visit her classroom, observe the students' behavior, and offer some recommendations to improve the situation.

The bell rings, class begins, and Mrs. Johnson guides her students through the lesson. As she teaches, the psychologist observes and takes notes. Sure enough, episodes of disrespectful behavior flare up.

At lunch, Mrs. Johnson meets with the psychologist to discuss the students' behavior. She speaks bluntly. She wants to see more behaviors such as supporting, encouraging, sharing, and helping, and fewer behaviors such as insults, put-downs, name-calling, and rude gestures. She and the psychologist come up with a plan. They decide that she will reward her students each time they display a desirable, prosocial behavior—supporting, encouraging, sharing, or helping. The reward will be the teacher's approval; she will smile warmly, give positive attention, and offer praise for a job well done. To monitor how well the plan is going, the psychologist promises to visit her class regularly.

Two weeks pass, and the pair are again eating lunch together. This time the psychologist shows Mrs. Johnson a number of charts and graphs. One chart shows how often students engage in desirable behaviors, and Mrs. Johnson is happy to see the line on the chart going up. Another chart shows how often students engage in the undesirable behaviors, and she is even happier to see this line going down. Rewarding desirable, prosocial behaviors has worked. The frequency of desirable behaviors increased and that of undesirable behaviors decreased. In addition, Mrs. Johnson says that she enjoys her time with these students even more than before.

The two agree that their goal should now be to find out whether the students can manage their own behavior. If so, Mrs. Johnson will no longer need to provide extensive attention every time she sees students behaving appropriately. It is time to determine whether students' newfound prosocial behavior can produce its own, natural consequences of greater friendship and lessened hostility. To see how well students can regulate themselves, the psychologist promises to return in two weeks and create a new set of charts.

Before we begin, consider the perspective of a school psychologist such as the one who visited Mrs. Johnson's class. School psychologists care deeply about students' misbehaviors and social skill deficits, especially when they interfere with learning and interpersonal relations. School psychologists can achieve their goals through the careful use of behavioral learning techniques (Bergan & Caldwell, 1995).

Behavioral, Cognitive, and Social-Constructivist Theories of Learning

There are numerous theories of learning, and it is important to have a clear understanding of the similarities and differences among them. In this section, we will briefly examine different approaches to learning, focusing on behavioral learning theories. Teachers attempt to create conditions in their classrooms that will promote and facilitate learning. To do this, they must have a theory of learning that guides their decisions about the kinds of learning environments they will create and the kinds of tasks they will assign to students in order to promote learning. Their ideas of what constitutes learning will also influence what they decide to measure in determining whether students have learned what the teacher intends them to learn. This section will also address how individual differences among learners might be viewed from a behavioral learning perspective.

Learning is a process through which relatively permanent changes in behavior or knowledge occur as a result of experience. Through experience, we learn behaviors such as writing our names, driving a car, and teaching a class, and we learn to understand theories of human behavior. In the classroom, teachers provide students with learning experiences. To help students learn particular behaviors and knowledge, teachers need to provide the kinds of experiences that will facilitate these types of learning. Because the kinds of experiences that foster the learning of behaviors are different from those that foster the learning of knowledge, different approaches to learning have emerged.

Contrasting Three Theories of Learning

The broadest definition of learning involves an interaction between the individual and the environment that results in some permanent change in behavior:

$$\text{Environment} \rightarrow \text{Individual} \rightarrow \text{Behavior}$$

The behavior can be covert or overt. Behavioral, cognitive, and social-constructivist or sociocultural theories of learning place different degrees of emphasis on these three components. From a *behavioral viewpoint*, the most important relationship is between the environment and behavior: Changes in the environment will result in changes in behavior. Individual differences are less important to this view of learning because the goal is to produce desirable behaviors or reduce the frequency of undesirable behaviors. From a behavioral viewpoint, individual differences may be seen as reflecting different histories of conditioning, reinforcement, or punishment.

Appendix
Understanding Learning

Many theories have attempted to explain learning (PRAXIS™, I.A.1; INTASC, Principle 2).

learning A relatively permanent change in behavior or knowledge that occurs as a result of experience.

In contrast, from a *cognitive viewpoint*, the individual plays a key role in learning. Two people can perceive the same environment differently, and as a result, the effects of their interactions with their environment on subsequent behavior may vary. For example, two children may watch the same movie; one may be enchanted by it, and the other may respond with fear. Their different reactions reflect not just the stimulus available in the environment (in this case, a movie) but also how that stimulus is understood by each child. Thus, the Environment → Individual relationship is emphasized over the Environment → Behavior relationship.

A *social-constructivist* or *sociocultural viewpoint* stresses the nature of the environment and its relationship to behavior, but this relationship is quite different from that which might be studied from a behavioral standpoint. The environment is not just the physical environment but includes the history of practice and expertise acquired by a community from which an individual might learn by becoming an apprentice in that community. A sociocultural viewpoint is concerned with the influence of the environment on the individual and his or her behavior.

Teachers pay different degrees of attention to characteristics of the environment, efforts to change the environment, the role of individual differences, and the outcomes of interactions between learners and the environment, depending on which of these theories of learning they favor. A teacher whose theory of learning is grounded in cognitive theory will be interested in children's prior experiences and knowledge as well as their individual interpretations of events in the classroom. Another teacher may emphasize a behavioral learning theory and focus on breaking curriculum units down into smaller units to provide opportunities for feedback and reinforcement.

Behavioral learning principles are used in a variety of instructional settings. They are used with children with special needs, in instruction using computer software, and in classroom management. Although cognitive approaches to instruction are more highly valued at present, behavioral learning theory can make useful contributions to classroom practice.

Kinds of Learning That Can Be Explained by Behavioral Learning Theory

Behavioral learning theory focuses on behavior—the kinds of behaviors that were the concern of Mrs. Johnson and the school psychologist. It also focuses on skills and self-regulatory capacities, as shown in Figure 5.1. Behaviors represent situationally appropriate and desirable actions, such as completing homework assignments, as well as situationally inappropriate and undesirable actions, such as fighting. Skills represent social skills, such as helping others, as well as motor skills, such as playing a musical instrument. Self-regulation represents such actions as goal setting, self-instruction, self-monitoring, self-evaluation, and self-consequences. Although self-regulatory behavior is also cognitive in nature, we focus here on its behavioral aspects. Behavioral learning theory does not focus on mental knowledge, such as learning information, using memory, understanding concepts, and creating meaning.

What all these behaviors, skills, and self-regulatory abilities have in common is that they represent voluntary, intentional, and purposive ways of trying to adapt to one's environment. Learning these behaviors, skills, and self-regulatory abilities enables one to gain rewards and favorable outcomes (e.g., praise, admiration) and avoid punishers and unfavorable outcomes

Figure 5.1 The Three Kinds of Learning Explained by Behavioral Learning Theory

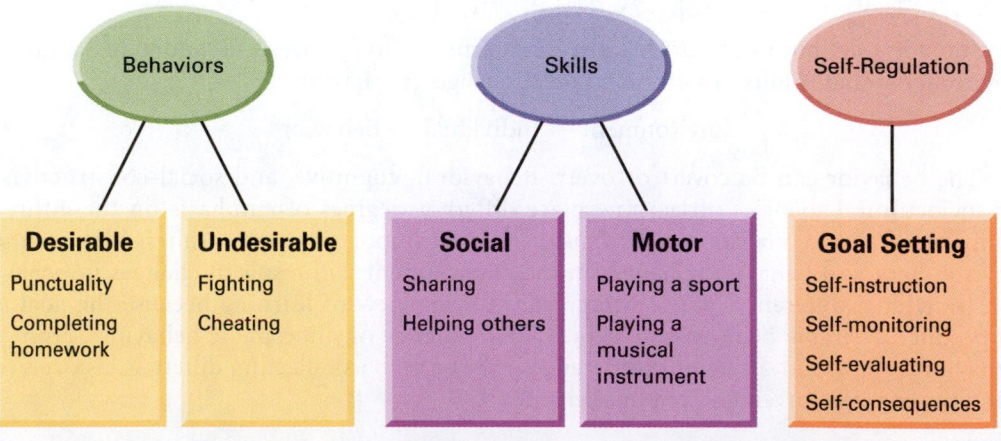

Behaviors		Skills		Self-Regulation
Desirable	**Undesirable**	**Social**	**Motor**	**Goal Setting**
Punctuality	Fighting	Sharing	Playing a sport	Self-instruction
Completing homework	Cheating	Helping others	Playing a musical instrument	Self-monitoring
				Self-evaluating
				Self-consequences

(e.g., criticism, being laughed at). That is, learning behaviors, skills, and self-regulation help promote students' personal competence, social welfare, and capacity to carry out activities on their own.

Principles of Behavioral Learning Theory

There are several types of behavioral learning theories, each associated with a set of specific principles. Many of these principles can be useful in the classroom.

Types of Behavioral Learning Theories

Early behavioral theorists proposed that learning occurs through a process of **contiguity**—that is, learning is the result of events occurring at the same time. For example, when you enter a store, you may hear a pinging noise. You soon learn to expect that such a noise will occur whenever you enter that store. The two events occur at the same time, and you learn that they are associated with each other.

The best-known contiguity theory is **classical conditioning**, which involves the pairing of a stimulus and a response. Some stimuli—for example, a loud noise—produce an automatic physiological response, such as a startle reflex. The stimulus leads to the response without any prior learning. The provocative stimulus (loud noise) and consequent response (startle reflex) are termed the **unconditioned stimulus (UCS)** and the **unconditioned response (UCR)**. The term *unconditioned* communicates that the student learns to pair the stimulus and response in a way that is automatic or involuntary.

It was the Russian physiologist Ivan Pavlov who discovered the phenomenon of classical conditioning. He was conducting research on the physiology of digestion. A dog in his laboratory salivated when food was presented to him. The drooling response was automatic. Pavlov began to ring a bell whenever food was presented to the dog, a contiguous pairing of events. Initially, the sound of the bell elicited no response from the dog. Gradually, the dog came to associate the sound of the bell with the food, an unconditioned stimulus (food) that produced an unconditioned response (drooling). The dog soon learned to drool at the sound of the bell. Through experience, the bell had become a **conditioned stimulus (CS).** The once-neutral stimulus (NS) of the bell gained the capacity to produce a **conditioned response (CR)** (drooling) as a result of the contiguous pairing of the two (Figure 5.2).

Students may have acquired certain responses through a process of classical conditioning. Most often, the behaviors that are learned are those that were once associated with a strong emotional response. For example, a teacher may pick up a note passed by one eighth-grade student to another and read it aloud to the class. The student whose note is read may experience embarrassment and humiliation. In such circumstances, the student's response is uncontrolled. In future encounters with this teacher, the student may experience embarrassment and withdrawal when the teacher asks for his or her homework assignments. Previously, the request for the homework would not have produced a response of embarrassment.

Associationist theories also depend on the principle of contiguity. When children memorize number facts (e.g., $4 \times 4 = 16$) by rote, they may be simply associating the words. For example, young children may learn songs by simple association of words without perhaps pronouncing the words as intended or without comprehending what they mean. Frequent pairings of stimuli and responses result in a stronger association between them. In theories of learning that depend on contiguity as the mechanism by which learning occurs, the learner is passive. Events occur, and because they occur together, the learner forms an association between them. The learner does not act on the environment. Instead, the learner rather passively and automatically learns *what goes with what* or what classroom events co-occur. Mrs. Johnson always smiles, the music room is always too hot, chalk on the chalkboard squeaks, and so forth.

contiguity A condition in which two events occur at the same time.

classical conditioning The association of automatic responses with new stimuli.

unconditioned stimulus (UCS) A stimulus that, without prior learning, produces an automatic physiological response.

unconditioned response (UCR) A behavior that is produced in response to a stimulus without prior learning. It is typically an automatic physiological response.

conditioned stimulus (CS) A stimulus that, with experience, produces a learned or acquired response.

conditioned response (CR) A response that is linked to a particular stimulus through conditioning by being paired with the stimulus.

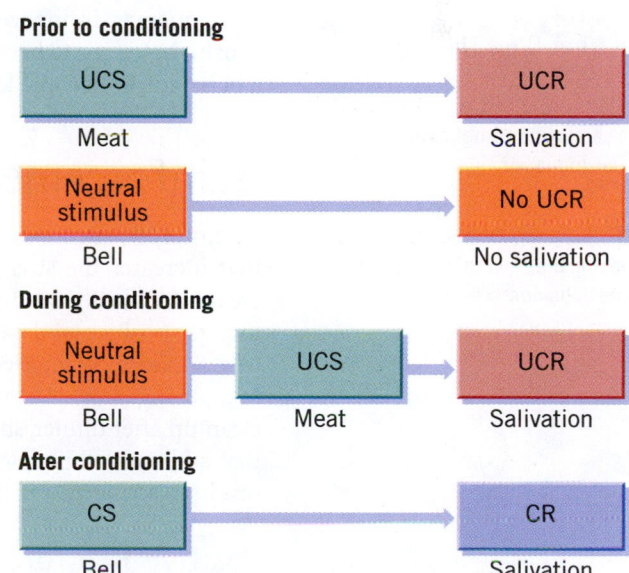

Figure 5.2 A Normal Distribution of IQ Scores
Source: Westen, D. (2002). *Psychology: Brain, Behavior, & Culture* (3rd ed.). Hoboken, NJ: John Wiley and Sons, p. 163.

operant learning Actions by a learner, the consequences of which influence further behavior.

An alternative theory of behavioral learning assumes a more active learner. In **operant learning**, the learner acts, or *operates*, on the environment, and depending on what happens as a result, the likelihood of the learner's repeating the behavior will either increase or decrease.

Operant Learning Theory

At recess, José and his friends are playing baseball. It is José's turn to bat. He grabs the bat and gets ready for the first pitch. The bat is rather heavy, so he holds his hands about a foot apart. Here comes the first pitch. He swings and misses. Strike one. That did not work, so he moves his hands closer together. Here comes the second pitch. He swings and misses. Strike two.

Eager to make contact with the ball, José moves his hands together. Here comes the third pitch. He swings, and "smack," he hits the ball right over the third baseman's head and runs happily to first base. While standing on the base, he decides that holding his hands apart is no good, whereas holding them together is good. When it is his turn to bat again, José will hold his hands close together.

Most behaviors are learned. We learn how to write our names, ride a bicycle, wait for our turn in line, raise our hand to ask a question, study for a test, and operate a Bunsen burner in chemistry lab. The process through which we learn such behaviors follows a set of principles. Behaviorists such as John B. Watson and B. F. Skinner focused on the objective data of behavior. Skinner's approach was to try to identify relationships between elements of the environment that would predict behavior (Skinner, 1950). His approach has often been described as a *black box* theory, with information from the environment going in to the individual, who then behaves. But nothing could be said about what occurred in the *black box* of the individual. This approach is in sharp contrast to cognitive approaches, which are very interested in what occurs in the individual as he or she receives and actively processes information from the environment.

law of effect The phenomenon in which behavior that produces good effects tends to become more frequent, while behavior that produces bad effects tends to become less frequent.

The Law of Effect   The law of effect was originally proposed by E. L. Thorndike (1913). According to the **law of effect**, behaviors that have good effects tend to become more frequent, whereas behaviors that have bad effects tend to become less frequent. Thus, if a child pets a dog and that petting produces good effects, such as tail wagging and companionship, the child will pet the dog more often. If petting the dog produces bad effects, such as growls and barking, the child will pet the dog less often. The point of the law of effect is that behavior is highly influenced by the effects that follow it.

consequences The good or bad effects that follow a person's behavior.

Consequences   **Consequences** are the good or bad effects that follow a person's behavior. They are important to learning because they influence the future frequency of the behavior. Good consequences influence the person to engage in the behavior more often, whereas bad consequences influence the person to engage in the behavior less often. Consequences that cause a behavior to become more frequent are called *reinforcers*, and consequences that cause a behavior to become less frequent are called *punishers*.

> **What Does This Mean to Me?**
> What kinds of events have you found to be reinforcing or punitive?

Reinforcement

reinforcer A consequence of behavior that increases or strengthens behavior.

A **reinforcer**, such as a sticker, a candy bar, or an approving smile, is an environmental event that increases the strength of a behavior. Reinforcers are consequences of behavior that increase the likelihood that the behavior will be performed again. There are two types of reinforcers: positive and negative. A positive reinforcer can involve adding something pleasant to a situation (e.g., a gold star on a homework paper) or removing something unpleasant (e.g., being allowed to rejoin classmates after a time-out). If John's mother wants him to help clean up after dinner, she might either praise him when he helps clean up (a positive reinforcer that adds something pleasant) or stop nagging him to help clean up (a negative reinforcer that results in an increase in the desired behavior because the unpleasant stimulus has been removed).

Positive Reinforcers to Strengthen Behaviors

positive reinforcer Any environmental event that, when given, increases the frequency of a behavior.

A **positive reinforcer** is any environmental event that, when given, increases the frequency of a behavior. In terms of the law of effect, a positive reinforcer follows the performance of a behavior and increases the probability that the behavior will be performed again. As an example, a teacher might notice that a student used proper punctuation in an essay and, therefore, places a happy-face sticker on the paper. The giving of the sticker acts as a positive reinforcer if it increases the student's use of proper punctuation in the future. Other common positive reinforcers in the classroom include praise, privileges, tokens, attention, high grades, scholarships, honors, certificates, trophies, prizes, food, awards, money, smiles, public recognition, and positive feedback. When teachers give students a special privilege for being quiet during study time and when schools place students' names on the honor roll for making good grades, they are reinforcing desirable behaviors (being quiet, making high grades) by making sure that those behaviors produce good effects that will strengthen them.

(Dynamic Graphics, Inc./Creatas)

Many times, a learner may use the opportunity to engage in a preferred activity as reinforcement for engaging in a less preferred activity. For example, a person may need to tidy his or her apartment (more preferred activity) and study for an exam (less preferred activity). The individual studies first and then "rewards" himself or herself by engaging in the more preferred activity. This is known as the **Premack principle** (Premack, 1959).

Undesirable behaviors can also be reinforced, and their frequency of occurrence can increase as a result. As a young child, the nephew of one of the authors was very good at imitating people. A next-door neighbor had a very high-pitched voice, and the boy would imitate him perfectly. His parents laughed when he did this, and he continued to imitate this individual until one day he replied to the neighbor using the same high-pitched voice. His parents were, of course, quite embarrassed. The neighbor thought the boy was making fun of him and, as a result, was angry. The boy's parents' laughter had served to reinforce the child's behavior.

Teachers often find that students have been reinforced previously for negative behaviors. Some children, for example, may have been reinforced by other students' approval for disobeying a teacher. It can be very difficult to change behaviors such as these.

Negative Reinforcers to Strengthen Behaviors

A **negative reinforcer** is any environmental event that, when removed, increases the frequency of a behavior. In terms of the law of effect, a negative reinforcer involves the removal of unpleasant events or experiences after a desired behavior has been performed. As an example, a teacher might stare at a student until the student begins working on an assignment. If the student wants the teacher to stop staring at her, she must increase her on-task behavior. The teacher's staring is an unpleasant event, and the teacher stops staring after the student gets to work on the assignment. What is being reinforced is the student's on-task behavior. Other common negative reinforcers in the classroom include nagging, deadlines, surveillance, threats, negative evaluations, criticizing, and yelling. When teachers stop pleading for students to answer their questions, they are attempting to increase (reinforce) the desirable behavior (answering questions) by removing the negative event (pleading).

Why Do Rewards Encourage Approach Behavior? A **reward** is anything given in return for another person's service or achievement (Craighead, Kazdin, & Mahoney, 1981). Thus, when a teacher promises students a prize if they will participate more or smiles when students perform well, he or she is giving them an extrinsic reward. Extrinsic rewards are often confused with positive reinforcers, which are defined by their effects on behavior. A focus on rewards highlights the instructional practice of soliciting students' participation or acknowledging their achievement, regardless of whether those rewards actually reinforce behavior. A reward functions as a reinforcer only when the learner values it. Sometimes teachers offer rewards that students do not value; such rewards do not increase the

---

A teacher's affection and approval can positively reinforce and strengthen a student's desirable behavior, such as reading.

Premack principle Using a more-preferred activity as a reward for doing a less-preferred activity.

RIDE Why might it be difficult for the committee to change the students' behavior?

negative reinforcer Any environmental event that, when removed, increases the frequency of a behavior.

reward Anything given in return for another person's service or achievement.

(© Media Bakery)

Receiving an extrinsic reward such as a trophy can be very reinforcing to students.

frequency of the desired behavior. For example, a teacher may praise a child publicly for his or her work, but the child may be embarrassed by the attention. The effect of the praise is punitive rather than reinforcing.

When they see a sticker attached to their latest homework effort, most children glow with pleasure. When offered the chance to obtain a special privilege, most adolescents perk up with interest. Why? Why do rewards give life to positive emotion and elicit approach behavior or engagement? Like all human beings, students are sensitive to signals of gain and pleasure. The physiological mechanism that makes students sensitive to rewards is release of the neurotransmitter dopamine (Mirenowicz & Schultz, 1994; Montague, Dayan, & Sejnowski, 1996), which triggers the behavioral activation system (BAS; Gray, 1990). Increased activity in the BAS generates positive feelings, such as hope and interest. It also triggers approach behavior, because students will move toward signals of personal gain. Knowing that one will receive a reward for completing a homework sheet may generate positive feelings of anticipation.

The mental event that activates the BAS is the perception that a situation is unfolding in a way that is better than expected (Montague et al., 1996). For instance, expected and predicted classroom situations have little effect on students' BAS. However, when a situation signals that things are taking an unexpected turn for the better, dopamine release and BAS activity increase. Unexpectedly receiving a sticker and becoming aware that one might obtain a special privilege are two examples of situations that have taken a turn for the better. In short, extrinsic rewards encourage approach behavior because they signal that personal gain is imminent (Mirenowicz & Schultz, 1994).

Why Are Extrinsic Rewards Prevalent in Schools?

School personnel take note as students display emotional and behavioral responses to extrinsic rewards. To capitalize on such responses, they often identify some desired target behavior and find a way to create a connection between the behavior and the reward. From a motivational (as opposed to behavioral) perspective, teachers use rewards to bolster students' otherwise low motivation (Boggiano et al., 1987). The idea is as follows: If the task itself cannot generate enough motivation for students to engage in it, what is needed is some added external gain that can give students the motivation they lack. For instance, if a poetry assignment fails to motivate students to read, perhaps bonus points for doing the assignment will provide the needed motivation. Hence, extrinsic rewards can have motivational value.

Do extrinsic rewards work? It is generally agreed that extrinsic rewards do encourage targeted behaviors, at least when teachers provide them in a sincere and contingent way (Baldwin & Baldwin, 1986; Skinner, 1953). Extrinsic rewards impose a structure on classroom behaviors by encouraging compliance and on-task behavior as well as countering random and off-task behavior. When extrinsic rewards are no longer offered in exchange for desired behaviors, however, their effectiveness declines and the once-contingent behavior quickly returns to its previous level.

> **How Can I Use This?**
> What alternatives can you think of to motivate behavior without resorting to extrinsic rewards?

Selecting Reinforcers

Not everyone experiences the same consequences in the same way. A teacher may attempt to reinforce a fourth grader's excellent written work by reading the child's story aloud to the class. The child is likely to derive some pleasure from this. The teacher's goal of reinforcing the child's work will probably be successful. However, if a middle school teacher attempts to reinforce a student's good written work by reading it aloud to the class, the student might experience this action as punitive. Middle school students are very conscious of their peers and may be embarrassed by the teacher's attention, or they may be ridiculed by peers as a *teacher's pet*. One way to decide what reinforcers to provide is to ask the students what they would value. Examples of some students' responses are presented in the nearby What Kids Say and Do box. Another strategy to identify reinforcers is to note what students elect to do when they have some free time. They will generally choose activities that are reinforcing to them.

Patterns of Reinforcement

Students come to class with a history of reinforcement and punishment that influences their behavior in the classroom. You may provide reinforcements and punishments with the goal of increasing the frequency of desirable behaviors or reducing that of undesirable behaviors, and sometimes you may wonder why your strategies are not working. It may be because of patterns of reinforcement and punishment that have been applied to the students' prior behaviors.

Consequences do not always follow behavior. Sometimes a student's on-task behavior goes unnoticed. Not every behavior needs to be followed by reinforcement. Patterns of reinforcement are called *schedules of reinforcement*. These refer to the frequency with which reinforcement is provided. Schedules of reinforcement influence the speed, continuity, and persistence of behaviors. When a behavior is acquired for the first time, it is often performed under a different schedule of reinforcement than when it is being maintained. **Continuous reinforcement** schedules provide reinforcement after every occurrence of a behavior. In trying to teach autistic children to focus on an aide's face, for example, the aide will provide reinforcement every time the child makes eye contact. Continuous reinforcement can be helpful in learning a new behavior.

Intermittent schedules of reinforcement provide reinforcement only some of the time. Such schedules can be either variable or fixed, as shown in Figure 5.3. A fixed schedule of

What Kids Say and Do

What We Find Reinforcing

Kindergarten students
- Being a messenger and leaving the class on my own
- Having lunch with the teacher in the classroom
- A special note home

Fourth-grade students
- Computer time
- Certificate to be the teacher's helper for a week
- Homework passes
- Certificate to select what the teacher brings for a snack for the children

Ninth-grade students
- Homework passes
- Chance to retake a quiz
- Pass from doing book report

continuous reinforcement Reinforcement that is provided after every performance of a behavior.

Figure 5.3 Schedules of Reinforcement

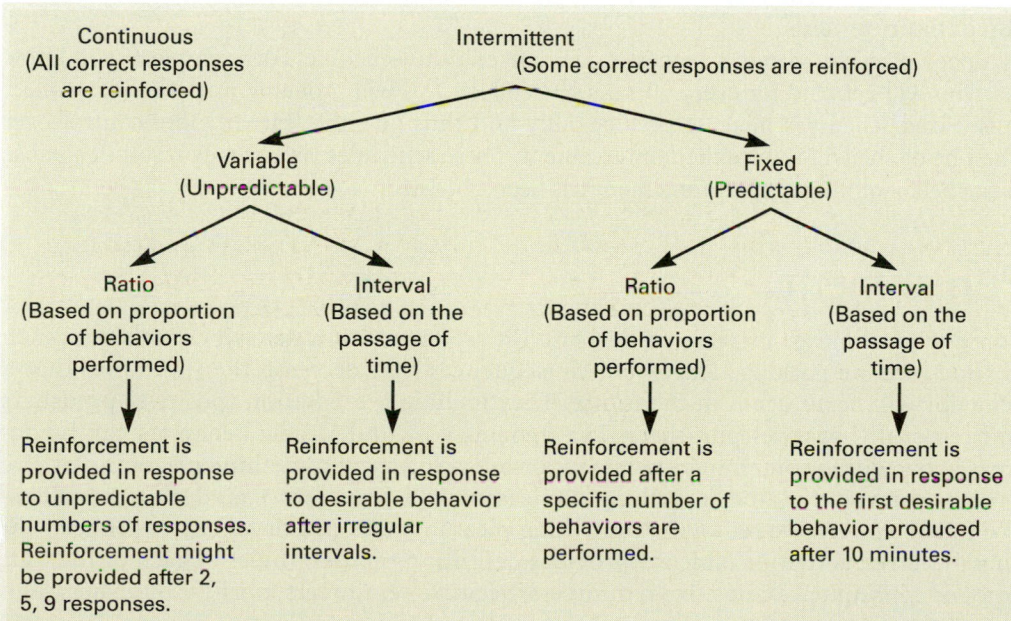

reinforcement allows the learner to predict when reinforcement will be provided. Because it is fixed, the learner knows when to expect reinforcement. The schedule can be based on the passage of time (e.g., the first desired behavior after a five-minute period) or on the number of behaviors performed (e.g., every five homework assignments submitted). When the schedule is based on *the passage of time*, it is called an **interval schedule**. When the schedule is based on *the number of behaviors performed*, it is called a **ratio schedule**. If students know that they will get a homework pass after turning in five homeworks on time, they can predict when they will get their next homework pass. Because reinforcement is predictable, learners have more control over when they receive reinforcement. During the early acquisition of behaviors, fixed schedules are helpful because they allow learners to predict when the next reinforcement will occur. They can quickly learn the relationship between the behavior and the consequence.

interval schedule A schedule of reinforcement based on time.

ratio schedule A schedule of reinforcement based on the number of behaviors.

Variable schedules of reinforcement are unpredictable. For example, if I press my garage door opener, I expect the door to open. Many times, however, it does not open. I may have to press the opener any number of times before it works. Because the door opens some of the time, I continue to press the opener rather than replacing it because it works often enough for my needs. The same pattern of reinforcement happens every day to students in the classroom, as their correct answer, punctuality, and offers of kindness are sometimes reinforced and sometimes not. Sometimes the teacher will provide praise for a correct answer and other times he or she will just move on to another question for another student. Like fixed schedules, variable schedules can be based on the passage of time (variable interval) or based on the number of responses variable ratio. Because the student cannot predict when he or she might be reinforced, and assuming that the possible reinforcement is in fact likely to increase the probability of performing the behavior again, the student will persist in the behavior.

fixed interval schedule A schedule of reinforcement based on the passage of a fixed amount of time.

fixed ratio schedule A schedule of reinforcement based on the number of behaviors performed.

variable interval schedule A schedule of reinforcement in which reinforcement is provided at irregular intervals based on the passage of time.

variable ratio schedule A schedule of reinforcement in which reinforcement is provided at irregular intervals based on the number of behaviors performed.

Effects on Performance The four schedules of reinforcement (**fixed interval, fixed ratio, variable interval, variable ratio schedules**) have very different effects on behavior. Fixed schedules give the learner the greatest control over the delivery of reinforcement. Reinforcement is unpredictable under a variable schedule. Variable schedules, whether based on the passage of time (interval) or on the number of responses (ratio), result in relatively consistent patterns of responses. Variable ratio schedules result in higher rates of response than do variable interval schedules. If you know that you will be reinforced after performing a certain behavior but don't know how many times you need to perform it before being reinforced, your rate of performance will be higher than it would be if you knew the actual schedule of reinforcement. Persistence in the performance of a behavior is higher when the behavior is reinforced on a variable schedule. If you cannot predict when you will be reinforced, you will likely continue to perform the behavior. For example, if your parents occasionally give you a gift when you get good grades, you may continue to work to keep your grades up in anticipation of future rewards.

Speed of performance is highest under a fixed ratio schedule. For example, if you know that you will get paid for every 10 cans you collect, you will probably work faster to collect cans. Fixed schedules increase predictability and thus give the learner more control over when he or she will receive the reinforcement. These schedules also usually result in a pause in the behavior after the reinforcement has been obtained.

Punishment

punisher A consequence of behavior that weakens or decreases behavior.

Consequences either increase or decrease the frequency of a behavior. **Punishers**, such as time-outs or parking tickets, are consequences that decrease the likelihood that a behavior will occur again in the future. They include presentation (positive) punishers and removal (negative) punishers. The frequency of undesirable behaviors can be decreased by adding something unpleasant or by taking away something pleasant. Positive punishers involve adding something unpleasant to a situation (e.g., detention). Negative punishers involve removing something pleasant (e.g., privileges such as time spent on a preferred activity). Table 5.1 provides definitions and examples of each of the four types of consequences: positive reinforcers, negative reinforcers, positive punishers, and negative punishers.

TABLE 5.1

Definitions and Examples for the Four Types of Consequences

Positive Reinforcer

Definition	Any environmental event that, when given, increases the frequency of a behavior.
Example	The teacher smiles when Sam raises his hand in class. Because he wants to get more smiles from the teacher, Sam will raise his hand more often in the future.

Negative Reinforcer

Definition	Any environmental event that, when taken away, increases the frequency of a behavior.
Example	The teacher stares coldly at Suzi to encourage her to answer a question. Because she does not like having the teacher stare at her, Suzi will answer questions more often.

Positive Punisher

Definition	Any environmental event that, when given, decreases the frequency of a behavior.
Example	The teacher reprimands John for horsing around during the lesson. Because he does not want to receive any more reprimands, John steps horsing around.

Negative Punisher

Definition	Any environmental event that, when taken away, decreases the frequency of a behavior.
Example	The teacher places Maria in a time-out for teasing a classmate. Because she does not want to be taken out of the class again, Maria stops teasing her classmates.

Positive Punishers to Suppress Behaviors

A **positive punisher** is any event that, when given, decreases the frequency of a behavior. In terms of the law of effect, a presentation punisher represents bad effects or consequence of behavior. As an example, a teacher might reprimand a student who cheated on a test. The teacher gives the reprimand in order to stop the student's cheating. Other presentation punishers that are often used in schools are giving detention, assigning extra homework, spanking, or sending the student to the principal's office. When a teacher gives a student a disapproving look because the student continually taps a pencil on his desk, the teacher's strategy is to punish the undesirable behavior by making sure that it has bad effects that reduce the likelihood that it will occur in the future.

Desirable behaviors may be reduced by inadvertent punishment. A child who is shy and desperate to fit in with peers may experience a teacher's praise and attention in response to an assignment as punitive. The child may be ridiculed by peers or may be embarrassed. The frequency of doing assignments may well decline as a consequence.

positive punisher Any environmental event that, when taken away, decreases the frequency of a behavior.

Negative Punishers to Suppress Behaviors

A **negative punisher** is any event that, when removed, decreases the frequency of a behavior. In terms of the law of effect, a negative punisher represents the termination of a behavior's good effects. For example, a teacher might remove a child from the playground after the child has pushed a classmate to the ground. The teacher takes away the child's playground privileges in order to punish (decrease) the aggression. This type of negative punisher is called a *response cost*, indicating that each occurrence of the undesirable behavior will cost the student some attractive resource, such as money (a fine or penalty), time on the classroom computer, the chance to watch a movie during the last 15 minutes of class, or a free Saturday morning (as with detention).

negative punisher Any environmental event that, when taken away, decreases the frequency of a behavior.

How Can I Use This?

If you wanted to teach students a new behavior, what schedule of reinforcement would you select?

RIDE Could the committee use reinforcement or punishment to help solve the problems in the lunchroom described at the beginning of the chapter?

A second type of removal (negative) punisher is a time-out from an opportunity for positive reinforcement. Students generally enjoy being with their friends during class, lunch, and recess. A time-out is a procedure in which the teacher directs the student to leave a highly reinforcing environment and go to one that offers little or no reinforcement. In a classroom, a student can be assigned to sit at a distance from other students. School suspensions and expulsions are also removal punishers. When teachers take away points from students who sleep in class and when schools suspend students for hitting others, the strategy is to punish the undesirable behaviors (sleeping, hitting) by making sure that they produce bad effects that make them less likely to occur in the future.

The Appeal of Punishers The benefit to teachers of using punishers is that they can gain students' immediate compliance (Gershoff, 2002b). A verbal reprimand can stop children's horseplay, and peer rejection can stop an adolescent's rudeness. This compliance effect is almost always temporary, however. When the punisher is removed, the undesirable behavior often returns and may even increase. This phenomenon is called *recovery*. As soon as the teacher leaves—and verbal reprimands cease—the child's horseplay resumes.

(Photo Disc, Inc./Getty Images)

A trip to the principal's office is a frequently used punishment to teach students that their undesirable behaviors will produce bad effects.

The Problem with Punishers It is understandable that people use punishers to try to prevent undesirable behaviors from recurring. They see others cheating, hitting, stealing, teasing, name-calling, arguing, damaging property, and committing acts of aggression, and they feel that they must do something about it. Usually, that means using a punisher. The punisher might be obvious, such as denial of privileges or a critical remark, or it might be subtle, such as a sigh of disappointment or a cold look. Classroom behaviors such as cheating, hitting, and stealing cannot be ignored; teachers need to act. Spending a day in a classroom watching teachers interact with misbehaving students will convince almost any observer that punishment is a common strategy. But is it effective? Does the use of a punisher—whether positive or negative—actually suppress undesirable behaviors?

Unlike the single benefit of punishment, the costs are many. Table 5.2 lists four problematic *side effects* of punishment. As shown in the table, using punishers to suppress misbehavior teaches aggression through a modeling effect. The child learns, for instance, that the way to cope with an irritating peer is to punish him or her. Punishment also produces negative emotions. Because punishers are aversive events, they open the door to emotions such as fear, anger, and anxiety and behaviors such as crying and hiding. These negative emotions are important not only in themselves but also because they undermine the relationship between teacher and student. The final side effect is that punishment often backfires and yields a vigorous protest response. Sometimes, using a punisher is like throwing fuel on the fire of misbehavior. These four side effects of punishment place teachers in a difficult dilemma—they need to stop undesirable behaviors, but the side effects are too troubling to accept. Fortunately, there are viable alternatives to punishment and negative control, such as ignoring behavior, substituting activities, and others.

Corporal Punishment in Schools It may surprise you to know that as many as 22 states allow corporal, or physical, punishment in schools. In the 1999–2000 school year, more than 300,000 students were paddled in school. The National Association of School Psychologists (NASP) opposes the use of corporal punishment in schools (NASP, 2002), and research on the use of such punishment by parents indicates that it increases immediate compliance but is linked to higher levels of aggression and lower levels of moral internalization (Gershoff 2002b). A disproportionate number of children who experience corporal punishment are minority students or students with disabilities (NASP, 2002). The NASP provides a number

TABLE 5.2

Four Side Effects of Punishment

1. Punishment teaches aggression.

   By using a punisher to suppress another person's behavior, the person administering the punisher is modeling aggression as a means of dealing with undesirable ways of behaving. This effect occurs through observational learning. A student who receives verbal or physical punishment for misbehavior often imitates this way of coping when interacting with others and later tends to use harsh words and behaviors in the hope of suppressing the misbehavior of others.

2. Punishment produces negative emotions.

   Punishment is an aversive behavioral strategy. When people receive aversive forms of stimulation, they often feel negative emotions such as fear, anger, distress, and worry. Punished students also report feeling embarrassed or humiliated in a public way. Understandably, students often associate these negative emotions with the person who is punishing them.

3. Punishment undermines the quality of the interpersonal relationship.

   People who are punished typically want to escape from the person who is punishing them. They also go out of their way to avoid coming into contact with the person who punishes. Thus, if a teacher uses punishment on students, students may be motivated to stay clear of the teacher.

4. Punishment often exacerbates misbehavior.

   Punishment suppresses behavior. But as one person punishes another, the person being punished experiences higher muscle tension, a raising of the voice, and a general increase in vigor of response. Being punished can sometimes throw fuel on the fire of misbehavior by producing shouting, threatening, protesting, and even acts of violence, counterresponse, and revenge. That is, punishment often makes matters worse, not better.

of alternative strategies for effective discipline that focus on positive behaviors; these are listed in the nearby Taking It to the Classroom box.

Can Punishment Be Used Effectively?

Most teachers will agree that punishment and negative control are not the best ways to manage students' behavior. They will say, however, that punishment is still necessary, at least under certain conditions. At the top of the list of those conditions are situations in which misbehavior threatens the safety or well-being of others. A child who hits another child is put into a time-out to protect the victim and the class as a whole.

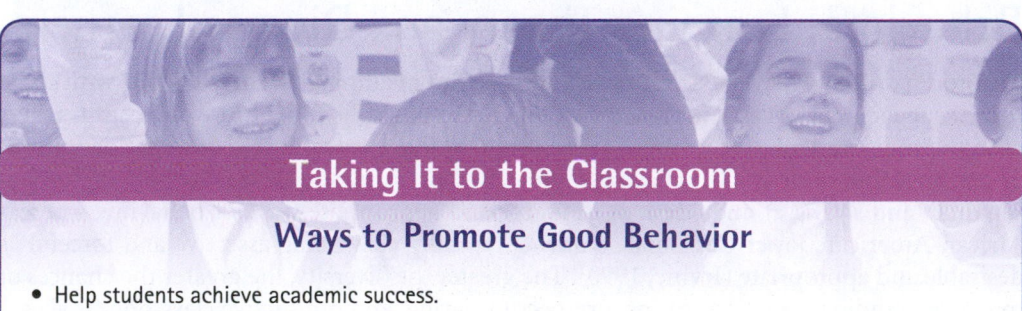

Taking It to the Classroom

Ways to Promote Good Behavior

- Help students achieve academic success.
- Use behavioral contracting.
- Encourage positive reinforcement of appropriate behavior.
- Use individual and group counseling.
- Encourage disciplinary consequences that are meaningful to students and have an instructional and/or reflection component.
- Provide social skills training.

Source: National Association of School Psychologists. (2002). *Position statement on corporal punishment in schools.* Retrieved October 10, 2004, from http://www.nasponline.org/about_nasp/pospaper_corpunish.aspx.

> ## Taking It to the Classroom
>
> ### Do You Know Jack? Ignoring Consequences
>
> *Jack often seems to ignore or disregard the consequences of his actions.* Despite various penalties, punishments, and other negative consequences, he persists in behaving in ways that cause problems both for himself and for others. He does not finish classwork; he teases his peers (or worse); he interrupts the teacher; he behaves immaturely during the change of classes between periods. What can you do to help Jack?
>
> 1. Try to find good behaviors to reinforce.
> 2. Ignore some of the less disruptive behaviors.
> 3. Observe Jack when he is happy and on-task. Note what events or interactions seem to please him.
> 4. Develop a behavior management plan for Jack (see later in this chapter or in Chapter 6).
> 5. Try taking Jack's perspective on the problem in an effort to develop some insight. Does he get teased as well? Is he looking for more attention from you?
> 6. Consult the school psychologist for assistance in developing alternatives for dealing with Jack's behavior.

In one sense, punishment whose goal is to protect others makes sense and is justified. For example, an upper-elementary school student of one of the authors once threw his chair, creating a risk for other students in the room. The student was immediately escorted to the principal's office. Punishment gives teachers a *last resort* to be used when other strategies are unsuccessful. A closer look at what happens in a classroom after a punished troublemaker has been removed (as through time-out, suspension, or expulsion), however, is revealing. More often than not, other students come forward to fill the void left by the absent troublemaker (Noguera, 2003). When this happens, should the teacher punish those students, too? As you can see, what teachers need are viable, effective alternatives to punishment, ones that succeed in suppressing undesirable behaviors without producing the harmful side effects identified in Table 5.2. The above Taking It to the Classroom box presents an example of how behavioral principles might be used in the classroom.

Appendix
Awareness of Difference

Differences among students can present challenges to the classroom teacher in managing behavior because of potential misunderstanding (PRAXIS™, I.B.4; INTASC, Principle 1).

Behavioral Learning Theory and Diverse Learners

Classroom diversity may make it more challenging for beginning teachers to cope with classroom management issues. This may be so for two reasons. First, the more different teachers are from their students, the greater is the likelihood that they will have different definitions of desirable and undesirable behaviors. White, middle-class, female teachers often view being quiet and sitting at one's desk as desirable and appropriate ways of behaving, whereas African-American, lower-class, male students typically view being assertive and forceful as desirable and appropriate (Irvine, 1990). The greater the diversity, the greater the chances of misunderstanding. Second, creating a respectful, caring, and productive classroom is always a challenge, and diversity in the classroom, in which students see differences all around them, can make this challenge even greater. Students sometimes interpret difference as inferiority; one student might think that another student speaks the "wrong" language, for instance. On the other hand, when teachers and students value and embrace diversity, they avoid such negative interpretations and develop productive relationships (Weiner, 2003).

Classroom diversity, therefore, places an obligation on teachers to understand their students' cultural, national, and ethnic backgrounds. They can do this by fostering relationships with parents and community representatives, reading and watching videotapes about their students' cultures, and familiarizing themselves with the countries and cultures from which their students have emigrated (Curran, 2003). Armed with such knowledge, they can better interpret and explain students' (mis)behavior (Norris, 2003).

Interviews and classroom observations of effective teachers in highly diverse schools reveal three principles of classroom management that work particularly well (Brown, 2003). First, culturally responsive classroom management involves communicating in culturally appropriate ways. One teacher who taught highly language-diverse students, for instance, made a special effort to greet each child in his or her native language. Such an action opens the door to two-way communication in which the minority culture is as valid and respected as is the majority culture. Second, culturally responsive classroom management establishes clear expectations for behavior. In many urban classrooms, establishing clear expectations means being assertive, establishing authority, enforcing rules, and reminding students with assurances such as, "I'm here to help you. I'm not going to let you slide! You're not going to get away with acting the wrong way or not doing the work" (Brown, 2003). Third, culturally responsive classroom management revolves around caring for all students. Teachers in diverse classrooms who have well-behaved, highly engaged students offer affection, warmth, and high-quality relationships to all students. What diverse students say when asked to describe caring teachers appears in the nearby What Kids Say and Do box.

What Kids Say and Do

Describing Caring Teachers

Here are examples of what middle school students in highly diverse schools say when asked to describe caring teachers:

Caring teachers ...
- are fair.
- ask me what I think.
- hold high expectations for what I can do.

Caring teachers do not ...
- yell.
- interrupt me.
- criticize me.
- hold low expectations for what I can do.

Applied Behavior Analysis

In addition to its consequences, behavior is also influenced by the situational cues that precede it. When particular behaviors are followed by reinforcements in situation A but not in situation B, the cues preceding each behavior signal whether reinforcement is likely or not. These cues become **discriminative stimuli**. A behavior such as petting a dog might have good effects in one situation but bad effects in another. Petting the family dog might produce tail wags, whereas petting the neighbor's dog might produce growls. As a result, people learn to be sensitive to the situational cues that help them determine whether a behavior is likely to produce good effects (reinforcement) or bad effects (punishment) in a certain situation. In this example, being with the family dog is a cue that petting will produce good effects, whereas being with the neighbor's dog is a cue that petting will produce bad effects. In the same vein, students learn that talking is good during lunch period but bad while taking a test. The point of situational cues is that people learn which behaviors do and do not work in one situation as well as which behaviors do and do not work in other, different situations.

discriminative stimuli Antecedent cues that allow the learner to predict the likelihood of reinforcement.

Because behavior is influenced both by the cues that precede it and by the effects that follow it, the following formulation can be used to summarize two basic principles of behavioral learning theory:

$$A : B \rightarrow C$$

In this formulation, A stands for antecedent cues, B for behavior, and C for consequences. Antecedents come before behavior; consequences occur after behavior. The arrow from B to C indicates that behavior causes the consequences to happen. Petting the dog causes the dog's good or bad reaction. The colon between the A and B means that antecedent cues set the stage for—but do not cause—the behavior.

Teachers can observe the kinds of cues that seem to precede desirable or undesirable behaviors. For example, a student may exhibit the undesirable behavior of shouting out answers in class, but only when he or she is seated beside a friend. When the child is seated beside other students, he or she may raise a hand to offer an answer. In this case, observation of the antecedents of the undesirable behavior would allow the teacher to identify the best course of action. The nearby Taking It to the Classroom box provides guidelines for applying behavioral learning principles to classroom problems.

Taking It to the Classroom

Guidelines for Applying Behavioral Learning Principles to Classroom Problems

Phase	Factors to Consider
Premodification phase	
Problem identification and definition	• Identify and describe the problem to be resolved and the behavior to be changed.
	• It is very useful to note antecedent events.
Recording	• Note the contexts in which the behavior occurs and how often it occurs.
	• Graphs often reveal patterns.
Modification plan	• Focus on a targeted behavior.
	• Devise a plan based on information revealed by records.
Modification phase	
Modification plan applied	• Ensure that when the targeted behavior occurs, it is followed by an appropriate consequence.
	• Note: In some cases, the behavior is addressed by changing antecedent conditions.
Recording	• Recording is necessary to determine the plan's effectiveness.
Evaluation	• In most successful interventions, there will be an abrupt change in the number of incidents.
	• Gradual change usually indicates that a better plan could be designed.
Postmodification phase	
Modification plan removed	• If the plan is successful, discontinue the intervention.
	• The plan can be considered successful when the student's behavior changes in the desired way and the change is extensive enough to resolve the problem for both the student and the teacher.
Recording	• Monitor the student's behavior after the modification.
Evaluation	• If the targeted behavior returns, decide whether to reapply the original plan or devise a new one.
	• If the plan is successful, it is a good idea to conduct a periodic spot check of behavior, especially if the student displays other undesirable behaviors.

Source: Based on Bergan, J. R., & Caldwell, T. (1995). Operant techniques in school psychology. *Journal of Educational and Psychological Consultation*, 6, 103–110. Copyright © 1995 by the Taylor and Francis Group.

In one study (Hall et al., 1970), teachers gave fifth-grade students a positive reinforcer if they returned promptly from recess and were inside the classroom door before the bell rang. The positive reinforcer was to have their name placed on a wall chart under the heading *Today's Patriots* (the students were learning about eighteenth-century patriots and saw the label as very positive). Figure 5.4 shows how effective the positive reinforcer was in increasing students' punctuality. Before the study (days 1–13), when no positive reinforcer was associated with being in the classroom on time, eight students on average were late returning from recess. During days 14–32, when punctuality earned the student a name on the Today's Patriots chart, lateness was rare, and 100% of the students were punctual during days 21–32. During days

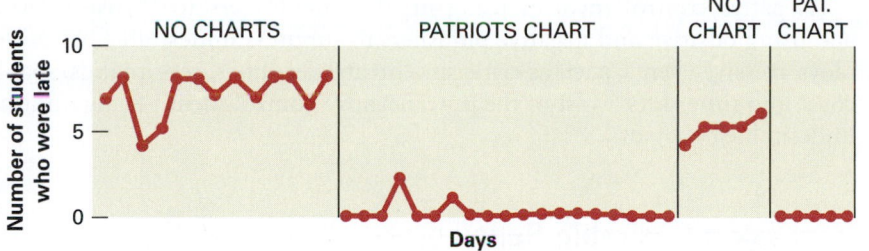

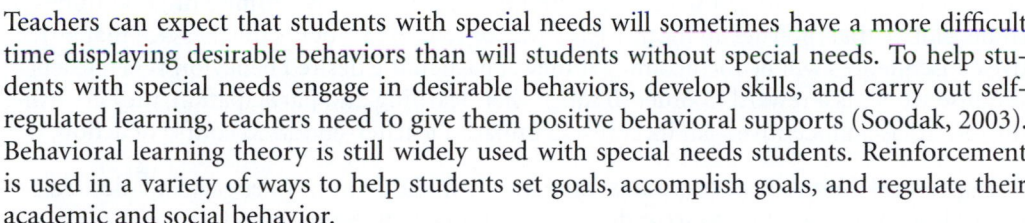

Days

Figure 5.4 Effects of a Positive Reinforcer on Students' Punctuality

Source: Hall, R. V., Cristler, C., Cranston, S. S., & Tucker, B. (1970). Teachers and parents as researchers using multiple baseline designs. *Journal of Applied Behavior Analysis,* 3, 247–255. Reprinted with the permission of IABA.

33–37, the wall chart was removed so that punctuality no longer earned the status of Patriot, and once again, on each of these days several students were late. Finally, during days 38–42, the wall chart was reinstated, and punctuality rates again returned to 100%. This study shows that giving a positive reinforcer can increase a desired target behavior such as punctuality.

Behavioral Learning Theory and Special Needs Students

Teachers can expect that students with special needs will sometimes have a more difficult time displaying desirable behaviors than will students without special needs. To help students with special needs engage in desirable behaviors, develop skills, and carry out self-regulated learning, teachers need to give them positive behavioral supports (Soodak, 2003). Behavioral learning theory is still widely used with special needs students. Reinforcement is used in a variety of ways to help students set goals, accomplish goals, and regulate their academic and social behavior.

Under the provisions of the reauthorized Individuals with Disabilities Education Act (IDEA) (2004), the right of a student with a disability to remain in his or her current educational setting pending an appeal was eliminated for violations that were serious enough to warrant a suspension of more than 10 days. Previously, a student was removed only pending appeal for violations involving drugs, weapons, or other dangerous behavior. The disruption of services to a child with a disability who is moved to a new educational placement may limit the child's progress. Prior to the reauthorization of IDEA in 2004, the school was required to show that the behavior that resulted in disciplinary action was not a manifestation of the child's disability before it could apply the kinds of disciplinary procedures that would be applied to nondisabled students. Under the new law, the burden has been shifted to the parents, who must prove that the behavior for which discipline is being considered was related to the child's disability.

Managing Behavior

Managing behavior means setting up conditions that make desirable behaviors more likely to occur and undesirable ones less likely to occur. Such conditions include strategic use of antecedent conditions to cue desirable behaviors and discourage undesirable ones, but for the most part managing behavior involves strategic use of behavioral consequences.

When it comes to managing behavior, students generally like positive control and dislike negative control. Positive control refers to instructional efforts to manage behavior through the use of rewards and positive reinforcement. Negative control refers to instructional efforts to manage behavior through the use of negative reinforcement, positive punishment, and negative punishment. Students also learn better and more efficiently under conditions of positive control than they do under conditions of negative control. All four types of consequences are important determinants of students' learning and behaving, but in practice, effectively managing students' behavior entails a liberal administration of positive reinforcers and minimal use of negative reinforcers, positive punishers, and negative punishers. Before discussing how to increase students' desirable behaviors, let us first wrestle with the problems and shortcomings associated with negative control. Negative control routinely leads to the sort of side effects listed in Table 5.2.

Negative control involves using negative reinforcers to increase desirable behaviors and using positive and negative punishers to suppress undesirable behaviors. Thus, it employs aversive events, such as criticism, threats, deadlines, reprimands, spankings, response costs, and time-outs. Most of the time, negative control means using punishers to suppress undesirable behaviors.

Increasing Desirable Behaviors

Teachers who use behavioral learning principles to increase students' desirable behaviors generally do so in three ways. First, they offer attractive incentives that elicit behaviors. Second, once a desired behavior has begun, they use prompts and behavioral supports to maintain it. Third, after an episode of desired behavior, they use positive reinforcers to strengthen that behavior and encourage its occurrence in the future. As part of this third course of action, they may use **shaping**, or reinforcement of gradual approximations of the desired behavior.

shaping Reinforcement of gradual approximations of the desired behavior.

incentive An environmental event that attracts a person toward a particular course of action.

Incentives   An **incentive** is an event that attracts a person toward a particular course of action. Incentives are antecedent conditions; therefore, they always precede desired behaviors. Some common classroom incentives include a smile, a surprise box that contains wrapped gifts from which a child can select, the sound of laughter, or any promise of good things to come. Notice that offering an incentive is a way of sending students the message that attractive consequences will be forthcoming if they engage in the desired behavior. When teachers promise students a reward in order to solicit their learning and participation, they are using the reward as an incentive—an incentive to initiate a teacher-endorsed course of action.

prompts Physical, verbal, or other assists that help a person perform a desired behavior that he or she would be unlikely to perform without such assistance.

Prompts and Behavioral Supports   Sometimes students want to engage in a desired behavior but either forget to do so or do not quite know how. Sometimes they need a reminder, as illustrated by the prompt shown in Figure 5.5.

Prompts are physical, verbal, or other assists that help a person perform a desired behavior that he or she might not have performed without such assistance. A teacher might, for instance, provide a student with the first three lines of a poem to get him or her started, or give the child a tip about how to proceed if he or she is stuck or confused. The teacher might also offer a gesture, picture, instruction, suggestion, or hint about how to proceed or how to get back on track. A sign, a note card, a string tied around the finger, or a verbal reminder from a cooperative learning partner, such as, "Okay, now we should paraphrase," are all ways of prompting desired behaviors. After the desired behavior has been prompted and performed, positive reinforcement can be used to strengthen it.

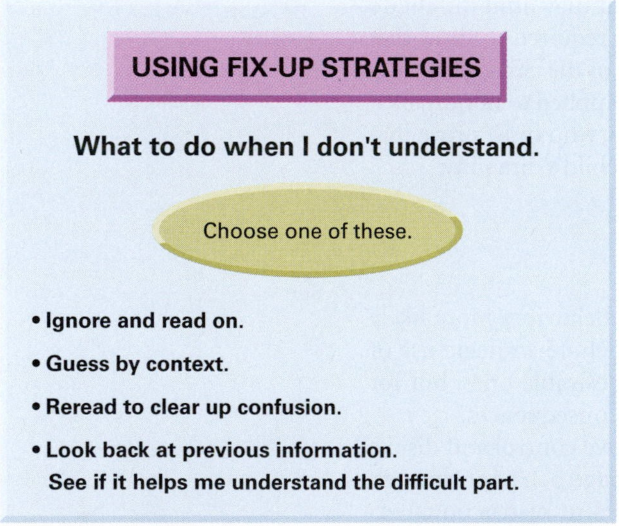

USING FIX-UP STRATEGIES

What to do when I don't understand.

Choose one of these.

- Ignore and read on.
- Guess by context.
- Reread to clear up confusion.
- Look back at previous information.
  See if it helps me understand the difficult part.

Positive Reinforcers   Using positive reinforcers to strengthen desired behaviors can be characterized as a strategy of "catching them being good." When a desired behavior occurs, the teacher gives the student a positive reinforcer—the sooner the better. The purpose is to help the student learn that this particular way of behaving has positive consequences. The more the student associates good effects with the behavior, the more frequently he or she will engage in that behavior.

Figure 5.5 A Behavioral Prompt for Readers

Source: Creating confident and competent readers: Transactional strategies instruction by C. P. Casteel, B. A. Isom, and K. F. Jordan, 2000, *Intervention in School and Clinic*, Vol. 36, 67–77. Copyright 2000 by PRO—ED, Inc. Reprinted with permission.

To use positive reinforcement effectively in the classroom, you can do the following:

- Ask students to identify effective reinforcers or observe what they choose to do during their free time.
- Establish a variety of reinforcers, because different children will be reinforced by different consequences.
- Be sure to reinforce behaviors in ways that students value; that is, ensure that the consequences you provide are actually reinforcing.

Uncommon Sense

Praise Is Always Good—Or Is It?

Praise is often used as a reinforcer in classrooms. Children respond positively to praise from their teachers. It is easy for teachers to use praise as a reinforcer because it does not require record keeping. But is praising students always a good idea?

Praise is given in an attempt to increase the probability that desired behaviors will be repeated. Consequences that are reinforcing are associated with pleasant feelings. Consequences are punitive if the frequency of the undesirable behavior decreases, and receiving a punitive consequence such as criticism is typically associated with unpleasant feelings.

Research on the use of praise and criticism (Meyer, 1992) has found some paradoxical effects. When praise is provided, the recipient often feels that the person providing the praise regards his or her ability as low. In contrast, the recipient of criticism feels that the person providing the criticism regards his or her ability as high. You should be clear and systematic in providing praise, pointing to the behavior that is praiseworthy. Genuine accomplishments should be praised; otherwise, it will not be effective. When providing praise, you should attribute the behavior to the child's efforts and ability.

- Give plenty of reinforcement when students are trying new skills or learning new material.
- When new behaviors have become established, provide reinforcement on an unpredictable schedule to encourage the persistence of those behaviors.
- Try to ensure that all students receive reinforcement.

Praise is frequently used by teachers as a positive reinforcer, and when praise is used successfully, positive behavior is likely to increase. To use praise appropriately, the teacher should not provide empty compliments. Instead, praise should be dependent on the performance of a desired behavior. In giving praise, the teacher should describe what behavior is praiseworthy. Teachers do not always use praise appropriately, however (see the nearby Uncommon Sense box).

Shaping If we waited for a child to perform a complex behavior before reinforcing that behavior, we might not provide much in the way of reinforcement. The child may not yet be able to perform such behaviors. For example, cursive writing is difficult for many young children and requires fine motor control and perception. The first time a child writes the letter *a*, it may not resemble what we consider a cursive *a*, and it would not be the desired behavior. However, if we reinforce the child's attempts to write the letter *a* as each one comes closer to the correct form, we are *shaping* the child's behavior. The child is gradually getting closer to performing the behavior at the standard we are aiming for.

Downsides of Rewards From the preceding discussion, the way to increase desired behavior is clear: Offer attractive incentives, provide prompts, and give positive reinforcers when the desired behavior occurs. But just as punishers have troubling side effects, so do incentives and reinforcers. These side effects are further discussed in Chapter 10. Incentives, rewards, and reinforcers can (1) undermine intrinsic motivation, (2) interfere with learning, and (3) hinder autonomous self-regulation.

Incentives, rewards, and reinforcers are designed to promote extrinsic motivation. Why a student who expects to be rewarded behaves in the desired way is clear—because of the offer of the attractive incentive or reward. So although they are not designed to promote intrinsic motivation, incentives and rewards *do* promote extrinsic motivation and, thus, place intrinsic motivation at risk.

Incentives and rewards can help students learn behaviors and factual knowledge (e.g., the right answer). But when educators want to promote other types of learning, such as conceptual understanding, they need other approaches to instruction; these are discussed in later chapters. Finally, incentives and rewards are intended as ways to regulate

Appendix
Positive Behavior

You can encourage and support positive behaviors that will facilitate students' learning and motivation (PRAXIS™, I.C.2; INTASC, Principle 5).

(© The New Yorker Collection 1986 Lee Lorenz from cartoonbank.com. All rights reserved.)

"That is the correct answer, Billy, but I'm afraid you don't win anything for it."

One downside of rewards is that students become overly dependent on rewards to motivate their classroom participation.

desirable and undesirable behaviors. When students learn to depend on incentives, prompts, and rewards to regulate their behavior, these external events can forestall the development of self-regulatory abilities (Joussemet et al., 2004). Educators need to make a special effort to promote students' capacity for self-management. This important topic will be discussed later in the chapter.

Decreasing Undesirable Behaviors

Teachers can prevent minor behavior problems from becoming more serious. Punishment produces a mixed response: It gains temporary compliance and thus stops the undesired behavior, but it does so at the expense of four troubling side effects (see Table 5.2). Nevertheless, the use of punishment is quite common. Fortunately, there are a number of effective alternatives to punishment. Let us take a brief look at some of them.

Verbal Reprimands One of the most common types of negative consequences (punishment) is verbal reprimands. Reprimands are a teacher's brief statement to draw attention to misbehavior, such as "no," "don't," "stop that," or "get back to work." Reprimands given in private are likely to be most effective in suppressing undesirable behavior (O'Leary et al., 1970). Some students may find that a scolding by the teacher is actually reinforcing because of the attention they receive, but many find it unpleasant. Depending on the situation, a scolding can be embarrassing as well as unpleasant.

Response Cost The following is an example of the use of response cost. A child in a first-grade class was constantly getting out of her seat without permission. The teacher found this behavior very disruptive, because the child talked to other children and took things from them. He decided to use a response cost system to reduce the incidence of this behavior. He gave the child a jar with 10 marbles in it and told her that she would lose a marble if she got up from her seat without permission. If there were 3 marbles left in the jar at the end of the day, she would receive a reward. As the marbles disappeared, the child became aware of the possible loss of the promised reward. The visible record of her misbehavior gave her a chance to exercise control over her own behavior.

Differential Reinforcement Differential reinforcement is a two-step strategy that captures the essence of the phrase "catch them being good." First, the teacher identifies both the undesired behavior and an alternative, desired way of behaving. For instance, during group work, if a student insults other students, the teacher might identify insults as the undesired behavior and giving encouragement as an alternative, desired behavior. Second, when the desired behavior occurs, the teacher provides a positive reinforcer to strengthen that behavior. At the same time, the teacher ignores the undesired behavior—neither punishing it nor reinforcing it. This differential reinforcement works to suppress the undesired behavior because the alternative way of behaving becomes more frequent and eventually replaces the undesired way of behaving. In other words, if the student encourages his or her peers more, he or she will spend less time insulting them. Through differential reinforcement, the teacher plays the constructive role of reinforcer and avoids the negative role of punisher.

Inductive Reasoning Inductive reasoning is a two-step strategy in which the teacher helps the misbehaving student understand the harmful effects of the misbehavior. The teacher holds a conversation with the student to identify and emphasize the suffering caused, intentionally or unintentionally, by the undesired behavior. For instance, if a child *borrowed* another child's pencil, he or she might imagine that little harm had been done. The teacher could describe the harm done to the child who now lacks a pencil and go on to try to induce perspective taking and empathy for the victim. For instance, the teacher might invite the child to imagine what it would be like to lack a pencil when the class was working on an assignment. The child cannot complete the work in time and may have to stay in at recess to complete the work. In general, inductive reasoning is an effective strategy for coping with misbehavior because it decreases future undesirable behaviors while avoiding harmful side effects and promoting beneficial effects (e.g., greater empathy, increased social skill).

An important extension of inductive reasoning—a third step—is to continue discussing perspective taking until the child generates a prosocial alternative way of behaving or solving the problem. The teacher might invite the child to answer the question, "Instead of taking Billy's pencil without his permission, what else could you have done that would have allowed you to have a pencil?" Often the child can readily generate prosocial responses, such as "I could ask his permission" or "I could keep a pencil in my desk" or "We could share his pencil—take turns using it." Teachers who use inductive reasoning believe that *being good* does not simply mean behaving well. It means that students are thinking and learning about their behavior and how it affects others. Through inductive reasoning, the teacher plays the constructive role of counselor and avoids the negative role of punisher. (See the Taking It to the Classroom box on the next page for strategies to prevent negative behavior from escalating.)

Observational Learning Experienced teachers can often anticipate misbehavior before it occurs. An experienced teacher, for instance, might anticipate that an elementary school student might shove others to get to the front of the lunch line or that a high school student might ridicule a peer who has difficulty making a classroom presentation. This foreknowledge comes from experience. If the teacher anticipates that such behaviors may occur, he or she can demonstrate what appropriate behavior looks like in these situations. After modeling the desired behavior, the teacher can invite students to imitate it. As students practice the desired behavior, the teacher can coach, refine, and positively reinforce it. Notice that if students are already behaving in the desired way, the teacher is never placed in the position of having to correct their misbehavior. Through observational learning, the teacher serves as a *role model* and avoids the role of *punisher*.

Scaffolding/Tutoring Sometimes students misbehave because they do not yet know how to behave in more appropriate ways. Bullies sometimes do not know how to make friends and resort to undesirable behaviors to gain attention and respect. Through scaffolding and tutoring, a teacher can assist students' efforts to learn desirable behaviors. The teacher can provide examples, clues, reminders, hints, tips, challenges—whatever the misbehaving student needs to "get over the hump" and learn more desirable and rewarding ways of behaving. Notice that this sort of coaching also involves the use of prompts and behavioral supports, such as questions, to lead the student to think about the needed content. Through scaffolding, the teacher plays the role of *tutor* or *coach* and avoids the role of *punisher*.

Why Do Students Misbehave?

The approach described in the previous paragraph might be summarized as "reinforce, explain, model, or coach desirable behavior so as to reduce and eliminate undesirable behavior." Such strategies replace undesirable behaviors with desirable ones. The question remains, however, as to why students engage in the undesirable behavior in the first place: Why do students misbehave?

One could equally well ask: Why don't students behave properly? The best way to promote on-task attention and desirable behaviors during a lesson is to provide high-quality instruction. That is, regardless of the discipline strategies a teacher employs (positive versus negative control), teachers who provide interesting activities, ask challenging

What Does This Mean to Me?
Did you misbehave in high school? Why? What could a teacher have done to prevent this misbehavior?

Taking It to the Classroom

Preventing Behavioral Escalations

Background

Most classroom problems are minor, and the teacher can easily work with the student to resolve the problem. However, there are times when a relatively minor incident (e.g., arguing, calling out) can escalate into a confrontation between student and teacher. This often results in challenges to the teacher or refusal to comply with the teacher's directives. Other students become anxious or curious onlookers, and instruction comes to a halt. Experts in classroom management recommend that teachers focus on preventing behavioral escalations instead of managing crisis situations once they occur (Shukla-Mehta & Albin, 2003). Following are some guidelines for preventing behavioral escalations in the classroom.

Guidelines for Preventing Behavioral Escalations in the Classroom

Strategy	Examples/Rationale
Reinforce calm and on-task behaviors.	• Provide positive attention. • Encourage peer approval. • Praise on-task behavior.
Know the triggers.	• Difficult academic tasks • Time pressure • Anxiety about an exam
Do not escalate along with the student.	• Remain calm when provoked. • Disengage from confrontation. • Give student time or space to disengage from confrontation.
Offer opportunities to display responsible behavior.	• Do not make demands on student while he or she is agitated. • Verbally prompt the student regarding appropriate choices. • Debrief student privately to point out consequences and explore suitable alternative behaviors.
Intervene early in the sequence.	Steps: • Recall/identify early problem behaviors in the escalation pattern. • Intervene with deescalation strategies. • Anticipate subsequent problem behaviors and be prepared to continue interventions.
Understand how such incidents ended in the past.	• Teacher should evaluate the effectiveness of a strategy on the basis of its effect on the student's previous behavior. ("Is my strategy serving my goal or an undesirable goal?")
Know the function of problem behaviors. (Problem behaviors often have underlying functions or goals.)	• Avoidance of work • Teacher attention • Peer attention
Use good judgment about which behaviors to punish.	• Match consequence to severity of problem behavior. • Avoid using same consequence (e.g., time-out) for all types of problem behaviors.
Teach students socially appropriate behavior to replace problem behavior.	• Teach and reinforce a more responsible behavior (e.g., asking for help) in place of a less desirable behavior (e.g., complaining) when a difficult task is assigned.
Teach academic survival skills and set students up for success.	• Teach effective learning strategies such as note taking and study skills. • Anticipate mistakes.

Source: Shukla-Mehta, S., & Albin, R.W. (2003). Twelve practical strategies to prevent behavioral escalation in classroom settings. Preventing School Failure, 47(3), 156–161. Reprinted with permission of the Helen Dwight Reid Educational Foundation. Published by Heldref Publications, 1319 Eighteenth St., NW, Washington, DC 20036-1802. Copyright © 2003 by the Taylor and Francis Group.

questions, and know how to engage students in learning will have students who display mostly on-task and desirable behaviors. Teachers who provide boring activities, ask only right-or-wrong factual questions, and do not know how to engage students in learning will have students who display mostly off-task and undesirable behaviors (Jeanpierre, 2004).

In a learning environment, being inattentive, lazy, and uncooperative are undesirable behaviors. If students are to learn, such behaviors must be replaced by more productive, desirable behaviors, such as being attentive and actively engaged. From this point of view, misbehavior is as much a quality-of-teaching issue as it is one of discipline. This is so because disengagement is a natural response to a lesson that is unchallenging, repetitious, or irrelevant to one's goals. To promote learning and on-task behavior, teachers need to provide effective teaching strategies, high-quality instruction, and a family-like environment in which students feel supported by a caring teacher (Cremin, 1988). Effective classroom management, therefore, requires not only positive control strategies but also high-quality instruction (Newmann, 1992; Noguera, 2003; Wong & Wong, 1998).

Another reason students misbehave is that they find themselves in environments that do not address their needs (Brown, 2003). (See the nearby Uncommon Sense box.) An interesting phenomenon occurs when a student's teacher, rather than his or her parents, explains the student's misbehavior. Teachers tend to invoke some shortcoming on the part of the student (e.g., "He doesn't like school," "She's angry"), whereas parents tend to invoke reasons such as boredom and frustration with instruction, the lack of a trusting relationship with the teacher, and school practices that they perceive as unfair and discriminatory (Weiner, 2003). Although this difference in emphasis may be somewhat unfair to the teacher, there is some truth in it, because the students who are punished the most are those with the greatest academic, social, economic, and emotional needs (Cartledge & Milburn, 1996; Irvine, 1990; Johnson, Boyden, & Pittz, 2001), particularly students who are low achievers, have learning disabilities, are minorities, are in foster care, or are entitled to free or reduced-price lunches (Meier, Stewart, & England, 1989; Skiba, 2000).

Uncommon Sense

Zero-Tolerance Policies Solve Problems of Aggression and Violence—Or Do They?

Zero-tolerance policies use exclusionary forms of discipline, such as suspension, when students behave in violent ways. Introduced in the 1990s, they are designed to send a clear and unambiguous message that no aggressive behavior will be tolerated in school (Ayers, Dorhn, & Ayers, 2001). Looking for ways to stop violence, many schools adopted a tough yet simple plan: Evict violent students (i.e., one strike and you're out).

Zero-tolerance policies have four major drawbacks (Noguera, 2003; Skiba & Peterson, 2001). First, they undermine their own purpose by eroding civility within the school. It is hard to promote caring and compassion by using punishment. Second, these policies penalize students who are most in need of emotional connectedness to the school. Third, zero-tolerance policies are rarely applied equally to all students. Students of color and students with disabilities are at the greatest risk of expulsion. Last, students who are suspended rarely change their behavior for the better.

Zero-tolerance policies have the same appeal that any punishment-based strategy has—namely, schools have to do something to protect students who behave properly. The assumption behind this *bad apple theory* is that safety and order can be achieved by removing *bad* individuals and keeping them away from the others, who are presumed to be *good*. Although there is some truth in this belief, it is equally true that aggressive students often abandon their behavioral problems when they are assigned to classes with highly effective teachers (McCarthy & Benally, 2003). The finding that zero-tolerance policies rarely work is uncommon sense because most teachers endorse this *bad apple* theory (Noguera, 2003). Careful analysis reveals, however, that the most common causes of students' misbehavior are classroom factors, such as (1) being bored and alienated from school, (2) learning from teachers who are disorganized or unmotivated, (3) believing that teachers have very low expectations of what the student can do and accomplish, and (4) having antagonistic relationships with teachers and administrators (Steinberg, 1996). Such findings offer educators a hint of hope because all these factors are, to some extent, under their control.

Promoting Self-Management

By using behavioral principles, teachers can influence students' behaviors. Often, however, they want to do more than that. They want to transfer the responsibility for managing behavior away from the teacher and onto the students themselves. In other words, they want to encourage self-management.

Effective self-management is a learned ability. Before students can be expected to manage their own behavior, they need to learn how to do so. Initially, many behaviors are teacher-regulated. For instance, many first-grade students have a difficult time using a quiet voice in class, just as many middle school students have a difficult time doing their homework on time, and many high school students have a difficult time reading assigned books during study hall. To self-manage such behavior, students need to learn the following abilities: (1) plan their behavior and set their own goals (goal setting); (2) provide self-instructions and constructive self-talk (self-instruction); (3) monitor how well or poorly they are behaving (self-monitoring); (4) evaluate the desirability of their behavior (self-evaluation); and (5) apply self-generated consequences to reinforce their desired behaviors (self-consequences).

Table 5.3 illustrates these aspects of self-management. Whether the person who engages in self-management is a writer, an athlete, a musician, or a student, each of the five regulatory processes contributes to self-management. The student, for instance, engages in self-management by first making a list of what is to be accomplished during the study session (goal setting), verbally prompting and praising desired study behaviors (self-instruction), keeping records of completed assignments (self-monitoring), checking work before handing it in (self-evaluation), and making watching TV or phoning friends contingent on completion of assignments (self-consequences).

How can teachers help students learn such self-regulatory abilities? Obviously, they need to encourage self-management and communicate its value. Some teachers ask students to follow strict routines, whereas others encourage them to be responsible for their own behavior (Bohn, Roehrig, & Pressley, 2004). One effective strategy is to teach students how to carry out a think-aloud analysis (Brown & Pressley, 1994; Pressley et al., 1992). In a think-aloud analysis, the teacher assigns the student a task such as reading a book. At different points in the task (e.g., before reading the book, while reading it, and after reading it), students are to ask themselves questions such as: What is my goal? What specifically will I do? How many pages have I read? Did I do well? What kind of reward do I deserve?

TABLE 5.3

Self-Regulatory Processes Underlying the Effective Self-Management of Writers, Athletes, Musicians, and Students

Self-Regulatory Processes	Domain			
	Writers	**Athletes**	**Musicians**	**Students**
Goal setting	Setting daily word or page goals	Setting specific and quantifiable daily goals for training	Setting daily practice session goals	Making lists of things to accomplish during study
Self-instruction	Saying aloud what will be written	Self-verbalizing confidence statements—for example, "Let's go!"	Verbally praising or prompting oneself	Rehearsing steps in solving a math problem
Self-monitoring	Keeping records of literary production	Keeping a daily record of goal accomplishment or filming matches for replay	Keeping daily records of performance—for example, stress levels	Keeping records of completed assignments
Self-evaluation	Putting off self-judgments	Breaking game into components and evaluating oneself after each performance	Listening to self-recording, setting realistic standards	Checking work before handing it in
Self-consequences	Putting off pleasurable events until writing is completed	Grading oneself after every match	Refusing to end practice until passage is played flawlessly	Making TV or telephoning contingent on completion of homework

Source: Adapted from Zimmerman, B. J. (1998). Academic studying and the development of personal skill: A self-regulatory perspective. *Educational Psychologist, 33,* 73–86. Copyright © 1998 by the Taylor and Francis Group.

Notice that these questions correspond to goal setting, self-instruction, self-monitoring, self-evaluating, and self-consequences, as illustrated in Table 5.3. With experience, students develop these self-regulatory abilities and become increasingly able to manage their own learning and behavior.

The Fundamental Task of Classroom Management

The fundamental task of classroom management is to create an inclusive, supportive, caring, engaging, and challenging community in which students frequently engage in desirable, constructive, and prosocial behavior (Good & Brophy, 1997; Weinstein, Curran, & Tomlinson-Clarke, 2003). For a teacher who thinks of classroom management as a system of rules, rewards, and penalties, this view may be puzzling at first. But creating a classroom environment that fully engages students in learning activities is the best antidote to misbehavior. It is also a proactive, preventive strategy, one that promotes and reinforces desirable behavior, rather than a reactive, remedial strategy that controls and punishes undesirable behavior. From this point of view, the ultimate goal of classroom management is not to achieve compliance and control, but rather to provide students with frequent opportunities for learning (Weinstein et al., 2003). The nearby Taking It to the Classroom box offers three suggestions for creating opportunities for students to learn and grow.

Appendix
Promoting a Positive Climate
You can promote positive social behavior, positive relationships, and cooperation among students that will result in more time available for learning (PRAXIS™, I.C.4; INTASC, Principle 5).

Contracts and Contingencies

One strategy for helping students regulate their behavior is to use behavioral contracts. Contracts can be used to promote new behaviors, increase the rate of performance of a behavior, maintain a skill, decrease undesirable behaviors, or monitor the completion of academic tasks (Downing, 2002). Teachers who wish to use such contracts need to make the decisions illustrated in Figure 5.6. An example of a contract is presented in Figure 5.7.

Sometimes teachers manage behavior by means of group contingencies—reinforcements or punishments that apply to the entire class. The goal is to encourage the use of peer pressure

Taking It to the Classroom

Three Suggestions for Creating Opportunities for Students to Learn and Grow

1. **Organize the physical environment in ways that will promote desirable behavior.**

   If the teacher values social interaction, desks should be arranged in clusters so that students can work together, share materials, have face-to-face discussions, and help one another with assignments. If the teacher values being kind to others, he or she can provide a *kindness box* into which students can drop brief notes about acts of kindness they witness; periodically, the teacher can pull a note from the box and read it aloud (Beane, 1999).

2. **Establish expectations for desirable behavior.**

   Effective teachers make certain that students know what is expected of them; they say clearly that students must listen to and respect one another. They also model these behaviors, and they explain why these rules of conduct are important, helpful, and constructive. Throughout the school year, these teachers give students opportunities to practice and develop these ways of behaving, even to the point of teaching classroom behaviors and norms in the same way that they teach academic subjects.

3. **Create caring, inclusive classrooms.**

   Misbehavior such as teasing, insulting, fighting, and bullying stems from disrespect and conflict between students. To prevent such misbehavior before it occurs, teachers can create caring, inclusive communities in their classrooms. One way to achieve this goal is to hold a *morning meeting* in which students greet each other, share news, and participate in a group activity (Kriete, 1999). A similar activity is a *sharing circle* in which students get together to brainstorm and generate solutions to problems such as conflicts that occur on the school bus (Norris, 2003). Notice that the teacher's attention is focused at least as much on promoting high-quality relations between students as it is on promoting specific desirable behaviors or preventing specific undesirable behaviors.

Figure 5.6 Creating an Individualized Contract

The teacher identifies specific behaviors to target.

The contract should:
- specify the goals for the student
- identify the rewards that the student will receive if the goals are met
- identify specific consequences that the student will receive if the goals are not met

The teacher discusses the contract with the student.

Both parties sign the contract.

to improve behavior. Often, students will be motivated not to let their peers down or to increase the reinforcements available to the group. Students in middle school and high school are particularly concerned about their peers' approval. An example of a group contingency strategy is the "Good Behavior Game" (Barrish, Saunders, & Wolf, 1969). The teacher divides

Figure 5.7 Example of an Individual Contract

My Contract

My Name: Elizabeth Jones

Grade: 7th Grade

My Goal:

1. Turn in my completed homework on time.

Consequences:

If I meet my goals:

If I complete my homework on time five days in a row, I will get a homework pass for one night.

If I do not meet my goals:

If I do not complete my homework on time on more than one of five days in a row, I will get extra homework for the weekend.

Signatures   _____ Student

              _____ Teacher

Monday	Tuesday	Wednesday	Thursday	Friday

The teacher will initial each day I am successful.

the class into two teams. Each time a rule is broken, the teacher makes a mark beside the name of the team whose member broke the rule. The goal is to have as few marks as possible beside the name of one's team. Research has shown that this approach is effective (Darveaux, 1984; Dolan et al., 1993).

A more recent example of a group contingency program is called "Anchor the Boat" (Lohrmann & Talerica, 2004). It involves (1) defining expectations for behavior in positive terms; (2) teaching the expectations, using direct instruction and role-play; and (3) reinforcing students when they have met the criteria for appropriate behavior. A picture of a boat positioned 20 inches above an anchor is attached to a board. If the class engages in 50 or fewer of the undesirable target behaviors during a class period, they earn 2-inch paperclips to make a chain to connect the boat to the anchor. When the chain is complete, they earn a reward.

> **How Can I Use This?**
> How can you minimize potential negative effects in using group contingency contracts?

Lohrmann and Talerico (2004) evaluated this technique in a multi-age classroom that provided learning support for students with learning disabilities. The participants were six boys and four girls. After three days of the intervention, the incidence of undesirable behaviors (talking out of turn, getting out of seats, and incomplete assignments) was reduced. The results were consistent with those of other studies of group contingencies.

The group contingency approach should be used with caution. Romeo (1998) points to a number of potentially negative outcomes: (1) It can model injustice and unfairness; (2) it can create a hostile classroom environment; and (3) other students may become surrogate punishers of children who do not comply with the rules. Students in middle school are particularly vulnerable to the negative effects of peers' disapproval or hostility. Furthermore, some children have poor impulse control and have difficulty regulating their personal behavior unless they receive substantial support. Such children can create problems for other students in a group contingency context because they may cause the group to lose privileges. In turn, the other students may become hostile toward a difficult student. Teachers should use group contingencies very carefully, especially when the class includes students with special needs.

Influences of Behavioral Learning Theory on Instruction

Behavioral learning theory can be used to foster particular kinds of learning. These theories imply that the experience of success is important in instruction because it results in reinforcement and increases the likelihood of continued effort. The focus on opportunities for success also implies that content be broken down in order to maximize opportunities to experience success. Simple skills should be taught before complex skills. Two areas of instruction that have been influenced by behavioral learning theory are mastery learning and instructional technology.

Mastery Learning

In 1968, Benjamin Bloom developed the concept that came to be known as *mastery learning* (Bloom, 1968). The basic principle of mastery learning is that all students can achieve a set of educational objectives with appropriate instruction and enough time to learn. The curriculum is divided into small units that have specific objectives, with formative assessments tied to them. Assessments are given, and further instruction or activities and feedback are provided to help the student overcome problems. A student does not progress to the next unit until he or she has reached a prescribed level of mastery (e.g., 80% correct on a test). Because the material is broken into smaller units, the focus is on success and consequent reinforcement before proceeding to the next unit.

Many studies of mastery learning programs have been conducted. A series of **meta-analyses** were conducted that synthesized the results of many of those studies (Guskey & Gates, 1986; Guskey & Piggot, 1988; Kulik, Kulik, & Bangert-Downs, 1990). The results of the analyses showed that, in general, mastery learning is an effective instructional strategy. Performance on achievement tests improved as a result of mastery learning, as did student

meta-analysis A quantitative review and summary of research on a topic.

Software programs routinely feature positive reinforcers, such as celebratory sights and sounds, to encourage and maintain students' on-task behavior.

(© Media Bakery)

attitudes toward learning. The positive results were also found to persist over time (Kulik et al., 1990). Not everyone agrees about the positive effects of mastery learning, however. One analysis concluded that mastery learning had few documented effects (Slavin, 1987b). Some of the differences in interpretation of the results of studies occur because researchers do not always include the same studies in their analyses.

Feedback and Knowledge of Results An important component of mastery learning is corrective feedback. One study compared mastery and nonmastery learning to find out how feedback was related to achievement (Wentling, 1973). Four outcomes were examined: immediate achievement, attitude toward instruction, time spent on instruction, and delayed achievement. Participants in both the mastery and nonmastery learning conditions were provided with no feedback, partial feedback in the form of information about the correctness of the response, or complete feedback that included provision of the correct response. The results indicated that participants who received partial feedback outperformed those in the nonfeedback and complete-feedback groups on measures of both immediate and delayed achievement. No differences were found in the time spent on instruction or attitudes toward instruction.

In sum, many aspects of mastery learning are influenced by behavioral learning theory. These include the division of content into small units and the use of formative tests that guide the use of corrective feedback and activities. The goal is to foster the experience of success, which is reinforcing and supportive of continued effort. It is useful to keep in mind that although there is much evidence in support of mastery learning as an instructional strategy, mastery learning is not widely used today. Instruction in today's classrooms is influenced more by other theories of learning, such as constructivism or information processing.

Instructional Technology

Behavioral learning theory has influenced some aspects of the design of software and computer-assisted instructional programs. Skinner (1958) was the first to propose applying behavioral learning principles to teaching academic skills by using programmed instruction. Content was arranged in small chunks, and progress was organized from simple to complex content. Computer-based instruction involved the use of a computer to deliver programmed instruction and maintain records of progress.

One example of the influence of behaviorism can be seen in software that provides drill and practice (Lockard & Abrams, 2004). A child may be presented with a picture, such as an apple, and asked to make a response, such as selecting the word *apple* from among a number

How does learning occur?	Law of effect; reinforcements and punishments	
Where does knowledge come from?	The same stimulus triggers the same response	
What is the student doing?	Acting on the environment; responding to consequences	
What is the role of the teacher?	Designer of the environment; provider of consequences	
What is the role of peers?	Sources of reinforcement or punishment	
If a teacher subscribes to this theory, what is he or she likely to include in a lesson plan?	Divide curriculum into small units with clear objectives; provide reinforcement	

Figure 5.8 Behavioral Learning Theory and Instruction

of words. Thus, the child is encouraged to associate the picture with the word *apple*. Success in these kinds of activities may be reinforced by flashing lights, bells, or other signals. The child may persist on the task in pursuit of such reinforcements.

Figure 5.8 summarizes some of the key questions that teachers might have with respect to how adopting a behavioral learning theory might influence decisions a teacher must make.

In addition, the negative effects of overreliance on tangible reinforcement or reward may actually decrease motivation and performance. Intrinsic motivation for participation in activities or tasks can be undermined.

REFLECTION FOR ACTION

The Event

Mr. Duba is the leader of a committee that has been appointed by the middle school principal to generate ideas and an action plan for reducing misbehavior during lunch period. Members of the committee have contributed ideas about how to solve the problem. Mr. Duba has written some of them on the chalkboard. Now it is time for the committee to make some recommendations.

Reflection RIDE

Why are the students behaving badly? How can the committee improve the situation in the lunchroom without also making the students resentful and angry?

What Theoretical/Conceptual Information Might Assist in Interpreting and Remedying This Situation? Consider the following:

Reinforcement of Desirable Behavior

The committee could recommend creating a system for rewarding good behavior. It might be possible to draw up contracts with different classes, with rewards contingent on improved behavior.

Punishment of Undesirable Behavior

The committee could recommend sanctions for bad behavior, such as detention, extra homework, or not allowing students who continually break the rules to go on school outings or to the school dance.

Monitoring of Antecedents and Consequences of Behavior

Antecedents precede behaviors. The behavior is followed by consequences that will either increase or decrease the likelihood that the behavior will occur again. Perhaps members of the committee should observe students in the lunchroom and try to identify the antecedents to behaviors, such as throwing food.

Information Gathering RIDE

What is the problem? The problem for the committee is to decide whether to try to improve students' behavior during the lunch period by using reinforcement or by using punishment. The committee should look at the research evidence related to the use of reinforcement and punishment. It will also be important for committee members to observe the situation in the lunchroom and determine whether a few students cause the problems or many students are involved in the disruptive incidents. A careful analysis of the antecedents of disruptive behaviors will be helpful to the committee in deciding how to tackle the problem. It will also be helpful to have more than one member of the committee observe at the same time and compare notes later. Do they observe the same behaviors?

Decision Making RIDE

The committee members may observe in the lunchroom. If they determine that the problems are largely caused by a small number of students who provoke other students, they may decide to reduce the opportunities for the disruptive students to provoke others. They may recommend that the lunch periods be staggered to limit the number of students in the lunchroom at any one time. They may also recommend assigning the disruptive students to different locations in the lunchroom to isolate them from one another.

If the disruptive behavior is not confined to a few students, the committee will need to consider reinforcement and punishment alternatives. Punishment does not extinguish behavior but merely suppresses it. Reinforcement can increase the incidence of positive behaviors, but the committee members will need to consider carefully what might be reinforcing to the students. The use of group contingencies (rewards and punishments) might be a useful strategy because middle school students care about the opinions of their peers. Every effort should be made, however, to focus on increasing positive behaviors rather than on punishment. The lunchroom aides might assist with recording incidents of bad behavior, and rewards could be assigned if the number of incidents remains below a certain threshold. The use of group contingencies can have negative outcomes if particular students are unresponsive to peer pressure or are unable to regulate their own behavior adequately (e.g., students with attention-deficit-hyperactivity disorder. Individual contingency contracts can also be used with specific students.

Evaluation RIDE

The lunchroom aides can provide reports of the number of disruptive incidents that occur. A decrease in the frequency of such incidents will indicate that the intervention was successful. If the misbehavior continues at the previous level, the committee will need to reconvene and develop a new strategy.

Further Practice: Your Turn

Here is a second event for you to reflect on. In doing so, generate the sequence used above in terms of reflection, information gathering, decision making, and evaluation.

The Event

Ms. Jefferson was concerned about her seventh graders' lack of interest in reading. She concluded that they needed more immediate and tangible rewards. She devised a program that would provide rewards for students' reading achievements. Classes in which each child read three books in a month would receive a free pizza party at a local pizzeria. After three months, book borrowing at the school and local libraries had increased dramatically.

Has Ms. Jefferson succeeded in increasing the frequency of students' reading? What about the quality of their reading?

SUMMARY

- **How do teachers who adhere to behavioral, cognitive, and social-constructivist approaches describe learning?**

  Behavioral, cognitive, and social-constructivist theories of learning place different emphases on the relationships among the environment, the individual, and behavior. Behavioral learning theories emphasize the connection between the environment and behavior. Cognitive theories emphasize the relationship between the individual and the environment. Social-constructivist theories also emphasize the relationship between the environment and the individual, and the environment includes the history of practice and expertise acquired by a community, from which an individual might learn by becoming an apprentice in that community.

- **What kinds of learning can be described by behavioral learning theory?**

  Behavioral learning theory focuses on behavior, skills, and self-regulatory capacities, as shown in Figure 5.1.

- **How do different forms of reinforcement affect behavior and performance?**

  Different forms of reinforcement influence the speed with which behaviors are performed, the continuity of the behavior after reinforcement, and the persistence of the behavior. Fixed schedules of reinforcement are the most predictable and are useful in the initial stages of acquiring a behavior. After receiving reinforcement on a fixed schedule, the learner is likely to pause before repeating the behavior. Speed of performance is highest under a fixed ratio schedule of reinforcement because the delivery of reinforcement is predictable, and the learner can control the timing of the behaviors necessary to obtain reinforcement. Variable schedules are unpredictable and result in the greatest persistence of the desired behavior.

- **How can teachers increase the frequency of desirable behaviors and decrease that of undesirable behaviors?**

  Desirable behavior can be increased and undesirable behavior decreased by a combination of reinforcement and punishment. An emphasis on positive behavior management is more likely to be successful than a focus on negative behavior. Positive reinforcements such as praise can be used to increase desirable behaviors. Undesirable behaviors can be decreased by means of such strategies as response cost, differential reinforcement, inductive reasoning about behavior, and the use of contracts.

- **How can teachers help students learn self-management?**

  To effectively manage their own behavior, students need to learn the following capabilities: (1) plan their behavior and set their own goals (goal setting); (2) provide self-instructions and constructive self-talk (self-instruction); (3) monitor how well or how poorly they are behaving (self-monitoring); (4) evaluate the desirability of their behavior (self-evaluation); and (5) apply self-generated consequences to reinforce desired behaviors (self-consequences).

- **How can teachers use behavioral learning principles in instruction?**

  Behavioral learning theory suggests that the experience of success, positive reinforcement, feedback, and gradual progress are important aspects of learning. Instructional strategies such as mastery learning and many kinds of programmed instruction are strongly influenced by behavioral learning theory.

- **How might teachers use behavioral learning theory with diverse learners and learners with special needs?**

  Behavioral learning principles are frequently used in instructional and behavior management programs for students with special needs (e.g., autistic or emotionally disturbed children). Positive behavioral intervention strategies may also be part of a student's individualized education plan, as required by IDEA 2004. Behavioral learning theory is concerned with the environment and behavior, not with mental states. It is important for a teacher to understand diverse learners' prior histories of reinforcement and punishment.

● **What are some limitations of behavioral learning theory?**

Behavioral learning theory cannot adequately explain complex learning. Complex learning is more than the sum of the parts of a task and involves cognitive, metacognitive, and affective or social skills. In addition, the negative effects of overreliance on tangible reinforcement or reward may actually decrease motivation and performance.

Key Terms

classical conditioning, p. 155
conditioned response (CR), p. 155
conditioned stimulus (CS), p. 155
consequences, p. 156
contiguity, p. 155
continuous reinforcement, p. 159
discriminative stimuli, p. 165
fixed interval schedule, p. 160
fixed ratio schedule, p. 160
incentive, p. 168

interval schedule, p. 160
law of effect, p. 156
learning, p. 153
meta-analysis, p. 177
negative punisher, p. 161
negative reinforcer, p. 157
operant learning, p. 156
positive punisher, p. 161
positive reinforcer, p. 156
Premack principle, p. 157

prompts, p. 168
punisher, p. 160
ratio schedule, p. 160
reinforcer, p. 156
reward, p. 157
shaping, p. 168
unconditioned response (UCR), p. 155
unconditioned stimulus (UCS), p. 155
variable interval schedule, p. 160
variable ratio schedule, p. 160

Exercises

1. *Observing the Use of Reinforcers and Punishers*

   Observe a teacher in a classroom. What kinds of reinforcers or punishers does the teacher provide? Make a list of these and classify each as an example of a positive (presentation) or negative (removal) punishment or positive or negative reinforcement.

2. *Reinforcement during the Use of a Computer Game*

   Observe a student playing a computer game. At what points in the game does the student smile or show pleasure? What happens after the student does this? Can you tell what behaviors are being reinforced? Can you tell which consequences are responsible for the student's smiles and sense of pleasure?

3. *Changing Behavior*

   Identify one behavior that you would like to change (e.g., getting up late in the morning). Develop a plan for how you will change the behavior and write it down. Over the course of a week, keep a record of what you did to try to change the behavior. At the end of the week, identify the reinforcers or punishers you used. Were they effective in increasing the frequency of desired behavior or reducing that of undesirable behavior?

4. *Evaluating Education*

   Read B. F. Skinner's "The Shame of American Education" (1984, *American Psychologist, 39*, 947–954) and summarize the criticisms that Skinner made of American education. How many of these criticisms are valid in describing the current status of American education?

Lesson Plans

The lesson plans on these pages are excerpts from more complete plans. They are included in this form to provide you with practice in examining a lesson from the perspective of the content of this chapter. The complete lesson plans are available at www.pbs.org. For both lesson plans, read the lesson plan excerpt and respond to the questions related to behavioral learning theories in the Ask Yourself! section at the end.

Lesson #1: "It's All about Word Play!"

GRADES: 1—4

SUBJECT AREAS: Language Arts, Technology, Visual Arts, Physical Education

URL: http://pbskids.org/mayaandmiguel/english/ parentsteachers/lessonplans/wordplay.html

I. SUMMARY

Maya and Miguel's first cousin, Tito, recently emigrated from Mexico. His native language is Spanish but his English is improving every day as he interacts with his multilingual American family. This lesson focuses on word play through conversational language activities that will help build confidence and increase proficient language skills for early English language learners.

II. OBJECTIVES

- Students will recognize and respond orally to picture—word associations.
- Students will develop visual recognition skills, model correct language usage, and identify specific graphics and words.
- Students will interpret conversational language through role-play.
- Students will use technology and art to create a picture—word collage.
- Second language students will share Spanish (or native language) translations with peers.

III. MATERIALS

- Picture cards, photos, or classroom posters
- Stickers (stars work great)
- Graphics, magazine pictures for cutting out
- Glue, scissors, and construction paper for extension activity

IV. PROCEDURE (SESSION ONE)

1. Instruct students that they are going to play a fun game called "Look, Say, Find!" Use hand motions as you say "Look, Say, Find!":

- "Look" with one hand in saluting position over eye
- "Say" by touching hand to mouth
- "Find" by extending arm and pointing from far left to right

2. Pronounce, then spell, the graphic or word. Repeat pronunciation and spelling. Encourage volunteers to independently model pronunciation and spelling. Be sure to ask second language learners to share oral and written Spanish (or their own native language) as you move through graphics.

3. Prompt thought about each graphic with age-appropriate vocabulary and conversational language. For example, show graphic of children playing and ask: What are these children doing? How many children are there? Where do you think they live? How old are they? How do you think they are feeling right now? Have you ever played like they are playing? What kind of weather are they playing in and what season does it seem to be where they live? Do you think you would have fun playing with these children? Continue by encouraging students to independently express their understanding of each graphic through conversational language.

4. Ask each student to take a turn at placing a sticker on the graphic you call out. Ask individual students to identify, pronounce, spell, and describe the graphic.

- Watch the *Maya and Miguel* episode "The Doubtful Prince" to experience more language skill building and fun word play.
- Incorporate technology by helping students print out a list of 5—10 familiar content words on the computer. Cut out each word, arrange, and glue onto construction paper (leaving space for illustrations). Cut out graphics for each word to reinforce picture—word associations. This can also be used to create a larger classroom collage or bulletin board.
- For early language learners, reinforce picture—word association by exploring these bilingual books:
- *No More Spanish* (Get Ready for Gabi Series #3) by Marisa Montes (ages 7—9)
- *A Crazy, Mixed-Up Spanglish Day* (Get Ready for Gabi Series #1) by Marisa Montes (ages 7—10)

Lesson continues . . .

> ## Ask Yourself!
>
> **1.** What could serve as reinforcers for the children in this lesson?
>
> **2.** How could you use your understanding of associationist theories in this lesson?

Published with the permission of Scholastic, Inc.

Lesson Plans

Lesson #2: "Fit Forever"

GRADES: 3–6

ESTIMATED COMPLETION TIME: 12–15 class periods

SUBJECT AREA: Health, Physical Education

I. OVERVIEW: With an increased awareness of childhood obesity and its many dangers, many schools are implementing fitness programs with their students in conjunction with regular fitness education.

II. OBJECTIVES: Students will be able to:
- Assess personal fitness level and capabilities
- Identify personal fitness goal
- Formulate and implement a fitness plan

III. MATERIALS:
- Basic fitness equipment (activities can be adjusted based upon availability)
- Music
- Fitness journals
- Clipboards/pencils

IV. PROCEDURE:

Class 1:

1. Have students brainstorm what they know about a healthy lifestyle (foods they should eat, how much activity level they should have).

2. Have students complete a self-assessment of their current fitness abilities. Items on the assessment can include:

    a. I can run at least 20 ft without stopping

    b. I can jump rope for 3 minutes straight

    c. I can do 30 sit-ups without stopping

3. After students complete self-assessment, do an actual assessment of what they can and cannot do.

Class 2:

1. Have students identify 3 goals based upon what their assessment showed (e.g., I will be able to jump rope for 5 minutes), taking into account things that are on the self-assessment that they can't already do.

2. Have students work to complete the following statement (you may want students to seek help from a partner or group): By being able to fulfill these goals, I will _____ (examples of what to fill in are things like "be a stronger baseball player; be healthier all around; etc).

3. Do a small or large group share in order for students to determine how realistic their goals are.

Class 3:

1. Students will work to create a daily fitness plan. This will involve instruction on how to create small goals (e.g., I will run 1 inch further every day for the next 5 days).

Classes 4–14:

1. Students will begin to implement their fitness plan, logging progress in a fitness journal. Give students time to share and reflect at the end of each session.

Class 15:

1. Have students share their project; this might be a fun time to do a celebration so that students can share their accomplishments.

Ask Yourself!

1. What kind of reinforcers could you use to help the students implement their fitness plans?

2. If you were to develop a fitness plan, what schedule of reinforcement would work best for you?

3. How would knowledge of the results of your efforts to improve your fitness change your behavior?

(Courtesy of Teddy Linenfelser, town of Grand Island N.Y. historian.)

Leah Aronds has just awakened on her first day as a new fourth-grade teacher. She had been dreaming that her classroom looked like the photo here. After a few deep breaths, she realizes that her classroom is not going to look like the photo. Besides the obvious differences in what Ms. Aronds and her students will be wearing, the walls of Ms. Aronds's classroom will not be quite as barren. But some things will be similar. Look at the children's faces. She can expect some of her students to display the eager anticipation shown by the girl in the front row on the right as well as the tall girl seated in the second row. And the boy in the far back on the right . . . he looks as though he is going to be a handful.

Managing Learning in Classrooms

 **Reflection for Action**

Today's classrooms come in all shapes and sizes. They are all fairly barren when not in use. Some stay that way even when teachers are using them; others come alive. Consider these questions: In what kind of classroom would you like to be a student? A teacher? What types of activities are facilitated in classrooms? What types of activities are hindered? How can classroom management be facilitated or hindered through classroom design?

Guiding Questions

- How can classrooms be organized to make it easier to achieve instructional goals?
- How can the first day of school set the tone for the rest of the year?
- How should rules be developed for classrooms?
- How do successful teachers create a learning community in their classrooms?
- How do instructional formats affect classroom management?
- How can I handle a really tough classroom?
- What can be done about problem behaviors that are more serious than occasional rule breaking?
- What is the proper balance between being sensitive to cultural differences and applying the same rules and expectations to all students?
- What kinds of classroom management policies can be used to address the special needs of certain learners?

CHAPTER OVERVIEW

This chapter looks at the opportunities, problems, and concerns associated with creating and managing successful learning communities in classrooms. We begin with the skeleton, discussing some of the concerns that teachers face in designing the physical environment of classrooms. Then we move into the areas that bring the bare bones to life: creating a learning community, establishing and enforcing norms and rules for behavior, and managing day-to-day classroom life. Teachers differ in how they deal with issues of classroom management, based on their needs and those of their students.

Designing the Physical Environment
- The Influence of the Environment on Behavior
- Designing the Elementary School Classroom
- Designing the Middle or Secondary School Classroom
- Addressing Student Diversity and Special Needs through the Physical Environment
- Using Technology to Design Your Classroom

Designing the Social Environment: Norms and Rules
- The Tension between Freedom and Structure
- Getting Started
- Establishing Procedures for Routines
- Misbehavior: Informal Correctives and Imposing Penalties

- Conclusions about Establishing Norms and Rules
- A Student-Centered Approach

Managing Day-to-Day Classroom Instruction
- Independent Work or Seatwork
- Small-Group Work
- Whole-Class Instruction
- Special Needs, Diversity, and Instruction

Dealing with Behavior Problems
- Chronic Problems
- Acute Problems
- Personal Problems
- Particular Problems

Designing the Physical Environment

Classrooms are like living organisms (Smith, Smith, & De Lisi, 2001). Their physical structure, furnishings, and state of repair are merely the skeleton, a starting point for classroom design. Classrooms have a life cycle, bursting into action in the fall with chaos, uncertainty, and excitement. By late fall, patterns have been established, and there is a familiar climate in the classroom that lasts through most of the school year, a steady hum of activity. Classrooms have rhythm, flow, and purposes. They have movement and life, moments of joy and despair. Then, in early summer, the activity closes down, and the classroom hibernates, waiting for the beginning of the next school year.

The nature and quality of the activity that occurs in classrooms depend largely on the teacher in charge of the room. Students affect classrooms as well. Some students can have large positive or negative effects on what happens in a classroom, but the key variable is the teacher. The teacher has the power to create a learning community. These communities not only produce learning and growth in children but also promote friendships that can last a lifetime. Teachers serve as models of how to behave in groups. Students' success depends on how well they function within a community: how smoothly they operate and whether they stay focused on the goals of the class.

For 180 days of the year, classrooms are where students live. The only other room where primary or elementary school students spend more time is their bedroom, and they are asleep for most of that time. So it is not surprising that the physical environment of the classroom has many effects on students, effects that we will describe in this section. Consider, too, how much time teachers spend in their classrooms over the course of a career. Making the classroom a positive and welcoming environment is well worth the investment of time and effort it will require.

According to Hickey and Schafer (2006), there are five ways to categorize actions that teachers undertake in the process of instruction: engagement, curriculum, relationships, development, and discipline. Each of these needs to be facilitated by the design of classroom spaces. Elementary and secondary school classrooms differ in a number of important ways. The two most basic differences, obviously, are the age of the children in them and the fact that at the elementary school level, students typically spend the entire day in one classroom, whereas high school students (and most middle school students) move from one classroom to another to take their various courses. Thus, the elementary school classroom is more of a home to students. At the middle and high school levels, the classroom is primarily a place to engage in academic work. Younger students will need more help in learning what is appropriate behavior, and older students are more likely to test rules and to display misbehavior of a more serious nature. Because of the magnitude of these differences, we devote separate sections to designing elementary and secondary school classrooms.

The Influence of the Environment on Behavior

Classroom management begins well before the first student enters the room on the first day of school. The influence of physical characteristics of the classroom on achievement is well documented (e.g., Slater, 1968; Tanner, 2000; Tinker, 1939; Weinstein, 1979). The attractiveness of the classroom, the arrangement of the furniture, the quality of the lighting, the ability of the walls to absorb sound, even the nature of the floor coverings have been shown to affect student achievement.

> **How Can I Use This?**
> Next time you are in a classroom, either as a student or a visitor, examine the room to see whether you can identify the influences in this list.

The classroom environment influences behavior, and therefore learning, by determining the following:

- Where students are located in the room and how close they are to other students
- What students are looking at—other students, the teacher, a computer monitor, a colorful picture, a blank wall, out the window
- How students get from one place to another and who and what they pass on the way there
- Whether students have a comfortable place to read a book or can find art materials easily
- Whether students are feeling inspired or excited by their surroundings, or tired and bored
- Whether students enter a class with eagerness and a sense of anticipation or with feelings of worry and anxiety

> **Appendix**
> **Environmental Influences on Behavior**
> Organizational theory and educational research support the argument that the environment has a strong influence on behavior (PRAXIS™, I.C.I; INTASC, Principle 5).

In addition to influencing behavior, the classroom environment communicates to students how teachers feel about them and about the tasks of schooling. Does the appearance of the classroom show that the teacher spent a lot of time and effort in thinking about how the classroom will look, or does it look as though the teacher entered the room for the first time on the same day as the students?

Working from a general theory of organizations developed by Fred Steele (1973), Weinstein, Romano and Mignano (2010) describe six basic functions of classroom environments:

> **What Does This Mean to Me?**
> How do you protect your personal space in rooms where you attend classes?

- **Security and shelter.** Classrooms need to be places where students feel safe and secure, where they know they will not be subject to physical or emotional distress. Because classrooms have very little inherent privacy, students need to have a place in the room that gives them a sense of security and **personal space**, a physical zone that is separate from those of other students and under each student's control. They also need to be as free as possible from the dangers posed by scissors, pencil points, electrical or chemical hazards, or loose objects in much-traveled pathways.

- **Social contact.** The design of the classroom will encourage certain kinds of interactions and discourage others. Teachers must decide how many and what kind of interactions students need to have in order to meet instructional goals.

personal space An area where an individual feels separate from other individuals and able to be in control.

social contact Interaction among students.

(© Media Bakery)

A well-designed classroom is attractive, safe, and allows multiple activities to occur at the same time.

RIDE Look at the photo of a classroom from the 1930s at the beginning of the chapter. Try to rate this classroom in terms of the six functions of classrooms just described. Would it provide the best sense of security and safety?

- **Symbolic identification.** People's homes tell you a great deal about the people who live there: what their interests are, what their tastes are—in short, who they are. What does a classroom say about the students in the class? Does it tell you who they are? Does it reveal anything about them as individuals? Do they have any sense of ownership of the classroom?

- **Task instrumentality.** A central factor in designing the physical environment of the classroom is the nature of the activities (tasks) that will occur there. Will students be working primarily in groups or by themselves? How much artwork is going to be done? How much seatwork? Will there be an emphasis on silent reading that will require quiet spaces set apart from the rest of the room? Do all the students need to have a clear sight line to the board and the teacher's desk?

- **Pleasure.** Teachers and students spend a great deal of time in classrooms. Classrooms should be pleasing in appearance and create a positive feeling. A mix of colors and textures helps, along with open spaces and *nooks and crannies*. Plants, and even a classroom pet or two (if possible), are welcome additions, particularly at the elementary and middle school levels.

- **Growth.** Young students can grow an amazing amount in the course of a school year. They grow physically, of course, but they also grow cognitively and emotionally, often in ways that are not related to the formal educational goals of the class. A well-designed classroom can promote such growth by providing materials and opportunities that intrigue, excite, and challenge students.

Designing the Elementary School Classroom

Look at the design for a second-grade classroom shown in Figure 6.1. Try to answer the following questions in relation to this design:

- What does this classroom reveal about the person who designed it?
- What will go on in this classroom?
- What kinds of learning and growth will be encouraged?
- What kinds of learning and growth will be hindered?
- What strengths and weaknesses can you spot in this design?
- What kinds of activities would be easy to conduct in this room?
- What kinds of activities would be harder to carry out?

What Does This Mean to Me?
What would you do to improve the arrangement of the classroom in Figure 6.1?

Among the positive aspects of this classroom is that the arrangement of the desks encourages cooperative work. The room has a library center, a separate area for working at the computer, and a table for artwork. Most students would have good sight lines to the teacher and the chalkboard. It also looks as though it would be fairly easy to enter the room and find one's seat. On the negative side, it looks as though the cubbies and cabinets might be difficult to get to, particularly if students are using any of the learning centers. Also, if students are actually seated around the desk sets, half of them will be facing away from the teacher.

Well-designed elementary school classrooms meet the six functions in ways that are appropriate for young children. Many elementary schools do not have lockers, for example, so desks and cubbies provide personal space. They should be clearly labeled and easily accessible, especially at the beginning and end of the day and during **transition times**; otherwise, valuable instructional time could be lost to traffic jams. Frequently used pathways need to be clear and open for young students, who often do not pay as much attention as adults do to where they are going or what they are doing.

transition times Times when students are changing from one activity to the next.

Figure 6.1 Map of a
Second-Grade Classroom

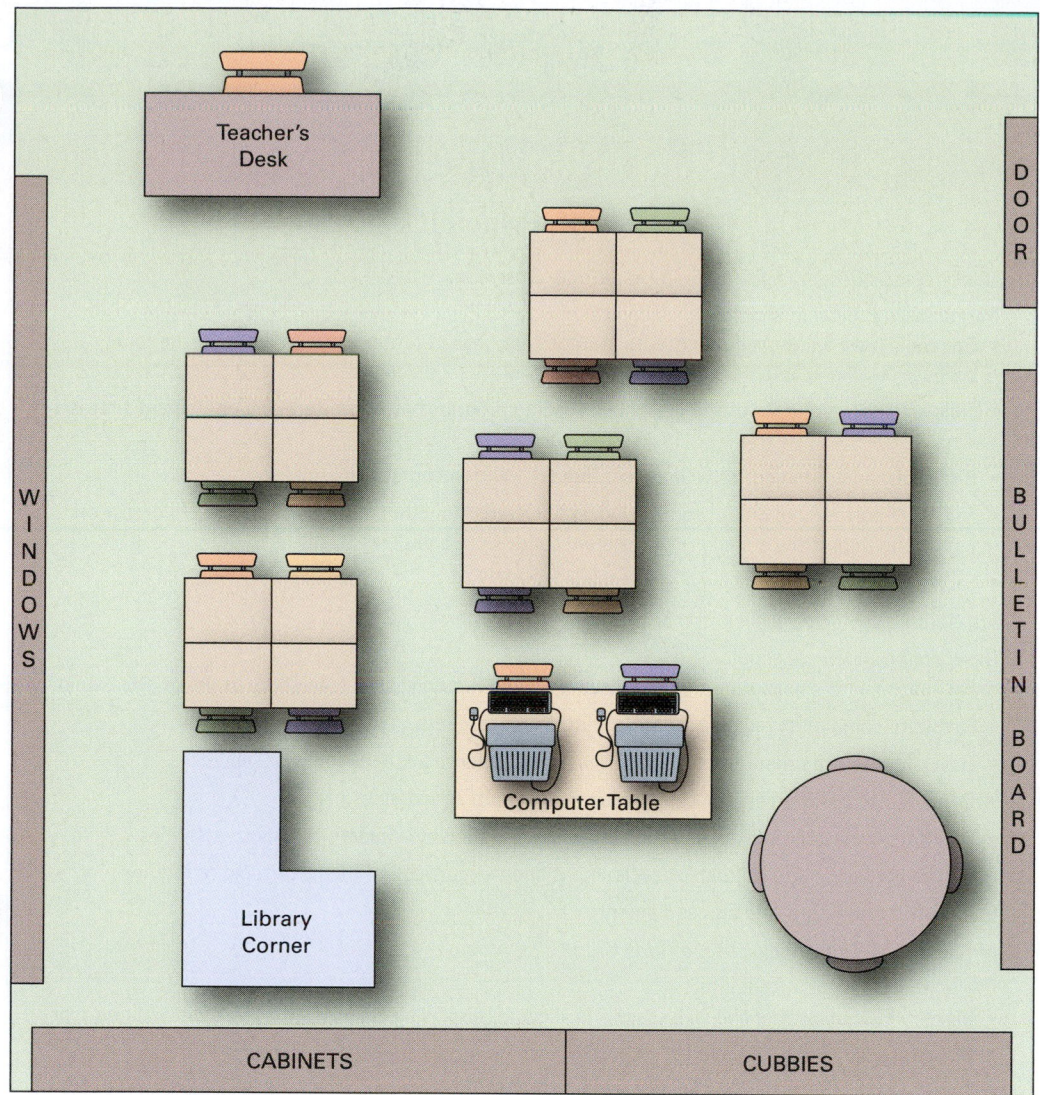

One of the critical tasks of childhood is to learn how to make friends and work with them. Teachers need to think carefully about arrangements of seating, working, and playing areas that will promote positive social interactions. This may mean assigning seats rather than letting children choose their own seats and rearranging seating when necessary. A judicious relocation of students can have a dramatic effect on the atmosphere in the classroom.

Learning centers are found in most elementary school classrooms, especially at the primary level. Library corners, science centers, and art areas can all be important parts of an elementary school classroom. The most recent addition to learning centers is computers. How they will be used needs to be thought through carefully and adjusted from one classroom to another, depending on the number and type of computers available, whether Internet access is available, and how the teacher wants to use these resources. Children in schools in poorer neighborhoods may have far less access to and familiarity with computers at home than children in schools in more affluent neighborhoods.

Much of the work that elementary school students produce is colorful and includes art. Displaying this kind of work on bulletin boards, clotheslines above the students' heads, or windows and doors helps them feel pride in and identify with their classroom, as well as making the room attractive to students. Teachers need to be careful to show each student's work and to change the displays frequently so that students can take their work home to their families.

Elementary school classrooms should be forward looking as well as outward looking. Teachers should consider what developmental challenges (both cognitive and physical) lie ahead for their students and what interests those students might have that are not directly related to the instruction they are receiving in the classroom. An aquarium or terrarium, juggling balls

learning center An area of a classroom specifically designed to facilitate exploration of a particular aspect of the curriculum.

Taking It to the Classroom

Design Principles

Mrs. Jackson's Design Principles for a First-Grade Classroom

The room arrangement should:

- Generally have wide-open space, with storage that does not interfere with space in the room, because "bigger is better"
- Follow the general rules of the prescribed reading program, with furniture and equipment that is flexible
- Be "bright and outgoing" as well as feel "homey," with a carpet and a rocker
- Facilitate partner and group work with desks clustered together, but also facilitate children working on the floor if the activity requires more space than a desk
- Facilitate social success as well as academic success

Ms. Abram's Design Principles for a Second-Grade Classroom

The room arrangement should:

- Facilitate hands-on learning through discovery- and inquiry-based teaching with learning centers
- Facilitate community building among children and teachers
- Have storage and organizational space that complements the need for floor space
- Contain alcoves that children can use for small-group activities
- Facilitate less structured activity than older grades, allowing children to choose activities
- Vary according to the children's development and the curriculum theme or topic of inquiry
- Include flexible furniture and equipment

Mr. Bower's Design Principles for a Third-Grade Classroom

The room arrangement should:

- Make full use of all floor and wall space and allow for displaying children's work without wasting space
- Be acoustically quiet but colorful and exciting to promote interest and learning
- Permit access to the outdoor environment or "outdoor classroom" to extend activities
- Provide quality "private" space for teacher–student or teacher–parent conferences
- Include accessible restrooms and a water fountain to minimize interruptions
- Provide flexible furniture and equipment with space to circulate as children are working

Source: Lackney, J. A., & Jacobs, P. J. (2004). *Teachers as placemakers: Investigating teachers' use of the physical learning environment in instructional design.* University of Wisconsin School Design Research Studio. Retrieved March 10, 2005, from http://schoolstudio.engr.wisc.edu/placemakers.html. Used with permission.

(soft sacks, actually), a telescope or microscope, or materials about careers might spark an interest in a child that will eventually become a vocation or a lifelong avocation.

Lackney and Jacobs (2004) researched the issues that elementary school teachers consider when designing their classrooms. They asked first-, second-, and third-grade teachers what principles they considered important for designing their classrooms. Some of the responses are listed in the above Taking It to the Classroom box.

Designing the Middle or Secondary School Classroom

The design of middle and secondary school classrooms shares some ideas and concerns with the design of elementary school classrooms, but there are significant differences as well. Students usually spend about 42–55 minutes a day in a secondary school classroom, as opposed to the whole day. Moreover, typically only one subject is taught in these classrooms, and the demands of that subject dictate the nature of the classroom design. English classes often need to be arranged so that students can readily see one another for purposes of interaction.

In addition to facilitating working in groups, math teachers generally want students to have clear sight lines to the chalkboard or projection screen. Science classes obviously need to be arranged so that students can conduct lab work safely. Another consideration for secondary school classrooms is that one teacher may not use the same classroom all day long. Classrooms may be shared by two or more teachers, and arrangements have to be worked out to meet the needs of all the classes meeting in that room.

Middle school classrooms may look more like elementary school classrooms or more like secondary school classrooms, depending on the structure of the classes and the school's instructional philosophy. In many schools, students are grouped into instructional teams and only occasionally move from one classroom to another. In other schools, students travel to each of their classes just as high school students do. Teachers in middle schools often draw ideas from both elementary and secondary school classrooms, as well as bringing their own ideas to bear on the unique challenges and opportunities of teaching middle school students.

Some aspects of classroom design are similar across all the school years. The general functions that Steele (1973) described for organizations apply to secondary school classrooms as much as they do to elementary school classrooms, but they play out differently. Issues of security and safety take on a different meaning as students grow older and are likely to use dangerous chemicals in chemistry classes; power tools in wood, metal, or auto shop courses; and knives in biology labs. There are other security issues as well. High school and even middle school students' disagreements may boil over into fights, sometimes with dramatic **consequences**. Also, particularly at the middle school level, students seem to go through an awkward period during which they are not fully in control of their movements. One way of dealing with this problem is to give students a little more physical space. Students will then be less likely to bump into one another as they walk down aisles to get to their seats and less likely to antagonize one another during instruction.

Social contact among students is not always desirable in instructional settings at the middle and secondary school levels. Much instruction at these levels requires that all the students pay attention to what is happening at the front of the room. Putting desks in rows limits interaction among students and the problems associated with it (Bennett & Blundell, 1983). Today, desks are not bolted down, as they were well into the second half of the twentieth century. It is possible to have desks in rows for some purposes and in groups, semicircles, pairs, or other arrangements for other purposes.

Secondary school classrooms are often rather sterile environments. Many rooms do not look as though anyone lives in them. In such cases, students feel little connection with the room; in Steele's terms, they lack any symbolic identification with the room. Students are likely to think, "This is just a place where I am for a while; it doesn't have anything to do with me." This does not have to be the case. Even if your classroom holds 120 students over the course of a day, you can display items that reflect the kinds of work and interactions that occur there. Even an amusing hat on the skeleton in the biology lab can help students feel more at home.

Efficiency in carrying out tasks is a key feature of the secondary school classroom. Students need to get into the classroom and get to work with a minimum of lost time. If a class loses two minutes a day due to a slow start, this can add up to almost nine days of lost instruction over the course of the year. Establishing and enforcing classroom rules provides much of what is needed to get students on-task quickly, but the classroom itself must be ready for the students when they enter. Class arrangements should not provide places where students can gather and chat before the class begins. Students should be easily able to get any supplies they need and get back to their seats quickly. Desks should be arranged so as to focus students' attention naturally where it needs to be focused for the class to begin.

Remember, however, that one of Steele's (1973) categories of the functions of organizations is pleasure. There is no reason for secondary school classrooms to be unattractive. Plants, posters, mobiles, and contrasting colors make a classroom more attractive and contribute to the quality of the interactions that occur within it. A strong effort at the beginning of the year

Appendix
Designing Classrooms

As children grow, their physical environments need to change to meet their changing physical, emotional, cognitive, and social needs (PRAXIS™, I.A.2; INTASC, Principle 2).

consequences The good or bad effects that follow a person's behavior.

(PhotoDisc, Inc./Getty Images)

For some instructional needs, such as administering assessments or having students focus on instruction at the front of the room, it can be useful to have student seating organized in rows.

to make a classroom attractive pays off in a more pleasant environment for the rest of the year. Teachers who are not particularly adept in the area of decoration can rely on friends, colleagues, and parents for help in creating an attractive classroom environment.

Steele's final category is growth. Students in middle or high schools often show remarkable physical growth over the course of the school year, but it is really academic growth that is of concern here. Most academic growth is the direct result of the curriculum. But classrooms can also provide opportunities for unplanned growth. Will a friendship develop between two students who are very different simply because they are seated next to each other? Will a student's interest be piqued by a poster or because the student was asked to help contribute to the appearance of the classroom? Will a book that you place in the class library change a student's life? It is hard to know what kinds of growth might occur due more to chance than to deliberate efforts, but a classroom with many things to capture a student's attention holds greater potential for such growth than a barren one.

Addressing Student Diversity and Special Needs through the Physical Environment

The design of the classroom takes care and consideration, as does the location of students within the classroom. For example, some students should not be seated next to certain other students. Some students need to be close to the action. Students with special needs may need to be close to the teacher or somewhere where it is quieter or where a paraprofessional can provide extra help unobtrusively. In an experimental study looking at students with emotional or behavioral problems, Kamps and colleagues (1999) found that environmental variables have a strong influence on both increasing positive student behavior and decreasing undesirable behavior.

Students who use wheelchairs need to have wide enough pathways to move where they need to without disrupting the class or feeling embarrassed. Students with physical challenges must be considered carefully in planning art, music, physical education, recess, and lunchtime activities. In thinking about students with special needs, do not hesitate to ask the students or their parents, assistants, or former teachers for advice.

Achieving the right classroom mix requires some trial and error. Sometimes opposites work well together; sometimes they are a recipe for disaster. In an ethnically diverse class, veteran teachers often encourage **cross-ethnic groupings**. At the same time, teachers must be sensitive to students who may feel isolated from friends with whom they feel secure.

cross-ethnic groupings Groupings of children from different ethnic groups.

Students should be told right away that the seating arrangement established at the beginning of the year may change as the year progresses. They should also understand that the purpose of the class is not social but academic. The most productive arrangement for learning may not be the most socially appealing one. (See the nearby What Kids Say and Do box.)

Using Technology to Design Your Classroom

www.wiley.com/college/odonnell

Designing classrooms and placing students in them is clearly an art, but as with almost all art, it involves a little science as well. Teachers need to think about the kind of learning community they want to build and the instructional tasks that will be carried out in the classroom. Students need to *be* safe and secure and to *feel* safe and secure. The classroom should also be a welcoming and attractive place. Some teachers are naturally better at classroom design than others. Most teachers are willing to share ideas and lend a hand in setting up a colleague's classroom, especially one who is less experienced.

The National Clearinghouse for Educational Facilities is an excellent place to find ideas about how to design a classroom (the Web address for its site can be found on the Web site for this text). A wealth of other resources are available online, including discussion groups, research literature, and software. A simple search on "classroom design" is an excellent way to start. There are also Web resources dealing with classroom design available on the Web site for this text.

What Kids Say and Do

A Painful Request

Two weeks after rearranging the seats in her eighth-grade honors algebra class, Mrs. Stevens was confronted by Angelo, who had what could have been the saddest face she had ever seen on a child

Mrs. Stevens: Angelo, what's the matter? I've never seen such a sad face.

Angelo: Mrs. Stevens, you have to move my seat. I can't sit next to Maria.

Mrs. Stevens: I thought you liked Maria.

Angelo: That's the problem, Mrs. Stevens. If I'm sitting next to Maria, there's no algebra going on in my head.

Designing the Social Environment: Norms and Rules

Good classroom management skills are important in building a successful career in teaching (Charles, 2002; Good & Brophy, 2000; Good et al., 1987). In fact, Wang, Haertel, and Walberg (1993, 1993/1994) argue, based on an extensive analysis of the research literature, that good classroom management has the greatest influence on student learning. The establishment of norms and rules for classroom behavior is an important component of classroom management. The next Taking It to the Classroom box provides an example of the need for establishing norms and rules.

When children enter a classroom at the beginning of the year, they enter a physical space that has been designed to encourage desirable behaviors and discourage undesirable ones. But as Mrs. Johnson discovered with her high school English class, they also enter a psychological and social space, and they do not yet know the **social norms** (typical behavior that is considered appropriate), rules, and expectations for that space. Will quiet talking to one's neighbor be permitted? What is the procedure for going to the bathroom? What is the first thing that the student is supposed to do on entering the classroom? What should students do if they see another student misbehaving?

Walter Doyle (1986) has described six features of classrooms that make them unlike almost any other setting. They may remind you of the idea of a classroom having a life of its own, which we described at the beginning of the chapter (Smith et al., 2001). Doyle's six features of classrooms are as follows:

1. **Multidimensionality.** In classrooms, students do not only read and write, they put on plays, do artwork, argue with one another, care for the class pet, hold elections and debates, conduct science experiments, make recitations in foreign languages, and explore the world through the Internet. Classrooms have to facilitate this multidimensionality.

2. **Simultaneity.** Rarely is only one thing going on in a classroom. At the same time that Mrs. Knowles is working with Marissa on initial estimation of long division, a group of students is writing a letter to the mayor to ask that the traffic light near the school stay red longer. Tory and Joaquim are checking out a Web site with information about an upcoming meteor shower, and Martin is trying to paste Lara's desk to the floor. And Mrs. Knowles *knows all of this*. Not only can exceptional teachers handle the multidimensional and simultaneous nature of activities in the classroom, they relish it.

3. **Immediacy.** The French have a saying: *l'esprit d'escalier*, or "the wit of the staircase." It refers to the really clever things people might have said *had they thought of them at the time*. With thousands of interactions with students each day, *l'esprit d'escalier* could become a teaching motto. Classroom life is a real-time event. Teaching occurs in real time. At the end of the day, a good teacher might come up with half a dozen better responses to certain situations than the one used at the time. There is no need to be upset about not always coming up with the perfect response. With experience, teachers develop the ability to make good decisions more quickly. This is one of the characteristics that distinguishes veteran teachers from novices.

4. **Unpredictability.** Related to immediacy is the notion of unpredictability. Although, in general, teachers have a good sense of what will happen each day, from an instructional perspective they do not know whether a student will come to class with a personal problem that makes him or her act out or whether a fire drill will occur in the middle of a lesson that is going very well. Teachers have to be calm in the face of such unpredictability.

Appendix
Classroom Rules
Establishing rules effectively early in the year is the key to a positive classroom community (PRAXIS™, I.C.4; INTASC, Principle 5).

social norms Expectations for proper behavior.

multidimensionality Having more than one characteristic (such as a purpose or an ability) at the same time.

(Dana White/Photo Edit)

This classroom illustrates the multidimensional nature of middle school life. How many different things are happening here?

immediacy In teaching, decisions and actions have to occur in the real time of classroom life, that is, immediately, not at a leisurely pace.

Taking It to the Classroom

Even the Brightest Kids . . .

Vernita Johnson was a first-year high school English teacher. The principal had assigned her the top honors English class in an effort to "give her one really positive experience in her first year of teaching." It was a noble idea, but it was not working. Six weeks into the school year, Mrs. Johnson was at her wit's end. She was seriously considering quitting at the end of the semester and going to graduate school in any field other than education. These were the brightest kids in the school, yet she found them uncooperative, uninterested, unmanageable, and generally unteachable. They were rude to one another and to her, did not hand in homework on time, and complained about almost every assignment.

At the end of a particularly vexing day, Sander showed up in her doorway. He was not one of the worst-behaving students in the class, but he did not contribute much. Most of the time, he sat and looked at his desk.

"Mrs. Johnson, can I talk with you?" asked Sander, surpassing the total number of words he had spoken in the class to date.

"Certainly, Sander, please come in and have a seat."

"Mrs. Johnson, this class isn't going very well."

She had to suppress a laugh. This was the understatement of all understatements. "No, Sander. It isn't. Do you have any thoughts on why that is?"

Sander paused for an uncomfortably long time. Then he said, "Well, I've been in school with these kids since we were in elementary school, and they're good kids. When your class is over, we all go down the hall to math class, and there aren't any problems there."

"Are you saying this is my fault?"

Another interminable pause, and then, "No. That's just what happens."

"Why did you come see me today, Sander?"

"Because I want this to be a good class. So do the other kids."

Sander had not uttered more than 100 words in the course of this conversation, but he had spoken volumes. First, even in an honors class, there need to be rules and expectations that are consistent with the goals of the course, and they need to be enforced. This has to start at the beginning of the school year. Second, the negative attitude that Mrs. Johnson had developed toward this class may have been unjustified. Maybe the students did want the class to be a good one, but they were not in charge. Third, if she was to salvage the year (and perhaps her teaching career), she needed to make some changes quickly. The first step would be to walk down the hall and have a chat with the honors math teacher.

See the next Taking It to the Classroom box for advice on remaining calm in unpredictable situations.

5. **Lack of privacy.** Classrooms are public places. There is no place to hide, especially for the teacher. Stuart Polansky (1986) captures this notion in his highly readable account of high school teaching, *900 Shows a Year: A Look at Teaching from a Teacher's Side of the Desk*. Lack of privacy plays out differently at different levels. Although elementary

Taking It to the Classroom

When the World Impinges on the Classroom

From time to time, something happens in the world or locally that brings the school day to a halt. Teachers have struggled with the task of talking to students about international tragedies, assassinations of presidents, disasters in space exploration, or local events that had significance for schoolchildren.

When such an event occurs, it is a good idea to talk things over, even if only briefly, with colleagues and supervisors so that the school, as a community, can take a consistent approach. Honesty, compassion, sincerity, willingness to listen and share feelings, and concern for the students should be guiding principles. It is important to keep in mind that how children handle the event depends in part on how it is presented to them and discussed by their teacher.

school teachers need to provide structure and monitoring for students during the entire day, middle and high school teachers are more likely to be the direct focus of the students' attention during each class period. Lack of privacy is a feature of classrooms for students as well as for teachers. In school, students are almost never alone.

6. **History.** Classrooms do not start from scratch each morning. Classroom interactions and their consequences have a history. Brad and Jessica may both fail to turn in homework on the same day. But Brad will be treated differently from Jessica if he has not turned in his homework on four consecutive days and this is the first time she has forgotten her homework all year. A history of events accumulates over the course of the year and affects how the teacher interacts with students and how they interact with one another.

The Tension between Freedom and Structure

Structure revolves around teachers clearly communicating what they expect students to do to achieve academic, social, and behavioral goals. In most societies and social activities, there is a certain degree of tension between freedom and structure. In highly structured settings where appropriate behavior is well understood, such as going to a movie or participating in a graduation ceremony, people often seek freedom from the regimentation. Thus, they may call out at the film or throw popcorn. They may decorate their mortarboard hats or wear shorts and sandals under their graduation robes. On the other hand, in highly unstructured settings, such as a free Saturday or a trip to a museum, people often seek to impose some structure on the setting (Smith & Wolf, 1996).

It might seem from this analysis that structure and freedom are opposite ends of the same continuum—that high structure means low freedom, and vice versa. But the point is that people value both structure and freedom *at the same time*. Those who study classroom management view structure and freedom as distinct aspects of classroom management strategy. Teachers can impose a highly structured classroom on students and offer them little or no freedom. Or they can impose a highly structured classroom on students and offer them a great deal of freedom by giving them choices, opportunities to be heard, and opportunities to take the initiative within the classroom structure. The worst classroom management strategy is to provide a classroom with little or no structure. This is a permissive environment. Students learn and function better in a highly structured environment. The optimal classroom management environment, however, is one that features both high structure (clear rules, procedures, goals) and considerable freedom within that structure (choices, opportunities).

First impressions are lasting. This teacher has a brightly colored shirt and decorations in the hallway to welcome students on the first day of school.

(© Syracuse Newspapers/Dick Blume/The Image Works)

Initially, a classroom is an unstructured setting. For students to feel comfortable and be productive, some sort of structure must be imposed on that setting. Students need to know what to do, how to do it, when to do it, and how to get help if they need it. Pace and Hemmings (2007) argue that establishing the authority of the teacher in the classroom and maintaining a positive classroom environment is a job that is never *done*, it is always in process. What this means is that the teachers must always consider how their actions affect not only the issue of the moment but how they might change the underlying dynamics and relationships in the classroom.

Getting Started

For a school year to be successful, it is essential to start setting rules and norms for classroom behavior on the first day of school. As Mrs. Johnson learned the hard way, time spent establishing clear expectations for classroom behavior more than pays off in time saved for learning during the rest of the school year (Evertson & Harris, 2003). Like classroom environments, rules and norms for behavior are different for elementary, middle, and secondary schools, even for different groups within those schools. Weinstein, Romano and Mignano (2010, p. 61) have developed an excellent set of principles for thinking about classroom rules:

- Rules should be reasonable and necessary.
- Rules need to be clear and understandable.
- Rules should be consistent with the instructional goals and with what we know about how people learn.
- Classroom rules need to be consistent with school rules.

Most teachers have a sense of the rules they want for their classrooms, but many find it effective to develop the rules jointly with the class. Needless to say, this requires some informal control on the part of the teacher, especially for younger children, but it is also good to let the children feel a sense of responsibility for how the classroom is run. It is also important to be sure that students understand the specifics of the rules. Exactly what is a violation of the rules and what is not?

The First Day of School No matter what happened the year before, students and their families approach the first day of a new school year filled with hope and some anxiety. The first day of school is critical for the teacher as well, especially the beginning teacher. Whether at the elementary or the secondary level, the first day must be well planned. First impressions are lasting ones. Research findings show clearly that the very beginning of the school year is the most important factor in how the whole year will go. Emmer, Evertson, and Anderson (1980), for example, observed a group of third-grade teachers for the first three weeks of school and found that effective teachers had clear rules for behavior and spent a good deal of time, from day 1, teaching these rules.

Teachers need to clarify on the first day their behavior expectations for the rest of the school year. For younger students, this focus will most likely be on helping them understand the rules. As described in the following sections, it takes a while for younger students to fully understand what is and is not appropriate. Time spent pointing out examples of appropriate and inappropriate behavior will be helpful. At the secondary school level, the issue will more likely be one of testing the rules. Students will be trying to discover what kinds of behavior will *sneak in* just under the limits and what kinds of behavior will be considered *crossing the line*. Burden (2000, p. 96) has developed the following list of guidelines for communicating classroom rules to students:

1. Plan to discuss and teach the rules during the first class session.
2. Discuss the need for the rules.
3. Identify specific expectations that are relevant to each rule; provide examples and stress the positive side of the rules.
4. Inform students of the consequences when rules are followed as well as when they are broken.
5. Verify understanding.
6. Send copies of your discipline policy to caregivers and to the principal.
7. Post the rules in a prominent location.
8. Remind the class of the rules at times other than when someone has just broken a rule.
9. Review the rules regularly.

The first day is not the day to become the students' friend: The first day is the day to communicate how the class is going to operate and to *nip in the bud* potential problem behaviors. This does not mean that the teacher cannot smile. It just means that the primary task of the day is to work toward establishing the sense of order that will permit the development of a learning community and last for the rest of the school year.

Rules for Elementary School Classrooms Elementary school students are typically more eager to please their teacher than are middle or high school students (Buzzelli & Johnston, 2002; Pace & Hemmings, 2007). This is particularly true of younger children. On the other hand, they know less about what is and is not appropriate classroom behavior. Also, they have more trouble simply understanding rules. Therefore, elementary school teachers need to make sure that rules are understood. They spend more time teaching the rules, demonstrating dos and don'ts, and providing corrective feedback than middle or high school teachers do, but less time dealing with defiant behavior. Establishing rules requires determining both what the rules should be and what the consequences of not following them should be. It is important to be certain that both the rules and the consequences are reasonable and enforceable.

Figures 6.2 and 6.3 show two sets of classroom rules. Figure 6.2 is a set of rules for a kindergarten, and Figure 6.3 is a set of rules for an upper-elementary school classroom. It is interesting to see that in the kindergarten, where the children participated in setting the rules, making noise with your shoes was a fairly serious concern, whereas niceness needed to be shown only to friends. Note that the kindergarten rules do not have a set of consequences associated with them.

As mentioned earlier, small children tend to be more anxious to please the teacher, so there might not be a need for a formal set of consequences (though in certain classrooms there may be). However, young children do not have as much experience with rules as older students do, and teachers must spend time instructing them in proper behavior. How would the teacher of this kindergarten class go about teaching students the specifics associated with some of these rules, such as "Help Mrs. Wade"?

At the upper-elementary school level, it is advisable to include clearly stated, enforceable consequences. Note that rules for students in the upper-elementary school grades and above should specify consequence for breaking the rules. Teachers must, however, consider whether they are willing to give up part of their lunch periods to spend time with misbehaving students, as this teacher apparently is. The lunchtime detention mentioned here might be problematic in several respects. First, it is also a type of detention for the teacher as well in that she loses her own free time—a break she might welcome in the

Mrs. Wade's Classroom Rules

This set of classroom rules were written by and agreed upon by Mrs. Wade's kindergarten class.

- Help Mrs. Wade.
- Don't hit or kick people.
- Play nicely on the playground.
- Be nice to your friends.
- Be quiet in the hallway.
- Raise your hand.
- Don't make fun of people.
- Don't be loud with your shoes.
- Clean up your mess.
- Don't run in the hallway.
- Don't run in the cafeteria.
- Behave.

Figure 6.2 Set of Kindergarten Rules

Taking It to the Classroom

Do You Know Jack? The Reluctant Misbehaver

Jack, an athletic student but a struggling learner, was prone to engage in behavior that would get him into trouble. Seated next to him was Melvin, a much stronger student academically but completely unaware of how irritating his behavior could be. During reading instruction, Jack has been working hard to pay attention while Melvin, who is bored, keeps launching his pencil into the aisle from the edge of his desk. Jack ignores the first several launches, but on about the fifth try, Melvin's pencil hits him in the side of the head. Jack gives out a huge and sincere sigh, picks up Melvin's pencil, and takes a big bite out of the middle. He returns the pieces to Melvin's desk saying, "I think these are yours."

As Jack and Melvin's teacher, what would you do about this situation?

1. Do not laugh, at least not until you make it to the teacher's lounge later in the day.
2. Point out to Jack that the pencil has been in Melvin's hands and on the floor and ask him whether he took that into consideration before putting the pencil in his mouth. Talk to him about more constructive ways to deal with a nuisance such as Melvin.
3. Tell Melvin to stop pestering Jack. Tell him you expect more mature behavior from him and offer some prosocial ways of behaving in that situation.
4. Keep Melvin from getting bored. Melvin needs more challenging work, not as punishment for this incident but to keep him more generally engaged.

**Figure 6.3 Set of Upper-
Elementary School Rules
and Consequences**

CLASSROOM RULES

**WHY we have classroom rules: To keep our classroom a
positive learning community where everyone can be
productive and feel safe and respected.**

1. Treat your classmates the way you would like them to
   treat you.
2. Listen carefully to directions as they are given.
3. Be in your seat and ready to learn when the bell rings.
4. Bring necessary materials to class.
5. When you want to contribute to the discussion, raise your
   hand to be called on.
6. No hitting, kicking, threatening, throwing of objects,
   making fun of, or teasing.
7. Follow all school rules as presented in the school handbook.

WHAT the consequences of not following the rules are:

1. A verbal warning that a rule has been broken.
2. A second warning and name written on the board.
3. A conference with the teacher about following rules and a
   written assignment for the student on how behavior will
   be improved.
4. Detention for part of lunch period and referral to
   principal's office.
5. Conference with student and parents.

FOR A SERIOUS VIOLATION, any of the steps of the
consequences may be skipped.

middle of the day. Second, it is important not to deny the student the opportunity to eat lunch (this detention comes during the recess portion of the lunch period). And third, for some students, taking away a time to go outside and burn off energy might not be an advisable approach to classroom management. (See the nearby Taking It to the Classroom box.)

Rules for Middle and High School Classrooms Like Vernita Johnson, teachers at the middle and high school levels may find that their students are somewhat less likely to behave appropriately simply to gain the teacher's approval but that they are better able than younger children to understand rules and consequences. The tone of the rules and consequences will probably have to be somewhat more firm than at the elementary and primary levels. For a beginning teacher, coming up with a list of rules that is comprehensive without being overwhelming may be challenging. General rules must be considered as well as rules that are specific to particular subjects. Lab or shop courses need different rules from foreign language or math classes. Safety is especially important in lab classes. Figures 6.4 and 6.5 show two examples of classroom rules and consequences.

Thinking about Difficult Situations Some classroom settings are simply more difficult than others. You may find yourself teaching in one someday. Ryan Del Guercio (2011, p. 40) offers the following tips for establishing control in challenging settings:

- Create a seating chart for students on day 1, and, if needed, change seats throughout the year.
- Be as organized as possible as you present a lesson. A seamless lesson provides students with little downtime and, therefore, fewer chances to misbehave.

Rules for Mr. West's Class

Our goal is to have a happy and productive classroom where students can learn and Mr. West can teach!

Six Easy-to-Follow Classroom Rules: *The "B" List!*

1. Be on time—that's in your seat and ready to go when the bell rings.
2. Be respectful—we are all equally important in this class and deserve respect.
3. Be ready to learn. Have your homework and other materials out and ready to go.
4. Be a follower (of classroom procedures).
5. Be safe. Don't create a hazard for yourself or your classmates.
6. Be thoughtful. Treat others as you would want to be treated.

Consequences *for Failing to Follow the Rules*

1st offense: Warning from Mr. West about the behavior and the rule.

2nd offense: Conference with Mr. West where the problem is explored.

3rd offense: Notification of parents of misbehavior.

4th offense: You and your problem go to the vice principal's office.

- Greet students as they enter the room and give them direction right away ("sit in your seats," "take out your homework," "find your folder," etc.).
- Identify class leaders and gain their respect. The behavior of kids that the other students admire sets the tone for the class. These students may even help you by telling classmates to "quiet down" or by modeling good behavior.
- Never argue with a student when addressing misbehavior. Arguing sends the message that students are your equal and that is not the case.
- Use the "broken record" technique:
- Give the student a direction, such as "Please have a seat."
- Be sure to use "please" and "thank you." Impolite behavior on your part gives the student license to behave badly.
- Don't argue with the students if they disobey.
- Repeat the direction two times, and then give the student a choice, such as "Sit in your seat, please, or you will receive detention for failure to follow the teacher's directions."
- Let the student take responsibility for his or her actions by choosing to take a detention. Most of the time students will want to avoid the consequence.
- Use positive/praise directions by recognizing students who are following directions, such as "I see Stephen has his book out and so does Marc—good job."

Figure 6.5 Set of Rules and Consequences at the High School Level

Source: Otay Ranch High School. Reprinted with the permission of Minako Oskay, www.injapanese.com, Otay Ranch High School.

Otay Ranch High School
Ms. Oskay
Classroom Rules

Please...
- Come to class on time, and be ready to study when the bell rings.
- Bring all the materials every class.
- Bring assignments ready to submit.
- Participate in the class activities.
- Do not sleep or chat.
- Be seated at your seat.
- Respect yourself, the classmates, and the teacher.
- No drinks, food, or chewing gum. Discard drinks in cups before you enter the classroom. Water bottles with caps are allowed. Any other drink bottles need to be put away in your backpack.
- Do not overuse the hall pass. Regular and/or repetitive use of the hall pass and/or not coming back to the classroom for more than maximum 5 minutes will be considered "truancy". (Please ask for a nurse pass if you are sick.)
- Put your cell phone in "silent mode." No phone calls and no photo-taking/videotaping using cell phones are allowed during the class. Keep your cell phone in your backpack.
- No music with headphones or earphones. Keep your CD player and headphone in your backpack.
- Take off your caps, hats, sunglasses, and hoods.

THANK YOU!!

Consequences:
If the above classroom rules are not followed, the following corrective steps will be taken.
(1) Warning to student and/or conference with student
(2) Call to parent
(3) Detention with the teacher, or campus/classroom beautification
(4) Parent/teacher conference with student present
(5) Referral to the school administration
(6) Withdrawal from the class
In case of serious offenses, some of the above steps will be skipped and/or immediate referrals may be written.

Establishing Procedures for Routines

RIDE Think about a new student joining a classroom in midyear. How hard would it be to learn classroom rules if they were not made explicit?

In classrooms, pencils have to be sharpened, assessments handed out, homework turned in, fire drills carried out, and the like. These activities do not need rules, but they do need procedures. Without procedures, time is lost, disturbances occur, and students may feel that they are being treated unfairly. Gaea Leinhardt and her colleagues (1987) at the University of Pittsburgh have developed categories of **routines**, and Weinstein, Romano and Mignano (2010) have converted them into a set of practical classroom applications. There are three broad categories of routines: class-running routines, lesson-running routines, and interaction routines. When routines are firmly established and running well, they almost become invisible. One of the characteristics of expert teachers is that their students seem to know what to do without the teacher telling them. It may seem like magic to someone entering the class for the first time in midyear, but it is, in all likelihood, the result of clear communication and consistent reinforcement. It helps provide a structure for students that makes them comfortable in understanding what they are to do.

How Can I Use This?

What procedures used by your teachers seemed to work especially well? Maybe you can adapt them to your own classes.

routines Activities that occur on a regular, ongoing basis and require the same or similar behavior on each occurrence (such as sharpening pencils and going to lunch).

- **Class-running routines.** These involve the everyday, nonacademic business of the classroom, including taking attendance, going to the bathroom, cleaning chalkboards, and leaving and entering the room at the beginning and end of the day. Creating effective routines for these types of activities can save teachers and students considerable time and aggravation.

- **Lesson-running routines.** These involve instruction. They specify such things as what students should bring to class every day, how to use language lab equipment, what should be included in homework and how it should be handed in, and procedures for using chemicals in the chemistry lab. The effectiveness of lesson-running routines will directly influence the quality of instruction.

- **Interaction routines.** These govern talking in the classroom. In a room filled with 30 or so people, talk affects the degree to which students can be heard, concentrate on their work, and engage in class discussions. There will be different routines for different instructional activities. For example, when the teacher is presenting information, students will probably be required to raise their hands if they wish to speak. On the other hand, in a small-group discussion, students need to be able to speak more freely without being impolite to others in the group.

Misbehavior: Informal Correctives and Imposing Penalties

One of the problems that novice teachers frequently run into is establishing and enforcing consequences and **penalties** when students misbehave. Mrs. Johnson, for example, was struggling in this area. Classrooms are filled with students who are engaging in minor infractions of rules or simply not paying attention. These situations call for teacher action that stops the behavior without interrupting the instruction.

We all remember from our own school days some of the more effective methods that our teachers used to keep students in line. Some teachers had a *look* that could stop misbehavior in midstream; others used a mild form of ridicule; still others merely moved toward the misbehaving student.

Something that all teachers need to attend to is who gets the look—or the reprimand, or the punishment—and who does not. Research indicates that boys' misbehavior is more likely than girls' to elicit a response from the teacher and that a student who is weaker academically is more likely to be punished for an infraction than a good student making the same infraction. Teachers also need to make certain that students who are different from themselves in ethnicity, religion, gender, or ability are receiving fair and equal treatment in terms of misbehavior and the imposition of consequences.

Weinstein, Mignano, and Romano (2010) have categorized a wide variety of teacher interventions and penalties. Drawing on this work, the following are some options for correcting misbehavior with minimal interruption of the flow of instruction. The nearby Uncommon Sense box discusses which ones teachers choose most frequently.

- Ignoring behavior. Sometimes misbehavior can be ignored in an obvious fashion to communicate that it has been observed and that the teacher considers the flow of instruction more important than one student misbehaving.
- Using facial expressions that let a student know a behavior is not appreciated.
- Making direct eye contact with the miscreant; also known as *the look.*
- Signaling to the offending student with a hand signal or a nod.
- Moving toward the student who is misbehaving.
- Stopping instruction in midsentence. (The pause usually attracts attention.)
- Increasing the volume of instruction noticeably (to let students know there is a disturbance that requires this modification).
- Saying the student's name. This can be done directly or as part of the flow of the instruction, as in "Let's say, David, for instance, wanted to know. . . ."
- Calling on the student. There is a fine line here between bringing the student back into the instruction and making him or her feel "picked on." The difference often lies in how the teacher handles the student's response. Students might feel that they are being treated unfairly, for example, if the teacher calls on them to answer a question they did not hear or cannot answer. A less punitive use of this approach is to call on the student first, then ask the question.
- Using humor. This can be directed toward the class as a whole or toward an individual student. It is important to differentiate between humor and sarcasm, however.
- Using an **I-message** or other indication of disappointment in the student behavior. I-messages involve describing the inappropriate behavior and its effect on the teacher or

penalties Consequences for misbehavior, such as loss of privileges, time-out, or a visit to the principal's office.

I-message A reaction to a behavior that describes the behavior and how it has affected a given situation as well as the individual's emotional response to the behavior.

What Does This Mean to Me?
Which of these options do you think you would be able to carry out? Which ones should you practice?

the class, followed by a statement of the teacher's feelings about the situation. For example, "Danielle, when you start putting things in your backpack before the bell rings, I feel that you don't care about what's happening in class." A less formal approach might be a statement such as, "It's hard for me to explain this properly with other people talking."

- Making a direct request to cease and desist.
- Reminding students that a rule is being broken. This has the additional benefit of letting students know that the teacher knows the rule is being broken.
- Raising the possibility of a penalty if the behavior does not stop. But it is important here not to threaten a penalty that you are not prepared to carry out if the misbehavior does not stop.

Sometimes misbehavior ranges beyond inattentiveness or distracting behavior, and a more significant intervention is necessary. This can be a particular problem for special needs students with behavioral problems. When misbehavior clearly violates class rules and informal correctives do not seem sufficient, penalties might be the next step in maintaining a productive learning community. There are a variety of possible penalties, which Weinstein et al. (2010) have organized into categories. These have been adapted to create the list that follows this paragraph. This list should not be interpreted as a hierarchy or a sequence; it is simply a list of possibilities. When they administer penalties, teachers should make a special effort to explain why the student is being penalized and what the student can do to avoid penalties in the future. By explaining the rationale behind the penalty and by offering students a more desirable and productive way of behaving, the teacher's goal is not so much to punish the student as it is to create a learning experience in which the misbehaving student has a chance to internalize the classroom rule and develop a more constructive way of behaving.

If it is necessary to punish a misbehaving student, these guidelines will be helpful:

- Assignment of points toward a penalty. Many teachers have a system in which a student receives a negative mark of some sort for misbehavior. These points have to accumulate for the student to reach the next level of punishment. Typically, improved behavior can reduce the number of points on the student's record.
- Loss of privileges. The privilege lost can be free time, use of the computer, choosing a game for the class to play, or something else that the student values.
- Time-out. This means removal from the flow of activity in the classroom for a specified period.
- Written reflections on the problem. Some teachers have students write about what happened, why it happened, what the consequences were, and how they can improve their behavior in the future. The writing assignment may include a letter of apology to an affected student. This is the journal version of having to write "I will not speak out of turn" 100 times on the chalkboard.
- Visits to the principal's office. Nobody wants to go to the principal's office. Teachers should keep in mind that the principal cannot take the time to attend to large numbers of misbehaving children. Furthermore, as a new teacher, you do not want to send a message to the principal that you cannot control children. If this seems to be where a situation is headed, talk to a colleague about it.
- Contact with parents. Contacting caregivers should not be used as a threat to students; it should be an admission that the child's behavior is sufficiently out of line that the school and the family need to work together to solve the problem. To prevent the situation from becoming this serious, teachers may wish to involve students' families in the classroom at a much earlier stage. Teachers need to be careful not to communicate the idea that a student needs to be punished by parents. Positive communication established to promote positive outcomes is the key.

MINDFUL HABITS OF EFFECTIVE TEACHERS

Effective teachers pick their battles carefully. Effective teachers know when to let something pass and when to insist on something. They know how to defuse potentially explosive situations and when to draw the line.

Conclusions about Establishing Norms and Rules

Setting rules and imposing consequences for not following them are critical elements of classroom management. Rules need to be taught to students in a conscientious fashion, and teachers must make sure that students—especially younger students—understand them.

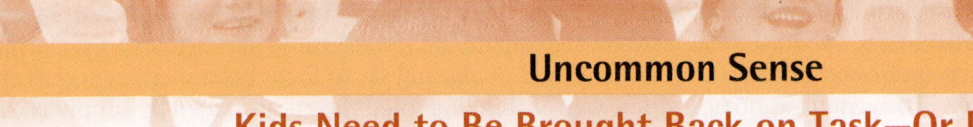

Uncommon Sense
Kids Need to Be Brought Back on Task—Or Do They?

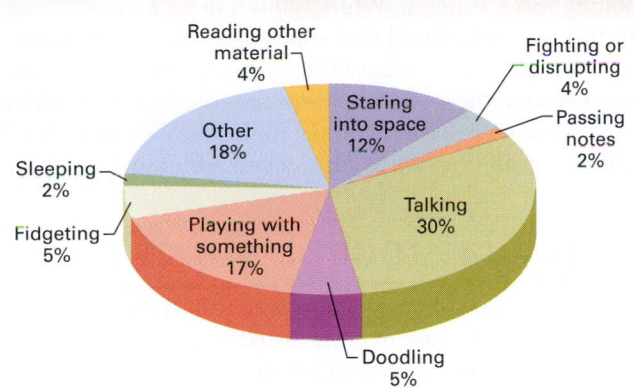

Reading other material 4%
Fighting or disrupting 4%
Staring into space 12%
Passing notes 2%
Other 18%
Sleeping 2%
Talking 30%
Fidgeting 5%
Playing with something 17%
Doodling 5%

Numbers have been rounded off.

Figure 6.6 What Students Do When They Are Off-Task

Source: Adapted from Escudero, J., Kim, Y., McGrath, M., Odabasi, P., So, E., & Vera, F. (2002). *What cues cause off-task students to get back on task?* Unpublished manuscript. New Brunswick, NJ: Rutgers University.

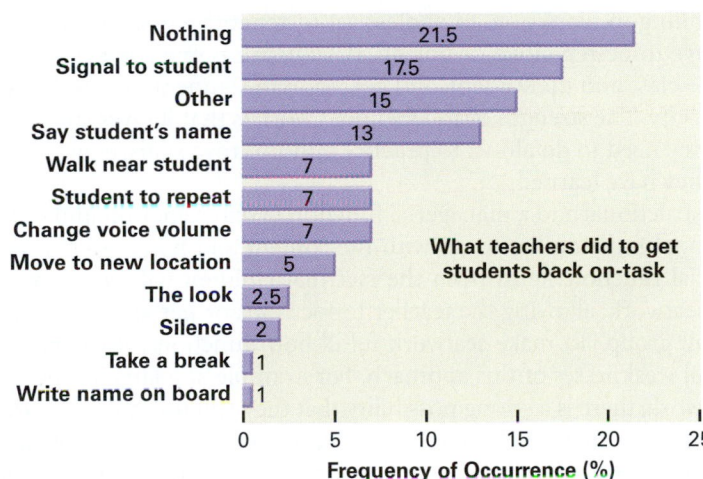

Nothing 21.5
Signal to student 17.5
Other 15
Say student's name 13
Walk near student 7
Student to repeat 7
Change voice volume 7
Move to new location 5
The look 2.5
Silence 2
Take a break 1
Write name on board 1

What teachers did to get students back on-task

Frequency of Occurrence (%)

Two of the authors of this text teach a course called "Teacher as Researcher" in which students who are preparing to become teachers collect and analyze data on topics of their choice. One group project focused on perhaps the most common form of misbehavior in classrooms: not paying attention, or being **off-task**. This research team (Escudero et al., 2002) went into 14 elementary school classrooms (grades 4–6) and observed a complete lesson in mathematics. Their task was to scan the classroom to find a student who was off-task. The researchers recorded what kind of off-task behavior the student engaged in and what the teacher did to bring the student back on task. Figure 6.6 shows the percentages of the different kinds of off-task behaviors in which students engaged.

Now look at Figure 6.7 to see what the teachers did to get the students back on-task. Somewhat surprisingly, the most frequent behavior that veteran teachers employed to get students back on-task was to do nothing. In almost 25% of the cases observed, students got themselves back on-task with no action by the teacher. The second most frequent occurrence is to signal to the student, either by nodding or by pointing at the student and the work, that he or she is off-task. The *other* category contained a variety of nonverbal and verbal behaviors, including using humor, tapping on the student's desk while passing by, and so forth. Perhaps the most direct intervention that was used with any frequency was simply saying the student's name.

The behavior of the teachers in this study demonstrates that their first priority was keeping the lesson on pace. Novice teachers sometimes expend too much effort dealing with inattention, disrupting the entire class in the process. This is not to say that teachers should rely on doing nothing, but rather that students will often get themselves back on task, and when an intervention is needed, it need not disrupt the flow of instruction.

Figure 6.7 Teachers' Most Frequent Responses to Students' Off-Task Behavior

Source: Adapted from Escudero, J., Kim, Y., McGrath, M., Odabasi, P., So, E., & Vera, F. (2002). *What cues cause off-task students to get back on task?* Unpublished manuscript. New Brunswick, NJ: Rutgers University.

There are a variety of *tricks* that teachers can use to stop minor misbehaviors before they become major disruptions. Successful teachers blend nonverbal cues, direct requests, humor, and occasionally penalties to keep the class on task. Establishing procedures for running the class, the lesson, and interaction routines is also an effective way to support good behavior and minimize misbehavior.

Developing a positive and productive classroom environment that has a minimum of behavioral problems is one of the biggest challenges that new teachers face (Smith, 2006; Smith, Mobley, & Klein, 2003). Help is available from Web sites and educators who have written about the topic. In addition, it is advisable for new teachers to ask how other teachers in their school deal with classroom management issues, what kinds of rules students have been required to follow in previous years, and what the most effective classroom routines are.

off task Not paying attention to instruction.

A Student-Centered Approach

Teachers adopt a general style or approach to working with their students. Some teachers take a more formal, or authoritarian, approach, while others are more student-centered. By student-centered, we mean that teachers are empathetic toward students, try to express warmth and genuine concern for their students' well-being, and try to focus on student concerns and issues. The general approach to this way of thinking might be encapsulated by simply taking the students' perspective on a given situation. Ask yourself: If I were the student here, what would I want? What would I be looking for? Cornelius-White (2007), in an extensive meta-analysis of the research literature in this area, has found that student-centered instruction is positively associated with a wide variety of positive student outcomes. Of course, at the same time that good teachers take into consideration the students' side of the equation, they will not lose sight of their responsibility as teacher, leader, and role model in the class. To consider the student perspective is not to abdicate responsibility; it is to consider an additional viewpoint.

Managing Day-to-Day Classroom Instruction

Day-to-day instruction can mean many different things. In the classroom from 1937 that is pictured at the beginning of the chapter, it looks as though most instruction will take the form of lectures and explanations by the teacher. Indeed, this is what teaching consisted of for many decades. In some classes, it still is. This approach can be very effective if the teacher's ability to explain is strong. However, most teachers instruct in a variety of formats and settings, using independent work (seatwork), small-group work, and whole-class instruction. This section describes those formats and examines the strengths and weaknesses of each.

Independent Work or Seatwork

seatwork Work that is done independently by students at their desks or seats.

Seatwork is independent work on some learning task that is done individually by a student in the classroom. This approach has been in disfavor in recent years because it is assumed to consist of little more than filling in blanks on an endless set of repetitive worksheets. Seatwork, however, does not have to be repetitive or boring. If seatwork is engaging, related to the instructional goals of the class and the student, and geared to the student's cognitive level, it can be a very useful activity. The strength of independent work is that it gives students a chance to work on things they need to do alone: to practice and improve skills, explore new areas, or consolidate what they have learned.

Seatwork has both an instructional and a managerial function (Weinstein, Romano & Mignano, 2010). The instructional function has to do with the content and nature of the seatwork, whereas the managerial function stems from the fact that children will be quiet and nondisruptive while doing seatwork, allowing the teacher to focus his or her attention on an individual student or a small group. To make seatwork fulfill both functions, teachers need to keep in mind the potential weaknesses of this approach. For example, if a large number of students are engaged in seatwork, there is a strong possibility that they will finish their work at different times. This can result in students with nothing to do, which is always a problem. In thinking about seatwork, the teacher needs to have an option for students who finish early, such as "When you're finished with this, please work on the geography assignment from yesterday."

Another seatwork concern is that, because the purpose is to have students work independently, if they get stuck on a problem, the teacher cannot always be there to help them. Several options are available for addressing this concern:

- Another student can provide help.
- Students can skip problems that they cannot figure out.
- Students can *hold* their help requests until the teacher is free to help them.
- Independent activities can be assigned that do not call for a series of correct answers. For example, independent work could involve writing in a journal about recently read material or editing a peer's essay.

Seatwork can also be blended with homework by giving students a problem set, allowing some seat time to work on the problems, and assigning as homework the problems not finished in class. This approach has several advantages. First, because every problem done in class means more free time in the evening, there is strong motivation for students to stay on-task. Second, if a student has a question about a particular problem, it can be asked while the teacher is available, and misunderstandings can be diagnosed and corrected quickly. Third, assigningle enough problems eliminates the possibility of some students finishing their seatwork and not having anything to do.

Another effective approach to seatwork is to have students study for an upcoming assessment. Many students are very poor at studying for exams. If the teacher is going to work with a small group or an individual student, the remaining students can be assigned study material. This studying can be structured so as to teach proper study techniques, such as outlining and condensing material and self-testing.

(© Media Bakery)

Students sometimes need to develop and reinforce skills through independent seatwork. It is important to make sure that this work is productive for students, not just a time filler.

Small-Group Work

Small-group work might be defined as work done independently by some subset of the entire class. This might be a form of cooperative or collaborative learning (see Chapter 9), or it might be a simple and short-term task that students can work on together or on which they can help one another. This instructional format has a number of strengths, including the following:

● Increased learning

● More interaction among students (Johnson & Johnson, 1989/1990)

● Development of friendships (perhaps across gender, racial, and ethnic lines)

● Greater productivity

Group work has potential weaknesses, as well. Among them are the following:

● Decreased learning (or no increase in learning) in some settings (O'Donnell & O'Kelly, 1994)

● Management problems in the classroom (children working in groups usually increases the noise and activity levels in the classroom, which may be a problem in some situations)

● Unequal participation among group members (Cohen, 1994)

● Difficulties in assigning grades fairly

● Student disaffection with group-based activities

Working in small groups has both strengths and weaknesses. Effective group work can turn out very well for both the teacher and the students, but group work is often done very poorly. Because it is such a challenging and important aspect of classroom learning today, we devote an entire chapter of this text (Chapter 9) to peer learning. The important point is that group work constitutes one useful option for teachers to consider in their efforts to manage classroom instruction.

small-group work Work being done independently by a group of students smaller than the whole class.

R I D E How does the organization of a classroom encourage or discourage working in small groups?

Whole-Class Instruction

In many classrooms, particularly at the secondary school level, whole-class instruction dominates instructional time. **Whole-class instruction** simply means that the whole class is participating in the same activity. The activity may be a lecture or explanation by the teacher; it may be a recitation (question by the teacher, answer by a student) or a class discussion. Each of these formats has its own unique strengths and can be very useful if done well. A weakness of much whole-class instruction, however, is that students are often passive in their learning, participating only occasionally at best.

whole-class instruction Working on instructional material with the whole class at the same time.

(© David Grossman/The Image Works)

Working in small groups can lead to improved skills, promote sharing of ideas, and enhance socialization among students. Make sure it is not simply a time to chat about school and friends.

lecturing Presenting information to a group of learners as a whole.

explaining Breaking down the concepts and ideas of a lesson to make them easier to understand.

Lecturing and Explaining Lecturing and explaining occur when the teacher is talking to the entire class about a subject, and the students are listening and taking notes. During a lecture, information is being provided, much as it would be in a text format. This does not mean that questions and answers cannot be posed and responded to, both teacher to student and student to teacher. Lecturing is the predominant mode of instruction in most college courses, especially large classes. More common in K–12 instruction is explanation. The difference between the two is that whereas lecturing is focused on the subject matter and the presentation of information, ideas, and concepts, explanation involves taking apart that information, those ideas and concepts, and putting them back together in such a way as to make them easier to understand. The focus is on the learner at least as much as on the subject matter. A lecture may be the best approach to use if you are trying to get across information that all the students need to know and is not available through other means, but often students need to have things explained to them rather than simply presented in a lecture.

The basic idea of an explanation can be illustrated in terms of explaining a concept such as Thanksgiving. How could Thanksgiving be explained to the following groups of people?

- A classroom full of kindergarten students
- A group of dignitaries visiting from Thailand (who speak English)
- A friend from Canada

In reflecting on how to go about this, consider the following:

- How much knowledge people have about the topic at the outset
- What you know and do not know about Thanksgiving
- How much information people have about related concepts
- How much information the group can process at one time
- The best way to convey information to the group
- Good metaphors, analogies, and examples to use

Explanations are almost always more interesting than lectures. Unless a person is truly prepared to listen to a lecture at the level at which it is given, it can be quite boring. If students are bored, they will find relatively more interesting diversions to pass the time. Explanations that are on target, anticipate the students' learning needs, and use bold metaphors and examples that are pertinent to students' lives can be very engaging. When presenting information to the class as a whole, make sure everyone is understanding it as you move along, and provide opportunities for interaction.

recitation An instructional approach where teachers ask closed-ended questions (questions with clear right answers) and students answer them.

Recitation and Discussion In **recitation**, the teacher asks questions, the students answer, and the teacher evaluates the quality of their responses (this is also called a *drill* or IRE discourse). The idea of recitation is to learn how well the students know the material, to assess whether there are specific areas of misunderstanding or lack of knowledge, and to give students a chance to show what they can do. The focus tends to be on correct answers, which leads to a public evaluation of the quality of the answer and of the student giving the response. Recitation is often criticized because of these two issues, but the recitation format has certain strengths as well. First, sometimes there *are* right answers. For example, if certain chemicals are mixed, either there will be a precipitate or there will not be one. Second, the recitation format is a good way to get an idea of how well the class understands certain concepts. Third, when the class is well prepared for a recitation, it can be a very positive experience. Here are some things that veteran teachers keep in mind when using this format:

- Every student should be called upon for a response. It is easy for some students to get lost in the shuffle. Having a sheet on which to check off names as students participate helps the teacher make sure that everyone is participating, thus avoiding a situation such as the one described in the nearby What Kids Say and Do box. The checklist also silently communicates to students that they will all be expected to participate.

- Pose the question and leave some **wait time** before calling on anyone for an answer. If a particular student is called upon before the question is posed, some of the other students will not try to come up with the answer. If the question is posed before calling on a student, all the students have to think about the question. This is especially true for questions where there might be a variety of good answers.

- Look for elements of correctness in responses that are not 100% on target. If a person is way off, some gentle humor can deflect embarrassment. Or simply say, "That's not really what I'm looking for here—who else would like to give this a try?"

- Remember that children from some cultures are not comfortable with public recitation or with receiving public criticism (or even praise). This can be a sensitive issue. It is best not to treat all members of a particular group the same way but instead to try to understand tendencies and look for solutions. Consult a veteran teacher or administrator to find out how teachers approach this issue.

- Recitation may not be fun, but a quiz show often is! Try turning your recitation into a version of a quiz show that is popular with the students. Forming teams can make this even more exciting.

Recitation can be an effective way to get an idea of how well the class is doing, but students usually like to express ideas more than to hunt for right answers. A related format is the *class discussion*. In class discussions, a topic is raised, and students offer ideas and opinions about it. Discussion questions generally do not have a single right answer, and the teacher does not evaluate students' responses for correctness, as in recitation. Teacher-led discussions can be exciting exchanges; students may come up with new ideas, and the teacher can get a sense of how much the class knows about a topic. The teacher also needs to take steps to avoid certain problems. First, make sure that a few students do not dominate the discussion and that other students contribute. Second, make certain that the topic is one that will generate interest. A common disaster, especially for beginning teachers, is the anticipated 20-minute class discussion that falls flat on its face after 3 minutes. This can be hard to predict. For secondary school teachers who are teaching several sections of the same class, the same topic can generate wildfire in the morning class and not even a spark in the afternoon. Teacher enthusiasm will play a part in how well the discussion goes, but it is hard to predict when a discussion will die out prematurely. The best course is to always have a backup plan.

Our discussion points out certain parallels between lecture and explanation on one hand and recitation and discussion on the other. Lecture and explanation represent two ends of a continuum, between a presentation focusing on subject matter and a more student-oriented presentation, a range from "this is what this is about" to "this is how best to understand this." Explanation focuses on the learner; lecture, on the topic. Similarly, recitation is directed toward getting right answers based on the material, whereas discussion is directed toward eliciting the ideas and opinions of the participants. Thus, the nature of a discussion is determined more by the group than by the topic, whereas a recitation session is oriented toward the topic. Figure 6.8 summarizes these contrasts.

What Kids Say and Do

Helping Out

Andy Mignano, one of the authors of the excellent book on classroom management mentioned earlier, was also the fourth-grade science teacher of a child of one of the authors of this text. When this parent told Andy how much his son, Ben, was enjoying science class, Andy asked, a bit puzzled, "How do you know? He *never* raises his hand in class."

Your author went home and asked his son, "Hey, Ben, how come you never raise your hand in Mr. Mignano's class?"

"Oh, Dad, Mr. Mignano *knows* I know the material," he replied. "I don't raise my hand so he can find out if the *other* kids know the material."

wait time The time between when a question is asked in a classroom and when a student is called upon to answer it.

Figure 6.8 A Continuum of Whole-Class Activities

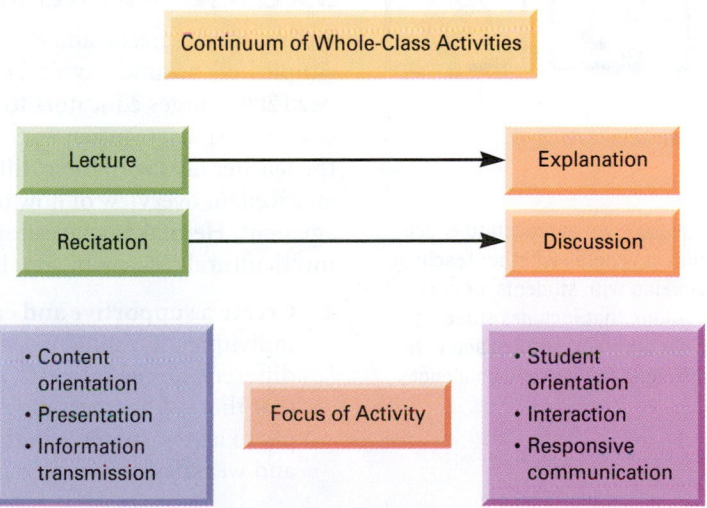

What Kids Say and Do

The Power of Open-Ended Questions

New Zealand's National Educational Monitoring Project assesses children in subject areas across the curriculum at ages 8 and 12. Most of the tasks are performance-based, administered in one-to-one settings; many of the children's responses are recorded on videotape. One of the tasks involved telling children to imagine that an elderly woman had just moved in next door and was living alone. Children were asked what they might do to help their new neighbor.

One 8-year-old Samoan boy went into deep thought about this question. After about 20 seconds, a smile came across his face. He turned to the teacher who was administering the assessment and said softly, "I could sing her a nice song. She'd probably like that."

This small interaction was telling in many respects. First, it is important to give children time to think about questions. This child not only had a beautiful response, it was also one he was clearly pleased about. He had put himself into the situation. His comment—"She'd probably like that,"—indicates that he had a virtual elderly lady in mind. Second, open-ended questions provide the opportunity for rich interaction and discussion. Imagine that response in a classroom setting and the springboard it could provide for discussion. Third, it allowed for an expression of the child's culture. Singing is an important aspect of Samoan life.

Open-ended, authentic questions with a wealth of possible good responses, time for children to think about what they want to say, and receptivity to using children's ideas are hallmarks of productive discussions.

All the instruction formats we have discussed have both strengths and weaknesses. There is no single approach that is best for all teachers, students, grade levels, or subject areas. Even for a particular teacher, there is no single approach that is best at all times. On the first day of school, for example, most teachers, especially beginning teachers, should use instructional activities that are readily managed, perhaps in a whole-class setting. But as could be seen in the What Kids Say and Do box about the power of open-ended questions, whole-class activities do not have to be impersonal. They can be an opportunity for all children to contribute thoughts and ideas.

Activities that do not involve the whole class usually require more planning and a higher level of energy on the part of the teacher. Organizing instruction to work with groups and individual students should not be viewed as an impossible task but as an opportunity to accomplish more than one thing at a time. A teacher cannot be everywhere at once, but that does not mean that learning should not be going on everywhere at once. It takes planning, careful and enthusiastic action, and reflection on what went well and what did not to develop the ability to blend different teaching formats. When the teacher is working with students individually or with groups, other students must be doing something else. This helps students learn how to work productively on their own or in small groups.

Each teacher has to find the mix of settings and approaches that seems to work best. The best advice is always to think through the possibilities of at least two different ways to approach a particular lesson and to look for opportunities to blend different formats.

Special Needs, Diversity, and Instruction

Taking special needs and diversity into consideration for classroom planning is critical. A simple look around a typical classroom will bring home the importance of that concept. Lopez (2007) urges educators to consider diversity in race and ethnicity, gender, ability, metacognitive skills, transiency, economic status, first language, and special needs. How should the teacher deal with these differences in planning instruction? Paul Burden (2003) provides an excellent overview of how to think about diversity as it relates to issues of classroom management. He makes suggestions in four major areas related to developing an **inclusive** and multicultural classroom (pp. 152–158):

inclusive An approach to education in general, whether teaching, working with students, or curriculum, that includes students from different cultures and with different abilities and challenges.

- **Create a supportive and caring environment.** Each student comes to class as a unique individual. If a student speaks a different language, observes different holidays, or has different special interests, celebrate those differences in the classroom. At the same time that those differences are recognized and honored, the same standards have to apply to all the students in the class. All students need to be encouraged, their strengths and weaknesses recognized and incorporated into instruction. This not only promotes academic growth but also shows students that the teacher cares about them. Experienced teachers occasionally look through their class roster and ask, "Am I more positive toward some students than others? Am I treating all the students fairly?" It is easy to slip into a habit of reacting negatively to some students and positively to others for the same or similar behavior.

- **Offer a responsive curriculum.** Make sure that instructional materials are inclusive and free from bias. This can be a particular problem if some materials are old. Even as recently as 10 years ago, instructional materials reflected certain groups in a less than positive light. (For example, does the science text describe both male and female scientists, include people with physical challenges, and portray individuals from a variety of cultures?) Web sites are available that provide materials with a multicultural and inclusive orientation.

- **Vary instruction.** Not all children learn equally well from any given approach to instruction. Be sure to use a variety of instructional approaches, including letting children work individually, both in terms of how they learn and, in some cases, what they choose to learn. Do not miss opportunities to include culturally relevant material and student choice in your instruction.

- **Provide needed assistance.** Some students need special assistance from time to time. This includes not only special needs children with individualized education programs but also students who are struggling with a particular task and students who need a push to achieve a high level of performance. Some children need extra help to follow the norms and rules of the classroom and to fit in with the group as a whole. Such children can be a particular challenge. In working with children who are having trouble, it is almost always useful to try to understand the situation from their perspective.

As a general rule, the teacher should try to understand who the students are and how they differ from one another. That information can then be used to benefit students as individuals as well as the class as a whole. Maintain high expectations for all students while recognizing that they are different. Check on a regular basis to make sure that students have equal opportunities to reach their goals. Other programs that might prove useful, particularly with students with emotional or behavioral problems, include Skillstreaming the Elementary School Child (McGinnis & Goldstein, 1997) and the Affective/Social Skills: Instructional Strategies and Techniques program (Huggins, 1995).

There is a tendency to focus on the problems of students with learning or behavior challenges in terms of what those challenges mean for others (e.g., disruptive behavior, need for additional attention). However, it is often useful to stop and think about life from the perspective of those who are facing the challenges. Bos and Vaughn (2002) have put together an excellent research summary of school life from the perspective of the learning-disabled student. Among their findings are that such students are not well accepted by their peers, have poor conversational skills, are less likely to be chosen in play settings, are more susceptible to peer pressure to engage in inappropriate behavior, and interact less often with their parents and teachers. Think about that list for a second. Put yourself in that situation. Who is most likely to be able to send out a lifeline to that student? It is important to remember that students who face these challenges live not only with these difficulties but with the consequences of the difficulties as well. That is, having fewer friends, less ability to express feelings appropriately, and a greater likelihood to behave inappropriately exacerbates all of the developmental social challenges faced by children. A great teacher can make all the difference in the world for such a child.

Dealing with Behavior Problems

Some problems are more serious than occasional misbehavior, periodic acting out, or a class that is rowdy on the Friday afternoon before a holiday. These problems move beyond the realm of classroom rules into serious issues. These issues are of four basic types: chronic problems, acute problems, personal problems, and particular problems.

What Does This Mean to Me?
If a child from the island nation of Palau is assigned to my class, does that mean I should look up Palau to see what that country is like?

Appendix
Behavior Problems
There are a variety of approaches for addressing behavior problems effectively (PRAXIS™, II.B.2; INTASC, Principle 4).

chronic problems Problems that persist over time, even though they may not be severe.

contingency contracting An approach to behavior management that involves a written agreement about behavior that makes rewards and punishments depend on the student's performance of that behavior.

self-management An approach to behavioral modification where students keep a written record of their behavior in an effort to increase desirable behaviors or decrease undesirable ones.

logical consequences An approach to classroom management that lets the natural outcomes of bad behavior serve as the punishment for that behavior.

Chronic Problems

Chronic problems are problems that, although they may not be serious in any one instance, persist over time. This might involve talking out of turn, failing to complete homework, or being unable to keep one's hands to oneself. Although these problems may seem small, even trivial when described on paper, they can become vexing when the usual classroom management techniques are not successful. A variety of approaches have been developed for handling chronic misbehavior problems. These include the following:

- **Contingency contracting.** This approach consists of negotiating and agreeing to a contract. The contract calls for appropriate modification of the behavior for a specified period and a reward for successful completion of the contract (the reward is *contingent* on the student's meeting the terms of the contract).

- **Self-management.** This approach involves having a child keep a record of certain behaviors that the teacher wishes to increase (such as raising a hand before speaking in a class discussion) or decrease (such as poking the child in the next seat). Recording desirable or undesirable behaviors to become more aware of how frequently they occur should enhance students' self-awareness and self-management skills.

- **Logical consequences.** This is a cognitive approach that involves tying consequences directly to behavior. For example, if a student misbehaves during recess, he or she must spend recess in the classroom. If a student is not working on completing tasks in class, those tasks can be assigned as homework. Vitto (2003) presents some useful suggestions for thinking about appropriate consequences, including asking, "Would this consequence cause *me* to change *my* behavior?"

These approaches, and other possibilities, are detailed interventions that need to be well understood before being carried out. A list of resources and programs for changing chronic behavior problems can be found at the Web site for this text.

www.wiley.com/college/odonnell

How Can I Use This?

What is a logical consequence for students who talk to their neighbors too much in class?

acute problems Problems that occur only infrequently but are severe.

Acute Problems

Acute problems are problems that do not occur on a regular basis but are serious and demand immediate attention. These might include abusive or defiant behavior, behavior that makes it impossible to go on with the lesson, or behavior that harms or endangers another student or the student who engages in it. Acute problems can occur at any grade level but are more likely to occur at the high school level. Two issues arise in connection with such behavior: how to prevent it and how to deal with it if it occurs.

Preventing Acute Problems Although some acute problems are completely unforeseen, many are escalations of minor issues (Weinstein, 2003). Thus, many **acute problems** can be prevented simply by not letting minor problems escalate. The key is to be aware of the potential for escalation and to defuse the problem. The tips listed in the nearby Taking It to the Classroom box may help prevent many acute problems.

It is important to remember that students spend the entire school day with very few opportunities to make choices. Earlier in the chapter, we discussed the tension between freedom and structure. Although students need structure, sometimes they also need a feeling of greater freedom, dignity, and autonomy. A student who behaves in a defiant or disruptive fashion may be expressing frustration over a lack of choice and control. That frustration may have little or nothing to do with the current situation. (We have all done things that we regretted later because we were upset over a completely different matter.) If, in an attempt to correct the misbehavior, the teacher challenges the student, it may push the student past his or her limits and turn a simple problem into a complex one. This might occur with any student, even one who is usually perceived as a *good* student, so it may come as a surprise to the teacher. When a teacher is frustrated, it can be hard for the teacher to see that a student is upset and try to understand why, thus allowing the problem to be worked out. It is always better to be on guard against such possibilities and to defuse potentially explosive situations before they occur.

Dealing with Acute Problems When a problem becomes acute, a teacher may be frustrated, angry, intimidated (even fearful), and in danger of losing emotional control. The

Taking It to the Classroom

Tips for Creating a Peaceful Classroom

This set of principles for working with students in classrooms, compiled by the Center for Adolescent and Family Studies at Indiana University, provides a helpful, commonsense way of looking at teaching as a profession.

1. **Have a genuine interest in your students.** Greet students at the door. Learn about their cultures. Be aware of teen slang terms. Offer praise and encouragement frequently. Attend to students as individuals, not just to the class as a whole.

2. **Communicate classroom rules clearly.** Enforce rules fairly and consistently. Consider each incident's unique circumstances while making discipline-related decisions.

3. **Be objective, not judgmental.** Try to adopt the students' perspective. Look at issues from a variety of perspectives.

4. **Show that you are human.** Be prepared to admit your mistakes. Use humor when appropriate.

5. **Minimize the power differential in everyday communication.** Sitting behind a desk or standing behind a podium can send the message that you want to create some distance between yourself and the students. Avoid language that tells students what they must, should, or have to do. Instead, explain the reasons behind your rules, requests, and assignments so that students understand that these really are for their own good.

6. **Address problem behavior directly and immediately.** Unresolved conflicts and issues often recur. Addressing a problem early lessens the chance that it will arise again.

7. **Take a collaborative approach.** Maximize opportunities for student choices within the classroom. Consider the perspective that this is *our* classroom, not *my* classroom. Actively solicit students' opinions and perspectives.

Source: Adapted from Center for Adolescent and Family Studies (1996). Tips for creating a peaceful classroom. *Teacher Talk, 2*(3), Indiana University, Bloomington, IN. Retrieved June 23, 2011, from http://www.drugstats.org/tt/v2i3/peaceful.html. Reprinted with permission.

irony here is that it is in these situations that the teacher most needs to be calm, flexible, and in control of his or her emotions. The first priority is to avoid imposing one's own will or trying to *save face*. Instead, it is far better to assess the situation and work to defuse it. Once the situation is calm, order can be reestablished.

If uninvolved students are in danger or are making the problem worse by paying attention to it, the teacher can either ask them to leave the room or tell them to work on something else. This not only removes part of the problem but also communicates to everyone the message that the teacher is in charge.

The next step is to give the problem student some way of exiting the situation. A teacher can ask the student to join him or her in the hallway for a minute in a voice that communicates firmness but also sympathy. Once there, the student can present his or her view of the problem. The focus should be on the student's concerns. The teacher can revisit the incident in the classroom when the student is calmer, and a less intense discussion can occur. These steps might not always work; in such cases, the teacher will have to seek help from someone in the school who is trained in and responsible for dealing with such situations, such as a principal, counselor, or school psychologist.

When the incident is over, it can be useful for the teacher to discuss it with colleagues. The very act of engaging in a discussion can be helpful emotionally. Moreover, the situation can be analyzed: What went wrong? What other forms of intervention might have been more successful? Finally, the teacher needs to follow up on the situation, talking to the student after things have cooled off—maybe even a day or two later. The incident can be used as an opportunity to help the student work on the underlying problem.

Personal Problems

At all levels, but particularly at the middle and high school levels, students may be dealing with serious problems of mental or physical health. A student might confide in the teacher about a problem—an unwanted pregnancy, an eating disorder, contemplation of suicide, extreme anger toward another student or group of students. Indications of a problem in a piece of written work or artwork might be noticed, or a teacher might overhear a troubling interaction between students. These interactions must be taken very seriously. Although the issues may be difficult to contemplate, teachers are often the first resource available to help deal with such problems.

At the same time, teachers need to remember that they are *not* the school counselor, the school psychologist, or the police. The teacher's role in this process is to work with people who are trained to handle such issues. Many states require that certain observations be reported to the police or other authorities. *It is absolutely essential that teachers understand clearly what their responsibilities are for such reporting.* When in doubt about a given situation, it is critical to find out what those responsibilities are.

In *Principles of Classroom Management: A Professional Decision-Making Model,* James Levin and James F. Nolan (2004) present a set of six warning signs indicating that a student is in distress. The following list is adapted from their work:

1. **Changes in physical appearance.** Changes in dress or grooming habits can be warning signs of deeper problems. Sudden weight loss or gain and problems with teeth can signal eating disorders. Cuts and scarring may indicate self-mutilation.

2. **Changes in activity level.** Students who are frequently tardy or absent, fall asleep in class, or are hyperactive may be expressing symptoms of a wide range of problems.

3. **Changes in personality.** Students who suddenly change from being outgoing and friendly to engaging in outbursts of inappropriate behavior or showing signs of depression need to be watched carefully.

4. **Changes in achievement status.** A decline in a student's performance in class may be a symptom of deeper problems—personal, interpersonal, or even physical.

5. **Changes in health or physical abilities.** If a student appears to be having trouble hearing or seeing, has difficulty speaking, or complains of physical illness, you need to be concerned about the student's overall health.

6. **Changes in socialization.** Children who are isolated and withdrawn and seem to have no or few friends are cause for concern.

Particular Problems

There are particular problems that do not fall neatly into any of the categories discussed thus far. These problems are cheating, violence, and bullying. Cheating and bullying are age-old problems that have recently gained the attention of researchers. Violence, too, is all too common in American schools.

Cheating   It is sad to say, but cheating is rampant in American schools. Ditman (2000) reports that four of five high achievers in a high school survey admit to having cheated at some point. Evans and Craig (1990) report similar levels of cheating by middle and high school students. In an excellent and highly readable work, *Cheating on Tests: How to Do It, Detect It, and Prevent It,* Cizek (1999) surveys the ways in which students cheat on all types of assessments. He has developed a **taxonomy**, an ordered categorization, of how students cheat. More recently Cizek (2003) has turned this research into a practical handbook for teachers who have discovered that their students are cheating.

Although it is difficult to prevent all forms of cheating, there are some simple steps that can minimize the likelihood that cheating will occur:

- Assign seats for exams that are different from the students' regular seats, and if possible, spread students out so that there is space between them, in order to cut down on opportunities for copying from other students' exams.

- If there are several sections of the same course, create multiple forms of exams or just mix up the order of the choices in the multiple-choice section.

- Give exams that require higher-order thinking skills rather than recall of information to reduce the utility of *crib sheets* for the exam. Eliminating hats, gum, cell phones, and PDAs will also cut down on opportunities to use crib sheets.

- Use software that has been specially developed to scan the Internet for plagiarized material in student papers. An alternative is simply to enter a suspicious phrase into a search engine and specify "exact phrase." This is likely to turn up an original source if the material is not orginal.

- Finally, if cheating seems to be a serious problem, use a reference such as one of the books by Cizek.

taxonomy A classification of objects according to a set of principles or laws.

Violence Violence has become a sad and frightening reality in American schools. One research team (Kaufman et al., 1999) found that in the mid-1990s, one in ten schools reported that a serious crime or act of violence had occurred in the school. Although, as a society, we focus on school violence for very long only when a tragedy such as the Columbine shootings occurs, lesser instances of violence occur all too often.

How Can I Use This?
What are some ways you feel that you could begin a discussion with a student whom you suspect of cheating?

A report issued by the U.S. Secret Service Safe School Initiative (2000) indicates that, in most cases, the perpetrators of school shootings felt that they were the victims of bullies (discussed later in the section) or other unfair treatment in school. As teachers, it is important to watch for signs that students are troubled. The warning signs described earlier under the heading Personal Problems can also indicate that a student may be considering committing a violent act. Teachers may notice troubling signals in students' appearance or behavior, or occasionally in the things they write for assignments. If a teacher is seriously concerned about a particular student, this concern needs to be communicated to a principal, to a school counselor or psychologist, or perhaps to legal authorities.

Bullying Bullying often does not appear to be a serious problem for most educators because it tends to occur on school buses, in hallways, on the playground, or after school. In a fascinating study, Barone (1997) found that although 60% of eighth-grade students said that they had been bullied while in middle school, their teachers expected that the percentage would be about 16%. There is clearly a lack of congruence between the magnitude of the problem and its perception by teachers.

Bullying usually involves what Vitto (2003) calls an *imbalance of power*. Students or groups of students who are stronger physically, emotionally, or intellectually, or who are higher in status, inflict some sort of hurtful behavior (teasing, taunting, physical abuse) on weaker students or groups of students (Smith & Brain, 2000). This hurtful behavior can turn everyday school life into torture for the victims. Bullies share a number of characteristics, both in terms of personality and in terms of home environment. They want to dominate their victims and show little regard or empathy for them. They tend to have poor academic records, and they are more likely than other students to smoke and consume alcohol (Roberts & Morotti, 2000). They tend to come from homes where aggression and negative attitudes are common (Glover et al., 2000). Different scholars view the problem of bullying differently, but most agree that there are multiple causes of bullying, including social pressures and rewards, personality problems, and family influences (Smith et al., 2004).

Bullying has recently gained the attention of educational researchers, and a number of anti-bullying programs have been developed. Perhaps the most widely studied program is the Olewus Bullying Prevention Program (Olewus, 1993, 1997), which involves a schoolwide approach to the prevention of bullying. The Olewus program emphasizes direct teaching on the issue of bullying; ongoing communication among school teachers, counselors, and administrators; and a team approach to the problem. Research conducted in Norway, where the program originated, has been quite promising, but efforts to implement the program elsewhere have been less successful (Smith et al., 2004). Allen (2010) found that bullying occurred more often in classroom environments that were disorganized or that involved harsh approaches to discipline.

A new and malicious form of bullying has accompanied technological development. Students are bullying other students through the use of text messages, sometimes called cyber-bullying (Bhat, 2008). Texting is particularly nasty because cell phones are ubiquitous, and text messages can be sent asynchronously and broadly. Thus, first, bullying is not limited to school hours, and second, an unkind message about someone can be sent to dozens of students. A victim of bullying can feel that there is no escape from the problem.

The issue for teachers concerns what to do in the classroom about bullying, because it does not usually take place there. The first thing teachers can do is bring the issue out into the open. Teachers need to talk about respect for others' feelings and point out that what is seen as teasing by the instigator is experienced as bullying by the victim. Also, teachers need to monitor potential bullies and clearly communicate to them that such behavior will not be tolerated. Several resources are listed on the Web site that accompanies this text, including such works as *Bully-Proofing Your School: A Comprehensive Approach for Middle Schools* (Bonds & Stoker, 2000) and *Bullying in American Schools: A Social-Ecological Perspective on Prevention and Intervention* (Espelage & Swearer, 2004).

REFLECTION FOR ACTION

The Event

Before children ever enter a classroom, the process of teaching and learning begins when a teacher designs the classroom. Now it is time to think seriously about the classroom you will design. What will it look like? What activities will it encourage or inhibit? How will students react to it?

Reflection RIDE

How good will you be at designing a classroom? Think about a particular classroom setting, such as a first-grade class with 25 six-year-olds or a high school class with 30 students learning about social studies. What do these classrooms need to convey to students? What should they encourage or restrict? Now turn to your future classroom and ask the same questions. Do not just think about this in the abstract. Make a list. Identify various options and think about the pros and cons.

What Theoretical/Conceptual Information Might Assist in Interpreting and Remedying This Situation? Consider the following:

Considering the Social Environment

What are the norms, rules, and patterns of social interaction you are trying to promote in your classroom? What do you have to pay special attention to in developing the learning community that is going to exist in your classroom? How might you facilitate progress in this area through the design of your classroom?

Influence on Learning and Managing the Classroom

How does classroom design influence learning? Cohen (1994), Morrow and Weinstein (1982), and Evertson and Harris (2003) have looked in detail at how the design of a classroom influences different approaches to learning and management problems.

Symbolic Representation

What does this classroom represent to you and your students? *Looking in Classrooms* by Good and Brophy (2000) offers an excellent vehicle for thinking about such issues.

Information Gathering RIDE

Some people are good at design, and others are not. If you are, please keep the ideas presented in the chapter in mind in making your decisions. If you are not, help is available. For practicing teachers, there are books and professional articles, other teachers, Web sites, students, parents, and others (e.g., friends with some knowledge of design). For the purposes of this assignment, books and articles, Web sites, and friends might be the best sources of information.

Decision Making

Try out your decision with a simulation. You can do this with a piece of graph paper, a classroom architectural Web site, or scale-level furniture purchased at a teachers' supply store. When you have a possible design, check it against your list of things it needs to accomplish. How is it stacking up? Ask a friend who is planning to become a teacher to try the same task, then compare notes. You will quickly realize that classroom design involves trade-offs and compromises. That is fine—it forces you to think hard about what is really important.

Evaluation

Without having real children in a real setting, it will be difficult to evaluate your classroom, but it would be fun to ask friends who are training to be teachers to give you an evaluation. When you design your actual classroom, remember to evaluate your physical environment on a regular basis to be certain that it is helping you in your teaching.

Further Practice: Your Turn

Now try to imagine how you would deal with a behavioral problem.

The Event

Lunchtime has arrived, and not a moment too soon. Two of your twelfth-grade English students came into class in the midst of an argument that almost escalated into a physical fight 15 minutes into the period. You were able to get one of the students down to the principal's office during the class and sent the other one there as soon as the period ended. You have a free period for lunch now, but you will see this class again tomorrow.

What are you going to do now? How should you follow up? What will you do when the students enter your classroom tomorrow? Was your reaction to the situation the best possible one? How would you know?

SUMMARY

- **How can classrooms be organized to make it easier to achieve instructional goals?**

  Good classroom management starts before the beginning of the school year, with the design of the classroom. Classrooms need to be organized in terms of what will take place in them. They need to be designed to support the primary tasks of the class yet be flexible enough to meet multiple demands. They need to provide security and safety while at the same time being pleasant places in which to spend the day.

- **How can the first day of school set the tone for the rest of the year?**

  The first day of school is one of anticipation and anxiety for students and teachers alike (not to mention parents). It is also a critical day in terms of setting the proper tone for the rest of the year. Time spent on the first day introducing and explaining class rules and behavior expectations will be more than repaid later in the year in time available for learning.

- **How should rules be developed for classrooms?**

  During the first few weeks of school, teachers need to establish rules for the classroom. They need to make sure that all the students understand them and the consequences for not complying with them. Teachers may want to involve students in helping to set the classroom rules. For younger students, the challenge will be to make certain that they understand the rules; for older students, the challenge will be to set limits as students try to find out how far rules can be bent.

- **How do successful teachers create a learning community in their classrooms?**

  The goal of setting rules for classrooms, and of classroom design as well, is to create a sense of community. Students should feel that they are all members of a learning community that is working together toward common goals. The establishment of rules and routines for getting work done lets students know what is expected of them, how to get along with one another, and how to get their work done. This structure gives the students the freedom they need to operate within specific limits.

- **How do instructional formats affect classroom management?**

  When students get off-task or start to misbehave, one of the first questions teachers should ask is whether their instructional activities are keeping the students engaged. Most classroom instruction combines individual or seatwork, small-group activities, and whole-group instruction, including lecture, explanation, recitation, and discussion. All these formats have both strengths and weaknesses, and teachers must determine the best mix and timing for using them.

- **How can I handle a really tough classroom?**

  Start by taking control of those things that you can control. Create a seating chart for students and change it if necessary. Always have your lessons well organized so that you are not losing time thinking of what you need to be doing. Greet students as they enter and give them something to do. Be polite but be insistent. Recognize students who are behaving appropriately.

- **What can be done about problem behaviors that are more serious than occasional rule breaking?**

  Behavior problems can arise in classrooms even when they are well managed. Chronic problems, such as not turning in homework or misbehaving on the playground, often need to be addressed with a program of remediation. A variety of such programs are available; they need to be carried out patiently and firmly. Sometimes a situation gets out of hand and calls for immediate attention. Teachers need to respond to acute situations calmly. The personal problems of students can range from mild to heartbreaking. While realizing that they are not counselors or school psychologists, teachers can be a significant source of support—and even inspiration—for a troubled student. It is important to keep an eye out for signs of personal problems as well as potential violence. Teachers have to inform school counselors, psychologists, or principals when a student is in danger. Two widespread problems also require vigilance on the part of the teacher: cheating and bullying.

- **What is the proper balance between being sensitive to cultural differences and applying the same rules and expectations to all students?**

  The key is to notice that there are differences and that these differences may influence how children behave, how you react to their behavior, and how they respond. There are no quick fixes or golden rules. It is inappropriate to conclude that all students of a certain ethnicity or religion will behave in the same way. It is appropriate to be aware that students may behave differently because of their background and to understand that behavior in the context of the school setting. This is not a situation that can be solved once and for all. It is an attitude toward teaching diverse groups of children that encourages continual learning and reflection on the part of the teacher.

- **What kinds of classroom management policies can be used to address the special needs of certain learners?**

  Once again, there is no easy solution. Teachers have to be sensitive, ask questions, get advice, and make adjustments accordingly. There is a broad literature on students with special needs and many places to get help. Many techniques recommended for students with disabilities would work for nondisabled students as well. In general, students with disabilities need clear instructions and guidelines, help in getting started, frequent feedback and correctives, and a system of record keeping that will help them monitor their progress toward learning and behavioral goals.

Key Terms

acute problems, p. 212
chronic problems, p. 212
consequences, p. 193
contingency contracting, p. 212
cross-ethnic groupings, p. 194
explaining, p. 208
I-message, p. 203
immediacy, p. 195
inclusive, p. 210

learning center, p. 191
lecturing, p. 208
logical consequences, p. 212
multidimensionality, p. 195
off-task, p. 205
penalties, p. 203
personal space, p. 189
recitation, p. 208
routines, p. 202

seatwork, p. 206
self-management, p. 212
small-group work, p. 207
social contact, p. 189
social norms, p. 195
taxonomy, p. 214
transition times, p. 190
wait time, p. 209
whole-class instruction, p. 207

Exercises

1. *Classroom Design*

   Design your classroom. Start with a statement of the level and subject areas you are going to teach and what you want your classroom to do for you. Then design your classroom with construction paper cutouts. When you are done, trade your work with one of your classmates and critique each other's work. Then consider the critique you have given and the one you have received. How has the feedback process helped you improve your design and helped you think about how to go about classroom planning?

2. *Instructional Style and Classroom Management*

   Think about your instructional style and approach to classroom management. Make a list of what you think your strengths and weaknesses are in terms of managing a group of children and adolescents. Are you a good organizer, a dynamic personality, patient, strong-willed, good at attending to details, fun to be with, and so forth? Think about how you use your strengths to be an effective classroom manager. If you have a friend in this course whose opinion you value, you might have him or her make the same list about you (and you about that person) to see whether your self-perceptions are shared by others. Then you can explore how your personal characteristics can be turned into management strengths.

3. *Working with Students with Special Needs*
A student who uses a wheelchair has been assigned to your class. What adjustments will you make to accommodate this student? Find at least two Web sites that provide help in this area and make a list of what you consider to be the three most important accommodations that you can make.

Lesson Plans

For each of these lesson plans, review the lesson plan excerpt and respond to the questions related to classroom management in the Ask Yourself! section at the end.

Lesson #1: "Immigrant Journeys"

GRADES: 9–12

SUBJECT AREA: Social Studies

ESTIMATED COMPLETION TIME: 90 minutes

I. OVERVIEW: Since the triumph of the Cuban Revolution in 1959, many immigrants have left Cuba and immigrated to the United States. The immigrants had various experiences that were dependent on the personal circumstances and historical context of the immigrant. In this lesson students will create a fictional biography of a Cuban immigrant who left Cuba for Miami in 1980.

II. OBJECTIVES: Students will be able to:
- Examine the relationship between historical context and the immigrant experience
- Propose reasons why individuals may choose to immigrate to the United States
- Consider the experience of immigrants to the United States

III. MATERIALS:
- World map
- Laptop computers with Internet access for all students

IV. PROCEDURE:

1. Have students fill out a KWL chart about immigration from Cuba to the United States.

2. Allow students time to use the laptop computers for 30 minutes to research the history of Cuba since 1959.

3. Tell students that we will be working in pairs and creating a fictional biography about someone who immigrated to the United States from Cuba in 1980.

4. Tell students that their biography should include:
   - Name, gender, age, occupation, and level of education of their fictional immigrant
   - How the immigrant traveled from Cuba to the United States
   - How the immigrant's family members viewed the immigrant's decision to leave Cuba
   - The immigrant's motivation for leaving Cuba
   - What was going on in Miami when the immigrant arrived
   - The similarities between the United States and Cuba in 1980
   - The differences between the United States and Cuba in 1980

5. Pairs will then share their biographies with the class.

6. The class will then have the opportunity to ask the authors additional questions about their fictional immigrant.

7. The class can then discuss the similarities and differences among all the fictional immigrants.

Ask Yourself!

1. What would be the strengths and weaknesses of this lesson as one to begin the school year with?

2. How might this lesson affect children in your classroom who themselves are immigrants? What areas of sensitivity or concern might exist?

3. How might this lesson plan be adapted if there were a large number of Asian students in your classroom?

4. *Starting the Year Right*
   The first day of school is critical in setting the tone for the school year. Review the material in the chapter dealing with the first day of school and develop your lesson plans for that day. How will your plans set the right tone for your class?

5. *Linking Motivation to Classroom Management*
   Motivation and classroom management go hand in hand. Go to Chapters 11 and 12, and examine the material on motivation. Which of the theoretical perspectives discussed there seem to be particularly important for classroom management? In what ways?

Lesson Plans

Lesson #2: "Wind Chill"

GRADES: 6–8

SUBJECT AREA: Math and Science

ESTIMATED COMPLETION TIME: 45 minutes

I. OVERVIEW: This lesson will help students understand wind chill factor and how wind speed affects wind chill.

II. OBJECTIVES: Students will be able to:
- Understand wind chill
- Analyze the relationship between temperature and wind speed
- Use understanding of graphs to create a visual representation of the relationship among wind speed, temperature, and wind chill

III. MATERIALS:
- Shallow pan or cookie sheet with raised edges
- Electric fan
- Timer
- Water (room temperature)
- Thermometer
- Chart (below)
- Graph paper

IV. PROCEDURE:

1. Fill the pan with water (no more than 1 cm).

2. Place the bulb of the thermometer in the water and leave it in, untouched, for five minutes, then record the temperature.

3. Place the electric fan a few centimeters from the pan.

4. Turn the fan on a low setting and record the temperature every five minutes. Repeat this step until the water temperature no longer changes.

5. Repeat step 4 on a higher fan speed (if applicable).

6. Allow time for students to fill in their charts.

7. Have students graph their results on a double bar (if different fan speeds are used).

Fan Speed	Temperature at 0 Minutes (record before fan is turned on)	Temperature after 5 Minutes	Temperature after 10 Minutes	Temperature after 15 Minutes
Low				
High	Not Applicable			

8. Have students discuss the following questions with their lab partner:
- How did placing the fan in front of the water affect the temperature?
- If the air moving through the fan is the same air (and thus the same temperature) as the air in the room, why did the temperature of the water change?
- If you were stuck in an area with a high wind chill, what do you think you could do to protect yourself from the negative impacts of the wind chill?
- (Optional) Have students show and compare graphs.

Ask: If we all were using the same materials, why do you think everyone had different results?

Ask Yourself!

1. How can this lesson be modified to be inclusive of a child with substantial learning challenges?

2. What areas of concern for safety might exist for a fifth-grade classroom?

3. How can this science demonstration be conducted so that all students in a class of 25 can get a good view and understanding of what is happening?

The Problem

The Cinema Club takes the money from their fund drive and puts half of it in the club treasury. They spend one-third of it on a trip to the movies and one-sixth of it on supplies. This year their fund drive was a car wash where they charged $5 to wash a car. They washed a total of 23 cars and got an additional $44 in tips. How much money will they be able to spend on going to the movies?

Be sure to show your work and explain your reasoning in a short paragraph.

Martin's Answer

$5 a car   23 cars
$ 44 in tips   movies

1/6   1/3 of 44   23+44   What are they doing!!

Why didn't they just spend all of the money on the movies—it's a Cinema club, isn't it? What are they saving for, a trip to a film festival? I'm not sure what I'm supposed to do here. I read the problem several times, but I just got lost and then I got upset. How much money for the movie is a third of the money, but what money are we talking about? Are there two different problems here? If I knew better how to set this up, I think I could do it, but I can't.

Tasha's Answer

$23 $23 $23   1/3   1/6
× 5   × 5   × 5
115   115   115
+ 44
$159   ? 115
            2)159   199
                                   2

Well, I started by trying to figure out how much money they made. I figured once I did that, then I could figure out how much they spent on three things. I multiplied 23 times 5 and got $115 and added $44 and got $159 for the total. But if they put half of the money in the bank, you can't divide $159 in half, so I couldn't figure out what they were supposed to do. I must be doing something wrong, but I checked my math three times and I can't figure out where my error is. I'm sorry but I can't make it work.

Mr. Gomez was going over the problem set for the unit on word problems with fractions on which his third-grade class was working. Generally speaking, he was pleased with his students' performance, but there were still a few weaknesses. He thought, "I want them to really understand how to solve these problems—to be confident in their abilities. If I'm teaching this well, and most of the kids are getting it, why aren't they all getting it? What can I do to reach the kids who need help right now?" Mr. Gomez decided to focus his attention on two students who were having trouble. Above is their performance on one particular problem.

Cognitive Learning Theory 7

R I D E Reflection for Action

Wrong answers can often be windows into the cognitive difficulties students are having with a new learning task. What kinds of problems do you see in the work of these two students? What kinds of larger problems do the students' difficulties with these math problems suggest? What kinds of things can you do as a teacher to help these students accomplish their goals in mathematics?

Guiding Questions

- How do cognitive and constructivist theories of learning differ?
- Why are attention, perception, and working memory important for learning?
- How is knowledge represented?
- What are the different kinds of long-term memory?
- How is encoding related to retrieval?
- Why and how do we categorize?
- How can teachers apply cognitive theories of learning in working with diverse students and students with special needs?

CHAPTER OVERVIEW

This chapter focuses on structures and processes of learning from a cognitive perspective, with special emphasis on information-processing theory. We describe the basic processes of encoding and retrieval as well as and the constraints of various components of the information-processing system, such as working memory, that limit processing. Each section also describes the instructional implications of those components. Throughout the chapter, particular attention is devoted to how we can understand the needs of exceptional children from a cognitive perspective and what teaching strategies might be helpful in reducing the difficulties experienced by all students in classrooms.

Cognitive Theories of Learning

The Information-Processing Model
- Perception
- Attention

Memory Systems
- Sensory Memory
- Short-Term Memory
- A Model of Working Memory
- Memory Difficulties of Children with Special Needs
- Long-Term Memory

Encoding, Retrieval, and Forgetting
- Types of Knowledge
- Organization, Practice, and Elaboration
- Mnemonic Strategies
- Imagery and Visual-Learning Strategies
- Retrieval and Forgetting

Categorization
- Teaching Concepts
- Diversity, Culture, and Experience in Developing Concepts and Categories

Cognitive Theories of Learning

In the example that follows, you can see that learning results from the interaction between the student's skills and the kind of instruction that a teacher provides. Jeff Morgan is a student who is having trouble processing information, and his efforts to acquire knowledge are not very successful. In this chapter, you will learn about how information is processed and the kinds of strategies a student can use to acquire knowledge.

Jeff Morgan was excited about taking social studies in his junior year. He really liked the subject matter and had done very well in the course he took in his sophomore year. His teacher last year was exciting, enthusiastic about teaching the content, eager for students to ask questions, and pleased to answer their questions after class. On the first day of the junior year social studies class, Jeff knew things were going to be different. The teacher spoke very rapidly, and the material he taught was not the same as in the textbook. Jeff struggled to take notes. He was not good at spelling, and when he paused to try to spell a word correctly, he could no longer make sense of what the teacher was saying. Unlike last year's teacher, this teacher did not write notes on the board or provide outlines. Jeff hoped that he would get used to the teacher's methods and that things would improve. After two weeks, he looked at his notes. He could hardly make sense of them. There were fragments of ideas that did not seem to be connected. He began to worry about how he would do on exams in this class.

In Chapter 5, we introduced a general definition of learning as an interaction between the individual and the environment that results in a relatively permanent change in behavior or knowledge. We also saw that a behavioral theory of learning focuses primarily on the relationship between the environment and behavior. In contrast, the relationship between the individual and the environment is the key focus of cognitive theories of learning. From a cognitive perspective, a person does not necessarily view the same environment in the same way as others. For example, two people may see the abbreviation *IRA*. One, who is a reading specialist, may interpret it to mean "International Reading Association." The other, who is nearing retirement, may instead interpret it as "individual retirement account." Although the same environmental stimulus is available to both individuals, they interpret it in different ways as a result of their own experiences and motivations. A cognitive approach to learning explores how individual differences in knowledge and experience influence the way we interpret the environment and, as a result, what we learn from that interaction.

Cognitive theories include a variety of approaches to understanding the relationship between the individual and his or her environment. At the heart of most cognitive approaches to understanding learning is the notion that knowledge is constructed by the learner and affected by the learner's prior experiences. All cognitive theories are constructivist in nature in that they all emphasize the active role of learners in making meaning out of their experience. This chapter focuses primarily on information-processing approaches to learning.

The Information–Processing Model

The learner interacts with the environment and receives information from the environment through the senses. The information-processing approach to learning describes the learner's development of internal representations of the external world. As you read the pages of this chapter, you first need to attend to words and images and perceive what these words and images mean to you. Attention and perception allow information written on the page to become cognitively represented in your mind as sensory memory. To go beyond sensory memory, you next need to process what you are seeing and reading in short-term memory. Here, you work on the information you see and read, making sense of it and relating it to what you already know about the topic. Finally, to remember the information well after you have closed the book and gone on to doing something else, you also need to transfer what you have processed from short-term to long-term memory, using the strategies we will introduce and discuss throughout the chapter. This brief example applies to making sense of and remembering information from reading a book, but the learning processes within the information-processing model apply equally well to a wide variety of learning experiences, such as making sense of and remembering a lecture, making sense of and remembering what you learned from a how-to videotape, or making sense of and remembering a conversation with a friend.

Perceptual and attentional processes limit the amount of information that is available. Not all the available information can be processed because of the limited capacity of various components of the memory system. Information is processed in working memory and potentially transferred to long-term memory, from which it can be retrieved later. This information-processing system is illustrated in Figure 7.1. In the next few sections of this chapter, we will discuss the components of the information-processing system more fully.

Perception

Perceptual and attentional processes are important to information processing. Students who have difficulty with them are at risk of failure in school. Awareness of these processes and how they affect other aspects of information processing may help teachers develop instructional strategies that will support students as they attempt to learn.

Perception involves giving meaning to sensory input. One of the difficult things for very young children to learn is that objects have permanence. The face that disappears behind a newspaper when one is playing peek-a-boo remains the same whether it can be seen or not or whether it is turned sideways or not. When children start to recognize letters, we ask them to perform a very complicated task. We ask them to recognize the letters *b, p, d,* and *q* as separate

Appendix
Memory

Understanding how memory works will help you tailor your teaching to your students' needs (PRAXIS™, I.A.1; INTASC, Principle 2).

perception The meaning attached to sensory information.

Figure 7.1 The Information-Processing Model

Source: Huffman, K. *Psychology in Action*, Seventh Edition. © 2004 John Wiley & Sons. Reprinted by permission of John Wiley & Sons, Inc.

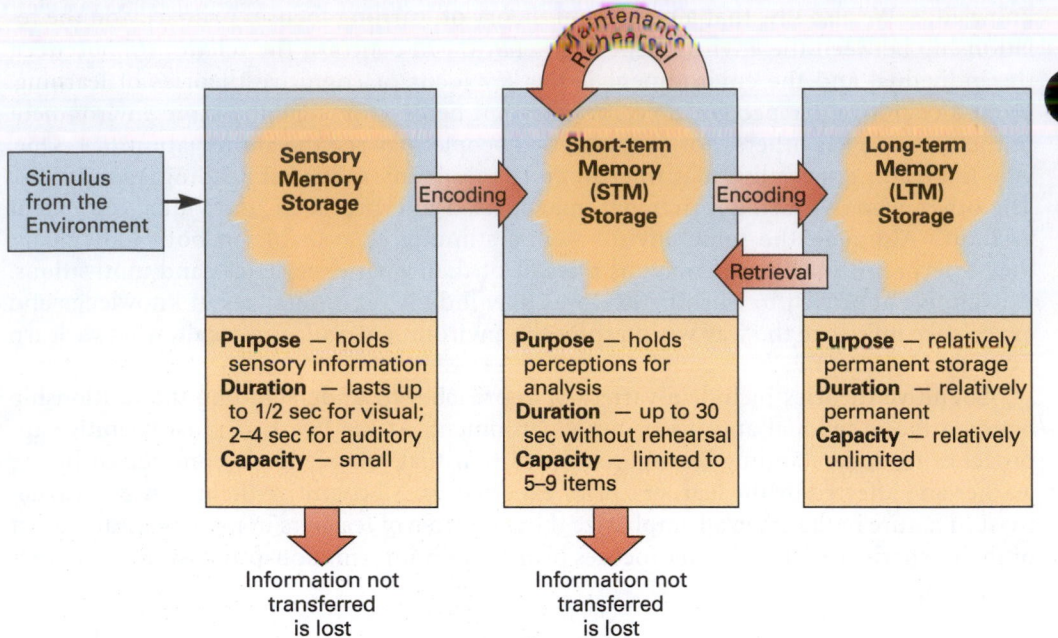

and distinct, even though they are very similar (Figure 7.2). We also can recognize different kinds of handwriting, as seen in Figure 7.3. The fact that we can learn to do these things suggests how powerful our perception system is.

Recognizing Objects   Two approaches are often used to describe how we recognize objects. The first of these, called **feature analysis** or **bottom-up processing**, involves identifying the component features of objects and building a representation of the object from them. An example of feature analysis is phonics, in which sounds associated with individual letters or phonemes are combined to make a word. For example, a child may view the word "Elmo" and sound out the components "L" + "MO" = "Elmo." Only when the features of the word are combined may a student recognize the word. Figure 7.4 presents examples of the letter *A*. If we could recognize objects only through feature analysis, we might recognize only the first example as an instance of the letter *A*. We would identify individual features (three lines, the angles at which the lines intersect) and assemble them to build a representation of the letter. Using this approach, we would be unlikely to recognize the other two examples.

An alternative approach to recognizing objects is to rely on context and fill in any missing information. This is called **top-down processing**. Figure 7.5 illustrates this approach. Although the letters in Figure 7.5 are incomplete, people typically read the words as THE CAT. Although some of the letters are incomplete, people fill in the missing information. If people relied on feature analysis to recognize the words, they would not recognize them: They could not combine the features effectively because necessary information is missing. Methods for teaching reading that rely on the use of context to infer what words mean use top-down processing.

feature analysis Identifying the component features of objects and building a representation of the object from them.

bottom-up processing A process in which a stimulus is analyzed into its components, then assembled into a recognizable pattern, also known as *feature analysis*.

top-down processing A type of perception in which a person uses what he or she knows about a situation to recognize patterns.

Figure 7.2 Perception of Similarly Shaped Letters

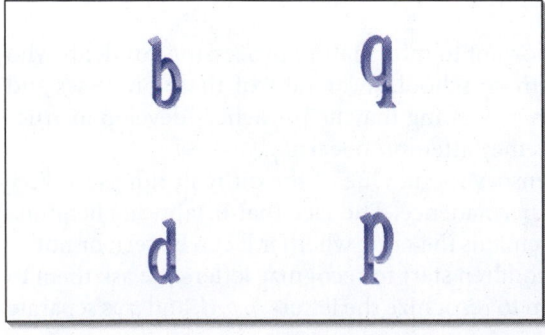

Figure 7.3 Variations in Handwriting

Source: From MAN MACH ENGRG—SEE 51B5501 1st edition by Chapanis. © 1966. Reprinted with permission of Wadsworth, a division of Thomson Learning: www.thomsonrights.com.

> We all read different styles of handwriting so easily and so commonly that it is easy for us to overlook what an extraordinary ability this is. Note the extreme discrepancies in the way different people write certain letters of the alphabet. Now consider what kind of a machine would be necessary to "recognize" all these LETTERS. IN PART, WE ARE ABLE TO READ THESE SAMPLES OF HANDWRITING because of the context and redundancy in the passage. But to a page type, our ability to read this passage is also due to the remarkable capacity the human organism has for "perceptual generalization".

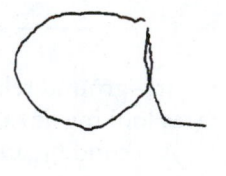

Figure 7.4 Perceiving the Letter *A*

Object Recognition Relies on Form Some psychologists believed that when viewing objects, the perception of the whole is greater than the sum of the parts. These psychologists were known as Gestalt psychologists. Objects are more easily perceived if they exhibit good form, or *pragnanz*. They also proposed a set of organizing principles that allow us to perceive objects. These are illustrated in Figure 7.6. Among the most important organizing principles is that of *figure–ground*: The figure is always seen as closer than the ground. We group together elements that appear similar (figure) and distinguish them from those that appear dissimilar (ground).

TAE CAT

Figure 7.5 Context

Source: Selfridge, O. G. (1955). Pattern recognition and modern computers. *Proceedings of the Western Joint Computer Conference.* New York: Institute of Electrical and Electronics Engineers (IEEE). Reprinted with the permission of the Association of Computer Machinery.

Figure 7.6 Gestalt Principles

Source: Huffman, K. *Psychology in Action*, Seventh Edition. © 2004 John Wiley & Sons. Reprinted by permission of John Wiley & Sons, Inc.

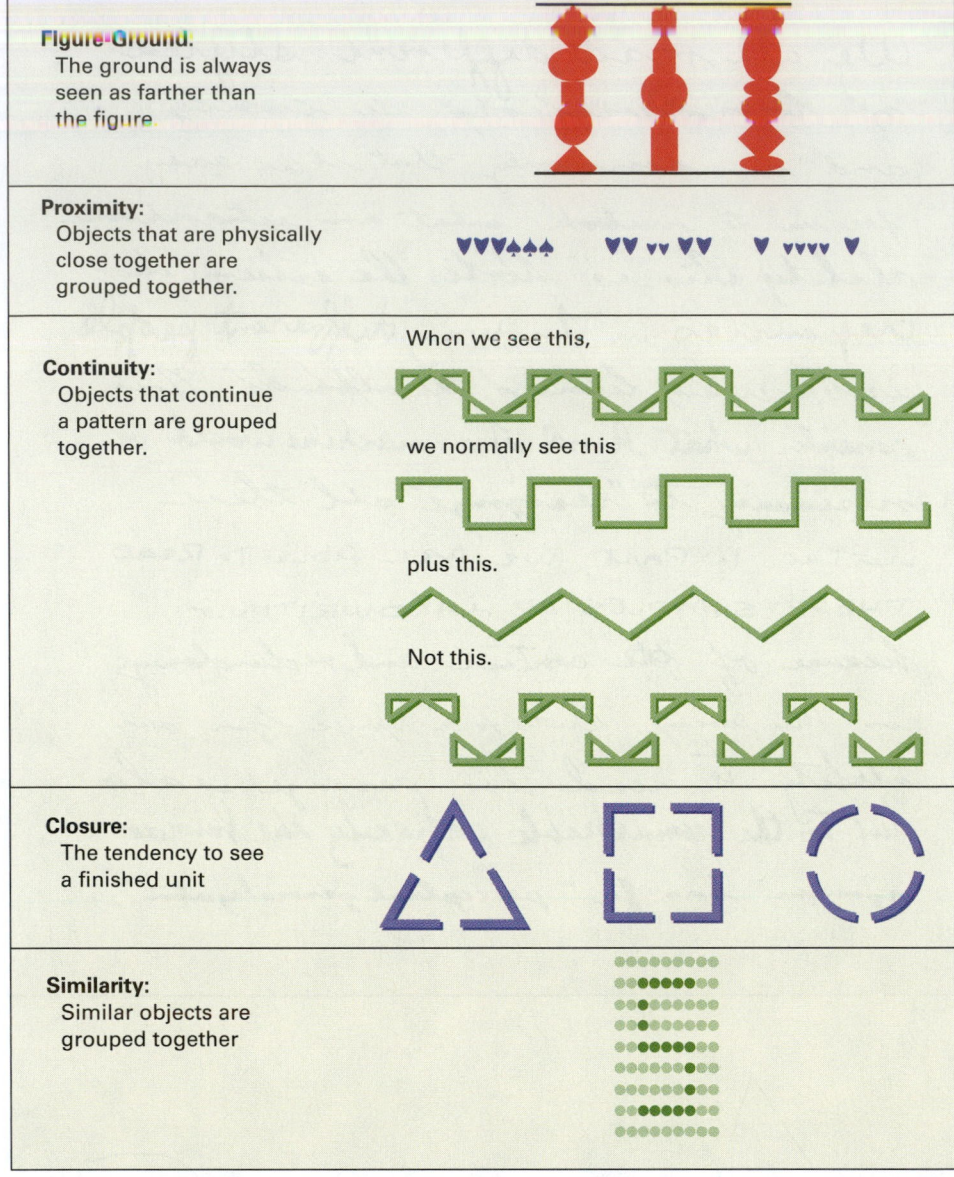

Figure–Ground:
The ground is always seen as farther than the figure.

Proximity:
Objects that are physically close together are grouped together.

Continuity:
Objects that continue a pattern are grouped together.

When we see this,

we normally see this

plus this.

Not this.

Closure:
The tendency to see a finished unit

Similarity:
Similar objects are grouped together

(© SSPL/The Image Works.)

Figure 7.7 What Do You See? A Vase or Two Faces?

attention Focus that is selective and limited.

Figure–ground relations are also illustrated in Figure 7.7. You can see either a vase or two faces looking at each other, but not both at the same time.

A second organizing principle is that of *proximity*. When things are close together, they are seen as belonging together (see Figure 7.6). The third principle is that of *continuity:* We prefer continuous forms. In Figure 7.6, you are more likely to see a continuous line than a segmented line. *Closure* is the fourth principle. This principle indicates that we tend to see completed figures rather than incomplete ones and to fill in the missing information (see Figure 7.6). *Similarity* also works as an organizing principle. In Figure 7.6, the dark green dots are seen to belong to one another and stand apart from the others because of their similarity in size and color. They are perceived in this example as the number 5. Visual displays such as concept maps that are prepared using Gestalt principles are more effective for learning than displays that do not use these principles (Wallace et al., 1998).

Attention

Some of the key features of **attention** are illustrated in the following quotation:

Everyone knows what attention is. It is the taking possession by the mind, in clear and vivid form, of one out of what seems several simultaneously possible objects or trains of thought. It implies withdrawal from some things in order to deal effectively with others, and is a condition which has a real opposite, in the confused, dazed, scatterbrained state . . . which is called distraction. (James, 1890, pp. 403–404)

This description has a number of noteworthy features: (1) Attention involves simultaneous experiences; (2) it is selective, withdrawing from some objects and focusing on others; and (3) lack of attention is characterized by confusion and diffusion. Perceptual processes enable us to organize sensory input, and attentional processes enable us to be selective. Children who suffer from attention disorders or attention-deficit/hyperactivity disorders are at risk for school failure. A child who exhibits six of the following characteristics for a period of six months or longer is considered likely to suffer from an attention-deficit disorder, according to the *Diagnostic and Statistical Manual of Mental Disorders*, fourth edition, of the American Psychiatric Association (as reported by Centers for Disease Control, 2004):

- Often does not give close attention to details or makes careless mistakes in schoolwork, work, or other activities
- Often has trouble keeping attention on tasks or play activities
- Often does not seem to listen when spoken to directly
- Often does not follow instructions and fails to finish schoolwork, chores, or duties in the workplace (not due to oppositional behavior or failure to understand instructions)
- Often has trouble organizing activities
- Often avoids, dislikes, or doesn't want to do things that take a lot of mental effort for a long period of time (such as schoolwork or homework)
- Often loses things needed for tasks and activities (e.g., toys, school assignments, pencils, books, or tools)
- Often is easily distracted
- Often is forgetful in daily activities

It is easy to see from these symptoms why a child who experiences six or more of these characteristics for an extended period of time would be at risk for low achievement. Pervasive attentional problems can interfere with a child's ability to respond to and benefit from instruction (Mercer & Pullen, 2009). Most children experience some of the difficulties listed above. Basic processes of attention and perception thus are very important in understanding individual learning and failure to learn.

Because people cannot attend to all the information that is available, they need some means to select the information that is important to them. Various theories have attempted to explain how selective attention works. One of the earliest theories of attention was the *filter theory* (Broadbent, 1958), in which attention was compared to a filter. Sensory information is processed but quickly reaches a bottleneck. Filter theory suggests that attention is an all-or-none phenomenon. An alternative theory of attention (Treisman, 1960) proposed that attention to one source of information is reduced, but not eliminated, when one pays attention to another source. This is known as an *attenuation model*. You have probably had the experience of being at a party, deeply involved in a discussion with a friend, and suddenly becoming aware that someone at the other end of the room has mentioned your name. A filter model of attention suggests that you would not hear your name being mentioned because your attention is focused entirely on the person with whom you are speaking. An attenuation model suggests that while you are focused primarily on your conversation, some attention remains available for other sources of information.

Attention can also be viewed as a limited resource, similar to a reservoir that can be filled up or emptied. This is known as a *capacity model* (Kahneman, 1973). Capacity models are concerned with the amount of mental effort needed to perform a task. If two tasks require the same kind of mental effort, they may interfere with each other. You may find it easy to visualize a scene (e.g., your apartment) and describe it in words. Doing two tasks that tap into the same resource can be very difficult. For example, reading a text and counting backward at the same time would be difficult. Both tasks require high mental effort via verbal processing.

As tasks are practiced, they become more automatic and require less attention—we acquire **automaticity**. Driving and riding a bicycle are examples. Once we acquire these skills, we can perform them without conscious attention. If a process is overlearned,

automaticity The ability to perform a task without having to think much about it.

however, there may be a tendency to engage in it whether we wish to or not. Automatic processes occur without conscious attention. Sometimes driving is performed automatically. Have you ever driven somewhere while thinking through a problem only to realize on your arrival that you do not remember the drive? You probably engaged in an automatic process. **Controlled processes**, in contrast, require conscious attention. For example, you are likely to be more deliberate and control your attention when you are driving in bad weather than you might otherwise do. Reading is typically an automatic process. Once we learn to read, we can do so automatically. The Stroop Test was used to investigate controlled and automatic processes (Schneider & Shiffrin, 1974). An example is presented in Figure 7.8, where you will find a list of words. If you simply read the words, you can no doubt do it quickly and easily. However, if you now try to name the colors in which the words are printed, you will be much slower in completing the task. In order to *name* the colors, you must prevent yourself from reading the words. This is more difficult when the word refers to a color that is different from the one in which it is printed. In performing these two tasks, you went from automatic processing to controlled processing. Children with learning disabilities may have difficulty with automatic processing (Lavoie, 1994).

controlled processes Cognitive processes that require conscious attention.

Figure 7.8 The Stroop Test

Source: Westen, D. *Psychology: Brain, Behavior and Culture*, Third Edition. © 2002 John Wiley & Sons. Reprinted by permission of John Wiley & Sons, Inc.

Memory Systems

Imagine what it would be like if you could not remember well. Alan Baddeley describes the case of Clive Wearing, a talented musician who fell ill with a viral infection (Baddeley, 1999). As a result of the encephalitis that developed from the infection, Wearing suffered extensive brain damage. He cannot remember what happened more than a few minutes before. He continues to believe that he has just regained consciousness and keeps a diary in which he constantly records that fact. Wearing has been in this condition since 1985. His case demonstrates how important memory is and how much we take it for granted. When we see examples of great deficiencies in memory, as in patients with Alzheimer's disease, we are reminded of its importance.

A variety of models of memory were proposed in the 1960s. In 1968, Atkinson and Shiffrin developed a model consisting of three different kinds of memory: sensory, short-term, and long-term (Atkinson & Shiffrin, 1968). This model is represented in Figure 7.1. The model remains useful to describe the general components of memory.

RIDE How might issues of attention and perception be related to the difficulties experienced by the students in Mr. Gomez's class?

Sensory Memory

Sensory memory is very brief. Memory for visual information is referred to as *iconic memory*, whereas memory for auditory information is called *echoic memory*. In a famous experiment, George Sperling provided empirical support for the capacity of sensory memory. Participants were shown three rows of letters for approximately one-twentieth of a second. After delays of varying length, participants were asked to recall one of the rows. Their recall worsened with longer delays. Based on these findings, iconic memory is thought to last about one-third of a second (Sperling, 1960).

sensory memory Brief memories associated with various senses.

Short-Term Memory

Short-term memory (STM) is a temporary memory storage. It has limited capacity and duration. Without active processing of information in short-term memory, the information will be lost.

short-term memory A temporary memory storage.

Figure 7.9 Digit Span

Source: Westen, D. *Psychology: Brain, Behavior and Culture*, Third Edition. © 2002 John Wiley & Sons. Reprinted by permission of John Wiley & Sons, Inc.

Capacity and Duration of Short-Term Memory George Miller wrote a classic paper on temporary memory. It was titled "The Magical Number Seven, Plus or Minus Two: Some Limits on Our Capacity for Processing Information" (Miller, 1956). Miller described the capacity of short-term memory storage as 7 ± 2 bits of information. Your telephone number most likely consists of 7 digits. Your Social Security number consists of 9 digits. Typically, the capacity of an individual's short-term memory is assessed by asking the person to recall a list of numbers such as those in Figure 7.9. An individual is presented with a sequence of digits and asked to repeat them back. (Try this with the list in Figure 7.9.) The length of the sequence is increased until a point is reached at which the individual always fails. The sequence length at which the individual is correct most of the time is considered to be his or her short-term memory capacity.

The duration of short-term memory is about 20 to 30 seconds if you do not make an effort to rehearse or elaborate on the material. Among the strategies available for keeping information in short-term memory are rehearsal and organization. There are two kinds of rehearsal: maintenance rehearsal and elaborative rehearsal. **Maintenance rehearsal** is what you do when you repeat information over and over without actually altering it. You may do this when you call directory assistance. When you are given the number you require, you repeat it over and over to yourself in order to maintain it in short-term memory. Unfortunately, you actually forget it much of the time. Today, many telephone companies compensate for this deficiency by offering to dial the number for you for a small fee. **Elaborative rehearsal** involves a deeper form of rehearsal that allows information to be transferred from short-term to long-term memory when an individual elaborates on information by connecting the to-be-remembered information to what he or she already knows. One way to reduce the demands on short-term memory involves **chunking** information, or grouping together bits of information. For example, a telephone number may be recalled as two *chunks* (732–7333) rather than as seven separate digits.

Information is lost from short-term memory through decay and interference. **Decay** occurs when information is not used and it simply fades from memory. **Interference** occurs when something else gets in the way of your recall. Have you ever gone into the kitchen to get something and found that, when you got there, you could not recall what you went in to get? If you have, you have experienced interference.

Phenomena Associated with Short-Term Memory When asked to listen to a list of words and recall them, one typically remembers some of the items at the beginning of the list and those at the end of the list. These are called *primacy* (heard first) and *recency* (just heard) effects. The probability that an item will be recalled depends on its position in the list, a phenomenon known as the **serial position effect** (Figure 7.10). Recognizing the limits of short-term memory, teachers can keep their instructions brief and provide opportunities for rehearsal.

A Model of Working Memory

Working memory is a term used to describe a limited, though active, memory system. Short-term memory refers to a short-term store. Working memory differs from short-term memory in that it includes both manipulation functions as well as storage functions. For example, if you attempt a mental arithmetic problem such as 456×8, you will need to store the information temporarily *and* keep track of the products of your computation. Thus, you are both storing and manipulating the information. Limited working memory capacity has important implications for learning. (See the nearby Taking It to the Classroom box).

Daneman and Carpenter (1980) devised a task to measure working memory span. Participants were shown sentences and asked to read each one. After reading the final sentence, they were asked to recall the last word in each sentence. An individual's working memory span was the number of words they recalled correctly.

The Phonological Loop System Baddeley proposed that working memory has a number of subsystems that are coordinated by a *central executive* (Baddeley, 1990). The first of these subsystems is the **phonological loop** system, which processes speech or auditory information. It consists of a passive phonological store and an articulatory rehearsal process. Several findings indicate that such a system does indeed exist.

First, people make more errors if the words they are asked to recall are similar in sound to one another. For example, it is harder to recall *man, can, an, map* than it is to recall *pen, day, cow, bar, rig* (Baddeley, 1993, p. 51). This phenomenon is called the **phonological similarity effect**.

Further evidence for the existence of a phonological loop comes from the **unattended speech effect**. When individuals are asked to perform a verbal task (e.g., reading) with speech in the background, performance is impaired. Performance is disrupted whether or not the background

---

maintenance rehearsal A cognitive process in which information in working memory is repeated to oneself frequently.

elaborative rehearsal A way of remembering information by connecting it to something that is already well known.

chunking The grouping of bits of data into larger, meaningful units.

decay Loss of memories because information is not used.

interference Loss or deficiency of memories because of the presence of other information.

serial position effect The fact that the likelihood of information being recalled varies according to its position in a list.

working memory A limited memory system that includes both storage and manipulation functions.

phonological loop The component of working memory that processes verbal information.

phonological similarity effect People make more errors recalling sets of words if the words they are asked to recall are similar in sound to one another.

unattended speech effect Verbal information automatically enters the phonological loop and can interfere with a person's verbal task performance even if that person is not paying attention to the information.

How Can I Use This?

Remember to keep your instructions brief so your students can recall what you want them to do.

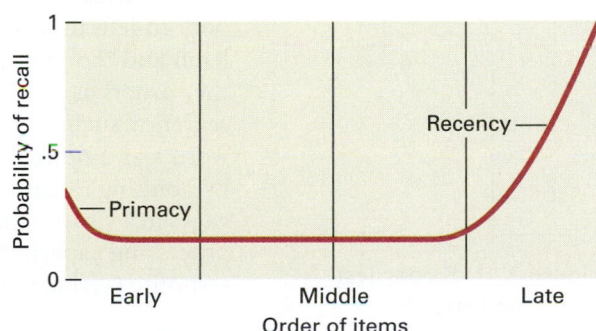

Figure 7.10 Serial Position Effect

Source: Reprinted from *The Psychology of Learning and Motivation,* Vol. 2, Atkinson, R. C., & Shiffrin, R. M. "Human memory: A proposed system and its control processes," 89–195, Copyright 1968, with permission from Elsevier.

Taking It to the Classroom

Do You Know Jack? Solving Word Problems

Jack is having trouble solving word problems in his algebra class. Some problems confuse him because of their wording. Other problems stymie him because he does not know what strategy to use to solve them. Sometimes he uses the wrong mathematical operation to solve the problem. What steps can you take to help Jack overcome this difficulty?

- Have Jack underline key words to help him focus on the important information in the problem.
- Pair him with another student and have them take turns telling each other what the problem is that they are being asked to solve.
- Show Jack how to draw a diagram that may help him keep the important information available to him rather than having him rely on his memory.
- Give Jack worked examples to follow.
- Provide Jack with lots of practice and feedback with similar problems.

---

speech is meaningful. You may have experienced this effect while studying difficult material. You may find that you have to turn off the radio because it is interfering with your task. Verbal information that is presented auditorily is processed automatically. Information in the working memory store is subject to both decay and interference from new material.

A third source of evidence in support of the phonological loop is found in the **word length effect**. There is a link between memory span and the length of words to be recalled. Verbal information that is presented auditorily gains direct access to the passive phonological store, which retains information in a phonological form.

Nick Ellis of the University of Bangor in Wales (Baddeley, 1993) administered a standardized IQ test to Welsh children. Their performance on the digit span was below the norms typically seen among American children (Ellis & Hennelley, 1980). Welsh words take longer to pronounce than their English equivalents. What appeared to be a difference in cognitive functioning between children from the two cultures was actually a difference in word length that affected performance on the digit span test. The results of this research suggest that cultural differences in basic processing should be interpreted with caution.

The Visuospatial Sketchpad A second subsystem in Baddeley's model is the **visuospatial sketchpad**, which is used for processing visual or spatial material or both. In Figure 7.11 you will see the letter *F*, a stimulus used in one of the tasks invented to explore the spatial and verbal components of recall (Brooks, 1968). In a study designed to test the processing of these components, participants were shown the letter and asked to keep it in mind. Starting at the bottom left, they were instructed to say "yes" if the corner was at the top or bottom of the letter and "no" if it was not. They found this much harder to do if they were asked to point to the corners as they announced their decisions. In contrast, when participants were shown a sentence, such as "A bird in the hand is not in the bush," and asked to indicate whether each word was a noun or not a noun, their performance was better if the responses were made by pointing rather than by speaking. These results demonstrate that when an individual engages in a visuospatial task such as pointing while performing a visual imagery task, the same processing capacity is being used. If the form of the task (verbal or visual) and that of the response (verbal or visual) are the same, performance is impaired.

The Executive System The central executive system of working memory controls the phonological loop and the visuospatial sketchpad. It is an attentional control system with limited capacity (Baddeley, 1993). Daneman and Carpenter (1983) explored the relationship between working memory and reading comprehension by asking individuals to read passages that contained inconsistencies due to the presence of words with more than one meaning. Here is an example:

word length effect The link between memory span and the length of words to be recalled.

visuospatial sketchpad The component of working memory that processes visuospatial content.

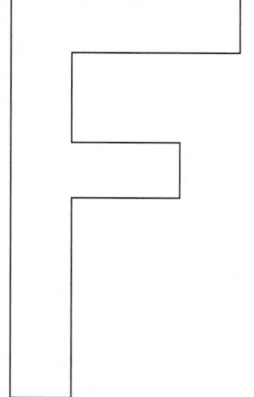

Figure 7.11 Brooks Test Using the Letter *F*

Source: Brooks, L. R. Spatial and verbal components of the act of recall. *Canadian Journal of Psychology, 22,* 349–368. Copyright 1968. Canadian Psychological Association. Reprinted with permission of the American Psychological Association.

There was a strange noise emanating from the dark house. Bob had to venture in to find out what was there. He was terrified: Rumor had it that the house was haunted. He would feel more secure with a stick to defend himself, so he went and looked among his baseball equipment. He found a bat that was very large and brown and was flying back and forth in the gloomy room. Now he didn't need to be afraid any longer.[1]

When reading this for the first time, most people assume that the *bat* is a baseball bat until information occurring later in the passage contradicts this notion. However, individuals with low working memory spans were able to come to the correct conclusion only 25% of the time. Individuals with high working memory spans are able to keep the initial information in working memory until they encounter the information that clarifies the passage. Additional research suggests that the functioning of the central executive system is the key difference between good and poor comprehenders (Oakhill, 1982, 1984; Oakhill, Yuill, & Parkin, 1986). Swanson and Sáez (2003) reviewed studies related to memory difficulties of learning-disabled students and concluded that they experience deficits in the executive control system and the phonological loop of the working memory system.

RIDE Think again about the students described at the beginning of the chapter. Are they exhibiting problems of working memory and executive control?

Memory Difficulties of Children with Special Needs

It is important for teachers to know that working memory is limited. When instructions are complicated or lengthy, there is a risk that students will not remember them. We may be disappointed when they do not follow instructions, but we may simply have exceeded their working memory's capacity for processing information.

Interruptions are frequent in elementary school classes and include such events as announcements from the administration, telephone calls, and visitors to the classroom. The effects of these disruptions on children's learning have not been studied. It seems reasonable to assume that the constant interruption can produce interference effects. Working memory is involved in such tasks as reading comprehension, writing, problem solving, and mathematics (Swanson & Siegel, 2001). Individuals with a large working memory span utilize cognitive resources more efficiently while reading and as a result have more resources for storage while comprehending the text (Swanson & Siegel, 2001). Students must also retrieve information from long-term memory to include in their writing. Maintaining ideas and choosing among them while actually producing text can make heavy demands on memory capacity. Some learners have difficulty writing because of limited working memory capacity.

When given a list of words to recall, learning-disabled children remember fewer words than normally achieving peers (Torgesen, 1977). Students with learning disabilities frequently have deficits in working memory (Swanson & Siegel, 2001). In particular, they have difficulty with reading comprehension because of deficits in the phonological loop—that is, the component of working memory that processes verbal information. Difficulties with working memory are problematic on tasks that require a learner to retain information in mind for a short period while also carrying out further activities. This skill is very important in reading tasks in which information that is coming in must be stored temporarily while other information is being processed (Swanson & Alexander, 1997). Difficulties with working memory can also interfere with writing because efforts to record ideas may interfere with maintenance rehearsal in working memory.

Students and teachers can use a variety of strategies to reduce the demands on working memory. Children often count on their fingers, thus giving themselves a visible record of their cognitive activity rather than relying on memory. Other strategies for supporting working memory include presenting information in **multiple modalities** presenting to various senses, allowing students to record their ideas before writing, or using speech-to-text software to reduce the burden on working memory. (See the next Taking It to the Classroom box.)

What Does This Mean to Me?
Think back to a time in a class when you felt that your working memory was overloaded. What could the teacher have done to make the situation better for you?

multiple modalities Various senses.

(Digital Vision)

Using an external representation can reduce the demands on working memory.

[1]From Daneman, M., & Carpenter, P. A. (1983). Individual differences in integrating information between and within sentences. *Journal of Experimental Psychology: Learning, Memory, and Cognition, 9,* 561–584. Reprinted with the permission of the American Psychological Association.

Taking It to the Classroom

Supporting Working Memory in the Classroom

Here are some guidelines for supporting students' working memory during instruction.

- *Keep directions simple.* Because working memory is limited, students may find it hard to follow complex directions. Simple directions are more likely to be followed correctly because students are more likely to remember what was said.

- *Provide information in both verbal and visual formats.* The working memory system has both verbal- and visual-processing components. Information that is provided in both visual and verbal formats is easier to process.

- *Teach students to create representations of problems.* Children often have difficulty solving word problems in mathematics. The limitations of working memory can contribute to these difficulties because children may forget important parts of the problem. Teaching children how to represent what the problem is asking them to do can help. For example, drawing a picture of the problem can be a very useful aid to problem solving.

- *Use tape recorders for children who have difficulties with writing.* Some students' writing may appear very disconnected and unstructured. The difficulties involved in producing writing or typing can interfere with working memory, and the student may simply forget his or her idea while trying to produce text. In such instances, you might have the student audiotape his or her verbally produced story and write it down later or assist the student in writing it down.

Long-Term Memory

long-term memory Memory of unknown, possibly unlimited, capacity and duration.

The capacity and duration of **long-term memory** (LTM) are not known, though it is clear that its capacity is very large and its duration is very long. It is also evident that the contents of long-term memory can include all kinds of information. Researchers have described several types of long-term memory. The Atkinson and Shiffrin model (see Figure 7.1 at the beginning of the chapter) was based on the duration of memory. In it, processing was divided among sensory, short-term, and long-term memory. This model was very useful, but it does not provide a complete description of how memory works. Sensory memory lasts half a second, short-term memory lasts about 30 seconds without rehearsal, and long-term memory may be unlimited. However, we have memories that last much longer than 30 seconds but are not indefinitely stored in long-term memory.

Types of Long-Term Memory   There are several ways to distinguish between various kinds of long-term memories. One important distinction is between episodic and semantic memory (Tulving, 1972). **Episodic memory** is memory of events and typically includes sensory information (things seen, heard, or smelled, etc.). Such memories often have heightened emotional content (happy, sad, or fearful). You need only consider events of your childhood (e.g., the first day of school) to generate an episodic memory. These memories are embedded in a specific context—a specific time and place.

episodic memory Long-term memory of particular places and events in a person's life.

In contrast, **semantic memory** is memory of verbal information or **declarative knowledge**—that is, knowledge about *what*. It is separate from sensory information and not tied to particular experiences. An example of an item that might be held in semantic memory is the answer to the question: In what city is the National Art Gallery? If you have visited that art gallery, you will have created episodic memories related to the content, and your combined semantic and episodic memory will make this information more memorable and retrievable.

semantic memory The memory a person has for meaning.

declarative knowledge Factual knowledge that can be expressed through verbal exchange, books, Braille, or sign language; knowing that something is true.

A second distinction is between declarative and procedural memory. **Declarative memory** is like semantic memory: It is memory about what. For example, you might have declarative memories about the structure of a bicycle. **Procedural memory** is memory about *how* to do something. You may remember how to ride a bicycle. These kinds of memory are also called *explicit* and *implicit memory,* respectively.

declarative memory Memory for abstract information.

procedural memory Memory for how to do things.

Brain Processes and Memory   A number of structures in the medial temporal lobes of the brain (Figure 7.12) are important for memory. They include the amygdala, the hippocampus, and the rhinal cortex that underlies the amygdala and hippocampus. The hippocampus plays a key role in the storage of new memories (Gazzaniga & Heatherton, 2003). The hippocampus and surrounding rhinal cortex are the most important areas for the consolidation of memory (Eichenbaum, 2002; Gazzaniga & Heatherton, 2003). The amydala is also involved in the consolidation of memories. In addition, the frontal lobes are considered important for memory; although people who experience damage to the frontal lobes do not suffer dramatic memory loss, they may have difficulty remembering the order of events. Brain-imaging studies show that when people try to remember a list of words, the frontal lobes light up (Buckner, Kelly, & Petersen, 1999). The frontal lobes are more active when a task requires deeper encoding.

Semantic Memory Semantic memory is memory for meaning and is thought to be organized like a network. Collins and Quillian (1969) proposed the earliest network model of semantic memory. In this model, semantic networks are made up of a network of related propositions. Such a network is analogous to a road map. On a map, cities, towns, and villages are linked to one another through a series of roads that vary in size and frequency of use. The same can be said for a semantic network. Figure 7.13 illustrates a network in which the basic unit of a semantic network is a **proposition**, the smallest unit of meaning that can be verified as true or false (Anderson, 2005). A proposition involves linking two concepts by a relationship. For example, the proposition *A bird is an animal* can be verified as true or false. According to Collins and Quillian, it should take longer to verify that *A wren is an animal* than it would to verify that *A bird is an animal* (Collins & Quillian, 1969). The word *wren* is two links away from *animal*, whereas the word *bird* is only one link away. However, based on this model, it should take as long to verify that *A wren is an animal* as it would to verify that *An eagle is an animal*. Most people in the United States will verify the latter proposition more quickly than the former because of familiarity. Connections between ideas also vary in strength and frequency of use. The more frequently connections between ideas are revisited, the stronger the connection becomes and the more quickly ideas can be retrieved. Frequency of use and strength of the connection between ideas are more important in understanding retrieval and speed of retrieval than the actual categorical structures.

Images When we think about an object that is not present, we experience an image of that object. Responding to a question about an image takes about the same amount of time as responding to a picture (Kosslyn, 1976). It appears as though people act on an image in the same way as they would act in response to an actual picture. In one study, participants were asked to form a mental image of a cat. They were then asked questions such as: Does the cat have a head? Does the cat have claws? Responses to the latter question took longer, as participants appeared to scan the image. In a related study, participants memorized a fictional map (Figure 7.14) and were asked to fixate on a specific landmark. A second landmark was mentioned, and participants were asked to imagine a small speck moving from the first

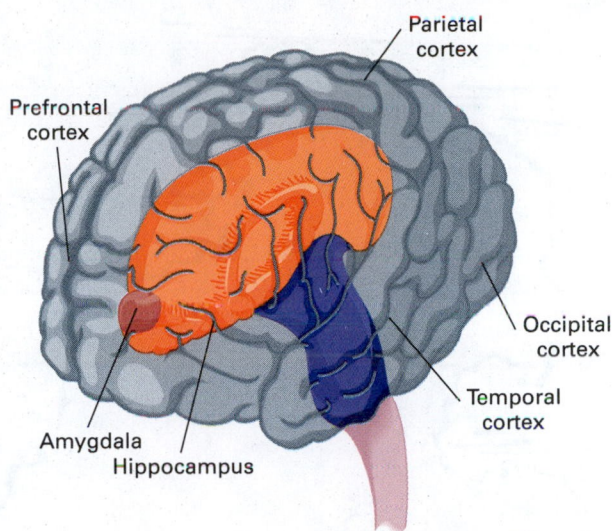

Figure 7.12 Major Regions of the Medial Temporal Lobe

Source: Westen, D. *Psychology: Brain, Behavior and Culture,* Third Edition. © 2002 John Wiley & Sons. Reprinted by permission of John Wiley & Sons, Inc.

proposition The smallest unit of knowledge that can be verified.

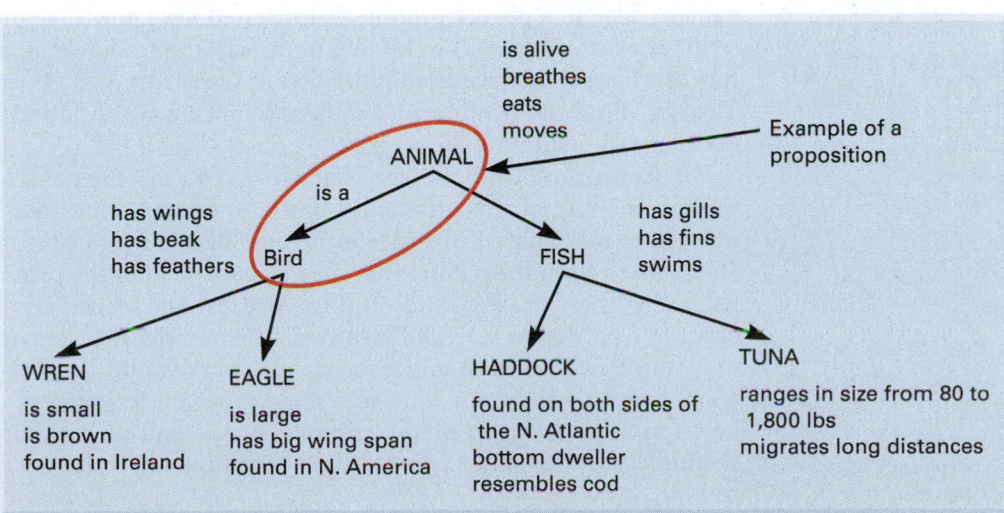

Figure 7.13 Network of Concepts and Example of a Proposition

Figure 7.14 Image Scanning with a Fictional Map

Source: Kosslyn, S. M., Ball, T. M., & Reiser, B. J. (1978). Visual images preserve metric spatial information: Evidence from studies of image scanning. *Journal of Experimental Psychology: Human Perception and Performance, 4,* 47–60. Reprinted with the permission of the American Psychological Association.

propositional network A set of interconnected pieces of information that contains knowledge for the long term.

schema The basic structure for organizing information.

script An event schema for the sequence of events in common situations, such as ordering food at a fast-food restaurant.

Figure 7.15 Mental Rotation

Source: Huffman, K. *Psychology in Action,* Seventh Edition. © 2004 John Wiley & Sons. Reprinted by permission of John Wiley & Sons, Inc.

landmark to the second. The greater the distance between the two landmarks, the longer it took participants to respond (Kosslyn, Ball, & Reiser, 1978).

In Figure 7.15, two shapes are presented. An individual is asked to determine whether the shape on the right is the same as the one on the left. In other words, is the shape on the right a rotated version of the one on the left? To do this task, individuals imagined rotating the shape on the left to determine whether it was the same as the one on the right. Response times were longer when the images were far apart in orientation.

Image information is thought to be stored in piecemeal fashion in long-term memory. Images are created by activating the overall or global shape of the image; elaborations are then added to create a complete image (Kosslyn, 1980, 1983). More detailed images take longer to retrieve. Images are thought to be stored in a nonimage format (Reisberg, 2001) that specifies a *recipe* for constructing the image. As with the processing of language, processing images takes time.

Schemas and Scripts Semantic memory is organized in complex networks. When people know isolated facts, representations of these facts in semantic memory may not be connected to many other ideas. In contrast, complex understanding of a domain will result in a dense network of interconnected propositions about that domain called a **propositional network**. **Schemas** refer to organized sets of propositions about a topic. A learner's available schemas influence how he or she interacts with the environment. The learner's schemas may be altered as a result of interacting with the environment. A schema of a teacher might include such propositions as "A teacher is a graduate" or "A teacher is kind." Figure 7.16 illustrates how a schema about colleges might be represented. Each proposition can be verified as true or false. For example, one proposition is "Colleges have buildings." This assertion can be verified as true or false.

A schema that describes the typical sequence of events in a situation is called a **script**, or *event schema*. For example, when you go to a restaurant, you usually expect actions to unfold in a particular way. Sometimes, however, they do not. On a recent occasion, one of the authors went to a restaurant with friends. Before long, the server appeared and asked us whether we would like drinks. One person asked for a cup of coffee. The server replied that she could not have the coffee now, because that was served after dinner. The server had a different script for how events should unfold than the customer did. This same conflict sometimes occurs between the teacher's classroom script and the students' classroom script.

In the nearby What Kids Say and Do box, you can read the response of a fourth grader named Chloe to a picture prompt that involved her knowledge of a script or event schema. The children in this class were shown a picture of a boy sitting outside an office that was labeled "Main Office." The boy's head was bent down, and he was looking at the floor. His bookbag was beside him.

In her account, Chloe showed knowledge of a schema or script related to being at the principal's office. She knew that a child must have misbehaved in order to be outside the office waiting. She inferred from the picture that the office was that of the principal, rather than another kind of office. Because she identified the office in a particular way, she activated schema-relevant elements of a story: The boy had misbehaved, and there would be consequences for his actions. Chloe also showed her understanding of how scripts allow us to predict actions. At the end of her story, she indicated that Billy repeated the actions for which he got in trouble.

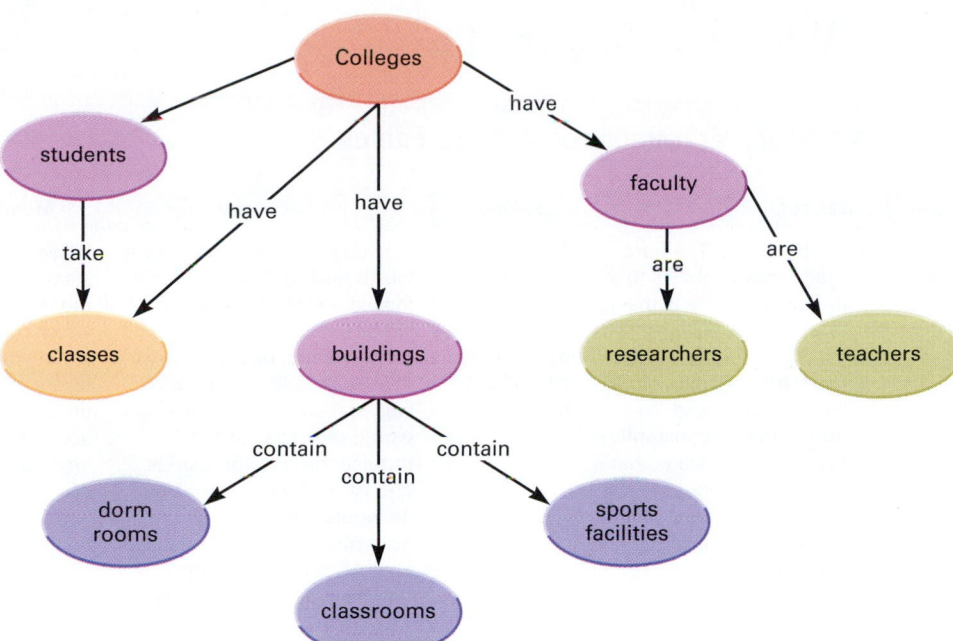

Figure 7.16 A partial schema for a college

Another type of script is a **story grammar** that can help students to understand and remember stories (Gagné, Yekovich, & Yekovich, 1993). In the next What Kids Say and Do box, Ms. D'Andrea taught her students the following story grammar to help them understand Aesop's fables: title, characters, setting, events, problem, solution, summary, and moral. You can see one child's response to the task of constructing a story grammar.

story grammar The typical structure of a category of stories.

Levels of Processing   Craik and Lockhart proposed an alternative theory of memory in 1972. They suggested that memory differences are not so much a function of *duration* as of *depth* of processing (Craik & Lockhart, 1972). In other words, the more deeply we process information, the more likely we are to remember it. A classic experiment compared the memory performance of three groups of students as they processed a word list. The first group was asked to determine whether a particular letter was present in a word as it was presented. These students attended to the structure of the word. The second group was asked to decide whether they liked the word when it was presented. Thus, they attended to the content on an affective level. The third group was asked to generate a word that was opposite in meaning to the presented word. These students attended to the meaning of the word. The results showed that students who attended to meaning performed significantly better than those who decided whether they liked a word. The latter group, in turn, did better than the students who only decided whether a particular letter was present. Craik and Lockhart argued that the differences in performance reflected differences in depth of processing.

What Kids Say and Do

Using a Script

"Ouch! That hurt, Billy. I'm telling the principal." Beep went the intercom. "Billy Smith, please come to the office *now*!" Billy went to the main office. He went inside. "The principal will see you in a few minutes. Sit down on the bench." Billy sat down and thought about what he did to Johnny. He said to himself, "My mom is going to kill me." It was now time to speak to the principal about what he had done.

After the conversation, he was suspended for three days. Johnny was doing fine in the hospital, and Billy promised himself that he would never hurt or beat someone up again. A few years later, he forgot about the promise and "Ouch!"[2]

[2] Written by Chloe Branch. Used with permission of Chloe Branch and Jeffrey Smith.

Craik and Lockhart's concept of **levels of processing** helped shift the emphasis in the study of memory from storage to processing. The Atkinson and Shiffrin model defined memory systems in terms of the storage/duration of memories and described very short-term stores (sensory and short-term memory) and very long-term stores (long-term memory). It did not include intermediate-length memories, such as the memory for course content one might have after cramming for a test. Such information lasts longer than the typical short-term memory storage would predict but is generally not available in long-term memory. The levels of processing theory focuses on the likelihood of retrieval as a function of how effortful and meaningful the initial encoding was. The limitation of this work is that it was impossible

levels of processing theory A theory that asserts that recall of information is based on how deeply it is processed.

What Kids Say and Do

Using a Story Grammar for Aesop's Fables

Title	Characters	Setting	3 Events	Problem	Solution	Summary	Moral
The Hare and the Tortoise	The hare and the tortoise	The woods	1. The hare challenges the tortoise to a race. 2. The hare takes a nap during the race. 3. The tortoise wins the race.	The hare thinks that he is the fastest animal in the woods and constantly brags that no one can beat him in a race.	The tortoise accepts the challenge because he has faith that he can win the race.	One day in the woods, a hare was boasting that he was the fastest animal in the woods. No one would take him up on his challenge, until one day a little voice said, "I will." So it was agreed that the hare would race against the tortoise through the woods and back. The hare, thinking he would win the race with no problem, decided to take a nap. All of a sudden, the tortoise passed the hare and won the race.	"Slow and steady wins the race," which means when you take your time, you can accomplish anything.

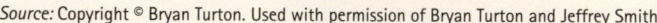

Source: Copyright © Bryan Turton. Used with permission of Bryan Turton and Jeffrey Smith.

---

procedural knowledge Knowledge about how to perform tasks.

conditional knowledge Knowledge that guides a person in using declarative and procedural knowledge.

TABLE 7.1

Organized and Disorganized Lists

List 1	List 2
Geneva	Banana
Orchid	Grape
Orlando	Melon
Geranium	Orange
Melon	Buttercup
Minnesota	Geranium
Orange	Mums
Buttercup	Orchid
Grape	Berlin
Mums	Geneva
Berlin	Milan
Banana	Orlando

to measure *depth*. Nevertheless, the emphasis on processing made an enormous contribution to the study of memory.

Encoding, Retrieval, and Forgetting

Encoding is the taking in of information. The probability that information will be retrieved or remembered depends on the quality of encoding. Different types of knowledge can be encoded.

Types of Knowledge

The kinds of encoding strategies that students use will vary as a function of the type of knowledge they are acquiring. Declarative knowledge is knowledge about *what*. Knowing history facts or being able to name the parts of a cell are examples of declarative knowledge **Procedural knowledge** is knowledge about *how*. Knowing how to set up the equipment in the chemistry lab is an example of procedural knowledge. **Conditional knowledge** involves knowledge of both *what* and *how*. It involves knowing the necessary information and how to apply it in the right situation. For example, knowing that a more active study strategy than underlining is necessary when studying complex material is an example of conditional knowledge.

Organization, Practice, and Elaboration

Remembering is best when information is encoded well. Key processes in good encoding are organization, practice, and elaboration. It is easier to learn organized material than it is to learn disorganized material. For example, Table 7.1 presents two lists of words. List

2 will be easier to learn because it is organized by category: fruits, flowers, and cities. List 1 contains the same information but will be harder to learn because it lacks organization.

Practice helps develop good memory. Material that is used more often is remembered more easily. However, there are different ways of practicing. **Distributed practice** is much more effective than **massed practice**. Distributed practice is done over a period of time, with varying intervals between rehearsals of the information. Rather than studying for an exam the night before, a learner might study for a few hours on alternating days in the week before the test. Distributed practice provides opportunities to practice retrieval after varying lengths of time. Remembering involves using the cues available to assist remembering but also involves generating cues that help remembering. Distributed practice allows students to practice both of these skills. These are processes that are necessary when taking an examination. Massed practice, in contrast, involves engaging in extensive practice at one time, such as studying all night before an exam. This can be somewhat effective for an immediate task but is unlikely to lead to long-term recall of information.

Elaboration also helps in encoding and retrieval. When you connect the information you are trying to learn to information you already know or to images or other enhancements of the information to be learned, you are elaborating on the material. Images in particular are powerful aids to memory and are frequently used to elaborate on information. Elaboration helps you extend a network of concepts and the relationships among them. When a concept is elaborated upon, connections are made to other concepts, thereby permitting more pathways to retrieval. Mnemonic strategies are one example of elaboration.

Mnemonic Strategies

Learning is much easier when information is meaningful. Although higher-order thinking skills are important, sometimes facts, concepts, relationships, and the like simply have to be memorized. In such cases, it is helpful to understand the processes through which memory works and what kinds of activities will enhance that process. Students enjoy learning memory tricks and are glad that they have learned them when they see how they can be applied to learning. Strategies for remembering information are known as **mnemonic strategies**. Such strategies include acronyms, the keyword strategy, the method of loci, and pegword mnemonics.

Acronyms In using the *acronyms* strategy, you would create a word in which each of the letters stands for one of the words to be remembered. For example, in this textbook, you are asked to engage in reflection, information gathering, decision making, and evaluation. The acronym RIDE makes this easy to remember. A common acronym is ROY-G-BIV for remembering the colors of the rainbow: **r**ed, **o**range, **y**ellow, **g**reen, **b**lue, **i**ndigo, and **v**iolet.

The Keyword Strategy Among the most helpful mnemonic strategies is the *keyword strategy* for learning vocabulary (particularly in a foreign language). A visual image is used to make a link between a word in the foreign language and its meaning in English. For example, the French word *sortir* means "to leave" and is pronounced somewhat like *sort tear* (*tear* as in crying, with apologies to native French speakers). The keyword strategy begins by the learner thinking of something that comes to mind easily when one sees the word *sortir*. For example, *sort tear* might suggest a postal worker sorting so many letters that he is crying. That could be the initial image. Now it has to be modified to put the definition "to leave" into it. This will not be very difficult. The postal worker could be crying, throwing the letters in the air, and leaving the post office. The keyword works by starting with the target word, then going to the image that it prompts—in which the definition is embedded—and retrieving the definition.

The Method of Loci The *method of loci* uses spatial imagery to assist memory. If you need to learn a list of words or concepts, you could visualize yourself walking around a familiar place, such as your apartment, and putting each word in a different place. For example, if you were trying to remember the assignments you needed to complete, you might imagine leaving your assignments in various locations in the apartment. Your assignment for your educational psychology class might be on the kitchen table, your assignment for English beside the TV, and so forth.

distributed practice Practice that is interspersed by unequal intervals.

massed practice Intense practice for a single period of time. Also known as *cramming*.

elaboration A process through which we add and extend meaning by connecting new information to existing knowledge in long-term memory.

mnemonic strategies Strategies for remembering nonmeaningful information by making it meaningful.

Pegword Mnemonics   *Pegword mnemonics* requires you to associate each new word with a word on a previously memorized list. For example, suppose that you wish to learn the following list of words: *battleship, volcano, ambulance, policeman, television, computer, calendar, mirror, flashlight, pencil.* First, you would memorize the following rhyme.

One is a bun.	Six is a stick.
Two is a shoe.	Seven is heaven.
Three is a tree.	Eight is a gate.
Four is a door.	Nine is a dime.
Five is a hive.	Ten is a hen.

This rhyme is easy to remember because you are depending on similar sounds to help memory. The next step in the strategy is to associate each of the words to be remembered with a line of this rhyme. The first word to be remembered is *battleship*. You now associate battleship with *One is a bun*. You might visualize a battleship between two parts of a hamburger bun.

One = Bun = Battleship

The second word to be memorized is *volcano*. Now you link volcano to *Two is a shoe*. You might imagine a shoe with a volcano in it, with lava pouring over the edges of the shoe. The process would continue until you had linked each word with a line of the rhyme. The strategy is very effective for remembering lists of words.

Imagery and Visual-Learning Strategies

A theory that explains why images are helpful in remembering is the dual-coding theory (Paivio, 1986). According to this theory, images and words are represented differently, as *imagens* and *logogens*. When the two forms of representations are linked, the memory for the information is stronger. Baddeley's findings on the separate working memory systems for visual and verbal information also support the importance of presenting and learning information in both visual and verbal forms (Baddeley, 1999). Visual strategies such as concept maps and graphic organizers integrate verbal, visual, and spatial information to enhance encoding and retrieval. (See the next Taking It to the Classroom Box.)

graphic organizer A visual display of verbal information.

Appendix
Visual Strategies

Using graphic organizers and concept maps in your teaching can help your students understand relationships among concepts they are learning (PRAXIS™, II.A.2; INTASC, Principle 4).

Graphic Organizers   A **graphic organizer** is a visual display of verbal information. The term *graphic organizer* includes such devices as concept maps, mind webs, semantic maps, knowledge maps, tables, and so forth. Graphic organizers are intended to help students to comprehend, summarize, and synthesize information. A well-designed graphic organizer can represent parts of a whole and show the relationships among those parts. In the example shown in Figure 7.17, a fourth-grade teacher used a graphic organizer to help her students use the KWLH strategy, a means of helping students activate existing knowledge. First, the students recall what they *know* (K) about the topic; then they identify what they *want* (W) to know, what they have *learned* (L), and *how* (H) they can learn more. By providing a graphic organizer, the teacher helps the students comprehend, summarize, and synthesize the day's lesson.

Concept Mapping   Concept mapping is a strategy in which students create diagrams or pictures to illustrate their understanding of a concept. A concept map (Figure 7.18) shows a set of concepts and the relationships between them. Concept maps are sometimes referred to as mind maps or knowledge maps. Concept maps are intended to mimic the ways in which schemas may be structured (see Figure 7.16). Research on the individual and collaborative use of concept mapping has shown them to be effective learning tools (Asan, 2007; Basque & Lavoie, 2006; Novak, 1993). The teacher can also use concept maps as teaching aids.

Students can be taught to label the relationships between ideas in a concept map. Figure 7.19 includes a list of typical links that might be used to connect ideas. The links are of three types: dynamic, static, and elaborative. Dynamic links show that the information in one node is the outcome of the previous node—for example, driving over nails and

What Does This Mean to Me?
Which are stronger, your verbal skills or your visual skills? How might a graphic organizer help you understand the content of this chapter?

Figure 7.17 Sample
K–W–L–H

Source: Donna Ogle. *K–W–L–H Technique.* Retrieved from the Web site of the North Central Regional Educational Laboratory at http://www. ncrel.org/sdrs/areas/issues/students/ learning/lr1kwlh.htm. Reproduced with permission.

Dinosaurs

What We Know	What We Want to Find Out	What We Learned	How Can We Learn More
Dinosaurs are large. Dinosaurs are dead. They lived a long time ago. There is a movie about dinosaurs.	How long ago did they live? Why did they die? How do we know what they looked like? Who are the people who study dinosuars?	An archeologist has an exciting life. Dinosaurs eat plants, and some eat meat. Some dinosaurs were gigantic, but had small brains. Fossils uncover dinosaur traits.	Research Museums Field trips Archeological digs Videos Internet computer search

Categories of information we expect to use:
A. Size

B. Career

C. Eating habits

D.

E.

F.

G.

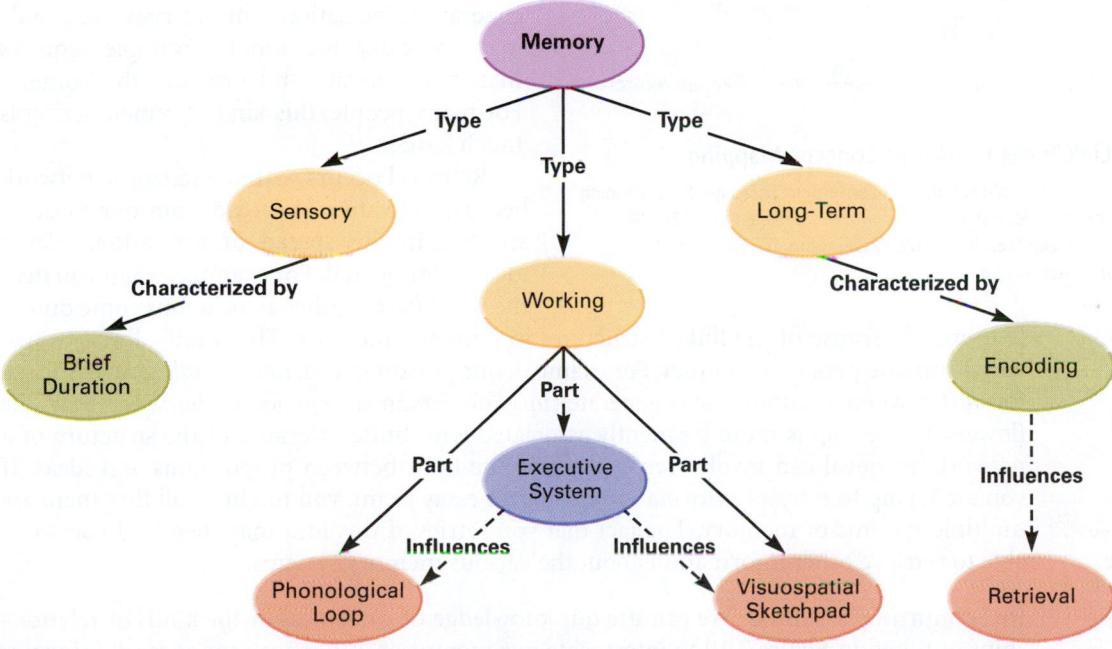

Figure 7.18 A Partial Concept Map of Memory Systems

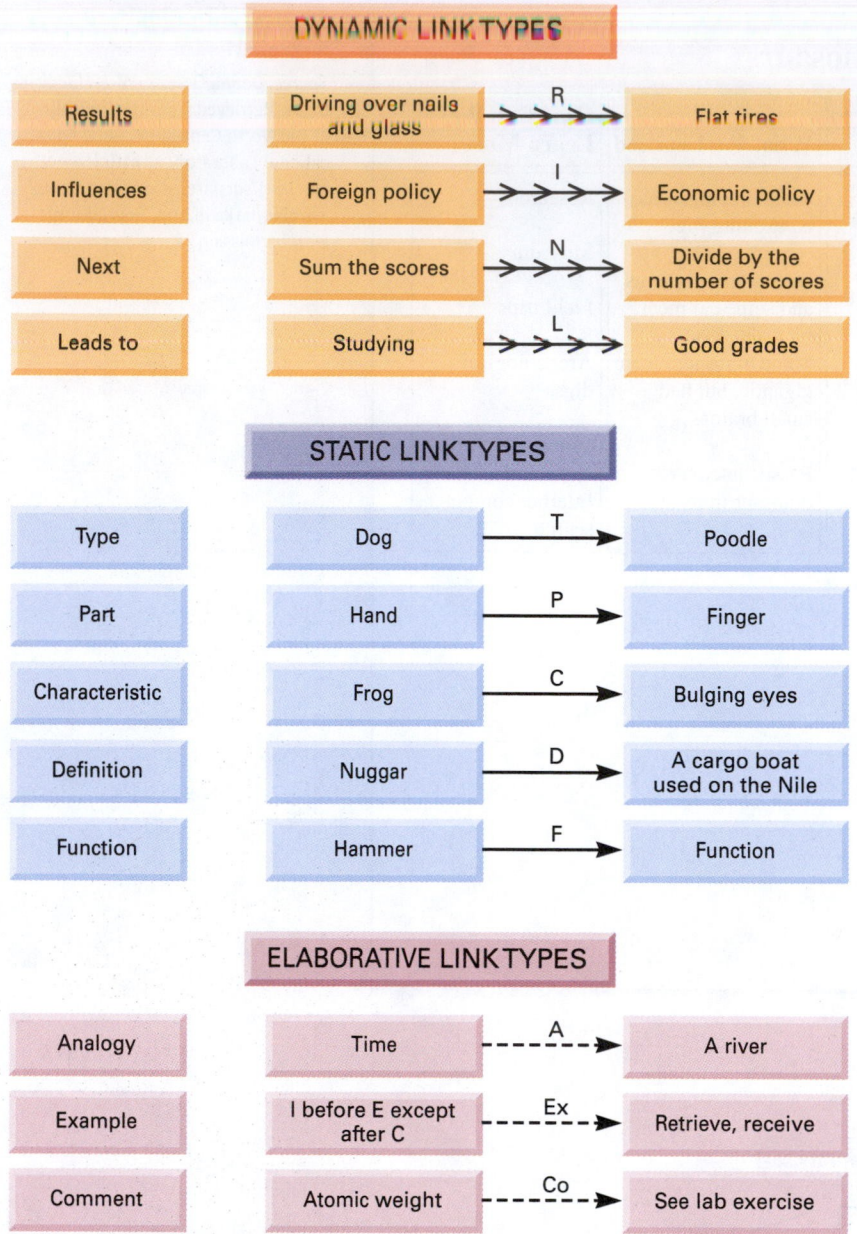

Figure 7.19 Examples of Link Types for Use in Concept Mapping

Source: McCagg, Edward C., & Dansereau, Donald F. (1991). A convergent paradigm for examining knowledge mapping as a learning strategy. *Journal of Educational Research, 84*(6), 317–324. Published by Heldref Publications, 1319 Eighteenth St., NW, Washington, DC 20036-1802. Copyright © 1991 by the Taylor and Francis Group.

recognition memory Memories are cued, then recognized.

recall Information is retrieved from long-term memory.

spread of activation The retrieval of bits of information on the basis of their relatedness to one another. Remembering one piece of information stimulates the recall of associated knowledge.

glass *results in* flat tires. Static links describe structural relationships between ideas—for example, a poodle is a type of dog. Elaborative links extend the information in one node by linking it to another—for example, time is *analogous* to a river. Younger students will experience great difficulty with using a complex set of links such as those found in Figure 7.19. Older students may also experience some difficulty. Therefore, it is best to introduce the various types of links slowly and show clearly how they describe structures of knowledge.

Knowledge Structures Graphic representations can also show the structure of knowledge. In Figure 7.20, three knowledge structures are illustrated. The first is a chainlike structure that clearly shows a sequence of events. Cluster structures show descriptive knowledge about a topic, and hierarchies show the relationships among parts of a system.

Retrieval and Forgetting

Remembering can occur through either **recognition memory** or **recall**. Recognition simply requires us to respond to information and recognize that we have seen it before. Recognition memory responds to cues. Responding to multiple-choice tests can require recognition memory because the cues provided by the options from which you may choose will provide some assistance to memory. When you are asked to recall information, on the other hand, you must generate information without cues. Responding to an essay question, for example, requires that you generate and organize the content. For many people, this kind of remembering is much harder.

Retrieval occurs within a semantic network because activation is spread from one node to another. In this **spread of activation**, related ideas are triggered. For example, when you hear the word *butter,* other associations come quickly to mind because of the linked structures in semantic memory. The specific linkages will vary from one person to another. For example, one person may generate *milk* as an associate for *butter,* whereas another may generate *cup.* The person who generates *buttercup* may like flowers; hence, *cup* is more frequently associated with butter. Because of the structure of a network, retrieval can involve reconstructing the links between propositions and ideas. If you are trying to retrieve information during an essay exam, you might recall that there are multiple systems of memory. The fact that you retrieved this idea may then lead you to be able to retrieve other information about the various memory systems.

Interrogating Memory We can use our knowledge of categories or the kinds of relationships outlined in Figure 7.19 to interrogate our memories. When we cannot recall information about a topic, we can conduct a *relationship-guided search.* A simple acronym for some

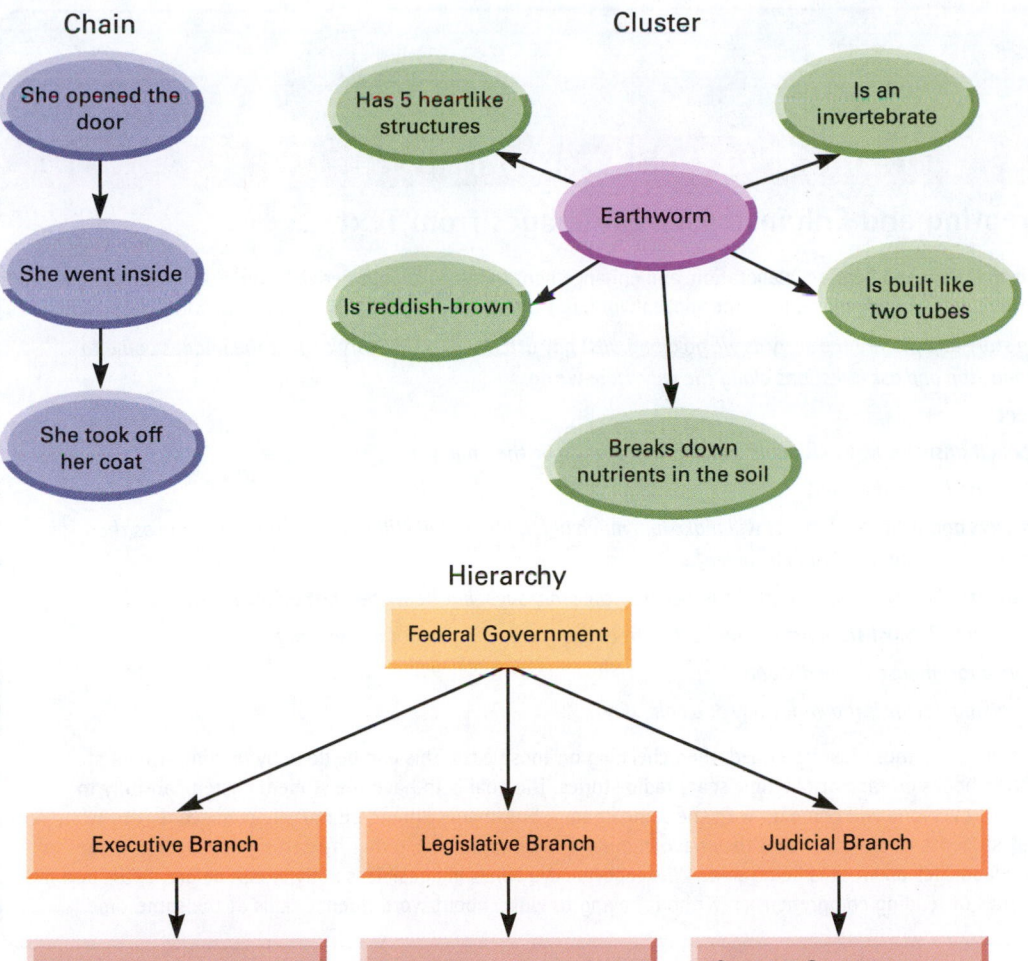

Figure 7.20 Knowledge Structures

of the types of links shown in Figure 7.19 is T-PLACE (for type, parts, leads to, analogy, characteristics, examples). If you were to interrogate your memory about a topic such as *famines*, you could ask yourself questions related to the various types of links. For example:

Question: What types of famines are there?

Answer: There are those caused by weather conditions, those caused by wars.

Question: What do famines lead to?

Answer: Starvation of many, likely leading to lots of deaths.

Forgetting   Forgetting occurs when there is interference or decay. When material is encoded in an organized manner, more cues are encoded, thus making retrieval easier. Also, information that is used more frequently is easier to recall. Material that is not encoded in an organized way and not used often is more likely to be forgotten. This is so because in a propositional network model of memory, retrieval occurs through a process of spreading activation. When one node in a network is triggered, related nodes are also triggered as activation spreads along the links to them. When these links are used often, less activation is needed to generate the connecting node. If the nodes are highly interconnected with many links, forgetting is less likely, but retrieval may take longer. In a curious irony, the more you know, the longer it may take you to verify that you know it.

Forgetting occurs when information is not used. If you have not practiced solving geometry problems for a year, you are likely to have forgotten the steps in doing so. Forgetting

What Does This Mean to Me?
Use some of the link types in Figure 7.19 to interrogate your memory of what you have read in this chapter.

What Does This Mean to Me?
Can you explain to yourself why these principles of multimedia learning might be true?

Taking It to the Classroom

Creating and Enhancing Visual Images from Text

Part of reading comprehension is the creation, modification, elaboration, and enhancement of visual images derived from text. An enjoyable approach to developing this skill involves working on images from the spoken word, not the written word. Consider the following class activity:

Today we are going to listen to a story and picture the story as we go along. Just pay attention to the story and let the images come to your mind. I'll tell you the story and stop and ask questions along the way. Here we go:

"Jack was walking down the street."

In your mind, how old is Jack? [Solicit answers. Most students will consider Jack to be their age.]

"He wished he had brought his cane and a warmer coat."

Now how old is Jack? [Solicit answers again. Some students will make him much older; others will still have him the same age as themselves even though the story now suggests that he should be older.]

Is Jack wearing a coat? [Most students will say no, but clearly he is, because the story says that he wished he had a warmer coat.]

What kind of street is Jack walking down? [Most students will make it a street like the one in front of the school.]

"Smoke was wafting skyward from a farmhouse in the distance."

Now what kind of street is Jack walking down? Is it a windy day or a calm day?

You can continue the story, providing cues like those just described, then checking on those cues. This can be done by reading from a story that is rich in such cues, or even getting books on tape or old-time scary radio stories. The goal is to have the students listen carefully to what the author is saying. Of course, not everyone will come up with the same images, but images should be roughly consistent with what the author is saying. You can also ask students to describe what they have in mind at a certain point, either by writing down their images or by sharing them with the class. Who elaborates on what is being said? Who reports *bare bones* images? This activity can be great fun, and it offers a way to help students with issues of reading comprehension without having to worry about word fluency skills at the same time.

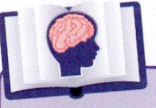

MINDFUL HABITS

Effective teachers promote active learning by their students by providing opportunities for deep processing of information, the use of prior knowledge, and diverse teaching strategies

concept An abstraction with which a person categorizes objects, people, ideas, or experiences by shared properties.

criterial attributes Attributes that must be presented for an instance to be a member of a particular category.

also occurs because of interference. If you go to the grocery store having made a mental list of what you need to purchase and you meet a friend, the discussion with your friend may interfere with your recall of your grocery list. (See the nearby Taking It to the Classroom box.)

Categorization

Earlier in the chapter, you saw how attention can be used to narrow the scope of the environmental input we receive. Categorization is another way in which we narrow the range of information available to us. Categorization helps us do the following:

- Reduce complexity
- Identify objects
- Devote less effort to learning
- Order and relate classes of objects and events

Concepts are abstractions that are the result of assigning objects, people, ideas, or experiences to categories. We can most readily distinguish between categories when they differ on a single dimension. For example, triangles can be distinguished from squares or rectangles because triangles have three sides, and squares and rectangles have four sides. Many categories differ in more than one dimension, however, and we learn to distinguish among them by applying logical rules.

To understand which instances are members of a concept category, we need to identify **criterial attributes**. These attributes are ones that must be present in order for the instance to be considered a member of the class. The process of including recurring attributes and excluding nonrecurring attributes is called *abstraction*. If a child is attempting to categorize shapes into rectangles or triangles, he or she learns to attend to the number of sides of the object (i.e., three or four) and ignore the varying colors of the shapes.

Concept Attainment Tasks The tasks used by Jerome Bruner and his colleagues (Bruner, Goodenow, & Austin, 1956) in their studies of concept attainment were of two kinds: reception and selection tasks. Reception tasks involve the development of hypotheses about the nature of the target concepts, with revisions and alterations to the hypotheses when the data do not fit. In a selection task, an individual is shown a positive instance of a concept, then asked to pick out another instance of that concept. The individual is then told whether the selection was correct. Strategies for completing selection tasks vary. They depend on the individual forming a hypothesis, testing its accuracy, and revising it in coherent ways. Young children are often asked to engage in selection tasks as they learn to classify. Selection strategies include the following:

- Focus gambling, in which the learner focuses on a certain attribute, gambling that it is the correct one. (See the nearby What Kids Say and Do box.)
- Simultaneous scanning, in which the learner keeps all attributes in mind. This strategy has the problem of being too complex and making heavy demands on working memory.
- Successive scanning, in which the learner tests a single hypothesis and persists until it has been proven wrong.

Teaching Concepts

A concept attainment model is often used to teach concepts. Typically, a lesson has four components. First, examples of the concept are presented; then nonexamples are presented. The teacher should lead a discussion of why the examples are good examples of the concepts and the nonexamples are not. If the target concept is *mountain*, children are shown examples and nonexamples. The nonexamples provided could include a hilly landscape and a lighthouse in its surrounding area. The children and their teacher discuss why these are nonexamples. Possible attributes of a mountain that children might identify as missing in the nonexamples include peaks. The teacher would test the children's understanding by providing them with new stimuli and asking them whether they are mountains. The students would test their hypotheses about what attributes make a mountain by answering the question. Errors can occur through **overgeneralization** when a student includes nonexamples in a category or **undergeneralization** when students fail to identify appropriate members of the category.

Criticisms of Classical Concept Research Not all concepts or categories can be described by defining attributes. As the number of attributes increases, the demands on working memory become excessive. For some categories, it is difficult to define a criterial attribute. Such categories are called **natural categories** (Rosch, 1973). For example, it is difficult to identify the criterial attribute that defines *dog*.

Real-world or natural categories are hierarchically organized (Rosch et al., 1976). There are three levels in such a hierarchy: superordinate, basic, and subordinate (see Table 7.2). The subordinate level contains the most specific examples of the general or superordinate category. The most important level is the basic level, because the examples at this level are most different from one another. A bus and a car, for instance, are more dissimilar than are a school bus and a city bus.

Some members of natural categories are better examples of the category than others. For example, an ostrich is not as good an example of the category *bird* as is a robin. A **prototype** is the best representative of its category. Other members of the category can be more or less similar to the prototype. For example, if the prototype of the category *dog* is an Alsatian, a Labrador retriever would be more similar to the prototype than a dachshund. Members of a category can be described as having **graded membership** in the category, which means that they may be closer or farther away from the prototype for the category. (See the nearby What Kids Say and Do box.)

overgeneralization Inclusion of a nonmember of a category or class in that category or class.

undergeneralization The exclusion of some instances from a category or group even though they are true members of that category or group.

natural categories Real-world categories.

prototype The best representative of a category.

graded membership The extent to which an object or idea belongs to a category.

TABLE 7.2

Examples of Superordinate, Basic, and Subordinate Categories

Superordinate	Basic	Subordinate	
Animal	Bird	Robin	Hummingbird
	Dog	Labrador	Poodle
	Fish	Tuna	Haddock
Furniture	Table	Kitchen table	Dining room table
	Lamp	Night lamp	Desk lamp
	Chair	Armchair	Kitchen chair
Vehicles	Car	Sedan	Convertible
	Truck	Pickup truck	Dump truck
	Bus	School bus	City bus

Taking It to the Classroom

Principles of Multimedia Learning

- *Multimedia Principle*: Students learn better from words and pictures than from words alone.
- *Spatial Contiguity Principle*: Students learn better when corresponding words and pictures are presented near each other on the page or screen.
- *Temporal Contiguity Principle*: Students learn better when corresponding words and pictures are presented simultaneously rather than successively.
- *Coherence Principle*: Students learn better when extraneous words, pictures, and sounds are excluded.
- *Modality Principle*: Students learn better from animation and narration than from animation and on-screen text.
- *Redundancy Principle*: Students learn better from animation and narration than from animation, narration, and on-screen text.
- *Individual Differences Principle*: Design effects are stronger for low-knowledge learners than for high-knowledge learners and for high-spatial learners rather than for low-spatial learners. Students who have prior knowledge of the content of a multimedia presentation perform better than those who do not. Furthermore, students with good spatial skills or those who are good at generating and using mental images perform better than those who are less skilled.

Source: Adapted from Mayer, R. (2001). *Multimedia Learning* (p. 184). New York: Cambridge University Press. Reprinted with the permission of Cambridge University Press.

Appendix
Cultural Differences

Diverse students will vary in their schemas, scripts, and categories of knowledge (PRAXIS™, III.B; INTASC, Principle 6).

Diversity, Culture, and Experience in Developing Concepts and Categories

A child's culture and experience influence the kinds of categories and concepts that he or she develops. One of the authors taught in an elementary school in a very poor inner-city district. She took her class on a field trip to a hilly area that had lots of trees and sheep. The children lived in a housing project, where the landscape was very flat and there were no trees, some grass, but mostly concrete. During the field trip, one of the second graders asked the teacher, "How come the sheep don't fall over?" The teacher looked where the child was pointing and observed a sheep about halfway up a very steep hill. The child had only seen pictures

What Kids Say and Do

Focusing on a Single Attribute

Ms. Nowicki has taught first grade for many years. For the last week, her class has been working on a science unit about *Living Things*. Among the first activities was a task in which the children looked through magazines for pictures of living and nonliving things that they could paste on the appropriate pages in their *Living Things* scrapbooks. The students would later compare their choices and note the shared characteristics of the living things. Ms. Nowicki thought this task would be easy for the children and a good introduction to a discussion of the differences among living things.

When Ms. Nowicki reviewed Anthony's scrapbook, she noticed that he had included a bus and a racing car on a page for living things. When she questioned him about these choices, he claimed that the vehicles were alive because they moved. He insisted on this category for the vehicles, even though he agreed that they did not have babies, did not need food, and so on.

The timing of the science unit coincided with parent–teacher conferences. Ms. Nowicki mentioned the situation to Mrs. Reynolds, Anthony's mother. "You should've simply told Anthony that vehicles aren't alive and why not—then he'd get it," Mrs. Reynolds stated. Ms. Nowicki replied, "I don't think that's the answer, Mrs. Reynolds. I want to think about this some more. Maybe I should address this situation a different way." "I think you should follow my advice," insisted Anthony's mother.

The next morning, Mrs. Reynolds and Anthony arrived at the classroom a few minutes before the official start of the school day. "Anthony would like to tell you something, Ms. Nowicki," announced Mrs. Reynolds. "Buses and cars aren't alive. Trains and boats aren't, either," he stated. "Now tell Ms. Nowicki why they can move," ordered Mrs. Reynolds. Anthony declared, "They have motors!"

Ms. Nowicki paused for a few moments, and asked, "Is the motor alive, Anthony?" Anthony glanced at his mother, looked back at the teacher, smiled, nodded his head, and said, "Yes!"

of sheep in books and did not understand that they had knees that could bend. The child's previous experience and categories thus influenced his ideas about how the world works.

Michael Cole (1996) described his experience with an educational project in Liberia in the 1960s. He had been hired as a consultant to help improve the learning of mathematics by children in the Kpelle tribe. Among the things he was told about Kpelle students was that they could not distinguish between geometric shapes because of perceptual problems, they could not classify, and they could not measure. Cole found that the Kpelle measured rice using a *kopi*, a tin that holds 1 dry pint of rice. They also stored rice in *boke* (buckets), *tins* (tin cans), and bags. There were 24 kopi to a bucket and 48 to a tin, and 2 buckets were equivalent to 1 tin. In a study that compared American adults and children with Kpelle adults and children, participants were given four mixing bowls of equal size holding different amounts of rice: 1.5, 3, 4, 5, or 6 kopi. They were shown the tin to be used as a unit of measurement and were then asked to estimate the number of kopi of rice in each bowl. Kpelle adults were extremely accurate, with an error rate of about 2% to 3%. The American adults greatly overestimated the amounts. The American children performed like the American adults with smaller amounts and like the Kpelle children with the larger amounts. Cole concluded that people develop cognitive skills in relation to the important activities in their lives. Kpelle children did not have difficulty with concepts of measurement, whatever the cultural differences between them and American children.

Figure 7.21 summarizes some of the key questions that teachers might have with respect to how adopting a cognitive learning theory might influence decisions a teacher must make.

What Kids Say and Do

What Pony?

Children like to categorize as much as adults do. They often categorize according to concepts that are important to them, even if those concepts do not correspond to adult notions.

On a class trip to the zoo, kindergarten teacher Malva Mulrooney eavesdropped on Marisa offering a carrot to a Shetland pony:

Marisa:	Here you go, Mr. Camel.
Mrs. Mulrooney:	"Mr. Camel" is a funny name for a pony. I like that.
Marisa:	What pony?
Mrs. Mulrooney:	This pony, Marisa, the one you're giving that nice carrot to.
Marisa:	[Almost in tears.] This isn't a camel?
Mrs. Mulrooney:	I'm afraid not, dear. It's a beautiful Shetland pony. Tell me, what made you think it's a camel?
Marisa:	Because it's small and brown like the camel in my favorite bedtime book. Camels are small and brown.
Mrs. Mulrooney:	Well, this camel is really a pony. Why don't we call him "Mr. Camel"?
Marisa:	Because his momma probably already gave him his name.
Mrs. Mulrooney:	You're probably right. He really likes that carrot.
Marisa:	Yes, ma'am.

How does learning occur?	Active learning using attention, perception, and memory processes including existing schemas
Where does knowledge come from?	External sources of information and activation of prior knowledge
What is the student doing?	Student interacts with the environment, develops internal representations of the external environment, is an active processor
What is the role of the teacher?	Provides information, designs activities to promote active processing on the part of the students
What is the role of peers?	Peers can promote active processing and different perspectives as well as provide opportunities for elaboration and rehearsal
If a teacher subscribes to this theory, what is he or she likely to include in a lesson plan?	The teacher will use verbal, visual, and other modalities to present information and include opportunities for practice and elaboration

Figure 7.21 Cognitive Learning Theory and Instruction

REFLECTION FOR ACTION

The Event

Recall that some of Mr. Gomez's students were having difficulty with some math problems. The solutions and explanations attempted by students were presented.

Reflection

What kinds of problems were these students having? What have you learned in this chapter that could be applied in these cases? What kinds of activities can Mr. Gomez provide for the students to work on that might improve their performance on these kinds of problems and enable them to generalize that learning to other areas and other types of tasks? Is it better to work harder with students on problems of this type or to try to uncover the root cause of their difficulties? (Note: This is not a trick question.)

What Theoretical/Conceptual Information Might Assist in Interpreting and Remedying This Situation? Consider the following:

Working Memory and Executive Control

How would limited working memory or difficulties with executive control influence the children's performance on the math problem? Was there any indication of such difficulties? What kinds of strategies would support students' working memory while they are doing word problems?

Visual Representation

Word problems can be difficult. Could the students have developed a visual representation that would have helped them understand the problem?

Retrieval

Have the students experienced similar mathematical problems before? Can they recall how they solved them? Do they have any examples available to them?

Information Gathering RIDE

There are a number of sources of information about this situation; which ones you use will depend on how the problem is framed. A very good source of information (as is often the case) is the student. How did the student do on similar problems? What might happen if the problem was simplified? If a student's difficulties seem to be due to difficulties with working memory, do the same kinds of difficulties show up in other areas of his or her work?

Once you have a better idea of what the problem is, there is the question of what to do about it. Here you might turn to the research literature on instructional techniques for improving working memory, executive control, or whatever the problem might be. It is important to keep in mind that if a broader approach is chosen, it will be necessary to show students how it applies to specific examples of tasks and problems.

Decision Making RIDE

Decision making in this situation involves two phases: diagnosing the problem and selecting a solution. In making a decision, Mr. Gomez needs to think about what he believes to be the most likely cause of a student's difficulties and what he can do about it. He also has to keep in mind that he has a whole class of students to be concerned about. He needs an approach that he can apply within the confines of his instructional setting.

Evaluation RIDE

If Mr. Gomez's approach is successful, he should see improved performance not only on the math problems that triggered his initial concern but on other problems that seem to be stemming from the same underlying difficulty. Of course, success on the math problems alone will be quite rewarding, but Mr. Gomez should watch for possible progress in writing, science experiments, and so forth. The point here is to maintain a broad focus on students' learning. Simply reviewing a specific type of math problem may help students learn to solve that type of problem but will not enable them to generalize that learning to any other kind of math problem, let alone other subject areas.

Further Practice: Your Turn

Here is a second event for consideration and reflection. In doing so, implement the processes of reflection, information gathering, decision making, and evaluation.

The Event

It happened to Melanie again. Her grades for the marking period did not reflect all the work she had done. Melanie was a serious student in her junior year of high school. She was attentive during her classes. She did her homework and prepared for the tests. But when it came time to take a test, she could not recall the information she had studied. Her grade point average was sinking with each marking period. What further distressed her was that her friends received better grades but spent less time and energy on schoolwork.

Melanie comes to her homeroom teacher, Mrs. James, to talk about how she might improve her grades. What can Mrs. James suggest to Melanie that will help her perform better on tests?

SUMMARY

- **How do cognitive and constructivist theories of learning differ?**

Cognitive theories of learning focus on the idea that each person does not necessarily view the same environment in the same way. They explore how individual differences in knowledge and experience influence how we interpret our environment and what we learn as a result. Knowledge is constructed by the learner and influenced by the learner's previous experience. Constructivist theories of learning share the idea that meaning is constructed by the learner.

- **Why are attention, perception, and working memory important for learning?**

Perception is important for learning because it involves giving meaning to the sensory input we receive. Gestalt psychologists have proposed a number of organizing principles that allow us to perceive objects. The principles are figure–ground, proximity, continuity, closure, and similarity. Attention is important to learning because it involves selection of information, withdrawing from some objects and focusing on others. Lack of attention is characterized by confusion and diffusion. Attentional processes allow us to be selective, and perceptual processes allow us to organize sensory input, two key aspects of learning. Working memory is a limited memory system that includes both storage and manipulation functions. Baddeley's idea of working memory consists of a number of subsystems that are coordinated by a central executive: the phonological loop system; the visuospatial sketchpad; and the central executive system, which controls both the loop system and the sketchpad.

Teachers must understand that working memory is limited and that short, concise, and clear instructions are most effective. Limiting the amount of classroom disruption is also important. Working memory is also implicated in such tasks as reading comprehension, writing, problem solving, and mathematics. Students with a larger working memory are more successful in the use of cognitive resources during reading comprehension and as a result have more resources for information storage while comprehending text. Teachers must remember that some learners have difficulty with writing because of limitations of working memory.

- **How is knowledge represented?**

Knowledge is represented in images, propositions, schemas, and scripts. Images and propositions are the basic units for storing visual and verbal information. Schemas represent organized sets of knowledge about a topic and can include both verbal and visual information. Scripts are event schemas. They include the steps needed to complete particular actions, such as dining at a restaurant.

- **What are the different kinds of long-term memory?**

There are several kinds of long-term memory. Episodic memory is memory for events and can include sensory information. Childhood memories are an example of episodic memory. Semantic memory is memory for verbal information, also known as *declarative knowledge*. Declarative memory is like semantic memory: It is memory about *what*. An example would be a memory about the structure of a bicycle. Procedural memory is memory about how to do something—for example, remembering how to ride a bicycle. These kinds of memory are also called *explicit* and *implicit memory*, respectively.

- **How is encoding related to retrieval?**

The processes of encoding are organization, elaboration, and practice. All three processes can aid in later retrieval of information. When you connect information that you are trying to learn with information that you already know or to images or other enhancements of the information to be learned, you are elaborating on the material and are more likely to remember it. When material is encoded in an organized manner, more cues are encoded, thus making retrieval easier.

● **Why and how do we categorize?**

Categorization is a way of narrowing the range of information available to us in order to reduce complexity, identify objects, reduce the need for constant learning, decide what actions are appropriate, and order and relate classes of objects and events. This allows us to be more cognitively efficient. Classic approaches to defining categories focused on the use of criterial attributes to assign members to a category. This does not work for natural or real-world categories. Membership in a natural category is best defined by a prototype, or best example, of the category. Other members of the category have graded membership in the category based on their similarity to the prototype.

● **How can teachers apply cognitive theories of learning in working with diverse students and students with special needs?**

The focus of a cognitive approach to learning is on the relationship between the individual and the environment. Children from different cultural or socioeconomic groups come to school with different experiences and knowledge. Teachers need to tap into what students already know in order to increase their understanding of the content being taught. Students with special needs may have impairments in various aspects of the information-processing system, including perception, attention, working memory, and retrieval. Diverse students may be expected to vary in the content of the knowledge structures they bring to class such as their schemas, scripts, and categories.

Key Terms

attention, p. 228
automaticity, p. 229
bottom-up processing, p. 226
chunking, p. 231
concept, p. 244
conditional knowledge, p. 238
controlled processes, p. 230
criterial attributes, p.244
decay p. 231
declarative knowledge, p.234
declarative memory, p. 234
distributed practice, p. 239
elaboration, p. 239
elaborative rehearsal, p. 231
episodic memory, p. 234
feature analysis, p. 226
graded membership, p. 245

graphic organizer, p. 240
interference, p. 231
levels of processing theory, p. 237
long-term memory, p. 234
maintenance rehearsal, p. 231
massed practice, p. 239
mnemonic strategies, p. 239
multiple modalities, p. 233
natural categories, p. 245
overgeneralization, p. 245
perception, p. 225
phonological loop, p. 231
phonological similarity effect, p. 231
procedural knowledge, p. 238
procedural memory, p. 234
proposition, p. 235
propositional network, p. 236

prototype, p. 245
recall, p. 242
recognition memory, p. 242
schema, p. 236
script, p. 236
semantic memory, p. 234
sensory memory, p. 230
serial position effect, p. 231
short-term memory, p. 230
spread of activation, p. 242
story grammar, p. 237
top-down processing, p. 226
unattended speech effect, p. 231
undergeneralization, p. 245
visuospatial sketchpad, p. 232
word length effect, p. 232
working memory, p. 231

Exercises

1. *Analyzing What You Know about How You Learn and Remember*

   Find a poem that is more than 12 lines long and try to memorize it. Note the strategies you use to encode information and whether they are effective. What modalities did you use? Did you engage in maintenance or elaborative rehearsal?

2. *Creating a Graphic Organizer or Concept Map*

   Create a graphic organizer or concept map about the attention information presented at the beginning of the chapter on pages 228–230. Analyze the skills you needed to be able to construct such an organizer or concept map.

3. *Culture, Concepts, and Categories*

   Generate five examples of how cultural background could influence the interpretation of information. For example, the word *pop* means soda to some individuals and a noise to other people.

4. *When a Schema Is a Stereotype*

A stereotype is a concept that individuals might have that is not completely accurate but is based on generally occurring characteristics. What are some features of a schema that are present in a stereotype you might have of a particular place?

Lesson Plans

The lesson plans on these pages are excerpts from more complete plans. They are included in this form to provide you with practice in examining a lesson from the perspective of the content of this chapter. For both lesson plans, read the lesson plan excerpt and respond to the questions related to cognitive development in the Ask Yourself! section at the end.

Lesson #1: "Molly and Her Pilgrim"

GRADES: 4–6

ESTIMATED COMPLETION TIME: 2–3 class periods

SUBJECT AREAS: Social Studies, Language Arts

I. OVERVIEW: This unit introduces students to the culture behind the Thanksgiving holiday. Activities encourage students to explore cultures outside of American traditions, investigate characteristics of Russian society, and understand what it truly means to be a Pilgrim.

II. OBJECTIVES: Students will be able to:
- Compare the characteristics of American Thanksgiving to those of Russian culture
- Analyze the traditions of American Thanksgiving

NOTE: This lesson calls for the use of a KWL chart. This chart will contain three columns. Column one will be titled "What We Know." Column two will be titled "What We Want to Know." Column three will be titled "What We Have Learned." Columns will be filled out accordingly based on the procedure.

III. MATERIALS:
- *Molly's Pilgrim*, by Barbara Cohen
- Internet connection and/or library access for research
- Books on Thanksgiving and Russian culture
- Pictures of Pilgrims and their traditional clothing
- Pictures of modern-day Russian students
- Large poster board/paper for KWL charts
- World map (to identify the location of Russia)

IV. PROCEDURE:

1. In their groups students will be given two large poster board/paper KWL charts. The first chart will cover information based on the American Thanksgiving holiday tradition.

The second chart will cover information based on Russian culture. Together, the students will complete columns one and two on the KWL chart.

2. One group at a time, students will take turns presenting the K and W components of their charts.

3. The teacher will read *Molly's Pilgrim* to the students.

4. Students will be given group time to research the history behind Thanksgiving and Russian culture. To assist with research, the teacher should provide the groups with prompting questions, such as:

- Why do Americans celebrate Thanksgiving?
- How did the Pilgrims contribute to the Thanksgiving holiday?
- What does it mean to be a "Pilgrim"?
- How does Russian culture differ from American culture in terms of schooling and dress/attire?

5. Students will revisit their KWL charts and fill in what they have learned about Thanksgiving and Russian culture.

6. Each student will submit a question to the teacher to be answered during a class discussion. Questions can be based on American culture versus. Russian culture and Thanksgiving. The teacher will spend time reading the questions to the class while the class engages in a group discussion to help answer the questions.

7. Students will write imaginary letters to students in Russia based on thoughts they have after reading *Molly's Pilgrim.*

Ask Yourself!

1. How will the materials needed for this lesson promote active information processing on the parts of the students?

2. How will the KWL chart support students' working memory?

5. *Problems with Memory*

Identify some things that you find hard to remember (e.g., people's names, formulas, appointments). For example, how difficult a task would it be to learn the names of all your classmates in this course? Develop a plan for how to improve your memory of these items.

Lesson Plans

Lesson #2: "European Vacation"

GRADES: 6–8

ESTIMATED COMPLETION TIME: 2–3 class periods

SUBJECT AREAS: Social Studies, Language Arts, Technology

I. OVERVIEW: This unit introduces students to various European world cultures. This particular lesson consolidates the cultures into three countries: Spain, Italy, and France. However, this lesson can be adapted to any region in the world.

II. OBJECTIVES: Students will be able to:
- Utilize technology to research various cultures.
- Investigate the cultures of three different countries, specifically focusing on food, music, clothing, education, major industries, religion, and lifestyles.
- Apply their persuasion, reasoning, logic, research, and creative skills by creating a brochure marketing the aspects of all three countries.

III. MATERIALS:
- Internet connection/library access for research
- Construction paper, glue, scissors, markers, and so forth for brochure construction
- Computer access for word processing/picture printing
- Books on Spain, Italy, and France

IV. PROCEDURES: Students will be divided into pairs to complete this project.

1. The activity will begin with a class discussion on what students currently know about the three different countries. The teacher can divide the board into three columns, each column representing a different country, thus creating a list of prior knowledge. The lists should remain throughout the activity.

2. Together, the students will research aspects of all three countries, keeping seven specific topics in mind:
- Food
- Music
- Clothing
- Education
- Major industries
- Religion
- Lifestyle

3. Students will assemble informational brochures based on their findings.

4. When the brochures have been assembled, they will be displayed in the form of a gallery throughout the classroom. Students will have time to view the gallery and compare what their classmates have learned.

5. To conclude, students will write a journal entry containing one interesting fact from each country based on what they learned from the brochures of their classmates. (These facts should be different from the ones used in their own brochures.)

Ask Yourself!

1. How does the teacher activate students' prior knowledge?

2. What strategies does the teacher use to encourage elaboration and/or rehearsal?

(© Media Bakery)

M s. Bernoulli had hoped that her fifth-grade students would learn a lot at the hands-on science museum and extend their knowledge of physical science. On the bus ride home from the museum, Ms. Bernoulli wondered about many things:

- How much noisier would her students have to be before the bus driver asked her again to calm them down?
- Would Martin become nauseated again, as he had on the way to the museum?
- Was there one child in the class who had had a positive experience at the museum?
- Did the students learn anything from the trip?
- Did the students help one another learn or just distract one another?
- Why had she thought this trip was a good idea, and would she ever think so again?
- Would the mustard stain come out of her sweater?

Ms. Bernoulli's first thoughts were about the specifics of the trip: Was the bus ride too long, was the museum a poor choice for these students (or for this grade level), and had she not done enough to prepare the students? Had she not succeeded in getting them interested in the kinds of things they would see and do at the museum? At first she thought the students were to blame, and she was going

Social Learning Theory, Complex Cognition, and Social Constructivism

8

to talk to them about it when they were safely back in the classroom. How could they be so well behaved in the classroom and so badly behaved in the museum? Then she turned to herself: Maybe this was actually her fault. Why did she fail to anticipate these problems? Why did the museum staff not provide more help? Ms. Bernoulli decided that this would be a good thing to think about over the weekend, after she took the sweater to the cleaners and made a mental note not to wear nice clothes on a field trip again.

R I D E Reflection for Action

Ms. Bernoulli pushed herself to think about what the real issues and underlying problems on the field trip might be. What do you think they were? How can she uncover the underlying cause of the problems? What could she have done to improve the situation? What could the students have done?

Guiding Questions

- What is social learning theory?
- What is necessary for observational learning to occur?
- How can teachers promote complex cognition?
- How can teachers promote problem solving?
- How is scaffolding used in instruction?
- How can teachers use scaffolding techniques to work with diverse learners?
- What kinds of instruction are influenced by social constructivism and sociocultural theory?
- Can learners with special needs benefit from social-constructivist or sociocultural approaches to learning?

255

CHAPTER OVERVIEW

We previously provided a description of many of the basic structures and functions of the human information-processing system. In this chapter, we extend this material by examining social learning theory, which provides one example of how we learn from others. We then focus on social-constructivist approaches to complex cognition. Like all cognitive theories that are constructivist in nature, social constructivism emphasizes the active role of learners in making meaning out of their experience and the contribution of the social world in doing so. The chapter describes examples of complex cognition and revisits the notion of scaffolding that was introduced in previous chapters. Examples of instruction that is influenced by social constructivism are also included.

Social Learning Theory
- Modeling
- Conditions Necessary for Observational Learning
- Modeling and TV Viewing

Complex Cognition
- Metacognition
- Self-Explanation
- Reasoning and Argumentation
- Problem Solving
- Transfer

Complex Cognition and Social Constructivism
- The Role of Experience

- Scaffolding
- Scaffolding with Technology
- Scaffolding for Students with Special Needs
- Scaffolding for Students from Diverse Backgrounds

Instruction Influenced by Social-Constructivist and Sociocultural Theory
- Cognitive Apprenticeships
- Reciprocal Teaching
- Problem-Based Learning
- Classroom Communities

Social Learning Theory

social learning theory A theory of how we learn from others.

Social learning theory was developed by Albert Bandura. The original theory (Bandura, 1977b) was considered a neobehavioral theory because it included concepts such as reinforcement and punishment. However, Bandura's theory added new cognitive elements, in which an observer engages in processes such as attention, encoding, and retrieval of a model's behavior, cognitive processes that were described in the previous chapter. Consequences follow appropriate and inappropriate behavior, and these consequences help the individual learn how to behave.

vicarious experience Learning from the experience of another person.

In addition to learning from direct experience, we learn through **vicarious experience**— that is, we substitute the experiences of others for our own direct experience. With vicarious experience, we watch what others do. *Vicarious* means that another person acts in our place. For instance, a young child stands on the playground staring at the dangerous-looking swing, not knowing what to do. An older child approaches, sits in the seat, and begins to swing. As the younger child watches, she begins to learn new ways to behave that had not occurred to her before, as well as the consequences of different types of behaviors. Just by watching, she sees how to sit in the seat, how to grip the rope, how to lean back and push off with her feet to get some speed, and to ask others for a push. Also, just by watching, she sees the consequences of all these behaviors. Thus, just by standing and watching, she learns how to swing.

The key characteristic of social learning is its efficiency. If the young child tried to learn how to swing on her own through trial and error, it would likely take her a long time to learn how to swing well. She might swing very poorly at first and possibly fall off. She might also

TABLE 8.1

Four Things That Students Learn through Vicarious Experience

1. *New Behaviors*

   In art class, students initially may have difficulty with painting or sculpting. By watching others, they can imitate what expert painters and sculptors do. In social settings, students might have a hard time knowing how to make friends or how to be popular. By watching popular kids, they can imitate what those kids say and do.

2. *New Consequences*

   Students who have never been on the honor roll can learn what the consequences of such an achievement are by watching what happens to students who make the honor roll. Students also typically learn the consequences of cheating by watching what happens to classmates who cheat. One student can learn how much fun computers can be by watching a cooperative learning partner play computer games.

3. *Performance Expectations*

   Students who have little experience on a task do not know what to expect when they are asked to engage in that task. By watching others, they can learn how hard or easy a course is, how likely success and failure are in some endeavor, or what emotions people typically feel during sports, dating, or a class presentation.

4. *Self-Talk*

   By watching others who use optimistic self-statements, students can learn how to talk positively to themselves, learning self-talk such as "I am sure I can do this. I just have to keep trying different ways so I can figure it out." By watching others who use pessimistic self-statements, students can learn how to talk negatively to themselves, learning self-talk such as "I don't think I can do this. I've tried everything, and nothing seems to work."

become discouraged. Through social learning, however, she can quickly and reliably learn how to swing well. Think for a minute how fast and effective it can be to learn the following skills by watching others and how slow and cumbersome it can be to learn them through trial and error: how to tie one's shoes, how to operate a camera, how to dress, how to behave with good manners, how to use a computer, and how to converse with a police officer.

Previously, you saw how the reinforcements and punishments that follow our actions influence our subsequent behavior. Consequences that others experience can also influence our behavior. When we observe someone being reinforced for particular behaviors, it may increase the chance that we will perform that behavior in the future. This is called **vicarious reinforcement**. For example, if a teacher smiles approvingly at a child who reports another child's misbehavior, other children are more likely to do the same in the future. If another person is punished for an action, we are less likely to perform the punished behavior. This is called **vicarious punishment**. If the teacher reprimands the child who reports another child for misbehavior, other children will be less likely to report others. Table 8.1 lists four examples of what students can learn vicariously. Teachers can take advantage of this kind of learning by directing students' attention to appropriate models.

Modeling

The girl learning how to swing by watching another child is an example of learning by observing a model (another person) performing a behavior. There are three types of **modeling** effects: (1) observational learning, (2) inhibitory and disinhibitory effects, and (3) response facilitation (Baldwin & Baldwin, 1986).

Observational Learning Observational learning involves the learning of behavior. Observers gather information about a behavior and use it to direct their own actions. Young children learn a great deal through observation and imitation. Parents often model behaviors (e.g., brushing one's teeth) and guide their child in imitating the behavior. Behaviors of a model that are reinforced are more likely to be imitated. Observational learning thus involves both an acquisition stage and a performance stage. To acquire a behavior, a person must attend to the behavior and remember it. Performance involves reproducing the behavior. Continued practice improves the performance of the behavior. Additional shaping and prompting of the behavior may be necessary before it is performed well.

vicarious reinforcement If another person is reinforced for a behavior, the likelihood of an observer engaging in that behavior is increased.

vicarious punishment If another person is punished for a behavior, the likelihood of an observer engaging in that behavior is decreased.

modeling Learning by observing a model.

observational learning Learning by observing other individuals.

Appendix
Learning from Others

Students can learn from others through observational learning and vicarious experience (PRAXIS™, I.A.1; INTASC, Principle 2).

(Corbis Digital Stock)

A number of factors influence whether a model's behavior will be imitated. A model that has prestige or status, such as this grandfather, is likely to be imitated.

A number of factors influence the likelihood that a behavior will be acquired through observational learning (Baldwin & Baldwin, 1986). First, the observer must see the model's behavior as positive or useful. If the observer does not see consequences as reinforcing, he or she is unlikely to acquire the behavior. A model that has status or prestige is more likely to be imitated. A second influence on whether the observer will learn from a model is the degree to which the model and the observer are similar. Children who experience high self-efficacy are more likely to learn from models (Linnenbrink & Pintrich, 2003). Children are also likely to select models that are similar to themselves. Third, an observer who is engaging in a task is more likely to learn from a model that is engaging in a similar task. Fourth, an observer who attends to a model's behavior closely is more likely to acquire that behavior.

Teachers can help students' observational learning by directing their attention to what the model is doing and by reinforcing them for paying attention. The visibility of the modeled behavior and the ease with which it can be performed also affect whether the observer will learn the model's behavior. For example, a teacher may model his or her thinking processes by engaging in a *think-aloud*.

Hallenbeck (2002) presents a teacher who modeled the writing process for a group of learning-disabled students by choosing a topic the students were familiar with: a concession stand fund-raising project in which all the students were involved. Students first learned how to brainstorm ideas. In a subsequent lesson, the teacher modeled the color-coding of his brainstormed ideas. Color-coding was the first step in organizing the paper. Using a felt-tipped marker, the teacher used the same color to mark ideas that seemed to belong together. His think-aloud enabled students to understand the process. In the following excerpt, the ideas in quotations were read directly from written work during brainstorming:

> I'm lookin' for things that have to do with the kinds of students involved [in the concessions stand fund-raising project]. Okay, "officers," I think I'll make that blue dot. That has to do with the students. Uh, "monster cookies, popcorn balls, puppy chow," no, "juice, fruit, popcorn." (Hallenbeck, 2002, p. 233)

The teacher modeled his thoughts about the items he read as he searched for content that had to do with students so he could color-code it in blue. (See the nearby Taking It to the Classroom box.)

One strategy for modeling a new skill is to have the teacher tutor a student and have other students observe (Chi, Roy, & Hausman, 2008). In a study conducted by Craig, Chi,

What Does This Mean to Me?

Think of a teacher you had whom you would like to imitate. What characteristics of the teacher made him or her a worthy model?

Taking It to the Classroom

Making Thinking Visible

Following are guidelines for promoting think-alouds so that thinking is visible and can be imitated:

- Tell students that their help is needed to learn more about something that is not well understood.
- Give them something concrete to talk about.
- Ask one student to tell another what he or she is thinking about while performing the task.
- Model the task of thinking aloud.
- Give plenty of practice at thinking aloud.
- Use probes or questions if a student becomes quiet.

and Van Lehn (2009), pairs of students watched videos of an expert tutoring a student in problem solving in physics. The tutee was an intermediate-level student who had completed an introductory physics course. The performance of the observers on subsequent measures of learning was contrasted with that of pairs of students who observed the same expert solve problems. A third group of students consisted of individuals who observed the expert solving problems. Although there were no significant differences between the three groups of students on immediate learning outcomes, measures of long-term retention and transfer showed consistent differences in favor of the collaborative observation condition. The authors interpret their results as showing support for an active learning hypothesis in which the collaboration between partners is more effective in the observation condition.

Inhibitory and Disinhibitory Effects Sometimes the observer does not acquire new behaviors by observing a model. Instead, the chances that a previously acquired behavior will be performed are enhanced, or *disinhibited*. If a teacher tells a student that she will give her extra homework if she gets out of her seat again, then fails to do so, the likelihood that other children will get out of their seats will be increased. The restraint they had shown will be disinhibited because of the teacher's actions. Likewise, if the teacher follows through on her warning and assigns extra homework to the child, other children's willingness to get out of their seats will be *inhibited*. Their behavior of staying in their seats has been vicariously reinforced. They are not acquiring new behaviors in this situation; instead, the likelihood of their performing a previously learned behavior is increased or decreased.

Response Facilitation Effects Sometimes a model's behavior can serve as a discriminative stimulus for the observer and thus facilitate the observer's response. In other words, the learner may perform a behavior that is already known. Observing others may simply facilitate the learner's performance of the behavior. If, for example, a number of people are looking up at the sky, the observer is likely to do so, too. No new behaviors are acquired. In a classroom context, a student may laugh when other students do because he or she realizes from observing others that it is appropriate to do so. (See the nearby Uncommon Sense box.)

Conditions Necessary for Observational Learning

Students can observe without learning. Observational learning occurs only when the learner pays attention to a model's behavior, retains the behavior, can produce the behavior, and is motivated to do so (Bandura, 1986a).

- **Attention.** The learner must attend to the important features of a model's behavior in order to learn from it. A teacher can help direct students' attention. For example, a student might be asked to show on the board how he solved a math problem. He might first draw a diagram of his understanding of the problem. The teacher can direct other students' attention to this aspect of his performance and point out how the diagram helped him keep track of important elements of the problem.

- **Retention.** The learner must retain the information that has been observed. A teacher can help students remember by teaching them strategies for retaining information. Examples of such strategies include mental rehearsal or creating acronyms to help in remembering specific steps.

- **Production.** The learner's efforts to imitate the model's behavior may be awkward at first. For example, if you watch a dancer you admire, your efforts to imitate the dancer's steps may be clumsy at first. However, with practice and feedback, your performance of the behavior will come closer and closer to that of the model.

- **Motivation.** A learner can observe a model, attend to specific features of the model's behavior, retain information about the behavior, and be able to produce the behavior. In addition, the learner must be motivated to perform the behavior. Before the learner will perform what has been learned, he or she must see the behavior as important or one that will lead to success or reinforcement.

Figure 8.1 summarizes some of the key questions that teachers might have with respect to how adopting social learning theory might influence decisions a teacher must make.

Uncommon Sense

Social Learning Always Has Positive Outcomes—Or Does It?

(Corbis Digital Stode)

Friendships do not always have positive effects on social development. During adolescence, some friendships may actually be harmful (Hartup, 1983). Thomas Dishion and his colleagues examined how *deviancy* training predicted future problem behaviors (Dishion, McCord, & Poulin, 1999). *Deviancy training* was defined as positive reactions by peers to discussions about breaking rules or engaging in inappropriate behavior. When boys aged 13–14 experienced deviancy training, they were more likely to use addictive substances (Dishion et al., 1995), report increased delinquency (Dishion et al., 1996), and engage in more violent behavior (Dishion et al., 1997). Peers who participate in interventions designed to reduce problem behavior may in fact encourage such behavior (Dishion et al., 1999) by providing support for deviant behavior. For example, if in a discussion of the inappropriateness of vandalism, a member of the group describes how his status increased among his peers, the other members of the group may end up seeking peer approval by engaging in the same kind of behavior.

Modeling and TV Viewing

Television can provide both positive and negative learning experiences. Parents and educators often express concern about whether children might learn to be aggressive or violent by watching television. They also expect that children will learn from instructional programs designed for them.

TV and Aggression The study of what children learn from television has focused primarily on the effects of watching violence on television. Interest in this topic goes back to a classic study conducted by Albert Bandura in 1965. Kindergarten children watched one of three

Figure 8.1 Social Learning Theory and Instruction

How does learning occur?	Learning occurs by observation, imitation, and vicarious reinforcement
Where does knowledge come from?	Modeling, observational learning, and vicarious reinforcement
What is the student doing?	The student attends to a selected model, observes and retains behavior, and may then reproduce the behavior
What is the role of the teacher?	The teacher models behavior or draws attention to other selected models, provides opportunities for practice of modeled behavior, and provides vicarious reinforcement
What is the role of peers?	Peers may serve as models
If a teacher subscribes to this theory, what is he or she likely to include in a lesson plan?	Opportunities for modeling behavior and practice of modeled behavior

films in which a child (the model) beat up an adult-sized toy called a "Bobo doll." In the first film, the model was rewarded with candy. In the second film, the model was criticized and spanked for the aggressive behavior. In the third film, nothing occurred in response to the model's behavior. After watching one of the films, each child was left alone in a room with some toys, including a Bobo doll, and researchers observed his or her behavior through a one-way mirror. A child who had seen a model being reinforced or not punished was more likely to beat up the Bobo doll—that is, to imitate the aggressive model. Boys were more aggressive than girls.

More recent research suggests that viewing violent television may have a number of negative outcomes. Viewers may engage in increased aggressive behavior, change their attitudes in favor of the use of aggression to solve problems, show decreased sensitivity to violence, and show increased tolerance for violence (Huston et al., 1992). Murray (2001) conducted a preliminary study of how the brain responds to violent and nonviolent imagery. He showed eight children between the ages of 8 and 13 a number of short segments of a violent or nonviolent film (Murray, 2001). The violent segments consisted of two 3-minute scenes of boxing from the movie *Rocky IV*. The nonviolent segments consisted of two 3-minute scenes from a nature program and from a children's literacy program. He found that areas of the brain involved in visual and auditory processing were activated when the children watched both kinds of films. However, watching violent film segments seemed to activate brain areas associated with arousal/attention, detection of threat, encoding and retrieval of episodic memories, and motor programming (Murray, 2001).

Watching violent television can have long-term effects. Huesemann and colleagues conducted a longitudinal study of the relationship between children's exposure to TV violence and their behavior in young adulthood (Huesemann et al., 2003). The participants were between 6 and 10 years old at the time of the initial data collection (1977–1978). In 1992–1995, additional data were collected about the same participants when they were between 20 and 22 years old. The results showed that children's viewing of violence on TV, their identification with same-sex violent TV characters, and their perceptions of the realism of the violence seen were significantly related to their level of aggression as adults. These results were true for both female and male participants and were the same regardless of how aggressive the participants had been as children.

Instructional Benefits and TV Viewing Television viewing can have positive effects. Teachers can use students' television-viewing experiences to increase their understanding of audience. Television advertisements are clearly intended for different kinds of audiences, and the scheduling of particular programs also targets particular kinds of audiences. Stevens (2001) showed that middle school students could identify the intended audience for the television program *South Park*. Teachers can also use students' television viewing to further their understanding of genre. Various kinds of programs are shown on television (e.g., soap operas, reality shows, documentaries), and discussions of the differences among them can enhance students' understanding of genre (Williams, 2003).

Television can also be used to teach positive skills. Over 99% of homes in the United States have television sets (*Statistical Abstract,* 2000). Mielke (1994) noted that television can be used to address the literacy needs of children with inadequate educational opportunities. Linebarger and her colleagues compared the emergent literacy skills of young children in kindergarten and first grade who viewed 17 episodes of the television program *Between the Lions* with those of children in the same grades who did not (Linebarger et al., 2004). The program incorporates emergent literacy processes (Strickland & Rath, 2000). Teachers in this study were required not to provide additional instruction on the content of the program and asked not to refer to the program in any other instruction. The results of the study showed that the children who viewed the program showed better literacy skills (higher word recognition, standardized test scores, and means on letter–sound and phonemic-awareness tasks) than those who did not. The findings did not extend to the children at greatest risk for reading failure. Those children may have needed more support from their teachers to benefit from viewing the program. The nearby Taking It to the Classroom box provides some ideas about how social learning theory can be used in everyday life.

Taking It to the Classroom

Social Learning Theory and Everyday Life

Consider the following everyday activities that involve acquiring skills and knowledge:

- Playing catch
- Riding a bicycle
- Playing chess
- Eating dinner
- Writing a story
- Doing a crossword puzzle
- Meeting people at a party

Which of these activities are learned from others? Which are learned more or less on one's own? Think about one of these activities that is by its nature a social event. Could it be done on one's own? If so, how would it change? Can you play chess by yourself? (You can on the Internet.) When children come to school, they are used to learning in and from social situations. Now think about some of the things that students learn in school. Do they lend themselves more to learning in social situations or to learning individually? How are they affected by modeling?

In thinking about how to develop lessons and activities for the classroom, it is useful to consider the nature of the task and how it might be influenced by social versus individual learning activities and by active modeling by an expert.

Complex Cognition

Previously, you read discussions of basic information-processing structures and functions. All of these play roles in complex cognitive processes, which are the subject of this chapter, such as metacognition, reasoning, argumentation, problem solving, and transfer.

Metacognition

metacognition Thinking about one's own thinking.

Metacognition is the process of thinking about thinking. John Flavell described it as follows: "Metacognition refers to one's knowledge concerning one's own cognitive processes or anything related to them, e.g., the learning-relevant properties of information or data. For example, I am engaging in metacognition if I notice that I am having more trouble learning A than B" (Flavell, 1976, p. 232). Metacognitive knowledge includes knowledge of oneself as a learner, knowledge of strategies for success, and knowledge of when one should use those strategies. The knowledge of oneself as a learner allows you to gauge how difficult a task might be for you. If you judge yourself to be a good learner, you will approach a task with confidence. Knowledge of strategies for success is also important. Knowing, for example, that the use of concept maps can assist encoding of information is an example of having knowledge of strategies for success. Conditional knowledge about when one should use particular strategies is also part of metacognitive knowledge. You might use a highlighter when studying a history text but judge that you do not need to use this strategy when reading a spy novel for entertainment. You are engaging in metacognition when you realize that you have understood something or have failed to do so. These moments of insight will most likely trigger the activation of strategies to complete the task at hand.

Metacognition has three basic aspects: planning, monitoring, and evaluating. Planning helps you articulate a goal or purpose for the task you wish to perform. There is an old proverb that states: *No wind helps a ship that sails for no port.* In other words, if you do not know your destination, it is difficult to determine whether you have arrived or how close to your destination you are. Once you have identified a plan, you begin to carry it out. If your goal was to read the first 10 pages of the chapter and you had identified existing knowledge that you thought might be useful, you would proceed to read. As you read, you would monitor whether you understood the material. Many students find themselves at the end of a chapter, feeling very proud that they persisted with the task, but when asked what they read about, they cannot offer an accurate response. Their self-monitoring shut down during their reading, and they failed to notice that they no longer understood the material. (See the nearby Taking It to the Classroom box.)

R I D E   Was Ms. Bernoulli at the beginning of the chapter having difficulty with metacognition? How do you know?

Self-Explanation

Self-explanations are a means by which students can test their comprehension of material. They are explanations that start with something such as, "Okay, let me see if I understand this." When used effectively, they offer more pathways for retrieving knowledge (Kintsch & Kintsch, 1995) and allow students to assess their competence in a given area. Chi and her colleagues (Chi et al., 1989, 1994) have shown that student self-explanations are useful in physics and biology. Palinscar and Brown (1984) have used a type of self-explanation to develop reading comprehension skills. O'Reilly, Symons, and MacLatchy-Gaudet (1998) demonstrated the greater effectiveness of self-explanations, compared with other instructional interventions, with college students in biology. Brewer, Chinn, and Samarapungavan (2000) compared children's explanations with those of scientists. They found that "while children's explanations of the natural world may have very different content from scientists' explanations of the same phenomena, the underlying form of children's explanations is similar in many respects to those of scientists" (p. 134). Teachers can include self-explanations in their instruction by asking students to explain their understandings on a regular basis.

Reasoning and Argumentation

Stanovich (2009) proposed the concept of "dysrationalia," meaning the inability to think and behave rationally. He notes that even individuals with high levels of measured intelligence have difficulty in thinking well. The two problems he identifies that result in the inability to think are what he refers to as "cognitive miserliness" (p. 35) and a mindware problem. Cognitive miserliness occurs when we choose a cognitive process that is computationally easier than alternative processes. A mindware gap occurs when we are unable to retrieve the rules, data, procedures, strategies, and other cognitive tools that would allow us to think and behave rationally. Among such cognitive tools are the ability to reason about probability and engage in scientific inference. Teachers must very deliberatively teach strategies for reasoning and argumentation.

Taking It to the Classroom

Guiding Questions for Promoting Metacognitive Thinking

Asking these questions can help students engage in metacognitive thinking:

- How much time and effort will this problem require?
- What do you already know about this problem or argument?
- What is the goal or reason for engaging in extended and careful thought about this problem or argument?
- How difficult do you think it will be to solve this problem or reach a conclusion?
- How will you know when you have reached the goal?
- What critical thinking skills are likely to be useful in solving this problem or analyzing this argument?
- Are you moving toward a solution?

When the task is completed, students should be asked to judge how well the problem was solved or how well the argument was analyzed. Well-structured questions will help them reflect on their learning and may provide insights that will be useful in the future.

Source: Halpern, D. F. (1998). Teaching critical thinking for transfer across domains. *American Psychologist, 53,* 449–455. Copyright © 1998 by the American Psychological Association. Reproduced with permission.

argumentation The process of taking a position, providing reasons for the position, and presenting counterarguments.

Teachers can promote reasoning and argumentation by having students engage in challenging tasks together. Chinn (2006) defines **argumentation** as discourse among students in which learners take positions, give reasons for those positions, and present counterarguments to each other's ideas when they have different views. Billig (1996) notes that learning to argue may be essential in learning to think. Argumentation has four instructional benefits: (1) understanding content, (2) increasing interest and motivation, (3) improving problem-solving skills, and (4) increasing argumentation skills.

An argument consists of claims, warrants, reasons, and evidence backing up the argument. Figure 8.2 illustrates a simple argument.

Individuals can generate arguments in writing, but much argumentation occurs in small discussion groups. The mere fact that children are assigned to groups does not mean that they will engage in meaningful discussions. The quality of the conversations students have together is associated with learning (Webb, 1992). Many factors, such as the nature of the task or the composition of the group, will influence the quality of conversation. For example, children tend to have less abstract conversations about math or technology tasks than they do about language-based tasks (Holden, 1993). Most students need assistance in generating the quality of discourse that is associated with learning. Teachers can promote higher-quality discourse by asking students questions that vary in complexity (King, 1991, 1999; King, Staffieri, & Adelgais, 1998). Asking a student *why* something occurs rather than *what* occurred will result in the student engaging in deeper thinking.

Collaborative reasoning (CR) is an approach to discussing literature whose purpose is to promote critical reading by students and to be personally engaging (Waggoner et al., 1995). In collaborative reasoning, students read a story silently and then gather as a group with the teacher. The teacher begins the discussion by posing a key question related to the story. In one study (Chinn & Anderson, 1998), students read a story about a family who must find a new home for an uncle with Down syndrome. The family finally takes the uncle into their own home. The key question posed by the teacher to the students is to decide if the family made the right decision. Students adopt positions in response to the question and collaboratively construct arguments. Students' discussions are focused on evidence for and against

Figure 8.2 An Argument

Source: Figure 14.1 from Chinn, C. A. (2006). Learning to argue. In A. M. O'Donnell, C. E. Hmelo-Silver, and G. Erkens (Eds.), *Collaborative learning, reasoning, and technology.* Mahwah, NJ: Lawrence Erlbaum. Reprinted with the permission of Springer Science & Business Media.

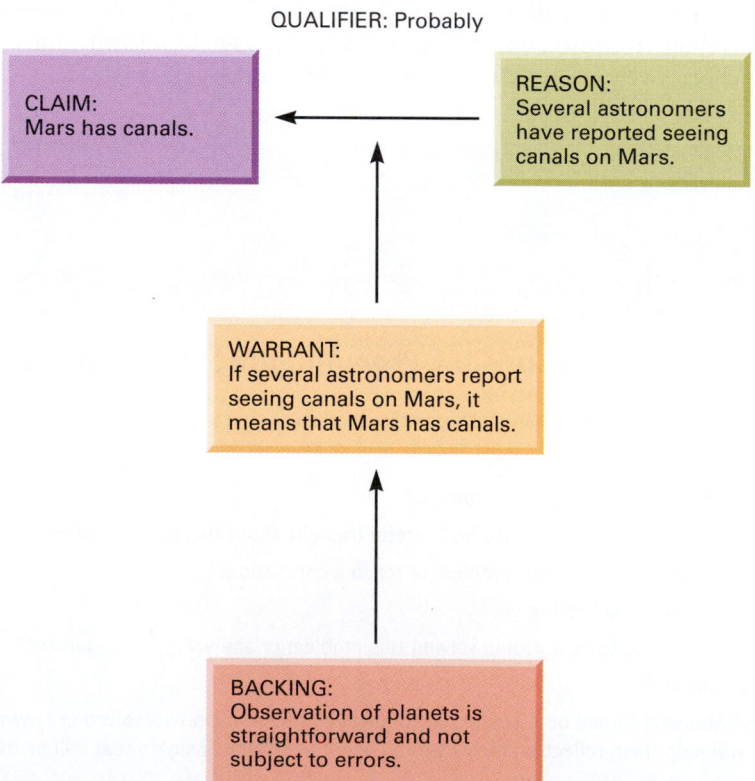

particular positions. The students' roles are central, and the authority for the direction of the discussion lies with them. In a comparison of collaborative reasoning with other discussion forms among fourth-grade students, Chinn, Anderson, and Waggoner (2001) found that students who used collaborative reasoning were more engaged and produced discussions that made more extensive use of high-level cognitive processes.

In a study of high-achieving sixth graders working together to solve problems, Barron found that success could not be accounted for by quality of discussion, prior achievement, or the generation of correct solutions (Barron, 2003). Less successful groups ignored or rejected correct proposals made by group members, whereas groups that were more successful discussed correct proposals or accepted them. Chinn and colleagues (Chinn, O'Donnell, & Jinks, 2000) found that fifth graders learned more when they engaged in deeper development of reasons during argumentation. For example, when children were asked to decide which of four conclusions from a science experiment was the best, they engaged in comparisons of the conclusions and produced more reasons for their decision. In comparison, students who were asked to decide whether the conclusions were good or not had discussions that were quite shallow.

Groups sometimes focus too much on procedural aspects of tasks (Erkens, Prangsma, & Jaspers, 2005), and even when participants list arguments, they may fail to coordinate their reasons and develop them fully (Andriessen, 2005). Successful discourse is coordinated among group members, with participants working together to construct knowledge rather than generating simple lists or arguments (King, 1994, 1999).

Efforts have been made to develop instruction that will promote the development of argumentation. Chinn (2006) outlines a number of strategies that have been used to promote reasoning and argumentation. One strategy is to provide students with lots of practice, but practice alone is associated with only modest effects (Kuhn et al., 2008). A second strategy is to provide prompts so that students provide particular components of arguments such as counterarguments. Closely related to the use of prompts is the requirement for students to evaluate their arguments. In one study (Chinn, O'Donnell, & Jinks, 2000), fifth-grade students conducted a series of experiments with batteries and resistors. They were then taught how to evaluate conclusions that might be drawn from such experiments. Students who were asked to decide which conclusion was best from a set of alternatives generated more complex arguments than did students who were asked to evaluate whether each conclusion was "okay/not okay." A fourth strategy is to provide students with model argument schemas and have them imitate these schemas in the generation of their own arguments.

A variety of other efforts have been made to support argumentation. The use of computerized argument diagrams to represent and support argumentation has received attention (Linn & Bell, 2000; Moor & Aakus, 2006). Chin and Osborne (2010) attempted to support students' argumentation through the use of questions. These served the kind of prompting function noted by Chinn (2006). The teachers in the study provided students with generic question prompts similar to those used by Alison King (1990). Students considered a scenario that described how some students were examining how water heats up. The scenario continues and illustrates two graphs that the students came up with to describe the relationship between time and water temperature. The target students in this research study were to decide which of the two graphs was most likely to show how the temperature of the water changes as the water heats up. The questions generated by the students helped them focus on the details of the data represented in the graphs and construct effective arguments.

Problem Solving

Problems have an initial state (where you are), a desired state (where you would like to be), and a path to follow in order to reach that state. The gap between the initial and desired states is called the *problem space*, and there can be many different paths across the space. Figure 8.3 depicts a physics problem in kinematics that was presented to high school students. The initial state of the problem is that the ball is placed on the ramp. The desired or end state is that the ball lands on the floor. The students must find a way to determine where the ball will land.

Appendix
Promoting Complex Thinking

Providing your students with opportunities to solve problems will allow them to engage in complex thinking (PRAXIS™, II.A.1; INTASC, Principle 4).

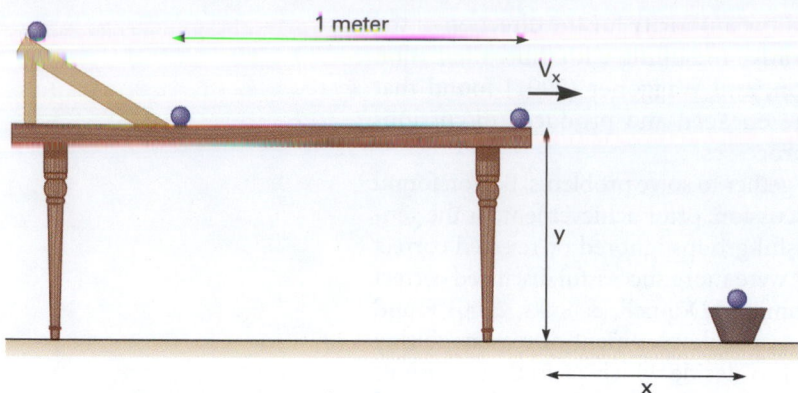

Figure 8.3 Problem Solving
Source: Copyright Michael Lawrence, Ed.D. Reproduced with permission.

algorithm A systematic and exhaustive strategy for solving problems.

heuristic A rule of thumb or shortcut for solving problems.

How Can I Use This?

How could you help a student represent a problem accurately? What strategies would you use?

means–end analysis A strategy for reducing the distance between the initial state and the goal state in problem solving.

functional fixedness Being able to consider only the typical function of an object.

response set The tendency to respond to different problems in the same way.

Problem solving involves five steps (Bransford & Stein, 1993), which can be remembered using the acronym IDEAL:

- Identifying problems and opportunities
- Defining goals and representing the problem
- Exploring possible solution strategies
- Anticipating, acting
- Looking back

The first step in problem solving is to recognize the nature of the problem. In the example in Figure 8.3, students need to recognize that the problem involves projectile motion and velocity. Experts in a domain typically spend much more time on the initial phases of problem solving than novices do (Bruning, Schraw, & Ronning, 1999). The second step is to define the goals and represent the problem. The problem solver must focus attention and understand the wording of the problem. If the learner has encountered similar problems in the past, he or she may draw on existing problem schemas for the problem.

The third step in problem solving is to explore possible solution strategies. These can include algorithms or heuristics. **Algorithms** are systematic and exhaustive procedures that are guaranteed to produce a solution. For example, if you have forgotten the three-digit combination for the lock on your briefcase, you might begin with 000 and systematically explore all possible combinations until you find the correct one. Alternatively, you could use a heuristic, or shortcut, and knock the lock off with a hammer. **Heuristics** can shorten the time needed to solve a problem, but they are not guaranteed to succeed.

One type of heuristic is **means–end analysis**. The problem solver decides what means would reduce the distance between the initial state and the goal state. For example, if the task is to write an essay for a language arts class, a problem solver might decide that he or she needs to make a detailed outline to help plan the essay. A second frequently used heuristic is *working backward*. This approach starts with the solution and works backward through the problem. For example, if you use this strategy to write a term paper, you might begin by noting the due date for the paper and work backward to determine what you would need in order to meet the due date.

Obstacles to Effective Problem Solving A number of factors can hinder problem solving. These factors include cognitive and social-emotional factors. One of the cognitive factors is cognitive rigidity, or lack of flexibility in thinking. Individuals who look at a problem from only one perspective are likely to have difficulty solving it because if the solution strategy they attempt does not work, they will have trouble considering alternatives. A specific kind of cognitive rigidity is **functional fixedness**. People who experience functional fixedness are unable to consider alternative uses for an object. For example, someone who is short may be unable to reach a book on the top shelf in a library. A small step is usually available in a library so that an individual can stand on it to reach the upper shelves. If an individual tends toward functional fixedness, he or she might not consider alternatives to using the step to reach the book. A more cognitively flexible individual might ask a tall person for help or use a book from a lower shelf to knock down the desired book.

A second cognitive impediment to problem solving is response set. An individual can be described as having a **response set** if he or she tends to respond to different problems in the same way or answer questions in the same way. For example, a student may learn to apply a particular strategy in solving ratio problems in mathematics. With practice, the student becomes very good at applying his strategy. However, he may become so accustomed to applying the same strategy that he may fail to notice when a new problem with which he is faced requires a different strategy.

A third cognitive impediment to problem solving is the limits of working memory capacity. Students may not be able to keep track of all the information they might need to solve a particular problem. They may not include all the necessary information from the problem in their representation of the problem. Students often have difficulty with mathematical word problems because of these limits. Teaching students how to diagram or construct representations of the problem can help them to support working memory while they engage in problem solving.

Noncognitive factors can also interfere with problem solving. Individuals who experience high levels of anxiety may be inhibited during problem solving. Students who have a high fear of failure will be reluctant to run the risk of being wrong.

Expert problem solvers have extensive knowledge in a particular domain. They recognize patterns and have access to large stores of information. They have a large repertoire of strategies, and their knowledge is refined, practiced, and organized. They spend more time planning for problem solutions and engaging in problem representation than they spend carrying out solution strategies. Problem-based learning is described later in this chapter.

Promoting Problem Solving in the Classroom   Each step of problem solving can pose difficulties for students. In order to promote effective problem solving in the classroom, a teacher must help students develop strategies for problem solving and create a supportive environment in which students are willing to take academic risks. The teacher should encourage students to generate different representations of the problem. Imagine students are given the following problem:

> *A man wishes to increase the amount of light in his room. He has one window that is 2 feet wide and 2 feet tall. He is not allowed by his landlord to change the dimensions of the window. What can he do?*

In attempting to answer the question, a student might represent the window as either a circular window or a square window. In both cases, the height and width of the window would be 2 × 2 feet.

A teacher can encourage students to experiment with different strategies for solving problems. In order to help them generate such strategies, she should encourage them to think of other ways to do things and have students explain their ideas to others. A teacher should also reduce anxiety about "being wrong" by providing positive feedback on efforts to generate alternatives or interesting strategies. Reducing the contingencies associated with "correct answers" will encourage more exploratory behavior on the part of students.

Transfer

The goal of learning is not only to be able to perform a strategy or skill or to remember something; it is also to be able to apply those skills, strategies, or knowledge in new contexts. This is called **transfer**, the ability to use previously learned skills or information in a new context. There are a number of ways in which to distinguish between types of transfer. **Low road transfer** is the automatic application of previously learned skills (Salomon & Perkins, 1989). An example of low road transfer would be using a pencil rather than a pen to write. In this example, a learner would give no conscious thought to the task and would not need to engage in metacognitive activity, such as monitoring, in order to accomplish the task. **High road transfer** involves deliberative application of knowledge learned in one context to another (Salomon & Perkins, 1989). An example of high road transfer would include trying to identify whether the math problem you are faced with is similar to one you have done before. In this example, you are deliberately searching for prior knowledge that might be useful to solve the current problem. **Positive transfer** occurs when prior knowledge or skill is successfully applied to a new context. For example, individuals easily transfer knowledge of one word-processing program to another. **Negative transfer** occurs when learning one skill impairs performance

transfer The ability to use previously learned skills or information in a new context.

low road transfer The automatic application of previously learned skills.

high road transfer Deliberate application of previously learned strategy or knowledge to a new problem.

positive transfer Successful application of prior knowledge or skill to a new context.

negative transfer Interference of prior learning with new learning.

on another. For example, learning one kind of notation for statistics may interfere with one's ability to learn effectively if a different teacher uses different notation.

Transfer does not readily occur (Gick & Holyoak, 1980). An example of the difficulties associated with transfer can be found in a study conducted by Carraher, Carraher, and Schliemann (1995). They investigated the mathematical strategies used by Brazilian children who worked as street vendors. After recording the nature and accuracy of the computations in which the children engaged while selling their goods, the researchers asked the children to come to their laboratory. The children took a variety of mathematics tests that included the same numbers and mathematical operations as those they used as street vendors. The results showed that the children were 98% accurate in the practical context of selling but only 37% accurate on the same operations in the laboratory context. This study showed the failure to transfer between real-life context and the classroom context. We are typically concerned about whether what is taught in school will transfer to real-life contexts.

The Cognition and Technology Group at Vanderbilt (CTGV, 1997) developed a set of problem-based curricula called *The Adventures of Jasper Woodbury*. Each Jasper adventure is situated in a real-life context and is complex, often including multiple subproblems. In one of the Jasper adventures, *Rescue at Boone's Meadow*, the focus is on mathematical concepts of distance, rate, and time. Jasper's friend Larry teaches Emily how to fly a plane. They also discuss their plans for a camping trip to Boone's Meadow. As the adventure develops, important embedded data are introduced. These data are facts and numbers that will be needed to solve the problem posed. For the Boone's Meadow problem, the embedded data include information on who knows how to fly an ultralight plane, their weight, the weight of the plane, the plane's payload, gas consumption, and so forth. The key problem to be solved in this adventure is how to transport a wounded bald eagle as quickly as possible to the veterinarian. By embedding mathematics in a real-life problem context, the CTGV group sought to improve students' ability to transfer their mathematical skills. Evaluations of the Jasper series showed that Jasper students do as well as non-Jasper students on assessments of basic mathematical knowledge but they score better on word problems testing transfer of the knowledge learned through Jasper and on their ability to identify what information needs to be considered in solving complex problems (CTGV, 1997).

> **How Can I Use This?**
>
> How can you transfer knowledge learned in this course or from this book to your teaching in an actual classroom?

Teachers can encourage students to transfer their knowledge and skills by reminding them to look for similarities between the tasks in which they are engaged and ones they have done previously. Students need opportunities to practice new skills. The teacher should provide feedback and remind students to consider the strategies they are using and how these strategies might be useful in the future. Finally, the teacher can provide problems that are very similar to one another (near transfer), then provide problems that are quite varied (far transfer). Students will need help to engage in the metacognitive activity necessary to do far transfer.

Complex Cognition and Social Constructivism

Social learning theory has its roots in behavioral learning theory; it describes how we learn from others, particularly by observing them and imitating their behavior. Social learning theory also includes cognitive elements, because we must encode, retain, and retrieve knowledge of the model's behavior in order to perform that behavior. A natural extension of social learning theory is social constructivism.

According to both social constructivism and sociocultural theory, learners construct knowledge in a social context. Constructivism is not a single theory of learning but includes a number of theories, all of which view learners as active participants in constructing understanding (Moshman, 1982). One kind of constructivism is similar to information processing in that the person creates a representation of what exists in the world. Moshman (1982) refers to this as exogenous constructivism. Students construct an understanding of what the teacher presents. Another form of constructivism describes the learner as constructing new knowledge from prior knowledge (endogenous constructivism). Piaget viewed conceptual development from this vantage point (De Lisi & Golbeck, 1999). Learners use prior knowledge to make sense of new information. A third form of constructivism describes knowledge being constructed by the learner as a result of the continual interaction between the individual and his or her social world and environment. This type of constructivism is best illustrated by Vygotsky's theory (Hogan & Tudge, 1999). The source of knowledge, from this perspective, is subjective experience in interaction with the environment. Social learning theory, social constructivism, and sociocultural theory are all concerned with how we learn from others.

Social constructivism and sociocultural perspectives on learning include both social and cognitive components. Vygotsky's theory of cognitive development argues for a **dialectical relationship** between the individual and the social context in which the child develops. The individual acts on the social context and changes it, and is subsequently changed by the new social context.

Cognitive processes are modeled in the social world before the child can internalize them (Hogan & Tudge, 1999). Children interact with the adults in their world and gradually acquire the skills available in the community. Table 8.2 compares different constructivist approaches.

Social-constructivist and sociocultural theories of human learning emphasize (1) social participation, (2) authentic tasks in which learning is embedded, and (3) tools to support learning. Both theories place special emphasis on social participation. Learners are social beings who develop competence through participation in valued activities from which meaning can be derived (Wenger, 1998). They integrate new knowledge with existing knowledge and actively interact with their environment. According to Vygotsky (1978), a developing child acquires the skills available in the community by participating in activities with adults. The cognitive skills modeled by skilled members of the community are imitated and eventually internalized.

The tasks in which learners engage are meaningful real-world tasks. In other words, they are **authentic**, and all participants have legitimate roles in performing them (Jonassen, Peck, & Wilson, 1999). For example, students might study the quality of the water in a local river. The Jasper Woodbury problem-solving series (CTGV, 1997) presents problems based on real-world situations. In one of Jasper's adventures, students see a video about how architects try

dialectical relationship A relationship in which the participants have mutual influence on one another or in which the actor changes the environment in some way, and that changed environment subsequently changes the actor.

How Can I Use This?

How will you know with what groups your students identify? In particular, consider how middle and high school students display a sense of collective identity.

authentic tasks Tasks that are connected to the real world.

TABLE 8.2

Comparison of the Major Characteristics of Constructivist Perspectives

Major Characteristics	Piagetian Perspective	Vygotskyian Perspective	Social-Constructivist-Perspective	Holistic Perspective
Goal	Develop logical thinking	Develop self-regulated attention, conceptual thinking, logical memory	Construct and reconstruct contexts, knowledge, and meanings through discourse communities	Student ownership of the learning process
Classroom focus	Spontaneous, student-directed experimentation	Interaction with subject matter concepts to develop advanced cognitive capabilities	Emergence of a community of participants that together re-create knowledge	Real-world communication tasks that build on children's strengths and interests
Role of the teacher	Create and organize challenging experiences; ask probing questions to facilitate learner rethinking	Model, explain, correct, and require the learner to explain	Create discourse communities	Generate and mediate tasks tailored to the needs of each learner in each learning situation
Role of the learner	Manipulate objects and ideas; experience cognitive conflict between one's ideas, experimental results, and teacher's questions; reorganize one's thinking	Interact with the teacher in instruction to develop conscious awareness of and mastery of one's thinking; learn to think in subject matter concepts	Participate in a system of practices that are themselves evolving; participate in the "co-construction" of knowledge	Interact with a variety of learning contexts to learn and communicate actively
Example	Some math and science curricula	Reciprocal teaching	Some elementary school and math classrooms	Whole language

Source: Green, S. K., & Gredler, M. E. (2002). A review and analysis of constructivism for school-based practice. *School Psychology Review, 31*, 53–70. Copyright 2002 by the National Association of School Psychologists, Bethesda, MD. Reprinted with permission of the publisher.

(Lawrence Migdale/Photo Researchers, Inc.)

Learners can experience a sense of community and collective efficacy when working on authentic tasks with experienced members of a community such as this research scientist.

collective efficacy A jointly held belief that the community is effective when working together.

affordance A property of a tool or artifact that allows a person to act in particular ways that would not be possible without using the tool.

to solve a community problem such as designing safe places in which children can play. The video ends with a challenge to design a safe playground for the neighborhood. To solve such problems, students must bring a complex set of skills to the task.

Identification with a community or group is a key element of sociocultural approaches to learning. When individuals participate in a valued activity together, they may experience **collective efficacy**, a jointly held belief that they are effective when they are working together (Bandura, 2000). The processes of identification and the experience of collective efficacy are important motivators for learning.

Sociocultural theories suggest that the tools found in a society (e.g., library corners in classrooms rather than desks bolted together in rows) reflect how the society solves problems and thinks about certain issues (Lebeau, 1998). The artifacts or products created by a community suggest the strategies developed by its members to solve particular problems and support the thinking and activities of its members. For example, most people in the United States know what a dishwasher is. It is a machine in which dishes can be placed after use. When operated, it cleans the dishes. The average American home may have a dishwasher. In such homes, the sink unit consists of a stainless steel basin with faucets embedded in a countertop. In countries where having a dishwasher is the exception rather than the rule, kitchen sinks include the standard basin and faucets but are also designed with a built-in draining board on one side of the basin. It is expected that dishes will be washed by hand and left to dry. In contrast, one might never see such a sink unit in an American home because it is expected that a dishwasher may be available. The construction of these sink units reflects how the cultural practices of a community influence the design of objects produced in that community. These, in turn, affect how activities are carried out in that community.

Development is assisted through the use of tools or artifacts generated by the culture. Previously you read that the primary tool by which meaning is communicated among members of a community is language.

Tools such as computers, video cameras, calculators, and mobile phones embody the expertise of their designers and the values of the culture in which they are used. Cognitive activity is distributed, or shared, between the individuals and the tools they use. The tools provide **affordances**, or support, for particular kinds of cognitive activity. They allow members of the community to act in ways that would not be possible without the tool. For example, a student who uses a calculator does not need to use working memory to engage in mental computations. The student thus frees up cognitive resources that can be devoted to other aspects of the task.

Consider how people's communications and activities have changed as a result of the continued development of the telephone. Early telephone systems had *party lines*. Numerous members of a community had access to the same phone line. These systems made possible not only the intended behaviors of communication but also unintended behaviors, such as eavesdropping on other people's conversations. Telephone booths were originally designed to enable two people to hold a private telephone conversation. This was particularly true in England and other countries, where telephone booths were enclosed boxes in which the person making a phone call could close the door and thus maintain privacy. The advent of cell phones has greatly changed the nature of communications. People can make phone calls whenever they wish and from almost any location. Their phones are not simply devices to allow one person to talk to another but may also include text-messaging systems, access to the Internet, music players, video cameras, and other functions. The cell phone no longer affords privacy as a necessary property of the communication between people as the phone booth once did. In sum, the tools or artifacts produced by a community support certain kinds of thinking and make it possible for its members to engage in activities in which they might otherwise be unable to participate.

Tools can also serve an important role in communications between the more competent and less competent members of a group. Learners can share knowledge and develop joint understanding more easily if there are visible, tangible objects that can serve as points of reference in solving problems or be used to assist communication. For example, if students in a high school chemistry lab can point to the effects of a chemical reaction, they have a shared representation of what occurred that will permit them to discuss their understanding of what happened.

In distributed systems, responsibility for a task is shared among participating individuals. The focus is on participants engaging in an activity, and the performance of the group as a whole can exceed that of each individual. Such a system is not simply a division of labor among members but a collaborative activity in which knowledge and expertise are shared: "Cognition in such instances is understood as jointly undertaken by individuals interacting with one another and with surrounding physical, social, and intellectual resources" (Lebeau, 1998, p. 3). The tools available to the group may scaffold its members' performance and support their activity. For example, a group's use of presentation software can help individual students offer new ideas that add to the collective slideshow prepared by the group for presentation to the class.

Examples of instructional forms that are influenced by sociocultural approaches to learning include the computer-supported intentional learning environment (CSILE; Scardamalia, Bereiter, & Lamon, 1994) and communities of learners (Brown & Campione, 1994). (See the nearby What Kids Say and Do box.)

The Role of Experience

The experiences that children have in their community make an important contribution to their cognitive development (Saxe, 1988). Their activities may help them develop complex understandings. For example, in the study of child street vendors in Brazil mentioned earlier in the chapter, Saxe (1988) found that unschooled child street vendors had developed usable strategies for solving arithmetic and ratio problems involving large numbers. A comparison group of nonvendors had not developed such strategies. The practical experiences of the child vendors had helped them develop strategies for carrying out their daily work.

Similarly, Jurdak and Shahin (1999) found that child vendors in Lebanon were more effective in using logical-mathematical skills in solving problems with transactions or word problems than they were when solving computation problems. Sociocultural theories of learning recognize the crucial role of the cultural practices to which children are exposed in their cognitive and social development.

Instruction is likely to be most effective when it takes account of students' previous experiences and interests. The Algebra Project (2005) is an example of an instructional project that is embedded in students' experience (Moses, 1994). The target students for the Algebra Project are students in underserved rural and inner-city areas, primarily African-American and Latino communities. The goal of the project is to help students gain the mathematical skills necessary for college preparatory math classes. The Algebra Project helps students develop mathematical understanding through a process that begins with familiar concrete experiences (e.g., taking a ride on the subway) and moves from there to more abstract mathematics (e.g., the concept of displacements). One of the curricular units developed by the Algebra Project is the African Drums and Ratios Curriculum (Algebra Project, 2005). It is based on the examination of rhythmic concepts and cultural features of African drum traditions. Students learn ideas about pulse, harmonic rhythm, and other rhythmic concepts, which are then used to help them understand such concepts as ratio and proportion, fractions, measurement, and equivalence. Students make their own drums and

How Can I Use This?

Walk into a K–12 classroom and identify the numerous cultural tools in that room, such as the chalkboard, iPads, computers, and wall charts.

RIDE What kinds of learning tools exist in museums that do not exist in classrooms?

What Does This Mean to Me?

Can you think of an example of working in a group in which you felt that cognition was distributed?

Appendix
Prior Experience

Students' prior experience and knowledge vary and influence their learning (PRAXIS™, I.B.6; INTASC, Principles 1, 2, 3).

What Kids Say and Do

The Benefits of Technology?

This exchange took place between a tutor and a student practicing for the SATs

Tutor: So what would you do now?
Student: Well, we've set this up as a series of simultaneous equations.
Tutor: That's right.
Student: And I think the equations are properly laid out.
Tutor: If so, what would you do next?
Student: We have to subtract the second equation from the first. This simplifies the problem to—let's see—6 times 8!
Tutor: And that is . . .
Student: Where's my calculator?

Figure 8.4 Learning Fractal Geometry Using Cornrow Braiding

Source: Eglash, R. Retrieved May 15, 2005, from http://www.ccd.rpi.edu/Eglash/csdt/pr/photos.html. Copyright Ron Eglash. Reproduced with permission.

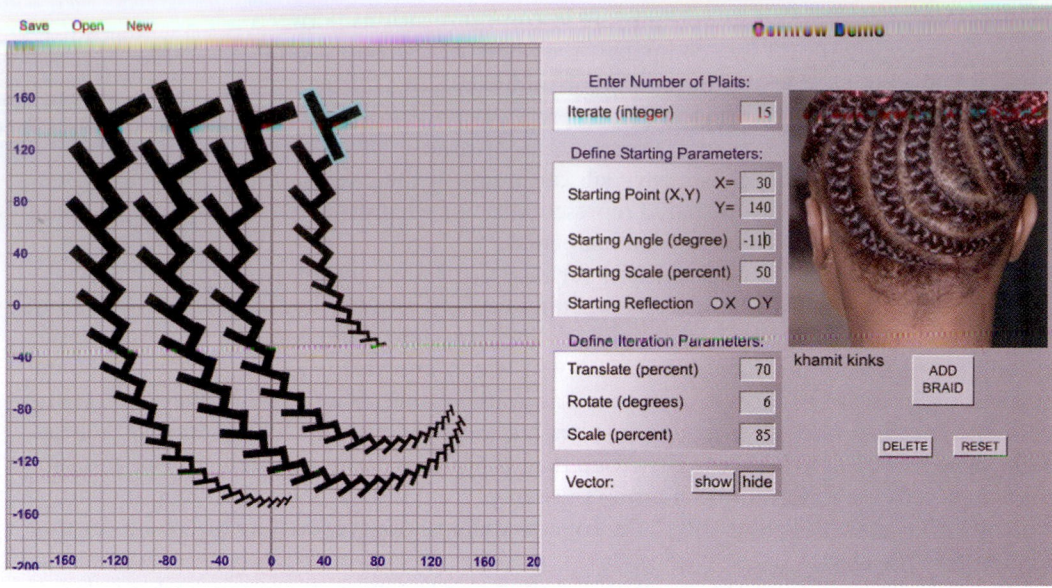

MINDFUL HABITS OF EFFECTIVE TEACHERS

Effective teachers provide appropriate and helpful scaffolding in support of students' learning.

create percussion compositions. They learn to recognize drum patterns and relationships and represent them in mathematical terms. The curriculum has high-interest value for students.

Efforts have also been made to engage students in learning by situating learning activities within their cultural experience. Eglash (1999) has described the presence of concepts of fractal geometry in many facets of African culture. He has been working with African-American math teachers to find ways to increase minority students' interest in math. In one example of a culturally situated instructional activity, Eglash (2005) describes how African cornrows, or braids, illustrate four geometric concepts: translation, rotation, reflection, and dilation. Figure 8.4 shows how students might use cornrow braiding to learn fractal geometry.

This and similar instructional approaches try to take advantage of the fact that students are likely to be more motivated when the content of instruction is personally relevant and meaningful to them.

Scaffolding

Sociocognitive development occurs at two levels. The first level is face-to-face interaction between less competent and more competent members of a group. The second way is through the culture's history and technology. The more competent member scaffolds the learning of the less competent member. The learner and guide jointly create a zone of proximal development in which the learner is able to perform at a level that he or she could not achieve without assistance. For example, a parent may steady a child's hand as she practices cursive writing, or an older sibling may steady a bicycle as a child learns to ride it.

Scaffolding is more than simply providing help. Wood and his colleagues described scaffolding as "a process that enables a child or novice to solve a problem, carry out a task, or achieve a goal which may be beyond his unassisted efforts" (Wood, Bruner, & Ross, 1976, p. 90). An important aspect of scaffolding is the eventual fading of the support so that the child can perform the task on his or her own. "Once the learner has a grasp of the target skill, the master reduces (or fades) his participation, providing only limited hints, refinements, and feedback to the learner, who practices successively approximating smooth execution of the whole skill" (Brown & Palinscar, 1989, p. 456). A child who is learning to ride a bicycle often begins with the aid of training wheels that provide balance. The child may be further supported by an adult who steadies the bicycle. As the child develops the skills needed to ride the bicycle, the supports are gradually removed. The adult may allow the child to depend solely on the training wheels; eventually these are taken off, and the child rides without support.

The guide who provides scaffolding does so by engaging in three activities: channeling, focusing, and modeling (Pea, 2004). **Channeling** (of the learner's activity) and focusing (of the learner's attention) involve providing constraints during the task so that the learner is more likely to perform it effectively. An example of software designed to channel and focus student learning is WorldWatcher (Edelson, Gordin, & Pea, 1999), a tool for displaying and analyzing gridded geographic data in the form of color maps. Students are given access to sets of climate data that are relevant and manageable in size. However, these data sets are constrained in that they are simpler than the complete data would be. The guide focuses the learner's attention by identifying important features of the task. This helps maintain the learner's progress toward completing the task. The guide also models some of the steps involved in completing the task. Previously, we discussed how students are able to learn from models. The guide who provides scaffolding to a learner takes advantage of this ability by modeling aspects of the task.

Two major steps are involved in scaffolding (Lipscomb, Swanson, & West, 2004): Instructional plans must be developed to lead students from what they already know to a deep understanding of new material, and the plans must be carried out, with the teacher providing support at each step. Applebee and Langer (1983) identified the following five features of appropriate instructional scaffolding.

1. *Intentionality*. Each instructional activity should help the learner accomplish the task.

2. *Appropriateness*. The task is difficult enough so that the learner needs help.

3. *Structure*. The teacher models strategies and asks questions that are examples of appropriate ways to approach the task.

4. *Collaboration*. The teacher is the learner's partner, not his or her judge. The teacher needs to welcome the learner's efforts and redirect the learner when necessary.

5. *Internalization*. The teacher's support is gradually withdrawn, and the learner can perform the task alone.

The concept of scaffolding is central to Vygotsky's theory and important for classroom teachers. It will be helpful to identify specific acts of instruction that constitute scaffolding. Carefully consider the following 18 scaffolding acts listed under the headings of *planning*— structuring the learning situation for the student and modeling expert skills; *coaching*—social guidance, instruction, and collaboration; and *fading*—the transfer of responsibility for problem solving from the teacher to the ever more proficient student (from Wood et al., 1976; Rogoff, 1990).

Planning

- Choosing activities—deciding which skills are to be encouraged, such as reading books and writing letters
- Planning and structuring—setting up the learning situation
- Selecting task difficulty—modifying or simplifying a complex task to adjust it to the student's current level of readiness and skill
- Defining the learning goal—"We're going to learn square roots today"
- Scripting task involvement—identifying the sequence of steps required for carrying out the task
- Modeling the activity for the novice

Coaching

- Offering tips, hints, pointers, and assistance
- Suggesting task strategies of which the student is unaware
- Helping the student maintain pursuit of the goal by calming frustration and supporting interest and effort

channeling Providing constraints during the task so that the learner has an increased likelihood of acting effectively.

RIDE In the account at the beginning of the chapter, how could Ms. Bernoulli have used scaffolding to improve the trip the class took to the museum?

(David R. Frazier/Photo Researchers, Inc.)

Scaffolding is more than help. It involves helping a learner perform a task with assistance that the learner could not do alone.

- Offering reminders, prompts—"What happens next?"
- Asking well-timed questions and making well-timed suggestions
- Explaining why a certain procedure will work best
- Showing nonverbal cues indicating proficiency and improvement—glances, smiles, and the like

Fading

- Monitoring the student's need for assistance
- Decreasing the explicitness of instruction
- Transferring the center of decision making from the teacher to the collaborative pair, then to the student
- Pausing more and talking less
- Listening and answering questions, rather than instructing and directing

How Can I Use This?

Tutor a novice in a task in which you are very competent. In doing so, use the scaffolding method of planning–coaching–fading. Is this the best way to teach another person a skill?

An Instructional Example of Scaffolding   Scaffolding can be carried out in a variety of ways. Pea (2004) noted that the term *scaffolding* is used very broadly to describe various kinds of support or help in a learning situation. In its most formal sense, the term refers to a process that includes deliberate fading of teacher support after some time. Informal uses of the concept of scaffolding involve assisting the student's current performance.

Figure 8.5 presents an example of instructional scaffolding. An additional example of scaffolding is the use of procedural facilitation (Scardamalia, Bereiter, & Steinbach, 1984) in writing instruction. **Procedural facilitation** is a structured approach to improving students' use of elements of the writing process. The goal is to help students move from knowledge telling to knowledge transformation. In one study, students were given cue cards that contained procedural prompts for each task goal. They were also given specific prompts in the form of starter sentences to help them think about their writing. For example, a cue card might list a task goal as "improving an idea," and the students might be given a specific prompt about how to do this—for example, "I can make my point clearer by . . ." The performance of sixth-grade students who used planning cues and think-aloud modeling strategies was compared to that of a comparison group of sixth graders who used more typical methods of generating ideas and producing text (Scardamalia et al., 1984). Students in the experimental group produced high-quality written compositions and were more reflective than students in the control group.

procedural facilitation A structured approach to improving students' use of elements of the writing process.

Scaffolding with Technology

Students need a great deal of assistance in learning how to give appropriate help to peers (Webb & Farivar, 1994). Efforts have been made to scaffold complex cognitive activities by providing support in computer-based environments (Guzdial, 1994). Technology-supported scaffolds can provide task structure or automate aspects of the task (de Jong et al., 1999). They can also be used to reduce the cognitive load involved in the task (Sweller & Chandler, 1994).

Web-Based Inquiry Science Environment   Inquiry-based, computer-supported science environments help students learn while doing. Students conduct investigations, interpret the results, and communicate them to others (Linn et al., 1994; Reiser et al., 2001). An inquiry-based environment allows students to engage in scientific processes that are similar to those in which scientists engage, as well as to develop a deep understanding of the nature of science (Tzou et al., 2002).

The Web-based inquiry science environment (WISE) is an online science-learning environment for use by students in grades 4–12 as they learn about and respond to scientific controversies. Software is provided to help students navigate through Web pages that contain content, notes, and hints. Together, these features of WISE guide students as they reflect on the content. An example of a WISE project involves cycles of malaria. Students learn about the nature of the disease, where it is found, and how it is spread. They compare a number of strategies for controlling the spread of malaria. Supports are provided in the

MEMORY SNAPSHOT LESSON

Prewriting

Sharing Pictures
- Ask the students to bring a picture to school that they would like to write about. The photograph could be of themselves, a family member, a special pet, an important event, a trip, or anything they have a special memory of.
- In small groups or with the whole class, have students share their photos and discuss why they chose them.

Snapshots and Thoughtshots
- Discuss the concept of snapshots and thoughtshots in writing. Explain that when the students write about their actual photograph, they will be creating a written picture, which can convey the writer's thoughts and feelings. "Writers have a magic camera that they can point at the world and create snapshots that contain smells and sounds as well as colors and light."
Bary Lane. *After the End: Teaching and Learning Creative Revision.*

Modeling by the Teacher: Cluster and Open Mind
- Share a photograph that you as a teacher plan to write about. In front of the class, start a cluster in which you generate descriptive language to capture your photograph in words. Then draw an Open Mind in which you draw and record your thoughts and feelings about the memory depicted in the photograph. (An Open Mind is simply a blackline drawing of the outline of a head. Inside the head, use words, pictures, or symbols, and colors to illustrate actions and feelings.)

Prompt
- Provide students with the prompt. Read it out aloud and discuss any questions the students have.

Your task will be to create a written mental snapshot that captures your photograph in words and creates a you-are-there feeling in the reader. Use the "magic camera" of your pen to zoom in on your subject and create rich sensory details (sight, sound, smell, taste, touch, and movement). Remember that you can make your snapshot a "moving picture" by adding action and dialogue. Also, give the reader more panoramic views of thoughts, feelings, and big ideas to create a frame for your specific details.

You will be writing an autobiographical incident about your memory snapshot. An autobiographical incident focuses on a specific time period and a particular event that directly involves you. Your goal is not to tell about your event but to show what happened by dramatizing the event. You may write in the present tense, as though your event were happening now, or in the past tense, to describe your incident as a recollection.

Your memory snapshot paper will have a setting that leaves the reader with a dominant visual impression, a plot or story line, and characters. However, the nature of your memory may cause you to place your emphasis on one of the elements over the others. Throughout your paper, and particularly in your conclusion, you should show (and not tell) the reader why this memory is so significant for you.

Precomposing
- Draw your mental snapshot. Tell the students: "The memory you have in your mind may not be identical to the actual snapshot. Draw the picture of the snapshot in your mind. It may include a number of significant details that are not in your actual photograph. After completing your drawing, write at the bottom of the drawing: *This snapshot memory is significant to me because_____*. Be sure you show the significance of this memory in your writing through the use of your snapshots and thoughtshots."
- Have the students discuss their drawing and the significance of the memory with a partner, then talk about how they might begin their essay, what portion of the memory might be an effective "hook" for the reader.

Modeling
- Before students write, read a model of a memory snapshot piece. Have them identify what makes the writing effective. These criteria might become the scoring guide or rubric.

Writing
- Give students ample time to write.

Sharing
- Give the students a memory snapshot response sheet to fill out in pairs or groups of three.
  - The most memorable part of your memory snapshot essay was . . .
  - The words or phrases that were especially vivid and created mental pictures for me were . . . because . . .
  - You made me feel like I was there when . . .
  - One thing I learned about you is . . .

Revising
- Have students revise with an eye toward enhancing snapshots, adding thoughtshots, or showing the significance of the memory.

Editing
- Have students edit for the conventions of English.

Evaluation
- A possible scoring rubric on a 6-point scale might be:
  - Uses rich, sensory/descriptive language (snapshots) to help the reader "picture" the snapshot memory
  - Adds action words and/or dialogue to make the snapshot a "moving picture"
  - Uses thoughtshots to show the characters' thoughts and feelings
  - Clearly demonstrates why the snapshot memory is significant
  - Follows the conventions of written English

Figure 8.5 Scaffolding a Writing Lesson

Source: Curriculum Futures: Preferred Practices. Copyright © 2000. Seventh-Day Adventist North American Division Office of Education. Retrieved May 15, 2005, from http://www.curriculumfutures.org/instruction/a06-06.html. Reproduced with permission.

Figure 8.6 A WISE Project Page, with Inquiry Map, a Note, and a Hint

Source: Figure 4.2 from O'Donnell, A., Hmelo-Silver, C., & Erkens, G. (2005). *Collaborative learning, reasoning, and technology.* Mahwah, NJ: Lawrence Erlbaum. Reproduced with permission of Springer Science & Business Media.

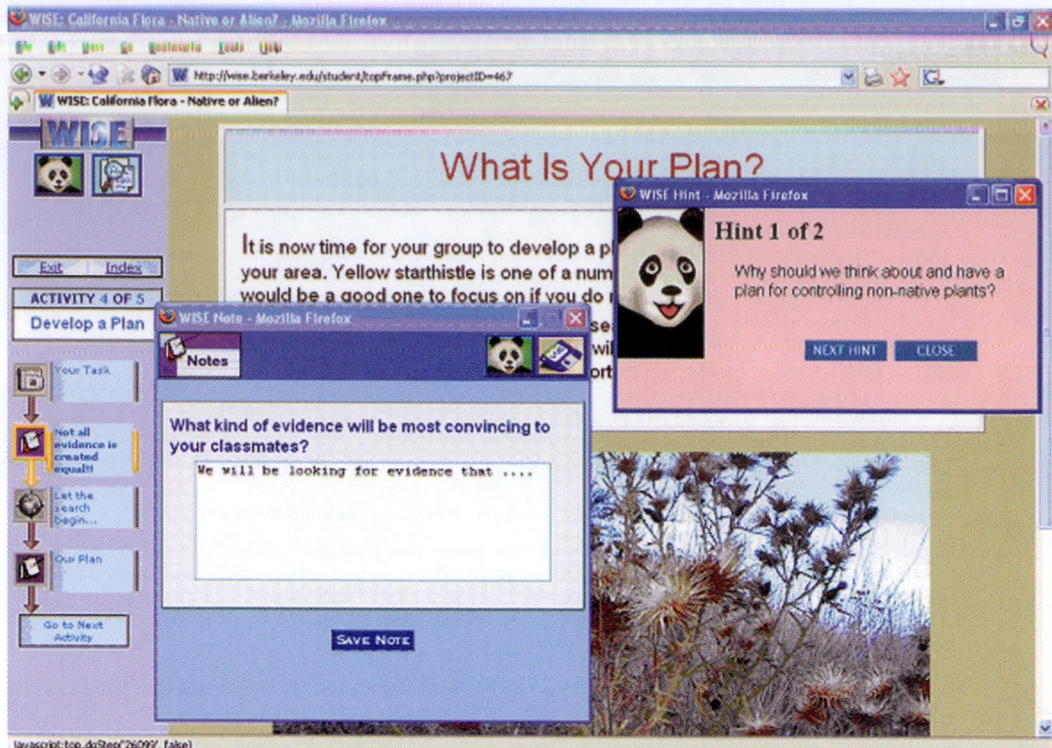

form of hints and tools for visualizing data. An example of a WISE environment can be seen in Figure 8.6

The goals of WISE are to make science accessible by using topics and models that students understand; to make thinking visible by using visualizations and representations; to help students learn from one another by using collaborative tools, online discussions, and group projects; and to promote autonomy with reflection, critique, argument comparison, and design activities. These features focus on authentic tasks, collaborative activity, and meaning.

Biology-Guided Inquiry Learning Environment BGuILE, the biology-guided inquiry learning environment, involves investigations in which students build empirically supported explanations from a computer-simulated data set. Scaffolding is provided by features of the environment that offer guidance about what actions to take, the order in which they are to be done, and the required aspects of work products, such as explanations (Reiser, 2002). The BGuILE software serves as the context for investigation, providing access to the primary data and tools for analyzing and explaining them. In addition, informal and structured discussions are interspersed throughout the activities to provide opportunities for reflection and for sharing and critiquing ideas (Reiser, 2002). For example, The Struggle for Survival, one of the BGuILE learning environments, helps middle school students learn about the ecosystem and natural selection by investigating a crisis in the Galapagos Islands. The students' task is to explore what is killing many of the animals on the islands and whether there is a pattern that explains how some of the animals have managed to survive the crisis. The problem gives students a chance to apply and extend their knowledge about species interactions, relationships between structure and function, and natural selection (Reiser, 2002). Figures 8.7 and 8.8 present examples of what students see as they work with BGuILE. Figure 8.7 shows the Explanation Constructor, a computer-based science journal that students use to construct scientific explanations. As students work on an investigation, they record their primary research questions and other questions as they emerge. They construct explanations and link them to the research questions and evidence that might be used to support the explanations. Figure 8.8 illustrates the artifacts created in the Animal Landlord software (Smith & Reiser, 1998). Using this software, students study examples of animal behavior. They isolate and analyze key components of the animal's behavior. Students select frames from a digitized video, categorize the behavior using a behavioral taxonomy, and annotate them with their interpretations.

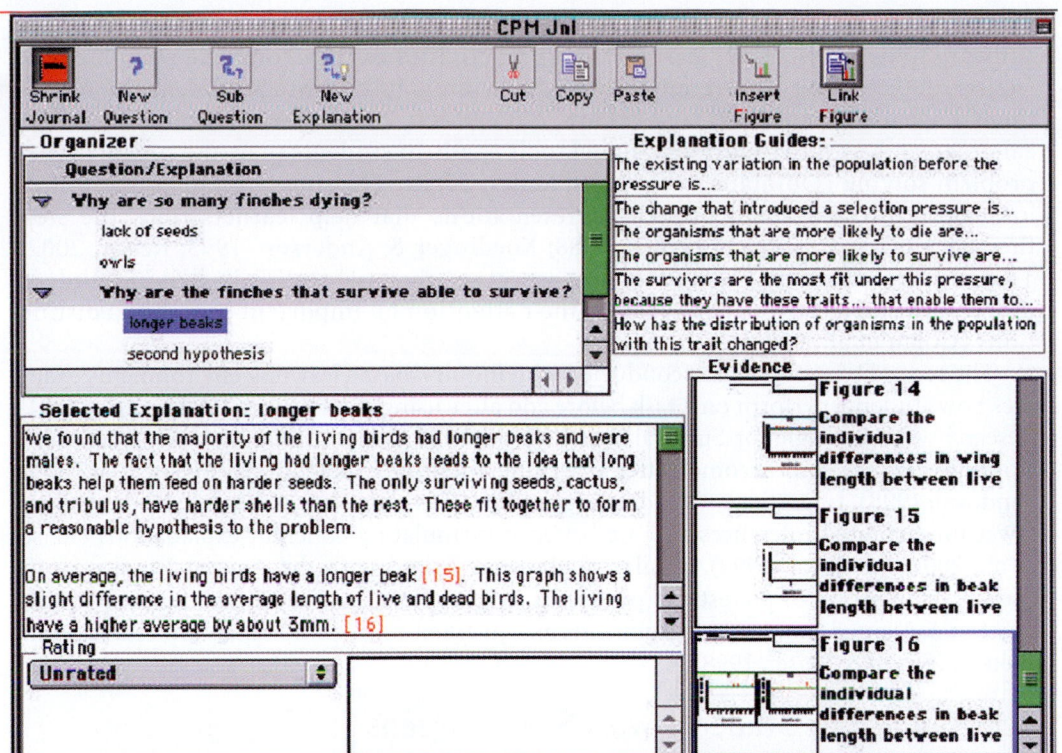

Figure 8.7 The Explanation Constructor

Source: Figure 1 from Reiser, B. J. (2004). Scaffolding complex learning: The mechanisms of structuring and problematizing student work. *The Journal of the Learning Sciences, 13*(3), 273–304. Copyright © by the Taylor and Francis Group.

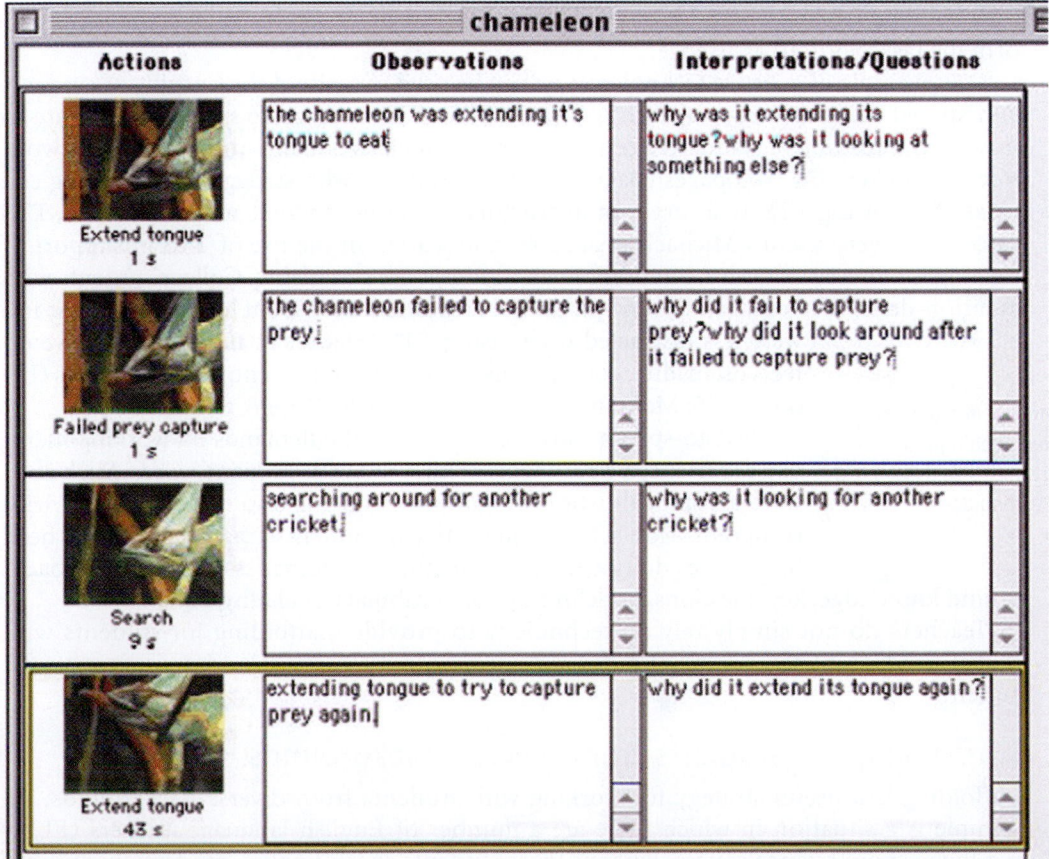

Figure 8.8 Artifacts Constructed in the Animal Landlord

Source: Figure 2 from Reiser, B. J. (2004). Scaffolding complex learning: The mechanisms of structuring and problematizing student work. *The Journal of the Learning Sciences, 13*(3), 273–304. Reproduced with permission of the Taylor and Francis Group.

Much of the research on inquiry-based learning environments focuses on how software tools can scaffold learners' inquiry activities as they complete complex tasks (Reiser, 2002). The software might provide prompts to encourage students or remind them of what steps to take (Davis & Linn, 2000; Reiser, 2002). The availability of graphical organizers or other representational tools can help students plan and organize their problem solving (Quintana et al., 1999; Reiser, 2002). The software can also automate lower-level processes and provide representations that help learners track the steps they have taken (Collins & Brown, 1988; Koedinger & Anderson, 1993; Reiser, 2002). The software makes the methodological aspects of the task explicit by helping students progress through the task and focusing their attention on important conceptual distinctions (Golan et al., 2001).

The second type of research conducted with inquiry-based learning environments examines how students perform on a task before and after using the software (Golan et al., 2001). Research with Struggle for Survival shows some initial evidence that high school students working with the unit become better at writing scientific explanations (Reiser et al., 2001; Sandoval, 1998). In particular, the data suggest that after completing the unit, students make fewer unwarranted inferences and are better at formulating coherent explanations (Reiser et al., 2001; Sandoval, 1998). Similar results were found with the Animal Landlord software. A comparison of pretest and posttest essay questions also found that the essays on the posttest contained more causal arguments and justified more points than did essays on the pretests (Smith & Reiser, 1998).

Scaffolding for Students with Special Needs

assistive technology Any piece of equipment that can improve the functionality of a child with a disability.

Students with special needs often need a great deal of support when performing academic tasks. One strategy for providing that support is to use assistive technologies. In Section 602 of the reauthorization of the Individuals with Disabilities Education Improvement Act (2004), **assistive technology** is defined as "any item, piece of equipment, or product system, whether acquired commercially off the shelf, modified, or customized, that is used to increase, maintain, or improve functional capabilities of a child with a disability." Many assistive-technology tools do not scaffold a student's learning in the way described by Vygotsky. They help the student communicate or participate, but the student remains unable to perform the tasks without assistance.

One example of assistive technology that can be used to scaffold the learning of students with special needs is text-to-speech software (TTS). TTS uses voice synthesis software to provide oral reading of standard electronic text files, such as documents prepared in a word processor or text on Web pages (Balajthy, 2005). Students who struggle with reading can benefit from using TTS. In a survey of instructors of college students with disabilities, TTS was rated as very useful (Michaels et al., 2002). Research on the use of TTS in support of learning is not very extensive, but preliminary findings are promising. College students with attention-deficit disorders and below-grade-level reading scores spent less time reading and were less distracted when using TTS (Hecker et al., 2002). Positive effects on reading comprehension were found in a number of studies (Leong, 1995; Montali & Lewandowski, 1996; Wise & Olson, 1994).

How Can I Use This?

When students cannot complete complex instructional activities (e.g., understand an assigned reading), they may feel inadequate. Look for opportunities to use electronic scaffolding and assistive technology to support their progress and learning.

Text-to-speech software can reduce the demands on working memory experienced by students as they struggle to learn words. Such software assists with word recognition. Students also need assistance with comprehension activities in particular content areas. Teachers may need to provide additional scaffolding for such activities in the form of background knowledge, key questions, or definitions of vocabulary (Balajthy, 2005).

Teachers do not simply rely on technology to provide scaffolding for students with special needs. The teacher plays a key role in providing support and assistance to the student.

Scaffolding for Students from Diverse Backgrounds

Scaffolding is a useful strategy for working with students from diverse backgrounds. An example is a situation in which there are a number of English language learners (ELLs) in a high school science course. Perhaps these students speak English moderately well but not fluently. They are very likely to have difficulty with some of the technical language used in scientific discussions (Buxton, 1998; Minicucci, 1996; Noguchi, 1998). That is, because ELL students learn the syntax and structure of a language mainly through interaction with their peers (Hawkins, 2001), they are often ill equipped to tackle the language of science instruction (and science assessment). This problem is not limited to science classes, but science instruction is a useful example.

Shaw (2002) shows how scaffolding, especially in dealing with the language used in science instruction, can greatly facilitate learning for ELL students. She presents the following suggestions:

1. Assess the difficulty of the language used in the instructional materials. Look for areas where extra assistance might be helpful.

2. Modify your language in discussing complex issues with students.

3. Help students address difficult language issues on their own. For example, work with them to understand the language associated with cause-and-effect relationships.

4. Encourage the use of metacognitive strategies with students. Have them think about what they know and do not know about a subject as well as reflect on and summarize what they have learned after instruction.

5. Use graphical organizers to help students to master material.

6. Explicitly teach the vocabulary that students will need to know for an instructional unit.

Figure 8.9 summarizes some of the key questions that teachers might have with respect to how adopting a social-constructivist theory might influence decisions a teacher must make.

(© Media Bakery)

Assistive technology can be used to scaffold the learning of students with special needs by providing supports of various kinds. Students often experience great satisfaction in being able to complete tasks with assistance.

Appendix
Responsive Teaching
You will need to be able to design instruction that is responsive to your students' needs and prior experiences (PRAXIS™, I.B.4, I.B.6, II.A.2; INTASC, Principles 1, 2, 3, 4).

Instruction Influenced by Social–Constructivist and Sociocultural Theory

The examples of scaffolded instruction described so far are clearly influenced by social-constructivist and sociocultural theory. Wenger (1998) listed the following implications of these perspectives for human learning:

● A central aspect of human learning is the fact that learners are social beings.

How does learning occur?	Learners use cognitive skills (e.g., metacognition, working memory) to engage in complex cognition, constructing knowledge and meaning by participating in a community of learners.
Where does knowledge come from?	Knowledge is built upon and constructed by individuals in a dialectical relationship between individuals and in interaction with the environment.
What does the student do?	Participates in a system of practices developed by the community. Constructs knowledge.
What is the role of the teacher?	Creates a discourse community through guided discovery. Serves as a facilitator, providing scaffolding and coaching.
What is the role of peers?	Participants have mutual influence on one another as members of a learning community.
If a teacher subscribes to this theory, what is he or she likely to include in a lesson plan?	The teacher will likely select authentic tasks, provide tools that afford complex cognition, and provide support for the students' efforts through guidance and prompts.

Figure 8.9 Social Constructivism and Instruction

- Knowledge reflects competence in some valued activity.
- The act of knowing involves participating in valued activities.
- Learning should produce meaning.

Examples of instructional strategies that have been influenced by this view of learning include cognitive apprenticeships, reciprocal teaching, and problem-based learning.

Cognitive Apprenticeships

cognitive apprenticeship An instructional strategy in which the learner acquires knowledge by modeling the activities of the teacher and is coached by the teacher.

Cognitive apprenticeships are an example of how scaffolding can be used in classrooms. A traditional apprenticeship involves an apprentice learning from a *master* craftsperson. The apprentice learns through observation, coaching, and practice (Lave & Wenger, 1991). Cognitive apprenticeships take advantage of these factors by having the teacher model cognitive strategies and make his or her thinking *visible* (Collins, Brown, & Holum, 1991; Collins, Brown, & Newman, 1989). The typical apprentice begins by doing simple tasks, gradually becomes more skilled, and finally engages in the most complex task. A cognitive apprenticeship has much in common with the traditional craft apprenticeship. It includes modeling, coaching, scaffolding, reflection, articulation, and exploration (Brill, Galloway, & Kim, 2001). At the beginning of this chapter, you learned that modeling is likely to result in the acquisition of a new behavior when the modeled behavior is visible, easy to observe, and easy to perform. Because cognitive activities lack these qualities, teachers must make explicit efforts to make thinking visible. Teachers can provide a model of how they are solving a problem and have students practice thinking aloud and describing their cognitive processes.

The nearby What Kids Say and Do box presents a story written by Noah, age 12, in which he displays his understanding of scaffolding and apprenticeship.

Appendix
Instructional Strategies

It is important for you to be knowledgeable about the appropriate use of a variety of instructional strategies (PRAXIS™, II.A.2; INTASC, Principle 4).

Reciprocal Teaching

Reciprocal teaching is an instructional strategy based on cognitive apprenticeship. Developed by Annemarie Palinscar (Palinscar & Brown, 1984), it was originally designed to improve reading comprehension. It consists of a dialogue between teachers and students regarding segments of text. "The purpose of these discussions is to achieve joint understanding of the text through the flexible application of four comprehension strategies: prediction, clarification, summarization, and question generation" (Palinscar & Klenk, 1991, p. 116). The teacher first models each of these component strategies. When reading a text, he or she summarizes the content of a segment of text, asks a question about the main idea, clarifies any part of the text that is difficult, and predicts what will come next. The teacher then gives students an opportunity to take on some of the responsibility for these strategies by coaching them as they practice the component skills. Gradually, responsibility is shifted from the teacher to the student, and eventually the teacher's involvement in the performance of the strategies is faded. The teacher will continue to monitor the students' performance as they use these cognitive strategies and will provide further coaching if needed.

A summary of 16 research studies on the use of reciprocal teaching provided support for its use as an instructional strategy (Rosenshine & Meister, 1994). Reciprocal teaching has been used with a broad range of students, from third grade through adulthood. It has been successfully used with middle school students who were identified as remedial or special education students (Palinscar & Klenk, 1992).

Reciprocal teaching illustrates several characteristics of cognitive apprenticeship. First, the teacher

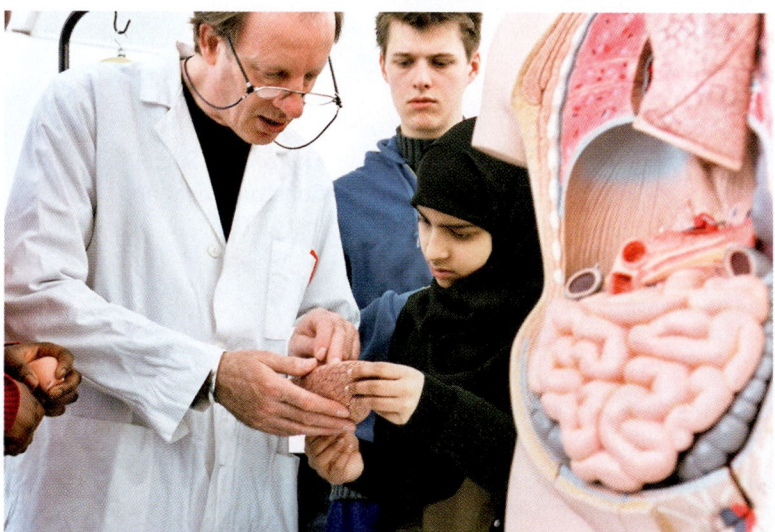

(© Media Bakery)

In a cognitive apprenticeship, the expert models the cognitive activity, coaches the learner in performance of the activity, guides the learner to reflect on the activity, articulates the cognitive processes involved, and guides further exploration.

What Kids Say and Do

Understanding Apprenticeship

The Boy Who Loved Stories, by Noah Rocklin

There once was a boy who loved stories. Any kind of story, books, plays, movies, even the plot of a video game as long as it was a good story.

One day The Boy tried to write a story (which was really just the story he saw on TV last night retold and set in a different place), but it wasn't as good as the stories he read so he tried again and again and again. After a while he realized he wasn't getting anywhere so he sent his story (or the eighth revision thereof) to ten of his favorite authors so they could offer advice.

In the coming weeks he received nine form letters apologizing about how busy the authors were and one very helpful letter from Gabriel Winters, his favorite young author. It made the story better without affecting the core plot.

The Boy kept sending stories and Gabe, as The Boy came to know him, kept helping until the letters became more like two friends getting each other's comments on a work than a famous author helping out a little kid.

As the years dragged on The Boy graduated from high school and went to a college with a good writing program (as an English major of course). He acted in plays (some of which he wrote), wrote stories for the school paper, but always, always wrote to Gabe.

The Boy graduated and became a man, but he still was The Boy. He got married young, became a well-known author himself and always, always wrote to Gabe. One morning The Boy was eating his breakfast in his new house when the phone rang.

"That's odd," he thought, "I just moved in."

The voice on the phone said, "Hello is this 334–5672?"

"Yes this is. Why are you calling?" asked The Boy.

"Gabriel Winters told me to tell you about his leukemia," stated the voice.

"Oh, my God, how long does he have?" The Boy asked anxiously.

"Until next month I'm . . . I'm very sorry," the voice said.

"Where is he staying? I need to get there right away."

"At the Mayo Clinic, I hope you arrive soon," said the voice solemnly.

The Boy got the first tickets to Rochester he could find. He didn't care about the baby crying, he didn't care about the cramped space, he didn't care about the person kicking his seat, he cared about Gabe and to The Boy that's all that mattered. He arrived at the hospital jetlagged and sure his pocket had been picked at least once, but he had gotten to Gabe and that's all that mattered.

As he walked through the hospital doors he realized this was the first time Gabe and him would meet face-to-face. He found Gabe's room and when he walked in he wasn't sure he was in the right room. The bed's occupant was a small frail man.

"Gabe?" The Boy asked obviously confused.

"Yep," said Gabe also a little confused.

They talked about how they had imagined one another different sizes and about the stories they wrote and the stories they wanted to write and in between The Boy thought, "He's going to be okay, no one who has a month to live can seem so . . . happy." The thought only lasted a millisecond, but it put The Boy's mind at ease and that was good.

The Boy stayed until a little after the funeral and on the way home thought about that one moment where everything was okay. When he arrived home he wrote a book about Gabe and him (changing the names of course). It received good reviews and finally let The Boy move on.

One day The Boy received a letter. It was from a little girl who wanted his advice on her story. The Boy smiled and began to write.

Source: Copyright Noah Rocklin. Reprinted with permission of the author.

models the cognitive strategies to be used, making his or her thinking visible and inviting students to join in. By giving students opportunities to practice each of the strategies under the teacher's guidance, he or she coaches them in the use of the strategies, providing assistance if they are having difficulty with any of them. For example, some students have difficulty summarizing content from a text, and the teacher needs to help them identify the key ideas that must be retained in a summary. Reciprocal teaching also includes other elements of coaching that are considered important, such as providing feedback, hints, and reminders (Brill et al., 2001).

Problem-Based Learning

In **problem-based learning (PBL)**, students work in collaborative groups to solve a complex and interesting problem that does not have a single correct answer (Hmelo-Silver, 2004). Students' learning is anchored to the problem posed. An example of a complex problem can be found in Alien Rescue (University of Texas at Austin, 2004), a problem-based hypermedia learning environment. The program, presented on a CD, is designed to engage middle school students in solving a complex problem. Students are told that six species of aliens are in earth's orbit but

problem-based learning (PBL) An instructional strategy in which students work in collaborative groups to solve a complex problem that does not have a single correct answer.

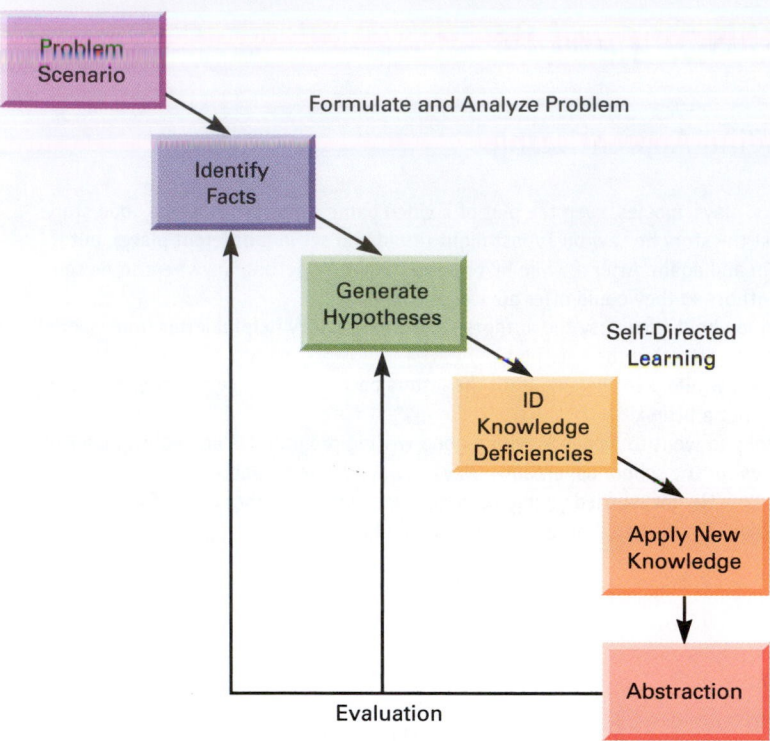

Figure 8.10 The Problem–Based Learning Cycle

Source: Figure 1 from Hmelo-Silver, C.E. (2004) *Educational Psychology Review*, Vol. 16. "Problem–based learning: What and how do students learn?" p. 237. Reprinted with permission of Springer Science & Business Media.

their spaceship is damaged. The aliens must find new homes on planets that can support their life-forms. Students are given the task of selecting the most suitable relocation site for each alien species. They must learn about each species and identify its basic needs. They must also learn about the solar system and the kinds of life that might exist on each of a number of planets. Students take on the role of scientists examining the solar system.

Alien Rescue provides a variety of tools to support learning, including databases of information about the solar system, the aliens, and probe missions carried out by NASA. It also includes a probe design tool, a notebook, tutorials, stories about how experts have handled similar problems, and tools that students can use to present their solutions to the class. With the aid of their teachers, students use technological tools and scientific procedures to help the aliens find new homes that can support them.

The goals of PBL are to engage students in a complex problem-solving process in order to foster the development of (1) flexible knowledge, (2) problem-solving skills, (3) self-directed learning skills, (4) effective collaboration skills, and (5) intrinsic motivation (Hmelo-Silver, 2004). These goals are consistent with the view of learning that is implied by sociocultural and social-constructivist theories. The teacher guides students through a process in which they are presented with the problem scenario, gain an understanding of the problem, and identify the relevant facts. They then generate hypotheses about potential solutions. They identify gaps in their understanding and engage in self-directed learning to fill those gaps. They apply their new knowledge and evaluate their original hypotheses on the basis of what they have learned. Upon completion of a problem, they reflect on what they have learned. This process is depicted in Figure 8.10.

Students engaged in PBL are initially given very little information about a complex problem. They must seek further information from the teacher or facilitator. For example, if the students were working on Alien Rescue, they would need to find out what kind of home was needed (air, water, etc.) for each alien species. Students work through what they know and what they still need to know, and they reevaluate their ideas and their progress toward solving the problem in light of the new information they acquire. Because the problem is complex and students often make false starts or need to revise their hypotheses, it is important for them to record their progress, using a whiteboard to keep track of facts they have uncovered or decisions they have made. Students keep track of (1) facts related to the problem, (2) ideas about solving the problem, (3) learning issues or concepts about which more information is needed, and (4) a plan for action. Figure 8.11 shows what one group of students wrote on a whiteboard as they tried to solve a problem about a chemical spill.

In an example of PBL in the sixth grade, students were assigned the task of designing a zoo. The class was divided into small groups, and each group selected a different climate zone (e.g., equatorial forest) whose animals would be represented at their section of the zoo. Students had to find out what kinds of food, temperature, and space their animals needed. The zoo would have limited space, and students needed to work together to make decisions about the limitations they would impose on their design. For example, they needed to agree on the height of the buildings they would include.

Characteristics of Good Problems To promote flexible thinking effectively, problems must be complex, open-ended, and ill structured (Barrows & Kelson, 1995; Kolodner, Hmelo, & Narayanan, 1996). For students to be intrinsically motivated by the task, it must also be interesting. Effective problems require knowledge from a variety of domains. When students

Facts	Ideas	Learning Issues	Action Plan
Hazardous chemical	Minimize on-site storage	What are the safety standards for cyanide storage?	Call EPA to find out standards
Near population center	Provide safety training Improve early warning system	What technology is available to safely store hazardous chemicals?	

Figure 8.11 Example of Using a Whiteboard while Determining the Cause of a Chemical Spill

Source: Figure 2 from Hmelo-Silver, C.E. (2004) *Educational Psychology Review*, Vol. 16. "Problem-based learning: What and how do students learn?" p. 243. Reprinted with permission of Springer Science & Business Media.

designed a zoo, for example, they used skills from language arts, mathematics, science, and art. Complex and interesting problems promote discussion and sharing of ideas and enhance the building of knowledge (Hmelo-Silver, 2004). When students need to seek new information as part of the PBL process, they engage in self-directed learning and learn to evaluate the state of their own knowledge.

The Role of the Teacher or Facilitator   The purpose of PBL is to engage students in self-directed learning, but the role of the teacher in supporting students as they do so is crucial (Hmelo-Silver, 2004). The teacher can model good strategies, as might be expected in a cognitive-apprenticeship model (Collins Brown, & Newman, 1989). The teacher scaffolds students' learning by modeling and using questioning strategies (Hmelo-Silver, 2002). As students become more skilled, the teacher begins to fade the explicit scaffolding of their activities. The teacher must monitor the progress of a PBL group, encouraging all students to participate and to talk about what they are thinking.

Classroom Communities

An important technique for building learning communities was developed by Ann Brown and Joseph Campione (Brown, 1992; Brown et al., 1993). A central feature of this approach is that students help design their own learning environment, including choosing curricula. The Communities of Learners model (Brown & Campione, 1994) includes the use of reciprocal teaching (described earlier) and a modified Jigsaw arrangement. Students work in small teams to prepare teaching materials. For example, high school students studying human migrations might divide the general topic into smaller ones (flight from war or famine, movement toward economic opportunity, seasonal migrations). The students then regroup into reciprocal teaching seminars in which each student is an expert in one subtopic. (All the students are experts in selected subtopics.)

According to Brown and Campione (1994), the ideal classroom environment has a number of important features:

- *Individual responsibility with communal sharing.* Students must take individual responsibility for their work but share their expertise with others.

- *Ritual, familiar, participant structures.* Students need to know what the participation frameworks are (e.g., reciprocal teaching).

- *A community of discourse.* A key component of a learning community is the building of a community of discourse (Fish, 1980) in which constructive discussions, questioning, and criticism can occur.

- *Multiple zones of proximal development.* Because students are working with several of their peers, they have opportunities to participate in multiple zones of proximal development. For example, a student may serve as the guide for one student's learning but may be the beneficiary of another student's guidance.

- *Seeding, migration, and appropriation of ideas.* Teachers and students *seed* ideas—that is, suggest them. If an idea is adopted by other members of the learning community, it *migrates* and persists over time. Participants can appropriate, or adopt, ideas and language and use them in their own learning.

R I D E Think back to Ms. Bernoulli's class trip to the hands-on science museum described at the beginning of the chapter. Museums are often places where different displays and exhibitions compete for visitors' attention. How can you get students to engage in complex cognition in such an environment?

REFLECTION FOR ACTION

The Event

Ms. Bernoulli had a rather trying day at the hands-on science museum. Her students were normally well behaved in class, but they were not during this visit. They were noisy at the museum and on the bus ride home. During the visit, they did not listen to her instructions or to those of the museum staff. She wondered what had gone wrong and how to make sure that the next visit would be more successful.

Reflection RIDE

Imagine that you are taking your class on a visit to the hands-on science museum. How would you avoid the problems experienced by Ms. Bernoulli? How can you make the trip an exciting learning experience while at the same time maintaining order? How will you keep the children interested?

What Theoretical/Conceptual Information Might Assist in Interpreting and Remedying the Problems Described in This Situation? Consider the following:

Goals

The goals of the visit were not clear to the students. Ms. Bernoulli had to think about what the trip to the museum was meant to achieve in terms of student learning. Why were they going there? Was it just a day off from school? All her colleagues plan class trips. What do they use them for? How are they supposed to fit in with the curriculum?

Planning

Ms. Bernoulli realized that she had not prepared her class for the visit. The children had little idea of what their day would be like. Moreover, they were in an environment that was completely different from the classroom: Museums are places to explore, roam around, and make choices. Ms. Bernoulli values these ideas as a teacher, but she now realizes that they need to be managed when one is dealing with 23 fifth graders.

Scaffolding

When visiting an unfamiliar learning environment, it helps to have a guide to assist you to learn. Ms. Bernoulli realized that she needs to include scaffolds—such as index cards with questions, partners, assistance from museum guides, and so on.

Information Gathering RIDE

How can Ms. Bernoulli gather information that will help her understand the field trip, set goals for students' learning, and plan better for the future? First, the field trip has a purpose and she should think about the learning goals and how to achieve them. Second, she can consult colleagues about trips to cultural institutions to assist her planning. What do they do that is effective, and what are some of their "disaster stories"? Also, she can look at some other cultural institutions and see what they do. She can read some of the research on children's learning in museums to find out what kinds of planning and postvisit activities seem to be most effective. Third, because the museum will be an unfamiliar learning environment for her students, she can assist her students by introducing scaffolding opportunities.

Decision Making RIDE

Fortunately for Ms. Bernoulli, she does not need to take any action right away. She may want to take some disciplinary actions, but she probably will not be going on another field trip in the near future. However, she needs to think about some of the following issues:

- What kind of institution would fit best with what the class is studying? How well does it match the age and nature of her students? What practical aspects of the trip need to be considered (how long will the bus ride be, can the students have lunch at the institution, etc.)?

- How does the institution work with school classes? Many institutions will tailor visits to the needs of the class. Some institutions are highly oriented toward visits by school groups; others are less experienced and less well suited to such visits.

- What should Ms. Bernoulli do to prepare for the visit? She should probably visit the institution on her own first; she should get in touch with the person giving the tour; she should visit the museum's Web site and get the museum's school-group materials so that she can prepare pre- and postvisit activities.

- She needs to set specific goals and objectives for the visit. These will lead to the development of specific activities for the students to engage in while visiting the museum.

Evaluation RIDE

A museum visit is different from other types of school activities. Often, a primary goal of such a visit is to get students excited about the specific museum and about museums in general. Fun, excitement, and engagement are perfectly valid goals. In addition, almost any museum has material that can be linked to instructional goals. For example, in a zoo (or even a natural history museum), the teacher can test students' classification skills by asking what other animals are most closely related to an animal that is new to most students (an ibex, platypus, or wallaby). Islamic art is highly patterned and geometric in nature and can be tied to mathematics instruction. Narrative art can be used to help develop a sense of story in students.

Evaluating the changes one makes in approaching visits to museums, or field trips in general, will depend to some extent on the goals, objectives, and sources of support for such a trip. There are other indicators as well. Is there a "buzz" about the trip in the classroom the day or two before the trip? What are students saying about it? Is it useful to discuss the visit? Are the students talking about what they might learn? This can be done informally during class discussion or through reflections in writing in which the students consider the visit. It will give you an opportunity to reinforce appropriate behavior, gain insight into the best and worst aspects of the day, and make adjustments for future trips. It will also be useful to look for ways to refer to the trip in upcoming lessons. Finally, it can be helpful to have a *discovery* or *exploration* sheet (some museums have these, called *museum hunts*) that can be discussed on the day after the visit. This will give you an idea of the level of students' engagement in the visit and provide a springboard for class discussion.

Further Practice: Your Turn

Here is a second event for you to reflect on. In doing so, generate the sequence used above in terms of reflection, information gathering, decision making, and evaluation.

The Event

Mr. Paine is a high school social studies teacher. He wants his students to learn how to do historical research. He intends to have his students select a period of history that is of interest to them, frame a specific question they would like to explore (e.g., How did Stalin come to power?), and use online resources, libraries, and so forth to locate information. He wants them to learn to be critical of the resources they locate. Jake is very resistant to the idea. He insists that all he needs is his textbook.

What should Mr. Paine do? Why do the other students imitate Jake? What can Mr. Paine do to utilize Jake as a constructive rather than destructive role model?

SUMMARY

● **What is social learning theory?**

Social learning theory was originally developed by Albert Bandura and includes such concepts as reinforcement and punishment. It also includes cognitive elements, because a learner must attend to, remember, and produce behavior that he or she has observed. According to social learning theory, individuals can learn vicariously from the experiences of others. The reinforcements or punishments that follow other people's behaviors will influence the likelihood that the observer will perform those behaviors.

● **What is necessary for observational learning to occur?**

The learner must attend to the critical features of a model's behavior. The behavior must be remembered. The learner must be able to produce the behavior, although initial efforts to perform it may not be completely correct. Finally, the learner must be motivated to perform the behavior. Vicarious reinforcement or punishment will influence the learner's motivation to perform the behavior.

● **How can teachers promote complex cognition?**

To promote metacognition in the classroom, the following information should be discussed: the amount of time and effort the problem or argument is worth, what you already know about it, the goal or reason for engaging in extended and careful thought about it, how difficult you think it will be to solve the problem or reach a conclusion, how you will know when you have reached the goal, the critical thinking skills that are likely to be useful in solving the problem or analyzing the argument, and whether you are moving toward a solution. A teacher can promote argumentation by requiring students to articulate and defend positions on topics. Transfer can be encouraged by asking students to look for the similarities between problems.

● **How can teachers promote problem solving?**

Teachers can help students develop strategies for problem solving and create an environment in which students are willing to take academic risks. Teachers can encourage students to generate different representations of the problem, explore alternative strategies, and focus on the process of problem solving and not on the outcome. They can encourage students by eliminating or reducing contingencies associated with problem solutions.

● **How is scaffolding used in instruction?**

Scaffolding can be used in a number of ways in instruction. Scaffolded instruction has two key elements: The learner's efforts are supported by a more skilled individual so that the learner can accomplish more than he or she might accomplish alone. With practice and feedback, the learner internalizes the new skill, and support is gradually faded.

● **How can teachers use scaffolding techniques to work with diverse learners?**

Scaffolding techniques are an excellent way to work with diverse learners. Scaffolding is based on the idea that teachers need to find students' strengths and weaknesses and attempt to build on the strengths and minimize the weaknesses. When working with students who have difficulties with English or students whose background in a subject area is weak, scaffolding can help bridge the gap between confusion and understanding.

● **What kinds of instruction are influenced by social constructivism and sociocultural theory?**

Potentially, all types of instruction can be influenced by social constructivism and sociocultural theory. Examples of particular instructional strategies that are influenced by social constructivism and sociocultural theory are cognitive apprenticeships, reciprocal teaching, and problem-based learning. These three strategies all assume that learners construct meaning in a social context and that such construction can be assisted by scaffolding learners' efforts.

● **Can learners with special needs benefit from social-constructivist or sociocultural approaches to learning?**

Behavioral techniques have been shown to be particularly effective for working with students with special needs. Social-constructivist approaches, which employ these techniques, hold strong promise for working with such students. In addition, assistive technology, such as TTS devices, can be a useful adjunct to regular instruction.

Key Terms

affordance, p. 270
algorithm, p. 266
argumentation, p. 264
assistive technology, p. 278
authentic tasks, p. 264
channeling, p. 273
cognitive apprenticeship, p. 280
collective efficacy, p. 270
dialectical relationship, p. 269

functional fixedness, p. 266
heuristic, p. 266
high road transfer, p. 267
low road transfer, p. 267
means–ends analysis, p. 266
metacognition, p. 262
modeling, p. 257
negative transfer, p. 267
observational learning, p. 257

positive transfer, p. 267
problem-based learning (PBL), p. 281
procedural facilitation, p. 274
response set, p. 266
social learning theory, p. 256
transfer, p. 267
vicarious experience, p. 256
vicarious punishment, p. 257
vicarious reinforcement, p. 257

Exercises

1. *The Downside of Metacognition*
   What might be some disadvantages of having good metacognitive skills?

2. *Learning or Not?*
   Visit a hands-on science museum or other cultural institution. Select an exhibit and make a list of features you think are helpful to complex learning and those that are not. Indicate why you have identified each feature as helpful or not.

3. *Scaffolding with Software*
   Select a piece of software that you use often—for example, your word-processing software. Identify characteristics of the software that seem to scaffold your learning or performance. In what sense do these features provide scaffolding? How is the scaffolding faded after use?

4. *Distributed Cognition*
   To gain a better understanding of distributed cognition, participate in an online message board. Notice how many individuals contribute. Does the collective membership of those who post messages know more than any individual participant?

Lesson Plans

The lesson plans on these pages are excerpts from more complete plans. They are included in this form to provide you with practice in examining a lesson from the perspective of the content of this chapter. The complete lesson plans are available at www.pbs.org. For both lesson plans, read the lesson plan excerpt and respond to the questions related to complex cognition and social constructivism in the Ask Yourself! section at the end.

Lesson #1: "Dinner Party"

GRADES: 7–9

SUBJECT AREA: Math

ESTIMATED COMPLETION TIME: One 90-minute class period

I. OVERVIEW: One of the most difficult tasks involved with teaching mathematics is showing students the real-world applications of the concept they are learning. This task has proven to be a fun way for students to be involved in planning an event while actually practicing their math skills!

II. OBJECTIVES: Students will be able to
- Work collaboratively to plan a "dinner party" for themselves and their closest friends
- Anticipate issues that might arise in executing a plan for a dinner party
- Apply principals of *unit price*
- Understand and apply the concept of sticking to a budget

III. MATERIALS:
- Copies of a grocery store weekly circular
- Calculators
- Paper
- Scissors/glue (optional)

IV. PROCEDURE:

1. Students will make a combined list with their groups of ten people they want to invite to their dinner party.

2. Students have $100 to spend on their party; however, offer an incentive for the party that is the cheapest *per person.*

3. Using the prices in the weekly circular, students will plan their party menu, taking into account how much multiple items will cost, how many pounds of weighable items there will be, etc.

4. Once students have their set menu/how much of everything they need, they will put these items into a circle graph to show how much of their $100 budget is going to which item/course.

5. Optional: Students can cut the items from the circular and glue them on the circle graph to create more of a display.

6. After students are done, offer the following scenario: 3 of your dinner guests wish to bring a "+1". How does this affect your budget? Will people have to eat less to stay within the $100, or can you reallocate certain items?

7. Have students write a response to the following question: How do you think this relates to what your parents have to do with their paycheck each month?

Ask Yourself!

1. What features of this lesson are influenced by a social learning theory of learning?

2. What kinds of thinking is the teacher trying to promote? Explain your answer.

3. What cultural tools are used in this lesson? What kinds of affordances do they provide?

Lesson Plans

Lesson #2: "Epidemic"

GRADES: 4–8

SUBJECT AREA: History, Epidemiology

I. OVERVIEW: Using the history of epidemics in the immigrant ghettoes of turn-of-the-twentieth-century New York and the public health measures they led to, this activity asks students to research recent episodes when diseases like colds or flus spread through their school. It also asks them to think of public health measures that might stop a disease from spreading again.

II. PREP: Start this activity off by getting your students to read the articles "The Battle with the Slum" and "Better Health for All."

Hold a class discussion about epidemics and pub-lic health. Begin with a discussion of the conditions that might have led to epidemics in the immigrant ghettoes of turn-of-the-twentieth-century New York: crowding, poor ventilation, inadequate diets, overwork, lack of vaccines and medicines, and so forth. How did each of these fac-tors contribute to the spread of disease? Next, you might have them think about epidemics today. What contributes to diseases like AIDS? What are the differences between the influenza and AIDS epidemics? What are some of the improvements we have made in the prevention and treat-ment of epidemics—both in terms of vaccines and cures, as well as in the realm of public health measures? You might also want your students to focus on their school. What are some of the factors that cause diseases like colds and flus to spread quickly: crowded classrooms, shared lunchrooms, winter conditions?

Once you have discussed the spread of disease, it's time to focus on public health measures. Have the students discuss some of the measures sought or taken by New York officials 100 years ago: education, housing reform, health clinics, home visits by public health officials, shorter work hours, and, in extreme cases, quarantine and isolation. Then have the students discuss some of the measures that could be used to stop a disease from spreading through their school. Remind them that public health measures have to be taken carefully so that they don't disrupt daily life too much or violate people's civil liberties.

III. STEPS: The activity is probably best done as a group or class project.

1. To research past epidemics at their school, students are asked in this activity to seek out information from ap-propriate officials—like the school attendance officer and the school nurse. You may want to talk to these people in advance and explain to them what the students are doing and what they are looking for. Essentially, the students are seeking to find answers to the following questions: When was the last epidemic, who got sick first, who got sick later, how many students were infected altogether, and when did the epidemic came to a halt? Obviously, privacy is an issue here. But students need not get names, just overall numbers and patterns.

2. If researching a past school epidemic is not an option, you might direct students to books or encyclopedia articles about famous epidemics of yesterday and today: The great influenza epidemic of 1918 is one possibility for yesterday; AIDS is the obvious choice for today.

3. Once they have researched epidemics, it's time for them to think of measures to prevent or control future ones.

4. Finally, students are asked to present the measures they would take to prevent or control an outbreak of disease at their school. There are several options, such as a report, a visual display of data, or an informational poster. You can put these on display in the classroom or school for oth-ers to look at. Another option is to put on a kind of class play. Have the students pretend that a disease is spreading through their school. Different students can play different roles: as sick students, healthy students, teachers, adminis-trators, maintenance and cafeteria people, and the school's nurse or nursing staff.

Ask Yourself!

1. What features of this lesson are influenced by a social-constructivist view of learning?

2. What kinds of thinking is the teacher trying to promote? Explain your answer.

3. What cultural tools are used in this lesson? What kinds of affordances do they provide?

Courtesy of Thirteen WNET New York.

M s. O'Neill organized her third-grade class into groups for mathematics. Each group was given a bag of money and asked to find out the total amount of money in the bag. The group you will read about had four members, two boys and two girls. Ms. O'Neill walked by the group and overheard the following interaction:

Maria: 8, 9, 9, and 8 . . . how much is it . . . 17, right?

Carla: Yeah, that's what I did.

Maria: Yeah, then you carry the 1, that's 9, and 9 is 18.

Wilson: *She wrote, "Oh, W . . , I like you."*

Maria: Carry the 1, is 2 . . . $2.89.

Andy: *You like her, too?*

Maria: $5.00 it says there.

Wilson: *No.*

Maria: Is 2 dollars 80 . . . 89 cents.

Carla: 89 cents?

Wilson: *You like, you like Andrea?*

Maria: Wait and that's a . . . 4 minus 2 equals 2.

Wilson: *She lives downtown.*

Maria: And 10 minus 7 is 3.

Carla: Okay.

Maria: So, erase the answer, just erase 8 and a 7 . . . that's it.

Andy: *I don't want her phone number. I hate . . . .*

Wilson: *You goin' crazy. You all crazy.*

Andy: *Like this. Me and J . . . we the only people that Andrea likes.*

Maria: And then write 13 cents.

Andy: *She don't like you.*

Maria: Wait, you don't have to write the cents.

Carla: Okay, I gotta go.

Wilson: *Then why's she always looking at me?*

 Reflection for Action

Maria, Andy, Wilson, and Carla were asked to work together on a math task. Ms. O'Neill hoped that they would learn from one another and help one another understand the task. Are they working together well? Is this group effective? Why do you think so? Do you think they are learning mathematics? Who is most helpful in the group? How might a teacher help students work together? What should you do with this particular group?

Guiding Questions

- How do various theoretical perspectives describe the means by which students can learn from peers?
- How effective is tutoring? What processes are involved?
- What do teachers need to consider when having students work in larger groups?
- What kinds of tasks are suitable for groups of students?
- What is the role of the teacher when using a peer-learning strategy?
- Do diverse learners benefit from peer learning?
- Can peer learning be used effectively with students who have special needs?

CHAPTER OVERVIEW

Learning from peers, as discussed in this chapter, can involve active information processing and the more complex cognition that is described earlier in this book. In this chapter, we lay out different theoretical perspectives on peer learning and describe how these perspectives define the means by which peers can promote learning. The purpose of the chapter is to help you understand how to select a peer-learning technique to fit your instructional goals. To assist you in doing so, the chapter explains the mechanisms and processes through which peer learning can lead to the acquisition of skills and knowledge in widely differing classroom situations. We discuss peer-learning techniques in the context of both one-on-one tutoring and larger, heterogeneous groups. We also consider key issues in the use of peer learning in the classroom, including the quality of students' discourse, the kinds of tasks that teachers may choose, the role of the teacher in using peer learning, and assessing the outcomes of peer learning.

Perspectives on Peer Learning

Most people have worked in groups, helped another student with schoolwork, received help with schoolwork, or had some experience with tutoring either as a tutor or a tutee. All these experiences involve peers working together to improve some aspect of academic performance. Another benefit of peer learning is that it fosters greater interaction and respect among diverse students. Peer learning is often recommended as a teaching strategy, and both students and teachers can respond well to its use. Many state and national curriculum standards include recommendations about the use of groups and other peer-learning situations to enhance critical thinking, conceptual understanding, and other higher-order skills. Students often enjoy interacting with one another. Teachers frequently find that the presence of other students can serve as a key instructional resource. Acceptance by peers is linked to many positive outcomes in school, such as satisfaction with school, high academic performance, and positive beliefs about academic competence (Hymel, Bowker, & Woody, 1993; Wentzel, 1994; Wentzel & Asher, 1995; Wentzel, Battle, & Looney, 2001). The use of collaborative and cooperative learning in classrooms has the potential to provide the social and emotional support students need from their peers.

Peer learning can be organized in a variety of ways. The tasks assigned, the rewards that are contingent on completion of the task, and the size and makeup of the group in which children work together influence the success of peer learning. Too often, however, teachers do not connect specific types of peer learning to instructional goals or give enough consideration to issues of assessment of student learning.

In the opening vignette, you were asked to decide whether the third-grade group was effective. You have only a brief sample of the children's conversation on which to base your decision. What did you think of the students' interactions? Were they on-task? What makes a group effective? Was the group effective as a social unit? Were the children learning? How can you tell? How can groups be formed so that they are effective for both social and cognitive outcomes? This chapter will provide some answers to these questions.

(Digital Vision)

The opportunity to exchange ideas and work with other students can have important social and cognitive outcomes.

Theoretical Orientations toward Learning from Peers

In this section of the chapter, we describe a variety of theoretical orientations toward learning from or with peers. These orientations are drawn from a variety of subdisciplines such as social, cognitive, and developmental psychology. Depending on the perspective adopted, the reasons for why peer learning might be effective differ. In the pages that follow, we will outline these perspectives and their implications.

Many of the original theories of cooperative learning were strongly influenced by social-psychological principles (Deutsch, 1949). The general principle underlying these theories is **interdependence** (Johnson & Johnson, 1991, 2008). Interdependence is a condition in which group members' goal accomplishments are linked together. According to social-motivational theory, cooperation and competition are two sides of the same coin. They are the **goal structures** of the task and characterize the manner in which students relate to others who are also working toward a particular goal. They both focus on the relationships among the goals of the participants in a group activity. In a competitive context, when one individual accomplishes his or her goals, other participants cannot. This is called **negative interdependence**. For example, when one individual is selected as the valedictorian of a high school class, others cannot be selected, because only one person can receive that honor. When one person succeeds, others must fail. This is the essence of competition. In a cooperative context, in contrast, no one can accomplish his or her goals unless everyone does. This is called **positive interdependence**. The success of the group is dependent on everyone in the group succeeding. A soccer team is an example of a cooperatively interdependent group. No one on the team succeeds unless everyone does.

Table 9.1 summarizes the kinds of positive outcomes that can result from cooperative learning. The table presents conclusions drawn from a review of more than 300 studies of cooperative, competitive, and individualistic learning. It is important to remember that positive outcomes such as those listed in the table do not occur without careful planning and implementation.

There are two different approaches toward creating the kind of interdependence that is necessary for a cooperative group: the social-motivational perspective and the social-cohesion perspective. In describing these perspectives, we give examples of specific techniques associated with each. Later in the chapter we refer back to these techniques to illustrate the kinds of decisions that teachers make when adopting a particular approach and their implications for other aspects of classroom practice.

The Social-Motivational Perspective

As you read about the various perspectives on peer learning, you will see that each of them fits with certain types of instructional goals. You will also see that many decisions a teacher makes are influenced by his or her perspective on peer learning. A social-motivational approach to

interdependence A condition in which group members' goal accomplishments are linked together.

goal structure The manner in which students relate to others who are also working toward a particular goal.

negative interdependence A condition that exists when, in order for one person to succeed in accomplishing his or her goals, others must fail to meet their goals.

positive interdependence A condition that exists when the success of each individual depends on all group members being successful.

TABLE 9.1
Outcomes of Cooperative Learning

Achievement Gains

Cooperative learning is more successful than individual learning.

Cooperative learning is more successful than competition among peers.

Individualistic learning and competitive learning produce similar results.

Additional Gains for Students Engaged in Cooperative Learning

Develop more positive relationships with peers.

Exhibit greater social competence.

Retain information longer.

Show higher levels of reasoning, critical thinking, and metacognition.

Show higher levels of creativity.

Exhibit more positive attitudes toward subject matter.

Source: Johnson, D. W., & Johnson, R. T. (1989). *Cooperation and competition: Theory and research.* Edina, MN: Interaction Book. Company. Reprinted with permission of D. W. Johnson.

individual accountability Each student is responsible for improving his or her performance.

creating interdependence relies on the use of rewards or recognition for group productivity. Individuals are motivated to work together to achieve rewards or attain recognition. Techniques derived from this perspective include Teams–Games–Tournaments, or TGT (De Vries & Edwards, 1973); Team-Accelerated Instruction, or TAI (Slavin, 1984); Cooperative Integrated Reading and Composition, or CIRC (Madden, Slavin, & Stevens, 1986); and Student Teams Achievement Division, or STAD (Slavin, 1986). The basic premise of these techniques is that students will be motivated to work together and help one another because the group as a whole will be rewarded or will receive recognition. Thus, if one person is not working to help the group, the whole group suffers. Interdependence is created by the use of rewards or the promise of recognition. STAD is one of the most thoroughly researched cooperative learning techniques.

The nearby Taking It to the Classroom box summarizes some of the key steps in using STAD. The cooperative aspect typically follows general instruction by the teacher and provides the students with an opportunity to rehearse that material. The teacher makes the key decisions about the content to be taught, the kinds of tests to be given, and the kinds of rewards or recognition that will be used. The teacher retains the primary responsibility for instruction.

In STAD, each student takes an individual test. The teacher ensures **individual accountability** through the use of improvement points. Each student is responsible for improving his or her performance. The teacher first calculates a baseline score for each student. The teacher then determines the numbers of improvement points necessary in order to earn specific numbers of team points. For example, students whose test performance exceeds their baseline score by 5 points may earn 3 team points. Students who already excel simply need to stay within a specified range of high performance in order to bring the maximum number of points to their team. Team scores are created by adding up the team points generated by each individual.

A reward or recognition is given to teams with high levels of achievement. Again, teachers must decide how many teams to reward or recognize and how to do so. The reward should be one that is valued by students. Although there is cooperation among members of a group, the groups compete with other groups in the class. Thus, there is within-group cooperation and between-group competition. The teacher's goal is to increase the students' motivation. If the success of only one group is acknowledged, some of the benefits of cooperation may be lost in the competition between groups.

Taking It to the Classroom

Implementing STAD

The following is a typical four-step procedure that teachers might use to implement STAD (Student Teams Achievement Division) cooperation in their classrooms:

1. *Before lesson.* Students are grouped into four- to six-member heterogeneous teams.

2. *During lesson.* The teacher presents the information to be learned, using various instructional strategies (e.g., lecture or videotape presentation).

3. *Peer learning.* After students have been exposed to the information, they work together to learn it. For example, the teacher gives the students a worksheet that reviews the lecture material. Students share information to help each other.

4. *After lesson.* The teacher gives each student an individual test. The tests are scored based on each student's improvement from a prior test performance. Teams with the highest improvement scores earn a reward of their choice.

Among the important features of the social-motivational approach to peer learning are the use of heterogeneous groups, individual accountability in the form of quizzes, improvement points for calculating overall group performance, and the use of recognition and reward in response to group performance. Interdependence is created and maintained by the use of team points for individual performance. All students are expected to help one another because it is in everyone's interest to gain as many points as possible. The key mechanism promoting interdependence is motivation. The strengths of STAD include successful motivation of all kinds of learners because each student has a reason to participate. The focus on improvement shifts attention from overall levels of performance to individual accountability for improvement. High-, low-, and average-achieving students have the opportunity to contribute equally to the team's points and subsequent recognition. A weakness of STAD is that it focuses on lower-level cognitive objectives. Because students use prepared answer sheets to respond to their peers' efforts to answer questions, the cognitive levels of the tasks may remain quite low, focusing on factual recall and basic comprehension rather than on higher-level abilities. It would be very challenging to prepare answer sheets for responses to more open-ended questions.

It is difficult to maintain interdependence if students believe that they are unequal contributors to the group's performance. High-achieving students sometimes believe that working in groups puts them at a disadvantage, even though there is no strong evidence to support this belief (Slavin, 1995). Interdependence can be maintained only if all the participating students believe that they can contribute without risking ridicule or pressure. High-achieving students need to believe that they do not bear all the responsibility for achievement, and lower-achieving students need to believe that they can contribute to the group. A key feature of STAD that serves to maintain interdependence is that each student has the same opportunity to contribute to the team score, regardless of his or her actual level of performance. Thus, the high achievers are required to maintain a high level of performance in order to contribute to the group. The average and low achievers need to improve on their previous performances in order to contribute.

Slavin (1986) outlined a number of other cooperative learning techniques, such as TGT, CIRC, and TAI, that all rely on increased motivation as a result of group goals and individual accountability to promote learning. Some of these techniques were developed for specific subject areas, such as mathematics (TAI; Slavin, 1984) or reading and writing (CIRC; Madden et al., 1986). The development of CIRC, for example, was based on an analysis of research on how to teach reading and writing. Although a particular technique may be primarily social or primarily cognitive, many cooperative learning techniques include both social and cognitive strategies.

The Social-Cohesion Perspective

A social-cohesion approach to cooperative learning also relies on the principle of interdependence. From this perspective, students are motivated to help one another succeed because they care about one another. David and Roger Johnson, directors of the Cooperative Learning Institute at the University of Minnesota (www.co-operation.org), have conducted research on cooperative learning techniques since the 1970s. They developed the technique known as *Learning Together* (Johnson & Johnson, 1991).

Cooperative learning has five basic elements (Johnson & Johnson, 1991): positive interdependence, face-to-face promotive interaction, individual accountability and personal responsibility, interpersonal and small-group skills, and group processing. In Learning Together, a great deal of attention is given to the role of social skills. Students may not display the care and concern for others that are central to a social-cohesion approach, and teachers may have to spend much time helping them see others' perspectives, teaching them how to show respect in their responses to others, and providing encouragement and feedback. In using Learning Together, a teacher selects a lesson and identifies objectives both for the content and for social skills. The teacher must make a number of important decisions about the size of each group and which students make up a group. Typically, the teacher will form groups that are heterogeneous with respect to ability or other characteristics. Heterogeneous groups allow students to appreciate different perspectives on a task. The teacher must ensure that adequate materials are available and that students are assigned particular roles within the group. The teacher explains the task to the students and establishes positive interdependence among group members. One function of assigning roles within the group is to maintain that interdependence as students work together. The teacher must also establish

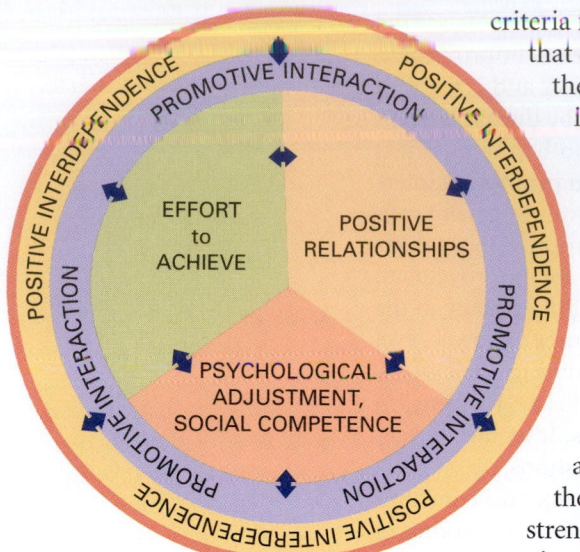

Figure 9.1 Outcomes of Cooperation

Source: Johnson, D. W., & Johnson, R. T. (1989). *Cooperation and competition: Theory and research.* Edina, MN: Interaction Book Company. Reprinted with the permission of D. W. Johnson.

criteria for evaluating the success of the group and develop a strategy for ensuring that each individual in the group is accountable for his or her performance. As the students work together on the task, the teacher needs to monitor their interactions and note any evidence of expected behaviors (e.g., providing encouragement to others). Once students have completed the assigned task, members of each group work together to discuss how well their group worked.

The focus of the group activity is on team building and the development of social skills. Roles are assigned to individuals (e.g., the *materials manager* is responsible for distributing and collecting materials). The roles are not necessarily cognitive in nature but often involve social management of the group. A group grade is assigned to the completed product. When they have finished their tasks, group members review the aspects of working together that they believed went well and try to identify areas of activity in which they might improve. For example, they might conclude that they asked good questions but did not provide enough encouragement. The strengths of Learning Together include its emphasis on social skills, the creation of a caring classroom climate, and students' involvement in evaluating how their groups work. It also stimulates many useful cognitive processes. Figure 9.1 shows that positive interdependence encourages interactions that have many favorable outcomes, such as increased effort, good social relations, and positive psychological adjustment and social competence.

You can see that if, as a teacher, you chose a social-cohesion perspective on cooperative learning, you would engage your students in very different activities (e.g., team building, social skill development) than you would if you chose a social-motivational perspective. If you adopted the latter approach, you would focus more on ways to provide recognition or reward. The tasks you assigned would also differ. If you chose a social-motivational perspective, you might assign tasks that require practice and rehearsal. If you chose a social-cohesion perspective, you might assign more open-ended tasks or tasks that require higher-order thinking skills.

Figure 9.2 presents an analysis of an example of Learning Together. The teacher of a fifth-grade class assigned the novel *Sara, Plain and Tall*. The academic objective was to have the students discuss and answer questions related to the main characters, the central theme of the story, the actions in the story, and the use of symbolism. The social objective was to have the students criticize ideas but not the students who proposed them.

The tasks on which children work using Learning Together can be complex, requiring students to coordinate their efforts in pursuit of a single goal, to monitor progress toward that goal, and to redirect their efforts if necessary. These are advanced cognitive skills, and if students do not also have good social skills and know how to disagree and question the direction of the group, many kinds of interpersonal issues can arise. Potential weaknesses of the technique include reliance on a group product, a form of assessment that can cause problems if parents or students object. The teacher needs to pay a great deal of attention to creating a classroom culture in which children treat one another with respect and care. Essentially, the teacher must help students develop the desire to help others. This can be quite difficult if the values experienced by children in their homes are also competitive and argue against helping others.

Among the important features of the social-cohesion approach to peer learning are the use of heterogeneous groups, face-to-face interaction, individual accountability, and group processing of the interactions that occur. This approach shares many features with the social-motivational approach, including its reliance on interdependence, its use of heterogeneous groups, and the use of group reward. Deliberate training of students in social skills offsets potentially negative group processes that may result from the heterogeneity of the group's members. The teacher also plays a key role in creating and maintaining a culture of care and respect. Group members' involvement in evaluating the interactions that occurred enhances their awareness of their behavior and contributes to positive interdependence.

The nearby What Kids Say and Do box presents the self-assessments of two groups of students working on a cooperative learning task. In this example, how students actually performed on the task is less important than their perceptions of how they worked together and how well they

Grade and Subject: Grade 5 language arts
Content: The novel *Sara, Plain and Tall*
Group Task: Using rotating roles, pairs answer questions on partner worksheets.

Grouping
- Students are assigned to heterogeneous groups.
- Pairs are selected by the teacher based on ability.
- Pairs work together for a single class period.

Positive interdependence
- Goal: to create one set of combined answers from the pair
- Reward: partner worksheets contribute to grade
- Role: assigned roles of Checker and Recorder

Individual accountability
- Each student has to write an answer for each question before the discussion begins.
- Each student is responsible for the pair's combined answer.
- Each student is responsible for a particular role within the pair.

Interpersonal and cognitive skills
- Direct teaching of the skill of criticizing ideas, not people
- Guided practice of the skill during the activity

Evaluation and reflection
- Each student is evaluated on his or her individual answers and on the pair's combined answer.
- There is an individual test on the content of the novel.
- Pairs reflect on their contributions using a self- and teammate-evaluation form.

Extension activity
- Students who complete the task before other pairs could help other pairs.
- Pairs who have completed the task could combine all the answers, then give a short oral presentation to the class.

Figure 9.2 Analysis of Learning Together Example
Source: From *Classroom connections: Understanding and using cooperative learning* by Abrami et al. © 1995. Reprinted with permission of Nelson, a division of Thomson Learning: www.thomsonrights.com. Fax 800 730–2215.

thought things were going. Students develop metacognitive skill slowly, and applying **metacognition**, or thinking about one's thinking, to complex social processes takes practice.

metacognition Thinking about one's own thinking.

Students in group 1 were positive in response to the question: What did your group do well? However, when asked how the group could better help them learn, their replies clearly indicated that there were problems. It is important to understand the nature of the question you ask as a teacher. Without asking the second question (What could your group do better to help you learn?), the teacher might not have understood that the students were having some difficulty.

In group 2, students did not just say that they were doing well. They were able to explain the processes that were going well (e.g., we take turns and answer questions). There was less conflicting information in the responses of group 2's members to the two questions. This kind of group processing is important in helping students regulate their behavior in the group in future interactions. This practice of self- and shared regulation is an important skill.

RIDE How do you think the group in the vignette at the beginning of the chapter would evaluate their interactions and performance?

Are These Approaches Effective?

Are social-motivational or social-cohesion approaches to peer learning effective? Experiments can be designed to determine whether one instructional intervention is better than another. The results of separate experiments can be combined through **meta-analysis**, a quantitative summary of a number of research studies that test the same hypotheses (e.g., is cooperative learning more effective than individualistic learning?). Meta-analyses of research studies that compared the effectiveness of cooperative, competitive, and individualistic learning conditions show strong support for the effectiveness of cooperative learning (Johnson & Johnson, 1989; see Table 9.1). Many of the studies included in these meta-analyses showed that cooperative learning techniques that reflected either a social-motivational or a social-cohesion perspective were more effective than other methods.

meta-analysis A quantitative review and summary of research on a topic.

What Kids Say and Do

Learning to Understand Group Processes

Students in a seventh-grade classroom provided the following comments about how they think they worked together on a cooperative learning task. Two groups evaluated how they worked.

Group 1
What did your group do well?

Sean: Our group took turns well and was quite organized.

Pablo: We did everything well.

Isabel: Well, kinda, we all answered the questions together in the first two sessions.

Stefan: Our group did well on everything.

What could your group do better to help you learn?

Sean: I think our group could work better together and others could contribute more.

Pablo: Pay attention to what is going on in the group.

Isabel: Well, some people could give other people a chance to answer the questions instead of just saying, "Well, she doesn't know it so I'll go." I thought that that was very rude and they should learn to give other people at least a minute instead of a second.

Stefan: I think if some people could pay attention to what we are discussing.

Group 2
What did your group do well?

Kirsten: Our group did a lot of things well. We work nicely together and never yell or call names (only if we are fooling around).

Kenisha: Our group did well answering open-minded questions and working as a group.

Brenda: I think so because we work well together and cooperate.

Tonya: My group is good because we work together and take turns answering questions. When we have to solve something and one of us doesn't agree, we try to talk about it.

What could your group do better to help you learn?

Kirsten: Our group sometimes needs to act more serious.

Kenisha: Our group could do better in staying on topic and not making so many weird jokes about it.

Brenda: I do not think that there was really anything the group can do to help me learn but we could be more serious.

Tonya: Our group could stay on topic and stop playing around a lot, but we still learned.

The research literature suggests that including group goals and individual accountability is necessary for successful peer learning. Slavin (1996) examined 52 studies of cooperative learning techniques and found that these techniques were particularly effective when they included group goals and individual accountability. When they did not include those factors, cooperative learning was no more effective than individualistic learning.

Despite the positive effects of cooperative techniques that include group goals and individual accountability, many teachers do not believe in using rewards (Antil et al., 1998) and therefore do not use these techniques exactly as recommended. The research evidence supports the effectiveness of the techniques when they are used as designed. When teachers deviate from the recommended procedures, it is unclear how effective the altered technique is. When teachers choose not to use rewards or recognition when implementing their version of STAD, for example, they are eliminating a key component of the technique that contributes to achievement and positive interaction in heterogeneous groups. If the group incentive required by a social-motivational approach is not replaced by the kinds of effort needed by a social-cohesion approach, problems in group processes and productivity are highly likely. Similarly, efforts to use cooperative learning techniques with students who have learning disabilities can be ineffective if they do not include individual accountability (Jenkins & O'Connor, 2003). Slavin (1992) reported that the positive outcomes of cooperative learning without individual accountability are minimal, and this finding is supported by more recent research by McMaster and Fuchs (2002).

How Can I Use This?

What aspects of using groups would vary if you chose a social-motivation or social-cohesion approach to peer learning?

Social perspectives on peer learning do not directly address cognitive processes. A basic assumption of such techniques is that if students are motivated, good things will result. It is true that motivation is an important element of effective learning. However, "will without skill" is unlikely to lead to successful outcomes. A focus on cognitive mechanisms for group learning is quite different from a focus on social-motivational mechanisms. In the next section, we describe several types of peer learning that are influenced by different cognitive or developmental theories.

Cognitive–Elaboration Perspectives

Cognitive-elaboration approaches to peer learning are based on an information-processing approach. Peer interaction is used to amplify, or cognitively elaborate, the performance of basic information-processing activities such as encoding, activation of schemas, rehearsal, metacognition, and retrieval.

Encoding involves actively processing incoming information. Students with prior knowledge of a topic are more likely to encode new information effectively because they can link it to information that they already understand. Teachers can help students encode information more effectively by reminding them of what they already know or helping them activate existing *schemas*, or organized sets of knowledge about the topic. **Schemas** are the basic cognitive structures for organizing information. By practicing or rehearsing the information, students process it more deeply, making it easier to retrieve the information later. Performing these activities in the presence of peers will result in deeper processing and more active engagement (O'Donnell, Dansereau, Hythecker, et al., 1987). The presence of a peer can help students stay on-task, and feedback provided by a peer can help students decide when they need to check their understanding of the content they are trying to explain (O'Donnell & Dansereau, 1992).

An example of a peer-learning strategy that is consistent with a cognitive-elaboration approach is O'Donnell and colleagues' **Scripted Cooperation** (O'Donnell & Dansereau, 1992; O'Donnell, Dansereau, Hall, et al., 1987), which is based on information-processing theory. The nearby Taking It to the Classroom box summarizes the technique. An important aspect of Scripted Cooperation is that cognitive activities that are typically done by an individual are divided between partners. Students actively elaborate on the information, connecting it to information that they already know and making an active effort to make the new information memorable. The technique improves text processing because it emphasizes cognitive processes that are known to increase learning, such as rehearsal, metacognition, and elaboration.

Research has shown that Scripted Cooperation is a very effective strategy (O'Donnell & Dansereau, 1992). Not only do students perform better on tests related to the material when they work together, but they also perform better on subsequent tasks when they work alone (O'Donnell, Dansereau, Hall, et al., 1987). Scripted Cooperation has been used successfully by students as young as third graders (Rottman & Cross, 1990) with reading tasks, and a modified version of the script was used successfully with fifth graders learning to solve math problems (Zuber, 1992). It can also be used with students in high school and college. The

schema The basic cognitive structure for organizing information.

Scripted Cooperation A learning strategy in which students take turns summarizing materials and criticizing the summaries.

RIDE Would a more structured technique for interaction have helped the group described in the vignette at the beginning of the chapter?

Taking It to the Classroom

Implementing Scripted Cooperation

The following script is a typical four-step procedure that teachers might use to implement Scripted Cooperation in their classrooms:

1. *Before lesson.* Students are grouped into pairs. The teacher assigns one student the role of Initiator and the other student the role of Elaborator.
2. *During lesson.* Both students read the text on their own.
3. *Peer learning.* After 10 minutes of independent reading time, the Initiator summarizes what was read (without referring to his or her notes). The Elaborator listens, detects errors, then adds new elaborations.
4. *After lesson.* Together, the Initiator and the Elaborator reflect on their conversation and discuss how the material covered is connected to other things they know.

technique is highly structured, and with younger children, the teacher must provide numerous opportunities to learn basic skills such as summarizing, error detection, and elaboration. The technique is focused less on what students teach one another than on how the cooperative context can stimulate deeper processing, more focused activity, and a less demanding cognitive load on an individual student.

Noreen Webb's work also stems from a cognitive-elaboration perspective (1989, 1991, 1992). Much of it focuses on students' learning of mathematics. Webb has explored the effects of various types of groupings (i.e., heterogeneous, homogeneous, female-dominated, male-dominated) on achievement. Webb's groups are more open-ended than the dyads that use Scripted Cooperation. The students decide how to participate, although training in how to do so is usually provided.

Webb and her colleagues found that students who participate actively in a group learn more than students who are passive, those who provide explanations achieve more than those who do not, and higher-quality explanations are associated with higher levels of achievement (Webb, 1989,1991,1992). High-level explanations are expressions of deeper processing and elaboration of content, and may aid in restructuring existing knowledge.

There are, however, a number of possible difficulties with this approach. First, not all students provide good explanations or are given an opportunity to do so. Typically, the more able students provide more explanations, and the less able or less experienced ones seek help and look for explanations. Webb and her colleagues have attempted to teach students how to seek appropriate help, with mixed success (Webb & Farivar, 1994). There is also the risk of amplifying differences in social status within a classroom. **Status differences** occur when peers see some students as being more valuable and having more to contribute than others. These differences may occur because of ability or because of more **diffuse status characteristics**, such as race, ethnicity, gender, or language of origin (Meeker, 1981).

Characteristics are considered *diffuse* if they have no direct bearing on task performance but are assumed to indicate greater or lesser capability to perform the task (Meeker, 1981). For example, girls might expect boys to perform certain tasks better than they do even though there may be no differences in performance based on gender. The reverse may also be true. Status differences and their implications are described in more detail later in the chapter.

Figure 9.3 compares social-motivational, social-cohesion, and cognitive-elaboration approaches to peer learning, along with their practical implications.

status differences Differences in status among individuals that influence their participation in group activities.

diffuse status characteristics Characteristics that have no direct bearing on task performance but are assumed to be indicators of greater or lesser capability to perform the task.

How Can I Use This?

When using cooperative learning in your class, what would you emphasize if you adopted a cognitive-elaboration approach to peer learning?

Cognitive-Developmental Perspectives

Peer learning includes cooperative learning, collaboration, and various forms of peer tutoring. Both Piagetian and Vygotskian theories provide a foundation for peer learning that focuses on development, but they differ in their emphasis on individual cognitive processes or social processes. The three theoretical perspectives described earlier (social motivational, social cohesion, and cognitive elaboration) all depend in part on Piagetian and/or Vygotskian theories. Both Piaget and Vygotsky stressed a constructivist approach to teaching and learning that involves both individual and social processes. A **constructivist perspective** suggests that individuals create meaning using their prior understandings to make sense of new experiences.

constructivist perspective A theoretical perspective that stresses the active role of the learner in building understanding and making sense of information.

assimilation An incorporation process in which an outside event is brought into one's way of thinking.

accommodation A modification process in which low-level schemas are transformed into higher-level schemas.

cognitive disequilibrium The experience of cognitive conflict.

Piagetian Theory Piaget developed a constructivist theory of cognitive development in which a child forms new conceptual structures as a result of interactions with his or her environment. Cognitive growth occurs through the process of adaptation and proceeds through the processes of **assimilation** (a process in which an outside event is brought into one's way of thinking) and **accommodation** (a process in which low-level schemas are transformed into higher-level schemas). Modifications to existing cognitive structures occur when a structure is changed in some way as a result of experiencing new objects or events. The individual seeks equilibrium or balance in the cognitive system, and when this balance is disrupted, he or she seeks to restore equilibrium. Peers may provide opportunities for others to experience **cognitive disequilibrium**, or cognitive conflict. For example, students may disagree about the solution of a problem. Through discussions and other activities, they may restore cognitive equilibrium by arriving at new understandings as they work together.

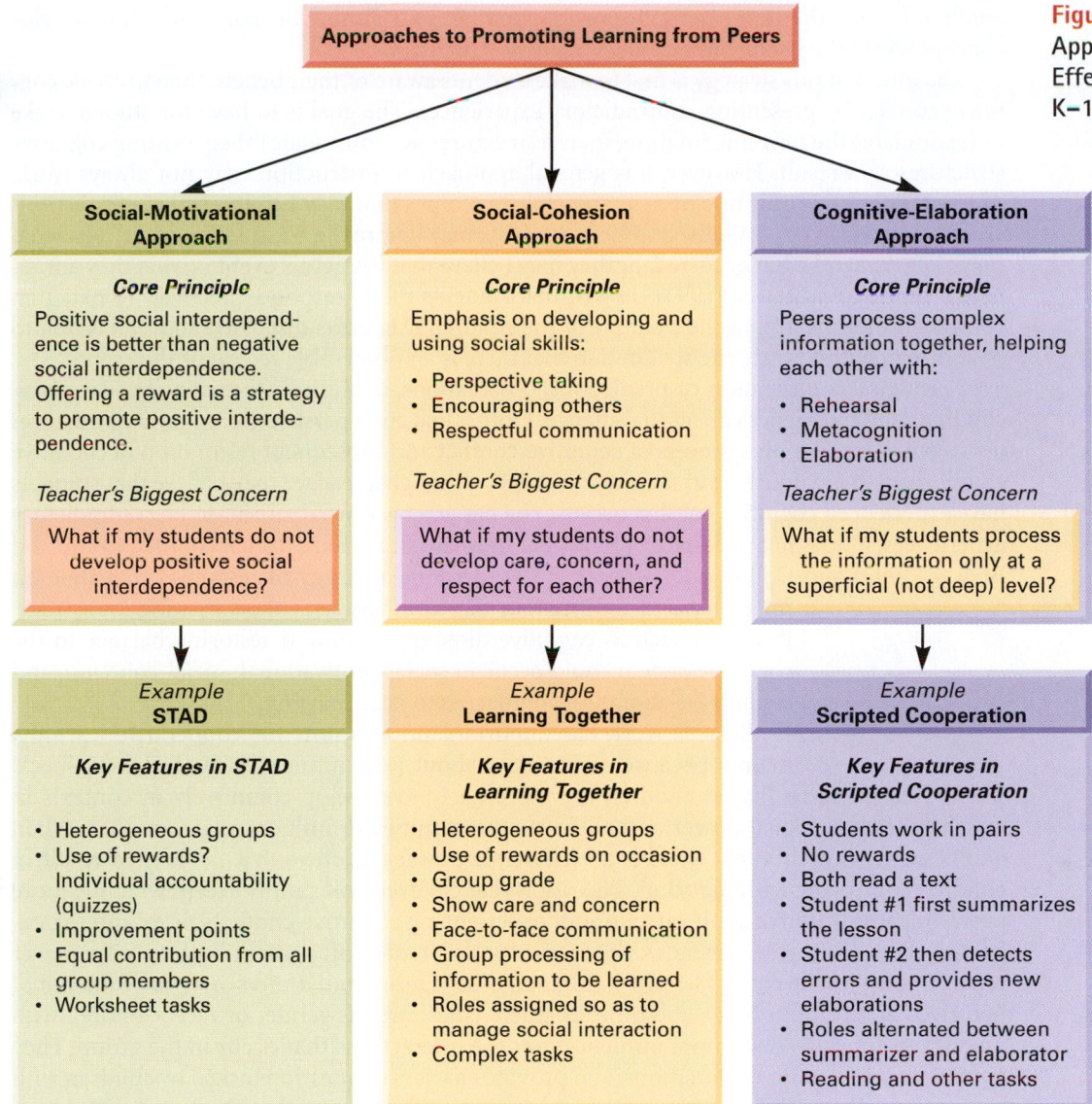

Figure 9.3 Three Theoretical Approaches to Implementing Effective Peer Learning in K–12 Classrooms

Approaches to Promoting Learning from Peers

Social-Motivational Approach	Social-Cohesion Approach	Cognitive-Elaboration Approach
Core Principle Positive social interdependence is better than negative social interdependence. Offering a reward is a strategy to promote positive interdependence.	***Core Principle*** Emphasis on developing and using social skills: • Perspective taking • Encouraging others • Respectful communication	***Core Principle*** Peers process complex information together, helping each other with: • Rehearsal • Metacognition • Elaboration
Teacher's Biggest Concern What if my students do not develop positive social interdependence?	*Teacher's Biggest Concern* What if my students do not develop care, concern, and respect for each other?	*Teacher's Biggest Concern* What if my students process the information only at a superficial (not deep) level?
Example **STAD**	*Example* **Learning Together**	*Example* **Scripted Cooperation**
Key Features in STAD • Heterogeneous groups • Use of rewards? Individual accountability (quizzes) • Improvement points • Equal contribution from all group members • Worksheet tasks	***Key Features in Learning Together*** • Heterogeneous groups • Use of rewards on occasion • Group grade • Show care and concern • Face-to-face communication • Group processing of information to be learned • Roles assigned so as to manage social interaction • Complex tasks	***Key Features in Scripted Cooperation*** • Students work in pairs • No rewards • Both read a text • Student #1 first summarizes the lesson • Student #2 then detects errors and provides new elaborations • Roles alternated between summarizer and elaborator • Reading and other tasks

Conceptual change teaching seeks to challenge students' existing concepts so as to create cognitive disequilibrium. Providing students with evidence that contradicts students' initial beliefs will require them to modify cognitive structures on the basis of new information. Through this process of adaptation, students build new cognitive structures.

A general approach to instruction that emerges from this notion is that the teacher first elicits students' expectations about a phenomenon, then gives them opportunities to test their predictions, uncover contradictory evidence, and contrast their expectations with their experiences (Neale, Smith, & Johnson, 1990). Teachers need to create conditions in which students are responsive to the data they gather. For example, in preparing for a unit of instruction on light and shadow, students might be asked to predict where their shadows will fall as they turn their bodies in the sunlight. Some students may respond with the expectation that their shadows will appear in front of their bodies. The teacher can challenge this expectation by providing experiences that contradict it. In this case, if the children are positioned sideways to the sun, their shadows will appear at their sides. The teacher needs to remind them that their predictions about what would happen were different from what actually happened. He or she must then ask them to think about why their predictions were not accurate. At the same time, the teacher should be aware that even though the contradictory information is available, students will not necessarily experience it as creating cognitive

conceptual change teaching A method of teaching that helps students understand concepts by challenging them to examine their ideas and identify shortcomings in them.

conflict. In fact, the new experience or information may simply be assimilated into a prior concept with little change in existing cognitive structures.

The intent of this strategy is first to make students aware of their beliefs, then to create cognitive conflict by presenting contradictory experiences. The goal is to have the students take in (assimilate) the new information, then restructure (accommodate) their existing cognitive structures as a result. However, this general approach to instruction may not always work. Accommodation is only one of many possible outcomes that may result when contradictions are presented (De Lisi & Golbeck, 1999). Students may ignore the contradiction between what they expected and what occurred, or they may believe that the actual event is what they anticipated. Chinn and Brewer (1993) showed that students rarely respond effectively to data that contradict their beliefs. In the example of the children's shadows discussed above, it is best to have other children trace the shadows so that there is an observable record of the event.

Through a combination of predictions, observations, and efforts to reconcile differences, children may experience conceptual change. From a Piagetian perspective, cognitive structures develop as a result of this process of **cognitive conflict** and subsequent restoration of cognitive equilibrium. It is important to keep in mind that, although a teacher may believe that students have experienced cognitive conflict because she has arranged what appear to be contradictory experiences, it does not necessarily follow that they have experienced such conflict. Chinn and Brewer (1993) and De Lisi and Golbeck (1999) describe a variety of responses that children might have to information that conflicts with their existing knowledge. Processes such as cognitive disequilibrium and restoring balance to the cognitive system could occur in social-motivational, social-cohesion, and cognitive-elaboration approaches to peer learning.

Piaget's work has important implications for cooperative learning, mainly because of his ideas about peer influence (De Lisi & Golbeck, 1999). According to Piaget, children are more likely to develop cognitively in contexts in which peers have equal power and all have opportunities to influence one another. When adults work with children, there is an inevitable power structure that is likely to result in children complying with the adult. The risk is that children will simply accept what the more powerful, authoritative adult says without experiencing cognitive conflicts or examining existing beliefs. Even when peers work together without an adult present in the group, power relations may not be equal. Certain children may have more status and power as a function of perceived ability, popularity, and other characteristics, such as gender or race. Children with high status typically have more influence over the interactions that occur in the group. They tend to say more, offer explanations, and provide answers to questions asked by children with lower status. Other children may simply go along with the ideas of these high-status children.

Vygotskian Theory A second approach to understanding collaboration is associated with Vygotskian theory. Vygotsky's perspective on development includes both cultural/societal and individual components.

There is a dialectical relationship between the child and the cultural environment: "In the process of development, the child not only masters the items of cultural experience but the habits and forms of cultural behavior, the cultural methods of reasoning" (Vygotsky, 1929, p. 415). Although the social environment provides models of performance and skill, children must still master the skills for themselves. Moshman (1982) refers to this mutual influence between the individual and the environment as **dialectical constructivism**; in this view, knowledge lies in the continual interaction between the individual and the environment.

The characteristics of a student's environment are very important. According to Hogan and Tudge (1999), "The presence or absence of certain types of institutions (e.g., schools), technologies, and semiotic tools (e.g., pens or computers) as well as variations in the values, beliefs, and practices of different cultural groups are interdependent with differences in ways in which children's development proceeds" (p. 41). An example of an effort to provide an environment that is conducive to positive development is the Head Start program. It was founded to improve the quality of the environments available to young children so that their cognitive development could be enhanced. The characteristics of the learner are also important, because traits such as motivation, work ethic, and curiosity affect the degree to which learners work to master the skills they need to participate in their community.

Appendix
Piaget's Contribution
Piaget is one of the theorists who describes how learning occurs and how students construct knowledge (PRAXIS™, I.A.1; INTASC, Principle 2).

cognitive conflict Experience of conflict when new information does not agree with existing knowledge.

How Can I Use This?
How would you determine whether a child has experienced cognitive conflict?

Appendix
Vygotsky's Contribution
Vygotsky is one of the theorists who describes how learning occurs and how students construct knowledge (PRAXIS™, I.A.1; INTASC, Principle 2).

dialectical constructivism The theory that considers knowledge to lie in the continual interaction between the individual and the environment.

What Does This Mean to Me?
Can you give an example of an occasion when you experienced dialectical constructivism?

A second key idea concerns what Vygotsky termed the **zone of proximal development.** According to Vygotsky, the zone of proximal development is a level of competence on a task in which the student cannot yet master the task on his or her own but can perform the task with appropriate guidance and support from a more capable partner. Assistance comes from a more competent child or adult who can recognize the learner's current level of functioning and the kind of performance that might be possible, and provide appropriate support. Cognitive development occurs as the child internalizes the processes that take place in the course of interacting with a more competent adult or peer. The child's cognitive structures are reorganized, and in later interactions the child may show evidence of having developed new cognitive structures by explaining his or her thinking or actions.

From a Vygotskian perspective, pairing an adult with a child is most likely to promote cognitive growth. The adult may be expected to have some skill in recognizing the child's current level of functioning and adjusting instruction to support the child's efforts. Webb (1991) noted that the kind of help a learner receives must match his or her needs. One might reasonably expect adults to more effectively provide the level of help needed by a learner. The zone of proximal development is jointly established by the participants (Hogan & Tudge, 1999) and is best accomplished when one partner is aware of the other's current level of functioning and is able to prompt, hint, or otherwise scaffold or support the other partner's developing competence. **Scaffolding** is the guidance, support, and tutelage (e.g., hints, tips, cues, reminders) provided by a teacher during social interaction designed to advance students' current level of skill and understanding.

If adults are not available, more competent peers can support the learning of a less competent student. However, peers need assistance in providing the appropriate level of help. Person and Graesser (1999) have shown, for example, that naive tutors are not very good at identifying the tutee's current level of functioning and scaffolding the tutee's efforts so that his or her performance improves. Webb and Farivar (1994) have clearly shown that it is difficult to train young students to identify or act within another learner's zone of proximal development. However, King and her colleagues (King, Staffieri, & Adelgais, 1998) show that with appropriate instructional support, peers can respond effectively to one another's efforts. We return to these issues later in the chapter when we discuss tutoring and strategies for assisting peers. Table 9.2 presents a summary of the different theoretical perspectives described thus far and the mechanisms through which peers can promote learning.

In the preceding sections, we have discussed various theoretical approaches to peer learning. The key difference among these perspectives is the mechanism that allows peer interaction to promote learning. This is important for teachers, because if they do not understand *how* peers promote learning, they will not make appropriate decisions about the size of groups, the kinds of skills needed, how to participate with groups, what kinds of tasks to assign, and other instructional choices. Table 9.3 summarizes the implication of the various theoretical perspective for classroom decisions.

In the next few sections, we will describe strategies for peer learning that range from working in pairs to working in complex heterogeneous groups. Many students have little experience working in groups, and new teachers are often reluctant to try group learning because of concerns about **classroom management** (Slavin, 1995). They fear losing control of the classroom or having a noisy room that might draw negative attention from the principal or other teachers. Organizing and managing students is easier when they are working in pairs than when they are working in larger groups, and managing pair learning is also easier than managing learning in more complex groups. There are some tasks (discussed later) that are best carried out by larger groups. However, if neither you nor your students have experience in working with or in groups, it is wiser to start with some simple structures and gradually build up to more complex ones once you are sure that the students have the skills (both cognitive and social) to coordinate their efforts.

zone of proximal development A level of competence on a task in which the student cannot yet master the task on his or her own but can accomplish that same task with appropriate guidance from a more capable partner.

scaffolding The guidance, support, and tutelage provided by a teacher during social interaction designed to advance the student's current level of skill and understanding.

classroom management Teacher behaviors and management techniques that result in a healthy learning environment, generally free of behavior problems.

TABLE 9.2

Mechanisms for Promoting Learning from a Variety of Theoretical Perspectives

Theoretical Perspective	Mechanism for Promoting Learning
Social motivational	Interdependence created through motivation
Social cohesion	Interdependence created through care and concern
Cognitive elaboration	Deeper processing of information
Cognitive development—Piaget	Adaptation as a result of cognitive conflict
Cognitive development—Vygotsky	Modeled behavior that is scaffolded and internalized

TABLE 9.3
Key Considerations in Cooperative Learning from a Variety of Theoretical Perspectives

	Theoretical Perspectives				
	Social–Behavioral		Cognitive		
				Developmental	
Considerations	Motivation	Social Cohesion	Elaboration	Piagetian	Vygotskian
Goals/incentives	Rewards essential	Rewards nonessential	Rewards nonessential	Rewards nonessential	Rewards nonessential
Group size	Large (4–6)	Large (4–6)	Small (2–4)	Small	Dyads
Group composition	Heterogeneous	Heterogeneous	Heterogeneous/ homogeneous	Homogeneous	Heterogeneous
Tasks	Rehearsal	Rehearsal/ integrative	Rehearsal/ integrative	Exploratory	Skills
Teacher role	Director	Facilitator	Facilitator	Facilitator	Model/guide
Potential problems	Use of reward Group size	Poor social skills Social loafing Cognitive loafing	Poor help-giving Unequal participation	Inactive No cognitive conflict	Poor help-giving Providing adequate time/dialogue
Averting problems	Improvement scores	Team building	Direct instruction in help-giving	Structuring controversy	Direct instruction in help-giving
	Simpler tasks	Conflict resolution strategies	Modeling help-giving		Modeling help-giving
	Social cohesion	Discuss group process	Scripting interaction		

Source: O'Donnell, A. M., & O'Kelly, J. B. (1994). Learning from peers: Beyond the rhetoric of positive results. *Educational Psychology Review, 6,* 321–349. Reprinted with the permission of Springer Science & Business Media.

Tutoring

tutoring An instructional experience in which one student typically teaches another student who is less skilled.

Tutoring is typically conducted by pairing one tutor and one tutee. Many students benefit from tutoring. Students who experience one-on-one tutoring gain greater understanding of content, report being more motivated, and work faster (Slavin, 1987a). According to Bloom (1984), students who receive one-on-one tutoring perform at levels significantly above those achieved by comparable students who experience regular instruction.

Evidence for the Effectiveness of Tutoring

There is a great deal of research evidence supporting the benefits of tutoring (Cohen, Kulick, & Kulick, 1982; Person & Graesser, 1999). In a meta-analysis conducted by Cohen and colleagues (1982), the benefits were particularly evident in studies that were of short duration, employed structured tutoring, focused on lower-level skills, used tests developed by the instructor, and typically focused on mathematics. Thirty-eight of the fifty-two studies examined by Cohen and colleagues (1982) found positive effects for the tutee. More recent evidence in support of tutoring comes from an evaluation of the America Reads tutoring program, a component of the AmeriCorps National and Community Service program. Students who participated in tutorial activities were generally in the low-to-average range in terms of reading skills. Students at all grade levels improved their reading performance over the course of their participation in the program. A number of practices were associated with positive outcomes: (1) Tutors met with their tutees at least three times a week, (2) formal evaluations of tutorial programs were conducted, (3) tutors received training beforehand and additional training during the course of the program, and (4) the programs were moderately or fully implemented as designed.

(PhotoDisc, Inc./Getty Images)

A learner's competence increases when another person is aware of the learner's current level of functioning and provides appropriate assistance.

Tutoring often takes place between more skilled and less skilled students. Typically, the goal is to improve the performance of the less skilled student. Vygotsky's theory of cognitive development is frequently drawn upon to explain the benefits of such tutoring. The tutor's efforts to scaffold the tutee's learning by modeling behaviors, offering prompts, and providing feedback are thought to be operating in the tutee's zone of proximal development. Chi and colleagues (Chi et al., 2001) define *scaffolding* as "any kind of guidance that is more than a confirmatory or negative feedback" (p. 473). It includes the kinds of prompts, hints, and splicing of information described by Graesser and colleagues (Graesser & Person, 1994; Graesser, Person, & Magliano, 1995; Person & Graesser, 1999). For example, the tutor might ask "What's going on here?" to prompt the tutee to describe a process. Tutoring is a skill that can be taught and can be progressively improved with further training and practice.

(Corbis Digital Stock)

Peers can support each other's learning by providing help but may need assistance in providing appropriate hints, prompts, or explanations.

Structured tutoring in particular is most effective in improving learning. It provides individualized instruction that is consistent across many educational settings (Lindren, Meier, & Brigham, 1991; Slavin & Madden, 1989) and reduces some of the variability in outcomes that occurs as a result of differences among tutors. Tutees' academic achievement increases more if they participate in a structured tutoring program (Lindren et al., 1991).

Tutoring also benefits the tutor (Chi et al., 2001). As they plan, prepare for, and carry out their tasks, tutors improve their understanding of the content they are teaching (Cohen et al., 1982). This is not unexpected. Tutors have opportunities to explain content to another person, and providing explanations has been shown to promote achievement (Webb, 1991, 1992). Moreover, tutors may gain metacognitive experience about their own understanding of the content (Baker & Brown, 1984). In other words, as a tutor tries to explain a concept to a tutee, she may realize that she does not understand it as well as she thought she did. For teachers worried that high-ability students might not receive the same benefits from tutoring that low-ability students receive, it is important to know that high-ability students—when asked which instructional practices seemed most fair to them—selected peer tutoring as the fairest way to help everyone learn (Thorkildsen, 1993).

What Does This Mean to Me?
Can you explain why different theoretical perspectives on peer learning might influence your decisions in the classroom? Refer to Figure 9.3.

Processes Involved in Tutoring

We know from the research literature that tutoring helps students; the literature also tells us that tutoring is a process that can be improved in most situations. Naive tutors may be inhibited by politeness rules (Person et al., 1995). For example, a tutor may be reluctant to tell a tutee that he or she is wrong. Tutors may also provide inappropriate feedback to their tutees (Person & Graesser, 1999). Despite these problems, one-on-one tutoring is effective. Person and Graesser (1999) describe tutoring in terms of five steps:

1. The tutor asks a question (or presents a problem for the student to solve).

2. The student answers the question.

3. The tutor gives feedback on the answer.

4. The tutor and the student collaborate to improve the quality of the answers.

5. The tutor assesses the student's understanding of the answer (Person & Graesser, 1999, pp. 71–72).

(Corbis Digital Stock)

Tutoring can provide a variety of benefits for both the tutor and tutee.

Steps 1–3 are typical of the kinds of interactions that may occur between a teacher and a student in the context of whole-class instruction. Steps 4 and 5 rarely occur in that context because of time constraints and the large number of students in most classrooms. Step 4 is the one in which the tutor is most likely to work with the tutee in the zone of proximal development. It is during this step that scaffolding is provided (Chi et al., 2001; Graesser et al., 1995).

In most tutoring situations, the tutor dominates the interaction. McArthur, Stasz, and Zmuidzinas (1990) analyzed the activities of tutors and found that 53% of them could have elicited responses from students. Tutees' responses are important because their quality contributes to the effectiveness of the tutoring process (Chi et al., 2001). The efforts of tutees to understand the content being taught, in light of their existing knowledge, may be the most valuable aspect of tutoring. However, if tutors are not trained, the quality of their instructional efforts will vary. Therefore, it is unlikely that the activities of the tutor alone are responsible for the benefits of tutoring (VanLehn et al., 2003). Indeed, the tutee's motivation may be very influential to the outcomes from tutoring (Derry & Potts, 1998).

Chi and her colleagues (Chi et al., 2001) conducted two studies to examine why tutoring works. The tutors were college students who tutored eighth-grade students about the circulatory system, using a prepared text consisting of 86 sentences. Each sentence was printed on a separate page. The tutor and the tutee worked on one sentence at a time. The tutors' explanations were correlated with student learning, as were the students' responses to scaffolding efforts (e.g., prompts, hints, comprehension questions). In a second study, tutors were trained to prompt tutees for knowledge construction responses, using a set of content-free prompts (e.g., What makes you say that? What happens next?). This procedure is similar to that used by King in her studies of peer tutoring (King, 1991; King et al., 1998), described later in the chapter. The use of prompts resulted in more episodes of deep scaffolding, in which there were longer exchanges between tutors and tutees. Students who were prompted were more constructive overall, displaying more of what they knew and putting more effort into the exchanges.

Figures 9.4 and 9.5 present examples of *shallow* and *deep* scaffolding. In the first episode (Figure 9.4), the tutor and the tutee are working with the statement "These arteries branch into arterioles and then capillaries." The exchange is described as *shallow* scaffolding because although the tutor asks questions, the questions do not seem to require deep processing. The exchange remains superficial, with the tutor asking questions whose answers do not require complex explanations or reasoning. The key question asked in this episode is "And what would you expect to be passed back and forth?" In this question, the tutor provides a description of what happens (something is passed back and forth). All the tutee needs to do is to identify a substance. The tutee in this example commented, "This is where diffusion happens." The tutor could have checked the tutee's understanding of this process by asking, "How does diffusion happen?" Instead, the tutor supplies a statement of what that process is. The tutor does not ask the tutee to explain it, then to work with him to improve the answer and describe what is being diffused.

In contrast, Figure 9.5 is an example of *deep* scaffolding. In the example of *shallow* scaffolding, the tutor and the tutee worked on a sentence that described part of the structure of the circulatory system. The statement itself focused them on a descriptive kind of exchange. In contrast, the interaction in Figure 9.5 focuses on a statement that describes a process. The tutor and the tutee are working on the statement "If a substance can pass through a membrane, the membrane is permeable to it." The first question asked by the tutor is "How would that relate back to the capillary walls?" To answer this question, the tutee must provide a response that shows connected knowledge. When the tutee struggles

Sentence 84) These arteries branch into arterioles and then into capillaries.

    S: Like arteries do.
    T: Uh-huh.
    S: And then.
    T: So what would you assume comes next?
    S: After capillaries?
    T: Uh-huh.
    S: Can I look? [Pause.] Venules. So then, you have venules because they go to the capillaries, to the venules, is that how you say it? To the veins.
    T: And we're inside the lungs now?
    S: What?
    T: Is where this, where the picture, is inside the lungs?
    S: Well this is here. This is where diffusion happens.
    T: **And what would you expect to be passed back and forth?**
    S: Oxygen and carbon dioxide. Do you want me to put that?
    T: You don't have to.
    S: O.k.

Note: S = student; T = tutor.

Figure 9.4 An Example of Shallow Scaffolding

Source: Chi, M. T. H., Siler, S. A., Jeong, H., Yamauchi, T., & Hausmann, R. G. (2001). Learning from human tutoring. *Cognitive Science, 25,* 526. Copyright by the Cognitive Science Society.

to respond, the tutor again asks whether the tutee can explain. After the tutee begins to explain, the tutor further probes the tutee's understanding. The tutor is able to draw out a complex explanation by asking high-level questions and prompting the tutee for more information. When tutors ask high-level questions, the result is greater depth of processing by the tutee.

In sum, one-on-one tutoring benefits both tutor and tutee and can be done with varying degrees of effectiveness. The outcomes of tutoring improve when tutors are trained to be less dominant in their interactions with tutees and to provide prompts and scaffold the tutee's learning. In the sections that follow, we will describe some specific examples of tutoring.

What Does This Mean to Me?
Have you ever tutored someone? What was difficult or rewarding about the experience?

Sentence 60) If a substance can pass through a membrane, the membrane is permeable to it.

    S: So, it explains itself: If something is permeable to something, then that thing can pass through the other thing.
    T: So how would the—
    S: And if it's impermeable, it can't.
    T: **And how would that relate back to the capillary walls?**
    S: Well the capillary walls. . . .
    T: Can you explain?
    S: Well this is how I learned it.
    T: Uh-huh.
    S: In the cell, it's made up of these things and then it has these protein things like this. They're really, really big. And then there's a little substance like oxygen and it can just go through here, but a big substance like sugar which is tons of letters has to go through the protein first.
        :
    T: **And how does, how does that relate to the cell membrane or the capillary?**
    S: Well if it's too big, if something's too big, to go into the capillary membrane through the capillary membrane, it can't because the capillary membrane is only one cell thick, but then maybe if it has protein, it can. O.k.
    T: O.k.
    S: Alright.

Note: S = student; T = tutor.

Figure 9.5 An Example of Deep Scaffolding

Source: Chi, M. T. H., Siler, S. A., Jeong, J., Yamauchi, T., & Hausmann, R. G. (2001). Learning from human tutoring. *Cognitive Science, 25,* 527. Copyright by the Cognitive Science Society.

Tutoring Diverse Learners

A number of tutoring programs have been developed for use with culturally and linguistically diverse students in urban areas. Two such programs are described in this section. Although they were developed for use with a very diverse group of students who were generally of low socioeconomic status (SES), the techniques can be used with all kinds of learners.

Classwide Peer Tutoring   Classwide peer tutoring (CWPT) was developed by researchers at the University of Kansas with the help of classroom teachers. This technique includes elements of both cooperation and competition, and is influenced by a social-motivational perspective on peer learning. Its purpose is to improve overall performance in basic academic skills (Delquadri et al., 1986), particularly for students who are culturally and linguistically diverse and come from poor families. Rather than having less skilled students tutored by more skilled peers, CWPT involves the entire class in tutoring activities. Students are either randomly paired or matched by ability or language proficiency. Students with limited English proficiency are initially paired with other students who speak their native language but whose English is better.

At the beginning of a week, all the pairs of students are assigned to one of two competing teams. One person serves as a tutor for the first 10 minutes, then the partners switch roles. The teacher initially presents the content to the whole class and uses the peer-tutoring sessions for practice and rehearsal. The tutor asks the tutee a question about an instructional item, such as a math fact or a spelling word. If the tutee answers correctly, he or she is awarded 2 points. The tutor has an answer sheet so that the answer can be checked. If the answer is incorrect, the tutor provides the correct response, asks the tutee to write or say the correct answer three times, thus providing **positive practice**, and gives the tutee 1 point for correcting the mistake. Positive practice involves practicing the correct answer after making a mistake. If the tutee fails to correct the answer, no points are awarded, and the tutor gives the tutee the answer both orally and visually. The tutor and the tutee are not competing with each other but are contributing to an overall team score. The team is made up of numerous tutor–tutee pairs. The goal is to go through the assigned material at least twice in the allotted time. The more work is completed correctly, the more points the pair contributes to their team. The team with the highest number of points earns recognition or rewards.

As the pairs work together, the teacher moves around the classroom and awards bonus points for appropriate tutoring behaviors (such as clear presentation of material), awards points based on performance and proper use of the error-correction procedure, and makes positive comments. Some elements of the Johnsons' social-cohesion approach may be seen in this aspect of the technique in that positive social behaviors are reinforced.

Arreaga-Mayer, Terry, and Greenwood (1998) summarized the research evidence supporting the effectiveness of this particular form of tutoring. They found positive effects of CWPT on a variety of measures of academic achievement, such as reading, spelling, vocabulary, and mathematics (Greenwood, Carta, & Kamps, 1990; Greenwood, Maheady, & Carta, 1991; Mathes & Fuchs, 1993). A four-year study examined the effects of using CWPT with low-SES students on the students' achievement in grades 1 to 4. The performance of these students was compared with that of a control group of children who moved through the same grades and experienced a teacher-designed instructional program. The results showed that CWPT significantly increased student achievement in comparison to that of students in the control group (Greenwood, Delquadri, & Hall, 1989). A follow-up of the students two years later when they were in the sixth grade found that the gains made by those who received CWPT were maintained (Greenwood & Terry, 1993). In addition, compared to students in the control group, fewer members of the CWPT group were placed in special education programs. An additional comparison group was also used, consisting of students from the same school district who were not considered at risk. The parents of students in both the experimental group and the control group of at-risk students had received much less formal education, had lower incomes, and held lower-status jobs than the parents of students in the nonrisk group. Students who had experienced CWPT performed as well as students in the nonrisk comparison group on half of the comparisons made.

---

positive practice Practicing the correct answer after making a mistake.

What Does This Mean to Me?
Why do you think these tutoring programs were effective?

Using Technology to Improve Implementation Children did not benefit as much from CWPT if they were absent from school, the content was not challenging, or the peer tutoring was of poor quality (Greenwood et al., 1993; Greenwood & Terry, 1993). In an effort to improve the implementation of CWPT, Greenwood and his colleagues developed the Classwide Peer Tutoring Learning Management System (CWPT-LMS; Greenwood et al., 1993, 2001), which allows teachers to set up classroom rosters and record outcomes. The system includes a data analysis module that enables teachers to chart individual and classroom progress over time. Tools are available that assist teachers in managing data and sharing, deleting, or modifying program information. The technology allows teachers to monitor the program more effectively and to use data from students to make decisions about instruction.

The CWPT-LMS system was evaluated in the classrooms of five teachers of English language learners (ELLs). The results showed that the teachers carried out the program as intended. Both students and teachers were satisfied with the program, and the students made progress in understanding the content being taught.

Reciprocal Peer Tutoring Reciprocal peer tutoring (RPT) was originally designed for pairs of low-achieving urban elementary school children (Fantuzzo, King, & Heller, 1992; Fantuzzo, Polite, & Grayson, 1990). As in most effective tutoring programs, students receive training before tutoring begins. They are first introduced to the concepts of teamwork, partnership, and cooperation. These efforts are intended to promote a sense of social cohesion. Students learn how to do RPT in two to three 45-minute sessions. RPT sessions occur twice weekly and to date have been applied primarily to the learning of mathematics. Students are assigned to pairs and work on computational problems for the first 20 minutes of a session, during which they play the roles of both teacher and student. The procedure used in RPT is similar to that used in classwide peer tutoring. Student dyads first select a team goal from among a number of available choices. The peer teacher is given a set of flashcards that designate areas in which the student's mathematical skills need improvement. These areas are identified through curriculum-based assessments. Each flashcard has a sample problem on one side and the steps for solving it on the other. The pair is given a worksheet on which they keep track of the number of attempts made to solve the problem. The student tries to solve the problem and receives feedback on the effort. If the student succeeds, he or she is praised. If the student does not, the peer teacher suggests that he or she try the problem again and records the answer in the second column of the worksheet, which is labeled "Try 2." After the first 20 minutes, the two students complete drill sheets, and at the end of the period, they check each other's papers, adding up the total number of problems that were answered correctly. The dyads compare their scores with their team's goals and decide whether they have succeeded. After a specified number of *wins*, student dyads choose rewards from a set of available choices.

Reciprocal peer tutoring combines many elements of both the social-motivational and the social-cohesion perspectives on peer learning. It uses elements of the social-motivational perspective because students are individually accountable for their performance, and teams are rewarded based on their performance. It uses elements of the social-cohesion perspective in its emphasis on preparing students for teamwork and cooperation. The teacher must do a great deal of preparation to provide flashcards and drill sheets for each dyad.

Reciprocal peer tutoring involves both structured interaction and the use of rewards. Are both necessary for this instructional strategy to be effective? Fantuzzo et al. (1992) examined this question in a study of at-risk fourth and fifth graders in an urban elementary school. Students who received both elements of RPT were most successful. These results are similar to those reported by Slavin (1996). Students who experienced structured conditions reported feeling higher levels of academic and behavioral competence. Teachers recognized that students who were eligible for rewards behaved better than students who were not. Overall, peer-assisted learning improves students' on-task behavior during a lesson (Ginsburg-Block & Fantuzzo, 1997). Reciprocal peer tutoring was more effective when parents were supportive (Fantuzzo, Davis, & Ginsberg, 1995; Heller & Fantuzzo, 1993).

Tutoring and Students with Special Needs

Tutoring initially was viewed as a process in which an older or more skilled student tutors a younger or less skilled student. This view was in line with Vygotskian theory in that a more competent individual was more likely to be able to provide scaffolding to support the creation of a zone of proximal development for a less competent individual. However, techniques such as CWPT, RPT, and structured tutorial interaction show that interactions between peers who are similar in age and ability can achieve similar outcomes.

Students with special needs benefit from tutoring (Cook et al., 1985–1986; Osguthorpe & Scruggs, 1986; Scruggs & Mastropieri, 1998). In general, they also benefit when they have a chance to serve as tutors. For example, students with learning and behavioral problems tutored non–special needs children in reading for four 20-minute sessions per week (Top, 1984). Both the tutors and the tutees improved their reading skills. Scruggs and Osguthorpe (1986) reviewed 26 studies of the effects of tutoring on the academic performance and social development of tutors and tutees. They concluded that students with mild disabilities can serve as effective tutors for both handicapped and normally achieving peers and that their success depends on careful training and supervision. Tutoring experiences had little effect on students' self-esteem. These results were similar to those found in a meta-analysis of studies in which students with mild disabilities served as tutors (Cook et al., 1985–1986). Peer tutoring in reading for such students is generally effective but is not more effective than teacher-led interventions, such as teacher-led small-group instruction (Mathes & Fuchs, 1993; Mathes et al., 2003).

Peer-assisted learning strategies, or PALS (Fuchs et al., 1997; Mathes et al., 2003), is a technique based on CWPT (Delquadri et al., 1986). Pairs of students work on a skill in which one student is more competent than the other. The main features of this technique include the following:

- The tutor models and gradually fades a verbal rehearsal routine that sets forth a series of steps for solving the problem.
- The teacher provides step-by-step feedback to confirm and praise correct responses, provide explanations, and model strategic behavior for incorrect answers.
- There are frequent verbal and written interactions between tutors and tutees.
- There are opportunities for tutees to apply explanations to subsequent problems.
- The process includes reciprocity, in which both children serve in the roles of tutor and tutee during each session (adapted from Fuchs & Fuchs, 1998 p. 27).

The PALS strategy is influenced by Vygotskian theory in that it involves the pairing of a higher-achieving student with a lower-achieving student, along with support for productive interactions. It is successful with mathematics (Fuchs, Fuchs, Yazdian, et al., 2002) and reading (Mathes et al., 2003). Learning-disabled students in elementary school classrooms that used PALS were more socially accepted than similar students in classes that did not use PALS, and they enjoyed the same social standing as most of their non–special needs peers (Fuchs, Fuchs, Mathes, et al., 2002).

Appendix
Students as Diverse Learners

Tutoring can be an effective strategy for addressing differences in how students learn. Children with special needs can benefit from being tutored and from providing tutoring to others (PRAXIS™, I.B.2; INTASC, Principles 2, 3).

Tutoring for Higher-Order Outcomes

Both CWPT and RPT were developed for use with learners who are at risk for academic failure as a result of poverty or difficulty with English. Both have been shown to help students succeed academically. The kinds of tasks in which students engage tend to be basic in nature, and assessments target lower-level skills. It is possible, however, for students with low skill levels to be involved in tasks that require higher-order skills. Examples of techniques that promote such skills are structured tutorial interaction (King et al., 1998) and complex instruction (Cohen et al., 1999). The role of the task on which peers work and how it fits with particular kinds of peer learning are discussed later in the chapter.

Structured Tutorial Interaction   Tutoring among same-age peers can result in higher-order learning. (See the nearby Taking It to the Classroom box for tutoring guidelines.) The performances of seventh-grade students assigned to three different peer-tutoring conditions were compared (King et al., 1998). The tutors were the same age as the tutees. The tutors were trained to use one of three strategies for tutoring: (1) explaining material to each other, (2) asking

Taking It to the Classroom

Guidelines for Effective Peer–Tutoring Sessions

1. Select the content and instructional materials for tutoring sessions.
2. Explain the purpose and rationale for the technique. Stress the idea of increased opportunities for practice and on-task behavior.
3. Stress collaboration and cooperation rather than competition.
4. Train students in the roles of tutor and tutee. Include specific procedures for (a) feedback for correct responses, (b) error correction procedures, and (c) score keeping.
5. Model appropriate behaviors for both tutor and tutee. Demonstrate acceptable ways to give and accept corrective feedback.
6. Provide sample scripts for students to use in practicing roles. Divide the class into practice pairs and teams.
7. Let pairs of students practice the roles of tutor and tutee as the teacher moves around the room, provides feedback, and offers reinforcement.
8. Conduct further discussion of constructive and nonconstructive pair behavior. Answer questions and solve problems as needed.
9. Let the pairs switch roles and practice the new roles as the teacher provides feedback and reinforcement. Repeat Step 8.

Source: From "Classwide peer tutoring at work" by B. M. Fulk & K. King, *Teaching Exceptional Children,* Vol. 34, 2001, 49–53. Copyright 2001 by The Council for Exceptional Children. Reprinted with permission.

comprehension and thought-provoking questions in addition to explaining, and (3) asking such questions in a particular sequence, as well as explaining. Every student was taught how to explain using the tell-why strategy. They *told* their partners what they knew, explained the *why* and *how* of something, and linked the information to what their partners already knew. The second part of the tutoring strategy required them to *tell why, tell how,* and *use their own words.* The goal of the strategy is to help students elaborate on ideas, explain their thinking rather than merely describe information, and connect the material to what they already knew. Students were also trained to ask comprehension and *thinking* questions. An example of a thinking question is: How is the circulatory system of the earthworm different from that of the grasshopper? (O'Donnell, 2003). We saw from Chi and colleagues' analysis of shallow and deep scaffolding that different kinds of questions elicit different qualities of thinking and response. Students in the question sequence group learned to ask comprehension questions, following up with a probing question if the answer was not complete. An example of a probing question is: How do the valves in the heart work—Can you say more? If the answer was incorrect, the students asked a *hint* question. Finally, they asked a thinking or knowledge-building question. An example of a hint question is: Why are the chambers of the heart important?

Students who asked questions, explained, and sequenced their questions and those who asked questions and explained performed better on inference and integration tasks than did those who engaged in explanation alone. They had no advantage on tests of literal comprehension. Eight weeks after the initial study, students in the two tutoring groups that included inquiry maintained their advantage on tests of inference and integration. This study shows that peer tutoring need not be limited to lower-level tasks or outcomes but can be used to promote higher-level knowledge.

Learning in Heterogeneous Groups

Many cooperative learning techniques were designed for use with groups of four to six students. Typically, these groups are heterogeneous with respect to academic achievement and other characteristics, such as race, gender, and ethnicity. Larger groups can be used for both simple and complex tasks. The heterogeneity of the group can foster the sharing of different perspectives on the academic content and promote social and affective outcomes such as increased appreciation for differences among students. Such groups can also be either tightly or loosely structured. In this section, we will first describe some commonly used cooperative techniques (in addition to STAD and Learning Together, described earlier).

Examples of Cooperative Techniques

A variety of cooperative techniques are described here. There are many more that could be included. As you read these examples, pay attention to the kinds of tasks for which the technique can be used, the role of the teacher, and the underlying view of peer learning. Each technique has a **participation structure**, or rules that define how to participate in an activity.

participation structures The rules that define how to participate in an activity. Such rules may be formal as well as informal.

Structural Approaches   The structural approach to cooperative learning provides flexible structures for interaction that can be fitted to a variety of tasks (Kagan, 1993). Kagan's structures (1989/1990) can be used to develop a sense of belonging to a team as well as to improve communication skills and mastery of content. In general, the structures for interaction are easily integrated into ongoing instruction. One of Kagan's structures that is easy to implement is the *Think–Pair–Share* technique. Before a lesson begins, students are grouped into pairs, sitting side by side. The teacher presents the lesson, which might be a lecture or demonstration, or might involve hands-on activities. After about 15 minutes, the teacher writes a question on the board or overhead transparency that requires students to reflect on some aspect of the material just presented. For example, a reflective question for a ninth-grade social studies class might be: What caused the American Civil War? Each student tries to answer the question, and then each pair of students discusses their answers with one another. They share their answers with the class. The teacher may conduct a whole-class discussion to hear different points of view. He or she might, for example, point to different answers provided by pairs of students and lead a discussion on why the answers are different.

Jigsaw   One of the original cooperative learning techniques is Jigsaw (Aronson et al., 1978). Students are divided into heterogeneous four-person groups and assigned topics on which they are to become experts. For example, if a group is learning about the rain forest, each of its members will be responsible for becoming an expert on a particular subtopic (e.g., birds and animals of the rain forest, people who live in the rain forest, plants, and the destruction of the rain forest). Each student has different reading material. Students with the same *expert topic* meet to discuss their topic. The *expert* groups consist of members of different teams. Their task is to learn as much as possible about their topic. They then return to their groups and teach the material to the other members of the group. Each student in turn teaches the group about his or her subtopic. Later, students take individual quizzes on the material, and individual grades are assigned.

In this technique, every student must participate. Each member of a group has access to materials that others in the group do not and is responsible for communicating that information to the others. Some students may have difficulty mastering the material and may be ineffective in communicating it to others in their group. From a cognitive-elaboration perspective, each student will process information more actively because of the need to *teach* it to others. The teacher needs to monitor students in expert groups and to make sure all the experts have mastered the material. One of the difficulties of using this technique is that the teacher must prepare different materials for different students. In addition, students may not be effective in seeking help when they are being taught material by their peers.

Jigsaw II   In Jigsaw II (Slavin, 1986), each student reads the same material. Students are assigned to expert groups and given an expert *sheet* to guide their study. This simplifies the task for the teacher in preparing for the use of cooperative learning. Slavin (1995) describes a Jigsaw II with a social studies unit about the Blackfoot Indian tribe that is used to teach about groups, group norms, and leadership. An expert sheet might be similar to the one shown in Figure 9.6. Students who have been assigned the same

(Richard T. Nowitz/Photo Researchers, Inc.)

Learners in heterogeneous groups have the opportunity to learn from students who differ in their skills and interests.

expert topic meet in groups to discuss it, using the expert sheet to guide their learning. Each student then returns to his or her team and teaches the topic to its members. The teacher can provide outlines to guide the discussions, in which each expert presents the information to the rest of the group. Students take individual quizzes, and teams are rewarded based on the team's performance.

Group Investigation Sharan and Hertz-Lazarowitz (1980) developed a technique known as group investigation that consists of six stages. Its key components (Sharan & Sharan, 1992) are interaction, investigation, interpretation, and intrinsic motivation. In the first stage (stage I), the teacher chooses a general topic to fit with the curriculum goals for the class. This topic is split into a number of subtopics. Students then organize themselves into research groups, each of which will focus on a particular subtopic. The teacher must ensure that there are adequate resources for students to use in the investigative part of the project. For example, an eighth-grade social studies teacher might assign the topic of famines. The students might organize their research around various countries that have experienced famines: Ethiopia, Ireland, North Korea, Somalia, Sudan, and Ukraine.

In stage II, students plan their research and decide how they are going to gather the information. They may write down a set of questions to be answered. For example, if students are designing a section of a zoo, they might develop some questions about what kinds of animals would be in a particular section. In stage III, they carry out the research, with each student contributing to the effort. They can use a variety of resources such as the Internet, encyclopedias, or videos for their research. In stage IV, the students share the information they have gathered and plan a presentation to the class. They identify the ideas they wish to communicate and develop a strategy for presenting them to the other groups in the class. Each group chooses a representative who works with other representatives to plan an overall strategy for the presentation. In stage V, the students make their presentations. In stage VI, the teacher and students evaluate them. They may, for example, jointly construct a test, based on the content of the presentations, to be given to the entire class. Students conducting a group investigation need to show high levels of self-regulated learning, coordination, and metacognition. One of the important potential outcomes from a group investigation is the development of community and shared goals within the classroom.

Evaluations of group investigations are typically done by comparing students who participated in group investigations with students who experienced whole-class instruction. They have found that most students in group investigation classes outperform their peers in comparable classes (Lazarowitz & Karsenty, 1990; Sharan & Shachar, 1988; Sharan & Shaulov, 1990). The assessments contain questions that require students not only to provide factual information but also to interpret information and apply it to new problems.

Structured Controversies Students often have difficulty expressing disagreement. Children and adolescents who are shy are unlikely to contradict the class or group leader. They may worry about having the wrong answer or appearing *stupid* to their peers. Others may not wish to appear critical of their peers. The ability to argue is an important skill and reflects the ability to reason and think critically. According to Johnson and Johnson (1995), academic controversy occurs when students disagree about ideas, information, opinions, theories, and conclusions. The controversy is resolved as students reach a consensus on a particular position. In the technique known as structured controversy, the teacher guides students through the steps outlined in Table 9.4.

**Expert Sheet
The Blackfoot**

To read: pages 3–9 and 11–12
Topics
1. How were Blackfoot men expected to act?
2. What is a group, and what does it do? What are the most important groups for the Blackfoot?
3. What did Blackfoot bands and clubs do?
4. What were the Blackfoot customs and traditions?

Figure 9.6 Expert Sheet for Jigsaw II

Source: From Robert E. Slavin, *Cooperative Learning*, 2e. Published by Allyn and Bacon, Boston, MA. Copyright © 1995 by Pearson Education. Reprinted by permission of the publisher.

TABLE 9.4

Structured Controversies

Step 1	Students research a position, learn the relevant information, and prepare a persuasive "best case possible" for the position.
Step 2	Students present the best case possible for the position in as persuasive and convincing a way as possible.
Step 3	Students engage in an open discussion in which they argue forcefully for their position and rebut attacks on it.
Step 4	Students reverse perspectives and present the opposing position as accurately, completely, persuasively, and forcefully as they can.
Step 5	Students drop all advocacies, create a synthesis or integration of the opposing positions, and reach a consensus as to the best reasoned judgment that may be made about the issue.

Source: Figure 1 from Johnson, D. W., & Johnson, R. T. (1995). *Creative controversy: Intellectual challenge in the classroom.* Edina, MN: Interaction Book Company. Reprinted with the permission of D. W. Johnson.

Appendix
Teaching Heterogeneous Students

The use of cooperative learning techniques is one approach to teaching heterogeneous students who differ in gender, ability, race, and ethnicity (PRAXIS™, I.B.4; INTASC, Principles 1, 3).

Students are placed in a four-person cooperative learning group, which is then divided into two pairs. A high school class might be asked to consider whether pollution regulations for cars should be eased. One pair of students is to make the case for keeping the regulations as they are, and the other pair is to make the case for easing them. All the students will do research to support their positions. At each step of the process, the teacher plays an important role. The students may need assistance in finding useful information and in distinguishing between good arguments and strong opinions. The students present their positions to one another, with each pair taking turns. They then engage in an open discussion of the ideas that have been presented, trying to convince one another of their point of view. The pairs then switch sides and present the opposing arguments. This causes them to focus on the arguments themselves and makes it easier to achieve consensus. The group then develops a report that summarizes the arguments for each perspective and the group's decision as to which position is best. Students need good social skills to engage in a structured academic controversy. It is important that they not criticize one another personally but instead criticize the arguments being made. (See the nearby Taking It to the Classroom box.)

Collaborative Reasoning Collaborative reasoning (CR) is an instructional strategy developed by researchers at the Center for the Study of Reading at the University of Illinois at Urbana–Champaign (Anderson, Chinn, Waggoner, & Nyguyen, 1998; Waggoner, Chinn, Yi, & Anderson, 1995). During collaborative reasoning, students work in small groups to discuss controversial issues that arise in their readings. The students work with high-interest materials and begin by taking positions on a "big" question. Such questions address social or moral dilemmas. Examples might include discussions of fairness, honesty, pollution, and so forth. As they engage in discussions, students are expected to provide reasons, evidence, and justifications for their positions. They are also encouraged to listen to one another's arguments, evaluate them, and consider multiple perspectives on the issue under discussion. As Reznitskaya and colleagues (2009) note: "the contestable nature of big questions, where nobody, not even the teacher knows the right answer, promotes the establishment of a truly egalitarian classroom community" (p. 33). It is precisely this kind of community in which Piagetian perspectives on peer learning may be found. The mutuality of influence experienced in these discussion groups permits each child to have an influence on the final decision. Teachers have an important role in promoting collaborative reasoning discussions. They must remind students to provide reasons for their opinions, draw attention to the evidentiary strategies that students are using, model reasoning processes by thinking aloud, provide counterarguments to those of the students, keep track of the positions proposed, and summarize the arguments. Research on collaborative reasoning has shown it to be effective in promoting critical thinking, reasoning, argumentation skills, and writing skills (Dong, Anderson, Kim, & Li, 2008; Li et al., 2007; Reznitskaya et al., 2001, 2009).

Collaboration and Technology

Changes in technology and widespread use of the Internet have made it possible to devise new forms of cooperative and collaborative learning. Some of these involve groups of students using online resources together, whereas others involve communication without face-to-face interaction. In this section, we discuss WebQuests, online mentoring, and computer-supported intentional learning environments (CSILE).

WebQuests

WebQuests use a central question based on a real-world issue and ask students to solve the problem or answer the question. Using the World Wide Web, students can contact experts and access searchable databases, current news reports, and other materials. In many WebQuests, students take on specific roles within a cooperative group and develop expertise (similar to

Taking It to the Classroom

Promoting Productive Interaction

- **Encouraging Respect**
  Discuss with students how they like to be treated and how they do not like to be treated. Have them explain how they might feel if others treat them badly. In some situations, you might ask students to draw up a contract stating how they will treat one another and have each of them sign it and keep a copy.

- **Encouraging Good Thinking**
  Encourage students to be critical of ideas, not of the people who propose them. You could assign one student to record ideas as they are proposed so that they can be discussed later. This will help the group avoid reacting to specific students.

- **Encouraging a Focus on Learning**
  Encourage students to consider different ideas so that they can improve on the arguments they might make. Remind them that it is better to change their minds and adopt a better position than to stick with a bad idea.

Jigsaw and Jigsaw II) in a particular aspect of the topic. The students can post their solutions or answers on a Web site for comments and evaluation.

An example of a WebQuest is one designed by eTeachers (2005) for high school social studies students. It is based on the Chinese Cultural Revolution; the question asked is: How did China's Cultural Revolution affect the lives of ordinary Chinese at home and abroad? The WebQuest provides background information. Students take on individual roles within a cooperative group: student, politician, dissident, Red Guard, propagandist, and housewife. Support is provided for each role in the form of questions that can be used to guide the students' analysis of the problem and collection of information. The students work together to respond to the question. They can then post their response or seek feedback from experts on the topic. This kind of activity not only promotes collaborative learning but also encourages students to learn from the community outside the classroom.

Online Mentoring

Online mentoring takes many forms. It can include one-on-one mentoring or groups of students working with a single mentor. Many online mentoring programs are available. A key consideration in using an online mentoring program is that learners can interact *safely* with adult volunteers. It is important to maintain the learner's privacy, limit access to the learner by undesirable individuals, and establish rules to govern interactions between learners and mentors.

Online mentoring can have many benefits for mentors, students, and teachers. Online communication may be the only way that some volunteers can interact with students because of their work schedules. Students can get more individual attention while working on a project than they might get in the classroom. Online communication gives them opportunities to hone their writing and reading skills. In addition, online mentoring can help students develop a caring relationship with an adult who takes an interest in their work. Teachers can also benefit from the availability of online mentors to provide expertise or resources for various curricular topics.

Knowledge Forum

Knowledge Forum was developed from the computer-supported intentional learning environment (CSILE; Scardamalia, Bereiter, & Lamon, 1994), which was designed for use by an entire class of students. Students worked on networked computers in a classroom that was

Appendix
Enhancing Learning
You can enhance students' learning by using a variety of resources and materials to support your instruction. Examples of such resources include computers, Internet resources, and other technology (PRAXIS™, II.A.4; INTASC, Principle 4).

connected to a server and maintained a communal database. The database included text and graphical notes that the students produced and could be accessed by all the students by means of database searches. Any student could add a note or a comment. Only the original writer of a note could delete it. CSILE was evaluated in four classrooms in the same school. Students who had used CSILE performed better on standardized tests of math and language arts than did students in a comparison group (Scardamalia et al., 1994). A study of explanations offered by fifth- and sixth-grade students found that the CSILE students attempted more coherent explanations when asked what they had learned from a particular unit. Knowledge Forum expands on this system and is designed to assist students in *knowledge building:* defining problems, generating hypotheses, collecting and analyzing information, and collaborating.

Influences on Effectiveness in Heterogeneous Groups

Heterogeneous groups have a number of advantages. They give students a chance to work with others who may differ from themselves. When such groups work well, students benefit both academically and socially. However, groups do not automatically work well. Without instruction in the cognitive skills needed for tasks or the social skills needed to coordinate their activities, students tend to work at the most concrete level or give each other only minimal support (Cohen, 1994). Group interaction is influenced by the goals and incentives associated with the assigned task, the nature of the task itself, and individual differences among the participants (O'Donnell & Dansereau, 1992).

Gender and Cooperative Groups

Previously, you read about the importance of teachers' beliefs and their influence on classroom practices. One area in which teachers appear to have strong beliefs is the role of gender in the classroom, particularly as it relates to interaction in cooperative groups. Many teachers, for example, believe that boys dominate interactions with girls. However, the findings of research on this question are mixed.

Questions of interest with respect to gender include the following: Do girls participate in group interaction at the same rates as boys? Does their participation depend on the balance between boys and girls in the group? Is the participation of boys and girls influenced by the nature of the task they are assigned?

Concerns are often raised about dominance in groups because some students might have limited opportunities to participate in ways that promote learning (Webb, 1989, 1992). Boys and girls in cooperative groups may not participate equally. Many high school teachers use same-gender pairings to limit the degree to which students avoid tasks that they consider gender-specific. One study (Webb, 1984) found that when boys in the group outnumbered girls, the boys dominated the interaction. When girls outnumbered boys, the girls still tended to defer to the boys, even if there was only one. In groups that were balanced with respect to gender, all the students tended to participate equally. However, this particular study is quite old and it is unclear whether similar results would be found now.

Other studies have found differences in the ways in which boys and girls interact in groups. For example, Underwood and Jindal (1993) found that mixed-gender pairs did not perform as well as same-gender pairs on a computer-based language task. Pairs of boys showed the greatest gains when told to cooperate. Similar results were found by Fitzpatrick and Hardman (2000). The kinds of tasks on which children work also play a role. Seven- and nine-year-old children worked in same- or mixed-gender pairs on a language-based computer task and on a noncomputer task (Fitzpatrick & Hardman, 2000). The mixed-gender pairs were less collaborative than the same-gender pairs. Girls in mixed-gender pairs were more assertive during the noncomputer task, whereas boys were more assertive during the computer-based task. Similar gender differences were found by Holden (1993), who examined boys' and girls' contributions to discussions in a language task and in a mathematics/technology task. When boys outnumbered girls in cooperative groups performing a language

What Does This Mean to Me?
Do you think that gender matters when one is working in a cooperative group? In what ways does it influence group interaction?

TABLE 9.5

Summary of Findings on the Role of Gender in Cooperative Groups

Researcher	Year	Findings
Webb	1984	• When boys outnumber girls in a group, boys dominate the interaction.
		• When girls outnumber boys in a group, girls defer to the boys.
Underwood	1993	• Mixed-gender pairs did not perform as well as same-gender pairs on a computer-based language task.
		• Pairs of boys benefited most from directives to cooperate.
Fitzpatrick	2000	• Mixed-gender pairs were less collaborative than same-gender pairs.
		• Girls in mixed-gender pairs were more assertive during a noncomputer task.
		• Boys in mixed-gender pairs were more assertive during a computer task.
Tolmie	1993	• Female pairs avoided conflict and focused on problems experienced.
		• Male pairs learned most when they discussed feedback.
		• Mixed-gender pairs were very constrained in their interactions.
Holden	1993	• When boys outnumbered girls in a group for a language task, girls contributed little abstract talk.
		• There was little abstract talk by either boys or girls on a math/technology task.

task, the level of abstract talk contributed by girls was low in comparison to groups whose composition was more balanced. There was little abstract talk in discussions of the mathematics/technology task. Holden concluded that the kind of talk in which students engage varies as a function of the task and the composition of the group.

Tolmie and Howe (1993) found that boys and girls did not differ in performance on a task in which they were asked to predict the trajectories of falling objects but found that they did differ in their interactions. Female pairs avoided conflict, focusing instead on what problems they had in common. Male pairs learned most when they discussed the feedback and referred to explanatory factors that might account for differences between predictions and actual events. Mixed pairs were very constrained in their interactions. Table 9.5 presents a summary of the findings we have described.

It is difficult to draw strong conclusions about the role of gender in cooperative groups based on the available evidence. Nevertheless, teachers should be sensitive to the possible influence of gender on group interaction and take it into account when assigning students to groups.

What Does This Mean to Me?
Look at Table 9.5. Which of these findings make sense to you? Why?

RIDE What role did gender play in the group interaction described in the vignette at the beginning of the chapter?

Race, Ethnicity, and Language

Cooperative learning is often promoted as an instructional strategy that can be used to integrate children from a variety of backgrounds. Slavin (1995) reviewed a number of studies that examined the effects of cooperative learning on intergroup relations. The findings indicate that children who experience cooperative learning report more cross-racial, cross-ethnic friendships than do children who experience whole-class instruction. It is important to note that although the research is promising, the conclusions drawn from it may not necessarily apply to today's classrooms, because their composition is quite different than it was 20 years ago. Creating positive interdependence would seem to be crucial to the effort to promote positive intergroup relations.

A more recent study examined the effects of a cooperative learning program, Bilingual Cooperative Integrated Reading and Composition (BCIRC), on the Spanish and English reading, writing, and language achievement of second and third graders with limited English proficiency (Calderon, Hertz-Lazarowitz, & Slavin, 1998). The BCIRC program consists of a set of activities that take place before, during, and after reading. They include building background knowledge and vocabulary, making predictions, reading a selection, partner reading and silent reading, story comprehension treasure hunts, story mapping, story retelling, story-related writing, saying words out loud and spelling them, checking the partner's work, putting new vocabulary into meaningful sentences, and tests. Three schools that used BCIRC were included in the study, and the performance of the students who participated in the program was compared to that of students in other schools in the district with similar demographic profiles. Second graders in BCIRC classrooms performed significantly better than students in comparison groups in writing on the Spanish Texas Assessment of Academic Skills. Third graders in BCIRC classrooms outperformed comparison students in reading but not in language. If the third graders had been in BCIRC for two years, they outperformed comparison students on both measures. Third graders in BCIRC classrooms met the criteria for exit from bilingual classes at much higher rates than did students in comparison classes.

Special Needs and Cooperative Learning

Do students with special needs benefit from cooperative learning? Cooperative learning was shown to have significant positive effects in only 50% of the studies reviewed by Tateyama-Sniezek (1990). Techniques that included rewards and methods for making sure that each child was responsible for his or her performance had the strongest effects (Stevens & Slavin, 1991). Jenkins and O'Connor (2003) cautioned against drawing firm conclusions from these findings. They point out that more and longer studies are required. In addition, they note that research done to date has not paid enough attention to whether students retain information and/or transfer the skills they acquire to new tasks.

> **How Can I Use This?**
>
> What kind of peer-learning situation would you use with learning-disabled children? Can you explain your reasoning?

There are, however, some notable successes in using cooperative learning when students with special needs participate in general education classrooms. Stevens and colleagues examined the effectiveness of Cooperative Integrated Reading and Composition (CIRC) with third and fourth graders. They evaluated the effect of the technique over a 12-week and a 24-week period; they found that academically handicapped students achieved more when they were mainstreamed into CIRC classes and received support from a special education teacher who collaborated with the general education teacher (Stevens et al., 1987). In a follow-up study conducted over a two-year period, Stevens and Slavin (1995) showed that students in CIRC classrooms showed higher achievement in vocabulary, comprehension, and language expression than did students in the matched schools. Academically handicapped students in CIRC classrooms showed significantly higher achievement in reading vocabulary, reading comprehension, and language expression than did the students in the pull-out programs.

Some students with learning disabilities prefer not to work in groups (Elbaum, Moody, & Schumm, 1999). In mixed-ability reading groups, the difficulties created by learning disabilities are more visible to classmates. Depending on how the group is structured, the attentional demands of working with a number of others may be too great for these students. Students with learning disabilities may lack the social skills to participate well in a cooperative task (Holder & Fitzpatrick, 1991; Pearl, 1992). However, cooperative learning or other peer-learning experiences can improve the classroom social standing of students with learning disabilities

(Bob Daemmrich/The Image Works)

Students with special needs can benefit from working with other students in cooperative groups.

Taking It to the Classroom

Do You Know Jack? Getting the Help He Needs

Jack needs help. Jack, who has a math learning disability, is in middle school. He goes to the resource room to get help with math, but he also participates in general education math classes taught by Mr. Kumar. Jack knows that he has trouble with math, and he feels intimidated when the teacher assigns the class to work in groups. He is afraid that the other students will make fun of him when he cannot do the problems. He does not ask for help because he does not want the others to know how much he is struggling. What can Mr. Kumar do to help Jack?

Mr. Kumar will need to intervene with the whole class to help Jack. Here are some things he can do:

1. Talk to the class about the importance of helping one another.
2. Teach the class communication skills (e.g., paying attention, not talking too loud, and asking one another whether they understand the material).
3. Teach students how to ask for help:
   - Choose someone to help you.
   - Ask for assistance and feedback (e.g., What should I do next? How does this look?).
4. Reward students for helping others (e.g., computer time, choosing library books).
5. Assign Jack to work with other students who are patient and kind.
6. Ask Jack to record on a simple chart the number of times he asks for help.

(Slavin, 1995). Teachers who wish to use cooperative learning as an instructional strategy need to plan the composition of the groups carefully, design tasks that can be done by students with special needs, and monitor the work of the group closely (see the nearby Taking It to the Classroom box).

Status Characteristics

Some students have high status in the classroom, and their peers defer to them, seek their help, and follow their example. Students with low status seek help and are often ignored, and their contributions may not be valued by their peers. Researchers have studied the cognitive consequences of these kinds of status differences (Cohen, 1982; Cohen & Lotan, 1995, 1997; Cohen, Lotan, & Catanzarite, 1990). When working in groups, higher-status students may have more opportunities to engage in the kinds of cognitive activities that promote elaborative processing and higher achievement (Cohen, 1982). Low-status students may not have many such opportunities.

Another problem may be posed by **stereotype threat**: "the threat of being viewed through the lens of a negative stereotype or the fear of doing something that would inadvertently confirm that stereotype" (Steele, 1999, p. 46). Minority and female students may perform less well than they are able to perform because of concerns that they might reinforce negative stereotypes about their racial group or gender (Inzlicht & Ben-Zeev, 2003).

Who has status in a group? It depends on the culture of the classroom or school. Students who are known to be successful in school often have high status in classrooms where achievement is valued. Other

status characteristics Characteristics of individuals that may signal that they have high or low status.

stereotype threat Concern about being viewed from the vantage point of a negative stereotype or acting to confirm such a stereotype.

Some students can feel left out of group activities or be deliberately excluded by their peers. Teachers need to be on the alert for such problems.

(Ellen B. Senisi/The Image Works)

Figure 9.7 Status Characteristics

Source: From Cohen, E. G., Lotan, R. A., Scarloss, B. A., & Arellano, A. R. (1000). Complex instruction: Equity in cooperative learning classrooms. *Theory into Practice, 38*(2), pp. 81–82. Copyright 1999 by the College of Education, The Ohio State University. All rights reserved.

"Let's use a tune we all know," suggests Veronica.

"Okay, but what will the song be about?" asks Hector. The group members fall silent for a moment. Carolina, recorder for the day, takes out a piece of paper and a pencil.

"Why don't we use some of the ideas from the song we heard!" Carolina suggests. "How about if we make it about Jose, who wants to come to Hollywood to be a movie star?" Veronica and Hector nod their heads in agreement.

Victor, the fourth member of the group, shrugs his shoulder, looks away, and as usual, mumbles something quietly. "I'm sure this guy didn't have too much fun. Sounds to me like he worked really hard. He fixed the rails and picked tomatoes and mixed cement. For only 50 cents an hour! I'd be tired and disappointed."

Carolina begins to write what she has decided will be the first line of their song. Ms. Garcia, who has been watching the group from a discreet distance, interjects:

"Victor, you listened to the song carefully and you clearly understood the deep message of the lyrics. This is important information for your group. What do you think your group's song should be about?"

"I'm not sure," Victor answers hesitantly. "I just know that my family didn't come here because they wanted to be movie stars. They came because there were no jobs in Mexico. My father says he wanted to work so we could have a better life."

"Maybe we can put those ideas in our song." Veronica is ready to compromise.

As the students offer examples of how they might do this, Ms. Garcia moves away, now reassured that Victor's contribution will be heard by his group.

characteristics of students, including athletic ability, popularity, and gender, may also be associated with high status.

Figure 9.7 illustrates some of the ways in which status characteristics operate. In the vignette, the children are discussing the question: Why do people move? Group members are trying to come up with a song in response to the question. Victor disagrees with their interpretation, but he does so quietly. Not until the teacher intervenes and points out the value of his contribution do other students pay attention to his ideas.

Limiting Status Effects in the Classroom Status differences affect interaction, rates of participation, and the kinds of cognitive activities in which students engage (e.g., providing explanations, asking questions). Peer-learning techniques that maximize participation by all students can limit the impact of status characteristics. A technique such as Scripted Cooperation can reduce inequalities in participation because all students must take turns engaging in specified cognitive activities. A cooperative learning technique that involves interdependence among group members can also reduce the effects of status differences. Petersen and colleagues (Petersen, Johnson, & Johnson, 1991) found that boys gained status over girls in an individualistic learning condition but that in a cooperative condition there were no perceived differences between boys and girls on measures of achievement, verbal participation in the group, leadership, or status.

Elizabeth Cohen developed the multiple-abilities treatment to minimize the differentiation among students in a classroom (Cohen, 1994; Cohen & Lotan, 1997). The intent of this program, called *Complex Instruction*, is to promote participation by all students. Students work on complex tasks to which all of them can contribute but which none of them can complete alone. Like the other approaches discussed in this section, Complex Instruction attempts to reduce the focus on a narrow set of skills and increase participation by all students.

In Complex Instruction, the teacher chooses a complex task that cannot be completed by a single student alone and to which *all* students can contribute. The teacher begins by discussing what abilities are needed to carry out a task. For example, the class may be asked to design a zoo. The abilities needed include being able to measure, write instructions, and research the housing and food requirements for animals in the zoo; artistic ability is required for creating the actual model, and many other specific abilities are involved. Students come to recognize that no single individual could complete the entire task alone and that each student has something to contribute while also recognizing that some students have many skills. The focus on the specific abilities needed to accomplish the task at hand allows for the inclusion of many children, whereas a narrow focus on traditional academic skills may exclude some children from actively participating. In addition, the focus on what students can contribute to a task encourages them to be task-oriented and to stress abilities rather than deficiencies.

In Figure 9.7, you saw the teacher, Ms. Garcia, intervene in Victor's group to point out how his contribution was valuable to the group. By **assigning competence** to Victor in this context, Ms. Garcia helped the group members accomplish their task and prevented status differences from interfering with the quality of their work.

assigning competence The teacher acknowledges the contribution of a student to the completion of a task.

Learning from Peers: Practices for Learning

The various theoretical perspectives described earlier in the chapter provide frameworks for making decisions when using cooperative or collaborative pairs or groups in the classroom. Three key dimensions of classroom practice are (1) the quality of students' discourse, (2) the role of the teacher in the collaborative classroom, and (3) the tasks selected.

The Importance of Discourse Quality

The mere fact that children are assigned to groups does not mean that they will hold meaningful discussions. The kinds of tasks on which they work will influence their talk. Children tend to engage in less abstract talk on mathematics/technology tasks than on language-based tasks (Holden, 1993).

If one adopts a Vygotskian view of peer learning, intellectual skills must be modeled before a child can internalize them. If the child's reasoning, explanation, or questioning is of very low quality, he or she may gain little practice in higher-level thinking in the context of the group. Most students need support in generating the quality of discourse that is associated with learning. Teachers can promote high levels of cognitive activity by asking questions that vary in complexity (King, 1991; King et al., 1998). As can be seen later in Table 9.6, asking increasingly complex questions results in higher-quality discourse.

The importance of discourse quality is not just true of interactions in the classroom. Research on learning in museums has focused on the kinds of conversations people have while viewing exhibits (Allen, 2002; Leinhardt, Crowley, & Knutson, 2002). Allen examined the conversations of 49 dyads (adult–adult, adult–child) as they viewed a large exhibit at the San Francisco Exploratorium (Allen, 2002). The exhibit was about frogs and consisted of 10 hands-on interactive elements, videos of frog activities, live frogs, an immersion experience involving sitting on a back porch listening to frogs at night, excerpts from children's books, and many other elements. The conversations of the dyads were recorded and later transcribed and coded for evidence of learning. The results showed that 83% of the talk between members of dyads was related to learning. Five categories of talk related to learning were identified: (1) *perceptual talk* (drawing attention to some element of the exhibit), (2) *conceptual talk* (interpreting the content of the exhibit, including inferences and predictions), (3) *connecting talk* (making connections to existing knowledge), (4) *strategic talk* (talk about how to use the exhibit), and (5) *affective talk* (references to emotions and feelings).

The dyads engaged in a great deal of conceptual talk, and this kind of talk was more frequent when the dyads were discussing the live animals in the exhibit than when they were engaging in hands-on activities. This is not entirely surprising, because involvement in an activity tends to distract individuals from discussions. Adult–child interactions produced less conceptual talk than did adult–adult interactions (Allen, 2002). The conversations often took place as people moved between elements of the exhibit.

The design of exhibits can have an important influence on what occurs when visitors interact with them (Allen, 2004). Exhibits that are created around issues promote a different kind of learning than do more expository exhibits. Issue-based exhibits often provoke controversy and can be emotionally charged (Pedretti, 2004). Pedretti (2004) conducted research on exhibitions of this type. One of the exhibits she studied was called Mine Games. The exhibit's designers intended to make science interesting by helping people feel that the issue had some connection to their lives. The exhibit was interactive and involved a simulation game that explored the consequences of building a mine in the imaginary town

Appendix
Appreciating Heterogeneous Students

Students who vary in gender, race, ethnicity, and ability or who experience special needs contribute to heterogeneity in the classroom. These differences can enhance learning, and you need to be aware of the influence of these differences on students' learning from particular instructional strategies (PRAXIS™, I.B.2, III. B; INTASC, Principles 2, 3, 6).

of Grizzly. Through video and computer simulations, visitors met the town's residents and heard their perspectives on the issues. In the final and unique feature of the exhibit, the Hot Seat, visitors sat in a tiered semicircle and, with the guidance of a mediator, held a discussion of the issue, using information learned from the exhibit. Students who visit such an exhibit have an opportunity to engage in argumentation and reasoning related to its content. The Hot Seat promotes many of the cognitive processes encouraged by the use of collaborative reasoning described earlier.

The Role of the Teacher

Teachers' roles are key components of effective peer learning. These roles can be very complex. Different peer-learning activities require different stances with respect to students, tasks, and outcomes. Teachers must take into account both the social context in which learning occurs and the cognitive processes that are either supported or hindered in that context. They need to analyze their classrooms to determine whether there may be obstacles that limit the cognitive opportunities available to students or prevent them from making use of those opportunities. Teachers can adopt many roles in relation to the use of peer learning. Table 9.6 presents a summary of these roles. In this section, we look briefly at each of them.

The quality of discourse from students is not the only discourse that is important. Webb, Nemer, and Ing (2006) found that students reproduce the discourse of teachers in the context of a semester-long program of cooperative learning in middle school mathematics classes. They concluded that the models of discourse presented by the teacher were imitated by students. Teachers experienced difficulty in changing their behaviors to ones in which they allowed students authority for discourse.

Preparer of Learning Activities   A critical role that teachers adopt is that of being a preparer of learning activities. The importance of planning was described in Chapter 2. Teachers identify their instructional goals and select learning tasks for their students that will allow them to accomplish these goals. Teachers need to analyze the complexity of the demands that any particular learning task will place on students' cognitive, emotional, and social resources. For example, if the task is too difficult, students may become easily frustrated and impatient with one another. Alternatively, if the task is too simple, students may become easily bored. As a preparer of learning activities, teachers will provide supports to students (e.g., roles, worksheets, questions, expert sheets) that will assist them as they engage in the task.

Community Builder   Most American classrooms are increasingly heterogeneous. The teacher may need to promote the experience of community actively in the classroom and the school so all students feel that they are valued and that the teacher supports their efforts. If they do not feel valued and supported, students may become alienated and have low expectations. As community builder, the teacher develops a context in which students show mutual respect, are willing to help one another, and recognize others' need for help. In adopting this role, the teacher may look to sociocultural theory, Vygotskian theory, or social-cohesion theory to understand the contribution that community can make to effective learning. Cohen's strategy of assigning competence to students is one way of recognizing the contributions of children with different skills.

Task Developer   Teachers in American classrooms must be aware of state and national standards for educational performance. They need to examine the curricular goals for the classes they teach and design tasks that are appropriate to those goals and might be facilitated by the use of some form of peer learning. They need to understand the students' current level of performance, the desired level of performance, and the kinds of tasks that will promote the transition from current to desired performance levels. They must understand the use of practice, feedback, examples, alternative representations, and many other features of instruction in order to develop tasks that can be carried out effectively by peers. The focus cannot be simply on *group performance* of a task but on each student's improvement in the skills required by the task.

MINDFUL HABITS OF EFFECTIVE TEACHERS

Effective teachers play many important roles in the classroom and thoughtfully move between various roles in response to changing circumstances in the classroom.

TABLE 9.6

Roles for Teachers during Cooperative Work

Teacher Role	Teacher Activity	Theoretical Perspective or Technique
Preparer of learning activities	• Selects the learning activity task, including its level of complexity and whether it should offer open-ended problems • Assigns students their roles and offers role training if needed	• All approaches
Community builder	• Helps students develop social skills necessary to work together • Emphasizes common purposes • Helps heterogeneous group become a community • Promotes mutual respect • Promotes willingness to help one another • Recognizes others' need for help	• Social cohesion • Social cohesion and social motivational
Task developer	• Designs group-worthy tasks	• Complex instruction • Group investigation
Model	• Models the use of cognitive and metacognitive strategies • Demonstrates how to engage in constructive social skills, such as encouraging others, taking turns, and elaborating on an idea	• Vygotskian theory • Reciprocal teaching • Cognitive elaboration
Coordinator of activities	• Assigns students to groups • Manages the classroom; creates a context in which work can be accomplished • Moves between groups and monitors social and cognitive activities	• All approaches

Evaluator	• Provides criteria for evaluation of students' work
	 • Leads students in evaluating their own work and group processes
	 • Includes measures of individual accountability
	 • Give students feedback on:
	   • Use of on-task behavior
	   • Products produced by group
	   • Contributions of individual members
		• Vygotskian
		 • Piagetian
		 • Cognitive elaboration
		 • Social motivational

The Teacher as Model Another role of teachers is that of model. Techniques such as reciprocal peer tutoring emphasize the role of the teacher as the initial model for complex cognitive activity. A skilled teacher is able to make her or his thinking visible, allowing students to practice increasingly complex skills and eventually decreasing the amount of support they need.

Coordinator of Activities Many teachers rely mainly on whole-class instruction, not because they necessarily believe in its efficacy but because they are concerned about managing the learning activities of multiple groups, limiting negative social processes, and "covering the curriculum." (See the nearby Taking It to the Classroom box.)

Evaluator The teacher can choose to evaluate many aspects of a peer-learning situation, including students' use of social skills, their on-task behavior, the products they produce, and individual contributions to the group product or other individual products that might be required. The feedback that teachers provide can enhance students' expectations of success or

Taking It to the Classroom

Management Issues to Consider

Here are some guidelines for managing multiple groups.

Getting Students into Groups

Do not have all the students moving at once. Make sure all students know who is in their group and where their group will meet. One strategy is to create four-person groups by handing out four #1 cards, four #2 cards, and so forth. Then call all the #1's together.

Distributing Materials

Designate one person in each group to be the materials person. Each *materials* person can collect and distribute worksheets or other materials to the members of the group. This strategy reduces the number of students moving around the classroom at any one time.

Too Much Noise?

Before asking students to move into groups, decide on a way to reduce the level of noise while they work in groups. Some teachers use *12-inch voices*—ones that can be heard only 12 inches away. Others use a card with a large red circle that they can hand to a group if it is too loud.

Getting the Children's Attention Back

Before you assign students to groups, describe the signal you will use when you want them to be quiet and look to you for the next instruction. You might, for example, raise your hand as a signal to be quiet. The students who notice your hand in the air might also be expected to raise their hands so that students around them will notice and quiet down.

What if the Groups Finish Their Work at Different Times?

First make sure that the students who claim to have finished have actually done so. They may have rushed through parts of a task and not understood the material. Have additional questions available that can be used to extend the work.

---

promote explanations of success or failure that are conducive to improved effort and performance. A teacher can also provide feedback that discourages a student and results in negative explanations of poor performance. A summary of how a teacher might play the roles just described appears in Table 9.6.

When more than one person is engaged in a learning task, social processes are involved. In using cooperative groups or other forms of peer learning, the teacher also needs to provide feedback on students' interactions. Cohen and colleagues have shown that when students are given criteria for an acceptable group product and use them to evaluate their work, their interactions improve and their learning increases (Cohen et al., 2002).

Classroom Tasks

Teachers need to set goals for any task they assign. They may select tasks with the goal of motivating or engaging students, providing a context for social interaction with a student who is having particular difficulties, getting students to learn factual material, or getting them to engage in higher-order reasoning and thinking skills. Depending on the goals of the task, the kind of peer learning employed will vary.

Not all tasks require the same level of effort, generate the same level of interest, or require the same cognitive processes. Tasks can be classified along a number of dimensions. The first dimension is complexity. Tasks can be simple and involve simple cognitive strategies, such as rehearsal. Memorizing the names of the capitals of states requires rehearsal. *Basic knowledge acquisition tasks* are those in which content is encoded into the student's memory for later recall. Strategies for helping students master such tasks include teaching them memorization and rehearsal strategies, such as the use of mnemonics, summarization, and elaboration strategies. Techniques such as STAD or Scripted Cooperation can be very useful in helping students perform these tasks effectively.

Other tasks require more complex cognitive skills. Such tasks require students to pose their own questions, explore alternatives, gather information, generate evidence or arguments in support of ideas, and draw conclusions. The techniques that support basic knowledge acquisition and rehearsal are not sufficient to promote these kinds of higher-order thinking. Tasks that are more open-ended or require more collaborative knowledge construction call for cooperative techniques that are less structured in order to permit the kinds of interactions that will result in the desired outcomes.

Consider an example: Students in a high school science class could be asked to conduct a chemistry experiment by following the directions in a lab notebook. This task is much simpler and requires lower-level cognitive skills than one in which students are asked to design an experiment to determine whether the water from the local lake is safe to drink.

Cohen (1994) distinguishes between individual and group tasks. According to Cohen, a group task is one that "requires resources (information, knowledge, heuristic problem-solving strategies, materials, and skills) that no single individual possesses so that no single individual is likely to solve the problems or accomplish the task objectives without at least some input from others" (p. 8). Such tasks are open-ended and require **problem solving**; students can approach them from a number of vantage points and have multiple opportunities to demonstrate their intellectual competence. These tasks are concerned with important content, require positive interdependence among group members and individual accountability of all members, and include clear criteria for how the group's product will be evaluated (Lotan, 2003). *Group-worthy tasks* (Lotan, 2003) require a great deal of time and expertise on the part of the teacher.

problem solving An activity in which a person uses knowledge to reach a specific goal but in which there is no clearly specified way of reaching the goal.

There are some risks associated with open-ended tasks. Students may be drawn into negative social interactions, some may be easily frustrated if the task is ambiguous, and some will not participate fully. Various strategies, such as the social skills training advocated by the Johnsons, the status interventions proposed by Cohen, and close monitoring of groups, can limit these negative outcomes.

It is important to note that not all students will be ready to assume complex roles and use complex strategies. Students who have not worked in cooperative groups will need training and gradual experience in taking more responsibility for their learning. Likewise, students who have not valued educational achievement in the past will not suddenly become passionate about learning without a major effort to change their values regarding achievement. Techniques such as STAD can be effective in reshaping classroom values so that group success is important. (See the nearby Uncommon Sense box.)

Uncommon Sense

Out-of-School Group Projects Are Always Cooperative—Or Are They?

Classroom time is limited, and it can be difficult to allocate the amount of time needed to carry out a complex group project. Mr. Johnson has worked very hard with his eighth-grade English class to create a climate of mutual respect. He holds a Piagetian view of the contribution of peer learning; that is, he believes that peer interaction is more likely to promote learning if students are equal in status and power. He has assigned students to five-person groups to prepare a computer-based presentation based on Shakespeare's *King Lear*. Each group has to prepare a presentation about Lear's disowning of Cordelia. Members of the group need to meet outside of school hours to discuss their strategy for doing the task, make work assignments, and complete the work.

The students are very busy after school with extracurricular activities and have difficulty arranging a time when they can get together. They need to find somewhere to work, but many of their parents are also very busy, and it is difficult to find a place to work, then arrange for someone to drive everyone to the agreed-upon location. Although the group's members work well together in class and have very trusting relationships, their parents are now involved in this project (and not happy about it). The task is no longer a cooperative one as intended because adults are involved and are putting pressure on their children to get the work done quickly. Mr. Johnson's intention to have students engage in a task that requires deep thought has backfired. By assigning the task to the students to do at home, he introduced elements (parents, transportation, scheduling difficulties) that changed the nature of their collaboration.

R I D E

REFLECTION FOR ACTION

The Event

A group of third graders have been given a bag of money and asked to find out the total amount of money in the bag. Maria, Carla, Andy, and Wilson are talking to one another. Part of their discussion was presented at the beginning of the chapter. Is the group effective? How would you know?

Reflection R I D E

The group is not acting like a group. The two girls, Maria and Carla, are talking to each other and trying to do the task that the teacher assigned. The two boys, Wilson and Andy, are not doing the task and are talking about a girl. They do not interact with the two girls in their group. What is this an example of? It could be an example of poor classroom management, because two of the children are not paying any attention to the task. It could be an example of ineffective instruction, because the teacher did not assign a task that engages the students. It could also be an example of the operation of status characteristics, because the girls do not interact with the boys. It is an example of a dysfunctional group because the two pairs of students do not interact, and one pair is behaving inappropriately. The students who are working on the task make no effort to engage the other students.

What Theoretical/Conceptual Information Might Assist in Interpreting and Remedying this Situation? Consider the following:

Group Structures

Slavin and the Johnsons describe many of the features of effective group structures. The participants' goals should be interdependent, and each student must be individually accountable for the group's achievement. Perhaps the teacher did not help the students develop a sense of interdependence.

Task Structures

Steiner (1972) describes several types of tasks on which groups work. Some of these tasks are completed by simply having a competent individual solve the problem. Some require coordination of the efforts of several members of a group. Cohen (1994) describes the kinds of cognitive processes that can be promoted using structured and unstructured tasks. The task of finding out how much money is in the bag is a procedural one that is not easily divided among group members.

Classroom Management

The teacher is not attending to the group's interaction and has not noticed the off-task behavior of two of its members. The teacher should draw on theories of reward and scaffolding to correct the problem.

Information Gathering R I D E

How would you decide which of the three possibilities listed above is the correct one? What else would you like to know? The group is not effective in that its four members are not working together. Two members are working on the assigned task, and the other two are off-task. It is almost as though there were two parallel conversations going on. You might like to know whether the two off-task children are typically off-task. You need to be careful if you determine that the two boys are typically off-task. You might attribute the problem to characteristics of the students and not to the nature of the task. It is possible that the teacher always assigns boring tasks that the boys are unlikely to pay attention to or the tasks might be very easy and not require much effort on the part of the boys, leaving them plenty of time to get into trouble.

You might also like to know whether this short segment of conversation is representative of the group's work or just a brief moment of distraction. Depending on the answers to these questions, you might make a different decision about how to solve the problem. If you were the teacher, you might ask the students' previous teacher about their typical behaviors. Do not rely solely on that teacher's comments because they may color your expectations about these students. You might consult the research literature and find out what it says about task structures that promote more effective engagement. You might also look at the literature on motivation to find out what it says about how to get students engaged in a task.

Decision Making R I D E

What is the best interpretation, given the available information? Without more information, you would conclude that the group is not working well. There are problems with the group's structure. The principles of cooperative learning suggest that heterogeneous groups can work effectively, but group members need to experience interdependence, and each member of the group needs to be individually accountable. The two on-task students in this group make no effort to engage the other students and do not try to redirect them, as might be expected if the students believed that their goals were intertwined. There may also be problems with the task structure. The task does not seem to require contributions by all the group's members, and it therefore facilitates cognitive and social loafing on the part of some of the students. To the extent that the two boys are off-task, there is a problem in classroom management, but this problem arises as a consequence of failing to structure the group properly and use a group-worthy task (Lotan, 2003) that would motivate all the members of the group.

Evaluation R I D E

Based on the available information, if you were the classroom teacher, you might decide to assign the students a new task that requires each participant to be involved. You should assign each student a role within the group and require that they all sign a contract that commits them to performing their assigned role. By doing this, you will help them understand the goals of the task and help them become more committed to completing the work. The two students who were on-task might encourage the others to perform their assigned roles. You might also find a more interesting task that requires the students to consider alternative solutions to a problem, and you could create a system of individual accountability that would require each student to be responsible for learning.

If you tried a new task or new procedures, would the group function better? You should monitor the group closely to determine whether the students participate more equally. At the end of the period, you might ask the students to assess how well they played their roles and how attentive to the task they were. If you find that the problem of unequal participation remains unsolved, you should engage in a new cycle of reflection, information gathering, decision making, and evaluation.

Further Practice: Your Turn

Here is a second event for you to consider. In doing so, carry out the processes of reflection, information gathering, decision making, and evaluation.

The Event

You have finally decided to have your sixth-grade students work in groups. You have 26 students in your class, 16 boys and 10 girls. Four of them have special needs. The project on which the children will work will take about two weeks. Tommy is often absent because of illness.

How many groups will you form? What will the composition of the groups be?

SUMMARY

● **How do various theoretical perspectives describe the means by which students can learn from peers?**

Much of the work on cooperative learning is based on a social-motivational perspective and relies on group goals, rewards, and individual accountability to ensure success. Social-cohesion perspectives also rely on positive interdependence among group members for successful peer learning. Interdependence in this case is created by developing social skills and encouraging care and concern for others. Alternative explanations for the efficacy of peer learning can be found in cognitive-developmental and cognitive-elaboration perspectives. The various perspectives on peer learning suggest different mechanisms through which peers may promote learning. The implications for the decisions teachers make vary accordingly. Key decisions involve those related to the size and composition of groups, the tasks on which they work, whether rewards or recognition are provided, and whether there is individual accountability.

● **How effective is tutoring? What processes are involved?**

Students have the greatest chance to participate when working with a single other student. In larger groups, there are fewer opportunities for each student to participate. It is also easier for teachers to organize pairs of students and maintain control of the classroom environment. This is particularly important if the teacher lacks experience in conducting groups or the students lack experience in working together. There are a variety of strategies for getting students to work effectively in pairs. Many of them involve various forms of tutoring; they include classwide peer tutoring, reciprocal peer tutoring, peer-assisted learning, Scripted Cooperation, and others. Tutoring is generally effective. Students can be trained in how to prompt their partners' understanding (by providing cues or hints) and in ways to reduce the tutors' dominance of the dialogue between tutor and tutee.

● **What do teachers need to consider when having students work in larger groups?**

When students are assigned to larger groups, the composition of the groups must be carefully considered. Techniques for use with larger groups include Jigsaw and Jigsaw II, group investigations, and structured academic controversies. Characteristics such as race, gender, ethnicity, and language of origin can have an effect on group interactions. The research evidence on the effects of gender on interaction is mixed. However, these variables should be considered when forming groups, and group interaction should be closely monitored. Status characteristics may operate in a larger group, with high-status students having more opportunities to participate and to do so in ways that promote learning. Low-status students have limited opportunities. Strategies for minimizing the effects of status characteristics include selecting peer-learning techniques that enable all students to participate.

● **What kinds of tasks are suitable for groups of students?**

Peer learning can be used with a range of tasks. Tasks vary in the complexity of the cognitive processes required, ranging from simple rehearsal strategies to complex higher-order reasoning, metacognition, and problem solving. Unstructured tasks permit more creativity but may also lead to negative social processes. Students typically need a great deal of support to engage in higher-level thinking. Such support can be provided through the use of questions written and prepared in advance. Teachers can provide students with question stems to help guide their discussions.

● **What is the role of the teacher when using a peer-learning strategy?**

The teacher must play a very active role when using peer-learning techniques in the classroom. The teacher's role includes many tasks: preparing learning activities, building community, designing tasks that are group-worthy, providing a model of cognitive activity, coordinating activities, and evaluating groups' products and processes.

● **Do diverse learners benefit from peer learning?**

Race, ethnicity, and gender may function as diffuse status characteristics and affect the interactions that occur within a group. Teachers need to monitor rates of participation by diverse students for evidence of effects of status characteristics and intervene to increase participation by lower-status students. Racial and ethnic minorities are thought to benefit from the use of cooperative learning methods, and intergroup relations are thought to improve as a result. However, few conclusions can be drawn about any benefits that might accrue to diverse learners that do not accrue to other participants in cooperative or other peer-learning techniques.

● **Can peer learning be used effectively with students who have special needs?**

The research evidence on the academic benefits of cooperative learning for students with special needs is mixed. There is stronger evidence that such students benefit both from being tutored and from serving as tutors.

Key Terms

accommodation, p. 300
assigning competence, p. 321
assimilation, p. 300
classroom management, p. 303
cognitive conflict, p. 302
cognitive disequilibrium, p. 300
conceptual change teaching, p. 301
constructivist perspective, p. 300
dialectical constructivism, p. 302
diffuse status characteristics, p. 300

goal structure, p. 293
individual accountability, p. 394
interdependence, p. 293
meta-analysis, p. 297
metacognition, p. 297
negative interdependence, p. 293
participation structures, p. 312
positive interdependence, p. 293
positive practice, p. 308
problem solving, p. 325

scaffolding, p. 303
schema, p. 299
Scripted Cooperation, p. 299
status characteristics, p. 319
status differences, p. 300
stereotype threat, p. 319
tutoring, p. 304
zone of proximal development, p. 303

Exercises

1. *Why Do You Like Working with Peers?*

   Find a number of students of different ages and ask them why they like working with their peers in a classroom setting. Make notes of their responses and try to categorize the reasons they give. Are the reasons related more to social and emotional processes than to cognitive processes?

2. *Why Do You Dislike Working with Peers?*

   Find a number of students of different ages and ask them why they dislike working with their peers in a classroom setting. Make notes of their responses and try to categorize the reasons they give. Are the reasons related more to social and emotional processes than to cognitive processes?

3. *Difficulties with Group Processes*

   Observe students in an elementary school classroom and a high school classroom in which group work or cooperative learning is being conducted. What difficulties do you see in the group process? Are the students on-task? Do they seem to understand what is being asked of them? Do you think they experience positive interdependence?

4. *Classroom Management of Group Work*

   Observe students in an elementary school classroom and a high school classroom in which group work or cooperative learning is being conducted. What aspects of the groups' behavior indicate whether the teacher is an effective classroom manager? What problems do you see? How could they be solved?

5. *Tutoring*

   Pair up with someone in your class and tutor your partner on content from this course. Make notes of the strategies you use to gauge your partner's understanding. What kinds of questions do you ask? What do you learn about your partner's understanding of the material from the answers provided? How do you adjust your strategies?

Lesson Plans

Lesson #1: "Traveling across Texas"

GRADES: 6–8

SUBJECTS: Geography, Math, Texas History

I. OVERVIEW: This activity cuts across several disciplines. It focuses on learning major Texas cities along with reasonable travel routes between cities. In addition to learning about the geography of Texas, students will also utilize valuable map skills, along with the concepts of measurement and mileage. Finally, students will investigate the history of various Texas cities.

While this particular activity is created for the state of Texas, the lesson can be modified for other states.

II. OBJECTIVES: Students will be able to:

- Demonstrate map skills, including distance, measurement, and locating
- Solve basic math computations, including measurement and conversions
- Demonstrate and refine communication skills while engaging in discussions regarding best travel routes

III. MATERIALS:

- Texas road maps
- Linear measurement conversion charts or prior conversion knowledge
- Rulers
- Books about Texas
- Internet connection/library access for research

IV. PROCEDURE:

1. Students will be assigned to groups of four. The task is to come up with the best travel route based on Texas highways.

2. The teacher will begin by asking a variety of questions to the class regarding the location of specific cities:

- Dallas
- Austin
- San Antonio
- Houston
- El Paso

3. Sample questions may include:

- Which city is the capital of Texas?
- Where is Dallas (San Antonio, Houston, or El Paso) in relation to the capital?
- What do we know about these cities?
- Why may we want to visit in these cities?

4. After the class discussion, the students will be asked to plan a trip across Texas, starting in San Antonio. The trip will include a visit to each major city listed above. While planning the trip, the following conditions apply:

- Students must determine the best order and routes to use in order to save time and mileage.
- Based on the highways chosen, students will document the directions and miles driven between cities.

5. While visiting each major city, the students should visit one historic destination. Students should be able to explain the significance and location of these destinations.

6. The final report should consist of the following:

- The route order
- The highways/directions between cities
- The number of miles between cities
- The number of miles converted to yards and feet
- The historic destination to be visited in each city, along with the significance behind these places

Ask Yourself!

1. What theoretical approach to peer learning do you think this teacher has adopted? Explain why.

2. What kinds of prerequisite skills (cognitive and social) do you think students would need to be able to do these tasks effectively?

3. What role(s) should the teacher play?

Lesson Plans

Lesson #2: "Paper Airplanes"

GRADES: 5–7

SUBJECT AREAS: Math, Science

I. OVERVIEW: Students will work in teams to construct the best paper airplane possible. Students will have time to test different folds and materials in order to reach ultimate flying distance. The activity will end with a flying competition and data analysis of the results.

II. OBJECTIVES: Students will be able to:
- Work in teams to construct a paper airplane.
- Conduct measurements and analyze data compiled from the flying distance of other teams.
- Convert their data into a visual representation in the form of a graph

III. MATERIALS:
- Variety of paper textures (printer paper, construction paper, cardboard, newspaper, etc.)
- Scissors
- Tape measures and rulers
- Chart paper

IV. PROCEDURES:

1. Students will be divided into groups of four. Together, the students will construct a paper airplane using the variety of paper provided. The airplane must be constructed out of paper and folds only (no glue/tape/weights/etc.). More than one type of paper may be used.

2. Students will engage in a flying competition. Each team will throw their airplanes from a designated starting point. The teams should leave their airplanes in place until all airplanes have been thrown.

3. As a team, the students will measure the distance of each airplane from the designated starting point. All information should be documented.

4. While still in teams, the students will create a chart or graph to document the distance of each flight. The students may use a chart or graph of their choice or the teacher may choose.

5. After the charts are complete, students will use the data to determine the mean, median, range, and mode of the separate distances. This information should be documented as well.

6. To conclude, each team should come up with a question they wish to ask an opposing team regarding plane construction or flying strategy. This activity should generate a class discussion.

Ask Yourself!

1. What theoretical approach to peer learning do you think this teacher has adopted? Explain why.

2. What kinds of prerequisite skills (cognitive and social) do you think students would need to be able to do these tasks effectively?

3. What role(s) should the teacher play?

> ### An Old Jewish Fable
>
> It seems that bigots were eager to rid their town of a Jewish man who had opened a tailor shop on Main Street, so they sent a group of rowdies to harass the tailor. Each day, the ruffians would show up to jeer. The situation was grim, but the tailor was ingenious. One day when the hoodlums arrived, he gave each of them a dime for their efforts. Delighted, they shouted their insults and moved on. The next day they returned to shout, expecting their dime. But the tailor said he could afford only a nickel and proceeded to hand a nickel to each of them. Well, they were a bit disappointed, but a nickel is after all a nickel, so they took it, did their jeering, and left. The next day, they returned once again, and the tailor said he had only a penny for them and held out his hand. Indignant, the young toughs sneered and proclaimed that they would certainly not spend their time jeering at him for a measly penny. So they didn't. And all was well for the tailor.

Like grades and extra-credit points, money is often used as a motivator. In the old Jewish fable above, once the tailor started handing out dimes, the ruffians came to believe they were jeering for the money. When the money dried up, so did the motivation to jeer. In schools, the currency is grades. To induce students to read, complete assignments, and participate in class, educators offer grades. Sometimes this leads students to think they are in it for the grade. Without a grade to justify their effort (Will this be on the test?), students' motivation can dry up in the same way that it did for the ruffians.

If students see their motivational resources evaporate, they will understandably have a difficult time generating motivation of their own to engage in lessons and activities. This state of affairs leads educators to search for engagement-fostering motivational strategies that do not involve external inducements to action.

Mrs. Watson is one such teacher. She loves teaching, and she invests herself heavily in the lessons she prepares. However, 20 minutes into the day's lesson, she sees her students staring blankly and giving only a half-hearted effort.

R I D E Reflection for Action

When looking back at her students' unengaged faces, what can Mrs. Watson do? Where does disengagement come from, and how can she counteract it? Where does enthusiastic engagement come from, and what can Mrs. Watson do during her instruction to promote it?

Guiding Questions

- What is engagement, what does it look like, and why is it important?
- How can teachers engage diverse learners and students with special needs?
- What is motivation?
- What is the difference between intrinsic and extrinsic motivation?
- How can teachers support students' psychological needs?
- In what ways can teachers spark students' motivated engagement?
- In what ways can teachers calm students' anxieties and fears?
- How can teachers motivate students during uninteresting activities?

CHAPTER OVERVIEW

Teachers care deeply about their students' engagement because they know that it predicts how much their students learn and how well they fare in school. In this chapter, we focus on students' engagement during learning activities. In doing so, we define engagement, identify what engagement versus disengagement looks like, explain why it is important, explain where it comes from, and identify instructional strategies for promoting it.

One source of engagement is intrinsic motivation, and we discuss intrinsic motivation, extrinsic rewards, and how extrinsic rewards affect intrinsic motivation. Psychological needs are another source of engagement, and we present three such needs: autonomy, competence, and relatedness. We also discuss curiosity, interest, and positive affect as ways to spark engagement during instruction.

The chapter also addresses student disengagement. We explain the roots of students' intentional and unintentional disengagement by focusing, first, on anxiety, self-worth protection, and self-handicapping as students' intentionally or strategically enact disengagement strategies and, second, on amotivation (the lack of motivation) as students sometimes react to unappealing learning activities with apathy. The chapter concludes by identifying ways teachers can calm these engagement-draining anxieties, defenses, and fears and also ways teachers can turn amotivation into motivated engagement.

Engagement

Motivation is a private experience. Teachers cannot *see* students' motivation directly. Instead, what they see during learning activities is how engaged or unengaged their students are. Thus, to understand motivation, it is first necessary to understand the outward manifestation of motivation—*engagement*.

What Engagement Looks Like

Engagement refers to the extent of a student's active involvement in a learning activity (Fredricks, Blumenfeld, & Paris, 2004; Furrer & Skinner, 2003; Jimerson, Campos, & Grief, 2003; National Research Council, 2004; Wellborn, 1991). It is a multidimensional construct, meaning that engagement consists of the four distinct but highly intercorrelated aspects of behavioral engagement, emotional engagement, cognitive engagement, and agentic engagement. To monitor how actively involved a student is during a learning activity, teachers can keep track of students' behavioral, emotional, cognitive, and agentic engagements, as summarized in Figure 10.1.

engagement How actively involved the student is during the learning activity.

Behavioral Engagement When they are highly engaged, students are active and they display strong and enduring effort. During learning activities, behaviorally engaged students show on-task attention, strong effort, and enduring persistence (Skinner, Kindermann, & Furrer, 2009; Wellborn, 1991). *Attention* represents the student's concentration and on-task focus. With *effort*, students invest a full measure of their capacities in what they are doing, rather than holding back and just going through the motions. With *persistence*, students invest their effort over time, even in the face of difficulties and setbacks. Whether the activity is completing a worksheet or writing a paper, the behaviorally engaged student is on-task, working hard, and keeping at the task over time.

behavioral engagement The extent to which a student displays on-task attention, strong effort, and enduring persistence on a learning activity.

Emotional Engagement Engagement involves more than just paying attention, working hard, and persisting in the face of obstacles. It also involves the presence of positive emotions that facilitate task engagement and the absence of negative emotions that take students away from task engagement (Furrer & Skinner, 2003; Miserandino, 1996). When emotionally engaged, students study and practice hard and long, but they do so within an emotional atmosphere of interest, curiosity, enthusiasm, enjoyment, and a sense of *wanting to*. In contrast, emotionally unengaged students might study or practice hard, but they do so under a cloud of negative emotion—tension, pressure, or stress—while experiencing task-withdrawing emotions such as distress, anger, or frustration as well as a sense of *having to* that gives them a sense of conflict or resistance to their behavioral engagement.

emotional engagement The extent to which a student displays task-facilitating emotions such as interest and does not display task-withdrawing emotions such as distress.

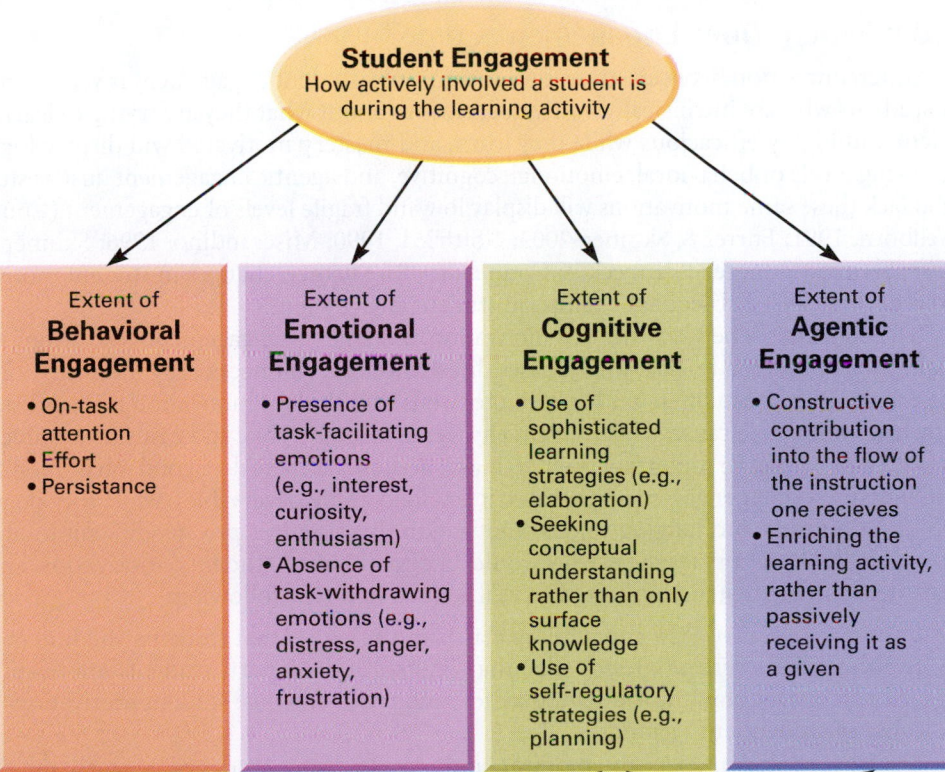

Figure 10.1 Four Interrelated Aspects of Engagement

(© Media Bakery)

When highly engaged, students show not only attention, effort, and persistence but also positive emotion.

cognitive engagement The extent to which a student displays the use of sophisticated learning strategies, such as elaboration, to conceptually understand the meaning of what he or she is trying to learn.

agentic engagement The extent to which a student contributes constructively into the flow of instruction he or she receives.

Cognitive Engagement Engaging oneself in a learning activity goes beyond effort and enjoyment to include the extent to which the student seeks to conceptually understand what he or she is trying to learn. To understand material at the conceptual level, students need to utilize sophisticated learning strategies such as elaboration and organization to try to understand and make sense of the material they are trying to learn (Elliot, McGregor, & Gable, 1999; Greene & Miller, 1996; Vansteenkiste et al., 2005; Walker, Greene, & Mansell, 2006). While learning, such **cognitively engaged** students paraphrase what they are learning, relate the new information to their prior knowledge, and think critically and deeply about what the information means. When cognitively unengaged, students learn with strategies such as rote memorization and basic rehearsal, as they read or copy the material over and over again or, perhaps, try to memorize the material in the exact way that the teacher presented it to them. That is, cognitively unengaged students might work on the lesson, but they do so in a shallow or rather superficial way.

Agentic Engagement **Agentic engagement** refers to the extent to which students contribute constructively into the flow of the instruction they receive (Reeve, 2011; Reeve & Tseng, 2011). Agentic engagement is the process in which students proactively and strategically try to enhance and personalize the conditions and circumstances under which they learn. For instance, upon hearing the teacher announce the learning objective for the day, highly agentically engaged students will offer their input, generate questions, express their interests and preferences, contribute something helpful, request examples, participate in and contribute to class discussions, and basically speak up whenever they can add something important and constructive into the ongoing flow of the instruction (Koenigs, Fiedler, & deCharms, 1977). Agentically unengaged students, in contrast, simply and passively let the teacher tell them what to do.

From Where Does Engagement Come?

The interconnection between student motivation and student engagement is very high. That is, students who are intrinsically motivated, curious about what they are trying to learn, confident and highly efficacious while they learn, and mastery motivated will display high and enduring levels of behavioral, emotional, cognitive, and agentic engagement, just as students who lack these same motivations will display low and fragile levels of engagement (Connell & Wellborn, 1991; Furrer & Skinner, 2003; Gottfried, 1990; Miserandino, 1996; Skinner et al., 2008; Skinner, Zimmer-Gembeck, & Connell, 1998). Further, changes in student motivation precede and cause subsequent changes in student engagement.

The connection between student motivation and student engagement is so strong that it is almost as though a teacher who focuses directly on one will necessarily indirectly focus on the other. The biggest difference between the two is that student motivation is the private and largely unobservable cause, while student engagement is the public and easily observable effect or outcome. This is an important point to make, because teachers do a good job of monitoring and judging student engagement (because it is public, easily observable), while they do a poor job of monitoring and judging student motivation (because it is private, difficult to observe; Lee et al., 2011). Thus, teachers who would like to enhance students' motivation and engagement during instruction would be well advised to do the following:

What Does This Mean to Me?
How engaged were you during your last class period? How could you tell?

- *Prior to instruction.* Plan and develop classroom activities that students will find motivating. That is, create a lesson plan that vitalizes and supports students' motivation. Prior to instruction, think about, plan for, and try to enhance student motivation—the cause of student engagement.
- *During instruction.* Focus on, monitor, and try to enhance students' engagement during the learning activities. Think about, keep track of, and try to enhance student engagement—the effect of student motivation.

Why Engagement Is Important

Engagement is important for four reasons. First, it makes learning possible. Learning a second language or developing the skill necessary to play a musical instrument is practically impossible without attention, effort, positive emotion, deep information processing and understanding, and a sense of personal agency. In effect, engagement is a necessary prerequisite for a productive learning experience. So, if educators want to promote students' learning and skill development, the path to do so goes right through engagement.

Second, engagement predicts students' academic progress and achievement (Ladd & Dinella, 2009). Engagement predicts achievement-related outcomes, such as grades and scores on standardized tests, and it does so across all grade levels (National Research Council, 2004). In one longitudinal study, students' engagement during elementary school predicted their achievement test scores and their decade-later decision to stay in high school or drop out (Alexander, Entwisle, & Dauber, 1993; Alexander, Entwisle, & Horsey, 1997). That is, engagement predicts how well students fare in school in terms of the grades they make, the gains they show in standardized test scores, and whether they complete school rather than drop out. Thus, engagement contributes to learning the day's lesson, but it further contributes to students' longer-term school functioning and achievement.

Third, engagement is malleable and, hence, open to a teacher's influence. Therefore, it makes sense to give serious consideration to school-based interventions that aim to enhance student engagement (Finn & Rock, 1997). For instance, engagement increases when teachers (1) relate to students in caring ways (Battistich et al., 1997; Birch & Ladd, 1997; Murray & Greenberg, 2000; Wentzel, 1997); (2) support students' autonomy or self-determination (Perry, 1998; Reeve, Jang, et al., 2004); (3) provide clear structure (Connell, 1990; Skinner et al., 2008); and (4) offer classroom activities that are interesting, optimally challenging, and provide opportunities to collaborate with peers (Davidson, 1999; Guthrie & Wigfield, 2000; Newman et al., 1992; Turner, Thorpe, & Mayer, 1998). Teachers might feel a bit frustrated that they cannot quickly change a student's ability level on a particular task, but engagement is different in that caring, supportive, structured, and challenging instruction can quickly change engagement for the better.

Fourth, engagement gives teachers the moment-to-moment feedback they need to determine how well their efforts to motivate students are working. For instance, when a teacher implements a motivational strategy, he or she can closely monitor the students for changes in their degree of engagement. Engagement is the telltale feedback about students' motivation.

What Kids Say and Do

What Engaged Students Say during Learning Activities

To communicate behavioral engagement:

I work hard in this class.

To communicate emotional engagement:

Class is fun—I enjoy it.

To communicate cognitive engagement:

When reading, I try to connect the things I am reading about with what I already know.

To communicate agentic engagement:

When I need something, I'll ask the teacher for it instead of just suffering quietly.

How Can I Use This?

The next time you help someone learn something, closely monitor that person's engagement and try to understand why it rises and falls during the lesson.

The Classroom Flow: Learning Environment → Motivation → Engagement → Student Outcomes

Student engagement comes from student motivation, so the next question to ask is: From where does student motivation come? This is a crucial question for every teacher to ask (and answer), as a teacher's answer to this question will influence the motivating style he or she relies on when trying to motivate and engage students in learning activities. For instance, some teachers believe that students generally lack motivation of their own and they therefore have to motivate students, as through offering attractive incentives, modeling desired behavior, or being highly enthusiastic about the lesson. Other teachers believe that students have their own motivation and the teacher's task is therefore to nurture and support the motivation students already have.

Those who study motivation generally agree that student motivation comes, in part, from the student himself or herself. That is, students walk into the classroom with a full repertoire of motivational resources that are fully capable of sparking their classroom engagement—

motivational resources such as interests, preferences, goals, and achievement strivings. From such a point of view, the teacher's role is to support the motivation students already have. That students have motivation of their own is only part of the story, however. Earlier, the point was made that student motivation needs supportive conditions, and that means that teachers and the classroom environment more generally also affect and contribute to student motivation. So, the two origins of student motivation are the students themselves and the learning environment, which of course includes the teacher.

The flowchart presented in Figure 10.2 summarizes the classroom flow that begins with the learning environment, extends into and influences students' motivation and engagement, and finally produces particular student outcomes. This chapter is essentially organized around the same top-to-bottom linear flow of activity that is depicted in Figure 10.2.

A good deal of research supports this basic "Learning Environment → Student Motivation → Student Engagement → Student Outcomes" model, but it is incomplete in some ways because students are, to some extent, architects of the classroom environment in which they learn as well as architects of their own classroom motivation and engagement. For this reason, the flowchart adds the small upward arrows that communicate that (1) student motivation (whether students are motivated or not, or whether students have one type of motivation or another) affects the teacher's motivating style and the classroom learning environment, (2) student engagement (whether students are engaged or unengaged in classroom activities) affects the teacher's motivating style and the classroom learning environment, and (3) student outcomes (the extent to which students learn, achieve, and develop skills) affect the teacher's motivating style and the classroom learning environment (Pelletier, Seguin-Levesque, & Legault, 2002; Skinner & Belmont, 1993). In addition, the outcomes students experience affect, at least in part, students' motivation and engagement. Further, student engagement also exerts some influence over student motivation, as students' high-quality engagement can produce motivation-enhancing experiences such as psychological need satisfaction or the sense of confidence that can grow self-efficacy beliefs (Reeve, 2011).

One way to use the flowchart depicted in Figure 10.2 to help understand student motivation and engagement is to work backwards in the chart to identify the causal source underlying each student variable. For instance, consider student outcomes. Most people involved in education (teachers, parents, administrators, the public) care deeply about student outcomes such as learning, achievement, and skill development. The question then becomes: From where do such positive student outcomes come? While many factors influence these outcomes, one fundamental cause that explains students' positive versus negative outcomes is the extent to which students are actively engaged in the classroom. That is, changes in student engagement cause changes in student outcomes. That of course raises the next question: From where does enthusiastic student engagement come? Student motivation is a strong cause of student engagement. This raises a final question: From where does constructive student motivation come? As discussed previously, student motivation comes from the students themselves, but the role of the learning environment and the role of a teacher's motivating style are important influences.

This latter point—that teachers and the learning environment affect student motivation—is so important to effective teaching that it deserves extra attention. As students express their inner motivations—their interests, their goals, and their sense of curiosity—the teacher reacts. To the extent that teachers can attend to, value, and support students' existing motivations and find ways to build on them, students have the opportunity to become increasingly energized and engaged. Similarly, to the extent that students lack motivation in the sense that they do not come to class with goals to strive for, a value for what is to be learned, or an interest in the subject matter, then students will need motivational support from their teacher. For instance, teachers can suggest meaningful goals for students to strive for (e.g., self-improvement), explain the value that lies behind the lesson, or present the

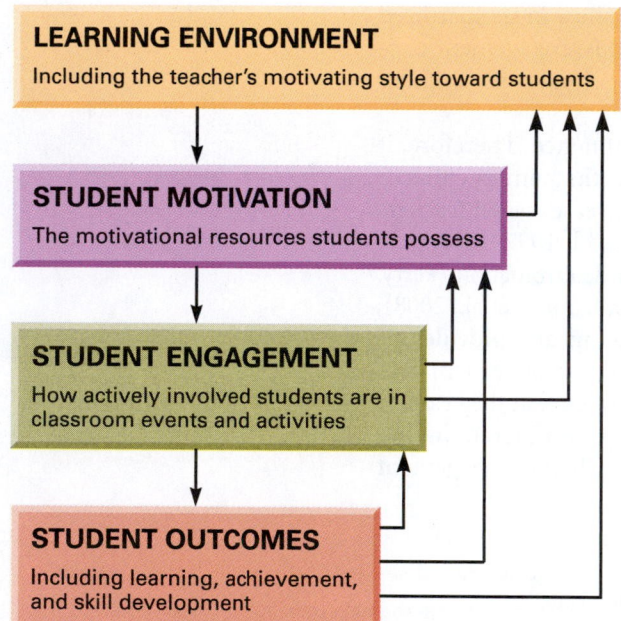

Figure 10.2 Depiction of the Classroom Flow That Begins with the Learning Environment and Extends to Student Motivation and Engagement to Produce Student Outcomes

lesson in a particularly interesting way. Such reasoning leads to three principles about the nature of motivation and how teachers can go about the task of motivating students.

Principle 1: Students have motivation of their own. The vitalization (versus hibernation) of these inner motivational resources explains why students willingly engage (or fail to engage) in learning activities.

Principle 2: Teachers motivate students when they provide classroom conditions that nurture students' motivation; teachers fail to motivate students when they provide classroom conditions that neglect or frustrate students' existing motivation.

Principle 3: How well or how poorly teachers involve and nurture students' inner motivational resources will be reflected on a moment-to-moment and on a day-to-day basis in how engaged versus unengaged students are during classroom activities.

Student–Teacher Dialectic A dialectical approach to motivation begins with the assumption that the student is inherently motivated and inherently active. Inner motivation is the source of that inherent activity (Deci & Ryan, 1985). The different motivational resources that students inherently have appear in the left-hand box in Figure 10.3. Notice that the eight different types of motivation shown in this Student Motivation box represent the contents of this chapter. That is, starting with the next section (on motivation), the chapter will discuss the engagement-facilitating motivations of intrinsic motivation, internalized extrinsic motivation, psychological needs, interests, values, curiosity, positive affect, and achievement strivings.

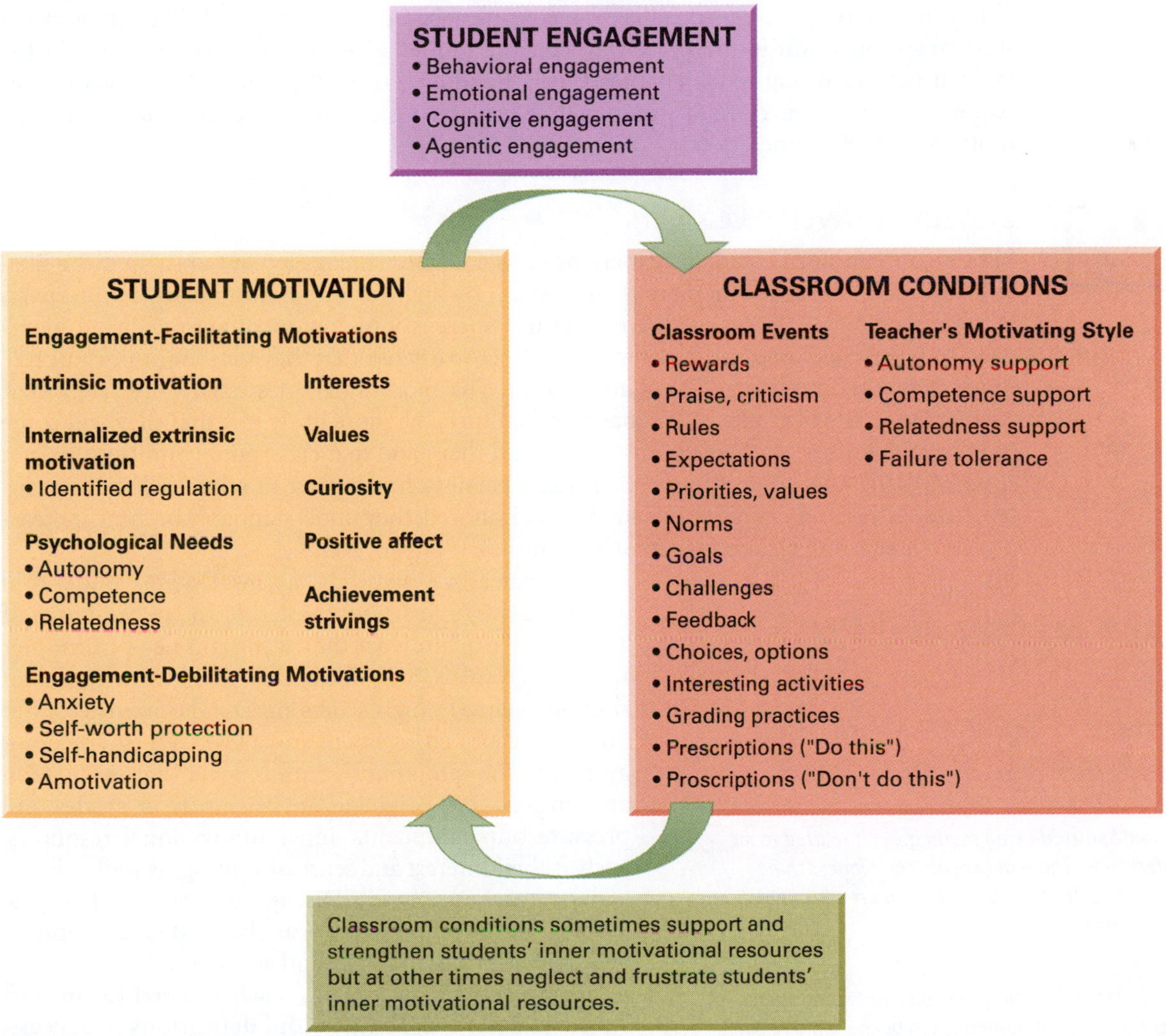

Figure 10.3 Student–Classroom Dialectic Framework

How well versus how poorly students experience these eight motivations can be tracked by teachers on a moment-to-moment basis by monitoring students' behavioral engagement, emotional engagement, cognitive engagement, and agentic engagement, as shown in Figure 10.3 by the upper green arrow that arises out of the Student Motivation box. A dialectical approach also assumes that people (teachers, parents, coaches, school administrators, peers), external events (rewards, rules, goals), and the teacher's motivating style (how supportive the teacher is) affect the student and introduce new forms of motivation for the student to internalize. These socialization demands and new sources of motivation are represented in the Learning Environment box on the right-hand side of the figure, and their influence on student motivation is shown by the lower green arrow in Figure 10.3.

Overall, a dialectical approach to motivation emphasizes the reciprocal and interdependent relationship between students' motivation and classroom conditions, such as a teacher's motivating style (Deci & Ryan, 1991; Reeve, Deci, & Ryan, 2004). In dialectic, both the student's motivation and the teacher's motivating style constantly change. The ongoing outcome of the student–classroom dialectic is an ever-changing synthesis in which the student's inner motivation is nurtured or thwarted by classroom conditions, and classroom conditions introduce new forms of motivation for students to internalize and accept as their own (Deci & Ryan, 1985).

As an example, consider the motivation to read. Interest and curiosity may lead a student to seek out and read a book (i.e., may lead to engagement). To support the student's interest and curiosity, the teacher might offer interesting books and time to pursue personal interests. Or the teacher might ask the student to read an assigned book. In doing so, the teacher will likely ignore or bypass the student's inner motivation and instead offer an external motivator—for example, a deadline or a test. If so, the student will likely gain a new motive to read. This deadline-based or test-based motivation will likely thwart the student's motivation in the same way that the money given to the hoodlums did in the fable at the beginning of the chapter. Overall and over time, the student's motivation becomes a changing mixture of inner factors (e.g., curiosity, interest) and socially acquired motives (e.g., deadlines, tests).

Engaging Diverse Learners

Low-income minority students experience less educational engagement and are more likely to drop out of school than are their middle- or high-income nonminority counterparts (Rumberger, 1987). To engage themselves in the classroom, low-income minority students need to feel understood and welcomed and to have a sense that they play an important role in the school community (Goodenow, 1993). The more different students are from their teachers in terms of ethnicity, language, and culture, the more likely it is that they will come to believe that their teachers do not understand them and that classroom conditions do not support their inner motivation. When students fail to find a place in school where their interests, abilities, and definitions of success are honored, they understandably become increasingly unengaged in classroom activities (Smith & Wilhelm, 2002).

In the nearby What Kids Say and Do box, students in an alternative high school located in the poorest area of a large city explain what they want and need from their teachers (Daniels & Arapostathis, 2005). Each student showed relatively high scores on standardized tests but poor classroom engagement and a low GPA (grade point average). The quotations communicate that motivation and engagement originate not so much in grades and pressure but in students' inner motivational resources, such as their interest and sense of valuing, as well as in the support teachers provide. Disengagement arose from the perception that the teacher was the student's opponent and enemy, rather than ally and advocate.

To promote engagement, teachers need to support students' interests, abilities, and definitions of success. Often, however, the approach teachers and schools take is to get tough. One approach, common in an era

What Kids Say and Do

What Unengaged Students Want Their Teachers to Know

Why I'm engaged:

I read that book, and I started liking reading.... It related to me a lot so it was interesting. The teachers are the biggest thing ... when the teachers pay attention to you like you're a student; like you're a person not a grade.

Why I'm unengaged:

You can't get good grades in something you can't stand. They blackmail you here to get your homework in because if you don't turn it in, you get an after-school detention.

of standardized tests and teacher accountability, is to pressure students into performing (Gratz, 2000; Thompson, 2001), as through grade-level retention, summer school remediation, and other similar strategies to improve students' abilities (Neill, 2003). While common, this approach fails to engage reluctant learners because compliance and obedience are poor replacements for the concept of engagement (see Figure 10.1). Compliance and obedience may tap somewhat into students' behavioral engagement, but they utterly fail in terms of tapping into and supporting students' emotional engagement, cognitive engagement, and agentic engagement. If teachers really want to engage students' positive emotions, conceptual learning, and personal agency, then they need to start by making a special effort to identify and support students' interests, abilities, and definitions of success.

Motivation

Motivation involves any force that energizes and directs behavior. *Energy* means that behavior is strong, intense, and full of effort. *Direction* means that behavior is focused on accomplishing a particular goal or outcome. The study of motivation is, therefore, the study of all the forces that create and sustain students' effortful, goal-directed action.

motivation Any force that energizes and directs behavior.

To understand students' motivation, consider three points. First, different types of motivation exist. In many teachers' minds, motivation is a unitary construct. Its key feature is its level, or amount. The question is "How much?" motivation does this student have, and the priority becomes: How can I foster more (or higher) motivation in my students? But there is more to motivation than "How much?" Watch as a student studies, paints, or reads a book, and you will see that motivation also varies in its type or quality. As you watch students study, paint, and read, ask: *Why* does this student work so hard? The answer to this *Why?* question reveals the student's type of motivation.

Second, some types of motivation produce better academic functioning than do other types (Vansteenkiste et al., 2009). For instance, intrinsic motivation is different from extrinsic motivation, and as we will see in Chapter 11, a goal to learn is different from a goal to perform (Ames & Archer, 1988; Ryan & Deci, 2000a, 2000b). Students who engage in learning activities out of intrinsic motivation and with the goal to learn consistently show a higher quality of engagement and learning than do those who study, paint, and read out of extrinsic motivation and with the goal to perform. This being the case, teachers need to focus not only on promoting high motivation but also on fostering productive types of motivation. A page from the diary of a class valedictorian in Milwaukee, Wisconsin, helps makes this point in the nearby What Kids Say and Do box.

A great deal of empirical evidence exists to support the conclusion that some types of student motivation produce better academic functioning than do other types (Vansteenkiste et al., 2009). But to understand this from a teacher's point of view (rather than from a researcher's point of view), try this thought experiment. For any classroom-based motivational strategy that comes to mind—including piquing curiosity, offering an optimal challenge, offering an attractive incentive if students will do what you ask them to do, or just yelling at students to get their work done—ask yourself how well that strategy can be expected to fully engage students in the learning activity. Relatively poor motivational strategies, like the third and fourth examples from the prior sentence, stir only students' behavioral engagement, as they leave students' emotional, cognitive, and agentic engagements either untouched or sacrificed so as to get the behavioral engagement. Relatively effective motivational strategies, like the first and second examples from the prior sentence, tap into and inspire the full range of students' engagement, including its behavioral, emotional, cognitive, and agentic aspects. Hence, a good question for any teacher to ask in selecting a classroom motivational

What Kids Say and Do

A Class Valedictorian Looks Back at the Quality of Her Motivation

Looking back on my high school career, I can see how extrinsically motivated I was. It has come to haunt me. I was seen as the smart girl in class. One of my best friends turned to competition to see who could be the highest achiever. She would focus solely on beating me in a test score or receiving the class award at the end of the year. I hated the competition, but I did not want to lose. I wanted to be the valedictorian and win all the awards. I was given worksheets upon worksheets for the majority of my classes. I spent hours at night doing tedious work. The whole school system should have taken the pressure off all the awards. It motivated me to do better in my classes but for all the wrong reasons.

How Can I Use This?

How will you motivate students? Which motivational strategies do you currently have high confidence in?

strategy is: Do I expect this motivational strategy to increase only students' behavioral engagement, or can I expect it to increase *all* aspects of students' engagement?

Third, to flourish, motivation needs supportive conditions. Each day, students walk into classrooms, relationships, and learning activities. The learning environment into which they walk can nurture and support their motivational strivings or it can neglect and frustrate those strivings. When students are surrounded by classroom environments that support and nurture their needs, wants, strivings, and constructive ways of thinking, they show greater engagement and learning.

Intrinsic and Extrinsic Motivation

As you watch students engage themselves in a learning activity, consider *why* they are engaged. Why is Mark reading that book? Why does Samantha answer questions in class? Why is Lamar a member of the school band?

Any such activity can be engaged in from two different motivations: intrinsic or extrinsic. On the one hand, a student might read a book because doing so produces an intrinsic sense of interest and enjoyment. On the other hand, a student might read a book because doing so produces an extrinsic reward, such as a sticker or public recognition in the school's Good Readers Club. *Any* activity, in fact, can be approached from either an intrinsic or an extrinsic motivational orientation (Pittman, Boggiano, & Ruble, 1983; Ryan & Deci, 2000a, 2000b).

Intrinsic motivation is the inherent desire to engage in one's interests and to exercise and develop one's capacities (Deci & Ryan, 1985). It emerges spontaneously out of the individual's needs for autonomy, competence, and relatedness. That these three psychological needs are the source of intrinsic motivation is shown in Figure 10.4. These three needs will be discussed in the next section, but the important point to mention now is that intrinsic motivation arises out of students' inherent psychological needs. Thus, to energize intrinsic motivation, teachers need to find ways to involve and nurture students' psychological needs. When teachers are able to do this—when students are offered classroom activities that allow them to feel free, capable, and accepted—then students say that class "is interesting, fun, and enjoyable."

Feelings of interest and enjoyment arise as *spontaneous satisfactions* from the experience of psychological need satisfaction (Ryan & Deci, 2000a, 2000b). So, whenever task engagement produces these experiences of spontaneous satisfaction ("its fun," "I like it," "it's so interesting"), then the task itself can generate student motivation ("reading is

intrinsic motivation The inherent desire to engage in one's interests and to exercise and develop one's capacities.

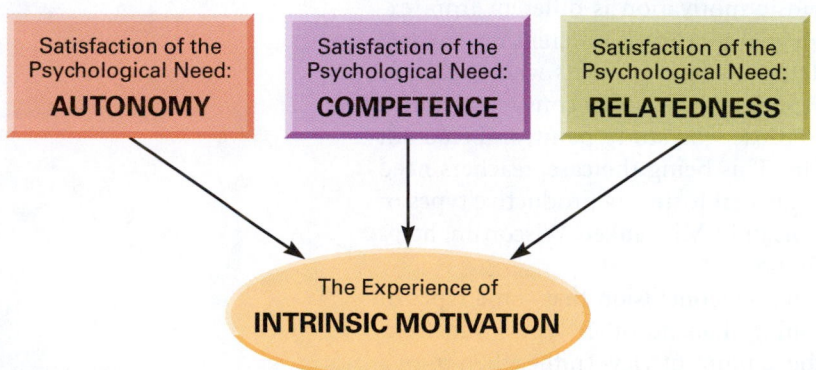

Figure 10.4 Psychological Need Satisfaction Is the Source of Intrinsic Motivation

fun," "I like reading," "reading is so interesting") to the point that students are intrinsically motivated to read. Student then say, "I want to read just because I enjoy it, and not necessarily for any other reason other than the experience of reading itself."

Intrinsic motivation yields numerous educational benefits. When students are intrinsically motivated, they exhibit healthy, productive functioning, such as initiative, persistence, creativity, high-quality learning, conceptual understanding of what they are learning, and positive well-being (Deci & Ryan, 1987; Ryan & Deci, 2000a, 2000b). To understand the constructive role of intrinsic motivation in students' lives, consider why students might want to read, play, exercise their skills, grow their competencies, make friends, learn to swim, explore learning materials, ask questions, learn to ride a bicycle, and a hundred of other such activities and personal competencies. It is intrinsic motivation that provides students with the naturally occurring motivation they need to engage in such initiative and learning.

Extrinsic motivation is a different type of motivation. It arises from outside incentives and consequences. Whenever students act to gain a reward, such as a high grade, or whenever students act to avoid a punishment, such as a teacher's criticism, their behavior is externally motivated. Students work hard not because they enjoy what they are doing but because they want to receive the reward or avoid the punishment. Extrinsic motivation

What Does This Mean to Me?

Do different types of motivation explain why you want to become a teacher?

exists as an *in-order-to* motivation (as in, Do this *in order to* get that). *This* is the behavioral request, whereas *that* is the incentive or consequence. In short, **extrinsic motivation** is an environmentally created reason to initiate or persist in an action.

Trying to extrinsically motivate students to engage in the school curriculum is a widely used strategy (Kohn, 1993). Common positive reinforcers in the classroom include praise, stickers, privileges, bonus points, tokens, marbles in jars, certificates, attention, high grades, scholarships, honors, trophies, prizes, public recognition (e.g., the school's honor roll), food, awards, money, and smiles of approval. The benefit of extrinsic motivation is that it elicits students' willing compliance. Generally speaking, students who are offered an attractive reward to engage themselves in a task are significantly more likely to do so than are students who are not offered a reward.

Hidden Costs of Rewards

Research on intrinsic and extrinsic motivation began with an intriguing question: "If a person is involved in an intrinsically interesting activity and begins to receive an extrinsic reward for doing it, what happens to his or her intrinsic motivation for that activity?" (Deci & Ryan, 1985, p. 43). For example, what happens to a child's motivation if she reads books for fun but then her parents see her reading and say, "Oh, look, Sarah is reading—let's show her how great we think that is and give her $5 for each book she reads!" One might suppose that rewarding Sarah's reading with an attractive prize would increase her motivation to read. It seems like common sense to think that if a student enjoys reading and is also rewarded for doing it, the intrinsic motivation (enjoyment) and extrinsic motivation (money) should work together to produce a sort of supermotivation. Indeed, if you ask teachers to make predictions about what would happen to students' motivation under these circumstances, almost every teacher will predict that student motivation would increase (Hom, 1994).

Supermotivation, however, does not occur. Rather, the imposition of an extrinsic reward in exchange for engaging oneself in an intrinsically interesting activity typically has a negative effect on future intrinsic motivation (Condry, 1977; Deci, Koestner, & Ryan, 1999; Kohn, 1993). This adverse effect is termed a **hidden cost of reward** (Lepper & Greene, 1978) because our society typically regards rewards as positive contributors to motivation (Boggiano et al., 1987). When people use rewards, they expect to gain the benefit of increasing motivation and behavior, but in so doing they often incur the hidden and unintentional cost of undermining intrinsic motivation (Deci et al., 1999; Kohn, 1993; Lepper & Greene, 1978; Rummel & Feinberg, 1988; Sutherland, 1993).

Teachers use rewards to motivate students, and they do so for the best of reasons—to increase students' motivation, engagement, and performance. But extrinsic motivation often carries a price in the form of three hidden costs. The first of those hidden costs is a loss of intrinsic motivation. As a case in point, consider the first school-based study to investigate whether extrinsic rewards undermine intrinsic motivation (Lepper, Greene, & Nisbett, 1973). Researchers visited a preschool and introduced a drawing game that the children found very interesting. The researchers observed the amount of time each child played with the drawing game during a free-play period. The researchers then randomly assigned each child into one of three groups. In an *expected-reward* group, children were promised an attractive Good Player award if they drew. In a *no-reward* group, children were simply asked whether they wanted to draw. Finally, in an *unexpected-reward* group, children were asked whether they wanted to draw but, after they had done so, were unexpectedly given the Good Player award. One week later, the experimenters returned to assess what had happened to the children's intrinsic motivation to draw. Children in the expected-reward group spent significantly less of their free-play time with the drawing game than did children in the other two groups. In effect, children in the expected-reward group lost some of their intrinsic interest in drawing. The no-reward and unexpected-reward groups showed no such decline.

In thinking about these findings, it helps to ask *why* the children wanted to draw during the second session. Children in the no-reward group drew because they wanted to— drawing was fun, an intrinsically motivating thing to do. Drawing itself was able to produce spontaneous satisfaction ("It's fun!") in these students. Children in the expected-reward group drew in order to get the Good Player award. During their free time, no additional Good Player award was promised and they had lost some of their intrinsic motivation to draw. Children in the unexpected-reward group drew for the same reasons that the children

extrinsic motivation An environmentally created reason to initiate or persist in an action or activity.

> **What Does This Mean to Me?**
> How is your type of motivation affecting the quality of your engagement with this book?

hidden cost of reward The unexpected, unintended, and adverse effects that extrinsic rewards sometimes have on intrinsic motivation, high-quality learning, and autonomous self-regulation.

in the no-reward group drew—because it was fun and an intrinsically motivated thing to do. Because these children were not induced to draw by an in-order-to promise, their intrinsic motivation was never put at risk.

Putting intrinsic motivation at risk is one cost of extrinsic reward, but there are two additional hidden costs (Deci & Ryan, 1987; Kohn, 1993). Extrinsic rewards also interfere with learning. They typically distract the learner's attention away from the material to be learned and toward getting the reward. As they learn, extrinsically motivated learners are generally passive information processors who attend to rote factual information (getting the right answer) at the expense of conceptual understanding (Vansteenkiste et al., 2005). Extrinsically motivated learners also prefer easy success and quick answers (conditions that make reward attainment more likely) over optimal challenge and the search for a creative solution (conditions that make learning most constructive). Thus, not only do extrinsic rewards put intrinsic motivation at risk, but they also take students away from learning per se and hence put the quality of their learning at risk (Benware & Deci, 1984; Harter, 1978; Pittman et al., 1983; Shapira, 1976).

The third hidden cost is that extrinsic rewards interfere with the development of autonomous self-regulation (Lepper, 1983; Ryan, 1993). After a history of always being rewarded for doing their schoolwork, students understandably begin to have difficulty regulating their behavior when not offered rewards for doing their schoolwork. Over time, the presence and absence of rewards, not interest and autonomous self-regulation, come to regulate the student's behavior—whether or not to study, when to study, what to study, how long to study, how hard to study, and so on.

In accepting the idea that extrinsic rewards produce worrisome costs, one might ask whether this is always the case. Extrinsic rewards generally produce these costs, but not always (Cameron, 2001; Deci et al., 1999). In particular, two factors explain when rewards undermine intrinsic motivation, interfere with learning, and derail autonomous self-regulation: reward expectancy and reward tangibility. Expected rewards engender an in-order-to approach to an activity. If teachers can find ways to give students unexpected rewards, these rewards do not produce hidden costs (Greene & Lepper, 1974; Orlick & Mosher, 1978; Pallak et al., 1982). For instance, *after* students have engaged themselves in a learning activity, the teacher might surprise them with, "Wow, in recognition of how well you all did today, you've earned a special privilege." Tangible rewards, such as food prizes, also tend to produce hidden costs, whereas verbal (i.e., intangible) rewards, such as praise, do not (Deci et al., 1999; Dollinger & Thelen, 1978). Thus, to reward a student, giving M&M candies is motivationally problematic, whereas giving "good job" praise is not.

Appendix
Effective Classroom Management

For effective classroom management, teachers need to learn when extrinsic rewards promote, and also when they undermine, students' motivation and engagement (PRAXIS™, I.C.4; INTASC, Principle 5).

That extrinsic rewards must be expected and tangible before they produce these three hidden and troublesome costs sounds like good news for educators who use rewards. The problem, however, is that schools so often and so routinely use expected and tangible rewards to motivate students. Stickers, tokens, food, prizes, trophies, scholarships, privileges, gold stars, marbles, awards, honor roll lists, and a dozen other such incentive plans are ubiquitous in schools (Kohn, 1993). In practice, therefore, it is not so comforting to say that only expected and tangible extrinsic rewards produce hidden costs because schools so often present rewards in expected and tangible ways. The nearby Uncommon Sense box examines whether extrinsic motivation is a useful tool in engaging students in routine activities.

Using Extrinsic Motivators Effectively

Not all extrinsic motivation is bad (Covington & Mueller, 2001). The problem lies in *how teachers use rewards*. A key question is why teachers use rewards. That is, for what purpose do teachers offer students stickers, incentives, and privileges?

Cognitive-evaluation theory is a theory of motivation designed to help teachers predict in advance what effect *any* extrinsic motivator will have on students' motivation and engagement. This theory is presented in graphical form in Figure 10.5. According to the theory, any extrinsic motivator—praise, money, grades, stickers, surveillance—can be administered either *to control behavior* or *to inform competence*. Offering rewards in a controlling way (saying, in effect, "If you do *X*, you'll get *Y*") increases compliance, but it routinely entails the three hidden costs of rewards as well. Controlling rewards interfere with students' need for autonomy and thus undermines motivation and engagement. Alterna-

Uncommon Sense

Using Rewards to Motivate Students Is a Good Strategy—Or Is It?

After some reflection, most educators will agree that rewards undermine student functioning when lessons are interesting and fun. What about when lessons are not inherently interesting? Perhaps rewards can motivate students to invest effort on worksheets, repetitive practice, and cleaning their desk space. What student would not like an extra 10 minutes at recess or a sticker for herself or a pizza party for the class? When rewards such as these are at stake, students come to life and eagerly complete even a routine assignment. If students begin a lesson with little intrinsic motivation, extrinsic rewards cannot be so bad, can they? After all, you cannot undermine something that is not there. Nevertheless, just as in other situations, compliance-pushing extrinsic motivators interfere with the process of learning and undermine the student's capacity for autonomous self-regulation. Ways to motivate students during uninteresting lessons exist, and these strategies (i.e., increase valuing, increase interest, promote intrinsic goals) promote—rather than undermine—students' inner motivational resources, learning, and autonomous self-regulation. (We discuss all three of these strategies at the end of the chapter.)

tively, offering rewards in an informational way (saying, in effect, "Good job, you're making progress") supports students' engagement without provoking the hidden costs of rewards. Informational rewards nurture students' need for competence and thus enhance motivation and engagement.

According to **cognitive-evaluation theory**, using extrinsic motivators effectively requires that extrinsic rewards be given to students in a way that is both noncontrolling and informational. Extrinsic motivators need to be noncontrolling so as not to interfere with students' need for autonomy, and extrinsic motivators need to be informational so as to support students' need for competence. What teachers say when they give students rewards in controlling versus informational ways can be seen in the nearby Taking It to the Classroom box.

cognitive-evaluation theory
A theory of motivation that explains how external events such as rewards affect students' psychological needs for autonomy and competence and, hence, their intrinsic motivation.

Praise Consider how one of the most frequently used rewards—**praise**—functions as an extrinsic motivator, sometimes to control students' behavior but at other times to nurture their competence (Brophy, 1981; Henderlong & Lepper, 2002; Ryan, Mims, & Koestner, 1983). To communicate a job well done in a noncontrolling and informational way, a teacher might say, "Excellent job; your pronunciation has improved since last week." Alternatively, the teacher

praise Positive verbal feedback.

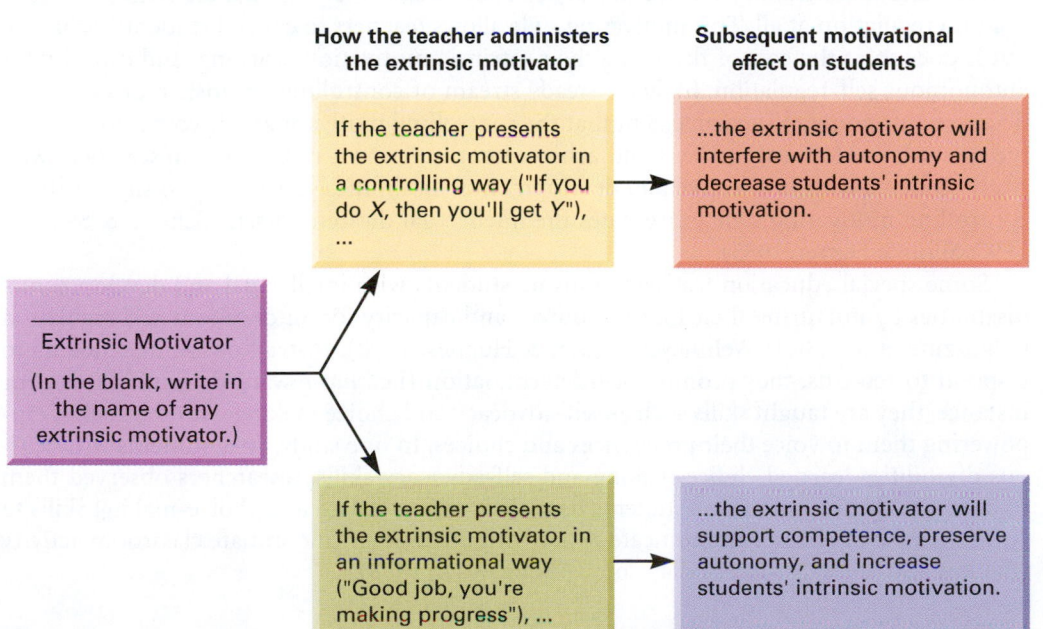

How the teacher administers the extrinsic motivator

Subsequent motivational effect on students

If the teacher presents the extrinsic motivator in a controlling way ("If you do X, then you'll get Y"), ...

...the extrinsic motivator will interfere with autonomy and decrease students' intrinsic motivation.

Extrinsic Motivator
(In the blank, write in the name of any extrinsic motivator.)

If the teacher presents the extrinsic motivator in an informational way ("Good job, you're making progress"), ...

...the extrinsic motivator will support competence, preserve autonomy, and increase students' intrinsic motivation.

Figure 10.5 Using Cognitive-Evaluation Theory to Predict How Any Extrinsic Motivator Will Affect Students' Motivation

Taking It to the Classroom

Communicating Extrinsic Rewards in Controlling versus Informational Ways

What controlling rewards sound like

If you do *X*, you'll get *Y*.

If you want a sticker, you'll have to come to class on time.

In order to earn points for your team, you have to turn your homework in on time.

Commentary:

Notice that each controlling reward bypasses the student's need for autonomy and instead focuses exclusively on gaining compliance.

What informational rewards sound like

Good job, you're making progess.

You're improving your skill so much that you've earned a sticker.

That's good work; you deserve an award.

Commentary:

Notice that each informational reward nurtures the student's need for competence and focuses on the message of a job well done.

How Can I Use This?

The next time you give someone a reward, ask yourself: Why am I giving this reward—to control behavior or to inform competence?

might communicate praise in a controlling way, saying, "Excellent job; you did just as you should." Tagging on phrases such as "as you should" and "as you ought to" conveys pressure, external evaluation, and doing what others tell you to do. From cognitive-evaluation theory, educators can conclude that the motivational effect of praise lies not so much in the praise itself as in the way it is administered by teachers (i.e., students ask themselves why the teacher is praising them: "Are you praising me to inform my competence, or are you praising me just to control my behavior?").

How to Motivate Students with Intellectual and Developmental Disabilities: Intrinsically or Extrinsically?

Two characteristics distinguish students with intellectual and developmental disabilities (formerly known as mental retardation) from students without such disabilities: diminished cognitive abilities and low autonomy. When teachers try to motivate and engage students with low autonomy and low cognitive abilities, they typically do so by employing extrinsic rewards and a **controlling motivating style**. They reason that external regulation is better than no regulation at all. This motivating style allows teachers to control students' behavior, but it does so at the cost of thwarting their intrinsic motivation, learning, and capacity for autonomous self-regulation. In fact, a steady stream of controlling extrinsic motivators can decrease autonomy to such an extent that the controlling motivating style comes to contribute to students' low engagement and achievement in its own right. Some researchers who study students with intellectual and developmental disabilities go so far as to suggest that a controlling motivating style exacerbates the intellectual disability itself (Schultz & Switzky, 1993; Silon & Harter, 1985).

Some special education teachers motivate students with intellectual and developmental disabilities by nurturing their inner resources and capacity for autonomous self-regulation (Algozzine et al., 2001; Wehmeyer, Agran, & Hughes, 1998). Instead of asking students to respond to rewards, they promote *self*-determination (i.e., *not* reward-determination). For instance, they are taught skills such as self-advocacy and choice making with the goal of empowering them to voice their preferences and choices. In one study, after students with various disabilities learned choice-making and self-advocacy skills, researchers observed them in inclusive classrooms. These students used their self-advocacy and choice-making skills to voice their preferences, communicate better with the teacher, and initiate classroom activity (Belfiore, Browder, & Mace, 1994; Cooper & Browder, 1998).

controlling motivating style
The interpersonal sentiment and behavior teachers provide during instruction to pressure students to think, feel, or behavior in a prescribed way.

Appendix
Motivating Students with Intellectual and Developmental Disabilities

Like all students, students with intellectual and developmental disabilities need and benefit from teachers' instructional strategies that promote their autonomy and instrinsic motivation (PRAXIS™, I.B.4; INTASC, Principle 3).

What happens when teachers provide autonomy support to students with intellectual and developmental disabilities? Like all other students, students with intellectual disabilities who have their autonomy supported rather than their behavior controlled develop a greater sense of autonomy, experience more positive well-being, and achieve higher standardized test scores (Deci et al., 1992). Motivations such as autonomy and intrinsic motivation exist in all students, but these motivations require nutriments from the social environment (i.e., autonomy support from teachers, parents). A teacher's autonomy support nurtures autonomy and intrinsic motivation in students with intellectual disabilities and, in doing so, promotes their learning, adjustment, and well-being (Deci, 2004). Clearly, it is easier for a teacher to say "You will get a candy bar if you clean up your desk now" than it is to take the student's perspective and encourage his or her autonomy and personal responsibility for cleaning. But autonomy can be supported. When it is, it allows students to develop a greater capacity to regulate their own behavior and display positive outcomes such as engagement, learning, and well-being. This statement is just as true for students with intellectual disabilities as it is for students without such disabilities.

Types of Extrinsic Motivation

External regulation via rewards is only one type of extrinsic motivation. There are two other types as well (Ryan & Deci, 2000a). All three types can be represented on a continuum, as shown in Figure 10.6.

On the far right-hand side of Figure 10.6 is intrinsic motivation, and on the far left-hand side is amotivation (literally, without motivation, or neither intrinsically nor extrinsically motivated). In the middle are three types of extrinsic motivation—external regulation, introjected regulation, and identified regulation.

According to self-determination theory (Ryan & Deci, 2000b, 2002), types of motivation can be distinguished on the basis of how autonomous (or self-determined) each type is. Amotivation is a lack of any sort of motivation—the student is neither intrinsically nor extrinsically motivated. Amotivation, which will be discussed at the end of the chapter, is associated with very negative outcomes, such as dropping out of school (Hardre & Reeve, 2003; Legault, Green-Demers, & Pelletier, 2006). External regulation represents extrinsic motivation that is not at all autonomous, introjected regulation represents extrinsic motivation that is somewhat autonomous, and identified regulation represents extrinsic motivation that is highly autonomous.

Identifying these different types of extrinsic motivation is important because the more autonomous students' extrinsic motivation is, the better they function in school (Gottfried, 1985; Grolnick & Ryan, 1987; Ryan & Connell, 1989). For instance, sixth-grade students who complete their homework because of identified regulation show greater effort, more positive emotion, and higher achievement than do sixth-grade students who complete their homework because of external or introjected regulation (Ryan & Connell, 1989). At the end of this

Not At All Autonomous		Somewhat Autonomous		Highly Autonomous
Amotivation	*Externally Regulated*	*Introjected*	*Identified*	*Intrinsic Motivation*
Lack of any type of motivation—neither intrinsic nor extrinsic	Motivation from an environmentally created reason to act, such as a reward	Motivation from an internalized but pressuring voice, indicating that one must act to avoid guilt or shame	Motivation from internalizing the way of behaving because it is a useful or important thing to do	Motivation from psychological needs that reflects interest and enjoyment
Source of Motivation				
Nothing	Rewards	Guilt/Shame	Importance	Interest

Figure 10.6 Degree of Autonomy (Self-Determination) in the Different Types of Motivation

What Kids Say and Do

Types of Motivation

Question: *Why do you do your homework?*

I don't know. Sometimes I do; sometimes I don't. I don't really see what good it does me. (Student with amotivation)

Because that's what I'm supposed to do. (Student with external regulation)

So I won't feel guilty about it. I'd rather just do it and get it over with rather than feel all guilty and worried about it. (Student with introjected regulation)

I do my homework because learning new things is important. (Student with identified regulation)

For fun. I do my homework because it's fun. (Student with intrinsic motivation)

psychological need An inherent source of motivation that generates a proactive desire to interact with one's environment to advance personal growth, social development, and psychological well-being.

autonomy The psychological need to experience self-direction in the initiation and regulation of one's behavior.

perceived locus of causality A person's understanding of whether his or her motivated action is caused by a force within the self (internal) or by some outside force (external).

chapter, in the section Motivating Students during Uninteresting Lessons, we highlight the motivational benefits of identified regulation and highlight instructional strategies to promote this autonomous type of extrinsic motivation. What students say when they experience each of these different types of motivation can be heard in the nearby What Kids Say and Do box.

Psychological Needs

A **psychological need** is an inherent source of motivation that generates a proactive desire to interact with the environment to advance one's personal growth, social development, and psychological well-being (Ryan & Deci, 2000b, 2002). The three psychological needs central to students in school are autonomy, competence, and relatedness (Deci et al., 1991). Autonomy, competence, and relatedness are referred to as "needs" because they represent conditions that are essential and necessary for growth, vitality, and psychological well-being. That is, students need to feel autonomous, competent, and related to others to grow and to be well.

Autonomy

Autonomy is the psychological need to experience self-direction in the initiation and regulation of one's behavior (Deci & Ryan, 1985). It represents the student's inner endorsement of his or her action—the sense that what one is doing emanates from the self and is one's own. When autonomous, students perceive that their behavior emanates from within themselves and is self-authored (Ryan & Deci, 2000). For example, when students feel they are doing something because they want to, they are experiencing high autonomy. Conversely, when students feel they are doing something because they have to or because others are making them do it, they are experiencing low autonomy.

An awkward but important term that underlies the experience of autonomy is **perceived locus of causality** (PLOC). It refers to the student's understanding of the originating source (or "locus") of his or her motivated actions (deCharms, 1976). PLOC exists on a continuum that ranges from internal to external. Students experience an internal PLOC when their behavior comes from within themselves—arising from their interests, wants, and desires. Students experience an external PLOC when some outside force—a teacher, test, or reward—causes the initiation and persistence of their behavior. With autonomy, students experience an internal PLOC and a high sense of freedom to choose and regulate their actions (Reeve, Nix, & Hamm, 2003). The nearby Uncommon Sense box presents the concept of autonomy in a classroom situation.

Teacher–Provided Autonomy Support Autonomy is a psychological need that requires support from environmental conditions. The key source of support for students' need for autonomy in the classroom is the teacher—and the teacher's motivating style toward them in particular. A teacher's motivating style toward students can be captured by the quality or tone of the interpersonal sentiment and behavior he or she displays when trying to motivate and engage students during learning activities (Deci et al., 1981). Teachers' motivating style can be understood along a continuum that extends from a highly autonomy-supportive style through a neutral style to a highly controlling style. When teachers are highly autonomy supportive toward students, they nurture and support students' psychological need for autonomy, but when teachers are highly controlling toward students, they neglect and frustrate students' need for autonomy.

Table 10.1 provides a definition for both types of teachers' motivating styles—controlling and autonomy supportive. The table also provides the set of enabling conditions that functionally orient teachers toward one motivating style or the other. The table further lists the instructional behaviors that are most closely tied to the two types of motivating styles.

Uncommon Sense

Giving Students Choices Increases Their Autonomy and Intrinsic Motivation—Or Does It?

If autonomy is an important motivational force, it makes sense that teachers should give students many choices. For instance, on a reading assignment the teacher might show students several books and ask them to choose one to read. On a writing assignment, the teacher might write a number of topics on the board and have students choose among them. Most teachers endorse the idea that choices promote motivation (Flowerday & Schraw, 2000), but not all choices are the same. Some choices involve the need for autonomy and promote intrinsic motivation, whereas others do not (Katz & Assor, 2007).

Asking students to choose among predetermined options is by far the most common type of choice teachers give. This is unfortunate though, because when students are offered choices among mandated options (e.g., Do you want to read book *A* or book *B*?), they generally do *not* experience autonomy and intrinsic motivation (Overskeid & Svartdal, 1996; Schraw, Flowerday, & Reisetter, 1998). Forced choices bear no motivational fruit (Flowerday, Schraw, & Stevens, 2004). However, when teachers offer students open-ended and authentic choices about what to do (e.g., Do you want to read a book?), they *do* experience autonomy and intrinsic motivation (Cordova & Lepper, 1996; Reeve et al., 2003). Choice is motivating when it offers students opportunities to act on their interests and preferences to decide for themselves what to do and how to do it (Patall, Cooper, & Wynn, 2010).

Teachers offer students an **autonomy-supportive motivating style** when they work to nurture and satisfy students' need for autonomy during instruction. Three conditions enable teachers to adopt an autonomy-supportive motivating style toward students: (1) Adopt the students' perspective; (2) welcome students' thoughts, feelings, and behaviors into the flow of instruction; and (3) support students' motivational development and capacity for autonomous self-regulation (Reeve, 2009). By taking students' perspective prior to and during instruction, teachers are better able to create classroom conditions that involve and nurture students' autonomy. By welcoming students' thoughts, feelings, and behaviors into the flow of instruction, teachers acknowledge the motivational importance of students' thoughts (goals), emotions (interests), and behaviors (initiative). By supporting students' capacity for

autonomy-supportive motivating style The interpersonal sentiment and behavior teachers provide during instruction to identify, nurture, and develop students' inner motivational resources (especially the need for autonomy).

TABLE 10.1

Definition, Enabling Conditions, and Instructional Behaviors Associated with Both the Controlling Motivating Style and the Autonomy-Supportive Motivating Style

Controlling	Autonomy Support
Definition	**Definition**
Interpersonal sentiment and behavior teachers provide during instruction to pressure students to think, feel, or behave in a specific way.	Interpersonal sentiment and behavior teachers provide during instruction to identify, nurture, and develop students' inner motivational resources.
Enabling conditions	**Enabling conditions**
Adopt the teacher's perspective.	Adopt the students' perspective.
Intrude into student's thoughts, feelings, or actions.	Welcome students' thoughts, feelings, and actions.
Pressure students to think, feel, or behave in a specific way.	Support students' motivational development and capacity for autonomous self-regulation.
Instructional behaviors	**Instructional behaviors**
Rely on outer sources of motivation.	Nurture inner motivational resources.
Neglect explanatory rationales.	Provide explanatory rationales.
Rely on pressure-inducing language.	Rely on noncontrolling and informational language.
Display impatience for students to produce the right answer.	Display patience to allow time for self-paced learning.
Assert power to overcome students' complaints and expressions of negative affect.	Acknowledge and accept expressions of negative affect.

Source: Reeve, J. (2009). Why teachers adopt a controlling motivating style toward students and how they can become more autonomy supportive. *Educational Psychologist, 44,* 159–175. Reprinted with the permission of the Taylor & Francis Group.

autonomous self-regulation, teachers build instruction around the goal of helping students generate and regulate **motivation** of their own. Alternatively, three conditions enable teachers to adopt a controlling motivating style toward students: (1) Adopt only the teacher's perspective; (2) intrude into students' thoughts, feelings, and behaviors; and (3) pressure students to think, feel, and behavior in a teacher-defined way. The starting point for a controlling style is to prioritize the teacher's perspective over that of the students' to the point that the goals, needs, and priorities of the teacher overrun those of the students. Being intrusive means rejecting students' existing ways of thinking, feeling, and behaving and, instead, trying to change them—to think differently, feel differently, and behave differently. Controlling further (and crucially) involves the application of pressure until students relent and change their opinions and behaviors to align with those prescribed by the teacher.

Why Supporting Autonomy Is Important   The more teachers support students' autonomy and the less they try to control students' behavior, the more positive are students' school-related outcomes. When students experience autonomy-need satisfaction from the teacher's nurturing autonomy-supportive motivating style, they function more positively and experience greater psychological well-being. Students who have their autonomy supported also show fundamentally important educational and developmental benefits, including greater classroom engagement, higher-quality learning, a preference for optimal challenge, enhanced intrinsic motivation, and higher academic achievement (deCharms, 1976; Deci et al., 1981; Guay et al., 2008; Reeve, Jang, et al., 2004; Vallerand, Fortier, & Guay, 1997; Vansteenkiste et al., 2004). Indeed, compared to students who have teachers who rely on a controlling motivating style, students of teachers who rely on an autonomy-supportive motivating style show educational benefits across the full range of positive student outcomes, including motivation, engagement, development, learning, performance, and well-being (Reeve, 2009).

How Teachers Can Support Students' Autonomy during Instruction   Table 10.1 listed the five instructional behaviors that are highly characteristic of a teacher who displays an autonomy-supportive motivating style. The first thing a teacher needs to do to be more autonomy supportive is to take the students' perspective, welcoming their thoughts, feelings, and behaviors into the flow of instruction, and support their developing capacity for greater autonomous self-regulation (the three enabling conditions listed in Table 10.1). In terms of specific and concrete instructional behaviors, teachers can support students' autonomy during instruction through the following five ways (Deci, 1995; Deci et al., 1994; Reeve, 1996, 2011; Reeve & Jang, 2006; Reeve, Jang, et al., 2004; Ryan & La Guardia, 1999).

1. *Nurture students' inner motivational resources.* Autonomy-supportive teachers motivate students by supporting their inner motivational resources, such as the psychological need for autonomy, intrinsic motivation, sense of curiosity, preference for optimal challenge, self-endorsed (intrinsic) goals, and self-endorsed (internalized) values. To do so, teachers need to find ways to build instruction around opportunities to have students' classroom engagement initiated and regulated by these inner motivational resources. The idea is to have students' sense of *wanting to* engage in and learn from lessons arise from of their own inner motivations. For instance, when asking students to begin a new lesson, teachers can solicit students' suggestions and preferences for how to proceed. Or a teacher might offer a curiosity-inducing question, "Which came first—dinosaurs or grass?" (This question is curiosity-inducing because, surprisingly, dinosaurs were extinct long before the first grass ever grew.). In contrast, a teacher with a controlling motivating style will ignore students' inner motivational resources and just push and pressure students to engage in the lesson (e.g., "C'mon, let's get to work.").

2. *Provide explanatory rationales.* Not all classroom activities can be intrinsically fun things to do. For those relatively uninteresting and less appealing activities and requirements, autonomy-supportive teachers make a special effort to communicate the value within the lesson by offering rationales that explain why the teacher is making such a request. A rationale is a verbal explanation of why putting forth effort might truly be a useful thing to do. It means communicating to students why an activity or course of action is useful to them. That is, instead of "Because I said so," teachers can provide explanatory rationales such as, "The reason we have this rule is so that everyone can be assured of feeling safe and respected."

RIDE   What role does an autonomy–supportive motivating style play in increasing students' engagement; what role does a controlling style play in decreasing it?

MINDFUL HABITS OF EFFECTIVE TEACHERS

Constantly monitoring and supporting students' inner motivational resources and engagement is a key habit of mind of effective teachers.

To the extent that students hear such a rationale and accept that it does justify their effort, they begin to say to themselves, "Yeah, okay, that makes sense; that *is* something I want to do." In contrast, a teacher with a controlling motivating style will make a request or tell students what to do and never explain the justifying *why* behind the request.

3. *Rely on noncontrolling language.* Noncontrolling language is communication that is nonevaluative, flexible, and informational. Autonomy-supportive teachers communicate classroom rules, requirements, and expectations with informational and noncontrolling language. Such language avoids rigid, pressuring phrases such as *have to* and *got to*. For instance, instead of saying "You must work harder" and hence closing down students' autonomy and communication, the teacher might openly invite the student into the problem-solving situation, saying, "You may want to participate" or "I've noticed that your writing doesn't quite have the same spark it did last week; would you like to talk about it?" In these two examples, the teacher supports both the classroom requirement and the student's autonomy. In contrast, a teacher with a controlling motivating style verbally pushes and pressures students toward compliance without enlisting the student's input or perspective (e.g., "You must improve your spelling.").

Appendix
Promoting Intrinsic Motivation
When teachers recognize how to promote students' autonomy and intrinsic motivation, they help students' capacity to become self-motivated learners (PRAXIS™, I.C.3; INTASC, Principle 5).

4. *Display patience to allow time for self-paced learning to occur.* All teachers encounter circumstances that challenge their patience, such as unforgiving time constraints and high-stakes testing requirements. It is therefore easy to understand why teachers are occasionally or even often impatient with students. But the reason autonomy-supportive teachers are so patient with students is because they hold a deep value for students' autonomy and an understanding that meaningful learning takes time. Displaying patience means creating the classroom conditions in which students will have the time and space they need to explore and manipulate materials and ideas, formulate and test hypotheses, make plans and set goals, monitor and revise their work and their thinking, and alter their problem-solving strategies. Under these conditions, student engagement aligns more with a sense of autonomy and interest than it does with a sense of pressure and evaluation. In contrast, a teacher with a controlling motivating style will impatiently rush in to tell or to show the student what the right answer is or how to solve the problem (e.g., "Here, we don't have much time; let me show you how to do it.").

5. *Acknowledge and accept students' expressions of negative affect.* Negative affect includes students' complaints, negative emotions and feelings, resistance, counterprotests, and generally "bad attitude" toward learning or school. Students show such resistance and negative affect because teachers and classrooms have rules, requests, and agendas that are sometimes at odds with their natural inclinations. When teachers acknowledge and accept such feelings, they acknowledge the students' perspectives; take students' suggestions to heart; and even welcome these expressions as potentially valid reactions to imposed rules, assignments, demands, and classroom structures. Acknowledging negative affect often takes the form of "I see that you are not very interested in today's lesson," while accepting negative affect often takes the form of "Okay, let's see; what might we do differently? Do you have any suggestions?" Soothing students' negative affectivity is often a prerequisite to students' engagement and learning, and the key step in soothing such negative affectivity is to acknowledge its existence and accept is as a potentially valid reaction. In contrast, a teacher with a controlling motivating style will counter and try to change students' complaining (e.g., "Oh, quit your complaining. You are so immature. Get to work, and do what you are supposed to do.").

Autonomy Support Is Hard to Do—Can Teachers Learn to Be Autonomy Supportive?

Intervention-based research in which both preservice teachers and experienced (veteran) teachers participate in informational and mentoring sessions on how to support students' autonomy during instruction shows that teachers can learn to become significantly more autonomy supportive (Su & Reeve, 2011). These studies show that when teachers are informed about the various ways to support students' autonomy (i.e., the five instructional behaviors just discussed), when they are given mentoring in how to implement these strategies in real classroom settings, and when they are given opportunities to discuss how things are going in their efforts to support students' autonomy with other teachers who are also trying to learn how to support students' autonomy, the training effect is very large, enduring, and highly beneficial to their students' motivation, engagement, and learning (Cheon, 2010; deCharms, 1976; Reeve, Jang, et al., 2004; Su & Reeve, 2011).

Competence

competence The psychological need to be effective during interactions with the surrounding environment.

Competence is the psychological need to be effective as one interacts with the surrounding environment (Deci & Ryan, 1985). In a hundred different ways, schools challenge students' skills, and competence is the need to develop mastery when challenged. For instance, in a Spanish class, one challenge that students encounter is to understand what Spanish speakers are saying to them; another is to produce the language themselves. As students try to master these challenges, the environment also provides guidance and feedback about how well or poorly they are meeting or exceeding the challenges, as represented by nods of approval or furrowed brows of confusion. Competence is the psychological need to seek out, take on, and master such challenges.

The Pleasure of Optimal Challenge To confirm that students do indeed derive need-satisfying pleasure from optimal challenges, Susan Harter (1974, 1978) gave school-age children a series of problems that varied in difficulty. Some problems were very easy, some easy, others hard, and still others very hard. The experimenter monitored each student's expressed pleasure (through smiling) after solving each problem. A curvilinear (inverted-U) pattern emerged in which students rarely smiled after solving the very easy and easy problems, smiled most after solving the moderately difficult problems, and smiled only mildly following success on the very hard problems. That is, based on how much or how little the children smiled, pleasure was greatest following success during moderate—or optimal—challenge. Easy tasks fail to involve the need for competence; moderately difficult undertakings fully involve the competence need; and very difficult tasks generate too much anxiety and frustration for students to enjoy them, even when they successfully solve them.

(© Media Bakery)

Students smile and derive need-satisfying pleasure from optimal challenge and positive feedback because these conditions best involve and nurture their underlying psychological need for competence.

How Teachers Can Support Students' Competence Optimal challenge is the key classroom condition that *involves* the need for competence; positive feedback is the key condition that *satisfies* it. Accordingly, in the classroom, teachers can support students' need for competence by offering lessons that begin with a challenge and, while students engage themselves in trying to master the challenge, provide positive feedback from making progress and from a job done well. For instance, teachers can challenge students by introducing a difficult math problem and then, throughout the problem-solving process, provide feedback about students' improvement, progress, and extent of mastery. It is not so much that the challenge is motivating or that the feedback is motivating; rather, challenge and feedback involve and satisfy the need for competence, and this experience of competence-need satisfaction is what is motivating and emotionally satisfying. Optimal challenge and positive feedback are the classroom conditions that make competence-need satisfaction likely.

How teachers can provide students with optimal challenges in a step-by-step fashion appears in Table 10.2. Before teachers can expect students to be enthusiastic about (rather than anxious about, or even afraid of) classroom challenges, a prerequisite condition is necessary in terms of establishing an emotionally safe learning environment. This is done through the teacher's motivating style, as in providing an autonomy-supportive learning environment (discussed earlier), but also by providing a mastery goal climate (discussed in the next chapter) and, perhaps most importantly, by providing an error-tolerant environment (discussed here). When teachers ask students to answer difficult questions, display their artwork, or go to the chalkboard to solve a problem, students are as likely to view these events as fearsome threats as they are to see them as attractive challenges. After all, one hallmark of an *optimal* challenge is that success and failure are equally likely outcomes. **Error tolerance** is the attitude of a teacher

error tolerance The attitude of a teacher who accepts errors and failures as a necessary, inherent, and even welcomed part of the learning process.

who accepts errors and failures as a necessary, inherent, and even welcomed part of the learning process (Clifford, 1988, 1990). It is rooted in the belief that students learn more from their failures than they do from their successes. Therefore, it emphasizes the constructive aspects of failure—identifying its causes, signaling the need to change one's strategies, and becoming aware of the need for further instruction (Clifford, 1984). It is only in this climate of error tolerance (even error valuing) that students experience an emotional green light to involve their need for competence in the challenges and feedback teachers provide.

For a practical feel as to how teachers might communicate and establish a highly error-tolerant learning environment, here are some of the things that highly error-tolerant teachers say:

TABLE 10.2

Anatomy of an Optimal Challenge

Prerequisite:	Provide an error-tolerant learning climate
Step 1:	State the challenge
Step 2:	Focus on improvement, progress
Step 3:	Nurture self-direction
Step 4:	Help students develop the capacity to enjoy a task and to enjoy a challenge for its own sake
Step 5:	Keep highly engaged self-direction going

- In this class, the goal is not to get a quick, fast answer—that just means the task is too easy; you aren't challenging yourself.

- I expect you to make mistakes, I expect you to have to work hard, I expect you to be confused, I expect you to run into obstacles and to run into dead ends. If you are not, we have a problem because that means the lesson is simply too easy for you.

- I want you to constantly revise your work. I want improvement. I want to see effort. I want to see you changing your strategies. I'm more interested in your final product than your first product.

- Risk failure. Risk making an error. Risk making a mistake. We are here to learn.

- Here is what making an error in this class means: *Ooo, I've got a challenge on my hands!*

Offering students a highly error-tolerant learning environment is just the prerequisite for accepting and seeking challenges. The actual offering of an optimal challenge starts with the teacher stating a challenge. For instance, a teacher might say:

- Here is a challenge, let's see if you can solve it.

- Tell me what excellence is, and let's see if you can produce it.

- Here is what one person did in the past. Can you come up with anything better?

- What would you like to do? What would you like to accomplish?

As students try to make progress on the challenge, the teacher focuses on signs that they are making progress, not on signs that they are getting the right answer. The focus on improvement and making progress is fundamentally important to promoting challenge seeking because competence satisfaction arises from an experience of making progress, of showing improvement, of doing a job well, and of gaining mastery and finding a solution where it did not exist before. These are the experiences that satisfy the psychological need for competence. To help students focus on improvement and mastery, teachers can help students focus less and less on their answers and more and more on their effort and strategy. In addition, the progress that students make needs to be authentic. That is, students need to feel that they earned or created their progress, rather than that the teacher or a peer handed it to them. To cultivate self-direction within the process of challenge seeking, the biology teacher, the band director, or the English teacher might follow up a challenge by saying, "You decide the goal, you decide the plan, you decide the strategy, you decide when to start, you decide when to change your course of action, you decide when to take a break, you decide…"

Steps 1–3 in Table 10.2 are the ways in which teachers can offer their students' optimal challenges during instruction. But teachers also need to think about helping students seek out and enjoy optimal challenges over the longer term. One way to do this is to help students develop the capacity to enjoy both (1) a task and (2) a challenge *for their own sake*. To do so, the teacher might take class time for a group discussion in which students think and talk about questions such as "Why do people enjoy science?" "Why do people enjoy playing music?" "Why do people feel so much satisfaction from a challenge—or get bored with being under-challenged?" Lastly, the teacher can focus on keeping students' highly

R I D E What role do perceived competence and flow contribute to students' engagement? How can teachers promote these motivations in students?

How Can I Use This?

Can you find ways to introduce challenges, goals, and feedback into one of your daily activities to support competence and flow?

engaged in self-directed challenge seeking throughout the school year. The best way to do this is to closely and continuously monitor (and support) students' expressions of behavioral, emotional, cognitive, and agentic engagement. The idea is to emphasize engagement and challenge seeking over the outcome or the end product (i.e., focus on effort and strategy, rather than the answer itself).

Learning how to provide students with optimal challenge is particularly important because only about one-half of students feel that they are challenged to do their best work in school, and this percentage gets smaller with each passing grade (McCarthy & Kuh, 2006). The trend in the later grades seems to be to provide students with easy success and tasks that allow them to confirm what they already know and can do.

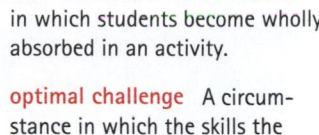
flow A state of concentration in which students become wholly absorbed in an activity.

optimal challenge A circumstance in which the skills the student possesses are equally balanced with the demands, difficulty, and complexity level of the task at hand.

Flow Flow is an absorbing state of concentration in which students become engrossed in the activity at hand (Csikszentmihalyi, 1975, 1990). If you have ever been so wrapped up in a challenging activity that you forgot to eat or failed to realize how much time had passed, you know firsthand what the flow experience is and how it can motivate engagement. The flow experience goes a long way in explaining why students stick with and develop their talents, such as in music, sports, mathematics, or art (Csikszentmihalyi, Rathunde, & Whalen, 1993).

Flow arises whenever students perceive that the challenges posed by the task nicely match with their current skills and competencies, as illustrated in Figure 10.7. The figure is important because it identifies the emotional consequences that arise from the different pairings of challenge and skill. When challenge exceeds skill, students worry that the demands of the task will overwhelm them. When challenge matches skill, **optimal challenge** occurs. With optimal challenge, students' concentration, involvement, and enjoyment all markedly rise as students experience flow. When skill exceeds challenge, students feel bored. Being underchallenged neglects one's need for competence, and that neglect manifests itself as boredom.

The practical implication of flow theory is that *any* activity can be made more enjoyable. Writing papers, debating issues, completing a worksheet, playing the same song for the 101st time, reviewing material for tomorrow's quiz, and other such activities are rarely at the top of students' lists of must-do activities, but the balance of skill with challenge adds the opportunity to experience flow and deep enjoyment. Consistent with this idea, Csikszentmihalyi found that students actually enjoy doing challenging homework more than they enjoy watching television (Csikszentmihalyi et al., 1993). Further, students actually experience flow more often in school than they do during their leisure hours (Csikszentmihalyi, 1982). Homework and schoolwork will be more enjoyable to the extent that students find more opportunities for challenge and feedback in these activities than they find while watching television and "hanging out."

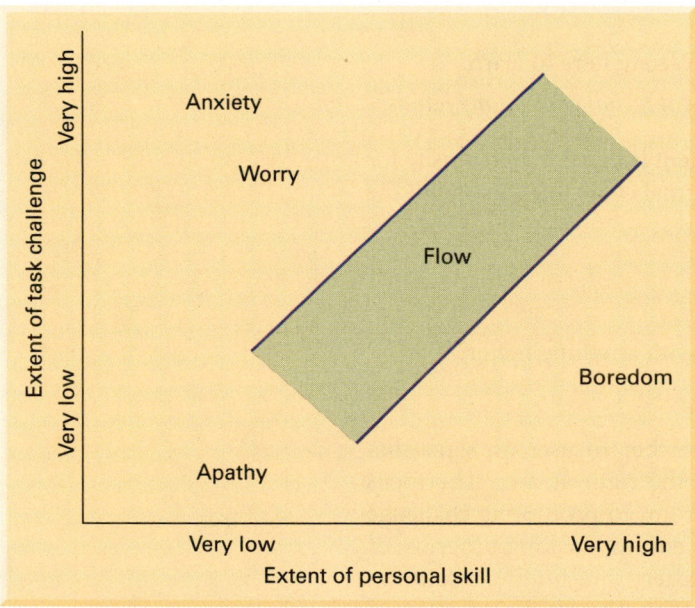

Figure 10.7 Model of Flow

Source: Adapted from Csikszentmihalyi, M. (1975). *Beyond boredom and anxiety: Experiencing flow in work and play.* San Francisco: Jossey-Bass. Reprinted with the permission of John Wiley & Sons, Inc.

Relatedness

relatedness The psychological need to establish close emotional bonds and attachments with other people.

Relatedness is the need to establish close emotional bonds with other people, and it reflects the desire to be emotionally connected to others and interpersonally involved in warm relationships (Baumeister & Leary, 1995; Ryan, 1991; Ryan & Powelson, 1991). Because students have a need for relatedness, they gravitate toward people they trust to care for them and away from people they fear will undermine their well-being. What students are looking for in a need-satisfying relationship is an opportunity to open up and relate to another person in an authentic, caring, and reciprocal way (Ryan, 1993).

The primary condition that involves the need for relatedness is social interaction, at least to the extent that such interaction takes place in a relationship characterized by warmth, care, and mutual concern. Merely creating opportunities for students to engage in social interaction will involve their need for relatedness. So, activities such as group work in class or conversation during lunch create opportunities for social interaction that involve students' psychological need for relatedness. Satisfaction of that need, however, requires more than mere interaction. Relatedness satisfaction requires the development of a social bond between the student and the other person. For a relationship to be need-satisfying, students must perceive that the other person (1) likes them, (2) cares about their welfare, and (3) accepts and values their *true self*, rather than a false social facade (Baumeister & Leary, 1995; Deci & Ryan, 1991; Ryan, 1993).

To get a feel for what students might say when they feel a high sense of relatedness at school, here are three items from a questionnaire to assess relatedness involvement and satisfaction (Goodenow, 1993):

- Most teachers at my school are interested in me.
- I am treated with as much respect as other students.
- Sometimes I feel as if I don't belong here (reverse scored).

Students' relatedness with the teacher is important because it supports engagement and internalization of the teacher's values and leadership.

Why Supporting Relatedness Is Important Supporting relatedness is important for two reasons. First, students who feel related to their classmates, related to their teachers, and related to their school community are more engaged in learning activities, (Furrer & Skinner, 2003; Goodenow & Grady, 1993). They also function better in school, because a sense of relatedness makes students more resilient to stress, less likely to drop out of school, and less vulnerable to emotional difficulties, such as depression (Battistich et al., 1997; Osterman, 2000; Ryan, Stiller, & Lynch, 1994).

Second, relatedness to teachers provides the context in which students will internalize their teachers' values (Goodenow, 1993; Grolnick, Deci, & Ryan, 1997; Ryan & Powelson, 1991). When students feel emotionally connected to and cared for by their teachers, relatedness is high and internalization occurs willingly. When deciding whether to do something or whether to believe something, students who feel close to their teachers say, "My teacher wants me to do this; I know [she] wants what is best for me so, okay, I'll do it." When students feel emotionally distant from and ignored or disrespected by their teachers, relatedness is low and internalization takes place at a snail's pace, if at all.

What Does This Mean to Me?
Notice the role that relatedness to others has played in the development of your own value system.

The Engagement Model

From a motivational point of view, high engagement arises from the psychological needs of autonomy, competence, and relatedness (Connell & Wellborn, 1991; Furrer & Skinner, 2003; Skinner & Belmont, 1993; Skinner et al., 1998, 2009). The extent to which students feel autonomous, competent, and related in the classroom depends on the extent to which their teachers find ways to involve and support these psychological needs during instruction. Specifically, as shown in Figure 10.8, (1) teacher-provided autonomy support enhances engagement because it nurtures students' need for autonomy, (2) teacher-provided structure (including the provision of optimal challenge) enhances engagement because it nurtures students' need for competence, and (3) teacher involvement and care enhances engagement because it nurtures students' need for relatedness.

As you look over and think about Figure 10.8, it might be helpful to return to Figure 10.2 earlier in the chapter to note the similarities between the two. In both figures, the essential message of how to motivate and engage students is the same and can be best be summarized by the flow of Learning Environment → Student Motivation → Student Engagement → Student Outcomes.

What Makes for a Good Day in School? As discussed earlier, when teachers nurture students' psychological needs, students experience a wide range of positive educational and developmental outcomes. An additional benefit from need-satisfying classrooms is psychological

What Does This Mean to Me?
Will teaching as a career generate a steady stream of psychological need satisfaction experiences for you?

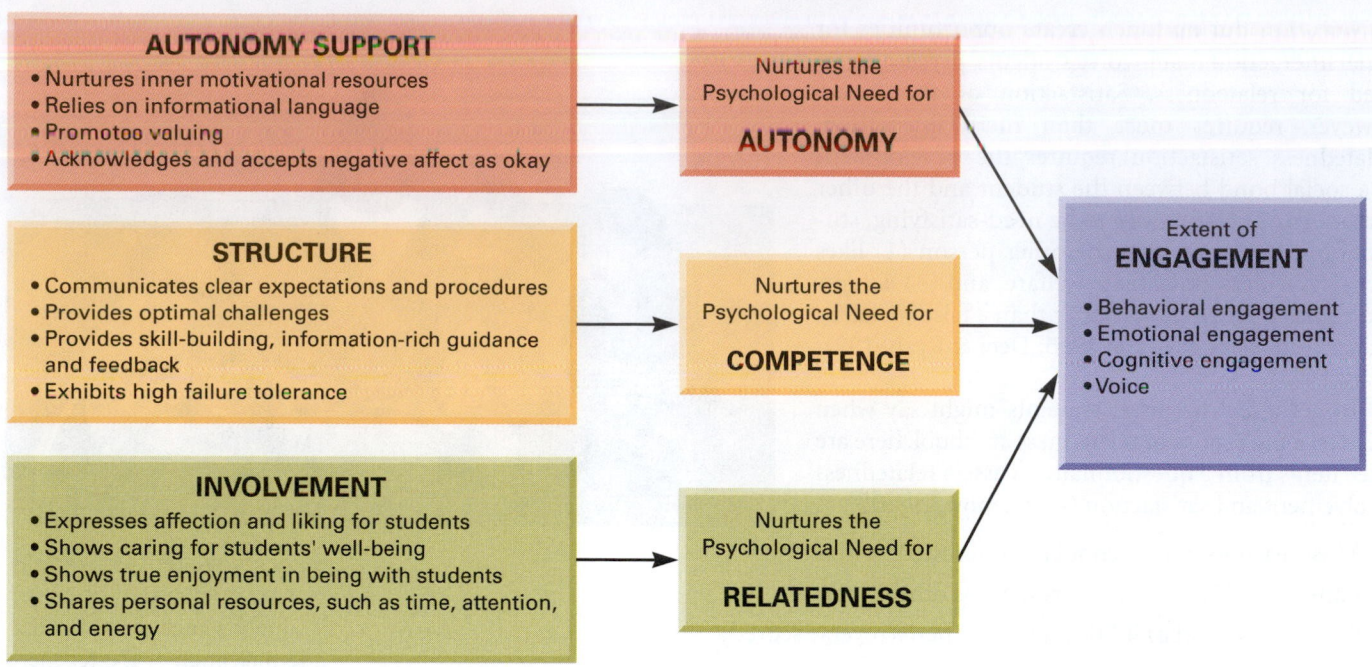

Figure 10.8 A Model of Engagement from Psychological Need Satisfaction

well-being (Reis et al., 2000; Ryan & Deci, 2001; Sheldon, Ryan, & Reis, 1996). Simply put, when students experience a need-satisfying classroom, they say they had a good day. When they experience a classroom that neglects and frustrates their needs, they say they had a bad day.

For instance, as students go about their school day, they engage in a variety of activities, such as attending classes, talking with friends, or playing a musical instrument. Students report having their best, happiest, and most fulfilling days when they experience high levels of autonomy, competence, and relatedness. That is, while in class, talking with friends, or playing an instrument, the more they feel that their behavior emanates from their own intentions (autonomy), the more mastery or flow they feel (competence), and the closer they feel to their teachers and classmates (relatedness), the more positive is their mood, and the greater is their well-being (Kasser & Ryan, 1993, 1996; Sheldon et al., 1996, 2001). These findings are important because they suggest that satisfaction of psychological needs supplies students with the *psychological nutriments* they need to experience good days (Sheldon et al., 1996).

What Does This Mean to Me?
What role has the satisfaction versus frustration of your needs for autonomy, competence, and relatedness played in your feelings of well-being today?

Curiosity, Interest, and Positive Affect

To learn something new, students need two things: new information and the motivation to seek out and learn that information. Teachers constantly give students new information, but the key motivational question is how they can motivate them to engage it—to seek it out and learn it. The study of curiosity, interest, and positive affect investigates how teachers can add some emotional punch to information so that students will truly *want* to seek it out and learn it.

To start, try this demonstration: Which of the 48 contiguous United States has the most miles of shoreline? (Alaska and Hawaii are excluded.) Upon first hearing this question, you might not feel very motivated to find the answer. But notice what happens as soon as you name a state only to learn that your guess is incorrect. Many people, for instance, will guess Florida. The answer is not Florida. Upon learning that Florida is not the state with the most shoreline, students' sense of curiosity ("Hmm, I wonder which state it is…") begins to slowly rise. If the answer is not Florida, it must be California, right? No, the answer is not California. Okay, Maine, right? The answer is not Maine. With each incorrect guess, curiosity rises a little more. The next guess might be New York, but New York is also incorrect. After learning that their answers are incorrect, most people undergo an interesting motivational shift as "I couldn't care less" slips into something closer to "Okay, now I care; I want to know which state it is." If you have been trying to guess which state has the most shoreline, you have probably experienced an increasing thirst for the answer—an increasing desire to seek out and find some new information. To determine whether your curiosity has increased enough to affect your behavior, let's see whether you are now curious enough to pull an atlas off the shelf or go online to look at a map. As a hint, your search might begin in a surprising place—namely, the upper midwestern states.

Sparking Curiosity

Curiosity is a cognitively based emotion that occurs whenever students experience a *gap* in their knowledge (Loewenstein, 1994). Students enter learning situations with knowledge and expectancies, and they use this information to make predictions about what will happen. When events unfold in unexpected ways, students experience curiosity. The cause of curiosity, therefore, is an *expectancy violation*, as in the following situations:

- I expected *X* to happen, but then *Y* actually happened.
- I predicted *X* would happen, but something else happened instead.
- I thought the answer would be *X*, but it wasn't. Now I'm wondering what the correct answer is.

Curiosity is important because it motivates engagement-rich exploratory behavior—the search for new information (Berlyne, 1966, 1978; Day, 1982; Loewenstein, 1994; Spielberger & Starr, 1994; Voss & Keller, 1983). When students are curious, they are more likely to ask questions, seek out resources, read books, and ask experts for assistance. Such exploratory behavior puts them in contact with the information they need to close their knowledge gaps. In sum, a knowledge gap causes curiosity, curiosity motivates exploration, and exploratory behavior yields the information students need to learn what will close their knowledge gaps (Berlyne, 1978; Kagan, 1972; Piaget, 1969). Two curiosity-inducing instructional strategies that teachers can integrate into almost any classroom lessons are guessing-and-feedback and suspense.

Guessing-and-Feedback   In **guessing-and-feedback**, the teacher first asks students a difficult question that is relevant to the lesson and has a factually correct answer. In a science class, the teacher might ask: What is room temperature on the Celsius scale? During a geography lesson, a teacher might ask: Which country has more landmass—China or the United States? Students then make guesses about the answer, and the teacher provides feedback about their accuracy. The disconfirming feedback (No, that's incorrect; it's *not* China) is crucial because it is the means by which teachers make students aware of the gaps in their knowledge. It is this awareness that sparks curiosity. As can be seen during any television quiz show, guessing combined with feedback makes people curious enough to engage in information-seeking exploratory behavior (Loewenstein, 1994).

Suspense   **Suspense** occurs as students await an outcome that they care about (Hitchcock, 1959; Zillman, 1980). While a person awaits an outcome, he or she hopes for a good outcome and fears for a bad one. In other words, suspense is hoping for a good outcome and fearing a bad one or, in classroom learning, hoping that your answer or solution is right and fearing that it might be wrong. The teacher can introduce a demonstration, ask students to write down their predictions, then carry out the demonstration as the students hope that their prediction is correct and fear that it is incorrect. Or the teacher can ask students to cast a vote for the answer they believe to be the correct one. A second-grade teacher can introduce the problem $26 - 17 = ?$; ask students to nominate possible answers, such as 18, 11, or 9; have the students vote for the answer they think is correct; then work out and solve the problem. Solving a problem with a suspense-filled answer on the line is more curiosity-inducing and engaging than is solving a routine or assigned problem.

Building Interest

Interest is a topic-specific motivational state that arises from attraction to a particular domain of activity (Silvia, 2006). When piqued, it creates alertness and attention, and it further enhances concentration, learning, and actions that are carried out to expand one's knowledge of and experience with the activity that aroused the interest (Fredrickson, 2001; Schraw & Lehman, 2001).

curiosity   A cognitively based emotion that occurs whenever students experience a gap in their knowledge that motivates exploratory behavior to remove that knowledge gap.

guessing-and-feedback   A curiosity-inducing instructional strategy in which the teacher asks students a difficult question, then announces that students' answers are incorrect so as to reveal a gap in their knowledge.

suspense   A curiosity-inducing instructional strategy in which the teacher asks students to predict an outcome before students engage in the work that will reveal that their prediction was right or wrong.

interest   A topic-specific motivational state that arises out of attraction to a particular domain of activity.

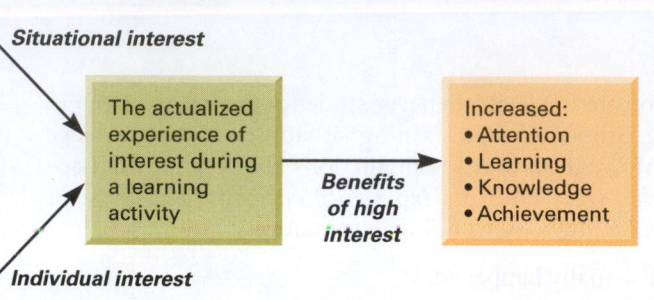

Figure 10.9 Origins and Educational Benefits of Interest

situational interest A topic-specific motivational state that is triggered by an external factor that produces a short-term attraction to the learning activity.

individual interest An enduring disposition in which one develops a clear preference to direct attention and effort toward a particular activity, situation, or subject matter.

In the classroom, interest appears in two forms, as summarized in the left-hand side of Figure 10.9. Situational interest is triggered by external factors and exists as a short-term attraction to a learning activity. For instance, a student might encounter a learning activity, such as a book, field trip, or class project, and notice that it is novel, surprising, or a particularly good fit with his or her needs and goals. That is, something sparks the student's interest, and this short-lived interest sparks engagement (Schraw & Lehman, 2001). Individual interest is more stable, enduring, and content-specific (Schiefele, 1999). It develops over time as a personal disposition. With individual interest, the student's unique developmental history creates a clear preference to direct his or her attention and effort toward a particular activity, situation, or subject matter (e.g., music, sports, learning about Mexico).

As shown on the right-hand side of Figure 10.9, interest has numerous benefits for learners (Alexander, Jetton, & Kulikowich, 1995; Alexander, Kulikowich, & Jetton, 1994; Hidi, 1990; Renninger, Hidi, & Krapp, 1992; Schiefele, 1991; Schraw & Lehman, 2001; Shirey & Reynolds, 1988; Silvia, 2006, 2008). Interest, for instance, directs the learner's attention to the task and away from distractors. It also improves later recall of that material, because interesting material is more deeply processed and more readily remembered than is uninteresting material. Interest in a particular subject also predicts a student's level of achievement in that subject. As shown in Table 10.3, interest correlates with students' achievement across all subject areas, and it does so for both elementary and high school students, and for both males and females (Schiefele, Krapp, & Winteler, 1992).

Several instructional strategies can be employed to pique students' classroom interest (Schraw, Flowerday, & Lehman, 2001). First, teachers can introduce learning activities in ways that involve students' inner motivational resources, such as autonomy (Danner & Lonky, 1981; Deci, 1992; Gibson, 1988; Malone, 1981). Second, teachers can use information (texts, handouts) that is already familiar to students before presenting the less familiar information about which the teacher wishes to enhance students' interest. Prior knowledge in a subject area predicts level of interest in that same area. That is, the more knowledge one has about a topic, the more interesting it tends to be (Alexander et al., 1995; Hidi, 1990; Hidi & Baird, 1986; Kintsch, 1980; Tobias, 1994). Having a well-developed level of background knowledge about a topic is a prerequisite for having a personal interest in that topic (Renninger, 2000; Tobias, 1994), and this is true for both the knowledge students possess prior to instruction and for knowledge supplied by the teacher prior to the lesson, as through a handout or videotape.

To help teachers integrate students' situational interests and individual interests, Hidi and Renninger (2006) proposed a four-stage model to guide instruction in which unengaged students become interested and engaged ones. In phase 1, teachers trigger situational interest, often through a puzzle or surprising information. In phase 2, teachers help students maintain their situational interest, often through setting a challenging goal or involving students in project-based learning to work through the puzzle or surprising information. In phase 3, the student begins to generate his or her own curiosity-based questions as individual interest begins to emerge. In phase 4, a well-developed individual interest takes root and allows students to sustain the long-term constructive and creative engagement that leads to knowledge building and deeper interest.

TABLE 10.3

Interest–Achievement Correlations for Seven Subject Areas

Subject Area	Interest–Achievement Correlation[a]
	r
Mathematics	.32
Science	.35
Physics	.31
Biology	.16
Social science	.34
Foreign language	.33
Literature	.17

[a] Numbers in the table represent the average study's correlation (denoted by the symbol r) between students' levels of interest and their achievement in that subject area. Higher numbers represent a stronger association between interest and achievement.

Source: Adapted from Schiefele, U., Krapp, A., & Winteler, A. (1992). Interest as a predictor of academic achievement: A meta-analysis of research. In K. A. Renninger, S. Hidi, & A. Krapp (Eds.). *The role of interest in learning and development.* Hillsdale, NJ: Lawrence Erlbaum Associates. Reprinted with the permission of Springer Science & Business Media.

Inducing Positive Affect

Positive affect refers to the everyday experience of feeling good (Isen, 1987). It is the mildly happy feeling students experience when the events in their lives unfold in ways that are better than expected. As unexpected and pleasant events unfold in the classroom—a compliment, making progress on a project, or seeing an amusing cartoon pop up on a PowerPoint or overhead slide—students experience a brief, mildly happy feeling.

positive affect The mild, subtle, everyday experience of feeling good.

Positive affect is important because students who are in a good mood think more flexibly and function more productively than do students who are in a neutral mood. Compared with when they feel neutral (which is most of the time), students who feel good are more creative, more efficient in their problem solving, more flexible in their thinking, more thorough in their decision making, more intrinsically motivated, more persistent in the face of failure, more accepting of risk, more cooperative, less aggressive, more sociable, more generous, and more willing to help others (Carnevale & Isen, 1986; Isen, 1987; Isen, Daubman, & Nowicki, 1987; Isen & Levin, 1972).

> **How Can I Use This?**
>
> Surprise someone with a small gift, such as a compliment or can of soda, then look for any subsequent increase in their creativity or sociability.

It is impressive that a small and unexpected event can have such a substantial and constructive effect on students' thinking, engagement, and sociability. To induce positive affect, teachers do not need to use big, attention-getting, entertainment-like events. Positive affect is subtle. It produces its benefits in thinking and productivity only when students are unaware of their elevated mood. It sounds paradoxical, but when students are made aware of their positive feelings (e.g., "Oh my, aren't we in a good mood today."), positive affect ceases to exert its constructive influence. So instead of entertaining students, the way to induce positive affect is through small, unexpected, and pleasant events, such as giving a small gift (Isen & Geva, 1987), providing refreshments (Isen et al., 1985), offering a cookie (Isen & Levin, 1972), showing a cartoon (Carnevale & Isen, 1986), giving a "Have a nice day!" card (Wilson et al., 2005), or just asking students to think about (Isen et al., 1985) or to write about (Johnson & Stapel, 2011) positive events.

Using Technology to Promote Motivation and Engagement

Technology is widely used in classrooms. Teachers use computers, Web sites, CD programs, videotapes, e-books, overhead slides, PowerPoint presentations, and so on. One appeal of technology is its potential to promote students' engagement. But not all technology necessarily promotes engagement. Here are four criteria a teacher can use to evaluate any piece of technology in terms of its capacity to motivate and engage students (Keller, 1983):

A = Attention (or curiosity, interest)

R = Relevance (or value, identified regulation)

C = Confidence (or competence)

S = Satisfaction (or intrinsic and extrinsic motivation)

Attention refers to whether the technology arouses the learner's curiosity and interest. *Relevance* refers to whether the learner perceives the technology to be connected to his or her personal goals—to the sort of things students care about. *Confidence* refers to the extent to which the learner expects to be able to cope with and successfully master the learning material. *Satisfaction* refers to the learner's intrinsic motivation and reactions to the rewards embedded in the technology (e.g., sound effects following a correct response).

The utility of the ARCS model is its capacity to answer the question: Will students find this technology motivating? According to the ARCS model, to the extent that the technology successfully addresses students' attention, relevance, confidence, and satisfaction, the answer will be yes. As a case in point, one teacher might consider using a computer software game to teach math or phonics skills, and another teacher might consider loading a foreign-language tutorial onto the school's computer network. Whether or not students will find the technology motivating and engaging can be estimated in advance in terms of its capacity to meet the ARCS criteria.

Different aspects of technology can stimulate and support different motivations. Multimedia learning environments that simulate authentic, or real-world, activities can spark curiosity and stimulate interest, as can those that embed learning activities within a fantasy context (Cordova &

Lepper, 1996; Loftus & Loftus, 1983; Maddux, Johnson, & Willis, 1997, Malone, 1981). Computer programs can offer learners a choice of difficulty levels and, therefore, provide optimal challenges to their skills. Technology is typically highly responsive and, therefore, can provide immediate feedback to nurture competence and flow experiences as well as informational extrinsic rewards, such as celebratory sound effects. The self-initiated and self-managed aspects of technology can support learners' autonomy. Teachers can stimulate all these motivational states without technology, but the point is that teachers can use technology to assist their efforts to create conditions in which students will find learning activities motivating and engaging.

Engagement–Draining Motivational Deficits

From a motivational perspective, the root cause of poor learning and underachievement is disengagement. Of course, many nonmotivational forces help explain underachievement, factors such as a lack of experience, a lack of resources, or a learning disability. That notwithstanding, it remains true that disengagement explains more than its fair share of poor learning and underachievement.

Students in secondary education often possess complex personal histories and problems. Some have accepted failure, and some suffer motivational deficits such as learned helplessness (discussed in Chapter 11). Others seek to avoid challenge and the possibility of failure and a harsh negative evaluation if they perform poorly. So disengagement is sometimes an intentional decision. Sometimes students become so fearful of the social and emotional consequences of failure and public shame that they would rather not take the risks involved in trying to succeed. Learning, success, and achievement are worthwhile, but in many students' minds, they are not worth the risk of opening the door to experiences such as shame, criticism, embarrassment, and loss of respect. When students decide that preserving their self-worth is more important than learning and achievement, withholding engagement becomes an intentional, even strategic, way of coping with academic challenges.

All academic standards of excellence are two-edged swords, motivationally speaking (Covington & Omelich, 1979). A standard of excellence simultaneously arouses in students both the desire to approach it and do well *and* the desire to avoid it and not embarrass oneself. When facing a standard of excellence (e.g., make a high score on a test, make a good class presentation, answer a question aloud in class, win a schoolwide election), the student feels excitement and hope and anticipates feeling pride in a job well done, yet simultaneously feels anxiety and fear and anticipates feeling shame and humiliation. Thus, as students decide whether to try hard or withhold their effort, they experience an emotional tug-of-war. Figure 10.10 depicts this

Figure 10.10 Positive and Negative Emotional Reactions to a Standard of Excellence

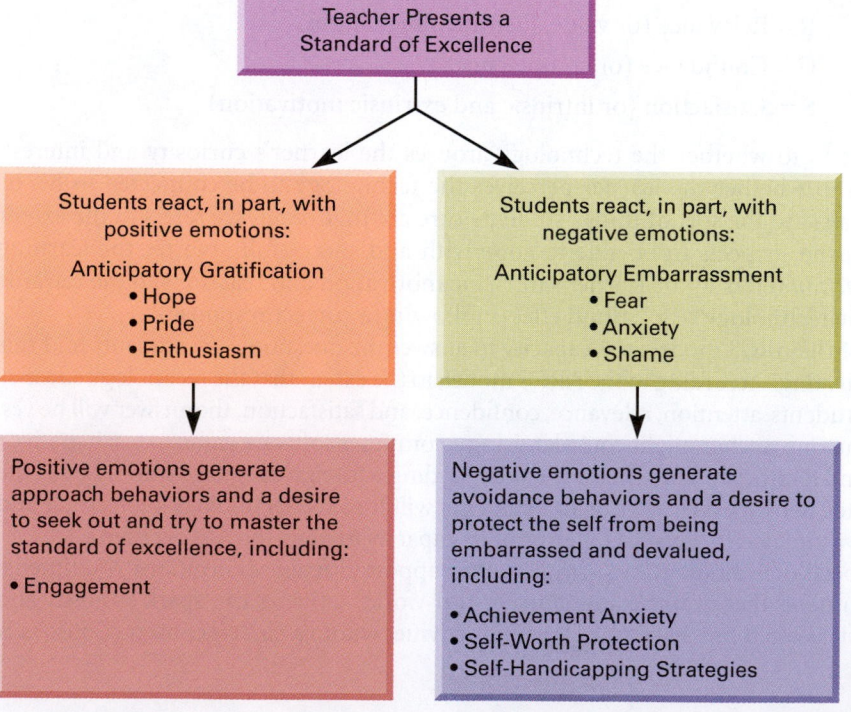

emotional conflict: It shows how the anticipation of hope, pride, and enthusiasm motivates approach and engagement, whereas the anticipation of fear, anxiety, and shame simultaneously motivates avoidance and disengagement.

During adolescence, self-consciousness reaches its peak. Adolescents care deeply about what their peers think of them and their abilities (Gray & Hudson, 1984; Riley, Adams, & Nielson, 1984). With each passing grade, self-consciousness rises, and adolescents gradually accumulate inhibitions against putting forth effort in achievement situations. Three of those inhibitions include the fear of being evaluated negatively (achievement anxiety), the concern with preserving self-worth in front of others (self-worth protection), and the desire to present oneself to others in a positive light (self-handicapping) (Baumeister, 1982). These are not engagement-facilitating motivational resources like the ones included in Figure 10.3. Instead, they are engagement-draining motivational deficits. These sources of inhibition and avoidance begin to rear their ugly heads in late elementary school and grow in strength during middle school, but they blossom into far-reaching, engagement-draining problems during the high school years.

Calming Anxiety, Protecting Self-Worth, and Overcoming Fear of Failure

Anxiety is the unpleasant, aversive emotion that students experience in evaluative settings, such as public speaking or taking a test (Dusek, 1980). When students are facing a standard of excellence, anxiety leads them to focus more on the threat of failure than on the hope of success. Anxious students, therefore, display effort-withholding, avoidance-based behaviors, such as making excuses, not participating, skipping classes, and pleading to be allowed to do something else (Smith, Snyder, & Handelsman, 1982). Test anxiety appears to undermine not only classroom engagement but also academic performance in general. Highly test-anxious students have lower GPAs than do non-test-anxious students (Seipp, 1991), and this poor achievement effect is found at every grade level (Hembree, 1988). That said, students' sensitivity to anxiety increases with each grade level, such that anxiety exerts relatively little effect on elementary school students, a moderate effect on middle school students, and a rather debilitating effect on high school students (Hill & Sarason, 1966). This is true irrespective of the student's race or gender (Hill, 1980; Willig et al., 1983). The classroom conditions that most commonly lead students to feel anxious include external evaluation, high-stakes testing, unrealistic performance demands, external pressures, interpersonal competition, and situations that exceed their coping capacities (Bandura, 1983; Eccles, Midgley, & Adler, 1984; Hill, 1980, 1984; Lazarus & Folkman, 1984).

anxiety The unpleasant, aversive emotion that students experience in evaluative settings.

Self-worth is an evaluation by others of one's personal worth. Appraisals of self-worth are based largely on three sources of information: perceptions of ability, perceptions of effort, and performance accomplishments (Covington, 1984a, then 1984b). Among elementary school children, each of these three sources contributes positively to an evaluation that a person is good and worthy of praise and respect. The solid lines in Figure 10.11a indicate that an elementary school student's praiseworthiness reflects high ability, high effort, and performance success. The more ability one has, the harder one tries, and the more successes one achieves, the more one deserves an appraisal of high self-worth.

self-worth An evaluation by others of one's personal worth.

Among adolescents, it is a different story. Adolescents come to understand that people who try hard are to be *pitied*, not praised. They come to believe that displays of great effort are a telltale sign that the person lacks ability (see the pair of negative signs in Figure 10.11b connecting effort to ability and effort to self-worth). The adolescent thinks that if someone has to try hard—study hard, prepare for hours, or practice diligently—that person surely must lack the ability that would otherwise allow him or her to breeze through the task with ease (Nicholls, 1978). In other words, great effort is a billboard advertisement that one possesses low ability (Covington, 1984a). For adolescents, any public display of classroom engagement all too often becomes a social threat to his or her self-worth.

Self-handicapping is a defensive self-presentation strategy that involves a deliberate effort to interfere with one's own performance so as to provide a face-saving excuse for failure—just in case one does indeed fail (Jones & Berglas, 1978). The goal of self-handicapping is to have others disregard low ability as a causal factor in one's poor performance. In doing so, the student protects his or her self-esteem from the potentially damaging effects of failure (Mc-Crea & Hirt, 2001). Often, students who use self-handicapping strategies are those with high

self-handicapping A defensive self-presentation strategy that involves intentionally interfering with one's own performance so as to provide a face-saving excuse for failure in case one does indeed fail.

Figure 10.11 Self-Worth Models of Children and Adolescents

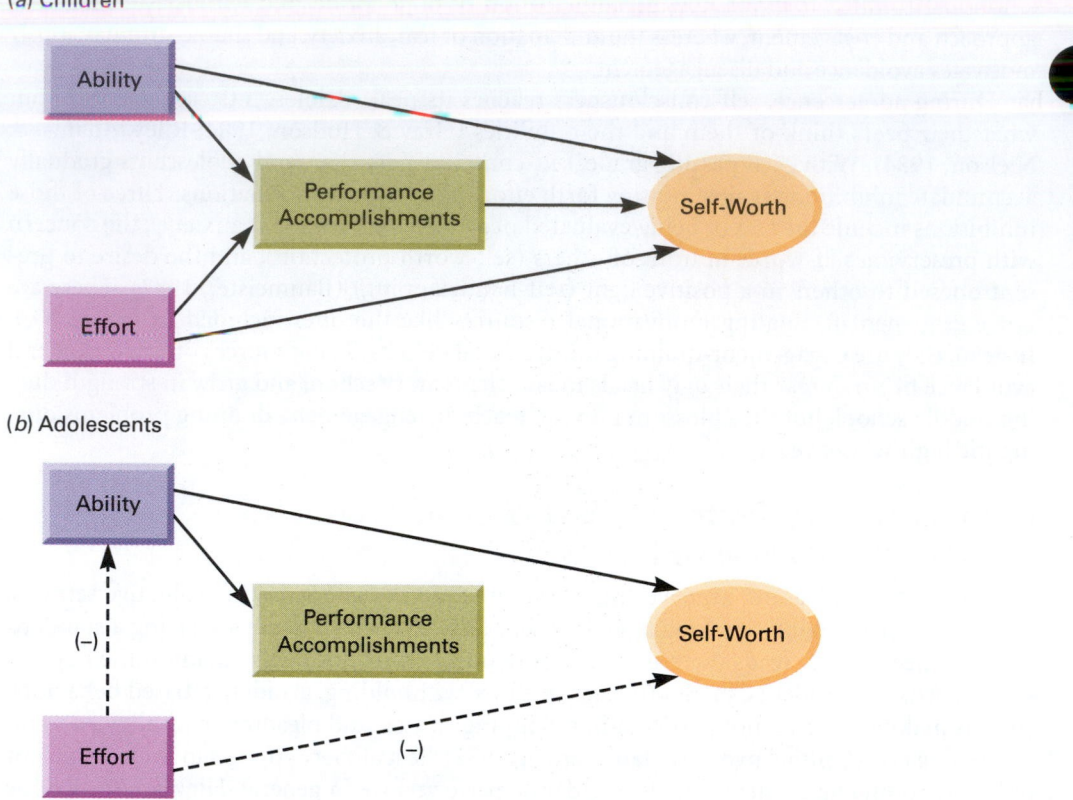

(a) Children

(b) Adolescents

ability or high self-esteem—high enough that these self-perceptions need to be protected (Arkin & Baumgardner, 1985; Baumeister, 1982).

The mental calculation that leads to self-handicapping is as follows: "Before I perform and risk failure and humiliation, I will find or create an obstacle to good performance. Then, if I perform poorly, it will be clear to everyone why I failed—namely, because of the obstacle. If I perform well, however, it will be easy to convince others that my high ability caused not only my success but also my triumph over the obstacle." The sorts of obstacles that students create to handicap themselves include procrastinating, goofing-off, adopting the sick role, reporting high stress, not getting enough sleep, being on medication, being in a bad mood, and avoiding necessary practice or preparation (Baumgardner, Lake, & Arkin, 1985; Covington, 1992; Covington & Omelich, 1979; Rhodewalt & Fairfield, 1991; Smith, Snyder, & Perkins, 1983; Snyder & Higgins, 1988). To become familiar with students' self-handicapping strategies, simply keep an open ear to what they say just prior to a public performance (e.g., "Oh, I'm not feeling well today, so don't expect too much, okay?").

The beneficial aspect of self-handicapping is that the self is protected, even immunized, against the possible humiliation of failure. The problem, however, is that sabotaging one's effort undermines performance and therefore makes success less likely and failure more likely.

Instructional Strategies to Ease Motivational Deficits

Anxiety, self-worth, and self-handicapping are problematic, self-defeating solutions to the motivational problem that students wrestle with each time they face a standard of excellence. The best way to help students adopt engagement-promoting solutions to these motivational dilemmas is to take an advanced peek into some of the instructional strategies that will be presented in the next chapter. First, consider anxiety. Student anxiety has a clear and reliable antidote. The antidote to anxiety is high self-efficacy (Bandura, 1983), the judgment that one has what it takes to cope well with the situation at hand (Bandura, 1993). As we shall see, as teachers find ways to increase students' sense of self-efficacy, students' anxiety decreases.

Second, consider protection of self-worth. Self-worth protection also has an antidote. The antidote to diminished self-worth is the awareness and adoption of an incremental self-theory. As we shall see in Chapter 11, adopting incremental thinking (the harder you work, the smarter you get) redefines effort so that it becomes a valued asset rather than a feared liability (i.e., a means to get smarter and to develop greater skill).

Third, consider the fear of failure. It, too, has a reliable antidote. The antidote to self-handicapping strategies is the establishment of a classroom learning (rather than performance) climate that is similar to a highly error-tolerant classroom climate. A learning goal is the goal to master the challenges of the task at hand—that is, to learn, improve, develop competence, and get better today at the task than you were at the task yesterday. Hence, teachers can help ease students' fear of failure by encouraging them to set and embrace learning goals during learning activities (as opposed to an obsession to get the right answer).

Perhaps the strategy that best captures the essence of the effort to calm anxiety, protect self-worth, and overcome the fear of failure is error tolerance, discussed earlier in this chapter. Recall that high error tolerance is a climate in which errors and setbacks are accepted, valued, even prized as an inherently *useful* and *constructive* aspect of the learning process (Clifford, 1990). This is so because the fundamental motivational problem that is so often embedded in the pursuit of a standard of excellence is this: What will others think of my ability when they see me put forth a great deal of effort on this task? To the extent that students expect others to use great effort as a cue to infer low ability, the motivation to use engagement-depleting defensive strategies will be strong. Error tolerance, however, represents a teacher's explicit attempt to solve students' risk-taking dilemma in a way that fosters engagement. To the extent that students find themselves in highly error-tolerant social climates, they can feel free to engage themselves fully in learning activities without the emotional distress created by anxiety, self-worth judgments, and the fear of failure.

R I D E Can a teacher's high error tolerance promote engagement by releasing students from the social pressures that breed intentional disengagement?

Understanding Amotivation

Another pervasive engagement-draining motivational deficit is amotivation. **Amotivation** literally means "without motivation" (Legault, Green-Demers, & Pelletier, 2006). It is a state of motivational apathy that arises when the student experiences unmet needs. When amotivated, students feel a lack of control over school-based outcomes and hence come to feel that there is little or no reason to invest effort and energy in trying to accomplish something. Hence, the amotivated student in a physical education class just sits bored on the sidelines, just as the amotivated student in a social studies class just "goes through the motions" or perhaps just sleeps (see the nearby photograph) or does not even come to class (Ntoumanis et al., 2004).

amotivation without motivation.

The model depicted in Figure 10.12 summarizes the basic profile of amotivation by identifying its underlying sources of unmet needs (based on Shen et al., 2010). The model shows the four elements of amotivation and adds a student quote to represent each element (Shen et al., 2010).

Part of the experience of amotivation comes from maladaptive ability beliefs, as the amotivated student believes that his or her actions will not be effective enough to produce a desired result. A second element within amotivation comes from maladaptive effort beliefs, as the amotivated student feels unable to generate and sustain the necessary effort to pursue a goal. A third element within amotivation comes from low value placed on the task at hand, as the amotivated student devalues it as simply an unimportant thing to do. Finally, a fourth element within the experience of amotivation comes from a sense that the task itself is unappealing, as the amotivated student sees the task as uninteresting or as lacking in any stimulating qualities.

(PhotoDisc, Inc./Getty Images)

Motivating Students during Uninteresting Lessons

A devalued, boring task does not have to remain boring, and students' functioning on relatively uninteresting tasks does not have to be poor (Sansone et al., 1992). After all, few people enjoy brushing their teeth, but most do it every day with care.

When a task is uninteresting (from the student's point of view), teachers have three fruitful means of engaging their students: increase valuing, increase interest, and promote

Figure 10.12 Maladaptive Beliefs and Unappealing Task Characteristics (with Illustrative Quotations) Are the Sources of Amotivation

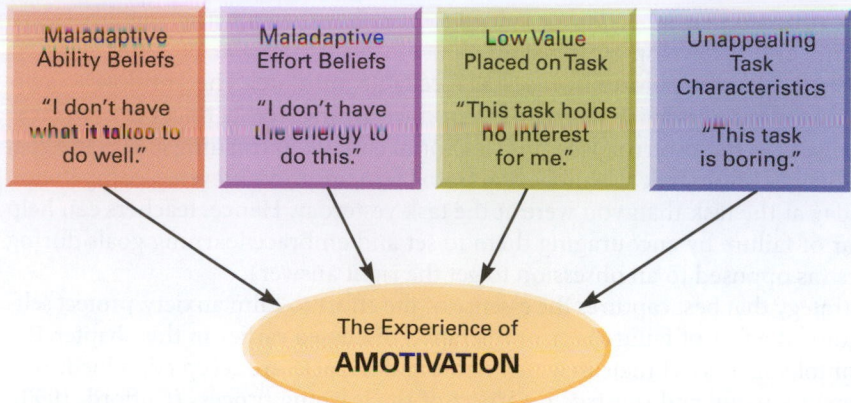

intrinsic goals. The nearby Taking It to the Classroom box supplements these three core engagement strategies with additional ways to motivate otherwise unengaged students.

Increase Valuing In general, the extent to which students value a subject matter decreases year after year from grade 1 to grade 12 (Archambault, Eccles, & Vida, 2010). Thus, classroom-based interventions to prevent decreases in the perceived value of school subjects and academic work are very important. In one such study, researchers asked students to reflect on how the material they were learning (e.g., math) was relevant to their lives (Hulleman, Godes, Hendricks, & Harackiewicz, 2010). Specifically, students engaged in a writing task to describe the potential relevance of what they were learning to their lives and also to give examples of how the lesson might be personally useful. The intervention was successful in boosting students' perceived value for the material. This "relevance intervention" not only increased students' sense of valuing, but that increased sense of value in turn increased students' interest and achievement as well.

The value of a task stems from its utility or usefulness to the student (Eccles et al., 1983). Brushing one's teeth and exercising at the gym are valuable because they enable good health. That is, brushing and exercising are personally useful things to do; hence, they are valuable. When students face an uninteresting (but important) lesson, they are often unaware of how that activity can help them attain goals that are important to them. If they don't understand a lesson's value, students experience a motivational problem. Therefore, the teacher needs to take the time to provide students with a **rationale** to explain why the lesson is worth their effort. The rationales that students find convincing or satisfying are those in which the teacher is able to connect the lesson with the student's future goals and strivings. For instance, preservice teachers generally take a course in educational psychology not necessarily because they think the course will be interesting and enjoyable but because they believe it will help them become more effective teachers. Providing rationales is an engagement-fostering motivational strategy, as students who receive teacher-provided rationales for why a lesson is truly worthwhile show significantly greater engagement than do students who receive no such teacher-provided rationales (Assor et al., 2002; Jang, 2008; Reeve et al., 2002). Students who sincerely value a lesson truly and willingly want to engage it, even if that lesson is an inherently uninteresting thing to do.

Increase Interest While students are engaged in relatively boring and uninteresting activities (e.g., completing worksheets, diagramming sentences, conjugating verbs in a foreign language), they can engage in a number of strategies to foster greater interest (Jang, 2008; Sansone et al., 1992; Sansone & Smith, 2000). One interest-enhancing strategy is to create a challenge or a goal to strive for. In trying to master a challenge or accomplish a goal, engagement is as much about mastering the challenge or achieving the goal as it is about the task itself. After all, what is so interesting about athletic activities such as hitting tennis balls or shooting basketballs, other than the pursuit of challenging goals?

A second interest-enhancing strategy is to mentally change the context of what one is doing—by adding a fantasy context, for instance (Cordova & Lepper, 1996). As an example, instead of just reading this book, use your imagination to place yourself in a context of trying to

rationale A verbal explanation as to why a task is important and worth one's attention, time, and effort.

Taking It to the Classroom

Do You Know Jack? Dealing with Disengagement

Jack is often unengaged. Jack does not participate in classroom activities that are interesting to his classmates. Grades appear to mean little to him. What practical and immediate approaches can you take to assist Jack?

- Ask Jack whether anything is wrong and whether you can help in any way.
- Support Jack's autonomy by integrating his interest or preference into the structure of the day's lesson (e.g., such as through a writing assignment).
- Provide Jack with a goal or optimal challenge to strive for and, as he works, immediate and authentic feedback that communicates progress and improvement.
- When communicating feedback to Jack, use informational language, such as "You're making progress," rather than controlling language, such as "Work faster."
- When Jack finds a lesson uninteresting, support his motivation either by explaining why the lesson is useful and truly worth his effort or by suggesting an interest-enhancing strategy, such as setting a goal to strive for.
- Spark Jack's curiosity and exploration with a curiosity-inducing strategy, such as guessing-and-feedback.
- Place Jack in an engagement-fostering role, such as a leader, detective, or presenter for his group.
- Adopt an error-tolerant attitude by communicating to Jack that failure is a useful, constructive, and beneficial aspect of the learning process.

motivate your future students. Preparing yourself to teach future students is likely to be a more interesting activity than simply reading this book. Using this interest-enhancing strategy, a foreign-language teacher might invite students to imagine being overseas and trying to communicate as they make their way around town.

> **How Can I Use This?**
>
> Try to increase your interest in this text by creating a goal to strive for or by imagining that you are the teacher in a class and trying to motivate students.

Promote Intrinsic Goals   Teachers often encourage student engagement by communicating the value and personal relevance and usefulness of an otherwise uninteresting task, and this strategy has been shown to be effective in sparking student engagement (Assor et al., 2002). A similar strategy is to refer students to a goal during their task engagements (Vansteenkiste, Soenens, Verstuyf, & Lens, 2009). That is, as teachers ask students to read a text about a particular topic, they can add how learning this knowledge might help students accomplish something that is important to them. But all goals are not equal, as encouraging students to pursue intrinsic goals (those that will satisfy their psychological needs) promotes greater engagement and learning than does encouraging students to pursue extrinsic goals (those that will help them attain extrinsic rewards; Vansteenkiste, Lens, & Deci, 2006). Those who recommend "intrinsic goal framing" as an engagement-fostering classroom strategy offer teachers the following guidelines (Vansteenkiste et al., 2009):

- Refer to the intrinsic, rather than extrinsic, benefits of an activity (e.g., "Here is a chance to learn something new or to make a friend" rather than "Here is a chance to make an A or to make some money.").
- Promote a specific, rather than vague, goal as meaningfully connected to the learning activity (e.g., "Use this assignment as an opportunity to develop your skills as a writer—to become a better writer"). This requires reflective thought, but research shows that teachers can do this with a brief, written note given at the start of the lesson.

By definition, any time a student pursues a need-satisfying personal goal, he or she cannot possibly experience amotivation. If they are to make the transition from an amotivated "Why should I do this?" to an intrinsic goal promoting "Here is a chance to improve myself," students will need help from their teachers to find meaningful goals to strive for.

REFLECTION FOR ACTION

The Event

As we saw at the start of the chapter, Mrs. Watson loves teaching, but she becomes discouraged when her students tune her out and disengage from the lesson she put so much time and heart into preparing. What can she do when they stare blankly and give only a half-hearted effort?

Reflection RIDE

Why are Mrs. Watson's students so disengaged from the lesson? How can she engage them more fully? What instructional strategies might she implement to promote active and enthusiastic engagement?

What Theoretical/Conceptual Information Might Assist in Interpreting and Remedying This Situation? Consider the following:

Autonomy and Intrinsic Motivation

From where do autonomy and intrinsic motivation come? If her students are extrinsically motivated, how can she nurture their autonomy and intrinsic motivation? Would it help if she adopted an autonomy-supportive motivating style?

Competence and Flow

How can she involve her students' need for competence? What if she redesigned her lessons to introduce a steady stream of optimal challenges?

Error Tolerance

Perhaps her students are disengaged for defensive reasons. What classroom conditions tend to put students on the defensive? How can she establish a classroom climate high in failure tolerance?

Information Gathering RIDE

How does Mrs. Watson know that her students are unengaged? What information does she need to evaluate the quality of her students' motivation? What information does she need to evaluate the quality of her own motivating style? To assess the quality of her students' motivation, she might ask students why they participate in class. To assess the quality of her motivating style, she might videotape a class to assess how much or how little she supports students' autonomy versus tries to control their behavior. She might ask a colleague to view the videotape for a second opinion. Are her lessons challenging? Has she established a highly error-tolerant learning climate for her students? How rarely does she utilize interest-enhancing strategies, such as guessing-and-feedback, and how much of a stranger is positive affect to her classroom? During lessons, do students typically experience flow, boredom, or anxiety? Are her students defensive? Are they holding back their engagement out of a sense of anxiety, self-worth protection, or a fear of failing? Are they amotivated? How fruitful would instructional strategies such as increasing valuing, increasing interest, and promoting intrinsic goals be?

Decision Making RIDE

With this information, Mrs. Watson needs to answer the following question:

- How engaged versus unengaged are her students?
- How much satisfaction of psychological needs do her students experience on a regular basis?
- Is her teaching style autonomy-supportive or controlling?
- How optimally challenging are her lessons?
- How interesting and curiosity-provoking do her lessons tend to be?
- What emotions do students typically experience in class—boredom, flow, or anxiety?
- What is the motivational status of her students' sense of valuing? Of interest? Of meaningful intrinsic goals to pursue?

She may need to find ways to introduce autonomy, intrinsic motivation, challenges, feedback, and error tolerance into her lesson plans. She needs to decide how often students feel flow, interest, and positive affect, and how often they feel anxiety, the need for self-worth protection, and the fear of failure.

Evaluation RIDE

With each adjustment she makes, Mrs. Watson needs to evaluate how closely her instructional adjustments correspond to rises and falls in her students' engagement. Mrs. Watson needs to evaluate the connections among how engaged her students are, as well as the following:

- The quality of their motivation
- The quality of her motivating style
- The extent to which her instructional strategies spark curiosity, interest, and positive affect versus anxiety, self-protection, and the fear of failure

Further Practice: Your Turn

Here is a second event for your consideration and reflection. In doing so, implement the processes of reflection, information gathering, decision making, and evaluation.

The Event

Mr. Marcus is a little worried about how today's lesson will go. Today's class features a lesson that students in the past have said was difficult and somewhat boring. The lesson, however, is important, even crucial, for students to learn if they are to master the course material and develop the skills they need.

What can Mr. Marcus do to add some motivational spark to today's lesson? What can he do to modify his existing lesson plan so as to more fully engage his students?

SUMMARY

● **What is engagement, what does it look like, and why is it important?**

Engagement refers to the extent of a student's active involvement in a learning activity. It is a multidimensional construct that consists of the four interrelated aspects of behavioral engagement, emotional engagement, cognitive engagement, and agentic engagement. Engagement is important for four reasons: It makes learning possible, it predicts how well students fare in school, it is malleable and therefore open to interventions, and it provides teachers the moment-to-moment feedback they need to diagnose how well their motivational strategies are working.

● **How can teachers engage diverse learners and learners with special needs?**

Diverse learners' interests and definitions of success sometimes clash with the school's expectations and priorities. When students fail to find a place in school where their interests and preferences are honored, they understandably decrease their engagement, especially when they perceive that teachers are their opponents and enemies rather than their allies and advocates. Special education teachers often rely on extrinsic motivators because they follow the motto that external regulation is better than no regulation at all. Some special educators, however, take a dialectical approach to motivating students by nurturing their capacity for autonomous self-regulation and, hence, their engagement.

● **What is motivation?**

Motivation is the study of the forces that energize and direct behavior. Energy means that behavior is strong, intense, and full of effort. Direction means that behavior is focused on accomplishing a particular goal or outcome. So any force that energizes and directs behavior constitutes motivation. This chapter highlighted the following motivations: intrinsic motivation, internalized extrinsic motivation, psychological needs, interests, values, curiosity, positive affect, and achievement strivings.

● **What is the difference between intrinsic and extrinsic motivation?**

Intrinsic motivation is the inherent desire to engage in one's interests and to exercise and develop one's capacities. It emerges spontaneously out of psychological needs and yields numerous educational benefits, such as high-quality learning. Extrinsic motivation is an environmentally created reason to initiate or persist in an action. It emerges from the offering of rewards and generally yields compliance, rather than engagement. Offering extrinsic rewards sometimes yields hidden and unintended costs, including undermining intrinsic motivation, learning, and autonomous self-regulation. Cognitive-evaluation theory explains how teachers can avoid these costs by giving extrinsic rewards in non-controlling and informational ways.

● **How can teachers support students' psychological needs?**

All students have three basic psychological needs: autonomy, competence, and relatedness. Autonomy is the need to experience self-direction in the initiation and regulation of one's behavior; teachers can support autonomy by relying on an autonomy-supportive motivating style. Competence is the need to be effective during environmental challenges; teachers can support competence by providing optimal challenges and a highly error-tolerant classroom climate. Relatedness is the need to establish close emotional bonds with others; teachers can support relatedness by providing warm, caring relationships.

● **In what ways can teachers spark students' engagement?**

Curiosity, interest, and positive affect can spark students' engagement. Curiosity occurs when students experience a gap in their knowledge; teachers can spark curiosity with instructional strategies such as guessing-and-feedback and suspense. Interest is a topic-specific motivational state that arises out of an attraction to a particular domain of activity; teachers can build students' interest through either situational or individual interest. Positive affect is the mild, subtle, everyday experience of feeling good; teachers can induce positive affect by offering students a small, pleasant, and unexpected event, such as refreshments.

- **In what ways can teachers calm students' anxieties and fears?**
Students experience standards of excellence as two-edged swords: challenges to their skills that arouse both the desire to approach them and do well and the simultaneous desire to avoid them and not embarrass oneself. The implementation of a highly error-tolerant classroom climate helps solves students' risk-taking dilemma by calming their anxiety, protecting their sense of worth, and overcoming their fear of failure.

- **How can teachers motivate students during uninteresting activities?**
Students find some learning activities uninteresting. Three instructional strategies to promote autonomy, avoid the hidden costs of rewards, and fully engage students in learning were identified. Teachers might increase students' sense of valuing by providing explanatory rationales that articulate the reason the lesson is truly worth the student's effort. Teachers might increase students' interest by offering interest-enhancing strategies, such as creating a goal or introducing an appealing fantasy context. Teachers might promote intrinsic goals to give students something meaningful and need-satisfying to pursue.

Key Terms

agentic engagement, p. 336
amotivation, p. 363
anxiety, p. 361
autonomy, p.348
autonomy-supportive motivating style, p. 349
behavioral engagement, p. 335
cognitive engagement, p. 336
cognitive-evaluation theory, p. 345
competence, p.352
controlling motivating style, p. 346
curiosity, p. 357

emotional engagement, p. 335
engagement, p. 335
error tolerance, p. 352
extrinsic motivation, p. 343
flow, p. 354
guessing-and-feedback, p. 357
hidden cost of reward, p. 343
individual interest, p. 358
interest, p. 357
intrinsic motivation, p. 342
motivation, p. 341
optimal challenge, p. 354

perceived locus of causality, p. 348
positive affect, p. 359
praise, p. 345
psychological need, p. 358
rationale, p. 364
relatedness, p. 354
self-handicapping, p. 361
self-worth, p. 361
situational interest, p. 358
suspense, p. 357

Exercises

1. *Monitoring Students' Engagement*
Use a 7-point scale (1 = *not at all*; 7 = *a great deal*) to create a rating sheet to measure the four aspects of behavioral engagement, emotional engagement, cognitive engagement, and agentic engagement. With this rating sheet in hand, observe a classroom and rate the class as a whole on each of these four aspects of engagement. After the class is over, use your ratings to decide whether the students were mostly engaged or mostly unengaged.

2. *Evaluating an Autonomy-Supportive Motivating Style*
Ask a teacher whether you can visit his or her classroom to make some ratings. Use a 7-point scale (1 = *not used at all*; 7 = *always used*) to score the following five aspects of an autonomy-supportive motivating style: nurtures inner motivational resources, provides explanatory rationales, relies on noncontrolling language, displays patience to allow time for self-paced learning to occur, and acknowledges and accepts students' expressions of negative affect. Was the teacher consistently high or consistently low on all five instructional behaviors, or was the teacher high on some behaviors but low on others? In what ways was the teacher's motivating style related to students' level of engagement?

3. *Providing Rationales*
Attend a class and write down all the rationales or explanations a teacher offers to explain why students are being asked to follow a rule, enact a procedure, comply with a request, or engage themselves in a learning activity. Some teachers offer no rationales, but many teachers will offer at least one rationale during the lesson. When you hear the teacher

voice a rationale, notice how students respond in terms of engaging in that task. Did the rationale help students generate the motivation they needed to engage in the activity?

4. *Observing Interest-Enhancing Strategies*
As you engage in a relatively uninteresting activity, pay close attention to anything you do to try to make the activity seem more interesting. For instance, while exercising, practicing a skill, or driving a long distance, do you use strategies such as setting a goal? Also, as you read this book, are you doing anything such as drinking a beverage, listening to music, or studying with a friend to boost your sense of interest and engagement?

Lesson Plans

Lesson #1: "The Blinking Bee"

GRADES: 4–6

ESTIMATED TIME: One 45-minute class period

SUBJECT: Math

I. OBJECTIVES: Students will be able to:
- Apply the principles and mathematics of sampling to make estimates
- Determine the reasonableness of an estimate in a structured setting

II. MATERIALS:
- Paper/pencil
- Calculator
- Timer
- Counting chart

III. PROCEDURE:

1. Ask students to guess how many times they blink in one year; place the guesses in a number-line format on the chalkboard so that students can see how broad their guesses are.

2. Have students guess how many times they think they will blink in one minute, and put the number on their *counting chart*; follow with the rest of their estimations.

How Many Blinks …	My Estimation	My Calculation
In a minute		
In an hour (times 60 minutes)		
In a day (times 24 hours)		
In a year (times 365 days)		

3. Students then need a partner to count how many times they blink in one minute (*if time is limited, have one partner be the official "blinker," one the "counter," and skip step 4*).

4. Have students average their blinks to put into "My Calculation."
Why? Because blinking is an inconsistent activity; taking an average will give a more accurate reading.

5. Students will calculate to fill in the rest of the second column.

6. Students will answer the following questions regarding this activity:

- How accurate were your estimations?
- Think about the difference between your and your partner's number of blinks. What does this tell you about your calculations for the number of times you blink in an hour? Is this number completely accurate or is blinking not consistent enough to be accurately calculated in this way?
- What effect do you think the activity itself has on your blinking (did you blink more or less than normal because you were suddenly aware of your blinking)?
- How would this activity be different (in terms of accuracy) if you were counting heart beats? Number of times you swallow?

Ask Yourself!

1. How can you promote students' intrinsic motivation during the lesson?
2. How can you help build students' sense of suspense so as to enhance their curiosity during the lesson?
3. For students who are anxious about mathematical calculations or answering questions aloud, how might you help minimize their anxiety and avoidance motivation?

5. *Observing Self-Handicapping Strategies*
   Observe any instance in which a person performs in an evaluative setting, such as making a speech in front of an audience. Both before and during the performance, listen carefully for any instances of self-handicapping that the person uses to deflect possible criticisms of the performance. Particularly listen for handicaps such as fatigue, lack of practice, lack of preparation, or lack of experience. Does it seem as though these self-generated obstacles help or hurt the person's performance?

Lesson Plans

Lesson #2: "Killer Disease on Campus"

GRADES: 9–12

SUBJECT: Science
URL: http://www.pbs.org/wgbh/nova/teachers/activities/2909_meningit.html

I. OBJECTIVE: To learn about the Food and Drug Administration's processes for new drug development.

II. MATERIALS: For each group:
- Copy of the "Evaluating Drug Development" student handout
- Copy of the "Development Steps" student handout
- Copy of the "Simplified New Drug Development Process" student handout
- Copy of the FDA's "New Drug Development Process" chart, found on the CDER (Center for Drug Evaluation and Research) Web site under the category "New Drug Development and Review," www.fda.gov/cder/handbook/
- Markers
- Large, poster-size paper

III. PROCEDURE:

1. Ask students why they think the government regulates the availability of new drugs.

2. Organize students into groups and provide each group with copies of the "Evaluating Drug Development" and "Development Steps" student handouts.

3. Have students read the definitions provided on the "Development Steps" student handout. Students should discuss with their group members the order they think the steps should follow. Once the order is agreed upon, have students draw a flowchart of the steps. Tell students they can cut out the steps and physically rearrange them if that will help them determine the sequence.

4. When all groups are done, have them share their results with the class. Have the class come to a consensus for the order of the steps.

5. Pass out copies of the "Simplified New Drug Development Process" student handout. Have students compare their final class chart to the simplified chart. Once they are done, hand out and discuss the actual FDA "New Drug Development Process" chart. Point out to students that the actual process doesn't happen sequentially, but that some steps overlap others. Also, the actual process involves additional application processes, review boards, and advisory committee overview.

6. Discuss the advantages and disadvantages to stringent, long-term studies of new drugs.

IV. ACTIVITY ANSWER:

Activity 1—New Drug Development Process
The FDA estimates that a drug is studied and tested for about 8.5 years before it can be approved for the general public. The steps in the flowchart should be arranged in the following order:

B: Synthesis and Purification
E: Short-Term Animal Testing
H: Long-Term Animal Testing
A: Phase One Clinical Studies
F: Phase Two Clinical Studies
I: Phase Three Clinical Studies
D: New Drug Application
G: Review Process
C: Legally Marketed in United States

Ask Yourself!

1. Some students might not find this information inherently interesting. How could you present the lesson in a way that would promote their sense of valuing of the information (i.e., how could you promote students' identified regulation, sense of importance, or sense of valuing)?
2. For each of the six steps of the lesson (under Procedure) generate what you could say to the students during the lesson to offer a convincing and satisfying rationale to students that could explain why that aspect of the lesson is important and truly worth their time and attention.

From Nova/WGBH Education Foundation. Copyright © 2002 WGBH/Boston.

In preparing today's lesson, Mr. Larsen cannot forget yesterday's. He introduced a difficult concept to his students. Some students showed confidence, tried hard, and persisted with enthusiasm until they understood the concept. Other students, however, did not. These students turned anxious, pessimistic, and psychologically abandoned the lesson at the first sign of difficulty. Mr. Larsen watched as these students' motivation wilted before his eyes. He watched as their mood turned negative, their thinking turned pessimistic, and their self-views turned defeatist (e.g., "I'm just not good at this.").

As you reflect on Mr. Larsen's teaching situation, consider your own motivational reaction as we invite you to take on the challenging task below. The coded message cannot be deciphered without an investment of attention, effort, and persistence. How will you react? Will your enthusiasm and optimism rise or will they go dormant as you quickly turn the page to leave the challenge, untouched, behind?

To reveal the teacher's secret, solve the coded message:

Jcokalokcx kr l wtbtbgnkrkob sct
ubltxkxi lxh rzkuu hbabucwjbxo.

Coded letter	Actual letter
l	a
b	e
o	t
r	s
c	o
t	r
a	v
x	n

Instructions
The teacher's secret is encrypted as a coded message in which one letter stands for another. Each time you see the coded letter *l*, for instance, replace it with the actual letter *a*; *lto* therefore translates into the word *art*. You have the codes for only eight letters. The remaining letters, like the message itself, need to be decoded.

Reflection for Action

Mr. Larsen wants to understand why some students react to lessons in ways that are so negative—so apathetic, pessimistic, helpless, and goalless. During today's lesson, he wants to see enthusiasm, optimism, resiliency, and goal striving. What might he do? How can Mr. Larsen motivate his students to engage fully in the lesson?

Guiding Questions

- How does quality of thinking explain quality of motivation?
- When students are hesitant, what can a teacher do to promote their confidence?
- How can teachers foster in students a constructive, mastery-oriented reaction to failure?
- How can teachers implement a goal-setting program?
- What can a teacher do to transform an anxiety-ridden classroom climate into a culture of eager learners?
- How can teachers help students become self-regulated learners?
- How can teachers support motivation in diverse learners and students with special needs?
- How does self-concept develop throughout the school-age years?

CHAPTER OVERVIEW

This chapter is based on the two fundamentals that, first, constructive thinking and productive motivation go hand in hand and, second, student motivation is rooted in how constructive versus destructive one's thinking is. The chapter explains where students' constructive and destructive ways of thinking come from, how these patterns of thinking change, what productive versus counterproductive thinking predicts, and why educators care so deeply about supporting students' constructive ways of thinking. In doing so, the chapter explains the constructive ways of thinking that underlie Mr. Larsen's motivated students—strong self-efficacy, a mastery of motivational orientation, an optimistic attributional style, hope, goal setting, goal striving, mastery achievement goals, effective self-regulation, and a positive self-concept. The chapter also explains the counterproductive ways of thinking that underlie Mr. Larsen's unmotivated students—self-doubt, helplessness, a pessimistic attributional style, a lack of goals, an absence of performance achievement goals, little capacity for self-regulation, and a negative self-concept. The chapter explains how these ways of thinking apply to different grade levels, to diverse learners, and to students with special needs. Intervention strategies are introduced that teachers can use to support their students' constructive patterns of thinking, including a mastery-modeling program, a goal-setting program, and a mastery-oriented classroom climate.

Motivation Is Rooted in Constructive Thinking
- A Social-Cognitive Approach to Thinking and Motivation

Self-Efficacy
- Why Self-Efficacy Is Important
- Sources of Self-Efficacy
- Mastery-Modeling Programs
- Technology, Socioeconomic Status, and Self-Efficacy
- Self-Efficacy in Students with Learning Disabilities

Mastery Beliefs
- Reactions to Failure
- Learned Helplessness
- Attributions
- Preventing Helplessness, Fostering Mastery
- Hope

Goals
- Difficult, Specific Goals Increase Performance
- Implementation Intentions
- Feedback
- A Caution before Assigning a Goal
- Goal-Setting Programs
- Possible Selves
- Achievement Goals
- Promoting Mastery Goals
- Grade-Level Effects on Achievement Goals

Self-Regulation
- Self-Regulatory Processes: Forethought through Reflection
- Promoting Self-Regulation
- Coregulation
- Self-Regulation for Students in Different Grades and for Learners with Special Needs

Self-Concept
- Enhancing the Self-Concept
- Self-Esteem

Motivation Is Rooted in Constructive Thinking

It is difficult, and probably impossible, to imagine a highly and productively motivated student whose thinking is characterized by doubt, fragility, pessimism, or a lack of goals. On the other hand, it is relatively easy to imagine a highly and productively motivated student whose thinking is characterized by confidence, hardiness, optimism, goals, and hope. Constructive thinking and productive motivation go hand in hand. The theme of this second chapter on motivation is that motivation is rooted in the degree of one's constructive thinking.

To clarify how student thinking contributes to student motivation, Figure 11.1 identifies the key thoughts students have during the ongoing flow of any learning activity. Typically, a lesson begins with an introductory period. It is during this period that students make initial judgments of how difficult and how interesting the task will be, while teachers state their expectations for students and identify the helpful resources that will be available. Crucially during this introductory period (left-hand side of Figure. 11.1), students will begin to think constructively and productively in that they will feel confident, optimistic, and set a goal for themselves. Alternatively, students might begin to think destructively and counterproductively in that they will feel anxious, pessimistic, and fail to set a goal for themselves. Already at this point in the lesson, the teacher will be able to see strong effects of students' thinking on their motivation and engagement. As the lesson continues, students more or less engage themselves in the learning activity (middle portion of Figure. 11.1). As students pay attention to how well or how poorly they are coping with the challenges in the lesson, they will continue to think constructively and productively in that they will feel a sense of competence, a sense of control, and actively regulate their learning. Alternatively, students might being to think destructively and counterproductively in that they will feel incompetent, overwhelmed and helpless, and fail to regulate their learning. As the lesson matures and comes to its conclusion, students evaluate whether they have learned or not, and they will make attributions for their success versus failure and will also make inferences for what this experience means for how they are (self-concept). During this reflective period (right-hand side of Figure 11.1), students think constructively and productively in that they attribute their learning to controllable causes and they see themselves as good at learning. Alternatively, students' reflections might lead them to think destructively and counterproductively in that they attribute their lack of learning to uncontrollable forces and see themselves as bad at learning.

A Social–Cognitive Approach to Thinking and Motivation

Student motivation is rooted in constructive thinking. Many of your future students will likely harbor destructive motivational thinking (e.g., doubt, helplessness), at least some of the time. So the question will arise as to how you, their teacher, can help support their constructive thinking during learning activities. A social-cognitive approach focuses on how students acquire patterns of thinking as a result of interacting with and observing role models (Pintrich & Schunk, 2002). Hence, the "social" in a social-cognitive approach to motivation refers to the influence that social models have on the quality of a student's own subsequent thinking.

Appendix
Understanding Students' Motivation

Chapters 10 and 11 help teachers understand the theoretical basis of where motivation comes from and offer instructional strategies to promote students' motivation, engagement, and learning (PRAXIS™, I.C.1; INTASC, Principle 5).

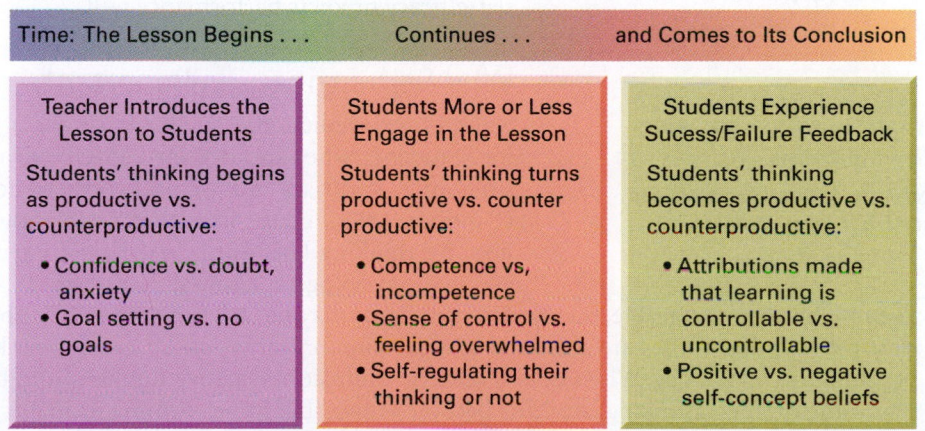

Figure 11.1 Patterns of Constructive versus Destructive Thinking during a Learning Opportunity

Time: The Lesson Begins . . .	Continues . . .	and Comes to Its Conclusion
Teacher Introduces the Lesson to Students	Students More or Less Engage in the Lesson	Students Experience Sucess/Failure Feedback
Students' thinking begins as productive vs. counterproductive:	Students' thinking turns productive vs. counter productive:	Students' thinking becomes productive vs. counterproductive:
• Confidence vs. doubt, anxiety • Goal setting vs. no goals	• Competence vs, incompetence • Sense of control vs. feeling overwhelmed • Self-regulating their thinking or not	• Attributions made that learning is controllable vs. uncontrollable • Positive vs. negative self-concept beliefs

So, where does a students' constructive versus destructive way of thinking come from? The principal sources of what and how students think are the people students respect the most (e.g., teachers, parents, societal role models). That is, students' thinking is heavily influenced and guided by the patterns of thinking they see in others. To guide their own thinking, students listen to, emulate, and internalize those ways of thinking that are modeled for them by the important people in their lives, as they "take on" and internalize the goals, values, and sense of optimism they see in others. This emulation process is what is meant by the term *social-cognitive* and means quite literally that student thinking begins at the social level before it becomes internalized as one's own, personalized way of thinking. Perhaps "social-cognitive" would be better presented as "social → cognitive." As you read the pages to come in this chapter, notice the key role that other people (e.g., teachers, peers, parents) are said to play in promoting students' constructive versus destructive thinking (e.g., efficacy versus doubt, mastery versus helplessness).

Self-Efficacy

self-efficacy One's judgment of how well one will cope with a situation, given the skills one possesses and the circumstances one faces.

Self-efficacy is a student's expectation or judgment of how well (or how poorly) he or she will cope with a situation, given the skills possessed and the circumstances faced (Bandura, 1986b, 1993, 1997). When they possess high self-efficacy in a given domain—when they feel they have sufficient skills to manage the existing situational circumstances—students believe they *have what it takes* to do well. When given a math problem, when trying to make friends at a party, or when trying to skip a fast-moving rope during physical education class, the belief that one *has what it takes* to do well is the belief of high self-efficacy.

Students with low self-efficacy doubt their ability to cope because they believe that the task before them will overwhelm their capacity to cope with it. What students say when they feel inefficacious (overwhelmed) can be seen in the nearby What Kids Say and Do box.

High self-efficacy is not high ability. A singer might have wondrous vocal talent but still sing poorly during a recital if he or she is nervous or if things go unexpectedly wrong. Ability helps performance, but the capacity to cope with the task and circumstances at hand are additionally important. This is so because *all* performance situations require coping and because *all* performance situations involve their fair share of distractions, obstacles, and potential setbacks. Whether taking a test, playing a sport, or trying to converse in a foreign language, all performance situations are at least somewhat stressful, unpredictable, and apt to have things go wrong (Bandura, 1997).

When things are going well, high ability and high self-efficacy seem to go together, just as do low ability and low self-efficacy. However, as soon as things start to go wrong, the obvious importance of self-efficacy quickly becomes apparent. When equipment suddenly fails, when one's partner surprisingly does not show up, when time runs short, or when the situation takes a surprising turn for the worse, self-efficacy matters most and foreshadows the extent to which the student will be able to turn things around for the better and still perform well. When things take a surprising turn for the worse (as they always do, at least to some extent), self-efficacy predicts performance well.

What Kids Say and Do

Self-Efficacy and Avoidance

In class, what makes you anxious or afraid? How do you cope? How do you handle the situation?

Having to read aloud . . . in front of the whole class. It's scary. I feel nervous. My stomach hurts. I always, always hope [the teacher] won't ask me to. (Fourth-grade student)

Doing hard stuff. It makes me feel dumb. I don't want to do it, so I get someone else to do it for me. (Tenth-grade student)

Why Self-Efficacy Is Important

Self-efficacy predicts the quality of students' functioning. Students who doubt their capacity to cope with situational surprises and setbacks experience anxiety (Bandura, 1988), confusion (Wood & Bandura, 1989), negative thinking (Bandura, 1983), bodily tension, and aversive physiological arousal (Bandura et al., 1985). Even highly knowledgeable, highly skilled students may be stricken with self-doubt during a class presentation if they are surprised by a question or unexpectedly asked to make the first presentation of the day. When doubt, anxiety, confusion, negative thinking, and bodily upset dominate their thinking, students become vulnerable to performing dismally. The same holds true for musicians, singers, athletes, and teachers. Self-doubt, erratic thinking, and negative emotion are the telltale warning signs that one's performance is on the verge of collapse and will soon spiral out of control. When self-doubt, erratic thinking, and negative emotion peak, the performer panics and "loses it." High self-efficacy is important because it keeps these debilitating thoughts and feelings quiet—even as things go wrong—so that the performer can continue to focus on the task at hand.

As shown in Figure 11.2, self-efficacy beliefs forecast three principal educational outcomes (Bandura, 1986b, 1997): (1) the decision to approach versus avoid a particular activity or particular environment, (2) how much effort and persistence to put forth, and (3) the quality of one's thinking and feeling during the performance.

Selection of Activities   Students continually make choices about what activities to pursue and which environments to spend time in. In general, students seek out, approach, and want to spend time in activities that they feel they can cope with or handle. They avoid activities that they fear might overwhelm their coping capacities (Bandura, 1977a, 1989). Simply put, low efficacy breeds high avoidance. If students believe that taking a math class, learning a foreign language, or socializing at the school dance will overwhelm their coping capabilities, they will actively and intentionally avoid such activities. Avoidance guards the self against being in a situation that can potentially overwhelm, stress, confuse, frustrate, or embarrass the self. When students shun an activity out of self-doubt, however, they unwittingly participate in an anti-educative process that arrests or retards their development (Holahan & Holahan, 1987). Not asking questions in class, not enrolling in an art or math class, or not accepting a social invitation can exert profound, detrimental, and long-term effects on development as avoidance decisions progressively restrict one's range of activities and settings (Bandura, 1982, 1986b; Betz & Hackett, 1986; Hackett, 1985).

Effort and Persistence   As students engage in a learning activity, their self-efficacy beliefs influence how much effort they exert and how long they continue to exert that effort (Bandura, 1989). Learning is always fraught with difficulties, obstacles, and setbacks, at least to a degree. Difficulties, such as unfamiliar words to pronounce, and setbacks, such as wrong answers, leave students vulnerable to doubt. Such self-doubt leads students to slacken their efforts, settle prematurely on mediocre solutions, or give up altogether

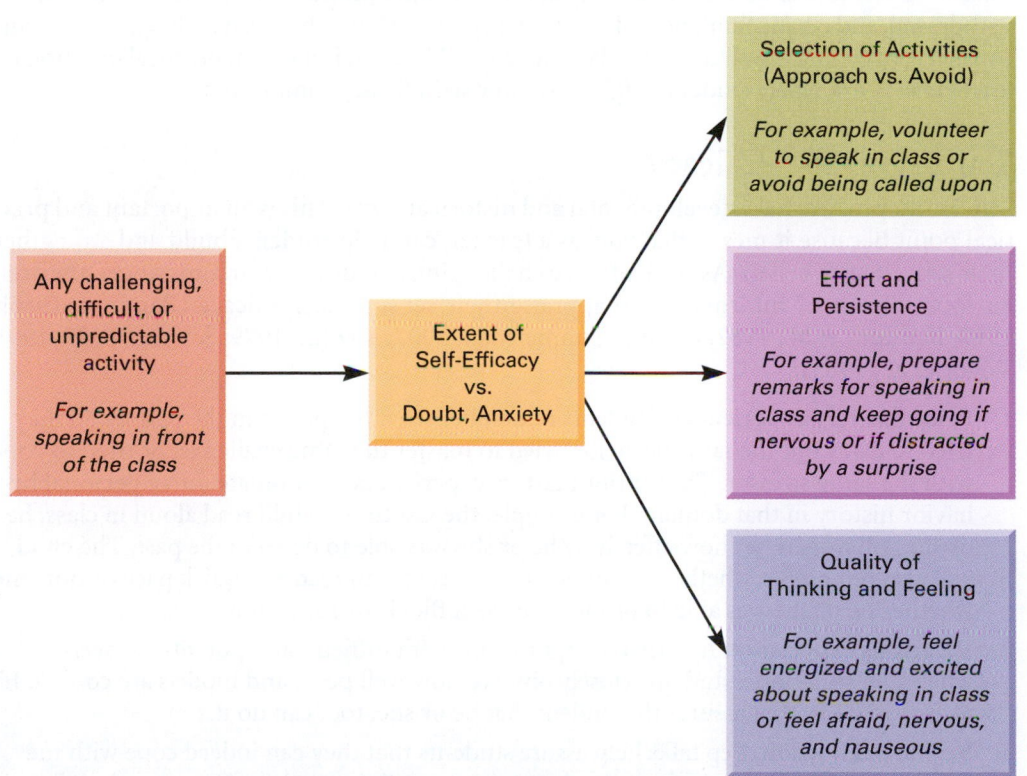

Figure 11.2 Consequences of Strong versus Fragile Self–Efficacy Beliefs

(Bandura & Cervone, 1983; Weinberg, Gould, & Jackson, 1979). In contrast, self-efficacy is a motivational resource that students can fall back on during difficult problems to offset doubt and preserve their effort and persistence. The reason self-efficacy plays such a pivotal role in facilitating effort and persistence is not that it silences self-doubt. Self-doubt is an expected, normal emotional reaction to failure. Instead, self-efficacy leads to *quick recovery* of self-assurance following such setbacks (Bandura, 1986b). It is the resilience of self-efficacy in the face of confusion, failure, and rejection that provides the motivational support students need to maintain their effort and persistence (Bandura, 1989).

Quality of Thinking and Feeling Students who believe strongly in their efficacy remain remarkably clear-headed (clear-thinking) during stressful episodes, whereas students with doubts think erratically (Bandura & Wood, 1989; Wood & Bandura, 1989). A strong sense of efficacy allows the student to remain *task*-focused, asking, "What is the question that I am being asked? What is the feedback telling me? Do I need to alter my strategy?" Self-doubt, on the other hand, distracts decision makers away from the task and toward thinking about deficiencies of the self, declaring, "I'm doing poorly. The audience is going to laugh at me. I'm such a loser." Dwelling on personal deficiencies opens the door to pessimism, anxiety, and depression (Bandura, 1983, 1986b; Bandura, Reese, & Adams, 1982; Bandura et al., 1985). Strong self-efficacy beliefs help keep doubt, anxiety, and distress at bay. Self-efficacy researchers go so far as to say that the root cause of anxiety is low self-efficacy (Bandura, 1983, 1988). If this is true, any sign of anxiety means that self-efficacy is slipping.

Self-Efficacy Promotes Achievement Self-efficacy is important because it promotes decisions to approach rather than to avoid, high effort, resilient persistence, and task-focused thinking and feeling. But, in some sense, these are merely the means to the end that many educators care strongly about—namely, achievement. Self-efficacy is a strong predictor of achievement (Pajares & Graham, 1999; Pietsch, Walker, & Chapman, 2003; Randhawa, Beamer, & Lundberg, 1993; Williams & Williams, 2010), and it is just as strong a predictor of achievement as is ability itself (Hailikari, Nevgi, & Komulainen, 2007; Pajares & Kranzler, 1995; Pajares & Miller, 1994).

Overall, a high and resilient sense of self-efficacy during an academic challenge helps students feel confident and optimistic and leads to a coping profile characterized by approach, effort and persistence, and task-focused thinking. A low and fragile sense of self-efficacy leads students to feel doubt and anxiety and to a coping profile characterized by avoidance, withdrawal, and erratic thinking and emotionality. This relation between high self-efficacy and constructive coping is well established (Bandura, 1997), so an important practical question for teachers is to ask where students' high versus low self-efficacy comes from.

Sources of Self-Efficacy

Self-efficacy beliefs have developmental and historical roots. This is an important and practical point because it means that you, as a teacher, can help students build and strengthen their self-efficacy beliefs. As students face challenging and difficult circumstances, they rely on four sources of information to appraise their sense of self-efficacy (Bandura, 1986b, 1997; Bandura et al., 1982; Chen & Zimmerman, 2007; Kazdin, 1979; Schunk, 1989, 1991; Taylor et al., 1985):

1. **Prior mastery experiences.** Students remember what happened in the past when they tried to carry out the same behavior, tried to master the same challenge, or tried to cope with the same stressor. These prior mastery experiences accumulate into a personal behavior history in that domain. For example, the last time a child read aloud in class, he or she will remember how effectively he or she was able to do so in the past. The child will also remember whether or not he or she was able to read at a quick pace or not, and whether he or she was able to pronounce the difficult words or not.

2. **Vicarious experience.** As they attempt to cope with difficult and potentially overwhelming situations, students closely observe how well peers and models are coping. If peers can do it, that assures the student that he or she, too, can do it.

3. **Verbal persuasion.** Pep talks help assure students that they can indeed cope with the situation at hand. The teacher or a classmate may tell the student, "You can do it."

4. **Physiological states.** Before and during their performance, students monitor what their body is telling them in terms of a racing heart versus a calm and steady one. A calm heart communicates a physiological message of confidence, while a racing heart communicates the opposite message.

The most important sources of efficacy are the first two—prior mastery experiences and vicarious experience (Schunk, 1989). Teachers are well advised to devote most of their attention to these first two sources of self-efficacy information, as discussed in the next section.

Mastery-Modeling Programs

Empowerment involves possessing the knowledge, skills, and beliefs needed to exert control over the situation at hand. Empowered students silence their doubts and fears, they persist in the face of adversity, and they think clearly about what they are doing and how they can do it well.

A formal program to empower students with resilient self-efficacy beliefs is a mastery-modeling program. In such a program, an expert works with a group of novices to show them how to cope effectively with an otherwise fearsome situation. Often, the expert is a teacher or a coach, and the novices are groups of students who are being exposed to lessons and skills that they are not yet familiar with, such as learning about computers, conversing in a second language, or developing talent in music or sport. The nearby Taking It to the Classroom box outlines the seven steps in a mastery-modeling program (based on Ozer & Bandura, 1990).

What Does This Mean to Me? How strong and resilient is your current self-efficacy for teaching? Which sources of self-efficacy have contributed to your current view?

empowerment Perceiving that one possesses the knowledge, skills, and beliefs needed to take control over one's learning.

RIDE Could a mastery-modeling program empower Mr. Larsen's anxious students?

Taking It to the Classroom
How to Implement a Mastery-Modeling Program

1. The teacher identifies the component skills that underlie effective coping in a particular situation. Through a questionnaire or interview, the teacher measures students' efficacy expectation on each component skill.

   Example: In a middle school computer course, the teacher first identifies three to five crucial skills that students need if they are to interact competently with the computer (e.g., use drop-down menus, edit a document, scan and import a photograph). The teacher asks students to write down their confidence versus doubt ratings on each of these component skills.

2. The teacher models competent functioning on each component skill, emphasizing those skill areas that students anticipate will be particularly fearsome.

3. Students emulate each modeled skill. The teacher provides corrective feedback as needed.

4. Students integrate these individual skills into one overall performance. During this simulated performance, the teacher introduces only mild obstacles as students enact the full range of their acquired skills in low-stress circumstances.

   Example: After practice and feedback, the teacher asks students to use their new skills, such as first scanning and importing a photograph, then using a drop-down menu to help write a paragraph about a favorite holiday.

5. Students practice in the context of cooperative learning groups. One student performs the activity while peers watch; provide support; and offer encouragement, tips, and reminders about how the performer might cope better. Students take turns until each has performed at least twice.

   Example: Students take turns revising their paragraphs. As they do so, their peers help by showing each other how to use each skill differently and more efficiently.

6. Students perform individually in a realistic situation, one that features authentic obstacles. The teacher provides further modeling and corrective feedback as needed.

   Example: Students are asked to create a two- to three-page presentation on a favorite topic, complete with photographs or illustrations imported from a scanner.

7. Throughout the mentoring, the teacher models confidence, especially in the face of stress.

   Example: As students learn how to control their anxiety, they will feel less vulnerable to being overwhelmed by the computer and thus begin to engage in (rather than avoid) the once-feared activity.

MINDFUL HABITS OF EFFECTIVE TEACHERS

Constantly monitoring and supporting students' constructive motivational thinking is a key habit of mind of effective teachers.

What Does This Mean to Me?

Could increased self-efficacy allow females to achieve as much or more than males in domains such as math, science, and technology?

calibration An ongoing corrective process in which the person adjusts his or her sense of confidence with a task to reflect most accurately the quality of his or her recent performances at that task.

The mastery-modeling program is a formal procedure designed to utilize all four sources of self-efficacy to advance anxious novices toward becoming confident experts. By performing each skill and receiving corrective feedback (steps 3, 4, and 6), students build efficacy through mastery experience that yields an accomplished personal behavior history. By watching the expert perform (step 2) and watching peers perform (step 5), students build self-efficacy through vicarious experience. By hearing peers' encouragement and tips (step 5), students build self-efficacy through verbal persuasion. By observing and imitating the teacher's ways of managing performance-debilitating arousal (step 7), students build self-efficacy through physiological states.

Technology, Socioeconomic Status, and Self-Efficacy

Electronic technologies are often new, complex, and apt to change. The key variable that determines whether students perceive educational technologies as welcome opportunities or as fearsome threats is self-efficacy. For instance, when exposed to Internet-based instruction, students with high self-efficacy learn and benefit from the experience, whereas those with low self-efficacy feel intimidated and learn little (Debowski, Wood, & Bandura, 2001). Engaging with technology can feel like risk-taking behavior. Thus, before students will approach, manage, and benefit from educational technology, they first need a firm sense of efficacy toward that technology (Krueger & Dickson, 1994).

Socioeconomic differences among students lead to inequitable access to electronic technology. Because technology is often expensive, students from high-socioeconomic families and school districts have greater access to it than do students from low-socioeconomic families and school districts. This access disadvantage means that low-income students are less able to use vast amounts of information found in world-class libraries and available via interactive multimedia instruction. It also threatens to reduce opportunities for low-income students to cultivate technology-based literacy, skills, and interests. Technology-based learning is, therefore, limited by at least two key factors: access to technology and the self-efficacy needed to take advantage of its opportunities. Schools can play an important role in helping all students—low-income students in particular—gain access to technology, and teachers can play an important role in building in students the sense of self-efficacy they need to take advantage of what technology has to offer them.

Self-Efficacy in Students with Learning Disabilities

Among students with learning disabilities, an interesting self-efficacy phenomenon sometimes occurs, called *calibration* (Klassen, 2002). **Calibration** involves, first, observing what one's true capabilities are, given recent performances, and, second, adjusting one's self-efficacy beliefs in accordance with that recent personal behavior history. Students with learning disabilities sometimes drastically overestimate their skills. In doing so, they exaggerate and inflate their self-efficacy beliefs.

High self-efficacy beliefs are motivational assets, but students with learning disabilities are often unable to translate their high confidence into effective coping. On writing assignments, for instance, they tend to focus excessively on lower-order processes, such as spelling and grammar, while ignoring writing's higher-order demands, such as organizing ideas or writing to an audience (Wong, Wong, & Blenkinsop, 1989). Competent functioning requires not only efficacy but also an honest understanding of task demands. (See the nearby Taking it to the Classroom box.)

When facing very high self-efficacy beliefs in learners with special needs, it makes little sense to try to lower their sense of self-efficacy (Pajares, 1996).

(Media Bakery)

In step 5 of a mastery-modeling program, peers provide support, encouragement, tips, and reminders while the teacher provides corrective feedback as needed

Taking It to the Classroom

Do You Know Jack? Reversing Students' Anxieties

Jack is anxious, very anxious. Jack is not always anxious; he is anxious only in your class. He finds the material particularly difficult, and he feels chronically overwhelmed and confused. Class is just too stressful, so Jack looks for any excuse he can to avoid volunteering or participating. What practical approaches can you take to assist Jack?

- Talk to Jack and try to pinpoint the source of his anxiety.
- Model for Jack what competent functioning in your class looks like and have Jack imitate your competent performance.
- Have one of Jack's able peers model what competent functioning looks like and have Jack imitate his classmate's competent performance.
- Before Jack performs, remind him of a time in the past in which he performed a similar behavior competently.
- Break the coursework into steps and make sure Jack can competently carry out step 1 before going to step 2.
- Form cooperative groups and have all group members offer tips, suggestions, and feedback to one another as they work on the lesson. Emphasize skill development over reproducing right answers.
- Offer Jack some coping strategies he can use to regulate his negative thoughts, emotions, and arousal better.

Rather, the unique challenge in this situation is to promote students' appropriate task analysis. From this point of view, teachers can embrace the high efficacy of their students with learning disabilities but focus on students' accurate task analysis, asking: How long do you estimate this writing assignment will take? How many drafts and revisions will be required? What does it take to grab and maintain a reader's attention?

Mastery Beliefs

During most educational endeavors, an outcome is at stake, such as a grade or the respect of one's peers. Before they begin, students forecast how controllable the sought-after outcome is likely to be. For controllable outcomes, students foresee a close relationship between their behavior and the outcome. For example, the student believes if he or she takes good notes and studies for hours, then a positive outcome, such as making an A, will happen. For uncontrollable outcomes, students foresee little or no relationship between their behaviors and outcomes. Good and bad outcomes happen, but not in ways that the student can influence or control. They think, "I'll take the test and see what happens; hopefully, Mr. Jones will give me a break." Students' beliefs as to how much control they have over the outcomes they seek are called *mastery beliefs* (Peterson, Maier, & Seligman, 1993). The opposite of a mastery belief is learned helplessness (discussed later).

Mastery beliefs are different from self-efficacy beliefs. Efficacy beliefs revolve around expectations of one's competence to do what is necessary to accomplish a given task, whereas mastery beliefs revolve around expectations of how controllable versus uncontrollable task outcomes are (Schunk & Zimmerman, 2005). Stated a little differently, as students try to attain some positive outcome, self-efficacy concerns the means to do so (the coping strategies) whereas mastery beliefs concern control over the end itself (the outcome).

As shown in Figure 11.3, efficacy beliefs explain students' motivation to initiate action and to try, whereas mastery beliefs explain students' motivation to gain control over outcomes. To see the distinction more clearly, imagine the thoughts of a student working on a math assignment. Efficacy beliefs concern the question of whether she can generate the needed coping behavior. She wonders, "Can I do this? Will I be able to remember the algebra formulas? If I get stuck, will I be able to get myself unstuck?" Efficacy beliefs help students get started, generate effort, and approach the task. Even students with high self-efficacy, however, can become passive and demoralized when outcomes are beyond their

mastery belief Extent of one's perceived control over a success/failure outcome.

Figure 11.3 Distinction between Efficacy Beliefs and Mastery Beliefs

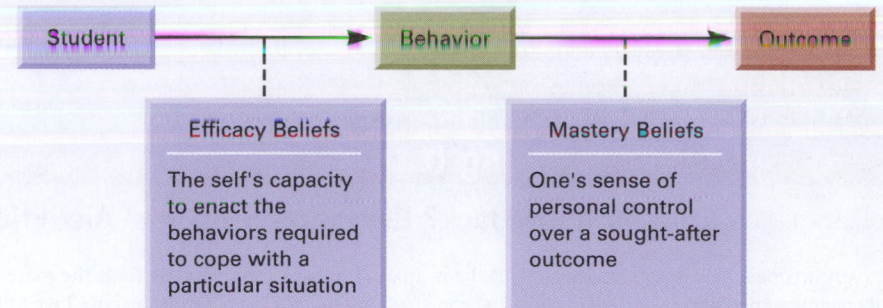

Figure 11.3 Distinction between Efficacy Beliefs and Mastery Beliefs

control. Mastery beliefs concern the question of how much control students have over how the assignment turns out. The student wonders, "What do I need to do to make an A? Will I succeed or fail? Does my grade really just depend on how difficult the assignment is or how leniently the teacher grades?" Mastery beliefs help students cope with outcomes.

Reactions to Failure

Many school-related outcomes center on success versus failure, acceptance versus rejection, or winning versus losing. Students with a strong sense of mastery over success, acceptance, and winning respond to an apparent lack of control by remaining task-focused and determined to achieve mastery over the outcome, despite the difficulties and setbacks (Diener & Dweck, 1978, 1980). At any sign of failure or rejection, mastery-oriented students adjust their behavior and strategies to regain control over the outcome. The opposite of mastery beliefs is helplessness beliefs. Students who feel helpless to prevent failure, rejection, and losing respond to an apparent lack of control by giving up and withdrawing, acting as though the outcome is beyond their control (Dweck, 1975; Dweck & Repucci, 1973). Rather than adjusting their behaviors and strategies, they accept the failure (because they believe that a positive outcome is uncontrollable).

When working with easy problems, most students perform well and stay task-focused and optimistic. When outcomes become harder to control, however, the motivational significance of mastery versus helplessness becomes clear. Mastery-oriented students are *energized* by setbacks or feedback that tells them they are not doing well. Given such feedback, they strive to improve their problem-solving strategies and try even harder than before they received the failure feedback (Dweck, 1999; Mikulincer, 1994). Helpless-oriented students fall apart in the face of setbacks because they first question and then outright deny their ability as they feel their control over the outcome slipping further and further away. In sum, in hard-to-control situations, mastery-oriented students have a hardy sense of self and focus on how to remedy failure (via effort or strategy); helplessness-oriented children have a fragile sense of self and focus on the punishing aspects of failing (Diener & Dweck, 1978).

The reason mastery-oriented and helplessness-oriented performers react so differently to failure emanates from their different interpretations of what failure means (Dweck, 1999). Mastery-oriented students do not see failure as an indictment of the self. Instead, they say things like, "The harder it gets, the harder I need to try" and "I love a challenge." For these students, failure feedback is information. Failure tells them that they need more effort, more resources, more enthusiasm, and a new-and-improved strategy. Helplessness-oriented individuals, however, view failure as an indictment of the self. They see failure as a sign of personal inadequacy. Helplessness-oriented students denigrate their abilities and even their self-worth (Diener & Dweck, 1978). They say things such as, "I'm no good at things like this" and "I guess I'm not very smart." Their problem-solving strategies virtually collapse into simply making wild guesses or picking answers at random. Their emotions quickly turn negative, and they cope via distraction, such as by acting silly (Diener & Dweck, 1978). The self-denigrating, negative mood and immature strategies signal the presence of helplessness, but the telltale sign of helplessness is simply how *quickly* and how *emphatically* the student gives up (Dweck, 1999).

R I D E Might Mr. Larsen's students be pessimistic because of their helpless reactions to failure?

What Does This Mean to Me?
Recall a recent failure. How did you react—with increased effort and an improved strategy, or with decreased effort and demoralized affect?

Learned Helplessness

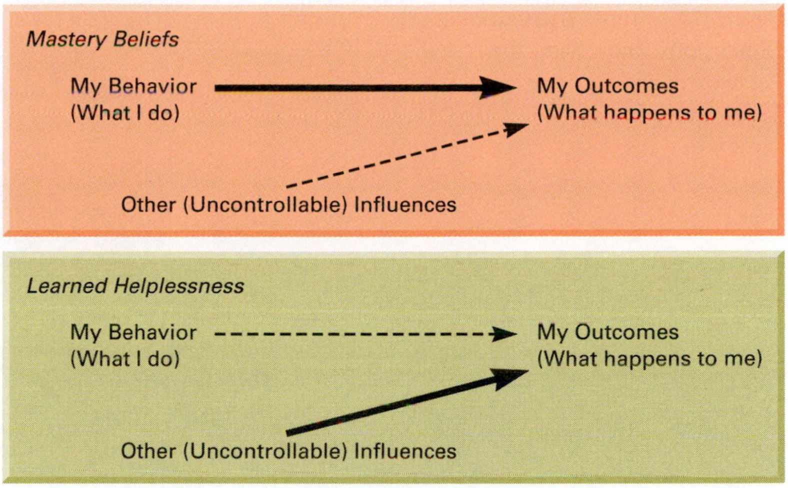

Helplessness is learned (Mikulincer, 1994; Peterson et al., 1993). Through personal experience, students learn that the strength of the relation between their behavior and their outcomes is strong versus weak, as shown in Figure 11.4. Imagine a high school student in a biology class who is trying to decide whether to invest effort in the day's lesson. Imagine also the three earlier lessons in which this student invested a good deal of energy to make a good grade by taking notes, asking questions, reading the textbook, and studying late into the night. These efforts make up *my behavior* in the figure. Over time and through experience, students learn how strong and how predictable the arrow is between *my behavior* and *my outcomes*. If the student comes to believe that a strong relation exist between how hard he works and the grade he receives, he will acquire mastery beliefs. If, however, the student comes to believe that there is little to no relationship between how hard he works and the grade he receives, he will begin to feel helpless, because his behavior does not cause his outcomes.

Learned helplessness is the psychological state that results when a student expects that school-related outcomes are beyond his or her control (Mikulincer, 1994; Peterson et al., 1993; Seligman, 1975). Learned helplessness occurs if experience teaches the student that the arrow from *my behavior* to *my outcomes* is weak to nonexistent, whereas the arrow from *other influences* to *my outcomes* is strong and determinate. When learned helplessness occurs, students turn markedly passive and display the three deficits listed in Table 11.1 (Alloy & Seligman, 1979).

Figure 11.4 Relationship between Behavior and Outcomes for Students with Mastery Beliefs and for Students with Learned Helplessness

learned helplessness The psychological state that results when a student expects that school-related outcomes are beyond his or her personal control.

Attributions

After a bad outcome, such as failing a test, students often try to explain why it turned out that way (Gendolla, 1997; Weiner, 1985). They may reason, "I failed the test because I didn't study" or "I failed because I didn't have enough time to finish." Whatever explanation follows the *because* constitutes an **attribution**, which is an explanation of why a particular outcome occurred (Weiner, 1986).

As shown in Figure 11.5, three key characteristics of attributions exist (Weiner, 1986, 2004). First, attributions can be internal or external. With an internal attribution, students explain the outcome as caused by forces in the self, such as effort or ability; with an external attribution, students explain the outcome as caused by forces in the environment, such as test difficulty or a noisy room. Second, attributions can be stable or unstable. With a stable attribution, students explain the outcome as caused by enduring forces, such as intelligence or personality; with an unstable attribution, students explain the outcome as

attribution An explanation of why an outcome occurred.

TABLE 11.1

Motivational Deficits: Three Telltale Signs of Learned Helplessness

Type of Deficit	Problem Area	Classroom Manifestation
Motivation	Unwilling to try	Students say "Why try?" and "What's the point?"
Learning	Pessimistic learning set	Once students learn that their behavior has little influence over their outcomes, they have a very difficult time relearning which behaviors can and do actually affect their future outcomes.
Emotion	Depressed emotionality	In the face of failure, students show passive, maladaptive, energy-depleting emotions, such as apathy and depression, instead of active, adaptive, energy-mobilizing emotions, such as frustration, anger, and assertiveness.

Figure 11.5 Three Attributional
Dimensions Underlying the
Pessimistic and Optimistic
Explanatory Styles

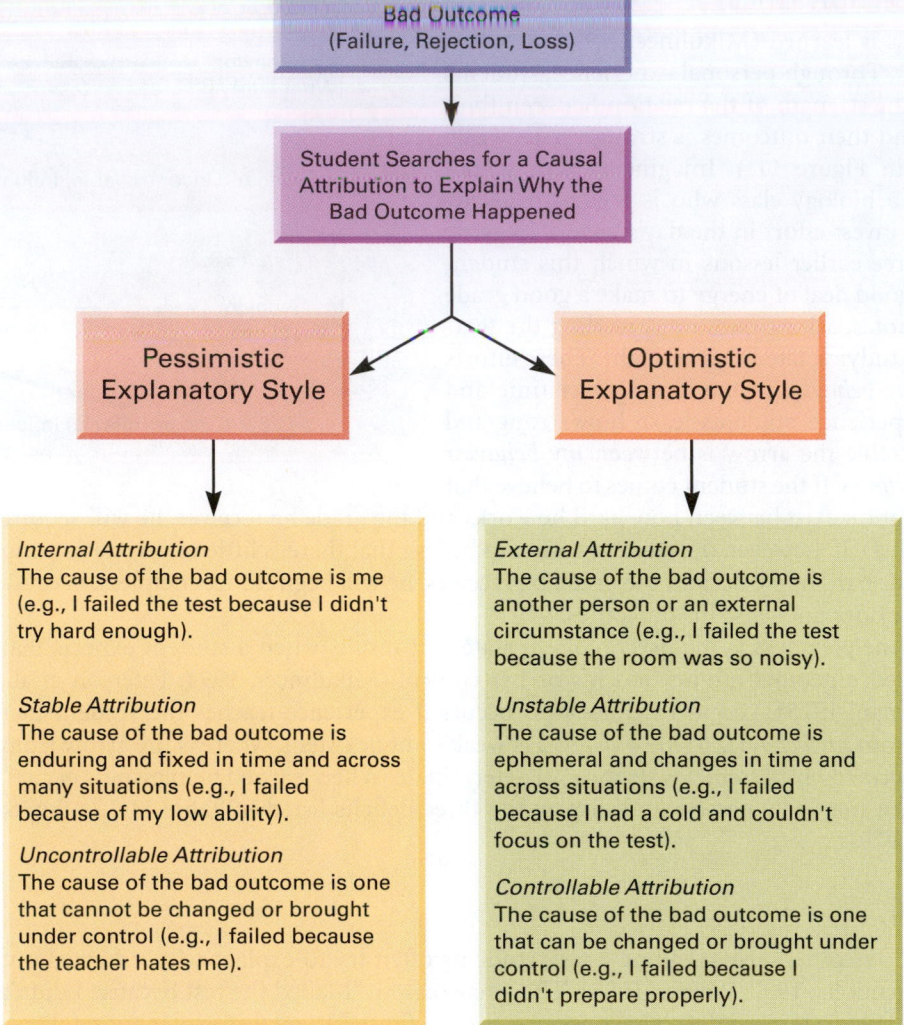

Figure 11.5 Three Attributional Dimensions Underlying the Pessimistic and Optimistic Explanatory Styles

caused by ephemeral forces, such as mood or luck. Third, attributions can be controllable or uncontrollable. With a controllable attribution, students explain the outcome as caused by forces under their direct influence, such as effort or strategy; with an uncontrollable attribution, students explain the outcome as caused by forces beyond their control, such as luck or difficult circumstances.

All attributions can be understood within this three-dimensional causal space: internal versus external (locus); stable versus unstable (stability); and controllable versus uncontrollable (controllability). For instance, the attribution of *intelligence* (e.g., I failed because I'm dumb) is internal, stable, and uncontrollable. The attribution of *luck* (e.g., I failed because I guessed all the wrong answers) is external, unstable, and uncontrollable. The same three-dimensional classification system can be applied to any attribution (effort, strategy, task difficulty, ability, etc.).

The reason it is worth a teacher's effort to see students' attributions in this three-dimensional space is because each dimension leads students to formulate a different expectancy regarding their future success. If failure is attributed to a stable influence (e.g., low ability, unfair teacher), students believe that the same outcome will recur in the future. If a failure is attributed to an unstable influence (e.g., low effort, poor strategy), students believe that a different outcome is likely to occur the next time. These forecasts about the likelihood of future successes and failures are the foundation of mastery versus helplessness beliefs. Helplessness-oriented thinkers fail and make stable, uncontrollable attributions that lead them to expect a future of chronic failure. They say, "Why try?" Mastery-oriented thinkers fail and make unstable, controllable attributions that lead them to generate the motivation they need to marshal the effort, strategy, preparation, and mentoring they need to remedy the failure. In each case, the failure outcome is the same, but what varies from one student to the next is the attribution being made. Importantly, different attributions foreshadow different motivational reactions.

Explanatory Style Bad events happen to everyone, but only sometimes do bad events ripen into helplessness. **Explanatory style** is a relatively enduring characteristic that reflects the way students explain why bad events happen to them (Peterson & Barrett, 1987; Peterson & Seligman, 1984). Students generally have a tendency to prefer certain kinds of attributions, and the pattern they habitually use characterizes their explanatory style as either optimistic or pessimistic.

An **optimistic explanatory style** is the tendency to explain bad events with attributions that are unstable and controllable, such as "I lost the contest because I didn't try hard enough." A **pessimistic explanatory style** is the tendency to explain bad events with attributions that are stable and uncontrollable, such as "I lost the contest because I have low ability." An attribution of low ability is pessimistic because it implies that failure is chronic (stable) and there is little that one can do about it (uncontrollable). It is also pessimistic because of what it implies about the future—namely, that failures in this domain are going to be both stable and uncontrollable. With such thinking, low effort and disengagement make sense, at least from the student's point of view. It is counterproductive, but it does make sense if one really and truly believes that effort and coping are futile.

Explanatory style predicts students' behavior in the face of failure. When students with a pessimistic style face educational failures, such as disappointing grades, they typically respond with a passive, fatalistic coping style that leads to decreased effort and even poorer grades (Peterson & Barrett, 1987). If the cause of one's setback is both stable and uncontrollable, it makes sense to withdraw effort and essentially give up because the poor outcome lies outside the student's control. Students with an optimistic explanatory style, however, see things differently. They see poor outcomes as being under their control and governed by their willful intent. To the extent that they feel that they can change the underlying cause of the poor outcome (i.e., effort is unstable and controllable), it makes sense to act constructively—increase effort, change strategy, prepare in a different way, or gain access to better mentoring and instruction.

Preventing Helplessness, Fostering Mastery

Learned helplessness is both preventable (Altmaier & Happ, 1985; Hirt & Genshaft, 1981; Jones, Nation, & Massad, 1977) and reversible (Miller & Norman, 1981; Orbach & Hadas, 1982). To prevent or reverse helplessness, teachers need to understand its two causes: an unresponsive environment and a pessimistic explanatory style (Peterson et al., 1993). The identification of underlying causes of helplessness suggests two ways to prevent or reverse helplessness: change the environment's responsiveness to the student's behavior or change the student's pessimistic explanatory style.

Changing an Unresponsive Environment into a Responsive One Sometimes students find themselves in an unresponsive classroom or school, perhaps because of discrimination, favoritism, or a bias of some sort. If teachers and schools wish to cultivate mastery beliefs in their students, they need to make sure that the environments they provide are responsive to students' initiatives and are indeed potentially controllable. That said, in most cases, students simply do not know which behaviors actually influence the outcomes they seek (Skinner, Wellborn, & Connell, 1990). Often, students do not really understand what it takes to do well in school, to make good grades, and to have friends. A teacher who carefully explains to students the reliable connections between *what to do* and *what subsequently happens* helps them build a mastery motivational orientation (Altmaier & Happ, 1985; Hirt & Genshaft, 1981; Jones et al., 1977). For instance, teachers can hold a classroom discussion to communicate what it takes to gain proficiency with a musical instrument or in a foreign language.

Too often, students remain unaware of the real keys to success. This lack of awareness of what works leads them to guess at what to do and to use relatively ineffective strategies.

explanatory style A personality-like characteristic that reflects the habitual way that students explain why bad events happen to them.

optimistic explanatory style The habitual tendency to explain bad events with attributions that are unstable and controllable.

pessimistic explanatory style The habitual tendency to explain bad events with attributions that are stable and uncontrollable.

Trying to gain control over valued outcomes by guessing and by using ineffective strategies leads students down a developmental road that too often ends in learned helplessness.

Changing a Pessimistic Explanatory Style into an Optimistic One   Students who embrace optimistic explanatory styles for the bad events that come their way are largely immunized against failure's demoralizing effects (Seligman, 1991). Such an immunization process occurs when teachers give students a small dose of failure that is quickly followed by training and coaching to identify the reliable connections between behaviors and outcomes (Klein & Seligman, 1976). A teacher might show students a difficult problem and, after they struggle in vain for a while, reveal the secrets of how to gain control over it. Students say, "Ah, it was solvable after all. I'll figure out the next problem." The logic of giving students an early dose of failure is that the immunization can foster personal control beliefs that are strong enough to prevent the onset of learned helplessness before it has a chance to occur (where there's a will, there's a way).

It is difficult to immunize a student against the demoralizing forces of failure once he or she already embraces a pessimistic explanatory style. For students with an already entrenched pessimistic style, attributional retraining is necessary. *Attributional retraining* is essentially teaching students a new way to explain the bad events that happen to them. The teacher can, for instance, attempt to expand the range of possible attributions students use to explain their academic failures (Wilson & Linville, 1982). A student might say, "I failed because I can't read as fast as everyone else; I'm just not a good reader." Given such pessimism, the teacher might offer alternative, *and equally valid*, attributions to rival and compete against the pessimistic attribution, such as an ineffective strategy, insufficient effort, or a lack of experience in the domain. In attributional retraining, the teacher does not deny or challenge the student's pessimistic attribution, which might very well be true. Instead, the teacher dilutes the potency of the pessimism by introducing alternative (and valid) explanations. It is important that the teacher's rival attributions be unstable and controllable. To the extent that teachers can help students embrace unstable and controllable attributions for their setbacks, they help students change a pessimistic and maladaptive explanatory style into a more optimistic and adaptive one.

Hope

Like your own reaction to the coded message in the opening vignette, students' motivation to undertake academic challenges can go either way. Under some conditions, students are filled with hope and confidence and act accordingly with efficacy and mastery. Under other conditions, students are filled with pessimism and doubt and act with anxiety and helplessness. The study of hope captures much of the essence of this motivational dilemma.

hope A motivational wish for an outcome that one expects to be fully capable of obtaining.

Hope is a motivational wish for a positive outcome that one expects to be able to attain (Snyder, Rand, & Sigmon, 2002; Snyder et al., 1991). When a student says "I hope to make an A" or "I hope to make the team," he or she expresses both coping confidence (self-efficacy) and optimism about the outcome (mastery beliefs). In other words, hope has two essential ingredients: high self-efficacy and high mastery beliefs.

Hope is important because the more hope students feel, the greater is their persistence (Snyder, Shorey, et al., 2002) and the better is their performance (Curry et al., 1997). Together, strong efficacy and strong mastery beliefs combine to give students the self-confidence and optimism they need to undertake academic and social challenges with healthy, constructive motivation.

Hope is highest when the student sees multiple pathways to a sought-after goal (Snyder et al., 1998). A student who wants to make an A on a homework assignment, for instance, might see the following four paths to an A:

- Personal effort: Invest time and effort to complete the assignment.
- Collaboration: Work on the assignment with a classmate.
- Computer: Use Internet resources for research.
- Help-seeking: Ask a parent for assistance.

The more viable routes the student can perceive to bring the positive outcome to fruition, the more hope that student will feel. Multiple pathways are important because environmental obstacles inevitably occur to close off one or more of these pathways. One's schedule might prevent sufficient time to master the assignment, a collaboration partner might not be at home, one's brother might monopolize the computer, or a helping parent might be called away to work. If the student has only one path to a goal, any obstacle that closes off that pathway kills hope—that is, the situation turns hopeless.

Multiple pathways to a goal sustain mastery motivation. Hope also, however, needs high self-efficacy (Snyder et al., 1998). For the student who wants to make an A on her homework, self-efficacy beliefs are important because she will need to cope effectively with the obstacles and setbacks that inevitably arise ("I'm not going to let this obstacle stop me"). Hope is strong when students know they have access to many routes to success and when they have the coping skills they need to capitalize on those available routes to success. Both mastery and efficacy levels must be reasonably high before a student will experience and maintain hope, because mastery beliefs keep learned helplessness at bay, and self-efficacy beliefs keep doubt and anxiety at bay.

To keep helplessness and anxiety from eroding students' hope, teachers can do two things. First, they can help students generate multiple pathways toward their goals. A student taking a foreign language gains hope when his teacher says that he can try to learn the language through his own efforts but, if he gets stuck, he can also go to the language lab to hear audiotapes or to the classroom computer to use software to practice. Knowing that he can fall back on the language lab and the computer preserves a student's hope for success. Still, the student needs to have a sense of self-efficacy to implement these alternative pathways. So the second thing the teacher can do to build hope is to walk students through a mastery-modeling program, as described earlier, to show them how to cope with the language, the language lab, and the computer software program. Equipped with the one–two punch of high efficacy and high mastery, students have hope.

Goals

A **goal** is whatever a student is striving to accomplish (Locke, 1996). It is the hoped-for end state that explains why one engages in a task. When a student tries to learn 10 new vocabulary words, read a book by Friday, or achieve a 4.0 GPA (grade point average), he or she is engaged in goal-directed behavior. Defined formally, a goal is a future-focused cognitive representation that guides behavior toward an attractive end state (Hulleman et al., 2010).

goal A future-focused cognitive representation that guides behavior toward an attractive end state.

Goals generate motivation by focusing students' attention on the *discrepancy* between their present level of accomplishment and their ideal level of accomplishment. As shown in Figure 11.6, the magnitude of the arrow between the present state and the ideal state represents the size of the discrepancy. A discrepancy between *what is* and *what can be* is a fundamental motivational principle (Locke & Latham, 1990, 2002). It stirs a desire to act, a desire to change what presently is into what ideally could be.

Figure 11.6 offers four ways of saying the same thing: The student envisions a future outcome that is better than is his or her present state. In the present, the student is aware of a C average, poor penmanship, not being a member of the team, or zero pages read in a book. Therefore, when the student asks himself "What can I do to increase my motivation?" the answer from a goal-setting perspective is very practical: Create an ideal state in your mind. That is, form a mental (cognitive) representation of an attractive end state in your mind that

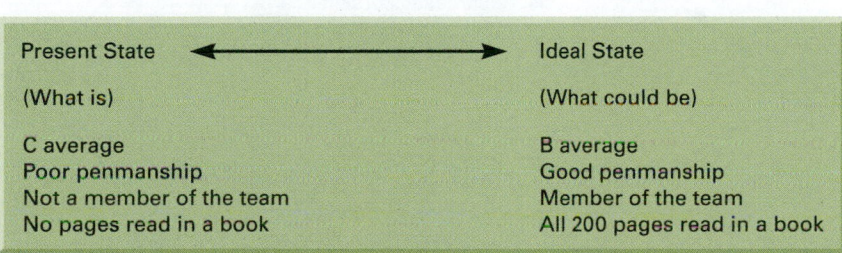

Present State		Ideal State
(What is)		(What could be)
C average		B average
Poor penmanship		Good penmanship
Not a member of the team		Member of the team
No pages read in a book		All 200 pages read in a book

Figure 11.6 Four Illustrations of Discrepancies between What Is (Present State) and What Could Be (Ideal State)

can guide your future action—a B average, good penmanship, being a member of the team, or having all 200 pages in the book read. So, practically speaking, when educators ask "What can I do to motivate my students?" the answer is equally practical: Offer them an attractive ideal state to shoot for.

Generally speaking, students with goals outperform students without goals (Locke, 1996; Locke & Latham, 1990), and the same student performs better with a goal than without a goal. So students who set goals for themselves and students who accept the goals others set for them outperform their no-goal peers.

Difficult, Specific Goals Increase Performance

Goals enhance performance, but the type of goal one sets determines the extent to which that goal translates into performance gains. The two key characteristics of a goal are how difficult and how specific it is (Earley, Wojnaroski, & Prest, 1987; Locke et al., 1981). Goals need to be difficult, because difficult goals energize the performer more than do easy goals. Goals need to be specific, because specific goals direct students' attention toward the desired course of action better than do vague goals. Figure 11.7 provides a summary of how and why difficult, specific goals enhance performance.

Goal Difficulty Goal difficulty refers to how hard a goal is to accomplish. *Do your best* and *pass the test* are easy goals. *Make a 90 on the test* and *improve your score by 10 points* are difficult goals, relatively speaking. As goals increase in difficulty, performance increases in a linear fashion (Locke & Latham, 1990; Mento, Steel, & Karren, 1987; Tubbs, 1986). Essentially, difficult goals enhance performance because they require more effort. Effort arises in proportion to what the goal requires: Having no goal stimulates no effort, an easy goal stimulates little effort, and a difficult goal stimulates great effort (Bandura & Cervone, 1983, 1986; Bassett, 1979; Earley et al., 1987; Locke, 2002; Locke & Latham, 1984, 1990). Difficult goals also increase the persistence of that effort, because effort continues over time and in the face of feedback until the sought-after goal is attained (LaPorte & Nath, 1976; Latham & Locke, 1975).

Goal Specificity Goal specificity refers to how clearly a goal informs students precisely what they are to do. *Do your best* and *study hard* sound like goals, but each is actually an ambiguous statement that does not make clear precisely what the student is to do. Most of the time, translating a vague goal into a specific one involves restating it in numerical terms, such as *make a 90, study for 1 hour, improve 10 points*, or *read pages 1 to 42*. Such specific goals enhance performance because they direct attention and encourage strategic planning. Specific goals direct attention toward the task and away from distractions (Kahneman, 1973; Klein, Whitener, & Ilgen, 1990; Locke et al., 1989; Rothkopf & Billington, 1979). They also encourage strategic thinking, as students wonder, "How am I going to get this done?" (Latham & Baldes, 1975; Terborg, 1976). With specific goals, students become strategic, focused, problem-solving thinkers.

> **How Can I Use This?**
>
> The next time a classmate says "I'll do my best," encourage him or her to set a difficult and specific goal.

Figure 11.7 How and Why Difficult, Specific Goals Enhance Performance

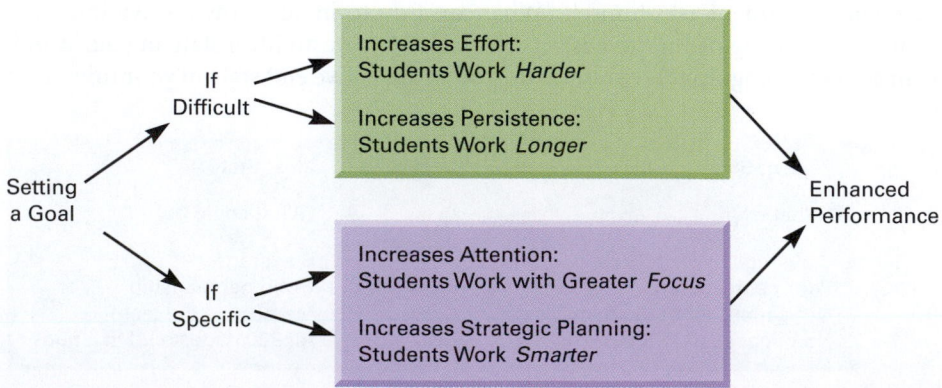

Implementation Intentions

When students fail to realize their goals, part of the problem can be explained by the type of goal. Was it difficult? Was it specific? But there is another critical part of the goal-setting process—namely, forming an implementation intention (Gollwitzer, 1996, 1999; Gollwitzer & Moskowitz, 1996). An **implementation intention** is a plan to carry out one's goal-directed behavior—deciding *in advance* when, where, and for how long goal-directed action will occur.

It is one thing to set a goal, yet another to actually carry it out and accomplish it. All goals take time, but time has a way of opening the door to distractions. An implementation intention links goal-directed behavior to a situational cue, such as a specific time or place, so that goal-directed behavior is carried out automatically, without conscious deliberation or decision making. For example, a student with a goal *to write a five-page paper* might form an implementation intention that "during study hall on Monday, Tuesday, and Wednesday, I'll write and revise my paper." Once the when–where–how long cue has been chosen and an intention to implement one's goal-directed action has been formed, the mere presence of the anticipated situational cue automatically initiates goal-directed action (Monday's study hall rolls around). If no such intention is formed, third-period study hall comes and goes without the goal-directed action ever taking place, because the student might not feel like writing, might have other things to do, or might be distracted by a conversation with a classmate.

Implementation intentions facilitate goal-directed behavior in two ways: getting started and finishing up (Gollwitzer, 1996; Orbell & Sheeran, 2000). Getting started is a problem when students let good opportunities to pursue their goals pass them by, as in "I had all day to read the chapter, but I just never sat down and actually read it." Finishing up is a problem when students suffer interruptions and distractions, as in "I started to read the chapter, but then the phone rang and I never did get back to it." With implementation intentions, students are significantly more likely both to start goal pursuit and to return to and complete it following an interruption.

implementation intention A plan to carry out goal-directed behavior.

Feedback

One additional variable is crucial in making goal setting effective—feedback (Erez, 1977). Goal setting enhances performance only in the presence of timely feedback. **Feedback**, or knowledge of results, allows students to evaluate and to keep track of their progress toward a goal (Bandura & Cervone, 1983; Becker, 1978; Erez, 1977; Strang, Lawrence, & Fowler, 1978; Tubbs, 1986).

Without feedback, goal-directed performance is emotionally unimportant. A student athlete can set a goal of *run a mile in six minutes*. But if she never has access to a stopwatch, she has no way to find out whether she is making progress. Feedback is information. It allows performers to judge their current level of performance: "Am I below goal level? At goal level? Above goal level?"

The combination of goals with feedback produces an emotionally meaningful mixture: Goal attainment breeds satisfaction, whereas goal failure breeds dissatisfaction (Bandura, 1991; Matsui, Okada, & Inoshita, 1983). Positive feedback—the news that one is performing at or above goal level—causes satisfaction and positive emotion. Negative feedback—the news that one is performing below goal level—causes dissatisfaction and negative emotion. Either way, effort increases because negative feedback gets students to work harder, and positive feedback gets students to set higher goals (Bandura & Cervone, 1983, 1986).

feedback Knowledge of results.

A Caution before Assigning a Goal

Generally speaking, interest in a task predicts how well a student will perform on that task (Renninger, 2000). Interest predicts performance because it focuses attention, encourages deep information processing, and heightens persistence (Hidi, 2000). Notice how these positive benefits of interests are very similar to the positive benefits produced by goal setting (see Figure 11.7). So, for highly interested students, teacher-set goals are largely superfluous, as students' own interests have already led them to set goals of their own and highly interested students do not perform any better when teachers assign them goals to pursue (Van Yperen, 2003). Goal setting most benefits less interested students, as assigning goals to students who lack interest in a task does tend to increase performance (Locke & Latham, 1990). So the caution to heed before assigning students a goal to pursue is that goal-setting programs work best (and maybe only) when tasks are relatively boring to start with, or at least when the tasks cannot generate motivation of their own. Stated differently, goal-setting programs work best when they are applied to those relatively uninteresting tasks in the curriculum.

Goal-Setting Programs

As a teacher, you will often set goals for your students. In general, the point of a goal-setting program is to raise students' performances—to generate higher test scores, to improve attendance, or to have students complete their homework more often. At one level, goal setting is simple. One person sets a goal for another. At another level, however, the overall goal-setting process is more complicated. When a teacher assigns a goal, several conditions need to be met before the assigned goal can be expected to improve students' performances. The nearby Taking It to the Classroom box outlines the steps involved in a successful goal-setting program.

The first four steps in a goal-setting program involve setting the goal. All goal-setting programs begin with the question: What do you want your students to accomplish? Once this fundamental question has been answered, the next step is to ensure that the goal is both difficult and specific, given students' abilities, experiences, and access to resources. In addition, the teacher announces when performance will be assessed. The last four steps in the goal-setting process help students accept the goal and actually pursue it. The goal needs to be transformed from a teacher-assigned goal into a student-internalized goal, one that has a measure of personal commitment associated with it (Erez & Kanfer, 1983; Erez & Zidon, 1984). To enhance goal acceptance, teachers typically need to negotiate with students and gain their participation in the process (Latham, Erez, & Locke, 1988; Latham & Saari, 1979). The next step is to discuss possible plans, strategies, and implementation intentions to advance students from goal setting to goal pursuing, from goal setting to goal striving. The teacher also needs to provide a

Taking It to the Classroom

Steps in a Goal-Setting Program

What a Teacher Might Say to Implement the Step

Part 1: Goal Setting

1. Specify the objective to be accomplished. — This week in biology, we are going to learn all the parts of a cell.

2. Define goal difficulty. — Try to learn all eight parts of the cell—not some parts, but all eight.

3. Define goal specificity. — Be able to locate, spell, and pronounce each part.

4. Specify the time span until performance will be assessed. — Next Monday, we will have a test to see how many parts you know.

Part 2: Goal Striving

5. Check on goal acceptance. — Does this sound like a reasonable goal for the week? Any suggestions?

6. Discuss goal-attainment strategies. — There are several ways you can learn about the parts of a cell. The textbook provides good pictures, you can make your own drawings, or you can work with a partner and quiz each other.

7. Create implementation intentions. — You have two days to learn the parts of a cell. By Thursday's class, know four parts; by Friday's class, know all eight.

8. Provide performance feedback. — At 1:30, I'll hand out a practice quiz that you can use to test your progress.

steady stream of feedback students can use to assess whether they are performing at, above, or below goal level.

Possible Selves

Possible selves represent students' long-term goals or strivings for what they would like to become (Markus & Nurius, 1986; Markus & Ruvolo, 1989). Some possible selves might include, for instance, honor roll student, high school graduate, successful artist, counselor, or state champion in a particular sport. Two of the most common possible selves embraced by elementary and middle school students include *good student* and *popular student* (Anderman, Anderman, & Griesinger, 1999).

An example of how possible selves originate and how they generate daily goals to pursue appears in Figure 11.8. Possible selves are almost always social in origin, as students observe successful others (Markus & Nurius, 1986). If the role model is attractive, such as the visiting police officer in Figure 11.8, the student might consider emulating the role model. The individual sees the current self as a *present self* and the role model as a possible future *ideal self* (recall Figure 11.6). To figure out how to become the desired future self, the student notices and learns about the attributes, characteristics, and abilities that he or she needs but does not yet possess. The student wonders, "If I am going to become my hoped-for possible self, what do I need to do? What education do I need? What activities should I pursue? How should I behave?" (Cantor et al., 1986; Markus & Nurius, 1986; Markus & Wurf, 1987). The answers to these questions generate goals (I will graduate high school; I will get in shape). Because of the processes identified in Figure 11.7 (effort, persistence, etc.), students accomplish their short-term goals and gradually make progress toward the long-term goal of possessing the attributes, characteristics, and abilities of the hoped-for (possible) self (Cross & Markus, 1994; Oyserman & Markus, 1990).

possible self A student's long-term goal representing what he or she would like to become in the future.

> **What Does This Mean to Me?**
> Does your possible self of *teacher* contribute to your interest, motivation, and daily goals in this course?

Figure 11.8 Illustration of How Possible Selves Stimulate Goal–Directed Behavior

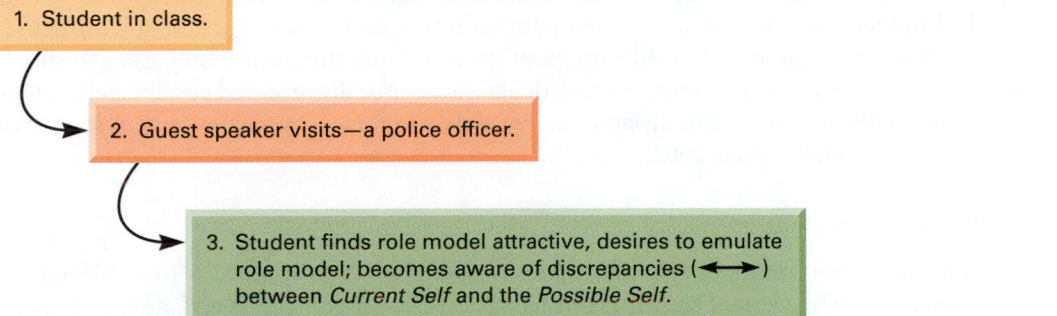

(Media Bakery)

Possible selves are almost always social in origin. This adolescent might consider becoming an artist by observing this practicing artist.

Possible selves play an important motivational role in the classroom, especially for adolescents (Oyserman & Markus, 1990). Without a possible self in a particular subject area, the student lacks an important cognitive basis for wanting to acquire knowledge and skill in that subject (Cross & Markus, 1994). A student who can envision a possible self in that subject, however, sees the events, knowledge, and skills featured as personally important (Cross & Markus, 1994; Markus, Cross, & Wurf, 1990). Thus, for a student enrolled in a foreign-language class who wants to realize possible selves, such as world traveler, French speaker, or foreign-language teacher, the desire to take notes, read books, watch foreign films, and participate in class comes easily. The same can be said for a would-be writer taking an English class, a would-be banker taking a math class, or a future teacher taking an educational psychology class. Consistent with this logic, students with classroom-relevant possible selves have higher grade point averages than do students without such possible selves (Anderman et al., 1999).

Possible Selves for Students in Poverty Students who live in poverty often lack role models and mentors who embody the importance of school and what it can do for them in their lives. As a consequence, these students often lack a clear understanding of how current school participation can help their future selves. One group of researchers developed and offered middle school students who lived in poverty a school-to-jobs intervention program to help develop clear and detailed possible selves. During the after-school intervention, early adolescents worked to identify attractive job-related possible selves, completed problem-solving activities in small groups, and interacted with guest speakers from the community. After the nine-week intervention, students were able to articulate academically oriented possible selves, they identified skills they needed and wanted to develop, and their school engagement improved (Oyserman, Terry, & Bybee, 2002).

Achievement Goals

achievement goal What the student is trying to accomplish when facing a standard of excellence.

standard of excellence Any challenge to the student's sense of competence that ends with a success/failure interpretation.

Certain goals are **achievement goals** because they apply specifically to achievement settings. In an achievement setting, performance is measured against a standard of excellence (Heckhausen, 1967). A **standard of excellence** is any challenge to the student's sense of competence that ends with a success/failure, right/wrong, or win/lose outcome, such as a score on a test, an answer to a question, or the outcome of an election or contest. As shown in Table 11.2, when facing a standard of excellence, students typically adopt one of two achievement goals: mastery goals or performance goals (Dweck, 1986; Elliot, 2005; Nicholls, 1979, 1984; Pintrich, 2000).

TABLE 11.2

Aims of Students with Mastery versus Performance Goals

Mastery (or Learning) Goal	Performance Goal
• Improve competence	• Prove competence
• Make progress	• Display high ability
• Acquire and develop skills	• Outperform others
• Gain understanding	• Succeed with little apparent effort
• Overcome difficulties through effortful learning	• Avoid activities in which one expects to do poorly

Mastery goals (which are also referred to as learning goals) focus attention on developing competence. Doing well means developing competence by improving, learning, and making progress. For a student with a mastery goal, the standard of excellence in an achievement situation is the development of competence, as in the effort to develop an ability, master a new skill, show improvement, accomplish something challenging, and understand the learning materials (Meece, Anderman, & Anderman, 2006). Students adopt mastery goals because they seek personal development and growth.

Performance goals focus attention on demonstrating or proving that one has high ability on the task. Doing well means demonstrating competence by doing better than others. For a student with a performance goal, the standard of excellence in an achievement situation is the perception of competence (by others), as in the effort to demonstrate high ability relative to others, to outperform others, and to exceed normative performance standards. Overall, with mastery goals, students strive to increase, develop, or improve their competence; with performance goals, they strive to demonstrate or prove their ability to an audience of others (Ames, 1992; Ames & Archer, 1988; Dweck, 1986, 1990; Meece et al., 2006; Nicholls, 1984; Spence & Helmreich, 1983).

The fundamental determinant of which type of achievement goal students embrace is their understanding of what constitutes competence (Elliot & McGregor, 2001; Nichols, 1984). Students define competence in two different ways as they ask themselves, "Am I good at math?" One way to assess competence is to judge the extent to which one has reached a certain maximum capacity in terms of knowledge or skills in that domain. A student is competent with a calculator, for instance, if he knows how to use all the available functions. Or a teacher is competent to the extent that she ably carries out the full range of classroom tasks (e.g., motivating, explaining, assessing). A second way to assess competence is to judge one's performance relative to the performances of peers. In this case, a student is competent with a calculator to the extent that he performs better on the calculator than do his peers. Or a teacher is competent to the extent that she performs better than do the other teachers in her school.

Students with different achievement goals want to know different things. Students with mastery goals want feedback that they can use to learn and improve, whereas students with performance goals want feedback that they can use to judge their ability and sense of superiority (Butler, 2000). Figure 11.9 shows a sample of one teacher's feedback on a high school student's writing assignment. A student with a mastery goal will likely focus on the teacher's

mastery goal The intention to develop competence by improving, learning, and making progress.

performance goal The intention to demonstrate competence by doing better than others.

What Does This Mean to Me?
What does competence in teaching mean to you—learning and improving or being better than your peers?

Grade: C

Teacher's Written Comments: The paper has a number of strengths. Your topic sentences in each paragraph were quite good—brief, clear, and foreshadowing the content of the paragraph to come. Your spelling was also excellent—no spelling errors.

The paper also has a number of weaknesses. Here are a couple of key points that you might want to use in thinking about how you might develop your writing skills in the future. In almost every sentence, you used the passive voice. By rewriting these sentences into the active voice, your writing will become livelier. Also, did you notice that your paper consisted of only two long paragraphs? I found five separate ideas in your paper, so a series of five shorter paragraphs might work better. And many of your sentences are very long—one is 36 words and another is 45 words. Long sentences contain multiple ideas and stress the reader's comprehension. One way to improve your writing would be to break down these long sentences into shorter ones.

Figure 11.9 A High School Teacher's Feedback on a Student's Essay

Figure 11.10 Positive
Educational Outcomes
Associated with the
Adoption of Mastery Goals

Source: Based on Ames, C., & Archer,
J. (1988). Achievement goals in
the classroom: Students' learning
strategies and motivation processes.
Journal of Educational Psychology, 80,
260–267. Copyright © 1988 by the
American Psychological Association.
Adapted with permission.

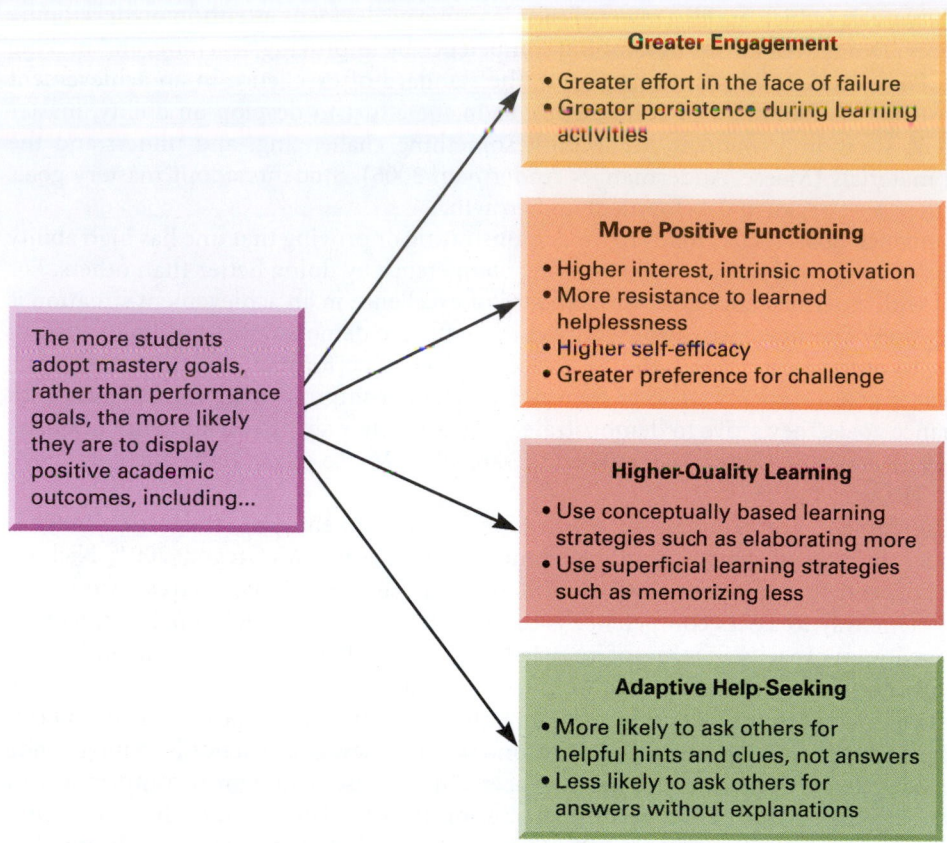

comments and double his effort to improve and develop his writing skills, thinking, "If I can improve on my use of the active voice, develop my paragraphs, and use shorter sentences, then I can improve my writing." A student with a performance goal, however, will likely focus only on the letter grade. He will be less interested in the written comments and may even submit later papers or a revision of this paper with the same weaknesses. What the student with a performance goal wants is a means to judge his ability relative to others—namely, the letter grade.

The distinction between mastery and performance goals is important because the adoption of a mastery goal is associated with constructive and productive ways of thinking and behaving, whereas the adoption of a performance goal is associated with relatively negative and unproductive ways of thinking and behaving (Anderman & Maehr, 1994; Dweck, 1999; Dweck & Leggett, 1988; Harackiewicz & Elliot, 1993; Midgley, Kaplan, & Middleton, 2001; Spence & Helmreich, 1983; Utman, 1997; Van Yperen, 2003). Students who adopt mastery goals—saying to themselves, "In this course, I am going to try to learn as much as I can"—cultivate a self-regulated type of learning in which they seek information in order to acquire, develop, and refine their knowledge and skill (Butler, 2000). As summarized in Figure 11.10, students who adopt mastery goals display more positive educational outcomes than do students who adopt performance goals, including greater engagement, more positive functioning, higher-quality learning, and more adaptive help-seeking (Ames, 1992; Ames & Archer, 1988; Dweck & Leggett, 1988; Elliot & Dweck, 1988; Elliot & McGregor, 2001; Linnenbrink, 2005; Meece, Blumenfeld, & Hoyle, 1988; Nolen, 1988; Stipek & Kowalski, 1989; Wolters, 2004).

Promoting Mastery Goals

Intervention studies to promote students' mastery goals show that students are more likely to adopt and to keep mastery goals when teachers enact the instructional strategies summarized in Table 11.3 (Maehr & Midgley, 1996; Meece & Miller, 1999). Following the entries listed in Table 11.3, classrooms that promote mastery goals have teachers who define success as improvement, value effort, communicate that satisfaction comes from

TABLE 11.3

Dimensions of Classroom Climate That Influence Students' Adoption of Mastery versus Performance Achievement Goals

Climate Dimension	For Teachers Who Promote Mastery Goals	For Teachers Who Promote Performance Goals
Success defined as	Improvement, progress	High grades
Value placed on	Effort, learning	Normatively high ability
Reasons for satisfaction	Working hard	Doing better than others
Teacher orientation	How students are learning	How students are performing
View of errors/mistakes	Part of learning	Source of anxiety
Focus of attention	Process of learning	One's performance relative to others' performances
Reasons for effort	Learn something new	Better performance than others
Evaluation criteria	Progress (grade on effort)	Normative (grade on ability)

Source: Based on Ames, C., & Archer, J. (1988). Achievement goals in the classroom: Students' learning strategies and motivation processes. *Journal of Educational Psychology, 80,* 260–267. Copyright 1988 by the American Psychological Association. Adapted with permission.

working hard, focus on how students learn, view errors as a natural part of learning, focus on the process of learning, explain the need for high effort while learning something new, and assign grades based on progress or improvement. Additional suggestions on how to promote mastery goals appear in the nearby Taking It to the Classroom box. Such teacher-led interventions have been shown to be especially helpful for low-ability students and for students with learning disabilities (Fuchs et al., 1997).

Teachers influence the type of achievement goals students adopt (Ames & Archer, 1988; Anderman & Midgley, 1997; Urdan, 2004; Wolters, 2004). For instance, in one study with elementary school children, students were asked to agree or disagree with questions assessing the extent to which their teachers promoted mastery goals ("The teacher pays attention to whether I am improving") or performance goals ("I work hard to get the highest grade"). The researchers then assessed students' learning strategies, willingness to be challenged, and attitude toward the class. Students with teachers who promoted mastery goals used more sophisticated learning strategies, were attracted to the challenge rather than threatened by it, and enjoyed the class more (Ames & Archer, 1988).

Higher teacher efficacy further helps in teachers' efforts to promote mastery goals. This is so because the effort to promote mastery goals represents relatively advanced or sophisticated instruction (Meece, 1991; Wolters & Daugherty, 2007), such as promoting meaningful learning by facilitating active participation and collaborative learning, making material interesting and important to students, offering complex and challenging tasks and problems, helping students make sense of and conceptually understand the lesson material, and using alternative forms of assessment (e.g., portfolios instead of multiple-choice exams).

> **How Can I Use This?**
> Use these two checks to determine which type of achievement goals are promoted in the course you are taking: evaluation (improvement versus "the curve") and recognition (private praise for improvement versus public praise for beating others).

Students Have Achievement Goals of Their Own Students' achievement goals often correspond to what is most emphasized in the classroom—mastery versus performance (Anderman & Midgley, 1997; Urdan, 2004). Despite the teacher's efforts to establish a mastery-oriented learning climate, however, students nevertheless harbor goals of their own (Kaplan & Maehr, 2007). Even when teachers enact the classroom strategies outlined in Table 11.3, some students will strive only for high grades and to beat others. Students generally bring performance goals of their own into the classroom when they have the following characteristics: competitiveness, pressure to excel, and parents who communicate conditional approval ("Do well and make us proud!") (Church, Elliot, & Gable, 2001; Elliot & McGregor, 2001).

One reason students adopt performance goals is that, often, embracing a performance goal predicts high achievement (Barron & Harackiewicz, 2001; Elliot & Church, 1997; Elliot,

Taking It to the Classroom

Teacher Discourse to Promote Mastery Goals

Introduce lessons as learning opportunities

- Introduce activities as learning opportunities ("This is a chance to develop a new skill"), rather than as ability assessments ("This is a test of your ability").

Focus on understanding

- Instead of asking students to produce correct answers, ask them to explain how they arrived at their answers. Encourage students to ask questions when they don't understand.

Provide worked-out, step-by-step solutions

- Provide correctly worked-out solutions to difficult problems so that students can focus on learning how to solve the problem, rather than on whether their answer is right or their ability is low.

Focus on improvement

- Give students comments and feedback about their progress, rather than judgments of their ability, such as who scored the highest or performed the best.

Support collaborative learning

- Encourage students to think of peers as helpful resources for learning, rather than as sources of competition and comparison.

McGregor, & Gable, 1999; Elliot & Murayama, 2008; Harackiewicz et al., 2000, 2002). The earlier discussion on goal-setting theory helps explain why performance goals facilitate achievement outcomes (recall Figure 11.7). The problem is that pursuing performance (rather than mastery) goals tends to yield some troubling side effects, such as a reliance on superficial learning strategies (Ames, 1992; Meece, Blumenfeld, & Hoyle, 1988), a poor long-term retention of knowledge (Midgley, Kaplan, & Middleton, 2001), use of self-handicapping strategies (Urdan, Midgley, & Anderman, 1998), and even cheating (Anderman, Griesinger, & Westerfield, 1998).

Two Types of Performance Goals Performance goals come in two varieties: approach and avoidance (Elliot, 1999; Elliot & Thrash, 2002). A performance-approach goal involves *approaching success*; it involves striving to show how smart one is and to attain positive judgments from others. A performance-avoidance goal involves *avoiding failure*; it involves striving to not look stupid and to avoid negative or unfavorable judgments from others. To clarify this distinction, Figure 11.11 lists sample items from a questionnaire to assess all three achievement goals. The distinction between types of performance goals is important because

Figure 11.11 Questionnaire Items to Assess the Three Types of Achievement Goals

Source: Middleton, M. J., & Midgley, C. (1997). Avoiding the demonstration of lack of ability: An underexplained aspect of goal theory. *Journal of Educational Psychology, 89,* 710–718. Copyright 1997, American Psychological Association. Adapted with permission.

Mastery Goal
____ An important reason I do my math work is because I like to learn new things.
____ An important reason I do my math work is because I want to get better at it.

Performance-Approach Goal
____ I want to do better than other students in my math class.
____ I would feel successful in math if I did better than most of the other students in the class.

Performance-Avoidance Goal
____ It's very important to me that I don't look stupid in my math class.
____ An important reason I do my math work is so I won't embarrass myself.

students who adopt performance-avoidance goals show the worst educational outcomes (Elliot, 1999; Elliot & Harackiewicz, 1996; Middleton & Midgley, 1997).

Multiple Achievement Goals Adopting a mastery goal does not necessarily mean that the student fails to adopt a performance goal; a student can hold multiple achievement goals (Ames & Archer, 1988; Harackiewicz, Barron, & Elliot, 1998; Harackiewicz et al., 2000; Meece & Holt, 1993; Pintrich, 2000). Hence, students are as likely to have *both* a mastery and a performance goal as they are to have *either* a mastery or a performance goal (Harackiewicz et al., 1997; Midgley, Anderman, & Hicks, 1995). One reason students often harbor both goals is that teachers (and parents) communicate mixed messages, telling students both to learn and to perform up to externally set standards (Turner et al., 2003).

In some ways, students benefit from adopting multiple goals (Harackiewicz et al., 2000; Pintrich, 2000). Mastery goals promote students' interest, positive affect, and deep understanding of what they are learning, and performance-approach goals promote making good grades and performing well when evaluated (Elliot & Murayama, 2008; Harackiewicz et al., 1997, 2000; Turner et al., 2003). No one, however, benefits from adopting performance-avoidance goals (Elliot, 1999), as performance-avoidance goals are associated with low self-efficacy, anxiety, self-handicapping, and poor grades (Urdan et al., 2002).

The dual benefit of harboring both mastery and performance-approach goals (high interest, high performance) is limited by two factors: age and ability. Only high school and college students benefit from multiple goals; elementary and middle school students benefit more from mastery goals alone (Bouffard, Vezeau, & Bordelau, 1998). For high-ability students—proficient writers, able artists, skilled athletes—multiple goals promote both interest and performance. But when students have less ability—that is, they do not yet have adequate capacities to meet the performance demands of the activity—mastery goals alone are more adaptive (Dweck & Leggett, 1988).

Grade-Level Effects on Achievement Goals

Generally speaking, the higher the grade level, the more likely it is that students will embrace performance rather than mastery goals. One reason for the developmental trend toward performance goals is that the culture of schooling becomes more performance-oriented (Eccles, 1993; Eccles & Midgley, 1989; Eccles, Midgley, & Adler, 1984). With each passing grade, the school culture shifts away from learning for its own sake and toward the products of learning—grades, evaluations, standardized test scores, scholarships, and the like. What this trend means is that primary school classrooms are more likely to promote mastery goals, whereas secondary school classrooms are more likely to promote performance goals (Lepper & Henderlong, 2000). Hence, high school teachers have a particularly pressing need to create classroom climates that value and promote mastery goals.

Self-Regulation

All the striving and planning that take place in the goal-setting process occur over time, and they need to be monitored and evaluated—that is, regulated. A self-regulated student is one who does the following:

- Sets goals
- Uses effective strategies
- Monitors effectiveness
- Makes adjustments as needed

Self-regulation is the deliberate planning and monitoring of one's cognitive and emotional processes during academic tasks, such as writing an essay, finishing homework, or completing a reading assignment in a timely and comprehensive manner (Boekaerts & Corno, 2005; Pintrich & De Groot, 1990; Zimmerman, 1986, 1989, 2002). As a student engages in an academic task, she sets a goal and makes plans and strategies to accomplish that goal. She also monitors feedback to assess how things are going.

self-regulation The deliberate planning, monitoring, and evaluating of one's academic work.

All students engage in some such planning and monitoring, but some students engage in this self-steering process better than others (Winne, 1997). Some students are more likely to activate and sustain goal-oriented thinking and behaviors than are other students, who are more likely to "wing it," or just see what happens. The more students regulate their own learning, the better they do in school. In one study, researchers predicted high school students' academic achievement with 93% accuracy simply on the basis of how extensively students regulated their learning (Zimmerman & Martinez-Pons, 1988).

Self-Regulatory Processes: Forethought through Reflection

As shown in Figure 11.12, self-regulation is an ongoing cyclical process involving forethought, performance, and reflection (Zimmerman, 2000). The quality of students' recurring forethought, performance, and reflection determines the quality of their self-regulation. **Forethought** encompasses task analysis (How difficult? How complex? How interesting?), goal setting, strategic planning, and the formation of implementation intentions. Forethought captures much of the essence of the goal-setting process. Following such forethought, performance begins as the student engages in the task and receives feedback about the quality of his performance. With feedback in hand, **reflection** follows in the form of self-monitoring and self-evaluating. Such reflection allows the student to construct more advanced forethought, and the self-regulation cycle repeats. As the cyclical phases of self-regulation repeat themselves, students learn and strategically improve how they manage their own learning and goal striving.

Self-monitoring is a self-observational process in which students keep track of the quality of their ongoing performances (Zimmerman, 2000). The student finds a way to assess performance, such as keeping score, taking a practice test, or making video or audio recordings of his performances. Such careful, consistent, and objective self-monitoring makes self-evaluation possible.

Self-evaluation is a judgmental process in which the student compares his or her current performance with the hoped-for goal state (Zimmerman, 2000). A biology student with the goal of making a B on Friday's test, for instance, monitors his study session by testing himself. If he can name 80% of the muscles in the human body, he realizes that he is making progress toward his goal. Together, feedback and self-evaluation open the door to emotional reactions, because students feel good when they make progress and distress when they fail to do so (Carver & Scheier, 1990). Hence, students need to regulate not only their thoughts but also their emotions.

Promoting Self-Regulation

Effective self-regulation involves the capacity to carry out the full goal-setting process *on one's own* (Schunk & Zimmerman, 1997; Zimmerman, 1998). When it is fully realized, students learn to regulate not only the goals they seek but also all of the elements that go into effective goal setting and optimization of performance—regulation of cognition (or thinking), regulation of motivation and emotion, regulation of behavior, and regulation of context or

forethought What one thinks prior to engaging in a task and prior to receiving feedback about the quality of one's performance on that task.

reflection Thinking critically about one's task performance after receiving feedback and while constructing more advanced forethought for a future performance.

self-monitoring A self-observational process in which students keep track of the quality of their ongoing performances.

self-evaluation A self-judgmental process in which students compare their current performance with a hoped-for goal state.

Figure 11.12 Cyclical Phases of Self-Regulation

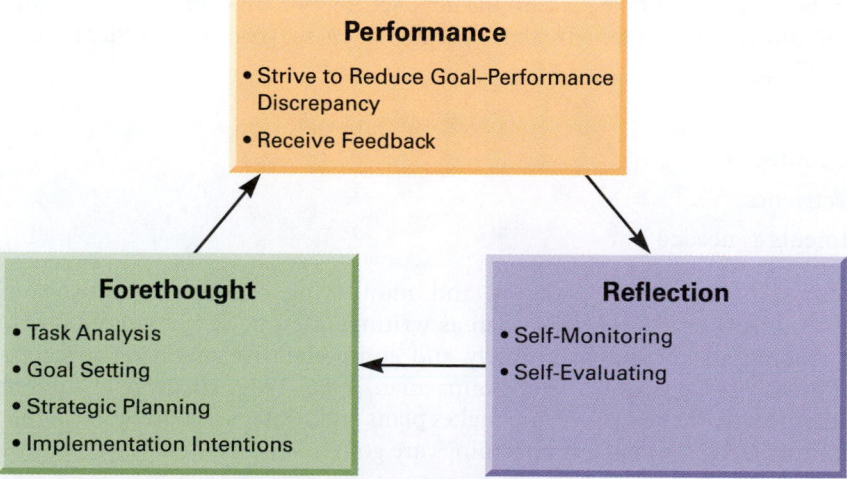

Performance
• Strive to Reduce Goal–Performance Discrepancy
• Receive Feedback

Forethought
• Task Analysis
• Goal Setting
• Strategic Planning
• Implementation Intentions

Reflection
• Self-Monitoring
• Self-Evaluating

Lack of Self-Regulation Skills	Social Learning Process	Acquisition of Self-Regulation Skills
Unable to regulate one's goals and behaviors in the new domain	1. Observation of expert model 2. Imitation, social guidance, feedback 3. Internalization of goals and standards 4. Self-regulatory process, including self-monitoring, self-evaluating	Now able to regulate one's own goals and behaviors in the domain

Figure 11.13 Summary of the Social Learning Process to Acquire Self–Regulatory Skills

environment (Pintrich, 2000). Effective self-regulation develops gradually through a social learning process, as illustrated in Figure 11.13.

On academic tasks that require unfamiliar goals and behaviors, students tend to display novice self-regulatory thinking (e.g., vague goals, no implementation intentions). In such a context, the student lacks self-regulatory skill and instead is dependent on others (teachers) for guidance. The social learning process begins at an observational level in which the novice observes the verbalizations, strategic planning, self-monitoring, problem solving, and self-evaluation of the expert. It continues with imitation, guidance, corrective feedback, and eventually with the novice's internalization of the expert's way of self-regulation. The novice begins to gain proficiency when he or she internalizes the expert's self-regulatory processes, such as forethought, monitoring, and evaluation.

The effort to become a competent, self-regulated writer illustrates how self-regulation skill is acquired (Zimmerman & Risemberg, 1997). To become proficient, would-be writers need answers to questions such as: If I'm going to become a good writer, what sort of goals do I set, when and where do I write, how do I obtain feedback, and what is good writing, anyway? Through observation of a proficient model, the novice receives preliminary answers to these questions and begins to act on them. Novice writers emulate the expert's style, standards, and even the physical environment in which writing takes place. With internalization, students are increasingly able to ask their mentors more sophisticated questions. They become increasingly able to generate their own planning and goal setting. The once-novice writer begins to set personal goals and to engage in self-monitoring and self-evaluation. Eventually, would-be writers reach the point that they no longer need the expert model; they can set their own goals, and they can monitor, evaluate, and carry out their own work.

Progression through the four phases of self-regulation—observation, imitation, self-control, and self-regulation—is only the beginning of expertise. Mastering complex skills such as reading, writing, and music is a time-consuming process that requires not only intensive mentoring but also countless hours of practice (Ericsson, Krampe, & Tesch-Romer, 1993; Ericsson & Charness, 1994). Deliberate practice is crucial. That said, research on self-regulation shows that students are more likely to develop expertise when they have the benefit of a mentor who models how to plan, monitor, and evaluate the overall goal-setting process.

Coregulation

When students are novices, teachers need to regulate learning activities on their behalf. That is, teachers often need to set the goal, make the plan, communicate a standard of proficiency, articulate the value of the activity, assess the learning, and so on. With observation and imitation, the quality of students' participation changes and becomes more active. In response, the teacher adapts by allowing the student greater autonomy. Eventually, learning becomes a co-regulated activity.

(Media Bakery)

Through observation, imitation, and internalization of a proficient model, the once-novice writer begins to set personal goals and engage in self-monitoring and self-evaluating.

coregulation A collaborative process in which the teacher and student jointly plan, monitor, and evaluate the academic work of the student.

During **coregulation,** the quality of the relationship between teacher and student is paramount. Students are more likely to become competent, self-regulated learners when they observe and emulate supportive teachers who provide choices; offer flexible decision making; create opportunities for the student to control task challenge and task difficulty; communicate rich verbal descriptions that answer the student's *what, how, why,* and *when* questions; share the responsibility for learning; make time for open-ended activities; and evaluate in nonthreatening and mastery-oriented ways (Perry, 1998; Perry, Nordby, & VandeKamp, 2003; Perry et al., 2002). When students have supportive models to observe, they quickly emulate and internalize the teacher's regulation strategies. Harsh, nonsupportive models take away students' willingness to emulate and internalize what they see. Without supportive models, students lack the critical support they need during the coregulation phase if they are to become sophisticated, self-regulated learners.

Self-Regulation for Students in Different Grades and for Learners with Special Needs

Effective self-regulation is learned. In learning how to regulate their own behavior, young or inexperienced students and learners with special needs typically need their teachers to provide them with needed "how-to" instruction and external support.

Grade Level Schools provide students in the early grades with substantial external support. In the early elementary school grades, teachers provide highly structured learning environments, including giving specific directions about what students should do. Little is expected of these students outside the classroom in terms of self-directed learning experiences, such as homework or independent study. By the late elementary school grades, teachers begin to assign homework and expect students to show personal responsibility in completing these assignments on their own. By the high school years, teachers expect students to engage in self-initiated studying and to assume full responsibility for completing assignments on their own.

Unfortunately, classroom observations show that teachers rarely teach students self-regulatory skills, such as goal setting or self-monitoring (Zimmerman, Bonner, & Kovach, 1996; Zimmerman & Risemberg, 1997). If students are going to develop the self-regulatory skills that are expected of them in each advancing grade, teachers need to integrate the teaching of self-regulatory skill into their regular classroom lessons (Martinez-Pons, 2002). For a sampling of what skills teachers might model, Table 11.4 provides a range of possible self-regulatory strategies (Zimmerman & Martinez-Pons, 1986, 1988).

TABLE 11.4

Ten Self-Regulatory Processes Used by Self-Regulated Learners

Self-Regulatory Process	Example
Goal setting	Make a list of things to accomplish while studying.
Task strategies	Create a mnemonic to remember information.
Imagery	Imagine the consequences of failing to study.
Self-instruction	Rehearse steps in solving a math problem.
Time management	Schedule daily studying and homework time.
Self-monitoring	Keep records of completed assignments.
Self-evaluation	Check work before handing it in to teacher.
Self-consequences	Make watching TV or telephoning contingent on homework completion.
Environmental structuring	Study in a secluded place.
Help-seeking	Use a study partner.

Source: Adapted from Zimmerman, B. J. (1998). Academic studying and the development of personal skill: A self-regulatory perspective. *Educational Psychologist, 33,* 73–86. Copyright © 1998 by the Taylor and Francis Group.

Students with Special Needs Self-regulatory skills predict students' level of academic achievement, and nowhere is this truer than when students face a personal obstacle, such as a learning disability. When an assignment is complex, students with learning disabilities often need added external support. Special education teachers often create self-regulation-boosting prompts that learners with special needs can use to plan, monitor, and evaluate their work. For example, the teacher might provide the student with a set of cue cards in which one card says *Use exciting, interesting words: Use synonyms for words occurring more than once* (De La Paz, 2001). Notice that such a prompt offers the student a goal (use exciting words), encourages monitoring one's writing (have you used the same word more than once?), and provides an evaluation of what good and bad writing look like. Without these sorts of prompts, students with attention-deficit/hyperactivity disorder (ADHD) fail to plan, monitor, or evaluate their writing. As a result, they tend to write low-quality essays. With the externally provided prompt in hand, however, the same students can generate plans for their writing, monitor what they write, and evaluate how well they are doing. They also write higher-quality essays.

Effective self-regulation requires planning, anticipating, allocating effort strategically (not impulsively), self-control, self-monitoring, and self-evaluation. Students with ADHD have difficulty with *all* of these skills (Barkley, 1997, 2004). Students with ADHD can therefore be expected to struggle with their academic self-regulation. The most pressing self-regulatory failure teachers can expect from students with ADHD, however, is a lack of planning. Thus, students with ADHD have a particularly difficult time with the first crucial phase of effective self-regulation—namely, forethought.

Students with learning disabilities have difficulty with the second phase of effective self-regulation—namely, reflection, as through self-monitoring and self-evaluating their work (Pintrich & Blazevski, 2004). For this reason, students with learning disabilities benefit greatly from both external prompts and a teacher's coregulation, two processes that are especially helpful during the performance phase of a self-regulated learning activity. With these supports—external prompts and supportive models to emulate—students with learning disabilities are able to better self-regulate themselves (Swanson, 2000).

> **What Does This Mean to Me?**
> Do you have difficulty completing assignments (papers, readings)? Are you regulated by the self or by deadlines and tests?

Self-Concept

Self-concepts are students' mental representations (mental models) of themselves. Accordingly, the **self-concept** is the set of beliefs that a student uses to understand his or her sense of self. More specifically, self-concept is the set of beliefs a student holds about his or her abilities in school subjects and academic domains. For instance, a student with a constructive self-concept will say, "I'm good at most school subjects," whereas a student with a counterproductive self-concept will say, "I'm hopeless in biology classes" (Brunner et al., 2010).

Developmentally, a child advances from a global, undifferentiated self-concept in preschool to a differentiated, complex, and multidimensional self-concept by high school (Harter, 1990; Marsh & Ayotte, 2003; Marsh & O'Neill, 1984; Montemayor & Eisen, 1977). (*Differentiation* refers to the number of different domains one incorporates into the self-concept.)

First graders show their first signs of differentiation by noticing distinctions in their competence in domains such as math versus English (Marsh, Smith, & Barnes, 1983). Throughout the elementary school grades, children's self-concepts continue to differentiate into at least three distinct areas—social, academic, and physical (Harter, 1983; Marsh & Shavelson, 1985)—and sometimes into six areas—relationship with parents, relationship with peers, math, reading, physical abilities, and physical appearance (Marsh, 1990; Marsh et al., 1983). By high school graduation day, the 12 differentiated domains listed in Table 11.5 are typical: math, verbal, general academics, problem solving, physical abilities, appearance, same-sex peers, opposite-sex peers, parents, religion, honesty, and emotionality.

The global, one-dimensional self-concept is not a very useful educational construct (Marsh & Craven, 1997; Yeung et al., 2000). Instead, educators emphasize the multidimensional,

self-concept Set of beliefs the individual uses to mentally represent or understand his or her sense of self.

TABLE 11.6

Twelve Domains of the Differentiated Self-Concept

Mathematics	I find many mathematical problems interesting and challenging.
Verbal	I am an avid reader.
General academic	I like most academic subjects.
Problem solving	I can often see better ways of doing routine tasks.
Physical abilities	I enjoy sports and physical activities.
Appearance	I have a good body build.
Same-sex peers	I am popular with other members of the same sex.
Opposite-sex peers	I make friends easily with members of the opposite sex.
Parents	My parents understand me.
Religion	Continuous spiritual/religious growth is important to me.
Honesty	I am a very honest person.
Emotionality	I tend to be high-strung, tense, and restless.

Source: Items from the 136-item Self-Description Questionnaire (SDQ-III) from Marsh, H. W., & O'Neill, R. (1984). Self-description questionnaire III: The construct validity of multidimensional self-concept ratings by late adolescents. *Journal of Educational Measurement, 21,* 153–174.

hierarchical self-concept (Byrne, 1996; Marsh, 1990; Shavelson & Marsh, 1986). This is so because how good students feel about themselves in subject areas such as math, science, and economics bears little or no relationship to how good they feel about themselves in subjects such as English, history, and foreign languages (Marsh, Byrne, & Shavelson, 1988). That is, self-concepts are specific to school subjects. For example, educators find little, if any, correlation between a student's math self-concept and his or her verbal self-concept (Marsh & Shavelson, 1985; Marsh et al., 1988). Findings such as these show that by adolescence, students no longer endorse a global self-view but instead understand the domain specificity within the self-concept.

Enhancing the Self-Concept

One goal of education is to promote in students a healthy sense of self—that is, a healthy self-concept (Australian Education Council, 1989; Marsh & Hau, 2003). Educators seek to boost students' self-concept for two reasons. First, they believe that enhancing the self-concept is a desirable educational goal in its own right. Second, they believe that an enhanced self-concept will spill over and enhance other valued educational goals, such as academic achievement (Craven, Marsh, & Burnett, 2003).

Enhancing the Self-Concept: Why? Educators seek to enhance students' self-concept because they generally believe that doing so will enhance students' academic achievement. When researchers tested whether changes in self-concept predicted students' subsequent grades, they found no such causal effect (Byrne, 1984). Researchers do, however, consistently find that the domain-specific areas of self-concept (math, English, etc.) do correlate with students' achievement in that domain. For instance, the more students achieved in mathematics, the more positive became their math self-concept, whereas their verbal self-concept remained unchanged (Marsh, Byrne, & Yeung, 1999; Marsh & Yeung, 1997a). Domain-specific self-concept beliefs (e.g., "I'm good in math") correlate positively not only with academic achievement in that domain (e.g., math grades, scores on standardized tests) but with other positive educational outcomes as well, including taking coursework and putting forth high effort in that domain (Byrne, 1996; Marsh & Yeung, 1997b). So, enhancing the (domain-specific) self-concept does not causally increase academic achievement, though increasing academic achievement does causally enhance the (domain-specific) self-concept.

Enhancing the Self-Concept: How? Designing educational interventions to bolster students' self-concept has been both a popular and a frustrating enterprise (Hattie, 1992). When teachers have tried to bolster students' global self-concept by administering a steady stream of praise or positive self-talk, these efforts have been unsuccessful (Burnett, 1999, 2003). Instead, change in students' self-concepts closely *follows* actual achievement gains in specific domains. For example, gains in English self-concept occur mostly in the wake of an achievement experience, such as making a good grade or having a poem accepted by a school publication. One popular intervention program designed to capitalize on this achievement-driven process is the Outward Bound program.

Outward Bound programs are designed to build a positive self-view in adolescents and young adults. The program exists in two versions. The Standard Course is a 26-day residential program comprising physically and mentally demanding outdoor activities for young adults. This program does not have academic goals, but it is mentioned here because the Standard Course is a well-known program whose goal is to provide the person the sort of achievements that bolster the self-concept.

The Bridging Course is a 36-day residential experience comprising academic activities for 13- to 16-year-old underachieving boys. This program has academic goals. It seeks to enhance academic aspects of the self-concept, and the course does generally boost adolescents' achievement in reading and math (Marsh & Richards, 1988). As they improve their reading and mathematics skills, adolescents report enhanced academic self-views after the program is over (Marsh & Richards, 1988). Successful intervention programs such as these show that (1) the self-concept is a multidimensional, not a global, phenomenon; (2) intensive intervention programs can boost students' domain-specific skills; (3) as students gain skills and achievements, they change their self-concept accordingly; and (4) these self-concept enhancements endure over time.

Social Comparisons How well one performs relative to one's peers is a potent source of information for the self-concept. The act of comparing one's personal characteristics, performances, and abilities to the characteristics, performances, and abilities of others is called **social comparison** (Ruble, 1983; Ruble & Frey, 1991; Wood, 1989). Without other students around, it can be difficult for a student to know whether he or she is smart, attractive, athletic, emotional, or friendly. It is handy to have other students around to compare how smart or attractive one is with how smart or attractive everyone else appears to be. Social comparison provides especially useful information for those abilities about which students are unsure: Am I artistic? Am I a good speaker? Am I a fast reader?

In most cases, social comparison is an intentional strategy. That is, students seek information about themselves for a reason (Swann, 1999). These reasons include wanting to (1) develop an accurate self-view, (2) enhance the self-view, and (3) learn what excellence is. When students want to develop an accurate self-view, they compare their characteristics, attributes, and abilities to their peers who share other qualities with them, such as age and gender (Zanna, Goethals, & Hill, 1975). When students want to enhance their self-view (e.g., after failure, rejection), they compare themselves to those they suspect will be less smart, less talented, and the like. Such downward social comparisons allow the student to appear in a favorable light. When students want to learn what excellence is, they compare themselves to others who they suspect possess greater ability than they do (e.g., experts, gifted students, students from higher grades; Gibbon, Benbow, & Gerrard, 1994).

In other cases, social comparisons just sort of happen to the student because of who is available to compare oneself to (Marsh et al., 2008). That is, depending on the school context, students might find themselves surrounded by other students who display very high or very low academic abilities. Comparing oneself to other students in the same school has been termed the *big fish in a little pond* effect (Marsh, 1991, 2007; Marsh & Hau, 2003). When students compare their own academic abilities with those of their not-as-able classmates, they tend to formulate a higher academic self-concept of themselves, which is a positive big fish in a little pond effect. On the other hand, when students compare their own academic abilities with those of their highly able classmates, they may formulate a lower academic self-concept for themselves, which is a negative big fish in a little pond effect.

social comparison The act of comparing one's personal characteristics, performances, and abilities to the characteristics, performances, and abilities of others.

What Does This Mean to Me?
The last time you failed at something, did you engage in downward social comparisons? If so, did it help protect your self-view?

Self-Esteem

self-esteem The evaluation of oneself as a person across multiple domains of functioning.

Self-esteem is the evaluation of oneself as a person. Whereas self-concept is a description of oneself, self-esteem is an evaluation of oneself (Rosenberg, 1979). Self-esteem is partly evaluated on the emotional basis of how others treat the self (acceptance versus rejection), but self-esteem is mostly evaluated on the basis of one's competence and achievement in different domains. Accordingly, self-esteem exists as the sum of evaluated domains of the self-concept. Self-esteem is, therefore, high in proportion to the extent to which students rate themselves positively across multiple domains of functioning: Am I good in math? Am I good in sports and athletics? Am I popular with members of the opposite sex? Do I make friends easily?

Students clearly vary in their levels of self-esteem, as some students think very highly of themselves while others do not. It seems logical, therefore, to want to intervene and boost the self-esteem of students who lack it. But motivation researchers do not recommend *boosting self-esteem* as a constructive intervention strategy (Baumeister et al., 2003). In the nearby Uncommon Sense box, we explain why self-esteem is *not* a crucial motivation and why boosting it is not a recommended motivational strategy. The basic problem with such a strategy is that self-esteem is a *consequence* of life going well (i.e., "I'm doing well; therefore I have high self-esteem"), not a *cause* of life going well (i.e., "If I would think more highly of myself, then I could make all sorts of wonderful things happen."). Instead of high self-esteem, this and the previous chapter have discussed the motivational constructs that underlie academic engagement and so cause students' lives to go well—namely, intrinsic motivation, psychological need satisfaction, flow, self-endorsed values, interest, curiosity, positive affect, achievement strivings, self-efficacy, mastery beliefs, controllable attributions, an optimistic explanatory style, hope, goals, implementation intentions, possible selves, achievement goals, and self-regulation.

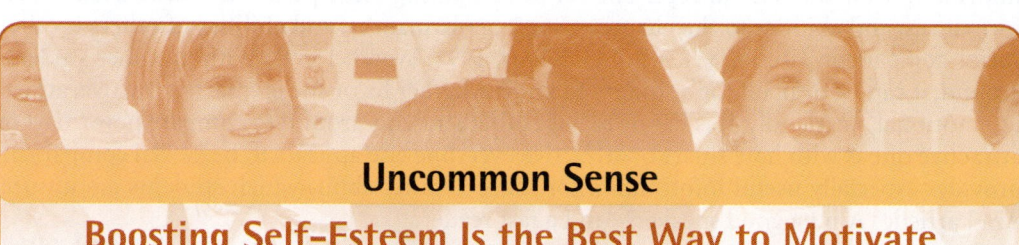

Uncommon Sense

Boosting Self-Esteem Is the Best Way to Motivate Students—Or Is It?

Boosting self-esteem is a popular motivational strategy, one that attempts to motivate students by helping them see the value in themselves. Praise them. Compliment them. Give them some affirmation that they are loved and are important—a sticker, a trophy, or a catchy slogan. Once students feel good about who they are, all sorts of good things will start to happen.

The self-esteem movement was essentially launched in 1986, when the state of California decided to boost the self-esteem of all state residents. In attempting to do so, it intended to reduce rates of school failure, unwanted pregnancy, welfare dependence, crime, and drug addiction. Advocates argued that "self-esteem has profound consequences for every aspect of our existence" (Branden, 1984, p. 5) and that virtually all psychological problems could be traced to low self-esteem. Following this lead, several self-esteem-boosting programs were initiated in schools. Empirical research showed that these programs failed to make students' lives better (Baumeister et al., 2003).

Students with high self-esteem function well in school, whereas students with low self-esteem generally do not (Bowles, 1999; Davies & Bremer, 1999). The reason these two variables are correlated, however, is because doing well in school boosts self-esteem (Byrne, 1996; Harter, 1993; Helmke & van Aken, 1995; Shaalvik & Hagtvet, 1990). Achievement causes self-esteem, but the reverse is not necessarily true. Increases in self-esteem do not cause corresponding increases in school performance. In fact, the typical finding is that an intervention to boost self-esteem is likely to decrease students' subsequent performances (Forsyth & Kerr, 1999)! This is so because self-esteem intervention programs interfere with the natural effort-to-achievement relationship by encouraging students to feel good about themselves regardless of their effort, improvement, or achievement.

Self-Esteem in Students with Learning Disabilities If self-esteem reflects one's evaluation of one's abilities in various domains, then students with learning disabilities might be at risk of low self-esteem. By definition, students with learning disabilities have difficulty learning. Because competencies in mathematics, reading, spelling, and writing represent the building blocks of learning, this is unfortunate for the construction of a healthy self-esteem in students with learning disabilities. Research confirms that students with learning disabilities score substantially lower on measures of self-esteem than do equally intelligent students who do not have learning disabilities (Chapman & Boersma, 1991). This shows both how competence and achievement evaluations of oneself in a domain shape self-esteem and how students with learning disabilities are at risk for low self-esteem precisely because their disability tends to interfere with their competence and achievement displays.

REFLECTION FOR ACTION

The Event

In preparing today's lesson, Mr. Larsen cannot forget yesterday. He introduced a difficult concept and observed that some students showed enthusiasm, optimism, resilience, goal striving, and regulated their own learning. Others, however, did not. These students turned apathetic, pessimistic, helpless, and quit working at the first sign of failure.

Reflection RIDE

Mr. Larsen wants to understand why some students are so negative—so apathetic, pessimistic, helpless, and goalless. During today's lesson, he wants to see these students display resilient and constructive motivation. What might he do? How can Mr. Larsen motivate his students to try hard?

What Theoretical/Conceptual Information Might Assist in Interpreting and Remedying This Situation? Consider the following:

Self-Efficacy

Where do confidence and eagerness to try come from? Can he turn students' anxiety into efficacy? Should he take precious class time to implement a mastery-modeling program?

Mastery Motivation

Perhaps his students act helpless because they do not know how to gain control over the difficult problems being presented to them. Perhaps they don't know what to do. What if they were presented with a series of difficult problems and discussed effective versus ineffective problem-solving strategies?

Goal Setting

Perhaps his students are trying to "do their best" but are not actually doing their best. To help his students work harder, longer, smarter, and with more focus, Mr. Larsen could implement a goal-setting program.

Information Gathering RIDE

What is the problem? How is Mr. Larsen to recognize motivational resources, such as high self-efficacy, mastery beliefs, and self-set goals? How is he to recognize motivational problems, such as low self-efficacy, helplessness, and a lack of goals?

- If confident, how do students show their confidence?
- If anxious, how do students express low self-efficacy?
- What do students with strong mastery beliefs do? How do they explain failure?
- How do students with a helplessness orientation behave? How do they explain failure?
- Do Mr. Larsen's students have any goals? Are those goals difficult? Specific?
- Do his students have any plans and implementation intentions to get their work done?

Decision Making RIDE

To decide on the best course of action, Mr. Larsen will need at least three kinds of information. First, do students *want* to try? If not, the problem is likely one of low self-efficacy. Students who want to try approach the task, display effort and persistence, and think clearly rather than defensively. Second, are students optimistic and mastery-oriented? If not, the problem is likely one of learned helplessness. Students with a mastery orientation try harder in the face of difficulties and make unstable and controllable attributions when things go wrong. Third, do his students have goals? If not, the problem is likely their lack of goals. Students with difficult and specific goals try hard, persist over time, think strategically, and devote their attention to the task at hand.

Evaluation RIDE

If Mr. Larsen's information gathering leaves him with the impression that his students approach the lesson with doubt and anxiety, he will need to implement a mastery-modeling program to boost his students' self-efficacy. If his information gathering leaves him with the impression that his students are helpless and pessimistic, he will need to point out to students how behaviors such as taking notes and forming cooperative learning groups can help them gain control over difficult assignments. He might also need to challenge their pessimistic explanatory styles. If his information gathering suggests that his students lack difficult and specific goals, he will need to introduce a formal goal-setting program into the structure of the lesson.

Further Practice: Your Turn

Here is a second event for you to reflect on. In doing so, generate the sequence used above in terms of reflection, information gathering, decision making, and evaluation.

The Event

Looking at the 28 faces in front of her, Mrs. Applesmith can feel the tension in the air. Her students are working on a week-long writing project, and she has noticed that what they care about is making a good grade, doing better than others, and not looking stupid. Few students are actually trying to learn, improve, and develop new skills. Mrs. Applesmith wants to transform this evaluative, competitive, and performance-driven classroom climate into a mastery-oriented, learning-based culture.

What can Mrs. Applesmith do to create a classroom climate that cultivates mastery goals rather than performance goals?

SUMMARY

- **How does quality of thinking explain quality of motivation?**

The theme of the chapter is that the quality of one's thinking predicts and explains the quality of one's motivation to learn. So, instructional efforts to support students' self-efficacy beliefs, mastery beliefs, optimistic attributions, hope, mastery goals, self-regulation, and healthy self-concept are simultaneous instructional efforts to support and build students' constructive and high-quality motivation.

- **When students are hesitant, what can a teacher do to promote their confidence?**

Self-efficacy reflects students' judgments of how well they can cope with a situation, given the skills they possess and the circumstances they face. Self-efficacy beliefs predict students' classroom functioning, especially their approach versus avoidance, extent of effort and persistence, and quality of their thinking and feeling. Self-efficacy beliefs arise from four sources: prior mastery experiences, vicarious experience, verbal persuasion, and physiological state. To promote students' self-efficacy beliefs, teachers can implement a seven-step mastery-modeling program.

- **How can teachers foster in students a constructive, mastery-oriented reaction to failure?**

Mastery beliefs reflect how much personal control students believe they have over the outcomes they seek. When students believe they have little control over their successes and failures, they experience learned helplessness. When they face outcomes that are difficult to control, mastery-oriented students and students with an optimistic explanatory style become energized and increase their effort, whereas helplessness-oriented students and students with a pessimistic explanatory style give up trying and self-denigrate their abilities. Hope is a motivational wish for an outcome that one expects to be fully capable of obtaining. For hope to be high, both self-efficacy and mastery beliefs must be reasonably high.

- **How can teachers implement a goal-setting program?**

A goal is whatever the student is trying to accomplish. It is a hoped-for end state that one strives to attain. Students with goals outperform students without goals. For a goal to enhance performance, it needs to be both difficult and specific because difficult goals energize students and specific goals direct their attention toward the desired course of action. In addition, students with goals need implementation intentions and feedback. To help students perform well, teachers can implement an eight-step goal-setting program.

- **What can a teacher do to transform an anxiety-ridden classroom climate into a culture of eager learners?**

Achievement goals are goals that students set in achievement settings. Students with mastery goals seek to develop their competence: Doing well means improving, learning, and making progress. Students with performance goals seek to prove their competence: Doing well means doing better than others. Mastery goals generally lead students toward more productive ways of thinking and behaving. To promote mastery goals, teachers can establish classroom climates that define success as improvement, value effort for its own sake, communicate that satisfaction comes from working hard, view errors as a natural part of learning, and assign grades based on progress or improvement.

- **How can teachers help students become self-regulated learners?**

Self-regulation involves planning, monitoring, and evaluating all aspects of the goal-setting process. With forethought, self-regulated learners analyze the task, create goals, make plans, develop strategies to overcome obstacles, and formulate implementation intentions. With reflection, self-regulated learners monitor feedback; evaluate their progress; reflect on how things are going; and continuously revise their goals, plans, and strategies. Teachers can help students advance from impulsive novices to self-regulating experts through social learning and coregulation processes.

● **How can teachers support motivation in diverse learners and students with special needs?**
Recognizing the high demands academic lessons place on students with learning disabilities, teachers can help students make accurate task analyses and hence appropriately calibrate their self-efficacy beliefs with the demanding lessons they face. When students lack possible selves, teachers and school-related programs can help bridge the motivational gap that separates their current schoolwork from their future selves. In terms of self-regulation, students in younger grades and students with special needs become more likely to show effective self-regulation when teachers provide external prompts and supportive models to emulate.

● **How does self-concept develop throughout the school-age years?**
The self-concept is the set of beliefs that students use to understand their sense of self. In the school, academic self-concept concerns students' beliefs about their abilities in school subjects. Developmentally, the self-concept differentiates throughout the school-age years from a childhood-based global self-view into an adolescent sense of self that is differentiated, complex, and multidimensional. It further develops in response to achievement gains in specific domains and to social comparisons of one's qualities compared to those of one's peers. Whereas self-concept is a description of oneself, self-esteem is an evaluation of oneself. The strategy of trying to boost students' self-esteem so as to motivate and engage students is not recommended. Instead, the chapter outlines how to promote students' constructive and productive thinking.

Key Terms

achievement goal, p. 392
attribution, p. 383
calibration, p. 380
coregulation, p. 400
empowerment, p. 379
explanatory style, p. 385
feedback, p. 389
forethought, p. 398
goal, p. 387

hope, p.386
implementation intention, p. 389
learned helplessness, p. 383
mastery belief, p. 381
mastery goal, p. 393
optimistic explanatory style, p. 385
performance goal, p. 393
pessimistic explanatory style, p. 385
possible self, p. 391

reflection, p. 398
self-concept, p. 401
self-efficacy, p. 376
self-esteem, p. 404
self-evaluation, p. 398
self-monitoring, p. 398
self-regulation, p. 397
social comparison, p. 403
standard of excellence, p. 392

Exercises

1. *What Is Motivation?*
Ask a group of students what motivates them—what energizes them to put forth effort, persist in the face of difficulty, and seek out challenges? What motives do students spontaneously name? Compare the list of motives generated by the group of students you interview with the motives highlighted in this chapter (i.e., self-efficacy, mastery beliefs, controllable attributions, an optimistic explanatory style, hope, goals, implementation intentions, possible selves, achievement goals, and self-regulation).

2. *Motivating Students*
Observe a couple of classrooms and pay close attention to those instances in which teachers try to motivate students. As you observe, compile a list of the different motivational strategies you observe. Also, note which of these strategies increase students' effort and initiative, and which do not. Do you see teachers trying to implement the type of intervention programs discussed in the chapter—mastery-modeling program, goal-setting program, mastery goal classroom climate, and so on.?

3. *Mastery-Modeling Program*
Tutor another person in an activity that is beyond their current skill level (e.g., speak a foreign language, use an unfamiliar computer software program). As you do so, ask about the person's existing anxiety and doubt, then create and implement a mastery-modeling program. After applying your mastery-modeling program, did you see a substantial increase in the person's confidence and hope? Did you see a substantial drop in his or her anxiety and doubt?

4. *Goal-Setting Program*
When a person says he or she would like to perform a particular task better, work with him or her to create a formal goal-setting program that includes the eight steps outlined in the text. Guide the other person through each step (e.g., Is that a difficult goal? Will you need your full capacity to achieve it?). After outlining the eight-step program, ask whether the other person is confident that it will yield an enhanced performance.

Lesson Plans

Lesson #1: "The Great Debate"

GRADES: 6–8

ESTIMATED COMPLETION TIME: Three 45-minute class periods

I. OVERVIEW: Students will participate in a mock presidential debate, focusing on students' concerns and school issues. Each student will be responsible for participating in the debate and for helping his or her teammates prepare as well.

II. SUBJECT AREAS: Civics, Government, Social Studies

III. OBJECTIVES: Students will be able to:
- Recognize and explain a major political issue
- Formulate an argument with supporting details
- Participate in a mock presidential debate

IV. MATERIALS: Teacher-created handouts:
- *Persuasive Language*
- *Forming an Argument*
- *Questions for the Candidate*

Helpful information for creating these handouts can be found at: http://www.changingminds.org/techniques/language/persuasive/persuasive.htm http://debate.uvm.edu/default.html

V. PROCEDURES: Before beginning, assign each student into one of the debate teams (4-5 students each).

Day 1:

1. Provide an introduction to the history and purpose of presidential debates.

2. View a 20-minute segment of the third presidential debate between Bush and Kerry (10/13/04). It can be found at: rtsp://cspanrm.fplive.net/cspan/project/c04/c04101304_debate4.rm?start=:48.0
- While viewing the video, students will recognize and record the issues and point of view of each candidate. Discuss the class findings.
- As a whole, create a class list of school issues and choose three topics for the debate. New questions may arise during the debate, so debate team members should be prepared to answer unexpected questions.

Day 2:

1. Review the *Persuasive Language* handout

2. Students complete teacher-created handouts
- Debate team: *Forming an Argument* handout
- Voters group: *Questions for the Candidate* handout

3. Debating begins (choose the first group at random). Students will follow a general debate format, presenting their arguments and then answering questions from the "voters" (classmates).

Day 3:

1. Given what they learned from the first day, students revise their handout responses.

2. Students continue to debate.

3. Leave 10–15 minutes for an end-of-class discussion on what the students learned about the process of debating.

VI. STANDARDS:
- National Council for the Social Studies Standards, X: Civic Ideals and Practices: g. practice forms of civic discussion consistent with the ideals of citizens in a democratic republic.
- National Standards for Civics and Government: "Political communication: television, radio, the press, and political persuasion," page 118.

Ask Yourself!

1. How important a role will students' self-efficacy for public speaking play in the successful implementation of this lesson plan?

2. Would it be a good use of class time to create a one-class mastery-modeling program to help build and strengthen students' self-efficacy for public speaking before proceeding with the lesson and its associated debate activity?

3. Would it be a good idea or a bad idea, motivationally speaking, to let students who fear debating choose a role such as making the opening statement because it can be prepared beforehand and simply read aloud?

5. *Quality of Self-Regulation*
Interview a student or a teacher about how he or she completes an important task, such as studying, writing, or teaching. Assess the quality of that person's forethought and reflection by asking about task analysis, self-efficacy, goal setting, strategic planning, implementation intentions, mood and anxiety, reactions to feedback, self-monitoring, self-evaluation, and general tendency to reflect on what he or she is doing. Once your interview is complete, how would you rate the quality of the person's self-regulation?

Lesson Plans

Lesson #2: "Which U.S. Historical Landmark Is the Best?"

GRADES: 7–12

ESTIMATED COMPLETION TIME: Two class periods

I. OBJECTIVES: Students will be able to:
- Gather information about a landmark, its location, and relevant historical information.
- Use knowledge of persuasion techniques to create and deliver a speech to the president (teacher) about why their landmark should be named "The Best U.S. Historical Landmark."

II. NATIONAL SOCIAL STUDIES STANDARDS:
Standard 2: Time, Continuity, and Change
Standard 6: People, Places, and Environment

III. MATERIALS:
- Books about each of the historical landmarks
- Materials such as pamphlets and brochures from each of several different historical landmarks
- Computer with Internet access
- Poster board for visual image(s) of historical landmark—students should create without using pictures printed from the Internet

IV. PROCEDURE:

1. Provide students with a list of important U.S. historical landmarks.

2. As an example, talk with students about the merits of the Statue of Liberty as an important historical landmark. It is best to provide students with a brief background article regarding the Statue of Liberty so that all students are able to participate in the activity.

3. Model for students how to research information about a landmark, and model for students what a speech arguing that the Statue of Liberty is the best U.S. historical landmark might include.

4. Guide students in their research and speech by providing focus questions.

- What is the history of the land or object that you are researching?
- Why is it a historical landmark?
- What does it represent or honor?
- How could you describe it to someone that has never been there?
- When did it become a historical landmark?
- Why should people visit the landmark?
- Why is this landmark so special that it should be voted the best in the United States?

5. Using their responses to the focus questions, students may work on creating their speech to present to the president. Students should keep in mind that they are trying to persuade the president to choose one landmark to be ranked number one against other landmarks that all have great value and significance in U.S. history. Therefore, their writing should include persuasive writing, details, and facts regarding their landmark. Students should show enthusiasm for their landmark and have a well-organized speech and visual to display during their presentations.

V. ASSESSMENT:
Speech:
- Accuracy and level of sophistication of historical information
- Organization and persuasiveness

Ask Yourself!

1. How would you structure the class so as to promote learning goals prior to and throughout the lesson?

2. How would you structure the class to minimize the likelihood that students might adopt performance goals (and performance-avoidance goals in particular) either prior to or during the lesson?

(Elizabeth Crows/The Image Works)

C arlos Morales is concerned about Jamie. It's just the second week of school and Jamie is new to the district from out of state. He is an extremely likable 9-year-old, but sometimes he just seems a bit out of control. Maybe it's because he is overly eager to please Mr. Morales, but he can't seem to wait to answer classroom questions and he is having difficulty making friends. It isn't for lack of trying; if anything, he seems to try too hard! Carlos really wants him to be successful, but this is only his second year of teaching, and he hasn't dealt with a situation like this one before. He doesn't want to complain to the principal because he once heard the principal complaining about a teacher who kept coming to him with "problem children." He decides to have a look at Jamie's file to see if there is any information there that might be of help. It turns out, there is no file! None accompanied him when he transferred into the district. Jamie's problems are starting to be class problems, and Carlos is not sure where to turn.

R I D E Reflection for Action

What should Carlos do? Does he ask for a conference with Jamie's parents? Should he talk to a senior teacher? Should he contact the school psychologist about a possible referral for Jamie? What would you do?

Guiding Questions

- How was intelligence understood initially, and how have views of intelligence changed over time?

- How is intelligence measured, and how is it related to achievement?

- How does talent develop?

- What happens when students are grouped by ability?

- In general, how do schools identify children with special needs?

- How are learning disabilities and attention-deficit/hyperactivity disorder identified?

- How can teachers bring students with physical challenges fully into classroom life?

- How do differences in socioeconomic status and culture affect students' success in school?

CHAPTER OVERVIEW

This chapter is concerned with how students differ from one another. The first part of the chapter focuses on intelligence and talent. It describes how the concept of intelligence evolved and introduces a number of theories of intelligence. The next part of the chapter discusses how talent is developed and the extremes of intelligence. Some instructional strategies for managing variation in students' ability are then described. The next part of the chapter focuses on children with special needs, including learning disabilities, physical challenges, attention-deficit disorder, autism, and attention-deficit/hyperactivity disorder.

Variability in the Classroom

Intelligence
- The History of Intelligence
- Controversies in Intelligence
- Current Thinking on Issues of Intelligence
- How Is Intelligence Measured?

Talent
- Deliberate Practice and the Monotonic-Benefits Assumption
- Effort Becomes Talent
- Early Talent and Developed Talent

Extremes of Intelligence
- Giftedness
- Intellectual and Developmental Disabilities

Differences in Ability and Instruction
- Between-Class Ability Grouping
- Within-Class Ability Grouping

Learners with Special Needs
- The Law and Special Education
- Identifying Children with Special Needs
- Inclusion

Prevalent Student Needs and Challenges
- Learning Disabilities
- Autism and Related Disorders
- Physical and Sensory Challenges
- Attention-Deficit Disorder
- Attention-Deficit/Hyperactivity Disorder
- Differentiating Instruction

Variability in the Classroom

Students are different from one another. Some are good athletes; others are popular. Some have a good idea of their strengths and weaknesses; others do not have a clue. What are your strengths and weaknesses? How do they compare to those of your best friend or your brother or sister? How do you know what your strengths and weaknesses are? Were you born with them, or did they develop as you grew? Did you work hard to build up your strengths, or did you just focus on what you seemed to be good at, or both?

Do you have any friends or relatives who face special challenges in life? These might be learning challenges, physical challenges, or emotional challenges. When you think about that person, do the challenges define that person for you, or are they just a part of a fuller image of who that person is? Does this person get support and encouragement from others, or does he or she experience discrimination?

As a teacher, how would you work with a diverse group of students? What is your responsibility in terms of understanding their strengths and weaknesses and making what you teach relevant to their lives? How would you work with a student whose life challenges greatly exceed those of the other children in the class? What about children with milder disabilities?

One of the great things about being a teacher is that no two days are the same, and no two children are the same. The challenge is to acknowledge and celebrate the differences among children, working to maximize the growth in each child. At the same time, there is a natural tension between the aspirations and abilities of students—their dreams and goals—on one hand and the requirements of teaching algebra, or French, or fourth grade, on the other. In his classic work, *The Child and the Curriculum*, John Dewey argues that "the child and the

Students in today's classrooms vary in their abilities, motivation, and backgrounds.

curriculum are simply two limits which define a single process. Just as two points define a straight line, so the present standpoint of the child and the facts and truths of studies define instruction" (Dewey, 1971, p. 11).

As Dewey points out, at one end of this continuum are subject areas, which are varied and complex. At the other end are children, who are also varied and complex. Children differ in temperament, enthusiasm, prior knowledge in different subjects, distractibility, self-concept, verbal ability, spatial reasoning, motivation, physical mobility, and on and on. And of course, there is not just one child; there is a whole classroom full of children or adolescents. But as a teacher, you should look at this situation not as hopelessly complex but as wonderfully rich. On one hand, you have students who bring a variety of strengths, ambitions, and backgrounds to the task of learning. On the other hand, you have a world of ideas, possibilities, knowledge, and skills to bring to your students. Your task as a teacher is to determine how to work with a roomful of highly diverse students to help all of them acquire the knowledge, skills, dispositions, and abilities that you wish them to obtain.

Intelligence

One characteristic on which students vary is intelligence. Intelligence is an idea that has been around for thousands of years. Plato identified *reason* as one of the three components of the soul (along with *will* and *appetite*). Aristotle linked intelligence to physiological processes. Intelligence is a theoretical concept that makes it easier to understand the (psychological) world. Like many such concepts, it has undergone challenges, rejections, and revisions over the course of the past century. Because intelligence is a controversial concept, it is important to understand how it originated and how it has changed over time.

The History of Intelligence

The modern interest in intelligence began in the late 1870s. The German philosopher and psychologist Wilhelm Wundt founded the first psychological laboratory, emphasizing **physiological psychology** (the study of the relationships among the brain, the nervous system, and behavior, sometimes called *psychophysics*) and making psychology more distinct from philosophy. He is often referred to as the father of modern psychology.

physiological psychology The study of the relationship among the brain, the nervous system, and behavior.

Alfred Binet and Francis Galton Probably the most important scholars in the early development of the concept of intelligence were Alfred Binet and the English psychologist

Francis Galton. A younger cousin of Darwin, Galton studied medicine, meteorology, biology, and statistics, among other fields. In addition to his work on intelligence, Galton invented weather maps, pioneered the use of fingerprints to identify individuals, and identified the ideas underlying correlation and regression analysis in statistics (McClearn, 1991). In the field of psychology, he was a pioneer in the area of individual differences. He was obsessed with the measurement of human characteristics and differences among them. He was the first psychologist to use the normal distribution of Gauss as a model for the distribution of human characteristics. His classic work *Hereditary Genius* (Galton, 1869) set forth his theory about the influence of genetics on mental abilities.

eugenics A political and scientific movement that argued for selective reproduction of individuals and immigration laws based on intelligence levels.

Galton's interest in mental abilities and the genetic influences on them led him to form the Eugenics Society, which argued for selective mating to improve the human race. The ideas associated with the **eugenics** movement are strongly disavowed today.

Alfred Binet came to the study of mental abilities from a very different perspective. In the early 1900s, he was asked to develop a set of measures, or *scales,* that could be used for the placement of low-achieving Parisian students into special schools for children with cognitive disabilities. Along with his assistant, Theodore Simon, he published his first set of scales in 1905. The tasks included in these scales focused on elements that Binet considered to be common sense or practical judgment. He tried them out on a sample of average students to determine which of them could be done by students at various ages. Examples of these tasks include touching various parts of the body on request, determining which of two lines is longer, repeating groups of numbers read by the examiner, and defining everyday words (Nunally, 1967). At higher levels, students were asked to repeat up to seven numbers backward and to find rhymes for multisyllabic words (Fancher, 1985).

If students could answer questions that a typical child could answer at a given age, Binet classified them at that mental level. Thus, if a 12-year-old child could answer the questions for 9-year-olds but not those for 10-year-olds, the child would be classified at the mental level of a 9-year-old. Binet's scales focused on the end product of intelligence rather than on its underlying nature (Nunally, 1967). Binet warned that although his scales seemed appropriate for the students he was working with—that is, students in Paris—he was cautious about the possibility of extending his work beyond that population.

Binet's scales became the basis for much of the subsequent work in intelligence testing. Psychologists Henry Goddard and Lewis Terman independently brought his work to the United States in the early 1900s. Terman, who taught at Stanford University, developed Binet's scales into what came to be known as the Stanford-Binet intelligence test.

Intelligence and IQ What exactly *is* intelligence? This question has been debated since the idea first arose and is still actively debated today. Binet felt that intelligence is "judgment, otherwise called good sense, practical sense, initiative, the faculty of adapting one's self to circumstances" (Binet & Simon, 1916). Goddard theorized that "the chief determiner of human conduct is a unitary mental process which we call intelligence" (Goddard, 1920, p. 1). Working with Terman, William Stern suggested that the age level of the tasks a child can perform **(mental age)** could be divided by the child's chronological age to form a ratio of mental age to chronological age. When multiplied by 100, this ratio became the child's **intelligence quotient,** or **IQ:**

mental age The age level associated with the ability to perform certain mental tasks. A mental age of 7 means that a person can perform the tasks of a typical 7-year-old but not those of a typical 8-year-old.

intelligence quotient (IQ) A method for communicating the level of a person's intelligence.

$$\text{IQ} = \frac{\text{mental age}}{\text{chronological age}} \times 100$$

In the early years of IQ measurement, IQ was thought to be a single, overarching ability that could be measured precisely; it was assumed that a two- or three-digit number, the IQ, could be used to represent the measurement. Terman focused on individuals with very high levels of intelligence, whereas Goddard focused on people with lower levels of intelligence. Some psychologists, including Goddard (1920), believed that intelligence is an **innate ability,** or present at birth.

innate ability The ability a person was born with.

The Development of the Idea of Intelligence A British psychologist, Charles Spearman, administered a large number of measures of various aspects of mental ability and subjected them to a statistical technique called *factor analysis,* a technique that groups related items together. The results of the analysis suggested that intelligence could be viewed as consisting of one broad, or general, factor, which Spearman labeled *g* (for general), plus a variety of individual, or specific, factors (Spearman, 1923, 1927). Psychologists still use *g* as a kind of shorthand for general intelligence.

As factor-analytic techniques progressed, L. L. Thurstone (1957) proposed a dramatically different approach to defining intelligence. Based on an extensive study of schoolchildren in Chicago, Thurstone proposed a model of intelligence consisting of seven **primary mental abilities:**

- Verbal comprehension (ability to understand verbal analogies and comprehend reading passages)
- Word fluency (ability to manipulate words, vocabulary)
- Number facility (speed and accuracy of computation)
- Spatial visualization (ability to do things such as mental rotation of objects)
- Associative memory (ability to remember words or objects presented in pairs)
- Perceptual speed (such as ability to find the number of times a specific letter appears on a printed page)
- Reasoning (ability to solve arithmetic or logical reasoning problems)

> **primary mental abilities** L. L. Thurstone's theory of intelligence as consisting of seven distinct abilities.

This view of intelligence, or *primary abilities*, was much broader than previous ones. Thus, a child could be strong in word fluency (have a large vocabulary) but not be good at visualizing or in perceptual speed. In other words, a child could show an uneven pattern of strengths and weaknesses. Thurstone's approach to mental abilities painted a richer picture of the individual, an idea that would appear again later in the development of thinking about intelligence.

Raymond Cattell made a highly useful contribution by proposing the terms *fluid* and *crystallized intelligence* (Cattell, 1963). **Fluid intelligence** refers to the ability to solve problems, figure out what to do when you are not sure what to do, and acquire new skills. **Crystallized intelligence** involves the use of acquired skills and knowledge, such as reading and language skills. Fluid intelligence tends to develop until early adulthood, then decline. Crystallized intelligence, on the other hand, tends to grow throughout adulthood. Note that this does not mean that older adults do not have any fluid intelligence; it just means that they do not have as much as they did when they were younger.

> **fluid intelligence** The ability to solve problems, figure out what to do when one is not sure what to do, and acquire new skills.

> **crystallized intelligence** The use of acquired skills and knowledge, such as reading and language skills.

Controversies in Intelligence

It would be hard to imagine an area of psychology that is more controversial than intelligence. The problem has to do with what is called the **nature/nurture** debate: Is intelligence developed by the individual's experiences within his or her environment, or is it basically genetic in nature and inherited? Early psychologists, such as Galton, Goddard, and Yale psychologist Robert Yerkes, were associated with the eugenics movement. They argued that intelligence is primarily genetic and that governments, therefore, should encourage the reproduction of individuals with higher levels of intelligence and discourage that of individuals with lower levels of intelligence. They also argued for selective immigration laws.

> **nature/nurture** A shorthand term for the debate over whether mental abilities are developed by the individual's environment (nurture) or are inherited (nature).

These issues were brought to a head in 1994 with the publication of a highly controversial book, *The Bell Curve*, by Richard Herrnstein and Charles Murray. The authors argued that intelligence, thought of as a single mental ability, is real; that differences among ethnic and racial groups exist; and that intelligence predicts a large number of life outcomes. Perhaps the most eloquent argument against this perspective was presented by evolutionary biologist Stephen Jay Gould in *The Mismeasure of Man* (1981). Gould argued against the notion of intelligence being a single trait as well as against a genetic basis for mental abilities.

Current Thinking on Issues of Intelligence

Building on the earlier work, two new and highly influential theories of intelligence have been proposed in recent years: Robert Sternberg's triarchic theory of intelligence and Howard Gardner's theory of multiple intelligences. The concept of **metacognition**, attributable primarily to John Flavell, has also strongly influenced research and scholarship on mental

> **metacognition** Thinking about one's own thinking.

abilities. These theories and related research have influenced not only how psychologists think about intelligence but also educational practice.

Sternberg's Triarchic Theory of Intelligence One of the most popular approaches to thinking about intelligence from a practical perspective is Sternberg's **triarchic** theory (Sternberg, 1985, 2000) and his more recent extension of it, which he calls *successful intelligence* (Sternberg, 1997; Sternberg & Grigorenko, 2000). The triarchic theory holds that intelligence has three main facets: *analytical*, *creative*, and *practical*. The analytical facet is the ability to respond effectively to problems. It has three components: metacomponents, performance components, and knowledge acquisition components. *Metacomponents* have to do with the ability to organize, execute, and evaluate one's cognitive resources in responding to a problem. This is very similar to the idea of metacognition, explained later in this section. *Performance components* are the specific abilities necessary to solve certain kinds of problems: abilities such as those involved in solving an algebra problem or making comparisons between objects. *Knowledge acquisition components* are the abilities involved in new learning—what you would do to memorize new information or perfect a new skill.

The creative facet of the theory involves generating new ideas, coming up with new approaches, taking a different look at a problem, or combining information in a novel way. This part of the theory has two components: novelty or insight, and **automaticity**. Automaticity is the ability to perform a task without having to think much about it. Ice-skating is a good example. When one first learns how to skate, it takes a great deal of cognitive effort just to remain upright. After some practice, however, maintaining balance becomes more automatic, and one can focus on other aspects of skating.

The practical facet of the theory involves the ability to handle everyday problems and issues. People who are able to adapt to changing aspects of their environment are strong in the practical aspect of intelligence. They are also able to change their environment to meet their needs or to realize that the environment they are in is not the best one for them and to seek out a new environment. The practical facet of the theory might be thought of as "street smarts."

To summarize the triarchic theory, it involves the ability to (1) solve problems, (2) generate new ideas, and (3) put one's ideas and solutions to purposeful use in the environment. A model of the theory is presented in Figure 12.1.

Sternberg's Idea of Successful Intelligence Based on his triarchic theory, Sternberg developed what he calls a theory of successful intelligence. In his words, "Successful intelligence is the ability to succeed in life, given one's own goals, within one's environmental contexts. Thus successful intelligence is a basis for school achievement, but also life achievement" (Sternberg, 1997, p. 12).

---

triarchic Composed of three components, each of which is at the top of a hierarchy.

automaticity The ability to perform a task without having to think much about it.

> **What Does This Mean to Me?**
> Which of Sternberg's facets is your strongest one? How can you use it to your advantage as a teacher?

R I D E   Might there be aspects of intelligence where Jamie is particularly strong?

Figure 12.1 Sternberg's Triarchic Theory of Intelligence

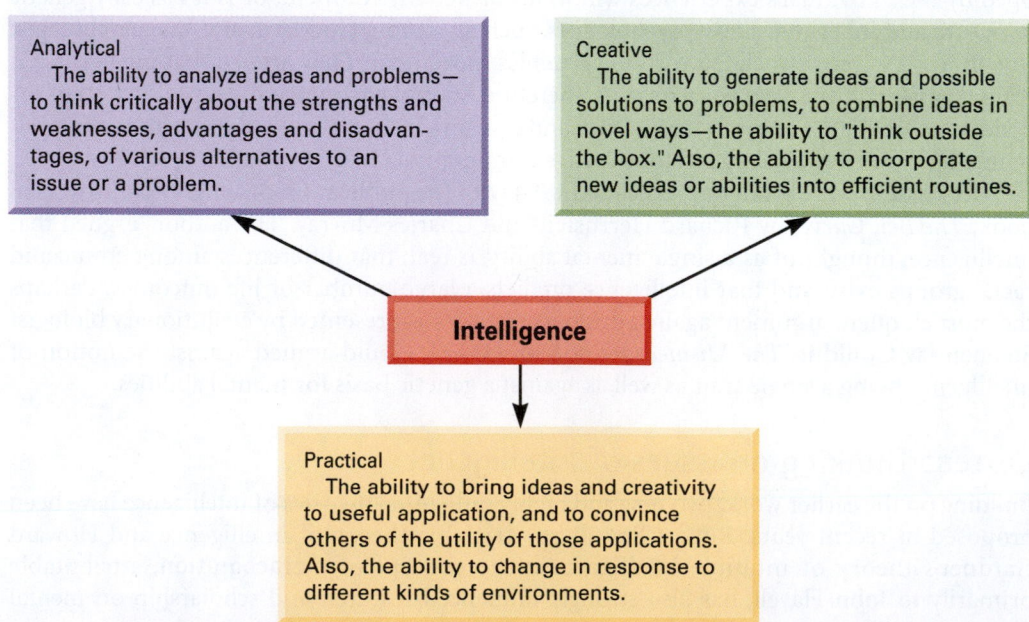

Analytical
   The ability to analyze ideas and problems—to think critically about the strengths and weaknesses, advantages and disadvantages, of various alternatives to an issue or a problem.

Creative
   The ability to generate ideas and possible solutions to problems, to combine ideas in novel ways—the ability to "think outside the box." Also, the ability to incorporate new ideas or abilities into efficient routines.

Intelligence

Practical
   The ability to bring ideas and creativity to useful application, and to convince others of the utility of those applications. Also, the ability to change in response to different kinds of environments.

This view of intelligence suggests that educational activities might mean different things for different students and that individuals bring different cognitive strengths and weaknesses to their learning efforts. Teaching designed to promote successful intelligence, according to Sternberg, has four key elements:

1. Teaching for memory learning: the acquisition of information—the who, what, where, when, and how of learning
2. Teaching for analytical learning: the ability to understand the reasons underlying issues and to explain, evaluate, or judge them
3. Teaching for creative learning: the inventive and creative aspect of learning—letting students explore new ideas of their own imagining
4. Teaching for practical learning: the practical application of knowledge and skills—making things work in the real world

Sternberg argues that it is not always necessary to emphasize all four of these elements but that attention to all of them on a regular, ongoing basis will help students enhance their strengths and overcome their weaknesses as they learn about themselves.

Gardner's Theory of Multiple Intelligences The most popular view of intelligence in schools is Howard Gardner's **multiple-intelligences (MI) theory**. Based in part on his observations of schoolchildren and individuals with brain damage, Gardner reasoned that abilities are more separate and isolated than other theories portray them. First presented in 1983 in *Frames of Mind*, Gardner's theory holds that any concept of intelligence as consisting of a single or small number of overarching abilities is too limiting. As an alternative, Gardner proposes that there are at least eight identifiable forms of intelligence, and possibly more (Gardner, 1993, 1995, 1998, 1999, 2003). Table 12.1 lists and describes these eight forms of intelligence.

Teachers have responded positively to Gardner's theory. It may fit well with their experiences of the different ways in which children learn. It also provides a framework for organizing curricula and assessment and focuses teachers on what children *can* do rather than on what they cannot. Gardner uses a number of criteria to decide whether an ability can be considered intelligence. The main criterion is the ability's contribution to solving genuine problems or difficulties. He has considered additional intelligences, such as **existential intelligence**—concern with larger questions of human existence, such as the meaning of life—but has chosen not to include them in his list of intelligences (Gardner, 1999).

Appendix
How Students Learn
Various theories of intelligence describe facets of students' learning. You may wish to encourage these varied facets in your classroom (PRAXIS™, I.A.1; INTASC, Principle 2).

multiple-intelligences (MI) theory A theory of intelligence that argues that individuals may exhibit multiple intelligences (possibly eight or more).

existential intelligence Concern with larger questions of human existence, such as the meaning of life.

TABLE 12.1

Gardner's Theory of Multiple Intelligences

According to Howard Gardner, an individual may exhibit the following types of intelligence.

Logical-mathematical: The ability to understand and use numerical patterns, carry out mathematical operations, and engage in the reasoning associated with logic. This is similar to quantitative ability in many theories of intelligence.

Linguistic: The ability to acquire and use the functions of language to express oneself and to comprehend others. This is similar to verbal ability in traditional theories of intelligence.

Spatial: The ability to recognize and manipulate patterns, spaces, and objects—for example, the ability to rotate objects mentally. This ability is found in some other theories of intelligence, notably Thurstone's primary mental abilities.

Musical: The ability to recognize and use the components of music (tones, pitches, rhythms, musical phrasing, etc.) in composing or performing music.

Bodily-kinesthetic: The ability to use the body in a coordinated and productive fashion, such as in athletics, dance, arts and crafts production, dentistry, surgery, and so on.

Interpersonal: The ability to interact with others in a positive and productive fashion, to recognize others' feelings, motivations, and intentions.

Intrapersonal: The ability to understand one's own motivations and abilities and use that information to guide one's own life in a productive fashion.

Naturalistic: The ability to understand the natural world, recognizing plant and animal species and the workings of the environment.

Gardner's theory has been adopted by a number of schools and educators, but it is not without its critics (Smith, 2002). The most consistent criticisms focus on the criteria he uses to identify intelligences, his conceptualization of intelligence, and the absence of empirical support for his conceptualization (Smith, 2002). Many educators have been very receptive to the ideas behind the theory of multiple intelligences. Some efforts to apply the theory involve either setting up a learning center for each of the intelligences or trying to include all or most of them in lesson plans. Others attempt to identify a child's strengths and emphasize them. Even though Gardner's original work is over 30 years old, its educational implications are still being explored and debated. Perhaps the strongest contribution of MI theory is that it has caused educators to take a different perspective on abilities. If interpersonal skills can be thought of as *intelligence*, rather than just as interpersonal skills, it is important to consider them as part of the educational process. Although other psychologists have considered intelligence to be multifaceted, Gardner's work is revolutionary in its inclusion of athletic and musical ability, and even the ability to understand oneself. It can be argued that these abilities are not really intelligence; it cannot be argued that they are unimportant, and Gardner's work offers a way to evaluate their importance.

How Can I Use This?
What classroom tasks could stimulate the use of Gardner's eight intelligences?

Views of Intelligence People have many different views of the nature of intelligence. Some individuals think that their abilities are determined at birth and cannot be altered in any major way. Carol Dweck describes this as an **entity view of intelligence** (Dweck, 1986, 2000). Others believe that basic abilities can be improved through hard work. This is known as the **incremental view of intelligence**. The idea that ability is fixed seems to change over time; as they grow older, children tend to take a more incremental view (Dweck, 2002). From a teacher's perspective, what is important about these different points of view is that the incremental perspective should be nurtured. When teachers emphasize a growth mindset—when they tell students that the brain is like a muscle that grows with use—students who adopt that mindset show dramatic improvements in their study habits and equally dramatic gains in their academic achievement (Dweck, 2006).

entity view of intelligence The belief that intelligence is genetically determined and not alterable.

incremental view of intelligence The belief that intelligence can be improved through effort.

What Does This Mean to Me?
Do you have an entity or an incremental view of your own intelligence? What does this mean for how hard you work at tasks?

If students believe that they can improve their abilities through hard work, they are much more likely to put forth the effort necessary for success in school. If, on the other hand, they feel that their successes and failures are determined by fixed abilities over which they have no control, they are much less likely to strive to succeed.

How Is Intelligence Measured?

As discussed earlier, there are many different ways of viewing intelligence. It follows that the types of measures used to assess intelligence differ as well. Another factor in the design of intelligence tests has to do with whether they are intended to be administered to individuals by trained psychologists or educators, or administered to groups. To assess children who may have special needs, individually administered tests are typically used.

Standardized IQ Tests Two of the most popular individually administered tests are the Wechsler Intelligence Scale for Children, fourth edition [referred to as the WISC-IV (Wechsler, 2003)], and the Kaufman Assessment Battery for Children, or K-ABC II (Kaufman & Kaufman, 2005). The WISC-IV is made up of 13 subtests, of which 6 are combined into a verbal IQ scale and 7 into a performance IQ scale. The subtests on the scales are as follows:

Verbal	Performance
Information	Picture Completion
Similarities	Coding
Arithmetic	Picture Arrangement
Vocabulary	Block Design
Comprehension	Object Assembly
Digit Span	Symbol Search
	Mazes

The K-ABC II is made up of two main scales, a sequential processing scale and a simultaneous processing scale. The sequential processing scale involves working with concepts or objects in order, whereas the simultaneous processing scale involves processing in which order is not a factor. The subtests on each of the scales are as follows:

Sequential Processing Scale	Simultaneous Processing Scale
Hand Movements	Magic Window
Number Recall	Face Recognition
Word Order	Gestalt Closure
	Triangles
	Matrix Analogies
	Spatial Memory
	Photo Series

The questions (called *items* by measurement specialists) on IQ tests take a wide variety of forms. On most scales, these items rely not so much on the individual's level of knowledge as on his or her ability to do something with the information or situation that is presented. Figure 12.2 provides examples of the types of items that are used in IQ tests.

Test Bias and Culture-Free Tests   A persistent criticism of intelligence tests is that they are biased against certain groups, notably African-Americans and individuals whose first language is not English (Joseph, 1977; Williams, 1974). Bias has both an everyday and a technical definition. In everyday language, it means a predisposition against a certain group of people based on irrelevant characteristics. Thus, one might say, "The teacher is biased against me because I play football and she doesn't like football players." In intelligence testing and other forms of standardized testing, **bias** refers to situations in which the same score would have different meanings for individuals from different groups. For example, if Harold and Maria both get 1140 on their SATs, one should be able to predict that they will do equally well in college. Put another way, if women who score 1140 do better overall in college than men who score 1140, we would conclude that the SATs are biased against men.

bias Systematic unfair treatment of a particular group of individuals.

Research on most intelligence and other standardized tests has not found this type of evidence for various groups of individuals (Hartigan & Wigdor; 1989; Linn, 1982). Bias, however, can occur either within the test itself or in how the test is used (Shepard, 1982). Measures such as intelligence tests, college admissions tests, and employment tests are all intended to be *part* of a decision-making process. When test scores are weighted too heavily relative to other factors, they can result in decisions that are biased even when the measures used in making them are unbiased.

A number of efforts have been made to develop tests that do not give undue advantage to particular cultural groups; these are known as **culture-free tests**. Raymond Cattell (1940) made some of the earliest efforts to produce a culture-free test. Among the best known of these is the Ravens Progressive Matrices (Raven, 1995), which consists of a series of increasingly complex matrices of shapes: The examinee has to determine which of a series of options would properly complete the matrix. The Ravens test is widely used, but its results show the same differences between whites and minorities as do other measures of intelligence (Veroff, McClelland, & Marquis, 1971).

culture-free tests Standardized tests that do not include items that might favor one culture over another.

Measures of New Approaches to Intelligence   Having looked at measures based on traditional views of intelligence, it is natural to wonder how the newer approaches, such as Sternberg's or Gardner's models, are measured. Sternberg's triarchic theory is more similar to traditional approaches than is Gardner's multiple-intelligences theory. Working with a team of colleagues, Sternberg has been developing the Sternberg Triarchic Abilities Test (Sternberg et al., 2001). The breadth of Gardner's approach to intelligence makes measurement more difficult. Shearer's Multiple Intelligences Developmental Assessment Scales is probably the most fully developed assessment for measuring Gardner's intelligences (Shearer, 2004). (See the nearby What Kids Say and Do box).

What Kids Say and Do

Messages Received by Children

This comes to us from one of our colleagues, who is a developmental psychologist:

It was the first day of third grade and I was walking to school with my best friend, Pete. I said, "Hey, who knows, maybe we'll have the same teacher this year. That would be great." When Pete heard what I said, he began to cry. I said, "Pete, what's the matter? Aren't you feeling good?" Pete's response was, "We're not going to be in the same class, Richard. You're smart. You're going to be in the smart kids' class. I'm dumb. I'm going to be in the dumb kids' class." It would be nice to say that we were in the same class, but we weren't. Pete was right. What kinds of messages do we send to children in school when their self-perception at age 7 is "You're smart, I'm dumb"?

Figure 12.2 Examples of
IQ Test Questions

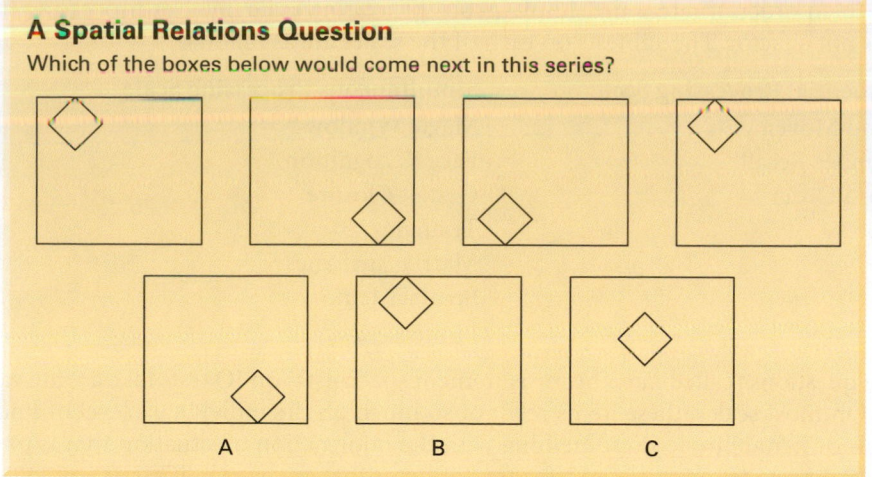

A Spatial Relations Question
Which of the boxes below would come next in this series?

(a)

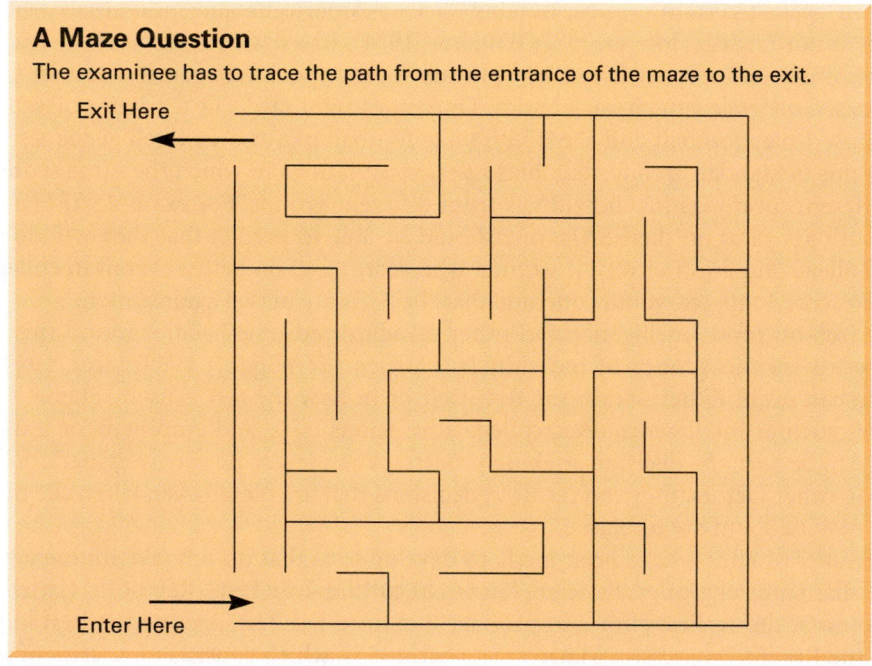

A Maze Question
The examinee has to trace the path from the entrance of the maze to the exit.

Exit Here

Enter Here

(b)

An Analogies Question
Grief is to sorrow as joy is to

    A. Tragedy   B. Remorse   C. Happiness   D. Excitement

(c)

A Quantitative Question
What number would come next in this series of numbers?

    2, 5, 9, 14...

    A. 9   B. 17   C. 20   D. 25

(d)

Talent

Talent is the capacity to produce exceptional performance. As mentioned previously, test scores are just one measure used to identify exceptional children. Abilities can develop over time. Sternberg (1999) describes intelligence as the development of expertise. During their school years, students often develop talent or expertise in such areas as music, mathematics, science, computers, writing, and athletics. As educators observe talented students in these domains, they frequently attribute the talent to an innate gift. But research shows that talent is often acquired and that practice plays a larger role in its development than is commonly believed (Bloom, 1985; Ericsson, Krampe, & Tesch-Romer, 1993). Figure 12.3 presents a model of how experience and practice contribute to the development of talent.

As shown at the top of the figure, the school curriculum asks students to engage in a variety of activities, such as practicing penmanship, writing essays, working on computers, and playing tennis. Most of the time, students quickly attain a level of proficiency in an activity that is "good enough." After that, their performance becomes routine, and they make little further progress in developing their talent in that domain. For instance, a student may think, "My penmanship is good enough the way it is." The dashed lines in the figure illustrate this normal course of events. Sometimes, however, students wish to increase their ability in a particular domain.

The left side of Figure 12.3 identifies three sources that spark students' desire to increase their talent: enjoyment, valuing, and external support (Csikszentmihalyi, Rathunde, & Whalen, 1993). Enjoyment typically arises when the task produces an optimal experience, such as when a student performs a difficult piece of music and has fun doing so. Valuing typically arises from wanting to improve one's skill in the domain for its own sake, such as wanting to improve one's writing skill just to become a better writer, not to make a better grade. External support typically takes the form of having access

talent The capacity to produce exceptional performance.

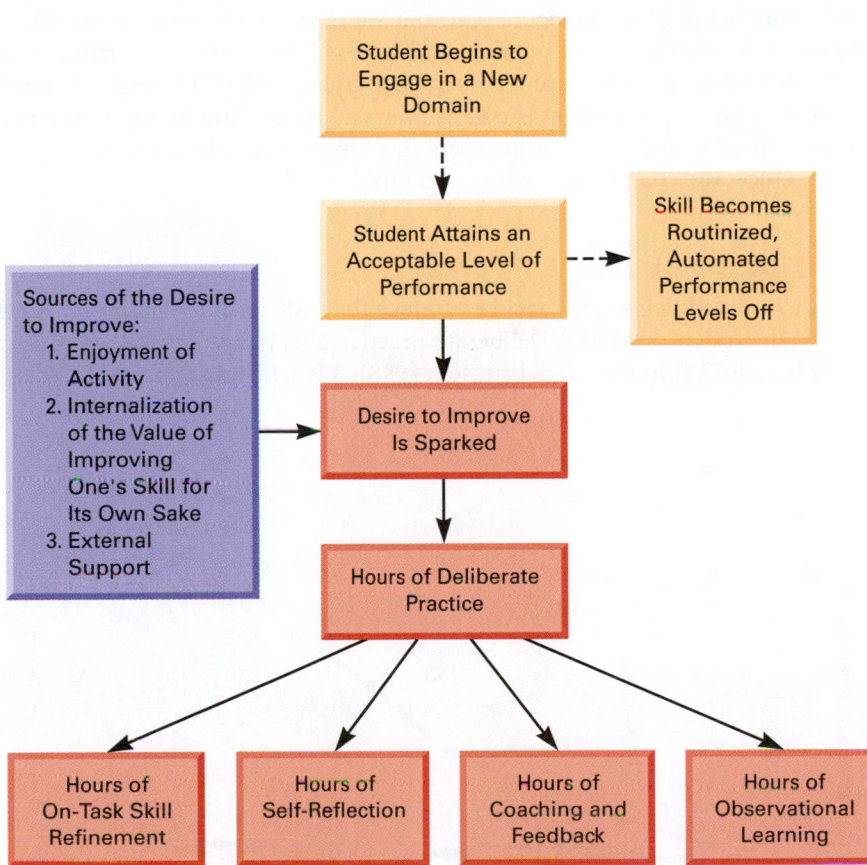

Figure 12.3 Factors That Contribute to the Development of Talent

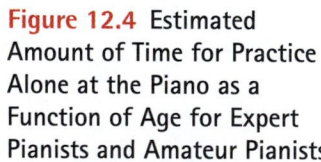

How Can I Use This?

How will you provide opportunities for deliberate practice to students with special needs?

to resources and social support, such as encouragement from one's teacher. Students with special needs will need a lot of support to engage in these activities.

Deliberate Practice and the Monotonic-Benefits Assumption

deliberate practice Activity that is designed to improve one's skills in a particular area.

The desire to increase one's talent leads one to engage in many hours of deliberate practice. **Deliberate practice** is activity whose main purpose is to attain and improve one's skills (Ericsson et al., 1993; Sosniak, 1985). It is not practice the way we understand it in connection with such activities as playing tennis or playing a musical instrument. Rather, deliberate practice involves repetitive work on a single aspect of the task, such as refining one's grip or finger position on the tennis racket or violin strings. The four boxes at the lower part of Figure 12.3 show what students do during deliberate practice. Some hours are spent on-task, directly refining one's skill. During these hours, students invest their full effort as they engage in aspects of the task that they cannot yet do. Other hours are spent in self-reflection. During this "time to think," students engage in mental simulations of what they might do to improve their technique. During self-reflection, performers mentally compare their actual performances against their ideal performance and try to figure out how to close the gap between the two. Other hours of deliberate practice are spent receiving coaching, instruction, and feedback. Improving one's skill and learning how to do what one cannot currently do require the insights and feedback of an expert. Lastly, many hours are spent observing experienced performers. During this observational learning, students gain exposure to highly skilled models and use this information to develop new ideas and hypotheses about what to try during their practice time.

monotonic-benefits assumption The argument that there is a one-to-one correspondence between one's effort and one's gains in a skill or ability.

Those who study the development of talent assume that deliberate practice produces **monotonic benefits**: The amount of time an individual spends in deliberate practice is monotonically (one-to-one) related to his or her acquired performance level in that domain (Ericsson et al., 1993; Reingold et al., 2001). This means that the number of hours of deliberate practice is a nearly perfect predictor of performance level, as shown in data such as those graphed in Figure 12.4. The figure plots the hours of weekly practice over the years from age 4 to age 20 for two groups of pianists—amateurs and experts. The amateurs practiced 2 or 3 hours each week for 16 years, and they became good pianists. The experts, however, practiced for about 5 hours per week at age 8, 12 hours at age 14, and about 23 hours at age 18. It is assumed that the number of hours spent in deliberate practice is the transformational event that produces the changes that allow talent to develop.

Effort Becomes Talent

How do hours of deliberate practice produce the wide individual differences that educators observe in students' talents? Deliberate practice alters a student's cognitive capacities and bodily functions (Bloom, 1985; Ericsson, 1998). A less talented chess player, for instance, will

Figure 12.4 Estimated Amount of Time for Practice Alone at the Piano as a Function of Age for Expert Pianists and Amateur Pianists

Source: Ericsson, K. A., Krampe, R. T., & Tesch-Romer, C. (1993). The role of deliberate practice in the acquisition of expert performance. *Psychological Review, 100,* 363–406. Copyright © 1993 by the American Psychological Association. Reprinted with permission.

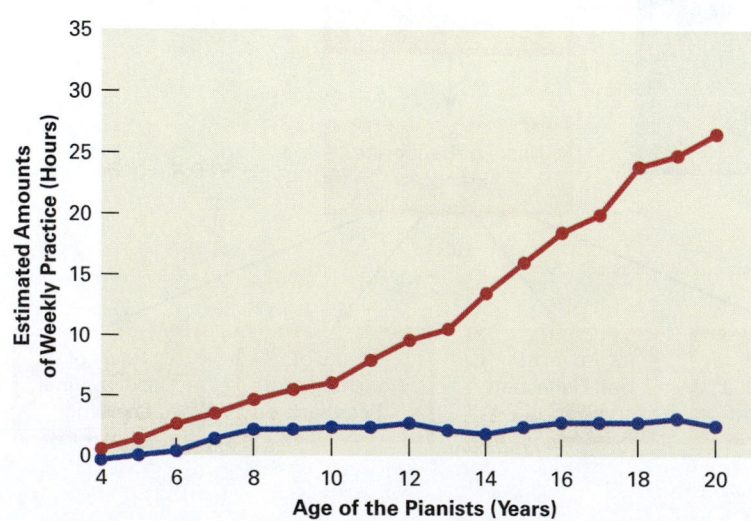

survey the pieces on the board, identify the merits of half a dozen possible moves, then select the best move from among the options. A more talented chess player has acquired much more elaborate chess schemas as a result of many hours of deliberate practice. With each turn, the expert makes an initial survey of the chess patterns, quickly explores as many as 40 or 50 possibilities, evaluates the merits of 5 or so of the best moves, and finally selects the best of those. Novice (less talented) and expert (more talented) teachers go through the same process when deciding what to do next in the classroom.

Deliberate practice also changes bodily functions: Piano players develop muscle patterns, such as finger rolls and reverse finger rolls, and long-distance runners grow new capillaries, break down and rebuild their leg muscles, and increase the capacity of their heart and lungs. Through these cognitive and physical means, effort becomes talent. Learners with special needs require a great deal of practice and may need to practice over a longer period.

The process through which writers' hours of deliberate practice help them develop talent illustrates this point. A typical classroom episode unfolds as follows: The teacher tells the students to write a 500-word persuasive essay; the students write their essays; they revise their essays; and finally, the teacher provides some feedback on the quality of the essays. Deliberate practice for talent development would involve a different lesson plan. The teacher might first identify the following writing skills as essential:

- Quality of topic sentences
- Active rather than passive voice
- Strong nouns and verbs
- Vocabulary
- Smooth transitions between paragraphs

The teacher would then highlight one skill to practice, such as the quality of topic sentences. On Monday, the students would write their topic sentences. On Tuesday, they would revise and improve those sentences. At this point, the students would generally feel that their topic sentences are "good enough," so the teacher would have reached the critical point in talent development: encouraging students to improve their topic sentences still further. If the students enjoyed writing, valued writing, and received support for writing, they would then spend Wednesday, Thursday, and Friday engaged in the four aspects of deliberate practice shown in the lower four boxes of Figure 12.3. During skill refinement, they could revise all aspects of their topic sentence in an effort to move closer to an ideal sentence. During self-reflection, they could think creatively and mentally try out different ways of improving their writing. During coaching and feedback, they could show their sentences to the teacher, peers, or even submit their work to computer software programs and receive suggestions. During observational learning, they could read topic sentences written by experts such as Hemingway or Salinger, or even articles in *Time* or *Sports Illustrated*. The idea is to have students spend time trying to do what they cannot currently do. Students with special needs will need a great deal of support to engage in these activities.

Early Talent and Developed Talent

Even a casual observation will confirm that students enter school with wide differences in many domains (Howe, Davidson, & Slobada, 1998). Some students are naturally better at math, others are better athletes, and so on. Before students begin investing many hours in deliberate practice, natural talent predicts performance rather well. As the number of hours of practice increases, however, developed talent becomes an ever-better predictor of a student's performance level. At some point—after years of deliberate practice—it becomes an even better predictor of performance than does natural talent (Ericsson et al., 1993; Monsaas, 1985).

Figure 12.5 helps explain the development of talent. During the first phase of talent development, students have not yet engaged in deliberate practice, and natural ability predicts performance very well. This is a period of play in a domain in which activity is spontaneous and motivation is not a problem. The student writes poetry for the fun of it, or the athlete dribbles, shoots free throws, and plays a game of *horse* for fun. Once students wish to improve their skills, they begin the second phase of talent development and engage in

What Does This Mean to Me?
On what tasks or activities do you engage in deliberate practice? What do you do to be "deliberate" about your practice?

RIDE Might Jamie's enthusiasm and willingness to please be harnessed into hard work in an area where Jamie has strong interest and, perhaps, talent?

Figure 12.5 Three Phases of Development Toward Adult Expertise

Source: Ericsson, K. A., Krampe, R. T., & Tesch-Romer, C. (1993). The role of deliberate practice in the acquisition of expert performance. *Psychological Review, 100,* 363–406. Copyright © 1993 by the American Psychological Association. Reprinted with permission.

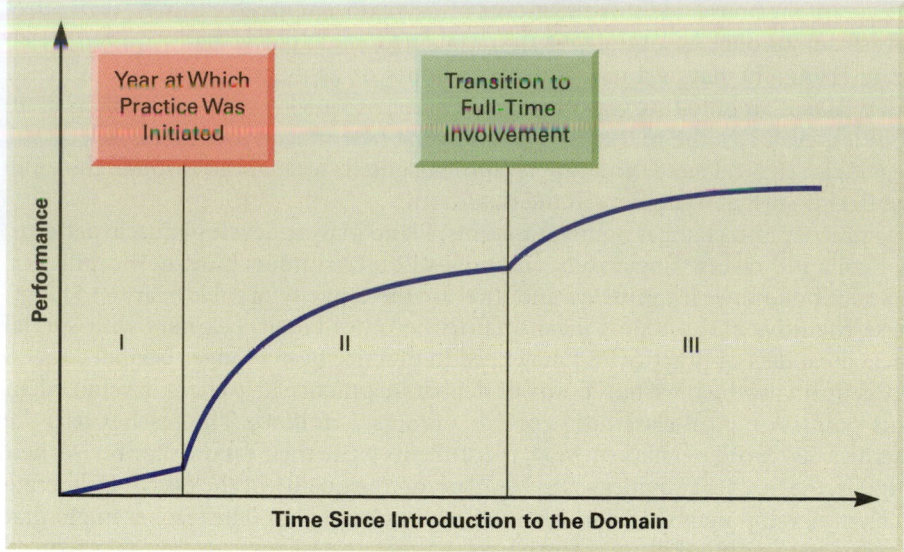

deliberate practice. Such activity requires intense concentration and effort, and motivation can become a problem. With deliberate practice, students see a large and immediate increase in their ability, as shown in Figure 12.5. Much schoolwork involves helping students make the transition from phase I to phase II, as illustrated by our earlier example of essay

Uncommon Sense

Talent Is Innate—Or Is It?

Many people believe that talent is genetically determined. To some extent, that is true, as students show wide individual differences in their performance across many domains. Math comes easily to some students; language or music comes naturally to others. But people also underestimate the individual's capacity for change and improvement. After all, some gold medalists from the Olympic Games held in the 1950s would not have enough talent to be selected for some of today's high school starting teams (Lehmann, 1998). This is so because talent is also rooted in hours of deliberate practice, instruction, coaching, feedback, and the kinds of activities identified in Figure 12.3. With more and more hours of deliberate practice, the relationship between natural ability and performance decreases whereas that between hours of deliberate practice and performance increases. For an example of this phenomenon, consider the words of three-time Olympic gold medalist Jackie Joyner-Kersee as she remembers her early years of deliberate practice:

If I know I've done the work, if I know I've done all the millions and millions of repeats and worked through all my mistakes, then I am confident I can give my best on the one shot that counts

(Joyner-Kersee, 1997)

(© AP/Wide World Photos)

writing. To attain an even higher level of proficiency, phase III is necessary. This phase features the decision to commit oneself to the domain and engage in many hours of deliberate practice in that domain.

Early talent plays into the model in Figure 12.5 because students who show early promise typically receive more encouragement to pursue deliberate practice. They may also receive more resources, such as books, tutors, and access to transportation so that they can spend time with coaches and attend events related to their area of interest (e.g., concerts, skating competitions). For these reasons, students who show early talent are likely to engage in more hours of deliberate practice over the years than are those who do not show early talent. But research on talent development makes it clear that number of hours of deliberate practice is at least as important as early talent. During deliberate practice, one's skill is constantly reorganized in response to instruction and feedback. The picture that emerges is that talent is not just a matter of genetic individual differences; rather, it reflects a combination of innate capacity, hours of deliberate practice, motivation to improve, and encouragement (van Lieshout & Heymans, 2000). (See the nearby Uncommon Sense box.)

Extremes of Intelligence

However one views intelligence, or intellectual ability, there are individuals whose performance on measures of intelligence is very strong or very weak. Different individuals have different strengths and weaknesses. Teachers can create a positive climate in their classroom by focusing on what students *can do* and using these strengths to address areas in which students are having difficulty.

The labels *gifted* and *intellectually disabled* have been used to describe people at the extremes of intelligence. There is a tendency to think of people in terms of such labels rather than as individuals with unique strengths and weaknesses. In part, this may be attributable to overreliance on the *normal curve*, a bell-shaped frequency distribution, to describe populations of individuals and their characteristics. Extremes of intelligence are identified in part by how far away from an average score an individual's IQ score is. A **standard deviation** is a measure of how far away from the average score a particular score is. A score that is two standard deviations away from the average score is an indicator of an extreme in intelligence (either high or low). Definitions of intellectual disability typically include an IQ below 70. At the other extreme, definitions of giftedness include an IQ of 130 or greater. Only about 5% of the population have IQ scores in the extreme range. The average IQ score is 100. Sixty-eight percent of the population have IQ scores within one standard deviation of the mean (between 85 and 115). Nearly 96% of the population have IQ scores within two standard deviations of the mean (between 70 and 130).

Figure 12.6 shows the normal curve, with IQ scores on the *x* axis. Look at the values of 70 and 130, the typical "cut points" for intellectual disabilities and giftedness. Does there seem to be anything special about them? Look just to the right and left of those points. Would you imagine that a person with an IQ of 129 is very different in terms of intellectual functioning than one with an IQ of 131? Scores on a standardized IQ test are only one of several criteria used for identifying students who are gifted or have intellectual disabilities.

standard deviation A measure of how far scores vary from the mean.

Giftedness

Psychologists have long been fascinated by exceptionally talented individuals. Ever since the publication of Galton's *Hereditary Genius* (1869), people with strong abilities or talents have been a focus of research. In education, separate programs for students with strong academic abilities are somewhat more recent. Laws in most states now require gifted education. One of the issues with regard to gifted education is the question of how to determine who is gifted. Most school districts base the decision on a combination of factors, including a measure of academic aptitude or intelligence, performance in school, and recommendations from teachers.

Approaches to gifted education vary widely. Some districts use *pull-out* programs in which gifted students are removed from their regular classes to receive special instruction. Other districts try to incorporate gifted instruction within general education classrooms. Still others accelerate

Figure 12.6 A Normal Distribution of IQ Scores

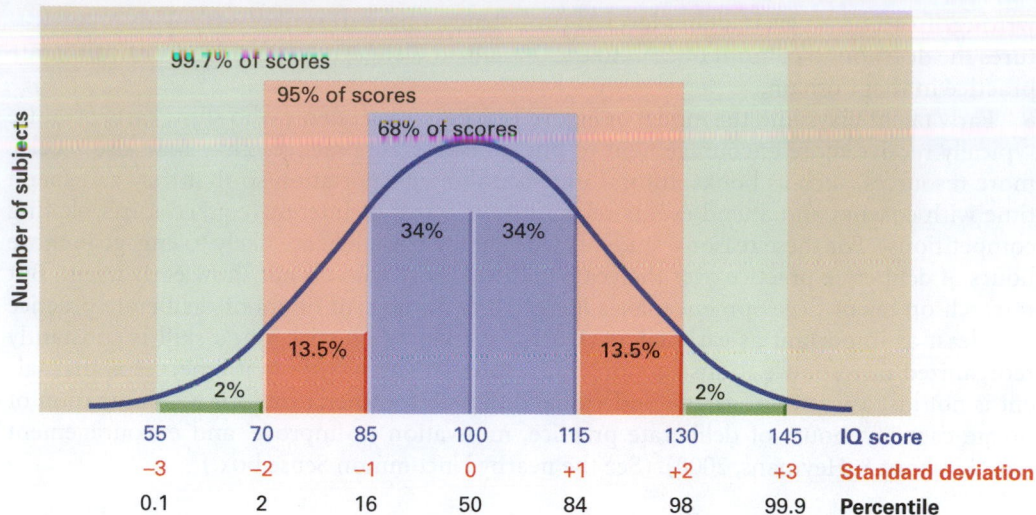

instruction in certain subject areas, such as mathematics or foreign languages. Gifted programs tend to be more common in elementary and middle schools than in high schools. At the high school level, students tend to "sort themselves out" through the selection of courses that interest them or for which they are judged capable. From the perspective of this chapter, it is important to keep in mind that even with a highly reliable measure, there is still a fair amount of error in tests of intelligence or ability. Decisions about a child's future should always be based on several sources of information. When different assessments of a child paint different pictures, it is necessary to obtain more information before making decisions.

Intellectual and Developmental Disabilities

The need to identify children with special needs properly and assess the level of those needs was the impetus for the first intelligence test (Binet & Simon, 1916). The American Association on Intellectual and Developmental Disabilities (AAIDD) defines the condition as follows:

> *Intellectual disability is a disability characterized by significant limitations both in intellectual functioning and in adaptive behavior, which covers many everyday social and practical skills. This disability originates before the age of 18. (AAIDD, 2011)*

The identification of individuals with intellectual disabilities typically includes an IQ score below the 70–75 range. It is important to understand that other factors are involved as well, including how well the individual adapts to new situations, functions in social settings, and handles day-to-day life. The information from this analysis needs to be combined with the test data in order to make an appropriate judgment about the person. The American Association for Intellectual and Developmental Disabilities focuses on the kinds of supports an individual will need in order to be able to function effectively.

Early research defined different levels of intellectual and developmental disabilities in terms of severity; in contrast, more recent work focuses on the type of support the individual needs. The individual with an intellectual disability experiences a mismatch between his or her competence and the demands made by the environment (AAIDD, 2011). The goal is to thoughtfully use social and cognitive supports to better align the individual's competence and the demands made on him or her. Examples of supports can include policies and procedures, behavioral contracts with the individual, and others (see AAIDD, 2011).

The American Association for Mental Retardation (AAMR) (now know as the American Association for Intellectual and Developmental Disabilities) described four levels of support (2002):

- Intermittent: The individual does not need constant, ongoing support, but rather needs support at certain times for certain tasks or transitions in life.
- Limited: The individual needs support in an ongoing and regular fashion, but the degree of support is not extensive.

RIDE Who would Mr. Morales, the teacher described at the beginning of the chapter, consult about Jaime?

Appendix
Extremes of Intelligence
You are likely to encounter students who vary greatly in their abilities. You will need to know how to accommodate these differences as you plan and implement your instruction (PRAXIS™, I.B.2, I.B.4; INTASC, Principles 1, 3).

- Extensive: The individual needs regular, ongoing support that is substantial. Individuals who require this level of support may need assistance in home or work settings on a daily basis.
- Pervasive: This level of support is ongoing and extensive. It is intense and is provided across different environments.

Differences in Ability and Instruction

However you define intelligence or ability, you can be certain that the students in your classroom will vary. From a practical standpoint, teachers must cope with variations in ability or intelligence, however they are defined. A number of options have been explored for managing variations in ability, achievement, or intelligence. One of them is to group children by ability. This is often done by assigning children to classes based on measured ability, a procedure known as **between-class ability grouping**. Low achievers are assigned to one class, average achievers to another, and high achievers to a third. All instruction occurs within these groups. In contrast, children can be assigned to ability groups *within* a class. In this approach, a child may be in the high-achievement group for reading but in the average-achievement group for mathematics. In other words, in **within-class ability grouping**, children are not permanently assigned to a particular group.

Between-Class Ability Grouping

Between-class ability grouping (also called "tracking" or "streaming") occurs when children are assigned to particular classes based on their performance or measured ability. This practice is not common in elementary schools at present. At the high school level, students are often *tracked* into advanced-placement courses, college preparatory courses, and more general courses. In 1990, the Second International Mathematics Study (SIMS) reported that ability grouping was used more frequently in the United States than in other countries that participated in the study (Oakes, 1990).

Ability grouping is controversial. Some who support it argue that gifted students should be educated together because they are not challenged enough in regular classes (Kulik, 1992). Other advocates of ability grouping point to the potential for providing more appropriate curricula and teacher attention to students at the same ability level. Those who oppose ability grouping emphasize the negative effects on low achievers. Students in low-ability tracks have difficulty moving into higher tracks and tend to receive lower-quality instruction (Dreeben & Gamoran, 1986; Gamoran & Mare, 1989; Oakes, 1990; Veldman & Sanford, 1984).

Robert Slavin conducted extensive reviews of the effects of ability grouping in comparison with heterogeneous grouping in both elementary and secondary schools (Slavin, 1987a, 1990). He concluded that there are no advantages associated with ability grouping. Others disagree (Gamoran, 1987; Hallinan, 1990; Hiebert, 1987). The topic thus remains controversial, and the available research has not shown conclusively how ability grouping influences student achievement (Sloane, 2003). A key factor that links grouping and achievement is the quality of the instruction provided (Gamoran, 1987).

The National Association of School Psychologists (NASP) recommends the use of heterogeneous grouping (NASP, 2002). *Multi-age grouping* (also called *nongraded classrooms*), in which classes include children of various ages (e.g., kindergarten through second grade), is one approach of this type. In this approach, children's abilities are less subject to social comparison within their age groups. Research studies show that students in nongraded classrooms perform as well or better than students in traditional classrooms (Anderson & Pavan, 1993; Gutierrez & Slavin, 1992). In addition to positive achievement effects, multi-age classrooms are associated with other gains, such as increases in students' self-esteem and willingness to take responsibility for their own learning (Gutierrez & Slavin, 1992; Mackey, Johnson, & Wood, 1995).

Elizabeth Cohen developed the multiple-abilities treatment to minimize the differentiation among students in a classroom (Cohen, 1994; Cohen & Lotan, 1997). The intent of this program, called *Complex Instruction*, is to promote participation by all students.

between-class ability grouping A procedure in which children are assigned to different classes based on measured ability.

within-class ability grouping A system in which children are assigned to ability groups within a class.

Appendix
Promoting Learning for All
You will need to consider your students' various skills, abilities, and interests and design instruction that is appropriate to their needs (PRAXIS™, I.B.4; INTASC, Principles 1, 3).

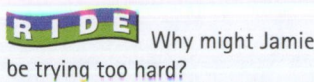

Why might Jamie be trying too hard?

Students work on complex tasks to which all of them can contribute but which none of them can complete alone. Like the other approaches discussed in this section, Complex Instruction attempts to reduce the focus on a narrow set of skills and increase participation by all students.

Within-Class Ability Grouping

Within-class ability grouping involves assigning students in a heterogeneous classroom to homogeneous groups for instruction in specific subjects, such as mathematics and reading. A child is assigned to a reading group, for example, based on his or her current functioning with respect to reading. The same child may be placed in a group at a different level for instruction in mathematics. In an analysis of various studies of within-class ability grouping, Slavin concluded that it can be effective if the instructional pace and materials are adapted to the students' needs (Slavin, 1987b). An important factor in the use of within-class ability grouping is the need for continued assessment so that children can move to another group when their competence increases.

Learners with Special Needs

This chapter has focused so far on the variability that we see in children. It has touched at several points on variability that is exceptional in one fashion or another. It has also looked at how factors such as practice and effort can affect one's capabilities. In looking at individual children, it is not difficult to see areas of strength and potential, and other areas where special efforts will be needed to reach desired goals.

One might reasonably say that every child has special needs. However, the term *special needs* is used in a specific sense to refer to children who have been identified by the school system as having needs that are significant enough to warrant special educational services. In 1976–1977, the number of students under age 21 who were being served in federally supported programs for individuals with disabilities was 3,694,000. In 2011, the number of students served had grown to 6.5 million. This change represented an increase in number served as a percentage of total enrollments from 8.32% to 13.01%. In the earlier time period, 26% of the students served had specific learning disabilities. In the 2004–2005 school year, the percentage had risen to 48% (U.S. Department of Education, 2006). This means that all teachers are likely to encounter students with special needs at some time in their careers.

The Law and Special Education

The Education for All Handicapped Children Act (Public Law 94-142) was passed in 1975. It required states to provide every child between the ages of 3 and 21 with a free and appropriate education, regardless of the severity of the child's handicap. PL 99-457 (1986) extended the requirement for a free and appropriate education to all handicapped children between the ages of 3 and 5. In 1990, the Americans with Disabilities Act extended the rights of individuals with disabilities in areas such as transportation, employment, and telecommunications. PL 94-142 was amended in 1990 by the Individuals with Disabilities Education Act (IDEA), which was reauthorized in 1997 and again in 2004.

The initial law (PL 94-142) required that students be educated in the least restrictive environment possible. The intent was to allow children to be educated with their peers as much as possible. The available options included in-class support, pull-out programs in resource rooms, self-contained classrooms, special day schools, residential schools, and hospitals or home. The further away from the normal classroom a student was placed, the more restrictive the environment was considered to be.

The 2004 IDEA legislation states that multiple measures must be used to identify children with disabilities and that these measures should be selected so as not to discriminate on a cultural or racial basis. The tests used must be valid and reliable.

A key change in IDEA 2004 is a statement of the qualifications required of special education teachers. They must demonstrate competence in all the core academic subjects they teach in the same manner as is required for an elementary, middle, or secondary school teacher.

Each child with a disability must be provided with an **individualized education program (IEP)** written by a child study team that includes the student's parents or guardians, the student's teachers, a school psychologist, and a special education supervisor. The IEP should include information about the following:

- The student's current level of performance
- Measurable educational or behavioral goals for the year
- A description of how the child's progress toward meeting the goals will be measured
- A statement of special education and related services, based on scientific research where possible, that will be given to the student
- A description of the student's participation in the regular school program
- An explanation of the child's nonparticipation with nondisabled children in the classroom (if applicable)
- For older students, descriptions of services that are needed to help the student make a transition toward further education or work in adult life

An example of an IEP is presented in Figure 12.7. Curt is a ninth-grade low achiever who was considered by the district to be a poorly motivated, disciplinary problem student with a "bad attitude." His parents recognized him as a very discouraged, frustrated student who had learning disabilities, especially in language arts.

The IEP team for a student should include no less than one regular teacher of the student, no less than one special education teacher, someone who can interpret the instructional implications of the evaluation, other people with appropriate expertise, and, when appropriate, the student. The team also needs to consider special factors, such as the student's language needs. Planning for the transition from school to work or other postgraduate activities begins when the child is 13, and implementation of the plan in terms of identifying and activating services begins when the child is 16. Members of the IEP team are required to consider the child's strengths; the concerns of his or her parents; the results of the evaluation; and the child's academic, developmental, and functional needs. Under the new law, states may propose to develop multiyear IEPs covering up to three years in order to provide long-term planning for a child.

A third provision of the initial PL 94-142 that remains in effect protects the rights of students and families. The Family Educational Rights and Privacy Act (FERPA; 1974) was written to ensure that schools do not release information about a child's educational records without the permission of his or her parents or guardians. Schools must have procedures for keeping students' records confidential. The aim of this law is to ensure that parents and guardians have access to their child's educational records and that schools do not give that information to others without permission.

Additional protection for students with disabilities is provided by Section 504 of the Rehabilitation Act, which was passed in 1973. This law bars discrimination against people with disabilities in any program that receives federal funds, including public schools. It guarantees that children with disabilities have a right to participate in school activities. Table 12.2 provides an overview of the differences between these two laws.

The No Child Left Behind Act of 2001 requires that students with special needs participate in statewide testing and that they meet state standards for achievement. In response to the National Survey of Public School Teachers 2003, 84% of teachers object to the idea that special education students should be expected to meet the same content standards as students of the same age in general education classes (McCabe, 2004).

Identifying Children with Special Needs

The identification of children with special needs may begin informally when a teacher sees that a child appears to be having difficulties relative to other children. The child may, for example, have trouble learning to read or have more behavioral problems than is typical. The teacher may begin a prereferral process in which efforts are made to address the child's needs in the classroom. If the problem continues, the child may be referred for a formal evaluation.

individualized education program (IEP) An educational and behavioral intervention plan for a student with special needs.

Unique Educational Needs, Characteristics, and Present Levels of Performance	Special Education, Related Services, Supplemental Aids & Services, Assistive Technology, Program Modifications, Support for Personnel	Measurable Annual Goals & Short-Term Objectives or Benchmarks •To enable student to participate in the general curriculum •To meet other needs resulting from the disability
(including how the disability affects the student's ability to progress in the general curriculum)	*(including frequency, duration, & location)*	*(including how progress toward goals will be measured)*
Present Level of Social Skills: Curt lashes out violently when not able to complete work, uses profanity, and refuses to follow further directions from adults.	1. Teacher and/or counselor consult with behavior specialist regarding techniques and programs for teaching skills, especially anger management.	*Goal:* During the last quarter of the academic year, Curt will have 2 or fewer detentions for any reason. Obj. 1: At the end of the 1st quarter, Curt will have had 10 or fewer detentions. Obj. 2: At the end of the 2nd quarter, Curt will have had 7 or fewer detentions. Obj. 3: At the end of the 3rd quarter, Curt will have had 4 or fewer detentions.
Special Needs: •To learn anger management skills, especially regarding swearing •To learn to comply with requests	2. Provide anger management instruction to Curt. Services 3 times/week, 30 minutes. 3. Establish a peer group which involves role playing, etc., so Curt can see positive role models and practice newly learned anger management skills. Services 2 times/week, 30 minutes. 4. Develop a behavioral plan for Curt which gives him responsibility for charting his own behavior. 5. Provide a teacher or some other adult mentor to spend time with Curt (talking, game playing, physical activity, etc.). Services 2 times/week, 30 minutes. 6. Provide training for the mentor regarding Curt's needs/goals.	*Goal:* Curt will manage his behavior and language in a reasonably acceptable manner as reported by faculty and peers. Obj. 1: At 2 weeks, asked at the end of class if Curt's behavior and language were acceptable, 3 out of 6 teachers will say "acceptable." Obj. 2: At 6 weeks, asked the same question, 4 out of 6 teachers will say "acceptable." Obj. 3: At 12 weeks, asked the same question, 6 out of 6 teachers will say "acceptable."

Study Skills/Organizational Needs:
How to read text
Note taking
How to study notes
Memory work
Be prepared for class, with materials
Lengthen and improve attention span and on-task behavior
 	
Present Level:
Curt currently lacks skill in all these areas.
	1. Speech/lang. therapist, resource room teacher, and content area teachers will provide Curt with direct and specific teaching of study skills, i.e.
	    Note taking from lectures
	    Note taking while reading text
	    How to study notes for a test
	    Memorization hints
	    Strategies for reading text to retain information
	
	2. Assign a "study buddy" for Curt in each content area class.
	
	3. Prepare a motivation system for Curt to be prepared for class with all necessary materials.
	
	4. Develop a motivational plan to encourage Curt to lengthen his attention span and time on task.
	
	5. Provide aide to monitor on-task behaviors in the first month or so of plan and teach Curt self-monitoring techniques.
	
	6. Provide motivational system and self-recording form for completion of academic tasks in each class.
		Goal: At the end of academic year, Curt will have better grades and, by his own report, will have learned new study skills.
		Obj. 1: Given a 20-30 min. lecture/oral lesson, Curt will take appropriate notes as judged by that teacher.
		Obj. 2: Given 10-15 pgs. of text to read, Curt will employ an appropriate strategy for retaining info.—i.e., mapping, webbing, outlining, notes, etc.—as judged by the teacher.
		Obj. 3: Given notes to study for a test, Curt will do so successfully as evidenced by his test score.
		
		Goal: Curt will improve his on-task behavior from 37% to 80% as measured by a qualified observer at year's end.
		Obj. 1: By 1 month, Curt's on-task behavior will increase to 45%.
		Obj. 2: By 3 months, Curt's on-task behavior will increase to 60%.
		Obj. 3: By 6 months, Curt's on-task behavior will increase to 80% and maintain or improve until end of the year.

Figure 12.7 Example of an IEP

(continued)

Source: Bateman, B. D., & Linden, M. A. (1998). *Better IEPS* (3rd ed.). Longmont, CO: Sopris West Educational Services.
Copyright 1998 by Sopris West Educational Services. Reprinted with permission.

Unique Educational Needs, Characteristics, and Present Levels of Performance	Special Education, Related Services, Supplemental Aids & Services, Assistive Technology, Program Modifications, Support for Personnel	Measurable Annual Goals & Short-Term Objectives or Benchmarks •To enable student to participate in the general curriculum •To meet other needs resulting from the disability
(including how the disability affects the student's ability to progress in the general curriculum)	*(including frequency, duration, & location)*	*(including how progress toward goals will be measured)*
Academic Needs/Written Language: Curt needs strong remedial help in spelling, punctuation, capitalization, and usage. Present Level: Curt is approximately 2 grade levels behind his peers in these skills.	1. Provide direct instruction in written language skills (punctuation, capitalization, usage, spelling) by using a highly structured, well-sequenced program. Services provided in small group of no more than four students in the resource room, 50 minutes/day. 2. Build in continuous and cumulative review to help with short-term rote memory difficulty. 3. Develop a list of commonly used words in student writing (or use one of many published lists) for Curt's spelling program.	*Goal:* Within one academic year, Curt will improve his written language skills by 1.5 or 2 full grade levels. Obj. 1: Given 10 sentences of dictation at his current level of instruction, Curt will punctuate and capitalize with 90% accuracy (checked at the end of each unit taught). Obj. 2: Given 30 sentences with choices of usage, at his current instructional level, Curt will perform with 90% accuracy. Obj. 3: Given a list of 150 commonly used words in writing, Curt will spell with 90% accuracy.

Adaptations to Regular Program:
- In all classes, Curt should sit near the front of the class.
- Curt should be called on often to keep him involved and on task.
- All teachers should help Curt with study skills as trained by spelling/language specialist and resource room teacher.
- Teachers should monitor Curt's work closely in the beginning weeks, months of his program.

Figure 12.7 (continued) Example of an IEP

Prereferral Processes In response to the rapid increase in the number of students in special education, prereferral intervention teams have become widespread (Buck et al., 2003). These teams (which go by a variety of names, such as pupil assistance committees, teacher intervention teams, or teacher assistance teams) have succeeded in reducing the number of inappropriate referrals for special education services (Kovaleski et al., 1999). Despite variations in how they function, the teams share a number of features (Buck et al., 2003):

- The process focuses on prevention.
- Interventions are designed, employed, and evaluated prior to a formal referral for special education.
- The team uses a problem-solving approach: It reviews information about the child, generates hypotheses about the causes of his or her problems, and designs strategies for intervention. (This process is not unlike the RIDE process you have used throughout this text.)
- The team develops a specific intervention that is implemented by the classroom teacher.
- The team evaluates the effectiveness of the intervention after a specified length of time.

Among the benefits associated with the use of prereferral teams is that a child receives assistance in his or her own class before being considered for special education. The fact that team members collaborate in the interests of the child is also a benefit. Effective interventions at an early stage reduce the number of inappropriate referrals for special education and result in cost savings (Buck et al., 2003).

Referrals If the child's problems persist despite the interventions proposed by the prereferral team, the child may be referred for evaluation for special education services. A school professional may request that a child be evaluated to determine whether he or she has a

TABLE 12.2

Understanding the Differences between IDEA and Section 504

	IDEA	Section 504
Purpose of law	Federal statute that governs all special education law in the United States.	Federal civil rights statute that requires all schools, public and private, that receive federal financial assistance not to discriminate against children with disabilities.
Identification	School districts are required to identify all children in the district who may have a disability. Children living in the district who do not attend public schools are included.	
Eligibility	(a) Child must meet eligibility requirements in one or more of 13 categories or (b) at the discretion of the state and school district, a child aged 3 to 9 may be eligible if he or she is experiencing delays in physical, cognitive, communication, social, emotional, or adaptive development; such delays require special education and related services.	The existence of an identified physical or mental condition (e.g., asthma, ADHD) substantially limits a major life activity. Among these activities are seeing, walking, breathing, working, speaking, learning, and caring for oneself. The school district is allowed to determine whether an impairment "substantially limits" a major life activity. Eligibility is broader under Section 504 than under IDEA.
Evaluation	• Full evaluation by a multidisciplinary team • Requires informed and written consent from parents/guardians • Reevaluation of each child if conditions warrant or if requested by teacher or parents, but at least once every three years • Provides for independent evaluation at district's expense if parents disagree with first evaluation	• Information gathered from a variety of professional sources (e.g., classroom teacher) • Requires notice to parents but not consent (although good practice indicates use of informed consent)
Appropriate education	• Requires an individualized education plan (IEP)	

Source: Adapted from "Understanding the differences between IDEA and Section 504" by Laurie deBettencourt, *Teaching Exceptional Children*, Vol. 34, 2002, 16–23. Copyright 2002 by The Council for Exceptional Children. Adapted and reprinted with permission.

disability. Parents may also initiate the request for evaluation. The parents or guardians of a child must consent to the evaluation. The evaluation may be conducted by a school psychologist and will include assessments in all areas that are related to the child's suspected disability. The results of the evaluation are used to determine whether the child is eligible for special education services. Parents who disagree with the results of an evaluation can request an independent educational evaluation (IEE). A group of qualified professionals, along with the parents, examine the evaluation results to determine whether the child is eligible for services. If the child is found to be eligible for services under IDEA, the IEP team has 30 days to write an IEP for the child. This process is outlined in Figure 12.8.

Some parents resist having their children declared eligible for special services because they may be concerned about the negative effects of the special needs label. Special services cannot be provided unless a child is found to be eligible for them, and this includes classifying or labeling the child's needs. Labels can both help and stigmatize a child (Heward & Orlansky, 1992; Keogh & MacMillan, 1996). The imposition of the label can result in services being provided. Sometimes, students with disabilities are regarded in a stereotypic manner. Teachers can reduce potential problems by modeling respect for students with disabilities and creating a classroom climate in which differences among students are valued.

Inclusion

The requirements of IDEA 2004 and Section 504 of the Rehabilitation Act of 1973 have increased the responsibilities of regular classroom teachers in implementing educational programs for classified and at-risk students. (Approximately 75% of the students served under

MINDFUL HABITS OF EFFECTIVE TEACHERS

Effective teachers are committed to their profession. They work to develop their skills and are dedicated to their students.

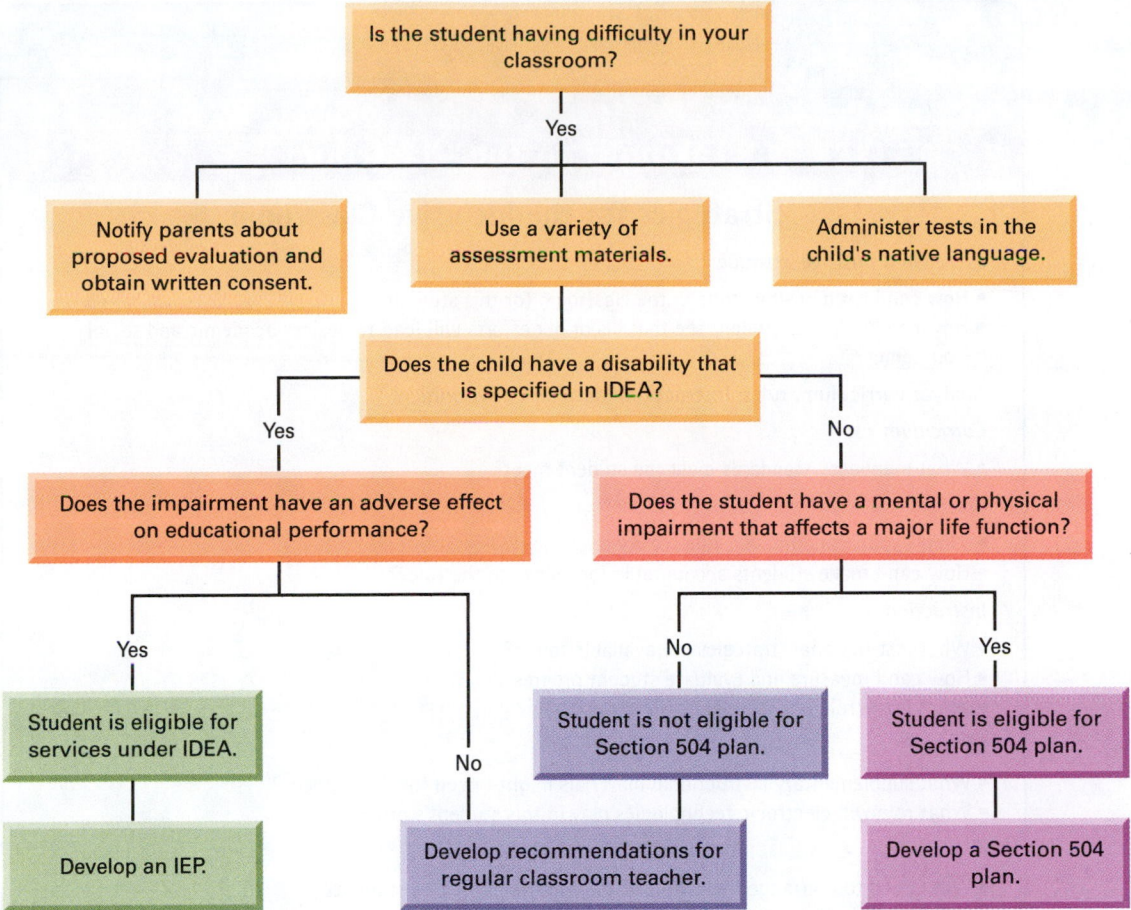

Figure 12.8 **Questions to Ask When Determining Appropriate Services**

Source: Adapted from "Understanding the differences between IDEA and Section 504" by Laurie deBettencourt, *Teaching Exceptional Children*, Vol. 34, 2002, 16–23. Copyright 2002 by The Council for Exceptional Children. Adapted and reprinted with permission.

IDEA are in general education classrooms for some part of the school day.) The reauthorization of IDEA in 1997 added the regular classroom teacher to the IEP team because that teacher would have a great deal of responsibility for implementing the program designed by the IEP team. This approach was maintained in the 2004 reauthorization of the law. These increased responsibilities make it necessary to develop strategies to help classified students adapt to a variety of classroom elements. Examples of such strategies are presented in the nearby Taking It to the Classroom box.

Prevalent Student Needs and Challenges

With changing laws related to special education, teachers encounter more students in their classes with special needs. Among the most prevalent kinds of students with special needs are those with learning disabilities and attention-deficit disorder.

Learning Disabilities

In 2004–2005, more than 2,800,000 children under age 21 were identified as having specific learning disabilities. Less than 1% of children between the ages of 6 and 21 diagnosed with specific learning disabilities were educated outside regular classrooms (U.S. Department of Education, 2000). Forty-four percent of students with learning disabilities spent 80% or more of each school day in their regular classrooms. An additional 39% spent between 40% and 79% of their time in their regular classrooms.

Taking It to the Classroom

Strategies for the Inclusive Classroom

Establish a positive attitude

- How can I set a positive tone in the classroom for this student?
- How can I help this student see that his or her efforts will lead to desired academic and social outcomes?

Analyze curriculum, rules, instruction, materials, environment

Curriculum

- What mandated standards must the student meet?

Rules

- What explicit and implicit rules of conduct should I establish for students?
- How can I make students accountable for following the rules?

Instruction

- What instructional strategies are available to me?
- How can I measure and evaluate student progress?
- What is the role of group work in my classroom?

Materials

- What supplementary instructional materials might I need for this student?
- What role will electronic technologies play in this student's program?

Environment

- Will I need to rearrange the layout of the classroom for this student?
- Will I need to adjust the daily instructional schedule?

Identify student characteristics (i.e., strengths and weaknesses)

- Academic skills
- Social skills
- Learning preferences

Learning disabilities are invisible. A student's low achievement in school may be an indicator of a learning disability, but not all learning problems are due to disabilities. Learning disabilities can be divided into three broad categories: (1) developmental speech and language disorders, (2) academic skills disorders, and (3) other disabilities [National Institute of Mental Health (NIMH), 2004]. Developmental speech and language disorders include disorders of articulation, expressive language, and receptive language. Problems with language are often the earliest indicators of a learning disability. Articulation disorders often can be corrected with speech therapy. Problems with expressive language or the communication of ideas or thoughts greatly hinder a child's ability to participate in school activities. Problems with receptive language or comprehending language produced by others are also major obstacles to cognitive development. Speech therapy can be successful in improving certain kinds of children's language difficulties. Achievement skills disorders include difficulties with reading, mathematics, and writing.

Under IDEA 2004, a team of qualified professionals and parent must determine that a

child does not achieve adequately for the child's age or to meet State-approved grade level standards in one or more of the following areas.(i) Oral expression. (ii) Listening comprehension. (iii) Written expression. (iv) Basic Reading skill. (v) Reading fluency skills. (vi) Reading comprehension. (vii) Mathematics calculation, (viii) Mathematics problem-solving or that the child does not make sufficient progress to meet State-approved grade-level standards in one or more of the area identified [above] when using a process based on the child's response to intervention... (34 C.F.R. 300.309)

One method of identifying students with specific learning disabilities is to look for a discrepancy between a student's measured IQ and his or her achievement. One of the problems with this approach to identifying learning disabilities is that the student may have experienced considerable failure before the disability is diagnosed. In 1996, 94% of states surveyed included the discrepancy component in their identification process (Mercer, Jordan, Allsopp, & Mercer,1996). Under IDEA 2004, states are not required to use the discrepancy factor.

Response to Intervention as an Identification Process The reauthorization of IDEA (2004) does not require schools to use a severe discrepancy between current achievement and measured intellectual ability to determine whether a child has a learning disability. The school may instead use an evaluation process to find out whether the child will respond to a scientific, research-based intervention. In other words, the child's response to instruction can become part of the evaluative process.

The **response to intervention (RTI)** as a process for identifying students with learning disabilities has resulted from concerns about the delay in identification of disabilities under the discrepancy model and the delay in initiation of remediation or early intervention (Mercer & Pullen, 2009). A number of tiers of instruction are involved. At tier 1, students are expected to receive high-quality instruction in the general education classroom. Such instruction should be the result of research-based practices. At tier 2, students are instructed in small groups. Progress is monitored carefully and judgments are made about the students' responses to the intervention. After an appropriate period of time has elapsed, a third tier of intervention is introduced. This often involves intensive one-on-one instruction. The goal of the response to intervention method of identifying specific learning disabilities is to maximize a student's likelihood of success by intervening early and intensively. Fuchs and Deshler (2007) argue that much remains to be known about the effectiveness of RTI.

Students with learning disabilities face increased cognitive challenges as they enter adolescence. Difficulties with executive functioning and working memory pose increased challenges as the middle school curriculum becomes more demanding. Students in middle school are required to increasingly extract information from texts, from lectures, and from discussions. The deficits these students experience in executive functioning make the tasks of selecting ideas to record, and actually recording them effectively, very difficult for them. Furthermore, students with learning disabilities encounter many challenges, both academically and socially, as they move into adolescence. They may also experience difficulty with expressing their ideas in writing. Because of deficits in working memory and central executive functioning, students with specific learning disabilities need support if they are to benefit from their classes.

response to intervention (RTI)
A method of providing early, high-quality academic intervention to students at risk for school failure.

Autism and Related Disorders

Autism has been a separate category under IDEA since 1990. Autistic children are characterized by extreme social withdrawal, deficiencies in cognitive processes, and language disorders. Symptoms such as the following must be present before the child is 3 years old: lack of eye contact, lack of reciprocal conversation, and atypical sensorimotor processing (National Education Association, 2006).

Approximately 7.5 cases of autism are found per 10,000 children (Hallahan & Kauffman, 2003), and the percentage of students with autism is growing at a rate of 10% to 15% new autism diagnoses each school year. Also, autism is more common in boys than in girls by a 4:1 ratio. Children do not outgrow autism, but its symptoms can be lessened over time with coping responses and treatment. Related disorders include Asperger's syndrome and pervasive developmental disorder (PDD), which is characterized by abnormal social relations and interactions. Autistic spectrum disorder describes a range of disorders that are indicative of symptoms of autism but may range in severity from mild to severe. No single behavior is always typical of autism, and the manifestation of autism is quite varied. Among the behaviors that may be present in autistic children are the following (Hallahan & Kauffman, 2003):

- Impaired social responsiveness. The child does not respond to other people in a typical fashion.
- Impaired communication. The child may have impaired verbal and nonverbal communication.

Taking It to the Classroom

Strategies for the Inclusive Classroom

Compare student characteristics with the learning environment

- Identify each significant student characteristic as either a "facilitator," a "barrier," or a "neutral" element within the classroom environment. (For example, poor social skills may be viewed as a barrier to group work.) Following is an example:

Category	My Classroom	Facilitators	Neutral	Barriers
Curriculum	State curriculum standards	Conceptual understanding; verbal expression		Reading; writing
Rules	Complete own work			Independent work
	Class on time		X	
	Homework on time			Forgetful
Instruction	Lecture	Auditory skills		
	Independent work			Reading; writing; not a learning preference
	Group work	Learning preference Gets along well with others		
	Chapter questions	Conceptual understanding		Reading; writing
	Weekly written tests	Conceptual understanding		Reading; writing
Materials Environment	Crowded room Auditory distractions			

Select small sets of

- Classroom elements that can be readily modified for the student
- Skills to develop in the student

Collaborate with other professionals who will be involved either directly or indirectly in the student's progress. Among these professionals are

- School nurses
- Therapists
- Psychologists
- Learning specialists
- Guidance counselors
- Social workers

Review and revise

- Examine the student's progress toward his or her targeted goals. Which adaptations in the program need to be adjusted? Which ones can be faded or eliminated?

Source: Adapted from "She will succeed! Strategies for success in inclusive classrooms" by M. A. Prater, *Teaching Exceptional Children*, Vol. 35, 2003, 58–64. Copyright 2003 by The Council for Exceptional Children. Adapted and reprinted with permission.

- Stereotypic or ritualistic behavior. The child may exhibit repetitive stereotypic behavior. Examples of stereotypic behavior may include rocking back and forth on one's heels or flapping one's hands.
- Preoccupation with objects and narrow range of interests. Autistic children may play with the same object for extensive periods. They may experience difficulty with changes (Adreon & Stella, 2001).

Teachers who have students in their classes with autistic tendencies will need to provide substantial support to these children. They will need to create a predictable environment and address issues of limited social awareness that these children may have, as well as other difficulties. Specifically, teachers can help meet the special needs of students with autism by giving them extra time to respond to questions and classroom events, identifying the important elements within a relatively complex task, sequencing information or projects into steps, respecting sensory sensitivities (e.g., flickering fluorescent lights, the ringing school bell), and helping students manage their time and make transitions between activities (Thiers, 2007).

Physical and Sensory Challenges

Some students face physical and sensory challenges in their day-to-day lives, including life in school. Sometimes these challenges are combined with cognitive impairments, sometimes not. How successful the children will be in any given year will depend, in large part, on their teachers.

If you wear glasses or contact lenses, then you have a sensory impairment (although probably a mild one). Visual impairment can range from easily correctable difficulties to total blindness. The same range of impairment occurs with hearing as well. Some students need a hearing aid, while others cannot hear at all. Other students have challenges with mobility or coordination. You are less likely to have a child with severe problems in these areas than mild ones, but you need to be sensitive to a host of issues related to these challenges.

From an instructional perspective, these challenges in the physical or sensory domains are substantial but well understood. In the physical domain, students may have problems with muscle tone, gross or fine motor skills, or communication skills, or they may have mobility problems requiring use of a wheelchair. Additionally, some students who are afflicted with chronic illness may have problems with stamina or the ability to attend to instruction for long periods of time.

Assistive Technology Most students with a physical or sensory challenge will use assistive technology of some sort. This might be as simple as a pair of glasses or a walker, but it might be more complicated and might be used only in certain settings or conditions. Assistive technologies might relate to everyday living, mobility, learning in school, sensory input, or communication. They might be as simple as a calculator or a set of symbols on cards to help in communication. They might be as complex as a motorized wheelchair or a keyboard adapted for special needs. As a teacher of a child who uses assistive technology, you will want to be familiar with the issues associated with that device. The following two Web sites are good places to start to look at issues related to assistive technology:

http://www.wati.org/ (Wisconsin Assistive Technology Initiative)

http://www.sc.edu/scatp/ (South Carolina Assistive Technology Program)

Classroom and Social Issues for Students with Physical and Sensory Challenges Students with physical and sensory challenges have to deal with these issues on a 24/7 basis. There is no time off from being hard of hearing or being a wheelchair user. Maes and Grietens (2004) point out that children with sensory problems included in regular classrooms are continually confronted with the differentness of their personal situation, potentially causing insecurity and a lack of confidence. Some children will have dealt with these issues from birth; others will have impairments as a result of injury or disease. These impairments often impact the child's social and emotional development as well as family relationships (Ammerman, Van Hasselt, & Hersen, 1986; Dote-Kwan, Hughes, & Taylor, 1997). Although some research has shown that students with sensory problems experience difficulty in school in a variety of spheres (academic, social, and behavioral), Maes and Grietens compared parent perceptions of children with sensory difficulties (hearing and seeing) to a matched sample of students without these difficulties. What parents report is that the primary problem has to do with the social life of the students.

Looking at elementary-grade students with physical challenges, Coster and Haltiwanger (2004) found that these students possessed what might be considered basic social skills but lacked the ability to demonstrate those skills consistently across a variety of school settings. In particular, there seemed to be a problem with social approach or initiation of social interaction. In a study comparing experiences of students with physical disabilities in regular schools or special schools for students with disabilities in Australia, Curtin and Clarke (2004) found that the special schools were generally easier from a social perspective for students with disabilities. This quote from a girl in a regular secondary school is typical of what they found:

"I have tried really hard to make friends. I used to go hell for leather and would smile and be nice but no one made any effort back towards me. ... they thought that I was going to tarnish their reputation or something because I was in a wheelchair or because I was a complete boff at most things." (p. 204)

Costner and Haltiwanger (2004) argue that teachers need to be highly sensitive to issues concerning social development for children with physical disabilities. This no doubt is true for students with sensory challenges as well.

Attention–Deficit Disorder

Two special needs that are not included in the official list of disabilities in IDEA 2004 are attention-deficit disorder (ADD) and attention-deficit/hyperactivity disorder (ADHD). Attention is needed for taking in information and also producing it when needed. Some students experience difficulty in managing their attention. **Attention–deficit disorder (ADD)** is a condition in which children experience persistent difficulties with attention span, impulse control, and sometimes hyperactivity. It is an emotional/behavioral disorder, not a learning disability. Between 3% and 5% of the school-age population is affected by ADD. According to the *Diagnostic and Statistical Manual*, fourth edition, of the American Psychiatric Association (APA, 1994), or DSM-IV, signs of inattention include the following:

- Becoming easily distracted by irrelevant sights and sounds
- Failing to pay attention to details and making careless mistakes
- Rarely following instructions carefully and completely
- Has difficulties organizing tasks and activities
- Losing or forgetting things such as toys, pencils, books, and tools needed for a task (NIMH, 2004)

Attention–Deficit/Hyperactivity Disorder

Attention–deficit/hyperactivity disorder (ADHD) is a neurological condition that involves problems with inattention, impulsivity, and self-regulation that are developmentally inconsistent with the student's age (Barkley, 1997). Typically, about one-third of students with ADHD have one of the other learning disabilities, usually either a specific learning disability or an emotional disturbance (Cantwell & Baker, 1991; Zentall, 1993). The critical question in determining whether ADHD constitutes a special need is whether it interferes with the student's learning (because it sometimes does not).

A child who cannot pay attention will have difficulty learning. Any classroom provides challenges to a child who is trying to focus on a learning task. The number of children in the room and the constant interruptions that occur in most classrooms make it difficult for any child to pay attention. For a child with ADHD, the challenge of attending to instruction is much greater. ADD and ADHD differ because of the presence of hyperactivity and impulsiveness in ADHD (NIMH, 2004). A hyperactive child is excessively active, may be unable to sit still, and may fidget even when seated. A child with ADHD may also be impulsive. Signs of hyperactivity and impulsivity include the following:

- Feeling restless, often fidgeting with hands or feet, or squirming
- Running, climbing, or leaving a seat in situations in which sitting or quiet behavior is expected
- Blurting out an answer before hearing the whole question
- Having difficulty waiting in line or for a turn

All children exhibit these kinds of behaviors from time to time. DSM-IV contains guidelines for identifying ADHD that include the requirement that the behaviors must appear before the age of 7 and continue for at least six months. An important aspect of determining whether a particular disorder exists is that the behavior must be observed over a specified period.

attention–deficit disorder (ADD) A condition in which children experience persistent difficulties with attention span, impulse control, and sometimes hyperactivity.

attention–deficit/hyperactivity disorder (ADHD) A condition in which children or adults consistently display inattention, hyperactivity, and impulsiveness.

The child's teacher may be the first person to notice that a child is hyperactive and may consult other school personnel about a possible evaluation. A prereferral process such as that described earlier may be the first course of action. Because teachers deal with a variety of children (and experienced teachers have encountered many hundreds of children), the teacher will probably have a good idea of what constitutes average behavior for a child of a particular age. Teachers of younger children will also be aware of different developmental patterns and will expect some variation in what constitutes average behavior. When such a teacher identifies a child as significantly different from the average, further analysis is required. A note of caution: Teachers are not immune from expectation effects and may misread a situation. A teacher could ask a colleague to observe a child in order to provide another perspective on the child's behavior. Observational studies of children who are diagnosed as hyperactive support the idea that there are readily observable differences in behavior between children who exhibit the disorder and those who do not (Luk, 1985). This advice is particularly important for beginning teachers, who have a smaller base of experience on which to judge how different a particular child's behavior is. Getting a colleague to "look in" on a class and pay particular attention to a child who has been a cause for concern can be particularly helpful.

R I D E Does Jamie fit the ADHD profile, or is he just someone who needs a little extra monitoring to keep him with the class?

Educational Options Table 12.3 includes descriptions of behaviors that may be characteristic of a child with ADHD and some general strategies for working with such a child. Children with ADHD vary in the severity of their disorder. Some may be unable to participate effectively in the classroom, whereas many others, given appropriate accommodations, can be very successful. In general, a teacher should try to minimize distractions and help the child regulate his or her behavior. (See the near by Taking It to the Classroom box.)

Children with ADHD are often treated with medication. A commonly prescribed medication is Ritalin, which is a stimulant. Such medications often reduce children's hyperactivity and improve their ability to pay attention. The use of medication to treat hyperactivity on a continuous basis is quite controversial, however. The NIMH conducted the most extensive study of treatments for ADHD to date: the Multimodal Treatment Study of Children with ADHD (MTA, 1999). Four treatments were compared: (1) medication management alone, (2) behavioral treatments alone, (3) a combination of medication and behavioral treatments, and (4) routine community care. A total of 579 elementary school boys and girls with ADHD were randomly assigned to one of the treatments. All the children were assessed at regular intervals throughout the study. The results showed that long-term combination treatments and medication management alone were superior to intense behavioral treatment and routine

Taking It to the Classroom

Do You Know Jack, the Disorganized?

Jack is disorganized. He often forgets where his materials are. He puts his papers in the wrong folders and binders, and loses them. He brings the wrong books and materials to various classes. He does not finish many of his in-class assignments because of his disorganized approach to them. He loses track of what homework he has, and he brings home the wrong items to do his homework. This disorganized approach affects nearly every aspect of his day at school. What practical and immediate steps can you take to help Jack? Here are some suggestions:

- Talk to Jack's parents about strategies that could help him be more organized.
- Provide Jack with a homework notebook to help him keep track of his assignments.
- Color code his books and notebooks for different subject areas so he can easily see which notebook and book he needs.
- Provide Jack with a list of what he will need for the next day's classes.
- Show Jack good models of how to organize materials.

TABLE 12.3

Behavioral Characteristics and General Strategies for Students with ADHD

Behavior	Characteristics of Child	General Strategies
Hyperactivity	1. Fidgets with hands/feet 2. Squirms in seat/leaves seat unexpectedly 3. Shows preference for gross motor activities 4. Shows frustration during fine motor tasks	1. Incorporation of gross motor activity and active responses into curriculum (e.g., role-play, hands-on activities) 2. Positive attention from peers 3. Attention and feedback from regular classroom teacher
Impulsivity	1. Inability to delay responding 2. Difficulty waiting for his or her turn in social and academic situations 3. Interrupts/intrudes on others 4. Emotional outbursts/reactions based on feelings, not facts 5. Poor performance on tasks that require planning	1. Cognitive-behavior therapy and self-monitoring of impulses 2. Time-outs 3. Positive reinforcement using tangible or material rewards 4. Response cost/removal punishment
Inattention/distractibility	1. Difficulty filtering irrelevant sensory information 2. Attraction to "novel" environmental conditions 3. Restriction of activity when experiencing excessive stimulation 4. Initiation of sensation-seeking activity when not sufficiently stimulated	1. Use of varied and interesting tasks (e.g., games, videos) 2. Use of novel qualities (e.g., color, size) to highlight important written task features 3. Moderate levels of noise (e.g., music, fan) during repetitious, familiar, and structured activities
Disorganization	1. Misplaces or loses belongings 2. Difficulty handling materials with multiple pieces 3. Messy desk 4. Difficulty completing tasks and tests within a time framework 5. Overestimates time intervals 6. Haphazard, illegible penmanship	1. Predictable location and labeling of classroom materials 2. Self-talk to monitor organization 3. Use of alternate means of producing responses (e.g., oral, transcribed)

Source: Adapted from "Arranging the classroom with an eye (and ear) to students with ADHD" by Eric Carbone, *Teaching Exceptional Children,* Vol. 34, 2001, 72–81. Copyright 2001 by The Council for Exceptional Children. Adapted and reprinted with permission.

community care. The combined treatment was superior on such measures as anxiety, academic performance, reduction of oppositionality or defiance, improved parent–child relations, and social skills.

Differentiating Instruction

Mainstreaming and inclusive classrooms are clear trends in contemporary K–12 education. Mainstreaming brings children and adolescents with defined disabilities and IEPs out of special education classrooms and into classrooms with students who do not have defined disabilities. The proportion of students with special needs who spend most of their school day (80% or more) in inclusive classrooms has grown every year since the enactment of IDEA to the point at which the majority of students with special needs now spend most of their school day in mainstream education.

differentiated instruction A teacher's response to the differing learning needs of a student.

Differentiated instruction—matching one's teaching to the needs of each learner—represents how teachers successfully adapt to the inclusive educational environment. Many educators, however, believe that differentiation means teaching each lesson in a variety of different ways—perhaps in as many different ways as there are students in the classroom.

But this approach to instruction is neither practical nor realistic. Instead, differentiated instruction involves offering a classwide lesson and then supplementing that lesson with instructional practices that allow it to be tailored to the individual needs of each student (Carolan & Guinn, 2007), including acts of instruction such as the following: (1) checking in with each student, (2) offering personalized scaffolding during one-on-one time, (3) using flexible means to reach defined ends (allowing multiple paths to accomplish educational objectives), and (4) creating a caring classroom in which differences are seen as assets (Carolan & Guinn, 2007).

Differentiated instruction is not easy; it is a teaching skill that needs to be learned and developed. Teachers who are experts in differentiated instruction suggest two ways to help novice teachers learn and develop such skill (Carolan & Guinn, 2007). First, novice teachers need opportunities to view concrete examples of differentiation, as by observing videotapes of a master teacher and then discussing the teacher's actions with either the master teacher or a small group of peer teachers. Second, novice teachers need mentoring relationships with master differentiation teachers so that they can experience firsthand observation and can participate in joint lesson-planning strategies on how to differentiate the curriculum and instruction to better meet the special needs of all students. Other recommendations for differentiating instruction include (1) providing clear directions and a lesson activity outline for students, (2) planning for frequent breaks, (3) developing tiered activities that involve the use of alternative assignments that cover the same material, (4) using clear worksheets, (5) decreasing task length, and (6) checking an assignment notebook (Bender, 2008).

Teachers as well as students need to adapt to the inclusive classroom. In one study, teachers responded to inclusion along two dimensions, hostility/receptivity and anxiety/calmness (Soodak, Podell, & Lehman, 1998). As we saw in Chapter 2, teachers' beliefs about their teaching efficacy has important influences on their effectiveness in the classroom. Teachers who teach in an inclusive classroom must feel efficacious if they are to effectively differentiate instruction. Soodak and colleagues (1998) found that teachers with high self-efficacy were more receptive to inclusion than less efficacious peers. Brownwell and Pajares (1996) examined the influence of teachers' efficacy beliefs on their perceived success with students with learning and behavior problems. One hundred twenty-eight general education second-grade teachers responded to a survey. The respondents were from a randomly selected sample. Teachers' efficacy beliefs had a strong direct effect on reported success, with higher expressed efficacy associated with higher levels of reported success. Experiences of collegiality with the special education teachers and quality professional development also were associated with reports of success. Teachers perceived themselves to be more successful if they had participated in service programs that address the needs of students with disabilities, curricular and instructional adaptations for students, and behavior management techniques. Preservice programs that included the same components were also associated with reported success.

In a study of 110 teachers, Soodak and Podell (2001) provided participants with a case that described a male third-grade student who was experiencing difficulty with reading. Teachers were asked to make suggestions about what to do and to note whether the suggested action would be effective. Thirty-four percent of the teachers made more suggestions that involved teacher-based actions, whereas 51% of the teachers suggested actions that involved resources outside the classroom. In general, teachers expressed little confidence in their suggested strategies. Teachers with higher levels of self-efficacy made significantly more teacher-based suggestions than those with lower levels of efficacy.

REFLECTION FOR ACTION

The Event

Carlos Morales is concerned about Jamie. Jamie is new to the district, and he seems to have trouble concentrating, is a bit out of control, and seems to have trouble operating within the norms of the class. Carlos suspects Jamie might have some serious challenges, but he is a new teacher and doesn't really have a strong idea of what the range of typical behavior is. What should he do?

Reflection RIDE

Carlos has a lot of issues to deal with here. He is a new teacher, so maybe he just needs a broader repertoire of instructional moves to rein Jamie in a bit. Perhaps he should go talk to the principal, but he fears the principal doesn't really want to hear about problems. He is also concerned that he has to deal with all of the problems of a first-year teacher and just can't devote enough time to this issue.

What Theoretical/Conceptual Information Might Assist in Interpreting and Remedying This Situation? Consider the following:

Attention-Deficit/Hyperactivity Disorder (ADHD)

Carlos's first suspicion is that Jamie has ADHD. But he is nervous about jumping to conclusions and starting a process that may unfairly lead Jamie to be labeled and consigned to a set of circumstances that are not in his best interest.

Maturity/Developmental Issues

Perhaps Jamie's problem is that he is just kind of young for his age. He's really not a bad kid, just what some people would call rambunctious. Maybe he just needs a little time and extra attention to adjust to the class. Maybe Carlos is getting too far down the road on this too early.

Prereferral

If a prereferral team exists in Carlos's school district, he might want to get in touch with the team members and learn about that process at some point.

Information Gathering RIDE

Carlos definitely needs more information. In fact, he has already tried to get more information but was unsuccessful. There was no file on Jamie. That would have been a good start. A second thing that he can do is try to observe Jamie's behavior a bit more systematically. He can start keeping records of the degree to which his behavior is inappropriate. Additionally, he can ask a colleague to come in and visit his class and get her impressions of Jamie. Furthermore, if he really suspects that ADHD might be a problem here, he can find out what behaviors he should be monitoring. He can also discuss the issue with the school psychologist.

Decision Making RIDE

What should Carlos do next? He probably first has to decide how severe a problem this is. If it really appears that Jamie is out of control and that this is impeding his progress and the progress of the class, then he needs to take action. If he thinks this is a minor problem that might resolve itself, then he probably simply wants to set up a monitoring system to keep track of the problem and be better able to describe what is going on should he need to at some point in the future. In either case, it wouldn't hurt to walk down the hall and consult with a trusted senior colleague.

Evaluation

If Carlos decides to take a "wait and see" approach to the problem, then he needs to develop a good system for seeing the problem. Does Jamie act out all of the time or just in certain settings? Is he truly disruptive or just on the fringe of the norms? Does he have any sense of his own behavior? If Carlos is going to describe the situation to others, he will need to be precise and talk about behaviors he has seen more than inferences he has made.

Further Practice: Your Turn

Here is a second event for consideration and reflection. In doing so, carry out the processes of reflection, information gathering, decision making, and evaluation.

The Event

Jorge is in the seventh grade. Mr. Jackson asks students in his language arts class to write a letter attempting to persuade the school board to allow them to have their own newspaper. After half an hour, he glances over Jorge's shoulder and notices that he has written very little. He reads Jorge's work quickly and notices that the ideas are quite disconnected.

Why is Jorge's production so poor? Why are his ideas so disconnected? How can you help him?

SUMMARY

● **How was intelligence understood initially, and how have views of intelligence changed over time?**

Spearman believed that intelligence could best be understood as consisting of one broad, or general, factor, which he labeled g (for general), and a variety of individual, or specific, factors. Thurstone proposed a different approach that involved seven "primary mental abilities": verbal comprehension, word fluency, number facility, spatial visualization, associative memory, perceptual speed, and reasoning. Thurstone's approach to mental abilities painted a richer picture of the individual. Cattell contributed the concepts of *fluid* and *crystallized intelligence*. Modern theories of intelligence include Sternberg's triarchic theory of intelligence; Gardner's theory of multiple intelligences; and the concept of metacognition, attributable primarily to Flavell. Sternberg's triarchic theory has three main facets: analytical, creative, and practical. Sternberg has also developed a theory of successful intelligence. Gardner's theory of multiple intelligences holds that abilities are more separate and isolated than other theories suggest. Gardner proposed that there are at least eight intelligences, including logical-mathematical, linguistic, spatial, musical, bodily-kinesthetic, naturalistic, interpersonal, and intrapersonal.

● **How is intelligence measured, and how is it related to achievement?**

Intelligence tests can be administered either to individuals or to groups. Two of the most popular individually administered standardized IQ tests are the WISC-IV and the K-ABC II. More recent theories, such as Sternberg's and Gardner's, require new ways to measure intelligence. Sternberg has developed the Sternberg Triarchic Abilities Test, and Shearer's Multiple Intelligences Developmental Assessment Scales is probably the most fully developed assessment based on Gardner's theory. Measured intelligence is positively correlated with school achievement. This may be because the kinds of skills sampled on an intelligence test are the skills that are valued in schooling. Binet's original task in 1905 was to develop tests that would distinguish between those who were likely to do well in school and those who were not. It is therefore not surprising that measures of achievement and intelligence are related.

● **How does talent develop?**

Talent is the capacity to produce exceptional performance. The desire to increase one's talent leads one to engage in many hours of deliberate practice. Deliberate practice is activity whose main purpose is to attain and improve one's skills. Students who engage in deliberate practice spend time refining their skills; engaging in self-reflection; receiving coaching, instruction, and feedback; and, finally, observing skilled and experienced performers. Deliberate practice alters a student's cognitive capacities and bodily functions (e.g., muscle patterns). The development of talent proceeds from a period of play in a domain, to deliberate practice, and, finally, to the decision to commit to the domain and engage in many hours of deliberate practice.

● **What happens when students are grouped by ability?**

Arguments against between-group ability grouping point to its negative effects on low achievers. Students in low-ability tracks have difficulty moving into higher tracks and tend to receive lower-quality instruction. Results for high achievers are less clear.

● **In general, how do schools identify children with special needs?**

Children who are thought to have special needs are initially screened through a prereferral process that results in an intervention within the child's classroom. If the problems persist, a formal evaluation for special education may be conducted. A team made up of school professionals and the child's parents or guardians meets to determine whether the child is eligible for special services. If the child is found to be eligible for services under IDEA, the team has 30 days to write an IEP for him or her.

- **How are learning disabilities and attention-deficit/hyperactivity disorder identified?**

  There is no objective way to determine whether a child has a learning disability. There are, however, signs that may indicate that the child has a problem that should be investigated. For example, low achievement may be a sign of a learning disability, but not all learning problems are due to disabilities. The recent reauthorization of IDEA (2004) states that schools are not required to use a discrepancy between achievement and intellectual ability in identifying learning disabilities. They can use a response to an intervention protocol to assist in diagnosis. DSM-IV contains guidelines for identifying ADHD; these include the requirement that the behaviors must appear before the age of 7 and continue for at least six months. An important aspect of determining whether a disorder exists is that the behavior must be observed over a specified period. A prereferral process such as that described earlier may be the first course of action. When a teacher identifies a child as significantly different from average, further analysis is required.

- **How can teachers bring children with physical challenges fully into classroom life?**

  Maes and Grietens (2004) point out that children with sensory problems included into regular classrooms are continually confronted with the differentness of their personal situation, causing insecurity and a lack of confidence. The primary problem children experience is social. Teachers need to be highly sensitive to issues concerning social development for children with physical disabilities and create a classroom environment to provide opportunites for interaction among students.

Key Terms

attention-deficit disorder (ADD), p. 440
attention-deficit/hyperactivity disorder (ADHD), p. 440
automaticity, p. 418
between-class ability grouping, p. 429
bias, p. 421
crystallized intelligence, p. 417
culture-free tests, p. 421
deliberate practice, p. 424
differentiated instruction, p. 442
entity view of intelligence, p. 420

eugenics, p. 416
existential intelligence p. 419
fluid intelligence, p. 417
incremental view of intelligence, p. 420
individualized education program (IEP), p. 431
innate ability, p. 416
intelligence quotient (IQ), p. 416
mental age, p. 416
metacognition, p. 417
monotonic-benefits assumption, p. 424

multiple-intelligences (MI) theory, p. 419
nature/nurture, p. 417
physiological psychology, p. 415
primary mental abilities, p. 417
response to intervention(RTI), p. 437
standard deviation, p. 427
talent, p. 423
triarchic, p. 418
within-class ability grouping, p. 429

Exercises

1. *Observation of "Abilities" in the Classroom*
   Visit an elementary or secondary school classroom. Your goal is to identify the abilities that are valued by the teacher or are called upon during the course of a class period. You might look for evidence of Sternberg's triarchic theory of intelligence or Gardner's theory of multiple intelligences.

2. *Resources on Special Needs*
   Identify five Web sites that provide helpful information about students with special needs. Indicate why these sites are useful and the criteria you used to select them.

3. *A Lesson Plan for Deliberate Practice*
   Create a lesson plan for a fifth-grade class in which you provide opportunities for deliberate practice. How will you support English language learners or individuals with special needs?

Lesson Plans

The lesson plans on these pages are excerpts from more complete plans. They are included in this form to provide you with practice in examining a lesson from the perspective of the content of this chapter. The complete lesson plans are available at www.pbs.org. For both lesson plans, read the lesson plan excerpt and respond to the questions related to cognitive development in the Ask Yourself! section at the end

Lesson #1: "Picture Scavenger Hunt"

GRADES: 1–3

SUBJECT AREA: Language Arts

ESTIMATED TIME: 45 minutes
URL: http://pbskids.org/wordgirl/parentsandteachers/pdf/lessons/scavenger_hunt.pdf

I. OBJECTIVES:
- Students will be introduced to new vocabulary.
- Students will use that vocabulary in context.
- Students will become aware of the connection between visual and written media.
- Students will practice observational and interpretive skills.

II. PROCEDURE:
Before the lesson, prepare a large example of a word caption and picture (illustration). Also prepare sets of three vocabulary cards for each student. Use a variety of words in each set, based on the suggested vocabulary below. Print the words on the bottom of the card so there is ample space left to glue a picture. On the back of the cards, provide the word's definition.

III. SAMPLE VOCABULARY TO BE PROVIDED:
1. Introduce the lesson by holding up the front page of a newspaper. Point to a photograph and ask students if they know what the words under the photograph are called. Explain that a caption is a very short explanation or description that accompanies a picture. Invite students to discuss why captions are important.

2. Now show students the example of the single-word caption and picture and discuss how this picture also illustrates the caption. Explain that students will be conducting a "scavenger hunt" to find pictures for word captions. Their challenge is to find the best matching visual examples of what their words mean.

3. Provide the class with many different magazines. Give each student scissors, glue, and three large, unlined index cards. Place dictionaries in central positions and tell students they are welcome to consult them if they need more information.

4. Once the students have found the best image(s) that conveys their word's meaning, they should glue their pictures onto the vocabulary cards above the word *caption*.

5. Invite students to choose their favorite caption and picture from the three they have completed to share with the class. Students should explain to the class what their word is, what it means, and then hold up their card to show the picture they've chosen to illustrate their capiton.

IV. ASSESSMENT:
Students should understand and be able to use new words in context. Students should become aware of the connection between visual and written communication. Students should comprehend the concepts of caption and illustrate.

Ask Yourself!

1. What kind of modifications of the lesson could you make for an English language learner?
2. What kinds of accommodations could you use for a child with a reading disability?

Published with permission from Scholastic, Inc. All rights reserved.

Lesson Plans

Lesson #2: "Deaf and Diverse, the Science of Sound"

GRADES: 9–12

SUBJECT AREA:
- Science—human biology, sound waves
- Social Studies—cultural awareness
- Writing—reflective, informational

URL: http://www.pbs.org/wnet/soundandfury/lesson2.html

LEARNING OBJECTIVES:
- Students will understand the cycle of how we listen and hear ourselves speak.
- Students will gain some knowledge about sound waves.
- Students will understand elements of the role that the nervous system plays in enabling humans to hear.
- Students will describe and explain some of the structures and functions of the human body.
- Students will understand that deaf people rely on other cues besides lip-reading for comprehension.

STEPS:

1. Divide students into pairs. Using the list of target words, students should draw a quick sketch of each target word on a separate piece of paper.

- While one student wears the headphones (listener), the other student (speaker) must read each word from the word list. The listener must try to repeat what the speaker said (no picture cues).
- Then the speaker should repeat each target word aloud while the listener points to the image of the word read by the speaker.
- Next, the listener should remove the headphones. The speaker will now put each target word in a sentence, saying the sentence aloud but omitting the target word. The listener should try to identify the target word.
- Last, the listener should put the headphones back on and read the word list aloud to experience the sensation of talking but not hearing the sound of her or his words through her or his ears.
- Discuss with the class the difficulties of (lip) speech-reading. Did the picture clues help to identify the target words? Did using the word in a sentence aid comprehension? How does it feel to not hear yourself talk?

2. Students will then write a composition on their personal experience during their trial "deaf" period. Describe the awareness of other senses, any uncomfortable feelings, frustrations, and means of communication.

3. Pass out five film canisters and five canister items (popcorn kernels, lentils, paperclips, dried peas, and grains of rice) to each student.

- Have each student place the popcorn into one film canister, the lentils into another, the paperclips into the third, the dried peas into the fourth, the rice into the fifth, and close the lids.
- Divide the students into pairs and have them listen to one another's shaking canisters. Working as a team, pairs will shake their canisters and try to match the canisters that sound the same. This exercise will demonstrate auditory discrimination. We need to distinguish sound in order to identify it and repeat it when speaking. Speech production is more than moving the lips and tongue; it is a process that involves the brain, the ear, the nervous system, and the vocal organs.

4. Work with the students to share their knowledge of the steps involved in communicating with others—speaking and listening.

5. Refer to the diagram of the ear on this Web site. Trace the path of the speaker's sound waves. Discuss the path of hearing.

- Sound waves enter the outer ear through the external auditory canal, or pinna.
- The waves or vibrations are funneled into the canal until they reach the tympanic membrane, or eardrum.

Ask Yourself!

1. What accommodations would you make for a student in your class who is hard of hearing?
2. What makes this lesson interesting?

Courtesy of Thirteen/WNET New York.

James climbed the steps to the entrance of Roosevelt High School brimming with optimism and hope. It was his first day as a history teacher at Roosevelt. Actually, it was his first day of teaching anything anywhere! He wasn't certain quite what to expect, as he had gotten the job rather late in the summer. But he had worked hard on learning the curriculum in the short time he had available and was eager to begin.

What he discovered on that first day was that he hadn't really thought too much about the students he would be teaching. He discovered that he had quite a mix. He had African-American students, Latino students, a few Asian-American students, and some of other nationalities and ethnicities. There were some kids who appeared to be poor and some who seemed wealthier. A number of children had disabilities of varying types and degrees. And some appeared to understand little of what he said because they were not native English speakers.

And yet his task was to teach history to all of them—American history to three of his four classes, and world history to the fourth. He thought hard about the task in front of him. As he headed to the parking lot, he saw Mrs. Martin, who was on the advisory committee that had selected him for the job. He asked her how she managed to adjust to the wide variety of students in the school. She smiled and said, "I don't teach kids, James, I teach algebra."

James walked over to the playing fields, sat down on the grass, and wondered just what he had gotten himself into.

R I D E Reflection for Action

What does it mean to teach children whose backgrounds and home lives are dramatically different from one anothers' and from your own? Mrs. Martin's statement seems harsh and uncaring. But is there one algebra for certain children and a different one for others? How can James address the issues of the diversity in his classes within the context of teaching history?

Guiding Questions

- What does diversity look like in the United States today?
- How can teachers best work with English language learners in regular classrooms?
- What is culture?
- What is multicultural education?
- How can teachers make their instruction inclusive of all learners in the class?
- How can a teacher learn about the students in his or her class and their culture?
- How can teachers recognize, adapt to, and respond to diverse learners?

CHAPTER OVERVIEW

This chapter focuses on the issues of diversity and how to teach children in diverse classrooms. Our society is a complex one, with individual backgrounds and ethnic differences from all over the world. As a teacher, you are called upon to teach *all* your students to read, write, develop their physical or artistic skills, become proficient in a foreign language, understand calculus or chemistry. But in order to do so, you have to understand your students—who they are as individuals, what their aspirations are, how their backgrounds have made them the people who they are as they enter your class. In this chapter, we look at the incredible diversity of the student population of the United States and consider ways that you can become an excellent teacher of all your students.

Diverse Learners
- Student Diversity in the United States
- The Relationships among Race, Ethnicity, and Socioeconomic Status
- Differences in Socioeconomic Status and Their Role in Learning
- Ethnicity and Learning

English Language Learners
- Using Technology to Support ELL Students' Learning

Multicultural Education: An Overview
- What Is Culture?

- Issues in Multicultural Education
- Advantages and Concerns of Multicultural Education
- Social Justice

Implementing a Multicultural Approach to Teaching
- Getting Started on a Multicultural Approach
- Digging Deeper: Looking at Various Multicultural Approaches to Education

Becoming a Teacher of Diverse Children
- Working in Culturally Different Contexts

Diverse Learners

pluralistic society A society made up of multiple groups, each of which has important contributions to make and perspectives to contribute to the whole.

The United States is a **pluralistic society** composed of identifiable ethnic groups. In schools, the meaning of diversity extends well beyond just ethnic and cultural groups to include diversity with respect to characteristics such as language, socioeconomic status, abilities, and even gender.

Two principles generally define a school's response to diversity. The first is equality, which is an explicit commitment to the ideal that all students are created equal and deserve the same high quality of instruction. Equality is a widely embraced ideal, and this is true irrespective of people's ethnic or cultural background (Schuman et al., 1997). With its emphasis on equality, multicultural education is an outgrowth of the civil rights movement (Sleeter, 1996). In this context, equality means recognizing and removing barriers that undermine a high-quality education, such as low teacher expectations, poverty, or differential access to programs and areas of study. For instance, students are typically selected into gifted and talented programs based on their high scores on tests written in English. Given that 11% of students do not consider English to be their first language, language becomes a barrier against English language learners' (ELL) access to gifted and talented programs. Indeed, ELLs are noticeably underrepresented in these programs.

The second response schools have to diversity is accommodation. Instead of forcing students of diverse backgrounds and characteristics to fit into a one-size-fits-all environment, schools commit to an open-armed embrace and appreciation for differences among students. The recent trends in state and national policy (e.g., No Child Left Behind), however, are to establish academic goals and standards that apply equally to all students and to teach students with special needs in regular classrooms. In this book, we try to address general issues related to diversity (and to special needs) in separate chapters, while at the same time embedding specific issues related to diversity and special needs within the other chapters of the book. Our rationale for this approach is that issues of diversity and special needs pervade many aspects of our classrooms but also warrant specific attention their own right. Our goal is to help preservice teachers develop the awareness and skills they will need to recognize, adapt, and respond to the diverse learners and students with special needs they will be teaching.

Student Diversity in the United States

Each year, schools become increasingly diverse. Figure 13.1 shows the demographics of the U.S. population. In the year 2000, a little over two-thirds of the population was Caucasian (i.e., non-Hispanic white), while one-third represented nonwhites: 13% African-American; 13% Hispanic; 4% Asian-American; 1% American Indian; and 1% other (U.S. Census Bureau, 2004). By the year 2020, multicultural households will account for more than 40% of the U.S. population. That percentage will likely grow to 50% by the year 2050 (Day, 1996).

The numbers in Figure 13.1 speak to the diversity of ethnic groups, but similar numbers also apply to other aspects of diversity, such as socioeconomic status and language spoken in the home, as shown in the state-by-state analysis that appears in Table 13.1. Today, about 40% of the 48 million students enrolled in public schools in the United States are minority students. Seventeen percent of public school students live in poverty. Eight percent speak little or no English in the home. Approximately 13% of these 48 million students have special needs that interfere with their ability to learn. These percentages are important to teachers

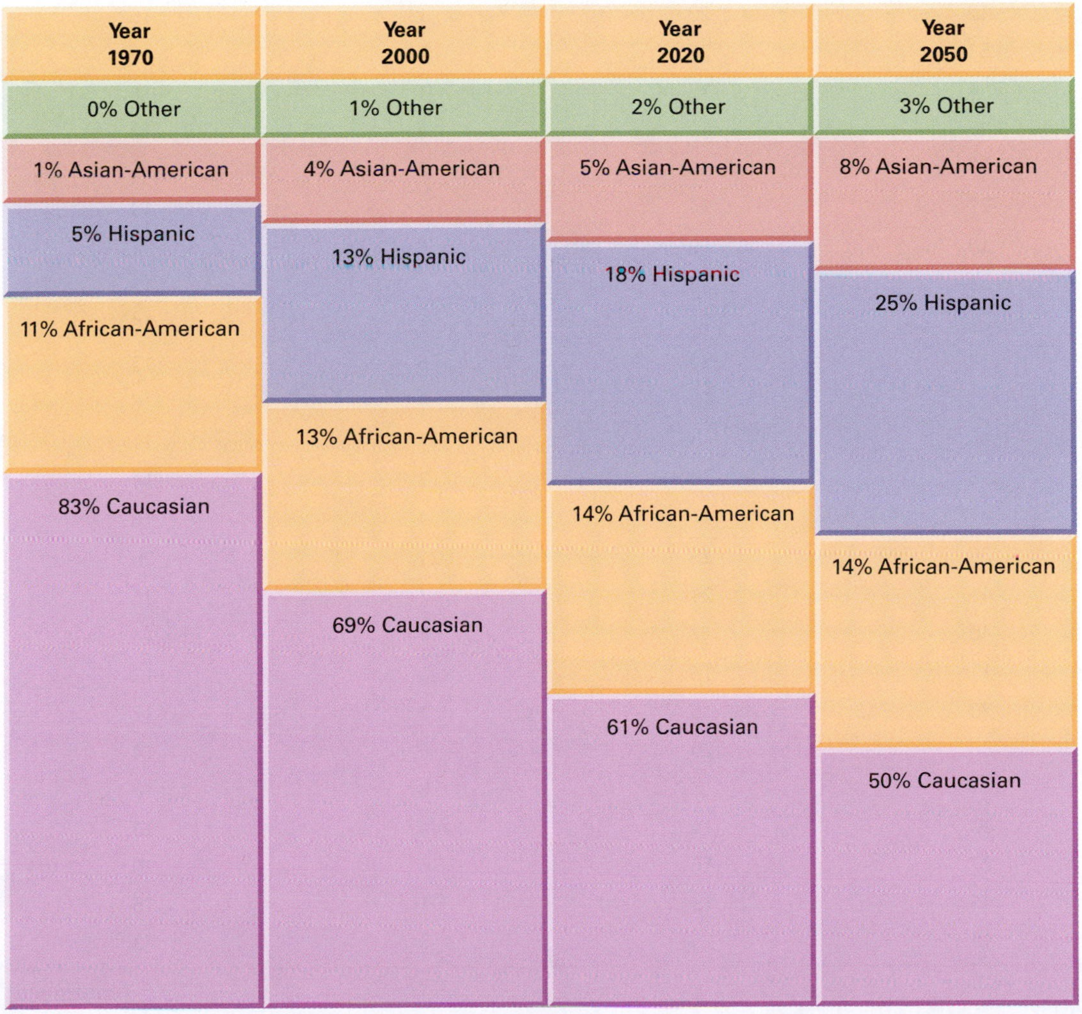

Figure 13.1 Diversity Trends in the U.S. Population: Actual and Projected Percentages for Major Ethnic Groups, 1970–2050
Source: U.S. Census Data

TABLE 13.1

State-by-State Information Summarizing Student Diversity and Special Needs

State	Minority Students (%)	Children in Poverty (%)	Non-English-Speaking Students (%)	Students with Special Needs (%)
Alabama	40	22	1	13
Alaska	40	11	15	13
Arizona	49	19	16	11
Arkansas	29	22	3	13
California	65	20	25	11
Colorado	33	12	10	10
Connecticut	31	10	4	13
Delaware	40	14	3	14
District of Columbia	95	29	11	17
Florida	48	19	8	15
Georgia	46	18	4	12
Hawaii	80	15	9	12
Idaho	15	17	7	12
Illinois	41	15	7	14
Indiana	17	12	4	16
Iowa	10	11	3	15
Kansas	22	14	4	13
Kentucky	12	20	1	15
Louisiana	51	26	2	13
Maine	4	15	1	16
Maryland	48	10	4	13
Massachusetts	24	15	5	15
Michigan	27	14	3	13
Minnesota	18	9	6	13
Mississippi	53	26	1	13
Missouri	21	17	1	15
Montana	14	20	5	13
Nebraska	18	13	4	16
Nevada	46	15	11	11
New Hampshire	5	8	2	14
New Jersey	41	11	4	16
New Mexico	66	26	21	20
New York	45	21	7	15
North Carolina	40	17	4	14
North Dakota	11	16	n/a	13
Ohio	20	16	1	12
Oklahoma	36	20	6	14
Oregon	21	16	8	13
Pennsylvania	22	14	n/a	13
Rhode Island	27	16	6	20
South Carolina	45	19	1	15
South Dakota	14	15	3	13

(continued)

TABLE 13.1

(continued)

State	Minority Students (%)	Children in Poverty (%)	Non-English-Speaking Students (%)	Students with Special Needs (%)
Tennessee	28	18	n/a	16
Texas	59	22	15	12
Utah	15	10	9	11
Vermont	4	12	1	13
Virginia	37	12	4	14
Washington	27	13	n/a	12
West Virginia	6	24	1	18
Wisconsin	20	11	3	14
Wyoming	13	18	3	13

Note. n/a, not available; minority students represents all PreK-to-12 students not classified as white, non-Hispanic; children in poverty represents all PreK-to-12 students living in families with annual incomes under $16,895; non-English-speaking students represents all PreK-to-12 students who receive English language learner (ELL) services; students with special needs represents all PreK-to-12 students who have individualized education programs (IEPs).

Source: Aggregated data from the *Digest of Education Statistics* Tables and Figures 2003, National Center for Education, U.S. Department of Education, available at http://nces.ed.gov/programs/digest/index.asp.

for at least two reasons. First, these percentages communicate the message that students enter school with different backgrounds, beliefs, and needs. Second, the extent to which classrooms are diverse communities of learners varies from state to state.

The Relationships among Race, Ethnicity, and Socioeconomic Status

Socioeconomic status (SES) is a term that scholars use to describe the combined effects of income, education, and occupational status in a single concept. People are usually described as being of high, middle, or low SES. In the United States, there is a fairly strong relationship between race and SES, and also between ethnicity in general and SES. Looking at the census data presented in Table 13.2, we see the differences in income levels for families in 2008 as reported by the U.S. Bureau of the Census in 2011.

It is clear that there is a strong relationship between ethnicity and income levels in the United States. This relationship has existed throughout the history of the country and remains a substantial issue today. The relationship between ethnicity and school performance is in part attributable to differences in SES. Table 13.3 shows the differences in graduation rates for students of different ethnicities.

Ethnicity, SES, and school achievement are intertwined in schools in the United States. The following section looks at the effects of SES on school achievement from an individual perspective.

socioeconomic status Socioeconomic status has to do with one's position in the social and economic hierarchy or structure in a society.

ethnicity Ethnicity concerns the classification of people into groups based on their race or national origin.

TABLE 13.2

Income and Poverty in the United States by Ethnic Group, 2008

	All Families	White	Black	Asian/Pacific Islander	Hispanic
Median income	$61,521	$65,000	$39,879	$73,578	$40,466
Percent of children below poverty level	18.5%	15.3%	34.4%	14.2%	30.3%

Source: U.S. Bureau of the Census (2011) Statistical Abstract.

TABLE 13.3

Differences in High School Graduation Rates by Racial/Ethnic Group

Racial/Ethnic Group	2007 Graduation Rate
Asian-American	80.7%
Black	53.7%
Hispanic	55.5%
Native American	50.7%
White	76.6%

Source: Phi Delta Kappan, Dropouts—By the Numbers, February, 2011, 92(5), p. 15. Reprinted with the permission of Phi Delta Kappan.

Differences in Socioeconomic Status and Their Role in Learning

When children walk in the school door in the morning, they come from different places. Some come from caring families with ample financial resources. Others may come from their mother's house on one day and their father's house on another. Some may come from extended families and others from a single-parent home where the parent is not far removed from childhood herself. Socioeconomic status is not just an academic term. It reflects what life is like for children. Consider the three children described below. Will they succeed in school?

Gary is a 7-year-old boy who lives with his siblings and parents in a three-bedroooom house in a low-income neighborhood. He has seven brothers and four sisters. One of his older brothers is in prison. He is often late for school. His clothing is very thin, as though it has been washed too much. His hair sticks out all over. Gary looks forward to lunch at school. His father is an alcoholic, and his mother does not work outside the home. His parents do not allow him to borrow books from the public library because they are afraid that he will damage the books and they will have to pay for them. They rarely spend time with him and never ask him about his schoolwork.

Darren is also 7 years old and is in the same class as Gary. He lives in the same neighborhood. His parents are also poor. He has three siblings, one sister and two brothers. His father works at a store. His mother does not work outside the home. Darren's clothes look warm and comfortable and fit him well. He is always on time for school and usually brings his own lunch. He loves to read and regularly goes to the public library to get books. His mother helps him with his homework every evening, and his father always reads a story to him before he goes to bed.

Miguel is 7 years old and lives in an upper-middle-class suburb. His school is brand new and has Internet access in every classroom. He already reads at the third-grade level. His father and mother both work in professional jobs, and they buy many books and educational toys for him. When he comes home, one of his parents helps him with his homework. His parents are always eager to find out what he learned in school.

How Can I Use This?

What strategies can you use to provide caring and support, high expectations, and opportunities for participating in your classroom?

A variety of family factors can put children at risk for developmental and learning problems. Poverty is one of the most serious of these. The official poverty rate in 2003 was 12.5%, up from 12.1% in 2002 (U.S. Census Bureau, 2011). In 2003, 35.9 million people were living in poverty, 1.3 million more than in 2002. The number of children living in poverty also rose between 2002 and 2003, increasing from 12.1 million to 12.9 million, or almost a full percentage point. A three-year average of poverty levels from 2001 to 2003 indicates that 10.2% of Caucasians, 24% of African-Americans, 11% of Asians, and 22% of Hispanic people were considered poor.

Family status is also associated with poverty. Of the families identified as poor in 2003, 5.4% were headed by married couples, 28% had a female householder with no husband present, and 13.5% had a male householder with no wife present. Children born into poverty are at greater risk for developmental problems (Hanson & Carta, 1996). Families who are poor are more likely to live in substandard or unsafe housing and to have high levels of stress. A child living in a poor home is less likely to receive the support needed for early learning. Problems that contribute to developmental or learning difficulties include poor nutrition, neglect, parents with substance abuse problems, child abuse, and violence in the home or neighborhood. Children in lower socioeconomic groups are less likely to have parents who are well educated.

Some researchers have studied the question of why some children in poor environments remain **resilient** (Werner, 1992). Many children do not succumb to the stresses of a deprived environment, and sometimes even thrive (Rak & Patterson, 1996). Among the factors that promote resilience are caring and supportive relationships, high expectations, and opportunities for meaningful participation in school activities (Benard, 1993). It is important to

resilient Having the ability to overcome handships and setbacks.

keep in mind that some children in all socioeconomic strata may not experience these three protective factors. At-risk students should be identified on the basis of demonstrated problems in school rather than exclusively on the basis of socioeconomic or sociocultural background (Benard, 1993).

Currently, about 40 school districts across the nation use SES to determine where children go to school (Tomsho, 2007). The Supreme Court (2007) struck down a law supporting voluntary desegration in Louisville, Kentucky, and in Seattle. Tomsho (2007) notes that more schools are likely to increase the economic diversity of their school populations.

The three children described at the beginning of this section differ in terms of the availability of the three protective factors. Darren is poor, which means that some resources are not available to him. However, he has supportive parents who help him with his homework or read to him, and he goes to the local library. Miguel experiences all three of the protective factors. Gary is the child who is most at risk for school failure, because his home does not protect him from the adverse effects of poverty. Each of these children has good days and bad, struggles and triumphs, and hopes for the future. Although their lives at home might be quite different, each deserves a teacher who will take their best interests to heart.

Ethnicity and Learning

An **ethnic group** is a collection of people who identify with one another on the basis of country of origin, race, religion, language, and/or behavioral rituals (Banks, 1994b; Biehler et al., 1999; Gollnick & Chinn, 1994). Such groups sometimes also share values and political interests.

As a teacher, you need to know how your students' ethnicity can affect student–teacher relationships. Christine Bennett (1995) identifies five aspects of ethnicity that are potential sources of student–student and student–teacher misunderstanding: verbal communication, nonverbal communication, orientation modes, social value patterns, and intellectual modes.

ethnic group A collection of people who identify with one another on the basis of race, country of origin, language, and/or behavioral rituals.

Verbal Communication Children who speak English as a second language may not hear or accurately discriminate among certain speech sounds. These students may be perceived as uneducated or less intelligent solely because they speak nonstandard English. Students may also speak the language with a *dialect*, an alternative form of speaking a particular language based on one's environment (Leu & Kinser, 1991). Because of these linguistic differences, students may be very reluctant to speak or perform in public. These students give public performances only after they attain a degree of mastery that is acceptable to them (Bennett, 1995; Vasquez, 1990). This approach is similar to domains such as music, whereby one practices in private until one has mastered a piece.

Eye Contact Direct eye contact is a form of nonverbal communication that is highly valued by mainstream American culture. Children are taught to look directly at people they speak to, in order to signify honesty and interest. But among many Aboriginal, Hispanic, and Asian cultures, averting one's eyes is a sign of respect for the other person, whereas looking directly at someone is a sign of defiance. Thus, some students who look down or away when being questioned or corrected are not necessarily hiding guilt, acting defiant, or communicating a lack of interest (Bennett, 1995; Bowd et al., 1994; Howe, 1994).

Time Mainstream American culture is also very time-oriented. People who organize their time and work efficiently are respected and rewarded. Statements such as "Time is money" and "Never put off until tomorrow what you can do today" are popular mainstream sayings. Moreover, classes begin and end at a specified time, with bells often interrupting a project or a discussion. But students who come from less time-oriented cultures may find such a time-bound approach to learning bewildering, and they might not cope well with rigid schedules (Bennett, 1995).

(Image Source)

Students whose first language is different from the language of instruction in the classroom may be reluctant to speak or perform in public until they have mastered the classroom language.

An effective teacher provides students with some flexibility, while at the same time impressing upon them that in mainstream American culture, getting things done on time and being punctual is important.

Competition and Individualism

Competition and individualism are two other cultural values central to mainstream American culture. Many people believe that competition brings out the best in people and that accomplishments should reflect an individual's efforts, rather than a group's efforts. Many classroom activities either implicitly or explicitly revolve around competition, and students attain grades for their own individual efforts. A responsive teacher needs to respect such **cultural differences** and make efforts to embrace noncompetitive and nonindividualistic learning styles, while at the same time informing students about the attitudes needed to survive in a competitive and individualistic society.

Knowledge and Learning Styles

Different ethnic groups value different types of knowledge and methods of learning. Some groups place a higher value on personal, communal, and spiritual knowledge than on scientific knowledge—a philosophy common in Asian, Native American, and Middle Eastern cultures.

(Media Bakery)

Teachers should try to be aware of the cultural differences in learning among their students and adjust their strategies accordingly.

Although constructivist and interactive approaches to teaching have increased over the past decade, teaching practices have not changed a great deal. Elementary teachers still employ a teacher-centered, large-group approach to instruction, with students all working from the same text, workbook, and worksheets (Sleeter & Grant, 2003). The typical classroom arrangement is still rows of chairs facing the front of the room, with the teacher asking questions, listening to answers, and guiding activity. These approaches to teaching are often in conflict with the learning styles of students from other cultural backgrounds. Learning in other cultures often focuses on cooperative arrangements, discussion, and hands-on learning. By using contextually rich approaches that allow for more input from the students' perspective, teachers can invite students to share their cultural priorities. Such active engagement will also be more motivating for these students.

Culture can also predispose certain groups toward particular ways of learning. Researchers have found that many Aboriginal students prefer visual rather than verbal methods of learning. In addition, they learn more effectively through deductive rather than inductive approaches. Thus, strategies that stress the details first and then lead to general conclusions can be ineffective with these groups. Interestingly, culture can predispose people to learning styles that contradict research. For example, in spite of the documented advantages of interactive learning techniques, Navajo students tend to believe that serious learning is private; they may not feel comfortable fully participating in discussions, debates, and contests (Bennett, 1995; Guild, 1994; Vasquez, 1990). A balance must be struck between respect for cultural differences and academic achievement.

Socioeconomic Factors

As discussed in Chapter 4, family socioeconomic status has always had a significant influence on a student's performance. Socioeconomic status includes factors such as annual income, occupation, level of education, place of residence, organizations to which family members belong, manner of dress, and material possessions. Socioeconomic factors often influence cross-cultural behavior. Student socioeconomic status can also have a significant impact on the predisposition and preparedness to engage (but not on ability).

Ethnicity, Social Background, and Teacher Expectations

Students' ethnic and social backgrounds influence their approach to and success with learning tasks. But lack of success is often influenced, consciously or unconsciously, by the **expectations** of teachers. Students whose teachers expect more of them and see them as capable tend to perform accordingly. In a similar way, ideas about ethnicity and social background influence teacher perceptions and teacher behavior.

Sonia Nieto's 1992 book, *Affirming Diversity: The Sociopolitical Context of Multicultural Education,* discusses teachers' tendency to form expectancies at the beginning of the school year. She describes a kindergarten teacher who apparently set expectations for each student

individualism The belief that each person should try to succeed on his or her own rather than focus on the development of society as a whole.

cultural differences Differences in the meaning and information systems that are transmitted from generation to generation in different cultural groups.

expectations One's beliefs about what will happen in a situation.

by the eighth day of the term. She did this by comparing each student to a hypothetical "ideal student," that is, one who conformed to middle-class characteristics. Children who closely matched this ideal were labeled "fast" learners, while the rest were the "slow" learners. The teacher interacted differently with students from each group during the school year. The "fast" learners received more attention, instructional time, and rewards. Both the teacher and the students were black, so her expectations were based on differences other than race. Remarkably, and tragically, after three years of similar behavior by other teachers, the children's actions more closely resembled the labels attached to them.

Research by Braun (1976), Brophy and Good (1974), Ladson-Billings (1994), and Nieto (1992) suggests the following:

- Attractive children are sometimes perceived by teachers to be brighter, more capable, and more social than unattractive children.
- Female teachers tend to perceive the behavior of girls as closer to the behavior of "ideal students" than do male teachers.
- Teachers tend to approve of girls' behavior more frequently than they do boys' behavior.
- Teachers are more influenced by negative information (for example, students' low test scores) than they are by neutral or positive information.
- Teachers tend to interact more frequently with high achievers than with low achievers.
- High-achieving students receive more praise than low-achieving students.
- Middle-class students are expected to achieve higher grades than low SES students, even when standardized achievement test scores are similar.

We review these factors because ethnic background, knowledge of siblings, and impressions of parents operate *together* to produce an expectancy. A single test score in unlikely to have much impact, but when combined with disruptive behavior, an expectancy may influence a teacher's future behavior. The nearby Taking It to the Classroom box provides suggestions for promoting multicultural understanding and classroom achievement.

What Does This Mean to Me?
Treat every student with a same high standards, but give all students the tools and time to achieve them.

Taking It to the Classroom

Teaching in Multicultural Classroom

1. Use a variety of strategies to motivate educationally disadvantaged students to do well in school, such as inviting them to design and undertake new activities.
2. Scaffold the achievement of educationally disadvantaged students by using a variety of instructional techniques.
3. Be conscious of the potential dangers of labeling, both in yourself and among your colleagues and other students. Concentrate on individuals while guarding against the impact of sterotyping.
   a. Remember that you are a human being who may at times react subjectively to students.
   b. Take concrete steps to ensure that you treat all students equitably, regardless of their backgrounds.
   c. Use information about students' backgrounds (e.g., cultural and social information) to help them become more effective learners and active members of the class.
4. Make students aware of the contributions of various ethnic groups to the history of the United States and the world, even if those groups are not represented in your class.
5. Assign group projects and activities that demonstrate culture-specific knowledge and skills and that encourage students to share the results with to whole class.
6. Help students to find and identify with successful representatives of their ethnic group. Allow students to create definitions of success, particularly if it differs from mainstream definitions. Dicuss the implications of deviations from the norm.
7. Use the Internet to find materials. Look for multicultural sites that capture the imagination and tell stories.

Source: Adapted from Biehler, R.F., Snowman, J., D'Amico, M., & Schmid, R.F. (1999). *Psychology applied to teaching* (Canadian edition). Toronto; ITP Nelson Canada.

English Language Learners

English language learners (ELLs) Individuals whose native language is other than English and who are learning English.

The number of students who are **English language learners (ELLs)** has grown substantially in the United States in recent years. According to estimates in the *Descriptive Study of Services to LEP Students and LEP Students with Disabilities* (Zehler et al., 2003), there were 3,977,819 ELL students in grades K–12 in the United States during the 2001–2002 school year, a 72% increase from the 1991–1992 estimate. These students represent a little over 8% of all students in schools. Spanish is the primary language of 77% of ELL students. Many districts have difficulty identifying English language learners who also have special needs, but Zehler et al. (2003) report that an estimated 375,325 ELL students also have special needs.

Clearly, the large number of students who do not speak English proficiently has important implications for teachers. Students' language skills affect every aspect of their learning, including the learning of mathematics. English language learners usually receive either some services or extensive services in English, or extensive English language learning services with significant native-language use. The study just mentioned found that English language learners scored below grade level in reading and mathematics but that students who completed language-learning programs typically were at grade level in those subjects (Zehler et al., 2003).

In a review of federally funded studies dealing with ELL students, 57 studies that focused on instructional services were included. The findings of these studies indicated that student outcomes could be improved by appropriate use of the native language and culture, adequate instruction in particular content areas, and an active learning environment [Special Issues Analysis Center (SIAC), 2003]. A trade association, Teachers of English to Speakers of Other Languages (TESOL), has established three main goals and standards for reaching them (TESOL, 1997). These are outlined in Table 13.4. Principles for teaching second-language learners are listed in Table 13.5.

Working with students who are ELLS will be challenging for you as a teacher, but seeing the development of such students is incredibly rewarding and enriching for teachers. Additionally, what you learn when working with ELL students will help you become a better teacher of all your students!

TABLE 13.4

ESL Standards for Pre-K–12 Students

Goals	Standards
To use English to communicate in social settings	• Students will use English to participate in social interactions.
	• Students will interact in, through, and with spoken and written English for personal expression and enjoyment.
	• Students will use learning strategies to extend their communicative competence.
To use English to achieve academically in all content areas	• Students will use English to interact in the classroom.
	• Students will use English to obtain, process, construct, and provide subject matter information in spoken and written form.
	• Students will use appropriate learning strategies to construct and apply academic knowledge.
To use English in socially and culturally appropriate ways	• Students will use appropriate language variety, register, and genre according to audience, purpose, and setting.
	• Students will use nonverbal communication appropriate to audience, purpose, and setting.
	• Students will use appropriate learning strategies to extend their sociolinguistic and sociocultural competence.

Source: Teachers of English to speakers of other languages. (1997). *ESL Standards for Pre-K–12 Students.* Alexandria, VA: Author. © 1997 Teachers of English to Speakers of Other Languages. Reprinted with permission.

TABLE 13.5

Principles for Teaching Second–Language Learners

Standard	Specific Example
Facilitate learning through joint productive activity among teacher and students.	Work on a common task (e.g., design of a Web page) and have opportunities to converse about it.
Develop competence in the language and literacy of instruction across the curriculum.	Use every opportunity to enhance language and literacy skills by having conversation about tasks, asking students to plan and explain activities.
Connect teaching and curriculum to students' experiences and skills of home and community.	Use students' prior knowledge and experience when designing tasks or assignments.
Challenge students toward cognitive complexity.	Have high standards and expectations, use assessments that allow you to provide meaningful feedback.
Engage students through dialogue, especially instructional conversation.	Use conversation to foster thinking skills by questioning, asking for explanations and elaborations of ideas.

Source: Standards from Center for Research on Education, Diversity, and Excellence (2002). Retrieved July 6, 2011, from http://gse.berkeley.edu/research/crede/standards.html.

Using Technology to Support ELL Students' Learning

Technology can be used to help ELL students meet the academic goals and standards set forth by TESOL (1997, see Table 5.4). García (1999) examined the effects of comic strip creation and animation software on the learning processes of bilingual children (Spanish and English) as they learned science and language simultaneously. The addition of visual representations of content being studied was helpful.

Tools such as email and the World Wide Web can help ELL students continue to develop competence in their first language, a skill that is vital to eventual success in their second language (Thomas & Collier, 2001). (See, however, the nearby Uncommon Sense box.) Padrón and Waxman (1996) argue that technology can be used to engage ELL students in the classroom learning environment because these learners are often disengaged and have generally experienced more failure than success in learning situations.

Teachers of English language learners can also take advantage of technology to improve their skills in working with students. The National Council of Teachers of English (NCTE) is preparing a professional development program for middle and high school English teachers to help them address the following questions:

- In what ways can we plan and facilitate students' language development while engaging learners in rigorous content?

- How can we create effective learning environments that facilitate student achievement?

- How can we provide opportunities for students to use language, learn language, and learn about language?

Appendix
Second Language Learning
Most teachers will encounter students who are learning English as their second language. Knowing some strategies for how to support their learning will be very helpful to you (PRAXIS™, I.B.5; INTASC, Principle 3).

R I D E Think back to James's problem in the introduction to the chapter. What are the problems that James is dealing with? Do these seem likely to be issues for James alone or for new teachers in diverse classrooms in general?

Multicultural Education: An Overview

Multicultural education is both a philosophical concept and an approach to education (Grant, Elsbree, & Fondrie, 2004). It is a philosophical concept because it is built on the ideals of equality, equity, justice, and human dignity. It is an approach to education because it helps students from diverse backgrounds experience educational equality. Those who study multicultural education are deeply interested in confronting social issues such as poverty, sexism, and bilingualism such that they seek to ensure that all students receive educational equality.

multicultural The perspective that cultural differences among several cultures are important and are deserving of consideration in a given setting.

Uncommon Sense

The Best Way to Learn a Language Is through Total Immersion—Or Is It?

Total immersion in a language means that a learner is completely immersed in a language. In other words, all communications are conducted in the language. Examples of immersion programs include ones in which one language (e.g., French) is spoken in a school in the morning and a second language (e.g., English) is spoken in the afternoon. The premise behind the belief that the best way to learn a language is through total immersion is that more time spent on a task leads to better learning. However, it is the quality of the exposure to the language, not merely the quantity of exposure, that matters (Crawford, 1998). In order to learn a second language, one must be able to understand what is being taught in that language (Krashen, 1996). A variety of instructional methods can help students learn a second language.

Thomas and Collier (2001) conducted a national study of long-term academic achievement by language-minority students. The strongest predictor of achievement in the second language was the amount of formal schooling in the first language. English language learners who were immersed in mainstream classes because their parents refused bilingual or English as a second language (ESL) instruction showed large decreases in reading and math achievement by grade 5. Some programs are more successful than others. Programs in which 90% of instruction is conducted in the child's native language in grades Pre-K–1, followed by a gradual transition to English by the fifth grade, are effective. Another effective type of program is 50–50 developmental bilingual programs. In those kinds of programs, children experience bilingual immersion in two languages. Thomas and Collier identified those two kinds of programs as the only ones that helped students reach the 50th percentile in both languages in all subjects. The fewest dropouts also came from those programs.

What Is Culture?

culture The meaning and information system that is transmitted from one generation to the next.

Culture exists as a meaning and information system that is transmitted from one generation to the next (Matsumoto & Juang, 2007). It provides both shared meanings (cultural interpretations) and shared activities (cultural practices) for its members (Greenfield et al., 2003). Communities create different cultures because they all face different problems (e.g., boys face different problems than do girls, low-SES students face different problems that do high-SES students), just as they possess different resources. People who share a commonality (those from the same social class, those with a shared history) generate different solutions to those problems, including different norms, rules, rituals, values such as collectivism, social hierarchies, and roles, all of which collectively define the culture.

One of the primary functions of any culture is to maintain social order and reduce social chaos. A culture does this by creating norms and expectations for behavior. Once established, norms provide guidelines for how members of the cultural group are to behave in given situations. These guidelines make it clear what is expected and what is accepted by the culture. So, culture is an asset, a meaning and information system people can rely on to solve the collective problems they face and interact successfully and amicably with one another.

A potential problem arises when members of a minority culture are placed into a social situation dominated by a majority culture. Under these conditions, the norms, guidelines, and expectations embraced by members of the minority culture might conflict with the norms, guidelines, and expectations of the majority culture. Such a circumstance places students from the minority culture at an academic disadvantage in terms of succeeding and thriving in school. Recognizing this, educators have embraced the need for multicultural education.

Issues in Multicultural Education

A multicultural approach to education fosters an understanding of and mutual respect for the values, beliefs, and practices of different cultural groups. The underlying assumption behind multicultural education is that only by understanding others' cultures can we, as

TABLE 13.6

Some Goals for Implementing Multicultural Education

- Show students how the past and present experiences of many ethnic groups, including their own, have had an impact on society. Help them develop both self-acceptance and respect for other ways.
- Show students how different cultural groups have influenced and perceived historical events and artistic creations, with the goal of reducing ethnocentrism and fostering productive relationships among members of those groups.
- Help students combat harmful stereotypes about ethnic groups.
- Support other teachers in developing attitudes, expectations, instructional practices, disciplinary policies and practices, and classroom climates that value and accept *all* students.
- Acknowledge the need for basic reading, writing, and computation skills and embed them in a personally meaningful cultural context.

> **What Does This Mean to Me?**
> Multicultural education means creatively selecting and inventing content, instruction, and learner-centered activities that promote cultural awareness and appreciation.

individuals and a society, prevent or overcome prejudice and discrimination. This concept has been around for many years and has sometimes created controversy. Many of the elements of contemporary multicultural programs were devised 60 to 70 years ago as part of a then-current emphasis on international education (Gollnick & Chinn, 1994).

The goals of a multicultural approach to education are rooted in the idea that we should acknowledge and celebrate the differences among us, use these differences to positive effect in our teaching, and encourage our students to understand and appreciate the differences we see among us. A set of goals for implementing a multicultural approach to education are presented in Table 13.6.

Advantages and Concerns of Multicultural Education

Multicultural approaches to education have been the source of some controversy in American society over recent years. There are several concerns with such an approach. Some people argue that a focus on multicultural issues detracts from more essential and more traditionally academic areas of focus in education. Another concern is that multicultural education favors some groups over other groups or caters to groups that are politically favored. There are also arguments that multicultural education promotes particular political views that are not a proper part of education for children. These are serious concerns deserving of consideration.

On the other hand, there are many strong arguments in favor of a multicultural approach to education. The arguments in favor of multicultural education (for example, Banks, 1994a, 1994c, 2006; Bennett, 1995; Garcia, 1994; Gollnick & Chinn, 1994; McAndrew, 1995; Ogbu, 1992) are based on the foundational principles listed in Table 13.7.

Working from these principles, a number of arguments can be made for taking a multicultural approach in the classroom. First, multicultural programs foster teaching practices that are effective in all classrooms, regardless of the extent or nature of diversity. For example, teachers can encourage students through verbal encouragement and smiling or can use peer tutoring, because research shows that all student are likely to benefit.

> **What Does This Mean to Me?**
> Have you always assumed that the way you were brought up was the "typical upbringing"?

TABLE 13.7

Foundational Principles of Multicultural Education

- The culture of America is positively influenced by contributions from many different cultural groups.
- Productive interaction with members of other cultures is enhanced if those people possess a degree of self- and group esteem.
- Learning about the achievements of one's own ethnic group enhances self- and group esteem.
- The United States has benefited and will continue to benefit from active interaction among members of culturally diverse groups.
- Cultural values and experiences lead to children thinking and behaving in particular ways. Students perform better academically once the teacher understands these values and experiences, accepts them as worthwhile, incorporates them into instructional lessons, and rewards them.

Uncommon Sense

That's True for Everybody—Or Is It?

Did you take it for granted that

• You were going to college?

• You could become what you wanted to become?

• Nobody would ever wonder what you were doing in a particular restaurant, neighborhood, or social setting because of your ethnicity or religious background?

• You would not have to check in advance that the establishment you were going to would have wheelchair access?

• Everyone would understand idiomatic speech in the same way that you do?

• Your academic strengths or weaknesses wouldn't be attributed to your gender or ethnicity?

Although these may or may not be true in your experience, they certainly are not true for everyone.

Source: Gay, G. The importance of multicultural education. *Educational Leadership, 61* (4), p. 32. Copyright © 2003 by the Association for Supervision and Curriculum Development. Reprinted by permission. The Association for Supervision and Curriculum Development is a worldwide community of educators advocating sound policies and sharing best practices to achieve the success of each learner. To learn more, visit ASCD at www.ascd.org.

What Does This Mean to Me?
In the section below on teacher expectations, you will see that it is often very difficult to avoid biases based on ethinic, social, or even acamedic grounds.

social justice Refers to the perspective that when considering issues such as education, human rights and the dignity of each human being should be a primary concern.

Second, all students profit from understanding different cultural values. For example, the respect for elders found in Native American and Asian cultures is likely to become increasingly desirable as the percentage of aging Americans increases over the years. Similarly, learning the Native American value of living in harmony with nature is increasingly important in this era of awareness of environmental impact (Biehle et al., 1999).

A third argument is that America is an increasingly diversified society, and students need to understand and know how to work with people of cultures other than their own. As can be seen in Table 13.1, we are clearly a broad mix of peoples.

A fourth argument is based upon the fact that "truth" is indeed in the eye of the beholder. Did Christopher Columbus *discover* a new world? From the perspective of Native peoples (from across North America), Columbus arrived in a world that was already populated.

Because the way we see the world is relative to who we are, we need multicultural programs to make the learning process meaningful and engaging. Well-designed programs have built-in respect for many cultures and teach about the contributions that various groups have made to American society.

A fifth argument emerges from statistics—the disappointing academic performance of many minority group students, frequently referred to as the "achievement gap" in academic performance. Multicultural researchers have shown that ethnically related content and activities can make classroom assignments more meaningful to minority students and can help them master basic skills (Banks, 1994a, 2006; Vasquez, 1990).

Social Justice

Social justice is a key element of multicultural education. According to Maxine Greene (1988), societies achieve social justice through the "dialectic of freedom." Freedom is defined here as growth, achieved together with others in social situations (Joshee, 2007). In schools, the growth process is fostered by creativity:

(Dynamic Graphics)

Different backgrounds result in different perspectives on school control and teaching methods.

Imagination allows us to break with those things are seen as "given" and to conceive of new ways of being. As she [Greene] noted, "There is no question but that some students face fearful obstacles due to inequities in this country [United States]. . . . It may be, however, that a general inability to conceive a better order of things can give rise to a resignation that paralyses and prevents people from acting to bring about change (Greene, 1995, pp. 18–19). (Joshee, 2007)

Multicultural approaches allow for a "public space," where creativity and imagination allow students to break free from prejudices, turning their cognitive capacity from self to community. Sleeter and Grant (2003) suggest that schools serve as a base for local social action projects, whereby diverse groups of students work together, encouraging an understanding of social justice and yielding concrete outcomes for a better society. As educators expand their programs to become more multicultural, they may find that respecting differences can cause conflict and contradiction. No one argues that schools should not teach arithmetic, but topics like language and history are confounded with social complexity. Multicultural education can help create bridges across the differences.

Implementing a Multicultural Approach to Teaching

What would implementing a multicultural approach to teaching mean in a classroom? How would one get started in adopting a multicultural (or *more* multicultural) approach to teaching? In this section, we start by looking at the rudiments of a multicultural approach and then dig deeper to look at a broader array of options.

Getting Started on a Multicultural Approach

We begin by looking at the basics of adopting a multicultural approach, the fundamentals of teaching in a culturally sensitive fashion. These basics might be summarized as in Figure 13.2: content integration, teaching accommodations, and prejudice reduction.

Integrate Culturally Relevant Content into Lesson Plans The goal of integrating culturally relevant content into one's lesson plans involves the question of what information should be included in instruction. For instance, which books should students read,

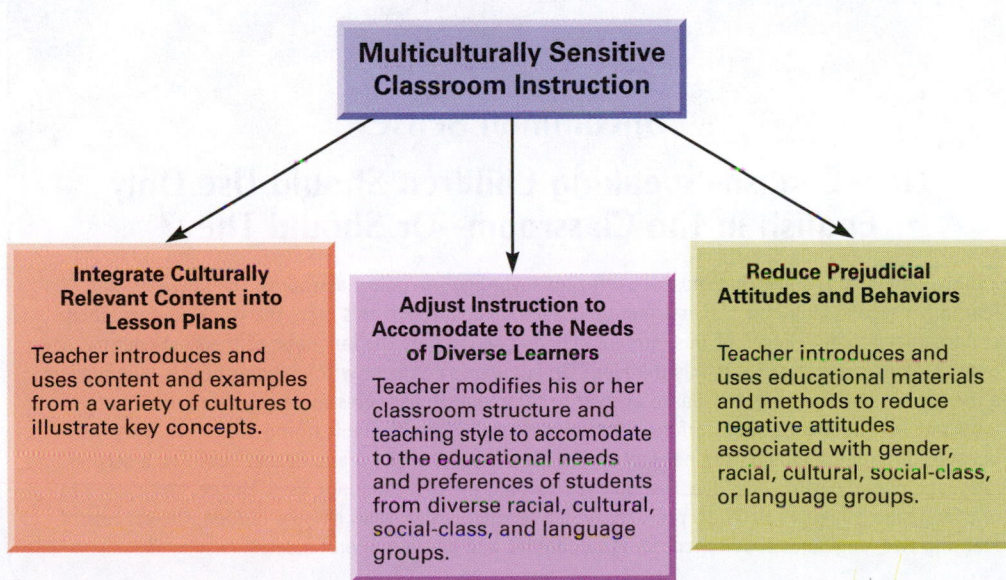

Figure 13.2 Basic Approaches to Multicultural Education

and which poems should be read, analyzed, and discussed? When they adopt the goal of multicultural education, teachers use examples, data, stories, and products from a variety of cultures and groups to illustrate key concepts, principles, generalizations, and theories in the subject matter of the course.

As is discussed in more detail later in the chapter, you can begin to work toward a more multiculturally sensitive approach to instruction by looking at what your students are already doing and trying to build more multicultural material into their efforts. There is ample help available on the Internet to get started on this approach. The lesson plans presented at the conclusion of this chapter will provide some ideas on how you can transform existing lesson plans into ones that are more multiculturally sensitive. As you develop your repertoire and stock of material, you may find yourself also developing a more sophisticated approach to multiculturally sensitive teaching.

Adjust Instruction to Accommodate to the Needs of Diverse Learners The early assumption behind equity-based instruction was that some students (e.g., low-SES students) were disadvantaged relative to their peers because of the socialization experience they receive in their homes and communities. The assumption was that, while all students have equally high potential for academic achievement, some cultural groups did not prioritize the internalization of the attitudes and skills that are essential for academic success. This assumption led to national programs such as the Head Start program for preschool students. More recently, however, those who study multicultural education underemphasize the "cultural deprivation perspective" and, instead, argue that students more typically suffer from a cultural clash. For instance, students from low-income and ethnic minority cultural groups often report that they encounter a majority culture that conflicts with their own (Gay, 2000).

It is difficult to prescribe specific instructional practices that promote equity. Instead, the general rule is for teachers to work hard to understand their students' perspective and goals and, once done, work equally hard to adapt the instruction they provide to the minority culture's strengths, interests, values, and aspirations. Adapting instruction to integrate students' primary language is one example of such accommodation (Beykont, 2000). The nearby Uncommon Sense box addresses this question of whether schools should require students to use the dominant culture's language only or should promote students' use of both the dominant language and the student's first language.

Reduce Prejudicial Attitudes and Behaviors The multicultural goal is to reduce prejudice by helping students develop democratic, rather than biased or negative, attitudes, values, and behaviors (Stephan, 1999). Racial attitudes begin to form early in life, even before

Uncommon Sense

Non-English-Speaking Children Should Use Only English in the Classroom—Or Should They?

Public opinion polls show that most U.S. citizens favor English-only classrooms. They believe that learning a second language places a mental burden on children. If this is so, the thinking goes, then children need to be relieved of this burden and educated in only the language of the host country, English. Does research support this thinking? Do languages compete with one another? Is bilingualism a mental burden? The research-based answer to these questions seems to be no. Using one's native language in school does not interfere in any meaningful way with the learning of English. This is so because different languages are not stored in different parts of the brain. Rather, learning a second language uses the same cognitive system that learning the first language uses. Hence, proficiency in one language is highly related to proficiency in a second. Rather than being a burden, the process of learning two languages simultaneously is a cognitive and developmental asset.

children enter the first grade, and they tend to reflect the attitudes in the majority culture. Nevertheless, teachers can help modify students' attitudes by integrating culturally relevant content and values into their lesson plans (McGregor, 1993), as discussed earlier. Teachers can also help modify students' attitudes through the use of cooperative learning.

As discussed in Chapter 9, cooperative learning generally enhances students' academic achievement, but it does more. It further helps students develop positive racial attitudes and cross-group (racial, gender) friendships (Aronson & Bridgeman, 1979; Slavin, 2001). Before teachers can expect cooperative learning to reduce prejudicial attitudes and behaviors, however, they need to prepare their students to interact in cooperative and constructive ways with students who are different from themselves. Without such pre-cooperative learning readiness, it is somewhat common for students to treat their peers unequally and for students with relatively high status (often boys or high-SES students) to dominate group dynamics at the expense of relatively lower-status students (often girls or low-SES students; Cohen, 1972).

Digging Deeper: Looking at Various Multicultural Approaches to Education

James Banks (1994a, 1994c, 2006; Banks & McGee Banks, 2010), a noted authority on multicultural education, discusses four **multicultural approaches** to education. Most multicultural programs adopt what he calls the *contributions approach*. These programs feature ethnic figures, both historical and present, who espouse values and behaviors consistent with those of mainstream American culture. Ethnic figures who challenge the dominant view are not included in these programs.

A second approach is called the *additive approach*, which expands the contributions approach. Ethnic concepts, themes, points of view, and accomplishments, as well as key ethnic figures, are added to the curriculum, but the perspective from which they are viewed is largely informed by mainstream values.

Banks refers to a third approach: *transformation*. This approach assumes that there is no single valid way of understanding people, events, concepts, and themes. Rather, each view or perspective has something of value to offer. For example, Duane Champagne (2006) describes the evolution of European settlers' perspective on Native rights. The attitude toward Native rights in the 1600s was "competitive colonialism." That later became "hegemony," and then finally "administrative colonialism" under the Indian Act. Remarkably, only since 1968 have Native peoples been able to exercise any decision-making autonomy over their lives and lands. Clearly, the perceptions of social justice during these periods were radically different.

Finally, Banks discusses the *social action approach*. It includes all components of the previous approaches. But students must also make decisions and take actions concerning the concepts, issues, or problems being studied.

multicultural approaches Approaches to education that include (1) contributions approach, (2) additive approach, (3) transformation approach, and (4) social action approach.

Key Concepts for Multicultural Education
The nearby Taking It to the Classroom box lists key questions to ask yourself when developing curriculum that uses facts and generalizations. These questions can also be used to analyze your response to particular ethnic groups or to compare and contrast the needs of different groups (Banks, 1994a).

The work of Eugene Garcia (1994) follows up on Banks's principles by offering instructional recommendations for implementing multicultural education (see the nearby Taking It to the Classroom box). But keep two points in mind when reviewing these recommendations. First, the recommendations are not unique to multicultural education: These are the things every teacher should do every day.

Second, Garcia's work focuses on bilingual education, which is of course important in America; so many of these recommendations apply well to bilingual contexts. While Garcia's recommendation for new teachers to find a mentor is wise, it is frequently problematic, since teachers are usually very busy and cannot spend very much time mentoring new teachers. As a result, teachers must draw upon the knowledge, skills, and values of their students to address diversity issues.

Taking It to the Classroom

Key Concepts that Guide the Teaching/Learning Process

- To what extent are your students aware of their ethnic identity, and how do they express that identity, if at all?
- What ethnic elements, such as values, customs, perspectives, are present in their group's culture today? How is their group's culture reflected in music, literature, art, and community activities?
- Immigration: From what country or countries do their groups originate? When and in what numbers did they immigrate to America?
- Community: To what extent are members of their groups concentrated within particular geographic regions?
- Racism and discrimination: In what ways have these groups been subjected to racism and discrimination?
- Communication: To what extent and for what reason do members any of these groups encounter problems when communicating with other ethnic groups?
- Self-concept: How have societal experiences affected the self-concepts of members of these groups?
- Power: What is the social, political, and economic status of their group? To what extent do they exercise power within the community? Within the larger society?
- Acculturation: To what extent have these groups influenced and been influenced by the mainstream society?

Source: Adapted from Biehler, R.F., Snowman, J., D'Amico, M., & Schmid, R.F. (1999). *Psychology applied to teaching* (Canadian edition). Toronto: ITP Nelson Canada.

Taking It to the Classroom

The Effective (Multicultural) Teacher

- Provides students with clear objectives.
- Continually communicates high expectations to every student. Remember: Differences aren't deficits!
- Monitors student progress and provides immediate feedback.
- Gets experience teaching culturally diverse students. New teachers should try to find a mentor.
- Clearly explains to students with specific instructional techniques. Winging it often does not work.
- Embeds instruction in a meaningful context, in part by getting students to help create the connections.
- Provides oppurtunities for active learning through small-group work and hands-on activities.
- Enchances students' self-esteem by having classroom materials and practices reflect their cultural and linguistic backgrounds.
- Develops a strong affinity for his or her students. Effective multicultural teachers describe their culturally diverse students in terms such as "We are all family here"
- Exhibits a high level of dedication. (Will often to be the first to arrive at school and among the last to leave, work weekends, constantly look for opportunities to improve instructional practices, and share successes and failures with colleagues). Every passion comes at a price, but with great rewards, too.
- And last but not least, has fun. Students don't laugh when they are bored or stressed, nor do they learn.

Source: Adapted from Biehler, R.F., Snowman, J., D'Amico, M., & Schmid, R.F. (1999). *Psychology applied to teaching* (Canadian edition). Toronto: ITP Nelson Canada. From Garcia, E.G. (1988). Attributes of effective schools for language minority children.

Becoming a Teacher of Diverse Children

In addition to the recommendations offered above, two strategies best help teachers become more multicultural (Grant et al., 2004). The first strategy is to ask teachers to become aware of and reflect on their attitudes toward others, and specifically on their attitudes toward others who are different from them, as in race or language. The second strategy asks teachers to become aware of and reflect on their instructional approach and how culturally relevant or sensitive it is to their students' diversity and cultural group memberships.

What Does This Mean to Me?
Am I an effective teacher? Which of the points in the box have I begun to work on? Which have I worked on the least?

Taking It to the Classroom

Connect With Kids and Parents of Different Cultures

By Linda Ross

As America's classrooms become increasingly diverse, many teachers face a culture gap that can hinder positive relationships with students and their families. In my work as a diversity trainer in schools, I help teachers begin bridging the gap by first taking a close look at their own assumptions and then finding new ways to reach out to those who are different. Here are some helpful hints for working successfully with a diverse student body.

Self-Quiz: What Are Your Assumptions?

Ask yourself . . .

- What are the different cultures in my school? (Include categories such as various ethnic groups, students with disabilities, new immigrants, residents of public housing, and any other relevant groupings.)
- What characteristics first come to mind when I think of each group?
- Where did these impressions come from? (Peers, family, media, religion, etc.) How reliable are these sources?
- How do I treat people based on these impressions?
- Can I remember a time when someone made assumptions about me based on a group I belong to? How did it make me feel?

Where Do Biases Begin?

How we react to people from different backgrounds is influenced by many factors:

- Our own personal experiences with people from that background.
- What we've heard about people from this background from our families, peers, the media, popular culture, school, religious institutions, and so on.
- Whether we see ourselves as sharing any values, goals, and ways of doing things with people of this background.
- Whether people from this background have any control over the things that make them different from us.
- How much power we believe people of this background have in our society and any laws or special programs we know about that affect how people of this background are treated.

How Culture Affects Behavior

- *Speaking up:* Sociologists draw a distinction between high-context societies in which there are many rules and people say less, and low-context societies that depend on explicit verbal messages.
- *Tracking time:* There are also different cultural takes on time: monochronic, meaning that people do one thing at a time and adhere to schedules, and polychronic, in which people do several things at a time, put interpersonal needs over schedules, and may view time as an invasion of self.
- *Physical self:* Culture shapes the kinds of gestures we use—for example, beckoning someone is offensive in some cultures—and the amount of personal space we need to feel comfortable.
- *Personal interaction:* Importantly for teachers, our cultures also contribute to how we view cooperation, competition, and discipline.

How to Build a Buffer against Bias

- Be aware of your assumptions.
  - We're all biased in one way or another. The key is to notice when you are making a judgment—positive or negative—about a child or parent, and then figure out what the judgment is based upon.
  - Invite an objective outsider to observe you in your classroom. You may suggest that the principal hire a professional to observe each teacher in the school.

(continued)

Taking It to the Classroom (continued)

- Be aware of cultural differences.
  - Everything we do—regarding time, personal space, body language, voice volume, small talk, and so on—is shaped by our culture. People from many cultures, including some Asians, Native Americans, Africans, and Hispanics/Latinos, don't make eye contact like Caucasian Americans do—in some cultures, in fact, making eye contact is considered an insult.
  - You can learn a lot about other cultures from your coworkers. Organize an after-school gathering for teachers and other school staff to bring in a favorite dish from their culture and to share cultural characteristics.
- Keep every student in mind.
  - Try to be sensitive to the cultural shock that new students experience.
  - It helps to be direct and deal with student biases right away. I recommend class discussions about why it is a mistake to judge people by their outer appearance.
  - When you create different standards for different groups, you do a disservice to everyone. Establish expectations and clearly communicate them—that way, no one will be made to feel second-rate or superior.
  - Familiarize yourself with all the holidays and traditions your students celebrate. Record important dates on a year-long calendar and check it before you schedule special events.
  - Encourage students to be honest about their own fears and misconceptions.
  - Make sure your classroom reflects diversity. Take a quick inventory. Do the pictures on your walls include a variety of cultures? Do you have a multicultural curriculum? One school got a grant to open up a Family Resource Center where parents could learn about the school and community and share information about their own cultures.
  - When in doubt about the appropriateness of certain materials, consult others. Think about forming a committee of parent volunteers to evaluate authenticity in questionable material.

Build Positive Communication with Parents

- Schools differ from culture to culture, as do parents' conceptions of the function of the school and the teacher. Before the school year begins, you might put together a newsletter describing the benefits of school, the opportunities that are available, what you expect of the students and parents, how the school operates, and how parents can get in touch with you if they have any problems or questions. Have volunteers translate the newsletter into the necessary languages.
- Establish rapport with parents. Encourage them to share about their cultures and experiences with you. They will feel more respected and will be more open to hearing about what you have to say. It is difficult for some parents to hear criticism of their children, so it will be easier to discuss a child when trust has been built.
- Let parents know that you care about their child, and suggest ways that they can help their child succeed in school. Demonstrate to the parents that a good education can make a difference in their child's life by citing examples of those who came from similar experiences and backgrounds and have been successful in America.
- Be consistent and honest. Teachers have told me that parents from certain cultures can be particularly unforgiving if they feel betrayed. It is often harder to reestablish trust after it's been damaged than to build it the first time.
- Help parents locate community resources. They may be keeping their child out of school to baby-sit or because they don't have appropriate clothing.
- Plan activities such as performances and parties to bring parents into the school.
- Recruit parent volunteers. Explain the benefits of their involvement and create a range of volunteer opportunities. If parents seem hesitant to volunteer, find out why. They may be embarrassed by their language skills or clothing, may need baby-sitting help, or may lack transportation. You may be able to encourage them or help them find solutions.

Source: These recommendations for working with kids and parents of different cultures were made by Linda Ross in Scholastic magazine. Retrieved from April 25, 2011, from http://www2.scholastic.com/browse/article.jsp?id=4426

Both of these strategies are surprisingly difficult for teachers to do, however, as expert observers rate the changes that teachers make as largely superficial rather than as truly transformational (Saldana & Waxman, 1997). The teachers who are able to transform their classroom instruction to reflect multicultural goals seem to do so by being specific in how they accommodate their lesson plans, doing so in depth rather than only at the surface, and linking the lesson plan of the day to the diverse students' goals, priorities, and concerns (Kitano et al., 1996).

Educators observe that "multilingual, multicultural, and multiethnic classrooms are here to stay. They are not a passing phenomenon" (Cohen & Lotan, 2004 p.736). In those classrooms where teachers use instructional strategies to create equity within heterogeneous (diverse) classrooms, students usually display a wide range of achievement, a wide range of literacy levels, and pronounced differences in English language proficiency. In the face of such student differences, the teacher needs to help all students feel that they are of equal status with their classmates. Teachers do this by believing that all students are capable of learning both basic skills and higher-level concepts, and also by creating conditions under which all students have equal access to challenging learning materials. One specific instructional strategy that these teachers use to create equality is cooperative learning, as mentioned earlier. Cooperative learning within heterogeneous student groups promotes not only greater social skills and academic achievement but also improved interpersonal relations among classmates (Slavin, 2001), at least to the extent that teachers help students to avoid negative and insensitive behaviors and encourage active oral participation among all group members. Teachers encourage active oral participation by placing students into rotating roles (e.g., facilitator, questioner, reporter; see Chapter 9) and by introducing skill-building activities such as how to ask for help from others and how to provide help to others (Cohen & Lotan, 2004).

Working in Culturally Different Contexts

Most beliefs that teachers hold about students, learning, and teaching come from their own experiences in life and as students. Because most prospective teachers are white and middle class, their beliefs typically reflect such an orientation. But many of these young people will be teaching in culturally diverse settings, or perhaps in settings that are not very diverse but represent a culture that is different from their own. This is simply a reflection of demographic changes in the United States. The issue of teaching in such settings is among the most important ones facing education today. Realizing the importance of the issue, however, is far from having a solid idea of what to do about it. Among the challenges that teachers face in diverse classrooms are these:

- Students with different backgrounds from their own—how to relate to these students, how to understand them
- Students with different backgrounds from those of other students in the class—how to create an environment in which students work well together and care about one another
- Poverty—working with students whose parents have very limited resources and with students whose parents are not present in the home
- Language—working with students who do not speak English (or do not speak it well) and with parents who do not speak English
- Numbers of students with special needs—working in urban school districts, which typically have much higher proportions of students who are classified as having special needs

This list may seem overwhelming, and indeed it would be unwise to underestimate the challenges associated with working with a diverse student body, particularly in a school with large numbers of students in or near conditions of poverty. However, the challenges are accompanied by rewards. A great teacher in a challenging setting can make a huge difference in hundreds of lives over the course of a career.

RIDE Mrs. Martin catches James in the hallway and says, "You know, James, I may have been a bit harsh the other day in saying that I don't teach kids, I teach algebra. What I mean by that is that I think all kids need to learn algebra, and I hold the same standards for all." How can James think productively not only about what he teaches but about how he teaches it?

Appendix
Influences on Learning
Students' learning is influenced by their experiences (PRAXIS™ I.B.6; INTASC, Principles 2, 3).

RIDE

REFLECTION FOR ACTION

The Event

James has discovered that he has an incredibly diverse set of students and he wants to be sensitive to all their needs in his instruction. He is trying to juggle his concerns over multiculturalism with his concerns for teaching the content he is assigned. How can he address the cultural diversity in his classes in a strong and positive way?

Reflection **RIDE**

What are the issues here? How can James possibly address the wide variety of differences among his students and retain his sanity?

What Theoretical/Conceptual Information Might Assist in Interpreting and Remedying This Situation? Consider the following:

The Press for Considering Diversity and the Press for Covering the Content

James needs to think about what the priorities are here. He should probably consult with the head of his department about where his focus should be for his teaching. How can he make sure that he is doing his job teaching his students the content they need to know and at the same time be a culturally responsible teacher?

What Is Reasonable to Accomplish in the First Year of Teaching

The first year of teaching is usually fairly stressful. Trying to be the best possible multicultural teacher may push James "over the edge." At the same time, he wants to do his best. He might think of his approach with regard to multicultural issues as taking "baby steps" in his first teaching year.

Being Student-Centered as an Overall Approach

Perhaps the best thing James can do is to take a very student-centered approach to his first year of teaching. That is, he can demonstrate his concern and interest to his students as he collects more information about the different cultures they bring to class. He can view this as a learning opportunity for himself as well as his students.

Information Gathering **RIDE**

James can look at some of the resources available in this chapter as well as others available on the Internet. He can also turn to his colleagues for help on this issue. His students and their families will also be able to help him.

Decision Making RIDE

James will need to make decisions about how much he can invest in making his teaching as multiculturally sensitive as possible and how much he will have to focus on other aspects of his teaching. He can certainly commit himself to holding high standards for his students and expressing his belief that they can be successful. He can also be honest about his interest in learning about his students and be frank about his responsibility to ensure that the material entrusted to him is taught to his classes.

Evaluation RIDE

James will need to conscientiously evaluate his progress in an ongoing fashion. Is he reaching out to all his students, or is he losing some? Does he really hold the same expectations for students regardless of their ethnic backgrounds? Is he engaging all his students or being selective? He might consider inviting a fellow teacher to observe his classes and give him feedback on it.

Further Practice: Your Turn

Here is a second event for consideration and reflection. In doing so, implement the processes of reflection, information gathering, decision making, and evaluation.

The Event

Working proactively is the best way to approach trying to be a good teacher of students from diverse backgrounds. But one of the issues when people come from different backgrounds is that sometimes they do not get along. Prejudices and biases often run strong. Imagine you have children in your class who come from groups that have long-standing disagreements with one another. There might be religious differences, differences relating to past or even current conflicts, or differences based on one group having oppressed the other. Imagine that these children refuse to work with one another or even acknowledge that the other children exist.

How would you approach this problem? Where would you go for help in this situation? What would you do if the problem escalates into verbal abuse or even physical threats? What is your role and responsibility in this situation for these students and for the class as a whole?

SUMMARY

● **What does diversity look like in the United States today?**

Each year, schools become increasingly diverse. In the year 2000, a little over two-thirds of the population was Caucasian, while one-third represented nonwhites: 13% African-American; 13% Hispanic; 4% Asian-American; 1% American Indian. By the year 2020, multicultural households will account for more than 40% of the U.S. population. The United States is also diverse in terms of socioeconomic status and language spoken at home. About 1 in 12 students come from homes where little or no English is spoken. About 1 in 8 students have special needs.

● **How can teachers best work with English language learners in regular classrooms?**

Teachers can work on tasks of interest to ELL students and where the opportunity for discussion of the tasks is strong. They can work on developing competence across the curriculum by remembering to take into account the needs of ELL students in all subject areas. They can use ELL students' knowledge and prior experience to build on their existing language competence. They can hold high standards for ELL students' ability to learn.

● **What is culture?**

Culture is a meaning and information system that is transmitted from one generation to the next. It provides both shared meanings (cultural interpretations) and shared activities (cultural practices) for its members. Communities create different cultures because they all face different problems (e.g., boys face different problems than do girls, low-SES students face different problems that do high-SES students), just as they possess different resources. People who share a commonality (those from the same social class, those with a shared history) generate different solutions to those problems, including different norms, rules, rituals, values such as collectivism, social hierarchies, and roles, all of which collectively define the culture.

● **What is multicultural education?**

Multicultural education is both a philosophical concept and an approach to education. It is a philosophical concept because it is built on the ideals of equality, equity, justice, and human dignity. It is an approach to education because it helps students from diverse backgrounds experience educational equality. Those who study multicultural education are deeply interested in confronting social issues such as poverty, sexism, and bilingualism such that they seek to ensure that all students receive educational equality.

● **How can teachers make their instruction inclusive of all learners in the class?**

Each year, schools become more diverse. Given such diversity, all students are different. Because teachers need to apply standards that apply equally to all students, they need to recognize, adapt, and respond constructively to students' diversity and special needs to help them overcome the unique obstacles they might face. Students from different cultural backgrounds hold different beliefs about learning, and no single approach to instruction will prove adequate in a culturally diverse classroom.

● **How can a teacher learn about the students in his or her class and their culture?**

There are a variety of approaches to this issue. To begin with, teachers need to know who their students are. Where do they come from, and what are their backgrounds? The Internet is an excellent resource for learning more about the cultural backgrounds of students once those backgrounds have been identified. And last, but certainly not least, there are the students themselves and their families. This is probably the best source of information because it is particular to the student and the student's family.

● **How can teachers recognize, adapt to, and respond to diverse learners?**

Each year, schools become more diverse. Given such diversity, all students are different. Because teachers need to apply standards that apply equally to all students, they need to recognize, adapt, and respond constructively to students' diversity and special needs to help them overcome the unique obstacles they might face. Students from different cultural backgrounds often hold different beliefs about learning, and no single approach to instruction will prove adequate to all students in a culturally diverse classroom.

Key Terms

cultural differences, p. 458
culture, p. 462
English language learners (ELLs),
    p. 460
ethnic group, p. 457

ethnicity, p. 455
expectations, p. 458
individualism, p. 458
multicultural, p. 461
multicultural approaches, p. 467

pluralistic society, p. 452
resilient, p. 456
social justice, p. 464
socioeconomic status, p. 455

Exercises

1. *Working in Culturally Different Contexts*
   How much experience do you have interacting with individuals who are different from you in race, ethnicity, or religious background? Have you spent time in settings in which you were in the minority with regard to any of these aspects? Make a list of significant and ongoing relationships you have with people whose cultural backgrounds are different from yours. What have you learned from these individuals (or settings) that you could apply to working with students who are different from you? Try to focus not just on particulars but also on broader issues of perspective taking, sensitivity, language, and assumptions that should be challenged. If your list is rather short, what can you do to gain broader experience in this area?

2. *Adapting Lesson Plans for a More Multicultural Approach*
   Try taking one of your lesson plans and altering it to be more multiculturally sensitive in the fashion that you see in the lesson plans at the end of this chapter. Ask yourself how you are going to get the necessary information and how you are going to incorporate it into your plan. This would also be something that would be great to do with a friend who is also becoming a teacher. Take the same plan and both of you make changes—and then compare your approaches.

3. *Learning about a Particular Culture*
   Consider a culture or ethnic group that is dramatically different from your own. You might want to pick one that you are likely to encounter in your teaching. Set yourself the challenge of becoming much more expert about that culture. What are the most interesting differences you see in how those cultural differences affect children of the age groups you anticipate teaching. Compare that culture to your own at the same age. What are the key differences and similarities you see?

4. *Compare Notes with a Friend Whose Upbringing Is Different from Yours*
   Get together with a friend whose culture or ethnicity is different from yours. Pick a number of issues or events to discuss where your different experiences growing up might be particularly strong. Good choices for this would be religion, parental expectations (are you expected to marry within the culture/religion?), family norms (did you typically have friends over to eat dinner with you or sleep over?), foods, important events such as birthdays, and so on. How has life been different for you and your friend, and how might that impact how you were as students?

5. *Biases*
   What biases do you hold? Think hard and stretch yourself on this one. Do you think certain groups of people tend to behave in certain ways? What is the difference between acknowledging differences between groups and holding biases or being prejudiced? How can you recognize biases that are affecting your ability to be a good teacher?

Lesson Plans

The lesson plans for this chapter are a little bit different from those in the other chapters. In this chapter, a lesson plan is presented as it might normally be, and then a revised version of the lesson plan is presented that looks at the same subject matter from a more multicultural perspective. These two examples are taken from an excellent resource: "Turning on Learning: Five Approaches for Multicultural Teaching Plans for Race, Class, Gender and Disability, fifth edition, by Carl A. Grant and Christine E. Sleeter.

Lesson #1: "Solving Two Equations with Two Unknowns"

BEFORE

SUBJECT AREA: Algebra

GRADES: 9–12

TIME: Four class periods

I. OBJECTIVE: Students will solve two equations with two unknowns using four methods: graphing, substitution, addition, and determinants.

II. SUGGESTED PROCEDURES:

1. Explain to students that they will learn how to solve two equations with two unknowns using four different methods: graphing, substitution, addition, and determinants.

2. Demonstrate a detailed example of how the graphing method is used. Be sure to encourage students to ask questions if they do not understand an aspect of the method. Work through one or two more examples, allowing students to give input as to how the problem should be solved using the method. When you feel that students can apply the method, assign homework from the textbook.

3. Teach the other three methods using the process outlined in step 2.

4. Prepare a worksheet with problems involving all four methods. Distribute the worksheet for students to use as a review for the quiz.

III. EVALUATIONS:

1. Listen to students' input when demonstrating the examples on the board to determine if they are grasping the methods.

2. Assess students' understanding of the methods by grading their homework assignments, worksheets, and exams.

AFTER

SUBJECT AREA: Algebra*

*Source: Robin White, Racine, Wisconsin.

GRADES: 9–12

TIME: Four class periods

I. OBJECTIVES:

1. Students will solve two equations with two unknowns using four methods: graphing, substitution, addition, and determinants.

2. Students will teach the methods they have studied to another student.

3. Students will interact with peers of the same and opposite sex.

4. Students will develop attitudes and skills for cooperation.

5. Students will develop planning skills.

6. Students will realize that both sexes are equally capable of learning and teaching math.

II. SUGGESTED PROCEDURES:

1. Divide students into four groups with equal numbers of girls and boys in each group. Separate the girls and the boys who associate with each other often. Separate students at the same skill levels.

2. Assign to each group one of the four methods for solving two equations with two unknowns.

3. Tell students to use their textbooks and the supplementary books to learn how to use this method. They should work together to apply the method to various problems in the books and to make sure that everyone in the group can solve the equations using the given method.

4. Once students feel confident about using the method being learned by their group, the teacher should check their problems to be sure they understand it. (Some sample problems are given in the figure on page 477.)

5. If the teacher feels that the students understand the method, the group can begin to design its mini-lesson, which they will use to teach the method to other students. The mini-lesson should have four parts—objectives, materials, procedure, and evaluation—to allow each student in the group to make some contribution to the plan. The mini-lessons can be as long or short as the group feels is necessary to teach the concept. The students may choose to explain the method and ask the other students to do problems, or they may assign homework and a quiz—the decision is to be made by the group. The students should make sure that each group member can teach the mini-lesson they have created.

6. The teacher should check each group's lesson plan to see how the methods will be taught and then make copies of the plan for each student in the group.

Lesson Plans

7. Divide students into four new groups with equal numbers of girls and boys in each group. Each group should have one or two students who can do one of each of the four methods. Separate the girls and boys who associate with each other often. Separate students at the same skill level.

8. Each student in the group should teach his or her method for solving equations to the other group members. The students should follow their lesson plans.

9. The students should make sure that all of the members of the group can perform the four methods. When the groups feel they are confident about the methods, the game begins.

10. Each student in the group should choose a number from 1 to 4 (or up to the number of students in the group), which will serve to identify the student from each group who will be competing.

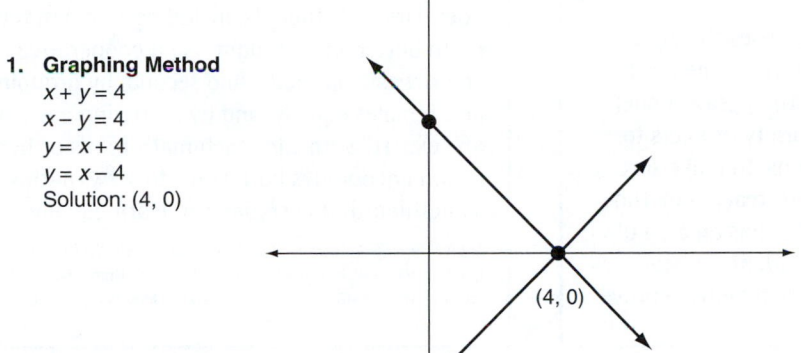

1. Graphing Method
$x + y = 4$
$x - y = 4$
$y = x + 4$
$y = x - 4$
Solution: (4, 0)

2. Substitution Method
$3x + 5y = 3$
$x = 8 - 4y$
$3(8 - 4y) + 5y = 3$
$24 - 12y + 5y = 3$
$-7y = -21$
$y = 3$
Solution: $(-4, 3)$
$x = -4$
Solution: $(-4, 3)$

3. Determinants Method
$3x - 2y = 7$
$3x + 2y = 9$

$D = \begin{vmatrix} 3 & -2 \\ 3 & 2 \end{vmatrix} = 6 - (-6) = 12$

$Dx = \begin{vmatrix} 7 & -2 \\ 9 & 2 \end{vmatrix} = 14 - (-18) = 32$

$Dy = \begin{vmatrix} 3 & 7 \\ 3 & 9 \end{vmatrix} = 27 - 21 = 6$

$x = \dfrac{Dx}{D} = \dfrac{32}{12} = \dfrac{8}{3}$

$y = \dfrac{Dy}{D} = \dfrac{6}{12} = \dfrac{1}{2}$

Solution: $\left(\dfrac{8}{3}, \dfrac{1}{2} \right)$

4. Addition Method
$x + y = 2$
$3x - 2y = 0$
$2x + 2y = 4$
$3x - 2y = 0$
$5x = 4$

$x = \dfrac{4}{5}$

$\dfrac{4}{5} + y = 2$

$y = \dfrac{10}{5} - \dfrac{4}{5}$

$y = \dfrac{6}{5}$

Solution: $\left(\dfrac{4}{5}, \dfrac{6}{5} \right)$

Sample Problems

11. Choose a number, and the student from each group with that number should come to the board. Read the problem, and the students must write and solve the problem. The problem must be solved by the method specified by the teacher.

12. The groups earn four, three, two, or one point for solving the problem first, second, third, or fourth, respectively. No points are given to a group that solves the problem incorrectly. All groups are required to keep score. The winning team may be given some reward, although the reward should not be overemphasized.

13. On the day after the game is played, give the students a quiz on which they must demonstrate their abilities to solve the equations.

III. EVALUATIONS:

1. Assess students' ability to solve the equations by correcting sample problems submitted by the initial groups and by observing their performance during the game and on the quiz.

2. Assess students' ability to teach the lessons by observing the second groupings.

(continued)

Lesson Plans

Lesson #1: "Solving Two Equations with Two Unknowns" (continued)

3. Observe the groups to determine if interaction and cooperation are occurring.

4. Listen to group conversations to determine if boys are treating girls equally and if girls are treating boys equally.

WHY THE CHANGES?

COOPERATION: The "After" lesson plan uses the jigsaw model of cooperative learning to teach the same math concepts taught in the "Before" plan. The jigsaw model involves students interacting with a variety of peers to figure out a method of solving equations, to make sure all group members understand it, and to teach a method to other peers. Since every class member has an area of expertise in the second grouping, all students appear valuable and capable to their peers, which helps improve students' perceptions of and interactions with each other. The "After" plan also helps students learn the content better than if the teacher simply delivers it to them, in that cooperative learning actively involves them in figuring it out themselves and in helping each other to learn.

STEREOTYPING: At the secondary grade level, students often begin to view math more as a male subject rather than as gender neutral, and many begin to doubt the competence of females in math. The "Before" lesson does not address this issue, whereas the "After" lesson does. First, all students, including females, tend to learn math better when taught using cooperative rather than competitive methods. And second, by grouping males and females equally, and by preparing each student to be an "expert" who can teach math to his or her peers, the lesson encourages both sexes to view math knowledge as something that everyone can learn equally well.

Source: Turning on Learning: Five Approaches for Multicultural Teaching Plans for Race, Class, Gender and Disability, 5th Edition, by Carl A. Grant and Christine E. Sleeter, pp. 115–118. Reprinted with the permission of John Wiley & Sons, Inc.

Lesson Plans

Lesson #2: Tie-Dyeing*

BEFORE

SUBJECT AREA: Art

GRADES: 4–6

TIME: Two class periods

I. OBJECTIVES:

1. Students will identify primary and secondary colors.
2. Students will produce patterns through tie-dyeing.

II. SUGGESTED PROCEDURES:

1. Show the color chart. Explain the meaning of primary and secondary colors.

    a. Primary colors—red, yellow, blue—are so called because they cannot be made by mixing any other colors.

    b. Secondary colors—orange, green, violet—are colors that come about from mixing the primary colors:
   Red + Yellow = Orange
   Yellow + Blue = Green
   Blue + Red = Violet

2. Explain to the class that they will be mixing secondary colors from primary colors. Pass out bowls of dye (one red, one yellow, one blue) and three empty bowls to each student. Have each student mix each of the three secondary colors.

3. Pass out 12-by-12-inch cloth and several pieces of string to each student.

4. Explain the concept of pattern. Pattern is the repetition of lines or shapes. The chief purpose of pattern is to provide a decorative quality to enrich the surface of the cloth.

5. Explain the principles of tie-dyeing. Cloth is wrapped in various ways with the pieces of string to make a pattern. The cloth is then put in the dye bath. The cloth underneath the string resists the dye and stays white, while the rest of the cloth turns the color of the dye, thus making a pattern.

6. Have each student wrap his or her cloth in the pattern desired; then dip all of it or sections of it in the dye.

7. When the cloth is dry, have each student unwrap his or her own piece, compare it with others in the group, and discuss how the pattern was obtained.

III. EVALUATION: Assess students' understanding of the concepts of color and pattern and of the process of tie-dyeing through the quality of their tie-dyed products.

AFTER

SUBJECT AREA: Art

GRADES: 4–6

TIME: Two or three class periods

I. OBJECTIVES:

1. Students will identify primary and secondary colors.
2. Students will appreciate the traditional Native American use of natural dyes to obtain various primary and secondary colors.
3. Students will produce patterns through tie-dyeing.
4. Students will appreciate the traditional Black/African use of pattern in clothing.
5. Students will work with peers of different races and gender.

II. SUGGESTED PROCEDURES:

1. Divide the class into groups of six students each. Groups should be as race and gender mixed as possible.

2. Show the color chart. Explain the meaning of primary and secondary colors.

    a. Primary colors—red, yellow, blue—are so called because they cannot be made by mixing any other colors.

    b. Secondary colors—orange, green, violet—are colors that come about from mixing the primary colors:
   Red + Yellow = Orange
   Yellow + Blue = Green
   Blue + Red = Violet

*Source: P. Lloyd Kollman, Kenosha, Wisconsin, and Debra Owena, Racine, Wisconsin.

(continued)

Lesson Plans

Lesson #2: Tie-Dyeing (continued)

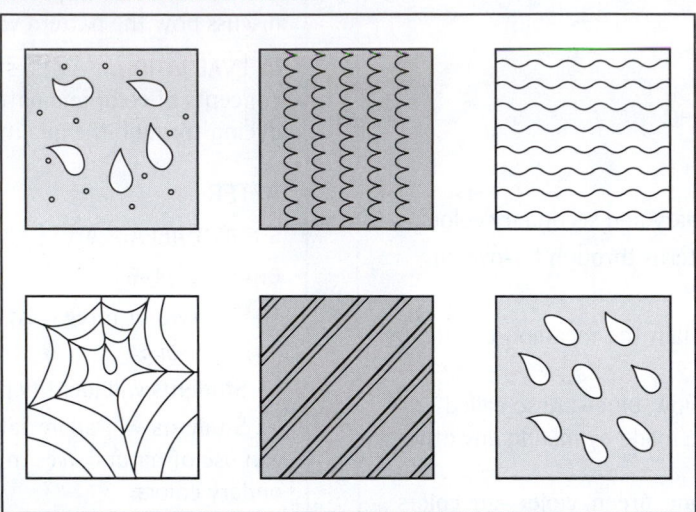

Wall Hanging

3. Explain that art for the Native American Indian was not separate from life; rather, it was a balance of tradition and spirituality. Color to the Native American Indian had energy and spiritual qualities. Read examples of American Indian poetry and traditional stories involving color, such as the following:

Prayer After Singing Gahe Songs (Chiricahua)

Big Blue Mountain Spirit,
The home made of blue clouds,
The cross made of the blue mirage,
There, you have begun to live,
There, is the life of goodness,
I am grateful for that made of goodness there.
Big Yellow Mountain Spirit in the south,
Your spiritually hale body is made of yellow clouds;
Leader of the Mountain Spirits, holy Mountain Spirit,
You live by means of the good of this life.
Big White Mountain Spirit in the west,
Your spiritually hale body is made of the white mirage;
Holy Mountain Spirit, leader of the Mountain Spirits,
I am happy over your words,
You are happy over my words.

Big Black Mountain Spirit in the north,
Your spiritually hale body is made of black clouds;
In that way, Big Black Mountain Spirit,
Holy Mountain Spirit, leader of the Mountain Spirits,

I am happy over your words,
You are happy over my words,
Now it is good. (Hoijer, 1938, p. 69)

Song of the Sky Loom (Tewa Indian Weaving Song)

Oh our Mother the Earth, oh our Father the Sky,
Your children are we, and with tired backs
We bring you the gifts that you love.
Then weave for us a garment of brightness;
May the warp be the white light of morning,
May the weft be the red light of evening,
May the fringes be the falling rain,
May the border be the standing rainbow.
Thus weave for us a garment of brightness
That we may walk fittingly where birds sing,
That we may walk fittingly where the grass is green,
Oh our Mother the Earth, oh our Father the Sky!
(Spinden, 1933, p. 94)

4. Explain that many Native American nations got the colors used in dyeing wool from natural plants. Give examples:

Red—Juniper ash (tree), bark of the root Cercocarpus parvifolius
Blue—Indigo (plant), blue corn, blue clay
Yellow—Rabbit weed (flower), Chamizo blossoms and twigs

Lesson Plans

5. Explain to students that they will mix secondary colors from the primary colors. Pass out three buckets of dye (one red, one yellow, one blue) and three empty buckets to each group. Have each group of six pair up (two-two-two). Each pair of students will mix a secondary color for their group (orange, green, violet).

6. Pass out 12-by-12-inch cloth to each student and several pieces of string.

7. Explain the concept of pattern. Pattern is the repetition of lines or shapes. The chief purpose of pattern is to provide a decorative quality to enrich the surface of the cloth.

8. Explain the principles of tie-dyeing. Cloth is wrapped in various ways with the pieces of string to make a pattern. The cloth underneath the string resists the dye and stays white while the rest of the cloth turns the color of the dye, thus making a pattern.

9. Explain to the class that in many Black/African cultures pattern and tie-dyeing are a way to decorate clothing. Show a sample of the loose-fitting garment called the *dashiki*, which probably originated in West Africa. Show examples of African animals as well.

10. Have each student wrap his or her cloth in the pattern desired; then dip all or sections of it in the dyes in the group.

11. When the cloth is dry, have each student unwrap his or her own piece, compare it with others in the group, and discuss how the pattern was achieved.

12. Pass out one 48-by-32-inch burlap piece and some glue to each group. Explain that each student in the group will contribute his or her tie-dyed cloth to make a large wall hanging for the class. It is up to the group members to decide on the design for the wall hanging. The figure on page 480 shows an illustration of a wall hanging made by one group. While the students are working on their wall hanging, play West African music.

13. When the wall hangings are finished, display one on each wall.

III. EVALUATIONS:

1. Through the quality of their tie-dyed products, assess students' understanding of the concepts of color and pattern and the process of tie-dyeing.

2. Through class discussion, assess students' appreciation of other cultures (Native American, Black/African).

3. Assess students' ability to work cooperatively and to contribute to the class through observation.

REFERENCES

Hoijer, H. (1938). *Chiricahua and Mescalero Apache texts.* Chicago: University of Chicago Publications in Anthropology, Linguistic Series.

Spinden, H.J. (1933). *Songs of the Tewa.* New York: Exposition of Indian Tribal Arts.

WHY THE CHANGES

CURRICULUM CONTENT

The "After" plan explores the cultural uses and origins of the concepts in the "Before" plan for the purpose of enhancing students' understanding of them and their knowledge and appreciation of other cultural groups. Content about how American Indians mixed color teaches students how colors can be achieved in ways other than using purchased dyes, as well as how color is derived from nature. The American Indian poetry teaches students to view color aesthetically and symbolically. Content about African use of tie-dyeing teaches students about the origins of this art form, as well as about the technique and thought behind one kind of African textile.

GROUPING OF STUDENTS

In the "Before" plan, each student works alone. The "After" plan encourages cooperation for reasons similar to those in the Human Relations approach: to encourage the appreciation of peers and the development of skills and attitudes for cooperating.

Source: Turning on Learning: Five Approaches for Multicultural Teaching Plans for Race, Class, Gender and Disability, 5th Edition, by Carl A. Grant and Christine E. Sleeter, pp. 203–207. Reprinted with the permission of John Wiley & Sons, Inc.

Mr. Antoine, Ms. Baldwin, and Mrs. Chambliss have all just finished teaching *The Scarlet Letter* in their ninth-grade English classes. Their classes are filing into their rooms to take the assessments that their teachers have developed. This is what they see:

Mr. Antoine

Examination
4th Period English
The Scarlet Letter

Instructions: You will have the entire period to complete this. There are 30 multiple-choice questions, two short essays, and one long essay. Each multiple-choice question is worth 2 points; the short essays are worth 10 points each, and the long essay is worth 20 points. If you have any questions, please come to my desk to ask them. Please make all your work be your own. Good luck.

1. Who is the protagonist in the novel?
   a. Arthur Dimmesdale
   b. Hester Prynne
   c. Nathaniel Hawthorne
   d. Pearl
   e. The Salem Witch Trials

Ms. Baldwin's Great *Scarlet Letter* Debate

Resolved: "Hester Prynne's treatment by the townspeople was basically fair given the social norms and values of rural Massachusetts at that time."

Pick a partner to work with on this project. Come up to the Great Debate Box and draw a lot that will tell whether you are going to argue to the pros or the cons of this debate, whom you are going to debate against, and when you will be scheduled to debate. Together, develop the arguments that support the position that you have been assigned. You may use the novel and your class notes from our discussion to develop your arguments. You will be graded on the logic of your argument, your ability to support your points from the novel and the writings we have read about the novel, and your speaking ability. You and your partner will receive the same grade for this work.

Chambliss Four-Star Productions
Casting Meeting for
The Scarlet Letter

Congratulations, you have been named Casting Director for Chambliss Four-Star Productions' filming of *The Scarlet Letter*. Your task over the next hour is to pick Hollywood stars to portray each of the following characters from *The Scarlet Letter*:

Rev. Arthur Dimmesdale
Hester Prynne
Roger Chillingworth
Pearl

For each character, pick a Hollywood star and write a brief essay explaining why you think the star would be the best person to play the role. In your essay, tell us what you know about the character and the star that makes the star the right person for the role. You may want to discuss other stars that you considered and decided against, and why.

R I D E Reflection for Action

Each of these assessments might be criticized for one reason or another. What strengths and weaknesses do you find in each of them? After you read the chapter, return to these assessments and answer the questions again. Have your answers changed?

Guiding Questions

- What assessments do we experience in everyday life and how do we react to them?

- What are the characteristics of assessment that make them most useful?

- What is the role of assessment in the instructional process?

- How can teachers devise assessments that facilitate instruction and at the same time provide information about students' progress?

- Of the many options teachers have for assessment, which are the best?

- How can a teacher develop a grading system that is fair and that lets students take responsibility for their own learning?

- How can assessment help students learn about their own strengths and weaknesses?

- How can teachers continually improve assessment and grading practices?

- How can teachers create and modify assessments to include learners who face special challenges?

- How do cultural differences among students and their parents affect the process of communicating progress?

CHAPTER OVERVIEW

Classroom assessments are an important form of communication. They inform teachers about student progress. They help students understand their own strengths and weaknesses. They are a critical communication between the student and the teacher. When used well, they give the teacher insight about the efficacy of her teaching and help her plan the next instructional steps. Carefully considered and well-constructed assessments promote the notion that classroom assessment is not just assessment *of* learning; it is assessment *for* learning. This chapter examines the critical issues of classroom assessment: It looks at reasons for assessment, assessment options, evaluation of results, and the relationship between assessment and instruction. The chapter concludes with a discussion of communicating with parents. In Chapter 15, we will focus on standardized and standards-based assessment; here we will concentrate on assessment used in the classroom.

Assessments in Everyday Life
- Assessments All around Us
- The Characteristics of Useful (and Welcome) Assessments

Assessment for Learning: Roles, Goals, and Audiences
- Student, Parent, and Teacher Concerns in Assessment
- Other Audiences and Areas of Concern
- Diversity among Students and Their Parents
- Formative and Summative Assessment

Principles of Assessment and Grading
- Communication
- Fairness
- Growth

Options for Assessment
- Recognition Format
- Generative Format
- Alternative, or Production, Format
- Informal Assessments

Developing and Using Assessments
- Determining What to Assess
- Rubrics
- Determining the Best Assessment Format
- Assessing Students with Special Needs
- Administering, Scoring, and Communicating Assessment Results

Interpreting Classroom Assessments
- Comparing Performance with Expectations
- Reflecting on Assessments to Improve Them
- The Student Role in Assessment

Developing a Grading System
- Options for Grading Systems
- Record Keeping for Grading

Communicating with Parents
- Parent/Teacher Conferences
- Parent/Teacher/Student Conferences
- Maintaining Communication

Assessments in Everyday Life

In everyday life, assessment involves taking stock of the current situation and determining the best course of action for the future. A painter makes a brushstroke or two, then assesses their effect on the overall composition. A teenager confronts a friend about a concern and wonders if she has been too harsh. A chef tries out a new dish and wonders what could be done to make it better. A family gathers to weigh the pros and cons of moving to a larger home in a neighboring town.

Assessments All around Us

What assessments do you experience in life? If you are an athlete, then every time you hit a golf ball, or shoot a free throw, or try to hit a softball, you receive feedback—an assessment—on how well you did. If you bake a cake, or drive a car, or call a girlfriend on the phone, you are bombarded with feedback, which is basically an assessment on how you are doing. Some of these assessments we eagerly seek out and welcome, some we approach with a sense of dread, and others depend entirely on what the feedback will be.

Why is that?

Why are some assessments eagerly sought after and others avoided? Why do we want to hear if people liked the dessert we made for them, but only want to hear from our dentist if the news is good. Why do we want to hear what our friends think about recently purchased clothes, but not so much what our parents think?

(Blend Images/ImageSource Limited)

The Characteristics of Useful (and Welcome) Assessments

We might start by thinking about shooting a free throw in basketball. If we see the ball bounce off the right-hand side of the rim near the front, we think: "Hmmmm . . . off to the right and not quite enough push on the shot." We don't think: "Well, I think it was a good shot no matter where it went. It must be the ball or the basket that is the problem here."

There are two interesting aspects to the feedback (the assessment results) that we get here. First, the information is objective. We need to know what occurred. There is little reason to doubt the feedback we got. If our dad says, "That was a very good free throw," we know the information is coming from our dad and we know he isn't always objective in how he sees his children and their efforts. Second, the feedback is timely. We know immediately what happened and can tie the feedback to what we just did. These are two very important characteristics of good assessments: objectivity and timeliness. We can have faith in the quality of the information, and it has been received soon enough to help us improve our performance.

So, we try to correct our form. We try to shoot a bit more to the left and a bit harder. But the results are disappointing. Our shots are going anywhere but in! We think: "I really wish my coach could take a look and give me some advice here." Sometimes we need expert help in order to improve. Some coaching (expert feedback with ideas on how to improve) would be greatly appreciated. A third characteristic of assessment is the degree to which interpretation of the feedback is necessary in order to improve. But it would be one thing for our coach to offer some help, as opposed to maybe our younger brother who is a "know-it-all" but really doesn't know much about basketball. A four characteristic of assessment is our confidence in the authority of the person giving the feedback.

Now imagine two different possibilities. The first is that we are trying out for the basketball team and really want to make it. Thus, we are very much interested in getting better at shooting free throws. In the second possibility, we are just having fun on a Saturday afternoon, and don't care all that much one way or the other about getting better. A fifth characteristic has to do with how important we think developing the skill is.

And finally, what if the free throw isn't in practice, but in a real game and at an important point? That changes the whole situation. The context of the assessment very much affects how we look at the feedback. If we make the free throw and win the game, then all feedback is welcome. If we miss the free throw and lose the game, we don't really want to hear from anyone for a while! The sixth characteristic is context.

Let's see what we have here. The characteristics of a good assessment relate to the following:

1. *Objectivity:* Can we rely on the information we have received?
2. *Timeliness:* Does the feedback come soon enough to be useful?
3. *Interpretation:* Do we need expert help to interpret the feedback in order to make good use of it?
4. *Source:* Do we trust the source of the information?

5. *Interest:* Do we see the feedback as helping us on a task at which we really want to get better?

6. *Context:* What are the consequences of our performance and the feedback we receive on it?

We will be looking at some more formal definitions of good assessments/feedback later in the chapter, but these commonsense notions of quality will be very helpful when you think about the assessments you are planning for your students. Try taking *their* point of view on each of these!

Assessment for Learning: Roles, Goals, and Audiences

assessment The process of coming to understand what students know and can do.

In education, **assessment** is the process of coming to understand what a student knows and can do. When we are engaged in *assessment for learning*, there is an additional step: determining what to do next. Thus, assessment is not an event; it is a process. Not only does the teacher gain this information, but in strong assessment programs the student does as well. And both obtain a sense of where to go next in the student's progress. Classroom assessment is one of the most important activities that teachers undertake.

Teachers want students to take pride in their work, to feel a strong sense of responsibility for it, to enjoy the efforts they put into it, and to learn about themselves as a result. When assessments provide the opportunity for students to rise to a challenge, cognitive and emotional growth results. Because of its potential to enhance or detract from learning, assessment must be carefully considered, planned, and executed. It should be caring, respectful, and professional. Developing an assessment program takes hard work, considerable thought, openness to new ideas, and the courage to reflect on and be critical of one's own ideas and actions.

Student, Parent, and Teacher Concerns in Assessment

The fundamental role of assessment in classrooms is to facilitate the growth of children. At the same time, there is often a need to provide feedback to students, their parents, the teacher, other educators, and the larger community. The three primary audiences are students, parents (or guardians), and teachers. Members of each group are likely to have different concerns about assessment.

Student Concerns in Assessment Questions or concerns that students might have as they approach an assessment include the following:

- Is the test/quiz/activity going to be fun?
- Am I going to do well on it? How good am I at this?
- What's going to be on this assessment?
- How will it be graded?
- How will it affect my grade?
- How will it affect what the teacher thinks of me?
- Am I going to be compared to other students, or maybe embarrassed in front of them?
- How much work is it going to be?
- Will this assessment help me get better at this?
- Will being successful be worth the effort?

Of course, students at different levels have different concerns. Young children seek their teacher's approval. A smile, a "good job," a sticker, a star, or a pat on the back can mean everything in the world to a young child. As children grow older, they still desire approval, but they also begin to develop concerns about grades. This development is not always simple, however. As discussed in Chapter 11, some students or even a whole class might wish to avoid publicly demonstrating a strong performance. In other cases, the desire for good grades becomes the primary motivation for students to achieve, crowding out any intrinsic love for learning.

Parent Concerns in Assessment   Some of the major questions and concerns that parents and caregivers bring to assessments are the following:

- How is my child doing?
- What can I do to help?
- What are my child's strengths and weaknesses?
- How is my child getting along socially?
- How is my child doing compared to the other children (in the class, in the school, in the nation)?
- Is my child working up to his/her potential?

(Mary Kate Denny/Photo Edit)

Teacher Concerns in Assessment   When considering assessment, teachers have to evaluate the progress of individual children as well as the class as a whole. They need to decide whether to move on to the next topic or to spend more time reviewing the current one. If they are about to start a new unit, they need to know how much the students already know about the new unit, how interested they are in the topic, and what approach might work best. Teachers are concerned with how to assess a child with special needs who has an individualized education program (IEP) that requires different assessment procedures from those of the rest of the children in the class. In addition to knowing how well children are doing on a specific task, teachers need to know whether students are developing broad skills that are transferable to a wide variety of tasks. Furthermore, teachers need to help children develop the ability to assess their own strengths and weaknesses. Some questions and concerns that teachers have about assessment are the following:

Whether an assessment is a cause for anxiety and frustration or an opportunity to show what you know depends on how the assessment setting is constructed by the teacher.

- Which assessment option would work best in this situation?
- When should assessment take place—before, during, or after instruction?
- How can this assessment promote students' ability to evaluate their own progress?
- How well does it match the statewide standards or assessments?
- How will I communicate the results to students and parents?
- How will students react to this assessment?
- How much work will it take to construct or select the assessment and to grade it?
- How is this assessment related to others in the class?
- How can students learn that they need to work more in this area without making them feel like failures?
- What if the results are really poor?
- How can this information improve instruction? What will I do next?
- Should this assessment count as part of the students' grades?

Other Audiences and Areas of Concern

Teachers also have to consider their responsibility to other audiences that receive and use assessment information. For example, colleges use high school transcripts to make admissions decisions. What should they expect from a course grade? What should employers expect? Should schools use eighth-grade report cards to determine whom to place in regular or in honors English classes in ninth grade?

There is substantial change and uncertainty in assessment today, not just for classroom assessment, but for annual **standardized assessment** on state-mandated tests as well (Cizek, 2001). State and federal concerns for educational achievement and the funding tied to that achievement have become matters of increasing importance for local school districts. The

standardized assessment A measure of student ability in which all students take the same measure under the same conditions.

No Child Left Behind federal legislation mandated not only standardized assessment but also regular progress of all groups of children on those assessments. State legislators, as representatives of the citizens who pay for schools, have a legitimate interest in how well students are doing (Phelps, 1998). More recently, the Race to the Top federal program requires standardized assessment related to a core set of standards (U.S. Department of Education 2009).

Diversity among Students and Their Parents

Not all students are the same. The student in a high school English class whose world will be crushed if she does not get into the Ivy League school of her dreams is sitting next to the boy who may be the first in his family to go to college. He is wondering whether instead of going to college, he should get a job to help his family. Next to them is a boy with special needs and next to him a girl for whom English is a second language. Their teacher is responsible for assessing each of these students fairly. That teacher must understand that children come from different cultural backgrounds that will influence not only their performances but also their parents' aspirations for them.

Increasingly, teachers work with students who are new arrivals to the United States. Parents who have recently immigrated to the United States may not understand our grading system. They may not realize that homework is expected of students or that parents are expected to be involved in education. Additionally, they may not be aware of what their rights are as parents (Almarza, as cited in Schneider, 2005).

Issues of acculturation and sensitivity to home cultures are important. Talking with parents about goals for their children can go a long way in establishing a strong basis for working with a child. A reference on an assessment to the child's home country tells the child that the teacher is thinking about him or her. Making sure the student understands assessments if the student is not a native English speaker is also essential.

Formative and Summative Assessment

formative assessment An assessment designed to inform teachers and students about student learning and to help improve instruction.

summative assessment Assessment designed to summarize student achievement.

Assessments can serve several purposes in instruction. Michael Scriven (1967) developed one of the most useful ways of distinguishing among assessments. He distinguished between assessments used primarily to help guide instruction and provide feedback to the teacher and the learner, and assessments used for grading or determining the amount of learning on an instructional unit. **Formative assessments** help to *form* future instruction, whereas **summative assessments** *sum up* learning. Formative assessments help us on our way and usually are not used for grading. Summative assessments determine whether a student has achieved the goals of instruction and are usually part of the grading system. When students engage in formative assessment not used as part of the grading system, they realize that the purpose of the assessment is to help them in their learning. Their reactions to this type of assessment are usually much more positive than with summative assessments, which frequently involve a level of anxiety (Wolf & Smith, 1995). Furthermore, formative assessments help students understand their own strengths and weaknesses without the pressures associated with grading. The following can help in differentiating formative and summative assessment:

Formative Assessment: Assessment *for* Learning

- Given prior to or during instruction
- Information the teacher can use to *form* forthcoming instruction
- Lets students see their strengths and weaknesses
- Not graded

Summative Assessment: Assessment *of* Learning

- Given after the conclusion of instruction or a lesson
- Information the teacher can use to *determine* what students have accomplished
- Infomation useful to broader audiences
- Graded

Principles of Assessment and Grading

In developing assessment and grading practices, teachers make a host of choices and decisions, including what to assess, which format to use, how to grade student work, whether an assessment should count for a grade, and how to communicate results to students. The research on classroom assessment shows that teachers' decisions are mixes of ideas and philosophical positions (Brown, 2004). Cross and Frary (1999) refer to the typical practices of teachers as "hodgepodge grading." In an effort to help teachers develop a coherent and internally consistent approach to assessment and grading, Smith and De Lisi (1998) have devised a set of principles to help teachers make choices about assessment and grading practices. The principles provide a framework for evaluating assessment and grading choices to see whether they are consistent from one choice to the next and with the teacher's instructional goals and teaching philosophy.

The three principles—communication, fairness, and growth—are equal in importance and, to some extent, conflict with one another because assessment choices, like instructional choices, often involve trade-offs. The principles provide a mechanism for examining trade-offs and deciding how to work toward the best assessment solutions.

Not surprisingly, the principles of assessment and grading begin with the premise that a specific set of instructional goals forms the basis of every teacher's instructional and assessment activities. Classroom assessments and grading practices should flow logically from the goals, objectives, or standards of the teacher and the school district. Briefly, goals are statements of what the teacher wants students to know and be able to do as a result of instruction. Goals are *not* statements of instructional activities or processes; they are statements of the intended endpoints of instruction. Clearly stated goals for students in a given middle or high school course or across the subject areas at the elementary level are essential as a guide to instructional practice and to assessment (Brookhart, 1999, 2001; Stiggins, 2004).

Appendix
Characteristics of Assessments

Teachers' choices of assessments should be made based on a set of principles that allow them to use assessments to promote student learning in addition to making judgments about the progress of students (PRAXIS™, II.C.2; INTASC, Principle 8).

R I D E   Why is the class reading *The Scarlet Letter*? What is the instructional goal of the unit? Is it concerned with the author's voice, literary style, use of language, historical context, or perhaps the novel's underlying moral implications?

Communication

Communication involves communication to oneself and communication with students. To communicate effectively, teachers must first understand what they are trying to accomplish in assessment and grading. Therefore, they should make assessment and grading explicit, writing out the decisions as they make them. Later, the teacher can examine them, reflect on them, and share them with others for comments and suggestions.

Once you have made your assessment program explicit, communicate it to the students. Communication is the key to letting students take ownership for their own achievement. Grades reflect that achievement. *Grades do not belong to teachers to give out; they are the students' to earn.* Teachers who make clear to students what they expect are much more likely to realize their expectations.

Communication is a two-way street. Just as teachers want to present clear expectations for student performance, students communicate with their teachers. Their performances on assessments, both formal and informal, tell the teacher about their strengths and weaknesses, interests (and lack of same), and concerns. Consider a high school English teacher who has five classes with roughly 20 students per class. How much time can he spend communicating directly, one-on-one, with each of his students? Yet when he assigns a paper to be done, and the student hands the paper in, that is a direct communication to the teacher. And the teacher's response to the student is a direct communication back to the student. It is a personal, one-to-one interaction between the student and the teacher about the student's progress and efforts in the course. It can have very powerful effects if used wisely. Consider for a minute that when the student is working on that paper, struggling over the best choice of a word or refining a sentence to have the greatest effect, the student realizes that the *only* audience for that paper, for all that time and effort, will be the teacher. The student is basically telling the teacher: "Here I am. Here is my best effort on this. I've worked hard to provide my best in this communication." We all have a need to be responded to (Cupchik, 2010). For work that is handed in and graded, the comments that a teacher puts on a paper are the only form of recognition, of acknowledgment, that a student might receive for a lot of hard work!

Effective teachers use the communication from students not only to tailor instruction but also to let students know that they are listening. For example, an assignment on how to search for information can just as easily use a topic of interest to students as not. Is a student more likely to be excited about searching for information on the development of hip-hop music or the Smoot Hawley tariff?

How Can I Use This?
How can you be certain that students understand what you expect of them?

Fairness

The second guiding principle of assessment is *fairness*, or the sense that the assessment or grade is just. Students' most frequent complaint about their courses is that the grades or assessments are not fair (Brookhart, 2004). The question of fairness can be broken down into three subcategories: validity, reliability, and freedom from bias. These terms have standard definitions among educational measurement specialists (Feldt & Brennan, 1989; Linn & Gronlund, 1995; Messick, 1989; Nunnally, 1967), but we rework them here to provide a better fit to classroom assessment and grading. They are essentially the same ideas presented in a different light.

validity The appropriateness of judgments about students based on assessment information. In classroom assessment, it is the correspondence between what an assessment measures and what was taught as part of instruction.

Validity When measurement specialists talk about **validity**, they are discussing whether an assessment provides useful and accurate information for making decisions (Messick, 1989). Classroom assessment is valid if it reveals student abilities and accomplishments relative to what is being taught. The phrase *what is being taught* is used rather broadly here; besides in-class instruction, it also includes learning that occurs outside the classroom that is part of the instructional process. For example, if a teacher asks students to do research at the library or on the Internet at home, that assignment would be part of *what is being taught*. Moreover, what is being assessed and what is being taught should be closely related to the instructional goals for the class. Goals, instruction, and assessment are tightly interwoven in successful classrooms (Brookhart, 1999, 2001; Stiggins, 2004), and only when they are can a teacher make decisions about how a class is progressing or whether a student has sufficient mastery of a topic to move on to the next topic.

 Look at Ms. Baldwin's debate assessment at the beginning of the chapter. What skills and knowledge would lead to the highest marks on that assessment? Are they closely related to how you would have taught the material?

Students are finely attuned to the validity of their assessments. If course content is not assessed, they will question the value of having worked to learn it and will develop similar doubts about future learning. If assessments include content that has not been taught, students will feel that the assessment is unfair. And if they feel that the assessment is unfair, they will feel that the course is unfair.

reliability Consistency over an aspect of assessment, such as over time and multiple raters. In classroom assessment, having enough information about students on which to base judgments is a concern of reliability.

Reliability Another aspect of fairness is **reliability**. Reliability is considered an issue of consistency of information (Feldt & Brennan, 1989). That is, a reliable assessment is one that will give much the same results about students if the same test or a very similar one is given again a few days after the first test or if different people grade it. With respect to classroom assessment, reliability means having enough information to make a good judgment about student achievement (Smith, 2003). If a grade is based solely on one short test, even if the test is related to instruction, the amount of information assesed may not be enough to make a good judgment.

Students should have a number of opportunities to show what they can do, and they should have the opportunity to do so in different modes, or formats. Varying the format or type of assessment has several benefits. First, many students perform better on certain kinds of assessment than on others. Second, the use of different formats helps students increase their ability to transfer their knowledge and skills and to demonstrate them in new and different venues. Third, teachers find it useful (and more interesting) to have different kinds of student work to evaluate; it is possible to gather information about students using one approach to assessment that might not have been available using a different approach. For example, a student who has difficulty in expressing his or her thoughts in writing in English might be able to demonstrate mastery of world history through a multiple-choice assessment.

bias Systematic unfair treatment of a particular group of individuals.

Freedom from Bias Freedom from **bias** is another issue in maintaining fairness. Typically, one thinks of bias as an unfair act against individuals who differ in race, gender, physical abilities, native language, or ethnic background. Teachers must be sensitive to these issues in designing assessment and grading practices. If students are going to write on an assigned topic, teachers should consider whether the topic—for example, American football—favors boys over girls or students who have grown up in the United States over immigrants.

Other issues of bias in assessment might not seem obvious at first. For example, if classroom participation is part of assessment, should shy students be at a disadvantage because of a personality characteristic that is unrelated to instructional goals? Bias can also become a critical issue in the grading of homework or the assignment of projects to be completed outside the classroom. When students bring in work from home, the teacher may wonder how much of the assignment was the student's own work and how much help parents, guardians, siblings, or friends provided. Further, is it easier for some students to revise their writing because they have access to good word-processing equipment at home and others do not? In designing a plan for an assessment and grading system, teachers should be sensitive to these issues. They must make very clear to students what they can receive help on and what they must do themselves, and teachers must clearly communicate which activities will count in determining grades.

Growth

The third of the three assessment principles is growth. A key purpose of schooling is to encourage students to grow—cognitively, emotionally, and socially. As an integral part of instruction, assessment and grading should enhance the instructional process and lead to student growth. In order to facilitate student growth, teachers need to find the right balance between too much assessment and too little. They need to develop assessments that are engaging and rewarding to students. They must provide rapid feedback that is focused on improvement. Teachers should consider whether an assessment is a good instructional device. They should ask: If the assessment is a test, will studying for it enhance learning? If it is a research paper, what skills will be developed by doing the work? If it is a group project, what will all students learn as a result of participating in it?

Teachers should also ask themselves: What is the quality and utility of the information that I will gain about my students as a result of this assessment? If students do not do well on this assessment, will I, and my students, learn about their strengths and weaknesses in relation to this goal? Will this assessment help me determine what further instruction is appropriate? In sum, will it facilitate students' future growth?

An often overlooked aspect of formative assessment is what is to be done with the results once they are obtained. Does the teacher have a plan of action for using the results of an assessment? Will instruction on the current unit continue? Will students be given individual activities to remediate weaknesses or build on strengths? Are there alternative approaches to teaching or learning the material that are available? When considering assessment from the perspective of assessment *for* learning, teachers think of assessment not just as an event, but as a process. Their assessment activity is forward looking, or *prospective*, as opposed to backward looking, or *retrospective*. In designing the assessment, they think about what they want to do with the results of the assessment as an important factor in developing the assessment.

Options for Assessment

As mentioned earlier, teachers should develop classroom assessments in varied formats. Some options mirror the formats of standardized tests; others derive from classroom-based practice. Each has its own strengths and weaknesses. This section looks at options for assessment under three general headings: recognition format (such as multiple choice), generative format (such as essays), and production format (such as research papers or presentations).

Recognition Format

The recognition format requires students to recognize the correct answer from a set of choices. Three types of recognition formats are multiple choice, matching, and true/false.

multiple choice An assessment item format consisting of a stem (question), a right answer, and a set of wrong answers (distracters). Students have to determine the best response to the stem.

stem The part of a multiple-choice item that asks a question.

distracter One of the options in a multiple-choice test.

item A test or assessment question, referred to as an *item* because not all test questions are actually questions.

Multiple Choice   The most common form of assessment used in U.S. schools is multiple choice. Developed for standardized tests because it can be scored quickly and consistently by machine, it continues to be the dominant format of standardized assessment. Teachers who have several sections of a course and dozens of papers to grade might benefit from using this format, but they need to be careful to make sure that the questions are not solely recall of information. Giving students practice in answering multiple-choice assessments can also be helpful to them when they have to take standardized assessments that rely heavily on this format.

The multiple-choice format consists of a question, or **stem**, followed by a list of options, sometimes called **distracters**, or foils. One of the options is the correct answer, and the remaining options are incorrect. Three-, four-, and five-option multiple-choice tests are the most common. The stem of the multiple-choice item can end in a question mark, or it can simply be an incomplete sentence that could be completed by any of the distracters. (Measurement specialists call test questions **items**, in part because not all test questions are actually questions.) The task of the student is to indicate which of the distracters is the correct choice. The question "Who is the protagonist in the novel?" presented at the beginning of the chapter is a simple example of the multiple-choice format. The stem can be a simple question based on a fact from the instructional unit, or it might require comprehension of information from the unit or an inference based on the unit:

- *When did the Civil War begin?* (Basic fact)
- *What was the major economic advantage the Union had over the Confederacy?* (Comprehension of information)
- *What would have happened to Reconstruction if Lincoln had not been assassinated?* (Inference from information in unit)

The stem of a multiple-choice question can also include information on which the question is based, such as:

> *Paul and Marie wanted to invite some friends over for a party. They thought that they would need three slices of pizza for each guest. If there are eight slices in a pizza, and if they have eight friends over, how many pizzas will they need?*

Once the stem, or question, has been written, the next step is to write an answer that is unambiguously correct or the best choice among alternatives (if there are several possible ways to construct a correct answer). A set of three or four plausible but clearly incorrect distracters then needs to be constructed. In mathematics items, this is usually accomplished by working through the problem in such a way that it includes a conceptual or mathematical error.

> *Paul and Marie wanted to invite some friends over for a party. They thought that they would need three slices of pizza for each guest. If there are eight slices in a pizza, and if they have eight friends over, how many pizzas will they need?*
>
> a. 3 (Would be enough for guests, but not for Paul and Marie)
> b. 4 (Correct answer)
> c. 5 (A reasonable guesstimate)
> d. 8 (The number of guests. Some students will just try to pick something from the problem.)

In verbal items, a good approach is to consider the correct answer and vary one or more of the characteristics of that answer to generate incorrect answers.

> When did the Civil War begin?
>
> a. 1861 (Correct answer)
> b. 1816 (Reversal of last two digits)
> c. 1917 (Beginning of WWI for the United States)
> d. 1865 (End of the Civil War)

One of the advantages of the multiple-choice format is that the teacher can control the difficulty of the item. Difficulty can come from a challenging stem or from the options. Consider the following:

Who was the 17th president of the United States?

Difficult answer set:

a. Andrew Johnson
b. Abraham Lincoln
c. Millard Fillmore
d. Ulysses S. Grant

Easier answer set:

a. Andrew Johnson
b. Thomas Jefferson
c. George Washington
d. William Clinton

Also keep in mind that, with some time and effort, multiple-choice items can be developed to assess **higher-order thinking skills** that require higher levels of cognitive processing in students. The following item requires some sophistication on the part of the student:

What would have happened to Reconstruction if Lincoln had not been assassinated?

a. It would have occurred very much the way it did. (Addresses the question but a poor choice)
b. The Confederacy would have re-formed to fight again. (A possibility and therefore attractive but clearly wrong)
c. It would have been more successful because of Lincoln's popularity. (Correct answer)
d. Because Lincoln opposed Reconstruction, it would not have happened. (Directly answers the question but facts are wrong)

In sum, the multiple-choice format allows teachers to closely control what they are assessing and is useful for assessing discrete pieces of knowledge or understanding. It needs to be developed carefully but is easily and rapidly scored (even without an electronic scanner). However, it does not permit the student to be very creative or imaginative. In addition, a student who does not know the answer to an item can guess the answer; he or she has a one-in-four chance of getting a four-option multiple-choice item correct. Some students take unusual and often not helpful approaches to answering multiple-choice questions (see the nearby Taking It to the Classroom box). Multiple-choice items can also be used to assess higher-order thinking skills, but creating such items requires substantial thought and work.

Matching **Matching** items are very popular with teachers. They have a gamelike quality that is appealing. In the matching format, two lists of concepts are presented side by side, and the student has to match the concept on the left with the corresponding concept on the right. Sometimes the nature of the required relationship is obvious; in other cases, the teacher specifies it, as in the following example:

Match the state with its capital city.

Nebraska	*Springfield*
North Dakota	*Trenton*
Illinois	*Bismarck*
New Jersey	*Lincoln*

The matching item is similar to the multiple-choice item in that students are required to recognize the correct answer rather than to generate the correct answer themselves. It requires a set of concepts, all of which are of the same type and have another specific concept associated with them. States and their capitals, parts of the body and their functions, and new vocabulary words and their definitions are all examples of concepts that can readily be assessed using the matching format. In the state capital example above, the teacher might want to consider omitting the capitals and requiring the students to fill in blanks. Consider for a

higher-order thinking skills Skills and abilities that go beyond recall and comprehension, including the ability to apply ideas and concepts, analyze and synthesize information, and evaluate complex information.

 Look at Mr. Antoine's assessment at the beginning of the chapter. What does that multiple-choice question say regarding what Mr. Antoine thinks is important about *The Scarlet Letter*? Use the example about Lincoln and create multiple-choice items for a work of literature that are more challenging and reflective of a higher set of expectations than Mr. Antoine's question.

matching An assessment item format that involves generating two sets of objects that are to be linked together, such as states and their capitals.

Taking It to the Classroom

Do You Know Jack? Multiple Choice or Multiple Guess?

Jack has a strange approach to multiple-choice questions. He answers them by looking at the choices first. He picks the two that seem to look the best to him, then reads the question to make a decision between his two options. His older brother told him this was the best way to do it. What can you do to convince Jack to keep all options open until he has read the question?

- Walk through a multiple-choice test with Jack, asking him to explain his approach as he answers several multiple-choice questions with you.
- Let Jack confront the illogic of his approach as he goes through the questions.
- If he does not see his problem, point it out with a more direct approach. Show him that there is usually no way to spot a right or wrong answer without first looking at the question.

minute how different these two formats would be. The matching format has limited applicability in most settings, but the puzzlelike nature of matching items can afford a nice break in an assessment, particularly for younger children.

True/False Another traditional approach to assessment is the true/false item. It consists of a factual statement that the student has to judge as true or false. The primary advantages of the true/false format are the number of items that can be included on the test (because it does not take long to answer them) and ease of scoring. For some types of information, the true/false format can be effective. For example:

Circle one.

The capital of North Dakota is Springfield.   T   F

This is a simple declarative statement that is false, and it assesses the student's knowledge of state capitals (or at least one of them).

Two significant problems, however, arise with true/false items. First, if students do not know the answer to the item, they still have a 50/50 chance of getting the item right. Second, some statements are not clearly true or false. For example:

Circle one.

The assassination of Archduke Ferdinand led to the start of World War I.   T   F

This, too, is a simple declarative statement, but it is not one on which all historians agree. For these reasons, it is probably better to avoid using true/false questions.

Generative Format

Items that require a student to generate an answer, or *generative* items, provide an alternative format for assessments. Two basic types of generative items are constructed response, or short answer, and essay.

Constructed Response (Short Answer) **Constructed response** is the term that measurement specialists use for what most people refer to as short-answer items. Students have to *construct* the answer rather than simply select it from a list as in multiple-choice items. Constructed-response items can take many forms. One very common use is the simple math problem. It can take the form of a story problem to which the student has to generate an answer, such as the following:

Appendix
Types of Assessments
It is useful to understand the strengths and limitations of different types of assessments. You should keep in mind that the assessments you choose should align with your instructional goals (PRAXIS™, II.C.1; INTASC, Principle 8).

constructed response A type of assessment format in which the student has to provide the answer to the question; more commonly referred to as *short answer*.

At 2 p.m., a 2-meter pole casts a 0.3-meter shadow. If there is a second pole next to it that is 10 meters high, how long a shadow will it cast?

Here is a simple calculation problem:

$$7\frac{7}{8}$$
$$-5\frac{3}{8}$$

Another version of the constructed-response format is the following:

In Niall's Saga, *what are the two underlying themes of the narrative?*

The constructed-response format is probably the one that teachers use most often. It is fairly easy to write constructed-response items, and they can be used in a wide variety of applications. Another advantage of the constructed-response format is that it requires the student to produce (i.e., construct) the correct response rather than simply to identify it, as in the multiple-choice format. Constructed-response items require *recall* rather than *recognition* of information.

Constructed-response questions seem like the simplest and most straightforward type of assessment format because they mimic questions asked in class. The teacher poses a question, and the student answers it. For many questions, the constructed-response format looks like a multiple-choice question without the choices. However, because there are no choices, care must be taken in creating constructed-response questions. For example, one can devise either a question that has a number of possible correct answers or a question that does not make sense without the options. Consider the following:

Which of the following is a prime number?

This question makes sense only if it is followed by a set of options. Or consider:

For what is William Henry Harrison known?

There are a number of possible answers to this question. Harrison is known for being the hero of the battle of Tippecanoe, his presidency was very brief due to his early death, and he was also known simply for being President of the United States. If these responses are all acceptable, the question will work well. But if a teacher really wanted to be certain that students knew that Harrison died early in his presidency, he or she would have to rephrase the question more precisely or turn it into a multiple-choice item.

Constructed-response questions should focus on unambiguous instructional content and should be specific enough that a student who knows the answer will get it right. Imprecisely worded questions can mislead students. If the question confuses students, no one can determine why they did not answer it correctly.

Essay Tests The essay format is a favorite of high school English teachers but is also widely used at earlier grades and in most subjects. Essay tests are rightly considered to be appropriate for meeting a variety of assessment needs. Further, the very act of writing an essay is a useful instructional activity. Practice in writing is practice in thinking.

The essay item requires the student to compose an essay in response to a question or *prompt*, which is the statement of what students must write. The tests on *The Scarlet Letter* handed out by Ms. Baldwin and Mrs. Chambliss and presented at the beginning of the chapter show two possible prompts for essays. The essay question can be graded on the information provided in the response, the quality of the writing in the essay, or other factors of concern to the teacher. Consider the following essay question and what it requires a student to do.

The first ten amendments to the United States Constitution are called the Bill of Rights and are considered to be a mainstay of our rights and freedoms as citizens. Some legal scholars have argued that we should eliminate the third amendment concerning the quartering of troops in private homes during peacetime. What is your opinion on this question? Write an essay of roughly 200 words defending your decision. Be sure to consider both the positive and negative effects of eliminating this amendment.

The strength of the essay format lies in what it requires of students. A well-constructed essay question requires students to consider the implications of the question, pull together the knowledge they have related to the question, and construct an essay presenting their points and supporting details. The essay format also gives the teacher considerable latitude in the construction of the assessment.

Because it takes a great deal of time for a student to complete an essay item, an assessment can contain relatively few of them. Thus, what is gained in depth of response can come at the cost of breadth. In addition, essay items conflate, or intertwine, several skills (such as organizational ability, recall of information, and the ability to make a good argument) that the teacher may want to assess separately. Students who write well, for example, are likely to do better on an essay test than students who do not write well. Even poor handwriting can interfere with performance on an essay test. Finally, teachers must spend a great deal of time grading essay tests and giving appropriate feedback to students. Essay testing has undergone substantial change in recent years, particularly with regard to the use of *rubrics*, scoring guides for essays (Danielson, 1997; Taggart et al., 2001). The use of rubrics is discussed later in the chapter.

As in all assessments, writing a good essay item begins with reflection on the instructional goal that is being assessed. One then constructs a prompt that requires the student to engage the instructional goal in a meaningful and important fashion. The teacher needs to think about what an excellent answer would include and how it would reflect the instructional goal.

The essay prompt must give students enough information about what a good essay must contain without at the same time providing the information or skills that the teacher is trying to assess. The teacher needs to remember that the open-ended nature of the essay question can leave the student anxious unless sufficient direction is provided in the question. Consider, for example, the following two versions of an essay question:

Version 1

In the mid-1400s, Johann Gutenberg developed a process for mass production of books through the use of movable type. Explain how the development of movable type influenced European society. Be sure to consider economic as well as religious developments.

Version 2

How did the development in the mid-1400s of movable type affect economic life in Europe? Write a three- to four-paragraph essay (roughly 300 words) examining the economic consequences of this invention, starting with its first uses and expanding its impact over the remainder of the century. Focus your essay on the changes that occurred in the European economy as a result of movable type. Discuss the economic and social context in Europe at the time of the development. The essay is worth twenty points on the exam. Fifteen points will be given to the quality of the content of your answer, and five points will be awarded based on the quality of the writing and grammar, punctuation, and spelling.

The first version is a reasonable essay prompt, but the second version gives a much clearer sense of what is expected of students and how they will be graded.

Student writing can be developed through prompts that include creativity and imagination along with demonstration of knowledge of instructional content. The prompt below allows students to use their imaginations. The teacher using this assignment chose not to count the responses toward the students' grades because she felt that although she wanted to encourage creativity on the students' part, she did not feel it fair to count that as part of a grade.

> We have been studying Greek gods and goddesses. Now it is your turn to "invent" a Greek god or goddess. Use what you know about Greek mythology to create a god or goddess. Determine what characteristics your god or goddess has and why. Present your god or goddess, locate him or her in the pantheon of gods (to whom is this god or goddess related?), and tell a story that involves your god or goddess. Your presentation should be about 200 words long. I will provide feedback on demonstrated knowledge of Greek mythology, creativity, and good essay-writing techniques.

Alternative, or Production, Format

The past decade has seen the development of a variety of new formats for assessment (Hargreaves, Earl, & Schmidt, 2002; Shepard, 2000). It might be more appropriate to say that experts in formal measurement have *discovered* a number of formats that teachers have been using for some time. These formats have been given many different names, including **authentic assessment** and the choice used here, **alternative assessment**. These approaches are more student-oriented than traditional assessments and less concerned with the formal characteristics of assessment formats. They also tend to relate more closely both to instruction and to real-life applications of the knowledge and skills involved. Types of alternative assessments include performance assessments, portfolios, journals, and informal assessments. One aspect most of these assessment approaches have in common is the idea that there is a student product, or production, involved. This might be a performance, a poster, a report, a journal, and so on. It might be something temporal, like a production, a skit, or a speech; or it might be something tangible, like a poster, or a research report, or a Web page. This type of assessment has become increasingly popular in classroom assessment because it relates more closely to things that one actually does in life. Thus, it can be thought of as being more authentic. Although educators typically refer to this type of assessment as alternative, or authentic, we think the term *production format* gives a better indication of what the format is all about.

Performance Assessments   The term **performance assessment** covers a wide array of assessment possibilities, but they can be grouped into two categories: those that involve a *performance* and those that result in an actual *product*.

Some performance assessments are literally real-time performances. Students must demonstrate proficiency or create and deliver a performance of some type; activities include class presentations, recitations in a foreign language, skits, and laboratory demonstrations in a science class (or the lab reports that accompany them).

This type of assessment has several advantages. First and foremost is the fidelity of the assessment to the skill being assessed. For example, the best way to determine whether students are pronouncing *l'œil* correctly is to have them pronounce it. Second, advocates of performance assessment argue that it causes students to prepare for the assessment in ways that are especially conducive to learning. Third, performance assessments tend to be more engaging for students.

The disadvantages of performances include difficulties in scoring, **objectivity** (fairness in grading), and correspondence between what is desired and what is obtained in the assessments. For example, if a talented student presents a speech that is well delivered, creative, and engaging but is somewhat off the assignment that had been given, how should a teacher grade it? Furthermore, with respect to objectivity, is everyone being graded fairly, or is there (perhaps unknowing) bias toward or against some students (perhaps a student with behavior problems)? Performance anxiety might also be a problem in this type of assessment because some students are very reluctant to engage in any kind of performance in front of their classmates. Remember that performances also occur in real time; if each student is to be assessed during a performance or a demonstration of ability, this can occupy an incredible amount of class time.

In the second type of performance assessment, students are given a task and must create a **product**, such as a travel promotion for visiting their hometown or a lab report on the

authentic assessment An assessment that is tightly related to the instruction that the students have received or to tasks that are relevant in real life.

alternative assessment A generic term referring to assessments that are different from traditional approaches, such as multiple choice and constructed response.

performance assessment An assessment in which students generate a product or an actual performance that reflects what they have learned.

objectivity Not having a direct interest or bias.

What Does This Mean to Me?
Do you think that you might tend to *play favorites* when you are assessing students' performance?

products Student creations that reflect their skills and abilities as well as their ability to create something new.

Mrs. Rinaldi's Fourth-Period Math Class

Imagine that you have been assigned the task of painting this classroom. You are going to do it over a weekend at the end of next month. By a week from Friday, you have to present the Board of Education with a plan and a budget for painting the room. You and one friend are going to do the painting, and you will be paid $7.50 an hour for your work. The custodian has cloths to lend you so that you will not spill paint on the desks and counters. Other than that, you must purchase all your materials and come up with a detailed plan for your work. You are to hand in the following:

1. A list of the activities that must take place in order to paint the room and a schedule of when they will occur.

2. A description of the type of paint and color or colors you wish to use and an explanation of why you made these choices.

3. A budget to cover all your expenses and a rationale for that budget.

Your report to the Board should be word-processed, should be free of errors, and should provide a convincing case that you can do the job. Good luck!

Figure 14.1 Thinking "Inside the Room": A Geometry and Planning Task

result of a titration experiment. (Assessing students as they conduct the experiment would be the other type of performance assessment.) In this type of performance assessment, the concept of performance does not mean a real-time performance but rather the demonstration of competence in accomplishing a goal or completing a project. Figure 14.1 presents a typical math performance assessment for fourth grade.

The strengths of this type of assessment are similar to those of real-time performances, but time limitations are less of a concern. The weaknesses are similar as well (except for performance anxiety), but there is one additional and important difficulty: As with any homework, if a performance assessment involves work conducted outside the classroom, it is difficult to know whether the student alone completed the work. Help from family members and friends can interfere with the fairness of the assessment. Performance assessment is a rapidly developing field in education today. The Web site associated with this text includes an up-to-date list of Web sites discussing the most current work in performance assessment. The nearby Taking It to the Classroom box presents ideas for developing alternative and performance assessments.

An excellent way to begin thinking about building a performance assessment is to view it not as an assessment per se but as an aspect of instruction related to instructional goals (Smith, Smith, & De Lisi, 2001). This idea actually works for a variety of assessment formats. Frequently, a strong instructional activity that involves independent work can be transformed into an assessment that has good instructional value as well. For example, having students plan for a

(Dennis MacDonald/Photo Edit)

Performance assessments engage students, encourage creativity, and tie closely to instructional goals.

Taking It to the Classroom
Developing Alternative Assessments

Developing alternative assessments can be a bit daunting at first. Here is a list of 10 ideas to use to get started.

1. Start by thinking not about assessment but about instruction. What good instructional activities do you have? Can any of them be turned into an alternative assessment? Develop your assessments as you develop your instruction.

2. Don't worry if an assessment is not alternative enough. Focus on the quality of the assessment, not how it would be described.

3. Use the Web. The Internet has thousands of Web sites with an enormous collection of alternative assessment ideas. Look not only for ideas that fit your purposes directly but also for other ideas that you can adapt to your needs.

4. Think about developing clear rubrics from the beginning. The rubric for an assessment should provide a definition of the assessment as well as your scoring system.

5. Share your work with colleagues. Ask them what they have that works well and ask them for suggestions on your work.

6. Your first efforts may not be brilliant. Do not get discouraged. At first, alternative assessments may take more time and may not deliver exactly what you want. You will get better with each new effort.

7. Keep a portfolio of your work. Maintain in the portfolio both the task and some student examples. Keep some of the best work but also same weak work that helped you diagnose student difficulties.

8. Make the assessment worth the students' effort. Let them know what you expect from them and how their work will be graded. Make it an important part of their grade if appropriate.

9. Consider having students grade one anothers' work as well as assessing their own. Alternative assessments are a great way to develop self-assessment skills in students.

10. Be reflective. At the end of an assessment activity, think about what went well and what did not. Takes notes and keep them in your assessment portfolio. Ask the students what they thought of the assessment. And keep trying!

trip to a different country as part of a social studies unit can have a rubric for grading developed for it. This will help students understand the nature of the project and provide the teacher with insight concerning their ability to seek out reference information.

Consider the performance assessments in Figures 14.2 and 14.3. These examples are taken from the National Educational Monitoring Project in New Zealand (you can find a wide range of performance assessments for roughly grades 3 through 8 at their Web site: http://nemp.otago.ac.nz). They are both excellent performance assessments. Consider the two tasks and the differences between them. The performance assessment in Figure 14.2 is an example of a performance as product. Students will hand in the results of their efforts. Although there are a number of possible answers here, they have more of a notion of answers that could be considered more or less appropriate. The performance assessment in Figure 14.3 requires both a product and the opportunity for group interaction and reflection. Here there are a wide variety of approaches to the task. Furthermore, students can see how effective their responses are from the reactions of their peers. This could be a great instructional or assessment task for either a writing lesson or a science lesson. See how each of these assessments could evolve from or lead into further instruction.

Portfolios Portfolios are collections of students' work. The concept of a portfolio originated in the field of art and spread to advertising and graphic design, where job seekers use their portfolios to demonstrate their abilities to potential employers. In classroom assessment, portfolios involve the collection of students' work over the course of a given period of time (e.g., a unit, a semester, or a year). This allows for an examination of the progress that a student has made in a given area. The audience for a student's portfolio might include the teacher, the student, the student's parents or guardians, or other concerned individuals. Portfolios are particularly effective for student/teacher and parent/teacher conferences about student progress.

portfolio A collection of students' work over time that allows for assessment of the development of their skills.

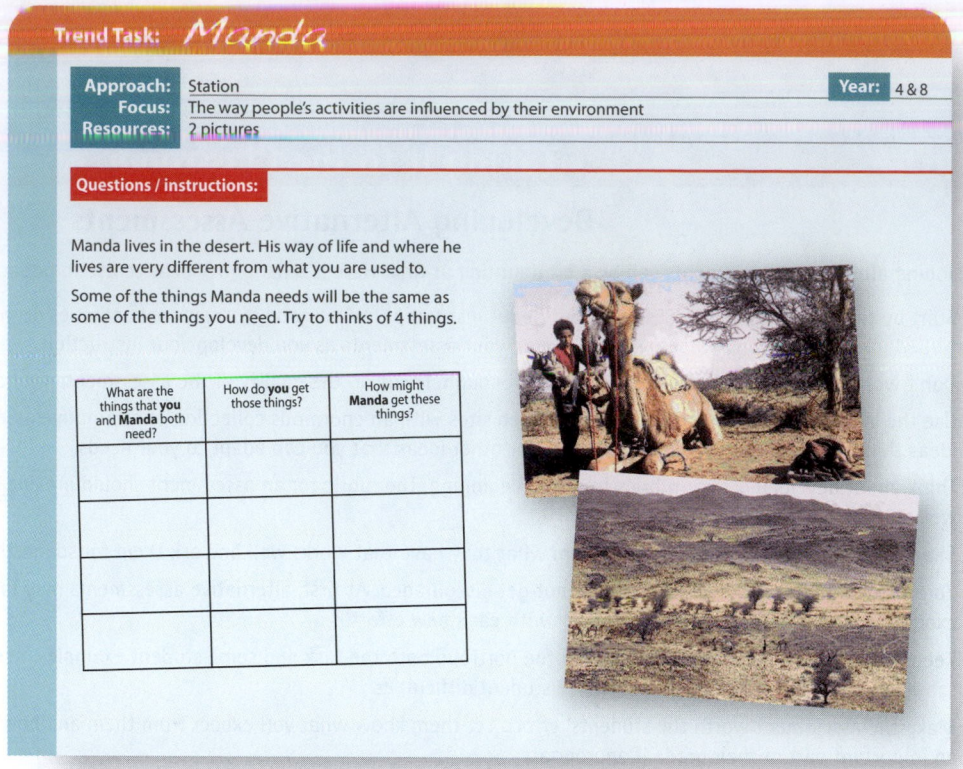

Figure 14.2 A Performance Assessment for Social Studies

Source: Crooks, T., Flockton, L., & Meaney, T. (2005). *National Educational Monitoring Project, Social Studies Assessment Results, 2005,* Report 36. Wellington, New Zealand: Ministry of Education.

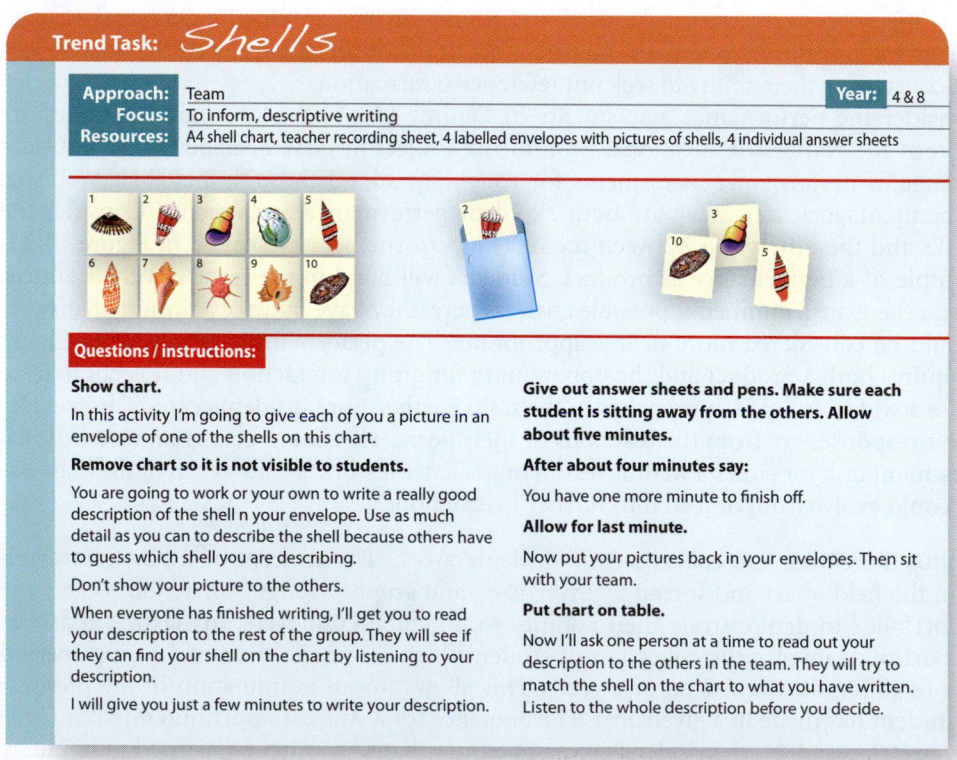

Figure 14.3 A Performance Assessment for Writing and/or Science

Source: Crooks, T., Flockton, L., & White, J. (2006). *National Educational Monitoring Project, Writing Assessment Results, 2006,* Report 41. Wellington, New Zealand: Ministry of Education.

The contents of portfolios can vary greatly. A high school writing portfolio might include several drafts or just a few representative works to show how well the student has mastered the writing process over time. An elementary school math portfolio might include samples that demonstrate the student's progress in problem-solving ability. Portfolios can include photographs, artwork, and notes from teachers to students as well as student work. Some teachers keep portfolios for several years and present them to students when they graduate from high school or move from one school to the next.

Some educators argue that portfolios are not assessments in and of themselves but rather materials on which to base assessments. Some consider a portfolio little more than a *folder* for keeping a student's work, something that teachers have always done (Smith et al., 2001). This does not minimize the potential value of the portfolio. Portfolios let students compare what they were doing earlier in the year to what they can do in the present. This helps students develop the ability to assess their own strengths and weaknesses, an invaluable learning tool. Thus, portfolio assessment is a process that involves using the portfolio to let the student and the teacher reflect on the progress that a student has made and jointly plot future activities and growth.

It is not necessary to put everything into a portfolio; in fact, it is probably detrimental, because it would soon become overwhelming. Instead, teachers develop a system for inclusion that will allow for the examination of growth over time. In some instances, all drafts of a piece of important writing are included in the portfolio, but not usually for all writing. All final products might be included, certainly in the case of substantial products. Preliminary notes for a project can give a student, upon reflection, a concrete example of how his or her thinking changed over the course of the project. This can be useful when brainstorming on subsequent projects. In a math class, students can follow the development of their own thinking on a certain topic and consider how this might be helpful as they work on their current math problems. Letting students join in the process of deciding what should and should not be included in their portfolios is usually a good idea because it promotes a sense of responsibility for one's own achievements.

The real strength of the portfolio lies in the ability of students, teachers, and parents to review progress (Gearhart & Osmundson, 2009). It helps all three audiences for assessment appreciate the learning process. Effective teachers regularly schedule conferences with students to go over their portfolios as a springboard for planning. Portfolios are also a great source of information and a discussion starter for parent/teacher conferences.

Journals Student **journals** offer great potential for gaining insight into the thought processes, ideas, concerns, and overall development of student abilities. A journal is a learning diary and can be structured in a number of ways. Some are free-form recordings of students' thoughts about their learning. Others include specific prompts, or requests, for the student to make entries in a journal. Teachers can choose to review them on a regular basis or give students the option of handing them in when they choose to do so.

Journals lie at the intersection of teaching and assessment. Teachers use them widely and for a variety of purposes (Trice, 2000). When students explain what they know, their understanding and difficulties with their understanding become clearer to them. When journals are designed to be shared with teachers, they can provide a rich source of information about how well the class and individual students are doing and where their difficulties lie.

> **journal** A running set of thoughts, responses to prompts, and reflections that students have concerning their learning in a particular area.

Informal Assessments

The assessment approaches presented so far are designed in advance. Another type of assessment is ongoing, fluid, and essential to teachers in making instructional decisions. Teachers use **informal assessment** to determine whether students understand a concept by asking probing questions or posing problems for them to solve. Equally important is the ability to evaluate the questions that students ask. What level of understanding and interest do they represent? Are the students exhibiting a solid understanding, or do they seem lost? What happens when the teacher changes the situation slightly and asks students to apply what they have learned?

Garnering useful information about students' progress during instruction is one hallmark of an exceptional teacher. This type of assessment informs teachers' decisions about

> **informal assessment** Classroom assessment activities used to get a quick and rough idea of student progress.

Taking It to the Classroom

Biology Bucks

A biology teacher at a teacher's workshop recently presented an innovative approach to rewarding students for participation in class discussion: *biology bucks*. Each year he printed a supply of fake dollars with his picture instead of George Washington's (note that it is illegal to copy real dollars). Whenever a student did something that contributed to the class, the teacher awarded him or her a biology buck, personalized with the student's name and validated with the teacher's signature. Each biology buck was worth one point added to any test score. A student could increase a B to a B+ or an A by cashing in biology bucks. For example, a student with a B+ score of 89 could hand in a biology buck and move that grade up to an A— score of 90. The system made it easy to communicate clearly to students what was and was not a good contribution, and record keeping was remarkably simple. Although not every teacher will want to use a system like this one, it is important to remember that creativity in assessment can be a powerful tool.

when to move on to the next topic, who might need extra help, and who can afford to take a few minutes to help a classmate. It can help the teacher determine whether a particular instructional approach is working well or not at all.

Although the use of informal assessments in a formative fashion to guide instruction is highly effective, the use of classroom participation and contribution as an informal part of an assessment and grading system has both strengths and weaknesses. Participation and contribution enhance instruction overall and teach students how to be good citizens in the classroom and in other settings. Classroom discussions can also be a rich source of informal assessment information for teachers to use in determining how well the class as a whole is progressing. However, they include a potential bias against students who are reluctant to speak up in class. This might be because of shyness, cultural differences, or disinclination to appear too smart to their classmates. Further, it is often hard to reconcile basing part of a student's grade on an assessment that is not part of the instructional goals for the class (few instructional goals include participation). Usually, teachers count participation toward grades because without it, students would participate less and learn less. Thus, counting participation facilitates growth (one of the principles of grading and assessment) but has strong potential to be biased and not directly related to instructional goals.

How can teachers encourage participation while minimizing the drawbacks of counting it as part of a grade?

- First, do not think of it as *participation*; think of it as *contribution*. Provide students with a variety of options for contributing to the class. Positive participation in classroom instruction is but one form of student contribution. They might also work with peers who are having problems in a certain area or bring in newspaper clippings or other illustrative materials, such as specimens of plants for a biology class.

- Second, limit the proportion of a grade that can be earned by participation, and inform the students what it is. Many teachers find that 5% of the total grade is sufficient to encourage contributions to the class.

- Third, develop a system for rewarding students that minimizes potential bias. Do not rely solely on your own judgment at the end of the grading term. (See the nearby Taking It to the Classroom box for a creative example of a rewards system.)

Developing and Using Assessments

Good assessments begin with a clear understanding of what is to be assessed. Then teachers have to determine the best format, how they will grade the assessments, how to take into consideration students with special needs, and how to address the diversity of the classroom.

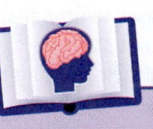

MINDFUL HABITS OF EFFECTIVE TEACHERS

The ability to use assessments (both formal and informal) to promote and enhance students' learning is a key habit of mind of effective teachers. This ability allows teachers to provide opportunities for students to demonstrate successful learning.

Another consideration in developing classroom assessments is to think about what students will be doing either to complete the assessment (for example, in the case of performance assessments) or to prepare for the assessment (in the case of in-class tests). Are these activities also good instructional experiences? Finally, teachers need to think about the students doing these assessments. Do they take students' interests into account? Will the students find them engaging or simply something that has to be done?

Determining What to Assess

The impetus for determining what to assess comes from the instructional goals for the class. With the advent of standards-based instruction and assessments, which exist in all states, teachers typically work from instructional standards that are state-mandated. But now the teacher needs to turn the standard into a more specific **achievement target** (Stiggins, 2004), a clear statement of what to assess. Consider this standard from the NJASK (New Jersey Assessment of Student Knowledge) in mathematics:

A Mathematics Instructional Standard

The students should be able to represent data using an appropriate graph and make inferences based on organized data and displays.

This is a reasonable standard. It seems perfectly clear and appropriate. But a number of issues lurk just beneath the surface:

- How good a graph should the student be able to make?
- Should the data be relevant to students? Should it be a frequency distribution or a cross-tabulation?
- How can this standard be developed into instructional or assessment materials so that students will be engaged in the activities? What kinds of data might be interesting to students: for example, preferences for video games, number of siblings, favorite movies?
- What is the basis for grading? What are the possible instructional ramifications of the results?

These questions are not criticisms of the standard, nor are they intended to demonstrate that the standard will be difficult to address in the classroom. They are issues that naturally concern teachers in the development of instruction and classroom assessment. The alignment of curriculum and instruction with the standards or objectives is a critical linkage in instruction (Martone & Sireci, 2009).

Test Blueprints Teachers start the development of an assessment by thinking about what they want to accomplish. What should the assessment be about, and why is it being given? When developing traditional assessment formats, such as multiple choice, constructed response, and essay, teachers rough out a table of specifications, or **test blueprint**, of what to include. The blueprint can be as simple and straightforward as an outline or it can be more sophisticated, such as the **content/behavior matrix** shown in Figure 14.4 (Bloom, Hastings, & Madaus, 1971). A content/behavior matrix is a form of test blueprint that crosses behaviors with subject headings to provide a matrix of possible instructional objectives.

achievement targets Well-specified statements of what teachers want to accomplish in a particular lesson or set of lessons.

test blueprint A statement of what a test will comprise, often in outline form.

content/behavior matrix A method for specifying what is to be assessed by making a matrix with expected student behaviors on one axis and the content on which that behavior will be observed on the other axis.

Content/Behavior Matrix in World History: World War I

Content/Behavior	Europe at the turn of the century	Relationships among European leaders	The beginnings of war	The reaction of the United States
Knowledge of people, facts, and dates	6 items	5 items	4 items	5 items
Understanding causes	0 items	2 items	5 items	3 items
Explaining/predicting outcomes	2 items	4 items	0 items	4 items

Figure 14.4 Content/Behavior Matrix

The content/behavior matrix in Figure 14.4 is particularly helpful in that it enables teachers to see all the possible areas for writing test questions. Not every possible cell has to have questions in it, however. If a particular combination of a content area and a cognitive behavior has not been taught, it should not be tested. The content/behavior matrix not only helps in test construction but also provides a useful way to reflect on instruction up to the point of the test. It can even lead teachers to a deeper understanding of their instruction ("I really haven't spent much time on this topic, have I?" or "This has turned out to be the real emphasis of this unit"). A good starting point for a test blueprint is the set of district or state standards for the unit being taught. The test blueprint is, in reality, a restatement and expansion of the goals for the unit, essential not just for assessment but for instruction as well.

A content/behavior matrix, with degrees of emphasis assigned, allows for the construction of an assessment in which the number of questions and the scoring weights given to those questions are based on the test blueprint. This ensures that the test reflects the most important elements of instruction.

Students can also use the test blueprint as a guide as they study (Smith & De Lisi, 1998). When students have a blueprint to study from, they can use their study time more efficiently. At the elementary level, a test blueprint can be a simple communication to students to help them prepare for a unit test.

Ms. Wade's "Be Ready" Sheet for Thursday's Geography Test

1. *Be able to identify all the countries of Europe.*
2. *Know all of their capitals.*
3. *Know which countries were formerly in the Soviet Union.*
4. *Be able to explain the European Union and how it came to be.*

Rubrics

When using an assessment such as a group project, journal entry, or performance assessment, it is particularly important to think carefully about what is being assessed. When educators ignore consideration of the underlying purpose of an assessment, the resulting assessments tend to lack reliability and validity (Baxter & Glaser, 1998; Shavelson, Baxter, & Pine, 1991). The need to be clear about the content of the assessment (what is being assessed) and the scoring of the assessment has led to the development of **rubrics**. (The word *rubric* comes from religious writings, in which headings, notes, and commentary were frequently written in red ink. *Rubric* has the same root as the word *ruby*.)

rubrics Explications of the criteria for a performance assessment or an essay that include specifications for how various levels of performance are to be graded.

Rubrics are specifications for how to score assessments, particularly assessments that do not lend themselves to simple right-or-wrong scoring. They are different from test blueprints in that they do not specify what is to be assessed but rather how to score what is being assessed. Thinking about scoring issues also helps the teacher define the nature of the assessment. For example, when planning an assessment that involves a class presentation, the teacher needs to determine how important the presentational style (as opposed to the content of the presentation) will be, how much the visual aids will count, and what the consequences will be for taking more than the allotted amount of time. In thinking about these issues, the teacher is defining the nature of the assessment.

criteria Specifications of what is expected of a student on an assessment.

A rubric typically consists of a set of **criteria** (statements about what is expected) combined with specifications for what levels of performance are required for various scores. This might be combined with a clear statement of what the assignment is (although some rubrics contain just the scoring criteria). Rubrics should clearly state the observable outcomes expected of students. They should describe what students should know and be able to do. Moreover, they should be defined in terms that students who are engaged in the assessment can readily understand.

Look at the example of a rubric for grading middle school science reports on boats and buoyancy presented in Figure 14.5. Does the rubric set clear expectations? As you can see, the rubric not only specifies the scoring but also defines the assignment. Rubrics assist in assessment and instruction by making clear what is to be learned. As you read through this well-designed rubric, you can see that it would make an excellent learning tool for students to use to look at their own work. The rubric *defines* the assignment.

	Beginning 1	Developing 2	Accomplished 3	Exemplary 4	Score
Introduction	Does not give any information about what to expect in the report.	Gives very little information.	Gives too much information—more like a summary.	Presents a concise lead-in to the report.	
Research	Does not answer any questions suggested in the template.	Answers some questions.	Answers some questions and includes a few other interesting facts.	Answers most questions and includes many other interesting facts.	
Purpose/Problem	Does not address an issue related to tidepools.	Addresses a tidepool issue which is unrelated to research.	Addresses an issue somewhat related to research.	Addresses a real issue directly related to research findings.	
Procedure	Not sequential, most steps are missing or are confusing.	Some of the steps are understandable; most are confusing and lack detail.	Most of the steps are understandable; some lack detail or are confusing.	Presents easy-to-follow steps that are logical and adequately detailed.	
Data & Results	Data table and/or graph missing information and are inaccurate.	Both complete, minor inaccuracies and/or illegible characters.	Both accurate, some ill-formed characters.	Data table and graph neatly completed and totally accurate.	
Conclusion	Presents an illogical explanation for findings and does not address any of the questions suggested in the template.	Presents an illogical explanation for findings and addresses few questions.	Presents a logical explanation for findings and addresses some of the questions.	Presents a logical explanation for findings and addresses most of the questions.	
Grammar & Spelling	Very frequent grammar and/or spelling errors.	More than two errors.	Only one or two errors.	All grammar and spelling are correct.	
Attractiveness	Illegible writing, loose pages.	Legible writing, some ill-formed letters, print too small or too large, papers stapled together.	Legible writing, well-formed characters, clean and neatly bound in a report cover, illustrations provided.	Word processed or typed, clean and neatly bound in a report cover, illustrations provided.	
Timeliness	Report handed in more than one week late.	Up to one week late.	Up to two days late.	Report handed in on time.	
				Total	

Figure 14.5 Rubric for Grading Science Reports

Source: Copyright Janice Thiel (1997). From the *Cabrillo Tidepool Study*, part of the Triton Project. Retrieved June 7, 2005, from http://edweb.sdsu.edu/triton/tidepoolunit/Rubrics/reportrubric.html. Reprinted with the permission of the author.

Rubrics also assist in creating valid assessments. Look at Figure 14.5 again. In this rubric, attractiveness, spelling and grammar, and timeliness will garner as many points as research, procedure, and conclusion. Is this truly desirable for this particular assignment? It may be, but it is important to understand the choices made in developing rubrics. A topic should not appear in a rubric just because it is easy to define and specify but because it supports the instructional goals.

Determining the Best Assessment Format

As you have seen, the various assessment options each have strengths and weaknesses. Therefore, consider the appropriateness of various alternatives to a specific assessment goal. For example, if the objective is to have students develop their own ideas in relation to an assigned task, an essay or a performance assessment is appropriate. Students should understand that the generation and execution of good ideas related to the task are important. If, on the other hand, a unit requires that students acquire and comprehend a large amount of information, a multiple-choice or short-answer test can provide a good sample of how much they have learned.

Appendix
Using Assessments

You should develop and use assessments that will allow you to understand students' current levels of performance and will allow you to design further instruction to help them progress to the next level (PRAXIS™, II.C.4, II.C.5; INTASC, Principles 2, 8).

Another consideration is the time and effort needed to build the assessment, administer it, grade it, and communicate the results to the students. Essay tests have many attractive features, but grading them and providing feedback to students take a great deal of time. Because feedback to students must be timely, teachers pressed for time or with large classes might consider an alternative form of assessment. Although it is desirable to try to develop the best possible assessment in every situation, veteran teachers understand that teaching decisions almost always involve trade-offs.

Typically, assessments should be closely linked to instruction. Sometimes teachers do move away from instruction, but they do so with a purpose. For example, most students have to take a **standards-based assessment** (mandatory assessment typically developed at the state level) at the end of the academic year. Often, teachers will build in some classroom assessment activities using assessment formats that are similar to the ones that will appear on the standards-based assessment.

Assessing Students with Special Needs

Many, if not most, classrooms today include students with special needs. These needs may be physical, cognitive, or affective; you might have a student who is visually challenged or has dyslexia or an emotional disturbance. Students with disabilities grow up to be scientists, authors, governors, diplomats, and highly successful businesspeople—as well as schoolteachers. The accomplishments of other students with disabilities are more modest, but each individual who faces a special challenge wants to live as full and productive a life as possible.

There are a host of issues that must be addressed when working with classified students; one of those is assessment. Kleinert, Browder, and Towles-Reeves (2009) present an excellent summary of the issues involved in the assessment of students with significant cognitive deficiencies that would apply to many situations where disabilities are not as severe. They focus on the cognitive demands that are made of students and the context in which students live their lives. Students with special needs, especially those with significant disabilities, have different, or sometimes modified, educational standards and objectives set for them, as detailed in individualized education programs.

Individualized Education Programs A student **classified** as having special needs has an **individualized education program (IEP)**, which is an educational and behavioral plan that specifies the student's annual goals. You can learn about IEPs by looking for the Individuals with Disabilities Act on the Internet (a link to the site can be found on the Web site for this text) and also by examining the IEP in Chapter 5 again. IEP goals are related to the general goals for the class, which have been modified in order to maximize the individual child's growth.

Teachers first need to review the IEP for classified children in their class. Assessments should be derived from instructional goals; if the goals for a given student are different from those for the rest of the class, it follows that the assessment may be different as well. Frequently the IEP will guide teachers regarding the **accommodations**, or modifications, that they should make for classified students. Table 14.1 lists some of these accommodations.

Classroom Assessments for Students with Special Needs Any element in the list of accommodations presented in Table 14.1 can be used in classroom assessment procedures. Often, however, it is necessary to think beyond this list and consider what a given assessment means for a student who has different instructional goals from those of the rest of the class. Here creativity, sensitivity, and communication with colleagues, school professionals, family members, and students are essential. Appropriate solutions will vary from one situation to the next. Information about working with students with disabilities is also available at the Web site for the National Center on Educational Outcomes (the link is provided on the Web site for this text).

Administering, Scoring, and Communicating Assessment Results

Once an assessment has been developed, a new phase begins. The teacher has to administer and score the assessments and provide feedback to students. This is a critical part of the assessment and instructional process. It is how teachers and students alike learn about student progress and determine what is to occur next.

---

standards-based assessment Assessments that are generated from a list of educational standards, usually at the state or national level; a form of standardized assessment.

classified A term used to refer to special education students who have been identified as having a particular disability.

www.wiley.com/college/odonnell

individualized education program (IEP) An educational and behavioral intervention plan for a student with special needs.

accommodations Modifications made in an assessment for students with disabilities.

www.wiley.com/college/odonnell

Administering Assessments Although as educators we want assessments to be engaging and appealing to students, students need to take assessments seriously, and, without engendering undue anxiety about the outcome, teachers need to make sure that they do. For in-class assessments, set aside a specific time and inform students of the schedule. When appropriate, specify time limits and follow them, but be sure to allow enough time for students to complete their work without feeling rushed. Classrooms should be quiet for in-class assessments and distractions minimized. Students should have a clean area to work on their assessment, and the necessary equipment (pens, pencils, erasers, rulers, calculators) should be readily available.

For projects or presentations, whether completed in class or out of class, rules and expectations need to be explicit. Communicate due dates to students as well as the consequences associated with failure to meet the deadline. Do not, however, establish a rule without considering possible exceptions and what to do about them. If points are to be deducted for overdue projects, what will happen, for example, if a student is ill or there is a death in the family? What about less serious impediments to progress ("We had to go to my grandmother's for her birthday")? If a project is to be completed largely outside of the classroom, the teacher should make clear the kinds of assistance that a student can appropriately receive.

Younger students are less able to allocate their time wisely than are older students. It is frequently helpful to build intermediate checkpoints into a longer project, such as the due dates for an outline and for a rough draft or for a schematic of a poster. We can all remember the last-minute panic of a neglected project. Help your students keep such experiences to a minimum.

Giving Feedback Assessment should be considered to be a *process*, not an event. An assessment is much more than the mechanism used to collect information. It is a vehicle to allow a teacher to communicate with students on a personal level (Bass & Glaser, 2004). This is particularly true at the secondary level. When a teacher has over 100 students, in five different courses or sections of a course, it is extremely difficult to personalize instruction. Some students may go days or even weeks without a personal interaction with the teacher.

Assessment allows teachers to break into that cycle. Think of a student handing in an assignment as a personal communication to you as to where that student is. As mentioned earlier in the chapter, the student is saying: "This is what I can do. Here is where I am with regard to this material." As a teacher, you can accept that communication and respond in kind: "Here is where I think you are doing really well. Here is where I think you are having some problems. This is what I think we can do about your problems and build on your strengths." And, importantly, you can say: "I really enjoyed reading about . . . I liked where you . . ."

When an assessment is handed back to students, it is a communication about how well they did on the particular assessment and how well they are doing in the class in general. Waiting for an assessment to be returned can be a source of anticipation, apprehension, or even anxiety for students. The communication itself can produce pride, excitement, disappointment, clarity, or confusion. If the assessment is a paper-and-pencil assessment (and the vast majority of formal and informal assessments in school are), this process begins with what a teacher writes on a paper. The effect on the student between "You missed the point here" and "This isn't exactly what I was looking for" is very different. The first communication finds fault with the student's response. The second accepts the response while indicating that there was an alternative closer to the mark. With forethought and awareness of some principles for marking papers, communications to students can engender a sense of self-efficacy and cognitive growth.

TABLE 14.1

Accommodations for Assessing Students with Special Needs

Accommodations related to time
- Providing extra time
- Allowing breaks as needed
- Administering the test in several sessions

Accommodations related to the setting
- Giving the test in a quiet, separate room
- Letting the student take the test at home

Accommodations related to the presentation of the assessment
- Using large print or magnification
- Having the test read aloud
- Using a helper
- Simplifying the directions

Accommodations related to the response format
- Letting the student write on the test instead of an answer sheet
- Letting the student use a computer or word processor
- Letting the student say answers rather than write them

Modifications of the assessment
- Simplifying the tasks according to the student's needs
- Allowing the student to use a dictionary or other resource

Be objective and specific. Students cannot learn from their mistakes or their successes unless they receive objective feedback about their efforts (Elawar & Corno, 1985; Sadler, 1989). This feedback must accurately reflect how well the student has done. In the abstract, it is easy to think that one would always grade accurately, not being overly generous or harsh about a certain answer on an assessment, but this can be difficult for teachers in individual cases. For example, if a student has worked very hard to master the material, it may be difficult to mark as wrong an answer that is nearly correct. But in order for the students to grow, they need honest feedback from their teachers.

Feedback should also be specific. Students need to know exactly what they have done well or poorly (Brookhart, 2001; Guskey, 2001). Merely telling students that they have done a good job is not enough to engender learning, particularly when the students can see that almost everyone else in the class has received the same response (Lipnevich, 2007; Lipnevich & Smith, 2009). Keep in mind that being specific does not necessarily mean providing the right answer. (See the nearby Uncommon Sense box for types of feedback.)

Focus on the positive and on growth. A paper that is returned with only criticisms on it can be very discouraging. If the teacher does not notice the really well-written paragraph that the student has struggled with or the math problem on which the student has worked through several false starts to reach a correct answer, the student may begin to wonder whether all the effort was worthwhile. Learning is the process of moving from one state to another. Therefore, whenever possible, try to think about students' past work in comparison to their current work. Students need to see and be reminded of the progress they are making, and portfolios can be valuable for this purpose. Two similar papers may mean very different things. Although they should receive the same grade (if they are being graded), the comments written on them might be quite different. For Martine, this paper may represent real progress, whereas for Edouard, it might be a disappointing effort. (See the nearby Taking It to the Classroom box for types of feedback.)

Student Conferences Without full and rich communication from a knowledgeable and concerned teacher, students are left on their own to interpret the success or failure of their efforts and can draw the wrong conclusions about their work. The best way to communicate with students is by means of a conference, or conversation. Conferences allow for finding common ground, for misunderstandings to be cleared up, for elaboration of issues and

> **What Does This Mean to Me?**
> How have you reacted to comments on papers from your teachers and professors?

Uncommon Sense

Mistakes Are Bad—Or Are They?

The British comedian and comic actor John Cleese of Monty Python fame has also starred in a film about making mistakes that is used in management courses. In the film, Cleese argues that mistakes are wonderful things because they let us know that we are off course in a certain endeavor and need to get back on course. Students' mistakes on assessments can be viewed in the same fashion. An incorrect solution to a mathematics problem is a message from a student. It says, "I'm not really sure how to work these problems, and here is the nature of the difficulty I'm having." This is a golden opportunity to intervene and provide the kind of feedback that will move the student from not knowing to knowing.

Sometimes all the teacher needs to do is let the student know an answer is wrong; the student may not have realized it. In other situations, a simple corrective suggestion is appropriate. This is particularly true in marking essays. Teachers are not the editors of student work; teachers provide feedback to make students better writers. The best comment on an essay may be something such as, "There are four grammatical errors on this page; find them and correct them." In still other situations, the teacher can point out that the student's solution leads to a logical inconsistency or is an unreasonable possibility (e.g., "But if Ed is 6 times as old as Mary, and according to your answer Mary is 34, how old would that make Ed?").

Wrong answers are a window into the student's cognitive processes. Take a look in.

Taking It to the Classroom

Marking Student Papers: Being Objective, Specific, and Growth–Oriented

Less Desirable Comments	More Desirable Comments
A lot of errors in this area.	See whether you can find four grammatical errors in this section and correct them.
This paragraph is poorly worded and unclear.	I think this paragraph makes the reader work too hard. See whether you can tighten it.
This is hardly your best work.	This looks a little hurried. It doesn't show the care I saw in your last paper.
This is not what we discussed in class.	You're off target somewhat here.
You can't reach the right answer if you are sloppy in your calculations.	You've got the idea, but check your work.
Awkward construction.	Reread this sentence and see whether it says what you want it to.
Redo this.	Try this again.
Excellent job here.	Your use of metaphor here is strong.
Great, I love this.	Think of how much more effective this argument is than in the paper you did last week.

concerns. They let the student respond to the feedback given by the teacher. Teachers often use conferences to discuss essays or other major projects, but it can also be very useful to talk with students about their performance on a test, even a multiple-choice test. The goal of a conference is to help students better understand their efforts, whether positive or negative. It can also help the teacher better understand students' progress and decide on the next set of learning steps.

Conferences involve communication in both directions. Avoid simply presenting opinions, pointing out weaknesses, and probing for information. Provide reactions, but also ask students for theirs. Stiggins (2004) does an excellent job of describing student/teacher conferences that are informative, positive, and student-centered. He recommends that teachers prepare for the conference by reviewing student work. Focus on listening, and make the conferences relatively brief—a few minutes might do.

Interpreting Classroom Assessments

Following some simple procedures can help ensure that assessments truly inform instruction. The first step in interpreting classroom assessments is to reflect once again on the purpose of the assessment. How closely is the content and format related to the instruction that it is designed to assess? Is there other information that can be gleaned from it (such as development of writing skills in an essay based on a social studies unit)? Keeping the overall purpose in mind prevents teachers from focusing on the readily accessible aspects of an assessment and losing sight of its overall goal. For example, when grading essays, teachers sometimes start grading primarily for grammar and lose sight of the development of ideas contained in that essay. On a mathematics assessment, it is possible to focus too heavily on computational issues and not enough on whether the student seems to understand the broader instructional ideas.

Appendix
Interpreting Assessments

The results of assessments are best understood in light of your instructional goals and help you focus on the kind of useful information that can be gleaned from the assessments (PRAXIS™, II.C.6; INTASC, Principle 8).

Just a few minutes in a one-to-one student conference can reap great rewards in terms of teacher understanding and student enthusiasm.

(Andrew W. Levine/Photo Researchers, Inc.)

Comparing Performance with Expectations

Children do not always perform as teachers expect they will on assessments. Surprises and disappointments are due in part to the students' performance and in part to the teacher's expectations. Expectations develop fairly naturally once a teacher has worked with a group of students. Although it is very important not to let such expectations affect the grading of student papers, they should affect the interpretation of the assessment and the communication to the student. The work that a student hands in at any given point in time is part of an ongoing thread of work that must be revisited from time to time to assess that student's growth properly. Remember, growth is one of the underlying principles of assessment. (See the nearby What Kids Say and Do box.) One of the real advantages of portfolios, as discussed above, is that they remind us of where a student was not too long ago.

Looking at Assessment Results for the Class as a Whole and for Individuals   In looking at assessments, teachers need to consider both the class as a whole and individual students. When the class in general does not do well on a particular aspect of an assessment, there could be a variety of explanations. First, perhaps the problem lies in the assessment itself. Did the students understand the instructions? Was there a mistake, a typographical error, or a possibility for misinterpretation? Second, perhaps the problem has to do not with the students but with the instruction. If there is nearly unanimity on a wrong response, it might be time to take a serious look at how the instruction was delivered with respect to this content. Finally, the problem may in fact have to do with the students. Perhaps they did not understand the expectations for performance, or there was simply a general letdown in performance. In situations such as this, it is often useful to look at how well the students who are usually at the top of the class performed. If the best-performing students did not do well, the problem probably lies in either the assessment or the instruction. If the problem seems to be with the class, ask them what went wrong.

Data-Based Determinations of Next Steps   The key to good classroom assessment is the use to which the information garnered is put (Bass & Glaser, 2004). Now that you know how well the individual students and the class as a whole did, what are you going to do about it? In large part, it is critical to ask this question *before* the assessment task is given. You should have some sense of where you are going with an assessment before you use it. Imagine, for example, that the class does much less well on an assessment than you thought they might. Unless you determine that this was just a problem with the assessment, you need to think seriously about what you are going to do with the class. Will you extend instruction on this unit, change your approach, focus on the specific, most important problems, and so on?

Evaluating how well the class performs overall and how well individual students perform is also useful for revising and refining the assessment. A useful tool for summarizing information from assessment data is the *stem-and-leaf diagram*. This tool was invented by John Tukey (1977), a remarkably creative statistician who is also credited with coining the computer terms *bit* and *software*. An example of how to construct a stem-and-leaf diagram is presented in the nearby Taking It to the Classroom box.

The results discussed in the box suggest that most students have a fairly solid understanding of the material but that some are struggling. In addition, many students may be having difficulty with one or two aspects of the unit. The teacher can investigate this by looking at the performance of the class on the various sections of the assessment and deciding to review some of the material with all of the class and to work more intensively with a few students.

What Kids Say and Do

Points of Departure

Addition and Subtraction Exercise Sheet

Name _____

6 +7 **13**	9 +2 **11**	8 +4 **12**
7 −4 **3**	28 −12 **16**	41 −20 **21**
13 −8 **5**	33 −7 **36**	52 −26 **6**

This is a math assessment from a young boy with moderate learning difficulties. It shows that he has acquired a good command of the addition problems and most of the subtraction problems. However, he still has some difficulty with subtraction problems in which the subtracting value is greater than the ones digit in the subtracted value. To understand the kind of performance this represents for this student (progress, no change, or decline), the teacher should have a very good idea of his recent progress and know what to expect.

Reflecting on Assessments to Improve Them

Once the assessment and feedback process has been completed, it is time to reflect on the assessment itself. In the first years of teaching, teachers feel they never have time to reflect on anything, but it is worthwhile to try to fit some reflection time into the schedule. Consider the following set of questions as a guide:

- How do the results look as a whole?
- What did I expect? Were there surprises?

Taking It to the Classroom

Using a Stem-and-Leaf Diagram

Mr. Locher has 23 scores from an assessment he has given: 78, 64, 94, 83, 80, 91, 84, 86, 83, 57, 88, 97, 62, 79, 70, 75, 82, 80, 93, 91, 89, 86, and 90. He wants to get an idea of how his class scored as a group, so he organizes them using a stem-and-leaf diagram. He begins by drawing a vertical line and entering the numbers from the tens column on the left of the line; this is the stem (Figure 14.6, Graph A).

Graph A	Graph B	Graph C	Graph D
9	9	9 | 7	9 | 7
9	9	9 | 41310	9 | 01134
8	8	8 | 6896	8 | 6689
8	8	8 | 304320	8 | 002334
7	7 | 8	7 | 895	7 | 589
7	7	7 | 0	7 | 0
6	6	6	6
6	6	6 | 42	6 | 24
5	5	5 | 7	5 | 7

Figure 14.6 High School Report Card

Mr. Locher then records the ones values at the appropriate spot in the chart for the respective tens values; these are the leaves. Graph B shows the first score in the list, 78, in its place in the middle part of the figure. Mr. Locher enters the remaining scores in the same fashion, which produces Graph C. He finalizes the stem-and-leaf diagram by arranging the numbers within a row from lowest to highest, as in Graph D. He can now examine the distribution of scores without losing any of the original values. Note that because there are no scores in the 65–69 range, he has left a blank space in the graph. Mr. Locher can now see at a glance that on this assessment, only one student did exceptionally well (a 97), a number of students had solid to strong scores (80–94), and a few had difficulty with the assessment (57, 62, 64).

- What was particularly difficult for students? For example, why did students pick a certain wrong option on a multiple-choice test?
- What seemed to confuse students? Are there items that students who really seemed to know the material got wrong? Why did some of the best students miss the idea behind an essay question?
- Did any of the students take an especially novel and/or useful approach to a performance assessment that I can incorporate next time around?
- How did the students respond to the assessment? Did they find it useful?
- How can I improve this assessment? Should I make changes in the instructions? In the actual tasks?

Good assessment practices now can help you in future years as well. Accumulate good assessments; measurement specialists call this an **item bank** or a **test bank**. Storing assessments electronically along with notes on what worked well and what needs to be revised saves a great deal of time later on. Remember to make revisions each year to ensure that the assessment matches the instruction for *that* year.

item bank A collection of test or assessment items for use in future assessments. Also called *test bank*.

The Student Role in Assessment

In keeping with one of the underlying themes of this chapter, it is important to consider the student role in assessment. This recommendation affects classroom life at the secondary and elementary levels in rather different ways. At the primary level, assessments tend to be more formative in nature and are seen by students in that fashion. This is not to say that students at the elementary level don't like grades, but much of what occurs at the elementary level is more typically formative in nature. At the high school level, students often see assessment as a rather mechanical and formal part of instruction that exists to assign grades (Levin & Kaner, 2007). Comments on papers and exams are viewed as justifications from the teacher for the grade received rather than help on how to improve.

Sense of Control, Motivation, and Anxiety In classroom assessment that is used for formative assessment, the goal is to find out about student learning in a fashion that can be used to enhance instruction and learning. In classroom assessments used for summative assessment, the goal is to make as fair an assessment as possible of the student's current state of knowledge and skills in the material covered in the class. One of the ways to promote the utility of an assessment in either situation is to make an effort to make the assessment meaningful to the students. To begin, when the assessment has a consequence such as a grade, students are more likely to take the assessment seriously (Wolf & Smith, 1995). This will increase the students' motivation to do well on the assessment, but will also increase their anxiety. For some students, the consequence of the assessment will have a net benefit (the increased motivation will outweigh the increased anxiety). But for some students, the anxiety associated with the exam counting for a grade will cause performance to decrease. There is no simple answer to this problem, except to be sensitive to the issue of test anxiety. It is real and, in some students, debilitating.

When students are in a situation where an assessment is important to them, but they don't feel they understand well what is expected of them, they feel out of control of the situation. Imagine a setting where an important exam is coming up, but the professor in the course has not provided any but the barest of details about what to expect. Your lack of direction as to what or how to study can cause anxiety, frustration, and ultimately anger. Clear communication to students about expectations can help greatly in increasing the students' sense of control.

Looking at Assessment from the Student's Perspective A good way to improve the quality of classroom assessment is to always take a minute to look at the assessment from the perspective of the student. As you develop an assessment, keep these "student questions" in mind:

- What is the teacher expecting on this assessment?
- Is this an assessment where I'll do well or will it be an embarrassment to me?
- If I work hard on this, will I do well?
- Is this going to be interesting or fun, or just a lot of work that will seem dumb to me?
- How much work will this be?
- Am I going to learn anything from this?
- What does this assessment mean to me?

Developing a Grading System

Grading occurs to some degree at all educational levels, but it differs markedly from the elementary to the secondary school levels. At the primary, elementary, and, to some extent, middle school levels, grading is mainly formative. At the secondary school level, grading is far more summative in nature and often plays a critical role in students' attainment of their college aspirations. The specific system teachers develop can have profound effects on both the affective and the cognitive growth of their students.

Teachers need to develop a system for grading that allows them to keep track of the progress of all their students and lets students know how well they are doing on an ongoing basis. Recall the three principles of grading and assessment described earlier in the chapter: communication, fairness, and growth. Keeping these principles in mind will help ensure that the grading system will be fair and encourage students' best efforts.

Options for Grading Systems

Ask your mom or dad if they still have your report cards from when you were in elementary school. Report cards are important, especially to parents! A remarkable number of options and alternatives are available (Brookhart, 2004; Guskey, 1994). Because grading systems differ substantially at different educational levels, it is useful to look at the options that are best suited to each level.

Grading Options at the Primary Level At the primary level, grading is concerned primarily with the development of the skills, learning behaviors, attitudes, and dispositions that will be necessary for student success in later years. Grading systems can be quite elaborate, as can be seen in the example presented in Figure 14.7. Each area of development, such as social skills, work habits, and the academic areas, is associated with a series of behaviorally oriented statements. These statements are rated by the teacher. Other ratings may include the following:

- Exceeds expectations
- Meets expectations
- Needs improvement

It may seem odd that the youngest children get the most detailed and complicated report cards. But young children's abilities and knowledge change dramatically from year to year. By the time children have completed their primary school years, kindergarten through third grade, they will have learned to read at a basic level and do mathematics through simple word problems and multiplication tables; they will be able to work together with other children and will understand the rules of proper school behavior; their vocabulary will have increased by thousands of words; and they will have figured out which bus to get on to come home. The changes that occur during this relatively short period are probably greater than those that will occur at any other time of their lives (except perhaps the five years before they entered school). A detailed grading and reporting system is entirely appropriate. The grades that students receive on report cards should always be based on real evidence from the classroom, not on impressions at the end of a marking period. Keeping good records for each child on a regular basis greatly facilitates accurate and productive communication on report cards.

Grading Options at the Upper-Elementary and Middle School Levels At the upper elementary and middle school levels, a shift usually occurs in grading and reporting systems. Letter grades are usually introduced in third or fourth grade, although they are often accompanied by comments about behavior and student growth as well. Work habits and social skills are also rated. This can be seen as a transitional report card, moving from the formative report cards of the primary years to the summative report cards of the secondary level. At the upper-elementary level, grades may not be seen as critical, but they set patterns and expectations and are sometimes used to determine access to special courses (e.g., advanced math courses) and gifted-and-talented programs. At the middle school level, some students will be taking high school–level courses, almost all students will have different teachers for each subject, and the transition to a high school type of report card will have been made in most districts.

Grading Options at the Secondary Level At the high school level, grading has become rather complicated in recent years. With the increased emphasis on applicants' high school record for college admissions, the importance of high school grades has grown markedly (Smith, 2003). Traditionally, high schools have used a grading system based on a five-point scale corresponding to the A–F grading system. The points possible are A = 4, B = 3, C = 2, D = 1, and F = 0. Decimals are used for plus or minus grades (e.g., B + = 3.2). The numerical values are combined into a grade point average, and the averages are ranked from highest to lowest to produce class rankings.

Most colleges use high school grade point averages or class rankings as an important factor in admissions decisions. In addition, admission to honor societies and the selection of valedictorians and salutatorians are determined by class rank. In recent years, many high schools have adopted systems in which additional points are given for performance in honors courses. In some high schools, it is possible to have a grade point average above 4.0 and still not be in the top 10% of the class. Each year, it seems, newspapers carry stories about

Figure 14.7 Primary School Report Card

New Carrington Elementary School
Pupil Progress Report   Student Name _____

Rubric for Effort in Class Activities			Rubric for Progress in Standards	
O	Consistently Outstanding	M	Displays Complete Mastery	
G	Good Effort Most of the Time	P	Progressing Toward Mastery	
N	Needs Improvement	N	Not Near Mastery at This Time	

English Language Arts	1	2	3	4	Final
Reading					
Sounding out words					
Fluency reading					
Working with text					
Extending meaning beyond text					
Mathematics					
Number Sense and Operations					
Knows numbers up to 1000					
Knows addition and subtraction facts					
Basic comprehension of fractions					
Measurement					
Can measure common objects with ruler					
Can tell time					
Understands basic concept of weight					

Classroom Behavior (Only Effort Marks Here)				
Takes responsibility for own behavior				
Works well with classmates				
Follows directions				
Hands in homework on time				
Follows rules and routines of the class				
Sustains effort to complete assignments				

students suing high schools over the selection of the valedictorian or how the grade point average was calculated in a given situation. For each story that reaches the news, dozens are battled out in the principal's office or a school board meeting. Grading at the secondary level is a serious matter.

Most reporting systems at the high school level are fairly similar. Figure 14.8 presents an example of a high school report card. As can be seen, the report card presents term and cumulative grade point averages.

Record Keeping for Grading

Good record keeping is one mark of a professional in almost any field; in teaching, it is absolutely critical. A high school math teacher with more than 100 students in a given year would find it impossible to keep track of their progress and assign grades fairly without a strong record-keeping system. A kindergarten teacher who observes a child reaching out to help another child for the first time wants to keep a record of that for a parent/teacher conference. If it were just one child and one event, the teacher could rely on memory. But with 24 children and hundreds of events, she must have a system for keeping track of this valuable information.

Figure 14.8 High School Report Card

Student report card
MARTINSDALE REGIONAL HIGH SCHOOL
HOME OF THE *PURPLE MARTINS*

Student Name: Henry Melton
Student ID: 100334

Grade: 10

Comment Codes:
1. Excellent work
2. Homework missing
3. Needs to try harder
4. Absent or tardy often
5. Behavior problems
6. Improving
7. Conference needed
8. Poor attitude

Marking System (Note: Plusses and minuses may be given for grades A–D.)

A	Superior performance
B	Above average
C	Average
D	Below average
F	Failing

				Marking Period				
Ref#	Title	Teacher	Period	1	2	3	4	Final
017	English 10 Honors	Arrone	1	A- 1				
043	Geometry CP	Fermat	2	B				
003	French 4	Velez	3	B- 3				
093	Chemistry I	Chandra	5	C- 2				
105	U.S. History	Johnson	7	B-				
607	Choral Music	Sills	9	B				

Term GPA: 2.90   Cumulative GPA: 3.12
Absent: 2 days   Tardy: 0

Record Keeping with Technology For centuries, grade books were the standard mechanism for record keeping, and they are still the most widely used method. However, electronic record books are replacing paper grade books. The Web site for this text lists some excellent resources in this area, although a teacher can benefit from the same flexibility and organization by using any standard spreadsheet program or even a basic word-processing program. Figure 14.9 shows an example of a simple but effective use of a spreadsheet program for record keeping.

Helping Students Develop a Sense of Responsibility for Their Grades As discussed earlier, one of the goals of a good assessment and grading system is to encourage students to take responsibility for their grades. To do this, they must fully understand the grading system and be kept up to date on their progress. This requires that students' work be graded and returned to them quickly and with appropriate comments. Teachers can help students keep track of their progress by providing them with a summary of their grades at several points during the marking system.

Teachers often assign more graded work toward the end of the marking period, leaving students in the dark about how well they are doing until late in the period. Regular evaluation, rapid and thorough feedback, and open communication are the mechanisms through which students can take responsibility for their grades.

Figure 14.9 Record Keeping with a Spreadsheet

Student Name	Start of Semester Comments	Knowledge of Math Facts/ Concepts		Mathematical Thinking			Homework Checks	End of Marking Period Comments
				Concept Tests	Journal Entries			
		Quiz 1 20	Quiz 2 20	1 50	1	2		
Adams, Nancy	Made good progress last marking period	18	20	44	3	3	YYYYNNYYYY	Working hard, progress continues. Need to focus on concepts.
Blanco, Maritizia	Still uncertain of some facts	14	14	42	2	2	YYNNNYYYYY	Picked up strongly near end of marking period. Increased parent support?
Caperton. Maurice	Very strong in all regards	19	19	48	3	2	YYYYYYYYYY	Continues excellent work. Maybe provide opportunities for enrichment.
Denali, Brooke	Needs to build confidence	17	15	41	2	2	YNYNYYYYYY	Still shaky on confidence level. Needs to experience success.
Hortons, Justin	Ability is there, but careless	13	14	44	2	1	NNYNYYNYYY	Needs a bit of a wakeup call. Enlist parent support. Emphasize potential.
Jackson, Renaldo	Needs a lot of review on facts	13	12	38	3	2	NNNYNNNYN	Still a lot of difficulty. May want to enlist school-based support on this.

Communicating with Parents

Imagine that the parent of Justin Traub, a fourth-grade student, is going to a parent/teacher conference. Compare the following two possible scenarios.

Conference 1

The teacher is writing at her desk as Mr. Traub stands in the doorway. Mr. Traub is not certain whether to walk in, knock on the open door, or just announce himself. A student desk is in front of the teacher's desk. Twenty seconds later, Ms. Wolf looks up.

Ms. Wolf:	Come in, please.
Mr. Traub:	Thank you. *[He is not certain where he is supposed to sit, but the desk in front of the teacher's desk seems to be the best choice.]*
Ms. Wolf:	Let's see. We're running a little late. You must be, let me see, Mr. Traub, Justin's father.
Mr. Traub:	Yes. Good evening.
Ms. Wolf:	Well. Justin. I have his materials here somewhere. Yes, here they are. Just a second. Well. Justin's not off to what I would call a terrific start. Although he seems quite good in math for the most part, he's really quite a weak writer. This is something that needs a lot of attention. He does have quite a sense of humor.

Conference 2

The teacher comes to the doorway to greet Mr. Traub. There is a table with three chairs around it that are big enough for adults to sit in. On the table is a set of student materials. There is also a coffee pot with a plate of Danish pastry nearby.

Ms. Wolf:	Hi, good evening. I'm Ms. Wolf, Justin's teacher. Please come in and have a seat.
Mr. Traub:	Thank you. I'm Jack Traub, Justin's dad.
Ms. Wolf:	Would you like some coffee and Danish? I'd join you, but in all honesty, you're my fifth conference of the night.
Mr: Traub:	No, thanks; I just ate.
Ms Wolf:	It's great having Justin in my class. He's got such a great sense of humor.
Mr. Traub:	He doesn't display it too often, I hope.
Ms. Wolf:	I rein him in from time to time, but he's got a pretty good sense of boundaries. I've got some of his work for you to look at. I thought we'd start with math; Justin is really progressing beautifully here. Here's his most recent assessment. Look at how he details all his responses.
Mr. Traub:	He talks a lot about being a scientist when he grows up. He says that way he'll get to do exciting stuff and not have to write a lot.
Ms. Wolf:	Writing *is* something we need to work on. I try to have students write in the areas of their interest. Perhaps we can find out which of the sciences Justin is most interested in and work on writing skills in that area.
Mr. Traub:	You know, he really loves astronomy . . .

Same child, same parent, same information, different Ms. Wolf: Which one would you like to have teaching *your* child?

Most beginning teachers are not parents themselves. Communicating with parents about student progress frequently means talking to people who might be closer to their parents' generation than their own. This can be a bit daunting and, unfortunately, sometimes causes beginning teachers to avoid communicating with parents. Parents and teachers are partners in the enterprise of helping children learn, and parents are often more nervous about conferences than teachers are.

Feedback on how well their child is doing in school is highly important to most parents. The girl who seems to fade into the background in a class, sometimes performing well, sometimes not, is the light of her parents' lives. A student who seems listless and bored may be caring for several younger siblings after school. A boy who is a behavior problem in school may be a model child at home. A teacher has a classful of students; parents, sometimes only one.

Parent/Teacher Conferences

The primary form of teacher-to-parent communication is the regularly scheduled parent/teacher conference. This is a very important interaction from several perspectives (Smith et al., 2001). First, it opens up communication between the parent and the teacher. Second, it is a communication between the teacher and the community. During parent/teacher conferences, a teacher might be talking to dozens of sets of parents or other caregivers. The success or failure of these conferences reflects on the role of the teacher in the community. Comments about them are almost certain to be passed on to a principal, supervisor, or board member. Following some simple rules can ensure successful parent/teacher conferences.

Successful teachers consider the classroom their home and parents their guests. They know who is coming into the room and make certain they feel welcome. More than anything else, the teacher wants parents to know he or she is *on the child's side*. Teachers and parents are a team working in the best interests of the child. If parents believe that the teacher likes their child and has the child's best interests at heart, they will be much better able to hear and process teacher perceptions of the child's strengths and weaknesses. If they sense that a teacher does not like their child or considers the child a burden, they will be defensive (and appropriately so). The teacher's first task, so to speak, is to bring the parents over to the teacher's side of the desk. It is wise (perhaps critical) to start on a positive note. Tell a story that puts the child in a good light. Focus first on the student's area of greatest strength. Keep in mind that even if the student is only average in this area, *it is the student's greatest strength* and, therefore, potentially the most important area of development for that student. Bring up issues that need to be worked on after you have developed rapport with the parents, and frame these not as problems but as challenges and areas for growth that you, the parents, and the student can work on together.

Note that the people coming for a conference about Heather Jackson may not be "the Jacksons." They may be Heather's mother and stepfather. Heather's mother may be using her maiden name. Neither of them may be Jacksons. There are probably records that include the names of each student's caregivers, or you can ask students who will be coming to the conference. When uncertainty arises, the following greeting should work: "Good evening. I'm Heather's teacher, Carmen Monroe. Please come in." This gives visitors a chance to explain who they are as they introduce themselves.

Parent/Teacher/Student Conferences

Many schools are moving toward the inclusion of students in the traditional parent/teacher conference (Stiggins, 1997, 2004). There are many approaches to such conferences, and issues to consider, but generally they are considered to be very worthwhile and effective in bringing all the pieces of student achievement together in the same place and at the same time. Students get the opportunity to discuss their work, "show off" their best efforts, and discuss what they are working on. Parents and teachers can review progress and set goals, with the student participating in the discussion. Clear agreements can be reached among all involved on how to proceed. Obviously, with the student present, if there are issues that are delicate in nature that need to be discussed just between parents and the teacher, such discussions cannot take place at that time. However, with this important caveat in mind, more and more schools are seeing the substantial advantages of moving to a parent/teacher/student conference as an important vehicle for establishing positive communication between school and home.

Parents' time is valuable. If it is necessary to finish notes from the conference with the previous set of parents, ask for the parents' indulgence, and finish up quickly. And do not forget to smile. (See the nearby Taking It to the Classroom box.)

www.wiley.com/college/odonnell

Appendix
Parents and Assessment Results

The results of your classroom assessments can provide you with important information that you will share with parents or guardians. Such communications will be an important part of your ongoing relationships with parents or guardians in working together to best help students. Awareness of the background of the family will help you to maximize the value of these communications (PRAXIS™, II.C.6, III.A; INTASC, Principles 6, 8).

(Bob Daemmrich/The Image Works)

Parent/teacher conferences provide the opportunity to learn more about students and to share hopes and concerns for students.

Taking It to the Classroom

What Makes a Good Conference?

Good parent/teacher conferences usually contain the following:

- A warm greeting for parents as soon as they come into the room
- A place for parents to sit (Anticipate that some of the parents are large; do not make them sit in a chair designed for a 6-year-old.)
- A welcoming demeanor on the part of the teacher
- A positive beginning
- An attitude of being *on the student's side*
- Notes on what the teacher wants to be sure to discuss
- Readily available student records and examples of student work (Note that if student work is displayed in the classroom, all students should be represented.)
- Specific, objective examples of problem areas that need to be addressed
- No comparisons to other students (even indirectly, such as, "Harley is the best math student in the class")
- An effort to work toward concrete suggestions and recommendations

Maintaining Communication

Many parents are eager to help their children in their schoolwork but are not sure what to do. During the parent/teacher conference, teachers need to gauge the parents' ability and willingness to work with their children. One approach is to set forth some options and see how the parents respond. For example, a parent with a strong mathematical background could help the child with math homework, and you could discuss with the parent the nature of that help. Another is to ask parents what thoughts or concerns they may have about how their child is progressing. The parent might provide a perspective on how to go about solving problems that is different from what has been presented in class and may be more helpful to the student. Some parents feel that helping their children with schoolwork is not their responsibility, or they simply do not have the time or academic ability. But most parents would like to contribute; finding a way for parents to work with their children can often be the most productive outcome of a parent/teacher conference.

Once established, the communication link should be maintained. This used to be quite difficult, because time during the workday usually is not available to either the teacher or the parent, and evening calls seem intrusive. Email, however, offers an effective way for parents and teachers to keep in touch. If possible, get parents' email addresses and have one to give to them, perhaps on a business card for safekeeping. Many school districts have a mechanism by which teachers can post homework assignments on the Internet. Teachers do not have enough time to email all students' parents every day or even every week but can achieve much with an occasional message such as, "Just wanted to let you know that I have read Ruby's essay on the Hubble telescope, and it shows some real growth in organization and style." It takes less than a minute and could truly brighten a parent's day. It can also help establish or reaffirm a positive parent/teacher relationship. Teachers can also provide the following via email or online (with passwords for parents):

- Course grades (assessments, quizzes, reports)
- Unexcused absences
- Missed assignments
- Disciplinary concerns

Do not put anything in an email that you would not like to see repeated or presented to someone else.

The lesson on parent/teacher communication is simple: Get in touch, stay in touch, and work together for the student's benefit.

REFLECTION FOR ACTION

The Event

At the beginning of the chapter, you saw assessments on *The Scarlet Letter* from three high school classrooms. You were asked to present a critique of these assessments by determining what they were trying to measure and how you might have gone about the task differently. Now we will look at this question more systematically. Think about those three approaches to assessment, how you would improve them, and, more important, what *your* approach would be.

Reflection RIDE

When you set out to construct an assessment, it is essential to begin with the goals or objectives for that assessment. If you do not know what the objective or achievement target (Stiggins, 2004) is, it is hard to evaluate the assessment. The goal or objective of reading literature is a particularly interesting problem. Why did these classes read *The Scarlet Letter*? To be able to say they read a classic piece of literature? To learn about the norms and mores of a different society? To see how an author can take an example from the past and impart lessons for today? To learn about literary style? To learn who Arthur Dimmesdale was?

What Theoretical/Conceptual Information Might Assist in Interpreting and Remedying This Situation? Consider the following:

Instructional Goals

Why do we read great literature? One source of information for thinking about the appropriate assessment approach is the set of goals or objectives related to the reading in question.

The Principles of Assessment and Grading

Do these assessments fairly represent what was taught in these classes? Does each student have an equal chance of doing well? Did the teacher clearly communicate expectations to the students? Do students know how they are to be graded on these assessments? How do the assessments promote the growth of the students? The principles of assessment and grading (communication, fairness, and growth) provide an excellent framework for assessing the assessments.

Assessment Options

What alternatives are there to the assessments presented at the opening of the chapter? Are the ones presented the best ones for assessing the goals of the instructional unit in relationship to the skills, knowledge, and abilities being taught?

Information Gathering RIDE

The easiest way to see whether the assessments reflect instructional goals and activities would be to visit the teachers and the classrooms. Of course, one can make a good guess at these goals and activities from the assessments themselves. It appears that Mr. Antoine is very much concerned about the students knowing the particulars of the novel. Ms. Baldwin's assessment focuses on applying information from the novel in a debate format. This emphasizes understanding broad themes in the novel and seeing how they relate to contemporary issues. Mrs. Chambliss's assessment looks at the issue of character development and appears to be an entertaining task. A potential problem in Mrs. Chambliss's approach is that some of the students may not have a strong background in modern American cinema; this might be particularly true of students from certain religious and ethnic backgrounds.

Decision Making RIDE

Each of the three assessment approaches has strengths and weaknesses.

- Mr. Antoine's approach will probably result in a thorough assessment of whether the students have read and understood the book. If he uses a good blueprint that is distributed to students before the assessment, it will help them to review the work and strengthen their comprehension of it. However, the assessment does not look very engaging and does not push the students to extend themselves in thinking about the novel.

- Ms. Baldwin's approach is novel and exciting, and it will encourage the students to look at the book from a new perspective and seek out other sources of information. However, it will not result in a broad assessment of students' comprehension of the material. Moreover, students who are good at seeking out and organizing information and are good debaters will have a distinct advantage over those who do not have those abilities. Were these skills taught as part of the unit that included reading the novel? Is this assessment fair?

- Mrs. Chambliss's very creative approach would probably be the most fun to do, especially for a film fan. However, it seems to rely heavily on a background in Hollywood cinema, and students may need to obtain outside help.

Each approach has its strengths and weaknesses. Using all three might be desirable, but the assessment would probably be unreasonably long. Perhaps you could use them in intervals throughout the unit. For example, you could break the traditional assessment into several quizzes. Perhaps you could assign and organize the debate at the beginning of the unit, with the actual debates being a cumulative activity. The casting assignment could be a homework assignment for students to do and share by presenting their choices and defending them in an end-of-unit social exchange.

Evaluation RIDE

Once you have made your choice or choices, you need to monitor your students' responses. How well did they seem to comprehend the material (based on the more traditional assessment)? Was the debate a source of excitement or just added work? Should you combine reading the novel with lessons on gathering information and debating the issues? Would it be better to save the debate for a later instructional unit on debates? Did the casting assessment go well, or did only some students participate? Did your approach to assessing students have them buzzing with excitement or dreading the activity? How well did your assessment enhance your instruction, and how much information did it add to your understanding of your students' progress? A good way to find out how well the assessments worked would be to ask the students. What did they like or not like? What did they think was fair or unfair? Do they have suggestions for modifications or alternatives for the future?

Further Practice: Your Turn

Here is a second event for consideration and reflection. In doing so, implement the processes of reflection, information gathering, decision making, and evaluation.

The Event

Imagine that you have just graded an assessment for your class, and constructed a stem-and-leaf diagram of the results. They are a disaster. The students did much worse than you had expected. Only the two best students in the class did well, although they did very well.

What might have gone wrong? How can you find out what happened, and how you can avoid repeating this situation?

SUMMARY

- **What assessments do we experience in everyday life and how do we react to them?**

  We experience assessments in the form of feedback to our actions all day long, every day. This might be when we are driving a car, talking to a friend, or playing a game. When people respond to what we post on a social network site or send out a tweet, we are getting an assessment from people who are important to us.

- **What are the characteristics of assessment that make them most useful?**

  We respond positively to assessments when we trust the information that we get from them, when the information is timely, when they concern issues of importance to us, and when we feel that they are being received in a supportive and positive environment.

- **What is the role of assessment in the instructional process?**

  Assessment is an integral part of the instructional process. Instruction and assessment should flow logically from clearly stated instructional goals, creating a seamless weave of learning and understanding of what has been learned.

- **How can teachers devise assessments that facilitate instruction and at the same time provide information about students' progress?**

  Teachers can use a set of principles (communication, fairness, and growth) in reflecting on their assessment decisions and the consequences of those decisions. The principles emphasize making sure students understand what is expected of them (communication), gathering information pertinent to instruction (validity), gathering enough information to make good decisions (reliability), and using assessment to enhance instruction (growth).

- **Of the many options teachers have for assessment, which are the best?**

  A wide variety of assessment options are available, some traditional and some more recent developments. These options have both strengths and weaknesses and are more or less useful for different purposes. For example, essays help teachers evaluate students' ability to pull material together, organize thoughts, and communicate clearly. However, they may not be as good for determining whether students have acquired a large and complex set of information. Performance assessments often allow students to display their creativity and how well they can apply the skills and knowledge they have acquired.

- **How can a teacher develop a grading system that is fair and that lets students take responsibility for their own learning?**

  Grades should be based on assessments that reflect instructional goals and the instruction that has taken place in the classroom. Students should understand clearly what teachers expect of them and how their work will be graded.

- **How can assessment help students learn about their own strengths and weaknesses?**

  Assessment provides students with the opportunity to demonstrate their accomplishments both to their teachers and to themselves. When teachers give, mark, and return assessments in a spirit of support for learning and growth, students will have the opportunity to view their strengths as areas to develop and their weaknesses as points for improvement.

- **How can teachers continually improve their assessment and grading practices?**

  Continuous improvement requires an open mind, a conscientious and ongoing effort to improve, and the willingness to reflect in a systematic and meaningful way on one's assessment efforts. The principles of communication, fairness, and growth provide a structure for improving assessments. In addition, at any grade level, asking the students what they thought about the assessment will provide useful feedback.

- **How can teachers create and modify assessments to include learners who face special challenges?**

  Teachers can make a variety of modifications in their assessments to give learners facing special challenges the opportunity to display their abilities. These modifications include extra time, a distraction-free place to work, and rewritten instructions to facilitate comprehension of the tasks on the assessment. They can also be certain that assessments align closely with the student's IEP.

- **How do cultural differences among students and their parents affect the process of communicating progress?**

  Parents and children from diverse cultural backgrounds may have different views of schooling and teachers, different aspirations for their children, and differing opportunities to participate in school events and activities. Teachers need to be sensitive to such differences and keep the lines of communication open. Teachers are accustomed to telling parents about their classrooms and expectations for students. With parents from different cultures, especially recent arrivals to the United States, it is important not to make assumptions about what parents know and to explain the instructional process thoroughly.

Key Terms

accommodations, p. 506
achievement targets, p. 503
alternative assessment, p. 497
assessment, p. 486
authentic assessment, p. 497
bias, p. 490
classified, p. 506
constructed response, p. 494
content/behavior matrix, p. 503
criteria, p. 504
distracter, p. 492
formative assessment, p. 488

higher-order thinking skills, p. 493
individualized education program
 (IEP), p. 506
informal assessment, p. 501
item, p.492
item bank, p. 512
journal, p. 501
matching, p. 493
multiple choice, p. 492
objectivity, p. 497
performance assessment, p. 497
portfolio, p. 499

products, p. 497
reliability, p. 490
rubrics, p. 504
standardized assessment, p. 487
standards-based assessment, p. 506
stem, p. 492
summative assessment, p. 488
test bank, p. 512
test blueprint, p. 503
validity, p. 490

Exercises

1. *Using the Principles of Assessment and Grading: Class Participation*

   Review the principles of assessment and grading presented in the chapter and determine how important class participation would be in determining the grades you would give your students. Consider the following:

   - How will you encourage classroom participation if you do not count participation toward grades?

   - If you do count participation, how will you take into consideration that some students are shy and do not want to participate?

   - How will you count participation so that you will have a system that is reliable, valid, and free from bias?

2. *Evaluating Assessment Quality*

   Think about the best assessment activity you have participated in as a student, whether in elementary school, high school, or college. Write down the characteristics of that assessment activity. What made it high in quality? What level of freedom and what constraints were there? Did you know you were doing well or poorly as you were working on the assessment? If you did, how did you know? Now think about the worst assessment you have ever had. What specifically did you dislike about that assessment? How could it have been turned into a positive experience?

3. *Comparing and Contrasting Your Assessments*

   With one or two classmates, choose a topic and grade level for which all of you feel comfortable in developing an assessment, perhaps using a statewide standard. Work out your plans individually, then meet to discuss your efforts. Who has the most creative idea? Whose assessment seems to cover the intended achievement targets best? Discuss how your work reflects your views about students and the content of the material.

4. *Improving Assessments*
   Working with a partner or a small group of classmates, examine several assessments that you have had in your college courses, based on what you have learned from the chapter. For example, look at a midterm examination or a writing assignment. How do they line up with the principles of assessment and grading? What would you do to improve them?

5. *Moving from Standards to Developing Assessments*
   On the Web, find the statewide standards for your state in the areas that you think you might want to teach. (Nearly all state departments of education include statewide stan-

Lesson Plans

Lesson #1: "Imitation Art"

GRADES: 6–12

ESTIMATED COMPLETION TIME: 3 class periods

SUBJECT AREAS AND NATIONAL STANDARDS:

World History:
- Understands significant aspects of Islamic civilization

Language Arts:
- Uses the general skills and strategies of the writing process
- Gathers and uses information for research purposes

Visual Arts:
- Identifies specific works of art as belonging to particular cultures, times, and places

I. OBJECTIVES: Students will be able to:
- Identify aspects of Islamic art in order to create their own replica
- Prepare a brief description of their piece that includes how it reflects ancient Islamic culture

II. PROCEDURE:

1. Review how ancient cultures used goods to trade with other peoples and discuss how trade influenced traditions and customs to spread.

2. Provide students with a brief explanation of the different types of art.

3. Give each student the rubric for their specific activity to help guide their work. Use the sample textile rubric provided.

4. Provide laptop computers, books, and class notes so students can research and develop their art piece. Include sample artwork for students to use to create pieces.

5. Assign students one of the four tasks below. Task should be assigned based on student level and ability:
- Patterned plate design—low level
- Architecture—high level
- Secular drawings—high level
- Textile design (rug)—on level

Written Component:
- Description should include:
  - Type of art
  - Origin (time/place)
  - Reflection of Islamic culture
- The description should be attached to the artwork.
- Students will create a brief presentation for their work.

III. ADAPTATIONS:

High-Level Students:
- Imitate the art of calligraphy, as it was an important part of Islamic culture
  - Can be used in their art piece, or in their written description

Lower-Level Students:
- Work with a partner or
- Provide the student with a sheet that already includes the design
  - Student will be responsible for creating a color scheme

IV. INTERNET RESOURCES FOR STUDENTS:
http://www.islamic-study.org/art.htm
http://www.historyforkids.org/learn/islam/art

V. ASSESSMENT:
- Art piece rubric
- Student's knowledge and understanding as expressed through the presentation
- Informal assessment during conferencing and observation during class

Ask Yourself!

1. How are the instructional objectives and the standards related?

2. Will you get enough information from the planned assessment to know if the objectives were met?

3. What would you add?

dards for each grade level and subject on their Web sites. A link to state departments of education is provided at the companion Web site for this book.) Choose one of your state standards and think about how you might assess that standard. Start by thinking about how you might teach that standard, then work from your instructional activities toward assessments. Try to develop assessment ideas using at least three of the assessment options discussed in the chapter. Even though the standard may seem to lend itself to a particular type of assessment, try to stretch your thinking to develop a second and a third approach.

Lesson Plans

Lesson #2: "Characteristics of Snakes and Turtles"

GRADES: 1–2

SUBJECT: Life Science, Geography, Literature
URL: www.pbs.org/wnet/nature/lesson_plans/reptiles1.html

I. LEARNING OBJECTIVES: Students will be able to:

- Name characteristics of snakes and turtles.
- Compare and contrast snakes and turtles.
- Name characteristics of reptiles.
- Compare and contrast reptiles and mammals.

II. STANDARDS LIFE SCIENCES:

Standard 5: Understands the structure and function of cells and organisms

Level I (Grade K–2):

1. Knows that plants and animals have features that help them live in different environments

Level II (Grade 3–5):

2. Knows that living organisms have distinct structures and body systems that serve specific functions in growth, survival, and reproduction (e.g., various body structures for walking, flying, or swimming)

3. Knows that the behavior of individual organisms is influenced by internal cues (e.g., hunger) and external cues (e.g., changes in the environment), and that humans and other organisms have senses that help them to detect these cues. Standard 6: Understands relationships among organisms and their physical environment

Level I (Grade K–2):

1. Knows that plants and animals need certain resources for energy and growth (e.g., food, water, light, air)

2. Knows that living things are found almost everywhere in the world and that distinct environments support the life of different types of plants and animals

Level II (Grade 3–5):

3. Knows that an organism's patterns of behavior are related to the nature of that organism's environment (e.g., kinds and numbers of other organisms present, availabil-

ity of food and resources, physical characteristics of the environment)

4. Knows that changes in the environment can have different effects on different organisms (e.g., some organisms move in, others move out; some organisms survive and reproduce, others die)

III. CULMINATING ACTIVITY/ASSESSMENT:

Grades 1 and 2:

Since the goals of the first two parts of the lesson are for the children to know the characteristics of snakes and turtles, assessment should be centered on those themes. Literature may be a good tool to find out if the students have learned the characteristics. There are many excellent books and stories that have snakes and turtles as protagonists. These include:

- For snakes, *Verdi* by Jannell Cannon, *Snakes Are Nothing to Sneeze At* by Gabrielle Charbonnet, and *Crictor* by Tomi Ungerer.
- For turtles, *The DancingTurtle*, a folktale from Brazil by Pleasant DeSpain; *Box Turtle at Silver Pond* by Susan Korman; *Box Turtle at Long Pond* by William T. George. Choose one story for snakes and another for reptiles. Read the story aloud to the class, asking leading questions about the characteristics mentioned in the story. For example: What do you think the snake is using its tongue for? How do you suppose the turtle heard that? How is that snake moving? As a final assessment, you may have the class write a story together about a snake

Ask Yourself!

1. What kind of assessment is this?
2. How can you use the information obtained to help students solidify their knowledge?
3. What kind of paper/pencil assessment could you develop?
4. Why might students be having difficulty with this lesson? What can you do about that?

Courtesy of Thirteen/WNET New York.

Memo

To: All Principals
From: Dr. Ramirez, Superintendent of Schools
Re: Statewide Testing Results
Date: September 15

Our analysis of the scores from the statewide testing program is complete. Although there are areas in which we are doing well and should take pride, there is also more work to be done. In particular, we see difficulties in fourth-grade language arts, eighth-grade science and mathematics, and eleventh-grade mathematics. Additionally, there are problems in various grade levels, especially when we disaggregate the test scores in different subject areas.

You will find attached to this memo an analysis for your school. Please review your results and write an action plan for your school. I think it would be best to form an advisory committee of teachers to participate in the development of your action plan. Dr. Novick, the test coordinator for the district, is available for consultation. We will hold a meeting of the executive staff in three weeks to review and discuss each school's plan.

Judy—
I'd like to have some "new blood" along with some veterans on this committee. Can I count on your participation?
Thanks- Marty

You are a new teacher in your school district, and you have just received a copy of this memo from the superintendent to your principal, along with the sticky note asking you to be a member of the advisory committee. First, this is not really an invitation; it is a directive. It is also a good opportunity for you—as well as a lot of work.

Standardized and Standards-Based Assessments

15

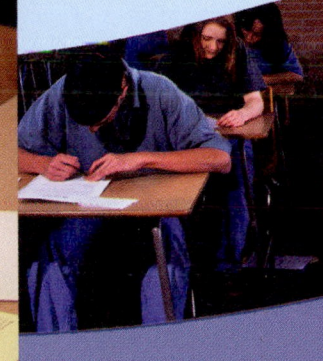

RIDE · Reflection for Action

Faced with a set of statewide assessment scores and a mandate for addressing problem areas in your school, your committee has to come up with an action plan. As you read this chapter, think about the following questions for the committee's work: What exactly is the situation for your school? Where are the strengths and weaknesses? How reliable and valid is the information that you have? What are some realistic options for improvement? How can you contribute to the work of the committee?

Guiding Questions

- What are standards and how do they influence what happens in schools?
- What are standardized assessments and where do they come from?
- How can a teacher make sense of the statistics and scales that come with these measures?
- What is the best way to interpret standardized test scores?
- How concerned should teachers be about issues of reliability and validity?
- How can teachers fairly assess students with learning and physical challenges?
- Is standardized assessment equally fair for students from different cultural backgrounds?

CHAPTER OVERVIEW

Standardized and standards-based tests are as much a fact of life in schools as taking attendance, recess, and water fountains. In this chapter, standardized and standards-based assessments are demystified. We will examine what these tests are, what they are used for, and how they are developed. We will consider the benefits gained from using such assessments as well as the problems associated with them. We will also look at the history of such tests and how to understand and interpret the scores, and we will consider controversies associated with standardized testing.

The Nature and Development of Standardized Assessments
- What Are Standards and Where Do They Come From?
- A Brief History of Standardized Assessments
- School and Statewide Testing Programs
- Standards-Based Assessment
- College Admissions Testing
- Intelligence Testing
- Selecting Standardized Assessments
- Categories of Assessments

Technical Issues in Assessment
- Statistics Used in Assessment
- Scales
- Norms and Equating
- Setting Passing and Other Proficiency Scores
- Validity and Reliability

Interpreting Standardized Assessments
- Finding the Child in the Data
- Demystifying the Assessment Report
- Combining Standardized Results with Other Information
- Bringing the Child to the Classroom
- Thinking about the Classroom, School, and District Levels
- Looking at Scores for English Language Learners
- Looking at Scores for Students with Special Needs

Controversies in Assessment
- Bias in Testing
- High-Stakes Testing and Its Implications

The Nature and Development of Standardized Assessments

standardized assessment A measure of student ability in which all students take the same measure under the same conditions.

Standardized assessments are tests given under standard conditions. That is, all students taking the test are given the same instructions, are tested in similar physical environments, have the same amount of time to complete the test, and have their tests scored in the same fashion. Standards-based assessments are a form of standardized test developed from a set of standards or objectives. Standardized tests serve a variety of purposes, ranging from seeing who is most ready for kindergarten to determining whether a school district is meeting statewide goals for performance. With the advent of the No Child Left Behind legislation, standards-based assessments are used in all states and have become an extremely important part of school life in America. Each state has developed its own program, and there are important differences among states. The Race to the Top legislation is changing the landscape of standards-based assessment, but the fact that all states give such assessments will remain for the foreseeable future, and thus teachers need to know about their state's program and how it affects their classrooms.

Educators refer to tests and assessments in somewhat different ways, and the differences are not completely clear. Generally speaking, a test consists of a set of questions that require student responses, which are graded as correct or incorrect, or scored according to a rubric. The point values are summed to create a total score. *Assessment* is a somewhat broader term that can include scores generated by performances or teacher judgments. Thus, a test is a type of assessment. A *measure*, or *measurement*, is any type of quantification of something. It can be a test, an assessment, or a measure of someone's height. Finally, *evaluation* is sometimes used to mean an assessment or a coordinated group of assessments toward a certain purpose (such as a special needs evaluation). Evaluation can also mean the process through which a program or activity is assessed in terms of its value (*evaluation* and *value* have the same root).

What Are Standards and Where Do They Come From?

Standards are statements of what we want students to be able to do. They often come in two basic forms: content standards and performance standards. Content standards focus on the knowledge and skills that we want to see in students, and performance standards focus on the levels of ability, or performance, that we want to see. Over the past 20 years, professional organizations related to curriculum areas and state departments of education have developed standards for learning in the various curricula from grades 1 to 12. In all likelihood, your state has such standards and has a Web site where you can see what they are. As mentioned in the chapter on classroom assessment, there are a number of different names for the same idea here. Sometimes they are called objectives, goals, achievement targets, or even WALTs (We Are Learning To)! But they are all basically the same idea: statements of what we want children to know or be able to do.

Most states have developed an extensive set of standards that essentially define the curriculum for the state in grades K–12 in all subject areas. They are usually quite extensive and are often based on standards developed by professional curriculum organizations. Even though most states have independently developed their own standards in areas such as literacy and mathematics, they are remarkably similar from one state to the next.

Why are they important? Because they essentially define what is to be taught in any given grade in school. That is, they determine what it is that *you* will be teaching.

A Brief History of Standardized Assessments

Although standardized assessment can trace its history back over 2,000 years to the civil service examinations given in China (Green, 1991), modern testing really began in the late 1800s. Developments occurring during that period (roughly the 1880s to the early 1900s) in Germany, France, England, and the United States led to the forms of standardized testing that exist today. In Germany, the pioneering psychologist Wilhelm Wundt and his students began the serious examination of individual differences among humans. In England, Charles Darwin's cousin and contemporary, Francis Galton, was interested in the inheritance of intelligence. In the United States, James Cattell focused his efforts on vision, reaction time, and memory, among other characteristics.

In France, Alfred Binet worked to develop a series of mental tests that would make it possible to determine the *mental age* of students who were not performing well in public schools so that they might be assigned to the proper school for remedial work. Binet's work led to two fascinating and quite divergent developments. The first was the creation of the **intelligence test**, and Binet is rightly called the father of intelligence testing. His initial measure, intended to assess abilities in children aged 3 to 13, consisted of a series of questions of increasing difficulty and can be considered the first intelligence test (Wolf, 1973). The American psychologist Lewis Terman expanded on Binet's work to create the Stanford-Binet intelligence test, which is still in use today (Terman, 1916).

intelligence test A measure of generalized intellectual ability.

The second development arising from Binet's work occurred shortly after his death at a relatively young age. A young Swiss researcher named Jean Piaget came to work in the laboratory that Binet had established with his colleague, Theodore Simon. Piaget used many of the tasks and experiments that Binet had developed but he was more interested than Binet in finding out *why* children answered questions the way they did—especially the characteristic mistakes they made. Thus, Binet's work spawned not only intelligence testing but also Piaget's theory of cognitive development.

All testing at this time was done individually with a trained specialist. A student of Lewis Terman, Arthur Otis, was instrumental in the development of group testing, including objective measures such as the famous (or infamous) multiple-choice item (Anastasi & Urbina, 1997). His work led to the development of the Army Alpha and Beta tests, which were used extensively in World War I. From the 1920s through the 1940s, college admissions testing, vocational testing, and testing for aptitudes and personality characteristics all flourished, bolstered by the belief that progress in the quantification of mental abilities could occur in as scientific a fashion as progress in mathematics, physics, chemistry, and biology.

School and Statewide Testing Programs

School testing programs began in the 1920s with the publication of the first Stanford Achievement Tests (Anastasi & Urbina, 1997). They were originally designed to help school systems look at the *overall effectiveness* of their instructional programs, *not the progress of individual children*. In keeping with the behaviorist approach to education and psychology that prevailed at the time, multiple-choice testing was favored because grading could be done in an objective fashion and machines could be used to score the tests. More programs developed over the decades, and from the 1960s on, the number of children taking standardized, end-of-year tests grew remarkably rapidly (Cizek, 1998). Although these programs usually provide tests for grades K–12, the primary focus has traditionally been on grades 2–8, with less emphasis on kindergarten, first grade, and the high school years.

Measurement specialists develop school testing programs by first looking at what schools teach and when they teach it. In recent years, the focus of this process shifted from school district curriculum guides to statewide assessment standards. These standards are examined and reduced to a common set of objectives, organized by the school year in which they are taught. Tests are then developed to reflect a common set of objectives. Historically, these tests consisted primarily of multiple-choice questions, but recent editions include more essay and constructed-response items.

norming study The administration of an assessment to a representative national sample to obtain a distribution of typical performance on the assessment.

standards-based assessment An assessments that is generated from a list of educational standards, usually at the state or national level; a form of standardized assessment.

The draft versions of tests go through a number of pilot tests to ensure that they have good technical qualities (discussed later in the chapter). The final version is then tested in a major nationwide **norming study**, in which a large group of students (tens of thousands) take the test to see how well a representative national sample performs on the test. The results of the norming study are used to determine scales, such as grade-equivalent scores and percentiles, all of which are discussed later in the chapter.

In the early 1970s, states began to develop their own testing programs, often selecting a limited number of grades at which to test and usually limiting testing to reading, mathematics, and sometimes science and/or writing. These *statewide testing programs* were intended to see how well school districts were doing and to provide benchmark information on the progress of individual children. They are usually developed by large testing companies and organizations under contract to state departments of education. Typically, a new version is developed each year and statistically equated to performance from previous years.

Standards-Based Assessment

The most recent development in standardized school testing is **standards-based assessment** (Briars & Resnick, 2000; Resnick & Harwell, 2000). This approach to assessment is based on the development of a comprehensive set of standards (which look much like objectives) for each grade level in each subject area. The standards are then used to develop instructional approaches and materials, as well as assessments that are clearly linked to the standards and to each other. The primary distinction between standards-based assessment and the commercial

(Media Bakery)

Standardized tests go through a number of trials with real children before the final forms are produced.

TABLE 15.1

Assessment Requirements of the No Child Left Behind Act

The No Child Left Behind Act requires the following:

- Testing in each year from grade 3 to grade 8 and once in high school in the areas of mathematics and language arts

- Testing at least once each in grades 3–5, 6–9, and 10–11 in science

- Student performance to be broken down by variables such as ethnicity, family income levels, English language proficiency, and disability to examine gains in performance

- English language learners have to become proficient in English

- A program for reaching high standards of achievement by the school year 2013–2014 has to be developed and approved by the federal government

- States must document annual growth toward these goals for all of their schools

NCLB also requires that all students be taught by highly qualified teachers and that students learn in schools that are safe and free from drugs and that promote learning. Schools that do not meet the standards of NCLB will initially receive support from their states to improve, but if improvement does not occur, a series of sanctions will take place that could include replacing the teaching staff and administration of the school. The implementation of the exact nature of the requirements can be found on the national NCLB Web site.

school testing programs described earlier lies in the notion that standards, instruction, and assessment are all linked together, that assessment is not something to be added on once goals and instructional programs have been established. Standards-based assessment programs at the state level are a key element in the federal No Child Left Behind legislation that so greatly influences assessment practices. It would be an excellent idea to look at the statewide assessment program in the state where you are planning to teach. The Web site that accompanies this text includes links to current information on standards-based assessment.

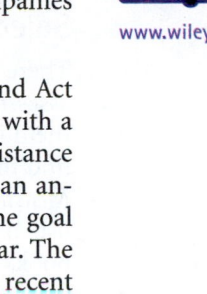

www.wiley.com/college/odonnell

The No Child Left Behind Act and Race to the Top The No Child Left Behind Act (NCLB) became federal law in January of 2002. NCLB mandates that states comply with a series of regulations and meet achievement standards in order to receive federal assistance in education. One of the primary requirements of the act is that each state develop an annual assessment program and that schools show regular progress toward meeting the goal that all students will reach high standards of achievement by the 2013–2014 school year. The requirements of NCLB as it pertains to assessment are presented in Table 15.1. More recent federal legislation, called Race to the Top, is now influencing educational practice. It may cause states to work together on common statewide assessment programs instead of each state having its own program.

College Admissions Testing

Whereas school testing programs have been very important in the pre–high school years, college admissions testing has been the primary assessment concern of high school educators and students alike. College admissions testing has been in existence for a long time, but only fairly recently has it taken the form in which it exists today. In the 1920s, the first version of the SAT was used for college admissions testing (Aiken, 2003); in 1947, the test began to look more like the one in use today (Haladyna, 2002). There are two major college admissions testing programs. The older of these is the SAT, which used to stand for Scholastic Aptitude Test, but the College Board, which runs the program, changed the name in 1994 to Scholastic Assessment Test. The College Board changed the name again in 2005 to simply the SAT. The SAT provides a verbal score, a quantitative score, and a writing score, each of which has a scale of 200 to 800. Each test has a *mean* (average) of 500 and a *standard deviation* (how far from the mean the scores tend to be) of 100. (Mean and standard deviation are explained further later in the chapter.) A companion set of measures assesses abilities in a variety of specific subject areas; scores use the same scale.

The other major college admissions testing program is the ACT Assessment. ACT is an acronym for American College Testing program, but the program is now called the ACT Assessment. It provides scores in English, mathematics, reading, and science reasoning, using a scale of 1–36 that has a mean of roughly 20 and a standard deviation of 4–5. Starting in 2005, there is also a writing assessment that is optional (some colleges will require it; some will not).

Colleges use admissions tests in different ways. Some large state universities combine them with high school grade point averages, using a mathematical formula. The results of the combination determine admissions. Other colleges and universities use the tests in combination with grades, letters of recommendation, extracurricular activities, and personal statements in a more subjective process to arrive at admissions decisions. Some colleges do not use them at all. Considerable controversy exists concerning the use of college admissions tests and the potential biases associated with them. This is undeniably a sensitive issue in American education; we discuss this in the Controversies in Assessment section later in the chapter. (See the nearby Uncommon Sense box.)

Intelligence Testing

If college admissions testing is a sensitive issue in American society, intelligence testing is a hypersensitive issue. Intelligence testing has a long and often not very attractive history. It began in the early 1900s with the work of Binet, described earlier, followed by that of Lewis Terman, Henry Goddard, and Charles Spearman in the United States. Originally designed for the admirable purpose of trying to help students with difficulties in learning, intelligence testing has been used for a host of less acceptable purposes, including prohibiting certain groups of people from immigrating to the United States (American Psychological Association, 1999). Today, intelligence testing in education revolves around the testing of students for purposes of special needs classification and selection for gifted-and-talented programs. The most widely used tests are the Wechsler Intelligence Scale for Children–Revised (WISC-R) and the Kaufman Assessment Battery for Children (K-ABC).

Selecting Standardized Assessments

There are standardized assessments for almost anything imaginable. There are standardized assessments for becoming a welder, for matching disabled people to animals that can help them in their lives (such as Seeing Eye dogs), or for determining people's lifestyles. You can find these and thousands of other assessments in a remarkable reference work titled *Mental Measurements Yearbook* (MMY; Plake, Impara, & Spies, 2003). MMY is a series of books published by the Buros Institute of Mental Measurements at the University of Nebraska. These books provide critical reviews of standardized assessments in all areas. Professionals in the field write the reviews, which are usually quite rigorous. MMY can be particularly helpful when a school or school district needs a standardized test for a particular reason. The Web site for this text lists the Web site for MMY, where you can find reviews electronically.

Categories of Assessments

In Chapter 14, differences between formative and summative assessment were discussed. Assessments can be categorized in a variety of other ways. Three of the most widely used categorization systems are the following:

- Norm- and criterion-referenced
- Achievement, aptitude, and affective measures
- Traditional and alternative assessments

Norm and Criterion Referencing   What does a test score mean? Is a 96 always a good score and a 32 always a poor one? In order to determine whether a score is good or bad, we need to compare it to something else (that is, provide a reference for it). If you compare a score to a fixed standard, or criterion (90% and above = A, 80–90% = B, etc.; or *passing* on the road test to get your driver's license), you are making a **criterion-referenced** interpretation of the score. If you compare a score to how well others did on the same test (70th percentile, above average, best in show), you are making a **norm-referenced** interpretation of the score. The concept of criterion versus norm referencing was developed in the early 1960s (Ebel, 1962; Glaser, 1963, 1968; Popham, 1978; Popham & Husek, 1969). The basic idea relates to the

RIDE Think back to the beginning of the chapter, where the superintendent and principal assigned you to a committee to look at your district's test scores. In all likelihood, your test was developed by your state department of education. There should be a Web site that provides technical information about the test and its development

www.wiley.com/college/odonnell

Appendix
Types of Assessments
The requirements of the No Child Left Behind Act have increased the importance of teachers' knowledge of various types of assessments and the kinds of information they can provide about students' progress (PRAXIS™, II.C.2; INTASC, Principle 8).

criterion-referenced Term describing a method for understanding what assessment scores mean by referring them to some arbitrary standard.

norm-referenced Term describing scores that are given meaning by referring them to scores from other individuals or sets of individuals.

Uncommon Sense

Technology Advances Testing—Or Does It?

Recent advances both in computers and in testing methodology have enabled computer administration of exams such as the Graduate Record Examination. Clear advantages to such administration exist, but so do disadvantages.

Among the advantages are the following:

- The test can be given at different times at different places.
- The selection of harder or easier items, depending on how well the examinee performs, reduces the time necessary to administer the test.
- Students receive their scores as soon as they finish the test.

Disadvantages include the following:

- On most computerized tests, the examinee cannot go back to reconsider a question after entering an answer into the computer.
- Reading passages require the examinee to scroll back and forth through the text.
- Test security is a big problem because examinees do not all take the test at the same time.
- Some examinees are far less familiar and comfortable with taking exams by computer than are others.

interpretation of the score. Consider, for example, that a student has just received a grade of 34 on an end-of-unit assessment in an algebra class. Is that grade good, okay, bad, or a disaster? It is hard to know without some sort of referencing system. If it is a percent-correct score, a 34 does not look very good. But if the test was the ACT with a maximum score of 36, a 34 might be terrific. Another way to think about a score would be to know how it stacked up against the other scores in the class. A 76 might be right in the middle (an okay score), the best in the class (excellent), or near the bottom (time to get some help).

When criterion-referenced tests (CRTs) were first introduced, they were relatively short; focused on a single, well-defined objective or achievement target; and accompanied by a passing score that certified the student as having *mastered* the objective. A CRT was often a one-page multiple-choice or short-answer test. Educators use CRTs in instructional programs that are objective-based and often developed from a behavioral perspective, such as mastery learning. Today, educators usually define the difference between criterion-referenced and norm-referenced testing in broader terms: Tests that use norm-based scores to give meaning to the results are norm-referenced tests; those that use an arbitrarily determined standard of performance to give meaning are criterion-referenced assessments.

Achievement, Aptitude, and Affective Tests Another way to classify tests is to decide whether one is assessing past achievement or predicting future achievement. An assessment that tries to measure what a student has been taught is called an *achievement test* (or assessment); one that is trying to predict how well students will do in future instruction is called an *aptitude test*. For example, the SAT, used by many colleges in deciding which applicants to admit, was originally called the Scholastic *Aptitude* Test. Intelligence tests are also used to predict future school achievement.

Assessment is not limited to what people know and can do; it also includes how they learn, how they feel about themselves, how motivated they are, and what they like and do not like. Issues related to an individual's attitudes, opinions, dispositions, and feelings are usually labeled *affective* issues. A large number of **affective assessments** are used in education, including measures of self-efficacy, self-esteem, school motivation, test anxiety, study habits, and alienation. Educational psychologists frequently use affective assessments to help them understand why some students do better in school than others. (See the nearby Uncommon Sense box.)

affective assessment An assessment related to feelings, motivation, attitudes, and the like.

Uncommon Sense

Aptitude Tests Predict Future Performance—Or Do They?

Recently, the idea of an aptitude test has fallen out of favor in educational circles, as has, to some extent, the distinction between achievement and aptitude tests. Scholars are concerned about whether students have had the opportunity to learn the material on an achievement test (and whether the test really measures achievement or instead measures the opportunity to have learned the material). They also question racial, ethnic, and gender differences in test results and whether tests whose results reveal such differences should be used for admissions and scholarship purposes. People now often talk about *ability* tests as simply a measure of a student's level of academic performance at a given point in time. Without knowledge of a student's educational history, a score on such a test does not imply a judgment about how the student attained his or her present level of performance.

Traditional and Alternative Assessments A third way of categorizing assessments is according to the form they take. When educators talk about traditional assessments, they are usually referring to multiple-choice tests, either standardized or for classroom use. Of course, teachers have used essay and short-answer tests for years; therefore, they might be considered traditional. As discussed in Chapter 14, a number of alternatives to traditional testing methods have evolved over the past 20 years. These include authentic assessment, performance assessment, portfolio assessment, and, more broadly, alternative, assessment.

Summary of Categories of Assessment You can classify any assessment using the following categories:

- Normative versus criterion-referenced
- Formative versus summative
- Achievement versus aptitude versus affective
- Traditional versus alternative

How Can I Use This?
How would you classify a multiple-choice midterm examination in a college history course?

For example, a teacher might use an assessment that requires students to make an oral presentation to determine the final grade in a French course; this would probably be a criterion-referenced, summative, achievement, alternative assessment. It would be criterion-referenced because each student would receive a grade that would not depend on how well other students did. It would be summative because it would be used for grading. It would be an achievement assessment because it would measure learning in the course, and it would be alternative because it uses a format that does not rely on paper-and-pencil approximation of a skill but rather measures the skill directly.

Appendix
Understanding Measurement
You will be better positioned to interpret the results from various assessments if you understand some basic concepts in measurement theory and assessment-related issues (PRAXIS™, II.C.5; INTASC, Principle 8).

Technical Issues in Assessment

The technical issues involved in assessment can be daunting to educators at all levels; consequently, some educators shy away from them. However, with some foundational knowledge, all teachers can understand and discuss these issues.

Statistics Used in Assessment

Understanding standardized assessment requires a basic knowledge of some rudimentary statistical concepts concerning summarizing and communicating information about a group of scores. The first has to do with the notion of a typical or average score of a group of people, or the *central tendency*. The second has to do with how much the scores differ from one

Figure 15.1
Calculating the Mean

The Scores	
8	
5	Total = 8 + 5 + 10 + 5 + 7 = 35
10	
5	Mean = $\dfrac{35}{5}$ = 7
7	

> There are five scores here. Add them and divide by 5, and you have the *mean* of the scores.

another, or their *variability*. The third concept is the *z-score*, a standardized numbering system for comparing individual scores. The fourth concept is the *normal distribution*, also known as the *normal curve* (and sometimes informally called the *bell curve*), which is a useful mathematical representation of groups of scores. A final useful statistical concept, the *correlation coefficient*, is discussed in Chapter 1. It has to do with how closely two scores measured on the same group are related (such as how closely related height and weight are for a particular group of people). These are not complex ideas, but the mathematics underlying them can get complex. The focus in this chapter is on the ideas, not the math.

Central Tendency: Mean, Median, and Mode The simplest way to convey information about the scores of a group of people on a test (or any other variable) is to describe what the middle scores are like. This is the **central tendency** of the scores. Using statistics, there are three measures of central tendency: the mean, the median, and the mode. The most widely used of these measures, the **mean**, is simply the arithmetic average of a group of scores. To obtain the mean, add all the scores together and divide by the total number of scores. Figure 15.1 presents a simple example.

The **median** is the middle score of a set of scores when they have been organized from the highest score to the lowest. It is very useful when a group of scores includes some extreme scores that might make the mean appear not to be representative of the set of scores as a whole. For example, the mean age of all the people in a kindergarten class is usually around 7. This is so because the children are around 5, and the teacher could be in her 30s or 40s. Therefore, the mean is not very useful in this case. The median (and the mode) would be 5, a number much more representative of the typical person in the class. Figure 15.2 shows how to obtain the median.

The **mode** is simply the score that occurs most frequently. Researchers use the mode in describing the central tendency of variables in situations in which the use of decimals seems inappropriate. For example, it is more reasonable to say that the modal family has 2 children, rather than saying that families have 2.4 children on average (Gravetter & Wallnau, 2004). In the example of the kindergarten classroom, the mode would be a good measure of the central tendency. (See the nearby Uncommon Sense box.)

Variability: Variance and Standard Deviations In addition to understanding where the center of a group of scores is, it is important to have an idea of their **variability**—that is, how they spread out, or differ from one another. Statisticians use several measures of variability. The focus here is on those that are most widely used and most important for assessment: the *standard deviation* and the *variance*. These both involve a bit more calculation than the measures of central tendency just discussed, but it is more important to understand the underlying concepts.

The **variance** is the average squared distance of each score from the mean. To obtain the variance, subtract each score in a group of scores, then square it. Do this for all the scores,

central tendency An indicator of the center of a set of scores on some variable.

mean The arithmetic mean of a set of scores.

median The middle score of a set of scores that have been rank-ordered from highest to lowest.

mode The most frequently occurring score in a set of scores.

variability The degree to which scores on an assessment (or other variable, such as height or weight) are spread out.

variance A measure of how much a set of scores is spread out.

Figure 15.2
Calculating the Median

The Scores	The Scores Reordered from Lowest to Highest
8	5
5	5
10	7
5	8
7	10

> There are five scores here. If they are put in order from lowest to highest, the middle score, 7, would be the *median*.

Figure 15.3
Calculating the Variance
and the Standard Deviation

Scores	Scores Minus the Mean (Deviations)	Deviations Squared
8	$8 - 7 = 1$	1
5	$5 - 7 = -2$	4
10	$10 - 7 = 3$	9
5	$5 - 7 = -2$	4

The squared deviations sum up to:
$1 + 4 + 9 + 4 + 0 = 18$
The variance is the sum of the squared deviations divided by the number of scores in the group:
$$\frac{18}{5} = 3.6$$

The standard deviation (SD) is simply the square root of the variance, or in this case:
$$SD = \sqrt{3.6} = 1.897$$

then add them and divide by the total number of scores in the group. Figure 15.3 provides an illustration of this.

The variance is widely used in statistical analysis, but it is not as practical as the standard deviation because the variance is in the form of squared units. That is, it tells you, on average, how far each score is from the mean *squared*. The standard deviation, on the other hand, provides a measure of the spread of the scores in the numbering system of the scores themselves. Calculating the standard deviation is easy once you have the variance: You simply take the square root of the variance to obtain the standard deviation, as shown in Figure 15.3

standard deviation A measure of how far scores vary from the mean.

The **standard deviation** provides an index of how far from the mean the scores tend to be. If, in a large set of scores, the distribution of scores looks roughly normal (or bell-shaped), about 95% of the scores will fall within 2 standard deviations on either side of the mean. That is, if one goes up 2 standard deviations from the mean, then down 2 standard deviations from the mean, about 95% of the scores will fall between those two values. If a particular set of scores had a mean of 38, a standard deviation of 6, and more or less a normal distribution, about 95% of the scores would fall between 26 (2 standard deviations below the mean) and 50 (2 standard deviations above the mean). If the standard deviation was 15, the bulk of the scores would range from 8 to 68. If the standard deviation was 2, the scores would range from 34 to 42. (More information about the normal curve appears later in the chapter.)

In essence, the standard deviation provides an idea of the numbering system of a set of scores. For example, SAT scores have a standard deviation of 100. Going up 10 SAT points is not a very big increase. ACT scores, on the other hand, have a standard deviation of roughly 4–5. Going up 10 points on an ACT score is a huge jump.

z-Scores   Earlier in the chapter we discussed norm-referenced testing as a way to give meaning to a score by comparing it to those of others who took the same assessment.

Uncommon Sense
We Are All Rich!—Or Are We?

Statistics can be used to confuse. If you were sitting in a room with a billionaire and 19 other people who made just a decent salary, *on average* you would all be millionaires. In reality, however, there would just be one billionaire and 20 people who had to work to earn a living. Combining information in an unreasonable fashion is a common way to trick people into believing a situation or to make an argument that otherwise would not stand up. If something seems too good to be true, it probably is.

Consider SAT scores again. They have a mean of roughly 500 and a standard deviation of roughly 100. A score of 550 would be one-half of a standard deviation above the mean. We could say that a score of 550 is +0.5 standard deviation above the mean. A score of 320 would be 1.8 standard deviations below the mean, or −1.8.

This concept is called a **z-score**; it is simply how many standard deviations away from its mean a given score is. If the score is above the mean, the z-score is positive. If the score is below the mean, the z-score is negative. The calculation for the z-score is simply the score minus its mean divided by its standard deviation. The formula looks like this:

$$z = \frac{(\text{score} - \text{mean})}{\text{standard deviation}}$$

For example, a student gets a score of 85 on a test. The mean for all the students in the class is 76, and the standard deviation is 6. The z-score is

$$z = \frac{(85 - 76)}{6} = +1.5$$

This means that a raw score of 85 is 1.5 standard deviations above the mean for this group of students. When combined with a working knowledge of the normal curve, presented below, z-scores provide a lot of information. For example, imagine Maria took a physical fitness test that had national norms that were roughly normal (bell-shaped). How well did Maria do? If Maria's z-score on the fitness test was +1.0, that would mean she outperformed roughly 84% of the students in the norming group. A z-score of −1.0 would mean she outperformed only 16% of the students. You can see that the raw score does not present much useful information, but the z-score tells us a lot.

Normal Distribution   The bell-shaped curve, often mentioned in conversations about testing and statistics, is more formally known as the **normal distribution**. It is actually a mathematical model or abstraction that provides a good representation of what data look like in the real world, particularly in biology and the social sciences. Many sets of test scores show a more or less normal distribution. The normal curve is depicted in Figure 15.4. Roughly speaking, normal distributions result when a number of independent factors contribute to the value of some variable.

In a perfectly normal distribution, 68% of the scores fall between 1 standard deviation above and 1 standard deviation below the mean; 96% of the scores fall between 2 standard deviations below the mean and 2 standard deviations above the mean. This can be seen in Figure 15.4. This figure provides a good reference for thinking about where scores are located in most roughly normal distributions. Many of the scales used in reporting standardized test scores are based on the concept of the z-score.

Using Statistics to Look at Groups of Scores   When looking at groups of scores, it is advisable to try to look at them from more than one perspective. The results presented on a standards-based assessment may highlight the number of students passing. But you should also look at the distribution of scores as a whole. How many students were close to passing? How many show substantial weaknesses? Are there any scores that have been included in the statistics that seem out of place? For example, are there any zero scores added into the mean? This could just be a student who did not take the assessment for some reason. Also, compare statistics across comparable groups. Are the means and standard deviations similar for all schools in your district? If one school is doing better than others on a given score, or subscale, that could be a clue to finding a particularly effective teaching strategy.

Scales

As mentioned earlier, most standardized assessment programs report results using one or more scales employed to transform the scores into numbering systems, or metrics, that are easier to understand. This section describes the most commonly used scales.

Raw Scores   **Raw scores** are usually obtained through the simple addition of all the points awarded for all the items (questions, prompts, etc.) on a test. For example, if an assessment

z-score A standard score that any set of scores can be converted to; it has a mean of 0.0 and a standard deviation of 1.0.

normal distribution A mathematical conceptualization of how scores are distributed when they are influenced by a variety of relatively independent factors.

What Does This Mean to Me?
An SAT verbal score of 650 is a z-score of roughly +1.5 (1.5 standard deviations above the mean). Check that against the figure of the normal curve in Figure 15.4, and you can see that this is higher than roughly 93% of the scores.

raw scores Scores that are simple sums of the points obtained on an assessment.

Figure 15.4
The Normal Curve and Assessment Scales

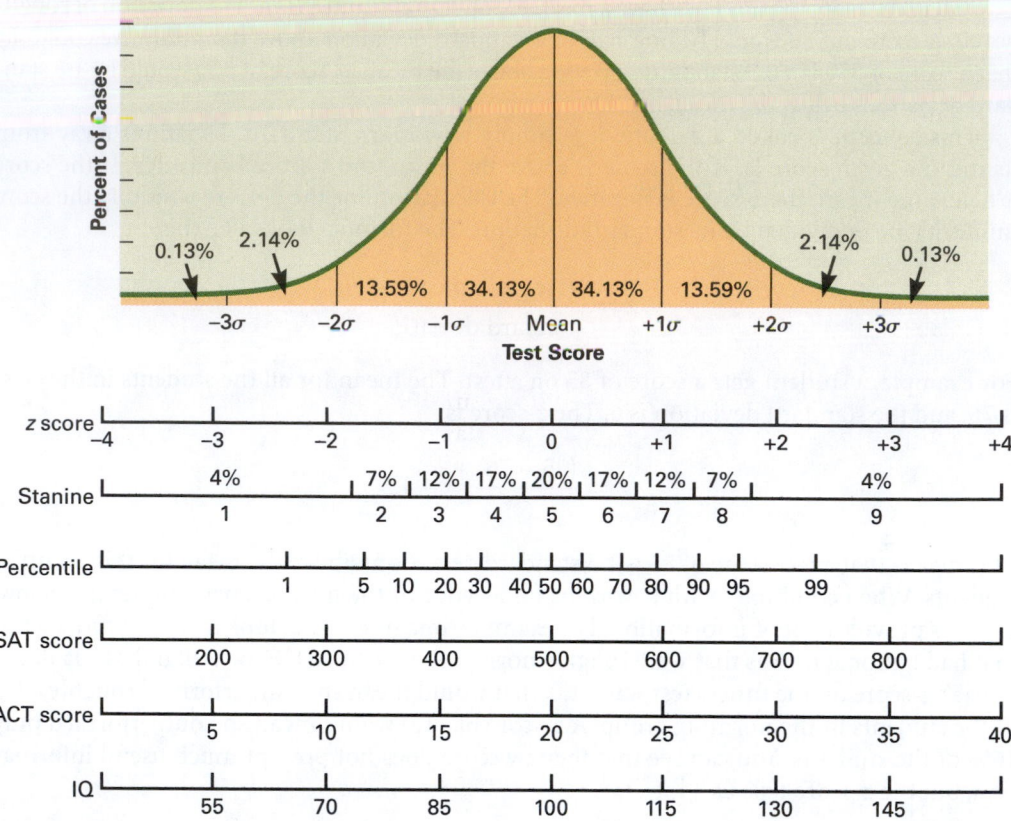

Note: SD stands for standard deviation. SAT and ACT scores are from the original scales. With each year's administration the means and standard deviations change slightly.

scaled scores Scores from an assessment that have been transformed into an arbitrary numbering system in order to facilitate interpretation.

has ten multiple-choice items worth 1 point each and five essays worth 5 points each, the maximum raw score would be 35, and each student's score would be the sum of the points attained on each item.

Scaled Scores Raw scores are useful in that they let students know how well they did against a total maximum score. They are not particularly useful in helping students (or teachers or parents) know how good a given score is. Moreover, assessment programs that test students on a yearly basis (such as the SAT or end-of-year standardized school assessment programs) usually construct a new assessment for each new cycle of the assessment. Testing companies try to make the new test produce scores that are as similar, or parallel, to the old one as possible. In testing, *parallel* means that the two tests have highly similar means and standard deviations, and there is a very high correlation between the two tests (usually, 80 or above). Even though two tests may be highly parallel, one test may be slightly easier than the other (or perhaps easier in the lower ability ranges and harder in the higher ability ranges). When this happens, a 64 on one test may be equivalent to a 58 on the other. In an effort to make scores more meaningful and to simplify equating scores from one form of a test to another, scores are often reported in terms of **scaled scores**. Scaled scores are mathematical transformations of raw scores into new scales, or numbering systems.

The first scaled score was the IQ score developed by Lewis Terman (1916). Terman took the French psychologist Alfred Binet's notion of *mental age* (the age associated with how well an examinee could perform intelligence-test tasks) and divided it by the examinee's chronological age to obtain an *intelligence quotient*, or IQ score. (IQ scores are no longer determined in this way.) The SAT (200–800) and ACT (1–36) are scaled scores. Most statewide stan-

(© Michael Nitzschke/Imagebroker/Age Fotostock America, Inc.)

When looking at a set of test scores, it is important not to lose sight of the individual children who produced them.

dards-based assessment programs have scaled scores that they report in addition to levels of performance, such as *proficient* and *advanced proficient*.

Percentiles Percentiles are the most straightforward scores other than raw scores. A percentile is the percentage of people who score less well than the score under consideration. For example, if 76% of the people who are tested score below a raw score of 59, the percentile score for a raw score of 59 is the 76th percentile. Percentiles are easy to interpret and are often used to report scores on school testing programs. Do not confuse *percentile* with *percent correct*. A second caution is that percentiles, along with the other scales described here, can drop or increase rapidly if the scale is based on only a few questions. Therefore, when looking at percentiles, always check to see how many questions were included in the scale being reported.

> **percentile** A number that indicates what percentage of the national norming sample performed less well than the score in question.

Stanines The U.S. Army developed **stanines** for use in classifying recruits in the armed services during World War II. Stanines (short for "standard nine") are scores from 1 to 9, with 1 being the lowest score and 9 the highest. They are calculated by transforming raw scores into a new scale with a mean of 5 and a standard deviation of 2. They are then rounded off to whole numbers. Therefore, a stanine of 1 would represent a score that is roughly 2 standard deviations below the mean, and a stanine of 6 would be 0.5 standard deviation above the mean. Look at Figure 15.4 to see how stanines work. The utility of the stanine is that it allows communication of a score with a single digit (number). In the days before the widespread use of computers, this was particularly useful, and stanines are still used in assessment programs today for quickly and easily providing an index of how well a student did on a test.

> **stanines** Short for "standard nine," scaled scores that run from 1 to 9 and have a mean of 5 and a standard deviation of 2.

Normal Curve Equivalent Scores Normal curve equivalent (NCE) scores were developed to provide a scale that looks like a percentile but can be used more easily in statistical analyses. NCE scores are transformed scores that have a mean of 50 and a standard deviation of 21.06. This spreads the scores out so that they can be interpreted in roughly the same way as percentile scores. School districts often use NCEs in evaluation reports for programs involving classified students. (See the nearby Taking It to the Classroom box.)

> **normal curve equivalent (NCE)** A scale related to the *z*-score that has a mean of 50 and a standard deviation of 21.06.

Developmental and Growth-Oriented Scales Some scale scores are based on where children fall within a particular cohort of students. They usually include some notion of the child being above or below the mean. A simple example of this is the *z*-score, where a positive score means above the mean and a negative score means below the mean. This often carries with it a negative connotation (who wants to be in the group with a minus sign?).

This can also be seen with percentiles or NCEs (being below the 50th percentile or NCE), stanines (below the 5th stanine), and so on. Other types of scales link scores across years and provide a developmental or growth-oriented picture of student progress. This can allow a teacher to focus on the growth of a given child over years rather than the fact that the child might currently be below national norms. A good example of this is a grade-equivalent score.

Grade-Equivalent Scores A useful but widely misunderstood scale is the **grade-equivalent score**. Grade-equivalent scores are often thought of as indicating how well students should be doing if they are on grade level. This is not true. A grade-equivalent score is the mean performance of students at a given grade level. That is, a grade-equivalent score of 5.4 is the performance obtained by an average student in the fourth month of fifth grade (like school years, grade-equivalent years contain only 10 months). But if this is the average performance, is it not the case that about half the students fall below this level? Yes. By the definition of grade equivalent, about half the students will always be below grade level. Do not interpret grade-equivalent scores as where students *ought* to be; instead, interpret them as average scores for students at that point in their school progress. The nearby Uncommon Sense box brings this point home. A teacher can also use them to show how much gain has been made in a particular year.

> **grade-equivalent scores** Assessment scores that are reported in terms of how well children did in the norming study at various grade levels.

Norms and Equating

Many of the scales discussed so far (e.g., stanines, NCE scores, grade equivalents) involve comparing a student's scores to scores that other students have received. Who are those

Taking It to the Classroom

Summary of Commonly Used Scores

Standardized assessment employs a variety of scores to present information. This table summarizes the definitions of the most common scores and their best usage.

Name	Definition	Best Use
Raw score	The total number of points earned on the assessment. This could be simply the total number of items correct or it could include questions scored according to a scoring rubric.	Simply looking at the number of items a student got right or, if a rubric is used, the number of points a student earned. This is often useful in combination with other scores.
Scaled score	An arbitrary numbering system that is deliberately designed not to look like other scores. The SAT, ACT, and IQ scores are examples of scaled scores.	Testing organizations sometimes use scaled scores to equate one form of a test to another.
Cut, passing, or mastery score	A score usually presented either as a scaled score or a raw score that indicates that students have exceeded a minimum level of performance on a test. This could be a high school graduation test or a formative test used as part of classroom instruction.	Usually used with criterion-referenced assessments, these scores are increasing in importance. They indicate that the student has met the minimal requirements, whether that be for a unit, for high school, or for a driver's license.
Percentile	Ranging from 1 to 99, percentiles indicate the percentage of test takers who got a score below the score under consideration. Thus, a raw score of 42 (out of a 50-point maximum) could have a percentile of 94 if the test was a difficult one.	Percentiles are very good for seeing how well a student did compared to other, similar students. It provides a norm-referenced look at how well a student is doing.
Normal curve equivalent score	Ranging from 1 to 99, normal curve equivalent scores (NCEs) are based on the normal curve and have a mean of 50 and a standard deviation of 21.06.	NCE scores were developed to look like percentiles but also have the statistical quality of being a linear scale, which allows for mathematical operations to be carried out on them.
Stanine	Ranging from 1 to 9, stanines (an abbreviation of "standard nine") are based on the normal curve. They have a mean of 5 and a standard deviation of 2, and are also presented rounded off to whole numbers. The U.S. military developed stanines to provide a score that could be presented in a single digit and compared across tests.	Stanines are good for quickly and easily providing an index of how well a student did on a test compared to other students.
Grade-equivalent score	Ranging basically from 1.0 to 12.9, they provide a score that indicates how well a typical student at that year and month of school would have done on the test in question. Imagine that a student had a grade-equivalent score of 5.4 on a given reading test. This would mean that this is how well a typical fifth grader in the fourth month of the school year would have scored.	Grade-equivalent scores give a quick picture of how well a student is doing compared to what students in the norming group did at a given grade level. Be cautious about grade-equivalent scores when they are far from the level of the test that has been given.

other students? They are what measurement specialists call the *norming group*, and there are several types. One such group would be a nationally representative sample of students who have taken the test under consideration. Commercially available testing programs use this approach. They select school districts in such a way as to produce a set of districts that are similar to districts in the nation as a whole. These districts are invited to participate in a *norming study*. If a district declines to participate, another similar district is invited. They continue this process until they have a representative sample. The schools all administer

Uncommon Sense

Marian Should Be in Seventh Grade—Or Should She?

Mrs. Roman, a fourth-grade teacher, receives a phone message from the mother of one of her students.

Marian's mom: Mrs. Roman, we just got the standardized test scores back for Marian, and the reading grade-equivalent score is 7.2. We were really pleased to see that and to see that Marian is doing so well. But we were wondering, if Marian is capable of doing seventh-grade work, should we be thinking about having her skip a grade next year? Can we come in and talk about this?

What should Mrs. Roman tell Marian's parents about her test score? First, it is important to understand that Marian took a fourth-grade test. She did very well on the reading portion of the test, as well as would be expected of an average student in the second month of seventh grade. This does not necessarily mean that Marian is ready for seventh-grade work. What it does mean is that she is progressing very well in reading in the fourth grade. What is essential is to make sure that Marian is receiving challenging and interesting assignments and activities in her reading instruction.

---

the test under standard testing conditions, even though the districts may or may not actually use the results. The scores of students produced by this norming study give the testing companies the information they need to develop the **norms** for the test. Norms are the information base that the companies use to determine such scales as percentiles and grade equivalents. Norms can also be developed from students who take the test under real conditions. This is how the SAT, ACT, and most statewide testing programs work. The percentiles for these tests are actual percentiles from people who took the test at the same time that the student did, not from a norming study (actually, the SAT and ACT accumulate information over several testings).

Setting Passing and Other Proficiency Scores

When a student is about to take an assessment, one question that is often in the student's mind is: How well do I have to do in order to get the grade I want? If the assessment is the driver's license test, the student is simply interested in passing. If the assessment is the final examination in a course, the student may want to know what the cut score will be for an A. In classroom assessment, these are the break points between an A and a B, a B and a C, and so forth. In statewide standards-based assessments, there are often two break points: one between passing and not passing, and another between passing and a high level of performance. The scores that determine whether a person passes or fails an assessment are called *passing scores, cut scores,* or *mastery scores.*

Setting **passing scores** on state and national assessments is a fairly sophisticated process that usually involves multiple steps. Setting levels for different grades in a classroom often involves the simple application of the "90 and above is an A . . ." system. With the prevalence of standardized and standards-based assessment in schools, it is important to understand the basic ideas behind how passing scores are set in standardized testing.

Passing Scores in Standardized Assessment In standardized assessment, passing scores are set in several basic ways, and new variations on these basic ideas are continually being developed (Cizek & Bunch, 2006; Impara & Plake, 1995; Plake & Hambleton, 2000). We describe some of these approaches here. The oldest and most common are called the Angoff (1971) approach and the Nedelsky (1954) approach. They share the following ideas.

The Angoff/Nedelsky Approach to Standard Setting The Angoff/Nedelsky approach to standard setting is described in the steps below and summarized in Figure 15.5.

---

norms A set of tables based on a representative national administration of an assessment that makes it possible to show how well particular students did compared to a national sample of students.

Appendix
Types of Scores
Standardized assessments report a variety of types of scores. It is helpful to understand the various types of scores when you attempt to interpret the results of these assessments (PRAXIS™, II.C.5; INTASC, Principle 8).

RIDE What kinds of scaled scores are used in the statewide assessment program in your state? Most state department of education Web sites will provide information on how to interpret the scales they use. Think back to the introductory material in this chapter. It would be good to go into the committee meeting with the principal understanding what the scaled scores are for your state. How are they determined and what do the results look like for the state as a whole?

passing scores The scores on an assessment that one needs to obtain or exceed in order to pass the assessment.

**Figure 15.6
Summary of Setting
Passing Scores**

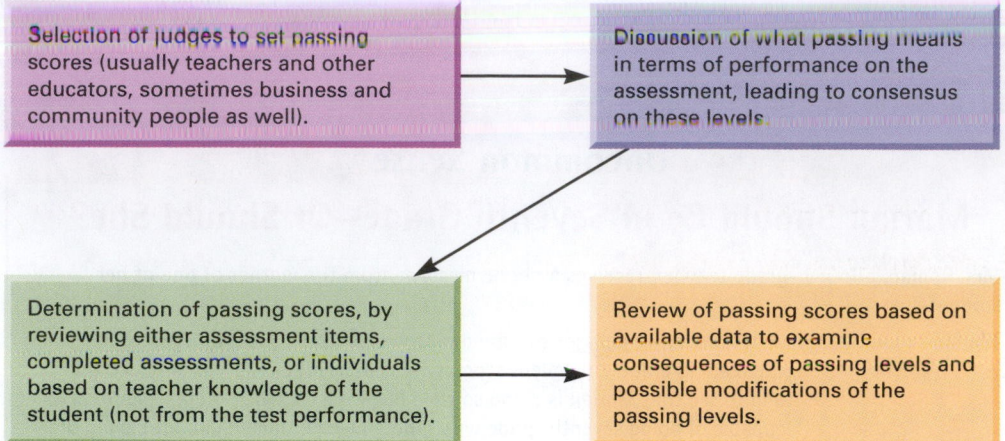

- A number of experts, called *judges*, in the area being tested (e.g., mathematics) are brought together for a standard-setting session.

- The group works with assessment specialists to agree on what general level of competence should determine a passing score (the minimal level of competence that would get a *pass* on the assessment).

- Each judge reviews each item on the assessment with this minimal level of competence in mind.

- Each judge determines how well the *minimally competent* student will perform on each item. For example, a judge may determine that on a 5-point short essay question, a minimally competent person should get at least a 3 on the item. Perhaps, on a 1-point multiple-choice item, the judge determines that the minimally competent person should have about an 80% chance of getting the item right (this is recorded as .8 in the standard-setting system).

- When the judges have assigned point values to how well they think the minimally competent person should do on each item, these values are added together, and the total becomes the estimated passing score for each judge.

- The judges' passing scores are combined to form an overall passing score. There are various ways of doing this, but taking the average of all the judges' scores is a frequently used approach.

This approach, or a variation on it, is the most common method used to set passing scores for standardized assessment. As can be seen, the score that is established will depend to a large extent on who is chosen to be on the judging panel and the choice of level of performance considered minimally acceptable. It is important to understand that this process is fundamentally subjective: Although technical issues are involved, the individuals' judgments are the basis for what the passing score should be.

The Student–Based Approach to Standard Setting   A second approach to setting passing scores uses classroom teachers as judges and asks them to make judgments about *students*, not assessments (Tindal & Haladyna, 2002). This is presented below and summarized graphically in Figure 15.6.

- A group of practicing classroom teachers and their students are selected to participate in the standard-setting process.

- The students take the assessment under standard conditions (the conditions under which the test would normally be administered).

- The teachers receive descriptions of the minimal level of competence required for the student to pass the assessment. This may be done in writing, or the teachers may be brought together to discuss what this level means (if two levels, minimal pass and advanced pass, are desired, both levels are discussed).

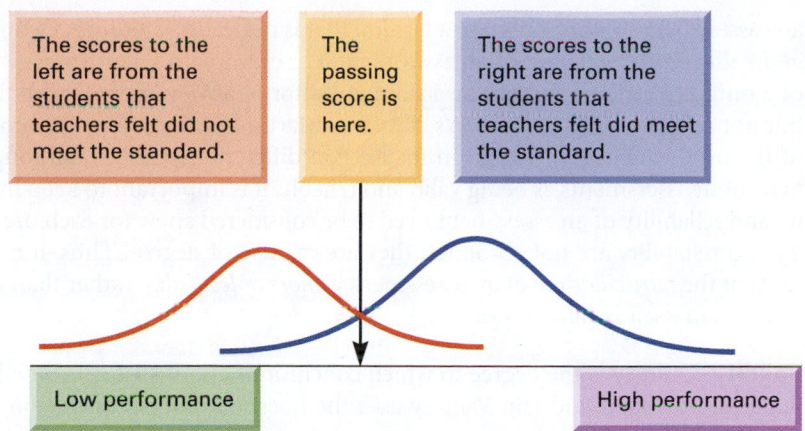

Figure 15.6
Student–Based Approach
to Standard Setting

- Without knowing how well their students did, each teacher rates each student as a *pass* or *not pass* (or on the two levels, if desired), based on knowledge about the student from work in the class.

- All the students who are rated *pass* are put into one group and all those rated *not pass* are put into a second group. The distribution of scores in each group is examined.

- The point where the two curves meet (see Figure 15.6) is the passing score for the assessment. It is the point that best differentiates minimally competent students from students who are not minimally competent, in the judgment of their teachers.

This approach is quite different from the Angoff/Nedelsky procedure, even though this approach also uses judgments to set passing scores. If three levels of performance are needed, the teachers are simply asked to rate their students as *not minimally competent*, *minimally competent*, or *advanced competent*.

The nearby Taking It to the Classroom box shows how you can use these ideas for setting passing scores or for setting standards for grading your classroom assessments.

The Bookmark Procedure   A third general approach to setting passing scores that has become popular recently is called the bookmark procedure (Karantonis & Sireci, 2006; Lewis et al., 1999). This approach works as follows:

- A panel of judges (as in the Angoff/Nedelsky procedure) is assembled to make decisions, and the ideas that underscore various levels of performance are discussed.

- The items on a test are ordered from the easiest to the hardest based on testing that has already occurred with students.

- Judges are told to think about a minimal passing student as one who had a 67% chance of performing successfully on a given item.

- Judges are asked to go through the ordered test and to place a "bookmark" at the point in the test where a minimal passing student would no longer have a 67% chance of successful performance.

- Once judges have made an initial determination of the passing level, their decisions are discussed in groups and refined through various procedures.

- This procedure has been described as if there was only one passing score to set, but the procedure could easily be extended to include several passing, or cut, scores.

The bookmark approach has gained rapidly in popularity with state testing programs designed to comply with NCLB requirements.

Validity and Reliability

A common statement associated with assessment is, "Of course, we want the assessment to be *valid* and *reliable*." What does that statement mean? The concepts of reliability and validity are simply formal refinements of commonsense notions of what assessments should be. To begin, any assessment might be used in a fashion that is not valid. Validity is technically a characteristic *of the use or interpretation* of an assessment. For example, a science assessment given at the end of a unit of instruction might be a valid indicator of achievement for Mr. Martin's science class but not as valid for Mrs. Jackson's class. Mr. Martin may have focused more on certain aspects of the unit, whereas Mrs. Jackson focused on different aspects. So although people frequently talk about assessments as being valid and reliable, it is important to keep in mind that the validity and reliability of an assessment need to be considered anew for each use. Furthermore, validity and reliability are not absolutes; they are matters of degree. Thus, it is more appropriate to say that the *particular use* of an assessment is *more or less valid*, rather than to say simply that the assessment itself is valid or not.

validity The appropriateness of judgments about students based on assessment information. In classroom assessment, the correspondence between what an assessment measures and what was taught as part of instruction.

Validity   **Validity** is the degree to which conclusions about students based on their assessment scores are justified and fair. Validity asks the question: Is the conclusion I am drawing about this student based on this assessment correct? In assessment, validity is the heart of the issue. If an assessment is valid, it actually has to be reliable. The concepts of antique and old provide an analogy. If something is antique, it has to be old, but not all old things are antique (rocks, for example). For standardized assessments, measurement specialists conduct studies to empirically validate that the assessment measures what it is intended to measure. These **validation studies** often include the following:

validation study A research study conducted to determine whether an assessment is valid.

- Having experts critically review the items on the assessment to ensure that they measure what is intended (this is called **content validity** evidence)

content validity An indicator of the degree to which the items on an assessment appear to fully cover the intended content of the assessment and whether there is any extraneous material.

- Statistically relating the scores from the measure with other, known indicators of the same traits or abilities (this is called **criterion-related validity** evidence)

- Conducting research studies in which the assessments are hypothesized to demonstrate certain results based on theories of what the assessments measure (called **construct validity** evidence)

criterion-related validity The degree to which an assessment correlates with an independent indicator of the same underlying ability.

For example, imagine that a state put a spelling test on its standards-based language arts/ literacy test for all fourth-grade children. A content validity study might consist of showing the words on the spelling test to fourth-grade teachers to see if they agreed that these were words that fourth graders should be able to spell (not too easy, not too hard). A criterion-related validity study might compare the scores obtained on this test to the number of spelling errors students made in their regular written work. A construct validity study might look at how the questions are asked on the test (do students have to pick the correctly spelled word out of a list of four options, or spell the words on their answer sheets after the teacher pronounces them?).

construct validity An indicator of the degree to which an ability really exists in the way it is theorized to exist and whether it is appropriately measured in that way by the assessment.

More recently, educators have become concerned about the consequences of using a particular assessment. For example, if a college highly values SAT scores as a determining factor in admitting students, what kind of a message does that send to high school students who want to go to that college with regard to how hard they should work on their school subjects? Concerns of this type assess the **consequential validity** of the assessment (Messick, 1994). In general, the issue of validity has to do with whether an assessment really measures what it is intended to measure and whether the conclusions or inferences that are made about students based on the assessment are justified. In the spelling test example above, the consequential validity question would center on how instruction in language arts/literacy would differ if the test was included or not.

consequential validity Concern for how the assessment will affect the person taking it.

reliability Consistency over an aspect of assessment, such as over time or over multiple raters. In classroom assessment, having enough information about students on which to base judgments.

Reliability   **Reliability** is the consistency or dependability of the scores obtained from an assessment. Reliability asks the question: Would I get roughly the same score for this student if I gave the assessment again? Imagine a group of high school students were given a grammar assessment in Spanish on a Friday and the same measure again on Monday (without learning how well they did in between). Correlating the scores between these two assessments would provide a measure of the reliability of the assessment Reliability is closely related to validity, but it is more limited in scope. In Chapter 14, we defined reliability in classroom assessment as having enough information to make a good judgment about student achievement. The definition presented here is a more formal definition of reliability, applicable to a wider range of assessment issues.

Taking It to the Classroom

Setting Standards on Classroom Assessments

Teachers set standards all the time. This might be as simple as determining what will be a check, a check-plus, or a check-minus, or as complicated as judging one paper an A– and another a B+. Frequently, teachers choose one of the following standard approaches to assigning letter grades to numerical scores:

Common Number-to-Letter Equivalence Systems

Letter Grade	Number Grade	System A	System B
A	4.0	93–100	95–100
A–	3.7	90–92	93–94
B+	3.3	87–89	90–92
B	3.0	83–86	87–89
B–	2.7	80–82	85–86
C+	2.3	77–79	83–84
C	2.0	73–76	80–82
C–	1.7	70–72	78–79
D+	1.3	67–69	76–77
D	1.0	63–66	73–75
D–	0.7	60–62	70–72
F	0.0	59 and below	69 and below

(Blair Seitz/Photo Researchers, Inc.)

Even when grades are disappointing, they can contain useful information for improvement and growth.

There is nothing wrong with using these systems, but they assume that a given percentage correct on an assessment always means the same thing. Some assessments are simply easier than others, even when they are measuring the same objective or achievement target. Consider the following math item from a fifth-grade assessment:

What three consecutive even integers add up to 48?

This is a moderately difficult item. But look what happens when the item becomes a multiple-choice item:

What three consecutive even integers add up to 48?

  a. 8, 10, 12   *b. 16, 16, 16*
  c. 15, 16, 17   *d. 14, 16, 18*

Now students do not have to generate an answer; they simply have to find a set that adds up to 48 and meets the criterion of consisting of even, consecutive integers. Here is yet another possibility:

What three consecutive even integers add up to 48?

  a. 4, 6, 8   *b. 8, 10, 12*
  c. 14, 16, 18   *d. 22, 24, 26*

Now all that students have to do is correctly add sets of three numbers and see which set totals 48. The difficulty of the items has been changed substantially, even though ostensibly they all measure the same objective. The point here is that a score of 90 (or 93) may not always represent an A level of performance.

Teachers can *recalibrate* their grading for an assessment by going through a procedure similar to the Angoff/Nedelsky procedure. After developing an assessment, go through it and determine how many points a minimal A student would receive on each item. Add up these points; this becomes the A/B break point. Then do the same thing for the minimally passing student to arrive at the D/F break point. Once these two break points have been determined, the B/C break point and the C/D break point can be determined just by making each grade range roughly equal. For example, this process might yield the following system:

A/B break point	86	(a difficult test)
D/F break point	64	

With this information, the B/C break point could be 78 and the C/D break point 71. The point to keep in mind is that the grades associated with an assessment should be the result of a thoughtful process rather than a predetermined system.

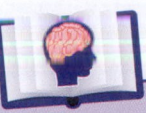

MINDFUL HABITS OF EFFECTIVE TEACHERS

Effective teachers are consistent: Effective teachers treat all students with respect and treat all students fairly. They teach in a manner that students can come to depend on. It might be said that effective teachers are reliable.

reliability study A study that is used to determine reliability coefficients.

reliability coefficient An index, ranging from .00 up to 1.00, of how reliable an assessment is.

split–half reliability A form of reliability coefficient, similar to coefficient alpha, that takes half of the items on an assessment, sums them into a score, then correlates that score with a score based on the other half of the item.

coefficient alpha An approach to assessing reliability that uses a single administration of the assessment and focuses on whether all the assessment items appear to be measuring the same underlying ability. Also called *Cronbach's alpha.*

inter–rater reliability A measure of the degree to which two independent raters give similar scores to the same paper or performance.

standard error of measurement An index of how high or low an individual's assessment score might change on a second testing.

true score The hypothetical true ability of an individual on an assessment.

As with validity, it is not the assessment itself but the particular application of the assessment that is reliable or not. Moreover, assessments are not either reliable or not reliable; they are either more reliable or less reliable. The essence of reliability is how certain one can be that the assessment would produce the same results on a second administration.

However, reliability is *not* related to the question of whether the assessment is really measuring what it is intended to measure. That is, just because a measure is reliable (i.e., produces consistent results) does not necessarily mean that it is valid (i.e., measures what is wanted or needed). *The SAT math score is just as reliable an assessment of artistic ability as it is of mathematics ability.* This seems astounding. But reliable is not the same thing as valid. The SAT math score is simply not a *valid* measure of artistic ability. Therefore, measures that do not provide validity evidence may or may not be measuring what you want. You need to carefully examine measures that do not provide supporting validity evidence to ascertain whether they are valid for your needs. Reliability is important, but validity is crucial. This point is important because assessments often have reliability evidence but no validity evidence.

The reliability of an assessment is determined in a **reliability study**. The simplest such study is one that assesses *test–retest* reliability by having a group of students take an assessment, then take it again a week or two later. Their scores on the two assessments are correlated, and the result would be the **reliability coefficient**. If the study involves using two different forms of the same test (such as with the SAT), the reliability would be called an *alternate form* reliability.

There are a number of other ways to calculate reliability coefficients. One very common approach is **split–half reliability**. In this approach, the assessment is given once to a group of students. Each student receives two scores, one based on performance on the even-numbered items and another based on performance on the odd-numbered items. These two scores are then correlated and adjusted using a formula that takes into account the fact that only half of the test has been used in obtaining each score. A variation on split-half reliability takes an average of all possible ways of splitting an assessment into two halves; this is **coefficient alpha**, or *Cronbach's alpha*. For multiple-choice assessments, a version of coefficient alpha called *KR-20* is often used. Finally, if a rater or judge is used to score the items on an assessment (such as on an essay assessment or a performance assessment), an index of **inter–rater reliability** is needed. Inter-rater reliability is assessed by having two raters score a set of assessments for a group of students, then correlating the scores produced by the two raters.

Teachers often ask how high a reliability coefficient should be. Generally speaking, an assessment that is used to make a decision about a child should have a reliability coefficient of .90 or above. If the assessment is going to be combined with other information, a slightly lower reliability (in the .80s) may be acceptable.

A concept closely related to reliability is very useful in understanding the scores students receive on assessments. This is the **standard error of measurement** (SEM). The SEM provides a way for determining how much variability there might be in a student's score. The best way to think about the SEM is to imagine that a student took the SAT 1,000 times. Each test included different items but measured the same thing. The student would get a somewhat different score on each administration of the test, depending on the specific items on that test, how the student was feeling, whether it was a lucky or unlucky day, and so forth. A plot of these scores would look like a normal distribution. The mean of that distribution is what measurement specialists call the **true score**. The standard deviation of that distribution would be an index of how much the student's score would vary. This standard deviation (of one student taking the test many times) would be the standard error of measurement.

Let's consider an example. Imagine that Martin received a 560 on his SAT verbal test. The SEM for the SAT is roughly 30 points. If he took the test again (without doing any additional preparation for it), he would have a two-thirds chance of scoring somewhere between 530 and 590, and a 95% chance of scoring between 500 and 620. That may seem like a large spread in the scores. Indeed it is, and the SAT has a reliability coefficient over .90. As the reliability gets lower, the SEM gets even higher, which is why it is recommended that assessments with low reliability not be used. Think back to the opening activity for this chapter. What evidence is available for the validity and reliability of the standards-based assessment used by your state?

Interpreting Standardized Assessments

Interpreting standardized assessments can be one of the most difficult things that teachers have to do. The difficulty might be attributable partly to the nature of the reports they receive, which can be hard to read, and partly to the love/hate relationship between educators and standardized assessment. That is, at the same time that many educators wish standardized tests would go away, they often put too much faith in them when making decisions about students.

Teachers encounter several problems when looking at standardized test reports. The first is that the teacher sees only the test report, not the actual efforts of students taking the test. On a classroom assessment, the teacher sees the work of each child on each problem or prompt. The teacher is able to gather information directly about the student on each problem, draw inferences, and make judgments about the student's overall performance on the assessment. With a standardized test, the teacher does not see the work itself, but rather a scaled score of some sort on a label, such as *interpreting text* or *process skills*. What does a score of 189 on *process skills* mean?

A related problem is that teachers do not usually get the results of an assessment until well after it was given. It may be months later; in fact, in some cases it may be after the end of the school year. It is difficult to have an influence on a student who is no longer in your class. Finally, the content of standardized assessments does not always line up directly with what was taught to all of the students. This can be a particular problem in mathematics, where different students can be working on very different material.

The purpose of this section is to see how looking at standardized test results can be a useful part of generating an overall picture of how well students are performing. For most teachers, standardized assessment results are available near the end of the school year. This section assumes that teachers looking at these results are considering students they have had in their classes during the year. They are assessing the progress those students have made, reflecting on the school year in terms of each child's growth, and perhaps putting together a summary communication to parents or to the child's teacher for the following school year.

Finding the Child in the Data

The first step in interpreting standardized assessment results is *not* to think of the process as one of interpreting standardized assessment results. Do not think of the task as trying to make sense out of a report; instead, think of it as getting some more information about a child you already know (or, if it is a new student, about a child you will be getting to know). Think of it as a snapshot of a real student, of Margaret. Maybe the picture is a bit blurred, and maybe it is not taken from a great angle. Maybe Margaret hates it. When looking at data from Margaret's standardized assessment results, combine *your* knowledge of Margaret with the assessment results (how well she did on her last classroom project, the kinds of questions she asks, a discussion with her parents at the parent/teacher conference). They are all snapshots of Margaret. None of them by itself gives a true image of Margaret, but in combination, they will get you pretty close to the real child. And that is the goal: *finding the child in the data*.

Demystifying the Assessment Report

Assessment reports come in all shapes and sizes. Figures 15.7 and 15.8 present the results of two standardized assessment reports, one from a statewide standards-based assessment and the other from a commercial testing program.

An Eighth-Grade Statewide Assessment At the top of the report from the New Jersey Statewide Assessment System (Figure 15.7), there is a set of information that tells:

- The child's name
- What school and school district he or she comes from

What Does This Mean to Me?
Did your SAT scores (or those of someone you know) change markedly from one testing to the next? How might the SEM help explain this?

What Does This Mean to Me?
A standardized assessment score is a picture of a child on a given day. How does this picture fit with what you know about the child? Where are the consistencies and inconsistencies with your image of the child? How can you reconcile them?

(Spencer Grant/Photo Researchers, Inc.)

Assessment results provide information about children that needs to be combined with other sources of information to get a useful overall picture of the child's strengths and needs.

New Jersey Statewide Assessment System
Grade Eight Proficiency Assessment
Individual Student Report

Test Date: March 2007

Country: 99 MIDSTATES
District: 9999 MIDSTATES
School: 99 MIDSTATES M.S.

Date of Birth: 01/11/YY
Gender: M

LEP:
SE:
APA:
Title I:

Test ID No: 002797000
Answer Folder No: 02466
District/School Student ID No:

Student Name: MARL, LZLF

Content Area	Your Scale Score	Proficiency Level
Language Arts Literacy	229	Proficient
Mathematics	204	Proficient
Science	256	Advanced Proficient

Partially Proficient: Scale Score BELOW 200

Proficient: Scale Score AT OR ABOVE 200 but BELOW 250

Advanced Proficient: Scale Score AT OR ABOVE 250

Language Arts Literacy

The Language Arts Literacy section assesses a student's abilities in the following clusters. A check mark indicates areas of possible strength.

Cluster	Your Points	Just Proficient Mean	
Writing	10.0 out of 18	9.2	✓
Reading	26.0 out of 36	20.3	✓
Interpreting Text	13.0 out of 15	8.8	✓
Analyzing/Critiquing Text	13.0 out of 21	11.5	✓

Mathematics

The Mathematics section assesses a student's abilities in the following clusters. A check mark indicates areas of possible strength.

Cluster	Your Points	Just Proficient Mean	
Number & Numerical Operations	8.0 out of 12	6.7	✓
Geometry & Measurement	5.0 out of 12	4.6	✓
Patterns & Algebra	4.0 out of 12	5.0	
Data Analysis, Probability, & Discrete Mathematics	9.0 out of 12	7.7	✓
Knowledge	26.0 out of 48	24.0	✓
Problem Solving Skills	19.0 out of 35	16.5	✓

Science

The Science section assesses a student's abilities in the following clusters. A check mark indicates areas of possible strength.

Cluster	Your Points	Just Proficient Mean	
Life Science	16.0 out of 22	9.2	✓
Physical Science	12.0 out of 16	6.4	✓
Earth Science	14.0 out of 16	6.3	✓
Knowledge	9.0 out of 11	4.8	✓
Application	33.0 out of 43	17.2	✓

Note: The scores in this report are for illustrative purpose only. For example, the raw score to scale score conversions are not necessarily the same as those used in the actual reports.

Source: New Jersey Department of Education. (2007). Grade 8 Proficiency Assessment (GEPA). Retrieved June 28, 2011, from http://www.state.nj.education/assessment/ms/gepa_score_interp_manual_07.pdf.

Figure 15.7 A Standards–Based Report

- Gender
- When he or she was born
- Whether he or she has limited English proficiency (LEP)
- Whether he or she is classified for special education (SE)
- Whether he or she is exempt from taking one or more of the assessments (IEP Exempt)
- Whether he or she is in a Title I remedial program (Title I)

There is a tendency to skip over such information, but that is not a good idea. Check this information to make sure that it is correct. For example, if this child is in fact classified LEP and this is not correctly indicated, that is an important mistake that the teacher needs to report.

Below the general information are the summary scores that Lzlf received in language arts literacy, mathematics, and science. As can be seen, Lzlf passed the mathematics, science, and language arts portions of the assessment. He needed to get a score of 200 on these assessments to pass. Although his language arts score (229) seems to have been well above the passing score, his mathematics score (204) just passed. His science score is well above passing and is listed as advanced proficient.

Moving from the overall summary scores, we see that each of the three main scores is broken down into subscales. In language arts literacy, there are writing cluster and reading cluster scores.

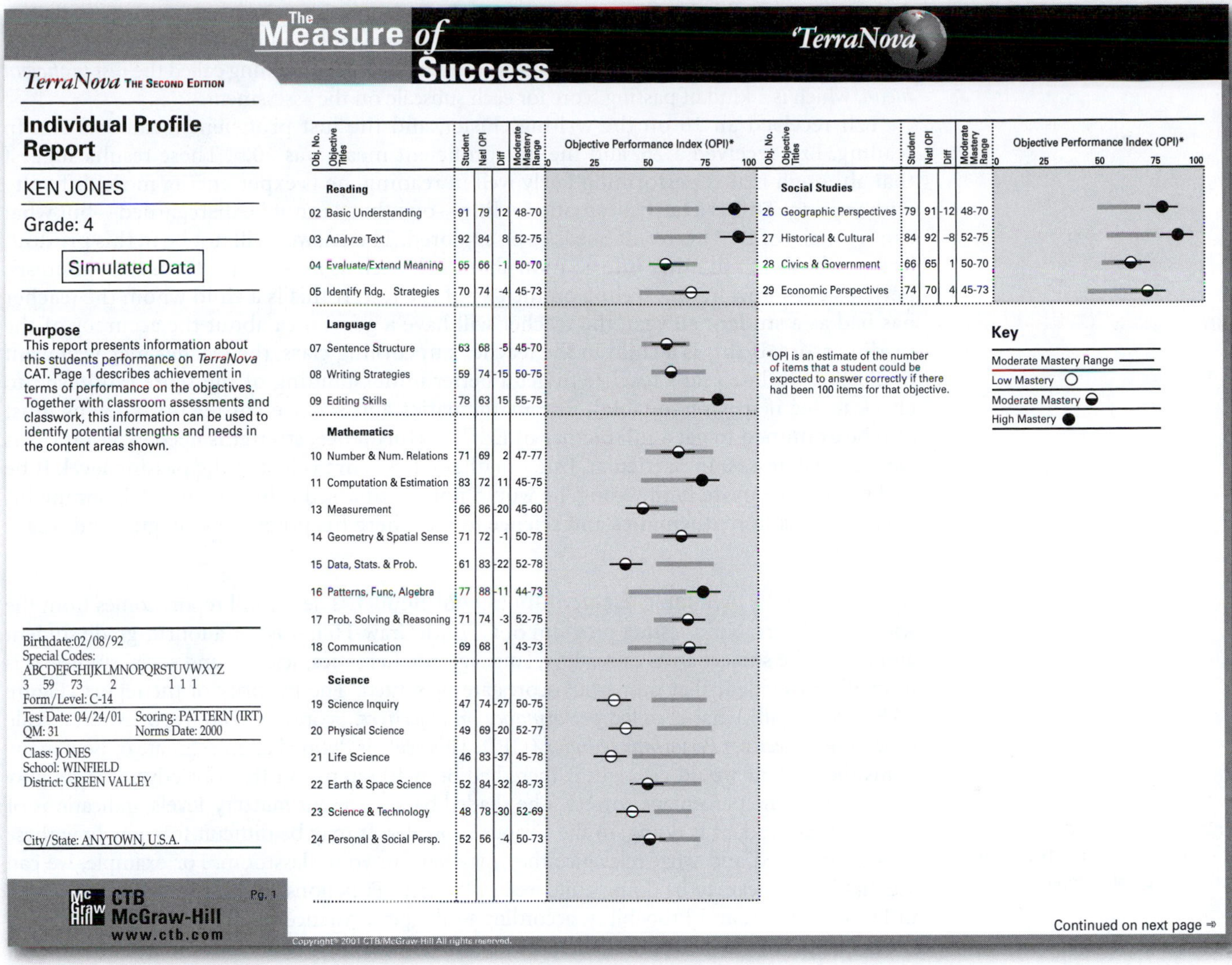

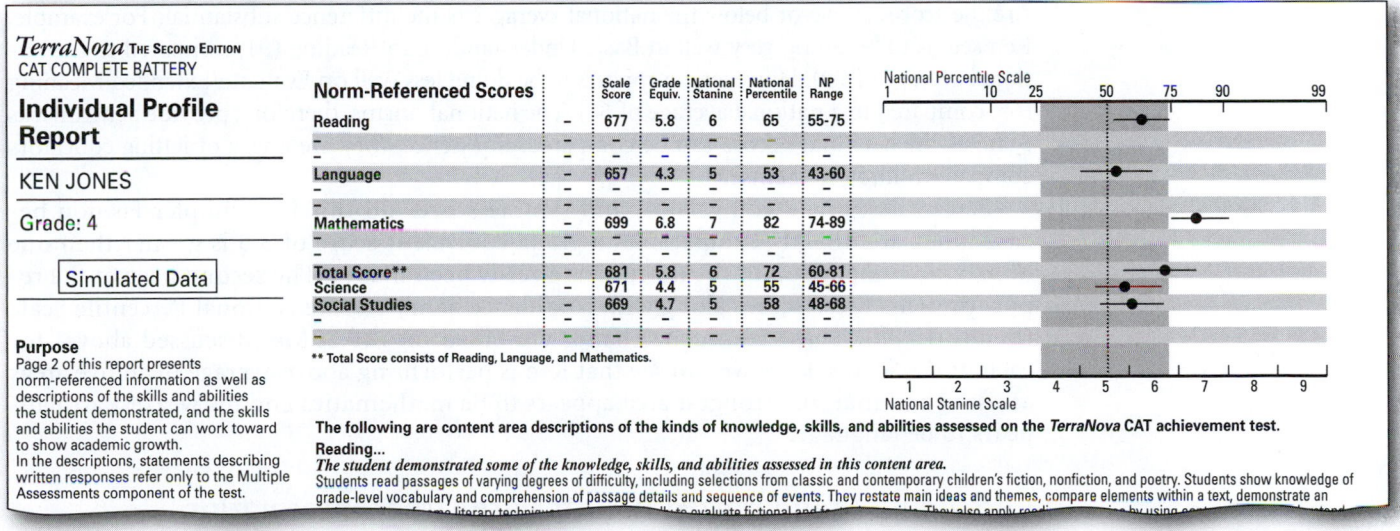

The Measure of Success

TerraNova THE SECOND EDITION

Individual Profile Report

KEN JONES

Grade: 4

Simulated Data

Purpose
This report presents information about this students performance on *TerraNova* CAT. Page 1 describes achievement in terms of performance on the objectives. Together with classroom assessments and classwork, this information can be used to identify potential strengths and needs in the content areas shown.

Obj. No.	Objective Titles	Student	Natl OPI	Diff	Moderate Mastery Range
	Reading				
02	Basic Understanding	91	79	12	48-70
03	Analyze Text	92	84	8	52-75
04	Evaluate/Extend Meaning	65	66	-1	50-70
05	Identify Rdg. Strategies	70	74	-4	45-73
	Language				
07	Sentence Structure	63	68	-5	45-70
08	Writing Strategies	59	74	-15	50-75
09	Editing Skills	78	63	15	55-75
	Mathematics				
10	Number & Num. Relations	71	69	2	47-77
11	Computation & Estimation	83	72	11	45-75
13	Measurement	66	86	-20	45-60
14	Geometry & Spatial Sense	71	72	-1	50-78
15	Data, Stats. & Prob.	61	83	-22	52-78
16	Patterns, Func, Algebra	77	88	-11	44-73
17	Prob. Solving & Reasoning	71	74	-3	52-75
18	Communication	69	68	1	43-73
	Science				
19	Science Inquiry	47	74	-27	50-75
20	Physical Science	49	69	-20	52-77
21	Life Science	46	83	-37	45-78
22	Earth & Space Science	52	84	-32	48-73
23	Science & Technology	48	78	-30	52-69
24	Personal & Social Persp.	52	56	-4	50-73
	Social Studies				
26	Geographic Perspectives	79	91	-12	48-70
27	Historical & Cultural	84	92	-8	52-75
28	Civics & Government	66	65	1	50-70
29	Economic Perspectives	74	70	4	45-73

*OPI is an estimate of the number of items that a student could be expected to answer correctly if there had been 100 items for that objective.

Key
Moderate Mastery Range
Low Mastery
Moderate Mastery
High Mastery

Birthdate:02/08/92
Special Codes:
ABCDEFGHIJKLMNOPQRSTUVWXYZ
3 59 73 2 1 1 1
Form/Level: C-14
Test Date: 04/24/01 Scoring: PATTERN (IRT)
QM: 31 Norms Date: 2000
Class: JONES
School: WINFIELD
District: GREEN VALLEY
City/State: ANYTOWN, U.S.A.

CTB McGraw-Hill www.ctb.com

Pg. 1

Copyright© 2001 CTB/McGraw-Hill All rights reserved.

Continued on next page ⇒

(*a*)

TerraNova THE SECOND EDITION
CAT COMPLETE BATTERY

Individual Profile Report

KEN JONES

Grade: 4

Simulated Data

Purpose
Page 2 of this report presents norm-referenced information as well as descriptions of the skills and abilities the student demonstrated, and the skills and abilities the student can work toward to show academic growth.
In the descriptions, statements describing written responses refer only to the Multiple Assessments component of the test.

Norm-Referenced Scores		Scale Score	Grade Equiv.	National Stanine	National Percentile	NP Range
Reading	–	677	5.8	6	65	55-75
Language	–	657	4.3	5	53	43-60
Mathematics	–	699	6.8	7	82	74-89
Total Score**	–	681	5.8	6	72	60-81
Science	–	671	4.4	5	55	45-66
Social Studies	–	669	4.7	5	58	48-68

** Total Score consists of Reading, Language, and Mathematics.

The following are content area descriptions of the kinds of knowledge, skills, and abilities assessed on the *TerraNova* CAT achievement test.

Reading...

The student demonstrated some of the knowledge, skills, and abilities assessed in this content area.

Students read passages of varying degrees of difficulty, including selections from classic and contemporary children's fiction, nonfiction, and poetry. Students show knowledge of grade-level vocabulary and comprehension of passage details and sequence of events. They restate main ideas and themes, compare elements within a text, demonstrate an

(*b*)

Figure 15.8 A Standardized Test Individual Report

Source: Individual Profile Report from TerraNova, The Second Edition. Published by CTB/McGraw-Hill LLC. TerraNova and CAT are registered trademarks of The McGraw-Hill Companies, Inc.

As is indicated in the descriptive note, the number in parentheses is the maximum number of points Lzlf could have received on this part of the assessment (36 in reading, 18 in writing). Lzlf received 10 points in writing and 26 in reading. Then there is something called the *just proficient mean,* which is a kind of passing score for each subscale on the assessment.

Lzlf received an 10 on the writing cluster, and the just proficient mean was 9.2. In reading, Lzlf received a 26, and the just proficient mean was 20.3. These results suggest that although Lzlf is performing fairly well in reading, he is experiencing more difficulty with writing. This is a fairly dramatic finding—one that cannot be disregarded—but what can we make of it? This result needs to be explored. The answer will not be in this printout but may be found in other information about Lzlf such as his class performance, interests, perhaps even how he was feeling on the day of the test. If this is a child whom the teacher has had as a student all year, the teacher will have a good idea about the accuracy of the reading score. If this is a child in the teacher's upcoming class, the teacher may well want to check with last year's teacher to get a better understanding of the score (and/even to check to see if it is reasonable). The mathematics and science cluster breakdowns must also be examined to get a full picture of Lzlf's performance; strengths need exploration as well as weaknesses. In particular, Lzlf's mathematics score is just at the passing level. If he had gotten one more item wrong, he would not have passed this assessment. Examine his cluster scores in mathematics and science to see where his potential strengths and weaknesses lie.

A Commercially Available Elementary School Report

The second report comes from the widely used TerraNova testing program of CTB/McGraw-Hill. It is for a fourth-grade student and covers the subject areas of reading, language, mathematics, science, and social studies. It is immediately evident that numerous scores are presented. The majority of the report (Figure 15.8a) deals with what is called *performance on objectives.* Scores here are reported on a scale called the *Objectives Performance Index* (OPI). This scale is defined as an estimate of how many items the student would get right if there had been 100 items on that objective. It is roughly equivalent to the percentage correct. The shaded bars represent **mastery levels**, indications of how well the student is doing, in the various subscales. It may be difficult to know how these were determined and what relevance they may have in your classroom. For example, we can see that Ken appears to be doing quite well in Patterns, Functions, and Algebra, but not as well in Data, Statistics, and Probability, according to the performance on objectives bars. Probably the best approach to interpreting these scores is to think of the national norming data as a set of baselines for looking at a student. Look at the national average OPI score in each subscale. That is how well the typical student did on that part of the assessment. Now look at how well Ken did. Are the scores above or below the national average? Is the difference substantial? For example, Ken seems to be doing very well in Basic Understanding in Reading (91, compared to the national average of 79). However, he appears to be doing less well on Evaluate/Extended Meaning (65, compared to a national average of 66). The national norms, therefore, provide benchmarks against which a child's score can be compared. In essence, they are a way of letting educators compare children to themselves.

Percentiles, grade equivalents, and stanine scores do this in a simpler fashion because they are directly comparable (a grade-equivalent score of 5.6 is greater than one of 5.2; the comparison to the norms has already been made). The second page of the report presents these scores along with confidence bands for the National Percentile Scale (Figure 15.8b). These confidence bands are based on the SEMs (discussed above) for each of the scores. Here we can see that Ken is performing above average in all five areas assessed and that his strongest area appears to be mathematics and his weakest area appears to be language.

Combining Standardized Results with Other Information

What conclusions should be drawn about Lzlf and Ken? None; at any rate, not yet. Although we have examined the standardized assessment scores for these two students, we need to consider a lot of other information. Remember, these are single snapshots of Lzlf and Ken taken on a given day, not complete pictures. This information needs to be combined with other information to arrive at a clearer and more useful evaluation. When

mastery levels Levels of proficiency, or mastery, determined for an assessment; related to cut scores and passing scores.

information from multiple sources converges, increased confidence can be taken in the interpretation. If the people looking at these results have just spent a year as Lzlf's and Ken's teachers, a great deal of other information needs to be considered in evaluating these students. For example:

- Do the scores on these assessments match the kinds of performances they displayed in their classroom work?
- Does a score that looks low actually reflect remarkable growth for a student who started the year with substantial difficulties in this area?
- Did the items on the assessment match well with the curriculum taught in the classroom (for example, in science for Ken)?
- Were there personal considerations, such as family problems or illness, that might have caused the day the assessment was given to have been an unusual one for the student?

The standardized assessment reports are just the beginning of the process of understanding a student's academic achievements; they are not the whole process. The class may have spent the year working on physics and astronomy, whereas the assessment may have addressed a variety of scientific ideas. If Ken is not very interested in science (which, as his teacher, you may know to be the case), perhaps the science score should be taken with a grain of salt. On the other hand, the relatively low score on Evaluate/Extended Meaning in reading may be a disappointment. Perhaps this was an area in which you thought Ken was making solid strides. It is important to remember that the assessment represents the efforts of a student on a particular day. It provides useful information, but information that must be interpreted in the context of what the student has done all year long. This is also true of the student whose classroom performance presents a different picture than his or her standardized test scores (see the nearby Taking It to the Classroom box).

Working from the Top Down The best way to look at standardized assessment results and combine them with other information is to begin with the highest level of information on the report. Most assessments provide a number of primary scores ranging from two (language arts and mathematics) to five or six (science, social studies, sometimes language arts

Taking It to the Classroom

Do You Know Jack? Test Taker Par Excellence

Jack does well—very well—on standardized tests. Often, children get test scores that are disappointing to teachers, parents, and the students themselves. Not Jack. Jack's test scores are always a surprise in the other direction: Jack regularly scores in the top 10% and occasionally gets a perfect score on a standardized assessment. But his classroom performance is sloppy, often nonexistent, and generally reflects great indifference to instruction.

What can be done to get Jack's classroom work up to his test performances?

- Have a discussion with Jack about why he is performing poorly in class and why he seems to do so well on standardized tests.
- Have a parent conference to go over Jack's test performance and school performance.
- See whether some more challenging assignments might increase Jack's interest level.
- Check with other teachers about how Jack is doing with them.
- Check Jack's attendance record.
- Allow Jack to choose some activities in which he is interested.

broken into reading and writing). These are the most reliable of the available measures and the best place to begin. Consider the following questions about the child:

- What are the child's strengths and weaknesses, according to the report?
- Do these strengths and weaknesses match what you know about the child?
- Are there any aspects of these scores that do not seem to make sense with regard to this child?

The next level to look at concerns the subscales that are provided within each primary score. If all these look similar, the primary score to which they are related can be considered the child's general ability level. If, however, there are strong discrepancies, this may be a good area for further investigation.

Making and Testing Hypotheses about the Child   Looking at the assessment report provides an opportunity to reflect on the progress the child has made during the year. Consider the scores for Ken. It appears that he is not as strong in Evaluate/Extended Meaning as he is in Basic Understanding in Reading. He also is not as strong in Problem Solving and Reasoning as he is in Computation and Estimation in Mathematics. These strengths and weaknesses suggest that Ken is missing some of the more subtle issues in both these areas. This is a general hypothesis about Ken. Is it a reasonable one? This probably cannot be determined just from looking at the assessment results, but a teacher who has had Ken as a student all year long probably has some insight into this hypothesis. Ken's teacher may think, "You know, that's pretty much what I see in Ken as well. He works hard and does well on the literal aspects of most of his work, but he is often reluctant to go beyond the literal to think of the broader possibilities. It almost seems like a personality characteristic more than an academic ability. I wonder what could be done to help bring his abilities out more?" Or the teacher may think, "Those results just aren't consistent with what I see in Ken on a day-to-day basis. I need to check out the types of questions that Ken had difficulty with to see what the problem is here. These data don't make sense to me." (See the nearby What Kids Say and Do box.)

Bringing the Child to the Classroom

Once one has looked at an assessment report and developed an overall picture of the student's achievement, the next step is deciding what to do about it. Sometimes this type of analysis results in a summary statement about the child provided to the teacher in the

What Kids Say and Do

Making the Data Make Sense

One standard rule for interpreting any score—or, for that matter, any report of data (from a newspaper article or television show, for example)—is that the data have to make sense. If the data do not make sense, be wary of putting too much faith in them. Here is a real example from the experience of one of the authors of this text.

A former graduate student who was a middle school principal called to ask about an assessment score in reading obtained by one of her students. Janell had almost always scored at the 95th percentile or above in every subject area on the commercial standardized assessment. This year was no different, except for the reading score, which placed Janell in the 43rd percentile. Before recommending the student to the child study team for review, the principal wanted to get an expert opinion on the assessment. "Doesn't make sense" was the response. "Bring it down to the university, and I'll have a look at it."

Upon review, an interesting pattern appeared. The answers to each question were given broken down by the subcategory on the assessment (literal comprehension, vocabulary in context, etc.). A plus was used if the item was correct, the letter of the multiple-choice response selected if the item was wrong, and a zero if the item was left blank. On Janell's answer sheet, of 60 questions, 29 were right, 1 was wrong, and 30 were blank. She had gotten only one question wrong but had failed to answer 30 items. Because the items were broken out by subscale, it was not immediately apparent that the 30 blank responses were from items 31–60. In other words, Janell had gotten 29 of 30 correct on the first 30 items and had left the last 30 blank. How could this be?

The principal was able to solve the problem by talking to Janell. Janell told her that on the day of the test she had become ill at lunchtime and had gone home. No one asked her to make up the second half of the test.

In sum, if the data do not make sense, be cautious about how much faith you put in them. There are many more simple mistakes in this world than there are truly amazing results.

subsequent year; sometimes it is used in a parent/teacher conference. Occasionally, the teacher uses it to plan further instruction for the child during the current school year; such would be the case if the assessment took place in the fall or if the teacher was looking at the results from the previous year's assessment. In this situation, the teacher has to *bring the child to the classroom.*

Bringing the child to the classroom means that the child's strengths, weaknesses, and goals must fit into the environment of the classroom as a whole. If there are 14 students in a self-contained fourth-grade classroom that emphasizes cooperative learning and problem-based instruction, fitting the child into the classroom will mean one thing. If there are 26 students—including 2 with special needs—in a more traditional setting, it will mean something quite different. If the child's parents are very involved in the child's education, their interest may be used to work on areas of need or strength that the teacher cannot address in the classroom. For example, if Ken is indeed having trouble with reading beyond the literal text, his parents might be interested in reading mysteries with him. This would give them an enjoyable vehicle to use in working with their child and helping him develop.

It would be wonderful if each child could get an education tailored to his or her unique needs, but that cannot happen with 20 other equally deserving children in the same classroom. Once the teacher has a good picture of the student and his or her needs, that student has to be brought into the educational and social structure of the classroom. Bringing the child to the classroom thus requires imagination and creativity on the part of the teacher.

Thinking about the Classroom, School, and District Levels

If we only ever had one child to think about, teaching would be a lot easier. But teachers work with classrooms full of children, and the group needs to be considered as well as the individual. Teachers can use many of the ideas presented in terms of interpreting scores for individuals for the class as a whole. Overall, what are the strengths of this class, what are the weaknesses? Are there issues that can be a focus for the class as a whole over the course of the year?

Perhaps a group of students appears to be stronger in reading than in mathematics. This might provide the teacher with an opportunity to allocate a little more instructional time to mathematics and perhaps to assess progress in mathematics within the classroom on a more regular basis.

Another possibility is that there are several students who are having difficulty with a particular aspect of the curriculum. These students might be grouped together for purposes of some special attention. It is important to reassess progress on a regular basis to make sure that instruction is attuned to students' current needs, not just where they were at the beginning of the year.

Although teachers focus primarily at the classroom level, they need to recognize that principals are concerned with the school as a whole and that district-level personnel need to think about the needs of all the children in the district. Coordination of instruction from one year to the next is a hallmark of a good instructional program. Careful examination of assessment scores across years and grades is an important component of such a program.

Looking at Scores for English Language Learners

Students who do not speak English well, ELL students, sometimes also referred to as LEP students, pose a major problem for the interpretation of assessments. The problem is easy to understand but difficult to solve. Language arts literacy scores may not be measuring the language arts abilities of these students at all but merely measuring their abilities in English. On the other hand, some ELL students speak English fairly well but may have deficiencies in language arts. How can the former situation be separated from the latter?

To begin with, there is research evidence showing that testing accommodations made for ELL students do not reduce the validity of the scores on the assessment (Abedi,

How Can I Use This?
In thinking about what you can do to tailor instruction to the needs of your students, consider the resources you have and try to match them to the students' needs.

RIDE Think back to the vignette at the beginning of the chapter. Where are the strengths in your district? Where are the weaknesses? Of the students who did not pass the test, how many need a lot of work, and how many need just a little more work? Be sure to keep your ideas tentative, as many seemingly strange results have simple explanations!

Courtney, & Leon, 2003; Abedi & Lord, 2001). Teachers should make sure that ELL students in their classes receive accommodations if they are entitled to them. Some state assessment programs have developed alternative forms of assessments for ELL students. Teachers should communicate across grades: A teacher who has an ELL student in third grade can communicate to the fourth-grade teacher about the language abilities of a particular student.

Looking at Scores for Students with Special Needs

Appendix
Careful Use of Assessment Results

The results of assessments completed by students with special needs or those with limited English proficiency should be interpreted with care and sensitivity. It is wise to gather multiple sources of information about students' level of performance (PRAXIS™, II.C.4; INTASC, Principles 2, 8).

Another group of students that should receive particular attention when one is interpreting assessment results consists of students who have special needs. Some of these students will be exempt from standardized assessments as part of their individualized educational program (IEP), which specifies the instructional goals, methods, and assessments appropriate for the child. However, the federal and many state governments place limits on the number of children who can receive such exemptions. Students with disabilities may be granted certain accommodations in the administration of an assessment (including, but not limited to, extra time, a quiet room, a helper to read to students with limited vision, and/or shorter testing sessions). Another possibility for students with disabilities is to take an alternative form of the assessment that minimizes the impact of the disability (see, e.g., the "DPI Guidelines to Facilitate the Participation of Students with Special Needs in State Assessments" of the Wisconsin Department of Public Instruction, 2002).

Interpreting the results of standardized assessments of students with special needs requires special sensitivity and care, particularly when discussing results with parents. There is a fine line between being sensitive to children's academic challenges and underestimating what they can do. Moreover, what is seen in the classroom environment or what may show up under the pressures of a standardized assessment may be quite different from what parents see in a more supportive and less chaotic home environment. It is particularly important for teachers to look for strengths in working with students and to see areas in which students are having difficulty as points of departure rather than as areas of weakness.

A major issue in interpreting the scores of students with special needs is the impact of the disability on performance. If a student is easily distracted or unable to concentrate for long periods of time, an assessment with a long reading passage may be particularly troublesome. Students who are good at mathematical ideas but weak on computation facts may not be able to demonstrate their abilities on multiple-choice mathematics items. Sometimes, assessment results for students with special needs are consistent with teacher expectations; at other times, they are baffling. This is one of the reasons why special education is a field of scholarly inquiry unto itself. There are resources available to help teachers work effectively with students with special needs. The Web site accompanying this text includes links to sites where you can find help. Some excellent text resources are also available (see Mastergeorge & Miyoshi, 1999; Mercer & Mercer, 2001; Venn, 2004).

www.wiley.com/college/odonnell

Assistive Technology and the Assessment of Learners with Special Needs Some students require technological assistance to demonstrate their abilities. Assistive technology devices help augment abilities where individuals face special challenges. This is more common than one might think. If you are wearing glasses or contact lenses to read this material, you are using assistive technology! The Florida Alliance for Assistive Services and Technology of the Florida Department of Education lists the following categories of assistive devices and services [1]:

- Augmentative communication devices, including talking computers
- Assistive listening devices, including hearing aids, personal FM units, closed-caption TVs, and teletype machines (TDOS)
- Specially adapted learning games, toys, and recreation equipment

[1]*Source:* Florida Alliance for Assistive Services and Technology. Retrieved June 14, 2005, from FAAST Web site at http://faast.org/atr_k12_rights.cfm. Used with permission.

- Computer-assisted instruction
- Electronic tools (scanners with speech synthesizers, tape recorders, word processors)
- Curriculum and textbook adaptations (e.g., audio format, large-print format, Braille)
- Copies of overheads, transparencies, and notes
- Adaptation of the learning environment, such as special desks, modified learning stations
- Computer touch screens or different computer keyboards
- Adaptive mobility devices for driver education
- Orthotics such as hand braces to facilitate writing skills

Controversies in Assessment

Assessment involves evaluating students' progress. Any form of evaluation or assessment holds the potential for controversy, and student assessment is no exception. Some issues in assessment have been controversial for decades; others have appeared within the last 20 years. Significant current controversies are discussed in this section.

Bias in Testing

Bias in testing has long been a topic of heated debate in the United States (Murphy & Davidshofer, 1994; Thorndike, 1997). Concerns about bias in testing often revolve around the highly verbal nature of some measures. Everyone who has taken the SAT verbal test acknowledges that a strong command of the English language is important in obtaining a good score. But the development of such language proficiency would seem to favor individuals who have greater access to the kinds of words that appear on the measure. Certainly, individuals who do not speak English as a first language would be at a disadvantage.

However, the situation is far from simple. Even the definition of **test bias** is a subject of debate among scholars. Some believe that whenever an assessment produces different results for members of different racial or ethnic groups, or between genders, that assessment is biased. Measurement specialists use a more refined definition: If individuals from different groups (racial groups, genders, etc.) obtain the same score on an assessment, it should mean the same thing for both individuals. If it does not, that is evidence that the test is biased. For example, if two students, one male and one female, get the same SAT scores, they should be predicted to do similarly well in college. Of course, the prediction is not made for one pair of individuals but for large groups.

Research on college admissions testing indicates that the tests typically do not show bias (Young, 2003). That is, the tests do an equally good job of predicting college performance for students from minority groups as they do for majority students. This finding is contrary to public opinion, but it has been shown to be true in a number of studies. This is not to say that there are no group differences in performance on these measures. Moreover, if colleges weigh the results of admissions tests too heavily, *the admissions process can still be biased even though the assessment is not.* This is somewhat akin to using height as the sole determinant of whom to select for a basketball team. All other things being equal, taller players tend to be better than shorter players. However, height is not the only factor that determines the quality of basketball players. In the same fashion, admissions test scores are not the only factor that determines success in college. Thus, an admissions system that relies too heavily on testing can be biased even though it may be hard to find bias in the measures themselves.

test bias The degree to which the scores from an assessment take on different meanings when obtained by individuals from different groups.

Assistive devices help special needs students demonstrate the achievements they have made.

(© Mugshots/Corbis Images)

Test bias means that different conclusions are drawn about students from different groups whose abilities are in fact the same.

(Media Bakery)

The situation is even more subtle for students who do not speak English as a first language. If a mathematics assessment contains a number of word problems, ELL students may fail to reach a correct answer not because of a deficiency in mathematics ability but because of difficulty understanding exactly what was being asked of them.

High-Stakes Testing and Its Implications

The increase in standardized assessment accompanying the federal No Child Left Behind Act has had a number of effects on educational practice—some intended, some not. Although the goal of having all children reach high standards of achievement is undoubtedly laudable, there are concerns associated with increased high-stakes standardized assessment that have an impact on classroom teachers, including the following (Cawthon, 2007; Porter, Linn, & Trimble, 2005):

- Standardization of curriculum
- Teaching to the test
- Increased emphasis on test performance in classrooms
- Increased reports of cheating on assessments, both by students and by educators

The standardization of the curriculum is not the purpose of standards-based instruction (Taylor et al., 2003); rather, it occurs as schools attempt to prepare their students for the assessment that accompanies the adoption of statewide standards. The problem this poses for classroom teachers is that the students in a classroom typically are not all at the same stage of ability or achievement in any given subject area. If they must all take the same test, the teacher must review this material prior to the assessment, thereby interrupting the natural progression of learning for many students. Thus, some students may end up reviewing material that they already know quite well and others may be exposed to material that is well beyond their abilities.

Education is a complex and multifaceted phenomenon. How children learn, the best conditions for learning, and how to maximize achievement for a class of students are all difficult issues to address. When issues of poverty, learning difficulties, unstable home environments, and limited English ability are thrown into the mix, the situation becomes even more challenging. Over the past several decades, education has become increasingly politicized at both the national and state levels. Typically, this gets played out as goals for increased achievement are made as policy decisions, with the problems associated

Appendix
High-Stakes Testing
Students may feel very pressured by the attention given to high-stakes testing in their classrooms, and their motivation for learning may be reduced as a result (PRAXIS™, I.C.3; INTASC, Principle 5).

with reaching those goals being left to educators. Standardized assessment is the vehicle through which accountability is checked.

Concomitant with the increased emphasis on attaining high scores on standardized assessments is a greater tendency to *teach to the test*. This phrase refers to the practice of primarily, or even exclusively, teaching those aspects of the curriculum that one knows are going to appear on the standardized assessment. The problem is that those aspects that do not appear on the test will disappear from the curriculum. In its extreme form, students are not just taught only the content that will appear on the test, they are taught that content only in the precise form in which it will appear on the test. For example, if a sixth-grade applied geometry standard is assessed by asking students how many square feet of wallpaper will be needed to paper a room with certain dimensions (including windows and doors), then eventually, in some classrooms, that is the only way in which that aspect of geometry will be taught.

However, as Popham (2001) points out, if the curriculum is well defined and the assessment covers it appropriately, teaching to the test can simply represent good instruction. Of course, this requires teaching the content of the assessment in such a way that students would be able to use it in a variety of situations, not just to do well on the assessment.

As can be seen, this is a complex problem with many facets and perspectives. How it will play out when *you* are teaching is hard to predict, but one thing is certain: *Teachers cannot afford simply to bury their heads in the sand and hope that all will turn out for the best with regard to testing.* Teachers must understand the political, educational, and assessment context in which they work. Teachers can be effective advocates for best practices in education for their students, both in the classroom and in the larger political and social context.

REFLECTION FOR ACTION

The Event

At the beginning of the chapter, you were assigned to a committee to consider how to improve the scores of students in your school on the statewide assessment program. Let us examine this issue, using the RIDE process.

Reflection RIDE

First, think about what your role is and what kinds of contributions you can make to this committee. You are a first-year teacher participating on a committee with teachers who are more experienced and have seen a number of innovations in education come and go. To begin with, do not try to be an expert; be a contributor. Listen to and respect more experienced teachers. Next, think about where you can make a contribution. Do your homework. Come to the meeting prepared.

What Theoretical/Conceptual Information Might Assist in Interpreting and Remedying This Situation? Consider the following:

The Validity of the Assessment and Curricular Alignment

How well does the district curriculum align with the statewide standards? If the alignment is poor, then the results may not be a valid picture of the students' achievement. However, since the statewide standards are set (fixed), the curriculum may be the thing that has to be adjusted.

Employing Statistical Analysis

What does the distribution of scores for the district look like, not just the percentages of students passing and failing? Are there areas where the district is close to having a lot more students pass the test? Are there areas of severe need?

Looking for Strengths and Weaknesses

Where do our strengths and weaknesses appear to be? What needs to be addressed? What strengths can be built upon?

Information Gathering RIDE

In this chapter, you have learned a great deal about how to look at assessment scores. Find the schoolwide report and examine it carefully before coming to the meeting. What are the school's strengths and weaknesses? How does this year's performance compare to last year's? Are there trends that are consistent over time? How does your school compare to others in the district or to similar schools in the state? The Web site for this text includes links to sites that will help you make such comparisons. You are not the only school facing this kind of problem. What have other schools done to improve scores? Some creative research on the Internet or in teachers' magazines may allow you to attend the meeting armed with good ideas. You might ask teachers you know from other districts what they are doing. You can be pretty certain the issues in your district exist in other districts as well.

Decision Making R I D E

There is a fable about mice being eaten by a cat. They decide to put a bell around the cat's neck so they can hear the cat coming and run away. The problem, of course, is how to get the bell on the cat. Ideas that sound great but cannot be accomplished are sometimes referred to as *belling the cat*. You need ideas that are practical and can be put into effect. In choosing among various options about what to do in your school, the solutions have to be reasonable, given your circumstances and resources.

Evaluation R I D E

Were you able to use your knowledge about standardized assessments to contribute to the committee's ideas, interpretations, and recommendations? The ultimate evaluation will occur when you look at the results for next year and the year after that. However, that is a long time to wait for results. You might want to suggest giving a midyear or even quarterly assessment that resembles the statewide assessment to provide an idea of how you are doing and where adjustments might be made.

Further Practice: Your Turn

Here is a second event for consideration and reflection. In doing so, implement the process of reflection, information gathering, decision making, and evaluation.

The Event

You are teaching fourth grade in your school for the first time. Three weeks before the statewide standardized assessments, you receive a set of materials to use in preparing your students for the test. In reviewing the materials, it seems to you that you are teaching what is going to be on the test in the same format as the test. Although these are not direct questions from the test, you are not sure whether this is ethical.

Teaching to the test is an issue of great concern in American education. On one hand, it seems unfair to expect children to show what they can do on an assessment without a solid understanding of what is expected of them and what will appear on the assessment. On the other hand, if you focus too heavily on what is on the assessment and how it is assessed, will you narrow what your students will learn and the contexts in which they can display their abilities? Will they know how to perform only on the assessment?

SUMMARY

- **What are standards and how do they influence what happens in schools?**

  Standards are statements of what we want children to know and be able to do. In this sense, they are very similar to objectives, goals, or achievement targets. Most state departments of education have developed sets of standards to guide instruction K–12 in the areas of reading, writing, mathematics, and often other subject areas. They influence schools because they basically determine what will be taught and when it will be taught. Statewide standards-based assessments, based on the standards, are taken by almost every student every year.

- **What are standardized assessments and where do they come from?**

  Assessment has a fairly short history, with the initial development of standardized assessment evolving from the need to determine appropriate educational placement for students with learning difficulties. Standardized school assessments and college admissions testing are both creations of the first half of the twentieth century. Most assessments used in schools today are required by federal legislation and are based on core curriculum standards developed by committees consisting of educators, businesspeople, and community members. Professional test development companies create most standardized assessments.

- **How can a teacher make sense of the statistics and scales that come with these measures?**

  To understand how standardized assessments are developed and how to interpret the scores, it is necessary to have a rudimentary command of statistics—primarily means, standard deviations, and correlation. The scores associated with standardized assessments are of three main types: scores based on a norming group of students (percentiles, NCE scores, grade-equivalent scores, stanines), scores that are independent of the norming group (SAT scores, scaled scores used in statewide assessment programs), and scores established by panels of experts.

- **What is the best way to interpret standardized test scores?**

  In interpreting standardized assessments, one should begin by thinking about the student, not the assessment. The purpose of looking at standardized assessment scores is to use the information they provide to refine and enhance your understanding of the progress your students have made. Standardized assessments should be combined with knowledge from classroom assessments and your personal knowledge of the student to generate the most complete picture of the student.

- **How concerned should teachers be about the issues of reliability and validity?**

  All assessments should be valid, reliable, and free from bias. *Valid* means that the interpretations based on the scores are appropriate and that the assessment is in fact measuring what it is intended to measure. *Reliable* means that the scores are consistent—that a similar score would be obtained on a second assessment. *Freedom from bias* means that the assessment does not favor one group over another—that the same interpretation of a score would hold, regardless of the race, gender, or ethnicity of a student.

- **How can teachers fairly assess students with learning and physical challenges?**

  Accommodations can be made for students who face special challenges that address their needs while maintaining the integrity of the assessment. Extra time, freedom from distractions, and the use of simpler language in math questions are frequently used accommodations. Assistive technology is also appropriate in some situations.

- **Is standardized assessment equally fair for students from different cultural backgrounds?**

  This is an issue of great concern for educators. Although research findings suggest that most assessments do not have substantial bias, the assessments can be used in such a way as to produce biased decisions. Special care must be taken in using and interpreting assessment results for students from differing cultural and ethnic backgrounds. At the K–12 level, this often can be seen in using standardized assessments with students who are English language learners (ELLs).

Key Terms

affective assessment, p. 533
central tendency, p. 535
coefficient alpha, p. 546
consequential validity, p. 544
construct validity, p. 544
content validity, p. 544
criterion-referenced, p. 532
criterion-related validity, p. 544
grade-equivalent scores, p. 539
intelligence test, p. 529
inter-rater reliability, p. 546
mastery levels, p. 550
mean, p. 535
median, p. 535

mode, p. 535
normal curve equivalent (NCE), p. 539
normal distribution, p. 537
norming study, p. 530
norm-referenced, p. 532
norms, p. 541
passing scores, p. 541
percentile, p. 539
raw scores, p. 537
reliability, p. 544
reliability coefficient, p. 546
reliability study, p. 546
scaled scores, p. 538
split-half reliability, p. 546

standard deviation, p. 536
standard error of measurement, p. 546
standardized assessment, p. 528
standards-based assessment, p. 530
stanines, p. 539
test bias, p. 555
true score, p. 546
validation study, p. 544
validity, p. 544
variability, p. 535
variance, p. 535
z-score, p. 537

Exercises

1. *Understanding Standards, Objectives, and Achievement Targets*
   Go to the Web or another source and find the statewide standards for your state in the areas that you think you might want to teach. (Nearly all state departments of education include statewide standards for each grade level and subject on their Web sites. A link to state departments of education is provided at the companion Web site for this book.) Print out the standards and review them.

   - What do you think about these standards overall? Do they seem thorough? Are they too detailed or not detailed enough? Do they seem to limit your creativity as a teacher?

   - If you had to eliminate one of the standards, which one would it be and why? If you could add one, what would it be? The purpose of this activity is to push yourself to think hard about whether the list is a thorough and exhaustive one.

2. *Standards and No Child Left Behind*
   How does your state meet the assessment mandates of the NCLB legislation? Go to your state department of education's Web site and find out what the assessment program looks like. Focus on the grade level and/or subject you are planning to teach. What are the standards for the grade and subject? How are the assessments constructed? Are they mostly multiple choice, or do they use alternative/authentic assessments? Write a summary of how your state addresses this important issue.

3. *Understanding Scales*
   What are the differences between grade-equivalent scores and percentiles? What are the strengths and weaknesses of each? If you could choose only one score to be reported for your students, which one would it be and why?

4. *Making the Data Make Sense*
   You are concerned about the test scores you have received for one of your students: They are not consistent with your expectations. What can you do about this now? What are some other sources of information you can turn to in order to assess the situation more fully?

5. *Relating Standardized Assessments to Classroom Assessments*
As a teacher, you will be developing classroom assessments for your students, but they will also be taking standardized assessments. These assessments have become very important in school districts in recent years. What do you think is the proper relationship between classroom assessments and standardized assessments? What types of assessments might you develop that would help your students perform at their best on standardized assessments? Is this goal (optimal performance on standardized assessments) a worthwhile one for your class? Why or why not?

Lesson Plans

Lesson #1: "Greek Mythology"

GRADES: 6–8

SUBJECT AREAS: World Cultures, Language Arts

I. OVERVIEW: Students will read a compilation of Greek myths and analyze how the myths have affected modern life. Students will then create myths of their own based on modern traditions.

II. OBJECTIVES: Students will be able to:
- Identify the steps of derivation of Greek mythology and its characters.
- Investigate and identify how Greek mythology has affected today's culture.
- Use creativity and knowledge of myth development to create their own myths based on modern culture.

III. MATERIALS:
- A variety of Greek myths (read either on the Internet or in books)
- Greek mythology videos (optional)

IV. PROCEDURE:

1. The teacher will begin by reading a myth to the class. The teacher will then prompt the class to discuss elements of the story and how they have affected how we live today.

2. The teacher will then divide the class into groups and assign different stories to each group. After reading the myths together, the groups will briefly present the myth to other members of the class.

3. In groups, students will compile a list of ways in which Greek myths may have affected/influenced modern traditions.

4. The groups will share their opinions with the class.

5. Finally, students will individually create their own myths based on any modern-day tradition. (Example: A myth of how we came to tie our shoes the way we do.)

Ask Yourself!

1. Read the objectives listed above. Are these objectives or instructional activities? Can you write some objectives that would be appropriate for this lesson plan?

2. Can you find standards from your state that are compatible with this lesson plan?

6. *Using Mental Measurements Yearbook Research as a Measurement Topic*
You might start with an assessment your district already uses, or you might pick an area of assessment you are interested in learning more about. You might also be able to find a copy of the assessment in a curriculum library. What can you learn about the validity of the assessment or whether there is evidence of ethnic bias?

Lesson Plans

Lesson #2: "Films Reels"

GRADES: 7–9

SUBJECT AREA: Math

I. OVERVIEW: Students will examine motion picture terminology, specifically focusing on film reels. On average, the length of a 35-mm motion picture reel is 1,000 feet. The reel itself has a cylindrical core and walls on the sides to hold the film, which is wound around the core. Using standard reel sizes, students will complete math computations.

II. OBJECTIVES: Students will be able to:
- Understand the basic principals of how film reels work.
- Demonstrate the ability to apply measurement, multiplication, and division concepts.
- Apply basic math formulas, including surface area of a cylinder and volume of a cylinder.

III. MATERIALS:
- Pictures of film reels
- Geometry formula chart

IV. PROCEDURE:

1. The teacher will explain the concept of film and film reels to students.

2. The teacher will review geometrical math computations involving cylinders, radius, diameter, surface area, and volume.

3. Students will answer the following questions based on film reels. Students can answer independently or work in groups.

V. QUESTIONS FOR DISCUSSION

1. The diameter of a 500-ft film reel is 8 inches. What is the radius of this reel?

2. If the diameter of a 500-ft film reel is 8 inches, how many feet of film would a reel with an 18-inch diameter hold?

3. What is the surface area of a reel with a diameter of 16 inches and a height of 2 inches?

4. Based on the numbers used above, what is the volume of a 1,500-ft film reel?

5. Based on the numbers used above, what is the surface area of a film reel with a diameter of 24 inches?

Ask Yourself!

1. How can you develop and extend some of the questions listed above?

2. What other kinds of media allow for mathematics to be used in this way?

3. How might you be able to use cooperative groups in this lesson

Appendix
Looking at the Praxis II™ Principles of Learning and Teaching Assessment and the INTASC Principles

In most states, part of the certification process for becoming a teacher includes an assessment of the aspiring teacher's knowledge, skills, and dispositions. This assessment is often based on what are known as the INTASC (Interstate New Teacher Assessment and Support Consortium) principles and/or involve the Praxis™ assessment developed by the Educational Testing Service.

The INTASC principles are a set of 10 statements that define what the consortium believes are exemplary instructional practices. They involve issues of motivation, collaborative activities, and appropriate assessment practices, among others. INTASC is in the process of developing an instrument that would assess mastery of these principles. It has also been working to develop model policies with respect to teacher preparation, teacher licensure, and professional development that states can use to align their own teaching standards.

Currently, 42 states use at least some part of the Praxis Series™ that consists of three sets of assessments: These are the Praxis I™ for college students wanting to study education to become teachers; The Praxis II™, which includes subject matter assessments as well as an assessment of subject-specific pedagogical skills and knowledge, called the Principles of Learning and Teaching (PLT); and the Praxis III™ for beginning teachers already working in classrooms. Of particular interest here is the PLT assessment, because many of the topics in the assessment parallel those in the text. There are four different levels for the PLT: Early Childhood, K–6, Grades 5–9, and Grades 7–12.

To help you prepare for the PLT and to help you better understand the INTASC principles, we developed a correspondence chart. In the following pages, you can examine the various areas of the PLT and locate in the text where those topics have been discussed. You can do the same for the INTASC principles. Both the Educational Testing Service and the INTASC consortium have Web sites where you can look in depth at these assessments and principles. For PRAXIS, see: www.ets.org/praxis. For INTASC, see: www.ccsso.org/projects/Interstate_New_Teacher_Assessment_and_Support_Consortium

The best way to prepare for any assessment is to test yourself on questions or prompts that are similar to the ones on the real assessment. You can find sample questions for the PLT on the ETS Web site. There are also commercially available practice assessments. Find your strengths and weaknesses, and work on those weaknesses by reviewing the appropriate material on the assessment. Do not hesitate to undertake a serious review. Doctors, lawyers, engineers—professionals in all fields—take special preparation to get ready for certification examinations. Take this preparation seriously—and good luck!

Praxis II™	Educational Psychology	INTASC
I. Students as Learners (approximately 35% of test)		
A. Student Development and the Learning Process		Principle #2: The teacher understands how children learn and develop and can provide learning opportunities that support their intellectual, social, and personal development.

Praxis II™	Educational Psychology	INTASC
1. Theoretical foundations about how learning occurs: how students construct knowledge, acquire skills, and develop habits of mind Examples of important theorists:		Principle #2 (Knowledge): The teacher understands how learning occurs—how students construct knowledge, acquire skills, and develop habits of mind—and knows how to use instructional strategies that promote student learning.
• Jean Piaget	Chapter 3/Cognitive development (pp. 72–85) Chapter 9/Piagetian theory (pp. 300–302)	
• Lev Vygotsky	Chapter 3/Sociocognitive development (pp. 85–93) Chapter 8/Complex cognition and social constructivism (pp. 268–278) Chapter 9/Vygotskian theory (pp. 302–303) Chapter 12/Gardner's theory of multiple intelligences (pp. 419–420) Chapter 12/Triarchic theory of intelligence (pp. 418–419)	
• Albert Bandura	Chapter 2/Teacher self-efficacy (pp. 41–43) Chapter 8/Social Learning Theory (pp. 256–262) Chapter 11/Self-efficacy (pp. 376–380)	
Important terms that relate to learning theory:		
• Adaptation	Chapter 3/Adaptation and schemas (pp. 73–76)	
• Conservation	Chapter 3/Concrete operations stage (pp. 78–81)	
• Constructivism	Chapter 7/Cognitive learning theory (pp. 264–265) Chapter 8/Complex cognition and social constructivism (pp. 268–279)	
• Private speech	Chapter 3/Role of language (p. 90)	
• Scaffolding	Chapter 3/Scaffolding in the zone of proximal development (pp. 86–90) Chapter 8/Scaffolding (pp. 272–279) Chapter 9/(pp. 339–342)	
• Zone of proximal development	Chapter 3/Scaffolding in the zone of proximal development (pp. 86–90)	
• Learning	Chapter 5/Behavior learning theory (entire chapter) Chapter 7/Cognitive and social cognitive learning (entire chapter) Chapter 8/Complex cognition and social constructivism (entire chapter)	
• Memory	Chapter 3/Brain structure and function (pp. 69–70) Chapter 7/Memory systems (pp. 270–278)	
• Schemas	Chapter 3/Adaptation and schemas: Piaget's theory (pp. 73–76) Chapter 7/Schemas and scripts (pp. 275–278)	
• Transfer	Chapter 8/Transfer (pp. 267–268)	
• Self-efficacy	Chapter 2/Teacher's self-efficacy (pp. 41–43)	

Praxis II™	Educational Psychology	INTASC
a. Human development in the physical, social, emotional, moral, speech/language, and cognitive domains.	Chapter 3/Cognitive development (entire chapter, includes language development) Chapter 4/Social development (entire chapter) Chapter 7/Cognitive and social cognitive learning (entire chapter) Chapter 11/Self-regulation (pp. 397–401)	Principle #2 (Knowledge): The teacher is aware of expected developmental progressions and ranges of individual variation within each domain (physical, social, emotional, moral, and cognitive), can identify levels of readiness in learning, and understands how development in any one domain may affect performance in others.
B. Students as Diverse Learners		Principle #3: The teacher understands how students differ in their approaches to learning and creates instructional opportunities that are adapted to diverse learners.
1. Differences in the ways students learn and perform	Chapter 12/Differences in ability and instruction (pp. 429–430) Chapter 12/Multiple intelligences (p. 419) Chapter 9/Status characteristics (pp. 319–321)	Principle #2 (Dispositions): The teacher appreciates individual variation within each area of development, shows respect for the diverse talents of all learners, and is committed to helping them develop self-confidence and competence. Principle #3 (Knowledge): The teacher understands and can identify differences in approaches to learning performance, including different learning styles, multiple intelligences, and performance modes, and can design instruction that helps use students' strengths as the basis for growth. Principle #3 (Performance): The teacher creates a learning community in which individual differences are respected.
2. Areas of exceptionality in students' learning: • Talent/Giftedness • Learning disabilities • ADHD • Functional and mental retardation • Autism	 Chapter 12/(pp. 412–449) Chapter 12/Extremes of intelligence (pp. 427–429) Chapter 12/Learners with special needs (pp. 430–435) Chapter 12/Learning disabilities (pp. 435–437) Chapter 11/Self-efficacy in students with learning disabilities (pp. 380–381) Chapter 12/Attention deficit hyperactivity disorder (pp. 440–442) Chapter 12/(pp. 412–449)	Principle #3 (Knowledge): The teacher knows about areas of exceptionality in learning—including learning disabilities, visual and perceptual difficulties, and special physical and mental challenges.
3. Legislation and institutional responsibilities relating to exceptional students • Americans with Disabilities Act (ADA); Individuals with Disabilities Education Act (IDEA); Section 504 Protections for Students • Inclusion, mainstreaming, and "least restrictive environment"	Chapter 12/The law and special education (pp. 430–435) Chapter 12/Inclusion (pp. 434–435)	

Praxis II™	Educational Psychology	INTASC
4. Approaches for accommodating various learning styles, intelligences, or exceptionalities	Chapter 2/Planning for students with special needs (pp. 51–52) Chapter 3/Technology support for young readers and readers with special needs (pp. 95–97) Chapter 5/Behavioral learning theory and diverse learners (pp. 164–165) Chapter 5/Behavioral learning theory and special needs students (p. 167) Chapter 6/Managing learning in classrooms (entire chapter) Chapter 8/Scaffolding for students from diverse backgrounds (p. 315) Chapter 8/Scaffolding for students with special needs (pp. 278–279) Chapter 9/Special needs and cooperative learning (pp. 318–319) Chapter 10/Engaging diverse learners (pp. 340–341) Chapter 10/How to motivate students with mental retardation: intrinsically or extrinsically? (pp. 346–347) Chapter 14/Classroom assessments for students with special needs (p. 506)	Principle #1 (Performance): The teacher can represent and use differing viewpoints, theories, "ways of knowing," and methods of inquiry in teaching of subject matter concepts. Principle #3 (Performance): The teacher identifies and designs instruction appropriate to students' stages of development, learning styles, strengths, and needs.
5. Process of second-language acquisition and strategies to support the learning of students for whom English is not a first language	Chapter 3/Second-language acquisition and bilingualism (pp. 97–99)	Principle #3 (Knowledge): The teacher knows about the process of second-language acquisition and about strategies to support the learning of students whose first language is not English.
6. Understanding the influence of individual experiences, talents, and prior learning, as well as language, culture, family, and community values on students' learning	Chapter 2/Teaching efficacy and diverse students (pp. 44–45) Chapter 3/Cultural tools (pp. 90–91) Chapter 3/Importance of peers (p. 91) Chapter 4/Culture, diversity, and special needs (pp. 115–119) Chapter 12/Talent (pp. 423–427) Chapter 12/Differences in ability and instruction (pp. 429–430) Chapter 12/Inclusion (pp. 434–435) Chapter 12/Educational options (pp. 441–442) Chapter 12/Differences in socioeconomic status and their role in learning (pp. 442–443) Chapter 8/The role of experience (pp. 271–272) Chapter 14/Diversity among students and their parents (p. 488)	Principle #1 (Knowledge): The teacher understands how students' conceptual framework for an area of knowledge, conceptions, and misconceptions can influence their learning. Principle #2 (Knowledge): The teacher understands that students' physical, social, emotional, moral, and cognitive development influences learning and knows how to address these factors when making instructional decisions. Principle #3 (Knowledge): The teacher understands how students' learning is influenced by individual experiences, talents, and prior learning, as well as language, culture, family, and community values. Principle #3 (Knowledge): The teacher has a well-grounded framework for understanding cultural and community diversity and knows how to learn about and incorporate students' experiences, cultures, and community resources into instruction. Principle #3 (Disposition): The teacher is sensitive to community and cultural mores. The teacher makes students feel valued for their potential as people and helps them to learn to value each other.

Praxis II™	Educational Psychology	INTASC
C. Student Motivation and the Learning Environment		Principle #5: The teacher uses an understanding of individual and group motivation and behavior to create a learning environment that encourages positive social interaction, active engagement in learning, and self-motivation.
1. Theoretical foundations of human motivation and behavior	Chapter 4/Psychosocial development (pp. 119–127) Chapter 5/Increasing desirable behaviors (pp. 168–170) Chapter 11/Motivation to learn (entire chapter)	Principle #5 (Knowledge): The teacher can use knowledge about human motivation and behavior drawn from the foundational sciences of psychology, anthropology, and sociology to develop strategies for organizing and supporting individual and group work.
2. How knowledge of human motivation and behavior should influence strategies for organizing and supporting individual and group work in the classroom	Chapter 10/Motivation and engagement (entire chapter) Chapter 11/Motivation to learn (entire chapter)	Principle #5 (Knowledge): The teacher understands the principles of effective classroom management and can use a range of strategies to promote positive relationships, cooperation, and purposeful learning in the classroom.
3. Factors and situations that are likely to promote or diminish student's motivation to learn and how to help students to become self-motivated	Chapter 5/Managing behavior (pp. 167–177) Chapter 5/Promoting self-management (pp. 174–175) Chapter 5/The fundamental task of classroom management (p. 175) Chapter 5/Feedback and knowledge of results (p. 178) Chapter 6/Managing learning in classrooms (entire chapter) Chapter 10/Two approaches to promoting motivation and engagement (pp. 342–348) Chapter 10/Using extrinsic motivators effectively (pp. 344–346) Chapter 10/The engagement model (pp. 355–356) Chapter 11/Motivation to learn (entire chapter) Chapter 11/Self-efficacy (pp. 376–381) Chapter 14/Communicating with parents (pp. 517–519)	Principle #5 (Knowledge): The teacher recognizes factors and situations that are likely to promote or diminish intrinsic motivation and knows how to help students become self-motivated. Principle #5 (Performance): The teacher analyzes the classroom environment and makes decisions and adjustments to enhance social relationships, student motivation and engagement, and productive work.

Praxis II™	Educational Psychology	INTASC
II. Instruction and Assessment (approximately 35% of test)		
A. Instructional Strategies		Principle #4: The teacher understands and uses a variety of instructional strategies to encourage student's development of critical thinking, problem solving, and performance skills.
1. Major cognitive strategies:		Principle #4 (Knowledge): The teacher understands the cognitive processes associated with various kinds of learning (e.g., critical and creative thinking, problem structuring and problem solving, invention, memorization, and recall) and how these processes can be stimulated.
• Critical thinking	Chapter 1/Critical thinking (pp. 3–5) Chapter 9/Perspectives on peer learning (pp. 292–304)	
• Inductive and deductive thinking	Chapter 3/Formal operations stage (pp. 81–83) Chapter 5/Inductive reasoning (p. 170) Chapter 8/Reasoning and argumentation (pp. 263–265)	
• Problem structuring and problem solving	Chapter 8/Problem solving (pp. 265–267)	
• Invention	Chapter 6/Misbehavior: Informal correctives and imposing penalties (pp. 203–204)	
• Encoding and Retrieval	Chapter 7/Encoding, retrieval, and forgetting (pp. 238–244)	
2. Major categories, advantages, and appropriate users of instructional strategies:		Principle #4 (Knowledge): The teacher understands principles and techniques, along with advantages and limitations associated with various instructional strategies (e.g., cooperative learning, direct instruction, discovery learning, whole-group discussion, independent study, interdisciplinary instruction).
• Cooperative learning	Chapter 3/Teacher as guide, mentor (p. 91) Chapter 9/Learning from peers (entire chapter)	
• Direct instruction	Chapter 2/Direct instruction (pp. 58–59) Chapter 3/Limitations of Piaget's theory (p. 85)	
• Expository teaching	Chapter 2/Expository teaching (p. 58)	
• Concept mapping	Chapter 7/Concept mapping (p. 240)	
• Questioning	Chapter 9/The importance of discourse quality (pp. 321–322)	
• Mastery learning	Chapter 5/Mastery learning (pp. 177–178)	
• Problem-based learning	Chapter 8/Problem-based learning (pp. 281–282)	
• Reciprocal teaching	Chapter 8/Reciprocal teaching (pp. 280–281)	
• Whole-group discussions	Chapter 6/Whole-class instruction (pp. 207–210)	
• Small-group discussions	Chapter 9/Learning in heterogeneous groups (pp. 311–314)	
• Independent work	Chapter 6/Small-group work (p. 207) Chapter 6/ Independent work or seatwork (pp. 206–207)	

Praxis II™	Educational Psychology	INTASC
3. Principles, techniques, and methods associated with major instructional strategies: • Direct instruction • Student-centered models	Chapter 2/Direct Instruction (pp. 58–59) Chapter 8/Complex cognition and social constructivism (entire chapter)	
4. Methods for enhancing student learning through the use of a variety of resources and materials: • Computers, Internet resources, Web pages, email • Audiovisual technologies, such as videotapes and CDs • Local experts • Field Trips • Libraries • Museums	Chapter 8/Instruction influenced by social-constructivist and sociocultural theory (pp. 279–283) Chapter 8/Scaffolding with technology (pp. 274–278) Chapter 2/Differences in knowledge between experts and novices (pp. 38–40)	Principle #4 (Knowledge): The teacher knows how to enhance learning through the use of a wide variety of materials as well as human and technological resources (e.g., computers, audiovisual technologies, videotapes and discs, local experts, primary documents and artifacts, texts, reference books, literature, and other print resources).
B. Planning Instruction	Chapter 2/Planning (pp. 48–57)	Principle #7: The teacher plans instruction based on knowledge of subject matter, students, the community, and curriculum goals.
1. Techniques for planning instruction, including addressing curriculum goals, selecting current topics, incorporating learning theory, subject matter, curriculum development, and student development and interests	Chapter 2/Planning (pp. 48–57) Chapter 6/Managing learning in classrooms (entire chapter) Chapter 14/Assessment for learning (entire chapter)	Principle #4 (Performance): The teacher carefully evaluates how to achieve reaming goals, choosing alternative teaching strategies and materials to achieve different instructional purposes and to meet student needs (e.g., developmental stages, prior knowledge, reaming styles, and interests). Principle #7 (Knowledge): The teacher understands reaming theory, subject matter, curriculum development, and student development and knows how to use this knowledge in planning instruction to meet curriculum goals.
2. Techniques for creating effective bridges between curriculum goals and students' experiences	Chapter 2/Guided discovery (p. 58) Chapter 8/Transfer (pp. 267–268)	Principle #4 (Performance): The teacher constantly monitors and adjusts strategies in response to learner feedback.

Praxis II™	Educational Psychology	INTASC
C. Assessment Strategies		Principle #8: The teacher understands and uses formal and informal assessment strategies to evaluate and ensure the continuous intellectual and social development of the learner.
1. Types of assessments	Chapter 14/Options for assessment (pp. 491–502) Chapter 15/(pp. 528–534)	Principle #8 (Knowledge): The teacher understands the characteristics, uses, advantages, and limitations of different types of assessments (e.g., criterion-referenced and norm-referenced instruments, traditional standardized and performance-based tests, observation systems, and evaluations of student work) for evaluating how students learn, what they know and are able to do, and what kinds of experiences will support their further growth and development.
2. Characteristics of assessments	Chapter 14/Principles of assessment and grading (pp. 489–491) Chapter 15/(pp. 528–534)	
3. Scoring assessments	Chapter 14/Administering, scoring, and communicating assessment results (pp. 506–509) Chapter 14/Developing a grading system (pp. 513–516)	
4. Use of assessments	Chapter 14/Developing and using assessments (pp. 502–509)	Principle #2 (Performance): The teacher assesses individual and group performance in order to design instruction that meets learner's current needs in each domain and that leads to the next level of development. Principle #8 (Performance): The teacher appropriately uses a variety of formal and informal assessment techniques (e.g., observation, portfolios of student work, teacher-made tests, performance tasks, projects, student self-assessments, peer assessment, and standardized tests) to enhance her or his knowledge of learners, evaluate student's progress and performances, and modify teaching and learning strategies.
5. Understanding measurement theory and assessment-related issues	Chapter 14/Data-based determinations of next steps (p. 510) Chapter 14/Developing a grading system (pp. 513–517) Chapter 15/(pp. 528–534)	Principle #8 (Knowledge): The teacher understands measurement theory and assessment-related issues, such as validity, reliability, bias, and scoring concerns.
6. Interpreting and communicating results of assessments	Chapter 14/Communicating with parents (pp. 517–519) Chapter 14/Administering, scoring, and communicating assessment results (pp. 506–509) Chapter 15/Interpreting standardized assessments (pp. 547–554)	Principle #8 (Performance): The teacher maintains useful records of student work and performance and can communicate student progress knowledgeably and responsibly, based on appropriate indicators, to students, parents, and other colleagues.

Praxis II™	Educational Psychology	INTASC
III. Communication Techniques (approximately 15% of test)		
A. Basic, Effective Verbal and Nonverbal Communication Techniques	Chapter 3/Transfer of responsibility (p. 88) Chapter 6/Taking it to the classroom: tips for creating a peaceful classroom (p. 213) Chapter 14/Principles of assessment and grading (pp. 489–491) Chapter 14/Communicating with parents (pp. 517–519)	Principle #6: The teacher uses knowledge of effective verbal, nonverbal, and media communication techniques to foster active inquiry, collaboration, and supportive interaction in the classroom. Principle #6 (Knowledge): The teacher recognizes the importance of nonverbal as well as verbal communication.
B. Effect of Cultural and Gender Differences on Communications in the Classroom	Chapter 2/(pp. 44–45) Chapter 6/ Taking it to the classroom: tips for creating a peaceful classroom (p. 213) Chapter 9/Taking it to the classroom: do you know Jack? getting the help he needs. (p. 319) Chapter 14/Principles of assessment and grading (pp. 489–491)	Principle #6 (Knowledge): The teacher understands how cultural and gender differences can affect communication in the classroom.
C. Types of Communications and Interactions That Can Stimulate Discussion in Different Ways for Particular Purposes		Principle #6 (Performance): The teacher knows how to ask questions and stimulate discussion in different ways for particular purposes, for example, probing for learner understanding, helping students articulate their ideas and thinking processes, promoting risk taking and problem solving, facilitating factual recall, encouraging convergent and divergent thinking, stimulating curiosity, helping students to question.
IV. Profession and Community (approximately 15% of test)		
A. The Reflective Practitioner	RIDE scenarios throughout the book Chapter 1/Reflective teaching (pp. 10–15)	Principle #9: The teacher is a reflective practitioner who continually evaluates the effects of his/her choices and actions on others (students, parents, and other professionals in the learning community) and who actively seeks out opportunities to grow professionally.
1. Types of resources available for professional development and learning: • Professional literature • Colleagues • Professional associations • Professional development activities	Chapter 2/Teacher development (pp. 33–41)	Principle #1 (Disposition): The teacher realizes that subject matter knowledge is not a fixed body of facts but is complex and ever evolving. He or she seeks to keep abreast of new ideas and understandings in the field. Principle #9 (Knowledge): The teacher is aware of major areas of research on teaching and of resources available for professional learning (e.g., professional literature, colleagues, professional associations, professional development activities).
2. Ability to read, understand, and apply articles and books about current research, views, ideas, and debates regarding best teaching practices		Principle #1 (Knowledge): The teacher understands major concepts, assumptions, debates, processes of inquiry, and ways of knowing that are central to the discipline(s) he or she teaches. Principle #1 (Performance): The teacher can evaluate teaching resources and curriculum materials for their comprehensiveness, accuracy, and usefulness for representing particular ideas and concepts.

Praxis II™	Educational Psychology	INTASC
3. Ongoing personal reflection on teaching and learning practices as a basis for making professional decisions		Principle #1 (Knowledge): The teacher can relate his or her disciplinary knowledge to other subject areas. Principle #9 (Performance): The teacher is committed to seeking out, developing, and continually refining practices that address the individual needs of students.
B. The Larger Community		Principle #10: The teacher fosters relationships with school colleagues, parents, and agencies in the larger community to support students' learning and well-being.
1. Role of the school as a resource to the larger community	Chapter 2/Teacher development (pp. 33–41) Chapter 8/Instruction influenced by social constructivism and sociocultural theory (pp. 279–283) Chapter 6/Managing learning in classrooms (entire chapter)	Principle #10 (Knowledge): The teacher understands schools as organizations within the larger community context and understands the operations of the relevant aspects of the system(s) within which he or she works.
2. Factors in the students' environment outside of school		Principle #3 (Disposition): The teacher is sensitive to community and cultural mores. The teacher makes students feel valued for their potential as people and helps them to learn to value each other. Principle #10 (Knowledge): The teacher understands how factors in the students' environment outside of school (e.g., family circumstances, community environments, health and economic conditions) may influence students' lives and learning.
3. Develop and utilize active partnerships among teachers, parents/guardians, and leaders in the community to support the educational process	Chapter 6/Managing learning in classrooms (entire chapter) Chapter 14/Communicating with parents (pp. 517–519)	Principle #10 (Performance): The teacher makes links with the learners' other environments on behalf of students by consulting with parents, teachers of other classes and activities within the schools, counselors, and professionals in other community agencies. Principle #10 (Performance): The teacher establishes respectful and productive relationships with parents and guardians from diverse home and community situations and seeks to develop cooperative partnerships in support of student learning and well-being.
4. Major laws related to students' rights and teacher responsibilities	Chapter 12/The law and special education (pp. 430–431)	Principle #10 (Knowledge): The teacher understands and implements laws related to students' rights and teacher responsibilities (e.g., for equal education, appropriate education for handicapped students, confidentiality, privacy, appropriate treatment of students, reporting in situations related to possible child abuse).

Glossary

accommodation A modification process in which lower-level schemas are transformed into higher-level schemas.

accommodations Modifications made in an assessment for students with disabilities.

achievement goal What the student is trying to accomplish when facing a standard of excellence.

achievement targets Well-specified statements of what teachers want to accomplish in a particular lesson or set of lessons.

action research A research method carried out by teachers in their own classrooms to inform and improve their classroom practice.

acute problems Problems that occur only infrequently but are severe.

adaptation Adjusting to the demands of the environment.

advance organizer A broad introductory statement of the information that will be presented in a lesson.

affective assessment An assessment related to feelings, motivation, attitudes, and the like.

affordance A property of a tool or artifact that allows a person to act in particular ways that would not be possible without using the tool.

agentic engagement The extent to which a student contributes constructively into the flow of instruction he or she receives.

aggression Any intentional behavior designed to harm another person or group physically or psychologically.

algorithm A systematic and exhaustive strategy for solving problems.

alternative assessment A generic term referring to assessments that are different from traditional approaches, such as multiple choice and constructed response.

amotivation Without motivation.

anxiety The unpleasant, aversive emotion that students experience in evaluative settings.

argumentation The process of taking a position, providing reasons for the position, and presenting counterarguments.

assessment The process of coming to understand what students know and can do.

assigning competence The teacher acknowledges the contribution of a student to the completion of a task.

assimilation An incorporation process in which an outside event is brought into one's way of thinking.

assistive technology Any piece of equipment that can improve the functionality of a child with a disability.

attachment A close emotional relationship between two persons that is characterized by mutual affection and the desire to maintain proximity with the other.

attention Focus that is selective and limited.

attention-deficit disorder (ADD) A condition in which children experience persistent difficulties with attention span, impulse control, and sometimes hyperactivity.

attention-deficit/hyperactivity disorder (ADHD) A condition in which children or adults consistently display inattention, hyperactivity, and impulsiveness.

attribution An explanation of why an outcome occurred.

attunement Sensing and reading another's state of being and adjusting one's own behavior accordingly.

authentic assessment An assessment that is tightly related to the instruction that the students have received or to tasks that are relevant in real life.

authentic tasks Tasks that are connected to the real world.

automaticity The ability to perform a task without having to think much about it.

autonomy The psychological need to experience self-direction in the initiation and regulation of one's behavior.

autonomy-supportive motivating style The interpersonal sentiment and behavior teachers provide during instruction to identify, nurture, and develop students' inner motivational resources (especially the need for autonomy).

behavioral engagement The extent to which a student displays on-task attention, strong effort, and enduring persistence on a learning activity.

behavioral schemas Mental representations of physical actions.

between-class ability grouping A procedure in which children are assigned to different classes based on measured ability.

bias Systematic unfair treatment of a particular group of individuals.

bilingualism The use of two or more languages in everyday life.

block scheduling An approach to scheduling at the middle and high school levels that allows for larger (but fewer) blocks of time to be scheduled for subjects.

bottom-up processing A process in which a stimulus is analyzed into its components, then assembled into *a recognizable* pattern, also known as feature analysis.

bullying An unprovoked physical, verbal, or psychological attack on a peer that is intended to harm, repeated over time, and involves a power differential between bully and victim.

calibration An ongoing corrective process in which the person adjusts his or her sense of confidence with a task to reflect most accurately the quality of his or her recent performances at that task.

care An emotional concern and sense of responsibility to protect or enhance another person's welfare or well-being.

central tendency An indicator of the center of a set of scores on some variable.

channeling Providing constraints during the task so that the learner has an increased likelihood of acting effectively.

chronic problems   Problems that persist over time, even though they may not be severe.

chunking   The grouping of bits of data into larger, meaningful units.

classical conditioning   The association of automatic responses with new stimuli.

classified   A term used to refer to special education students who have been identified as having a particular disability.

classroom management   Teacher behaviors and management techniques that result in a healthy learning environment, generally free of behavior problems.

coefficient alpha   An approach to assessing reliability that uses a single administration of the assessment and focuses on whether all the assessment items appear to be measuring the same underlying ability. Also called *Cronbach's alpha*.

cognitive apprenticeship   An instructional strategy in which the learner acquires knowledge by modeling the activities of the teacher and is coached by the teacher.

cognitive conflict   Experience of conflict when new information does not agree with existing knowledge.

cognitive disequilibrium   The experience of cognitive conflict.

cognitive engagement   The extent to which a student displays the use of sophisticated learning strategies, such as elaboration, to conceptually understand the meaning of what he or she is trying to learn.

cognitive-evaluation theory   A theory of motivation that explains how external events such as rewards affect students' psychological needs for autonomy and competence and, hence, their intrinsic motivation.

collective efficacy   A jointly held belief that the community is effective when working together.

committed compliance   Cooperatively carrying out a teacher's request to "do this" or "don't do that" with an eager, willing, and sincere commitment to the action.

comparative organizer   A broad statement that reminds the student of what he or she already knows.

competence   The psychological need to be effective during interactions with the surrounding environment.

concept   An abstraction with which a person categorizes objects, people, ideas, or experiences by shared properties.

conceptual change teaching   A method of teaching that helps students understand concepts by challenging them to examine their ideas and identify shortcomings in them.

conditional knowledge   Knowledge that guides a person in using declarative and procedural knowledge.

conditioned response (CR)   A response that is linked to a particular stimulus through conditioning by being paired with the stimulus.

conditioned stimulus (CS)   A stimulus that, with experience, produces a learned or acquired response.

conscience   The capacity to use one's moral cognition, moral emotions, and moral self to inhibit aggression and to initiate altruism and helping.

consequences   The good or bad effects that follow a person's behavior.

consequential validity   Concern for how the assessment will affect the person taking it.

conservation   Understanding that appearance alterations (e.g., an object's length, height, or width) do not change the essential properties of an object (e.g., its amount).

construct validity   An indicator of the degree to which an ability really exists in the way it is theorized to exist and whether it is appropriately measured in that way by the assessment.

constructed response   A type of assessment format in which the student has to provide the answer to the question; more commonly referred to as *short answer*.

constructivist perspective   A theoretical perspective that stresses the active role of the learner in building understanding and making sense of information.

content knowledge   Knowledge about the subject matter being taught.

content validity   An indicator of the degree to which the items on an assessment appear to fully cover the intended content of the assessment and whether there is any extraneous material.

content/behavior matrix   A method for specifying what is to be assessed by making a matrix with expected student behaviors on one axis and the content on which that behavior will be observed on the other axis.

contiguity   A condition in which two events occur at the same time.

contingency contracting   An approach to behavior management that involves a written agreement about behavior that makes rewards and punishments depend on the student's performance of that behavior.

continuous reinforcement   Reinforcement that is provided after every performance of a behavior.

control group   The group of participants in an experimental study who are randomly assigned not to receive exposure to the independent variable.

controlled processes   Cognitive processes that require conscious attention.

controlling motivating style   The interpersonal sentiment and behavior teachers provide during instruction to pressure students to think, feel, or behave in a prescribed way.

coregulation   A collaborative process in which the teacher and student jointly plan, monitor, and evaluate the academic work of the student.

correlation coefficient   A statistical value that ranges from −1 to +1 to describe both the direction and extent of the relationship between two variables.

correlational studies   A research method used to measure two naturally occurring variables and summarize the nature and magnitude of their relationship in numerical form.

criteria   Specifications of what is expected of a student on an assessment.

criterial attributes   Attributes that must be presented for an instance to be a member of a particular category.

criterion-referenced   Term describing a method for understanding what assessment scores mean by referring them to some arbitrary standard.

criterion-related validity   The degree to which an assessment correlates with an independent indicator of the same underlying ability.

critical thinking   Critical thinking is the process of telling fact from opinion, seeing holes in an argument, spotting illogic, evaluating evidence, and telling whether or not cause and effect have been established.

cross-ethnic groupings   Groupings of children from different ethnic groups.

crystallized intelligence   The use of acquired skills and knowledge, such as reading and language skills.

cultural differences   Differences in the meaning and information systems that are transmitted from generation to generation in different cultural groups.

cultural tools   Products created and designed by advanced members of a culture to help less advanced members of the culture learn and solve problems.

culture   The meaning and information system that is transmitted from one generation to the next.

culture-free tests   Standardized tests that do not include items that might favor one culture over another.

curiosity A cognitively based emotion that occurs whenever students experience a gap in their knowledge that motivates exploratory behavior to remove that knowledge gap.

decay Loss of memories because information is not used.

declarative knowledge Factual knowledge that can be expressed through verbal exchange, books, Braille, or sign language; knowing that something is true.

declarative memory Memory for abstract information.

deductive reasoning Drawing a valid conclusion out of a general premise or a sample of evidence.

deliberate practice Activity that is designed to improve one's skills in a particular area.

descriptive studies A research method used to describe the educational situation as it naturally occurs—what typically happens, how teachers teach, and how students learn and develop.

dialectical constructivism The theory that considers knowledge to lie in the continual interaction between the individual and the environment.

dialectical relationship A relationship in which the participants have mutual influence on one another or in which the actor changes the environment in some way, and that changed environment subsequently changes the actor.

differentiated instruction A teacher's response to the differing learning needs of a student.

diffuse status characteristics Characteristics that have no direct bearing on task performance but are assumed to be indicators of greater or lesser capability to perform the task.

direct instruction A systematic form of instruction that is used for mastery of basic skills and facts.

discovery-based learning Students work on their own to grasp a concept or understand a lesson.

discriminative stimuli Antecedent cues that allow the learner to predict the likelihood of reinforcement.

disequilibrium A state of cognitive conflict in which one's existing schema or way of thinking is not confirmed by experience.

distracter One of the options in a multiple-choice test.

distributed practice Practice that is interspersed by unequal intervals.

dual representation All symbolic objects have a dual nature, as they are simultaneously objects in their own right and representations of something else.

educational objectives Explicit statements of what students are expected to be able to do as a result of instruction.

educational psychology The scientific study of psychology in education.

elaboration A process through which we add and extend meaning by connecting new information to existing knowledge in long-term memory.

elaborative rehearsal A way of remembering information by connecting it to something that is already well known.

emotion regulation The capacity to modulate or calm internal emotional reactivity during stressful situations.

emotional engagement The extent to which a student displays task-facilitating emotions such as interest and does not display task-withdrawing emotions such as distress.

empowerment Perceiving that one possesses the knowledge, skills, and beliefs needed to take control over one's learning.

engagement How actively involved the student is during the learning activity.

English language learners (ELLs) Individuals whose native language is other than English and who are learning English.

entity view of intelligence The belief that intelligence is genetically determined and not alterable.

episodic memory Long-term memory of particular places and events in a person's life.

error tolerance The attitude of a teacher who accepts errors and failures as a necessary, inherent, and even welcomed part of the learning process.

ethnic group A collection of people who identify with one another on the basis of race, country of origin, language, and/or behavioral rituals.

ethnicity Ethnicity concerns the classification of people into groups based on their race or national origin.

eugenics A political and scientific movement that argued for selective reproduction of individuals and immigration laws based on intelligence levels.

existential intelligence Concern with larger questions of human existence, such as the meaning of life.

expectations One's beliefs about what will happen in a situation.

experimental group The group of participants in an experimental study who are randomly assigned to receive exposure to the independent variable.

experimental studies A research method used to test for a cause-and-effect relationship between two variables.

explaining Breaking down the concepts and ideas of a lesson to make them easier to understand.

explanatory style A personality-like characteristic that reflects the habitual way that students explain why bad events happen to them.

expository organizer A broad statement of what is to be learned in a lesson.

expository teaching A type of teaching in which the teacher provides an exposition of how a particular set of information is structured and organized.

extrinsic motivation An environmentally created reason to initiate or persist in an action or activity.

feature analysis Identifying the component features of objects and building a representation of the object from them.

feedback Knowledge of results.

fixed interval schedule A schedule of reinforcement based on the passage of a fixed amount of time.

fixed ratio schedule A schedule of reinforcement based on the number of behaviors performed.

flow A state of concentration in which students become wholly absorbed in an activity.

fluid intelligence The ability to solve problems, figure out what to do when one is not sure what to do, and acquire new skills.

forethought What one thinks prior to engaging in a task and prior to receiving feedback about the quality of one's performance on that task.

formative assessment An assessment designed to inform teachers and students about student learning and to help improve instruction.

functional fixedness Being able to consider only the typical function of an object.

generativity The sense of being productive in one's work and in looking after and guiding others.

gentle discipline A socialization strategy that revolves around explaining why a way of thinking or behaving is right or wrong.

goal A future-focused cognitive representation that guides behavior toward an attractive end state.

goal structure The manner in which students relate to others who are also working toward a particular goal.

graded membership The extent to which an object or idea belongs to a category.

grade-equivalent scores Assessment scores that are reported in terms of how well children did in the norming study at various grade levels.

graphic organizer A visual display of verbal information.

guessing-and-feedback A curiosity-inducing instructional strategy in which the teacher asks students a difficult question, then announces that students' answers are incorrect so as to reveal a gap in their knowledge.

guided discovery Students work under the guidance of a capable partner to grasp a concept or understand a lesson.

guided participation Having one's engagement in a learning activity encouraged, supported, and tutored by a skilled partner.

heuristic A rule of thumb or shortcut for solving problems.

hidden cost of reward The unexpected, unintended, and adverse effects that extrinsic rewards sometimes have on intrinsic motivation, high-quality learning, and autonomous self-regulation.

high road transfer Deliberate application of previously learned strategy or knowledge to a new problem.

higher-order thinking skills Skills and abilities that go beyond recall and comprehension, including the ability to apply ideas and concepts, analyze and synthesize information, and evaluate complex information.

hippocampus Seahorse-shaped structure in the limbic area of the brain involved in the formation of new memories.

hope A motivational wish for an outcome that one expects to be fully capable of obtaining.

hostile aggression The anger-driven impulse to inflict intentional harm on another person.

hypothesis A hypothesis is something that is believed to be true about life. Hypotheses allow for predictions about what will happen in an experiment, such as what effect an independent variable will have on a dependent variable.

identity The sense of being a distinct and productive individual within the larger social framework.

I-message A reaction to a behavior that describes the behavior and how it has affected a given situation as well as the individual's emotional response to the behavior.

immediacy In teaching, decisions and actions have to occur in the real time of classroom life, that is, immediately, not at a leisurely pace.

implementation intention A plan to carry out goal-directed behavior.

incentive An environmental event that attracts a person toward a particular course of action.

inclusive An approach to education in general, whether teaching, working with students, or curriculum, that includes students from different cultures and with different abilities and challenges.

incremental view of intelligence The belief that intelligence can be improved through effort.

individual accountability Each student is responsible for improving his or her performance.

individual interest An enduring disposition in which one develops a clear preference to direct attention and effort toward a particular activity, situation, or subject matter.

individualism The belief that each person should try to succeed on his or her own rather than focus on the development of society as a whole.

individualized education program (IEP) An educational and behavioral intervention plan for a student with special needs.

inductive reasoning The abstraction of a general principle from a variety of examples.

informal assessment Classroom assessment activities used to get a quick and rough idea of student progress.

initiative The child's capacity to use a surplus of energy to plan and constructively carry out a task.

innate ability The ability a person was born with.

instructional goal A statement of desired student outcomes following instruction.

instrumental aggression Strategic behavior to obtain something one desires that results in harm inflicted on another person.

intelligence quotient (IQ) A method for communicating the level of a person's intelligence.

intelligence test A measure of generalized intellectual ability.

interdependence A condition in which group members' goal accomplishments are linked together.

interest A topic-specific motivational state that arises out of attraction to a particular domain of activity.

interference Loss or deficiency of memories because of the presence of other information.

inter-rater reliability A measure of the degree to which two independent raters give similar scores to the same paper or performance.

intersubjectivity The unique product that arises from social interaction in which the interaction partners come to a shared understanding of how to manage the problem-solving situation.

interval schedule A schedule of reinforcement based on time.

intervention research An experiment-based research design in which a group of participants receive a particular instructional program or type of training to see if their performance on a desired outcome improves in a causal way.

intrinsic motivation The inherent desire to engage in one's interests and to exercise and develop one's capacities.

item A test or assessment question, referred to as an *item* because not all test questions are actually questions.

item bank A collection of test or assessment items for use in future assessments. Also called *test bank*.

journal A running set of thoughts, responses to prompts, and reflections that students have concerning their learning in a particular area.

language The use of agreed-on rules to combine a small number of symbols (sounds, letters, gestures) to produce a large number of meaningful messages.

language acquisition device Inborn capacity that enables children to understand grammar and produce language.

law of effect The phenomenon in which behavior that produces good effects tends to become more frequent, while behavior that produces bad effects tends to become less frequent.

learned helplessness The psychological state that results when a student expects that school-related outcomes are beyond his or her personal control.

learning A relatively permanent change in behavior or knowledge that occurs as a result of experience.

learning center An area of a classroom specifically designed to facilitate exploration of a particular aspect of the curriculum.

lecturing Presenting information to a group of learners as a whole.

levels of processing theory A theory that asserts that recall of information is based on how deeply it is processed.

logical consequences An approach to classroom management that lets the natural outcomes of bad behavior serve as the punishment for that behavior.

long-term memory Memory of unknown, possibly unlimited, capacity and duration.

low road transfer The automatic application of previously learned skills.

maintenance rehearsal   A cognitive process in which information in working memory is repeated to oneself frequently.

massed practice   Intense practice for a single period of time. Also known as *cramming*.

mastery belief   Extent of one's perceived control over a success/failure outcome.

mastery goal   The intention to develop competence by improving, learning, and making progress.

mastery levels   Levels of proficiency, or mastery, determined for an assessment; related to cut scores and passing scores.

matching   An assessment item format that involves generating two sets of objects that are to be linked together, such as states and their capitals.

mean   The arithmetic mean of a set of scores.

means–end analysis   A strategy for reducing the distance between the initial state and the goal state in problem solving.

median   The middle score of a set of scores that have been rank-ordered from highest to lowest.

mental age   The age level associated with the ability to perform certain mental tasks. A mental age of 7 means that a person can perform the tasks of a typical 7-year-old but not those of a typical 8-year-old.

mental models   Students' enduring beliefs and expectations about what they are like and what other people are like.

meta-analysis   A quantitative review and summary of research on a topic.

metacognition   Thinking about one's own thinking.

mnemonic strategies   Strategies for remembering nonmeaningful information by making it meaningful.

mode   The most frequently occurring score in a set of scores.

model testing   A correlation-based research method in which an entire system of variables included in a theoretical model are intercorrelated and presented pictorially to show the big picture of how all the variables relate to one another.

modeling   Learning by observing a model.

monotonic-benefits assumption   The argument that there is a one-to-one correspondence between one's effort and one's gains in a skill or ability.

moral development   Changes in students' reasoning as to why one action is right and another is wrong.

motivation   Any force that energizes and directs behavior.

multicultural   The perspective that cultural differences among several cultures are im-portant and are deserving of considerate in a given setting.

multicultural approaches   Include (1) contributions approach, (2) additive approach, (3) transformation approach, and (4) social action approach.

multidimensionality   Having more than one characteristic (such as a purpose or an ability) at the same time.

multiple choice   An assessment item format consisting of a stem (question), a right answer, and a set of wrong answers (distracters). Students have to determine the best response to the stem.

multiple modalities   Various senses.

multiple-intelligences (MI) theory   A theory of intelligence that argues that individuals may exhibit multiple intelligences (possibly eight or more).

natural categories   Real-world categories.

nature/nurture   A shorthand term for the debate over whether mental abilities are developed by the individual's environment (nurture) or are inherited (nature).

negative interdependence   A condition that exists when, in order for one person to succeed in accomplishing his or her goals, others must fail to meet their goals.

negative punisher   Any environmental event that, when taken away, decreases the frequency of a behavior.

negative reinforcer   Any environmental event that, when removed, increases the frequency of a behavior.

negative transfer   Interference of prior learning with new learning.

neurons   Nerve cells that receive and transmit the neural impulses underlying thinking.

normal curve equivalent (NCE)   A scale related to the z-score that has a mean of 50 and a standard deviation of 21.06.

normal distribution   A mathematical conceptualization of how scores are distributed when they are influenced by a variety of relatively independent factors.

norming study   The administration of an assessment to a representative national sample to obtain a distribution of typical performance on the assessment.

norm-referenced   Term describing scores that are given meaning by referring them to scores from other individuals or sets of individuals.

norms   A set of tables based on a representative national administration of an assessment that makes it possible to show how well particular students did compared to a national sample of students.

object permanence   Understanding that objects continue to exist even when they cannot be seen or detected by other senses.

objectivity   Not having a direct interest or bias.

observational learning   Learning by observing other individuals.

off-task   Not paying attention to instruction.

operant learning   Actions by a learner, the consequences of which influence further behavior.

operation   A mental action or a mental manipulation carried out to solve a problem or to reason logically.

optimal challenge   A circumstance in which the skills the student possesses are equally balanced with the demands, difficulty, and complexity level of the task at hand.

optimistic explanatory style   The habitual tendency to explain bad events with attributions that are unstable and controllable.

overgeneralization   Inclusion of a nonmember of a category or class in that category or class.

participation structures   The rules that define how to participate in an activity. Such rules may be formal as well as informal.

passing scores   The scores on an assessment that one needs to obtain or exceed in order to pass the assessment.

pedagogical content knowledge   Knowledge about how to make a particular subject matter understandable to particular students.

pedagogical knowledge   Knowledge about how to teach.

penalties   Consequences for misbehavior, such as loss of privileges, time-out, or a visit to the principal's office.

perceived locus of causality   A person's understanding of whether his or her motivated action is caused by a force within the self (internal) or by some outside force (external).

percentile   A number that indicates what percentage of the national norming sample performed less well than the score in question.

perception   The meaning attached to sensory information.

performance assessment   An assessment in which students generate a product or an actual performance that reflects what they have learned.

performance goal   The intention to demonstrate competence by doing better than others.

personal space   An area where an individual feels separate from other individuals and able to be in control.

pessimistic explanatory style   The habitual tendency to explain bad events with attributions that are stable and uncontrollable.

phonological awareness   The ability to identify the specific sound units in spoken language.

phonological loop   The component of working memory that processes verbal information.

phonological similarity effect   People make more errors recalling sets of words if the words they are asked to recall are similar in sound to one another.

physiological psychology   The study of the relationship among the brain, the nervous system, and behavior.

plasticity   The brain's capacity for structural change as the result of experience.

pluralistic society   A society made up of multiple groups, each of which has important contributions to make and perspectives to contribute to the whole.

portfolio   A collection of students' work over time that allows for assessment of the development of their skills.

positive affect   The mild, subtle, everyday experience of feeling good.

positive interdependence   A condition that exists when the success of each individual depends on all group members being successful.

positive practice   Practicing the correct answer after making a mistake.

positive punisher   Any environmental event that, when taken away, decreases the frequency of a behavior.

positive reinforcer   Any environmental event that, when given, increases the frequency of a behavior.

positive transfer   Successful application of prior knowledge or skill to a new context.

possible self   A student's long-term goal representing what he or she would like to become in the future.

power assertion   A socialization strategy designed to gain compliance through coercion, pressure, forceful insistence, and a negative or critical interaction style.

PQS discourse model   Conversation during instruction in which the teacher follows a script of probe, question, and scaffold.

praise   Positive verbal feedback.

prefrontal cortex   Cortical area of the brain lying behind the forehead that is responsible for the cognitive control of action and the planning of complex behaviors.

Premack principle   Using a more preferred activity as a reward for doing a less preferred activity.

primary mental abilities   L. L. Thurstone's theory of intelligence as consisting of seven distinct abilities.

private speech   Spoken-aloud thought, especially during the engagement of a learning activity.

problem solving   An activity in which a person uses knowledge to reach a specific goal but in which there is no clearly specified way of reaching the goal.

problem-based learning (PBL)   An instructional strategy in which students work in collaborative groups to solve a complex problem that does not have a single correct answer.

procedural facilitation   A structured approach to improving students' use of elements of the writing process.

procedural knowledge   Knowledge about how to perform tasks.

procedural memory   Memory for how to do things.

products   Student creations that reflect their skills and abilities as well as their ability to create something new.

prompts   Physical, verbal, or other assists that help a person perform a desired behavior that he or she would be unlikely to perform without such assistance.

proposition   The smallest unit of knowledge that can be verified.

propositional network   A set of interconnected pieces of information that contains knowledge for the long term.

prototype   The best representative of a category.

psychological need   An inherent source of motivation that generates a proactive desire to interact with one's environment to advance personal growth, social development, and psychological well-being.

psychosocial development   A broad term to describe the quality of a person's social development as a function of past relationships in that person's life.

punisher   A consequence of behavior that weakens or decreases the behavior.

qualitative research   A research method in which the researcher collects narrative-based data, such as quotations from interviews, to understand an educational phenomenon or to answer a practical question.

ratio schedule   A schedule of reinforcement based on the number of behaviors.

rationale   A verbal explanation as to why a task is important and worth one's attention, time, and effort.

raw scores   Scores that are simple sums of the points obtained on an assessment.

recall   Information is retrieved from long-term memory.

reception learning   A type of learning in which the learner acquires the structure of knowledge set forth by the teacher.

recitation   An instructional approach where teachers ask closed-ended questions (questions with clear right answers) and students answer them.

recognition memory   Memories are cued, then recognized.

referral   Educators' shorthand for the recommendation that a child be evaluated for possible special education classification.

reflection   Thinking critically about one's task performance after receiving feedback and while constructing more advanced forethought for a future performance.

reflective teaching   Generating conjectures to explain a surprising or negative event in the teaching situation, then gathering the information needed to make a decision about what would constitute the most effective course of action to pursue.

reflective thinking   Questioning why a surprising or negative outcome occurred and then searching for the information one needs to confidently understand why it occurred.

reinforcer   A consequence of behavior that increases or strengthens behavior.

relatedness   The psychological sense of having close emotional bonds and attachments with other people.

relationship   Interaction between two people in which the actions of one person affect the thoughts, feelings, and actions of the other person and vice versa.

reliability   Consistency over an aspect of assessment, such as over time and multiple raters. In classroom assessment, having enough information about students on which to base judgments is a concern of reliability.

reliability coefficient   An index, ranging from .00 up to 1.00, of how reliable an assessment is.

reliability study   A study that is used to determine reliability coefficients.

resilient   The ability to overcome handships and setbacks.

response set   The tendency to respond to different problems in the same way.

response to intervention (RTI)   A method of providing easy, high-quality academic intervention to students at risk for school failure.

reward   Anything given in return for another person's service or achievement.

routines   Activities that occur on a regular, ongoing basis and require the same or similar behavior on each occurrence (such as sharpening pencils and going to lunch).

rubrics   Explications of the criteria for a performance assessment or an essay that include specifications for how various levels of performance are to be graded.

scaffolding   The guidance, support, and tutelage provided by a teacher during social interaction designed to advance the student's current level of skill and understanding.

scaled scores Scores from an assessment that have been transformed into an arbitrary numbering system in order to facilitate interpretation.

schema The basic cognitive structure for organizing information.

script An event schema for the sequence of events in common situations, such as ordering food at a fast-food restaurant.

Scripted Cooperation A learning strategy in which students take turns summarizing materials and criticizing the summaries.

seatwork Work that is done independently by students at their desks or seats.

self-concept Set of beliefs the individual uses to mentally represent or understand his or her sense of self.

self-efficacy One's judgment of how well one will cope with a situation, given the skills one possesses and the circumstances one faces.

self-esteem Trust applied to oneself; an attitude that one is worthy of a positive rather than a negative self-evaluation.

self-evaluation A self-judgmental process in which students compare their current performance with a hoped-for goal state.

self-handicapping A defensive self-presentation strategy that involves intentionally interfering with one's own performance so as to provide a face-saving excuse for failure in case one does indeed fail.

self-management An approach to behavioral modification where students keep a written record of their behavior in an effort to increase desirable behaviors or decrease undesirable ones.

self-monitoring A self-observational process in which students keep track of the quality of their ongoing performances.

self-regulation The deliberate planning, monitoring, and evaluating of one's academic work.

self-worth An evaluation by others of one's personal worth.

semantic memory The memory a person has for meaning.

sensory memory Brief memories associated with various senses.

serial position effect The fact that the likelihood of information being recalled varies according to its position in a list.

shaping Reinforcement of gradual approximations of the desired behavior.

short-term memory A temporary memory storage.

situational compliance Cooperatively carrying out a teacher's "do this" or "don't

do that" request with a sense of obligation rather than a sincere commitment to the action.

situational interest A topic-specific motivational state that is triggered by an external factor that produces a short-term attraction to the learning activity.

small-group work Work being done independently by a group of students smaller than the whole class.

social comparison The act of comparing one's personal characteristics, performances, and abilities to the characteristics, performances, and abilities of others.

social competence How skilled children and adolescents are at managing the often frustrating and challenging experiences they have with other people.

social contact Interaction among students.

social justice Refers to the perspective that when considering issues such as education, human rights, and the dignity of each human being should be a primary concern.

social learning theory A theory of how we learn from others.

social norms Expectations for proper behavior.

socially shared cognition A shared understanding of a problem that emerges during group interaction that would not have been achieved by any individual member of the group acting alone.

socioeconomic status Socioeconomic status has to do with one's position in the social and economic hierarchy or structure in a society.

split-half reliability A form of reliability coefficient, similar to coefficient alpha, that takes half of the items on an assessment, sums them into a score, then correlates that score with a score based on the other half of the item.

spread of activation The retrieval of bits of information on the basis of their relatedness to one another. Remembering one piece of information stimulates the recall of associated knowledge.

standard deviation A measure of how far scores vary from the mean.

standard error of measurement An index of how high or low an individual's assessment score might change on a second testing.

standard of excellence Any challenge to the student's sense of competence that ends with a success/failure interpretation.

standardized assessment A measure of student ability in which all students take the same measure under the same conditions.

standards A comprehensive set of educational objectives organized by subject matter and grade level.

standards-based assessment An assessment that is generated from a list of educational standards, usually at the state or national level; a form of standardized assessment.

stanines Short for "standard nine," scaled scores that run from 1 to 9 and have a mean of 5 and a standard deviation of 2.

status characteristics Characteristics of individuals that may signal that they have high or low status.

status differences Differences in status among individuals that influence their participation in group activities.

stem The part of a multiple-choice item that asks a question.

stereotype threat Concern about being viewed from the vantage point of a negative stereotype or acting to confirm such a stereotype.

story grammar The typical structure of a category of stories.

summative assessment Assessment designed to summarize student achievement.

supportiveness An affirmation of the other person's capacity for self-direction and contribution to help realize his or her self-set goals.

suspense A curiosity-inducing instructional strategy in which the teacher asks students to predict an outcome before students engage in the work that will reveal that their prediction was right or wrong.

symbolic schemas Language-based representations of objects and events.

syntax The structure of a language, including sentence formation rules, such as noun–verb–object.

talent The capacity to produce exceptional performance.

taxonomy A classification of objects according to a set of principles or laws.

teaching The interpersonal effort to help learners acquire knowledge, develop skill, and realize their potential.

teaching efficacy A teacher's judgment of, or confidence in, his or her capacity to cope with the teaching situation in ways that bring about desired outcomes.

technical teaching Relying on routine knowledge and tried-and-true solutions to manage classroom problems.

test bias The degree to which the scores from an assessment take on different meanings when obtained by individuals from different groups.

test blueprint A statement of what a test will comprise, often in outline form.

theory   An intellectual framework that organizes a vast amount of knowledge about a phenomenon so that educators can understand and better explain the nature of that phenomenon.

top-down processing   A type of perception in which a person uses what he or she knows about a situation to recognize patterns.

transfer   The ability to use previously learned skills or information in a new context.

transition times   Times when students are changing from one activity to the next.

triarchic   Composed of three components, each of which is at the top of a hierarchy.

true score   The hypothetical true ability of an individual on an assessment.

trust   Confidence that the other person in the relationship cares, is looking out for your welfare, and will be there when needed.

tutoring   An instructional experience in which one student typically teaches another student who is less skilled.

unattended speech effect   Verbal information automatically enters the phonological loop and can interfere with a person's verbal task performance even if that person is not paying attention to the information.

unconditioned response (UCR)   A behavior that is produced in response to a stimulus without prior learning. It is typically an automatic physiological response.

unconditioned stimulus (UCS)   A stimulus that, without prior learning, produces an automatic physiological response.

undergeneralization   The exclusion of some instances from a category or group even though they are true members of that category or group.

validation study   A research study conducted to determine whether an assessment is valid.

validity   The appropriateness of judgments about students based on assessment information. In classroom assessment, the correspondence between what an assessment measures and what was taught as part of instruction.

variability   The degree to which scores on an assessment (or other variable, such as height or weight) are spread out.

variable interval schedule   A schedule of reinforcement in which reinforcement is provided at irregular intervals based on the passage of time.

variable ratio schedule   A schedule of reinforcement in which reinforcement is provided at irregular intervals based on the number of behaviors performed.

variance   A measure of how much a set of scores is spread out.

vicarious experience   Learning from the experience of another person.

vicarious punishment   If another person is punished for a behavior, the likelihood of an observer engaging in that behavior is decreased.

vicarious reinforcement   If another person is reinforced for a behavior, the likelihood of an observer engaging in that behavior is increased.

visuospatial sketchpad   The component of working memory that processes visuospatial content.

wait time   The time between when a question is asked in a classroom and when a student is called upon to answer it.

whole-class instruction   Working on instructional material with the whole class at the same time.

within-class ability grouping   A system in which children are assigned to ability groups within a class.

word length effect   The link between memory span and the length of words to be recalled.

working memory   A limited memory system that includes both storage and manipulation functions.

zone of proximal development   A level of competence at which a student cannot yet master a task on his or her own but can accomplish it with appropriate guidance from a more capable partner.

z-score   A standard score that any set of scores can be converted to; it has a mean of 0.0 and a standard deviation of 1.0.

References

Abedi, J., Courtney, M., & Leon, S. (2003). *Effectiveness and validity of accommodations for English language learners in large-scale assessments* (CSE Report 608). Los Angeles: National Center for Research on Evaluation, Standards, and Student Testing, University of California.

Abedi, J., & Lord, C. (2001). The language factor in mathematics. *Applied Measurement in Education, 14,* 219–234.

Abrami, P.C., Chambers, B., Poulsen, C., De Simone, C., d'Appollonia, S., & Howden, J. (1995). *Classroom connections: Using and understanding cooperative learning.* Toronto: Harcourt Brace.

Adreon, D., & Stella, J. (2001). Transition to middle and high school: Increasing the success of students with Asperger syndrome. *Intervention in School and Clinic, 32,* 266–271.

Aiken, L. R. (2003). *Psychological testing and assessment* (11th ed.). Boston: Allyn & Bacon.

Ainsworth, M. D. S. (1989). Attachments beyond infancy. *American Psychologist, 44,* 709–716.

Ainsworth, M. D. S., Blehar, M. C., Waters, E., & Wall, S. (1978). *Patterns of attachment: A psychological study of the strange situation.* Hillsdale, NJ: Erlbaum.

Alexander, K. L., Entwisle, D. R., & Dauber, S. L. (1993). First-grade classroom behavior: Its short- and long-term consequences for school performance. *Child Development, 64,* 801–814.

Alexander, K. L., Entwisle, D. R., & Horsey, C. S. (1997). From first-grade forward: Early foundations of high school dropout. *Sociology of Education, 70,* 87–107.

Alexander, P. A., Jetton, T. L., & Kulikowich, J. M. (1995). Interrelationship of knowledge, interest, and recall: Assessing a model of domain learning. *Journal of Educational Psychology, 87,* 559–575.

Alexander, P. A., Kulikowich, J. M., & Jetton, T. L. (1994). The role of subject-matter knowledge and interest in the processing of linear and nonlinear text. *Review of Educational Research, 64,* 201–252.

Algozzine, B., Browder, D., Karvonen, M., Test, D. W., & Wood, W. M. (2001). Effects of interventions to promote self-determination for individuals with disabilities. *Review of Educational Research, 71,* 219–277.

Algozzine, B., Christenson, S., & Ysseldyke, J. E. (1982). Probabilities associated with the referral to placement process. *Teacher Education and Special Education, 5,* 19–23.

Allen, J. P., & Hauser, S. T. (1996). Autonomy and relatedness in adolescent-family interactions as predictors of young adults' states of mind regarding attachment. *Development and Psychopathology, 8,* 793–809.

Allen, J. P., & Land, D. (1999). Attachment in adolescence. In J. Cassidy & P. R. Shaver (Eds.), *Handbook of attachment: Theory, research, and clinical applications* (pp. 319–335). New York: Guilford.

Allen, J. P., McElhaney, K. B., Land, D. J., Kuperminc, G. P., Moore, C. W., O'Beirne-Kelly, H., & Kilmer, S. L. (2003). A secure base in adolescence: Markers of attachment security in the mother-adolescent relationship. *Child Development, 74,* 292–307.

Allen, J. P., Moore, C. W., Kuperminc, G., & Bell, K. (1998). Attachment and adolescent psychosocial functioning. *Child Development, 69,* 1406–1419.

Allen, K. P. (2010). Classroom management, bullying, and teacher practices. *Professional Educator, 34*(1), 1–15.

Allen, S. (2002). Looking for learning in visitor talk: A methodological exploration. In G. Leinhardt, K. Crowley, & K. Knutson (eds.), *Learning conversations in museums* (pp. 259–304). Mahwah, NJ: Lawrence Erlbaum.

Allen, S. (2004). Designs for learning: Studying science museum exhibits that do more than entertain. *Science Education, 88,* S17–S33.

Allinder, R. M. (1994). The relationship between efficacy and the instructional practices of special education teachers and consultants. *Teacher Education and Special Education, 17,* 86–95.

Alloy, L. B., & Seligman, M. E. P. (1979). On the cognitive component of learned helplessness and depression. *The Psychology of Learning and Motivation, 13,* 219–276.

Almog, O., & Shechtman, Z. (2007). Teachers' democratic and efficacy beliefs and styles of coping with behavioural problems of pupils with special needs. *European Journal of Special Needs Education, 22,* 115–129.

Alsaker, F., & Nagele, C. (2008). Bullying in kindergarten and prevention. In D. Pepler & W. Craig (Eds.), *Understanding and addressing bullying: An international perspective* (PREVNet Series No. 1, pp. 230–248). Bloomington, IN: AuthorHouse.

Altmaier, E. M., & Happ, D. A. (1985). Coping skills training's immunization effects against learned helplessness. *Journal of Social and Clinical Psychology, 3,* 181–189.

Alvermann, D. E., & Hayes, D. A. (1989). Classroom discussions of content area reading assignments: An intervention study. *Reading Research Quarterly, 24,* 305–335.

Alvermann, D. E., O'Brien, D. G., & Dillon, D. R. (1990). What teachers do when they say they're having discussions of content area reading assignments: A qualitative analysis. *Reading Research Quarterly, 25,* 296–322.

Al-Yagon, M., & Mikulincer, M. (2004). Socioemotional and academic adjustment among children with learning disorders: The mediational role of attachment-based factors. *Journal of Special Education, 38,* 111–123.

American Association on Intellectual and Development Disabilities (2011) Re: Definition of intellectual disability. Retrieved from http://www.aamr.org/content_100. ctm?navID=21

American Association of Museums. (2003). Museum Financial Information, 2003. Washington, DC: Author.

American Association on Mental Retardation. (2002). *Mental retardation: Definition, classification, and systems of support* (10th ed.). Washington, DC: Author.

American Psychiatric Association. (1994). *Diagnostic and statistical manual of mental disorders* (4th ed.). Washington, DC: Author.

American Psychological Association. (1999). Controversy follows psychological testing. *APA Monitor Online, 30*(11). Retrieved August 12, 2005, from http://www.apa.org/monitor/dec99/554.html

Ames, C. (1992). Achievement goals and the classroom motivational climate. *Journal of Educational Psychology, 84*, 261–271.

Ames, C. A., & Archer, J. (1988). Achievement goals in the classroom: Student learning strategies and motivational processes. *Journal of Educational Psychology, 80*, 260–267.

Anastasi, A., & Urbina, S. (1997). *Psychological testing* (7th ed.). Upper Saddle River, NJ: Prentice Hall.

Anderman, E. M., Anderman, L. H., & Griesinger, T. (1999). The relation of present and possible academic selves during early adolescence to grade point average and achievement goals. *Elementary School Journal, 100*, 3–17.

Anderman, E. M., Griesinger, T., & Westerfield, G. (1998). Motivation and cheating during early adolescence. *Journal of Educational Psychology, 90*, 84–93.

Anderman, E. M., & Maehr, M. L. (1994). Motivation and schooling in the middle grades. *Review of Educational Research, 64*, 287–309.

Anderman, E. M., & Midgley, C. (1997). Changes in achievement goal orientations, perceived academic competence, and grades across the transition to middle-level schools. *Contemporary Educational Psychology, 22*, 269–298.

Anderson, C. A. (1983). Imagination and expectation: The effect of imagining behavioral scripts on personal intentions. *Journal of Personality and Social Psychology, 45*, 293–305.

Anderson, C. A., & Bushman, B. J. (2001). Effects of violent video games on aggressive behavior, aggressive cognition, aggressive affect, physiological arousal, and prosocial behavior: A meta-analytic review of the scientific literature. *Psychological Science, 12*, 353–359.

Anderson, C. A., & Bushman, B. J. (2002). Human aggression. *Annual Review of Psychology, 53*, 27–51.

Anderson, C. A., & Dill, K. E. (2000). Video games and aggressive thoughts, feelings, and behavior in the laboratory and in life. *Journal of Personality and Social Psychology, 78*, 772–790.

Anderson, D., Lucas, K. B., & Ginns, I. S. (2000). Development of knowledge about electricity and magnetism during a visit to a science museum and related post- visit activities. *Science Education, 84*, 658–679.

Anderson, D., Lucas, K. B., & Ginns, I. S. (2003). Theoretical perspectives on learning in an informal setting. *Journal of Research in Science Teaching, 40*, 177–199.

Anderson, L. W., & Bourke, S. F. (2000). *Assessing affective characteristics in the schools.* Mahwah, NJ: Erlbaum.

Anderson, L. W., & Krathwohl (Eds.) (2001). *A taxonomy for learning, teaching, and assessing: A revision of Bloom's taxonomy of educational objectives.* New York: Longman.

Anderson, R. C., Chinn, C., Waggoner, M., & Nguyen, K. (1998). Intellectually stimulating story discussions. In J. Osborn & F. Lehr (Eds.), *Literacy for all: Issues in teaching and learning* (pp. 172–186). New York: Guilford.

Anderson, R., Greene, M., & Loewen, P. (1988). Relationships among teachers' and students' thinking skills, sense of efficacy, and student achievement. *Alberta Journal of Educational Research, 34*, 148–165.

Anderson, R. H., & Pavan, B. N. (1993). *Nongradeness: Helping it to happen.* Lancaster, PA: Technomic Publishing.

Anderson-Inman, L., & Horney, M. (1999). Electronic books: Reading and studying with supportive resources. Retrieved from http://www.readingonline.org/electronic/ebook/index.html

Andriessen, J. (2005). Collaboration in computer conferencing. In A. M. O'Donnell, C. E. Hmelo-Silver, & G. Erkens (Eds.), *Collaborative learning, reasoning, and technology* (pp. 197–231). Mahwah, NJ: Erlbaum.

Angoff, W. H. (1971). Scales, norms, and equivalent scores. In R. L. Thorndike (Ed.), *Educational measurement* (2nd ed., pp. 508–600). Washington, DC: American Council of Education.

Anning, A. (1988). Teachers' theories about children's learning. In J. Calderhead (Ed.), *Teacher's professional learning* (pp. 128–145). London: Falmer.

Antil, L. R., Jenkins, J. R., Wayne, S. K., & Vadasy, P. F. (1998). Prevalence, conceptualizations, and the relation between research and practice. *American Educational Research Journal, 35*, 419–454.

Applebee, A. N., & Langer, J. (1983). Instructional scaffolding: Reading and writing as natural language activities. *Language Arts, 60*, 168–175.

Archambault, I., Eccles, J. S., & Vida, M. N. (2010). Ability self-concepts and subjective value in literacy: Joint trajectories from grades 1 through 12. *Journal of Educational Psychology, 102*, 804–816.

Arkin, R. M., & Baumgardner, A. H. (1985). Self-handicapping. In J. Harvey & G. Weary (Eds.), *Basic issues in attribution theory and research* (pp. 169–202). New York: Academic Press.

Arnett, J. J. (2000). Emerging adulthood: A theory of development from the late teens through the twenties. *American Psychologist, 55*, 469–480.

Arnett, J. J. (2004). *Emerging adulthood: The winding road from the late teens through the twenties.* New York: Oxford University Press.

Arnett, J. J. (2007). Emerging adulthood: What is it, and what is it good for? *Child Development Perspectives, 1*, 68–73.

Aronson, E., Blaney, N., Stephan, C., Sikes, J., & Snapp, M. (1978). *The Jigsaw classroom.* Beverly Hills, CA: Sage.

Aronson, E., & Bridgeman, D. (1979). Jigsaw groups and the desegregated classroom: In pursuit of common goals. *Personality and Social Psychology Bulletin, 5*(4), 438–446.

Arreaga-Mayer, C., Terry, B. J., & Greenwood, C. R. (1998). Classwide peer tutoring. In K. Topping & S. Ehly (Eds.), *Peer-assisted learning* (pp. 105–119). Mahwah, NJ: Erlbaum.

Artzt, A. F., & Armour-Thomas, E. (1999). A cognitive model for examining teachers' instructional practices in mathematics: A guide for facilitating teacher reflection. *Educational Studies in Mathematics, 40*, 211–235.

Asan, A. (2007). Concept mapping in science class: A case study of fifth grade students. *Educational Technology & Society, v10 n1 p186-195 2007.*

Ashton, P. T., & Webb, R. B. (1986). *Making a difference: Teachers' sense of efficacy and student achievement.* New York: Longman.

Assor, A., Kaplan, H., & Roth, G. (2002). Choice is good, but relevance is excellent: Autonomy-enhancing and suppressing teaching behaviors predicting students' engagement in schoolwork. *British Journal of Educational Psychology, 27*, 261–278.

Atkinson, R. C., & Shiffrin, R. M. (1968). Human memory: A proposed system and its control processes. In K. W. Spence & J. T. Spence (Eds.), *The psychology of learning and motivation* (Vol. 2, pp. 89–195). Orlando, FL: Academic Press.

Australian Education Council. (1989). *The common and agreed national goals of schooling.* Canberra: AGPS.

Ausubel, D. P. (1961). In defense of verbal learning. *Educational Theory, 11*, 15–25.

Ausubel, D. P. (1965). A cognitive structure view of word and concept meaning. In R. C. Anderson & D. P. Ausubel (Eds.), *Readings in the psychology of cognition.* New York: Holt, Rinehart and Winston.

Ausubel, D. P., Novak, J. D., & Hanesian, H. (1978). *Educational psychology: A cognitive view* (2nd ed.). New York: Holt, Rinehart and Winston.

Ayers, W., Dorhn, B., & Ayers, R. (2001). *Zero tolerance: Resisting the drive for punishment in our schools.* New York: The New Press.

Azmitia, M. (1988). Peer interaction and problem solving: When are two heads better than one? *Child Development, 59*, 87–96.

Bacon, C. S. (1993). Student responsibility for learning. *Adolescence, 28*, 199–212.

Baddeley, A. (1990). *Human memory.* Needham Heights, MA: Allyn & Bacon.

Baddeley, A. (1993). *Using your memory: A user's guide.* London: Penguin.

Baddeley, A. (1999). *Essentials of human memory.* Hove, UK: Psychology Press.

Badian, N. A. (1998). A validation of the role of preschool phonological and orthographic skills in the prediction of reading. *Journal of Learning Disabilities, 31,* 472–481.

Baillargeon, R. (1987). Object permanence in 3½ and 4½-month-old infants. *Developmental Psychology, 23,* 655–664.

Baker, L., & Brown, A. L. (1984). Metacognitive skills and reading. In P. D. Pearson (Ed.), *Handbook of reading research* (pp. 353–394). New York: Longman.

Bakermans-Kranenburg, M. J., & Van Ijzendoorn, M. H. (2009). No reliable gender differences in attachment across the lifespan. *Behavioral and Brain Sciences, 32,* 22–23.

Balajthy, E. (2005, January/February). Text-to-speech software for helping struggling readers. *Reading Online, 8*(4). Retrieved January 3, 2005, from http://www.readingonline.org/articles/art_index.asp?HREF5balajthy2/index.html

Baldwin, J. D., & Baldwin, J. I. (1986). *Behavior principles in everyday life* (2nd ed.). Englewood Cliffs, NJ: Prentice Hall.

Bandura, A. (1965). Influence of models' reinforcement contingencies on the acquisition of imitative responses. *Journal of Personality and Social Psychology, 1,* 589–595.

Bandura, A. (1977a). Self-efficacy: Toward a unifying theory of behavioral change. *Psychological Review, 84,* 191–215.

Bandura, A. (1977b). *Social learning theory.* Englewood Cliffs, NJ: Prentice Hall.

Bandura, A. (1981). Self-referent thought: A developmental analysis of self-efficacy. In J. H. Flavell & L. Ross (Eds.), *Social cognitive development: Frontiers and possible futures* (pp. 200–239). Cambridge, UK: Cambridge University Press.

Bandura, A. (1982). Self-efficacy mechanism in human agency. *American Psychologist, 37,* 122–147.

Bandura, A. (1983). Self-efficacy mechanisms of anticipated fears and calamities. *Journal of Personality and Social Psychology, 45,* 464–469.

Bandura, A. (1986a). *The social foundations of thought and action.* Upper Saddle River, NJ: Prentice Hall.

Bandura, A. (1986b). Self-efficacy. In *Social foundations of thought and action: A social cognitive theory* (pp. 390–453). Englewood Cliffs, NJ: Prentice Hall.

Bandura, A. (1988). Self-efficacy conception of anxiety. *Anxiety Research, 1,* 77–98.

Bandura, A. (1989). Human agency in social cognitive theory. *American Psychologist, 44,* 1175–1184.

Bandura, A. (1991). Self-regulation of motivation through anticipatory and self-regulatory mechanisms. In R. A. Dienstbier (Ed.), *Nebraska symposium on motivation: Perspectives on motivation* (Vol. 38, pp. 69–164). Lincoln: University of Nebraska Press.

Bandura, A. (1993). Perceived self-efficacy in cognitive development and functioning. *Educational Psychologist, 28,* 117–148.

Bandura, A. (1997). *Self-efficacy: The exercise of control.* New York: Freeman.

Bandura, A. (2000). Exercise of human agency through collective efficacy. *Current Directions in Psychological Science, 9,* 75–78.

Bandura, A. (2002). Growing primacy of human agency in adaptation and change in the electronic era. *European Psychologist, 7,* 2–16.

Bandura, A., & Cervone, D. (1983). Self-evaluative and self-efficacy mechanisms governing the motivational effects of goal systems. *Journal of Personality and Social Psychology, 45,* 1017–1028.

Bandura, A., & Cervone, D. (1986). Differential engagement of self-reactive influences in cognitive motivation. *Organizational Behavior and Human Decision Processes, 38,* 92–113.

Bandura, A., Reese, L., & Adams, N. E. (1982). Microanalysis of action and fear arousal as a function of differential levels of perceived self-efficacy. *Journal of Personality and Social Psychology, 43,* 5–21.

Bandura, A., Taylor, C. B., Williams, S. L., Mefford, I. N., & Barchas, J. D. (1985). Catecholamine secretion as a function of perceived coping self-efficacy. *Journal of Consulting and Clinical Psychology, 53,* 406–414.

Bandura, A., & Wood, R. E. (1989). Effect of perceived controllability and performance standards on self-regulation of complex decision making. *Journal of Personality and Social Psychology, 56,* 805–814.

Banks, J. A. (1994a). *An introduction to multicultural education: Theory and practice* (3rd ed.). Boston: Allyn & Bacon.

Banks, J. A. (1994b). *Multiethnic education: Theory and practice* (3rd ed.). Boston: Allyn & Bacon.

Banks, J. A. (1994c). Transforming the mainstream curriculum. *Educational Leadership, 51,* 4–8.

Banks, J. A. (2006). *Race, culture and education: The selected works of James A. Banks.* Florence, KY: Routledge.

Banks, J. A., & McGee Banks, C. A. (2010). *Multicultural education: Issues and perspectives* (7th ed.). Hoboken, NJ: Wiley.

Barkley, R. A. (2004). Attention-deficit hyperactivity disorder and self-regulation: Taking an evolutionary perspective on executive functioning. In R. F. Baumeister & K. D. Vohs (Eds.), *Handbook of self-regulation: Research, theory, and applications* (pp. 301–323). New York: Guilford.

Barnes, J. (1985). Experience and student achievement/teacher effectiveness. In T. Husen & T. N. Postlethwaite (Eds.), *International encyclopedia of education: Research and studies* (pp. 5125–5128). Oxford, UK: Pergamon.

Barron, K. E., & Harackiewicz, J. M. (2001). Achievement goals and optimal motivation: Testing multiple goal models. *Journal of Personality and Social Psychology, 80,* 706–722.

Barone, F. J. (1997). Bullying in school: It doesn't have to happen. *Phi Delta Kappan, 79,* 80–82.

Barrett, H. (2000). Create your own electronic portfolio: Using off-the-shelf software to showcase your own student work. *Learning & Leading with Technology, 27*(7), 15–22.

Barrish, H. H., Saunders, M., & Wolf, M. M. (1969). Good Behavior Game: Effects of individual contingencies for group consequences on disruptive behavior in a classroom. *Journal of Applied Behavior Analysis, 2,* 119–124.

Barron, B. (1993). When smart groups fail. *Journal of the Learning Sciences, 12,* 307–359.

Barron, B. (2003). When smart groups fail. *The Journal of the Learning Sciences, 12,* 307–359.

Barrows, H. S., & Kelson, A. C. (1995). *Problem-based learning in secondary education and the problem-based learning institute* (Monograph 1). Springfield, IL: Problem-Based Learning Institute.

Bartholomew, K., & Horowitz, L. M. (1991). Attachment styles among young adults: A test of a four-category model. *Journal of Personality and Social Psychology, 61,* 226–244.

Bass, K. M., & Glaser, R. (2004). *Developing assessments to inform teaching and learning* (CSE Report 628). Los Angeles: Center for the Study of Evaluation, National Center for Research on Evaluation, Standards, and Student Testing.

Bassett, G. A. (1979). A study of the effects of task goal and schedule choice on work performance. *Organizational Behavior and Human Performance, 24,* 202–227.

Basque, J., & Lavoie, M. C. (2006). Collaborative concept mapping in education: Major research trends. In A. C. Cañas and J. D. Novak (Eds.), *Proceedings of the 2nd International Conference on Concept Mapping,* San José, Costa Rica.

Bateman, B. D., & Linden, M. A. (1998). *Better IEPS* (3rd ed.). Longmont, CO: Sopris West.

Battistich, V., Solomon, D., Watson, M., & Schaps, E. (1997). Caring school communities. *Educational Psychologist, 32,* 137–151.

Baumeister, R. F. (1982). A self-presentational view of social phenomenon. *Psychological Bulletin, 91,* 3–26.

Baumeister, R. F. (1986). *Identity: Cultural change and the struggle for self.* New York: Oxford University Press.

Baumeister, R. F. (1987). How the self became a problem: A psychological review of historical research. *Journal of Personality and Social Psychology, 52,* 163–176.

Baumeister, R. F., Campbell, J. D., Krueger, J. I., & Vohs, K. D. (2003). Does high self-esteem cause better performance, interpersonal success, happiness, or healthier lifestyles? *Psychological Science in the Public Interest, 4,* 1–44.

Baumeister, R., & Leary, M. R. (1995). The need to belong: Desire for interpersonal attachments as a fundamental human motivation. *Psychological Bulletin, 117,* 497–529.

Baumeister, R. F., Tice, D. M., & Hutton, D. G. (1989). Self-presentational motivations and personality differences in self-esteem. *Journal of Personality, 57,* 547–579.

Baumgardner, A. H., Lake, E. A., & Arkin, R. M. (1985). Claiming mood as a self- handicap: The influence of spoiled and unspoiled public identities. *Personality and Social Psychology Bulletin, 11,* 349–357.

Baxter, G. P., & Glaser, R. (1998). Investigating the cognitive complexity of science assessments. *Educational Measurement: Issues and Practice, 17*(3), 37–45.

Bean, T. W., & Stevens, L. P. (2002). Scaffolding reflection for preservice and inservice teachers. *Reflective Practice, 3,* 205–218.

Beane, A. L. (1999). *The bully-free classroom: Over 100 tips and strategies for teachers K–8.* Minneapolis, MN: Free Spirit.

Becker, L. J. (1978). Joint effect of feedback and goal setting on performance: A field study of residential energy conservation. *Journal of Applied Psychology, 63,* 428–433.

Beijaard, D., Meijer, P. C., & Verloop, N. (2004). Reconsidering research on teachers' professional identity. *Teaching and Teacher Education, 20,* 107–128.

Beilin, H. (1992). Piaget's enduring contribution to developmental psychology. *Developmental Psychology, 28,* 191–204.

Bell, P., & Linn, M. C. International Journal of Science Education, v. 22, n. 8, p. 797–817, Aug. 2000.

Belfiore, P. J., Browder, D. M., & Mace, C. (1994). Assessing choice making and preference in adults with profound mental retardation across community and center-based settings. *Journal of Behavioral Education, 4,* 217–225.

Belsky, J., & Cassidy, J. (1994). Attachment: Theory and evidence. In M. Rutter & D. Hay (Eds.), *Development through life: A handbook for clinicians* (pp. 373–402). Oxford, UK: Blackwell Scientific.

Benard, B. (1993). Fostering resiliency in kids. *Educational Leadership, 51,* 44–48.

Bennett, N., & Blundell, D. (1983). Quantity and quality of working rows and classroom groups. *Educational Psychology, 3,* 93–105.

Benware, C., & Deci, E. L. (1984). Quality of learning with an active versus passive motivational set. *American Educational Research Journal, 21,* 755–765.

Berg, T., & Brower, W. (1991). Teacher awareness of student alternate conceptions about rotational motion and gravity. *Journal of Research in Science Teaching, 2,* 3–18.

Bergan, J. R., & Caldwell, T. (1995). Operant techniques in school psychology. *Journal of Educational and Psychological Consultation, 6,* 103–110.

Berk, L. E., & Garvin, R. A. (1984). Development of private speech among low-income Appalachian children. *Developmental Psychology, 20,* 271–286.

Berliner, D. (1992). The nature of expertise in teaching. In F. Oser, A. Dick, & J. Patry (Eds.), *Effective and responsible teaching* (pp. 227–248). San Francisco: Jossey-Bass.

Berliner, D. (1994). Expertise: The wonders of exemplary performance. In J. Mangieri & C. Block (Eds.), *Creating powerful thinking in teachers and students* (pp. 161–186). Fort Worth, TX: Holt, Rinehart and Winston.

Berliner, D. C. (1986). In pursuit of the expert pedagogue. *Educational Researcher, 15,* 5–13.

Berliner, D. C. (1990). If the metaphor fits, why not wear it? The teacher as executive. *Theory into Practice, 29,* 85–93.

Berliner, D. C. (2001). Learning about and learning from expert teachers. *International Journal of Educational Research, 35,* 463–482.

Berliner, D. C. (2006). Educational psychology: Searching for essence throughout a century of influence. In P. A. Alexander & P. H. Winne (Eds.), *Handbook of educational psychology* (2nd ed., pp. 3–27). Mahwah, NJ: Erlbaum.

Berlyne, D. E. (1966). Curiosity and exploration. *Science, 153,* 25–33.

Berlyne, D. E. (1978). Curiosity and exploration. *Motivation and Emotion, 2,* 97–175.

Berndt, T. J. (2004). Children's friendships: Shifts over a half-century in perspectives on their development and their effects. *Merrill-Palmer Quarterly, 50,* 206–223.

Betz, N. E., & Hackett, G. (1986). Applications of self-efficacy theory to understanding career choice behavior. *Journal of Social and Clinical Psychology, 4,* 279–289.

Beyer, B. K. (1988). *Developing a thinking skills programme.* Boston: Allyn & Bacon.

Bhat, C. S. (2008). Cyber bullying: Overview and strategies for school counsellors, guidance officers, and all school personnel. *Australian Journal of Guidance and Counselling, 18*(1), 53–66.

Bialystok, E. (2001). *Bilingualism in development: Language, literacy, and cognition.* New York: Cambridge University Press.

Biehler, R. G., Snowman, J., D'Amico, M., & Schmid, R. F. (1999). *Psychology applied to teaching* (Canadian edition). Toronto: ITP Nelson Canada.

Biklen, D. (1992). *Schooling without labels: Parents, educators, and inclusive education.* Philadelphia, PA: Temple University Press.

Binet, A., & Simon, T. (1916). *The development of intelligence in children.* Baltimore, MD: Williams & Wilkins.

Birch, S. H., & Ladd, G. W. (1997). The teacher-child relationship and children's early school adjustment. *Journal of School Psychology, 35,* 61–79.

Birch, S. H., & Ladd, G. W. (1998). Children's interpersonal behaviors and the teacher-child relationship. *Developmental Psychology, 34,* 934–946.

Bjorklund, D. F. (1995). *Children's thinking: Developmental function and individual differences* (2nd ed.). Pacific Grove, CA: Brooks/Cole.

Bjorklund, D. F., Miller, P. H., Coyle, T. R., & Slawinski, J. L. (1997). Instructing children to use memory strategies: Evidence of utilization deficiencies in memory training studies. *Developmental Review, 17,* 411–441.

Blasi, A. (1980). Bridging moral cognition and moral action: A critical review of the literature. *Psychological Bulletin, 88,* 1–45.

Bloom, B. (1968). Learning for mastery. *Evaluation Comment, 1*(2), 1–5.

Bloom, B. S. (1984). The search for methods of group instruction as effective as one-to-one tutoring. *Educational Leadership, 41*(8), 4–17.

Bloom, B. S. (1985). *Developing talent in young people.* New York: Ballantine.

Bloom, B. S., Engelhart, M. D., Furst, E. J., Hill, W. H., & Krathwohl, D. R. (Eds.) (1956). *Taxonomy of educational objectives: Handbook I. Cognitive domain.* New York: David McKay.

Bloom, B. S., Hastings, J. T., & Madaus, G. F. (1971). *Handbook on formative and summative evaluation of student learning.* New York: McGraw-Hill.

Bloom, L., Margulis, C., Tinker, E., & Fujita, N. (1996). Early conversations and word learning: Contributions from child and adult. *Child Development, 67,* 3154–3175.

Boekaerts, M., & Corno, L. (2005). Self-regulation in the classroom: A perspective on assessment and intervention. *Applied Psychology: An International Review, 54,* 199–231.

Boggiano, A. K., Barrett, M., Weiher, A. W., McClelland, G. H., & Lusk, C. M. (1987). Use of the maximal-operant principle to motivate children's intrinsic interest. *Journal of Personality and Social Psychology, 53,* 866–879.

Bohn, C. M., Roehrig, A. D., & Pressley, M. (2004). The first day of school in the classrooms of two more effective and four less effective primary grade teachers. *Elementary School Journal, 104,* 269–287.

Bohrnstedt, G. W., Stecher, B. M., & Wiley, E. W. (2000). The California class size reduction evaluation: Lessons learned. In M. C. Wang & J. D. Finn (Eds.), *How small classes help teachers do their best* (pp. 201–225). Philadelphia: Temple University Center for Research in Human Development and Education.

Bonds, M., & Stoker, S. (2000). *Bully-proofing your school: A comprehensive approach for middle schools.* Longmont, CO: Sopris West.

Bondy, E., & McKenzie, J. (1999). Resilience building and social reconstructionist teaching: A first-year teacher's story. *The Elementary School Journal, 100,* 129–150.

Borich, G. D. (1988). *Effective teaching methods.* Columbus, OH: Merrill.

Bornstein, M. H., Cote, L. R., Maital, S., Painter, K., Sung-Yun, P., Pascual, L., Pecheux, M.-G., Ruel, J., Venuti, P., & Vyt, A. (2004). Cross-linguistic analysis of vocabulary in young children: Spanish, Dutch, French, Hebrew, Italian, Korean, and American English. *Child Development, 75,* 1115–1140.

Bos, C. S., & Vaughn, S. (2002). *Strategies for teaching students with learning and behavior problems.* Boston: Allyn & Bacon.

Bosma, H. A., & Kunnen, E. S. (2001). Determinants and mechanisms in ego identity development: A review and synthesis. *Developmental Review, 21,* 39–66.

Bouffard, T., Vezeau, C., & Bordelau, L. (1998). A developmental study of the relation between combined learning and performance goals and students' self-regulated learning. *British Journal of Educational Psychology, 68,* 309–319.

Bowlby, J. (1982). *Attachment and loss: Vol. 1. Attachment.* New York: Basic Books. (Original work published 1969)

Bowlby, J. (1984). *Attachment and loss: Vol. 1. Attachment* (2nd ed.). London: Penguin.

Bowlby, J. (1988). *A secure base: Clinical applications of attachment theory.* London: Routledge.

Bowles, T. (1999). Focusing on time orientation to explain adolescent self concept and academic achievement: Part II. Testing a model. *Journal of Applied Health Behavior, 1,* 1–8.

Boyer, J. B., & Baptiste, Jr., H. P. (1996). The crisis in teacher education in America: Issues of recruitment and retention of culturally different (minority) teachers. In J. Siklua (Ed.), *Handbook of research on teacher education* (2nd ed., pp. 779–794). New York: Simon & Schuster Macmillan.

Boyle, E. A., Washburn, S. G., Rosenberg, M. S., Connelly, V. J., Brinckerhoff, L. C., & Banerjee, M. (2002). Reading SLiCK with new audio texts and strategies. *Teaching Exceptional Children, 35,* 50–55.

Boz, Y., & Boz, N. (2010). The nature of the relationship between teaching concerns and sense of efficacy. *European Journal of Teacher Education, 33,* 279–291.

Brabeck, M. (1983). Moral judgment: Theory and research on differences between males and females. *Developmental Review, 3,* 274–291.

Bradley, C. L. (1997). Generativity—stagnation: Development of a status model. *Developmental Review, 17,* 262–290.

Brand, S., Felner, R., Shim, M., Seitsinger, A., & Dumas, T. (2003). Middle school improvement and reform: Development and validation of a school-level assessment of climate, cultural pluralism, and school safety. *Journal of Educational Psychology, 95,* 570–588.

Branden, N. (1984). *The six pillars of self-esteem.* New York: Bantam.

Bransford, J. D., & Stein, B. S. (1993). *The ideal problem-solver: A guide to improving thinking, learning, and creativity* (2nd ed). New York: Worth.

Brendgen, M., Wanner, B., & Vitaro, F. (2006). Verbal abuse by the teacher and child adjustment from kindergarten through grade 6. *Pediatrics, 117,* 1585–1598.

Brendgen, M., Wanner, B., Vitaro, F., Bukowski, W. M., & Tremblay, R. E. (2007). Verbal abuse by the teacher during childhood and academic, behavioral, and emotional adjustment in young adulthood. *Journal of Educational Psychology, 99,* 26–38.

Brennan, S. W., Thames, W., & Roberts, R. (1999). Mentoring with a mission. *Educational Leadership, 57*(3), 49–52.

Bretherton, I. (1990). Open communication and internal working models: Their role in the development of attachment relationships. In R. A. Thompson (Ed.), *Nebraska Symposium on Motivation: Vol. 36. Socioemotional development* (pp. 57–113). Lincoln: University of Nebraska Press.

Brewer, W. F., Chinn, C. A., & Samarapungavan, A. (2000). Explanation in scientists and children. In F. C. Keil & R. A. Wilson (Eds.), *Explanation and cognition* (pp. 279–298). Cambridge, MA: MIT Press.

Briars, D. J., & Resnick, L. (2000). *Standards, assessments—and what else? The essential elements of standards-based school improvement* (CSE Technical Report 528). Los Angeles: National Center for Research on Evaluation, Standards, and Student Testing.

Brill, J. M., Galloway, C., & Kim, B. (2001). *Cognitive apprenticeship as an instructional model.* Retrieved November 26, 2004, from http://www.coe.uga.edu/epltt/CognitiveApprenticeship.htm

Broadbent, D. E. (1958). *Perception and communication.* New York: Pergamon.

Brody, G. H., & Flor, D. L. (1998). Maternal resources, parenting practices, and child competence in rural, single-parent African-American families. *Child Development, 69,* 803–816.

Brody, G. H., & Shaffer, D. R. (1982). Contributions of parents and peers to children's moral socialization. *Developmental Review, 2,* 31–75.

Brookfield, S. D. (1995). *Becoming a critically reflective teacher.* San Francisco: Jossey-Bass.

Brookhart, S. M. (1999). Teaching about communicating assessment results and grading. *Educational Measurement: Issues and Practice, 18*(1), 5–14.

Brookhart, S. M. (2001). Successful students' formative and summative use of assessment information. *Assessment in Education, 8,* 153–169.

Brookhart, S. M. (2004). *Grading.* Upper Saddle River, NJ: Pearson Education.

Brooks, L. R. (1968). Spatial and verbal components in the act of recall. *Canadian Journal of Psychology, 22,* 349–368.

Brophy, J. (1981). Teacher praise: A functional analysis. *Review of Educational Research, 51,* 5–32.

Broudy, H. S. (1980). What do professors of education profess? *Educational Forum, 44,* 441–451.

Brown, A. (1992). Design experiments: Theoretical and methodological challenges in creating complex interventions in classroom settings. *The Journal of the Learning Sciences, 2,* 141–178.

Brown, A. C. (1992). Design experiments: Theoretical and methodological challenges in creating complex interventions in classroom settings. *Journal of the Learning Sciences, 2,* 141–178.

Brown, A. L. (1992). Designing experiments: Theoretical and methodological challenges in creating complex interventions in classroom settings. *Journal of the Learning Sciences, 2,* 141–178.

Brown, A. L., & Campione, J. C. (1994). Guided discovery in a community of learners. In K. McGilly (Ed.), *Classroom lessons: Integrating cognitive theory and classroom practice* (pp. 229–272). Cambridge, MA: MIT Press.

Brown, A. L., & Palincsar, A. S. (1989). Guided, cooperative learning, and individual knowledge acquisition. In L. B. Resnick (Ed.), *Knowing, learning, and instruction: Essays in honor of Robert Glaser* (pp. 393–451). Hillsdale, NJ: Erlbaum.

Brown, D. F. (2003). Urban teachers' use of culturally responsive management strategies. *Theory into Practice, 42,* 277–282.

Brown, G. T. L. (2004). Teachers' conceptions of assessment: Implications for policy and professional development. *Assessment in Education, 11*(3), 301–318.

Brown, R., & Pressley, M. (1994). Self-regulated reading and getting meaning from text: The transactional strategies instructional model. In D. H. Schunk & B. J. Zimmerman (Eds.), *Self-regulation of learning and performance: Issues and educational implications* (pp. 155–179). Hillsdale, NJ: Erlbaum.

Brownell, M. (1997). *Coping with stress in the special education classroom: Can individual teachers more effectively manage stress?* ERIC Digest #E545. ERIC Clearinghouse on Disabilities and Gifted Education, Reston, VA.

Bruinsma, M., & Jansen, E. P. W. A. (2010). Is the motivation to become a teacher related to pre-service teachers' intentions to remain in the profession? *European Journal of Teacher Education, 33,* 185–200.

Bruner, J. S. (1961). The act of discovery. *Harvard Educational Review, 31*, 21–32.

Bruner, J. S. (1966). *Toward a theory of instruction.* Cambridge, MA: Harvard University Press.

Bruner, J. S., Goodenow, J. J., & Austin, G. A. (1956). *A study of thinking.* New York: Wiley.

Brunetti, G. J. (2001). Why do they teach? A study of job satisfaction among long-term high school teachers. *Teacher Education Quarterly, 28*(2), 49–74.

Bruning, R. H., Schraw, G. J., & Ronning, R. R. (1999). *Cognitive psychology and instruction* (3rd ed.). Columbus, OH: Merrill.

Brunner, M., Keller, U., Dierendonck, C., Reichert, M., Ugen, S., Fischbach, A., & Martin, R. (2010). The structure of academic self-concepts revisited: The nested Marsh/Shavelson model. *Journal of Educational Psychology, 102*, 964–981.

Bryan, T., & Nelson, C. (1995). Doing homework: Perspectives of elementary and middle school students. *Journal of Learning Disabilities, 27*, 488–499.

Buck, G. H., Polloway, E. A., Smith-Thomas, A., & Cook, K. W. (2003). Prereferral intervention processes: A survey of state practices. *Exceptional Children, 69*, 349–360.

Buckner, R. L., Kelly, W. M., & Petersen, S. E. (1999). Frontal cortex contributes to human memory formation. *Nature Neuroscience, 2*, 311–314.

Budig, G. A. (2006). A perfect storm. *Phi Delta Kappan, 88*, 114–116.

Bullough, R. V. (1991). Exploring personal teaching metaphors in preservice teacher education. *Journal of Teacher Education, 42*, 43–51.

Bullough, R. V., Jr. (1989). *First year teacher: A case study.* New York: Teachers College Press.

Bullough, R. V., Jr., & Stokes, D. K. (1994). Analyzing personal teaching metaphors in preservice teacher education as a means of encouraging professional development. *American Educational Research Journal, 31*, 187–224.

Burden, P. R. (2000). *Powerful classroom management strategies: Motivating students to learn.* Thousand Oaks, CA: Corwin.

Burden, P. R. (2003). *Classroom management: Creating a successful learning community* (2nd ed.). New York: Wiley.

Burghardt, G. M. (2005). *The genesis of animal play: Testing the limits.* Cambridge, MA: MIT Press.

Burnett, P. (1999). Children's self-talk and academic self-concepts: The impact of teachers' statements. *Educational Psychology in Practice, 15*, 195–200.

Burnett, P. (2003). The impact of teacher feedback on self-talk and self-concept in reading and mathematics. *Journal of Classroom Interaction, 38*, 11–16.

Bushman, B., & Anderson, C. A. (2001). Is it time to pull the plug on the hostile versus instrumental aggression dichotomy? *Psychological Review, 108*, 273–279.

Butler, R. (2000). What learners want to know: The role of achievement goals in shaping information seeking, learning, and interest. In C. Sansone & J. M. Harackiewicz (Eds.), *Intrinsic and extrinsic motivation: The search for optimal motivation and performance* (pp. 161–194). San Diego: Academic Press.

Buxton, C. (1998). Improving the science education of English language learners: Capitalizing on educational reform. *Journal of Women and Minorities in Science and Engineering, 4*(4), 341–369.

Buzzelli, C., & Johnston, B. (2002). *The moral dimensions of teaching: Language, power, and culture in classroom interaction.* New York: Routledge Falmer.

Bylsma, W. H., Cozzarelli, C., & Sumer, N. (1997). Relation between adult attachment styles and global self-esteem. *Basic and Applied Social Psychology, 19*, 1–16.

Byrne, B. M. (1984). The general/academic self-concept nomological network: A review of construct validation research. *Review of Educational Research, 54*, 427–456.

Byrne, B. M. (1996). *Measuring self-concept across the life span: Issues and instrumentation.* Washington, DC: American Psychological Association.

Byrnes, J. P. (1988). Formal operations: A systematic reformulation. *Developmental Review, 8*, 1–22.

Byrnes, J. P. (2003). Factors predictive of mathematics achievement in white, black, and Hispanic 12th graders. *Journal of Educational Psychology, 95*, 316–326.

Cain, T., & Milovic, S. (2010). Action research as a tool of professional development of advisers and teachers in Croatia. *European Journal of Teacher Education, 33*, 19–30.

Calderhead, J. (1989). Reflective teaching and teacher education. *Teaching and Teacher Education, 5*, 43–51.

Calderhead, J., & Robson, M. (1991). Images of teaching: Student-teachers' early conceptions of classroom practice. *Teaching and Teacher Education, 7*, 1–8.

Calderon, M., Hertz-Lazarowitz, R., & Slavin, R. E. (1998). Effects of bilingual cooperative integrated reading and composition on students' making the transition from Spanish to English reading. *The Elementary School Journal, 99*, 153–165.

California Department of Education. (1998). *History-social science content standards for California public schools.* Retrieved June 2, 2005, from http://www.cde.ca.gov/re/pn/fd/documents/histsocsci-stnd.pdf

Cameron, J. (2001). Negative effects of rewards on intrinsic motivation—a limited phenomenon: Comments on Deci, Koestner, and Ryan (2001). *Review of Educational Research, 71*, 29–42.

Cantor, N., Markus, H., Niedenthal, P., & Nurius, P. (1986). On motivation and the self-concept. In R. M. Sorrentino & E. T. Higgins (Eds.), *Handbook of motivation and cognition* (Vol. 1, pp. 96–121). New York: Guilford.

Caprara, G. V., Barbaranelli, C., Borgogni, L., & Steca, P. (2003). Efficacy beliefs as determinants of teachers' job satisfaction. *Journal of Educational Psychology, 95*, 821–832.

Carbone, E. (2001). Arranging the classroom with an eye (and ear) to students with ADHD. *Teaching Exceptional Children, 34*, 72–81.

Carbonneau, N., Vallerand, R. J., Fernet, C., & Guay, F. (2008). The role of passion for teaching in intrapersonal and interpersonal outcomes. *Journal of Educational Psychology, 100*, 977–987.

Carlo, G., Fabes, R. A., Laible, D., & Kupanoff, K. (1999). Early adolescence and prosocial moral behavior. II: The role of social and contextual influences. *Journal of Early Adolescence, 19*, 133–147.

Carnevale, P. J. D., & Isen, A. M. (1986). The influence of positive affect and visual access on the discovery of integrative solutions in bilateral negotiation. *Organizational Behavior and Human Decision Processes, 37*, 1–13.

Carraher, T. N., Carraher, D. W., & Schliemann, A. D. (1995). Mathematics in the streets and in the schools. *British Journal of Developmental Psychology, 3*, 21–29.

Carter, K. (1990). Meaning and metaphor: Case knowledge in teaching. *Theory into Practice, 29*, 109–115.

Carter, R. (1998). *Mapping the mind.* Berkley: University of California Press.

Cartledge, G., & Milburn, J. F. (1996). *Cultural diversity and social skills instruction: Understanding ethnic and gender differences.* Champaign, IL: Research Press.

Carver, C. S., & Scheier, M. F. (1990). Origins and functions of positive affect: A control-process view. *Psychological Review, 97*, 19–35.

Case, R. (1992). *The mind's staircase: Exploring the conceptual underpinnings of children's thought and knowledge.* Hillsdale, NJ: Erlbaum.

Case, R., & Okamoto, Y. (1996). The role of central conceptual structures in the development of children's thought. *Monographs of the Society for Research in Child Development, 61*, No. 1–2, Serial No. 246.

Caspi, A., Henry, B., McGee, R. O., Moffitt, T. E., & Silva, P. A. (1995). Temperamental origins of child and adolescent behavior problems: From age three to age fifteen. *Child Development, 66*, 55–68.

Caspi, A., Moffitt, T. E., Newman, D. L., & Silva, P. A. (1996). Behavioral observations at age 3 predict adult psychiatric disorders. *Archives of General Psychiatry, 53*, 1033–1039.

Casteel, C. P., Isom, B. A., & Jordan, K. F. (2000). Creating confident and competent readers: Transactional strategies Instruction. *Intervention in School and Clinic, 36,* 67–77.

Cattell, R. B. (1940). A culture-free intelligence test: Part 1. *Journal of Educational Psychology, 31,* 161–179.

Cattell, R. B. (1963). Theory of fluid and crystallized intelligence: A critical experiment. *Journal of Educational Psychology, 54,* 1–22.

Cavanaugh, T. (2002). Ebooks and accommodations: Is this the future of print accommodation? *Teaching Exceptional Children, 35,* 56–61.

Cawthon, S. W. (2007). Hidden benefits and unintended consequences of No Child Left Behind policies for students who are deaf or hard of hearing. *American Educational Research Journal, 44*(3), 460–492.

Center for Adolescent and Family Studies. (1996). *Teacher talk, 2*(3), Indiana University. Retrieved March 25, 2005, from http://www.education.indiana.edu/cas/tt/v2i3/peaceful.html

Center for Research on Education, Diversity, and Excellence (CREDE). (2002). Retrieved July 6, 2005, from http://www.crede.org/standards/standards_data.html

Centers for Disease Control. (2004). *Attention-deficit/hyperactivity disorder—Symptoms of ADHD.* Retrieved October 28, 2004, from http://www.cdc.gov/ncbddd/adhd/symptom.htm

Champagne, D. (2006). Native-directed social change in Canada and the United States. *American Behavioral Scientist, 50,* 429–450. Abs.sagepub.com/cgi/reprint/50/4/428.pdf

Chapanis, A. (1965). *Man machine engineering.* Belmont, CA: Wadsworth.

Chapman, J. W., & Boersma, F. J. (1991). Assessment of learning disabled students' academic self-concepts with the PASS: Findings from 15 years of research. *Developmental Disabilities Bulletin, 19,* 81–104.

Charles, C. M. (2002). *Building classroom discipline* (7th ed.). Boston: Allyn & Bacon.

Chase, W. G., & Simon, H. A. (1973). Perception in chess. *Cognitive Psychology, 4,* 55–81.

Cheek, J. M., & Smith, L. R. (1999). Music training and mathematics achievement. *Adolescence, 34,* 759–761.

Chen, P., & Zimmerman, B. (2007). A cross-national comparison study of self-efficacy beliefs of middle-school mathematics students. *Journal of Experimental Education, 75,* 221–244.

Chen, W. (2002). Six expert and student teachers' views and implementation of constructivist teaching using a movement approach to physical education. *The Elementary School Journal, 102,* 255–272.

Cheon, S. H. (2010). *The experimental test of an intervention program to help physical education teachers better support students' autonomy, positive class functioning, and future physical activity.* Unpublished doctoral dissertation, Korea University, Seoul, Korea.

Chera, P., & Wood, C. (2003). Animated multimedia "talking books" can promote phonological awareness in children beginning to read. *Learning and Instruction, 13,* 33–52.

Chi, M. T. H., Bassok, M., Lewis, M. W., Reimann, P., & Glaser, R. (1989). Self-explanations: How students study and use examples in learning to solve problems. *Cognitive Science, 13,* 145–182.

Chi, M. T. H., de Leeuw, N., Chiu, M. H., & LaVancher, C. (1994). Eliciting self-explanations improves understanding. *Cognitive Science, 18,* 439–477.

Chi, M. T. H., Feltovich, P. J., & Glaser, R. (1981). Categorization and representation of physics problems by experts and novices. *Cognitive Science, 5,* 121–152.

Chi, M. T .H., Roy, M., & Hausmann, R. G. M. (2008). Observing tutoring collaboratively: Insights about tutoring effectiveness from vicarious learning. *Cognitive Science, 32*(2), 301–341.

Chi, M. T. H., Siler, S. A., Jeong, H., Yamauchi, T., & Hausmann, R. G. (2001). Learning from human tutoring. *Cognitive Science, 25,* 471–533.

Chiappe, P., Glaeser, B., & Ferko, D. (2007). Speech perception, vocabulary, and the development of reading skills in English among Korean- and English-speaking children. *Journal of Educational Psychology, 99,* 154–166.

Chinn, C. A., & Anderson, R. C. (1998). The structure of discussions that promote reasoning. *Teachers College Record, 100,* 315–368.

Chinn, C. A., Anderson, R. C., & Waggoner, M. A. (2001). Patterns of discourse in two kinds of literature discussion. *Reading Research Quarterly, 36,* 378–411.

Chin, C., & Osborne, J. (2010). Supporting argumentation through students' questions: Case studies in science classrooms. *Journal of the Learning Sciences, 19*(2), 230–284.

Chinn, C. A., & Brewer, W. F. (1993). The role of anomalous data in knowledge acquisition: A theoretical framework and implications for science instruction. *Review of Educational Research, 63,* 1–49.

Chinn, C. A. (2006). Learning to argue. In A. M. O'Donnell, C. E. Hmelo-Silver, & G. Erkens (Eds.), *Collaborative learning, reasoning and technology.* Mahwah, NJ: Lawrence Erlbaum.

Chinn, C. A., O'Donnell, A. M., & Jinks, T. S. (2000). The structure of discourse in collaborative learning. *Journal of Experimental Education, 69,* 77–97.

Chomsky, N. (1959). A review of B. F. Skinner's *Verbal behavior. Language, 35,* 26–129.

Chomsky, N. (1968). *Language and mind.* San Diego: Harcourt Brace Jovanovich.

Chomsky, N. (1980). Rules and representations. *Behavioral and Brain Sciences, 3,* 1–161.

Church, M. A., Elliot, A. J., & Gable, S. L. (2001). Perceptions of classroom environment, achievement goals, and achievement outcomes. *Journal of Educational Psychology, 93,* 43–54.

Cizek, G. J. (1998). *Filling in the blanks. Putting standardized testing to the test.* Washington, DC: Thomas B. Fordham Foundation.

Cizek, G. J. (1999). *Cheating on tests: How to do it, detect it, and prevent it.* Mahwah, NJ: Erlbaum.

Cizek, G. J. (2001). More unintended consequences of high-stakes testing. *Educational Measurement: Issues and Practice, 20,* 19–27.

Cizek, G. J. (2003). *Detecting and preventing classroom cheating: Promoting integrity in assessment.* Thousand Oaks, CA: Corwin.

Cizek, G. J., & Bunch, M. B. (2006). *Standard setting: A guide to establishing and evaluating performance standards.* Thousand Oaks, CA: Sage Publications.

Clarke, E. A., & Kiselica, M. S. (1997). A systemic counseling approach to the problem of bullying. *Elementary School Guidance and Counseling, 31,* 310–326.

Clarke, S. (2005). *Formative assessment in action: Weaving the elements together.* United Kingdom: Hodder Education.

Clermont, C. P., Borko, H., & Krajcik, J. S. (1994). Comparative study of the pedagogical content knowledge of experienced and novice chemical demonstrators. *Journal of Research in Science Teaching, 31,* 419–441.

Clifford, M. M. (1984). Thoughts on a theory of constructive failure. *Educational Psychologist, 19,* 108–120.

Clifford, M. M. (1988). Failure tolerance and academic risk-taking in ten- to twelve-year-old students. *British Journal of Educational Psychology, 58,* 15–27.

Clifford, M. M. (1990). Students need challenge, not easy success. *Educational Leadership, 48,* 22–26.

Cognition and Technology Group at Vanderbilt. (1997). *The Jasper Project: Lessons in curriculum, instruction, assessment, and professional development.* Mahwah, NJ: Erlbaum.

Cohen, E. G. (1982). Expectation states and interracial interactions in school settings. *Annual Review of Sociology, 8,* 209–235.

Cohen, E. G. (1994). Restructuring the classroom: Conditions for productive small groups. *Review of Educational Research, 64*(1), 1–35.

Cohen, E. G., & Lotan, R. A. (1995). Producing equal-status interactions in the heterogeneous classroom. *American Educational Research Journal, 32,* 99–120.

Cohen, E. G., & Lotan, R. A. (1997). *Working for equity in heterogeneous classrooms: Sociological theory in practice.* New York: Teachers College Press.

Cohen, E. G., Lotan, R. A., Abrams, P. L., Scarloss, B. A., & Schultz, S. E. (2002). Can groups learn? *Teachers College Record, 104,* 1045–1068.

Cohen, E. G., Lotan, R. A., Scarloss, B. A., & Arellano, A. R. (1999). Complex instruction: Equity in cooperative learning classrooms. *Theory into Practice, 38,* 80–86.

Cohen, E. G., Lotan, R. A., & Catanzarite, L. (1990). Treating status problems in the cooperative classroom. In S. Sharan (Ed.), *Cooperative learning: Theory and practice* (pp. 203–229). New York: Praeger.

Cohen, P. A., Kulick, J. A., & Kulick, C. C. (1982). Educational outcomes of tutoring: A meta-analysis of findings. *American Educational Research Journal, 19,* 237–248.

Coladarci, T. (1992). Teachers' sense of efficacy and commitment to teaching. *Journal of Experimental Education, 60,* 323–337.

Colangelo, N., & Davis, G. A. (Eds.) (2003), *Handbook of gifted education* (3rd ed.). Boston: Allyn & Bacon.

Colby, A., Kohlberg, L., Gibbs, J., & Lieberman, M. (1983). A longitudinal study of moral development. *Monographs of the Society for Research in Child Development, 48* (1–2, Serial No. 200).

Cole, M. (1990). Cognitive development and formal schooling: The evidence from cross-cultural research. In L. C. Moll (Ed.), *Vygotsky and education* (pp. 89–110). New York: Cambridge University Press.

Cole, M. (1996). *Cultural psychology: A once and future discipline.* Cambridge, MA: The Belknap Press of Harvard University Press.

Collins, A., & Brown, J. S. (1988). The computer as a tool for learning through reflection. In H. Mandl & A. Lesgold (Eds.), *Learning issues for intelligent tutoring systems* (pp. 1–18). New York: Springer-Verlag.

Collins, A., Brown, J. S., & Holum, A. (1991). Cognitive apprenticeship: Making thinking visible. *American Educator, 15*(3), 38–39.

Collins, A., Brown, J. S., & Newman, S. E. (1989). Cognitive apprenticeship: Teaching the crafts of reading, writing, and mathematics. In L. B. Resnick (Ed.), *Knowing, learning, and instruction: Essays in honor of Robert Glaser* (pp. 453–494). Hillsdale, NJ: Erlbaum.

Collins, A. M., & Quillian, M. (1969). Retrieval time from semantic memory. *Journal of Verbal Learning and Verbal Behavior, 8,* 240–247.

Collins, N. L. (1996). Working models of attachment: Implications for explanation, emotion, and behavior. *Journal of Personality and Social Psychology, 71,* 810–832.

Collins, N. L., Guichard, A. C., Ford, M. B., & Feeney, B. C. (2004). Working models of attachment: New developments and emerging themes. In W. S. Rholes & J. A. Simpson (Eds.), *Adult attachment: Theory, research, and clinical implications* (pp. 196–239). New York: Guilford.

Condry, J. (1977). Enemies of exploration: Self-initiated versus other-initiated learning. *Journal of Personality and Social Psychology, 35,* 459–475.

Conger, R. D., Conger, K. J., Elder, G. H., Jr., Lorenz, F., Simons, R., & Whitbeck, L. (1993). A family process model of economic hardship and adjustment of early adolescent girls. *Developmental Psychology, 29,* 206–219.

Connell, J. P. (1990). Context, self, and action: A motivational analysis of self-system processes across the life-span. In D. Cicchetti (Ed.), *The self in transition: From infancy to childhood* (pp. 61–97). Chicago: University of Chicago Press.

Connell, J. P., & Welborn, J. G. (1991). Competence, autonomy, and relatedness: A motivational analysis of self-system processes. In M. R. Gunnar & L. A. Sroufe (Eds.), *Self processes in development: Minnesota symposium on child psychology* (Vol. 23, pp. 167–216). Chicago: University of Chicago Press.

Connolly, J. A., & Doyle, A. (1984). Relation of social fantasy play to social competence in preschoolers. *Developmental Psychology, 20,* 797–806.

Connor, C. M., Morrison, F. J., & Slomiski, L. (2006). Preschool instruction and children's emergent literacy growth. *Journal of Educational Psychology, 98,* 665–689.

Conway, P. F., & Clark, C. M. (2003). The journey inward and outward: A re-examination of Fuller's concerns-based model of teacher development. *Teaching and Teacher Education, 19,* 465–482.

Cook, S. B., Scruggs, T. E., Mastropieri, M. A., & Casto, G. C. (1985–1986). Handicapped students as tutors. *The Journal of Special Education, 19,* 155–164.

Cook-Sather, A. (2005). *Putting student voices at the center of teacher preparation.* Paper presented at the annual meeting of the American Educational Research Association, Montreal, Canada.

Cooper, H. (2006). Research questions and research designs. In P. A. Alexander & P. H. Winne (Eds.), *Handbook of educational research* (pp. 849–877). Mahwah, NJ: Erlbaum.

Cooper, K. J., & Browder, D. M. (1998). Enhancing choice and participation for adults with severe disabilities in community-based instruction. *Journal of the Association for Persons with Severe Handicaps, 23,* 252–260.

Cordova, D. I., & Lepper, M. R. (1996). Intrinsic motivation and the process of learning: Beneficial effects of contextualization, personalization, and choice. *Journal of Educational Psychology, 88,* 715–730.

Cornelius-White, J. (2007). Learner-centered teacher student relationships are effective: A meta-analysis. *Review of Educational Research, 77*(1), 113–143.

Covington, M. (1984a). The self-worth theory of achievement motivation: Findings and implications. *Elementary School Journal, 85,* 5–20.

Covington, M. (1984b). Motivation for self-worth. In R. Ames & C. Ames (Eds.), *Research on motivation in education* (Vol. 1, pp. 77–113). New York: Academic Press.

Covington, M., & Omelich, C. L. (1979). Effort: The double-edged sword in school achievement. *Journal of Educational Psychology, 71,* 169–182.

Covington, M. V. (1992). *Making the grade: A self-worth perspective on motivation and school reform.* Cambridge, UK: Cambridge University Press.

Covington, M. V., & Mueller, K. J. (2001). Intrinsic versus extrinsic motivation: An approach/avoidance reformulation. *Educational Psychology Review, 13,* 157–176.

Craighead, W. E., Kazdin, A. E., & Mahoney, M. J. (1981). *Behavior modification: Principles, issues, and applications.* Boston: Houghton Mifflin.

Craig, S., Chi, M. T. H., & VanLehn, K. (2009). Improving classroom learning by collaboratively observing human tutoring videos while problem solving. *Journal of Educational Psychology, 101*(4), 779–789.

Craik, F. I. M., & Lockhart, R. S. (1972). Levels of processing: A framework for memory research. *Journal of Verbal Learning and Verbal Behavior, 11,* 671–684.

Craven, R. G., Marsh, H. W., & Burnett, P. (2003). Cracking the self-concept enhancement conundrum: A call and blueprint for the next generation of self-concept enhancement research. In H. W. Marsh, R. G. Craven, & D. M. McInerney (Eds.), *International advances in self-research* (pp. 91–126). Greenwich, CT: Information Age Publishing.

Cremin, L. (1988). *American education.* New York: Harper & Row.

Crick, N. B., Bigbee, M. A., & Howes, C. (1996). Gender differences in children's normative beliefs about aggression: How do I hurt thee? Let me count the ways. *Child Development, 67,* 1003–1014.

Crockenberg, S., & Lourie, A. (1996). Parents' conflict strategies with children and children's conflict strategies with peers. *Merrill-Palmer Quarterly, 42,* 495–518.

Crocker, J. (1981). Judgment of covariation by social perceivers. *Psychological Bulletin, 90,* 272–292.

Cross, L. H., & Frary, R. B. (1999). Hodgepodge grading: Endorsed by students and teachers alike. *Applied Measurement in Education, 12*(1), 53–72.

Cross, S. E., & Markus, H. R. (1994). Selfschemas, possible selves, and competent performance. *Journal of Educational Psychology, 86,* 423–438.

Csikszentmihalyi, M. (1975). *Beyond boredom and anxiety: The experience of play in work and games.* San Francisco: Jossey-Bass.

Csikszentmihalyi, M. (1982). Toward a psychology of optimal experience. *Review of Personality and Social Psychology, 3,* 13–36.

Csikszentmihalyi, M. (1988). The flow experience and its significance for human psychology. In M. Csikszentmihalyi & I. S. Csikszentmihalyi (Eds.), *Optimal experience* (pp. 15–35). Cambridge, UK: Cambridge University Press.

Csikszentmihalyi, M. (1990). *Flow: The psychology of optimal experience.* New York: Harper & Row.

Csikszentmihalyi, M., & Nakamura, J. (1989). The dynamics of intrinsic motivation: A study of adolescents. In C. Ames & R. Ames (Eds.), *Research on motivation in education* (Vol. 3, pp. 45–71). San Diego: Academic Press.

Csikszentmihalyi, M., Rathunde, K., & Whalen, S. (1993). *Talented teenagers: The roots of success and failure.* New York: Cambridge University Press.

Culbertson, J. L. (1998). Learning disabilities. In T. H. Ollendick & M. Hersen (Eds.), *Handbook of child psychopathology* (pp. 117–156). New York: Plenum.

Cummins, J. (1979). Linguistic interdependence and the educational development of bilingual children. *Review of Educational Research, 49,* 222–251.

Cummins, J. (1981). The role of primary language development in promoting educational success for language minority students. In California Department of Education, *Schooling and language minority students: A theoretical framework* (pp. 3–50). Sacramento: Author.

Cupchik (2010). *The digitized self in the internet age.* Rudolph Arnheim Award Lecture, Annual Meeting of the American Psychological Association, San Diego, August, 2010.

Curran, M. E. (2003). Linguistic diversity and classroom management. *Theory into Practice, 43,* 334–340.

Curry, L. A., Snyder, C. R., Cook, D. L., Ruby, B. C., & Rehm, M. (1997). The role of hope in student-athlete academic and sport achievement. *Journal of Personality and Social Psychology, 73,* 1257–1267.

Dalbey, J., & Linn, M. C. (1985). The demands and requirements of computer programming: A literature review. *Journal of Educational Computing Research, 1,* 253–274.

Daneman, M., & Carpenter, P. A. (1980). Individual differences in working memory and reading. *Journal of Verbal Learning and Verbal Behavior, 19,* 450–466.

Daneman, M., & Carpenter, P. A. (1983). Individual differences in integrating information between and within sentences. *Journal of Experimental Psychology: Learning, Memory, and Cognition, 9,* 561–584.

Daniels, E., & Arapostathis, M. (2005). What do they really want? Student voices and motivation research. *Urban Education, 40,* 34–59.

Danielson, C. (1997). *Performance tasks and rubrics: Upper elementary school mathematics.* Larchmont, NY: Eye on Education.

Danner, F. W., & Lonky, E. (1981). A cognitive-developmental approach to the effects of rewards on intrinsic motivation. *Child Development, 52,* 1043–1052.

Darling-Hammond, L., & McLaughlin, M. W. (1995). Policies that support professional development in an era of reform. *Phi Delta Kappan, 76,* 597–604.

Darveaux, D. X. (1984). The Good Behavior Game plus merit: Controlling disruptive behavior and improving student motivation. *School Psychology Review, 13,* 510–514.

Davidson, A. (1999). Negotiating social differences: Youth's assessments of educator's strategies. *Urban Education, 34,* 338–369.

Davies, J., & Bremer, I. (1999). Reading and mathematics attainments and self-esteem in years 2 and 6—An eight-year cross-sectional study. *Educational Studies, 25,* 145–157.

Davis, E. A., & Linn, M. C. (2000). Scaffolding students' knowledge integration: Prompts for reflection in KIE. *International Journal of Science Education, 22,* 819–837.

Davis, S. H. (2007). Bridging the gap between research and practice: What's good, what's bad, and how can one be sure? *Phi Delta Kappan, 88,* 569–578.

Day, C. (2004). *A passion for teaching.* London: Routledge Falmer.

Day, H. I. (1982). Curiosity and the interested explorer. *Performance and Instruction, 21,* 19–22.

Day, J. C. (1996). *Population projections of the United States by age, sex, race, and Hispanic origin: 1995–2050.* U. S. Bureau of the Census, Current Population Reports (P-25-1130). Washington, DC: U. S. Government Printing Office.

Deater-Deckard, K., Dodge, K. A., Bates, J. E., & Pettit, G. S. (1996). Physical discipline among African American and European American mothers: Links to children's externalizing behaviors. *Developmental Psychology, 32,* 1065–1072.

deBettencourt, L. U. (2002). Understanding the differences between IDEA and Section 504. *Teaching Exceptional Children, 34,* 16–23.

Debowski, S., Wood, R. E., & Bandura, A. (2001). Impact of guided mastery and enactive exploration on self-regulatory mechanisms and information acquisition through electronic search. *Journal of Applied Psychology, 86,* 1129–1141.

deCharms, R. (1976). *Enhancing motivation: Change in the classroom.* New York: Irvington.

Deci, E. L. (1992). The relation of interest to the motivation of behavior: A self-determination theory perspective. In K. A. Renninger, S. Hidi, & A. Krapp (Eds.), *The role of interest in learning and development* (pp. 43–70). Hillsdale, NJ: Erlbaum.

Deci, E. L. (1995). *Why we do what we do: The dynamics of personal autonomy.* New York: Penguin.

Deci, E. L. (2004). Promoting intrinsic motivation and self-determination in people with mental retardation. In H. N. Switzky (Ed.), *International review of research in mental retardation* (Vol. 28, pp. 1–29). New York: Elsevier Academic Press.

Deci, E. L., Eghrari, H., Patrick, B. C., & Leone, D. R. (1994). Facilitating internalization: The self-determination theory perspective. *Journal of Personality, 62,* 119–142.

Deci, E. L., Hodges, R., Pierson, L., & Tomassone, J. (1992). Autonomy and competence as motivational factors in students with learning disabilities and emotional handicaps. *Journal of Learning Disabilities, 25,* 457–471.

Deci, E. L., Koestner, R., & Ryan, R. M. (1999). A meta-analytic review of experiments examining the effects of extrinsic rewards on intrinsic motivation. *Psychological Bulletin, 125,* 627–668.

Deci, E. L., & Ryan, R. M. (1985). *Intrinsic motivation and self-determination in human behavior.* New York: Plenum.

Deci, E. L., & Ryan, R. M. (1987). The support of autonomy and the control of behavior. *Journal of Personality and Social Psychology, 53,* 1024–1037.

Deci, E. L., & Ryan, R. M. (1991). A motivational approach to self: Integration in personality. In R. Dienstbier (Ed.), *Nebraska symposium on motivation: Perspectives on motivation* (Vol. 38, pp. 237–288). Lincoln: University of Nebraska Press.

Deci, E. L., Ryan, R. M., & Williams, G. C. (1995). Need satisfaction and the self-regulation of learning. *Learning and Individual Differences, 8,* 165–183.

Deci, E. L., Schwartz, A., Sheinman, L., & Ryan, R. M. (1981). An instrument to assess adult's orientations toward control versus autonomy in children: Reflections on intrinsic motivation and perceived competence. *Journal of Educational Psychology, 73,* 642–650.

Deci, E. L., Vallerand, R. J., Pelletier, L. G., & Ryan, R. M. (1991). Motivation and education: The self-determination perspective. *Educational Psychologist, 26,* 325–346.

de Jong, Martin, E., Zamarro, J., Esquembre, F., Swaak, J., & van Joolingen, W. R. (1999). The integration of computer simulation and learning support: An example from the physics domain of collisions. *Journal of Research in Science Teaching, 36,* 597–615.

De La Paz, S. (2001). Teaching writing to students with attention deficit disorders and specific language impairment. *The Journal of Educational Research, 95,* 37–47.

De Lisi, R., & Golbeck, S. (1999). Implications of Piagetian theory for peer learning. In A. M. O'Donnell & A. King (Eds.), *Cognitive perspectives on peer learning* (pp. 3–37). Mahwah, NJ: Erlbaum.

De Lisi, R., & Staudt, J. (1980). Individual differences in college students' performance on formal operations tasks. *Journal of Applied Developmental Psychology, 1*, 201–208.

DeLoache, J. S. (1987). Rapid change in the symbolic functioning of very young children. *Science, 238*, 1556–1557.

DeLoache, J. S. (1991). Symbolic functioning in very young children: Understanding of pictures and models. *Child Development, 62*, 736–752.

DeLoache, J. S. (2000). Dual representation and young children's use of scale models. *Child Development, 71*, 329–338.

Delquadri, J. C., Greenwood, C. R., Whorton, D., Carta, J. J., & Hall, R. V. (1986). Classwide peer tutoring. *Exceptional Children, 52*, 535–542.

DeMontebello, P. (1998, June). *Museums in a new millennium.* Presentation to the Association of Art Museum Directors, Providence, RI.

Derry, S. J., & Potts, M. K. (1998). How tutors model students: A study of personal constructs in adaptive tutoring. *American Educational Research Journal, 35*(1), 65–99.

Deslandes, R., Royer, E., Potvin, P., & Leclerc, D. (1999). Patterns of home and school partnership for general and special education students at the secondary level. *Exceptional Children, 65*, 496–506.

Deutsch, M. (1949). A theory of cooperation and competition. *Human Relations, 2*, 129–152.

De Vries, D. L., & Edwards, K. J. (1973). Learning games and student teams: Their effects on classroom process. *American Educational Research Journal, 10*, 307–318.

Dewey, J. (1910). *How we think.* New York: D. C. Heath and Co.

Dewey, J. (1933). *How we think.* New York: D. C. Heath.

Dewey, J. (1971). *The child and the curriculum.* Chicago: University of Chicago Press.

Dewey, J. (1990). *The child and the curriculum: The school and society.* Chicago: University of Chicago Press.

De Wolff, M., & van Ijzendoorn, M. H. (1997). Sensitivity and attachment: A meta-analysis on parental antecedents of infant attachment. *Child Development, 68*, 571–591.

Diamond, K. E., Huang, H.-H., & Steed, E. A. (2010). The development of social competence in children with disabilities. In P. K. Smith & C. H. Hart (Eds.), *The Wiley-Blackwell handbook of childhood social development* (2nd ed., pp. 627–645). Hoboken, NJ: Wiley.

Diaz, R. M. (1983). Thought and two languages: The impact of bilingualism on cognitive development. In E. W. Gordon (Ed.), *Review of research in education* (Vol. 10, pp. 23–54). Washington, DC: American Educational Research Association.

Diaz, R. M. (1985). Bilingual cognitive development: Addressing three gaps in recent research. *Child Development, 56*, 1376–1388.

Dicker, M. (1990). Using action research to navigate an unfamiliar teaching assignment. *Theory into Practice, 29*, 203–208.

Diener, C. I., & Dweck, C. S. (1978). An analysis of learned helplessness: Continuous changes in performance, strategy, and achievement cognitions following failure. *Journal of Personality and Social Psychology, 36*, 451–462.

Diener, C. I., & Dweck, C. S. (1980). An analysis of learned helplessness: II. The processing of success. *Journal of Personality and Social Psychology, 39*, 940–952.

Di Lalla, L. F., Marcus, J. L., & Wright-Phillips, M. V. (2004). Longitudinal effects of preschool behavioral styles on early adolescent school performance. *Journal of School Psychology, 42*, 385–401.

Dishion, T. J., Capalsi, D. M., Spracklen, K. M., & Li, F. (1995). Peer ecology of male adolescent drug use. *Development and Psychopathology, 7*, 803–824.

Dishion, T. J., Eddy, J. M., Haas, E., Li, F., & Spracklen, K. (1997). Friendships and violent behavior during adolescence. *Social Development, 6*, 207–223.

Dishion, T. J., McCord, J., & Poulin, F. (1999). When interventions harm: Peer groups and problem behavior. *American Psychologist, 54*, 755–764.

Dishion, T. J., Spracklen, K. M., Andrews, D. W., & Patterson, G. R. (1996). Deviancy training in male adolescent friendships. *Behavior Therapy, 27*, 373–390.

Ditman, O. (2000, July/August). Online termpaper mills produce a new crop of cheaters. *Harvard Education Letter, 16*(4), 6–7.

Dolan, L. J., Kellan, S. G., Brown, C. H., Werthamer-Larsson, L., Rebok, G. W., & Mayer, L. S. (1993). The short term impact of two classroom-based preventative interventions on aggressive and shy behaviors and poor achievement. *Journal of Applied Developmental Psychology, 14*, 317–345.

Doll, B. (1996). Children without friends: Implications for practice and policy. *School Psychology Review, 25*, 165–183.

Dollinger, S. J., & Thelen, M. H. (1978). Overjustification and children's intrinsic motivation: Comparative effects of four rewards. *Journal of Personality and Social Psychology, 36*, 1259–1269.

Dong, T., Anderson, R. C., Kim, I.-H., & Li, Y. (2006). *Collaborative reasoning in Asia: Discourse mismatch reconsidered* (pp. 289–302). Champaign, IL: Center for the Study of Reading.

Donmoyer, R. (1989). Theory, practice, and the double-edged problem of idiosyncrasy. *Journal of Curriculum and Supervision, 4*, 257–270.

Doty, D. E., Popplewell, S. R., & Byers, G. O. (2001). Interactive CD-ROM storybooks and young readers' reading comprehension. *Journal of Research on Computing in Education, 33*, 374–384.

Downing, J. A. (2002). Individualized behavior contracts. *Intervention in School and Clinic, 37*, 168–172.

Doyle, W. (1986). Classroom organization and management. In M. C. Wittrock (Ed.), *Handbook of research on teaching* (pp. 392–431). New York: Macmillan.

Doyle, W. (1990). Themes in teacher education research. In W. R. Houston, M. Haberman, & J. Sikula (Eds.), *Handbook of research on teacher education* (pp. 3–23). New York: Macmillan.

Draganski, B., Gaser, C., Busch, V., Schuierer, G., Bogdahn, U., & May, A. (2004). Neuroplasticity: Changes in grey matter induced by training. *Nature, 427*, 311–312.

Drake, S. G. (1834). *Biography and history of the Indians of North America.* Boston: Perkins and Hilliard, Gray.

Dreeben, R., & Gamoran, A. (1986). Race, instruction, and learning. *American Sociological Review, 51*(5), 660–669.

Duncan, M. J., & Biddle, B. J. (1974). *The study of teaching.* New York: Holt, Rinehart and Winston.

Duncan, R. M. (1995). Piaget and Vygotsky revisited: Dialogue or assimilation? *Developmental Review, 15*, 458–472.

Dusek, J. (1980). The development of test anxiety in children. In I. Sarason (Ed.), *Test anxiety: Theory, research, and applications* (pp. 87–110). Hillsdale, NJ: Erlbaum.

Dweck, C. S. (1975). The role of expectancies and attributions in the alleviation of learned helplessness. *Journal of Personality and Social Psychology, 31*, 674–685.

Dweck, C. S. (1986). Motivational processes affecting learning. *American Psychologist, 41*, 1040–1048.

Dweck, C. S. (1990). Motivation. In R. Glaser & A. Lesgold (Eds.), *Foundations for a cognitive psychology of education.* Hillsdale, NJ: Erlbaum.

Dweck, C.S. (1999). *Self-theories: Their role in motivation, personality, and development.* Philadelphia: Psychology Press.

Dweck, C. S. (2000). *Self-theories: Their role in motivation, personality, and development.* Philadelphia: Psychology Press.

Dweck, C. S. (2002). The development of ability conceptions. In A. W. J. Eccles (Ed.), *The development of achievement motivation.* San Diego: Academic Press.

Dweck, C. S., & Leggett, E. L. (1988). A social-cognitive approach to motivation and personality. *Psychological Review, 95*, 256–273.

Dweck, C. S., & Repucci, N. D. (1973). Learned helplessness and reinforcement responsibility in children. *Journal of Personality and Social Psychology, 25*, 109–116.

Earley, P. C., Wojnaroski, P., & Prest, W. (1987). Task planning and energy expended:

Exploration of how goals influence performance. *Journal of Applied Psychology, 72,* 107–113.

Ebel, R. L. (1962). Content standard test scores. *Educational and Psychological Measurement, 22,* 15–25.

Eccles, J. S. (1993). School and family effects on the ontogeny of children's interests, self-perceptions, and activity choices. In J. E. Jacobs (Ed.), *Nebraska symposium on motivation: Developmental perspectives on motivation* (Vol. 40, pp. 145–208). Lincoln: University of Nebraska Press.

Eccles, J. S., Adler, T. F., Futterman, R., Goff, S. B., Kaczala, C. M., Meece, J. L., et al. (1983). Expectations, values and academic behaviors. In J. T. Spence (Ed.), *Achievement and achievement motivation* (pp. 75–146). San Francisco: Freeman.

Eccles, J. S., & Midgley, C. (1989). Stage/environment fit: Developmentally appropriate classrooms for early adolescents. In R. E. Ames & C. Ames (Eds.), *Research on motivation in education* (Vol. 3, pp. 139–186). New York: Academic Press.

Eccles, J. S., Midgley, C., & Adler, T. (1984). Grade-level changes in the school environment: Effects on achievement motivation. In J. G. Nicholls (Ed.), *The development of achievement motivation* (pp. 283–331). Greenwich, CT: JAI Press.

Edelson, D. C., Gordin, D., & Pea, R. (1999). Addressing the challenges of inquiry-based learning through technology and curriculum design. *The Journal of the Learning Sciences, 8,* 391–450.

Eglash, R. (1999). *African fractals: Modern computing and indigenous design.* New Brunswick, NJ: Rutgers University Press.

Eglash, R. (2005). *Culturally situated design tools: Teaching math through culture.* Retrieved July 12, 2005, from www.rpi.edu/eglash/csdt.html

Eichenbaum, H. (2002). *The cognitive neuroscience of memory.* Boston: Oxford University Press.

Eisenberg, N. (1992). *The caring child.* Cambridge, MA: Harvard University Press.

Eisenberg, N. (2000). Emotion, regulation, and moral development. *Annual Review of Psychology, 51,* 665–697.

Eisenberg, N., & Fabes, R. A. (1998). Prosocial development. In W. Daman & N. Eisenberg (Eds.), *Handbook of child psychology: Social, emotional, and personality development* (Vol. 3, pp. 701–778). New York: Wiley.

Eisenberg, N., Fabes, R. A., Bernszweig, J., Karbon, M., Poulin, R., & Hanish, L. (1993). The relation of emotionality and regulation to preschoolers' social skills and sociometric status. *Child Development, 64,* 1418–1438.

Eisenberg, N., Fabes, R. A., Shepard, S. A., Murphy, B. D., Guthrie, I. K., Jones, S., et al. (1997). Contemporaneous and longitudinal prediction of children's social functioning from regulation and emotionality. *Child Development, 68,* 642–664.

Eisenberg, N., Guthrie, I. K., Fabes, R. A., Reiser, M., Murphy, B. C., Holgren, R., Maszk, P., & Losoya, S. (1997). The relations of regulation and emotionality to resiliency and competent social functioning in elementary school children. *Child Development, 68,* 295–311.

Eisenberg, N., Lennon, R., & Roth, K. (1983). Prosocial development: A longitudinal study. *Developmental Psychology, 19,* 846–855.

Eisenberg, N., & Shell, R. (1987). Prosocial moral judgment and behavior in children: The mediating role of costs. *Personality and Social Psychology Bulletin, 12,* 426–433.

Eisenberg, N., Spinrad, T., & Sadovsky, A. (2006). Empathy-related responding in children. In M. Killen & J. G. Smetana (Eds.), *Handbook of moral development* (pp. 517–550). Mahwah, NJ: Erlbaum.

Elawar, M. C., & Corno, L. (1985). A factorial experiment in teachers' written feedback on student homework: Changing teacher behavior a little rather than a lot. *Journal of Educational Psychology, 77*(2), 162–173.

Elbaum, B., Moody, S. W., & Schumm, J. S. (1999). Mixed ability grouping for reading: What students think. *Learning Disabilities Research and Practice, 14,* 61–66.

Elbert, T., Pantev, C., Wienbruch, C., Rockstroh, B., & Taub, E. (1995). Increased cortical representation of the fingers of the left hand in string players. *Science, 270,* 305–307.

Elliot, A. J. (1999). Approach and avoidance motivation and achievement goals. *Educational Psychologist, 34,* 169–189.

Elliot, A. J. (2005). A conceptual history of the achievement goal construct. In A. Elliot & C. Dweck (Eds.), *Handbook of competence and motivation* (pp. 52–72). New York: Guilford.

Elliot, A. J., & Church, M. A. (1997). A hierarchical model of approach and avoidance achievement motivation. *Journal of Personality and Social Psychology, 72,* 218–232.

Elliot, E., & Dweck, C. (1988). Goals: An approach to motivation and achievement. *Journal of Personality and Social Psychology, 54,* 5–12.

Elliot, A. J., & Harackiewicz, J. (1996). Approach and avoidance goals and intrinsic motivation: A mediational analysis. *Journal of Personality and Social Psychology, 70,* 461–475.

Elliot, A. J., & McGregor, H. (2001). Test anxiety and the hierarchical model of approach and avoidance achievement motivation. *Journal of Personality and Social Psychology, 76,* 628–644.

Elliot, A. J., McGregor, H. A., & Gable, S. L. (1999). Achievement goals, study strategies, and exam performance: A meditational analysis. *Journal of Educational Psychology, 91,* 549–563.

Elliot, A. J., & Murayama, K. (2008). On the measurement of achievement goals: Critique, illustration, and application. *Journal of Educational Psychology, 100,* 613–628.

Elliot, A. J., & Thrash, T. M. (2002). Approach-avoidance motivation in personality: Approach and avoidance temperaments and goals. *Journal of Personality and Social Psychology, 82,* 804–818.

Ellis, N. C., & Hellelley, R. A. (1980). A bilingual word-length effect: Implications for intelligence testing and the relative ease of mental calculation in Welsh and English. *British Journal of Psychology, 71,* 43–52.

Emmer, E. T., Evertson, C. M., & Anderson, L. (1980). Effective classroom management at the beginning of the school year. *The Elementary School Journal, 80*(5), 219–231.

Endresen, I. M., & Olweus, D. (2002). Self-reported empathy in Norwegian adolescents: Sex differences, age trends, and relationships to bullying. In A. C. Bohart & D. J. Stipek (Eds.), *Constructive and destructive behavior: Implications for family, school, and society* (pp. 147–165). Washington, DC: American Psychological Association.

Ennemoser, M., & Schneider, W. (2007). Relations of television viewing and reading: Findings from a 4-year longitudinal study. *Journal of Educational Psychology, 99,* 349–368.

Epstein, R. L. (2006). *Critical thinking.* Belmont, CA: Wadsworth Thomas Learning.

Erez, M. (1977). Feedback: A necessary condition for the goal setting performance relationship. *Journal of Applied Psychology, 62,* 624–627.

Erez, M., & Kanfer, F. H. (1983). The role of goal acceptance in goal setting and task performance. *Academy of Management Review, 8,* 454–463.

Erez, M., & Zidon, I. (1984). Effects of goal acceptance on the relationship to goal difficulty and performance. *Journal of Applied Psychology, 60,* 69–78.

Ericsson, K. A. (1998). Basic capacities can be modified or circumvented by deliberate practice: A rejection of talent accounts of expert performance. *Behavioral and Brain Sciences, 21,* 413–414.

Ericsson, K. A., & Charness, N. (1994). Expert performance: Its structure and acquisition. *American Psychologist, 49,* 725–747.

Ericsson, K. A., Krampe, R. T. C., & Tesch-Romer, C. (1993). The role of deliberate practice in the acquisition of expert performance. *Psychological Review, 100,* 363–406.

Erikson, E. H. (1959). Identity and the life cycle. *Psychological Issues, 1,* 1–171.

Erikson, E. H. (1963). *Childhood and society* (2nd ed.). New York: Norton.

Erikson, E. H. (1964). *Insight and responsibility.* New York: Norton.

Erikson, E. H. (1968). *Identity, youth, and crisis.* New York: Norton.

Erikson, E. H. (1982). *The life cycle completed.* New York: Norton.

Erkens, G., Prangsma, M., & Jaspers, J. (2005). Planning and coordinating activities in collaborative learning. In A. M. O'Donnell, C. E. Hmelo-Silver, & G. Erkens (Eds.), *Collaborative learning, reasoning, and technology* (pp. 233–263). Mahwah, NJ: Erlbaum.

Errington, E. (2004). The impact of teacher beliefs on flexible learning innovation: Some practices and possibilities for academic developers. *Innovations in Education and Teaching International, 41,* 39–47.

Escudero, J., Kim, Y., McGrath, M., Odabasi, P., So, E., & Vera, F. (2002). *What cues cause off-task students to get back on task?* Unpublished manuscript, Rutgers University, New Brunswick, NJ.

Espelage, D. L., & Swearer, S. M. (2004). *Bullying in American schools: A social-ecological perspective on prevention and intervention.* Mahwah, NJ: Erlbaum.

eTeachers. (2005). *The Chinese cultural revolution WebQuest.* Retrieved May 8, 2005, from http://www.eteachers.com.au/samples/int/sec/china/studyroom/6cultrev/webcultural.htm

Evans, E. D., & Craig, D. (1990). Teacher and student perceptions of academic cheating in middle and senior high schools. *Journal of Educational Research, 84,* 44–52.

Evans, E. D., & Tribble, M. (1986). Perceived teaching problems, self-efficacy and commitment to teaching among preservice teachers. *Journal of Educational Research, 80,* 81–85.

Evertson, C., & Harris, A. (2003). *Classroom organization and management program (COMP): Creating conditions for learning.* Nashville, TN: Vanderbilt University Press.

Evertson, C. M., & Weinstein, C. S. (2006). *Handbook of classroom management: Research, practice, and contemporary issues.* Mahwah, NJ: Erlbaum.

Falk, J. H., & Dierking, L. D. (2002). *Learning without limits: How free-choice learning is transforming education.* Walnut Creek, CA: AltaMira Press.

Family Educational Rights and Privacy Act of 1974. Retrieved April 10, 2005, from http://www.ed.gov/policy/gen/guid/fpco/ferpa/index.html

Fancher, R. E. (1985). *The intelligence men: Makers of the IQ controversy.* New York: Norton.

Fantuzzo, J. W., Davis, G. Y., & Ginsberg, M. D. (1995). Effects of parent involvement in isolation or in combination with peer tutoring on student self–concept and mathematics achievement. *Journal of Educational Psychology, 87,* 272–281.

Fantuzzo, J. W., Polite, K., & Grayson, N. (1990). An evaluation of reciprocal peer tutoring across elementary school settings.

Journal of School Psychology, 28(4), 309–323. doi:10.1016/0022-4405(90)90021-X

Fantuzzo, J. W., King, J. A., & Heller, L. R. (1992). Effects of reciprocal peer tutoring on mathematics and school adjustment. *Journal of Educational Psychology, 84,* 331–339.

Feldt, L. S., & Brennan, R. L. (1989). Reliability. In R. L. Linn (Ed.), *Educational measurement* (3rd ed.). New York: Macmillan.

Feng, H. (1996). Social skill assessment of inner city Asian, African, and European American students. *Social Psychology Review, 25,* 228–239.

Ferguson, T. J., Stegge, H., & Damhuis, I. (1991). Children's understanding of guilt and shame. *Child Development, 62,* 827–839

Finn, J. D., Pannozzo, G. M., & Achilles, C. M. (2003). The "why's" of class size: Student behavior in small classes. *Review of Educational Research, 73,* 321–368.

Finn, J. D., & Rock, D. A. (1997). Academic success among students at risk for school failure. *Journal of Applied Psychology, 82,* 221–234.

Fischer, K.W. (1980). A theory of cognitive development: The control and construction of hierarchies of skills. *Psychological Review, 87,* 477–531.

Fischer, K. W., Kenny, S. L., & Pipp, S. L. (1990). How cognitive processes and environmental conditions organize discontinuities in the development of abstractions. In C. N. Alexander & E. J. Langer (Eds.), *Higher stages of human development: Perspectives on adult growth.* New York: Oxford University Press.

Fischer, K. W., & Rose, S. P. (1995, Fall). Concurrent cycles in the dynamic development of the brain and behavior. *SRCD Newsletter,* pp. 3–4, 15–16.

Fish, S. (1980). *Is there a text in this class? The authority of interpretive communities.* Cambridge, MA: Harvard University Press.

Fisher, C., Wallace, S., & Fenton, R. (2000). Discrimination distress during adolescence. *Journal of Youth and Adolescence, 29,* 679–694.

Fiske, S. T. (2004). Mind the gap: In praise of informal sources of formal thinking. *Personality and Social Psychology Review, 8,* 132–137.

Fitzpatrick, H., & Hardman, M. (2000). Mediated activity in the primary classroom: Girls, boys, and computers. *Learning and Instruction, 10,* 431–446.

Flavell, J. (1976). Metacognitive aspects of problem-solving. In L. B. Resnick (Ed.), *The nature of intelligence.* Hillsdale, NJ: Erlbaum.

Flavell, J. H., Miller, P. H., & Miller, S. A. (1993). *Cognitive development* (3rd ed.). Englewood Cliffs, NJ: Prentice Hall.

Floden, R. E., & Clark, C. M. (1988). Preparing teachers for uncertainty. *Teachers College Record, 89,* 505–524.

Flowerday, T., & Schraw, G. (2000). Teacher beliefs about instructional choice: A phenomenological study. *Journal of Educational Psychology, 92,* 634–645.

Flowerday, T., Schraw, G., & Stevens, J. (2004). The role of choice and interest in reader engagement. *Journal of Experimental Education, 72,* 93–114.

Forsyth, D. R., & Kerr, N. A. (1999). *Are adaptive illusions adaptive?* Poster presented at the annual meeting of the American Psychological Association, Boston, MA.

Fox, B. A. (1988). *Interaction as a diagnostic resource in tutoring* (Technical Report No. 88-3). Boulder, CO: University of Colorado, Institute of Cognitive Science.

Fox, S. E., Levitt, P., & Nelson, C. A., III. (2010). How the timing and quality of early experiences influence the development of brain architecture. *Child Development, 81,* 28–40.

Francis, W. S. (1999). Cognitive integration of language and memory in bilinguals: Semantic representation. *Psychological Bulletin, 125,* 193–222.

Fredricks, J. A., Blumenfeld, P. C., & Paris, A. H. (2004). School engagement: Potential of the concept, state of the evidence. *Review of Educational Research, 74,* 59–109.

Fredrickson, B. L. (2001). The role of positive emotions in positive psychology: The broaden-and-build theory of positive emotions. *American Psychologist, 56,* 218–226.

Fuchs, L. S., & Fuchs, D. (1998). General educator's instructional adaptation for students with learning disabilities. *Learning Disabilities Quarterly, 21,* 23–33.

Fuchs, L. S., Fuchs, D., Karns, K., Hamlett, C., Katzaroff, M., & Dutka, S. (1997). Effects of task-focused goals on low-achieving students with and without learning disabilities. *American Educational Research Journal, 34,* 513–543.

Fuchs, D., Fuchs, L. S., Mathes, P. G., & Martinez, E. A. (2002). Preliminary evidence on the social standing of students with learning disabilities in PALS and no-PALS classrooms. *Learning Disabilities Research, 17,* 205–215.

Fuchs, D., Fuchs, L. S., Mathes, P. G., & Simmons, D. C. (1997). Peer-assisted learning strategies: Making classrooms more responsive to academic diversity. *American Educational Research Journal, 34,* 174–206.

Fuchs, L. S., Fuchs, D., Yazdian, L., & Powell, S. R. (2002). Enhancing first-grade children's mathematical development with peer-assisted learning strategies. *School Psychology Review, 31,* 569–583.

Fulk, B. M., & King, K. (2001). Classwide peer tutoring at work. *Teaching Exceptional Children, 34*(2), 49–53.

Fuller, F. F., & Brown, O. H. (1975). Becoming a teacher. In K. Ryan (Ed.), *Teacher education.* Chicago: University of Chicago Press.

Furlong, J., & Sainsbury, J. (2005). Best practice research scholarships: An evaluation. *Research Papers in Education, 20*, 45–83.

Furrer, C., & Skinner, E. A. (2003). Sense of relatedness as a factor in children's academic engagement and performance. *Journal of Educational Psychology, 95*, 148–162.

Fuster, J. M. (2008). *The prefrontal cortex* (4th ed.). San Diego: Academic Press.

Gagné, E. D., Yekovich, C. W., & Yekovich, F. R. (1993). *The cognitive psychology of school learning* (2nd ed.). Boston: Little, Brown.

Gallagher, J. M., & Easley, J. A., Jr. (1978). *Knowledge and development: Piaget and education* (Vol. 2). New York: Plenum.

Gallagher, K. C. (2002). Temperament and parenting style—adjustment. *Developmental Review, 22*, 623–643.

Galton, F. (1869). *Hereditary genius*. New York: Macmillan.

Gamoran, A. (1987). Organization, instruction, and the effects of ability grouping: Comment on Slavin's best evidence synthesis. *Review of Educational Research, 57*, 341–345.

Gamoran, A., & Mare, R. D. (1989). Secondary school tracking and educational inequality: Compensation, reinforcement, or neutrality. *American Journal of Sociology, 94*, 1146–1183.

García, E. E. (1999). Attributes of effective schools for language minority students. *Education and Urban Society, 20*, 387–398.

Gardner, H. (1985). *Frames of mind*. New York: Basic Books.

Gardner, H. (1993). *Multiple intelligences: The theory in practice*. New York: Basic Books.

Gardner, H. (1995). Reflections on multiple intelligences. *Phi Delta Kappan, 77*, 200–208.

Gardner, H. (1998). Are there additional intelligences? The case for naturalist, spiritual, and existential intelligences. In J. Kane (Ed.), *Education, information, and transformation* (pp. 111–131). Upper Saddle River, NJ: Merrill/Prentice Hall.

Gardner, H. (1999). *Intelligence reframed: Multiple intelligences for the 21st century*. New York: Basic Books.

Gardner, H. (2003). *Multiple intelligences after twenty years*. Paper presented at the annual meeting of the American Educational Research Association, Chicago.

Garlick, D. (2002). Understanding the nature of the general factor of intelligence: The role of individual differences in neural plasticity as an explanatory mechanism. *Psychological Review, 109*, 116–136.

Gauvain, M., & Rogoff, B. (1989). Collaborative problem solving and children's planning skills. *Developmental Psychology, 25*, 139–151.

Gay, G. (2003). The importance of multicultural education. *Educational Leadership, 61*(4), 30–35.

Gazzaniga, M. S., & Heatherton, T. F. (2003). *Psychological Science*. New York: Norton.

Gearhart, M., & Osmundson, E. (2009). Assessment portfolios as opportunities for teacher learning. *Educational Assessment, 14*(1), 1–24.

Golaheiser, L. M. (1990). Reducing the number of students identified as learning disabled: A question of practice, philosophy, or policy? In S. B. Sigmon (Ed.), *Critical voices in special education: Problems and progress concerning the mildly handicapped* (pp. 43–50). Albany, NY: State University of New York Press.

Gendolla, G. H. E. (1997). Surprise in the context of achievement: The role of outcome valence and importance. *Motivation and Emotion, 21*, 165–193.

Gershoff, E. T. (2002a). Corporal punishment by parents and associated child behaviors and experiences: A meta-analytical and theoretical review. *Psychological Bulletin, 128*, 539–579.

Gershoff, E. T. (2002b). Corporal punishment, physical abuse, and the burden of proof: Reply to Baumrind, Larzelere, and Cowan (2002), Holden (2002), and Parke (2002). *Psychological Bulletin, 128*, 602–611.

Gersten, R., & Vaughn, S. (2001). Meta- analyses in learning disabilities: Introduction to the special issue. *Elementary School Journal, 101*, 247–249.

Gettman, D. (1987). *Basic Montessori*. New York: St. Martin's Press.

Ghera, M., Marshall, P., Fox, N., Zeanah, C., Nelson, C. A., & Smyke, A. (2009). Social deprivation and young institutionalized children's attention and expression of positive affect: Effects of a foster care intervention. *Journal of Child Psychology and Psychiatry, 50*, 253–256.

Gibbon, F. X., Benbow, C. P., & Gerrard, M. (1994). From top dog to bottom half: Social comparison strategies in response to poor performance. *Journal of Personality and Social Psychology, 67*, 638–652.

Gibson, E. J. (1988). Exploratory behavior in the development of perceiving, acting, and the acquiring of knowledge. *Annual Review of Psychology, 39*, 1–41.

Gibson, S., & Dembo, M. H. (1984). Teacher efficacy: A construct validation. *Journal of Educational Psychology, 76*, 569–582.

Gilligan, C. (1993). *In a different voice: Psychological theory and women's development*. Cambridge, MA: Harvard University Press.

Gini, G., Pozzoli, T., Borghi, F., & Franzoni, L. (2008). The role of bystanders in students' perception of bullying and sense of safety. *Journal of School Psychology, 46*, 617–638.

Ginsburg, H. J., & Opper, S. (1988). *Piaget's theory of intellectual development* (3rd ed.). Englewood Cliffs, NJ: Prentice Hall.

Ginsburg-Block, M., & Fantuzzo, J. W. (1997). Reciprocal peer tutoring: An analysis of "teacher" and "student" interactions as a function of training and experience. *School Psychology Quarterly, 12*, 134–149.

Gladstone, G. L., Parker, G. B., & Malhi, G. S. (2006). Do bullied children become anxious and depressed adults?: A cross-sectional investigation of the correlates of bullying and anxious depression. *Journal of Nervous and Mental Disease, 194*, 201–208.

Glaser, R. (1963). Instructional technology and the measurement of learning outcomes. *American Psychologist, 18*, 519–522.

Glaser, R. (1968). Adapting the elementary school curriculum to individual performances. *Proceedings of the 1967 Invitational Conference on Testing Problems 3–36*. Princeton, NJ: Educational Testing Service.

Glassman, M. (1994). All things being equal: The two roads of Piaget and Vygotsky. *Developmental Review, 14*, 186–214.

Gick, M. L., & Holyoak, K. J. (1980). Analogical problem solving. *Cognitive Psychology 12*, 306–355.

Glickman, C., & Tamashiro, R. (1982). A comparison of first-year, fifth-year, and former teachers on efficacy, ego development, and problem solving. *Psychology in Schools, 19*, 558–562.

Glover, D., Gough, G., Johnson, M., & Cartwright, N. (2000). Bullying in 25 secondary schools: Incidence, impact and intervention. *Educational Research, 42*, 141–156.

Goddard, H. H. (1920). *Human efficiency and levels of intelligence*. Princeton, NJ: Princeton University Press.

Goddard, R. D., Hoy, W. K., & Woolfolk Hoy, A. (2000). Collective teacher efficacy: Its meaning, measure, and impact on student achievement. *American Educational Research Journal, 37*, 479–507.

Golan, R., Kyza, E. A., Reiser, B. J., & Edelson, D. C. (2001, March). *Structuring the task of behavioral analysis with software scaffolds*. Paper presented at the annual meeting of the National Association for Research on Science Teaching, St. Louis.

Gollnick, D . M ., & Chinn, P . C .(2009). *Multicultural education in a pluralistic society*. Upper Saddle River, NJ: Pearson Prentice Hall.

Gollwitzer, P. M. (1996). The volitional benefits of planning. In P. M. Gollwitzer & J. A. Bargh (Eds.), *The psychology of action: Linking cognition and emotion to behavior* (pp. 287–312). New York: Guilford.

Gollwitzer, P. M. (1999). Implementation intentions: Strong effects of simple plans. *American Psychologist, 54*, 493–503.

Gollwitzer, P. M., & Moskowitz, G. B. (1996). Goal effects on action and cognition. In E. T. Higgins & A. W. Kruglanski (Eds.), *Social psychology: Handbook of basic principles* (pp. 361–399). New York: Guilford.

Gondoli, D. M., & Silverberg, S. B. (1997). Maternal emotional distress and diminished responsiveness: The mediating role of parenting efficacy and parental perspective taking. *Developmental Psychology, 33,* 861–868.

Gonzalez, L. E., & Carter, K. (1996). Correspondence in cooperating teachers' and student teachers' interpretations of classroom events. *Teaching and Teacher Education, 12,* 39–47.

Good, T. L., & Brophy, J. E. (1997). *Looking into classrooms.* New York: Addison-Wesley.

Good, T. L., & Brophy, J. E. (2000). *Looking in classrooms* (8th ed.). New York: Longman.

Good, T. L., Slavings, R., Harel, K., & Emerson, H. (1987). Student passivity: A study of question-asking in K–12 classrooms. *Sociology of Education, 60,* 181–199.

Goodenow, C. (1993). Classroom belongingness among early adolescent students: Relationship to motivation and achievement. *Journal of Early Adolescence, 13,* 21–43.

Goodenow, C., & Grady, K. E. (1993). The relationship of school belonging and friends' values to academic motivation among urban adolescent students. *Journal of Experimental Education, 62,* 60–71.

Gopnik, A. (1984). The acquisition of *gone* and the development of the object concept. *Journal of Child Language, 11,* 273–292.

Goswami, U. (2011). Inductive and deductive reasoning. In U. Goswami (Ed.), *The Wiley-Blackwell handbook of childhood cognitive development* (2nd ed., pp. 399–419). Hoboken, NJ: Wiley-Blackwell.

Gottfried, A. E. (1985). Academic intrinsic motivation in elementary and junior high school students. *Journal of Educational Psychology, 77,* 631–645.

Gottfried, A. E. (1990). Academic intrinsic motivation in young elementary school children. *Journal of Educational Psychology, 82,* 525–538.

Gould, S. J. (1981). *The mismeasure of man.* New York: Norton.

Graesser, A. C., & Person, N. (1994). Question-asking during tutoring. *American Educational Research Journal, 31,* 104–137.

Graesser, A. C., Person, N., & Magliano, J. (1995). Collaborative dialog patterns in naturalistic one-on-one tutoring. *Applied Cognitive Psychology, 9,* 359–387.

Graham, S., Bellmore, S., & Mize, J. (2006). Aggression, victimization and their cooccurrence in middle school. *Journal of Abnormal Child Psychology, 34,* 349–364.

Grant, C. A., & Sleeter, C. E. (2009). *Turning on learning: Five approaches for multicultural teaching plans for race, class, gender, and disability* (5th Ed.) Hoboken, NJ: John Wiley and Sons, Inc.

Gratz, D. (2000). High standards for whom? *Phi Delta Kappan, 81,* 681–687.

Gravetter, F. J., & Wallnau, L. B. (2004). *Statistics for the behavioral sciences.* Belmont, CA: Wadsworth/Thompson Learning.

Gray, J. A. (1990). Brain systems that mediate both emotion and cognition. *Cognition and Emotion, 4,* 269–288.

Gray, W. M., & Hudson, L. M. (1984). Formal operations and the imaginary audience. *Developmental Psychology, 20,* 619–627.

Green, K. E. (1991). *Educational testing: Issues and applications.* New York: Garland.

Green, S. K., & Gredler, M. E. (2002). A review and analysis of constructivism for school-based practice. *School Psychology Review, 31,* 53–70.

Green, T. (1971). *The activities of teaching.* New York: McGraw-Hill.

Greene, B. A., & Miller, R. B. (1996). Influences on achievement: Goals, perceived ability, and cognitive engagement. *Contemporary Educational Psychology, 21,* 181–192.

Greene, D., & Lepper, M. R. (1974). Effects of extrinsic rewards on children's subsequent intrinsic interest. *Child Development, 45,* 1141–1145.

Greenfield, P. M., Keller, H., Fuligni, A., & Maynard, A. (2003). Cultural pathways through universal development. *Annual Review of Psychology, 54,* 461–490.

Greenough, W. T., & Black, J. E. (1992). Induction of brain structure by experience: Substrates for cognitive development. In M. R. Gunnar & C. A. Nelson (Eds.), *Minnesota symposia on child psychology: Developmental neuroscience* (Vol. 24, pp. 155–200). Hillsdale, NJ: Erlbaum.

Greenough, W. T., Black, J. E., & Wallace, C. S. (1987). Experience and brain development. *Child Development, 58,* 539–559.

Greenwood, C. R., Arreaga-Mayer, C., Utley, C. A., Gavin, K. M., & Terry, B. J. (2001). Class-wide peer tutoring learning management system. *Remedial and Special Education, 22,* 34–47.

Greenwood, C. R., Carta, J. J., & Kamps, D. (1990). Teacher versus peer-mediated instruction. In H. Foot, M. Morgan, & R. Shute (Eds.), *Children helping children* (pp. 177–206). London: Wiley.

Greenwood, C. R., Delquadri, J. C., & Hall, R. V. (1989). Longitudinal effects of classwide peer tutoring. *Journal of Educational Psychology, 81,* 371–383.

Greenwood, C. R., Finney, R., Terry, B., & Arreaga-Mayer, C. (1993). Monitoring, improving, and maintaining quality implementation of the classwide peer tutoring program using behavioral and computer technology. *Education and Treatment of Children, 16,* 19–47.

Greenwood, C. R., Maheady, L., & Carta, J. J. (1991). Peer tutoring programs in the regular classroom. In G. Stoner, M. R. Shinn, & H. M. Walker (Eds.), *Intervention for achievement and behavior programs* (pp. 179–200). Washington, DC: National Association of School Psychologists.

Greenwood, C. R., & Terry, B. (1993). Achievement, placement, and services: Middle school benefits of classwide peer tutoring used at the elementary school. *School Psychology Review, 22,* 497–516.

Grolnick, W. S. (2003). *The psychology of parental control: How well-meant parenting backfires.* Mahwah, NJ: Erlbaum.

Grolnick, W. S., Deci, E. L., & Ryan, R. M. (1997). Internalization within the family: The self-determination perspective. In J. E. Grusec & L. Kuczynski (Eds.), *Parenting and children's internalization of values: A handbook of contemporary theory* (pp. 135–161). New York: Wiley.

Grolnick, W. S., & Ryan, R. M. (1987). Autonomy in children's learning: An experimental and individual differences investigation. *Journal of Personality and Social Psychology, 52,* 890–898.

Grosjean, F. (1992). Another view of bilingualism. In R. Harris (Ed.), *Cognitive processing in bilinguals* (pp. 51–62). Amsterdam: Elsevier.

Grotevant, H. D. (1987). Toward a process model of identity formation. *Journal of Adolescent Research, 2,* 203–222.

Grusec, J. E. (1997). A history of research on parenting strategies and children's internalization of values. In J. E. Grusec & L. Kuczynski (Eds.), *Parenting and children's internalization of values: A handbook of contemporary theory* (pp. 3–22). New York: Wiley.

Grusec, J. E., & Goodnow, J. J. (1994). The impact of parental discipline methods on the child's internalization of values: A reconceptualization of the current points of view. *Developmental Psychology, 30,* 4–19.

Guay, F., Ratelle, C. F., & Chanal, J. (2008). Optimal learning in optimal contexts: The role of self-determination in education. *Canadian Psychology, 49,* 233–240.

Guercio, R. D. (2011). Back to the basics of classroom management. *Education Digest, 76*(5), 39–43.

Guskey, T., & Gates, S. (1986). Synthesis of research on the effects of mastery learning in elementary and secondary classrooms. *Educational Leadership, 43,* 73–80.

Guskey, T., & Piggot, T. (1988). Research on group-based mastery learning programs: A meta-analysis. *Journal of Educational Research, 81,* 197–216.

Guskey, T. R. (1984). The influence of change in instructional effectiveness upon the affective characteristics of teachers. *American Educational Research Journal, 21,* 245–259.

Guskey, T. R. (1988). Teacher efficacy, self-concept, and attitudes toward the implementation of instructional innovation. *Teaching and Teacher Education, 4,* 63–69.

Guskey, T. R. (1994). Making the grade: What benefits students. *Educational Leadership, 52*(2), 24–27.

Guskey, T. R. (2000). *Developing grading and reporting systems for student learning.* Thousand Oaks, CA: Corwin.

Guskey, T. R. (2001). Helping students make the grade. *Educational Leadership, 59*(1), 20–27.

Guthrie, J. T., & Wigfield, A. (2000). Engagement and motivation in reading. In M. Kamil & P. Mosenthal (Eds.), *Handbook of reading research* (Vol. 3, pp. 403–422). Mahwah, NJ: Erlbaum.

Guthrie, J. T., Wigfield, A., Barbosa, P., Perencevich, K. C., Taboada, A., Davis, M. H., Scafiddi, N., & Tonks, S. (2004). Increasing reading comprehension, motivation, and strategy use through Concept Oriented Reading Instruction. *Journal of Educational Psychology, 96*, 403–423.

Gutierrez, R., & Slavin, R. F. (1992). Achievement effects of the nongraded elementary school: A best evidence synthesis. *Review of Educational Research, 62*, 333–376.

Guzdial, M. (1994). Software-realized scaffolding to facilitate programming for science learning. *Interactive Learning Environments, 4*, 1–44.

Hackett, G. (1985). The role of mathematics self-efficacy in the choice of math-related majors of college women and men: A path analysis. *Journal of Counseling Psychology, 32*, 47–56.

Haft, W. L., & Slade, A. (1989). Affect attunement and maternal attachment: A pilot study. *Infant Mental Health Journal, 10*, 157–172.

Hagger, H., & Malmberg, L.-E. (2011). Preservice teachers' goals and future-time extension, concerns, and well-being. *Teaching and Teacher Education, 28*, 1–11.

Haidt, J. (2001). The emotional dog and its rational tail: A social intuitionist approach to moral judgment. *Psychological Review, 108*, 814–834.

Hailikari, T., Nevgi, A., & Komulainen, E. (2007). Academic self-beliefs and prior knowledge as predictors of student achievement in mathematics: A structural model. *Educational Psychology, 28*, 59–71.

Haladyna, T. M. (2002). *Essentials of standardized achievement testing: Validity and accountability.* Boston: Allyn & Bacon.

Halford, G. S., & Andrews, G. (2011). Information-processing models of cognitive development. In U. Goswami (Ed.), *The Wiley-Blackwell handbook of childhood cognitive development* (2nd ed., pp. 697–722). Hoboken, NJ: Wiley-Blackwell.

Hall, G. E., & Loucks, S. F. (1982). Bridging the gap: Policy research rooted in practice. In A. Lieberman & M. W. McLaughlin (Eds.), *Policy making in education* (81st Yearbook of the National Society for the Study of Education, Part 1, pp. 133–158). Chicago: University of Chicago Press.

Hall, R. V., Cristler, C., Cranston, S. S., & Tucker, B. (1970). Teachers and parents as researchers using multiple baseline designs. *Journal of Applied Behavior Analysis, 3*, 247–255.

Hallahan, D. P., & Kauffman, J. M. (2003). *Exceptional learners* (9th ed). Boston: Allyn & Bacon.

Hallam, S., & Ireson, J. (2003). Secondary school teachers' attitudes towards and beliefs about ability grouping. *British Journal of Educational Psychology, 73*, 343–356.

Hallenbeck, M. J. (2002). Taking charge: Adolescents with learning disabilities assume responsibility for their own writing. *Learning Disabilities Quarterly, 25*, 227–246.

Hallinan, M. T. (1990). The effects of ability grouping in secondary schools: A response to Slavin's best-evidence synthesis. *Review of Educational Research, 60*, 501–504.

Halpern, D. (2003). *Thought and knowledge* (4th ed.). Mahwah, NJ: Erlbaum.

Halpern, D. F. (1998). Teaching critical thinking for transfer across domains. *American Psychologist, 53*, 449–455.

Hamre, B. K., & Pianta, R. C. (2001). Early teacher-child relationships and the trajectory of children's school outcomes through eighth grade. *Child Development, 72*, 625–638.

Hanish, L. D., & Guerra, N. G. (2000). A longitudinal analysis of patterns of adjustment following peer victimization. *Development and Psychopathology, 14*, 69–89.

Hanson, M. J., & Carta, J. J. (1996). Addressing the challenges of families with multiple risks. *Exceptional Children, 62*, 201–212.

Harackiewicz, J. M., Barron, K. E., Carter, S. M., Lehto, A. T., & Elliot, A. J. (1997). Predictors and consequences of achievement goals in the college classroom: Maintaining interest and making the grade. *Journal of Personality and Social Psychology, 73*, 1284–1295.

Harackiewicz, J. M., Barron, K. E., & Elliot, A. J. (1998). Rethinking achievement goals: When are they adaptive for college students and why? *Educational Psychologist, 33*, 1–21.

Harackiewicz, J. M., Barron, K. E., Pintrich, P. R., Elliot, A. J., & Thrash, T. M. (2002). Revision of achievement goal theory: Necessary and illuminating. *Journal of Educational Psychology, 94*, 638–645.

Harackiewicz, J. M., Barron, K. E., Tauer, J. M., Carter, S. M., & Elliot, A. J. (2000). Short-term and long-term consequences of achievement goals in college: Predicting continued interest and performance over time. *Journal of Educational Psychology, 92*, 316–330.

Harackiewicz, J. M., & Elliot, A. J. (1993). Achievement goals and intrinsic motivation. *Journal of Personality and Social Psychology, 65*, 904–915.

Hardre, P. L., & Reeve, J. (2003). A motivational model of rural students' intentions to persist in, versus drop out of, high school. *Journal of Educational Psychology, 95*, 347–356.

Harford, J., & MacRuairc, G. (2008). Engaging student teachers in meaningful reflective practice. *Teaching and Teacher Education, 24*, 1884–1892.

Hargreaves, A., Earl, L., & Schmidt, M. (2002). Perspectives on alternative assessment reform. *Educational Researcher, 39*(1), 69–95.

Harper, L. V., & McCluskey, K. S. (2002). Caregiver and peer responses to children with language and motor disabilities in inclusive preschool programs. *Early Childhood Research Quarterly, 17*, 148–166.

Hart, B., & Risley T. (1995). *Meaningful differences in the everyday experiences of young American children.* Baltimore: Paul H. Brookes Publishing.

Hart, D., & Fegley, S. (1995). Altruism and caring in adolescence: Relations to moral judgment and self-understanding. *Child Development, 66*, 1346–1359.

Hart, S., Brassard, M., & Germain, R. (1987). Psychological maltreatment in education and schooling. In M. Brassard, R. Germain, & S. Hart (Eds.), *Psychological maltreatment of children and youth* (pp. 217–242). Elmsford, NY: Pergamon.

Hartas, D., & Donahue, M. L. (1997). Conversational and social problem-solving skills in adolescents with learning disabilities. *Learning Disabilities Research and Practice, 12*, 213–220.

Harter, S. (1974). Pleasure derived by children from cognitive challenge and mastery. *Child Development, 45*, 661–669.

Harter, S. (1978). Pleasure derived from optimal challenge and the effects of extrinsic rewards on children's difficulty level choices. *Child Development, 49*, 788–799.

Harter, S. (1983). Developmental perspectives on the self-system. In E. M. Hetherington (Ed.) & P. H. Mussen (Series Ed.), *Handbook of child psychology: Socialization, personality, and social development* (Vol. 4, pp. 275–386). New York: Wiley.

Harter, S. (1990). Causes, correlates and the functional role of global self-worth: A lifespan perspective. In R. J. Sternberg & J. Kolligian, Jr. (Eds.), *Competence considered* (pp. 67–97). New Haven, CT: Yale University Press.

Harter, S. (1993). Causes and consequences of low self-esteem in children and adolescents. In R. F. Baumeister (Ed.), *Self-esteem: The puzzle of low self-regard* (pp. 87–116). New York: Plenum.

Hartigan, J. A., & Wigdor, A. K. (1989). *Fairness in employment testing: Validity generalization, minority issues, and the General Aptitude Test Battery.* Washington, DC: National Academy Press.

Hartup, W. W. (1983). Peer relations. In P. H. Mussen (Series Ed.) & E. M. Hetherington (Vol. Ed.), *Handbook of child psychology: Vol. 4. Socialization, personality, and social development* (pp. 103–196). New York: Wiley.

Hattie, J. A. (1992). *Self-concept.* Hillsdale, NJ: Erlbaum.

Hattie, J., & Timperley, H. (2007). The power of feedback. *Review of Educational Research, 77*(1), 81–112.

Hatton, N., & Smith, D. (1995). Reflection in teacher education: Towards definition and implementation. *Teaching and Teacher Education, 11,* 33–49.

Hawker, D. S. J., & Boulton, M. J. (2000). Twenty years' research on peer victimization and psychosocial maladjustment: A meta-analytic review of cross-sectional studies. *Journal of Child Psychology and Psychiatry, 41,* 441–455.

Hawkins, B. (2001). Supporting second language children's content learning and language development in K–5. In M. Celce-Murcia (Ed.), *Teaching English as a second or foreign language* (pp. 367–383). Boston: Heinle & Heinle.

Hawkins, J., Pea, R., Glick, J., & Scribner, S. (1994). "Merds that don't like mushrooms": Evidence for deductive reasoning by preschoolers. *Developmental Psychology, 20,* 584–594.

Hazan, C., & Shaver, P. (1987). Romantic love conceptualized as an attachment process. *Journal of Personality and Social Psychology, 52,* 511–524.

Hazler, R. J. (1996). *Breaking the cycle of violence: Interventions for bullying and victimization.* Washington, DC: Taylor & Francis.

Hecker, L., Burns, L., Elkind, J., Elkind, K., & Katz, L. (2002). Benefits of assistive reading software for students with attention disorders. *Annals of Dyslexia, 52,* 244–272.

Heckhausen, H. (1967). *The anatomy of achievement motivation.* New York: Academic Press.

Heller, L. R., & Fantuzzo, J. W. (1993). Reciprocal peer tutoring and parent partnership: Does parent involvement make a difference? *School Psychology Review, 22,* 517–534.

Helmke, A., & van Aken, M. A. G. (1995). The causal ordering of academic achievement and self-concept of ability during elementary school: A longitudinal study. *Journal of Educational Psychology, 87,* 624–637.

Hembree, R. (1988). Correlates, causes, effects, and treatment of test anxiety. *Review of Educational Research, 58,* 47–77.

Henderlong, J., & Lepper, M. R. (2002). Effects of praise on children's intrinsic motivation: A review and synthesis. *Psychological Bulletin, 128,* 774–795.

Heron, J., & Reason, P. (1997). A participatory inquiry paradigm. *Qualitative Inquiry, 3,* 274–294.

Herrnstein, R. J., & Murray, C. (1994). *The bell curve: Intelligence and class structure in American life.* New York: Free Press.

Hersh, R., & Walker, H. M. (1983). Great expectations: Making schools effective for all students. *Policy Studies Review, 2,* 147–188.

Heward, W. L., & Orlansky, M. D. (1992). *Exceptional children* (4th ed.). Columbus, OH: Merrill.

Hickey, D. T. (1997). Motivation and contemporary socio-constructivistic instructional perspectives. *Educational Psychologist, 32,* 175–193.

Hickey, D. T., & Schafer, N. J. (2006). Design-based, participation-centered approaches to classroom management. In C. M. Evertson & C. S. Weinstein (Eds.), *Handbook of classroom management: Research, practice, and contemporary issues* (pp. 281–308). Mahwah, NJ: Erlbaum.

Hidi, S. (1990). Interest and its contribution as a mental resource for learning. *Review of Educational Research, 60,* 549–571.

Hidi, S. (2000). An interest researcher's perspective: The effects of extrinsic and intrinsic factors on motivation. In C. Sansone & J. M. Harackiewicz (Eds.), *Intrinsic and extrinsic motivation: The search for optimal motivation and performance* (pp. 309–339). San Diego: Academic Press.

Hidi, S., & Baird, W. (1986). Interestingness—a neglected variable in discourse processing. *Cognitive Science, 10,* 179–194.

Hidi, S., & Renninger, K. A. (2006). The four-phase model of interest development. *Educational Psychologist, 41,* 111–127.

Hiebert, E. (1987). The context of instruction and student learning: An examination of Slavin's assumptions. *Review of Educational Research, 57,* 337–340.

Higgins, N., & Hess, L. (1999). Using electronic books to promote vocabulary development. *Journal of Research on Computing in Education, 31,* 425–430.

Hightower, A. D., Work, W. C., Cowen, E. L., Lotyczewski, B. S., Spinnell, A. P., Guare, J. C., & Rohrbeck, C. A. (1986). The Teacher-Child Rating Scale: A brief objective measure of elementary children's school problem behaviors and competencies. *School Psychology Review, 15,* 393–409.

Hill, K. T. (1980). Motivation, evaluation, and educational testing policy. In L. J. Fyans (Ed.), *Achievement motivation: Recent trends in theory and research* (pp. 34–95). New York: Academic Press.

Hill, K. T. (1984). Debilitating motivation and testing: A major educational problem, possible solutions, and policy applications. In R. Ames & C. Ames (Eds.), *Research on motivation in education: Student motivation* (Vol. 1). New York: Academic Press.

Hill, K. T., & Sarason, S. (1966). The relation of test anxiety and defensiveness to test and school performance over the elementary-school years: A further longitudinal study. *Monographs of the Society for Research in Child Development, 104,* 31 (Whole No. 2).

Hill, K. T., & Wigfield, A. (1984). Test anxiety: A major educational problem and what can be done about it. *The Elementary School Journal, 85,* 105–126.

Hirt, M., & Genshaft, J. L. (1981). Immunization and reversibility of cognitive deficits due to learned helplessness. *Personality and Individual Differences, 2,* 191–196.

Hitchcock, A. (1959, July 13). Interview by H. Brean. *Life,* p. 72.

Hmelo-Silver, C. E. (2002). Collaborative ways of knowing: Issues in facilitation. In G. Stahl (Ed.), *Proceedings of CSCL 200* (pp. 199–208). Mahwah, NJ: Erlbaum.

Hmelo-Silver, C. E. (2004). Problem-based learning: What and how do students learn? *Educational Psychology Review, 16,* 235–266.

Hoffman, M. L. (1975). Moral internalization, parental power and the nature of parent-child interaction. *Developmetal Psychology, 11,* 228–239.

Hoffman, M. L. (1982). Development of prosocial motivation: Empathy and guilt. In N. Eisenberg (Ed.), *Development of prosocial behavior* (pp. 281–313). New York Academic Press.

Hogan, D. M., & Tudge, J. R. H. (1999). Implications of Vygotsky's theory of peer learning. In A. M. O'Donnell & A. King (Eds.), *Cognitive perspectives on peer learning* (pp. 39–65). Mahwah, NJ: Erlbaum.

Hogan, T., Rabinowitz, M., & Craven, J. A. (2003). Problem representation in teaching: Inferences from research of expert and novice teachers. *Educational Psychologist, 38,* 235–247.

Holahan, C. K., & Holahan, C. J. (1987). Self-efficacy, social support, and depression in aging: A longitudinal analysis. *Journal of Gerontology, 42,* 65–68.

Holden, C. (1993). Giving girls a chance: Patterns of talk in cooperative group work. *Gender and Education, 5,* 179–189.

Holder, H., & Fitzpatrick, H. (1991). Interpretation of emotion from facial expressions in children with and without learning disabilities. *Journal of Learning Disabilities, 24,* 170–177.

Hollon, R. E., Roth, K. J., & Anderson, C. W. (1991). Science teachers' conceptions of teaching and learning. In J. Brophy (Ed.), *Advances in research on teaching, 2* (pp. 145–185). Greenwich, CT: JAI Press.

Holt-Reynolds, D. (1992). Personal history-based beliefs as relevant prior knowledge in coursework: Can we practice what we teach? *American Educational Research Journal, 29,* 325–349.

Hom, H. L., Jr. (1994). Can you predict the overjustification effect? *Teaching of Psychology, 21,* 36–37.

Hourbe, B., Targuinio, C., Thuillier, I., & Hergott, E. (2006). Bullying among students and its consequences on health. *European Journal of Psychology of Education, 21,* 183–208.

Housner, L. D., & Griffey, D. (1985). Teacher cognition: Differences in planning and interactive decision making between experienced and inexperienced teachers. *Research Quarterly for Exercise & Sport, 56,* 44–53.

Howe, M. J. A., Davidson, J. W., & Slobada, J. A. (1998). Innate talents: Reality or myth? *Behavioral and Brain Sciences, 21,* 399–442.

Howes, C. (1999). Attachment relationships in the context of multiple caregivers. In J.

Cassidy & P. R. Shaver (Eds.), *Handbook of attachment: Theory, research, and clinical applications* (pp. 671–687). New York: Guilford.

Hoy, W. K., & Woolfolk, A. E. (1993). Teachers' sense of efficacy and the organizational health of schools. *Elementary School Journal, 93,* 355–372.

Hubbard, J. A., & Cole, J. D. (1994). Emotional correlates of social competence in children's peer relationships. *Merrill-Palmer Quarterly, 40,* 1–20.

Huesemann, L. R., Moise-Titus, J., Podolski, C. L., & Eron, L. D. (2003). Longitudinal relations between children's exposure to TV violence and their aggressive and violent behavior in young adulthood: 1977–1992. *Developmental Psychology, 39,* 201–221.

Huffman, K. (2004). *Psychology in action* (7th ed.). Hoboken, NJ: Wiley.

Huggins, P. (1995). *The ASSIST program—affective/social skills: Instructional strategies and techniques.* Seattle: Washington State Innovative Education Program.

Hughes, C., Rodi, M. S., Lorden, S. W., Pitkin, S. E., Derer, K. R., Hwang, B., et al. (1999). Social interactions of high school students with mental retardation and their general education peers. *American Journal on Mental Retardation, 104,* 533–544.

Hulleman, C. S., Godes, O., Hendricks, B. L., & Harackiewicz, J. M. (2010). Enhancing interest and performance with a utility value intervention. *Journal of Educational Psychology, 102,* 880–895.

Hulleman, C. S., Schrager, S. M., Bodmann, S. M., & Harackiewicz, J. M. (2010). A meta-analytic review of achievement goal measures: Different labels for the same constructs or different constructs with similar labels? *Psychological Bulletin, 136,* 422–449.

Hulshof, H., & Verloop, N. (2002). The use of analogies in language teaching: Representing the content of teachers' practical knowledge. *Journal of Curriculum Studies, 34,* 77–90.

Huston, A. C., Donnerstein, E., Fairchild, J., Feshbach, N. D., Katz, P. A., Murray, J. P., et al. (1992). *Big world, small screen: The role of television in American society.* Lincoln: University of Nebraska Press.

Huttenlocher, P. R. (1994). Synaptogenesis, synapse elimination, and neural plasticity in human cerebral cortex. In C. A. Nelson (Ed.), *Minnesota symposia on child psychology: Threats to optimal development: Integrating biological, psychological, and social risk factors* (Vol. 27, pp. 35–54). Hillsdale, NJ: Erlbaum.

Hyman, I., Kay, B., Tabori, A., Weber, M., Mahon, M., & Cohen, I. (2006). Bullying: Theory, research, and interventions. In C. M. Evertson & C. S. Weinstein (Eds.), *Handbook of classroom management: Research, practice, and contemporary issues* (pp. 855–884). Mahwah, NJ: Erlbaum.

Hymel, S., Bowker, A., & Woody, E. (1993). Aggressive versus withdrawn unpopular children: Variations in peer and self-perceptions in multiple domains. *Child Development, 64,* 879–896.

Impara, J. C., & Plake, B. S. (Eds.). (1995). Standard setting for complex performance tasks (Special Issue). *Applied Measurement in Education, 8*(1).

Individuals with Disabilities Education Act Amendments of 1997. Retrieved April 10, 2005, from http://www.ed.gov/policy/speced/leg/idea/idea.pdf

Individuals with Disabilities Education Improvement Act of 2004. Retrieved April 10, 2005, from http://thomas.loc.gov/cgibin/query/z?c108:h.r.1350.enr

Inhelder, B., & Piaget, J. (1958). *The growth of logical thinking from childhood to adolescence.* New York: Basic Books.

Inzlicht, M., & Ben-Zeev, T. (2003). Do high-achieving female students underperform in private? The implications of threatening environments on intellectual processing. *Journal of Educational Psychology, 95,* 796–805.

Irvine, J. J. (1990). *Black students and school failure: Policies, practices, and prescriptions.* New York: Greenwillow.

Isen, A. M. (1987). Positive affect, cognitive processes, and social behavior. In L. Berkowitz (Ed.), *Advances in experimental social psychology* (Vol. 20, pp. 203–253). New York: Academic Press.

Isen, A. M., Daubman, K. A., & Nowicki, G. P. (1987). Positive affect facilitates creative problem-solving. *Journal of Personality and Social Psychology, 51,* 1122–1131.

Isen, A. M., & Geva, N. (1987). The influence of positive affect on acceptable level of risk: The person with a large canoe has a large worry. *Organizational Behavior and Human Decision Processes, 39,* 145–154.

Isen, A. M., Johnson, M. M. S., Mertz, E., & Robinson, G. F. (1985). The influence of positive affect on the unusualness of word associations. *Journal of Personality and Social Psychology, 48,* 1413–1426.

Isen, A. M., & Levin, P. F. (1972). Effects of feeling good on helping: Cookies and kindness. *Journal of Personality and Social Psychology, 21,* 384–388.

Jackson, P. W. (1968). *Life in classrooms.* New York: Holt, Rinehart and Winston.

Jaffee, S., & Hyde, J. (2000). Gender differences in moral orientation: A meta-analysis. *Psychological Bulletin, 126,* 703–726.

James, W. (1890). *Principles of psychology.* New York: Holt.

James, W. (1912). *Talks to teachers on psychology: And to students on some of life's ideals.* New York: Holt.

Jang, H. (2003). *Providing a rationale as a motivational model to engage students in an uninteresting lesson: A test of multiple models.*

Unpublished doctoral dissertation, University of Iowa, Iowa City.

Jang, H. (2008). Supporting students' motivation, engagement, and learning during an uninteresting activity. *Journal of Educational Psychology, 100,* 798–811.

Jeanpierre, B. J. (2004). Two urban elementary science classrooms: The interplay between student interactions and classroom management practices. *Education, 124,* 664–675.

Jenkins, J. R., & O'Connor, R. E. (2003). Cooperative learning for students with learning disabilities: Evidence from experiments, observations, and interviews. In H. L. Swanson, K. R. Harris, & S. Graham (Eds.), *Handbook of learning disabilities* (pp. 417–430). New York: Guilford.

Jenlink, P. M., Kinnucan-Welsch, K., & Odell, S. J. (1996). New directions for professional development: Designing professional development learning communities. In D. J. McIntyre & D. M. Byrd (Eds.), *Preparing tomorrow's teachers: The field experience* (pp. 63–86). Thousand Oaks, CA: Corwin.

Jimerson, S. J., Campos, E., & Grief, J. L. (2003). Toward an understanding of definitions and measures of school engagement and related terms. *The California School Psychologist, 8,* 7–27.

Johnson, C. S., & Stapel, D. A. (2011). Happiness as alchemy: Positive mood leads to self-serving responses to social comparisons. *Motivation and Emotion, 35,* 165–180.

Johnson, D. W., & Johnson, F. P. (2008). *Joining together: Group theory and group skills* (10th ed.). Boston: Allyn & Bacon.

Johnson, D. W., & Johnson, R. T. (1979). Conflict in the classroom: Controversy and learning. *Review of Educational Research, 49,* 51–69.

Johnson, D. W., & Johnson, R. T. (1987). *Learning together and alone: Cooperative, competitive, and individualistic learning* (2nd ed.). Englewood Cliffs, NJ: Prentice Hall.

Johnson, D. W., & Johnson, R. T. (1989). *Cooperation and competition: Theory and research.* Edina, MN: Interaction Book.

Johnson, D. W., & Johnson, R. T. (1989/90). Social skills for successful groupwork. *Educational Leadership, 47*(4), 29–33.

Johnson, D. W., & Johnson, R. T. (1991). *Learning together and alone: Cooperative, competitive, and individualistic learning.* Englewood Cliffs, NJ: Prentice Hall.

Johnson, D. W., & Johnson, R. T. (1995). *Creative controversy: Intellectual challenge in the classroom.* Edina, MN: Interaction Books.

Johnson, D. W., Johnson, R. T., & Holublec, E. (1993). *Circles of learning: Cooperation in the classroom* (5th ed.). Edina, MN: Interaction Books.

Johnson, J. S., & Newport, E. L. (1989). Critical period effects in second language learning: The influence of maturational state on the acquisition of English as a second language. *Cognitive Psychology, 21,* 60–99.

Johnson, S. C., Dweck, C. S., & Chen, F. S. (2007). Evidence for infants' internal working models of attachment. *Psychological Science, 18*, 501–502.

Johnson, T., Boyden, J. E., & Pittz, W. (2001). *Racial profiling and punishment in U.S. public schools: How zero tolerance policies and high stakes testing subvert academic excellence and racial equity.* Oakland, CA: Applied Research Center.

Jolliffe, D., & Farrington, D. P. (2006). Examining the relationship between low empathy and bullying. *Aggressive Behavior, 32*, 540–550.

Jonassen, D. H., Peck, K. C., & Wilson, B. G. (1999). *Learning with technology: A constructivist perspective.* Upper Saddle River, NJ: Merrill/Prentice Hall.

Jonassen, D. H., Tessmer, M., & Hannum, W. H. (1999). *Task analysis methods for instructional design.* Mahwah, NJ: Erlbaum.

Jones, B. F., Pierce, J., & Hunter, B. (1989). Teaching students to construct graphic representations. *Teaching Exceptional Children, 46*(4), 20–25.

Jones, E. E., & Berglas, S. (1978). Control of attributions about the self through self-handicapping strategies: The appeal of alcohol and the role of underachievement. *Personality and Social Psychology Bulletin, 4*, 200–206.

Jones, S. L., Nation, J. R., & Massad, P. (1977). Immunization against learned helplessness in man. *Journal of Abnormal Psychology, 86*, 75–83.

Joseph, A. (1977). *Intelligence, IQ, and race—when, how and why they became associated.* San Francisco: R & E Research Associates.

Joussemet, M., Koestner, R., Lekes, N., & Houlfort, N. (2004). Introducing uninteresting tasks to children: A comparison of the effects of rewards and autonomy support. *Journal of Personality, 72*, 139–166.

Joyner-Kersee, J. (1997). *A kind of grace: The autobiography of the world's greatest female athlete.* New York: Warner.

Juel, C. (1996). What makes literacy tutoring effective? *Reading Research Quarterly, 31*(3), 268–289.

Jurdak, M., & Shahin, I. (1999). An ethnographic study of the computational strategies of a group of young street vendors in Beirut. *Educational Studies in Mathematics, 40*, 155–172.

Juvonen, J. (2006). Sense of belonging, social bonds, and school functioning. In P. A. Alexander & P. H. Winne (Eds.), *Handbook of educational psychology* (2nd ed., pp. 655–674). Mahwah, NJ: Erlbaum.

Juvonen, J., & Graham, S. (Eds.). (2001). *Peer harassment in school: The plight of the vulnerable and victimized.* New York: Guilford.

Juvonen, J., Graham, S., & Schuster, M. (2003). Bullying among young adolescents: The strong, weak, and troubled. *Pediatrics, 112*, 1231–1237.

Kagan, D. M. (1992). Implications of research on teacher belief. *Educational Psychologist, 27*, 65–90.

Kagan, J. (1972). Motives and development. *Journal of Personality and Social Psychology, 22*, 51–66.

Kagan, S. (1989/1990). The structural approach to cooperative learning. *Educational Leadership, 47*(4), 12–15.

Kagan, S. (1993). *Cooperative learning.* San Juan Capistrano, CA: Kagan Cooperative Learning.

Kahneman, D. (1973). *Attention and effort.* Englewood Cliffs, NJ: Prentice Hall.

Kaiser, B., & Rasminsky, J. S. (2003). *Challenging behavior in young children: Understanding, preventing, and responding effectively.* Boston: Pearson.

Kamps, D., Kravits, T., Stolze, J., & Swaggart, B. (1999). Prevention strategies for at-risk students and students with EBD in urban elementary schools. *Journal of Emotional & Behavioral Disorders, 7*(3), 178–188.

Kandel, E. R., Schwartz, J. H., & Jessell, T. M. (1991). *Principles of neural science* (3rd ed.). New York: Elsevier.

Kaplan, A., & Maehr, M. L. (2007). The contributions and prospects of goal orientation theory. *Educational Psychology Review, 19*, 141–184.

Karantonis, A., & Sireci, S. G. (2006). The bookmark standard-setting method: A literature review. *Educational Measurement: Issues and Practice, 25*(1) 4–12.

Kasser, T., & Ryan, R. M. (1993). A dark side of the American dream: Correlates of financial success as a central life aspiration. *Journal of Personality and Social Psychology, 65*, 410–422.

Kasser, T., & Ryan, R. M. (1996). Further examining the American dream: Differential correlates of intrinsic and extrinsic goals. *Personality and Social Psychology Bulletin, 22*, 80–87.

Katz, I., & Assor, A. (2007). When choice motivates and when it does not. *Educational Psychology Review, 19*, 429-442.

Kaufman, A. S., & Kaufman, N. L. (2005). *KABC-II: Kaufman Assessment Battery for Children* (2nd ed.). Circle Pines, MN: AGS Publishing.

Kaufman, P., Chen, X., Choy, S., Chandler, K., Chapman, C., Rand, M., & Ringel, C. (1999). Indicators of school crime and safety, 1998. *Educational Statistics Quarterly, 1*(1), 42–45.

Kaukiainen, A., Bjorkqvist, K., Lagerspetz, K., Osterman, K., Salmivalli, C., Rothberg, S., et al. (1999). The relationships between social intelligence, empathy, and three types of aggression. *Aggressive Behavior, 25*, 81–89.

Kazdin, A. E. (1979). Imagery elaboration and self-efficacy in the covert modeling treatment of unassertive behavior. *Journal of Consulting and Clinical Psychology, 47*, 725–733.

Keller, J. M. (1983). Motivational design of instruction. In C. M. Reigeluth (Ed.), *Instructional design theories and models* (pp. 383–434). Hillsdale, NJ: Erlbaum.

Kemmis, S., & McTaggart, R. (1988). *The action research planner* (2nd ed.). Geelong, Victoria, Australia: Deakin University Press.

Keogh, B. K., & MacMillan, D. L. (1996). Exceptionality. In D. Berliner & R. C. Calfee (Eds.), *Handbook of educational psychology* (pp. 311–330). New York: Macmillan.

King, A. (1989). Effects of self-questioning training on college students' comprehension of lectures. *Contemporary Educational Psychology, 14*, 366–381.

King, A. (1991). Effects of training in strategic questioning on children's problem-solving performance. *Journal of Educational Psychology, 83*, 307–317.

King, A. (1994). Guiding knowledge construction in the classroom: Effects of teaching children how to question and how to explain. *American Educational Research Journal, 31*, 111–126.

King, A. (1999). Discourse patterns mediating peer learning. In A. M. O'Donnell & A. King (Eds.), *Cognitive perspectives on peer learning* (pp. 87–115). Mahwah, NJ: Erlbaum.

King, A., Staffieri, A., & Adelgais, A. (1998). Mutual peer tutoring: Effects of structured tutorial interaction to scaffold peer learning. *Journal of Educational Psychology, 90*, 134–152.

Kintsch, E., & Kintsch, W. (1995). Strategies to promote active learning from text: Individual differences in background knowledge. *Swiss Journal of Psychology, 54*, 141–151.

Kintsch, W. (1980). Learning from text, levels of comprehension, or: Why anyone would read a story anyway? *Poetics, 9*, 87–98.

Klahrl, D., & Nigam, M. (2004). The equivalence of learning paths in early science instruction. *Psychological Science, 15*, 661–667.

Klassen, R. (2002). A question of calibration: A review of the self-efficacy beliefs of students with learning disabilities. *Learning Disability Quarterly, 25*, 88–102.

Klassen, R. M., & Chiu, M. M. (2010). Effects on teachers' self-efficacy and job satisfaction: Teacher gender, years of experience, and job stress. *Journal of Educational Psychology, 102*, 741–756.

Klein, D. C., & Seligman, M. E. P. (1976). Reversal of performance deficits in learned helplessness and depression. *Journal of Abnormal Psychology, 85*, 11–26.

Klein, G. A., & Hoffman, R. R. (1993). Seeing the invisible: Perceptual-cognitive aspects of expertise. In M. Rabinowitz (Ed.), *Cognitive science foundations of instruction* (pp. 203–226). Hillsdale, NJ: Erlbaum.

Klein, H. J., Whitener, E. M., & Ilgen, D. R. (1990). The role of goal specificity in the goal-setting process. *Motivation and Emotion, 14*, 179–193.

Kleinert, H. L., Browder, D. M., Towles-Reeves, E. A. (2009). Models of cognition for students with significant cognitive disabilities: Implications for assessment. *Review of Educational Research, 79*(1), 301–326.

Klomek, A. B., Sourander, A., Kumpulainen, K., Piha, J., Tamminen, T., Moilanen, I., et al. (2008). Childhood bullying as a risk for later depression and suicidal ideation among Finnish males. *Journal of Affective Disorders, 109,* 47–55.

Kochanska, G. (2002). Mutually responsive orientation between mothers and their young children: A context for the early development of conscience. *Current Directions in Psychological Science, 11,* 191–195.

Kochanska, G., & Aksan, N. (2004). Conscience in childhood: Past, present, and future. *Merrill-Palmer Quarterly, 50,* 299–310.

Kochanska, G., Aksan, N., & Koenig, A. L. (1995). A longitudinal study of the roots of preschoolers' conscience: Committed compliance and emerging internalization. *Child Development, 66,* 1752–1769.

Kochanska, G., Aksan, N., & Nichols, K. E. (2003). Maternal power assertion in discipline and moral discourse contexts: Commonalities, differences, and implications for children's moral conduct and cognition. *Developmental Psychology, 39,* 949–963.

Kochanska, G., Coy, K. C., & Murray, K. T. (2001). The development of self-regulation in the first four years of life. *Child Development, 72,* 1091–1111.

Kochanska, G., Friesenborg, A. E., Lange, L. A., & Martel, M. M. (2004). Parent's personality and infant's temperament as contributors to their emerging relationship. *Journal of Personality and Social Psychology, 86,* 744–759.

Kochanska, G., Gross, J. N., Lin, M.-H., & Nichols, K. E. (2002). Guilt in young children: Development, determinants, and relations with a broader system of standards. *Child Development, 73,* 461–482

Kochanska, G., & Murray, K. T. (2000). Mother-child mutually responsive orientation and conscience development: From toddler to early school age. *Child Development, 71,* 417–431.

Kochanska, G., Padavich, D. L., & Koenig, A. L. (1996). Children's narratives about hypothetical moral dilemmas and objective measures of their conscience: Mutual relations and socialization antecedents. *Child Development, 67,* 1420–1436.

Kochanska, G., & Thompson, R. A. (1997). The emergence and development of conscience in toddlerhood and early childhood. In J. E. Grusec & L. Kuczynski (Eds.), *Parenting and children's internalization of values: A handbook of contemporary theory* (pp. 53–77). New York: Wiley.

Kochenderfer, B., & Ladd, G. (1996). Peer victimization: Manifestations and relations to school adjustment in kindergarten. *Journal of School Psychology, 34,* 267–283.

Koedinger, K. R., & Anderson, J. R. (1993). Reifying implicit planning in geometry: Guidelines for model-based intelligent tutoring system design. In S. J. Lajoie & S. J. Derry (Eds.), *Computers as cognitive tools* (pp. 15–45). Mahwah, NJ: Erlbaum.

Koenigs, S. S., Fiedler, M. L., & deCharms, R. (1977). Teacher beliefs, classroom interaction, and personal causation. *Journal of Applied Social Psychology, 7,* 95–114.

Kohlberg, L. (1963). The development of children's orientations toward a moral order. I: Sequence in the development of moral thought. *Human Development, 51,* 8–20.

Kohlberg, L. (1975). The cognitive-developmental approach to moral education. *Phi Delta Kappan,* 670–677.

Kohlberg, L. (1981). *Essays on moral development: Vol. 1. The philosophy of moral development.* San Francisco: Harper & Row.

Kohlberg, L. (1984). *Essays on moral development: Vol. 2. The psychology of moral development.* San Francisco: Harper & Row.

Kohlberg, L., & Candee, D. (1984). The relationship of moral judgment to moral action. In W. Kurtines & J. Gewirtz (Eds.), *Morality, moral behavior and moral development* (pp. 52–73). New York: Wiley.

Kohn, A. (1993). *Punished by rewards: The trouble with gold stars, incentive plans, A's, praise, and other bribes.* Boston: Houghton Mifflin.

Kohn, A. (2006). Abusing research: The study of homework and other examples. *Phi Delta Kappan, 88,* 8–22.

Kolis, M., & Dunlap, W. P. (2004). The knowledge of teaching: The K3P3 model. *Reading Improvement, 41,* 97–107.

Kolodner, J. L, Hmelo, C. E., & Narayanan, N. H. (1996). Problem-based learning meets case-based reasoning. In D. C. Edelson & E. A. Domeshek (Eds.), *Proceedings of ICLS 96* (pp. 188–195). Charlottesville, VA: AACE.

Kosslyn, S. M. (1976). Can imagery be distinguished from other forms of internal representation? Evidence from studies of information retrieval times. *Memory and Cognition, 4,* 291–297.

Kosslyn, S. M. (1980). *Image and mind.* Cambridge, MA: Harvard University Press.

Kosslyn, S. M. (1983). *Ghosts in the mind's machine.* New York: Norton.

Kosslyn, S. M., Ball, T. M., & Reiser, B. J. (1978). Visual images preserve metric spatial information: Evidence from studies of image scanning. *Journal of Experimental Psychology: Human Perception and Performance, 4,* 1–20.

Kovaleski, J. E., Gickling, E. E., Morrow, H., & Swank, P. R. (1999). High versus low implementations of instructional support teams: A case for maintaining program fidelity. *Remedial and Special Education, 20,* 170–183.

Kowalski, R., Limber, S., & Agatston, P. (2007). *Cyber bullying: Bullying in the digital age.* Malden, MA: Blackwell.

Kowaz, A. M., & Marcia, J. E. (1991). Development and validation of a measure of Eriksonian industry. *Journal of Personality and Social Psychology, 60,* 390–397.

Krashen, S. D. (1996). *Under attack: The case against bilingual education.* Culver City, CA: Language Education Associates.

Kriete, R. (1999). *The morning meet book.* Greenfield, MA: Northeast Foundation for Children.

Krueger, N., Jr., & Dickson, P. R. (1994). How believing in ourselves increases risk taking: Perceived self-efficacy and opportunity recognition. *Decision Sciences, 25,* 385–400.

Kruger, A. C., & Tomasello, M. (1986). Transactive discussions with peers and adults. *Developmental Psychology, 22,* 681–685.

Kuhn, D. (2011). What is scientific thinking and how does it develop? In U. Goswami (Ed.), *The Wiley-Blackwell handbook of childhood cognitive development* (2nd ed., pp. 497–523). Hoboken, NJ: Wiley-Blackwell.

Kuhn, D., Kohlberg, L., Langer, J., & Haan, N. (1977). The development of formal operations in logical and moral judgment. *Genetic Psychology Monographs, 95,* 97–188.

Kuhn, D., & Phelps, E. (1982). The development of problem-solving strategies. In H. Reese (Ed.), *Advances in child development and behavior* (Vol. 17, pp. 1–44). New York: Academic Press.

Kuhn, D., Goh, W., Jordanou, K., & Shaenfield, D. (2008). Arguing on the computer: A microgenetic study of developing argument skills in a computer-supported environment. *Child Development, 79,* 1310–1328.

Kulik, C., Kulik, J., & Bangert-Downs, R. (1990). Effectiveness of mastery learning programs: A meta-analysis. *Review of Educational Research, 60,* 265–306.

Kulik, J. A. (1992). An analysis of the research on ability grouping: Historical and contemporary perspectives. *Communicator: The Journal of the California Association for the Gifted, 22*(5), 29–34.

Kurland, D. M., & Pea, R. D. (1985). Children's mental models for recursive Logo programs. *Journal of Educational Computing Research, 2,* 235–244.

Labbo, L. D. (2000). 12 things you can do with a talking book in a classroom computer center. *The Reading Teacher, 53,* 542–546.

Lackney, J. A., & Jacobs, P. J. (2004). *Teachers as placemakers: Investigating teachers' use of the physical learning environment in instructional design.* University of Wisconsin School Design Research Studio. Retrieved March 10, 2005, from http://schoolstudio.engr.wisc.edu/placemakers.htm

Ladd, G. W., & Dinella, L. M. (2009). Continuity and change in early school engagement: Predictive of children's achievement trajectories from first to eighth grade? *Journal of Educational Psychology, 101*, 190–206.

Ladd, G. W., Kochenderfer-Ladd, B., & Rydell, A.-M. (2010). Children's interpersonal skills and school-based relationships. In P. K. Smith & C. H. Hart (Eds.), *The Wiley-Blackwell handbook of childhood social development* (2nd ed., pp. 181–206). Hoboken, NJ: Wiley-Blackwell.

Landry, S. H., Anthony, J. L., Swank, P. R., & Monseque-Bailey, P. (2009). Effectiveness of comprehensive professional development for teachers of at-risk preschoolers. *Journal of Educational Psychology, 101*, 448–465.

Lane, K. L., Falk, K., & Wehby, J. (2006). Classroom management in special education classrooms and resources rooms. In C. M. Evertson & C. S. Weinstein (Eds.), *Handbook of classroom management: Research, practice, and contemporary issues* (pp. 439–460). Mahwah, NJ: Erlbaum.

Lane, K. L., Givner, C. C., & Pierson, M. R. (2004a). Teacher expectations of student behavior: Social skills necessary for success in elementary school classrooms. *Journal of Special Education, 38*, 104–110.

Lane, K. L., Givner, C. C., & Pierson, M. R. (2004b). Secondary teachers' views of social competence: Skills essential for success. *Journal of Special Education, 38*, 174–186.

Lanza, E. (1992). Can bilingual 2-year-olds code-switch? *Journal of Child Language, 19*, 633–658.

LaPorte, R. E., & Nath, R. (1976). Role of performance goals in prose learning. *Journal of Educational Psychology, 68*, 260–264.

Latham, G. P., & Baldes, J. J. (1975). The practical significance of Locke's theory of goal setting. *Journal of Applied Psychology, 60*, 122–124.

Latham, G. P., & Locke, E. A. (1975). Increasing productivity with decreasing time limits: A field replication of Parkinson's law. *Journal of Applied Psychology, 60*, 524–526.

Latham, G. P., Erez, M., & Locke, E. A. (1988). Resolving scientific disputes by the joint design of crucial experiments by the antagonists: Application to the Erez-Latham dispute regarding participation in goal setting. *Journal of Applied Psychology, 73*, 753–772.

Latham, G. P., & Saari, L. M. (1979). Importance of supportive relationships in goal setting. *Journal of Applied Psychology, 64*, 151–156.

Larrivee, B. (2006). The convergence of reflective practice and effective classroom management. In C. M. Evertson & C. S. Weinstein (Eds.), *Handbook of classroom management: Research, practice, and contemporary issues* (pp. 983–1001). Mahwah, NJ: Erlbaum.

Lave, J., & Wenger, E. (1991). *Situated learning: Legitimate peripheral participation.* New York: Cambridge University Press.

Lavoie, R. (1994). *Last one picked, first one picked on: Learning disabilities and social skills.* Available from http://ricklavoie.com/videos.html

Lay, K. L., Waters, E., & Park, K. A. (1989). Maternal responsiveness and child compliance: The role of mood as mediator. *Child Development, 60*, 1405–1411.

Lazarowitz, R., & Karsenty, G. (1990). Cooperative learning and students' academic achievement, process skills, learning environment, and self-esteem in a 10th grade biology classroom. In S. Sharan (Ed.), *Cooperative learning: Theory and research* (pp. 123–149). New York: Praeger.

Lazarus, R. S., & Folkman, S. (1984). *Stress, appraisal, and coping.* New York: Springer-Verlag.

Leagerspetz, K. M. J., Bjorkquist, K., & Peltonen, T. (1988). Is indirect aggression typical of females? Gender differences in aggressiveness in 11- to 12-year-old children. *Aggressive Behavior, 14*, 403–414.

Lebeau, R. B. (1998). Cognitive tools in a clinical encounter in medicine: Supporting empathy and expertise in distributed systems. *Educational Psychological Review, 10*, 3–34.

Lederman, N. G. (2001). A partial list of the empirical theoretical literature on subject-specific pedagogy. *School Science & Mathematics, 101*(2), 61–80.

Lee, H.-J. (2005). Understanding and assessing preservice teachers' reflective thinking. *Teaching and Teacher Education, 21*, 699–715.

Lee, W., & Reeve, J. (2011). *Teacher accuracy in judging students' motivation and engagement.* Manuscript submitted for publication.

Lee, W. O. (1996). The cultural context for Chinese learners: Conceptions of learning in the Confucian tradition. In D. A. Watkins & J. B. Biggs (Eds.), *The Chinese learner* (pp. 45–67). Hong Kong, China: Comparative Education Research Centre and the Australian Council for Education Research Ltd.

Legault, L., Green-Demers, I., & Pelletier, L. G. (2006). Why do high school students lack motivation in the classroom? Toward an understanding of academic motivation and social support. *Journal of Educational Psychology, 98*, 567–582.

Lehmann, A. C. (1998). Historical increases in expert performance suggest large possibilities for improvement of performance without implicating innate capacities. *Behavioral and Brain Sciences, 21*, 419–420.

Leinhardt, G. (1983, April). *Routines in expert math teachers' thoughts and actions.* Paper presented at the annual meeting of the American Educational Research Association, Montreal, Canada.

Leinhardt, G. (1993). Instructional explanations in history and mathematics. In W. Kintsch (Ed.), *Proceedings of the fifteenth annual conference of the Cognitive Science Society* (pp. 5–16). Hillsdale, NJ: Erlbaum.

Leinhardt, G., Crowley, K., & Knutson, K. (2002). (Eds.). *Learning conversations in museums.* Mahwah, NJ: Erlbaum.

Leinhardt, G., & Greeno, J. G. (1986). The cognitive skill of teaching. *Journal of Educational Psychology, 78*, 75–95.

Leinhardt, G., Putnam, R. J., Stein, M. K., & Baxter, J. (1991). Where subject knowledge matters. In J. Brophy (Ed.), *Advances in research on teaching* (Vol. 2, pp. 145–185). Greenwich, CT: JAI Press.

Leinhardt, G., Weidman, C., & Hammond, K. M. (1987). Introduction and integration of classroom routines by expert teachers. *Curriculum Inquiry, 17*(2), 135–175.

Leong, C. K. (1995). Effects of online reading and simultaneous DECtalk auding in helping below average and poor readers comprehend and summarize text. *Learning Disabilities Quarterly, 19*, 101–116.

Lepper, M. R. (1983). Social-control processes and the internalization of social values: An attributional perspective. In E. T. Higgins, D. N. Ruble, & W. W. Hartup (Eds.), *Social cognition and social development.* New York: Cambridge University Press.

Lepper, M. R., & Greene, D. (Eds.). (1978). *The hidden costs of reward.* Hillsdale, NJ: Erlbaum.

Lepper, M. R., Greene, D., & Nisbett, R. E. (1973). Undermining children's intrinsic interest with extrinsic rewards: A test of the "overjustification" hypothesis. *Journal of Personality and Social Psychology, 28*, 129–137.

Lepper, M. R., & Henderlong, J. (2000). Turning "play" into "work" and "work" into "play": 25 years of research on intrinsic versus extrinsic motivation. In C. Sansone & J. M. Harackiewicz (Eds.), *Intrinsic and extrinsic motivation: The search for optimal motivation and performance* (pp. 257–307). San Diego: Academic Press.

Leu, D. J., Jr. & Kinzer, C. K. (1991). *Effective reading instruction: K–8* (2nd ed.). New York: Macmillan.

Lever-Duffy, J., McDonald, J. B., & Mizell, A. P. (2005). *Teaching and learning with technology* (2nd ed.). Boston: Allyn & Bacon.

Levin, J., & Nolan, J. F. (2004). *Principles of classroom management: A professional decision-making model* (4th ed.). Boston: Pearson.

Levin, T., & Kaner, H. (2007). *High-school student views on classroom assessment practices.* Paper presented at the annual meeting of the American Educational Research Association, Chicago.

Levine, M. (2002). *A mind at a time.* New York: Simon & Schuster.

Levinson, D. J. (1986). A conception of adult development. *American Psychologist, 41*, 3–13.

Lewis, C. C. (2002). *Lesson study: A handbook of teacher-led instructional change.* Philadelphia: Research for Better Schools.

Lewis, D. M., Mitzel, H. C., Green, D. R., & Patz, R. J. (1999). *The bookmark standard setting procedure.* Monterey, CA: McGraw-Hill.

Lewis, M. (1987). Social development in infancy and early childhood. In J. D. Osofsky (Ed.), *Handbook of infant development* (2nd ed., pp. 419–493). New York: Wiley.

Li, Y., Anderson, R. C., Nguyen-Jahiel, K., Dong, T., Archodidou, A., Kim, I., Kuo, L.-J., Clark, A.-M., Wu, X., Jadallah, M., & Miller, B. (2007). Emergent leadership in children's discussion groups. *Cognition and Instruction, 25*(1), 75–111.

Lillard, A., Pinkham, A. M., & Smith, E. (2011). Pretend play and cognitive development. In U. Goswami (Ed.), *The Wiley-Blackwell handbook of childhood cognitive development* (2nd ed., pp. 285–311). Hoboken, NJ: Wiley-Blackwell.

Lim, K.-M., & Tan, A.-G. (2010). *Student teachers' perceptions of the importance of theory and practice.* Unpublished manuscript, Nanyang Technological University, Singapore.

Lindren, D. M., Meier, S. E., & Brigham, T. A. (1991). The effects of minimal and maximal peer tutoring systems on the academic performance of college students. *Psychological Record, 41*, 69–77.

Linebarger, D. L., Kosanic, A. Z., Greenwood, C. R., & Doku, N. S. (2004). Effects of viewing the television program *Between the Lions* on the emergent literacy skills of young children. *Journal of Educational Psychology, 96*, 297–308.

Linenfelser, T. (2005). *Grand Island's pictures from the past* (Vol. 3). Retrieved March 25, 2005, from http://www.isledegrande.com/picpage03.html

Linn, M. C. (1986). Science. In R. Dillon & R. Sternberg (Eds.), *Cognition and instruction* (pp. 155–197). Orlando, FL: Academic Press.

Linn, M. C., diSessa, A., Pea, R., & Songer, N. (1994). Can research on science learning and instruction inform standards for science education? *Journal of Science Education and Technology, 3*, 7–15.

Linn, M. C., & Slotta, J. D. (2005). Enabling participants in online forums to learn from one another. In A. M. O'Donnell, C. Hmelo-Silver, & G. Erkens (Eds.), *Collaborative learning, reasoning, and technology* (pp. 61–97). Mahwah, NJ: Erlbaum.

Linn, R. (1982). Ability testing: Individual differences, prediction, and differential prediction. In A. Wigdor & W. Garner (Eds.), *Ability testing: Uses, consequences, and controversies* (Part II, pp. 335–388). Washington, DC: National Academy Press.

Linn, R. L., & Gronlund, N. E. (1995). *Measurement and assessment in teaching* (7th ed.). Englewood Cliffs, NJ: Prentice Hall.

Linnenbrink, E. A. (2005). The dilemma of performance-approach goals: The use of multiple goal contexts to promote students' motivation and learning. *Journal of Educational Psychology, 97*, 197–213.

Linnenbrink, E. A., & Pintrich, P. R. (2003). The role of self-efficacy beliefs in student engagement and learning in the classroom. *Reading and Writing Quarterly: Overcoming Learning Difficulties, 19*, 119–137.

Lipnevich, A. A., & Smith, J. K. (2009). The effects of differential feedback on student examination performance. *Journal of Experimental Psychology: Applied, 15*(4), 319–333.

Lipscomb, L., Swanson, J., & West, A. *Scaffolding* (2005). Retrieved July 13, 2005, from http://www.coe.uga.edu/epltt/scaffolding.htm

Livingston, C., & Borko, H. (1989a). Expert-novice difference in teaching: A cognitive analysis and implications for teacher education. *Journal of Teacher Education, 40*(4), 36–42.

Livingston, C., & Borko, H. (1989b). Cognition and improvisation: Differences in mathematics instruction by expert and novice teachers. *American Educational Research Journal, 26*, 473–498.

Lo, J., & Hyland, F. (2007). Enhancing students' engagement and motivation in writing: The case of primary students in Hong Kong. *Journal of Second Language Writing, 16*, 219–237.

Lochman, J. E., Burch, P. R., Curry, J. F., & Lampron, L. B. (1984). Treatment and generalization effects of cognitive-behavioral and goal-setting interventions with aggressive boys. *Journal of Consulting and Clinical Psychology, 52*, 915–916.

Lockard, J., & Abrams, P. D. (2004). *Computers for the twenty-first century educators* (6th ed.). Boston: Allyn & Bacon.

Locke, E. A. (1996). Motivation through conscious goal setting. *Applied and Preventive Psychology, 5*, 117–124.

Locke, E. A. (2002). Setting goals for life and happiness. In C. R. Synder & S. J. Lopez (Eds.), *Handbook of positive psychology* (pp. 299–312). New York: Oxford University Press.

Locke, E. A., & Bryan, J. F. (1996). Motivation through conscious goal setting. *Applied and Preventive Psychology, 5*, 117–124.

Locke, E. A., Chah, D. O., Harrison, S., & Lustgarten, N. (1989). Separating the effects of goal specificity from goal level. *Organizational Behavior and Human Decision Processes, 43*, 270–287.

Locke, E. A., & Latham, G. P. (1984). *Goal-setting: A motivational technique that works!* Englewood Cliffs, NJ: Prentice Hall.

Locke, E. A., & Latham, G. P. (1990). *A theory of goal setting and task performance.* Englewood Cliffs, NJ: Prentice Hall.

Locke, E. A., & Latham, G. P. (2002). Building a practically useful theory of goal setting and task motivation. *American Psychologist, 57*, 705–717.

Locke, E. A., Shaw, K. N., Saari, L. M., & Latham, G. P. (1981). Goal setting and task performance: 1969–1980. *Psychological Bulletin, 90*, 125–152.

Loeber, R., & Hay, D. F. (1994). Developmental approaches to aggression and conduct problems. In M. Rutter & D. F. Hoy (Eds.), *Development through life: A handbook for clinicians* (pp. 488–516). Malden, MA: Blackwell Scientific.

Loevinger, J. (1976). Stages of ego development. In J. Loevinger (Ed.), *Ego development* (pp. 13–28). San Francisco: Jossey-Bass.

Loewenstein, G. (1994). The psychology of curiosity: A review and reinterpretation. *Psychological Bulletin, 116*, 75–98.

Loftus, G. R., & Loftus, E. F. (1983). *Mind at play: The psychology of video games.* New York: Basic Books.

Lohrmann, S., & Talerico, J. (2004). Anchor the boat: A classwide intervention to reduce problem behavior. *Journal of Positive Behavior Interventions, 6*, 113–120.

Lopez, O. S. (2007). Classroom diversification: A strategic view of educational productivity. *Review of Educational Research, 77*(1), 28–80.

Lotan, R. A. (2003). Group-worthy tasks. *Educational Leadership, 60*(6), 72–75.

Loughran, J. (2002). Effective reflective practice: In search of meaning in learning about teaching. *Journal of Teacher Education, 53*, 33-43.

Lourenco, O., & Machado, A. (1996). In defense of Piaget's theory: A reply to 10 common criticisms. *Psychological Review, 103*, 143–164.

Loveless, T. (2003). How well are American students learning? With special sections on homework, charter schools, and rural school achievement. *The 2003 Brown Center Report on American Education, 1*(4). Washington, DC: The Brookings Institution.

Luk, S. (1985). Direct observation studies of hyperactive behavior. *Journal of the American Academy of Child Psychiatry, 24*, 338–344.

Mabry, L. (1999). *Portfolios plus: A critical guide to alternative assessment.* Thousand Oaks, CA: Corwin.

Maccoby, E. E. (1992). The role of parents in the socialization of children: An historical overview. *Developmental Psychology, 28*, 1006–1017.

Mackey, B., Johnson, R., & Wood, T. (1995). Cognitive and affective outcomes in a multiage language arts program. *Journal of Research in Childhood Education, 10*, 49–61.

Madden, N. A., Slavin, R. E., & Stevens, R. J. (1986). *Cooperative integrated reading and comparison: Teacher's manual.* Baltimore, MD: Johns Hopkins University, Center for Research on Elementary and Middle Schools.

Maddux, C. D., Johnson, D. L., & Willis, J. W. (1997). *Educational computing: Learning with tomorrow's technologies* (2nd ed.). Boston: Allyn & Bacon.

Maehr, M. L., & Midgley, C. (1996). *Transforming school cultures*. Boulder, CO: Westview.

Magee, J. C., Galinsky, A. D., & Gruenfeld, D. H. (2007). Power, propensity to negotiate, and moving first in competitive interactions. *Personality and Social Psychology Bulletin, 33*, 200–212.

Mahoney, J. L., Cairns, B. D., & Farmer, T. W. (2003). Promoting interpersonal competence and educational success through extracurricular activity participation. *Journal of Educational Psychology, 95*, 409–418.

Main, M., Kaplan, N., & Cassidy, J. (1985). Security in infancy, childhood, and adulthood: A move to the level of representation. In I. Bretherton & E. Waters (Eds.), *Growing points of attachment theory and research. Monographs of the Society for Research in Child Development, 50* (1–2, Serial No. 209), 66–104.

Malmberg, L.-E., Hagger, H., Burn, K., Mutton, T., & Colls, H. (2010). Observed classroom quality during teacher education and two years of professional practice. *Journal of Educational Psychology, 102*, 916–932.

Malone, T. W. (1981). Toward a theory of intrinsically motivating instruction. *Cognitive Science, 4*, 333–369.

Marchant, G. J. (1992). A teacher is like a …: Using simile lists to explore personal metaphors. *Language and Education, 6*, 33–45.

Marcia, J. E. (1966). Development and validation of ego identity status. *Journal of Personality and Social Psychology, 3*, 551–558.

Marcia, J. E. (1994). The empirical study of ego identity. In H. A. Bosma, T. L. G. Graffsma, H. D. Grotevant, & D. J. de Levita (Eds.), *Identity and development: An interdisciplinary approach* (pp. 67–80). Thousand Oaks, CA: Sage.

Marder, C. (1992). Education after secondary school. In M. Wagner, R. D'Amico, C. Marder, L. Newman, & J. Blackorby (Eds.), *What happens next? Trends in postschool outcomes of youth with disabilities* (The second comprehensive report from the National Longitudinal Transition Study of Special Education Students, pp. 313-319). Menlo Park, CA: SRI International.

Markus, H., Cross, S., & Wurf, E. (1990). The role of self-esteem in competence. In R. J. Sternberg & J. Kolligian (Eds.), *Competence considered* (pp. 205–225). New Haven, CT: Yale University Press.

Markus, H., & Nurius, P. (1986). Possible selves. *American Psychologist, 41*, 954–969.

Markus, H., & Wurf, E. (1987). The dynamic self-concept: A social psychological perspective. *Annual Review of Psychology, 38*, 299–337.

Markus, H. R., & Ruvolo, A. P. (1989). Possible selves: Personalized representations of goals. In L. A. Pervin (Ed.), *Goal concepts in personality and social psychology* (pp. 211–241). Hillsdale, NJ: Erlbaum.

Marsh, H. W. (1990). The structure of academic self-concept: The Marsh/Shavelson model. *Journal of Educational Psychology, 82*, 623–636.

Marsh, H. W. (1991). The failure of high-ability high schools to deliver academic benefits: The importance of academic self-concept and educational aspirations. *American Educational Research Journal, 28*, 445–480.

Marsh, H. W. (2007a). Do university teachers become more effective with experience? A multilevel growth model of students' evaluations of teaching over 13 years. *Journal of Educational Psychology, 99*, 775–790.

Marsh, H. W. (2007b). *Self-concept theory, measurement and research into practice: The role of self-concept in educational psychology.* Leicester, UK: British Psychological Society.

Marsh, H. W., & Ayotte, V. (2003). Do multidimensional dimensions of self-concept become more differentiated with age? The differential distinctiveness hypothesis. *Journal of Educational Psychology, 95*, 687–706.

Marsh, H. W., Byrne, B. M., & Shavelson, R. J. (1988). A multifaceted academic self-concept: Its hierarchical structure and its relation to academic achievement. *Journal of Educational Psychology, 80*, 366–380.

Marsh, H. W., Byrne, B. M., & Yeung, A. S. (1999). Causal ordering of academic self-concept and achievement: Reanalysis of a pioneering study and revised recommendations. *Educational Psychologist, 34*, 155–167.

Marsh, H. W., & Craven, R. G. (1997). Academic self-concept: Beyond the dust-bowl. In G. Phye (Ed.), *Handbook of classroom assessment: Learning, achievement and adjustment* (pp. 131–198). Orlando, FL: Academic Press.

Marsh, H. W., & Hau, K. T. (2003). Big-fish-little-pond effect on academic self-concept: A cross-cultural (26-country) test of the negative effects of academically selective schools. *American Psychologist, 58*, 364–376.

Marsh, H. W., & O'Neill, R. (1984). Self description questionnaire. III: The construct validity of multidimensional self-concept ratings by late adolescents. *Journal of Educational Measurement, 21*, 153–174.

Marsh, H. W., & Richards, G. (1988). The Outward Bound Bridging Course for low achieving high-school males: Effects on academic achievement and multidimensional self-concepts. *Australian Journal of Psychology, 40*, 281–298.

Marsh, H. W., & Shavelson, R. J. (1985). Self-concept: Its multifaceted, hierarchical structure. *Educational Psychologist, 20*, 107–125.

Marsh, H. W., Smith, I., & Barnes, J. (1983). Multitrait-multimethod analyses of the self-description questionnaire: Student-teacher agreement on multidimensional ratings of student self-concept. *American Educational Research Journal, 26*, 333–357.

Marsh, H. W., Trautwein, U., Ludtke, O., & Koller, O. (2008). Social comparison and big-fish-little-pond effects on self-concept and other self-belief constructs: Role of generalized and specific others. *Journal of Educational Psychology, 100*, 510–524.

Marsh, H. W., & Yeung, A. S. (1997a). The causal effects of academic self-concept on academic achievement: Structural equation models of longitudinal data. *Journal of Educational Psychology, 89*, 41–54.

Marsh, H. W., & Yeung, A. S. (1997b). Coursework selection: The effects of academic self-concept and achievement. *American Educational Research Journal, 34*, 691–720.

Marshall, H. H. (1990). Metaphor as an instructional tool in encouraging student teacher reflection. *Theory into Practice, 29*, 128–132.

Martin, J. E., Marshall, L. H., & Sale, P. (2004). A 3-year study of middle, junior high, and high school IEP meetings. *Exceptional Children, 70*, 285–297.

Martin, T. (2009). A theory of physically distributed learning: How external environments and internal states interact in mathematics learning. *Child Development Perspectives, 3*, 140–144.

Martinez-Pons, M. (2002). Parental influences on children's academic self-regulatory development. *Theory into Action, 41*, 126–131.

Martone, A., & Sireci, S. G. (2009). Evaluating alignment between curriculum, assessment, and instruction. *Review of Educational Research, 79*(4), 1332–1361.

Mastergeorge, A. M., & Miyoshi, J. N. (1999). *Accommodations for students with disabilities: A teacher's guide* (CSE Technical Report 508). Los Angeles: CRESST/University of California.

Mastropieri, M. A., & Scruggs, T. E. (1998). Enhancing school success with mnemonic strategies. *Intervention in School & Clinic, 33*, 201–208.

Mathes, P. G., & Fuchs, L. S. (1993). Peer mediated reading instruction in special education resource rooms. *Learning Disabilities Research and Practice, 8*, 233–243.

Mathes, P. G., Torgeson, J. K., Clancy-Menchetti, J., Santi, K., Nicholas, K., Robinson, C., & Grek, M. (2003). A comparison of teacher-directed versus peer-assisted instruction to struggling first-grade readers. *Elementary School Journal, 103*, 459–479.

Matsui, T., Okada, A., & Inoshita, O. (1983). Mechanism of feedback affecting task performance. *Organizational Behavior and Human Performance, 31*, 114–122.

Matsumoto, D., & Juang, L. (2007). *Culture and psychology* (4th ed.). Belmont, CA: Wadsworth.

Matthew, K. I. (1997). A comparison of the influence of interactive CD-ROM storybooks and traditional print storybooks on reading comprehension. *Journal of Research on Computing in Education, 29,* 263–275.

Mayer, R. (2001). *Multimedia learning.* New York: Cambridge University Press.

Mayer, R. E. (1988). *Teaching and learning computer programming.* Hillsdale, NJ: Erlbaum.

Mayer, R. E. (2004). Should there be a three-strikes rule against pure discovery learning? The case for guided methods of instruction. *American Psychologist, 59,* 14–19.

McAdams, D. P., Diamond, A., du St. Aubin, E., & Mansfeld, E. (1997). Stories of commitment: The psychosocial construction of generative lives. *Journal of Personality and Social Psychology, 72,* 721–731.

McAdams, D. P., & du St. Aubin, E. (1992). A theory of generativity and its assessment through self-report, behavioral acts, and narrative themes in autobiography. *Journal of Personality and Social Psychology, 62,* 1003–1015.

McAlpine, L., Weston, C., Beauchamp, J., Wiseman, C., & Beauchamp, C. (1999). Building a metacognitive model of reflection. *Higher Education, 37,* 105–131.

McArthur, D., Stasz, C., & Zmuidzinas, M. (1990). Tutoring techniques in algebra. *Cognition and Instruction, 7*(3), 197–244.

McCabe, M. (2004, January). Teachers: Special ed. students should meet own standards. *Education Week, 23,* 20–21.

McCagg, E. C., & Dansereau, D. F. (1991). A convergent paradigm for examining knowledge mapping as a learning strategy. *Journal of Educational Research, 84,* 317–324.

McCarthy, J., & Benally, J. (2003). Classroom management in a Navajo middle school. *Theory into Practice, 42,* 296–304.

McCarthy, M. M, & Kuh, G. O. (2006). Are students ready for college? What student engagement data say. *Phi Delta Kappan, 87,* 664–669.

McClearn, G. E. (1991). A trans-time visit with Francis Galton. In G. A. Kimble, M. Werheimer, & C. L. White (Eds.), *Portraits of pioneers in psychology* (pp. 1–11). Hillsdale, NJ: Erlbaum.

McCord, J. (1995). *Coercion and punishment in long-term perspectives.* New York: Cambridge University Press.

McCrea, S. M., & Hirt, E. R. (2001). The role of ability judgments in self-handicapping. *Personality and Social Psychology Bulletin, 27,* 1378–1389.

McCutcheon, G. (1980). How do elementary teachers plan? The nature of planning and influences on it. *Elementary School Journal, 81,* 4–23.

McCutcheon, G., & Milner, H. R. (2002). A contemporary study of teacher planning in a high school English class. *Teachers and Teaching: Theory and Practice, 8*(1), 81–94.

McGinnis, E., & Goldstein, A. (1997). *Skillstreaming the elementary school child: A guide for teaching prosocial skills* (rev. ed). Champaign, IL: Research Press.

McKenna, M. C., Reinking, D., Labbo, L. D., & Watkins, J. H. (1996). *Using electronic storybooks with beginning readers* [Instructional Resource]. Athens, GA, and College Park, MD: National Reading Research Center.

McLaughlin, B. (1987). *Theories of second-language learning.* London: Arnold.

McMaster, K. N., & Fuchs, D. (2002). Effects of cooperative learning on the academic achievement of students with learning disabilities: An update on Tateyama-Sniezek's review. *Learning Disabilities: Research and Practice, 17,* 107–117.

Meece, J. L. (1991). The classroom context and students' motivational goals. In M. L. Maehr & P. R. Pintrich (Eds.), *Advances in motivation and achievement* (Vol. 7, pp. 261–285). Greenwich, CT: JAI Press.

Meece, J., Anderman, E. M., & Anderman, L. H. (2006). Classroom goal structure, student motivation, and academic achievement. *Annual Review of Psychology, 57,* 505–528.

Meece, J., Blumenfeld, P., & Hoyle, R. (1988). Students' goal orientations and cognitive engagement in classroom activities. *Journal of Educational Psychology, 80,* 514–523.

Meece, J. L., & Holt, K. (1993). Variations in students' achievement goal patterns. *Journal of Educational Psychology, 85,* 582–590.

Meece, J. L., & Miller, S. D. (1999). Changes in elementary school children's achievement goals for reading and writing: Results from a longitudinal and an intervention study. *Scientific Studies in Reading, 3,* 207–229.

Meehan, B. T., Hughes, J. N., & Cavell, T. A. (2003). Teacher-student relationships as compensatory resources for aggressive children. *Child Development, 74,* 1145–1157.

Meeker, B. (1981). Expectation states and interpersonal behavior. In M. Rosenberg & R. H. Turner (Eds.), *Social psychology: Sociological perspectives* (pp. 290–319). New York: Basic Books.

Mehan, H. (1979). *Social organization in the classroom.* Cambridge, MA: Harvard University Press.

Meier, K., Stewart, J., & England, R. (1989). *Race, class, and education: The politics of second generation discrimination.* Madison: University of Wisconsin Press.

Meilman, P. W. (1979). Cross-sectional age changes in ego identity status during adolescence. *Developmental Psychology, 15,* 230–231.

Mento, A. J., Steel, R. P., & Karren, R. J. (1987). A meta-analytic study of the effects of goal setting on task performance: 1966–1984. *Organizational Behavior and Human Decision Processes, 39,* 52–83.

Mercer, C. D., & Mercer, A. R. (2001). *Teaching students with learning problems* (6th ed.). Upper Saddle River, NJ: Merrill/Prentice Hall.

Mercer, C. D., & Pullen, P. C. (2009). *Students with learning disabilities* (7th ed). Upper Saddle River, NJ: Merrill.

Merrell, K. W., Gueldner, B. A., Ross, S. W., & Isava, D. M. (2008). How effective are school bullying intervention programs? A meta-analysis of intervention research. *School Psychology Quarterly, 23,* 26–42.

Messick, S. (1989). Validity. In R. L. Linn (Ed.), *Educational measurement* (3rd ed.). New York: Macmillan.

Messick, S. (1994). The interplay of evidence and consequences in the validation of performance assessments. *Educational Researcher, 23*(2), 13–23.

Meyer, J. (2004). Novice and expert teachers' conceptions of learners' prior knowledge. *Science Education, 88,* 970–983.

Meyer, W. (1992). Paradoxical effects of praise and criticism on perceived ability. In W. Stroebe & M. Hewstone (Eds.), *European review of social psychology* (Vol. 3, pp. 259–283). Oxford, UK: Wiley.

Michaels, C. A., Prezant, F. P., Morabito, S. M., & Jackson, K. (2002). Assistive and instructional technology for college students with disabilities: A national snapshot of postsecondary service providers. *Journal of Special Education Technology ejournal, 17.* Retrieved November 11, 2005, from http://jset.unlv.edu/17.1/michaels/first.html

Middleton, M. J., & Midgley, C. (1997). Avoiding the demonstration of lack of ability: An underexplained aspect of goal theory. *Journal of Educational Psychology, 89,* 710–718.

Midgley, C., Anderman, E., & Hicks, L. (1995). Differences between elementary and middle school teachers and students: A goal theory approach. *Journal of Early Adolescence, 15,* 90–115.

Midgley, C., Feldlaufer, H., & Eccles, J. (1989). Change in teacher efficacy and student self- and task-related beliefs in mathematics during the transition to junior high school. *Journal of Educational Psychology, 81,* 247–258.

Midgley, C., Kaplan, A., & Middleton, M. (2001). Performance approach goals: Good for what, for whom, under what circumstances, and at what cost? *Journal of Educational Psychology, 93,* 77–86.

Mielke, K. (1994). *Sesame Street* and children in poverty. *Media Studies Journal, 8,* 125–134.

Mikulincer, M. (1994). *Human learned helplessness: A coping perspective.* New York: Plenum.

Mikulincer, M. (1995). Attachment style and the mental representation of the self. *Journal of Personality and Social Psychology, 69,* 1203–1215.

Mikulincer, M. (1998). Attachment working models and the sense of trust: An exploration of interaction goals and affect regulation. *Journal of Personality and Social Psychology, 74,* 1209–1224.

Miller, G. A. (1956). The magical number seven, plus or minus two: Some limits on our capacity for processing information. *Psychological Review, 6,* 81–97.

Miller, I. W., & Norman, W. H. (1981). Effects of attributions for success on the alleviation of learned helplessness and depression. *Journal of Abnormal Psychology, 90,* 113–124.

Miller, P. H. (2011). Piaget's theory: Past, present, and future. In U. Goswami (Ed.), *The Wiley-Blackwell handbook of childhood cognitive development* (2nd ed., pp. 649–672). Hoboken, NJ: Wiley-Blackwell.

Miller, P. J., Fung, H., & Mintz, J. (1996). Self-construction through narrative practices: A Chinese and American comparison of early socialization. *Ethos, 24,* 237–280.

Minicucci, C. (1996). *Learning science and English: How school reform advances scientific learning for limited English proficient middle school students* (National Center for Research on Cultural Diversity and Second Language Learning, Educational Practice Report 17). CA: Berkeley.

Mirenowicz, J., & Schultz, W. (1994). Importance of unpredictability for reward responses in primate dopamine neurons. *Journal of Neurophysiology, 72,* 1024–1027.

Miserandino, M. (1996). Children who do well in school: Individual differences in perceived competence and autonomy in above-average children. *Journal of Educational Psychology, 88,* 203–214.

Mishna, F. (2003). Learning disabilities and bullying: Double jeopardy. *Journal of Learning Disabilities, 36,* 336–347.

Molnar, A., Smith, P., & Zahorik, J. (2000). *1999–2000 evaluation results of the Study Achievement Guarantee in Education (SAGE) program.* Milwaukee: University of Wisconsin, School of Education.

Monsaas, J. A. (1985). Learning to be a world class tennis player. In B. S. Bloom (Ed.), *Developing talent in young people* (pp. 211–269). New York: Ballantine.

Montague, P. R., Dayan, P., & Sejnowski, T. J. (1996). A framework for mesencephalic dopamine systems based on predictive Hebbian learning. *Journal of Neuroscience, 16,* 1936–1947.

Montali, J., & Lewandowski, L. (1996). Bimodal reading: Benefits of a talking computer for average and less skilled readers. *Journal of Learning Disabilities, 29,* 271–279.

Montemayor, R., & Eisen, M. (1977). The development of self-conceptions from childhood to adolescence. *Developmental Psychology, 13,* 314–319.

Montessori, M. (1917). *The advanced Montessori method.* New York: Frederick A. Stokes.

Moor, A. de & Aakhus, M. (2006). Argument support: From technologies to tools. *Communications of the ACM 49*(3), 93–98.

Moore, M., & Smith, L. (1996). Interactive computer software: The effects on young children's reading achievement. *Reading Psychology, 17,* 43–64.

Moore, W., & Esselman, M. (1992, April). *Teacher efficacy, power, school climate and achievement: A desegregating district's experience.* Paper presented at the annual meeting of the American Educational Research Association, San Francisco.

Morine-Dersheimer, G. (1979). *Teacher plan and classroom reality* (The South Bay Study, Part 4, Research series number 60). East Lansing: Institute for Research on Learning, Michigan State University.

Morris, R. D., Stuebing, K. K., Fletcher, J. M., Shaywitz, S. E., Lyon, G. R., Shankweiler, D. P., Katz, L., & Francis, D. J. (1998). Subtypes of reading disability: Variability around a phonological core. *Journal of Educational Psychology, 90,* 347–373.

Morrow, L. M., & Weinstein, C. S. (1982). Increasing children's literature use through program and physical design changes. *Elementary School Journal, 83*(2), 131–137.

Moses, R. P. (1994). Remarks on the struggle for citizenship and math/science literacy. *Journal of Mathematical Behavior, 13,* 107–111.

Moshman, D. (1982). Exogenous, endogenous, and dialectical constructivism. *Developmental Review, 2,* 371–384.

Muehlenhard, C. L., & Kimes, L. A. (1999). The social construction of violence: The case of sexual and domestic violence. *Personality and Social Psychology Review, 3,* 234–245.

Multimodal Treatment Study of Children with ADHD. (1999). A 14-month randomized clinical trial of treatment strategies for attention-deficit hyperactivity disorder (ADHD). *Archives of General Psychiatry, 56,* 1073–1086.

Murdock, T. B. (1999). Discouraging cheating in your classroom. *Mathematics Teacher,* October, 587.

Murphy, K. R., & Davidshofer, C. O. (1994). *Psychological testing: Principles and applications* (3rd ed.). Englewood Cliffs, NJ: Prentice Hall.

Murphy, P. K., & Edwards, M. (2005, April). *What the studies tell us: A meta-analysis of discussion approaches.* Paper presented at the Annual Meeting of the American Educational Research Association, Montreal.

Murray, C., & Greenberg, M. T. (2000). Children's relationship with teachers and bonds with school. *Journal of School Psychology, 38,* 423–445.

Murray, C., & Greenberg, M. T. (2001). Relationships with teachers and bonds with school: Social emotional adjustment correlates for children with and without disabilities. *Psychology in the Schools, 38,* 25–41.

Murray, J. P. (2001). TV violence and brain-mapping in children. *Psychiatric Times, 18*(10). Retrieved December 9, 2004, from http://www.psychiatrictimes.com/p011070.html

Museum Financial Information. (2003). Washington, DC: American Association of Museums.

Nansel, T., Overpeck, M., Pilla, R., Ruan, W., Simon-Mortton, B., & Scheidt, P. (2001). Bullying behaviors among U.S. youth: Prevalence and association with psychosocial adjustment. *Journal of the American Medical Association, 285,* 2094–2100.

National Association of Psychologists. (2002). Position statement on ability grouping. Retrieved October 21, 2004, from http://www.nasponline.org./information/pospaper_ag.html

National Association of School Psychologists. (2002). Position statement on corporal punishment in schools. Retrieved October 10, 2004, from http://www.nasponline.org/information/pospaper_corpunish.html

National Commission on Teaching and America's Future (2003). *No dream denied: A pledge to America's children.* Retrieved February 10, 2005, from http://www.nctaf.org/dream/dream.html

National Council on Education Standards and Testing. (1992). *Raising standards for American education: A report to Congress, the Secretary of Education, the National Education Goals Panel, and the American people.* Washington, DC: Author.

National Institute of Mental Health. (2004). Attention deficit/hyperactivity disorder. Retrieved October 24, 2004, from http://www.nimh.nih.gov/publicat/adhd.cfm

National Research Council. (2004). *Engaging schools: Fostering high school students' motivation to learn.* Washington, DC: National Academies Press.

Neal, L. I., McCray, A. D., Webb-Johnson, G., & Bridgest, S. T. (2003). The effects of African American movement styles on teachers' perceptions and reactions. *The Journal of Special Education, 37,* 49–57.

Neale, D. C., Smith, D., & Johnson, V. G. (1990). Implementing conceptual change teaching in primary science. *Elementary School Journal, 91,* 109–131.

Nedelsky, L. (1954). Absolute grading standards for objective tests. *Educational and Psychological Measurement, 14,* 3–19.

Neill, M. (2003). The dangers of testing. *Educational Leadership, 60,* 43–46.

Neimark, E. D. (1979). Current status of formal operations research. *Human Development, 22,* 60–67.

Nelson, C. A., & Bloom, F. E. (1997). Child development and neuroscience. *Child Development, 68,* 970–987.

Newby, T. J. (1991). Classroom motivation: Strategies of first-year teachers. *Journal of Educational Psychology, 83,* 195–200.

Newmann, F. (1992). *Student engagement and achievement in American secondary schools.* New York: Teachers College Press.

Newman, F. M., (1981). Reducing student alienation in high schools: Implications of theory. *Harvard Educational Review, 51,* 546–564.

Newman, R. S. (2008). Adaptive and nonadaptive help seeking with peer harassment: An integrative perspective of coping and self-regulation. *Educational Psychologist, 43,* 1–15.

Newmann, F., Wehlage, G. C., & Lamborn, S. D. (1992). The significance and sources of student engagement. In F. Newmann (Ed.), *Student engagement and achievement in American Secondary Schools* (pp. 11–39). New York: Teachers College Press.

Newton, D. P., & Newton, L. D. (2001). Subject content knowledge and teacher talk in the primary science classroom. *European Journal of Teacher Education, 24,* 369–379.

Nicholls, J. G. (1978). The development of the concepts of effort and ability, perceptions of academic achievement, and the understanding that difficult tasks require more ability. *Child Development, 49,* 800–814.

Nicholls, J. G. (1979). Development of perception of own attainment and causal attributions for success and failure in reading. *Journal of Educational Psychology, 71,* 94–99.

Nicholls, J. G. (1984). Achievement motivation: Conceptions of ability, subjective experience, task choice, and performance. *Psychological Review, 91,* 328–346.

Nieto, S. (1992). *Affirming diversity: The sociopolitical context of multicultural education.* New York: Longman.

Nishina, A., Juvonen, J., & Witkow, M. (2006). Sticks and stones may break my bones, but names will make me sick: The consequences of peer harassment. *Journal of Clinical Child and Adolescent Psychology, 34,* 37–48.

Noddings, N. (1984). *Caring: A feminine approach to ethics and moral education.* Berkeley: University of California Press.

Noguchi, J. (1998). "Easifying" ESP texts for EFL science majors. *Proceedings of The Japan Conference on English for Specific Purposes.* Aizuwakamatsu City, Fukushima, Japan. (ERIC Document Reproduction Service No. ED 424 776).

Noguera, P. A. (2003). Schools, prisons, and social implications of punishment: Rethinking disciplinary practices. *Theory into Practice, 42,* 341–350.

Nolan, S. A., Flynn, C., & Garber, J. (2003). Prospective relations between rejection and depression in young adolescents. *Journal of Personality and Social Psychology, 85,* 745–755.

Nolen, S. B. (1988). Reasons for studying: Motivational orientations and study strategies. *Cognition and Instruction, 5,* 269–287.

Norris, J. A. (2003). Looking at classroom management through a social and emotional learning lens. *Theory into Practice, 42,* 313–318.

Ntoumanis, N., Pensgaard, A. M., Martin, C., & Pipe, K. (2004). An ideographic analysis of amotivation in compulsory school physical education. *Journal of Sport and Exercise Psychology, 26,* 197–214.

Nunally, J. C. (1967). *Psychometric theory.* New York: McGraw-Hill.

Nunes, T. (1999). Mathematics learning as the socialization of the mind. *Mind, Culture, and Activity, 6,* 33–52.

Oakes, J. (1990). *Multiplying inequalities: The effects of race, social class, and tracking on opportunities to learn mathematics and science* (No. ED 329615). Santa Monica, CA: Rand Corporation.

Oakhill, J. V. (1982). Constructive processes in skilled and less skilled comprehender's memory for sentences. *British Journal of Psychology, 73,* 13–20.

Oakhill, J. V. (1984). Inferential and memory skills in children's comprehension of stories. *British Journal of Educational Psychology, 54,* 31–39.

Oakhill, J. V., Yuill, N., & Parkin, A. (1986). On the nature of the differences between skilled and less skilled comprehenders. *Journal of Research in Reading, 9,* 80–91.

Oberg, A., & McCutcheon, G. (1987). Teachers' experience doing action research. *Peabody Journal of Education, 64,* 116–127.

O'Donnell, A. M., & Dansereau, D. F. (1992). Scripted cooperation in student dyads: A method for analyzing and enhancing academic learning and performance. In R. Hertz-Lazarowitz & N. Miller (Eds.), *Interaction in cooperative groups: The theoretical anatomy of group learning* (pp. 120–141). New York: Cambridge University Press.

O'Donnell, A. M., Dansereau, D. F., Hall, R. H., & Rocklin, T. R. (1987). Cognitive, social/affective, and metacognitive outcomes of scripted cooperative learning. *Journal of Educational Psychology, 79,* 431–437.

O'Donnell, A. M., Dansereau, D. F., Hythecker, V. I., Larson, C. O., Skaggs, L., & Young, M. D. (1987). The effects of monitoring on cooperative learning. *Journal of Experimental Education, 54,* 169–173.

O'Donnell, A., Hmelo-Silver, C., & Erkens, G. (2005). *Collaborative, learning reasoning, and technology.* Mahwah, NJ: Erlbaum.

O'Donnell, A. M., & King, A. (1999). *Cognitive perspectives on peer learning.* Mahwah, NJ: Erlbaum.

O'Donnell, A., & O'Kelly, J. (1994). Learning from peers: Beyond the rhetoric of positive results. *Educational Psychology Review, 6*(4), 321–349.

O'Donnell, A. M. (2003, August). *Promoting understanding through collaborative questioning and use of graphic organizers.* Paper presented at the Annual Meeting of the American Psychological Association.

Ogle, D. (2007). *K-W-L-H technique.* Retrieved November 19, 2007, from North Central Regional Laboratory at http://www.ncrel.org/sdrs/areas/issues/students/learning/lr1kwlh.htm

Ohio Department of Education (2003). *Academic content standards, K–12 science: Benchmarks and indicators by grade level.* Retrieved June 2, 2005, from http://www.ode.state.oh.us/academic_content_standards/ScienceContentStd/RTF/g_Science_by_Grade_Level.rtf

O'Leary, K. D., Kaufman, K. F., Kass, R. E., & Drabman, R. S. (1970). The effects of loud and soft reprimands on the behavior of disruptive students. *Exceptional Children, 37,* 145–155.

Oliver, R., Hoover, J. H., & Hazler, R. (1994). The perceived role of bullying in small town Midwestern schools. *Journal of Counseling & Development, 72,* 416-420.

Olweus, D. (1980). Familial and temperamental determinants of aggressive behavior in adolescent boys: A causal analysis. *Developmental Psychology, 16,* 644–660.

Olweus, D. (1993). *Bullying at school: What we know and what we can do.* Oxford, UK: Blackwell.

Olweus, D. (1997). Bully/victim problems in school: Facts and intervention. *European Journal of Psychology of Education, 12,* 495–510.

Orbach, I., & Hadas, Z. (1982). The elimination of learned helplessness deficits as a function of induced self-esteem. *Journal of Research in Personality, 16,* 511–523.

Orbell, S., & Sheeran, P. (2000). Motivation and volitional processes in action initiation: A field study of the role of implementation intentions. *Journal of Applied Social Psychology, 30,* 780–797.

O'Reilly, T., Symons, S., & MacLatchy-Gaudet, H. (1998). A comparison of self-explanation and elaborative interrogation. *Contemporary Educational Psychology, 23,* 434–445.

Orlick, T. D., & Mosher, R. (1978). Extrinsic rewards and participant motivation in a sport-related task. *International Journal of Sport Psychology, 9,* 27–39.

Osguthorpe, R., & Scruggs, T. E. (1986). Special education students as tutors: A review and analysis. *Remedial and Special Education, 7*(4), 15–26.

Osterman, K. F. (2000). Students' need for belonging in the school community. *Review of Educational Research, 70,* 323–367.

Overskeid, G., & Svartdal, F. (1996). Effects of reward on subjective autonomy and interest when initial interest is low. *Psychological Record, 46,* 319–331.

Oyserman, D., & Markus, H. (1990). Possible selves and delinquency. *Journal of Personality and Social Psychology, 59,* 112–115.

Oyserman, D., Terry, K., & Bybee, D. (2002). A possible selves intervention to enhance school involvement. *Journal of Adolescence, 25,* 313–326.

Ozer, E. M., & Bandura, A. (1990). Mechanisms governing empowerment effects: A self-efficacy analysis. *Journal of Personality and Social Psychology, 58,* 472–486.

Pace, J. L., & Hemmings, A. (2007). Understanding authority in classrooms: A review of theory, ideology, and research. *Review of Educational Research, 77*(1), 4–27.

Padilla, A. M. (2006). Second language learning: Issues in research and teaching. In P. A. Alexander & P. H. Winne (Eds.), *Handbook of educational psychology* (2nd ed., pp. 571–591). Mahwah, NJ: Erlbaum.

Padrón, Y. N., & Waxman, H. C. (1996). Improving the teaching and learning of English language learners through instructional technology. *International Journal of Instructional Media, 23*, 341–354.

Paivio, A. (1986). *Mental representation: A dual coding approach.* New York: Oxford University Press.

Pajares, F. (1996). Self-efficacy beliefs in academic settings. *Review of Educational Research, 66*, 543–578.

Pajares, F., & Graham, L. (1999). Self-efficacy, motivation constructs, and mathematics performance of entering middle school students. *Contemporary Educational Psychology, 24*, 124–139.

Pajares, F., & Kranzler, J. (1995). Self-efficacy beliefs and general mental ability in mathematical problem-solving. *Contemporary Educational Psychology, 20*, 426–443.

Pajares, F., & Miller, M. D. (1994). Mathematics self-efficacy and mathematics outcomes: The need for specificity of assessment. *Journal of Counseling Psychology, 42*, 190–198.

Palincsar, A. S., & Brown, A. L. (1984). Reciprocal teaching of comprehension-fostering and comprehension-monitoring activities. *Cognition and Instruction, 1*, 117–175.

Palincsar, A. S., & Klenk, L. J. (1991). Dialogues promoting reading comprehension. In B. Means, C. Chelemer, & M. S. Knapp (Eds.), *Teaching advanced skills to at-risk students* (pp. 112–140). San Francisco: HarperCollins.

Palincsar, A. S., & Klenk, L. J. (1992). Fostering literacy in supportive contexts. *Journal of Learning Disabilities, 25*, 211–225.

Pallak, S. R., Costomiris, S., Sroka, S., & Pittman, T. S. (1982). School experience, reward characteristics, and intrinsic motivation. *Child Development, 53*, 1382–1391.

Park, L. E., Crocker, J., & Mickelson, K. D. (2004). Attachment styles and contingencies of self-worth. *Personality and Social Psychology Bulletin, 30*, 1243–1254.

Parke, R. D., & Slaby, R. G. (1983). The development of aggression. In P. Mussen (Series Ed.) & E. M. Hetherington (Ed.), *Handbook of child psychology: Socialization, personality, and social development* (Vol. 4, pp. 547–641). New York: Wiley.

Patall, E. A., Cooper, H., & Wynn, S. R. (2010). The effectiveness and relative importance of providing choices in the classroom. *Journal of Educational Psychology, 102*, 896–915.

Patterson, G. R., Debaryshe, B. D., & Ramsey, E. (1989). A developmental perspective on antisocial behavior. *American Psychologist, 44*, 329–335.

Paul, R. W. (1988). Critical thinking in the classroom. *Teaching K–8*, 49–51.

Paulsen, M. B. (2001). The relation between research and the scholarship of teaching. *New Directions for Teaching and Learning, 86*, 19–29.

Pea, R. (2004). The social and technological dimensions of scaffolding and related theoretical concepts for learning, education, and human activity. *Journal of the Learning Sciences, 13*, 423–451.

Pedretti, Erminia G. (2004). Perspectives on Learning through Research on Critical Issues-Based Science Center Exhibitions. Science Education, v88 nS1 pS34-S47 Jul 2004.

Pearl, R. (1992). Psychosocial characteristics of learning disabled students. In N. Singh & I. Beale (Eds.), *Current perspectives in learning disabilities: Nature, theory, and treatment* (pp. 96–117). New York: Springer-Verlag.

Pelletier, L. G., Seguin-Levesque, C., & Legault, L. (2002). Pressure from above and pressure from below as determinants of teachers' motivation and teaching behavior. *Journal of Educational Psychology, 94*, 186–196.

Pellegrini, A. D. (2005). Research and policy on children's play. *Child Development Perspectives, 3*, 131–136.

Pellegrini, A. D., & Smith, P. K. (1998). Physical activity play: The nature and function of a neglected aspect of play. *Child Development, 69*, 577–598.

Penner, S. G. (1987). Parental responses to grammatical and ungrammatical utterances. *Child Development, 58*, 376–384.

Pepler, D. J., Craig, W. M., Connolly, J. A., Yuile, A., McMaster, L., & Jiang, D. (2006). A developmental perspective on bullying. *Aggressive Behavior, 32*, 376–384.

Perry, G., & Talley, S. (2001). Online video case studies and teacher education. *Journal of Computing in Teacher Education, 17*, 26–31.

Perry, N. E., Nordby, C. J., & VandeKamp, K. O. (2003). Promoting self-regulated reading and writing at home and school. *Elementary School Journal, 103*, 317–338.

Perry, N. E., VandeKamp, K. O., Mercer, L. K., & Nordby, C. J. (2002). Investigating teacher-student interactions that foster self-regulated learning. *Educational Psychologist, 37*, 5–15.

Perry, N. (1998). Young children's self-regulated learning and contexts that support it. *Journal of Educational Psychology, 90*, 715–729.

Person, N. K., & Graesser, A. C. (1999). Evolution of discourse during cross-age tutoring. In A. M. O'Donnell & A. King (Eds.), *Cognitive perspectives on peer learning* (pp. 69–86). Mahwah, NJ: Erlbaum.

Person, N. K., Kreuz, R. J., Zwaan, R., & Graesser, A. C. (1995). Pragmatics and pedagogy: Conversational rules and politeness strategies may inhibit effective tutoring. *Cognition and Instruction, 13*, 161–188.

Petersen, R. P., Johnson, D. W., & Johnson, R. T. (1991). Effects of cooperative learning on perceived status of male and female pupils. *The Journal of Social Psychology, 113*, 717–735.

Peterson, C., & Barrett, L. C. (1987). Explanatory style and academic performance among university freshmen. *Journal of Personality and Social Psychology, 53*, 603–607.

Peterson, C., Maier, S. F., & Seligman, M. E. P. (1993). *Learned helplessness: A theory for the age of personal control.* New York: Oxford University Press.

Peterson, C., & Seligman, M. E. P. (1984). Causal explanations as a risk factor for depression: Theory and evidence. *Psychological Review, 91*, 347–374.

Pettit, G. S., Dodge, K. A., & Brown, M. M. (1988). Early family experience, social problem solving patterns, and children's social competence. *Child Development, 59*, 107–120.

Phelps, R. P. (1998). The demand for standardized testing. *Educational Measurement: Issues and Practice, 17*, 5–23.

Piaget, J. (1951). *Play, dreams, and imitation in childhood.* New York: Norton.

Piaget, J. (1954). *The construction of reality in the child.* New York: Basic Books.

Piaget, J. (1963). *Origins of intelligence in children.* New York: Norton.

Piaget, J. (1969). *Psychology of intelligence.* New York: Littlefield, Adams.

Piaget, J. (1970). *Genetic epistemology.* New York: Norton.

Piaget, J. (1971). *Science of education and the psychology of the child.* New York: Viking.

Piaget, J. (1973). *To understand is to invent: The future of education.* New York: Viking.

Piaget, J. (1980). Introduction. In J. Piaget (Ed.), *Les forms elementaires de la dialectique* (pp. 9–13). Paris: Editions Gallimard.

Pianta, R. C., Nimetz, S. L., & Bennett, E. (1997). Mother-child relationships, teacher-child relationships, and school outcomes in preschool and kindergarten. *Early Childhood Research Quarterly, 12*, 263–280.

Pianta, R. C., & Steinberg, M. (1992). Teacher-child relationships and the process of adjusting to school. In R. C. Pianta (Ed.), *New directions for child development: Vol. 57. Beyond the parent: The role of other adults in children's lives* (pp. 61–80). San Francisco: Jossey-Bass.

Pianta, R. C., Steinberg, M. S., & Rollins, K. B. (1995). The first two years of school: Teacher-child relationships and deflections in children's classroom adjustment. *Development and Psychopathology, 7*, 295–312.

Pietsch, J., Walker, R., & Chapman, E. (2003). The relationship among self-concept, self-efficacy, and performance in mathematics during secondary school. *Journal of Educational Psychology, 95*, 589–603.

Pigge, F. L., & Marso, R. N. (1997). A seven year longitudinal multi-factor assessment of teaching concerns development through preparation and early years teaching. *Teaching and Teacher Education, 13*, 225–235.

Pinnegar, S., Mangelson, J., Reed, M., & Groves, S. (2011). Exploring preservice teachers' metaphor plotlines. *Teaching and Teacher Education, 28*, 1–9.

Pintrich, P. R., & De Groof, E. (1990). Motivation and self-regulated learning components of academic performance. *Journal of Educational Psychology, 82*, 33–40.

Pintrich, P., & Schunk, D. (2002). *Motivation in education: Theory, research, and applications.* Upper Saddle River, NJ: Merrill Prentice Hall.

Pintrich, P. R. (2000). Multiple goals, multiple pathways: The role of goal orientation in learning and achievement. *Journal of Educational Psychology, 92*, 544–555.

Pintrich, P. R., & Blazevski, J. L. (2004). Applications of a model of goal orientation and self-regulated learning to individuals with learning problems. In L. M. Glidden (Ed.), *International review of research in mental retardation* (pp. 31–83). San Diego: Elsevier Academic Press.

Pittman, T. S., Boggiano, A. K., & Ruble, D. N. (1983). Intrinsic and extrinsic motivational orientations: Limiting conditions on the undermining and enhancing effects of reward on intrinsic motivation. In J. Levine & M. Wang (Eds.), *Teacher and student perceptions: Implications for learning* (pp. 319–340). Hillsdale, NJ: Erlbaum.

Plake, B. S., & Hambleton, R. K. (2000). A standard setting method designed for complex performance assessments: Categorical assignments of student work. *Educational Assessment, 6*(3), 197–215.

Plake, B. S., Impara, J. C., & Spies, R. A. (2003). *The fifteenth mental measurements yearbook.* Lincoln: University of Nebraska Press.

Polansky, S. B. (1986). *900 shows a year: A look at teaching from a teacher's side of the desk.* New York: Random House.

Popham, W. J. (1978). *Criterion-referenced measurement.* Englewood Cliffs, NJ: Prentice Hall.

Popham, W. J. (2001). Teaching to the test? *Educational Leadership, 58*(6), 16–20.

Popham, W. J., & Husek, T. R. (1969). Implications of criterion-referenced measurement. *Journal of Educational Measurement, 6*, 1–9.

Porter, A. C., Linn, R. L., & Trimble, C. S. (2005). The effects of state decisions about NCLB adequate yearly progress targets. *Educational Measurement: Issues and Practice, 24*(4), 32-39.

Prater, M. A. (2003, May/June). She will succeed! Strategies for success in inclusive classrooms. *Teaching Exceptional Children,* pp. 58–64.

Premack, D. (1959). Toward empirical behavior laws. 1. Positive reinforcement. *Psychological Review, 66*(4), 219–233.

Pressley, M., El-Dinary, P. N., Gaskins, I., Schuder, T., Bergman, J., & Almasi, L. (1992). Beyond direct explanations: Transactional instruction of reading comprehension strategies. *Elementary School Journal, 92*, 511–554.

Proctor, C. P., August, D., Carlo, M. S., & Snow, C. (2006). The intriguing role of Spanish language vocabulary knowledge in predicting English reading comprehension. *Journal of Educational Psychology, 98*, 159–169.

Putnum, R. T., & Borko, H. (2000). What do new views of knowledge and thinking have to say about research on teacher learning? *Educational Researcher, 29*, 4–15.

Quintana, C., Eng, J., Carra, A., Wu, H. K., & Soloway, E. (1999). Symphony: A case study in extending learner-centered design through process space analysis. In M. Willians & M. W. Alton (Eds.), *Proceedings of CHI 99 conference on human factors in computing systems* (pp. 473–480). New York: ACM Press.

Rak, C., & Patterson, L. (1996). Promoting resilience in at-risk children. *Journal of Counseling and Development, 74*, 368–373.

Ramus, F., Rosen, S., Dakin, S. C., Day, B. L., Castellote, J. M., White, S., & Frith, U. (2003). Theories of developmental dyslexia: Insights from a multiple case study of dyslexic adults. *Brain, 126*, 841–865.

Randhawa, B., Beamer, J., & Lundberg, I. (1993). Role of mathematics self-efficacy in the structural model of mathematics achievement. *Journal of Educational Psychology, 85*, 41–48.

Reeve, J. (1996). *Motivating others: Nurturing inner motivational resources.* Boston: Allyn & Bacon.

Reeve, J. (2005). Teachers as facilitators: What autonomy-supportive teachers do and why their students benefit. *Elementary School Journal, 105*, 381–391.

Reeve, J. (2006). Teachers as facilitators: What autonomy-supportive teachers do and why their students benefit. *Elementary School Journal, 106*, 225–236.

Reeve, J. (2009). Why teachers adopt a controlling motivating style toward students and how they can become more autonomy supportive. *Educational Psychologist, 44*, 159–175.

Reeve, J. (2011). A self-determination theory perspective on student engagement. In S. L. Christenson, A. L. Reschly, & C. Wylie (Eds.), *The handbook of research on student engagement.* New York: Springer Science.

Reeve, J., Deci, E. L., & Ryan, R. M. (2004). Self-determination theory: A dialectical framework for understanding sociocultural influences on student motivation. In D. M. McInerney & S. Van Etten (Eds.), *Big theories revisited: Research on sociocultural influences on motivation and learning* (Vol. 4, pp. 31–60). Greenwich, CT: Information Age.

Reeve, J., & Jang, H. (2005). *What autonomy-supportive teachers say and do during instruction.* Unpublished manuscript, University of Iowa, Iowa City.

Reeve, J., Jang, H., Carrell, D., Barch, J., & Jeon, S. (2004). Enhancing high school students' engagement by increasing teachers' autonomy-supportive instructional strategies. *Motivation and Emotion, 28*, 147–169.

Reeve, J., Jang, H., Hardre, P., & Omura, M. (2002). Providing a rationale in an autonomy-supportive way as a strategy to motivate others during an uninteresting activity. *Motivation and Emotion, 26*, 183–207.

Reeve, J., Nix, G., & Hamm, D. (2003). The experience of self-determination in intrinsic motivation and the conundrum of choice. *Journal of Educational Psychology, 95*, 375–392.

Reeve, J., & Tseng, C.-M. (2011). Agency as a fourth aspect of students' engagement during learning activities. *Contemporary Educational Psychology, 36*, 257–267.

Reglin, G. L., & Adams, D. R. (1990). Why Asian American high school students have higher grade point averages and SAT scores than other high school students. *High School Journal, 73*, 143–149.

Reich, P. A. (1986). *Language development.* Englewood Cliffs, NJ: Prentice Hall.

Reingold, E. M., Charness, N., Pomplun, M., & Stampe, D. M. (2001). Visual span in expert chess players: Evidence from eye movements. *Psychological Science, 12*, 48–55.

Reis, H. T., Sheldon, K. M., Gable, S. L., Roscoe, J., & Ryan, R. M. (2000). Daily well-being: The role of autonomy, competence, and relatedness. *Personality and Social Psychology Bulletin, 26*, 419–435.

Reiseberg, D. (2001). *Cognition: Exploring the science of the mind* (2nd ed.). New York: Norton.

Reiser, B. J. (2002). Why scaffolding should sometimes make tasks more difficult for learners. In G. Stahl, (Ed.), *Computer support for collaborative learning foundations for a CSCL community: Proceedings of CSCL 2002* (pp. 255–264.). Mahwah, NJ: Erlbaum.

Reiser, B. J. (2004). Scaffolding complex learning: The mechanisms of structuring and problematizing student work. *The Journal of the Learning Sciences, 13*, 273–304.

Reiser, B. J., Tabak, I., Sandoval, W. A., Smith, B. K., Steinmuller, F., & Leone, A. J. (2001). BGuILE: Strategic and conceptual scaffolds for scientific enquiry in biology classrooms. In S. M. Carver & D. Klahr (Eds.) *Cognition and instruction: Twenty-five years of progress* (pp. 263–305). Mahwah, NJ: Erlbaum.

Renninger, K. A. (1996). Learning as the focus of the educational psychology course. *Educational Psychologist, 31*, 63–76.

Renninger, K. A. (2000). Individual interest and its implications for understanding intrinsic motivation. In C. Sansone & J. M. Harackiewicz (Eds.), *Intrinsic and extrinsic motivation: The search for optimal motivation and performance* (pp. 373–404). San Diego: Academic Press.

Renninger, K. A., Hidi, S., & Krapp, A. (Eds.). (1992). *The role of interest in learning and development.* Hillsdale, NJ: Erlbaum.

Repetti, R. L., Taylor, S. E., & Seeman, T. E. (2002). Risky families: Family social environments and the mental and physical health of offspring. *Psychological Bulletin, 128,* 330–366.

Resnick, L., & Harwell, M. (2000). *Instructional variation and student achievement in a standards-based education district* (CSE Technical Report 522). Los Angeles: National Center for Research on Evaluation, Standards, and Student Testing.

Resnick, L., Levine, J. M., & Teasley, S. D. (Eds.). (1991). *Perspectives on socially shared cognition.* Washington, DC: American Psychological Association.

Resnick, L. B. (1981). Instructional psychology. In M. R. Rosenzweig & L. W. Porter (Eds.), *Annual review of psychology* (Vol. 32). Palo Alto, CA: Annual Reviews (pp. 659–704).

Revans, R. W. (1982). *The origins and growth of action learning.* Bromley: Charwell-Bratt Ltd. Bromley, UK.

Revans, R. W. (1984). *The sequence of managerial achievement.* Bradford: MCB University Press. UK.

Reznitskaya, A., Anderson, R. C., McNurlen, B., Nguyen-Jahiel, K., Archodidou, A., & Kim, S. (2001). Influence of oral discussion on written argument. *Discourse Processes, 32,* 155–175.

Reznitskaya, A., Kuo, L., Clark, A., Miller, B., Jadallah, M., Anderson, R. C., & Nyguyen, Jahiel, K. (2009). Collaborative reasoning: A dialogic approach to group discussions. *Cambridge Journal of Education, 39,* 29–48.

Rhodewalt, F., & Fairfield, M. (1991). Self-handicapping in the classroom: The effects of claimed self-handicaps in response to academic failure. *Basics of Applied Social Psychology, 16,* 397–416.

Rice, M. L. (1986). Children's language acquisition. *American Psychologist, 44,* 149–156.

Richardson, V. (1990). The evolution of reflective teaching and teacher education. In R. T. Clift, W. R. Houston, & M. C. Pugach (Eds.), *Encouraging reflective practice in education: An analysis of issues and programs* (pp. 3–19). New York: Teachers College Press.

Richardson, V. (1996). The role of attitudes and beliefs in learning to teach. In J. Sikula, T. Buttery, & E. Guyton (Eds.), *Handbook of research on teacher education* (2nd ed., pp. 102–119). New York: Macmillan.

Rigby, K. (2002). Should we make our school a telling school? *Prime Focus, 30,* 34–36.

Riley, T., Adams, G. R., & Nielson, E. (1984). Adolescent egocentrism: The association among imaginary audience behavior, cognitive development, and parental support and rejection. *Journal of Youth and Adolescence, 13,* 401–417.

Rimm-Kaufman, S. E., & Sawyer, B. E. (2003). Primary-grade teachers' self-efficacy beliefs, attitudes toward teaching, and discipline and teaching practice priorities in relation to the responsive classroom approach. *Elementary School Journal, 104,* 321–341.

Roberts, W. B., Jr., & Coursol, D. H. (1996). Strategies for intervention with childhood and adolescent victims of bullying, teasing, and intimidation in school settings. *Elementary School Guidance and Counseling, 30,* 204–213.

Roberts, W. B., & Morotti, A. A. (2000). The bully as victim: Understanding bully behaviors to increase the effectiveness of interventions in the bully-victim dyad. *Professional School Counseling, 4,* 148–155.

Roeyers, H. (1996). The influence of nonhandicapped peers on the social interactions of children with a pervasive developmental disorder. *Journal of Autism and Developmental Disorders, 26,* 303–320.

Rogers, C. E. (1969). *Freedom to learn: A view of what education might become.* Columbus, OH: Merrill.

Rogers, D. L., Noblit, G. W., & Ferrell, P. (1990). Action research as an agent for developing teachers' communicative competence. *Theory into Practice, 29,* 179–184.

Rogoff, B. (1990). *Apprenticeship in thinking: Cognitive development in social context.* New York: Oxford University Press.

Rogoff, B. (1998). Cognition as a collaborative process. In D. Kuhn & R. S. Siegler (Eds.), *Cognition, language, and perceptual development: Vol. 2. Handbook of child psychology* (5th ed., pp. 679–744). New York: Wiley.

Rogoff, B. (2003). *The cultural nature of human development.* New York: Oxford University Press.

Rogoff, B., & Gardner, W. (1984). Adult guidance of cognitive development. In B. Rogoff & J. Lave (Eds.), *Everyday cognition: Development in social context* (pp. 95–116). Cambridge, MA: Harvard University Press.

Rogoff, B., Turkanis, C. G., & Bartlett, L. (2002). *Learning together: Children and adults in a school community.* New York: Oxford University Press.

Romeo, F. (1998). The negative effects of using a group contingency system. *Journal of Instructional Psychology, 25,* 130–134.

Roness, D. (2011). Still motivated? The motivation for teaching during the second year in the profession. *Teaching and Teacher Education, 27,* 628–638.

Rosch, E. (1973). Natural categories. *Cognitive Psychology, 4,* 328–349.

Rosch, E., Mervis, C. B., Gray, W. D., Johnson, D. M., & Boyes-Braem, P. (1976). Basic objects in natural categories. *Cognitive Psychology, 8,* 382–440.

Rosenberg, M. (1979). *The conceiving self.* New York: Basic Books.

Rosenholz, S. (1987). Education reform strategies: Will they increase teacher commitment? *American Journal of Education, 95,* 534–562.

Rosenshine, B. (1979). Content, time, and direct instruction. In P. Peterson & H. Walberg (Eds.), *Research on teaching: Concepts, findings, and implications* (pp. 28–56). Berkeley, CA: McCutchan.

Rosenshine, B. (1987). Explicit teaching. In D. Berliner & B. Rosenshine (Eds.), *Talks to teachers* (pp. 75–92). New York: Random House.

Rosenshine, B., & Meister, C. (1994). Reciprocal teaching: A review of the research. *Review of Educational Research, 64,* 479–530.

Rosenshine, B., Meister, C., & Chapman, S. (1996). Teaching students to generate questions: A review of the intervention studies. *Review of Educational Research, 66,* 181–221.

Rosenshine, B., & Stevens, R. (1986). Teaching functions. In M. Wittrock (Ed.), *Handbook of research on teaching* (3rd ed., pp. 376–391). New York: Macmillan.

Ross, J. A. (1992). Teacher efficacy and the effect of coaching on student achievement. *Canadian Journal of Education, 17,* 51–65.

Rothbard, J., & Shaver, P. R. (1994). Continuity of attachment across the lifecourse: An attachment-theoretical perspective on personality. In M. Sperling & W. Berman (Eds.), *Adult attachment* (pp. 31–71). New York: Guilford.

Rothkopf, E. Z., & Billington, M. J. (1979). Goal-guided learning from text: Inferring a descriptive processing model from inspection times and eye movements. *Journal of Educational Psychology, 71,* 310–327.

Rottman, T. R., & Cross, D. C. (1990). *Scripted cooperative reading: Using student-student interaction to enhance comprehension.* Paper presented at the annual meeting of the American Educational Research Association, San Francisco.

Ruben, D. H. (1990). *Explaining explanation.* London: Routledge.

Ruble, D. (1983). The development of social comparison processes and their role in achievement-related self-socialization. In E. T. Higgins, D. N. Ruble, & W. W. Hartup (Eds.), *Social cognition and social development: A sociocultural perspective* (pp. 134–157). New York: Cambridge University Press.

Ruble, D., & Frey, K. S. (1991). Changing patterns of comparative behavior as skills are acquired: A function model of self-evaluation. In J. Suls & T. A. Wills (Eds.), *Social comparison: Contemporary theory and research* (pp. 79–107). Hillsdale, NJ: Erlbaum.

Rumberger, R. W. (1987). High school dropouts: A view of issues and evidence. *Review of Educational Research, 57,* 101–121.

Rummel, A., & Feinberg, R. (1988). Cognitive evaluation theory: A meta-analytic review of the literature. *Social Behavior and Personality, 16,* 147–164.

Rushton, J. P., Brainerd, C. J., & Pressley, M. (1983). Behavioral development and construct validity: The principle of aggregation. *Psychological Bulletin, 94,* 18–38.

Rushton, S. P. (2000). Student teacher efficacy in inner-city schools. *Urban Review, 32,* 365–375.

Ryan, R. M. (1991). The nature of the self in autonomy and relatedness. In J. Strauss & G. R. Goethals (Eds.), *The self: Interdisciplinary approaches* (pp. 208–238). New York: Springer-Verlag.

Ryan, R. M. (1993). Agency and organization: Intrinsic motivation, autonomy and the self in psychological development. In J. Jacobs (Ed.), *Nebraska symposium on motivation: Developmental perspectives on motivation* (Vol. 40, pp. 1–56). Lincoln: University of Nebraska Press.

Ryan, R. M., & Connell, J. P. (1989). Perceived locus of causality and internalization: Examining reasons for acting in two domains. *Journal of Personality and Social Psychology, 57,* 749–761.

Ryan, R. M., & Deci, E. L. (2000a). Intrinsic and extrinsic motivations: Classic definitions and new directions. *Contemporary Educational Psychology, 25,* 54–67.

Ryan, R. M., & Deci, E. L. (2000b). Self-determination theory and the facilitation of intrinsic motivation, social development, and well-being. *American Psychologist, 55,* 68–78.

Ryan, R. M., & Deci, E. L. (2001). To be happy or to be self-fulfilled: A review of research and eudaimonic well-being. In S. Fiske (Ed.), *Annual review of psychology* (Vol. 52, pp. 141–166). Palo Alto, CA: Annual Reviews.

Ryan, R. M., & Deci, E. L. (2002). An overview of self-determination theory: An organismic-dialectical perspective. In E. L. Deci & R. M. Ryan (Eds.), *Handbook of self-determination research* (pp. 3–33). Rochester, NY: University of Rochester Press.

Ryan, R. M., & Grolnick, W. S. (1986). Origins and pawns in the classroom: Self-report and projective assessments of individual differences in children's perceptions. *Journal of Personality and Social Psychology, 50,* 550–558.

Ryan, R. M., & La Guardia, J. G. (1999). Achievement motivation within a pressured society: Intrinsic and extrinsic motivations to learn and the politics of school reform. In T. Urdan (Ed.), *Advances in motivation and achievement* (Vol. 11, pp. 45–85). Greenwich, CT: JAI Press.

Ryan, R. M., Mims, V., & Koestner, R. (1983). Relation of reward contingency and interpersonal context to intrinsic motivation: A review and test using cognitive evaluation theory. *Journal of Personality and Social Psychology, 45,* 736–750.

Ryan, R. M., & Powelson, C. (1991). Autonomy and relatedness as fundamental to motivation and education. *Journal of Experimental Education, 60,* 49–66.

Ryan, R. M., Stiller, J., & Lynch, J. (1994). Representations of relationships to teachers, parents, and friends as predictors of academic motivation and self-esteem. *Journal of Early Adolescence, 14,* 226–249.

Rymer, R. (1993). *Genie: A scientific tragedy.* New York: HarperCollins.

Sadler, D. R. (1989). Formative assessment and the design of instructional systems. *Instructional Science, 18* (2), 119–144.

Salmivalli, C., Kaukiainen, A., & Voeten, M. (2005). Anti-bullying intervention: Implementation and outcome. *British Journal of Educational Psychology, 75,* 465–487.

Salmivalli, C., Peets, K., & Hodges, E. V. E. (2010). Bullying. In P. K. Smith & C. H. Hart (Eds.), *The Wiley-Blackwell handbook of childhood social development* (2nd ed., pp. 510–528). Hoboken, NJ: Wiley-Blackwell.

Salomon, G., & Globerson, T. (1987). Skill may not be enough: The role of mindfulness in learning and transfer. *International Journal of Educational Research, 11,* 623–637.

Salomon, G., & Perkins, D. N. (1989). Rocky roads to transfer: Rethinking mechanisms of a neglected phenomenon. *Educational Psychologist, 24,* 113–142.

Sanchez, E., Rosaes, J., & Canedo, I. (1999). Understanding and communication in expositive discourse: An analysis of the strategies used by expert and pre-service teachers. *Teaching and Teacher Education, 15,* 37–58.

Sandoval, W. A. (1998). *Inquire to explain: Structuring inquiry around explanation construction in a technology supported biology curriculum.* Unpublished doctoral dissertation. Evanston, IL: Northwestern University.

Sansone, C., & Smith, J. L. (2000). Self-regulating interest: When, why, and how. In C. Sansone & J. M. Harackiewicz (Eds.), *Intrinsic motivation: Controversies and new directions* (pp. 343–373). New York: Academic Press.

Sansone, C., Weir, C., Harpster, L., & Morgan, C. (1992). Once a boring task always a boring task? Interest as a self-regulatory mechanism. *Journal of Personality and Social Psychology, 63,* 379–390.

Sardo-Brown, D. (1988a). Experienced teachers' planning practices: A U. S. survey. *Journal of Education for Teaching, 16,* 57–71.

Sardo-Brown, D. (1988b). Twelve middle school teachers' planning. *Elementary School Journal, 89,* 69–87.

Saxe, G. B. (1988). The mathematics of child street vendors. *Child Development, 59,* 1415–1425.

Scardamalia, M., Bereiter, C., & Lamon, M. (1994). The CSILE project: Trying to bring the classroom into World 3. In K. McGilley (Ed.), *Classroom lessons: Integrating cognitive theory and classroom practice* (pp. 201–228). Cambridge, MA: MIT Press.

Scardamalia, M., Bereiter, C., & Steinbach, R. (1984). Teachability of reflective processes in written composition. *Cognitive Science, 8,* 173–190.

Schatschneider, C., Fletcher, J. M., Francis, D. J., Carlson, C. D., & Foorman, B. R. (2004). Kindergarten prediction of reading skills: A longitudinal comparative analysis. *Journal of Educational Psychology, 96,* 265–282.

Schellenberg, E. G. (2004). Music lessons enhance IQ. *Psychological Science, 15,* 511–514.

Scherf, K. S., Behrmann, M., Humphreys, K., & Luna, B. (2007). Visual category-selectivity for faces, places and objects emerges along different developmental trajectories. *Developmental Science, 10,* F15–F30.

Schiefele, U. (1991). Interest, learning, and motivation. *Educational Psychologist, 26,* 299–323.

Schiefele, U. (1999). Interest and learning from text. *Scientific Studies of Reading, 3,* 257–280.

Schiefele, U., Krapp, A., & Winteler, A. (1992). Interest as a predictor of academic achievement: A meta-analysis of research. In K. A. Renninger, S. Hidi, & A. Krapp (Eds.), *The role of interest in learning and development* (pp. 183–212). Hillsdale, NJ: Erlbaum.

Schlaefli, A., Rest, J. R., & Thoma, S. J. (1985). Does moral education improve moral judgment? A meta-analysis of intervention studies using the Defining Issues Test. *Review of Educational Research, 55,* 319–352.

Schneider, A. J. (2005). Cultural differences in school expectations for Latino parents. *Parenting.* Retrieved March 20, 2004, from http://missourifamilies.org/features/ parenting-articles/index.htm

Schneider, B., & Lee, Y. (1990). A model for academic success. The school and home environment of East Asian students. *Anthropology and Education Quarterly, 21,* 358–377.

Schneider, W., & Shiffrin, R. M. (1974). Controlled and automatic processing I: Detection, search, and attention. *Psychological Review, 84,* 1–66.

Schon, D. A. (1983). *The reflective practitioner.* New York: Basic Books.

Schon, D. A. (1987). *Educating the reflective practitioner.* San Francisco: Jossey-Bass.

Schraw, G., Flowerday, T., & Lehman, S. (2001). Increasing situational interest in the classroom. *Educational Psychology Review, 13,* 211–224.

Schraw, G., Flowerday, T., & Reisetter, M. (1998). The role of choice in reader engagement. *Journal of Educational Psychology, 90,* 705–714.

Schraw, G., & Lehman, S. (2001). Situational interest: A review of the literature and directions for future research. *Educational Psychology Review, 13,* 23–52.

Schuele, C. M., Rice, M. L., & Wilcox, K. A. (1995). Redirects: A strategy to increase peer initiations. *Journal of Speech and Hearing Research, 38*, 1319–1333.

Schulman, M., & Mekler, E. (1986). *Bringing up a moral child*. Reading, MA: Addison-Wesley.

Schultz, G. F., & Switzky, H. N. (1993). The academic achievement of elementary and junior high school students with behavior disorders and their nonhandicapped peers as a function of motivational orientations. *Learning and Individual Differences, 5*, 31–42.

Schuman, H., Steeh, C., Bobo, L., & Krysan, M. (1997). *Racial attitudes in America: Trends and interpretation*. Cambridge, MA: Harvard University Press.

Schumm, J. S., & Vaughn, S. (1992). Planning for mainstreamed special education students: Perceptions of general classroom teachers. *Exceptionality, 3*, 81–98.

Schumm, J. S., Vaughn, S., Haager, D., McDowell, J., Rothlein, L., & Saumell, L. (1995). General education teacher planning: What can students with learning disabilities expect? *Exceptional Children, 61*, 335–352.

Schunk, D. H. (1989). Self-efficacy and achievement behaviors. *Educational Psychology Review, 1*, 173–208.

Schunk, D. H. (1991). Self-efficacy and academic motivation. *Educational Psychologist, 26*, 207–231.

Schunk, D. H., & Zimmerman, B. J. (1997). Social origins of self-regulatory competence. *Educational Psychologist, 32*, 195–208.

Schutz, P. A., Crowder, K. C., & White, V. E. (2001). The development of a goal to become a teacher. *Journal of Educational Psychology, 93*, 299–308.

Schwartz, D., Gorman, A., Nakamoto, J., & McKay, T. (2006). Popularity, social acceptance, and aggression in adolescent peer groups: Links with academic performance and school attendance. *Developmental Psychology, 42*, 1116–1127.

Schwartz, J. M., & Begley, S. (2002). *The mind and the brain: Neuroplasticity and the power of the mental force*. New York: HarperCollins.

Scriven, M. (1967) The methodology of evaluation. In R. W. Tyler (Ed.), *Perspectives of curriculum evaluation* (pp. 39–83). Chicago: Rand McNally.

Scruggs, T. E., & Mastropieri, M. A. (1998). Tutoring and students with special needs. In K. Topping & S. Ehly (Eds.), *Peer-assisted learning* (pp. 165–182). Mahwah, NJ: Erlbaum.

Scruggs, T. E., & Osguthorpe, R. (1986). Tutoring interventions within special education settings: A comparison of cross–age and peer tutoring. *Psychology in the Schools, 23*, 187–193.

Seals, D., & Young, J. (2003). Bullying and victimization: Prevalence and relationship to gender, grade level, ethnicity, self-esteem, and depression. *Adolescence, 38*, 735–747.

Seipp, B. (1991). Anxiety and academic performance: A meta-analysis of findings. *Anxiety Research, 4*, 27–41.

Selfridge, O. G. (1955). Pattern recognition and modern computers. *Proceedings of Western Joint Computer Conference* (pp. 92–93). New York: Institute of Electrical and Electronics Engineers.

Seligman, M. E. P. (1975). *Helplessness: On depression, development, and death*. San Francisco: Freeman.

Seligman, M. E. P. (1991). *Learned optimism*. New York: Knopf.

Serpell, R. (1993). *The significance of schooling life-journeys in an African society*. Cambridge, UK: Cambridge University Press.

Shaalvik, E. M., & Hagtvet, K. A. (1990). Academic achievement and self-concept: An analysis of causal predominance in a developmental perspective. *Journal of Personality and Social Psychology, 58*, 292–307.

Shapira, Z. (1976). Expectancy determinants of intrinsically motivated behavior. *Journal of Personality and Social Psychology, 34*, 1235–1244.

Sharan, S., & Hertz-Lazarowitz, R. (1980). A group investigation method of cooperative learning in the classroom. In S. Sharan, P. O'Hare, C. Webb, & R. Hertz-Lazarowitz (Eds.), *Cooperation in education* (pp. 14–46). Provo, UT: Brigham Young University Press.

Sharan, S., & Shachar, H. (1988). *Language learning in the cooperative classroom*. New York: Springer-Verlag.

Sharan, S., & Shaulov, A. (1990). Cooperative learning, motivation to learn, and academic achievement. In S. Sharan (Ed.), *Cooperative learning: Theory and research* (pp. 173–202). New York: Praeger.

Sharan, Y., & Sharan, S. (1992). *Expanding cooperative learning through group investigation*. New York: Teacher's College Press.

Shavelson, R. J., Baxter, G. P., & Pine, J. (1991). Performance assessment in science. *Applied Measurement in Education, 4*(4), 347–362.

Shavelson, R. J., & Marsh, H. W. (1986). On the structure of self-concept. In R. Schwarzer (Ed.), *Anxiety and cognitions* (pp. 305–330). Hillsdale, NJ: Erlbaum.

Shaw, J. (2002). Linguistically responsive science teaching. *Electronic Magazine of Multicultural Education, 4*(1). Retrieved July 13, 2005, from http://www.eastern.edu/publications/emme

Shaw, S. M., Walls, S. M., Dacy, B. S., Levin, J. R., & Robinson, D. H. (2010). A follow-up note on prescriptive statements in nonintervention research studies. *Journal of Educational Psychology, 102*, 982–988.

Shearer, C. B. (2004). Using a multiple intelligences assessment to promote teacher development and student achievement. *Teachers College Record, 106*, 147–162.

Sheldon, K. M., Elliot, A. J., Kim, Y., & Kasser, T. (2001). What is satisfying about satisfying events? Testing 10 candidate psychological needs. *Journal of Personality and Social Psychology, 80*, 325–339.

Sheldon, K. M., Ryan, R. M., & Reis, H. T. (1996). What makes for a good day? Competence and autonomy in the day and in the person. *Personality and Social Psychology Bulletin, 22*, 1270–1279.

Shen, B., Li, W., Sun, H., & Rukavina, P. (2010). Amotivation and teachers' inadequate social support in physical education. *Journal of Teaching in Physical Education, 29*, 417–432.

Shepard, L. (2000). *The role of classroom assessment in teaching and learning* (CSE Technical Report 517). Los Angeles: National Center for Research or Evaluation, Standards and Student Testing.

Shepard, L. A. (1982). Definitions of bias. In R. Berk (Ed.), *Handbook for detecting test bias* (pp. 9–30). Baltimore: Johns Hopkins University Press.

Shirey, L. L., & Reynolds, R. E. (1988). Effect of interest on attention and learning. *Journal of Educational Psychology, 80*, 159–166.

Shuell, T. J. (1996). The role of educational psychology in the preparation of teachers. *Educational Psychologist, 31*, 5–14.

Shukla-Mehta, S., & Albin, R. W. (2003) Twelve practical strategies to prevent behavioral escalation in classroom settings. *Preventing School Failure, 47*, 156–161.

Shulman, L. S. (1981). Educational psychology returns to school. In A. G. Kraut (Ed.), *G. Stanley Hall lecture series* (Vol. 2). Washington, DC: American Psychological Association.

Shulman, L. S. (1986). Those who understand: Knowledge growth in teaching. *Educational Researcher, 15*(2), 4–14.

Shulman, L. S. (1987). Knowledge and teaching: Foundations of the new reform. *Harvard Educational Review, 57*(1), 1–22.

Sigman, M., & Ruskin, E. (1999). Continuity and change in the social competence of children with autism, Down syndrome, and developmental delay. *Monographs of the Society for Research in Child Development, 61* (1, Serial No. 256).

Silon, E. L., & Harter, S. (1985). Assessment of perceived competence, motivational orientation, and anxiety in segregated and mainstreamed educable mentally retarded children. *Journal of Educational Psychology, 77*, 217–230.

Silvia, P. J. (2006). *Exploring the psychology of interest*. New York: Oxford University Press.

Silvia, P. J. (2008). Interest, the curious emotion. *Current Directions in Psychological Science, 17*, 57–90.

Simmons, P. E., Emory, A., Carter, T., Coker, T., Finnegan, B., Crockett, D., et al. (1999). Beginning teachers: Beliefs and classroom actions. *Journal of Research in Science Teaching, 36*, 930–954.

Skiba, R. J. (2001), When is disproportionality discrimination? The overrepresentation of blacks in school suspension. In W. Ayers, B. Dohrn, & R. Ayers (Eds.), *Zero tolerance: Resisting the drive for punishment in our schools* (pp. 165–175). New York: New Press.

Skiba, R. J., & Peterson, R. L. (2001). School discipline at a crossroads: From zero tolerance to early response. *Exceptional Children, 66,* 335–346.

Skinner, B. F. (1950). Are theories of learning necessary? *Psychological Review, 57,* 193–216.

Skinner, B. F. (1953). *Science and human behavior.* New York: Macmillan.

Skinner, B. F. (1958). Reinforcement today. *American Psychologist, 13,* 94–99.

Skinner, E. A., & Belmont, M. J. (1993). Motivation in the classroom: Reciprocal effects of teacher behavior and student engagement across the school year. *Journal of Educational Psychology, 85,* 571–581.

Skinner, E. A., Furrer, C., Marchand, G., & Kindermann, T. (2008). Engagement and disaffection in the classroom: Part of a larger motivational dynamic? *Journal of Educational Psychology, 100,* 765–781.

Skinner, E. A., Kindermann, T. A., & Furrer, C. J. (2009). A motivational perspective on engagement and disaffection: Conceptualization and assessment of children's behavioral and emotional participation in academic activities in the classroom. *Educational and Psychological Measurement, 69,* 493–525.

Skinner, E. A., Wellborn, J. G., & Connell, J. P. (1990). What it takes to do well in school and whether I've got it: A process model of perceived control and children's engagement and achievement in school. *Journal of Educational Psychology, 82,* 22–32.

Skinner, E. A., Zimmer-Gembeck, M. J., & Connell, J. P. (1998). Individual differences and the development of perceived control. *Monographs of the Society for Research in Child Development, 63* (2–3, Whole No. 204).

Slater, B. (1968). Effects of noise on pupil performance. *Journal of Educational Psychology, 59,* 239–243.

Slavin, R. E. (1984). Combining cooperative learning and individualized instruction: Effects on students' mathematics achievement, attitudes, and behaviors. *Elementary School Journal, 84,* 409–422.

Slavin, R. E. (1986). *Using student team learning* (3rd ed.). Baltimore, MD: The Johns Hopkins University Press.

Slavin, R. E. (1987a). Making Chapter 1 make a difference. *Phi Delta Kappan, 69,* 110–119.

Slavin, R. E. (1987b). Mastery learning reconsidered. *Review of Educational Research, 57,* 172–213.

Slavin, R. E. (1987c). Ability grouping and student achievement in elementary schools: A best evidence synthesis. *Review of Educational Research, 57,* 293–336.

Slavin, R. E. (1987d). Ability grouping and its alternatives: Must we track? *American Educator, 11*(2), 32–36.

Slavin, R. E. (1990). Achievement effects of ability grouping in secondary schools: A best-evidence synthesis. *Review of Educational Research, 60,* 471–499.

Slavin, R. E. (1995). *Cooperative learning* (2nd ed). Boston: Allyn & Bacon.

Slavin, R. E. (1996). Research on cooperative learning and achievement: What we know, what we need to know. *Contemporary Educational Psychology, 21*(1), 43–69.

Slavin, R. E., & Madden, N. A. (1989). What works for students at-risk: A research synthesis. *Educational Leadership, 46*(5), 4–13.

Sleeter, C. E. (1996). Multicultural education as a social movement. *Theory into Practice, 35,* 239–247.

Sloane, F. C. (2003). *An assessment of Sorenson's model of school differentiation: A multilevel model of tracking in middle and high school mathematics.* Unpublished doctoral dissertation, University of Chicago.

Slobin, D. I. (1985). Crosslinguistic evidence for the language making capacity. In D. I. Slobin (Ed.), *The crosslinguistic study of language acquisition: Theoretical issues* (Vol. 2). Hillsdale, NJ: Erlbaum.

Smith, B. K., & Reiser, B. J. (1998). *National Geographic* unplugged: Designing interactive nature films for classrooms. In C. M. Karat, A. Lund, J. Coutaz, & J. Karat (Eds.), *Proceedings of CHI 98* (pp. 424–431). New York: ACM Press.

Smith, E. L., & Sendelbach, N. B. (1979, April). *Teacher intentions for science instruction and their antecedents.* Paper presented at the annual meeting of the American Educational Research Association, San Francisco.

Smith, J. D., Schneider, B. H., Smith, P. K., & Ananiadou, K. (2004). The effectiveness of whole-school antibullying programs: A synthesis of evaluation research. *School Psychology Review, 33*(4), 547–560.

Smith, J. K. (2003). Reconceptualizing reliability in classroom assessment. *Educational Measurement: Issues and Practice, 22*(4), 82–88.

Smith, J. K., & DeLisi, R. (1998). *Co-principal investigators. Making the grade: Improving postsecondary grading and assessment practices* (Final Report, Fund for the Improvement of Postsecondary Education). New Brunswick, NJ.

Smith, J. K., Smith, L. F., & DeLisi, R. (2001). *Natural classroom assessment.* Thousand Oaks, CA: Corwin.

Smith, J. K., & Wolf, L. F. (1996). Museum visitor preferences and intentions in constructing aesthetic experience. *Poetics: A Journal of Empirical Research in the Arts and Literature, 24,* 219–238.

Smith, J. K., & Wolf, L. F. (2004). The influence of test consequence on national examinations. *North America Journal of Psychology, 5,* 13–26.

Smith, L. F. (2006). *Great expectations: Perceptions of teacher efficacy in teaching practicum students in the United States and New Zealand.* (Proceedings of the annual meeting of the New Zealand Association for Research in Education, Rotorua, New Zealand.)

Smith, L. F., Mobley, M. M., & Klein, P. (2003, April). *Multiple perspectives of preservice teacher efficacy.* Poster presented at the annual meeting of the American Educational Research Association, Chicago.

Smith, M., & Wilhelm, J. (2002). *Reading don't fix no Chevys: Literacy in the lives of young men.* Portsmouth, NH: Heinemann.

Smith, M. K. (2002). Howard Gardner and multiple intelligences. *The encyclopedia of informal education.* Retrieved April 6, 2005, from http://www.infed.org/thinkers/gardner.htm

Smith, P. K., & Brain, P. (2000). Bullying in schools: Lessons from two decades of research. *Aggressive Behavior, 26,* 1–9.

Smith, T. W., Snyder, C. R., & Handelsman, M. M. (1982). On the self-serving function of an academic wooden leg: Test anxiety as a self-handicapping strategy. *Journal of Personality and Social Psychology, 42,* 314–321.

Smith, T. W., Snyder, C. R., & Perkins, S. C. (1983). The self-serving function of hypochondriacal complaints: Physical symptoms as self-handicapping strategies. *Journal of Personality and Social Psychology, 44,* 787–797.

Snow, C. E., Arlman-Rupp, A., Hassing, Y., Jobse, J., Joosken, J., & Vorster, J. (1976). Mother's speech in three social classes. *Journal of Psycholinguistic Research, 5,* 1–20.

Snyder, C. R., Harris, C., Anderson, J. R., Holleran, S. A., Irving, L. M., Sigmond, S. T., Yoshinobu, L., Gibb, J., Langelle, C., & Harney, P. (1991). The will and the ways: Development and validation of an individual-differences measure of hope. *Journal of Personality and Social Psychology, 60,* 570–585.

Snyder, C. R., & Higgins, R. L. (1988). Excuses: Their effective role in the negotiation of reality. *Psychological Bulletin, 104,* 23–35.

Snyder, C. R., Lapointe, A. B., Crowson, J. J., Jr., & Early, S. (1998). Preferences of high- and low-hope people for self-referential input. *Cognition and Emotion, 12,* 807–823.

Snyder, C. R., Rand, K. L., & Sigmon, D. R. (2002). Hope theory: A member of the positive psychology family. In C. R. Snyder & S. J. Lopez (Eds.), *Handbook of positive psychology* (pp. 257–276). New York: Oxford University Press.

Snyder, C. R., Shorey, H. S., Cheavens, J., Pulvers, K. M., Adams, V. H., III, & Wiklund, D. (2002). Hope and academic success in college. *Journal of Educational Psychology, 94,* 820–826.

Soodak, L. (2003). Classroom management in inclusive settings. *Theory into Practice, 42*, 327–333.

Soodak, L. C., & Podell, D. M. (1993). Teacher efficacy and student problem factors in special education referral. *The Journal of Special Education, 27*, 66–81.

Sosniak, L. A. (1985). Learning to be a concert pianist. In B. S. Bloom (Ed.), *Developing talent in young people* (pp. 19–68). New York: Ballantine.

Sourander, A., Elonheimo, H., Niemala, S., Nuutila, A. M., Helenius, H., et al. (2006). Childhood predictors of male criminality: A prospective population-based follow-up study from age 8 to late adolescence. *Journal of American Academy of Child and Adolescent Psychiatry, 45*, 578–586.

Spalding, E., & Wilson, A. (2002). Demystifying reflection: A study of pedagogical strategies that encourage reflective journal writing. *Teachers College Record, 104*, 1393–1421.

Spearman, C. (1923). *The nature of "intelligence" and the principles of cognition.* London: Macmillan.

Spearman, C. (1927). *The abilities of man.* New York: Macmillan.

Special Issues Analysis Center. (2003). *Literature review of federally funded studies related to LEP students.* Washington, DC: Office of Bilingual and Minority Languages Affairs.

Spence, J. T., & Helmreich, R. L. (1983). Achievement-related motives and behavior. In J. T. Spence (Ed.), *Achievement and achievement motives: Psychological and sociological approaches* (pp. 10–74). San Francisco: Freeman.

Sperling, G. (1960). The information available in brief visual presentations. *Psychological Monographs: General and Applied, 74*, 1–29.

Spielberger, C. D., & Starr, L. M. (1994). Curiosity and exploratory behavior. In H. F. O'Neil, Jr. & M. Drillings (Eds.), *Motivation: Theory and research* (pp. 221–243). Hillsdale, NJ: Erlbaum.

Sullivan, B. (1999). Professional development: The linchpin of teacher quality. *Infobrief*, No. 18. Retrieved Oct. 4, 2011 From www.ascd.org/publications/newsletters/policy-priorities/aug99/number18/Toc.aspx.

Stanford-Binet (5th ed.). (2003). Itasca, IL: Riverside Publishing.

Stanovich, K. E. (2009, Nov/Dec). The thinking that IQ tests miss. *Scientific American Mind, 20*(6), 34–39.

Statistical abstracts. (2000). Washington, DC: U.S. Government Printing Office.

Stavrinides, P., Georgiou, S., & Theofanous, V. (2010). Bullying and empathy: A short-term longitudinal investigation. *Educational Psychology, 30*, 793–802.

Steele, C. M. (1999, August). Thin ice: "Stereotype threat" and black college students. *Atlantic Monthly*, pp. 44–54.

Steele, F. I. (1973). *Physical settings and organization development.* Reading, MA: Addison-Wesley.

Steinberg, L. (1996). *Adolescence* (4th ed). New York: McGraw-Hill.

Steiner, I. D. (1972). *Group process and productivity.* New York: Academic Press.

Stern, D. N., Spieker, S., Barnett, R. K., & MacKain, K. (1983). The prosody of maternal speech: Infant age and context related changes. *Journal of Child Language, 10*, 1–15.

Sternberg, R. J. (1985). *Beyond IQ: A triarchic theory of human intelligence.* New York: Cambridge University Press.

Sternberg, R. J. (1997). *Successful intelligence.* New York: Plume.

Sternberg, R. J. (2000). Patterns of giftedness: A triarchic analysis. *Roeper Review, 22*, 231–235.

Sternberg, R. J., Castejon, J. L., Prieto, M. D., Hautamaki, J., & Grigorenko, E. L. (2001). Confirmatory factor analysis of the Sternberg Triarchic Abilities Test in three international samples: An empirical test of the triarchic theory of intelligence. *European Journal of Psychological Assessment, 17*(1), 1–16.

Sternberg, R. J., & Grigorenko, E. L. (2000). *Teaching for successful intelligence.* Arlington Heights, IL: Skylight.

Sternberg, R. J., & Zhang, L. F. (1995). What do we mean by giftedness? A pentagonal implicit theory. *Gifted Child Quarterly, 39*, 88–94.

Stevens, L. P. (2001). *Southpark* and society: Instructional and curricular implications of popular culture in the classroom. *Journal of Adolescent and Adult Literacy, 44*, 548–555.

Stevens, R. J., Madden, N. A., Slavin, R. E., & Farnish, A. (1987). Cooperative integrated reading and composition: Two field experiments. *Reading Research Quarterly, 22*, 433–454.

Stevens, R. J., & Slavin, R. E. (1991). When cooperative learning improves the achievement of students with mild disabilities: A response to Tateyama-Sniezek. *Exceptional Children, 57*, 276–280.

Stevens, R. J., & Slavin, R. E. (1995). Effects of a cooperative learning approach in reading and writing on academically handicapped and nonhandicapped students. *The Elementary School Journal, 95*, 241–262.

Stevens, T., Olivarez, A., Jr., Lan, W. Y., & Tallent-Runnels, M. K. (2004). Role of mathematics self-efficacy and motivation in mathematics performance across ethnicity. *Journal of Educational Research, 97*(4), 208–221.

Stiggins, R. (2004). New assessment beliefs for a new school mission. *Phi Delta Kappan, 86*, 22-33.

Stiggins, R. J. (1997) *Student centered classroom assessment.* Upper Saddle River, NJ: Prentice Hall.

Stiggins, R. J. (2001). *Student-centered classroom assessment* (3rd ed.). Upper Saddle River, NJ: Merrill/Prentice Hall.

Stiggins, R. J. (2004). *Student-involved assessment for learning.* Upper Saddle River, NJ: Merrill/Prentice Hall.

Stipek, D. J., & Kowalski, P. S. (1989). Learned helplessness in task-orienting versus performance-orienting testing conditions. *Journal of Educational Psychology, 81*, 384–391.

Stofflett, R. T. (1996). Metaphor development by secondary teachers enrolled in graduate teacher education. *Teaching and Teacher Education, 12*, 577–589.

Storch, S. A., & Whitehurst, G. J. (2002). Oral language and code related precursors to reading: Evidence from a longitudinal structural study. *Developmental Psychology, 38*, 934–947.

Strain, P. S., Schwartz, I. S., & Bovey, E. H. (2008). Social competence interventions for young children with autism. In W. H. Brown, S. L. Odom, & S. R. McConnell (Eds.), *Social competence of young children: Risk, disability, and intervention* (pp. 253–272). Baltimore: Brookes.

Strang, H. R., Lawrence, E. C., & Fowler, P. C. (1978). Effects of assigned goal level and knowledge of results on arithmetic computation: A laboratory study. *Journal of Applied Psychology, 63*, 446–450.

Strauss, A., & Corbin, J. (1998). *Basics of qualitative research: Grounded theory procedures and techniques* (2nd ed.). Newbury Park, CA: Sage.

Strickland, D. S., & Rath, L. K. (2000, August). *Between the Lions*: Public television promotes early literacy. *Reading Online, 4*(2). Retrieved January 3, 2005, from http://www.readingonline.org/articles/art_index.asp?HREF5strickland/index.html

Su, Y., & Reeve, J. (2011). A meta-analysis of the effectiveness of intervention programs designed to support autonomy. *Educational Psychology Review, 23*, 159–188.

Sutherland, S. (1993). Impoverished minds. *Nature, 364*, 767.

Swann, W. B., Jr. (1999). *Resilient identities: Self, relationships, and the construction of social reality.* New York: Basic Books.

Swanson, H. L. (2000). What instruction works for students with learning disabilities? Summarizing the results from a meta-analysis of intervention studies. In R. Gersten, E. Schiller, & S. Vaughn (Eds.), *Contemporary special education research: Syntheses of the knowledge base on critical instructional issues* (pp. 1–30). Mahwah, NJ: Erlbaum.

Swanson, H. L., & Alexander, J. E. (1997). Cognitive processes as predictors of word recognition and reading comprehension in learning-disabled and skilled readers: Revisiting the specificity hypothesis. *Journal of Educational Psychology, 89*, 128–158.

Swanson, H. L., & Siegel, L. (2001). Learning disabilities as working memory deficit. *Issues in Education, 7,* 1–48.

Sweller, J., & Chandler, P. (1994). Why some material is difficult to learn. *Cognition and Instruction, 12,* 185–233.

Taggart, G. L., Phifer, S. J., Nixon, J. A., & Wood, M. (2001). *Rubrics: A handbook for construction and use.* Lanham, MD: Scarecrow Press.

Tanner, C. K. (2000). The influence of school architecture on academic achievement. *Journal of Educational Administration, 38,* 309–330.

Tateyama-Sniezek, K. M. (1990). Cooperative learning: Does it improve the academic achievement of students with handicaps? *Exceptional Children, 54,* 426–437.

Taylor, C. B., Bandura, A., Ewart, C. K., Miller, N. H., & DeBusk, B. F. (1985). Capabilities soon after clinically uncomplicated acute myocardial infarction. *American Journal of Cardiology, 55,* 635–638.

Taylor, G., Shepard, L., Kinner, F., & Rosenthal, J. (2003). *A survey of teachers' perspectives on high stakes testing in Colorado: What gets taught, what gets lost* (CSE Technical Report 588). Los Angeles: Center for the Study of Evaluation, University of California.

Teachers of English to speakers of other languages. (1997). *ESL standards for pre-K–12 students.* Alexandria, VA: Author.

Terborg, J. R. (1976). The motivational components of goal setting. *Journal of Applied Psychology, 61,* 613–621.

Terman, L. M. (1916). *The measurement of intelligence: An explanation of and a complete guide for the use of the Stanford revision and extension of Binet-Simon intelligence scale.* Boston: Houghton Mifflin.

Texas Education Agency. (2003). *8th grade TAKS objectives and TEKS student expectations.* Retrieved June 2, 2005, from http://staff.banqueteisd.esc2.net/J_RCanales/scope%20and%20sequence.htm

The Algebra Project. (2005). Retrieved March 21, 2005, from http://www.algebra.org.

The Rehabilitation Act of 1973. Retrieved April 10, 2005, from http://www.nationalrehab.org/website/history/act.html

Thiel, J., (1997). From the *Cabrillo Tidepool Study,* part of the Triton Project. Retrieved June 7, 2005, from http://edweb.sdsu.edu/triton/tidepoolunit/Rubrics/reportrubric.html.

Thomas, G. (1997). What's the use of theory? *Harvard Educational Review, 67,* 75–104.

Thomas, W. P., & Collier, V. P. (2001). *A national study of school effectiveness for language minority students' long-term academic achievement.* Retrieved January 30, 2005, from http://www.crede.org/research/llaa/1.1_es.html

Thompson, R. A. (1994). Emotion regulation: A theme in search of definition. *Mono-graphs of the Society for Research in Child Development, 59* (2–3, Serial No. 240).

Thompson, R. A. (1998). Early sociopersonality development. In W. Damon (Series Ed.), N. Eisenberg (Ed.), *Handbook of child psychology: Social, emotional, and personality development* (Vol. 3, pp. 25–104). New York: Wiley.

Thompson, R. A. (1999). Early attachment and later development. In J. Cassidy & P. R. Shaver (Eds.), *Handbook of attachment: Theory, research, and clinical applications* (pp. 265–286). New York: Guilford.

Thompson, S. (2001). The authentic standards movement and its evil twin. *Phi Delta Kappan, 82,* 358–362.

Thorkildsen, T. A. (1993). Those who can, tutor: High-ability students' conceptions of fair ways to organize learning. *Journal of Educational Psychology, 85,* 182–190.

Thorndike, E. L. (1903). *Educational psychology.* New York: Lemcke & Buechner.

Thorndike, E. L. (1910). The contribution of psychology to education. *Journal of Educational Psychology, 1,* 5–12.

Thorndike, E. L. (1913). *Educational psychology* (3 vols.) New York: Teachers College, Columbia University Press.

Thorndike, R. M. (1997). *Measurement and evaluation in psychology and education* (6th ed.). Upper Saddle River, NJ: Merrill.

Thurstone, L. L. (1957). *Primary mental abilities.* Chicago: University of Chicago Press.

Tindal, G., & Haladyna, T. H. (2002). *Large-scale assessment programs for all students.* Mahwah, NJ: Erlbaum.

Tinker, M. A. (1939). The effect of illumination intensities upon speed of perception and upon fatigue in reading. *Journal of Educational Psychology, 30,* 561–571.

Tobias, S. (1994). Interest, prior knowledge, and learning. *Review of Educational Research, 64,* 37–54.

Tobin, K. (1990). Changing metaphors and beliefs: A master switch for teaching? *Theory into Practice, 29,* 122–127.

Tobin, K., & LaMaster, S. U. (1995). Relationships between metaphors, beliefs, and actions in a context of science curriculum change. *Journal of Research in Science Teaching, 32,* 225–242.

Tolmie, A., & Howe, C. (1993). Gender and dialogue in secondary school physics. *Gender and Education, 5,* 191–209.

Tomasello, M. (1992). *First verbs: A case study of early grammatical development.* Cambridge, UK: Cambridge University Press.

Tomasello, M. (1995). Language is not an instinct. *Cognitive Development, 10,* 601–609.

Tomlinson-Keasey, C., & Keasey, C. B. (1974). The mediating role of cognitive development in moral judgment. *Child Development, 45,* 291–298.

Top, B. L. (1984). *Handicapped children as tutors: The effects of cross-age, reverse role tutoring on self-esteem and reading achievement.* Provo, UT: Brigham Young University Press.

Torff, B. (2003). Developmental changes in teachers' use of higher order thinking and content knowledge. *Journal of Educational Psychology, 95,* 563–569.

Torff, B., & Sessions, D. N. (2005). Principals' perceptions of the causes of teacher ineffectiveness. *Journal of Educational Psychology, 97,* 530–537.

Torgesen, J. K. (1996). Thoughts about intervention research in learning disabilities. *Learning Disabilities: A Multidisciplinary Journal, 7,* 55–58.

Torgesen, J. K. (1977). Memorization processes in reading-disabled children. *Child Development, 48,* 56–60.

Tower, C. C. (1996). *Understanding child abuse and neglect.* Needham Heights, MA: Allyn & Bacon.

Tramontana, M. G., Hooper, E. P., & Selzer, S. C. (1988). Research on the preschool prediction of later academic achievement: A review. *Developmental Review, 8,* 89–146.

Treisman, A. M. (1960). Contextual cues in encoding listening. *Quarterly Journal of Experimental Psychology, 12,* 242–248.

Triandis, H. C. (1989). The self and social behavior in differing cultural contexts. *Psychological Review, 96,* 506–520.

Trice, A. D. (2000). *A handbook of classroom assessment.* New York: Longman.

Trickett, P. K., & McBride-Chang, C. (1995). The developmental impact of different forms of child abuse and neglect. *Developmental Review, 15,* 311–337.

Tripp, D. H. (1990). Socially critical action research. *Theory into Practice, 29,* 158–166.

Trope, Y. (2004). Theory in social psychology: Seeing the forest and the trees. *Personality and Social Psychology Review, 8,* 193–200.

Trushell, J., Burrell, C., & Maitland, A. (2001). Year 5 pupils reading an "interactive storybook" on CD-ROM: Losing the plot? *British Journal of Educational Technology, 32,* 389–401.

Tschannen-Moran, M., & Hoy, A. W. (2001). Teacher efficacy: Capturing an elusive construct. *Teaching and Teacher Education, 17,* 783–805.

Tschannen-Moran, M., & Hoy, W. K. (2000). A multidisciplinary analysis of the nature, meaning, and measurement of trust. *Review of Educational Research, 70,* 547–593.

Tschannen-Moran, M., & Woolfolk Hoy, A. (2001). Teacher efficacy: Capturing an elusive construct. *Teaching and Teacher Education, 17,* 783–805.

Tschannen-Moran, M., & Woolfolk Hoy, A. (2007). The differential antecedents of self-efficacy beliefs of novice and experienced teachers. *Teaching and Teacher Education, 23,* 944–956.

Tubbs, M. E. (1986). Goal-setting: A meta-analytic examination of the empirical evidence. *Journal of Applied Psychology, 71,* 474–483.

Tudge, J. R. H. (1989). When collaboration leads to regression: Some negative consequences of socio-cognitive conflict. *European Journal of Social Psychology, 19*, 123–138.

Tudge, J. R. H. (1992). Processes and consequences of peer collaboration: A Vygotskian analysis. *Child Development, 63*, 1364–1379.

Tukey, J. W. (1977). *Exploratory data analysis.* Reading, MA: Addison-Wesley.

Tulving, E. (1972). Episodic and semantic memory. In E. Tulving & W. Donaldson (Eds.), *Organization of memory* (pp. 381–403). New York: Academic Press.

Turiel, E. (1983). *The development of social knowledge: Morality and convention.* Cambridge, UK: Cambridge University Press.

Turiel, E. (2008). The development of children's orientations toward moral, social, and personal orders: More than a sequence of development. *Human Development, 51*, 21–39.

Turner, J., Thorpe, P., & Mayer, D. (1998). Students' reports of motivation and negative affect: A theoretical and empirical analysis. *Journal of Educational Psychology, 90*, 758–771.

Turner, J. C., Meyer, D. K., Midgley, C., & Patrick, H. (2003). Teacher discourse and sixth graders' reported affect and achievement behaviors in two high-mastery/high- performance mathematics classrooms. *Elementary School Journal, 103*, 357–382.

Tye, B. B., & O'Brien, L. (2002). Why are experienced teachers leaving the profession? *Phi Delta Kappan, 84*, 24–32.

Tyler, R. (1949). *Basic principles of curriculum and instruction.* Chicago: University of Chicago Press.

Tzou, C. T., Reiser, B. J., Spillane, J. P., & Kemp, E. K. (2002, April). *Characterizing the multiple dimensions of teachers' inquiry practices.* Paper presented at the annual meeting of the American Educational Research Association, New Orleans.

Underwood, B., & Moore, B. (1982). Perspective-taking and altruism. *Psychological Bulletin, 91*, 143–173.

Underwood, G., & Jindal, N. (1993). Gender differences and cooperation in a computer-based language task. *Educational Research, 36*, 63–74.

University of Texas at Austin. (2004). *Alien rescue.* Retrieved May 16, 2005, from http://jabba.edb.utexas.edu/liu/aliendb/home.htm

Urdan, T. (2004). Predictors of academic self-handicapping and achievement: Examining achievement goals, classroom goal structures, and culture. *Journal of Educational Psychology, 96*, 251–264.

Urdan, T., & Mestas, M. (2006). The goals behind performance goals. *Journal of Educational Psychology, 98*, 354–365.

Urdan, T., Midgley, C., & Anderman, E. (1998). The role of classroom goal structure in students' use of self-handicapping strategies. *American Educational Research Journal, 35*, 101–122.

Urdan, T., Ryan, A. M., Anderman, E. M., & Gheen, M. H. (2002). Goals, goal structures, and avoidance behaviors. In C. Midgley (Ed.), *Goals, goal structures and patterns of adaptive learning* (pp. 55–83). Mahwah, NJ: Erlbaum.

U.S. Census Bureau. (2004). U. S. interim projections by age, sex, race, and Hispanic origin. Retrieved from Jan. 4, 2005. http://www.census.gov/ipc/ww/usinterimpro.

U.S. Census Bureau. (2011). The 2011 Statistical Abstract: The National Data Book. http://www.census.gov/compendia/statab/cats/income_expenditures_poverty_wealth.html. Retrieved April 22, 2011.

U.S. Census 2000. Retrieved April 7, 2005, from 2005. http://www.census.gov/main/www/cen2000.html

U.S. Department of Education. (2001). *National assessment of educational progress, 1984 and 1999 long-term trend assessment.* Washington, DC: National Center for Education Statistics.

U.S. Department of Education, Institute of Education Sciences. (2003). Digest of Education Statistics. Retrieved Sept. 30, from http://nces.ed.gov/programs/digest/d03tables/dt052.asp

U.S. Department of Education. (2003). Office of Special Education Programs, Data Analysis System, 2002–2003. Washington, DC: Author.

U.S. Department of Education. (2005). Retrieved from Apr 7. 2005. http://www.ed.gov/rschstat/research/pubs/research.html

U.S. Department of Education. (2009). "Race to the Top Program Executive Summary." Washington, DC: US Department of Education.

U.S. Secret Service Safe School Initiative. (2000). *An interim report on the prevention of targeted school violence in schools.* Washington, DC: Author.

Utman, C. (1997). Performance effects of motivational state: A meta-analysis. *Personality and Social Psychology Review, 1*, 170–182.

Uttal, D. H., Scudder, K. V., & DeLoache, J. S. (1997). Manipulatives as symbols: A new perspective on the use of concrete objects to teach mathematics. *Journal of Applied Developmental Psychology, 18*, 37–54.

Vaillant, G. E., & Milofsky, E. (1980). The natural history of male psychological health. IX. Empirical evidence for Erikson's model of the life cycle. *American Journal of Psychiatry, 137*, 1348–1359.

Vallerand, R. J., Fortier, M. S., & Guay, F. (1997). Self-determination and persistence in a real-life setting: Toward a motivational model of high school dropout. *Journal of Personality and Social Psychology, 72*, 1161–1176.

VanLehn, K., Siler, S. A., Murray, C., & Bagget, W. B. (2003). Human tutoring: Why do only some events cause learning? *Cognition and Instruction, 21*, 209–249.

van Lieshout, C. F. M., & Heymans, P. G. (2000). *Developing talent across the lifespan.* Hove, UK: Psychological Press.

Van Manen, M. (1990). Beyond assumptions: Shifting the limits of action research. *Theory into Practice, 29*, 152–157.

Vansteenkiste, M., Lens, W., & Deci, E. L. (2006). Intrinsic versus extrinsic goal contents in self-determination theory: Another look at the quality of academic motivation. *Educational Psychologist, 41*, 19–31.

Vansteenkiste, M., Seonens, B., Verstuyf, J., & Lens, W. (2009). What is the usefulness of your schoolwork? The differential effects of intrinsic and extrinsic goal framing on optimal learning. *Theory and Research in Education, 7*, 155–163.

Vansteenkiste, M., Sierens, E., Soenens, B., Luyckx, K., & Lens, W. (2009). Motivational profiles from a self-determination perspective: The quality of motivation matters. *Journal of Educational Psychology, 101*, 671–688.

Vansteenkiste, M., Simons, J., Lens, W., Sheldon, K. M., & Deci, E. L. (2004). Motivating learning, performance, and persistence: The synergistic role of intrinsic goals and autonomy-support. *Journal of Personality and Social Psychology, 87*, 246–260.

Vansteenkiste, M., Simons, J., Lens, W., Soenens, B., & Matos, L. (2005). Examining the impact of extrinsic versus intrinsic goal framing and internally controlling versus autonomy-supportive communication style upon early adolescents' academic achievement. *Child Development, 76*, 483–501.

Van Yperen, N. W. (2003). Task interest and actual performance: The moderating effects of assigned and adopted purpose goals. *Journal of Personality and Social Psychology, 85*, 1006–1015.

Vaughn, S., & Linan-Thompson, S. (2003). What is special about special education for students with learning disabilities? *The Journal of Special Education, 37*, 140–147.

Vaughn, S., & Schumm, J. S. (1994). Middle school teachers' planning for students with learning disabilities. *Remedial & Special Education, 15*, 152–161.

Veenman, S. (1984). Perceived problems of beginning teachers. *Review of Educational Research, 54*, 143–178.

Veldman, D. J., & Sanford, J. P. (1984). The influence of class ability level on student achievement and classroom behavior. *American Educational Research Journal, 21*, 629–644.

Venn, J. J. (2004). *Assessing students with special needs* (3rd ed.). Upper Saddle River, NJ: Merrill/Prentice Hall.

Venn, M. L., & McCollum, J. (2002). Exploring the long- and short-term planning practices of Head Start teachers for children with and without disabilities. *The Journal of Special Education, 35*, 211–223.

Veroff, J., McClelland, L., & Marquis, K. (1971). *Measuring intelligence and achievement motivations in surveys.* Ann Arbor: University of Michigan. Ann Arbor.

Virginia Education Association and the Appalachia Educational Laboratory. (1992). Recommendations for teachers. Author.

Virginia Standards of Learning Algebra I Blueprint. (2003). Richmond, VA: Commonwealth of Virginia Department of Education.

Vitto, J. M. (2003). *Relationship-driven classroom management: Strategies that promote student motivation.* Thousand Oaks, CA: Corwin.

Voss, H. G., & Keller, H. (1983). *Curiosity and exploration: Theory and results.* San Diego: Academic Press.

Vygotsky, L. S. (1929). The problem of the cultural development of the child. *Journal of Genetic Psychology, 36*, 415–434.

Vygotsky, L. S. (1962). *Thought and language.* Cambridge, MA: MIT Press. (Original work published 1934.)

Vygotsky, L. S. (1978). *Mind in society: The development of higher psychological processes.* Cambridge, MA: Harvard University Press.

Vygotsky, L. S. (1987). Thinking and speech. In R. W. Rieber & A. S. Carton (Eds.), *The collective works of L. S. Vygotsky* (N. Minick, Trans.). New York: Plenum.

Wadsworth, B. J. (1996). *Piaget's theory of cognitive and affective development: Foundations of constructivism* (5th ed.). White Plains, NY: Longman.

Waggoner, M., Chinn, C. A., Yi, H., & Anderson, R. C. (1995). Collaborative reasoning about stories. *Language Arts, 72*, 582–589.

Walker, C.O., Greene, B.A., & Mansell, R.A. (2006). Identification with academics, intrinsic/extrinsic motivation, and self-efficacy as predictors of cognitive engagement. *Learning and Individual Differences, 16*, 1–12.

Walker, H. M., Irvin, L. K., Noell, J., & Singer, G. H. S. (1992). A construct score approach to the assessment of social competence: Rationale, technological considerations, and anticipated outcomes. *Behavior Modification, 16*, 448–474.

Walker, L. (2006). Gender and morality. In M. Killen & J. G. Smetana (Eds.), *Handbook of moral development* (pp. 93–118). Mahwah, NJ: Erlbaum.

Wallace, D. S., West, S., Wandell, C., Ware, A., & Dansereau, D. F. (1998). The effect of knowledge maps that incorporate Gestalt principles on learning. *Journal of Experimental Education. 67*, 5–16.

Wang, J. (1998). Opportunity to Learn: The impacts and policy implications. *Educational Evaluation and Policy Analysis, 20*(3), 137–156.

Wang, J., & Goldschmidt, P. (1999). Opportunity to Learn, language proficiency, and immigrant status: Effects on mathematics achievement. *Journal of Educational Research, 93*(20), 101–111.

Wang, M. C., Haertel, G. D., & Walberg, H. J. (1990). What influences learning? A content analysis of review literature. *Journal of Educational Research, 84*, 30–43.

Wang, M. C., Haertel, G. D., & Walberg, H. J. (1993). Toward a knowledge base for school learning. *Review of Educational Research, 63*(3), 249–294.

Wang, M. C., Haertel, G. D., & Walberg, H. J. (1993/94). What helps students learn? *Educational Leadership, 51*(4), 74–79.

Ward, J. R., & McCotter, S. S. (2004). Reflection as a visible outcome for preservice teachers. *Teaching & Teacher Education, 20*, 243–257.

Warton, P. M. (2001). The forgotten voices in homework: Views of students. *Educational Psychologist, 36*(3), 155–165.

Waterman, A. S. (1982). Identity development from adolescence to adulthood: An extension of theory and a review of research. *Developmental Psychology, 18*, 341–358.

Waterman, A. S. (1985). Identity in the context of adolescent psychology. In A. S. Waterman (Ed.), *Identity in adolescence: Processes and contexts: New directions for child development* (Vol. 30). San Francisco: Jossey-Bass.

Waters, E., Wippman, J., & Sroufe, L. A. (1979). Attachment, positive affect, and competence in the peer group. *Child Development, 50*, 821–829.

Watzke, J. L. (2007). Longitudinal research on beginning teacher development: Complexity as a challenge to concerns-based stage theory. *Teaching and Teacher Education, 23*, 106–122.

Webb, N. M. (1984). Sex differences in interaction and achievement in cooperative small groups. *Journal of Educational Psychology, 76*, 33–44.

Webb, N. M., Nemer, K. M., & Ing, M. (2006). Small-group reflections: Parallels between teacher discourse and student behavior in peer-directed groups. *Journal of the Learning Sciences, 15*(1), 63–119.

Webb, N. M. (1989). Peer interaction and learning in small groups. *International Review of Educational Research, 13*, 21–40.

Webb, N. M. (1991). Task-related verbal interaction and mathematics learning in small groups. *Journal of Research in Mathematics Education, 22*, 366–269.

Webb, N. M. (1992). Testing a theoretical model of student interaction and learning in small groups. In R. Hertz-Lazarowitz & N. Miller (Eds.), *Interaction in cooperative groups: The theoretical anatomy of group learning* (pp. 102–119). New York: Cambridge University Press.

Webb, N. M., & Farivar, S. (1994). Promoting helping behavior in cooperative groups in middle school mathematics. *American Educational Research Journal, 31*, 369–395.

Wechsler, D. (2003). *Wechsler Intelligence Scale for Children* (4th ed). San Antonio, TX: Psychological Corporation.

Wehmeyer, M. L., Agran, M., & Hughes, C. A. (1998). *Teaching self-determination to students with disabilities: Basic skills for successful transition.* Baltimore: Brookes.

Weinberg, R. S., Gould, D., & Jackson, A. (1979). Expectations and performance: An empirical test of Bandura's self-efficacy theory. *Journal of Sport Psychology, 1*, 320–331.

Weiner, B. (1985). An attributional theory of achievement motivation and emotion. *Psychological Review, 92*, 548–573.

Weiner, B. (1986). *An attributional theory of motivation and emotion.* New York: Springer-Verlag.

Weiner, B. (2004). Attribution theory revisited: Transforming cultural plurality into theoretical unity. In D. M. McInerney & S. Van Etten (Eds.), *Big theories revisited: Research on sociocultural influences on motivation and learning* (Vol. 4, pp. 13–29). Greenwich, CT: Information Age.

Weiner, L. (2003). Why is classroom management so vexing to urban teachers? *Theory into Practice, 42*, 305–312.

Weinstein, C. (1979). The physical environment of the school: A review of the research. *Review of Educational Research, 49*(4), 577–610.

Weinstein, C., Curran, M. E., & Tomlinson-Clarke, S. (2003). Culturally responsive classroom management: Awareness into action. *Theory into Practice, 42*, 269–276.

Weinstein, C. S. (2003). *Secondary classroom management: Lessons from research and practice* (2nd ed.). Boston: McGraw-Hill Higher Education.

Weinstein, C. S., Romano, M., Jr., & Mignano, A. J., Jr. (2003). *Elementary classroom management: Lessons from research and practice* (3rd ed.). Boston: McGraw-Hill Higher Education.

Weinstein, C. S., Mignano, A., & Romano, M. (2010). *Elementary classroom management: Lessons from Research and Practice, Edition 5.* New York: McGraw-Hill.

Weinstein, C. S., Romano, M., & Novodvorsky, I. (2010). *Middle and secondary management: lessons from research and practice, Edition 4.* New York: McGraw-Hill.

Weiss, B., Dodge, K., Bates, J. E., & Pettit, G. S. (1992). Some consequences of early harsh discipline: Child aggression and a maladaptive social information processing style. *Child Development, 63*, 1321–1335.

Wellborn, J. P. (1991). *Engaged and disaffected action: The conceptualization and measurement of motivation in the academic domain.* Unpublished doctoral dissertation, University of Rochester, Rochester, NY.

Wenger, E. (1998). *Communities of practice.* Cambridge, UK: Cambridge University Press.

Wenner, G. (2001). Science and mathematics efficacy beliefs held by practicing and prospective teachers: A five-year perspective. *Journal of Science Education and Technology, 10,* 181–187.

Wentling, T. (1973). Mastery versus nonmastery instruction with varying test item feedback treatments. *Journal of Educational Psychology, 65,* 50–58.

Wentzel, K. R. (1994). Relations of social goal pursuit to social acceptance, classroom behavior, and perceived social support. *Journal of Educational Psychology, 86,* 173–182.

Wentzel, K. R. (1997). Student motivation in middle school: The role of perceived pedagogical caring. *Journal of Educational Psychology, 89,* 411–419.

Wentzel, K. R., & Asher, S. R. (1995). Academic lives of neglected, rejected, popular, and controversial children. *Child Development, 66,* 754–763.

Wentzel, K. R., Battle, A., & Looney, L. (2001, April). *Classroom support in middle school: Contributions of teachers and peers.* Paper presented at the annual meeting of the American Educational Research Association, Seattle, WA.

Werner, E. E. (1992). The children of Kauai: Resiliency and recovery in adolescence and adulthood. *Journal of Adolescent Health, 13,* 262–268.

West, L. H. T., & Fensham, P. J. (1976). Prior knowledge or advance organizers as affective variables in chemical learning. *Journal of Research in Science Teaching, 13,* 297–306.

Westen, D. (2002). *Psychology: Brain, behavior, and culture* (3rd ed.). Hoboken, NJ: Wiley.

Whitbourne, S. K., Zuschlag, M. K., Elliot, L. B., & Waterman, A. S. (1992). Psychosocial development in adulthood: A 22-year sequential study. *Journal of Personality and Social Psychology, 63,* 260–271.

Whitehead, J. (1999). Educative relations in a new era. *Pedagogy, Culture, and Society, 7,* 73–90.

Whitehead, J., & McNiff, J. (2006). *Action research: Living theory.* London: Sage.

Wiggins, G. P. (1999). *Assessing student performance: Exploring the purpose and limits of testing.* Hoboken, NJ: Wiley.

Williams, B. T. (2003). What they see is what we get: Television and middle school writers. *Journal of Adolescent and Adult Literacy, 46,* 546–554.

Williams, R. L. (1974). Scientific racism and IQ: The silent mugging of the black community. *Psychology Today, 7*(12), 32–41.

Williams, T., & Williams, K. (2010). Self-efficacy and performance in mathematics: Reciprocal determination in 33 nations. *Journal of Educational Psychology, 102,* 453–466.

Willig, A. C., Harnisch, D. L., Hill, K. T., & Maehr, M. L. (1983). Sociocultural and educational correlates of success-failure attributions and evaluation anxiety in the school setting for black, Hispanic, and Anglo children. *American Educational Research Journal, 20,* 385–410.

Wilson, T. D., Centerbar, D. B., Kermer, D. A., & Gilbert, D. T. (2005). The pleasures of uncertainty: Prolonging positive moods in ways people do not anticipate. *Journal of Personality and Social Psychology, 88,* 5–21.

Wilson, T. D., & Linville, P. W. (1982). Improving the academic performance of college freshmen: Attribution therapy revisited. *Journal of Personality and Social Psychology, 42,* 367–376.

Windsor, J., Glaze, L. E., Koga, S. F., & the BEIP Core Group. (2007). Language acquisition with limited input: Romanian institution and foster care. *Journal of Speech, Language, and Hearing Research, 50,* 1365–1381.

Winne, P. H. (1997). Experimenting to bootstrap self-regulated learning. *Journal of Educational Psychology, 88,* 397–410.

Wisconsin Department of Public Instruction. (2002). *DPI guidelines to facilitate the participation of students with special needs in state assessments.* Madison: Wisconsin Department of Public Instruction.

Wise, B. W., & Olson, R. K. (1994). Computer speech and the remediation of reading and spelling problems. *Journal of Special Education Technology, 12,* 207–220.

Wittrock, M. C. (1992). An empowering conception of educational psychology. *Educational Psychologist, 27,* 129–141.

Wolf, L. F., & Smith, J. K. (1995). The consequence of consequence: Motivation, anxiety, and test performance. *Applied Measurement in Education, 8,* 227–242.

Wolf, S. A., & Gearhart, M. (1997). New writing assessments: The challenge of changing teachers' beliefs about students as writers. *Theory into Practice, 36,* 220–230.

Wolf, T. H. (1973). *Alfred Binet.* Chicago: University of Chicago Press.

Wolters, C. A. (2004). Advancing achievement goal theory: Using goal structures and goal orientations to predict students' motivation, cognition, and achievement. *Journal of Educational Psychology, 96,* 236–250.

Wolters, C. A., & Daugherty, S. G. (2007). Goal structures and teachers' sense of efficacy: Their relation and association to teaching experience and academic level. *Journal of Educational Psychology, 99,* 181–193.

Wong, B. Y. L., Wong, R., & Blenkinsop, J. (1989). Cognitive and metacognitive aspects of learning disabled adolescents' composing problems. *Learning Disability Quarterly, 12,* 300–322.

Wong, H. K., & Wong, R. T. (1998). *The first days of school: How to be an effective teacher.* Mountain View, CA: Harry K. Wong Publications.

Wood, D., Bruner, J., & Ross, G. (1976). The role of tutoring in problem solving. *Journal of Child Psychology and Psychiatry and Allied Disciplines, 17,* 89–100.

Wood, J. V. (1989). Theory and research concerning social comparisons of personal attributes. *Psychological Bulletin, 106,* 231–248.

Wood, J. W. (2002). *Adapting instruction to accommodate students in inclusive settings.* Upper Saddle River, NJ: Merrill/Prentice Hall.

Wood, R. E., & Bandura, A. (1989). Impact of conceptions of ability on self-regulatory mechanisms and complex decision making. *Journal of Personality and Social Psychology, 56,* 407–415.

Woolfolk, A. E., & Hoy, W. K. (1990). Prospective teachers' sense of efficacy and beliefs about control. *Journal of Educational Psychology, 82,* 81–91.

Woolfolk Hoy, A. (2004). The educational psychology of teacher efficacy. *Educational Psychology Review, 16,* 153–176.

Woolfolk Hoy, A., & Spero, R. B. (2005). Changes in teacher efficacy during the early years of teaching: A comparison of four measures. *Teaching and Teacher Education, 21,* 343–356.

Wright, J. (2005). Behavior contracts. Retrieved April 25, 2005, from http://www.interventioncentral.org/htmdocs/interventions/ behcontr.shtml

Yerkes, R. M. (1941). Man-power and military effectiveness: The case for human engineering. *Journal of Counseling Psychology, 5,* 205–209.

Yeung, A. S., Chui, H.-S., Lau, I. C., McInerney, D. M., Russell-Bowie, D., & Suliman, R. (2000). Where is the hierarchy of academic self-concept? *Journal of Educational Psychology, 92,* 556–567.

Yinger, R. J. (1980). A study of teacher planning. *Elementary School Journal, 80,* 107–127.

Yost, R. (2002). "I think I can.": Mentoring as a means of enhancing teacher efficacy. *Clearing House, 75,* 195–197.

Young, J. W. (2003). *Validity in college admissions testing.* New York: The College Board.

Zahokri, J. A. (1987). Teachers' collegial interactions: An exploratory study. *Elementary School Journal, 87,* 385–396.

Zanna, M. P., Goethals, G. R., & Hill, J. F. (1975). Evaluating a sex-related ability: Comparison with similar others and standard setters. *Journal of Experimental Social Psychology, 11,* 86–93.

Zehler, A. M., Fleischman, H. J., Hopstock, P. J., Stephenson, T. G., Pendzick, M. L., & Sapru, S. (2003). *Descriptive study of services to LEP students and LEP students with disabilities.* Washington, DC: Office of the Department of Education.

Zeichner, K. M. (2003). Teacher research as professional development for P–12 educators in the USA. *Educational Action Research, 11,* 301–325.

Zeichner, K. M., & Liston, D. P. (1987). Teaching student teachers to reflect. *Harvard Educational Review, 57*, 23–48.

Zeichner, K. M., & Liston, D. P. (1996). *Reflective teaching: An introduction.* Mahwah, NJ: Erlbaum.

Zhou, Q., Eisenberg, N., Losoya, S. H., Fabes, R. A., Reiser, M., Guthrie, I. K., Murphy, B. C., Cumberland, A. J., & Shepard, S. A. (2002). The relations of parental warmth and positive expressiveness to children's empathy-related responding and social functioning: A longitudinal study. *Child Development, 73*, 893–915.

Zillman, D. (1980). Anatomy of suspense. In P. H. Tannenbaum (Ed.), *The entertainment functions of television* (pp. 133–163). Hillsdale, NJ: Erlbaum.

Zimmerman, B. J. (1986). Becoming a self-regulated learner: Which are the key subprocesses? *Contemporary Educational Psychology, 11*, 307–313.

Zimmerman, B. J. (1989). A social cognitive view of self-regulated academic learning. *Journal of Educational Psychology, 81*, 329–339.

Zimmerman, B. J. (1998). Academic studying and the development of personal skill. A self-regulatory perspective. *Educational Psychology, 33*, 73–86.

Zimmerman, B. J. (2000). Attaining self-regulation: A social cognitive perspective. In M. Boekaerts, P. R. Pintrich, & M. Zeidner (Eds.), *Handbook of self-regulation* (pp. 13–39). San Diego: Academic Press.

Zimmerman, B. J. (2002). Becoming a self-regulated learner: An overview. *Theory into Practice, 41*, 64–70.

Zimmerman, B. J., Bonner, S., & Kovach, R. (1996). *Developing self-regulated learners: Beyond achievement to self-efficacy.* Washington, DC: American Psychological Association.

Zimmerman, B. J., & Martinez-Pons, M. (1986). Development of a structured interview for assessing student use of self-regulated learning strategies. *American Educational Research Journal, 23*, 614–628.

Zimmerman, B. J., & Martinez-Pons, M. (1988). Construct validation of a strategy model of student self-regulated learning. *Journal of Educational Psychology, 80*, 284–290.

Zimmerman, B. J., & Risemberg, R. (1997). Become a proficient writer: A social cognitive perspective. *Contemporary Educational Psychology, 22*, 73–101.

Zimpher, N. L., & Ashburn, E. A. (1992). Countering parochialism in teacher candidates. In M. E. Dilworth (Ed.), *Diversity in teacher education: New expectations* (pp. 40–41). San Francisco: Jossey-Bass.

Zins, J., Weissberg, R., Wang, M. C., & Walberg, H. J. (2004). *Building academic success on social and emotional learning (SEL): What does the research say?* New York: Teachers College Press.

Zirkel, P. (2007). Building bridges. *Phi Delta Kappan, 88*, 562.

Zuber, R. I. (1992). *Cooperative learning by fifth-grade students: The effects of scripted and unscripted cooperation.* Unpublished doctoral dissertation, Rutgers, The State University of New Jersey, New Brunswick, NJ.

Name Index

A

Aakus, 265
Abedi, J., 553–554
Abrami, P. C., 297
Abrams, P. D., 96, 178
Achilles, C. M., 3
Adams, D. R., 115
Adams, G. R., 361
Adams, N. E., 378
Adelgais, A., 264, 303
Adler, T., 361, 397
Adreon, D., 438
Agatston, P., 139
Agran, M., 346
Aiken, L. R., 531
Ainsworth, M. D. S., 111, 112, 116
Aksan, N., 113, 119, 131, 132
Albin, R. W., 172
Alexander, J. E., 233
Alexander, K. L., 337
Alexander, P. A., 358
The Algebra Project, 271
Algozzine, B., 44, 346
Allen, 215, 321
Allen, J. P., 112, 119
Allen, S., 321
Allinder, R. M., 43
Alloy, L. B., 383
Allsopp, 437
Alsaker, F., 140
Altmaier, E. M., 385
Alvermann, D. E., 89
Al-Yagon, M., 116
American Association on Intellectual and
    Developmental Disabilities, 428
American Association on Mental Retardation, 428
American Psychiatric Association, 440
American Psychological Association, 532
Ames, C., 393, 394, 396
Ames, C. A., 341, 393–395, 397
Ammerman, 439
Anastasi, A., 530
Anderman, E., 396, 397
Anderman, E. M., 391–396
Anderman, L. H., 391, 393
Anderson, 314
Anderson, C. A., 137–139
Anderson, J. R., 278
Anderson, L., 198

Anderson, R., 43
Anderson, R. C., 264, 265, 314
Anderson, R. H., 429
Anderson-Inman, L., 97
Andrews, G., 85
Andriessen, J., 265
Angoff, W. H., 541
Anning, A., 20
Antil, L. R., 298
Applebee, A. N., 273
Arapostathis, M., 340
Archambault, I., 364
Archer, J., 341, 393–395, 397
Arellano, A. R., 320
Arkin, R. M., 362
Armour-Thomas, E., 40
Arnett, J. J., 126
Aronson, E., 312
Arreaga-Mayer, C., 308
Artzt, A. F., 40
Asan, 240
Asher, S. R., 292
Ashton, P. T., 43
Assor, A., 349, 364, 365
Atkinson, R. C., 230, 231
Austin, G. A., 245
Australian Education Council, 402
Ausubel, D. P., 57, 58
Ayers, R., 173
Ayers, W., 173
Ayotte, V., 401
Azmitia, M., 91

B

Bacon, C. S., 9
Baddeley, A., 230–232, 240
Badian, N. A., 95
Baillargeon, R., 85
Baird, W., 358
Baker, 440
Baker, L., 305
Bakermans-Kranenburg, M. J., 118
Balajthy, E., 278
Baldes, J. J., 388
Baldwin, J. D., 158, 257, 258
Baldwin, J. I., 158, 257, 258
Ball, T. M., 236
Bandura, A., 41, 43, 45, 256, 259, 260, 270, 361, 362, 376–380, 388, 389

Bangert-Downs, R., 177
Banks, J. A., 457, 463, 464, 467
Barkely, 440
Barkley, R. A., 401
Barnes, J., 40, 401
Barone, F. J., 215
Barrett, L. C., 385
Barrish, H. H., 176
Barron, 265
Barron, K. E., 395, 397
Barrows, H. S., 282
Bartholomew, K., 116, 118
Basque, 240
Bass, K. M., 507, 510
Bassett, G. A., 388
Bateman, B. D., 432
Battistich, V., 337, 355
Battle, A., 292
Baumeister, R., 354, 355
Baumeister, R. F., 116, 123, 361, 362, 404
Baumgardner, A. H., 362
Baxter, G. P., 504
Beamer, J., 378
Bean, T. W., 21
Beane, A. L., 175
Becker, L. J., 389
Begley, S., 71
Beijaard, D., 36
Beilin, H., 85
Belfiore, P. J., 346
Bell, 265
Bellmore, S., 114
Belmont, M. J., 338, 355
Belsky, J., 112
Benally, J., 173
Benard, B., 456, 457
Benbow, C. P., 403
Bender, 443
Bennett, 458, 463
Bennett, C., 457
Bennett, E., 94
Bennett, N., 193
Benware, C., 344
Ben-Zeev, T., 319
Bereiter, C., 271, 315
Berg, T., 37
Bergan, J. R., 153, 166
Berglas, S., 361
Berk, L. E., 90
Berliner, D., 39
Berliner, D. C., 33, 36, 46

Subject Index

A

AAIDD (American Association on Intellectual and Developmental Disabilities), 428
Abandonment, 75
Ability:
  differences in, 429–430
  innate, 416
Abstraction, 244
Abuse, 114
Accommodation, 74, 300, 506
Accountability, individual, 294
Achieved identity, 124, 125
Achievement gap, 464
Achievement goals, 392–394
  defined, 392
  grade-level effects on, 397
  multiple, 397
  of students, 395–396
Achievement targets, 48–50, 503
Achievement tests, 533
Acronym mnemonic strategy, 239
ACT Assessment, 531–533, 536, 538, 541
Action, reflecting in, on, and for, 21–23
Action research, 8, 9, 15–17
Actual development, 86
Acute problems, 212–213
Adaptation, 74, 75
ADD (attention deficit disorder), 229, 440
Addition, 74
Additive approach (multiculturalism), 467
ADHD, see Attention deficit hyperactivity disorder
Adolescence, attachment in, 118
Advance organizers, 58
Affect, positive, 359
Affective assessments, 533
Affective talk, 321
Affordances, 270
Agentic engagement, 7, 336
Aggression, 136–141
  bullying, 139–141
  and punishment, 162
  and TV viewing, 260–261
  and video games, 138–139
Algebra Project, 271–272
Algorithms, 266
Alien Rescue, 281–282
Alternative assessments, 497–501
American Association on Intellectual and Developmental Disabilities (AAIDD), 428

Americans with Disabilities Act, 430
America Reads tutoring program, 304
Amotivation, 347, 363
Amygdala, 69, 234–235
Analysis:
  in Bloom's taxonomy, 49
  meta-, 177, 297
Analysis level (reflection), 21
Anchor the Boat program, 177
Angoff/Nedelsky approach (standard setting), 541–543
Animal Landlord software, 276, 277
Animism, 78, 79
Anxiety, 361, 362, 513
Application (in Bloom's taxonomy), 49
Apprenticeships, cognitive, 280, 281
Appropriateness (in scaffolding), 273
Aptitude tests, 533–534
ARCS model, 359
Argumentation, 263–265
Aristotle, 415
Army Alpha/Beta tests, 530
Asperger's syndrome, 437
Assessment(s), 483–525. *See also* Standardized assessment(s)
  administering, 507
  alternative (production), 497–501
  authentic, 497
  communicating about, 489–490, 517–519
  as concern for beginning teachers, 33, 34
  concerns in, 486–488
  defined, 486
  developing and using, 502–509
  and diversity, 488
  fairness in, 490–491
  feedback from, 507–508
  formative vs. summative, 488
  generative formats for, 494–497
  grading system for, 513–516
  improving, 511, 512
  informal, 501–502
  interpreting results of, 509–513
  for learning, 486
  parent concerns in, 487
  performance, 497–500
  principles of, 489–491
  as process, 507–508
  recognition formats for, 491–494
  student concerns in, 486–487
  for student growth, 491
  student role in, 512–513

of students with special needs, 506, 507
  teacher concerns in, 487
Assessment reports, 547–550
Assigning competence, 321
Assimilation, 74, 300
Assistive technology, 278, 439, 554–555
Associationist theories, 155
Attachment(s):
  defined, 115
  for learners with special needs, 118–119
Attachment styles, 116–119
Attention, 228–230
  and behavioral engagement, 335, 359
  and observational learning, 259
Attention deficit disorder (ADD), 229, 440
Attention deficit hyperactivity disorder (ADHD), 229, 401, 440–442
Attenuation model, 229
Attitudes:
  prejudicial, 466, 467
  in Stiggins's taxonomy, 50
Attributions, 383–385
Attributional retraining, 386
Attunement, 112–113
Authentic assessment, 497
Authentic tasks, 269
Autism (autism spectrum disorders), 71, 136, 437–439
Automaticity, 229–230, 418
Autonomy, need for, 348–352
Autonomy-supportive environment, 348–352
Autonomy-supportive motivating style, 349–350
Avoidance, 75
Avoidant style attachment relationships, 116

B

Bad apple theory, 173
Bandura, Albert, 256, 260
Banks, James, 467
BAS (behavior activation system), 158
Basic knowledge acquisition tasks, 324
BCIRC (Bilingual Cooperative Integrated Reading and Composition) program, 317–318
Beginning teachers:
  concerns of, 33–34
  expert teachers vs., 35–36, 38–40
  goals of, 34–35
  teaching efficacy of, 43, 44

Social environment (of classroom), 195–206. *See also* Instruction
on first day of school, 198
freedom vs. structure in, 197
handling misbehavior in, 203–204
routines in, 202–203
rules for, 198–202, 204–205
student-centered approach in, 206
unique features of, 195–197
Social justice, 464–465
Social learning theory, 256–262
and everyday life, 262
modeling, 257–261
Socially shared cognition, 89
Social-motivational approach (peer learning), 293–295, 297–299
Social norms, 195
Sociocognitive development, 85–93
applications of theory of, 91–93
and apprenticeship, 86
and cultural tools, 90, 91
and instructional conversation, 89–90
and peers, 91
role of language in, 90
and zone of proximal development, 86–89
Sociocultural theory, 154
cultural practices in, 271
instruction influenced by, 279–283
social contract in, 268
Socioeconomic status (SES). *See also* Poverty
defined, 455
and engagement, 340
and ethnicity and income, 455, 458
and learning, 456–457
and possible selves, 392
and self-efficacy, 380
and tutoring, 308, 310
Spatial intelligence, 419
Spearman, Charles, 416–417, 532
Special education, social competence in, 135–136
Special needs (term), 430
Special needs, students with, 430–443
assessing, 506, 507
attachment for, 118–119
attention deficit disorder, 440
attention-deficit/hyperactivity disorder, 440–442
autism and related disorders, 437–439
and behavioral learning theory, 167
as concern for beginning teachers, 33, 34
and cooperative learning, 318–319
differentiated instruction for, 442–443
English language learners, 460–461
identifying, 431, 433, 434
inclusion of, 434, 435
instruction for, 210–211
learning disabilities, 435–437
legal requirements, 430–434
memory difficulties in, 233
physical and sensory challenges, 439–440
and physical environment, 194
planning for, 56–57
scaffolding for, 278
self-regulation for, 401
teaching efficacy with, 44, 45
technology support for language development, 95–97
test scores of, 554–555
tutoring, 310

Sperling, George, 230
Split-half reliability, 546
STAD, *see* Student Teams Achievement Division
Standards, 49, 529
Standards-based assessment, 506, 530–531
Standard Course, 403
Standard deviation, 423, 427, 531, 535–536
Standard error of measurement (SEM), 546, 550
Standardized assessment(s), 487–488, 527–563
categories of, 532–534
college admissions testing, 531–532
controversies in, 555–557
defined, 487, 528
equating scores in, 539–541
history of, 529–530
intelligence testing, 532
interpreting, 547–552
and norms, 541
scales used in, 537–539
and school testing programs, 530
selecting, 532
setting passing/proficiency scores for, 541–543, 545
standards-based assessment, 530–531
statewide, 530
statistics used in, 532–537
using results of, 552–555
validity/reliability of, 543–544, 546
Standardized tests, 74
Standards of excellence, 392
Stanford Achievement Tests, 530
Stanford-Binet intelligence test, 416, 529
Stanines, 539, 540
Statewide testing programs, 530
Statistics, 534–537
Status characteristics, 319–321
Status differences, 300, 320–321
Stems, 492
Stem-and-leaf diagrams, 510, 512
Stereotype threat, 319
Stern, William, 416
Sternberg, Robert, 418–419
Stiggins's taxonomy, 49–50
STM (short-term memory), 230–231
Story grammar, 237, 238
Strategic talk, 321
Strategies, teaching, 57
Streaming, 427
Stroll (walking style), 14
Stroop test, 230
Structure:
freedom vs., 197
in scaffolding, 273–274
Structured controversies, 313–314
Structured tutorial interaction, 310–311
Students:
as component in teaching model, 32
virtual, 31
Student-based approach to standard setting, 542–543
Student-centered approach, 206
Student conferences, 508, 509, 518–519
Student engagement, *see* Engagement
Student/teacher/curriculum models, 32, 33
Student–teacher dialectic, 339–340
Student Teams Achievement Division (STAD), 294–295, 311, 324, 325
Subtraction, 74
Successful intelligence, 418, 419

Successive scanning, 245
Summative assessment, 488
Supportiveness, 113, 119, 210–211
Suspense, 84, 357
Suspensions, 162
Symbols, 77
Symbolic identification, 190
Symbolic problem solving, 77
Symbolic schemas, 74
Sympathy, 134, 135
Syntax, 93–94
Synthesis, in Bloom's taxonomy, 49
Systematic problem solving, 82

T

Tactics, 57
TAI (Team-Accelerated Instruction), 294, 295
Talent, 423–427
defined, 423
development of, 425–426
early vs. developed, 425–427
Talking books, 96–97
Tapped In (online community), 40–41
Tasks:
authentic, 269
classroom, in peer learning, 324–325
Task developer, teacher as, 322
Task instrumentality, 190
Taxonomies, 48–50, 214
Teacher(s):
and assessment, 487
concerns of beginning teachers, 33–34
expert vs. novice, 35, 36, 38–40
goals of beginning teachers, 34–35
and language development, 94–95
learning by, xxx
online communities of, 40–41
peer learning role of, 322–324
professional development of, 40–41
professional growth phases of, 35–36
and relationships, 114–115
as researchers, 15–16
research knowledge of, 17
self-efficacy of, 41, 42
and sociocognitive development, 91
students' attachment styles with, 116–119
verbal abuse from, 114
Teacher beliefs, 20, 36–38
Teachers of English to Speakers of Other Languages (TESOL), 461
Teaching, 30–32. *See also* Instruction
applying theories in, 17–19
approaches to, 57–59
beliefs about, 36–38
components of, 31–32
of concepts, 245–246
defined, 31
direct instruction, 58–59
discovery learning, 58
expository, 57, 58
multicultural approach to, 465–471
of problem-solving skills, 267
reciprocal, 280, 281
reflective, 19–25
rewards of, 47–48
teachers' beliefs about, 36–38
technical, 19–21